T0163271

N. F. S. Grundtvig

A life recalled

*Grundtvig in English is a series commissioned by the Centre for
Grundtvig Studies, University of Aarhus, Denmark; this volume in
collaboration with the Department of English & Related Literature,
University of York, England*

N. F. S. Grundtvig

A life recalled

An anthology of biographical
source-texts translated from the Danish
and edited by S. A. J. Bradley

Grundtvig in English Series: Volume I
General Editor : S. A. J. Bradley

Aarhus University Press

Dedication

Hvad er en Dag? Et Øieblik
Vi neppe Tid at skue fik
Og dog af lutter slige Dage
Vor Levetid bestaar.
Hvo er vel den som fræk tør klage
Han ikke nok af Dage faar
Lad han dem sammen regne!
Og ved enhver antegne
Hvad han paa dem har gjort.
Da skal han see hvis Skyld det er
Hans Levetid var kort.

What is a day? A moment's span
we hardly had the time to scan.
Yet of such days, and such days purely,
our living-time is wrought.
Whoever dares bemoan, so surly,
his sum of days as all too short,
let him but count their tally
and for each one tell fully
what from those days he won.
Then he shall see whose blame it is
his time so soon seemed done.

Grundtvig, Dagbog begyndt i København
Den XXVIII^de November MDCCCII

Verse prefacing Grundtvig's diary
begun in Copenhagen, 28 November 1802

Kimer, I Klokker! nu sluktes en Sol over Mulde,
længe den kæmped mod Mørket med Straalerne fulde;
sildig den sank,
stor i sin Nedgang og blank.
Æren er Guds i det høje.

Ring out, O bells! now a sun over earth is grown darkling,
long though it fought with the murk, in full radiance sparkling;
late sunk in night,
grand was its setting, and bright!
God's upon high is the glory!

Jens Christian Hostrup (1818-92), Ved N. F. S. Grundtvigs Jordefærd [At N.F.S.G.s Funeral] (1872)

N.F.S Grundtvig: A life recalled

© Aarhus University Press and S.A.J. Bradley 2008

Cover design: Lotte Bruun Rasmussen

Cover illustrations: N.F.S. Grundtvig, 1843 by C.A. Jensen.
    Courtesy of Hirschsprungske Samling

Altarpiece (1732) by Nicodemus Tessin, Vor Frelsers Kirke,
    Copenhagen, Photo: Ole Frederiksen

Graphic design and typesetting: Anne Marie Kaad

Printed in Denmark by Narayana Press

ISBN 978 87 7288 969 6

Aarhus University Press

Langelandsgade 177

DK-8200 Aarhus N

Denmark

www.unipress.dk

Gazelle Book Services Ltd.

White Cross Mills,

Hightown

Lancaster,

LA1 4XS

www.gazellebooks.co.

The David Brown Book Company (DBBC)

P.O. Box 511

Oakville CT 06779

USA

www.oxbowbooks.com

For generous grants given in support of the English Translation Project
to the Centre for Grundtvig Studies in the University of Aarhus,
Denmark, in collaboration with the Department of English
and Related Literature in the University of York, England,
grateful acknowledgment is made to:

Carlsbergfondet

Forskningsministeriet

Undervisningsministeriet

The University of Aarhus Research Foundation

Foreword

The projected series of English translations of writings of N. F. S. Grundtvig, of which this is the first volume, was devised as an essential corollary to the work of the Centre for Grundtvig Studies in the University of Aarhus, Denmark, which in 1990 committed itself to a reassessment of the Grundtvig legacy on the threshold of a new millennium and in an international perspective. As the Centre developed its programme of research, publications and conferences and seminars in venues as diverse as Aarhus and Copenhagen, Chicago, Kolkata and Darjeeling, Durham and York, it became ever more apparent that the Centre itself would have to take an initiative in supplying the acutely felt want of English translations of the works of Grundtvig in those parts of the world where there was an expressed interest in Grundtvig but little knowledge of the Danish language. Accordingly, with the generous support of grant-awarding bodies an English Translation Project was established. While work on this first volume was in progress, indications came from among its potential readership that there was also a greater need of supporting apparatus – in particular, contextual information in the English language – than it had originally been the intention to provide. It had indeed been planned from the outset that the first volume should be biographical in order to establish the figure of Grundtvig for such readers as could not access Danish sources, but it was decided in the light of this intimated need to augment very considerably the Index, in such a way as to furnish a reasonably broad sketch of the contemporary background of institutions, events, circumstances, personalities and ideas against which Grundtvig lived out his life and pursued his various causes and interests, great and small. Consequently, the completion of the work was protracted; but it is hoped that the resulting volume will therefore prove not only to be sufficiently informative for the general reader but also serviceable for use in university programmes and schools curricula; and that it will also serve to supplement future volumes published in this series.

During frequent research visits to Denmark in the course of this task I have received a great deal of hospitality. In Vartov, that priceless asset of Kirkeligt Samfund, Hans and Kirsten Grishauge and the staff who there give such practical daily meaning to the Grundtvigian concept of *det folkelige* have virtually become a surrogate family to me in my many stays and visits. Kurt Johannes Dokkedahl and Birgitte Amdisen have been extraordinarily generous in opening their home to me as often as I needed to be in Copenhagen, even to the extent of providing me with a book-lined study, where much of this volume was drafted. My good friends Theodor and Lise Jørgensen and Eyvin (K. E.) and Ilse Bugge have also extended warm hospitality and the encouragement of their interest in the ongoing project.

For the collaborative agreement whereby I was seconded for a period from my post at the University of York to join the Centre for Grundtvig Studies in Aarhus University, I warmly thank my former Department and the University authorities at York. My adoptive colleagues in Aarhus could not have been more unstinting in their readiness to help an English Anglo-Saxonist learn more about Grundtvig, theology and the nineteenth century. I must especially name Kim Arne Pedersen than whom few people, if any, know more about Grundtvig and none could be more altruistic in sharing that knowledge with others; but I am also greatly indebted for the privilege of the wise conversations and hospitality of Jakob Balling and Christian Thodberg. To Jette Holm and her colleagues in the Grundtvig Sermons project, I am grateful for permission to make use of the transcription of Grundtvig's sermon of 1 May 1844 that is used in item 53. To the younger generation in the Centre I am also indebted. Anja Stokholm most generously found time amid a busy professional and domestic life to draft the selection of significant dates. From conversations with Anders Eskedal, Anders Holm and Ulrik Overgaard I have gleaned more than they may have been aware of. It goes without saying that the way has many a time been smoothed by the admirable competence of the secretaries at the hub of the organisation: Birgit Winther-Hansen and her successor Anne-Grethe Dion Jørgensen. When the day's work was done, I was often revived by the warmth of hospitality offered in the charming home of Jette and Jens Holger Schjørring: they know how much their friendship has meant to me.

There are many others to whom I am indebted for something gleaned from discussions: I am grateful to them all. Those to whom I owe sincere thanks for help with particular aspects of the book include Niels Jørgen Cappelørn, K. E. Bugge, Flemming Lundgreen-Nielsen and Benedict Bradley.

It is right to recall and record what a privilege it is in Denmark and in England to have access to so many fine libraries and to be assisted by sufficient trained and dedicated staff – a hallmark, one might say, of a humane modern society, expensive though these resources are to maintain. Thanks be for the Royal Library in Copenhagen and the British Library in London. At the Grundtvig Bibliotek in Vartov, Liselotte Larsen, its librarian, has all along been a valued source of ever ready help both for on the spot searches and through email enquiries: I thank her for her good-humoured efficiency and encouragement. The Danish online Biblioteksvagt has never let me down: long may this excellent service be allowed to continue. In particular I have to thank Birgitte Langkilde of the Statsbibliotek in Aarhus in whose mailbox my enquiries tended to land and who answered them all with exemplary promptness and thoroughness.

At Aarhus University Press Pernille Pennington was my first, ever encouraging editor and valued sounding-board for ideas in progress: I am grateful to her – as I am also to her successor, Mary Waters Lund, for her adoptive enthusiasm for the project.

There will be errors, perhaps many of them, in so fact-fraught a book. To those people who have so charitably helped me avoid a number of them in the course of writing I owe much, especially to Mette Windfeld Bradley for discussing early stages of the translations, to Jakob Balling for patiently sampling their penultimate draft and making various suggestions for their improvement, and to Søren Jensen and Susanne Gregersen who heroically scanned an earlier draft of the Index with an impressive *falkeblik* and spared me various embarrassments. For surviving errors I alone am to be reproached.

There are three names I reserve for especially grateful mention. The first is that of Kurt Dokkedahl, whose voluntary and enthusiastic role as research assistant has been of the greatest practical benefit to me throughout. For his command of our materials, to which I could appeal when I needed to clarify my own mind, and for his assiduous labours which have spared me hours of toil, I am enormously grateful. The other two are those of Jens Holger Schjørring and Donald (A. M.) Allchin. My deep indebtedness to these two finest of colleagues and friends is indicated in the dedication of this book.

S.A.J. Bradley,
February 2008

Contents

Student years in Copenhagen

Part two – Memoirs of Grundtvig

Names or initials in square brackets are those which are most commonly used by Danish convention in reference to the informant concerned (thus, for example, Frederik Hammerich, F. C. Sibbern). Brief biographical notes on the informants, if not in the headnotes, are to be found in the Index

Student Years 1800-1803

The philosopher Steffens, Grundtvig's older cousin, recalls their first meetings as adults in 1802.

Obsequies 1872

Part three – Index

Introduction

"The writings of Grundtvig, whether in prose or verse, have never been attractive to me. They are so exclusively national as to be scarcely intelligible to a foreigner; they lie, if I may say so, outside the European tradition. But as a human being, as a documentary figure in the history of his country, no one could be more fascinating."

Since Edmund Gosse (*Two Visits to Denmark 1872, 1874*, London 1911) presented this view of Grundtvig to his English-speaking readership at the end of the first decade of the twentieth century, fascination with Grundtvig "as a human being" has continued to endure undiminished for nigh on a hundred years more, and it is likely to continue as long as human beings feel drawn in that universal human manner to experience vicariously, through reading of it, the drama, great or small, of another human being's life.

Grundtvig's long life incorporated drama on a large scale. At a personal level, its peaks and troughs were determined in part by his vulnerability to a manic-depressive disorder which three times brought him into serious crisis; but the age through which he lived was itself as dramatically turbulent for the Danes as for others across Europe. Grundtvig's adult life covered three-quarters of the nineteenth century, and it was hardly possible that anyone so seriously engaged in the issues of those decades – determined to play his part in his country's destiny under God and the worldly powers, willing to accept the burdens of responsibility, to face the exposure, the opposition, the penalties, the defeats, in the hope of also sharing in the victories great and small – could have a life that was anything other than dramatic.

It is a life abundantly documented. As well as writing books in prose and in verse, most of which have considerable personal and autobiographical content (though he never wrote a full formal autobiography), Grundtvig published periodicals of his own and contributed frequently to others. Sermons from almost every Sunday of his pastoral life and a great number of hymns help chart the course of his spiritual development and furnish a record of his pastoral teaching. The huge archive of personal papers in the Royal Library, Copenhagen, contains everything from his passport with its details of height and eye colour, through diaries and notebooks, teaching materials, texts of speeches and lectures, letters received, copies of his correspondence with others, and progressive drafts of subsequently published works, to the voluminous raw materials of works which did not reach publication. There are also, of course, the many published memoirs by people upon whose life his life impinged.

In Gosse's day, as he rightly observes, Grundtvig had significance "as a documentary figure in the history of his country" by virtue of his struggle to reawaken the Danish national congregation, to revitalise the Danish Church, to establish principles of individual liberty of conscience and of speech, to redefine the goals of education and give a hitherto disempowered majority access to an appropriate education, and to promote – through poetry and song as well as through more direct polemic and action – a historically-rooted idea of nationhood and community that was inclusive and faced outwards to the world with a well-defined threshold but an open door. Since then, his iconic figure has been invoked in circumstances as diverse as neutrality in one world war, enemy occupation in another, construction of a welfare state, conflict over the ordination of women as priests and bishops, the wider debate on equal rights for women, strife over student demands for university reform, participation in a European union and in a declaration of common ground among the Protestant churches, recurrent educational debate upon the evolving character, role and relevance of the Danish folk-highschools, political debate on immigration and cultural debate upon Danishness in an age of globalisation – not to mention the multitude of public and private occasions, from birth to death, when the sacred or secular ceremonies of the season and the rites of passage are given definitive expression in a hymn or a song by Grundtvig. Few are the Danish contexts in which Grundtvig has not been invoked by one opinion-group or another and few, if any, are the Danes who have held such a position in the modern period of Denmark's history.

This situation in a sense also reflects that thoroughgoing *national* character of Grundtvig's writings, which Gosse for his part found "scarcely intelligible." It is not the national*ism* of Grundtvig that defeats his understanding: Grundtvig's nationalism has solid theoretical and circumstantial grounds familiar to anyone who knows the basics of eighteenth- and nineteenth-century European cultural and political history. It is the national – that is, the internally-referential – nature of the stock of narratives, images and idiom used by Grundtvig to articulate his commitment to Denmark and Danishness that baffles Gosse. Admittedly, there are passages in Grundtvig's writings, especially in his poetry, that tax even the best-informed and friendliest Danish critics; but one might suspect that when Gosse's mind, intelligent, sophisticated and broadly Danish-sympathetic though it was, failed to flood with the light of recognition, the problem lay elsewhere than in the fact that sometimes Grundtvig allowed his ideas and images to flow too thick and fast for clarity to be the result. It is significant that one of the virtues esteemed by Gosse in Henrik Ibsen (whose work he pioneeringly mediated in critical writing and translation to a British public) was the amenability of his plays to an approach via contemporary European or cosmopolitan norms. What Gosse required of a modern writer was recognisable affiliation to the prevailing European critical canon – which traditionally gave little place to minority cultures and their literatures. Grundtvig, with all his personal and artistic idiosyncrasies, his dedication to the Danish language and Danish cultural orientation, his devotion to the historical identity of a people who, tallied in millions, numbered less than a handful, hardly fitted the bill.

No less awkward to fit into contemporary categories was Grundtvig's universal perspective, the uncompartmentalised structure of his mind. For him, theology and history together presented a self-revelation of the nature, purposes and provisions of the Christians' God through all the ages and among successive dominant cultures of the world into present time; they located the Danish people strategically within this temporal progression towards eternity; they affirmed the authenticity of the Church which lived by virtue of its divinely instituted nurture of the Living Word, and they obligated pastor and layman alike to be ever prepared to fight the good fight against those who would rationalise scripture and sacrament into intellectual vapidities or who would constrain by law, edict and hierarchical privilege that precious freedom of conscience which alone allowed individual exercise, for better or for worse, of free will. Theology and history together endorsed a certain ideal of nationhood – not that of a militaristic and expansionist worldly empire (though, like the Israelites of old, a nation may have to take to arms to defend its territory and its way of life) but that of a national congregation fulfilling its divine and historical destiny as it embraced the coming of God's kingdom on earth. The literary celebration of heroic antiquity consolidated this national identity, enshrined anew in the mother-tongue traditional values and ethical principles, and kept alive the guiding record of good and ill conduct. Literary celebration of the Danish landscape likewise tuned the rich resources of the mother-tongue to offer direct or implicit homage to the creator-God, and linked the natural seasons with the liturgical seasons of the Church which themselves kept believers mindful of both the past and the future of God's dispensation. For Grundtvig, the Bible, poetry, psalmody and prophecy remained dynamically linked in this latter age as in the age of David the psalmist, the Anglo-Saxon poet Cædmon or the Norse poet Bragi. Myth and metaphor continued to render the mother-tongue serviceable for the articulation of visions, mysteries, intuitions, revelations and insights as they had done in the world of the ancient Norsemen and the ancient Greeks and among the Hebrew congregation of biblical antiquity. Education, suitably constituted and presented, could open all this knowledge and understanding to all, offering all such enlightenment as would enable them to live the life they were given to the fullest, as mutually obligated members of one folk, so that, among the rest, democracy might become something loftier, more altruistic and unifying, than a competition for supremacy between sectional groups.

Thus Grundtvig the politician, the advocate of *folkelighed*, the educationist and teacher, the mythologist, the poet, the preacher, the hymn-writer, the prophet, the philologist, the antiquarian, the ecclesiologist, the polemicist and controversialist, the nationalist, the historian and the theologian, was guided by a comprehensive vision for the material and spiritual wellbeing and destiny of the Danish folk.

This vision was not given him ready-made in its entirety but rather emerged and was expanded and consolidated from his tireless and lifelong engagements, planned or accidental but always pursued with an awe-inspiring fervour and doggedness, in a wide range of the issues of church and state, especially as they bore upon personal freedom of the enlightened conscience in action and in expression. In part the vision was the outcome of profound personal spiritual crisis. In part it was realised (or constructed) retrospectively. In the usual way of autobiographers (a particularly conspicuous example was his contemporary, Hans Christian Andersen) Grundtvig in his various memoirs sought to elicit patterns from past life-events, taking the opportunity to put on record a retrospective justification and vindication of past choices, suggesting a clear-sighted informing purpose amidst what might otherwise have seemed to be a more passive response to circumstances. He also worked at the literary character of his narratives. But scepticism can be an over-blunt instrument of criticism, particularly if the scepticism rests upon twentieth or twenty-first-century premises while the object of the scepticism is a mind shaped by the eighteenth and nineteenth centuries. In Grundtvig's Christian perception the interventions of divine providence and such gifts of the spirit as prophecy were realities, manifest and to be sought in the daily workings of the world. If the biographical records reveal him from time to time reconstructing the record of his life, he is not engaged in brazen falsification but is persuaded, in the light of review, that there was greater cohesion, clearer progression, firmer direction in his diverse affairs than at the time had been evident to him. But even if convictions about mystical causations are set aside, the life-records of Grundtvig (like the life-records of Andersen) still present a genuinely remarkable story. Out of his vision which others, including many of Denmark's most able men and women, learned to see through his eyes and thenceforth espoused, Grundtvigianism was born within his own lifetime, and a Grundtvigian viewpoint upon the central departments of Danish national life, secular as well as religious, emerged and endured.

Sofus Høgsbro (1822-1902; see the Index entry), a leading Danish politician during and after the bitter struggle over the anti-democratic revision of the Constitution of Denmark in 1866, wrote (12 February 1869) to J. L. Knudsen: "We shall not all be quarriers like Grundtvig; on the contrary, *we* must strive to make the precious metal he quarried into current coin, even if it therefore becomes necessary to alloy it with copper. In no other way can it become the possession of the people." (*Sofus Høgsbro, Brevveksling og Dagbøger 1858-1873* [Correspondence and diaries], edited by Hans Lund, Copenhagen 1923, pp. 47-8; my translation) Many who have contributed to the shaping of modern Denmark, in many other fields besides the political, could endorse Høgsbro's profession of a Grundtvigian idealism albeit alloyed with pragmatism.

It is a widely held judgment that no other Dane of modern times has so comprehensively furnished Danish society with viable criteria for debating issues relative to state and church in both domestic and international fields, and for taking a particular personal stance in matters of conscience, whether in private or public life, and whether in matters worldly or spiritual. Grundtvig is still widely invoked in public debate of all sorts, and where the concept of Danishness is an issue he is not easily circumvented. To belong in the centre of one's national cultural heritage as Grundtvig does is to occupy a seriously exposed position. Having survived the cultural confrontations of the transition from the nineteenth into the twentieth century he is now embroiled in the confrontations – the *kulturkamp* as it is sometimes rather luridly called – of the twenty-first, where he is variously perceived as being at once a national touchstone and a millstone around the national neck, a guiding beacon of traditional values in an increasingly multicultural and multi-faith society and a bastion of conservatism which serves, as did the old city walls of Copenhagen, as much to shut the citizens in as to shut foreigners out. The fact remains that whoever wishes to understand Denmark and the Danes, or indeed the Danish legacy in other societies to which Danes have migrated, would do well to study the legacy of Grundtvig.

The Europe of Gosse's lifetime was largely swept away by two great wars, and a consequent economic, political and cultural reordering of the hierarchy of world powers. In the Europe emergent from postwar progression towards economic and political union, cultural differentiations have (to some extent paradoxically) commanded fresh attention, and the intellectual history of the individual nation has become part of the collective heritage of the united whole. Today, Grundtvig is properly to be approached as a genius within the European inheritance, even though the parameters of his mission and his *œuvre* were so specifically and wilfully Danish.

The label 'minority culture' sometimes stuck on Denmark is in any case far too facile. Only in a narrow numerical sense and with specific reference to the language can Danish culture of the modern period meaningfully be called a minority culture. This is not the place for attempting a catalogue of Denmark's participation in and contribution to those mainstream activities in the fields of the arts, sciences and religion, and of political, social and educational theory and practice which we conventionally regard as characterising civilised modernity across the western world; but it was in many of these respects a highly distinguished era in Denmark through which Grundtvig lived; indeed in some fields it was a Golden Age; and Grundtvig was integral to it, in part defined by it, in part one of those who formed its definition.

Furthermore, Grundtvig *has* gone forth into the world. As Danish culture has historically travelled abroad, as for example through emigration into America and Canada, Grundtvig as church reformer, theologian, poet, educationist has become part of the cultural heritage of other nations, even though currency of the Danish language itself, as vehicle of this cultural heritage, has all but ceased in the communities thus formed. Wherever the Lutheran Calendar of Saints is observed, as published for example in *Evangelical Lutheran Worship* (2006) by the Evangelical Lutheran Church in America, Grundtvig is commemorated on 2 September as "bishop, renewer of the church." Still other communities and cultures have turned to Grundtvig and the Grundtvigian legacy primarily for his educational ideas. In the first quarter of the twentieth century, for example, the Nobel prizewinner Rabindranath Tagore visited Copenhagen, asked to be shown a Grundtvigian highschool, and took the model and its informing philosophy back with him, to adapt it to Indian needs. Nearer home, the Baltic countries, recently freed from Soviet domination, have revived an old interest in the Grundtvigian educational ideals: schools, independent of the prescriptive State, where pupils are prepared for life rather than trained as a professional and administrative elite and encouraged by incentives of pay, privileges and honours to sustain unquestioned the system which favours them; and where the nurture of *folkelighed* and cultivation of mother-tongue and national history are perceived as a means of re-establishing previously eroded national identity and cohesion.

Despite interest in Grundtvig in these and in various other parts of the globe as distant from Denmark as the Far East, it is rather unlikely he will ever command the attention given to his compatriot and contemporary Søren Kierkegaard (the study of whose writings has benefitted enormously from their translation into many other languages). Yet wherever Kierkegaard is seriously studied, there some study of Grundtvig should also hold a significant place- and will surely come to do so, as translations of his works become more widely available. Allusions to Grundtvig in Kierkegaard's writings are probably to be numbered not in scores but in hundreds. In various fundamental respects these two Christian polemicists, though born a generation apart, were confronted in their formative years and in their maturity by the same institutions of the absolutist establishment, and their tracts, books and sermons were addressed to the citizens of the same small city. They knew each other, met in the street, and read and pronounced upon each other's published opinions. If, as a contemporary Dane, you rejected the path illumined by the one, its was probably to the path illumined by the other that you would have turned. Not to study these two towering nineteenth-century figures together makes poor sense, and it is a cheering symbol of a new impetus towards collaboration that the leading centre for Kierkegaard scholarship has recently taken up residence in Vartov, from the pulpit of whose church Grundtvig preached weekly for over thirty years.

It is for all these reasons that English-language translations of the principal writings of Grundtvig have become increasingly sought after. In addressing this demand, one cannot help but be conscious of the irony that only by translation into the *lingua franca* of English can Grundtvig, the passionate champion of the Danish mother-tongue, be made more fully known to the readership that desires to know him. By way of apology to the ghost of Grundtvig one can only appeal, in all modesty, to the cited words of Høgsbro: *Paa anden maade kan det ikke blive folkets ejendom.*

This choice of texts has been very largely governed by the selection in Steen Johansen and Henning Høirup, *Grundtvigs Erindringer og Erindringer om Grundtvig* (Copenhagen 1948; reprint 1983) – the intention being to ensure that readers who may wish to consult the Danish source text alongside the translations have a reasonably accessible Danish edition available to them. Johansen and Høirup were leading scholarly figures in a revitalisation of Grundtvig studies marked by the founding of the Grundtvig Selskab in 1948. Their selection of texts of course tends to reflect a certain favoured image of Grundtvig; but it is very far from being an act of undiscriminating hero-worship, and with the addition of a few supplementary passages (notably from Søren Kierkegaard's private fulminations over Grundtvig's dialectical failings) it may be claimed that the spectrum of opinion in the present volume is representatively wide.

It should also be noted that the present anthology consists of prose texts, and only token reference is made in these pages to autobiographical material which Grundtvig recorded in poetic form. A comprehensive biography of Grundtvig would draw extensively upon this poetic material where many a felicitously worded cameo is to be found – as for example in his poem upon the death of his mother published in *Nyeste Skilderie af Kjøbenhavn*, 1822: *O Moder-Støv og Moder-Aand! / Mit Hjertes Tak Du have, / Som lærde mig, i Lede-Baand, / Paa Herrens Ord at stave, / At stave, grunde, bygge paa / Det Ord, som aldrig skal forgaae!!* [O mother, dust and spirit both, / with all my heart I thank you, / who taught me, still in infant reins, / to spell upon the Bible, / to spell, to found and build upon / the Word which never shall decay].

Though there is a broadly chronological arrangement of texts, the chief principle of selection (following Johansen and Høirup) is by topic rather than by date; and in any case a strictly chronological criterion would have been impossible to achieve, given the wide sweep of some of the memoirs. It is hoped that the headnotes and the Selection of Significant Dates will assist the reader to keep a chronological structure in mind, if that is what is required.

I have made free use of the notes provided by Johansen and Høirup (who themselves appear to have drawn a great deal of their biographical material from H. P. G. B. Barfod's *Minder fra gamle Grundtvig'ske Hjem* [Memories from old Grundtvigian homes], 8 vols., Copenhagen 1921-28. Where occasionally they are the sole source of my information I have acknowledged them as '(*GEEG*)' but because their notes were written for a Danish readership in whom a degree of familiarity with personalities, institutions and such could (apparently) be assumed, it has been felt necessary greatly to augment the information supplied, for the sake of an international readership. Some of this information is in the form of endnotes to the individual texts, but the bulk of it is in the Index.

The very copious Index has been provided in order to enhance the *biographical* objectives of this volume as being the first in the intended series of translations. It might be protested it is neither fish nor fowl: it is much more than a strict list of references to the texts but it is much less than a comprehensive concordance or gazetteer. Needless to say, it was never an option, in a book already on the brink of becoming unwieldy, to aim at such comprehensiveness. Rather, I have sought regularly to provide the reader of this and subsequent volumes with primary pointers from prompts within this particular selection of texts onwards to a higher level of enquiry.

Since this is a work of translation, not of editing primary source material, I have not attempted what would as often as not have been impossible: a systematic and scrupulous reproduction of the authors' punctuation and presentational conventions. Grundtvig's sentences, for example, are often very long indeed. Trust in his usually lucid syntax and you can follow him to the end; but where his long-sustained constructions and his conventions of punctuation have occasionally seemed to me too unwieldy in translation I have taken the liberty of repunctuating. In common with other writers of the period he often makes profuse use of *spatiering* (double spacing between characters, for which, in modern editions and scholarly quotation of Grundtvig's writings, italic is conventionally used) for emphasis – such profuse use that the exasperated Søren Kierkegaard quipped that in the end it is the *un*emphasised words which stand out in Grundtvig's discourses; and the editors of *GEEG* themselves concede a problem. In this as in other respects (for example, Grundtvig's frequent use of the long dash as punctuation), I have felt free to substitute modern English conventions of punctuation. Within the translated texts I have used italic sparingly for emphasis and, in texts and editorial apparatus, regularly for the titles of literary texts and for quoted original Danish words and Danish titles. Square brackets in texts signify my editorial insertions.

In an attempt to make acknowledgement of Grundtvig's dedication to his mother-tongue, various strategies have been adopted to keep the user of this volume in some degree of contact with the Danish language. Hence, for example, many Danish terms have been preserved in the texts alongside their English translation (which, together with the running page references shown in square brackets, may also assist anyone wishing to follow the original Danish texts with the aid of the translations), and extensive quotation in Danish (in parallel with English translation) has been included in Index and notes.

Inevitably, historical cultural shifts in Denmark as well as cultural differences between Danish and English societies and institutions render a number of terms difficult to translate with exactitude. For example, 'priest' as a translation of Danish *præst* worries some Danes who feel it carries cultural nuances of Roman Catholicism or High Church Anglicanism, thus misrepresenting a Lutheran concept of the pastor. I have occasionally used 'pastor' to translate *præst*, though I have more generally settled for 'priest' intending it as a denominationally neutral generic term – encouraged not least because the translation 'parish priest' seems so absolutely natural for Danish *sognepræst*. A more serious standing problem is the appropriate translation of the central and recurrent Danish term *folk* together with its derivatives and compounds. The English (-American) usage 'folk' with its suggestion of a peasant or working-class or popular cultural alternative to a classical and established cultural canon can be fundamentally misleading. In Grundtvig's usage it is much closer to German *Volk* and it relates directly and specifically to nineteenth-century philosophy of a nation-like community or society defined by certain shared fundamental characteristics and conditions. Undoubtedly it is something of a portmanteau word in Danish, and no single English word will answer to all its Danish usages alone and in composite words. Another example of such a frequently used portmanteau word which seems to me to have no single English equivalent term is *aand* (and its various derivatives and compounds) with its core sense of 'spirit'. An attempt is made in the Index to explain the problems with such terms; and within the texts the Danish term is often given (in square brackets) alongside the English translation felt to be appropriate for the context in the hope that the reader can build up an understanding of the nuances of the term. Very occasionally, as in the case of Grundtvig's terms *folkelig* and *folkelighed*, I have not translated the Danish term at all, thinking it marginally better that readers should familiarise themselves with the Danish word and its nuances through the Index and thereafter let it stand for itself instead of being represented by misleadingly approximate or cumbrous English translations.

As regards the forms of names, for better or for worse I have generally retained the variations found in the sources, reflecting the then-prevailing lack of fixity of spelling, but perhaps requiring the reader occasionally to exercise a little ingenuity in finding an Index entry. I have also chosen to keep the more Danish-looking forms of some names such as Jylland rather than Jutland and Sjælland rather than Zealand although this sometimes leads to inconsistencies as when, for example, I translate *Jyde* as 'Jutlander' or indeed use the English forms for *Danmark*, *Norge*, *Island* and such.

Abbreviations

Albeck 1979 = Gustav Albeck, *N. F. S. Grundtvig: Dag- og Udtogsbøger* [NFSG: Diaries and Notebooks] (Copenhagen 1979).

Arkiv = The Grundtvig Archive in The Royal Library [Det kongelige Bibliotek], Copenhagen; see *Registrant*.

Bibliografi = Steen Johansen, *Bibliografi over N. F. S. Grundtvigs Skrifter* I-IV, 1948-54.

Breve = *Breve fra og til N. F. S. Grundtvig* [Letters from and to NFSG], ed. Georg Christensen and Stener Grundtvig, 2 vols., Copenhagen 1924-26.

DDS 2002 = *Den Danske Salmebog* [The Danish Hymnal] authorised 2002 .

GEEG = Steen Johansen, Henning Høirup (eds), *Grundtvigs Erindringer og Erindringer om Grundtvig* (Copenhagen 1948; reprint 1983).

MM = Svend Grundtvig (ed.), *Mands Minde 1788-1838. Foredrag over det sidste halve Aarhundredes Historie, holdte 1838 af Nik. Fred. Sev. Grundtvig* [Within living memory, 1788-1838. Lectures on the history of the last half-century, given 1838 by NFSG], Copenhagen 1877.

Molbech-Gr = Christian K. F. Molbech og Ludvig Schrøder (eds), *Christian*

Molbech og N. F. S. Grundtvig. En Brevvexling [A correspondence], Copenhagen 1888.

Registrant = *Registrant over N. F. S. Grundtvigs Papirer* [Descriptive catalogue of NFSG's papers], I-XXX (by Gustav Albeck, K. E. Bugge, Uffe Hansen, Henning Høirup, Steen Johansen, Niels Kofoed, William Michelsen, Kaj Thaning, Helge Toldberg and Albert Fabritius), 1957-64; and the supplement, S. A. J. Bradley, *N. F. S. Grundtvig's Transcriptions of the Exeter Book, Grundtvig Arkiv Fascicle 316, nrs 1-8*, 1998.

Rönning = F. Rönning, *N. F. S. Grundtvig: Et Bidrag til Skildring af Dansk Åndsliv i det 19. Århundrede* [A contribution to the depiction of Danish intellectual life in the 19th century], 8 parts, Copenhagen 1907-13.

US = *Nik. Fred. Sev. Grundtvigs Udvalgte Skrifter* [NFSG's selected writings], I-IX, ed. Holger Begtrup, 1904-09.

VU = *Værker i Udvalg* [Selected works], I-X, ed. Georg Christensen and Hal Koch, Copenhagen, 1940-49.

Bibliography

Bibliographical references to the relatively few English language studies of Grundtvig may be found in the following works:

A. M. Allchin, *N. F. S. Grundtvig: An introduction to his life and work*, Aarhus and London 1997. The present volume is envisaged as a kind of companion to this excellent English-language characterisation of Grundtvig and his work.

Christian Thodberg, Anders Pontoppidan Thyssen (eds), *Tradition and Renewal: Grundtvig's Vision of Man and People, Education and the Church, in Relation to World Issues Today*, Copenhagen 1983.

A. M. Allchin, David Jasper, J. H. Schjørring, Kenneth Stevenson (eds), *Heritage and Prophecy: Grundtvig and the English-speaking World*, Aarhus and Norwich 1993.

A. M. Allchin, S. A. J. Bradley, N. A. Hjelm, J. H. Schjørring (eds), *Grundtvig in International Perspective*, Aarhus 2000.

Grundtvig-Studier, the annual journal of the Grundtvig-Selskab (Copenhagen), carries some articles in English and maintains a current bibliography of Grundtvig-related publications.

Online Grundtvig-resources in English are relatively few, though increasing. No attempt is made here to list current sites, because online sites often prove ephemeral (a search engine will always yield abundant results for 'N. F. S. Grundtvig') but two good starting-points are the excellent Wikipedia entry and the Danish-language site *Arkiv for Dansk Litteratur* which has a major authoritative contribution on Grundtvig by Flemming Lundgreen-Nielsen and provides online texts based upon Holger Begtrup's *Udvalgte Skrifter* as well as valuable bibliographical information.

A Selection of significant dates, 1783-1872

Compiled in collaboration with Anja Stokholm
*Select titles of Grundtvig's works are shown in **bold italic***

1783 Gr is born in Udby Parsonage on island of Sjælland, 8 September. His mother teaches him reading and rudiments of Christian learning. American War of Independence ends; when Danish neutral merchant ships consequently lose rich earnings, temporary economic crisis follows in Dk.

1784 Dk consolidates colonial tenure along Gold Coast in West Africa.

1785 Jens Baggesen enters Danish literary scene with highly successful collection of poems, *Comiske Fortællinger* (Comic Tales). The Societas Disputatoria Medica Hauniensis (Medical Debating Society of Copenhagen) is established.

1786 Count Ditlev Reventlow and Norwegian jurist Christian Colbjørnsen convince Crown Prince Frederik to set up major commission on agricultural reform which would lead to *stavnsbåndets ophævelse* (abolition of adscription).

1787 First nominative census of Denmark. Rasmus Rask, outstanding Danish philologist, born.

1788 With abolition of adscription (*Stavnsbåndets ophævelse*; repeal of law of 1733 tying peasantry to district of birth), movement towards emancipation of Danish peasants and petty farmers from severe legal and social inequalities begins. New schoolmaster arrives in Udby and occasions "a complete revolution" in the young Gr's "little brain."

1789 Outbreak of French Revolution. Impressed by quarrels between pro-revolutionary schoolmaster and anti-revolutionary parish clerk, Gr begins to read "Berling's newspaper" and provisionally takes parish clerk's side. Danish poet B. S. Ingemann is born; later in life becomes close friend of Gr.

1790 Danish-born Jørgen Zoega, archaeologist and pioneering numismatist, resident and eventually Danish consul in Rome, and recipient of state stipendium from Dk, is elected honorary member of Academy of Arts (and later of Academy of Sciences), Copenhagen.

1791 Dk's first establishment for training of teachers, Blaagaards Seminarium, is opened just outside Copenhagen.

1792 Gr is sent away to Jylland for his primary education with parish priest of Thyregod. First European coalition is formed against France; Dk maintains neutrality and gains from trading with France. Trafficking in slaves is forbidden by royal decree in Dk and Danish colonies, with (intended, though not actual) effect from 1802, though ownership of slaves continues lawfully until abolition in 1848.

1793 Reign of terror prevails in France; Louis XVI and Marie Antoinette are guillotined. Dk's foreign minister A. P. Bernstorff resists pressure from Britain and other coalition members to join economic blockade of France.

1794 Dk and Sweden renew a pact of armed neutrality, primarily to protect their merchant fleets against British and allied interference at sea.

1795 Major fire, out of control for two days, wreaks much destruction in Copenhagen.

1796 Mary Wollstonecraft, sometimes labelled first modern feminist, publishes *A Short Residence in Sweden, Norway and Denmark*. Paul 1 becomes Czar of Russia; his proposal of treaty of armed neutrality among Baltic states, in order to exclude expansionist Great Britain from Baltic, contributes to British decision to attack Copenhagen 1801.

1797 Napoleon Bonaparte leads French army to victories which effect break-up of first European coalition; directs his attention to crippling chief remaining adversary, Britain.

1798 Gr, reaching confirmation age, is admitted to Latin School at Aarhus. *The Evangelical-Christian Hymnal (Den Evangelisk-Christelig Psalmebog)* becomes new official hymn book in Dk, replacing *The new appointed church-hymnal (Den Forordnede Ny Kirke-salme-Bog)* (1699) also called *Kingos Salmebog*. Various discriminations against Jews in Dk (including prohibition against Jewish-Christian marriage) lifted. Battle of Aboukir (Battle of the Nile), in which British fleet under Nelson thwarts Napoleon's attempts to cut off British trading routes, by destroying Napoleon's fleet.

1799 For printing criticism of absolute monarchy, Danish satirical writer P. A. Heiberg – previously fined for writing (of elaborate Danish honours system) that "Orders are pinned upon idiots" – is exiled for life.

1800 Gr matriculates from Cathedral School in Aarhus, which he would later call 'The black-school' (*Den sorte Skole*), and is admitted to University of Copenhagen to read theology. Malthe Conrad Bruun is exiled from Dk for satirical writings against absolute monarchy, aristocracy and establishment.

1801   Battle of Reden, off Copenhagen, between British and Danish fleets; episode in Napoleonic wars. Gr joins student militia formed in Copenhagen. Danish and Norwegian ships in English ports are seized and British blockade forces surrender of Danish Tranquebar on Bay of Bengal, and of Danish West Indian islands. Dk compelled to withdraw from anti-British neutrality pact; Britain ends occupations and permits Dk free mercantile passage at sea.

1802   Henrik Steffens gives series of lectures at Copenhagen University on German Romantic movement. Gr attends the lectures, but is not immediately affected by their content. Through friendship with fellow-student P. N. Skougaard his zeal for Saxo, Snorri and medieval Icelandic literature is fired. He tries his hand as dramatist. Two richly decorated gold horns found at Gallehus, southern Jylland, dated to period 400-450, are stolen from the Kunstkammer in Copenhagen and melted down. Adam Oehlenschläger, inspired by meeting with Steffens, composes poem *Guldhornene* (The Gold Horns) and establishes reputation as pioneer of national-romantic poetry in Dk.
        The Letter (Brevet)
        The Schoolmasters (Skoleholderne)

1803   Gr graduates from the university in Copenhagen as *candidatus theologiae*; returns briefly to Udby and makes extended visit to brother's family in Torkilstrup Parsonage on Falster, working intermittently on ambition to get writing published. National (standing) army is promulgated, though obligatory service (for six-year period) imposed upon peasantry alone.
        Ulfhild, a historical Tale (Ulfhild, en historisk Fortælling)

1804   Gr divides time between Udby, Torkilstrup and Copenhagen, now with aim of writing academic thesis on King Canute (*Knud*), but abandons plan, not least for want of income. Gr gets his name into print for first time with critique of educational provision on Falster, published in popular weekly journal *Politivennen*. Napoleon crowns himself emperor. German philosopher Immanuel Kant dies.
        Et Særsyn i det nittende Aarhundrede (A rare sight in the nineteenth century)

1805-08   Gr secures position as resident tutor at manor of Egeløkke, Langeland, where he subsequently falls deeply in love with his pupil's mother, Constance de Leth. Traumatic experience serves to open his sensibilities to Romanticism and themes of Steffens's lectures of 1802.

1805   British fleet under Admiral Nelson defeats Napoleonic fleet at Battle of Trafalgar but Nelson is killed. Danish poet and writer H. C. Andersen is born in Odense on Fyn.

1806   Final dissolution of the German so-called Holy Roman Empire clears way for Dk, with Napoleon's support, to incorporate duchy of Holsten within the kingdom. Gr, in relative isolation of Egeløkke, reads widely and furthers both learned and literary aspirations in his writings.
        Brief Comment on the Songs of the Edda (Lidt om Sangene i Edda)

1807   After failure of British proposal of alliance with Dk, entailing temporary neutralising of Danish naval fleet, Britain attacks Dk by land and sea. Copenhagen is bombarded and set ablaze and most of Danish fleet destroyed or seized. Royal Commission for the Preservation of Antiquities (Den Kongelige Commission til Oldsagers Opbevaring) is established in Dk, an enquiry is sent to all parish priests concerning antiquities in their parish, and foundations are laid of a national collection of antiquities.

> *On the Lore of the Aesir (Om Asalæren)*
> *On Schiller and The Bride from Messina (Om Schiller og Bruden fra Messina)*
> *On Religion and Liturgy (Om Religion og Liturgi)*
> *On Scholarship and its Encouragement, with particular regard to the Fatherland (Om Videnskabelighed og dens Fremme, især med Hensyn til Fædrelandet)*
> *Journey in the Summer of 1807 (Rejsen i Sommeren 1807)*

1808-11   Gr leaves Egeløkke, moves to Copenhagen and begins teaching at grammar school, the Schouboe Institute.

1808   Dk is much harassed by presence of mutinous French-Spanish army intending (but abortively) to attack Sweden. Christian VII dies, apparently from stroke brought on by shock of foreign troops entering Dk, and is succeeded by Frederik VI who has in effect ruled in stead of his insane father for two decades. Battle of Sjællands Odde, naval incident in Napoleonic Wars in which Peter Willemoes, friend of Gr, is killed aboard Dk's last surviving warship defying superior force of British ships. Oehlenschläger makes debut as tragic dramatist with *Hakon Jarl* at Royal Theatre Copenhagen.

> *Gunderslev Forest (Gunderslev Skov)*
> *The Masked Ball in Denmark (Maskeradeballet i Danmark)*
> *Willemoes (Villemoes)*
> *On Oehlenschläger's Balder the Good (Om Oehlenschlägers Baldur hin Gode)*
> *Freyr's Love (Freis Kærlighed)*
> *Textbook in World History (Lærebog i Verdenshistorien)*
> *Mythology of the North or Overview of the Eddic Lore (Nordens Mytologi eller Udsigt over Eddalæren)*

1809   Dk and Sweden sign peace treaty; subsequent upheaval in Swedish royal succession ends with Frederik VI missing chance of uniting Scandinavian kingdoms and succession is eventually (1810) vested in French Marshal Bernadotte as Crown Prince Karl Johan. Protective scheduling of ancient monuments begins in Dk.

> *In Praise of Freyja (Freias Pris)*
> *Scenes from the Decline of heroic Life in the North (Optrin af Kæmpelivets Undergang i Norden)*

1810   Gr preaches and publishes his probationary sermon, entitled *Why has the Word of the Lord disappeared from His House? (Hvi er Herrens Ord forsvundet af Hans Hus)*, an attack on rationalist preachers of the time. Gr begins to believe he is called to be a reformer of the Danish Church but is cast into violent self-questioning, as to whether he himself is a Christian. As a result of the crisis and attendant depression he is escorted by friends home to Udby. Here he regains his strength, returning spiritually to orthodox, pietistic Christianity embodied in his father. Napoleon's Marshal Jean-Baptiste Bernadotte is elected as Swedish Crown Prince, subsequently (1818-44) rules in Sweden as King Karl XIV Johan and in Norway as Karl III Johan.

> *Idun. A New Year's Gift (Idunna. En Nytaarsgave)*
> *Gather round, you lassies small (Kommer hid I Piger Smaa)*
> *New Year's Eve, or a Brief Glance at Christianity and History (Nytaarsnat eller Blik paa Kristendom og Historie)*
> *Odin and Saga (Odin og Saga)*

1811 Gr is ordained in Trinitatis Kirke Copenhagen in May and in June inducted as his father's personal curate in Udby. University of Kristiania (Oslo) is founded.

> *Scenes from the Battle of the Norns and Aesir (Optrin af Norners og Asers Kamp)*
> *The Hill by the Sea at Egeløkke (Strandbakken ved Egeløkke)*
> *Saga (Saga)*
> *Udby Garden (Udby have)*

1812 Danish Royal Commission for the Preservation of Antiquities publishes first number of *Antiquariske Annaler* (Antiquarian Annals), containing listings of ancient monuments and articles concerning them.

> *Brief Concept of the World Chronicle in Context (Kort Begreb af Verdens Krønike i Sammenhæng)*
> *Why are we called Lutherans (Hvorfor kaldes vi Lutheraner?)*

1813 Gr's father dies and Gr, his curacy terminated, moves back to Copenhagen. Søren Kierkegaard is born in Copenhagen. Frederik VI refuses to cede Norway to Sweden in exchange for promise of North German territories and possibly Holland, as conditions of admission to Coalition against Napoleon, and commits Dk to support of Napoleon's collapsing fortunes. Cessation of hostilities 15 December leaves Dk on wrong side.

> *The Chronicle's Retort (Krønikens Gienmæle)*
> *On the Conditions of Man (Om Menneskets Vilkaar)*
> *To the Fatherland on its Need and Peril (Til Fædrelandet om dets Tarv og Fare)*

1813-21 Gr, unable to secure an incumbency in city, makes precarious living as poet and writer.

1814 State bankruptcy is declared in Dk, 5 January. As result of peace-settlement in Kiel, 14 January, Dk is compelled to relinquish Norway to Sweden and Helgoland to Britain. At assembly in Eidsvold, Norwegians defy union with Sweden by adopting own constitution with outgoing Danish vice-regent, Christian Frederik (later Christian VIII of Dk) as king; but Kiel terms are soon conceded under threat of Swedish military occupation. Napoleon abdicates and is banished to Elba. Two royal decrees provide universal free but mandatory elementary education between ages 7-14 in *Almueskoler*.

Jews are admitted to full citizenship in Dk, though under various conditions.

> *Roskilde Rhymes (Roskilde-Riim)*
> *Roskilde Saga, in Clarification of the Roskilde-Rhymes (Roskilde-Saga til Oplysning af Roskilde-Riim)*
> *Brief View of the World Chronicle considered in its Context (Kort Begreb af Verdens Krønike betragtet i Sammenhæng)*
> *A little Bible-History for Children and the general Reader (En liden Bibelkrønike for Børn og Menigmand)*
> *A strange Prophecy (En mærkelig Spaadom)*
> *On the Prospects for Christ's Church (Om Udsigterne for Christi Kirke)*
> *On Polemics and Tolerance (Om Polemik og Tolerance)*

1815   Congress of Vienna reorders Europe after Napoleonic Wars. Though little more than a powerless observer there, Frederik VI returns home to hero's welcome. Hostile demonstrations outside British envoy's Copenhagen residence, following Napoleon's defeat at Waterloo, reveal popular Danish sympathy for Napoleon, but his brief resurgence ends in exile to St Helena. Gr learns Anglo-Saxon, and in *Latest Depiction of Copenhagen (Nyeste Skilderie af Kjøbenhavn)* acrimoniously (but informedly) disputes over *Beowulf* with that poem's first editor, G. J. Thorkelin.

> *Against the Little Accuser (Imod den lille Anklager)*
> *Commemorative Song at the Ancestors' Grave (Mindesang paa Fædres Gravhøi)*
> *Specimens from the Chronicles of Snorri and Saxo (Prøver af Snorres og Saxos Krøniker)*
> *Little Lays or Short Songs (Kvædlinger eller Smaakvad)*
> *Heimdall (Heimdall)*
> *Europe, France and Napoleon (Europa, Frankrig og Napoleon)*

1816-19   Gr publishes periodical *Dannevirke (Danne-Virke)*.

1816   Regulations are issued encouraging use of corporal punishment in Danish schools.

> *The 'Literary Times' Broadside in Respect of the Specimen of Saxo and Snorri (Litteraturtidendes Skudsmaal i Henseende til Prøverne af Saxo og Snorre)*
> *Biblical Sermons according to the Need and Occasion of the Time (Bibelske Prædikener efter Tidens Tarv og Leilighed).*

1817   On 300th anniversary of Luther's publication of his 95 theses against Rome, Danish bishops publish pastoral letter *Den hellige Skrift forklaret efter Fornuftens Love* (The Holy Scriptures clarified according to the laws of reason), entrenching rationalism – which Gr was to spend much of his life opposing – in Danish church.

> *On Revelation, Art and Knowledge (Om Aabenbaring, Kunst og Videnskab)*
> *Ragnarok (Ragna-Roke)*
> *The Daffodil [Easter-lily] (Paaske-Lilien)*
> *Prospect of the World Chronicle especially in the Age of Luther (Udsigt over Verdens-Krøniken fornemmelig i det Lutherske Tidsrum)*

1818   Gr receives public stipendium in recognition of his writing. His improved economic circumstances allow him to marry Elisabeth (Lise) Christina Margaretha Blicher after seven years of engagement. The Rigsbank, established after national bankruptcy, is reconstituted as Nationalbanken operating independently of national government.

1818-22   Translations of *Saxo's Chronicle of Denmark (Saxos Danmarks Krønike)* and of *Snorri's Chronicle of the Kings of Norway (Snorres Norges Konge-Krønike)*

1819   With gatherings initiated in his own home by Christen Madsen, beginnings of *det gudelige vækkelse* (religious revivalism) are laid in Fyn, and such *gudelige forsamlinger* (religious gatherings), held elsewhere than in churches and led by others than incumbent pastors, are ever more rigorously opposed by authorities.

1820   Danish scientist H. C. Ørsted discovers electromagnetism. Danish political agitator J. J. Dampe is sentenced to death (commuted to life imprisonment) for advocating end of absolute monarchy.
        Translation of the Old English poem *Beowulf (Bjowulfs Drape)*

1821   Gr at last receives pastoral appointment to parish of Præstø in southern Sjælland, not as he hoped to city church. Lay preacher Christen Madsen is sentenced to prison for illegally preaching to unauthorized religious gathering.

1822   Gr's first son, Johan, is born. His mother, Kathrine Marie Bang, dies. He is appointed curate of Church of Our Saviour (Vor Frelsers Kirke) in Christianshavn, Copenhagen, where he serves until his resignation in 1826.

1823   Political, economic and cultural implementation of Norway's separation from Dk continues to generate tension and adversely affect Dk's frail national economy. Rasmus Rask, Danish pioneer of comparative linguistics, returns from visit to India and Ceylon with invaluable Sanskrit and other manuscripts collected for University Library; but is only belatedly awarded professorship and dies prematurely in 1832.

1824   Gr's second son, Svend, is born. H. C. Ørsted establishes Society for the Promotion of Natural Science (*Selskabet for naturlærens udbredelse*) in Copenhagen.
        New Year's Morn (Nyaars-Morgen)
        The Land of the Living (De Levendes Land)
        The Danish Shield (Danne-Skjolds-Drape)
        Exchange of Letters (Brevvexling)

1825   Whilst reading Irenaeus, Gr formulates new theology of "the living Word" [Det levende Ord] as historical core of Church's confession– his so-called matchless discovery [*den mageløse Opdagelse*]. This view on the Church he asserts in *The Church's Retort (Kirkens Gienmæle)*, which is a reply to *The Church Constitution, Teaching and Ritual of Catholicism and Protestantism (Catholicismens og Protestantismens Kirkeforfatning, Lære og Ritus)* published 1825 by H. N. Clausen, professor in Copenhagen University.

Sued by Clausen for libel which is also deemed a breach of laws governing freedom of print, Gr is heavily fined and sentenced to lifelong censorship (revoked, however, in 1837).

> *The 18th Century Enlightenment in the Service of Salvation (Det attende Aar-hundredes Oplysning i Saligheds-Sag)*
> *Rome and Jerusalem (Rom og Jerusalem)*
> *On the Christian Struggle (Om den Christelige Kamp)*
> *On War and Peace (Om Krig og Fred)*

1826 Partly as a result of the lawsuit, partly because authorities refuse to allow use of his hymn *Den signede Dag (The blessed day)*, written specially for 1000th anniversary of Danish Church, Whitsunday 1826, Gr resigns his post. Various younger people, including Jacob Christian Lindberg, support and collaborate with Gr in his view of the church. Lindberg successfully forms a link between Gr and influential groups of lay people, thus laying first foundations of movement later known as Grundtvigian-ism. Sorø Academy reopens with appointment of distinguished professors including B. S. Ingemann.

> *Important Questions for Denmark's Jurists (Vigtige Spørgsmaal til Danmarks Lovkyndige)*
> *What is Christianity in Denmark (Hvad er Christendom i Danmark)*
> *On true Christianity and on the Truth of Christianity (Om den Sande Christen-dom og om Christenhedens sandhed)*

1827 Gr's daughter, Meta, is born. H. C. Ørsted devises process for making aluminium. Philosopher Friedrich Schlegel dies.

> *The literary Testament of the Writer N. F. S. Gr (Skribenten N. F. S. Grundtvigs literaire Testamente)*
> *On Freedom of Religion (Om Religions-Frihed)*

1827-31 *Christian Sermons or The Sunday Book I-III (Christelige Prædikener eller Sønd-ags-Bog I-III)*

1828 First Danish steam-engine, key to industrialisation, is built.

> *The Christian Faith (Den kristne Tro)*

1829 Adam Oehlenschläger is crowned with laurel in Lund Cathedral and paid homage as supreme poet of the North. H. C. Ørsted is appointed director of newly established Polytechnic College (*Polyteknisk Læreanstalt*) in Copenhagen. Scandinavia's first mechanised production of paper begins in Dk.

> *Chronicle in Rhyme for living School Usage (Krønike-Rim til levende Skole-Brug)*
> *The River of Time or Outline of Universal History (Tidens Strøm eller universal-historisk Omrids)*
> *Chronicle in Rhyme for Childhood Teaching (Krønike-Riim til Børne-Lærdom)*
> *Historical Teaching for Children (Historisk Børne-Lærdom)*

1829-31   Gr makes three journeys to England to study medieval, especially Anglo-Saxon, manuscripts in which he subsequently retains lifelong interest. His encounter with English sense of religious and secular freedom is of great significance for whole of latter part of his life and work.

1830-31   *Should the Lutheran Reformation really continue? (Skulle den Lutherske Reformation virkelig fortsætte?)*

   Books and Ideas on Naturalism in the North, past and present (Bøger og Ideer om Naturalisme i Norden før og nu)

1830   July-revolution in France heightens international awareness of issues of democracy. Under pressure from federation of German states, duchy of Holsten is given own consultative assembly [*stænderforsamling*] – which only serves to provoke 'schleswig-holsteinism' (agitation for union of Slesvig and Holsten and independence from Danish crown). In Dk, new ideas coincide with broad economic recovery and with emergence of a peasantry showing benefits of 1814 provision of free primary education.

1831   As gesture towards democratisation within Kingdom of Dk, and to avoid implication of separate status of duchy of Holsten, four Provincial Consultative Assemblies (*provinsstænderforsamlinger*) are established, on model of developments in Germany and Holsten. Gr publishes in London his **Bibliotheca Anglo-Saxonica**, inviting subscriptions to publication of surviving Anglo-Saxon manuscripts. Rasmus Rask, Danish pioneer of comparative linguistics, dies. German philosopher G. W. F. Hegel dies.

   On the Clausen Libel Case (Om den Clausenske Injurie-Sag)
   Political Considerations with an Eye to Denmark and Holsten (Politiske Betragtninger med Blik paa Danmark og Holsteen)

1832   Unlawful religious gatherings (*forsamlinger*), organised by J. C. Lindberg and other associates of Gr to challenge laws on parish ties, attract police intervention. Gr's *Nordens Mythologi* is a landmark in exposition of his integrated standpoints upon religion, education, society.

   Mythology, or Metaphorical Language, of the North (Nordens Mythologi eller Sindbilled-Sprog)
   Hagen's Hymnal (Hagens Salmebog) in collaboration with Laurits Christian Hagen.

1832-39   In attempt to evade confrontations over unlawful religious gatherings, authorities permit Gr to preach at evensong (and thus to establish own congregation) in Frederik's Church (Frederiks Kirke) in Christianshavn, suburb of Copenhagen.

1833-41   Publication of the Nordic Church Times (*Den Nordiske Kirke-Tidende*) is undertaken by J. C. Lindberg with contributions by Gr, as a means of disseminating his concept of the Church (*kirkelige anskuelse*).

1833-43 *Handbook on World History. According to the best Sources. An Attempt by N. F. S. Gr I-III (Haandbog i Verdens-Historien. Efter de bedste Kilder. Et Forsøg af N. F. S. Gr I-III)*

1834 *Fædrelandet*, a Danish newspaper voicing emergent moderate liberalism and responsible concern for public affairs, is founded, and subsequently harassed by the authorities.

> *The Danish State Church impartially viewed (Den danske Stats-Kirke upartisk betragtet)*
> *The Spirit of the Age (Tids-Aanden)*
> *Northern Gold (Nordens Guld)*
> *Education for State Affairs (Statsmæssig Oplysning)*

1835 Frederik vi famously epitomises absolutist doctrine when, in response to suggestion from various state officers that action be taken over insolent and seditious *Fædrelandet*, he declares: We alone can be in a position to judge what is of true benefit and best for the people (Vi aleene kan være i Stand til at bedømme, hvad der er Folkets sande Gavn og Bedste). Provincial Consultative Assemblies (*rådgivende stænderforsamlinger*) meet.

> The golden Mean (Den gyldne Middelvej)

1836 *The Danish Four-Leaf Clover (Det danske Fiir-Kløver)*, first of series of educational writings in which Gr presents concept of *skolen for livet* (School for life) which would "awaken and nourish love of the fathers' land and secure strength and richness of the mother-tongue" (*vække og nære fædrelandskærligheden og skaffe styrke og rigdom i modersmålet*), providing education based less upon traditional canon of schoolbooks than upon dialogue over real-life experience, Danish history and Danish literature including myths, mediated by spoken word and in mother-tongue.

1836-37 *Song-Work (or Carillon) for the Danish Church (Sang-Værk til den danske Kirke)*, containing some 400 of Gr's own hymns, plus reworkings of hymns from other Christian cultures and periods; second volume subsequently published 1870.

1837 Gr is freed from sentence of lifelong censorship. Provision is made for elected town representatives alongside king's magistrates in Danish local government. Accession of Queen Victoria (dies 1901).

> *This Night came a Knock at the Portals of Hell (I Kvæld blev der banket paa Helvedesport)*
> *First a Man – then a Christian (Menneske først og Kristen saa)*
> *To the Norwegians concerning a Norwegian Highschool (Til Nordmændene om en norsk Højskole)*

1838   In part to mark lifting of personal censorship, Gr gives series of public lectures on modern history, held at Borchs Kollegium, Copenhagen, later published as *Within living Memory (Mands Minde)*: lectures are great success in consolidating his popular reputation and giving expression to Danish sense of national identity. He publishes landmark exposition of ideas upon 'school for life' including advocacy of residential schools where community of teachers and pupils are in dialogue through spoken word and education is training for fulfilment in life. Advance of industrialisation in Dk is marked by establishment of The Industrial Association (*Industriforeningen*). Bertel Thorvaldsen, Danish sculptor renowned throughout Europe, returns to Dk after 41 years in Italy; a museum is built to house his huge collection, which he presents to the state. Søren Kierkegaard publishes *Af en endnu Levendes Papirer*.

   The School for Life (Skolen for Livet)

1839   Frederik VI dies, to be succeeded by Christian VIII. Gr shares optimism that a "new year" is dawning for the nation. With royal support, he is appointed to church at Vartov, charitable institution for elderly and impoverished women. Here a steadily growing free congregation, which comes to include Dowager Queen Caroline Amalie, gathers around him, and here he remains until his death in 1872. He is appointed member of a small anti-slavery committee, working for the abolition of slavery in the Danish West Indian Colonies. As means of both circumventing and challenging censorship laws, but also and primarily as means of promoting Danish cultural identity, formation of new societies becomes popular: The Scandinavian Association (*Det Skandinaviske Selskab*) with Gr as chairman; The Danish Historical Association (*Dansk historisk Forening*) founded by Christian Molbech with the objective of awakening Danish historical spirit and interest; The Danish Society (*Det danske Samfund*) for advancement of Danishness at *folkelig* level, through lectures and communal singing, with which Gr is closely associated. *Brage and Idun*, quarterly journal dedicated to cultural exchange between the Scandinavian countries, is launched by Frederik Barfod with Gr's active participation. Danish writer Steen Steensen Blicher initiates popular gathering on Himmelbjerg in Jylland, to arouse and celebrate Scandinavian consciousness.

   To my two Sons (Til mine to Sønner)
   Open Letter to my Children (Aabent Brev til mine Børn)
   Speech to the People's Council (Tale til Folkeraadet)

1840   Population of Dk reaches 1.3 million. Satirical journal *Corsaren* is launched in Copenhagen by Meir Aron Goldschmidt, in which many public figures will be pilloried, a notable victim who suffered greatly from its ridicule being Søren Kierkegaard. Authority responds with stringent application of censorship laws.

   The Phoenix-Bird. An Anglo-Saxon Lay (Phenix-Fuglen. Et angelsachsisk Kvad)

1840-42   *Church Enlightenment, especially for Lutheran Christians (Kirkelige Oplysninger især for Lutherske Christne)*
   Petitions and Ideas for a Danish University in Sorø (Bønner og Ideer for en dansk Højskole i Sorø)

1841 At bidding of Dowager Queen Caroline Amalie, Gr forms part of official reception committee to meet Elizabeth Fry, English prison reformer and Quaker, and her brother Joseph Gurney, emancipationist. Meir Aron Goldschmidt, publisher of satirical journal *Corsaren*, is sentenced to imprisonment and lifelong censorship for criticising system of absolutist government which, to disappointment of many, Christian VIII shows no sign of renouncing. Kierkegaard publishes *Om Begrebet Ironi*.

1842 Orla Lehmann, National-Liberal politician and fervent opponent of absolutism, is imprisoned for three months for spreading hatred and suspicion of government in a speech during 1841 elections to *stænderforsamling* (provincial advisory council), and thereby becomes popular martyr. Refusal of Peter Hiort Lorenzen to speak German in Slesvig's regional assembly turns status of duchy into national and nationalistic issue in Dk. Danish National Liberals formulate *Ejderpolitik* (claiming natural frontier for Kingdom of Dk on river Eider and thus splitting off Holsten and Lauenburg from Slesvig) which, revived in 1863, contributes to disastrous war with Prussia, 1864. *Almuevennen* (Peasants' friend), paper demanding social justice for lower agricultural classes, is launched.
   On religious Persecution (Om Religions-Forfølgelse)

1843 Gr makes his fourth visit to England, in order to contact leaders of the Oxford Movement; meetings however work out badly and Gr's respect for contemporary English Church henceforth diminishes. First of annual series of open-air mass-meetings at Skamlingsbanken (by Kolding, Jylland) is held, to assert cause of Danishness in Slesvig. Kierkegaard publishes *Enten/Eller* and *Frygt og Bæven*.

1844 Spring 1844, Gr once again (as in 1810 and later in 1867) enters period of deep and morbid depression, exacerbated by attack of mumps, which for a while renders him unable to work. However, by 4 July he has so far recovered that, as chief speaker, he addresses huge audience at second open-air gathering (of some 12,000 people) in support of Danish Slesvig, on Skamlingsbanken, and is greatly elated by experience. Kierkegaard publishes *Begrebet Angest*. Polarisation of factions in duchies sharpens appreciably. First folk-highschool opens in Rødding in North Slesvig on initiative of Christian Flor, professor in University of Kiel; school later moves northwards to Askov following loss of Sønderjylland to Prussia 1864. V. A. Borgen, appointed as king's candidate to overhaul Copenhagen's provision of child education, embarks upon successful programme of educational reform. Dk's first railway, between Kiel and Altona, opens. *Det Asiatiske Kompagni* (The Asiatic Company) goes into liquidation, reducing Dk's already small colonial presence abroad.
   Sleep sweet, little Babe (Sov sødt, Barnlille)
   The Waldhorn's Clarion among the Skamling Hills (Skov-Hornets Klang mellem Skamlings-Bankerne) and Rune-sliver aboard the Christian the Eighth for young Denmark (Rune-Bladet med Christian den Ottende til Det unge Danmark)
   Poetic Chat on Greek and Norse Myths and Ancient Legend for Ladies and Gentlemen (Brage-Snak om Græske og Nordiske Myther og Oldsag for Damer og Herrer)
   The little Ladies (Smaa-Fruerne)

1845   Launch of journal *The Danish Church Times* (*Dansk Kirketidende*), a chief mouthpiece
        for Gr's views on the Church and the *folkelige*. Henrik Steffens, philosopher and Gr's
        cousin, dies. Gr and H. N. Clausen are guests of honour at grand student-arranged
        dinner in Copenhagen to promote ideal of Scandinavian unity. Alliance is formed
        between increasingly prominent *bønder*-party (politicising cause of small farmers)
        and National Liberals. Danish colonies on Indian mainland are sold to British East
        Indian Company.

1846   Association of Friends of the Farmer (*Bondevennernes Selskab*) is formed out of al-
        liance between farmers and National Liberals, with aim of using political means to
        remove legal, political and social disadvantages attaching to petty farmers and peas-
        ants. Many supporters of Gr's theology and ideas on Church and on education are
        now to be found in the rising class of small farmers. Largely fired by National-Liberal
        Orla Lehmann's speeches and writings, agitation for a constitution continues to grow.
        In response to dissatisfaction with existing hymnal of State Church, draft of a new
        Kirke-salmebog (Church Hymnal) is tabled by appointed committee though largely
        Gr's work, but is rejected by Copenhagen's *Præstekonvent* (Clerical Convention).

1847   Railway between Copenhagen and Roskilde is inaugurated, the first locomotive be-
        ing named Odin. Royal ordinance declares that all native children henceforth born to
        slaves in Danish West Indies shall be free, and slavery abolished within twelve years.
        Danish warship is used to repress anti-colonial disturbances in Gold Coast (Ghana)
        colony.

1848   Christian VIII suddenly dies of blood-poisoning, to be succeeded by son Frederik
        VIII to whom, according to later report, dying king urged granting of free Constitu-
        tion for Dk. Outbreak of February-revolution in France gives further momentum
        to revolutionary and separatist movement in duchies of Holsten and Slesvig. Three
        Years War, first of two wars with the German confederation over the duchies Slesvig
        and Holsten, breaks out, with battles occurring across Slesvig and north to Århus.
        Day after a public meeting (20 March) at the Casino, Copenhagen, fifteen thousand
        people march to palace to demand democratic constitution, only to find king has
        already conceded end of absolute monarchy. Threatened by mass uprising of slaves in
        St Croix West Indian colony, governor General Peter von Scholten, who already had
        humane record of alleviating status of slaves, on own authority declares all slaves free.
        Dk vacates its colony in Nicobar Islands, Bay of Bengal. Gr, though initially pessimis-
        tic over actual fairness of democratic process of government, is elected member of
        Constituent National Assembly (*Den grundlovgivende Rigsforsamling*) to draft Con-
        stitution, and subsequently to new parliament. He launches *The Dane* (*Danskeren*),
        weekly periodical on topical issues, using it also for publication of his poems and
        songs; publication continues until 1851. Student Frederik Dreier publishes socialist
        vision for Dk, including commune-based social structuring, displacement of private
        by communal and collective, exploitation of industrialisation and mechanisation to
        disburden both women and men, and multiracial and multiethnic society (explicitly
        denouncing Gr's brand of nationalism); but seems to have been little read.

1849 Constitution (*Grundloven*) is finally signed by Frederik VII on 5 June, ending era of absolute monarchy and instituting a version of parliamentary government. The State Church (*Statskirken*) is reordered as the Folk (or National)-Church (*Folkekirken*). At December elections to the *Folketing* (lower house), number of votes cast by those eligible to vote corresponds to some 14.5 per cent of population. Kierkegaard publishes *Sygdommen til Døden*.

1850 Included in first acts of the new *Rigsdag* are laws empowering tied peasantry to buy themselves free from obligations to landlords and enabling them to do so by facilitating their access to credit. Gr supports Mathilde Lucie Fibiger, forerunner of women's emancipation, when popular indignation is expressed against her book *Clara Raphael. Tolv Breve* (CR. Twelve Letters), in which (fictive) letters from a governess pose such questions as: What right have men to subordinate us? Has Our Lord really created us of inferior stuff than men? As part of slowly ongoing humanitarian reform of Danish penal system, hard labour in the *Rasphus* ('filing house' – prison where male delinquents were set to rasping logwood imported from West Indies into purple textile dye powder), is abolished. Major battles continue in uprising of schleswig-holsteiners. Frederik VII, twice divorced, enters into morganatic marriage with Louise Rasmussen who receives title Countess Danner. Danish poet Adam Oehlenschläger dies.

1851 Gr's wife Elisabeth dies on 14 January; on 24 October he marries Marie Toft. The Three Years War over status of duchies of Slesvig and Holsten is ended without settlement of any of old issues. A folk-highschool is opened in Ryslinge on Fyn by Chresten Kold (1816-70), with financial support from Gr and his circle. Civil marriage is permitted to those not belonging to the Danish *Folkekirke*. Laws are passed to implement constitutional warranty of freedom of press.

1852 Following shift of political power in Dk, royal proclamation declares that Constitution of June 1848 shall be binding only upon Kingdom of Dk, and that duchies of Slesvig, Holsten and Lauenburg shall each have representation through own regional consultative Assembly (*stænderrepræsentation*) – thus acknowledging quadripartite character of Dk's monarchy and (temporarily) abandoning *Ejderpolitk* in favour of 'whole-state' doctrine (*Helstaten*). Law permitting building development on land outside Copenhagen's ramparts results in surge of speculative building and establishes future slums.

1853 Establishment of The Danish Association (*Dansk Forening*) with Gr as president, aiming at advancement of Danishness among the people and founding of a peoples' university (*en dansk folkelig Højskole*). Gr is elected as member of *Folketing*. On assumption of Frederik VII leaving no direct heir, right of succession is declared to pass from House of Oldenborg to male line of House of Glücksborg. Severe epidemic of cholera ravages Copenhagen.

1854   Gr's second wife, Marie, dies on 9 July after bearing a son, Frederik Lange. A. S. Ørsted, first minister, attempts partial restoration of absolutist rule but is forced to resign; at huge popular meeting a society for defence of the constitution is formed. Gr is again elected as member of *Folketing*, serving until 1858. Bishop J. P. Mynster dies. Prompted by eulogy upon Mynster by his successor Bishop H. L. Martensen, Kierkegaard unleashes vitriolic attack upon Danish national Church. Philosopher F. W. J. von Schelling dies.

1855   Further limitations upon 1849 Constitution are enacted with marked tendency towards restored absolutism. Law is passed intended to achieve degree of curriculum conformity between independent schools (including folk-highschools) and publicly-funded *almueskoler*. Law is passed permitting members of Danish *folkekirke* to choose which congregation they join, regardless of their parish of birth; a victory for Gr's party. Kierkegaard publishes number 1-9 of journal *Øieblikket*, sustaining his attack against Danish church from Christian existentialist standpoint. Gr responds, emphasizing significance of Church as historical entity, and as community of the faithful. On 11 November, aged 42, Kierkegaard dies after brief illness.
   The Danish Cause (Den Danske Sag)
   On the Resurrection of the Flesh and the Life everlasting (Om Kiødets Opstand-else og det evige Liv)

1856   Folk-highschool which comes to be known as *Grundtvigs Højskole* is inaugurated at Marielyst (named by Gr after his wife Marie) near Copenhagen, the property purchased with gifts from Gr's supporters in Dk and Norway in honour of his seventieth birthday, September 1853. Gathering of Scandinavian students in Uppsala, where Carl Parmo Ploug is notable speaker, urges union of Scandinavian kingdoms. Dismantling of city gate at Nørreport symbolises continuing progress of modernisation of Copenhagen's ancient fortified enclave, opening way to further expansion of city beyond ramparts.

1857   Dk agrees, in return for compensation, to forego ancient claim to take toll from ships passing through Øresund. Law passed ending civil sanctions against members of *folkekirke* refusing or neglecting to have children baptised; intention is that church should decide upon and exercise own sanctions in such cases. Danish women granted equal rights of inheritance and bequest; age of majority for unmarried women is set at 25 on par with that of men; law rescinding town trading monopolies has consequence that widows and unmarried women can own and run own businesses. J. C. Lindberg dies. Christian Molbech dies.

1858   Gr is married for third time on 6 April, to aristocratic widow, Asta Reedtz, born Countess Asta Tugendreich Adelheid Krag-Juel-Vind-Frijs. Slesvig-Holsten question continues to dominate government business.

1859   Relations with Holsten continue to deteriorate when Holsteners propose new constitution giving Kingdom of Dk no more than equal status with minor duchy of Lauenburg. King's morganatic wife, Countess Danner, encourages dismissal of National Liberal government in favour of one supported by Farmers' party, and is esteemed as champion of the people among pro-democracy groups. Publication of Darwin's *Origin of Species*.

1860   Gr's second daughter, Asta, is born. Tension over Slesvig sharpens when Prussia supports new surge of opposition to Danish rule in duchy.
        The Seven Stars of Christendom (Christenhedens Syvstjerne)

1861   On fiftieth anniversary of his ordination as priest Gr is given title of Bishop and ranked alongside Bishop of Sjælland. Prussian King Vilhelm insists that Slesvig-Holsten dispute must be resolved: there is talk of war on both sides. From among Grundtvigians, *Bondevenner* party and National Liberals signatories are recruited for a *Dannevirke-forening* (Dannevirke association; alluding to name of ancient southerly Danish frontier-fortification) to assert Danish sovereignty over all Slesvig to the Ejder frontier; though Gr himself is no supporter of *Ejderpolitik* or idea that German-speaking population in Slesvig should be required to use Danish. Vilhelm Beck and others found evangelical *Indre Mission* (Inner, or domestic, mission) for spreading and witnessing to the Gospel, which becomes and remains significant, parish-based force in Danish life. First formally qualified female teachers appointed in Copenhagen's public-funded schools.
        Beowulfes Beorh

1862   Otto von Bismarck becomes Prussian chief minister, ambitious to extend Prussian interests, not least by incorporation of Holsten. Britain, Prussia and Dk fruitlessly negotiate options in Slesvig-Holsten crisis. Danish poet and Gr's friend B. S. Ingemann dies.

1863   In climate of increasing hostility over constitutional status of duchies, Frederik VII suddenly dies, to be succeeded by conservative Christian IX who favours one constitution for kingdom and duchies alike. Rigsdag however approves plan to give Holsten and Lauenburg own separate constitution, thus separating the historically inseparable Slesvig and Holsten. Despite pressure from European powers, Dk can find no other way forward. Hopes of Scandinavian alliance coming to assistance of Dk in event of conflict are dashed when Sweden eventually declines to sign treaty. Friends of Gr gather at his home to honour his eightieth birthday (8 September) and establish annual gathering which subsequently takes formal shape of *Vennemøderne* (The friends' meetings) and continues until his death in 1872.

1864   When new constitution comes into force, 1 January, Prussia and Austria deliver ultimatum demanding its immediate suspension. Dk's first minister, D. G. Monrad, attempts to win time but on 1 February army of 57,000 Prussians and Austrians invades Slesvig from Holsten. Series of battles goes tragically badly for Dk. International conference in London eventually leads to signing of peace-treaty in Vienna (30

October), by terms of which Dk loses Slesvig, Holsten and Lauenburg. Dk's territory and population are both thereby reduced by roughly one-third, and psychological effect of losses is profound. First folk-highschool in Norway is established by Herman Anker and Olaus Arvesen. First International (International Workingmen's Association) is formed in London.

1865   Following calamitous outcome of war, D. G. Monrad, having resigned July 1864, emigrates to New Zealand. Folk-highschool originally established in Rødding, North Slesvig, to uphold Danishness is closed, but re-inaugurated in Askov, Jylland. Between now and 1869 some 53 similar highschools on Grundtvigian principles are established, and movement extends to Norway and Sweden. *Dansk Folketidende* (Danish folk-news), weekly journal edited by Sofus Høgsbro with support from Gr, is launched, reflecting political agenda of Liberal (*Venstre*) grouping. Constitutional issues, including reactionary bid to return to form of absolutism, continue to dominate politics. Deputation of loyalists from Prussian-annexed Slesvig is warmly received at open-air gathering in Dyrehaven, Copenhagen.

1866   Gr enters upper house (*Landsting*) of parliament. After major struggle, including Gr's failed last minute bid to persuade King Christian ix against signing bill, Constitution of 1849 is revised so as to place the greater landowners, king's appointees and conservatives in permanent majority in upper house, though *folketing* is little changed; *Danmarks riges gjennemsete grundlov* (Revised Constitution of the Kingdom of Dk) *af 28. juli 1866* remains in force until overturned 1901. Establishment in Ryslinge of first *valgmenighed* (congregation opting to elect and pay own pastor but remaining within established Church), though at odds with law. Heathland Reclamation Association (*Hedeselskabet*) is formed on initiative of E. Dalgas, partly to compensate for territorial and population losses following war of 1864. Following war between Prussia (victorious) and Austria, provisions of Treaty of Prague incorporate Slesvig in Prussia but allow for possibility of popular referendum in North Slesvig to decide national affiliation (finally enacted in *Genforeningen* (The reunion) 1920).

1867   Gr suffers another major manic-depressive breakdown on Palm Sunday. His proferred resignation is declined. After convalescence away from Copenhagen he recovers and resumes ministry. Seventeen new highschools are established within the year. Karl Marx publishes first volume of *Das Kapital*.

1868   Law enabling establishment of *valgmenigheder* (congregations within the *Folkekirke* which opt to elect and pay own priest) is passed after bitter dispute. Annual formalised Grundtvigian *Vennemøde* [meeting of friends] is inaugurated (8 September) at Gr's home in Store Tuborg outside Copenhagen, to honour Gr and to debate issues of church and state according to principles of Gr's perception of church, *folkelighed* and historic fatherland. In acknowledgment of economic significance of Dk's trade westwards with Britain and beyond, decision is taken to build deep-water port at Esbjerg in Vestjylland.
    Christian Childhood Teachings (Den christelige Børnelærdom)

1869   D. G. Monrad returns to Dk , is reappointed bishop 1871 and seeks election to Rigsdag 1872 (unsuccessfully, to Gr's great satisfaction). Dk acknowledges cessation of sovereignty over Nicobar Islands (Bay of Bengal) which is forthwith assumed by Britain.

1870   Outbreak of Franco-Prussian war which is over by following year. Gr and his supporters are bitterly disappointed at French failure to deliver crippling blow to increasingly powerful Prussia and open way for restoration of lost duchies or at least implementation of referendum in North Slesvig. Foundation of the United Liberal (*Det forenede Venstre*), grouping in parliament with historical roots in Association of Friends of the Farmers (*Bondevennerne*) and with strong Grundtvigian support. Chresten Kold, educational pioneer of the Danish independent schools (*friskoler*), dies.

   Song-Work or carillon for the Danish Church-School (Sang-Værk til den Danske Kirke-Skole), second part of Gr's *Sang-Værk*, is completed and published, being largely comprised of songs by Gr relating to Biblical and Church history.

1871   Foundation of German Empire with King of Prussia as emperor. Danish literary critic Georg Brandes gives his first highly controversial lectures at Copenhagen University ushering in movement later known as Cultural Radicalism (*Kulturradikalisme*), challenging old cultural and religious order by radical criteria and liberal patterns of behaviour. Long-standing conflict develops between this culturally radical movement and more traditional and conservative Grundtvigianism. Branch of the *Internationale* is established in Dk and socialist agitation advances amongst workforce.

   Church Mirror or Survey of the Course of the Christian Church (Kirke-Speil eller Udsigt over den christen Menigheds Levnedsløb)

1872   Significance of industrialisation in Danish economy is marked by rapid expansion of share-capital principle. In May a socialist-inspired mass-meeting of workers on the *Fælled* (Common, Stray) outside Copenhagen, forbidden by police, nevertheless proceeds; ensuing violence between crowd and police supported by mounted soldiers becomes popularly known as *Slaget paa Fælleden* (The Battle of the *Fælled*). A political gathering of Scandinavian' 'folk-parties' is held at Hammer in Norway (*Hammermødet*), its proceedings followed with interest by Gr, to whom leading politicians report. On 2 September, barely a week before his eighty-ninth birthday, Gr dies suddenly and peacefully at home.

   Brief Writings on the historical Highschool (Smaaskrifter om den historiske Høiskole)
   Old enough have I become now (Gammel nok er jeg nu blevet)

Part one – Grundtvig's memoirs

An autobiographical sketch

1. Papers of Thomas Hansen Erslew; Royal Library
Copenhagen; GEEG Stk. 1, pp. 15-16.

The extract is from a copy of an autobiographical sketch by Grundtvig, preserved among the papers of the biographical scholar Thomas Hansen Erslew (1803-70). Having given it a more formal and less personal tone by making slight alterations (such as removal of reference to the beauty of south Sjælland and the blackness of the Jutish heath and to Grundtvig's burial of his mother, addition of the classification of Grundtvig's *Attestats* examination 1803, and addition of a reference to Grundtvig's *Mands Minde* lectures 1838), Erslew published the text in a fascicule (1843) in his *Almindeligt Forfatter-Lexikon for Kongeriget Danmark med tilhørende Bilande fra 1814 til 1840* [General encyclopaedia of authors for the kingdom of Denmark with appertaining dependencies from 1814 to 1840], vols. 1-6, 1843-68, where it comprises pp. 508-509 of vol.1 (A-J) of the *Lexikon*. By 1840 when Erslew was compiling this volume, Grundtvig already featured in several Danish and German biographical handbooks, notably including Hans Ancher Kofod's *Conversations-Lexicon eller encyclopædisk Haandbog over de i selskabelig Underholdning og ved Læsning forekommende Genstande, Navne og Begreber* etc [Conversation-lexicon or encyclopaedic handbook of subjects, names and concepts occurring in social entertainment and in reading, etc.], XXII, 398-9 (1828); Brockhaus's *Conversations-Lexicon der neuesten Zeit und Literatur* (1833); Christian Molbech's *Dansk poetisk Anthologi* (I-II and IV, 1, 1830-40), IV, 3-30; and the *Conversations-Lexicon der Gegenwort* (1838-41), fascicule 12 (1839). In Grundtvig Arkiv Fasc. 431, 1.a is a printed draft, in French, of a brief and bland biography (1843) of Grundtvig as "Président de la société scandinave" (which he was) and "curé à la cathédrale de Copenhague" (which he was not), together with correspondence relating to the Paris-based Archives Historiques publication, *Inscriptions Historiques des Hommes Vivants*.

[GEEG p. 15] Grundtvig, Nikolai Frederik Severin, was born in Udby near Vordingborg in lovely South Sjælland (8 September 1783) where his parents were clergy-folk: Johan Grundtvig (son of O. Grundtvig, priest on Sejerø) and Kathrine Marie Bang (daughter of *kammerraad* N. Bang of Egeberg in Odsherred), but aged nine years he went over to Jylland's black heathland where (1792-98) he grew up with the priest L. Feld in Thyregod, amused himself among the Jutish peasants, the bees, Hvitfeld's Chronicles, Holberg's Church History, comedies and Niels Klim, *A Thousand and One Nights* and an annual trip back home. In two years he went through the top form in Aarhus Latin school, under [Thure] Krarup and [Jens] Stougaard, and strove to drive away the boredom by writing verse and by reading in the Chronicles of Charlemagne and of Holger Dansk and in [P. F.] Suhm's book on Odin. He took the first examination (1800) and the Theological *Attestats* (1803) in Copenhagen, but could not bear to listen to any lecture-series to the end apart from his cousin H. Steffens's on Goethe's poetry, and only because of the Bornholmer P. N. Skougaard did he become familiar with [Anders Sørensen] Vedel's Saxo, [Peder] Clausen's Snorro and [Bertel Christian] Sandvig's Edda and the Real Presence of an Icelandic book-treasure from the Middle Ages. Later (1805-08) he was resident tutor on Langeland at the lovely Egelykke (at Captain Steensen Leth's), and here the die was cast for the whole of his future in intellectual intercourse with Shakespeare, Goethe, [Friedrich] Schiller and [Adam] Oehlenschläger, [Johan Gottlieb] Fichte, [Henrik] Steffens and [Friedrich] Schelling. At Valkendorfs Kollegium (1808-11) "Hersleb-and-Sibbern"[1] treated him with unforgettable friendship, and through them he was introduced to N. Treschow, G. Sverdrup and the brothers Ørsted, but with his 'Dimis-Prædiken' [probational sermon] he quite unexpectedly stirred up a row with the capital's clergy, [**GEEG p. 16**] which had an incalculable influence upon his ensuing career and gave it, for the time being, a gloomy hue and a skewed direction. Only with much difficulty, through the help of the old Bishop [Nicolaj Edinger] Balle, did he become personal curate to his father (1811-13) who, after all, was by then a jubilarian, and for a long time afterwards (1813-21), could not, even by grace of the King, acquire any ecclesiastical appointment but led a kind of eremitic life in the capital among the books and a few good friends such as F. V. Treschow and B. S. Ingemann. Then (1821), without applying, he was nominated priest in Præstø, where he interred his mother, but in accordance with his own wish was moved (1822) to become resident curate at Frelserens Kirke in Christianshavn and there he worked until, in connection with his prosecution for *Kirkens Gjenmæle* (1826) he resigned his office and on the same occasion came under police censorship, the grievousness of which, even for the most unoffending writers, he, from ten years experience, thoroughly got to know. By the ever-constant grace of Frederik the Sixth he meanwhile not only retained the royal pension he had enjoyed (since 1818) as a national writer but was also supported by His Majesty for three journeys to England (1829-31), with special regard to the Anglo-Saxon manuscripts in London, Exeter, Oxford and Cambridge, where he got to know civic and academic life from (for him) a brand-new angle. With royal permission he subsequently (1831-39) became the *free* evensong-preacher at Frederiks Kirke in Christianshavn, and (1839) priest at the Hospital of the Holy Spirit or Vartou, as well as (1840) Knight of Dannebrog. From (12 August) 1818 he has been married to Elisabeth Christine Margrethe Blicher (daughter of *Provst* D. N. Blicher of Gunslev on Falster) and they have three children together, two sons and one daughter.

N. F. S. Grundtvig.

1. S. B. Hersleb (1784-1836) and F. C. Sibbern (1785-1872); hyphenated together into a unit to indicate the closeness and solidarity of their friendship together and with Grundtvig at that time.

Childhood and early youth

2. Grundtvig's Diary, reworked version (1804); Grundtvig Arkiv Fasc. 497; GEEG Stk. 2, p. 17; US I, p. 13.

On 28 November 1802, while studying at the University, nineteen-year-old Grundtvig began to keep a diary, which he prefaced with a summary review of his life to date, written as though an account of a third person, Frederik (the name by which he was known to the family). He referred to it as his *curriculum vitæ*. The surviving fragmentary portions of this diary are preserved in Grundtvig Arkiv Fasc. 496. From 27th to 29th May 1804 he revised the *curriculum vitæ* of 1802, preserving intact the prefatory poem (*Hvad er en Dag?*), and added a selection of the more important entries from that earlier diary, covering the years 1802-03. The reworked text thus produced is in Grundtvig Arkiv Fasc. 497 from which the following extract and a number of subsequent extracts are drawn. Grundtvig maintained the diary, albeit irregularly, through 1804-07, using it as a commonplace book in which, for example, to note and often quote from his reading (such as Holberg's epigrams, and Icelandic poetry and sagas). The reworked sections in particular display the young Grundtvig's literary aspirations. In referring to himself in the third person (correcting his text when he has inadvertently slipped back into I-narrative) and in setting up a "dear Reader" he creates scope for an amusing, detached (though usually affectionate) irony around the figure of Frederik and for a witty, irreverent attitude towards the solemnities (for example, of the educational process) through which Frederik is milled as his world grows wider and he passes from childhood to adolescence and early manhood. Other entries in the diaries are shorter or longer *tours de force* in the rhetoric of (often desperate) romantic passion; but to recognise that Grundtvig has opened himself to the influence of the writers he was reading over this period is in no way to demean the integrity of the experiencings he narrates; indeed, the varying degrees of rhetorical investment he makes in various narrations help more clearly to reveal to the reader (as good autobiographical writing should) the complex, and the complexity, of motivations (one of which is actually the desire to become a writer) that govern the subject's life.

———

[GEEG p. 17] Of what went on until his fourth year Frederik himself knows nothing. Presumably like others he got the stick and sugar-candy, though hardly indiscriminately, if he knows his mother aright. The said mother kept the old-fashioned custom of herself teaching her children to read. So Frederik too had to get going, but he could not be bothered to get to know his letters; he would rattle them off by rote well enough, but no more. Spanking was the order of the day; and he distinctly recalls that the letter O was close to earning him a whacking, had not a peasant turned up at that moment and a good friend in the meantime whispered a kindly deception in his ear.[1] *Per varios casus, per tot discrimina rerum* [Through various mishaps, through so many crises[2]] he at length learned his letters.

He is supposed to have regarded spelling as beneath his dignity and never to have given others time to persuade him to it. He had no siblings at home except for a slightly older sister. He could never find himself in agreement with her, and as the weakest he would get away with the advantage. This he sees as one of the most important reasons why he turned to reading, since he had never otherwise been any good at doing things with his hands, except turning pages. He now read a whole heap, of which he understood nothing, such as [Ludvig] Holberg's Church History, [Claus Christoffer] Lyskander's Genealogy of Danish Kings, etc; for as long as it was a book which had something to tell, he was after it like the Devil after a soul.

1. The Danish *veninde* signifies that the friend was female, presumably Grundtvig's sister, Ulrikke Eleonora, one year older than he, who benignly taught him to cheat by whispering "a kindly deception" [*en god Djævel*; literally, a good devil] in his ear.

2. Vergil, *Æneid* I, 204; the sentence, from the heroic speech of Aeneas to his demoralised men shipwrecked in Carthage and losing confidence in the vision of a new Troy, concludes *tendimus in Latium* [we progress towards Latium].

3. Mands Minde (1838, 1877): Grundtvig's draft for the second lecture; Grundtvig Arkiv Fasc. 359.1, 2; GEEG Stk. 3, pp. 17-18; MM p. 529.

The work from which this passage (and a number of following passages) is excerpted holds an important place in Grundtvig's authorship for several particular reasons. When he lost the lawsuit brought against him by Professor H. N. Clausen in 1826 lifelong censorship was imposed upon him. Though only rarely, in practice, was this more than a tedious formality (requiring him to submit proposed publications for the *imprimatur* of the Chief of Police), it was a relief to him and his supporters when in 1837 the situation was reviewed and the penalty lifted. It was to some extent in celebration of a restored personal freedom (though censorship remained a powerful instrument of the *enevælde* [absolute monarchy] until abandoned under the 1849 Constitution) that Grundtvig undertook preparation of a series of fifty-one public lectures, delivered to ever-increasing audiences at Borchs Kollegium in Copenhagen over the second half of 1838. The lectures, comprising a personal review of historical events in his own lifetime (he was then in his fifty-fifth year), were hugely successful in tacitly defining an ideal of Danishness which caught the enthusiasm of a new young generation of Danes, many of whom would become leading figures in Danish public life over the following years. "If, as we all hope and believe, a genuine Nordic *folkeliv* [national life] comes to be developed amongst us, we know this: Grundtvig was one of its great awakeners, just as he was its visionary." declared Frederik Hammerich from the rostrum after the final lecture, while Frederik Barfod (like Hammerich, then in his twenties), adding his vote of thanks, exclaimed: "We have seen a glimpse of Valhall! for does he not stand here before us, who pledged himself in order to lay in chains darkness and the children of darkness, Valhalla's most vicious foes, prejudices and a thrall-born faith in the wondrous saving powers of foreign gods – of Latin, German and French? Yes, gentlemen! we have seen a glimpse of Valhalla, a colossal glimpse!" (narrated by Rönning, VI, 205-6). The lectures are also important as autobiographical material for it is Grundtvig's express purpose to recount history as it impacted upon him both materially and spiritually. He lectured from his own handwritten drafts and notes. The lectures were not published in printed form until an edition was undertaken by Svend Grundtvig in 1877, five years after Grundtvig's death. The title is essentially Grundtvig's own, being written on the first lecture and elsewhere, though in the hyphenated form *Mands-Minde*.

This excerpt, recalling the young Grundtvig's dawning awareness of the outside world, and of history in the making, is from the draft of the second lecture (Svend Grundtvig usefully included a selection of Grundtvig's draft versions [*Udkastene*] in *MM*, Tillæg [Supplement], 505-596) and its style may be compared with the effect of vivid immediacy conveyed in the finalised version briefly excerpted in item 4.

⌒

It was [...] in the severe winter of [seventeen] eighty-eight and nine in the last century [...] that I first became aware of what was going on in the world outside the quiet village parsonage where for me – once I had made the giant step I almost never accomplished: of learning letters – everything went its even, orderly way except when I joined battle with my sister (naturally, by the way, my firm friend). What first awakened me, about half a century ago now, [**GEEG p. 18**] from my deep unconcern for the big world was in itself a very small circumstance, namely a loud outburst from our part-educated parish clerk[1] who used to come over to the parsonage of a Sunday afternoon and read the newspapers, and who now made known to all that the Russians had taken Oczakov by storm and would be in Constantinople before Easter. If the parish clerk's or the journalist's prophecy had been fulfilled then perhaps I would have continued to afford the activities of the great powers a little attention; but now, though I registered an impression of the parish-clerical outburst so that I can still almost hear it, yet I soon forgot both Russians and Turks in favour of a copper coin on the beautifully frosted windowpanes, a game of *Hanrej* or whatever other domestic events occupied me during the peace.

1.   Christian Valdemar Nohr.

4. Mands Minde (1838, 1877); GEEG Stk. 4, p. 18; MM, p. 16.

See the first paragraph of the headnote to item 3, to which this is a supplementary anecdote.

Here it was neither the parish clerk nor the Russian or Oczakov but *Easter* and *Constantinople* which struck me and wakened in the country parson's child a vivid image of a "joyous celebration" and a victorious entry into "the infidels' capital," an image which, like bathing oneself in the River of Life as it is found in a child's Paradise, was in a way imperishable, so that after the course of fifty years it is just as fresh as though it had first been born this evening.

See the first paragraph of the headnote to item 3. This passage, continuing Grundtvig's account of his earliest erratic acquisition of historical awareness, well illustrates the tone of light irony characterising the lectures.

⌒

When I now recollect to myself how, down here in South Sjælland, I first became aware of what was going on in France and especially in Paris, then I find that it happened rather late – not before the new French army was standing at the frontiers ready for the fray, under Lafayette, Luckner and Rochambeau, that is, in 1791; for though I told you that the capture of Oczakov by storm and even more the prophecy of the Russians' entry for Easter in Constantinople suddenly moved me to set up a small Foreign Department in my brain, yet when I heard nothing about the prophecy coming to fulfilment it was inevitably the case with me as we read every moment in the newspapers about much different – clever and political – folk: I occupied myself with matters that had only local interest […] Although I cannot promise you anything very interesting from my little village, yet the revolution there made a much more vivid and lasting impression upon me than the entire French one; and, just for once I think, you can [**GEEG p. 19**] bear to hear a short description of it, since basically one can just as well see one's reflection in what the peasant girls call a 'Sunday-eye' as in a floor-to-ceiling mirror.

In the severe winter of '88 there in fact came a new schoolmaster[1] to our village, who occasioned a complete revolution, not only in my little brain but even more in the old people's; for hitherto even the parish-clerk had been called "*Mosjø*" [Monsieur] and the schoolmaster did not come into account at all unless he had talents of his own either as a teller or an auctioneer, etc; but the new schoolmaster was an old *attestatus* who for many years had been a French language teacher in the capital, so that he became "*Herre*" [Sir] right away without the parish-clerk daring to grumble, since he was unwilling to hear that despite the preliminary examination which he had, he was an idiot and a dolt. This retired French teacher was in fact as complete a Jacobin as he could be, being born in Fyn, and was so enthusiastic [*sværmede*] for his own liberty that he never took time to think about that of others; but it was a matter of pride to him that he had scolded counts and barons alike and had said to a professor, who, into the bargain, was pro-Chancellor: "Thou whited wall!"[2] So naturally he was jubilant over the outbreak of the Revolution, but I hardly paid any attention to this before he came over to squabble with the parish-clerk over the likely outcome of the war; it was then I first noticed that the whole world was in commotion, so I too must be involved; and from that time I began to read Berling's newspaper, for the time being on the parish-clerk's side, partly because the revolutionary schoolmaster seemed to me half mad, and partly because I had read that in ancient days the Franks had been nasty to the Visigoths who, though distantly, were of our family.

1. Bertel Faurskov.

2. Faurskov was casting himself in the role of St Paul in Jerusalem who (Acts 23:1-5) rebuked the high priest Ananias for ordering him to be struck on the mouth: "(3) Then said Paul unto him, God shall smite thee, thou whited wall: for sittest thou to judge me after the law, and commandest me to be smitten contrary to the law?" (King James Bible).

6. Grundtvig's Diary, reworked version (1804); Grundtvig
Arkiv Fasc. 497; GEEG Stk. 6, pp. 19-20; US I, pp. 13-14.

On the source, see the headnote to item 2. Grundtvig here recalls the beginnings of what, by the time of writing, further experience had consolidated into an entrenched resentment of rote learning unmediated by any enlightening dialogue with the teacher. Nevertheless the foundations of a lifelong engagement with history, particularly world (or universal) history, were perhaps being laid at the same time.

In the year 1789 – no doubt – he began attending school, with a schoolmaster, newly arrived in the village, by the name of [Bertel] Faverskov, about 60 years old. He was by the way *Cand. S. S. Minist.*, had been tutor at *Grev* [Count] Ahlefeld's, Norwegian post-courier [*Norsk Post-fører*[1]], etc, etc, etc. Here he [Frederik] was to start learning Latin; he learnt Donatus, Aurora together with *colloqvier* [colloquies], a certain amount of a small dictionary and [Jacob] Baden's Grammar by rote, but did not understand a word of it because the deeply learned preceptor explained almost nothing, and if he did, he never lowered himself to his capacity to understand. Sometimes he would ask where the subject or the predicate lay in a sentence, without having imparted to him the slightest idea of what these things were. [**GEEG p. 20**] Here he also laid the foundations of his handwriting; how this went he does not need to say: these crows' claws themselves bear witness to it. From all that by-rote nonsense Frederik had no other benefit than that his memory was sharpened at the expense of his judgment, if one wants to call that beneficial. Meanwhile he read [Abraham] Kall's History of the World, and that was good, because it ought to be taught before one's judgmental ability begins to sprout. So it went on until: [Laurits] Feld, the priest with whom his elder brothers had been[2] (for I was my parents' fourth surviving son) came visiting in 1791 and promised Frederik a silver watch if by next year he could have learnt, in his free time, the above-mentioned book. He learnt it and when Herr Laurits Feld came again in 1792 Frederik's schooltime with Faverskov was at an end and he passed under private instruction with the said Jutlandic priest.

1. Though protected by royal authority and diplomatic agreements, the official carriage of mails outside Denmark in the 18th and part of the 19th century was licensed to contractors. The Norwegian route overland was somewhat bedevilled by touchy relations with Sweden through whose sovereign territory the mails had to pass; and sea-routes, which were in any case hazardous and costly, could also be affected by circumstances of war.

2. That is, they had boarded in Tyregod Parsonage with Laurits Feld (1751-1803) who prepared them for admission to the grammar school.

7. Grundtvig's Diary, reworked version (1804); Grundtvig
Arkiv Fasc. 497; GEEG Stk. 7, pp. 20-21; US I, pp. 14-16.

On the source, see the headnote to item 2. Grundtvig records his early encounter (at Thyregod) with deadening instruction in the sphere of religion as he had already encountered it in the teaching of other such staple subjects of the conventional curriculum as Latin and grammar. At the same time the wider reading permitted by Laurits Feld's liberal-mindedness (or laxity) was, in Grundtvig's retrospective view, all-redeeming.

⁓

Tyregod, whose nearest major town is Vejle, became his new place of residence. Here besides himself were P. H. Balle, a son of the Bishop of Sjælland,[1] who, since he wished it, became a soldier, together with two sons of a *Provst* [Niels Christian] Stjernholm, of which the eldest died in 1793 and the youngest, who had neither desire nor aptitude for study, is now, if I understand correctly, his father's son. Frederik therefore was the only one out of this group who matriculated [*blev Student*], although the eldest Stjernholm lived long enough to arouse his competitive spirit, and the mediocre genius of the younger, whom he (F.) had as companion over four years, afforded him (F.) the opportunity of repeating everything he had read.

Frederik now progressed with slow but sure steps and regrets nothing of the time he spent in Tyregod, except that which was squandered on chewing over, *usque ad infinitum* [interminably], the Catechesis, [Ove Jørgensen Høegh-] Guldberg's revealed theology[2] and everything connected with this commonsense-destroying apparatus. But he does not say this to disparage Hr. [Laurits] Feld, far from it. As a priest and as one who had studied Theology in times of high orthodoxy he was bound to believe it beneficial that his pupils should be secured against heresy, and he believed besides that the reading and learning of these books would be put to the test if he should at some time get into a grammar-school. That he was not mistaken, the following will demonstrate. Even though he himself was rather zealously orthodox yet tolerance was a chief trait in his character. "I have myself experienced doubt," he would often say, "therefore I sympathise with and do not despise those in doubt." Neither did he himself avoid heretical writings like the plague nor, which was even more remarkable, did he hide [**GEEG p. 21**] them from Frederik. No, far from it: he was in a reading-circle, and everything that arrived Frederik was allowed to read. Thanks be to him for this! Here was originally sown the seedling of a never-dying (until it should die together with his mental faculties or with his own self) lust for learning. He admired the authors of everything witty which then, in that golden age of the freedom of the pen, came out: the writings of a [Peter Andreas] Heiberg, a [Knud Lyhne] Rahbek, an M. C. Bruun whose *Aristokraternes Katekismus* [Aristocrats' Catechism] he greatly loved in as far as it was political, T. C. Bruuns *Særsyn* and all that had to do with those geniuses and products of genius which Denmark boasted from '93 to '98. Meanwhile Frederik steadily grew strongly orthodox, first because his faculty of judgment still lay dormant, secondly because he was early made aware that the mysteries were not the subjects of our knowledge but of faith. He found it so natural to believe in God, so shameful to cast doubt upon what he to whom we owe all had spoken to us as truth, that he was keenly vexed over the faithless endeavours of the neologists, and promised within himself that he would one day become one of the sturdily striving champions of the faith, and was already practising. Thus he recalls, after reading Bruun's *Særsyn*, having started upon something that was in rhyme – for from early on he was a rhymster, though without letting any human eye light upon his productions.

Yet, however, there expressed itself in the boy a certain spirit of contradiction. With his teachers – who treated him in the most friendly manner and readily teased out his opinion in order to teach him to think – he often contended in Religion. He still recalls the Fall and human Free Will as points of dispute. Frederik could not understand why God created humankind when he foresaw its fall; and Free Will appeared to him in Dogmatics altogether too restricted, which is why he asserted that, were it not otherwise, Man had no will at all. I Corinthians 15:28[3] caused Frederik much fruitless headache since he wished that this passage of Scripture should harmonise with the doctrine of the Trinity. But he never asked his teachers about this, because he would never have tampered with so fundamental an article.

1. Bishop Nicolaj Edinger Balle (1744-1816).

2. It is unclear here (though hardly important) which Grundtvig intends: the subject or the actual title of the book, *Den aabenbarede Theologi* [Revealed Theology; 1773], in which Høegh-Guldberg (1731-1808) expounded his theology.

3. I Corinthians 15:28 reads: And when all things shall be subdued unto him, then shall the Son also himself be subject unto him that put all things under him, that God may be all in all (King James Bible). The young Grundtvig evidently understood the text as contradicting the theological doctrine of the co-equal status of the Three Persons of the Holy Trinity as stated in the Athanasian Creed: And within this Trinity none comes before or after; none is greater or inferior, but all three persons are coequal and coeternal, so that in every way, as stated before, all three persons are to be worshipped as one God and one God worshipped as three persons.

8. Mands Minde (1838, 1877); GEEG Stk. 8, p. 21 (extended); MM, pp. 442-43.

See the first paragraph of the headnote to item 3. In his *Mands Minde* lecture of 14 November 1838, Grundtvig begins by correcting (not without the usual ironical tone) his own lapse in his previous lecture when he compared the industriousness of the English to that of an ant-hill – which simile, he now says, might well have suited the industriousness of Holland, but not of England. Instead, he finds a more appropriate metaphor in the bees of Jylland's heather-clad heath. The passage affords a striking if minor example of how Grundtvig, in *folkelig* fashion, drew upon the lessons of his own life to illustrate larger matters.

[…] The simile was not only […] very low, but much too low for others than those who, as [Ludvig] Holberg says, live below the sea[1] which, conversely, Englishmen quite literally fly over; so it must always be something flying and not something creeping that one compares the English with, if the simile is not to be as ill-suited as honour-impugning; so I myself am surprised that I could be so thick-headed (*stupid*)[2] as not to see at the time that England's everyday industriousness is naturally mirrored by bees – these marvellous insects which from my childhood I have loved as much as I hated the others. Yes, gentlemen, doubtless not all of you have been as intimate with bees from your childhood as I, among whose greatest amusements on the brown heathland it belonged to watch them migrate and watch them swarm; but we all know that the bee distinguishes itself above the ant not only by flying but – by building for itself and gathering in for its own benefit – it also toils for mankind and renders an historic yield; and precisely thus does English industriousness distinguish itself above that of Holland or the Netherlands.

1. Grundtvig refers of course to the inhabitants of the Lowlands, whose dykes hold back the sea.

2. The English word is included in parenthesis in the (Danish) printed text.

9. Sermon in Frederiks Kirke, New Year's Day 1834; Danske Kirketidende 1874, cols. 1 -2; GEEG Stk. 9, p. 22.

Though its topic here is a recollection from his young years at Thyregod Parsonage, the sermon itself dates from a period when Grundtvig, though still under censorship and still (since his resignation from Vor Frelsers Kirke in 1826) without any formal church appointment, had some grounds for satisfaction in the struggle over church freedoms in which he had increasingly engaged since his visits to England (1829-31). In 1832, after a highly risky contest of wills with the authorities of church and state, he succeeded (in collaboration with J. C. Lindberg, Lorenz Siemonsen and others connected with unlawful religious gatherings defiantly held at Lindberg's home), in wringing permission from them to preach on Sunday evenings in Frederiks Kirke to a free congregation, whilst not being granted the formal incumbency. *De facto*, a link had thus been fractured in the shackles preventing priests and people from forming free congregations within the State Church. In Frederiks Kirke (subsequently refurbished as Christians Kirke) the position of the pulpit, high above the altar (as is the pulpit in Vartov Kirke), symbolises the significance of the sermon in the Lutheran tradition. For Grundtvig in particular the sermon was a means of working out theological ideas and then teaching them by a popular medium. It was also a medium he associated closely with another great medium of expression in Lutheran congregational worship, the hymn. A number of his sermons drew upon the rhetorical register of poetry and became in effect prose-poems; and a number of his own hymns were composed from out of the context of a sermon so that there was potential for a coherent and dynamic interplay between sermon and hymn in the framework of the church service.

It is presumably the 16th c. translation by Rasmus Katholm (d. 1581) of the German hymn by Paul Eber (1511-69) which Grundtvig here recalls. This, and many other "old hymns" from across the Christian world, he found, translated and reworked and put into fresh currency in the service of the Danish congregation, chiefly through his forthcoming *Sang-Værk til den danske Kirke* (1837).

[GEEG p. 22] Among the old hymns which during my adolescence resounded so lively in my ears that they needs must grow old with me, there was also a New Year hymn – to be sure, humble to look at and in many ways only a poor translation of the German, but yet one which, when, as was the custom in the heathlands of Jylland, it was sung at house-prayers on New Year's Eve, cheered me and delighted me more than the best songs I have either heard or seen since. It was just the truth and the simplicity which made the old New Year's hymn so dear to me, when it said at the start:

Guds Godhed ville vi prise,	God's goodness, fain would we praise it,
vi Christne, store og smaa …	we Christians great and small …

and above all when it said at the end:

I Jesu Christi Navn	In Jesus Christ his name
vi bede dig saa saare:	so earnestly we pray thee:
giv os et fredeligt Aare,	a peaceful year do thou grant us
dig til Ære og os til Gavn!	to thy glory and to our gain!

10. Grundtvig's Diary, reworked version (1804); Grundtvig Arkiv Fasc. 497; GEEG Stk. 10, pp. 22-24; US I, pp. 16-19.

On the source, see the headnote to item 2. Grundtvig was admitted to Aarhus Cathedral (Latin, or Grammar) School at Michaelmas (29 September) 1798, in order to be prepared for university entrance. He hoped to be able to complete the *Mesterlektie* syllabus within two years. The *Konrektor* [Deputy Principal] Jens Stougaard was dubious of the youth's capacity to do so, and was inclined to place him in the lowest of the three grades in the *Mesterlektien* (with some 20-25 pupils in the three sections, below which there were also three lower classes, the second, third and fourth *lektien*); but *Rektor* Thure Krarup, after interviewing Grundtvig, deemed him fit to join the middle grade of the *Mesterlektien*. In his determination to prove Stougaard's estimation of him wrong, Grundtvig applied himself hard to his work and justified his place. He joined four other new boys, he being the only one from an 'academic' family – little practical advantage though this perhaps meant, given that he was sent from home as a child of eight, and that his debt-burdened father left his son short of money at school (Grundtvig earned a small *stipendium* – thirty *rigsdaler* in 1799 – to set off against school fees, by enrolling in the cathedral choir). His four fellows were sons of a grocer, a weaver, a hired-cab driver and a cooper. Two of them matriculated with Grundtvig at Michaelmas 1800 and went on with him to Copenhagen University and took the preliminary philosophical examination in April 1801. The social environment is noteworthy: Grundtvig lodged with a cobbler's family; Stougaard himself was a carpenter's son who had been educated at the school through an uncle's benevolence; at one time there was a so-called 'mulatto' in the school from the Danish West Indies. Teaching was both learned and slovenly, discipline both harsh and lax. The Latin garnishings of this passage, so uncharacteristic of Grundtvig, are doubtless meant to reflect, mockingly, the affected latinity of the school; and similarly the image of the partition-wall may reflect the physical partitioning of the ground floor of the school into zones of academic competence.

⌐⌐

The years slipped by. In 1798, in October, Frederik was to go to Aarhus grammar-school [...] With pounding heart he plodded along behind Hr. Feld with his books under his arm to Rektor Thure Krarup who was to examine him and determine his position in the school. This funny old man found that he came out with no more than he could give a good account of, but there were various things which were required in order to be admitted into the top form – and that is where I was supposed to go – which Frederik had never seen, such as Horace's Letters, the fourth book of Ovid, the first book of Cicero, Cicero's Epistles, [Johann Andreas] Danz's *Grammar* and the first four chapters of Genesis. If the Rektor had made a *Fux* [dunce] of him – *ut ajunt* [as they say] – in the lowest division he could really not have complained, but when he found his newly arrived pupil far from being any *hospes* [stranger] to Theology, which he greatly loved, he did not hesitate to place him as a *paries intergerinus* [partition-wall, borderliner] between the middle and the lowest division and to leave it to his industry as to whether he became *Fux* [dunce] of the former or *Dux* [leader] of the latter. Hebrew he undertook *privatim* [privately] to *instruere* [instruct] the fellow in.

Here *Mosjø*[1] Frederik was in a completely new world where at the start he did not particularly enjoy himself because his honest ambition did not permit [GEEG p. 23] him to belong to the lower section and it was hard keeping up with the middle one which for a year had already been scanning Greek and Roman epic, going through Rome's most out-standing speeches and speakers etc. The *Rektor* was well disposed towards him and in those parts he taught he was at home. But the *Konrektor*, Jens Stougaard, made various attempts to move the newcomer into the lowest division. This he did with good intentions, because he believed it better for him, but Frederik's sense of ambition was wounded and he did not soon forgive the worthy teacher this affront. Stougaard soon desisted however, partly when he realised he was not achieving anything, partly because he felt maybe it could turn out alright. In this, it helped that both [Abraham] Kall's World History and [P. F.] Suhm's small Danish History lay *in promptu* [readily to hand] in the archive of my memory. He himself loved history but his pupils were for the most part great ignoramuses in it, because their desire to know the past had never been awakened and probably never could be awakened by Kall's History. This somewhat secured me my teacher's favour.

At Easter 1799 Frederik committed a sin which brought many embarrassments as a consequence. From what little money he owned, ministering spirits had parted him by gam-bling, and now Easter arrived. In Aarhus it was the highly laudable custom that the pupils of the school should make an offering. Frederik owned no more than two Danish shillings. He had heard that the pupils' offering was made in order to set the congregation a good example; he took this exactly according to the letter and thought it was enough if he attended there. So he bought, for half of his fortune, a sheet of paper, divided it into its individual pieces and – made it his offering. There was a bit of an uproar, but – who had done it? Now Whitsunday arrived. Frederik had not become richer, on the contrary, poorer: he had only one shilling, and this he offered – converted into paper. Right enough, he was afraid of discovery, but he pacified himself with the thought: the clergy are after all followers of Jesus; he thought better of the woman who gave her last mite than of the lavish rich; *ergo* [therefore] they must also be pleased when they get everything that I own. Although the premises were correct, the conclusion was a dreadfully fatal error since, after all, the clerical gentlemen could not know whether the Mr Anonymous, who always sealed the envelope, had nothing, really nothing, or whether he meant to play jokes on them. Suffice it to say the facts were discovered. Publicly, the *Rektor* rebuked him; privately, the *Konrektor* interviewed him because he believed that either others [**GEEG p. 24**] had led him astray or else he did have no money. Frederik would not claim the former, because it was untrue, and the latter his pride forbade him to admit – or perhaps it was the awareness that he could have had the necessary money if he had not been gambling which hindered him from throwing the blame upon poverty; he himself believes both things conspired together. But this was the least part of the consequences of the sin. His fellow pupils viewed him almost as a church-robber, a detractor of the sacred, and a cheat. At every opportunity he had to hear this until Michaelmas when those belonging to the senior division left school and he himself came to sit upon the judgment throne.

In the first school examination Frederik took as a *proper* participant he was to some extent reconciled with the *Konrektor* when the latter publicly praised him in front of the exalted Very Reverend personage of that place. Frederik's second and final school-year had now begun. In the previous year he had done little; in this he did less, because his easy comprehension skills and good memory made up for his idleness. We had, for example, six reading preparations a day under the *Konrektor*. Frederik never read more than one of them – *Quintillian* or *Vergil*. He did read Sahl's version of Herodotus while the Latin author was being explicated and the rest he never looked at because he had learnt them with Hr. Feld, and he could rely upon what he had with him from Tyregod. The *Konrektor* tolerated this bad practice because he seldom found him unprepared when his turn came to be examined – because analysis of the Greek language, except for the dialects, was from Tyregod. Nothing further of note occurred except that meanwhile Frederik nevertheless made use of the school's not inconsiderable library: he read, for example, Suhm on Odin, his minor writings, etc. The former especially appealed to him, for which reason he also made a small extract from it for his own use – for he, led astray by [Arild] Hvitfeld, laboured under the false idea that we knew nothing about the mythology of our fathers, something he had always yearned to know.

1. Mosjø: Monsieur, used jocularly.

11. Annotations on a biography in *Conversations-Lexicon der Gegenwort* (1839) in Christian Molbech og Nikolai Frederik Severin Grundtvig. *En Brevvexling (1888); GEEG Stk. 11, pp. 24-25 (extended).*

The correspondence between Christian Molbech (1783-1857) and Grundtvig was collected by Molbech's son, Christian Frederik Molbech, and published by Ludvig Schrøder (1888). Molbech wrote to Grundtvig (3 August 1839) asking him to provide a few lesser-known facts about his life for inclusion in a biographical sketch which Molbech intended to use in the section on Grundtvig in his *Dansk poetisk Anthologie*, vol. IV (published the following year). Molbech mentions that he has just come across the biographical item on Grundtvig in the *Conversations-Lexicon der Gegenwart* (vols. 1-4 published in Leipzig 1838-41), vol.2 (1839). The excerpted passage (p. 219 in Schrøder's edition) is taken from Grundtvig's supplementary comments.

⌣

As empty and colourless as the recollection of my two years in the senior class [*Mesterlectien*; at Aarhus Latin School] is, just as rich and lively do I find, in contrast, that of the six years on the heath [at Thyregod Parsonage]: for the yearly summer-journeys to Udby sustained not only my active connection with the region of my birth and my parental home but widened my field of vision and enlivened my thinking, so that I would wish for all boys in their adolescence such inland journeys both by land and by water, as the best means to that universalism [*Universalisme*] in the home and the mother-tongue which in my view is all, at that age, one should either demand or desire of them. However, if on the whole I have to call my recollection of school-days in Aarhus empty and colourless, there are nonetheless individual exceptions, for in the first winter I regularly spent my evenings giving readings aloud in a little cobbler's workshop in the house where I was lodged, and thereby first learnt to know our old *Almue-bøger* [popular books, folk-books]; just as it [**GEEG p. 25**] was "Suhm on Odin" in the school library which first taught me that the memory of the old gods was far from being as obliterated as Arild Hvitfeld had told me on the Jylland heath.

12. Grundtvig's Diary, reworked version (1804); Grundtvig Arkiv Fasc. 497; GEEG Stk. 12, p. 25; US I, p. 20.

On the source, see the headnote to item 2. Much has been made, in popular accounts of Grundtvig's life, of his unhappiness in the 'black school' at Aarhus; and he himself, when it suited the context, knew how to blacken the reputation of the old curriculum based on Greek, Latin and Hebrew, and the antiquated teaching methods which put a premium upon a good memory and left undeveloped the faculty of judgment and the natural spirit of enquiry. Nevertheless, as this tribute indicates, he met with, and fully appreciated, humane pastoral care and affection among his teachers there, which continued to shape the man he was after his schooldays were over.

⁓

In September 1800 Frederik left Aarhus with a very laudatory testimonial.[1] In October the same year he was examined by the professors. He was declared *laudabilis præ ceteris* [commendable beyond others, distinction] in Latin, and *Laudabilis* [commendable] in the other languages and sciences except for Hebrew, in which he was adjudged *haud illaudabilis* [not uncommendable], and I reckon *haud* could well be deleted. Frederik was a duffer at reading Jewish [*Jødelæsning*] even though [Thure] Krarup, who was no mere dabbler in the Lord's own language, had worked hard upon him.

Before I go further I would like to glance back to Frederik's valediction from Aarhus; and he admits that the *Konrektor*'s oral was to him many percent more precious and more efficacious than the *Rektor*'s written.[2] Anyone who saw the former's eye glisten with tears whilst in the strongest terms he reminded his departing disciple of what his duties and his well-being demanded of him, anyone who heard him warn against the temptations of the King's and the vices' capital city which he had so often painted in the most vivid colours, would have to assume [Jens] Stougaard to be what he is: his disciples' nurturing father more than their strict teacher. And anyone who stood before him, who was now the object of his emotion and affectionate admonitions as previously of his teaching, would have to be worse than anyone at that age, except by great effort, can be, if he did not blush at the thought of having failed to appreciate this noble man and having sometimes done what lay within his small power to annoy him; or if there had not been laid down in his soul the enduring foundation of a warm reverence and an unfeigned veneration for this man who as it were extended his guiding hand in order to be of still further use beyond his own circle; or if he were not filled with the eager intention to prove good and capable and not to disappoint the hopes and wishes of such a man who had only pure humanity at heart and his disciple's true well-being as his goal. Nay, noble Stougaard! so despicable Frederik was not: often has his remembrance of you strengthened him against temptations, often has it called him back to the path of virtue when at times he has, alas, strayed from it.

So now Frederik was a *Student*.[3]

1. The testimonial, published by Vilhelm Grundtvig (*Gads danske Magasin*, 1928, 175 ff.; and *Arosia*, 1928, 38 ff.), mentions that Grundtvig the young man has, "by successfully developing that fortunate intellectual aptitude which has been his portion, truly contributed more than the early performance of the boy to a later reputation which grew with his age."

2. The *Rektor* [Head] was Thure Krarup, the *Konrektor* [Deputy Head] was Jens Stougaard. Appointment to the posts of *Rektor* and *Konrektor* in Latin Schools was formally in the hands of the monarch.

3. In the Danish sense, meaning that having been examined and satisfactorily passed by "the professors" at the University (not until 1850 was the university's management of this examination transferred to individual schools in the form of a school-leaving examination) he was now formally qualified to proceed to study at the University of Copenhagen.

Student years in Copenhagen

13. Grundtvig's Diary, reworked version (1804); Grundtvig Arkiv Fasc. 497; GEEG Stk. 13, pp. 26-28; US I, pp. 20-23.

On the source, see the headnote to item 2. Unlike Hans Christian Andersen who similarly arrived in Copenhagen (1819) penurious and proclaiming his provincial origins in dress and speech to the amusement of the sophisticated Copenhageners, Grundtvig, arriving to take up his university place, had family in the city, and like many another poor student (including his friend Christian Molbech) could bank on regular free meals from relatives and family friends, eked out with foodstuffs sent from home. Nevertheless the experience of being made to feel a cloddishly provincial outsider by urbane city and university folk whom he did not wholly respect evidently rankled more than a little; but like Andersen he would rise triumphantly above his disadvantaged beginnings.

⁓

[GEEG p. 26] For the first half year, except for a month when he was with his father and his brother Otto, priest at Torkilstrup on Falster, he resided in Copenhagen in order to prepare himself for the philosophy examination. He was not industrious, played cards and *Gnav* quite a bit, and much frequented public places, though without sacrificing there to Venus or Bacchus so that it had damaging consequences solely for his purse which that winter was in the best circumstances it had ever known; for I had about twenty *rigsdaler* a month, free dinners, and dry foodstuffs from home. No wonder then that I had little time to achieve much. My father had previously spent ten years in a small living, had expended a lot on his parsonages, and I was the fourth son he had allowed to study: understandable therefore why his financial circumstances were poor. My secure income amounted to two *rigsdaler* from my father, two from my brother Otto, two from my former teacher Hr. [Laurits] Feld, and two from my very rich maternal uncle Captain [Carl Vilhelm] Bang, monthly. My other maternal uncle, Professor [Frederik Ludvig] Bang, gave me dinner at his house [...].

... And there [Frederik] experienced his most tedious hours, not only at first but constantly. The reasons were various. He will give some as a sample. When he came from town in Jylland to town in Sjælland, his wardrobe was in a very parlous condition, to put it bluntly. On the quiet, I can easily give an inventory because I know it: he had (1) a blue homemade tailcoat with a Jutish cut – this, like a general, has to stand in the vanguard and show off a bit because, between the two of us, it was his only intact overcoat; (2) An old yellow one, with ditto, which was too skimpily cut at backside and elbows; (3) A red-spotted cashmere waistcoat which served him nigh on three years as its second owner; (4) A pair of black trousers, turned and threadbare, also darned on the one knee; (5) a homemade jacket which had been brown of which the arms *in genere* [in general] witnessed that there had been dust on the school-table and grease on his own, and of which the elbows *in specie* [in particular] with abundant testimony – sewn-on patches – confirmed that its owner had followed the highly laudable custom of adding buttresses – *ut ajunt* [as they say] – to a new house. Now add to this a black tail-coat and ditto waistcoat both of which had for a long time [**GEEG p. 27**] clothed his father's torso, and now for two years – every Sunday and at other solemnities – his, along with a pair of well-greased leather trousers;[1] and now consider that the unenumerated articles, along with jacket, the yellow and black tail-coat, were quite unusable, then you have a wardrobe which the blessed Diogenes would not have been ashamed of, and the usable part of it would certainly never – not, at least, for its showiness – attract attention. Now imagine to yourself a person – for convenience you can take the one just mentioned – in this dress coming tramping in with a pair of durable square-toed boots, into a circle of perfectly (in metropolitan fashion) well-dressed people and if you do not have much partiality for viewing comic situations you will not ask for any more laughable figure to be sketched out for your imagination.

Now turn Hr. Frederik round to a different angle and you will see that with this reorientation – he gains very little. Here you find a person, seventeen years old, who through eight years' dwelling in *Jydepot*-land[2] has gathered that knowledge which is required for Academia, whose intellect cannot exactly be called entirely uncultivated and who has acquired an interest in and a passion for the fine arts, but you will also find a person void of all that outward culturedness which everywhere commends one but which especially in Copenhagen families cannot be dispensed with by anyone who is to be acceptable. Do not forget that a goodly share of shyness hindered him from allowing the little internal culture he possessed from making its way out into the exterior personality. Remember! that every word he spoke had to expect criticism from the positively and negatively witty fellows amongst whom he found himself – even if only because they were dragged forth in a Jutish dialect which was not free from a certain jarring effect. What wonder if this deprived him of all courage to try an approach to the conversational tone of those more fully endowed creatures?

In short, he could not but believe that there was a whole world as a dividing-wall between them and him. From this it followed that in this house Grundtvig – I do not dare to call him Frederik now that he is become a student – must seem to each and every one like a lump of wood whose big protruding knots had never been removed by the broad-axe and that they therefore let the smoothing-plane of their mouth glide across his knotty form, not so much to attempt the impossible and seek to shape a person after their own likeness as to let him feel – if he could feel anything – how far he was beneath them. Hardly strange if, in consequence of this treatment, Grundtvig became – at [**GEEG p. 28**] least ostensibly – what he was seen as being: a clod. He appeared like an old folio volume which as it were assiduously traps the dust between its leaves whilst one dusts its edges. It was not because he believed he needed no polishing but because the way in which it was applied did not suit his character. To be sure, his polishers could not do anything about that – no, had he known how to take advantage of the treatment he got, he could really have become quite a lad in the fashionable world. The weapons were given into his hands: if only he had been willing to pay heed to the slaps he received on the one day, then on the following – since it was the *loci communes* [the local mode of discourse] – he could have applied them, to the enchantment of his instructors and instructresses. But to take witticisms on credit seemed to him an affidavit of stupidity and to borrow unwitty crudities and offer them back as it were in return for the food he received struck him as not only stupid but also bad, for he believed that he who is condemned to live off charity must practise self-denial.

All this meant that Grundtvig remained the person he was. One thing only he changed. He got himself such clothes as he need not, according to his status, be ashamed of.

1. "*et par dygtig fittede skindbukser*" – Museum experts confirm that at this time a young man from the country might have worn leather breeches which were periodically deliberately greased (*fittede*; modern Danish *fedtede*), in order to maintain their suppleness. More probably, Grundtvig's trousers were shiny with the grease and dirt which leather garments might naturally acquire with age; but either way, they were a conspicuous and embarrassing sign of an impoverished rural or provincial background.

2. *Jydepotters Land* is Jylland (Jutland) – a *Jydepot* being a Jutlander.

14. Grundtvig's Diary, reworked version (1804); Grundtvig Arkiv Fasc. 497; GEEG Stk. 14, p. 28 (extended); US I, p. 24.

On the source, see the headnote to item 2. A few months after Grundtvig's arrival in the University, a volunteer student militia, *Kronprindsens Livcorps*, was formed against the threat of a British sea and land assault upon Copenhagen in the course of the Napoleonic war, which culminated in the battle of Reden (in English naval annals, the battle of Copenhagen), April 1801. Though royal gratitude was expressed for their loyalty the students were never engaged in the action – and in this account Grundtvig is not slow to see the absurd side to his military adventurism. The exciting distraction unfortunately coincided with Grundtvig's examinations. The most significant outcome for him was probably the formation of his friendship with Peter Nikolai Skovgaard (1783-1838), as mentioned further below.

⌐⌐⌐

After having thus long looked upon Grundtvig as completely passive it is surely time also to view him as active – for he was in certain ways a *deponens*.[1] In Spring 1801, along with the other students, he took up arms. Here I am reminded of the following verse from an old folk-song:

Der var engang en Hare,	Once on a time a hare was,
Den vænte sig til Fare,	that lost its fear of danger:
Thi den vild' op i Herrefærd	for it would fain a-warring go
Og stride med Kong Valdemar	and fight beside King Valdemar,
Den ædelbaarne Herre.	that lord of noble birth.

But let this be without any application! However, this battle-play was responsible for Grundtvig being declared, in April, only *haud illaudabilis* in Mathematics and Astronomy, although since [Børge] Risbrigh said he was *laudabilis præ ceteris* and since [Thomas] Bugge and [Anders] Gamborg, except for the *præ*, said the same, he had the majority of votes in his favour and became *laudabilis*.[2]

Without letting himself be impeded by the continuing warlike exercises which Minerva's sons[3] were undertaking, he went home. But, dear reader! – if anyone, as I hope is not the case, gets to see this (but it is good to have someone one can talk to) – you now have before you a heretic. You will probably cross yourself and ask in holy zeal how Satan could achieve anything against one who was so well bedecked with shield and helm against his red-hot arrows? That is exactly what I had almost forgotten to recount. That the Devil is not stupid I do not need to tell you: he foresaw that Grundtvig would be hard on him if he did not manage to seduce him. Now the evil foe knew that the aforementioned person, however orthodox he was, liked to read what was witty, so on Falster[4] he put into his hands T. C. Bruun's *Skriftemaal*[5] and – *proh dolor*[6] – kaput went the orthodoxy. But one could also say a serious word here: Grundtvig recognises the fortunate revolution this book effected within his notions of religion but he believes it would not have been so if he had not come to study theology. However much he wished to be in another discipline, he is nevertheless glad of it in this respect. Now he began the study of theology without prejudice, and could therefore weigh the *pro* and the *contra*; but had he not become a theologian he too would surely have become a Bible-scoffer.

1. The Latin grammatical term for a deponent verb: one which has a passive form but an active sense.

2. In summary, with one examiner awarding *haud illaudabilis* [not uncommendable], one awarding *laudabilis præ ceteris* [commendable beyond the rest; distinguished] and two awarding *laudabilis* without the qualification *prae ceteris* – that is, plain *laudabilis* [commendable] – Grundtvig's final average was a *laudabilis*.

3. Over this period, Grundtvig made various visits to the island of Falster where his older brother Otto was parish priest of Torkildstrup.

4. Minerva was the Roman goddess of wisdom, protectress of teaching, with some of the characterisics of *Victoria*, personification of victory. Her sons, here, are of course the volunteer students.

5. Thomas Christopher Bruun (1750-1834) throughout his writing career flirted unrepentantly with the risk of censorship and other penalties for publications which many thought offensive to public morality, monarchy and religion. Grundtvig himself, who as an undergraduate enjoyed Brun's irreverent wit, later condemned him as a 'Bible-scoffer'). His *Skriftemaalet* [The confession] was published in 1798. See further the Index entry **Bruun,** Thomas Christopher.

6. Latin: Oh woe! The words of Grundtvig's original are: *proh dolor – Kaput var Ortodoxien*.

15. *Mands Minde (1838, 1877); GEEG Stk. 15, pp. 28-29; MM, pp. 530-531.*

See the first paragraph of the headnote to item 3. For Denmark, the naval Battle of Reden (2 April 1801) was in all political reality a humiliation; nevertheless it was successfully represented domestically as a kind of triumph of which one symbol was the heroic defiance displayed by the young Peter Willemoes (1783-1808) towards the attacking British fleet, led by the formidable victor of the recent Battle of the Nile, Nelson. Later, after the second British assault on Copenhagen (1807) and the battle of Sjællands Odde (1808) had stirred him to both anger and pride over the nation's response, Grundtvig was to ensure the Danish sea-hero's fame for ever, in patriotic song; but at the time of the first assault, as a student of the same age as Willemoes, there was little for him to contribute to the national cause (since the student militia was not actually deployed in action) other than refuse to be impressed by the British cannonade, and there was little patriotic zeal aroused either in himself or (he says) in his fellow-countrymen (Willemoes and his heroic companions excepted – whose feat "surprised us just about as much as it surprised the enemy") – as the following laconic reminiscences (15, 17) tell.

⌒

That it takes more than cannon-shots to awaken people I conclude from the fact that I really did listen to them on that famous Second of April with all attentiveness without their once making so enduring an impression upon me as the parish clerk's outburst over the capture of Oczakov or the schoolmaster's jubilation over the French Revolution.[1] To be sure now, this was a big failing in me, whom it had heartily delighted, in Jylland's heath-lands, to hear an ordinary New Year fired in on a simple firearm and who therefore surely ought to have been enthused at hearing a new century, a new World-Year fired in, to the undying honour of my fatherland. But this is one of the greatest delusions of our age, that it can benefit us to know how we and everything *ought to be*, when nevertheless everything *is* very different, [GEEG p. 29] and we have neither desire nor strength nor intelligence to improve it. However bad it was of me, therefore, that I took absolutely no live part in the fatherland's perils, battle and victories, it is nonetheless absolutely true; and as far as I could observe it was much the same with all academic folk, both young and old; for, that a proportion of us young ones would have dared to risk our necks, had there been the opportunity, *that* belongs in the nature of youth as long as there is the slightest strength remaining, and so the zest for a fresh brouhaha is never lacking, nor courage in the face of unknown dangers.

1. Christian Valdemar Nohr was the parish clerk, Bertel Faurskov Grundtvig's schoolmas-
    ter, at Udby. Concerning the impression these two village worthies made upon the child
    Grundtvig's awareness of the great dramas of the outside world, see items 3, 4 and 5.

16. Grundtvig's Diary, reworked version (1804); Grundtvig Arkiv Fasc. 497; GEEG Stk. 16, p. 29; US I, p. 28.

On the source, see the headnote to item 2. Having completed the first part of the second exami-nation at the University of Copenhagen in April 1801, Grundtvig (ill able to afford residential expenses in Copenhagen) went home to stay with his parents in Udby while concentrating on his theological studies – and composing rhyming verse narratives on legendary-historical sub-jects. In late June he returned for a few weeks to Copenhagen with (short-lived) good intentions to attend lectures in preparation for the next batch of examinations. Three decades onwards he is still defensive over his mixed results; but of much greater consequence than these was the formation, that summer, of his lifelong friendship with P. N. Skougaard.

⌒

But to get back to the Persona (again) simply as a person: On the twenty-first of June he went to Copenhagen to let himself be seen in the philological auditoriums; but he never got there, idling the time away until the beginning of August when he went home again.

However, during this stay in the capital the foundation was laid of an acquaintance-ship which he has since steadily maintained with pleasure, with a Bornholm student *cui nomen* [whose name is] Peter Nikolai Skougaard. The reason why this acquaintanceship did not like so many others arise and disappear, from the start lay fundamentally in the fact that Grundtvig loved the history of the North and was therefore extremely pleased to meet one of the few who both loved and knew it. Grundtvig was partly at home, partly on Falster[1] until the beginning of October when he travelled again to the capital in order to submit to the philological test.

So Grundtvig came to Copenhagen, was declared *laudabilis* [commendable] for History, *haud illaudabilis* [not uncommendable] for Greek since he offered two prose but no poetic authors, and *haud illaudabilis* for Latin – something for which he still cannot really forgive Hr. Professor [Jacob] Baden, since he had never been a dunderhead in this language and he had put in a lot of effort on the pieces he offered of Cicero's Epistles and Ovid's Metamorphoses, pieces which more than once exceeded in size the course which the Professor had run through – or rather crept through – during the semester, and which were no less instructive in the language than a Satire of Juvenal, or the *Agricola* of Tacitus. Anyway, he got, as they say, *haud [illaudabilis]* as his final classification.

1. Grundtvig was visiting his older brother Otto, parish priest of Torkildstrup on Falster.

17. Mands Minde (1838, 1877); GEEG Stk. 17, pp. 29-31; MM, pp. 270-272.

See the first paragraph of the headnote to item 3. In this retrospect, Grundtvig recalls a time of comprehensive stultification in Danish life. This he diagnoses as being in part the inheritance from eighteenth century Enlightenment, operative through the baneful effect of the Latin schools; he finds it in the lamentable intellectual torpor of the University, in the people's choice of blinkered lethargy when called to heroism and national pride, even in his own deadened spirit. The stage is set for revival.

I was at the time eighteen years old; and even though until I had [GEEG p. 30]reached fifteen I had more or less preserved, in a corner of the Jylland heath, a lively sense as well for the grand as for the homely and for the natural and the living as a whole, yet in much less than two years the Latin school had transformed me into so cold, self-opinionated and earth-bound a person that I did not even care how it was going with the great conflict I had been following with lively interest literally up to the day I set foot in that witch-cursed Latin school; for to me the battle of Abukir which took place a couple of months previously, I remember clearly, was remarkable in the extreme; but down in the classical tilth I noticed scarcely at all the homecoming of Napoleon or even the battle of Marengo; so in my memory Nelson's exploits at Abukir and at Copenhagen fuse together as though I had slept away the intervening time. And basically that is what I had done; for however our Latin schools might be now, the one I went to was so dull, so empty and boring that I either had to run away from it the day after my arrival or learn to be ashamed of my love of history as a whole and of the fatherland's in particular, indeed of every flicker of spirit and every spark of holy fire that yet existed within me; and though it is to my own lasting shame that I chose the latter, yet it was also a dreadful blindness in our naive fathers who threw us, at the most unstable and dangerous age, into a sphere so hostile to everything natural and living in a loftier sense, so devoid of everything that ennobles, so full of everything that can debase, deaden and deprave a person.

I surely do not need to tell you [...] that it is not the classics and not the involvement with antiquity's foremost monuments that I hereby censure, but only our Latin schools as I have known them, and that scholarship-for-boys [*Drenge-Videnskabelighed*] which is a pestilence to the intellect, because a boy's understanding cannot possibly grasp anything of all that belongs to the intellect and must therefore, when it achieves self-confidence, throw the whole lot away and pride itself in a currish cleverness [*Hundeklogskab*] like that which in the Eighteenth Century was customarily called Enlightenment. With *this* I came in the century's last hour, in October 1800, to the University, and only *this* did I find there, alongside antiquated ingenuousness, and both combined with that intellectual torpor and impotence which just about makes the battle of 2nd April [1801] into one of the greatest marvels in Denmark's and an exceptional event in the whole world's history.

[GEEG p. 31] Despite the fact therefore that precisely this battle in the Kongedyb, so honourable and yet unlucky, cheated if not of the garland then of the fruits, was particularly fitted to fan every slumbering spark of love of the fatherland and to rouse especially the young lads to exert all their abilities, for once to win back for Denmark her lost glory, yet it did not at all have this effect upon me, nor upon my contemporaries nor upon the people as a whole. It was much more the case that the feat surprised us just about as much as it surprised the enemy; and it so far exceeded what we ourselves felt ourselves inspired to that we were glad it had passed off so well that we could now expect peace and quiet in our day just as our fathers, except for these moments, had had in theirs; so that instead of arousing us from our unworthy slumber, the swiftly passing thunder in fact lulled us even more, since it seemed to us proven that we ourselves (with all our fatuity and pettiness) could yet, at whatever moment we wished, measure ourselves in strength and sacrifice along with our most distinguished fathers.

18. Mands Minde (1838, 1877); GEEG Stk. 18, pp. 29-31; MM, pp. 531-532.

See the first paragraph of the headnote to item 3. Grundtvig here recalls the impact of his friendship with P. N. Skovgaard: amid the comprehensive stultification of the times, new motivations stir a new intellectual momentum in Grundtvig.

As soon as the fight was over and peace concluded, everything returned to its usual course, and within my circle it was the most wearisome I can readily imagine, though I had not the slightest reason to believe that, humanly speaking, it was any more amusing outside it; for the revolutionary war was ended with the start of the new century when Napoleon set about giving France a new ruling dynasty whose difference from the old ones would lie chiefly in the name; literature, which had played a lively enough role and afforded me priceless amusement in my youth, among us was completely deceased; the University was stone dead, and I lay [kept residence], as they say, read for one examination after the other and merely wanted it to be over – though without knowing: what then? The only mortal amusement I had was in reading older Danish books (and among the Danish books from the previous century which fell into my hands I found vitality only in [Ludvig] Holberg's, [Johan Herman] Vessel's and [Jens] Baggesen's early works where the jesting is good enough but all of life's serious questions are passed off in jest); in writing bad verse; and in chatting about the warriors of the North with one of Bue Digre's fellow-countrymen and great admirers, a Bornholmer who, to be sure, made fun of my verse and exalted Mathematics to the skies but was a man of honest and robust character who cared nothing for examinations[1] or the daily bread but applied himself life and soul to what he fancied and [GEEG p. 32] was therefore so completely at home in his chosen sphere of knowledge that I could not but help find his company both amusing and instructive in a way different from theirs whom I knew by heart along with my school-books.

1. Peter Nikolai Skovgaard (1783-1838). Skovgaard sat no examination beyond the preliminary philological-philosophical, was harshly punished for publications deemed offensive to the monarchy, exiled from Copenhagen, and after 1807 earned his living as teacher and translator in Aalborg.

19. Mands Minde (1838, 1877); GEEG Stk. 19, p. 32; MM, pp. 272-273.

See the first paragraph of the headnote to item 3. Here Grundtvig pays homage to the memory of Peter Nikolai Skovgaard who had recently died (17 June 1838) in straitened circumstances in Aalborg.

I must therefore call it a stroke of luck that my love of the history of the North awoke again at that time and my real acquaintance with the old gods and heroes of the North was established; for the battle on Kongedybet gave at least the occasion for this, when, in the Studenterkorps [student-corps], I bumped into a Bornholmer of the same age, P. N. Skougaard (subsequently so unfortunate, and recently deceased in the deepest misery); for compared with him it was not, as in Aarhus School, for my strength but for my ignorance in history I had to be ashamed. Saxo and Snorri, the Eddas and the whole range of Iceland's sagas which I knew only by name were a sphere of knowledge in which he moved about as freely and easily as in his own home territory; and though he could not have been less poetically inclined and was heart and soul a mathematician yet the whole of world history was so familiar to him and thus seemed to have been conquered by him like a Napoleon in the world of books, that I had never before so admired anyone; and so I must thank my acquaintance with him not only for my relatively early acquaintance with the antiquity of the North but more broadly for this vivid awareness: that outside the round of examinations there lay a world of knowledge which it was well worth the trouble of travelling. I was thereby saved from the abyss of indolence and boredom into which the pedantry of school and the routine of examinations had come within a hair's breadth of pitching me; and if my life has or shall have any scholarly significance, then that was plainly the key factor – though not however the basis of its strength nor the source of its vitality, for that is alone the spirit [Aanden]; and of spirit my Bornholmer friend had just as little concept as I did, if spirit is supposed to be something other than on the one hand our commonsense and intelligence, and on the other a flashy wit.

20. *Mands Minde (1838, 1877); GEEG Stk. 20, pp. 32-35; MM, pp. 273-276.*

See the first paragraph of the headnote to item 3. On 11 November 1802 Henrik Steffens, Grundtvig's cousin though as yet they were barely known to each other, began a series of lectures at Elers' Kollegium which was in effect an introduction to German Romanticism. His *Indledning til philosophiske Forelæsninger* [Introduction to philosophical lectures] was published in Copenhagen in 1803. Grundtvig refers to the impact of the lectures upon him in his *Verdenskrønike* (1812), 353 ff., and in Letter 523 in *Breve*, vol. 2. Initially the impact, immediate though it was on the poet and dramatist Adam Oehlenschläger, upon Grundtvig himself (and, according to him, upon his fellow students) was slight ("This evening I understood no more than that the lecturer said he would tear down Kant and Fichte and raise himself up on their ruins" [Ieg ikke i Aften forstod meer af end at Docenten sagde han vilde rive *Kant* og *Fichte* ned og hæve sig paa deres Ruiner] (*Dag- og Udtogsbøger*, ed. G. Albeck, vol. 1, 1979, p. 16), but later, at Egeløkke, the ideas of Steffens began to furnish him with a new intellectual framework.

It was in these circumstances within my little circle that Henrik Steffens came to town, after having resided so long in Germany that I at least had quite forgotten that he existed, even though, by the way, I can well remember from my childhood that he showed me pictures in the first perspective-box my eyes ever saw. He was now twenty-eight years old, had been in close connection with the philosopher [Friedrich] Schelling, the authors [Ludwig] Tieck and Novalis [Friedrich von Hardenberg] and the brothers [August Wilhelm and Friedrich] Schlegel, put briefly, with all the leaders of the so-called New School in Germany which had established itself in the very last years of the eighteenth century and here in this country was [GEEG p. 33] known to very few except by rumour – as a raving mad antithesis to the whole of the eighteenth century's Poesy, History, Physics, Philosophy, Theology, Art and Science, and this an antithesis with gigantic strength such as one gains when one loses one's sanity; put briefly: a German revolution in the educated world even more gruesome than the French one in civil society – and this, into the bargain, in direct antithesis to the French, which was presented by the New School as a gross tragicomedy, staged by the inmates of that madhouse which Voltaire and his cronies had built and called the Temple of Wisdom.

 Of all this I however knew nothing, partly because I rarely if ever attended lecture courses, where I had soon learnt what at that age was enough for me – that I was bored; and partly because there was certainly not a hint of such novel goings-on anyway; for in those days our professors only indifferently kept pace with the times, so that our theologians knew but very little about [Immanuel] Kant, and our philosopher [Børge Riisbrigh] confined himself strictly to [Gottfried Wilhelm] Leibniz and [Christian von] Wolff; so most likely it would have turned out for me as for so many of my fellow-students who, when [Henrik] Steffens had gone away again, were hardly aware that he had been here, had not our family connection meant that I saw him frequently and naturally was curious to hear what he had to tell. But this I did not get to know quite so immediately; for besides the dropped-from-the-clouds novelty of the whole of his perception of things and the unillumined destitution in the Latin school, there lay another impediment in his style – rather German in various respects and full of all kinds of art terms I had never seen or heard; but the language he used, the tone he spoke in, the fire he breathed, this struck me at once so that I felt that in the world of the word too there is a heaven-high difference, as between fire and water, so that the enthusiastic word, even if one does not or cannot understand what it has to convey, as long as it has a ring to it, will prevail like a king in the midst of his foes.

Thus I had hereby gained, without being aware of it myself, a vivid conception of spirit and a respect for it as the marvellous life-force of the word whose influence compels us to the conviction that there is, in the invisible, a reality of a higher sort than that we can take hold of and feel, dissect and understand; and although many years were to pass before it made any discernible difference to my view on life and learning, yet this impression of a living word concerning the invisible and the homage to the spirit springing therefrom was evidently [GEEG p. 34] the first, that is to say the great step for me from the eighteenth into the nineteenth century, within the world of the spirit.

But this apart, there was still also something in the Steffens lectures which I, if not wholly then half, understood; which, even if I could not yet appropriate it to myself, still imprinted itself in me for closer contemplation: and this was on the one hand his conception of history as this is found in the Introduction to his philosophical lectures, the only Danish book he has published, and on the other his evaluation of the famous writers of the new age, in a lecture-series on Goethe he never wrote down, let alone had printed.

His historical perception of human life – as divine in its obscure eastern origin; as fallen but yet as though celestially consoled by the Greek Muses and Graces; but crucified by the uninspired, downright ungodly Romans who achieved in Nero, as the ultimate, that devilish perfection they had aspired to and fought for; the resurrection of this life from the dead with Christianity; but resurrection to another world which it could not manage and which therefore could only seem laughable to the ordinary understanding, so that the witty Frenchmen got the whole world on to their side; and now at length the new-German School's serious effort to raise the generation to a higher plane from which antiquity, the Middle Ages and Modernity might be surveyed, the secret connection discovered, and a new construct of the splendours from all ages be prepared – this perception was so free, so new and grand and yet so like our ideas from childhood and the Bible that it could not possibly fail to have its effect upon me at least, could only attract me and eventually take me over.

And then the evaluation of the famous authors, the praise of Shakespeare and Cervantes, Goethe, Tieck and Novalis, whom I did not know at all, praise from such eloquent lips and with an enthusiasm which gave itself the right to a voice about enthusiasm, that necessarily had to engross my attention, and this all the more so because Steffens straightaway gave a good drubbing to most of what, here at home, was called high poesy, and which I myself had found deeply dreary whilst for me it was a delight to read [Ludvig] Holberg and [Johan Herman] Wessel whom Steffens also called masters of their kind.

[GEEG p. 35] Yet, as mentioned, whatever effect Steffens worked upon me it necessarily took time and opportunity to teach me and others; but upon Oehlenschläger, who was not only older and enjoyed a friendly connection with him but differed from me in being both volatile and better prepared, it became instantly visible; and although it was naturally not Steffens who delivered to him that great talent by which, according to my thinking, he became the greatest poet not only of Denmark but of his age, yet without Steffens he would probably never have become this. This Oehlenschläger himself concedes[1] in his autobiography, from which we see that he had a volume of poems at press when he became acquainted with Steffens but which he then simply discarded and wrote instead the collection from 1803 with which there undeniably begins a new epoch in the history of our poetic art.

It is most remarkable that it was in the same year that [Bertel] Thorvaldsen's Jason towered aloft and established an epoch in the art of sculpture; indeed, the coincidence becomes even more curious since we know that as early as 1801 Thorvaldsen had shaped a Jason in natural size but which he then smashed to pieces in order to produce the *colossal* scale which Europe now admires; therefore we can thus conclude from Oehlenschläger's song *Sving dig glade Sang fra Jorden, højt til Himlens hvalvte Buer* [Joyous song! from earth go soaring, high to heaven's vaulted arches] and his *Anden April* [Second of April][2] that the poems which he discarded were good enough according to the customary measure but had to make way for those colossal works which Denmark regenerated in the world of the spirit as Napoleon did in the material world.

1. In his autobiography (*Levnet fortalt af ham selv* [His life, told by himself], 2 vols. 1830-31; vol. 1, 205 ff.) Oehlenschläger tells of the meeting with Steffens and records that he subsequently withdrew his partially printed work *Erik og Roller* and an unprinted volume of poems.

2. The first of these two pieces was Oehlenschläger's *Høitidssang for Kronprindsens Livcorps i Andledning af den 2den April 1802* [Festival song for the Crown Prince's Lifeguard in connection with 2nd April 1802]; the other was *Anden April 1801. En dramatisk Situation* [The second of April 1801. A dramatic situation] (1802); both related to the attack of the British fleet on Copenhagen, 2 April 1801.

21. Grundtvig's Diary, reworked version (1804); Grundtvig Arkiv Fasc. 497; GEEG Stk. 21, p. 35; US I, p. 29.

On the source, see the headnote to item 2. Grundtvig presents himself as a penniless, hungry, cold and disadvantaged student, compelled by economic circumstances to retreat home, and reading unguided by a tutor and in undisciplined fashion; nevertheless he will eventually win through to a firstclass degree.

⌐

Now he had to start reading for the *Attestats*, but he had only four *rigsdaler* a month, and since he paid more than half of it for lodgings he could neither pay for a tutor nor buy coals, and studying in a cold attic never works out well. For nearly two months he was in the country.

Over that winter [1801-02], incidentally, he read the poetry of [Johan Herman] Wessel, [Jonas] Rein, [Edvard] Storm, T. C. Brun and several others, along with a dreadful quantity of novels, since there were no other books in the reading-library, the use of which a friend granted him, and since he did not yet know how easy it was to get access to the University's book-collection.

22. Grundtvig's Diary, reworked version (1804); Grundtvig Arkiv Fasc. 497; GEEG Stk. 22, pp. 35-36; US I, p. 32.

On the source, see the headnote to item 2. Though Theology was his chosen academic discipline, Grundtvig aspired at this time to a literary career. Influenced by authors he was currently reading, such as the poets J. H. Wessel and T. C. Bruun, he experimented with verse in their style. The dream of many an aspiring author was to have a play accepted by the management of the Royal Theatre in Copenhagen, and Grundtvig, after reading the work of Ole Johan Samsøe (1759-96; notable for the loosely historical tragedy *Dyveke, et Sørgespil*, concerning Dyveke, mistress of Christian II), tried his hand with *Skoleholderne*. Still suffering from the constraints and indignities of a meagre budget, he returned home to Udby for a period, at the busy time of harvest.

[GEEG p. 36] We are now in August 1802. It is plain that Grundtvig, as a consequence of the preoccupations stated above, did not read much theology, though in April he had engaged a tutor[1] which he was put in a position to do because his brother who became a priest in Guinea[2] arranged for him a monthly subvention of four *rigsdaler*. His childless, exceedingly rich maternal uncle gave two. This is noted merely for the sake of comparison.

At the beginning of August Grundtvig travelled home on foot, except for the last two miles.[3] In the latter part of September he busily read theology, for in that month he went through, besides a quantity of dogmatics, the whole of the New Testament, except Mark, Luke and the Acts of the Apostles – these we do not read – and exegeses. But in November he took it into his head to try his luck with the management of the Theatre. With [P. C.] Skougaard's help he copied out and added a deal to the above-mentioned *Skoleholderne*, squeezed it into three acts and sent it in on 28 November.

1. A *Manduktør* was a privately hired tutor, often a recent graduate in the field of studies concerned who was earning a living while seeking a career appointment.

2. This brother Niels Christian Bang (b. 1777) was to die the following year (1803), stricken by disease in the Danish colony on the Guinea coast. Another brother, Jacob Ulrich Hansen had already (1800) died in the colony at the age of twenty-five.

3. Danish miles: one Danish mile was approximately 4.7 English miles.

23. Grundtvig's Diary, reworked version (1804); Grundtvig Arkiv Fasc. 497; GEEG Stk. 23, p. 36; US I, p. 34.

On the source, see the headnote to item 2. In the lethargic summer heat of 1803, up to a month before his final examination, Grundtvig is still postponing his theological study in favour of nurturing his ambitions to become a writer of historical romance and dramatic comedy.

In December 1802 Grundtvig went home. Towards the end of February 1803 he returned [to Copenhagen]. He now started upon his prose story *Ulfhild* which, except for the completion of *Brevet* and some small rhyming pieces, was the only bit of writing that distracted him from theology. But lethargy, reading historical writings from the public libraries and the heat did not leave theology very much more time, until the beginning of September when he put all such things away – except for the heat which went away by itself.

24. Grundtvig's Diary, reworked version (1804); Grundtvig Arkiv Fasc. 497; GEEG Stk. 24, p. 36; US I, p. 34.

On the source, see the headnote to item 2. In October 1803, Grundtvig not only successfully graduated as *cand. theol.* but, despite the record of distractions, impediments and wavering motivation, managed to secure a first-class degree. In this further extract from his *'curriculum vitae'* he records the occasion of his first getting into print. Symptomatically, perhaps, the published piece is not one of his newly-written literary works but a controversial accusation against the authorities for neglecting educational provisions on the island of Falster where his older brother Otto was pastor of the parish of Torkildstrup.

Towards the end of October he travelled home; towards the end of November to Falster. Here he polished up his *Ulfhild* as best he could, and decided upon this as his debut in his scholarly career. Early in January he travelled to Udby and sent the manuscript to [P. C.] Skougaard. This though was not the first printed piece under which his name came to stand, for in *Politivennen* nos. 299 and 300, if I remember rightly, he got inserted, under the headline 'Et Særsyn i det nittende Aarhundrede' [An uncommon sight in the nineteenth century], a report of the deplorable state of a Falster school because for ten years it has been lacking a teacher. This step won the approval, as far as he knows, of those informed in the matter, but it secured for him, when in mid-January he was again in Falster, a letter from the newly appointed Bishop [Andreas] Birch who quite took exception to his conduct.

25. Grundtvig's Diary, entry dated 31 December 1804; Grundtvig Arkiv Fasc. 497; GEEG Stk. 25, p. 37; US I, pp. 65-66.

This extract and the two following form part of Grundtvig's review of his past year (1804), on New Year's Eve 1804/5. Much of his time had been spent on Falster. Younger brother to the Grundtvig-family in Torkildstrup, fresh from University with a distinguished degree, entitled to speak of himself as an author (albeit as yet unpublished), and now a controversialist with a social conscience: it is little wonder that Grundtvig cut a very interesting figure in the neighbouring parish of Gundslev where *Provst* D. N. Blicher and his wife had a family of two sons and four daughters. Before long, Grundtvig was nursing romantic feelings for two of the sisters, one of whom, Lise, subsequently became his wife. His writing advanced little, though his manners were becoming more refined; however, his return to the parental home at Udby quickly reminded him that time on this earth is not to be wantonly frittered away.

[GEEG p. 37] The hour of midnight draws near, and here in the stillness of the evening I know nothing better than to review in thought the last three hundred and fifty days.

At the start of the year, then, I was in Torkilstrup and left Falster for only a few but all too busy days, in order to spend the rest of the winter here. I remained here until April and in this long period I really accomplished nothing, as is glaringly enough obvious from my diary, the pages of which I am now exasperatedly turning but seek almost in vain for anything other than these as evidence that I did not sleep away both day and night. And yet I cannot call my stay here altogether useless. Amongst much poor stuff I did nevertheless read something good; and – if I dare call it a gain – my manners became a little less unlike those of the more refined world than they previously were.

In April I travelled to Udby and – I am embarrassed, not to admit it but to acknowledge it as the truth – I was bored being with my good parents; because here there was not a scrap to be found of that recreation, that cheerful conversation and time-killing amusement to which I had grown accustomed. Though, not to do myself an injustice (something which one is rarely tempted to do, and which I, in the judgment of those that know, am supposed to be all too disinclined to), not more than a fortnight had passed before I found myself again. I was ashamed at having frittered away a period which perhaps comprises a very important portion of my earthly life, and I happily got started upon serious undertakings.[1]

1. He records that he felt summoned back to history and resolved to write a corrective doctoral thesis on "Canute the so-called Great … who laid the foundations of my native land's thraldom and besmirched his daily life with base cruelties" [Knud den – saakaldte – store […] denne fejge usling, der lagde grunden til mit fødelands trældom, og besmittede sit daglige liv ved nedrige grusomheder] (Grundtvig's diary, cited Rönning I, 131). Lacking research facilities, however, he set this project aside in favour of writing historical narratives drawn from Norse sagas – which he will later (item 29) refer to dismissively as his hobby-horse [Kephest].

26. Grundtvig's Diary, continuation of entry dated 31 December 1804; Grundtvig Arkiv Fasc. 497; GEEG Stk. 26, pp. 37-38; US I, pp. 69-70.

Grundtvig's diary records that a return to Copenhagen in late July 1804 was curtailed for want of financial resources. His hope of earning an income from teaching part-time at Borchs Kollegium came to nothing. He abandoned a planned doctoral thesis, returned to Udby in September and settled down to working on his Norse-historical narratives. Then came the fateful offer of an appointment as resident tutor in the Steensen-Leth household at Egeløkke. His disappointment on finding that this would take him to the island of Langeland rather than, as he was first informed, to Falster and the congenial social life of the parsonages at Torkildstrup and Gundslev, did not deter him from accepting the post.

In October I received a letter from my altruistic friend, the good-hearted madcap (and incidentally my cousin) Jakob Thomas Trojel, in which he informed me that a job on Falster was available to me if I would make a visit to the capital. I gladly complied, and set off. Upon my arrival I found that [J. H.] Edsberg, with whom I was almost totally unacquainted, had secured me the promise of a job; but I likewise discovered, and was not overcome by joy, that far from being on Falster it was not even in Lolland, as I imagined, but on [GEEG p. 38] Langeland, far away not only from town but from all the people who are dear to me.

However, little though I relished this twist in the matter I nevertheless decided, compelled by necessity, to accept the offer which, even if it upset all my plans and somewhat ruined my good cheer, nevertheless put me in a position to live unobligated to all, and to pay off the debt I had been forced to take upon myself.

When I visited *Generaladjutant* [Hans] Lindholm who, as brother-in-law to my prospective employer, was to sanction my engagement, his wife asked me (what to me was a strange question), whether I knew French, since her sister much desired it. (I had specifically enquired of Pastor [Christian Frederik] Brorson, who was Lindholm's plenipotentiary in this matter, what was required and in particular whether they were asking for a modern language). I said no, and so Lindholm thought it would be best to write first to Captain [Carl Frederik Steensen-] Leth – this is what my Langelandish head of household was called – and hear whether I, being unFrench, could be taken on. Angry at being led up the garden path I forgot my modesty and, telling them to consider that on Herr Brorson's specification which excluded modern languages I had travelled twelve miles, I declared that I must have a definite answer, and added that it was no indifferent matter to me what answer it was, unless, in the event of a rejection, I received compensation for my travel.[1]

So I was taken on with a salary of 150 *rigsdaler* a year, and when I was now informed that my new pupil[2] had not yet learnt the very first elements I could not restrain myself from remarking, in respect of what had gone before, that he would surely have to learn the mother-tongue before he could receive tuition in other living languages.

1. The 12 Danish miles approximately equalled 56 English miles – a considerable journey for the time.

2. Carl Frederik Steensen-Leth, the young son of Captain Carl Frederik Steensen-Leth and the Lady of Egeløkke, Constance Henriette.

27. Grundtvig's Diary, continuation of entry dated 31 December 1804; Grundtvig Arkiv Fasc. 497; GEEG Stk. 27, pp. 38-39; US I, pp. 70-71.

The significant role played by women in Grundtvig's life and the significant status given to female figures and feminine concepts in his thought and his writings have rarely been considered without reference to the circumstances of his upbringing: to the early influence of his mother and the old family servant Malene, to the fact that his male-dominated education entailed his home becoming a place he only revisited at intervals over part of his childhood and his adolescent years, and to his claim that as a student he sacrificed to neither Bacchus nor Venus. His visits as a 21-year-old to his brother Otto's family home at Torkilstrup Parsonage on Falster, as he admits, taught him social skills and graces otherwise lacking. Opportunities included supervised flirtations with the daughters of a neighbouring clergyman, one of which was Elisabeth Blicher. In due course he married Elisabeth. An endearing person in the eyes of most of those who came into the home, she made a touchingly loyal and long-suffering wife and affectionate mother to the three children. The diary-declaration of his half-sober 'intoxication' with Elisabeth makes an interesting juxtaposition to the later outpourings over Constance Leth – and yet: on this and the next page of the diary (476-7) several completely uncharacteristic large splashes and smudgings occur. At the year's end, Grundtvig seems to have been moved to tears in lonely reflection upon his dilemma.

Already in the Spring [of 1804] L. B. [Lise Blicher] interested me, though not to such a degree that the interest could be called by any other than its own name. When in the latter part of November I arrived in Falster I found her much as I had left her. Through individual small things she seemed to show that I was not a matter of indifference to her but her modesty ensured that she never allowed me to do more than suspect it. Only when, on 4 December, I was in G. [Gundslev] it seemed that a certain sadness shadowed her beautiful face and I was proud enough to believe that my departure, which was to take place the next day, was the cause of this. When I came back from my Don Quixotic [**GEEG p. 39**] journey she was happy. I myself have now reached thus far, whether it be through seeing her more often and being more in her company or through constant thought: that I for my part can imagine myself happy at her side even in poverty as long as it does not become altogether too crushing. That is to say, this is how I thought in my steadier periods. In my steadiest on the other hand it seemed to me utterly crazy to engage oneself to a penniless girl at my age and with my prospects. I am in my twenty-second year. I will assume that I am lucky enough to get an appointment in my twenty-sixth year – but then I can assume with certainty that the appointment will not bring in more than two to three hundred *rigsdaler*. Nothing is more reasonable than that I should get married, for if one has been engaged for four years and denied oneself the gratification of sensuality, that in itself would be sufficient explanation for wanting to get into the bridal bed even if there were many other more sensible reasons for the alliance. Now what would the consequence be? In the four to five years I would have to remain in such an appointment it is to be expected I would get into such debt that financial difficulties would be my lot for the rest of my life.

But when I am with her – oh, then my gaze hangs so fixedly upon her, then my heart beats with fear that she will deprive me of the sight of her, and then when at times she lifts up her beautiful gaze, when fair and full of love it meets mine and seems to demand of me a declaration concerning my enigmatic bearing, then I forget prospects and everything. Then with a feeling of the most intoxicating rapture I could enfold her in my arms and say out of the fulness of my heart: I love you, fair lass! Be mine, and I am happy!

Thus my head and my heart do battle.

Egeløkke (1805-1808)

28. Grundtvig's Diary, from the entry dated 20 November 1805;
Grundtvig Arkiv Fasc. 497; GEEG Stk. 28, pp. 39-40; US I, p. 86.

Grundtvig takes up his post at Egeløkke in March 1805 and is gratified to find himself treated as a member of the family.

[In November 1805] I was in Fyn for a week with Fru [Constance] Leth and my pupil, and there I found many occasions to esteem myself happy in my post, in so far as external circumstances can make a mortal happy. In comparing my position with that of other tutors in noble houses it became quite evident to me what great precedence I enjoy. I am a member of the family whilst the others are humble servants; if from time to time I get a sharp look when my ideas on upbringing do not coincide with the lady's not over-judicious love for the boy, nonetheless my will is not so very often ineffective even though it cannot completely make its influence felt through my rules of conduct. Now more than ever I feel the impossibility of taking a domestic-tutorship when I leave the Leths' house, for it would be altogether too unlikely that I should find one where I am surrounded by [GEEG p. 40] so much kindness and respect, where I, in the midst of my slavery, might enjoy so much freedom as here.

29. Grundtvig's Diary, from entries dated 5 December and 31 December 1805;
Grundtvig Arkiv Fasc. 497; GEEG Stk. 29, pp. 40-41 (extended); US I, p. 88 f.

"The three years as house-tutor at Egeløkke were, spiritually viewed, an extraordinarily rich and turbulent time for Grundtvig. He entered into a period of ferment which shook him to his innermost soul" (*GEEG*, 40). The following impassioned entry in Grundtvig's diary is incomplete – apparently by an act of censorship. Grundtvig's sexuality seems to have proved an embarrassment to the responsible party – whether himself or a member of his family – as it has proved to many of his followers and to some who have written on his life; but to take the option of not exploring it would be to forego access to a determining personal dynamic within Grundtvig, the varied expressions of which many of his contemporaries encountered and noted with more or less understanding. There can be no doubting the powerful and consequential reality of the passion he felt for Constance Leth; but one may at the same time observe that his written representation of it is something of an act of biographical self-construction. Goethe's romantic tale of obsessive unrequited love, profound melancholy, despair and suicide, *Die Leiden des jungen Werther* [The Sorrows of Young Werther] (1774), had given rise to a "Werther-period" with Werther as a template upon which the self-diagnosis of rejected lovers could be patterned.

There are examples close to hand on either side of Grundtvig's crisis: in the 1780s, it has been suggested, the friends Ole Johan Samsøe (1759-96) and Knud Lyhne Rahbek (1760-1830) had cast their respective sufferings in such a pattern (stopping short, however, of self-destruction); and when Grundtvig's friend Christian Molbech (1783-1857) suffered an unrequited love-affair in 1809 what did he do in his melancholy state but embark upon a translation of *Die Leiden des jungen Werther*? Grundtvig enjoyed and wrote in various forms of the role of women in his life but this rhetorically florid passage remains a rare attempt among his writings to record the rational mind struggling with unmanageable romantic emotion. From the experience he certainly emerged a changed person.

I sometimes marvel that I now neither rhyme nor write historical narratives or such things as were previously my hobby-horse. I cannot even bear to read what I have churned out of such stuff. Everything strikes me as so empty, so banal, that I am disgusted. Either all my productions really are like this, or else it arises from the total disharmony which continuously screeches out from my inward strings. Perhaps a bit from both.

Oh God! what am I doing here? Why should I have my bold doubts about the reality of love thus dissipated? Why should I learn to know this enchanting ethereal form only to see it flee? Why was I not, why am I not, as I formerly believed, cold and unfeeling? Why did your hand thrust me out upon the raging ocean and command that I be rolled away by the foaming waves without even having a landfall in sight that, by my struggle and striving, I might hope to gain? And yet, bold questions: do I, a mite, dare then to dispute with the Eternal? Have I read in the book of the future or seen through His plan?

What changes, without and within, have befallen me since, and by reason of, my coming hither? When I came here my happiness lay in flashing my small portion of wit and misusing it for unwarranted satire, in being able to flaunt my superficial abilities, in reading and writing in the glad hope of becoming a writer of renown. All other joys that had their well-spring in the heart and its more tender feelings were to me unknown; I believed I was wanting in the stuff of these and was glad of it, for to me it seemed they beckoned me away from my glorious glittering course. Love seemed to me a fool's game and I thought that none but weak-headed folk could have that feeling in any degree. I desired marriage only for the sake of companionship and the sexual urge and I could imagine myself without pain parted from the one who had thus become my mate, indeed at times I was even so bold as to desire this so as to achieve a change. When in my dreams of the future I came to the point where I was supposed to live quietly as a public servant with wife and children I was not satisfied. I [GEEG p. 41] had no concept of domestic happiness and I believed the boredom would kill me in such a situation where I should miss books and communion with men of learning. In short, my happiness was dependent upon my fortune and my place of residence.

I came here. I read into the fair woman's eyes and what were all the world's books to this? What could I get to know in those that were as dear to me as the sight of her glance resting with tenderness upon me? What were reading and talking against silent gazing upon the fair one? – it is as the dim lamp against the streaming sun.

What were my highest triumph, even as foremost of authors, against one firm squeeze of her hand at which my every gland trembled with joy, at which a heaven of bliss seemed to pour forth from each of her fingertips into my open swelling breast?

O, still bleeds my heart, still run the tears upon my pale cheek at the memory of that nameless joy I was careless enough to grasp.

Books and everything lay idle; she became to me more and more precious, more and more indispensable to my happiness. I hardly noticed it, and if I ever asked myself: what will the outcome be? then I would lay the question to rest, or rather suppress it, with the twisted reply: it is not vice I seek; it is only innocent enjoyment which, without leaving consequences, shall sweeten my life of the present moment. O fool that I am who with an impotent word, a feeble will, thought myself able to dam that ocean which from drops of love …

[Ten pages are missing from the diary at this point. The next surviving page contains an entry for 31 December, noting the death of his older sister Ulrikke Eleonora (born 1782). Its crafted elegiac rhetoric stands in some contrast to the more pragmatic entry of the previous March 7 recording that his sister was suffering from internal inflammation of the abdomen: "I should be extremely sorry if my sister died, not so much for her sake – since, lacking money, beauty, talents beyond the ordinary, and even a warm cheerfulness of soul, she would hardly be happy – as partly for my own, partly for my aged parents' sake: for who should then manage their house? Who should then look after my invalid mother? It would be extremely distressing, and were I to become sisterless I should certainly also soon become motherless."]

December XXXI.

You?
My sister, the only one, is dead. She was good; this thought comforts me, and she could as little perish as her memory can be erased from my heart.

Hereafter shall we meet and be together again.

O may, in that moment when death's bell tolls for me, as hollow as the one which now casts away the vanished year into the ocean of bygone time, may in that hour my soul be uninfected with the blemishes of sin. May the Lord, the almighty and all-good, grant me will, strength and courage to fight, success to prevail over all those temptations which my own inclinations and people might cause to appear around me!

Give me wisdom and understanding to educate the mind of the young one who has been entrusted to my guidance, to improve his heart and instil in it a warm love for you and his fellow men! Then shall I cheerfully lay myself to rest if I can take with me the conviction that I worked here with word and deed for the spread of your kingdom of truth and of virtue.

30. Grundtvig's Diary, from the entry dated 10 September 1806;
Grundtvig Arkiv Fasc. 497; GEEG Stk. 30, pp. 41-42; US I, pp. 107-108.

Erotic imaginings continued to disturb the young house-tutor's nights but it is clear from the notebooks' judicious reflections upon the theory and practice of teaching his pupil that talk of insanity was rather a flirtation with literary rhetoric than confession of a serious fear. This excerpt affords a telling example of Grundtvig turning to contemporary German literature in order to find self-expression, self-identification and to some extent, perhaps, self-construction, during the hitherto unexperienced turbulence stirred by his passion for Constance Leth.

⌒

I came here looking for good cheer, with a yearning for the opposite sex. Had I not fallen in love, my pupil would not have got so far,[1] and I would already have adorned a rather elevated place in the school of carnal lust.

I had often resolved to learn modern languages by self-help but I had never had the necessary patience. Now I was in love, and had my love been lucky then studies would have gone dormant, at least for a very long time: of this the first months' stay here convince me, my life's golden days, the home of my blissful dreams whose faint recall still makes my cheek glow and makes me happier than the whole world's idolisation could make me – when it does not call forth the streaming tears of loss upon the pale cheek.

[GEEG p. 42] Oh I can do no other: I must yet sacrifice a thought to that happy time. The day would fly by with cheerful jesting and the blissful exchange of loving glances and intoxicating squeezing of hands. For me, the night would cover the world with its dark blanket only to conjure forth in dreams a new one, more beautiful and blossoming. The hand I warmly kissed by day in dreams clasped round my bending neck, close joined my beating breast to the swelling bosom which by day but enchanted my eye, and pressed my mouth tight upon those blushing lips which poured forth kisses tenfold sweeter that the harmonious sounds which by day intoxicated my ear.

[Grundtvig now splices into his narrative three passages (not included in the *GEEG* excerpts) quoted in German from Friedrich Schiller (1759-1805), *Die Braut von Messina oder die feindlichen Brüder* [The bride of Messina or The enemy brothers] (1803). All three are from speeches of Don Manuel (Act 1, Scene 7). The first[2] quotation echoes the enraptured sentiments just stated by Grundtvig. Before the second,[3] Grundtvig writes "I cried out in a feeling of inexpressible joy: [Quotation]" and before the third[4] "My life was a song of praise to the Father of love; and, lifted aloft to him above the bounds of time, I dreamed myself into eternal pleasure. But ah! – soon, with more justification, I was obliged to burst forth: [Quotation]."]

Yes, it vanished, that blissful time, swift as a man's life before the Almighty's eye, and alone, abandoned I stand in the wilderness of creation like the faint glimmering star upon the dark sky, which wished to vanish, enshrouded in the black garment of everlasting night, but must live, robbed of its radiance. Oh though had I learnt to speak with all tongues, how could it make up for the loss of life's only love worthy of being spoken?

But back to the more even path of sanity! Treading this path, I may well call it fortunate that my love was so unfortunate since it rendered me productive and contributed to the increase of my insights.

1. Whatever bearing his passion for the mother may have had upon it, his approach to tutoring the son is conscientiously thought out in theory and in practice: his notes from this period show some evidence of Grundtvig the educationist in the making. His pupil's memory of the experience is recorded in item 60.

2. The quotations are here taken from the online Projekt Gutenberg text. *"Das unstet schwanke Sehnen war gebunden, / Dem Leben war sein Inhalt ausgefunden. / Und wie der Pilger sich nach Osten wendet, / Wo ihm die Sonne der Verheißung glänzt, / So kehrte sich mein Hoffen*

und mein Sehnen / Dem einen hellen Himmelspunkte zu." [My restless, formless yearning had been sealed, / The meaning of my life had been revealed. / And as the pilgrim travels toward the east / Where he beholds his sun of promise shine, / So did my hope and yearning turn to face / That one resplendent quarter of the sky. (tr. Charles E. Passage 1962)].

3.   *"[Denn] über allen ird'schen Dingen hoch / Schwebt mir auf Freudenfittigen die Seele, / Und in dem Glanzesmeer, das mich umfängt, / Sind alle Wolken mir und finstre Falten / Des Lebens ausgeglättet und verschwunden."* [(For) over all the things of earth my soul / Floats high aloft on pinions of sheer joy, / And in the sea of radiance around me / All clouds have disappeared and all the dark / Umbrageous folds of life have been smoothed out. (tr. Charles E. Passage, 1962)].

4.   *"Geflügeltist das Glück und schwer zu binden, / [...] / [Nicht] Blitzen gleich, die schnell vorüber schießen / Und plötzlich von der Nacht verschlungen sind."* [Swift-winged is Happiness and hard to bind, / (...) / Not like the lightning-streaks that flash and pass, / Devoured by darkness swifter than a look, (tr. Charles E. Passage, 1962)].

31. From a memorandum dated 30 December 1806; GEEG Stk. 31, pp. 42-43; US I, pp. 112-113.

Grundtvig ceased maintaining a diary in the Autumn of 1806, about the time when he seriously committed himself to writing for publication; but among his papers survive various diary-like notes or memoranda (*Optegnelser*) – dated 30 December 1806 and 24 June 1807 – upon the literary activities now preoccupying him and the recent history of his maturing sensibilities. During the emotionally turbulent year 1806, he noted, a chance event reminded him of another, previous love-affair of his – namely with the ancient literature of the North. That literature was now demeaned by a frivolous parody published in the literary journal *Minerva*. In rallying indignantly to its defence he also discovered how, for the better, his feeling for antiquity had changed in the interval. His revitalised sense of the intellectual and artistic richness of the ancient Northern literature, and of its dignity, was to inspire him to much important literary work over the coming years.

I came now to where my new life began,[1] where my eye was opened to love's sacred mysteries, whereby it was whetted to survey the wondrous works of poesy and antiquity, their temporal archetype. But I served long in the temple's forecourt without once daring to seek out with my eyes the shining cherubs, for the very thought of them set before me only that heavenly beauty I was doomed never to enjoy. I had a feeling for poesy; but that unfortunate bond which shackled me to actuality's poetic object[2] did not allow me to enjoy in a higher state of existence what yet I constantly felt the want of here. Øhlenschläger wrote *Vaulundurs Saga* and it made a deep impression upon me; but the same lack of courage, the same total commitment to one object, still hindered me from inwardly embracing an active form, and the constant alternation of momentary intoxication with months of despair rendered me completely unfitted to enter alone into the world of ideas.

Eventually I got so far as to become aware of this truth: actuality holds no pleasure for me. I read [GEEG p. 43] [Johan Gottlieb] Fichte's fine book on man's vocation [*Die Bestimmung des Menschen* (1800)], the splendid plays and deep speculations of [Friedrich] Schiller. I forsook life with [Friedrich] Schelling in his *Bruno*. I now stood at a point where only one push was needed to propel me into the antiquity of the North, to cause me to embrace it with the same love that I had always felt for it, and with a more cheerful eye. The push was a reworking of the Edda-poem *Skirnirs Rejse* [Skirnir's Journey] which was included in the May volume of [Knud Lyhne] Rahbek's *Minerva*, 1806. With my spontaneous indignation over this production I first learnt properly to appreciate how different my present standpoints were from those from which I had previously peered through the darkness towards the ancient North.

I seized my pen; my soul had to follow on – and it could, partly because after all it now enjoyed the freedom of the moment, and partly because right then the mistress of my being was far distant. Intellectual occupation was now as easy as it was necessary to me and step by step by the end of this reappraisal I arrived at a standpoint I merely sensed at the outset. From now on I shall live in antiquity, and actuality shall no more be able to make me its slave, unless, in acknowledgment of a lack of means to remain in a land into which I have ventured without certainty of gaining citizenship, I have to return – and then, O woe is me!

1. Grundtvig refers to Egeløkke.

2. What Grundtvig calls in rather unpoetic terms "actuality's poetic object" [*Virkelighedens poetiske Genstand*] is presumably the Lady of Egeløkke, Constance Leth.

32. Letter to Christian Molbech; in Christian Molbech og Nicolai Frederik Severin Grundtvig. En Brevvexling samlet af Chr. K. F. Molbech, og udgivet af L. Schrøder (1888), pp. 12-14 ; GEEG pp. 43-45.

In May 1808, having resigned his post at Egeløkke, Grundtvig returned to Copenhagen where he succeeded in securing a room in Valkendorfs Kollegium and a post teaching history and geography at the Schouboeske Institut. In a letter written the same month to his exact contemporary and friend Christian Molbech, he gives this report of how things stood with him.

To love and to live are one thing. I grew up unfamiliar with Nature, without love for anything living or dead that moved besides myself. Only the vanished ages did I love, only in them did I live, and when I was not there my life was that of a vegetable. Childish games were to me almost a burden; and only then was I really happy, when I could take refuge from them in my [Arild] Hvitfeld, [Claus Christoffer] Lyskander and [Ludvig] Holberg, stand in the ancient North and behold the lofty warriors or contemplate the lively contest between emperors and popes. It was as though, by this coldness towards everything around me, Nature wished to protect me from the frightful epoch through which I must needs make my way if I were ever to dare to commit myself to anything living. Thus flowed hence the interval of time from my eighth to my twenty-first year, and even my sickly existence, as something which in my world was no burden, could not disturb my peace. In company I was the stupidest, dumbest and most tedious creature, and in the [GEEG p. 44] same moment my heart was laughing within my breast because I was not what I seemed to be. Happily would I return to my loneliness and an almost incredible cheerfulness animated me.

But – now the time was come. I saw a woman; and I, love's coldest, bitterest disparager, was in love from the first instant, as deeply, as ardently as is possible for a mortal. Antiquity vanished from my sight or more correctly it merged with the present which appeared in my beloved. Yes, I have lived, lived in this world and embraced everything about me with love, for everything seemed to exist for the sake of the One and to revolve about the one point wherein my ideas and my feelings united. But brief was the bliss; for I needed only to know that I was in love to become as unhappy as I could be. Society's conventions stood as an insurmountable wall between us, and Nature had moreover fixed an engulfing chasm between our beings. Oh how I struggled with that burgeoning, growing passion! With what strength did I subjugate my mind under the most exhausting occupations in order to subdue the storm that raged within me! But all was in vain: it was as though a man sought to dam with his hand the rushing mountain stream. The years passed away and I sank, weak, into the darkest melancholy. Ah, I wandered dark, uncharted paths, for I had no home. That world was closed to me and my spirit lacked strength and, what was more, desire to shape itself a new one.

Then I saw the parody upon the momentous lives of the gods.[1] Anger wakened the slumbering strength; and antiquity – the beloved of my childhood and youth – again appeared before my eyes. The deep emotion had sharpened my vision and where before I had seen only an agreeable game, there I now became aware of a brilliant and perfect image of the most High. Now, but also perhaps now for the first time, you will be able to read what stood written in my heart, when I wrote: I once saw an image of the Eternal.[2] Had I been able, had I dared to paint it as it appeared to me then you would have worshipped kneeling; had I been able, had I dared to express the pain I felt when it was no longer before me then your joints would have trembled and your face would have paled. I cannot regret having seen it but unceasingly it floats before my eyes like the Olympian Jupiter's before the ancient Greeks' and its harmonious sublimity I must rediscover in the ancient North, or else my life is done." In antiquity I live and wander, but little as even the greatest poet can achieve an uninterrupted life in his self-created world as little can I forever enclose myself in the one I strove to have reborn within myself. And now, my friend! when that existence which surrounds me prevails upon me to contemplate it, indeed to contemplate myself within it, oh it is a good thing that speech lacks the sounds to express the emptiness and the pain to which I am the prey, for otherwise I should make everyone unhappy for whom I described my condition. Existence can have no worth, no reality in my eyes, except it manifests itself in her whom I eternally adore, and how can I gaze upon that point without despairing?! As long as I can make antiquity throw up its fortifications about me, both without and within, then I can live; but if I am torn out of that encirclement then there is nothing to hinder the pursuing Fury from entwining and crushing me in her arms.

1. *Skirnirs Reise* by Jens Møller published in May issue of *Ny Minerva* 1806.

2. Grundtvig alludes to his article *Om Asalæren* [On the lore of the Æsir] in the periodical *Ny Minerva* 1807, II, 156-88 (*US* I, 204-23; where the quotation, slightly differently phrased, is on p. 206).

Denmark c. 1807-1814

33. Mands Minde (1838, 1877); GEEG Stk. 33, pp. 45-46; MM, pp. 326-327.

See the first paragraph of the headnote to item 3. The capital to which Grundtvig returned in 1808 lay extensively in burnt-out ruin following the British incendiary bombardment of Copenhagen in 1807, and the unhappy foundations had been laid for the calamity of State bankruptcy which finally came about in 1814. He had been on (relatively remote) Langeland at the time of the British attack but, however preoccupied he had been with his feelings for Constance Leth, he had nevertheless been in some contact with military events: there he met Peter Willemoes who was transporting Danish troops between Langeland and Lolland, and there he had also served as military chaplain to the island's *Landeværn* (Home guard); but though it could not be other than a harrowing experience to return to the shattered streets of his student years, yet he now experienced "two of the happiest and proudest, most productive and educationally profitable years of my life" which he warmly recalled thirty years on, in his lectures at Borchs Kollegium 1838.

⌒

A writer, naturally, always finds it a miserable time when people will not read *his* books; and if he also believes as I long believed that books make people then the time from 1807 to 14 necessarily seem to him, by the side of that from 1820 to 30, as Heaven against Hell, since that was plainly the situation in our literature; but yet I must observe that a rich literature reveals that there are both great forces stirring and much participation, and I must add that from 1807 to 14 there was as much vitality in our seamen as in our writers: the only two kinds of people who had the freedom to bestir themselves; so whether it was a state of overwroughtness which had to be relieved by an excessive listlessness, or whether it was a new life which unfortunate circumstances almost strangled at birth, that year was all the same a little Danish Heroic Age which we who entered into the spirit of it have since painfully missed and now, when the worst part of the ordeal seems to be over, happily recall and commend to the young for closer consideration.

It was in May 1808 I returned to the capital in my twenty-fifth year, when strength is close to being at its greatest and hope therefore naturally has its brightest moment, so that adversity and [GEEG p. 45] difficulties do not depress but uplift and ennoble us; and even though Copenhagen lay for a large part in rubble yet in my eyes it was delightfully different from when I left it after the business of my examinations.[1] As a young writer who showed promise, I got a place in Valkendorfs Kollegium without particular difficulty and there lived out, in the daily company of [F. C.] Sibbern, the recently deceased Professor [S. B.] Hersleb from Norway[2] and a couple of others, two of the happiest and proudest, most productive and educationally profitable years of my life. It was a significant contribution to this that through Sibbern I made the acquaintance of the Ørsteds and Øhlenschläger, and through

Hersleb of the professors [Niels] Treschow, [Georg] Sverdrup and the whole Norwegian circle which at that time was the ornament of our university; but this circle, as well as Øhlenschläger and his circle, were also *Danish* innovations – expressions of that same new, vigorous life which at the beginning of the century, through Steffens and Thorvaldsen, had by hand and mouth witnessed to its real existence, and had now already created for itself distinguished circles in Denmark's capital city where one did not need to kill time with the ace of clubs and the queen of diamonds but strove to get out of it all possible benefit before it disappeared, had no need of wine to become cheerful but oneself sparkled with the best of them, in order to cheer up folk who were themselves half-dead.

1. *Examens-Driveri* appears to be an ironical pun: *driveri* could mean the conducting of business (from one sense of the verb *at drive*) but 'idleness, idling about' is a common meaning of the word, and so Grundtvig may be alluding to his admittedly casual approach to examination preparation. The further implication that examinations were in themselves an unproductive and time-wasting process is consistent with Grundtvig's expressed views elsewhere.

2. Hersleb had died in 1836, two years before Grundtvig gave this lecture.

34. *Mands Minde (1838, 1877); GEEG Stk. 34, pp. 46-47; MM, pp. 328-330.*

See the first paragraph of the headnote to item 3. In what he now sees in retrospect as "a little Heroic Age for Denmark" (coinciding with his own youth and the emergence of Oehlenschläger as poet) Grundtvig locates his realisation that "*the ancient North* was my poetic home" where he would be free from the tyranny of classical "rules of art" and free to use the Northern myths where classical convention alluded to the mythology of Greece and Rome.

We may [...] never expect from anyone, least of all from more poetic natures, an *objective* portrayal of their youth, but only a lively account, true according to their own feeling; for not only does it require fairness, but it is a benefit to our own selves since we learn by this to know a really living moment from the time that is past, to see a radiance which actually belongs to it and can, if we wish it, shed daylight upon the dark side; and should you sometime discover upon closer investigation that, not without justification, I regard the years of my youth as a little Heroic Age for Denmark as a whole, this does not come out of my impartiality but out of that historical nature which is in us and our nation, so that whatever was outwardly incidental to the resurrection of a national life [*Folkelivets Opstandelse*] happily coincided with the poetic Spring which our literature undeniably heralded in those years.

That a poetic star of the first magnitude has risen over our fatherland with this century, this I say boldly, certain that even foreigners who have the poorest eye for such heavenly portents either have seen or else will soon be obliged to see it; so it is merely a question [**GEEG p. 47**] of what this brilliance signifies: whether it was at the rising of the folk-sun [*Folkesolens Opgang*][1] or at its setting that the clouds so delightfully blushed and met so beautifully together with the billows blue. What Oehlenschläger's short poems in fact prophesied, this his *Poetiske Skrifter* [Poetic Writings] 1805 – in which *Vavlunder* and *Aladdin* alone would have been enough to render two poets immortal – his *Nordiske*

Digte [Nordic poems], or *Tors Rejse* [Thor's Journey], *Hakon hin rige* [Haakon the rich] and *Balder hin gode*, 1807, *Palnatoke* 1809, *Axel og Valborg* 1810, *Corregio* 1811, *Stærkodder* 1812 – not only fulfilled but vastly exceeded. This alone constitutes a poetic wealth which undoubtedly, when it becomes properly known, will arouse the envy even of the likewise poetically rich England (but luckily does not lend itself to being seized with steel glove or red-hot pincers).[2]

And now I began to join in, not in any way to contend for rank with Oehlenschläger or in general to win a poet's wreath: no, in my eyes Oehlenschläger, from the moment I saw his *Poetiske Skrifter*,[3] was a bard to whose shoulder I could hardly reach and whose wreath I did not covet at all – but *the ancient North* which he, in *Vavlunder* and the *Nordiske Digte* had visited upon the wings of an eagle and surveyed with the eye of a falcon, *this*, I felt, was my poetic home: a long-slumbering warrior-strain from the pagan past had, under the loud din of battle and the song of the skald, awakened in me, and meant to be heard without accommodating or correcting itself to any of all those valid or invalid rules of art that had been framed upon the writings of the ancient Greeks and Romans. That precisely these writings, however good they might be, should be *our* ideals, and that the myths and ancient poems of the North should yield place among North-dwellers to those of foreigners, this, in my eyes, was so unnatural a prejudice and so unreasonable a demand that if I did not treat them exactly as Thor treated the giants it was only because I lacked the strength or at any rate the intelligence to use it properly.

1. *Folkesolen* alludes back to *Folkelivets Opstandelse* in the previous paragraph: the vitality of the nation is likened to the sun. The terminology has (presumably deliberate) religious overtones.

2. Grundtvig's allusion is to the British fire-bombing of Copenhagen (1807).

3. It was in the romantic isolation of Egeløkke that Grundtvig first read Oehlenschläger's *Poetiske Skrifter* (1805), and then by chance, for the book had been erroneously dispatched from Copenhagen instead of Oehlenschläger's *Digte* (1803), as Grundtvig tells Christian Molbech in a letter (*Molbech-Gr*, 221).

Probational sermon and Christian breakthrough

35. Om Religions-Frihed. (Tredie og Sidste Stykke). Af N. F. S.
Grundtvig (1827, 1866); GEEG Stk. 35, pp. 47-50 (extended).

After his return to the city, the realities and figments of romantic passion in the seclusion of Langeland were relentlessly displaced by Grundtvig's necessary engagements with adulthood, duty to his family, career considerations and the politics of action within the small, tight, hierarchical and authoritarian society then prevailing in Copenhagen. Having accepted an obligation to go back to Udby and assist his aged father as curate, he was first obliged to qualify for ordination by preaching (on 17 March 1810) a probational or dimissory sermon before an official censor, Professor Peter Erasmus Müller. The sermon was deemed, as delivered, to have achieved distinction; but when Grundtvig subsequently published it under the rather provocative title "Hvi er Herrens Ord forsvundet af Hans Hus?" [Why has the word of the Lord vanished from his house?] six of Copenhagen's clerics made formal complaint to the Chancellery that Grundtvig had libellously defamed the clergy. The consequences of this embroilment were considerable and costly: not least was the breakdown and spiritual crisis which Grundtvig suffered in December 1810 (on which, see item 65 below). On the source-text, written at a later time of even greater conflict with the authorities, and partly suppressed by the censor, see the headnote to item 46.

I was at that time an *alumnus* at Valkendorfs Kollegium, and how this circumstance was used against an old [GEEG p. 48] theology *Candidat* and a young poet I cannot be bothered to tell here[1] but I mention it only in order to say: my close friends there, and particularly [S. B.] Hersleb in Norway and [F. C.] Sibbern here, know as well as I how far it was from my thoughts to cause a stir, namely, with my probational sermon, and how reluctantly I made my entry into the State Church's teaching profession;[2] so if my accusers had known me they would surely not have taken offence over a piece of work which, as such, was in my eyes the most insignificant I had written and which I only had printed because young authors would rather save their trivia in print than in the desk, and because I knew it would please my old father who just that year reached his fiftieth pastoral year in the State Church. It was solely and alone to stand by him in his high and venerable age that I preached for dimission and desired ordination; for in common with all poetic natures I had a secret horror of professional positions in the prosaic world, and besides, the scholarly field in which I wished both to work and to distinguish myself in writing was not Theology but the history and antiquities of the North; so every professional post I coveted was desirable to me only because I was poor and could not help but feel that one does not live off air however poetically one processes it, nor easily or long off one's pen in Denmark these days, especially if one is in the habit, as I am, of chewing the cud over it.

A formal difficulty, which I with my disinclination towards holding priestly office in the middle of nowhere was unwilling to fight to the bitter end, had resulted in my old father deciding to resign;[3] and so my probational sermon would probably have been the last sermon, as it was the first, that I would have had printed, if I had been left in peace; but it was not meant to be so, this is the only reason I can still think of for the public attack upon the young poet and slightly fanatical [sværmende] mythologist who – from earlier days, for example when as preacher in the open field to the militia on Langeland[4] he had seen the common folk flock about him at the voicing of ancient Denmark's danger and of the divine strength of the ancient faith – might well have had some opinion of his speaking-talents, but who had never taken one step towards ascending a pulpit in the capital or put pen to paper in order to apply for anything other than a place in Valkendorfs Kollegium and a travel grant which he did not get.

Now however, now when it has to be labelled a civil offence even [GEEG p. 49] literarily to lament the decline of the old Christianity, yes now might the blood well boil for once, even in the coldest veins, within a freeborn poetic nature, within the son of a jubilarian priest [Jubel-Lærer] in the State Church, the son of [Bishop N. E.] Balle's brother-in-law, with kinsmen in the Danish Church, even upon episcopal thrones and chairs of Theology, right back to Martin Luther's days, whose family name in so many parishes awoke the remembrance of venerable, zealous, free-speaking, well-gifted priests, and whose maternal lineage is traceable right back in the obscurity of the Middle Ages where Absalon radiantly shone! What wonder that the man born of the stock of the old priests, who even in his childhood glowed when he read of Luther, and in his adolescence, when he read Jesus og Fornuften [Jesus and Reason], dreamed of growing up only so that he might be Balle's armour-bearer, that he who for a little while was driven by the tide from his fathers, from his childhood faith and heroic dreams, from Balle's footsteps, from his mother's heart and his father's blessing but, when the critical hour struck in the school of life, had turned back, had scanned in history the triumph of ancient Christianity through the ages, had deeply felt, in those heavy days of Denmark's death-struggle, what he was lacking, but had now near forgotten it, in favour of dreams of nordic heroics; what wonder that he suddenly awoke in horror, in fright, in fiery indignation, since it could not even be allowed him, when in dreams he visited the ruinous church with his fathers' graves, to offer it and their memory and the grey-haired ones who vainly sought their faith and their consolation from the young priests, to offer all this a tear – which I still clearly remember involuntarily trickling and falling upon the paper when, in my dream-sermon, my eye fell upon these. This tear – the first truly pious one I had let fall in many a year – I could not possibly regret, even were it to become the source of many bitter ones; and even now, when it has become such, when only He who counts the stars can count the tears which ran down these pale cheeks and upon most of the books I have written, even now be it far from me as man, as Christian and as priest to regret my first tear or to complain over what it cost.[5]

What would have become of me if they had got me deleted from the list of graduands, or if only the grievous mental illness into which I fell had not deeply humbled me,[6] and [Bishop N. E.] Balle's recommendation to a gracious King had not secured my old father his position again and my ordination, this only He knows who has the heart of kings as well as of commoners in his hand; but it is not only in secular terms that I must shudder to think of what, to human eyes, had been done to a hopeful young writer who in his secular life certainly did not wilfully arouse anybody's anger and even when he was a heathen could never let the sun go down upon his own anger. They had come within a [GEEG p. 50] hair's breadth, to mortal eyes, of turning me into an unnatural zealot [*unaturlig Sværmer*] – unnatural in all respects, since it was the faith of our fathers and the religion of the State that I wanted to be zealous for; and since, even so, I would surely have found just as much of an inroad into the Danish populace as [H. N.] Hauge found into the Norwegian, and yet there was no freedom of religion here, it is likely that the prison-house would soon have become my church; and even if (though implausible to imagine) the uproar had thereby been stilled, yet I should have brought shame upon my good name, upon my honoured family, upon a fatherland I was neither unwilling nor unfitted to serve as priest and to honour as writer.

1. Though Grundtvig was no longer formally studying at the university he had secured residence (May 1808 to May 1811) in Valkendorfs Kollegium while he sought to establish himself as a writer. It was his status as *alumnus* here, Grundtvig suggests, which the university used against him in summoning him (12 January 1811) before the *Consistorium* to receive a reprimand relating to his probational sermon.

2. That is, the role of preacher in the State Church.

3. Johan Ottesen Grundtvig, burdened by both age and debt, had formally applied to have Grundtvig appointed as his curate but his bishop, short of candidates to fill vacant regular incumbencies, disallowed the request. Grundtvig also wrote to his father that he had decided he was not yet ready to take priestly office. Johan, disappointed, embittered and anxious about the future financial position of himself and his wife, resolved to force the situation by resigning (November 1810) in the hope that Grundtvig might be offered and would accept appointment as his successor. In the outcome, Johan's resignation was reversed and Grundtvig was appointed as his personal curate and ordained in Trinitatis Kirke Copenhagen on 29 May 1811; but there is every indication that the conflict of loyalties, duties and ambitions cut very deep and contributed to Gr's dramatic breakdown in December 1810.

4. In 1807 at the time of the British assault upon Copenhagen Grundtvig, who was then at Egeløkke on Langeland, was appointed by the chief military commander on Langeland, *Grev* Ahlefeld-Laurvig, as field-priest for the defence force stationed there, although he had not yet been ordained. Grundtvig preserved among his papers his farewell sermon preached to the soldiers and resident population on the First Sunday in Advent (28 November) 1807.

5. "This tear [...] cost." is omitted from *GEEG* but merits inclusion for the further glimpse it gives of the powerful emotional disturbances Grundtvig suffered amidst controversy. As is also clear from other contexts, mention of tears shed is, in Grundtvig's case, not to be dismissed as mere metaphorical usage: the confrontations in his life were not addressed without considerable cost of this kind.

6. One of three particularly severe breakdowns in Grundtvig's life (others in 1844 and 1867), usually attributed to a chronic tendency to a bipolar (manic-depressive) disorder. His father did not hesitate to see the crisis of December 1810 in terms of a Luther-like struggle against besetting doubts (*anfægtelser*). Grundtvig himself felt it had deeply humbled – or humiliated – him, and certainly, over the years, there were those who permitted themselves to make capital out of his weakness; but it is an heroic aspect of Grundtvig's life that he returned after each crisis in defiance of gossip, tales and sneers, to resume his ministry and to continue to work for his causes.

36. Fragment of a note apparently from the end of 1810; GEEG Stk. 36, pp. 50-51; US II, pp. 29-31.

Over the summer of 1810 Grundtvig was under great stress, awaiting the excessively protracted judgment of the University *Consistorium* on the affair of his dimissory sermon, reconciling himself with the prospect of leaving the city for rural Udby to assist his father, and finding himself unable to apply himself to writing, fluctuating between torpor and bursts of inspiration. Then, with a sudden urge to return to reading history came a clear realisation that his fellow Danes were generally oblivious to their own history. At the same time it occurred to him that a national sense of history (and therefore the national consequences of a people having, or not having, a current consciousness of its own history) came and went in phase with the waxing and waning of a people's Christian awareness. The two things together lent strength to the realm. Thus the conviction formed in him that he must share his own growing Christian (universal) understanding of history with a wider public. Despite the breaking of the crisis in December 1810, by 1812 he was ready to publish his *Verdenskrønike* [World, or Universal, History].

⌒⌐

The whole of that summer I lay as though in a torpor, and my poem upon Prince Christian together with my address to the Swedish people[1] are more or less all that I took on apart from my fixed occupations; but in the latter my perspective upon the history of the North developed itself, especially through the viewpoint upon the Kalmar Union [*Kalmarunionen*] which I then formed. Without being able to explain to myself why, I suddenly got an irresistible desire to read history, and [Arnold Herman Ludwig] Heeren's prize essay on the history of the crusades, which I had long been thinking about, unexpectedly fell into my hands. It was especially his perspective upon the hierarchy which gripped me, for although I had let myself be carried away by the hullabaloo over Papal authority into not drawing a distinction between the various periods, yet I had already, whilst working in the Spring upon the history of Henry the Fourth, developed a great respect for Gregory, of which my *dictata* from that period bear witness. It was likewise pleasing to me, in so unimpugnable an author, to find my own overview of the crusades which, however, I knew only in their merest outline. The consequences of the crusades I found unsatisfactorily and worryingly developed, as had to be the case with a man who combines great perspicuity with broad historical learning but lacks the religious-historical eye, which means that he sees clearly in detail but dimly in the entirety, and he himself notes this.

It now became an urgent need for me to know the crusades more closely; I got Hake's exposition which naturally much exasperated me; I got [Karl August Wilhelm] Spalding's History of the Kingdom of Jerusalem, and his wretchedly low perspective on the crusades also exasperated me but, since he then allows himself to be steered by his material and simply narrates, I saw him as expounding those expeditions, without his knowing it, in all their wondrousness. Alongside these I read [Jean Charles Leonard Simonde de] Sismondi's excellent work on the Italian republics, and although he too [**GEEG p. 51**] lacks a religious eye yet his narrative is so free from wretched pragmatism and so clear that in the reading there inevitably had to emerge in my mind a different picture of that period from the one he had, and yet up to a point I acknowledge his profundity.

I also read a portion of [Johan von] Müller's History of Switzerland and found myself for the first time in the company of a comparatively historical mind whose perspective upon the hierarchy was for me like an old painting, and his exposition of the horror which made all Europe shudder when the Pope no longer showed himself to be nor was respected as Christ's viceregent thoroughly shook me and planted the shoot of that application of the thesis concerning the necessity of Christianity in the history of the nations which subsequently followed. That Müller himself was not Christian, however, but only observed with his clear historical eye the close connection between religious ideas and the lives of the peoples, is clearly seen from his half-mocking cry: believe single-mindedly, or believe nothing! I saw that he fixed his gaze upon the Romans; I gazed there too, and I saw – sure enough, not that it was the same thing [as Müller saw], but certainly that one must heartily wish that just one single idea had asserted itself upon the sleeping races of Europe.

A new translation of Saxo was announced;[2] I perceived that it could not be what it was supposed to be, and I set myself the task of telling my nation that [Anders Sørensen] Vedel's translation, somewhat adapted in its language, was the one they ought to have, and I set forth the way by which it could again become popular reading,[3] as well as the importance of a nation knowing and loving the history of its land; but even as I wrote, the insight tormented me that it was not in fact the age of the language but the extinct feeling for the lives and achievements of the forefathers that had dispossessed Vedel and Snorri: this then is what was at issue, not a book. I sketched out a picture of Denmark's bygone life and with astonishment I saw for the first time, absolutely transparently, that feeling for the fatherland's history slept and was awakened along with Christianity. I resolved then to give a depiction[4] of what we are now and what the consequence may be, but here the clarity which I saw in the bygone age would not emerge and the task languished. I now read [August Friedrich Ferdinand] Kotzebue's History of Prussia which properly exasperated me, when – on the ninth of October – I was wondrously, inexpressibly affected: and from that time all fear was averted from me and, just like a mist, gone from my eyes.

1. *Sørgekvad ved Prins Kristjans Død* (1810) and *Er Nordens Forening ønskelig? Et Ord til det svenske Folk* [Is a Nordic union desirable? A word to the Swedish people] (1810); the text of which is in *US* II, 21-28.

2. The proposal was made by Gustav Ludvig Baden (1764-1840).

3. There is uncertainty whether Grundtvig wrote *Almuelæsning* or *Almenlæsning* but the sense is the same for either.

4. The draft survives among Grundtvig's papers in the *Grundtvig Arkiv* in the Royal Library Copenhagen.

Two glimpses from 1812-1814

37. Roskilde-Saga (1814), pp. 105-106; GEEG Stk. 37, p. 52.

In October 1814 Grundtvig attended the *Roskilde Landemode*, a biannual convention for dioc-esan clergy in Roskilde, Sjælland, recently reformed by Bishop Friederich Münter to provide a platform for learned papers to be read to the assembled clergy. Grundtvig, who had presented papers in 1811 and 1812, decided this year to read aloud a poetic composition of his own, the *Roskilde-Riim* [Roskilde Rhymes] (see item 71). The work, dedicated to Frederik VI, drew upon some eight centuries of the real and legendary history of Roskilde as a vehicle for exhorting the whole clergy to vigilance and integrity in their ministry and custodianship of the Christian heritage. Because his ailing father had been unable to attend the gathering, Grundtvig found an opportunity to read the poem to him at home in Udby in December. The old man, who had been a pupil at Roskilde Latin School, was deeply moved and gave his son a patriarchal blessing in gratitude. Poignancy is added to Grundtvig's account of that occasion by the fact that only a few months later his father died. The account is part of the *Roskilde-Saga*, an explanatory prose introduction (published separately in October 1814) which Grundtvig wrote to supplement the revised version of the *Roskilde-Riim*, completed on Christmas Eve 1813 and published in Febru-ary 1814. The curious chronicle-style of the excerpted passage is attributable to its source in the *Saga*.

[**GEEG p. 52**] It was a morning in Advent-tide, the second thereafter, when this same clerk saw his aged father for the last time sitting in the living room which had been his room for approaching forty years. He had been here in the world nigh on four score, and had duly proclaimed the word of God for more than two score and ten. There he sat, like an image of the Word's tongue which had bestirred itself for two score years and ten; there he sat in his mortal sickness, pale and feeble, and his son saw him silent and sorrowful. But when the old man asked after yesterday's gospel,[1] whether it did not speak of John's proclamation of the Saviour, and went on: I too am called John, and prisons are of many kinds and I too am in prison, then the heart was touched in the young clerk. And the *Rhyme* lay there right to hand, to be ready for his travels, and it had so wondrously chanced that contrary to custom the greybeard priest had heard nothing of it. Now it came into the son's head that mayhap the rhymes upon the church which was dear to the old man and familiar from the years of his youth, and upon his father, old Otto, whom he honoured in his grave and loved so pass-ing greatly, and upon the star above the graves of Christians which led and which lighted the brethren to their rest – that these rhymes mayhap could yet refresh the aged one. The young man read, the old man listened, and the cherished memories of youth came to life and the heart opened itself to the consolation of the word which was its familiar angel, and the dark night of the grave vanished before the star, and gentle tears ran upon cheek, and happy as a child and deeply affected the old man leaned over his son, gave him his blessing and said: So shall the Lord comfort you in your last hour, as you have comforted me here, because you sang hymns to the God of Israel.

1. The Third Sunday in Advent, 13 December 1812; the text was Matthew 11:2-10 and concerns John the Baptist who had been imprisoned by Herod.

38. *Mands Minde (1838, 1877); GEEG Stk. 38, pp. 52-53; MM, pp. 331-332.*

See the first paragraph of the headnote to item 3. The foreign policy of Frederik VI proved exceedingly costly to Denmark over the first fifteen years of the nineteenth century. Two land and sea assaults on Copenhagen by British forces (1801, 1807) wreaked great material and economic damage, exacerbated by Britain's command of the seas and capacity to interfere with merchant shipping. In 1813 the survival of Denmark's sovereignty itself was placed at risk. Sweden had laid claim to the northern part of Norway (at that time under Danish dominion), backed by Britain and Russia; and in response Frederik had entered into an alliance with Napoleon in July 1813. In reaction to this, a Swedish-led force supplied by the Allies entered Holsten (also under the dominion of the Danish crown) . A Danish army was mustered on the island of Fyn and for a time the country anticipated war, which it was assumed would be fought out in Jylland. Although since Napoleon's defeat at Leipzig in October 1813 (”The Battle of the Nations”) alliance with him was a less secure affair, a great surge of patriotism and loyalty to the king arose among the students of Copenhagen University to which Grundtvig (who in August 1813 had moved with his widowed mother from Udby to Copenhagen) gave a voice. His *Helligtrekongerlyset eller Tre Dages Hændelser paa Dannemarks Høiskole. En Beretning ved Nik. Fred. Sev. Grundtvig, Præst* [The Holy Three Kings (Epiphanytide) light or The events of three days at Denmark's University. An account by NFSG Priest] (1814), reporting the events of 4-7 January 1814, was printed under the motto *Vi have seet Hans Stjerne* [We have seen his star] (Matthew 2:2), and "in a unique manner maintains a diary over some of the most turbulent days in his, and the nation's, life" (*US* 3, 5). The students' offer to fight for Denmark was not taken up. Frederik VI could not risk battle in Jylland. On 14 January by the Treaty of Kiel he ceded Norway to Sweden, ending four centuries of union between Denmark and Norway. The following passage is from a retrospective summary of the crisis drawn from Grundtvig's lectures in Borchs Kollegium 1838.

⌣⌐

[GEEG p. 53] All through 1813 there had been plenty of talk about the Swede wanting to have Norway; but anyone who bothered at all about it doubtless thought as I did: yes, let him take it – if he can! without it occurring to us that Norway should be conquered in Holsten. Not until December, when [Louis Nicolas] Davout stormed into Hamburg and the enemy pursued our troops to Rendsborg, captured Glykstad and overran the land right up to Kolding River – not until then did we wake up to what was happening; but ever since the start of the year and the monetary upheaval there had been such widespread despondency and bewildered indifference everywhere that as far as I know it was only among the students, especially the Jutlanders, that things began to heat up; but there it was also deadly seriousness: they really had the courage to go through fire for Jylland's honour and for the foster-brotherhood with ancient Norway; they wanted me to join them and as it was a matter of rousing the Jutish militia to the defence of Norway surely no one could have been more eager than I. It was in the first days of 1814 that we gathered in crowds for meetings about this cause at Ehlers' Kollegium; in all respects it had been taken up too late, and without doubt, even if things had turned out as well as they could, it would only have cost Denmark more than it could spare, without benefit to Norway; but in just the same way as His Majesty declared to us that he would never forget the students' sentiment on that occasion, so shall I never forget those solemn evenings in that circle of young men minded to make the great sacrifice on the altar of the fatherland; for such hours are in my eyes worth many years; and even though I was far from getting thereby a permanent position on the speaking platform, yet I have always found that it could never be ascended under happier omens.

The "seven lean years" 1813-1820

39. Om Religions-Frihed, (Tredie og Sidste Stykke). Af N. F. S. Grundtvig, pp. 216-217; GEEG Stk. 39, pp. 53-54.

Still paying the price for offending the ecclesiastical establishment with his probationary sermon, and doing himself no favour by engaging in excessively abrasive public dispute (in the periodical *Nyeste Skilderie af Kiøbenhavn*, 1815) with the venerable scholar, State Archivist Grímur Jónsson Thorkelin (1752-1829) over the latter's *editio princeps* of *Beowulf*, Grundtvig passed what he called in biblical allusion his seven lean years without official appointment to a church living and without significant fixed income. It was far from being a period of idleness, however. Over this period he was working on three major medieval literary monuments, Saxo's legendary-history of the Danes, Snorri's History of the Norse kings, and the Anglo-Saxon poem *Beowulf*, alongside which he single-handedly published his periodical *Danne-Virke* (1816-19). For the time being, however, the interest of the book-buying public remained low.

⌐

That the seven years (1813-20) were in no respect to me as seven days will readily be believed, for my books from this period not only bear witness that I busied myself about becoming busier than I was inclined by temperament to be for so long, but unfortunately they also show [**GEEG p. 54**] that in the end it seemed to me so long a time that I had enough trouble making it pass for my own sake, not to mention for my readers, who felt neither inclination nor need to seek their pastime so far back in the North nor so deeply in the sepulchre of thought as I did. That not even for seven days, let alone seven years, can one live on fresh air even if one can make do with little; that a poet, if he is to be a bookworm [*Bog-Orm*], wants to be able to sink his teeth into what tastes good to him – especially if it is expensive; that longtime sweethearts, if they continue to be such, would like to be wedded; that one cannot get married, not to mention keep house, without money; and that precisely during those years it was a treacherous time for money – this is partly so natural, partly so familiar, and partly so prosaically trivial that at that time I was ashamed to talk about it, as being some-thing which ought not to cost a poet, and a Christian priest moreover, one single sigh or unquiet moment; but naturally it cost me many all the same, both then and subsequently, even though the generosity of outstanding friends performed miracles, and our still more outstanding King would hardly let the skald, who nonetheless had at length come to feel the pinch, sigh starving over his art before the royal word created for him a livelihood![1]

1. As the following passage tells, in the Spring of 1818 the king (Frederik VI) noted Grundtvig's hardship and granted him an annual 'Gratifikation' [honorarium] of 600 *rigsdaler* in recognition of his commitment to the translations. That August, Grundtvig at last felt financially secure enough to marry Lise Blicher to whom he had by then been engaged for seven years.

40. Kiærminder til Kong Frederik den Sjettes Krands (1840), pp. 75 -76; GEEG Stk. 40, p. 54.

From a speech made in the Danske Samfund, 28 January 1840, which Grundtvig also published to accompany the poem he composed, honouring the memory of the king who died 3 December 1839, whom he recalls in particular as the generous patron of *Skjalderne* [the poets] including Grundtvig himself. *Kiærminder* are both 'cherished memories' and the flower forget-me-not (species *Myosotis*; Danish *forglemmigej*) thus Grundtvig's title '*Kjærminde* for King Frederik the Sixth's wreath' has deliberately dual signification. The extract gives a glimpse of the culture of the *enevælde* [absolute monarchy] from both sides: the subject's access to the King, the King's personal power to grant Grundtvig an annual '*Gratifikation*' [honorarium], and Grundtvig's uncritical reverence for the monarch, whom he here casts as a latter-day Scylding (ancient Danish royal dynasty, patrons of poets, as celebrated in *Beowulf*, the Anglo-Saxon poem which Grundtvig was studying and translating over this same period).

When I […] was sitting, as good as excommunicated, and working on the translation of the folk-chronicles of the North [*Nordens Folke-Krøniker*], I found it impossible without special support to continue and complete the work, and I therefore approached the incomparably [*mageløs*] accessible absolute monarch and said to the just as incomparably [*mageløs*] natural and homely man: "His Majesty probably knows that I have been occupying myself a good deal with the ancient skalds." "Yes," was the answer, "and with great success." "I would hope not without success," I continued, "but one thing I have not been able to learn from the ancient skalds, and that is to manage without a livelihood." "Then we shall have one created" replied King Frederik the Sixth – and beneath whose sceptre should the song of the skalds be as much for the people as for the king, if not under that of the King who had such words upon his lips, and had a heart to match them?

41. Om Religions-Frihed. (Tredie og Sidste Stykke). Af N. F. S. Grundtvig; conclusion of an article in Theologisk Maanedsskrift, vol. 8 (Copenhagen 1827, suppressed by censor same year, eventually published 1866), pp. 217-219; GEEG Stk. 41, pp. 54-56; US V, pp. 115-117.

In the substantial article from which this excerpt is taken, Grundtvig based a significant discussion of religious liberty upon his own experiences between preaching his dimissory sermon (1810) and his resignation from Vor Frelsers Kirke in 1826. His conviction that there was a personal conspiracy against him in high places is supported by external evidence; in particular, *Provst* H. G. Clausen, powerful archdeacon of the diocese, was a dogged adversary. Ironically, this reasoned and reasonable challenge to the authorities was itself partially suppressed under the terms of the censorship imposed upon Grundtvig following his prosecution (1825) for libel against *Provst* Clausen's son, Professor H. N. Clausen.

Assuredly, I still belong as little as ever either to those curates or to those skalds who think one gets a special claim upon the State if one writes verse, and a double claim if one furthermore lets oneself be ordained; for this way of thinking is just as unreasonable and grossly egotistic as it is unpoetic and unchristian; but nevertheless it was neither fair, politically wise, nor consistent with the Danish government's (elsewhere in this matter) incomparably liberal spirit, [GEEG p. 55] manifestly to set aside, over a stretch of years, one of the most senior theological graduates who, although he was a personal curate, had after all completed his academic course with the best, had a reputation for preaching with excellent abilities and had made headway on the path of Danish authorship which even attracted His Majesty's most gracious notice and created a stir in the whole Nordic reading world. I really think that even if this curate and writer had held political principles which struck the Danish State as somewhat dubious, and had a reputation for being rather heterodox, yet it would have been wise to promote him, especially in the capital where ecclesiastical anomalies signify but little and where the government has a surveillance over all sorts of movements quite different from that outside; but then, since this curate in fact had a reputation for being hyper-orthodox in matters both ecclesiastical and secular, it cannot be denied that his calculated setting-aside until he could literally get a dry crust only through His Majesty's singular grace, or by emigrating, is a riddle in Danish history which presupposes a powerfully working personal antipathy towards the curate, either in the Royal Danish Chancellery or in someone who had a uniquely overbearing influence upon it.

Given, therefore, that in the Chancellery I constantly had to hear for one thing that I was a religious fanatic [*en Sværmer*] and for another that I must not allow myself the slightest hope of a clerical appointment within the city walls even if it were only at the church in the Citadel, for which unenviable position I competed three times;[1] given indeed that the President, as he himself openheartedly told me, as late as 1818 asked *Geheimeraad* [Frederik] Moltke whether the diocesan authority in Aalborg would have anything against my being presented to a vacant curacy there; given furthermore that I know that the President of the Chancellery got me (1817), through my supporter Abraham Kall, to petition him in order, as he himself said, to reconcile myself with the Chancellery; given that I know from several lengthy conversations with this recently deceased Minister what little secret he made of it, that my difference of opinion with the Copenhagen clergy was in his eyes not a political offence at all, but only an insuperable impediment to the advancement I sought; given that I know all this and much more like it – was it then a rash conclusion that the same hand which in 1810 laid the whole public esteem of the Copenhagen clergy in the balance against [GEEG p. 56] my public insignificance, that the same hand maintained that attitude until seven lean years had brought about a famine which the personal curate could not take nearly so lightly as the *Stiftsprovst*,[2] and until His Majesty cut through the knot the Chancellery could not untie, by nominating me – against my wishes but to my benefit – as a provincial town-priest in Sjælland,[3] and in the following year by calling me back – at my earnest request but, as it appears, to my public ruin[4] – as curate at Vor Frelsers Kirke in the *provsti* [deanery] of Vor Frue Kirke.

1. Grundtvig unsuccessfully applied for appointment to the church in the Citadel (now called Kastellet) in 1817, 1819 and 1820.

The seven lean years

2. Though phrased as a reference to 'deans' in general, this surely points at a specific *Stifstprovst*, namely H. G. Clausen, Grundtvig's adversary who obstructed him in various ways.

3. Without having applied for the position, Grundtvig was appointed (2 February 1821) to the incumbency of Præstø in southern Sjælland (where in 1822 he conducted the funeral of his widowed mother), but on 1 November 1822 his attempts to gain an appointment in a city church at last succeeded.

4. Grundtvig makes anticipatory allusion to the troubles which led to his resignation from Vor Frelsers Kirke in 1826.

42. Mands Minde (1838, 1877); GEEG Stk. 42, pp. 56-58; MM, pp. 475-476 and 481-482.

See the first paragraph of the headnote to item 3. On various occasions, Grundtvig returns to the theme of the insular-mindedness of Denmark in the first quarter of the century, at least in the ambiences that then most concerned him, in school and at university and in the Copenhagen literary world in which he hoped to make his way (though the view does not entirely square with, for example, the record of the many Danes who travelled abroad as part of their education or professional development, often with royal grants). Here he recalls what he sees as an example of parochialism in student circles and the literary life of the capital. In Germany and in Austria, especially among students, agitation for the concession of new liberties reached a peak when (October 1817) a *Studentenzug* (Danish *studentertog* 'student rally') gathered at Wartburg to commemorate Luther and the Protestant Reformation, to found a students' union in all German universities, and to protest against official suppression of activists by burning symbols of oppression and tyranny. A period of even more severe suppression and escalation of the confrontation followed, and in 1819 the German dramatist, satirist and historian A. F. F. Kotzebue who polemicised against demands for press freedom and democratic government was murdered by a student activist. In Copenhagen, says Grundtvig, solidarity extended only so far as the establishment (1820) of a *Studenterforening* [students' union] on Holmens Kanal in Copenhagen and "a little pen-feud" [*en lille Pennefejde*] involving a group of students and the poet Jens Baggesen.

⌒

I myself had a small hand in both but I would hardly have mentioned them were it not for Jens Baggesen's sake, who became a thorn in the flesh to our students just as [A. F. F.] Kotzebue to the Germans, although in a far more innocuous way and in a far milder degree. This same Jens Baggesen was, as you doubtless know, a poet from the last century who found himself practically homeless on our Parnassus in the new century, and was naturally a bit disgruntled with all us young ones over this, and especially with our master, *Aladdin*-Oehlenschläger. However, it was not at all due to the nature of the matter, but merely to the circumstances, that Baggesen found himself poetically homeless here in Denmark, for he was a master in his profession, not only in the art of verse-making but in everything that the most sparkling and at times brilliant wit can create, finding no rival among the younger skalds, let alone a superior. So it was only because in Germany and France, where Baggesen lived for many years, he had been led to believe that he was also, seriously speaking, a great poet, but found when he came home in the new century that at this people laughed all the louder – it was only because of this, and through his consequently low perception of high poesy, that he came to see in all of us barbarous forces which profaned the classical ground, and in Oehlenschläger a merely over-lucky rival for the bardic throne. War first broke out between him and me in 1815, when in *Rimelige Strøtanker* [Equitable aphorisms] I took the liberty of making slightly rough fun of his classical exclusiveness; but since it did not fail to proclaim how high he stood above the little people who wanted to elevate themselves above him, he soon found himself in agreement, and conceded me my little corner on Parnassus: among the standing stones where [GEEG p. 57] I was not in his nor anybody's way. But now he formed the desperate idea of wanting to knock Oehlenschläger off his perch, and took occasion for this partly from what was too deep for him and therefore seemed to him enormously stupid, and partly from some of his less successful work, over which the students got so furious that twelve of them – named therefore The Twelve [*Tylvden*] – challenged him not exactly to pistols but nor yet to the pen, which was *his* weapon; no, to a mouthful of cloister-Latin which they presumed that he understood. Now this I found both a bit impudent and very unchivalric, therefore I took Baggesen's part and I venture to believe that I contributed to damping down the excitability of youth.

The worst was that Baggesen, by suing one of his young reviewers who among other things had accused him of plagiarism,[1] initiated those literary Court and Municipal lawsuits which I call our literature's Descent into Hell from which it has hardly yet returned; for when writers become such philistine artisans that they sue each other for defamatory remarks and words of abuse where one is merely talking of intellectual vices and bookish sins, then no living soul can involve himself with any but the thoroughly dead who at least have the virtue of being long-suffering.

A modicum of the foregoing more than likely had its share in the fact that as early as 1817 I so to speak laid down weapons and pilgrim's staff and entombed myself in a burial mound with Saxo, Snorri and the ancient Anglo-Saxon who sang of Beowulf the Goth and Hrothgar *Danedrot*; although it was plainly done in order, if possible, to tempt or to drag *them* up with me into the light of day, in order to get a little companionship which was, to my mind, a cut above the ordinary. Lo, there I sat for seven years and did not know a great deal of what in the meantime was happening in our little world, not more than what I told about Baggesen and The Twelve; but then when I surfaced again in 1823 and began to look about me, then I cannot tell you how dismayed, dispirited and almost completely despairing I was; but if you care to see a picture of me in those days, then it is to be found in my *Forsetes-Kvide ved Grev Danneskjolds Grav* [Forsete's lament at the grave of Count Danneskjold]; for I really did feel as one who believed that he had slept for just one night but had unknowingly been dead a hundred years and therefore discovered an utterly strange world in his old home. No one talked of anything but what they had eaten yesterday and what they would have tomorrow, and where on earth one would get hold of the money for everything one ate in the course of time [GEEG p. 58] even if one was willing to drink water with it which, though, was a bit austere. *Bjovulvs Drape*, which I had truly believed would amuse people, nobody was bothering to read; the *Chronicles* of which I had expected heroic deeds simply did not budge.[3] Our great master of languages, Professor [Rasmus] Rask, came home from Persia and India and Ceylon with great literary treasures, with a name renowned over the whole of Europe and half of Asia and with knowledge unparalleled in his field; but after the banquet at the Skydebane I barely heard his name mentioned, and the University administration did not even find time to make him Professor in Oriental Languages before he was half dead. Not even German novels were translated any more but people made do with [Adolf Frederik] Elmqvist's *Læsefrugter* [Reading-fruits], gathered upon literature's Jutish common-lands. Was that not something to despair over, if one had believed it was the pen that was supposed to achieve wondrous works, and books to shape people!

But, as I have observed once before, the skalds have free access to Olympus so when it gets altogether too tedious down on the plain they know where they can get an encouraging view and a cheerful evening; and the situation endured until no later than 1824; then Ingemann sent me his *Valdemar den store og hans Mænd* [Valdemar the Great and his men] which maybe offended me with the jester's bells it hung on Saxo Grammaticus but yet soon carried me along with it so that I forgot both Saxo and Valdemar with the joyous sight, that the national heart had again turned to its historical heroes; because for me Ingemann was already by that time the thermometer of Denmark's heart.

1. The reviewer was Peter Hjort (1793-1871) who in February 1817 accused Baggesen of plagiarism in his *Trylleharpen* [The enchanting harp].

2. Grundtvig uses, no doubt for the ponderous effect, the formal title of the law-processes – Court and Municipal Lawcourts Processes (*Hof- og Stadsrets-Processer*) – invoked by Baggesen against his rash young reviewer.

3. Less than half of the 3000 copies of Gr's translation of Saxo printed 1818-23 were sold; the remaining 1700 were distributed free in connection with the 50th anniversary of the reign of Frederik vi (1834).

1824 – Retrospect and new ferment

*43. Brevveksling mellem Nørrejylland og Christianshavn
(1823-24) [An exchange of letters between North Jylland and
Christianshavn]; GEEG Stk. 43, pp. 58-66; US IV, pp. 229-235.*

In February 1821, after years of being passed over for clerical preferment, and dispirited by the failure of his translations of *Beowulf* and Saxo to immediately revive public interest in Denmark's history and destiny, Grundtvig was unexpectedly appointed parish priest of Præstø with Skibbinge, not far from his birthplace in southern Sjælland. In the following year his widowed mother died and Grundtvig, approaching his fortieth year, now married and father of a newborn son, was left with only one brother (Otto) out of the Udby family of seven. In the same year (1822) he was granted what he had so long desired and been denied – a *præstekald* [benefice] in the capital city, as *kapellan* [curate] at Vor Frelsers Kirke in Christianshavn, Copenhagen: "that city from which unbelief spread itself across the land, and whence everything which is going to spread itself across the land must flow." The turbulence of peaks and troughs, however, continued. Though he had looked forward to being able "for a time, uninterrupted, in peace, to proclaim the Gospel of Christ" from his own pulpit in the capital, he encountered almost everywhere an inert spiritual indifference (which he often associated with pervasive Rationalism) towards all that he regarded himself as standing for. In response he resolved to write an apologia contrasting the defensibility of Christianity with the indefensibility of indifference. Many drafts of it survive among his papers, showing that he had entered upon a new period of intellectual and spiritual ferment, entailing a retrospective clarification of the directions his own life had taken, and of the coherent objectives of his own actions and activities which had brought him to his present position and intimated his future. As a vehicle for this autobiographical approach he adopted the device of an exchange of letters. A serious and open-minded man from North Jylland writes to him in Christianshavn asking him for his thoughts upon the age and upon the course of his life, both viewed in relation to what Grundtvig understands to be human well-being. This potentially huge philosophical and historical undertaking was never brought to completion. The following text is from one of the last (Spring 1824) and most developed of the drafts as edited by Begtrup (*US* IV, 229-35) under the title *Brevveksling mellem Nørrejylland og Christianshavn* [An exchange of letters between North Jylland and Christianshavn]. It comprises all but an introductory paragraph of the first letter from Christianshavn.

⌒

[GEEG p. 59] I grew up on the Jutish heath under old-fashioned tuition in Christianity and languages but from my own experience I know not the slightest thing about that oppression and thraldom of spirit which has been so dearly sworn to be inseparably bound to it. On the contrary, I have never seen, and cannot imagine a freer development into something other than a loafer than that I have enjoyed, and therefore as long as I live I must now feel indignant, now smile, at the fuss that is made over the new methods, as though free development had been conjured to reside within them; indeed, as though one cannot be beaten just as tyrannically and just as casually over whatsoever last it might be.

From childhood my fancy impelled me mostly towards history, especially of the Church and the fatherland, and since in this I became almost exclusively a disciple of [Ludvig] Holberg and [Arild] Hvitfeld you will readily see that I was educated neither into ecclesiastical zealot [*kirkelig Zelot*] nor into fanatic [*Svœrmer*] over the antiquity of the North; on the contrary, such reading, in association with a liberal upbringing, inevitably gave me a boldness in following and defending my own convictions without any regard to what others thought – which, in the boy, was never in its proper place and which, grown to be second nature, gives offence even in the man, and at the very least easily leads to rashness. So from my own experience I know the weak sides as well as the good sides of a liberal upbringing and thus it comes about that I, who otherwise do not seem disposed towards the middle road, nonetheless in everything that in any way concerns development and upbringing, in major matters as well as in minor, am disposed towards this alone.

After this glimpse of my boyhood years during which I made the acquaintance of the daily papers and the tone prevailing in them, it will hardly surprise you that in the Latin school I keenly championed the old-time Christianity that mine then still was, and that as student not only did I immediately get swept away by the current and chose a way of thinking that advanced a bold freedom beneath its shield, but seized upon it to its full extent and was one of its most eager protagonists. I also therefore know from my own experience how it affects heads that are no better than mine, that is to say probably the majority, to exist in the midst of a naturalistic way of thinking which is called 'free' – and properly so, insofar as within it one bothers but little about Thought's eternal [**GEEG p. 60**] laws but boldly opposes one's own thinking, as an infallible conviction, against all laws. I know from my own experience (though it does not need experience in order to confirm it) that even if one has appropriate basic proficiency, much enthusiasm for reading, and a goodly share of ambition, the scientific disciplines have no right to congratulate themselves on the thoroughness to which that so highly renowned freedom from prejudice leads; and since I have subsequently learnt where a Christian way of seeing things will impel one I must needs smile, at least, when there is talk of Christian one-sidedness as a hindrance to true enlightenment and scholarly thoroughness.

When I reached the age of twenty-two my naturalism destroyed itself; and I know this arose from the fact that beneath my low esteem for all other laws I maintained a veneration for the sovereign law of conscience, and so I needs must declare it to be an unquestionable experiential truth that if one is willing just a little seriously to take stock of oneself, one will soon discover that it is hot air, all that is said about our natural powers of satisfying the unalterable law of purity and love, and that it is mindless parroting or base slander to say that by believing in the Saviour one becomes either indifferent to the law or feebler in its fulfilment. On the other hand, it is surely enough undeniable that if one is irresponsible or false enough for it, one can be just as wicked when one prays to as when one mocks Christ; but this proves nothing other than what Christ himself expressly bears witness to: that it depends not only upon the seed but also upon the soil, whether the harvest be blest.

As soon as I was cured of that unfortunate fallacy that it touches too closely upon men's honour to acknowledge their weakness and to pray God to help them, then Christianity appeared to me in all its lustre and I must needs bow deeply before the Cause of all those great undeniable Effects which I knew from the history of the Christian Church; for, God be praised! I have only a very dim notion of the possibility of defying truth clear as day and thus saying, when one sees Christ's miracles: he drives out devils through Beelzebub [Luke 11:15]; for is one really doing anything other than this if one says that belief in Christ – which, everywhere that it has been received, has destroyed the kingdom of the Devil – is nevertheless itself a superstition, a child of darkness!

I now became a writer and to this extent the die was cast, that, no matter what I said or involved myself with, I was obliged, in proportion to that degree of [GEEG p. 61] seriousness I now possessed, to be on my guard against contradicting, and to seize every opportunity of extolling, Christianity; and my observant readers know that all my writing has this in common – but that otherwise it consists of three principal components: a *mythological*, a *theological* and an *historical*.[1]

To the *mythological* section belongs not only my *Nordens Mythologie* [Mythology of the North] but everything that I wrote before 1811 – my probational sermon itself only half excepted. Others will perhaps rather call this stretch of my path the *poetic* – but I do not, for actually what I believe one ought to call 'poet' I have scarcely ever been, and a poetic element is to be found neither in any one of my writings, nor in their totality. On the other hand, my whole view of human life was at first mythological, for the verity that everything that is noble, great and strong in man is a divine effect, and that the corporeal first acquires its worth and significance when it is viewed as an image and an instrument of the spiritual, this verity, which actually all mythologies have in common with Christianity, was manifestly the centre point about which all my discourse revolved; and even the view, more peculiar to Christianity, of this temporal existence as a preparation for the eternal, was with me more Eddic than Biblical. Christianity then appeared to me as the ideal of all mythologies to which they had more or less approximated but which was unattainable by natural means and therefore, in the fulness of time, they had declined from the sublime. If one understands by mythology merely a collection of tales or even a mixture of true and false conceptualisations of the spiritual, then certainly Christianity was no such thing for me; for I took both the whole wondrous life of Christ to be historical truth and Christianity to be a pure uncorrupted manifestation of the spiritual; but by mythology I understood a map of the kingdom of the spirit and of the route to it which could be more or less incomplete, and in this sense Christianity was for me neither more nor less than a *complete mythology*. Therefore, what I could not allow myself as regards the story of Christ, which had to be pure historical truth in order to print the seal upon his teaching, this on the contrary I allowed myself as regards the teaching itself and as regards the history of the Old Testament, in that here I viewed the words as riddle-pictures whose meaning it was a duty to work out; and this is the proper distinction between a mythology and a [GEEG p. 62] *Revelation*, that in the former it must, and in the latter it may by no means be so. Where in fact one has to guess one's way concerning the import of the words there one has no revelation but a myth or a hieroglyph on its own, and therefore as long as one builds one's so-called Christian view of God's counsels for our salvation upon one's own interpretation or rewriting of the word of the Bible one is manifestly treating Christianity as a mythology and thereby destroying the advantage of the historical sealing; for a word we ourselves have to interpret must necessarily, according to the difference of the people and the times, be extremely differently interpreted and cannot possibly then be a sure guiding star for any of us. The divine sealing of such a word could not possibly occur, since in order to have faith in that which oneself finds reasonable one certainly does not need to regard it as a word of God any different from all the other words he has laid upon human tongues.

If you know anything about church-history you will probably be half shocked over the boldness with which I hereby declare a whole host of famous theologians, and even the Fathers of the Church, to be Christian mythologists – although you will readily see that since I must in all seriousness include myself there is no basis for unfairness; and if, as I believe, the proposed distinction between *Revelation* and *Myth* is illuminating, there is little purpose in blinding oneself.

My second period, up to 1815, I call the *theological*, even though it is hardly likely that anything of what I wrote, except my sermons (which anyway were published later), will be counted as theology; but I call it so because all my writing from that time has to do with simple belief in Scripture as the revealed word of God, and, springing from this, belief in Jesus Christ as the sole means of salvation for sinful human beings. On this part of my path my writings basically give all the information I can give; for whosoever, having read these, doubts that *I spoke because I believed*,[2] him my repeated assurance will surely not satisfy and he belongs all in all with those people to whom I have nothing to say. But among ourselves there can be no question about this, and what you will want to know must therefore be either whether I still have the same belief or what I now think about my way of proceeding with the proclamation and defence of this despised belief.

As regards the first, since you have heard that I still preach much as previously, you can hardly be in doubt [**GEEG p. 63**] as to my answer; but I think that even if you have heard nothing other than that I am a priest, this must be testimony enough for you, as long as you believe I am worth talking with; for you are no doubt familiar enough with the *Augsburg Confession* to know what it teaches concerning Scripture and belief in Christ; and what a scoundrel I would have to be if, after a path like mine, I were willing to sneak myself into a church whose loftiest premise I did not assent to from the bottom of my heart. I can at least assure you that I, as priest, would resign my post in the same moment that I was required to teach something that in my eyes was error; and now, when in 1821 I stood outside the church, busied with tasks which I loved and with the freedom to choose my place of residence where I could most freely busy myself to earn my bread, was I now supposed to sell soul and salvation for a crust of bread? No! such a paltriness with no other grounding than the desire to be paltry you cannot possibly believe of me, and your question must therefore surely concern only my manner of proceeding or at any rate only my subordinate premises as well, which you do not regard as being inseparable from the fundamental premise of my belief. That there can indeed be subordinate premises, such as those I once more or less expressly asserted, but now no longer acknowledge, I hardly dare to deny, since the infallibility of Scripture in every way reduces ours to nothing; but certainly I know of no premises of belief where this is the case, and I must therefore wait until such a thing confronts me. Nor of my manner of proceeding do I have much to say, for as far as I know there is no common rule given in this respect except the one, that we must proceed with propriety, and this I believe I have followed.

Or is it in fact improper in a Christian, when he writes a Brief Outline of World History, first and foremost to consider from a Christian standpoint the relationship of peoples and writers with Christianity, and to judge this according to the clear word of the Bible. And what other [than this] have they found to blame upon my book? or what else could they be impugning, other than that book [the Bible] – unless they were to expect that I should let it [the Bible] be torn down and my faith scorned without making a response.[3]

If you would have me say that it was a very imperfect attempt at an historical apologia for Christianity, which revealed that there were many gaps in the author's knowledge and much lacking in his insight, then you forget that I said all this in the preface and demonstrated in the supplement. But [GEEG p. 64] perhaps it was all too imperfect, immature, even as an attempt? Perhaps; but I do not believe it; for all such must be judged relatively, and a book which met with so much opposition among the learned and so little mastery must, viewed in its time, have been a defensible piece of work; this I would say if the book were another's; I must say the same though it be my own. I could not write it that way now: for that I have, if not too much knowledge, at least too little fire; but precisely for that reason I am glad I did not tarry until now, when a comparable book from me would probably be more difficult to attack but also far less worth defending.

My third period, from 1815, I call my *historical*, and in this there will be agreement with me since everything I have subsequently written turns upon the standpoint that it is also, in the main, only by experience one becomes wise, and that therefore History is something which as far as possible everyone should be familiar with, so that History, which uniquely embraces everything human, can and must connect and interpret it.

Here you see the link which binds together *Danne-Virke* with *Bjovulfs Drape*, and *Udsigten over Verdens-Krøniken* [The survey of world history], for learned folk, with the Danish translation of the Chronicles of the North, for the common man; and if my standpoint on History is as irrefutable as I regard it then it must be easy to discover the cohesion between my last periods because they relate to each other as enlightenment does to edification.

What no doubt surprises you however is partly that I could break off so important a struggle as that over the Faith in an age of professed unbelief, partly that I could calmly settle myself down and translate not Eusebius's Ecclesiastical History or Irenaeus's book against the heretics but Saxo's and Snorri's half-heathen folk-chronicles and a ditto Anglo-Saxon fable. Nor shall I deny that it rings a little strangely and, taken out of its context, it could appear to be proof that my struggle for Christianity was only an episode in my battle for the ancient North and indeed perhaps something I myself perceived as an over-enthusiasm. All this I admit, but the fact is: I did not break off the struggle, but only left the battleground, since they would not stand their ground once they had given up refuting me and were bored with insulting me. These were the circumstances under which I burned the midnight oil over Angul's song and the Chronicles of the North;[4] but yet continued right up to 1819, especially in *Danne-Virke*, to throw down the gauntlet to anyone who [GEEG p. 65] would do battle with me in the field of history, over the honour of the Church and the integrity of my Christianity. Nobody would; nobody now seemed to be in the least bothered any more as to whether belief was true or false, wise or stupid: and what then should a Christian priest, being without a church as though *in partibus infidelium* [in the lands of the unbelievers], not find time for, as long as it was innocuous, even if it had no other benefit than to keep him occupied and in cheerful state? If I had used these years to make matchsticks I could have defended to my contemporaries without anyone being able with justice to say that it demonstrated that I had changed faith or was afraid to hold a tug-of-war with the strong; so how much more should I not have been able to defend using them upon a labour which according to my conviction ought to be performed at some time, which I would perhaps have rather kept until last but ought to perform as soon as I had nothing else to do. I will not try to persuade you of the importance of the labour for I see ever more clearly that it came too early to be liked by many others than children, but that is better than if it had come too late to be liked by others than the elderly; and since I have overcome my own impatience I consign its judgment to time just as serenely as I consigned my time to its accomplishment.

My view of the past, you see, is serene; but now my view of the future – what is this? On the whole, God be praised, also serene, although in many respects mixed. Over human well-being as a whole, and over all the means thereto, that Father disposes, from whom everything father-like in heaven and in earth takes its name: and who can be his child in Christ and yet fear for those who are without God in the world, or sorrow as those that have no hope?[5] If however I view the present moment as something I will improve upon or, what is basically the same thing, as something which of its own self shall be good, then I am close to sinking into the ground; for I know of no time when it has seemed a matter of such indifference what one says and writes, what one does or leaves undone, whether one laughs or cries, sleeps or wakes, as right now. In the time I can remember, which history indeed teaches me belongs to the most intellectually moribund it knows, things have grown more and more moribund year upon year and it seems to me I have myself contributed just as much to this as my diametrical opponents and, according to the natural course of things, one would therefore have to expect, by living out one's span, to experience a time when one would preach if not to empty seats then at least to snoring listeners and when one would write [GEEG p. 66] only for oneself and one's censor.[6] Everywhere I turn my eyes it seems to me I see in the realm of the intellect only sleepwalkers and night-wanderers, skeletons and ghosts, so that I am on the brink of believing that it is also only one of the prime-signed warriors,[7] or ancient Lutheran priests, who walks again in me. Believe me, this is more than a joke, for it is manifestly the difference between the eighteenth and nineteenth centuries that folk of the former age wanted nothing grand but knew what they wanted and did not particularly want more than they could achieve; we on the other hand hardly know what we want and want nothing but impossible things. Now people want to bury themselves in the soil and yet have a lofty poetic outlook, to be free-thinkers and yet enjoy the consolations of religion, raise a rebellion without putting their life at risk, have representatives of the people [Folke-Repræsentanter] without listening to counter-argument; and who can count up all the impossibilities people want, right up to those which I want myself – for do not I wish for no less than that the blind shall see, the dumb speak and the dead arise?[8] For men it is impossible but with God all things are possible; and that my hope in him is not ill-founded, whatever dubious things may happen before it is fulfilled, of this I am, at least for my own part, a valid witness; for what I hope he will do for my kin is only what he has done for me. Many a time I can be too lethargic trustingly to say: "Thou sendest forth thy spirit, they are created; and thou renewest the face of the earth"[9] – but I would have to be a different person to give up the hope that it will happen.

1   "den i Øvrigt bestaaer af tre Hovedstykker: et *mythologisk*, et *theologisk*, og et *historisk*." To some extent this valuable analysis and classification is no doubt Grundtvig's retrospective imposition of seeming orderliness and systematic advance upon what, at the time, was hardly a planned progression. Even so, there is significant coherence in his undertakings in this important phase of his life. An opportunistic and perhaps over-zealous self-immersion in northern myth, which brought him to the point of rationalising Christ as a son of Odin, seems to have helped precipitate in him a remarkable resurgence of Christian orthodoxy which, when brought under control and harmonised with what remained tenable to him of his mythology, led him towards a certain inclusive view of world history (universal history) which he held, in essence, through the rest of his life.

2. Psalm 116:10; and cp. 2 Corinthians 4:13.

3. Grundtvig's Danish is not perfectly translucent here. His (quite important) argument seems to be as follows. (1) He defends his Christian-orientated universal historical stance in *Et kort Begreb* on the grounds that it is incumbent upon a Christian historian – as a testimony of Christian faith – to found his interpretation of history upon the basis of the Christian truths declared in the Bible. His book and his faith are in this sense identified with each other, and both are guaranteed by "the lucid words of the Bible" [*Bibelens klare Ord*]. (2) He asks (rhetorically) what else in his book his critics have attacked other than this expression of his Christian faith. The implicit answer is "Nothing" – all attacks on his book boil down to this single issue. (3) But the critics are attacking not just one book: they are attacking two. In impugning his book which draws its authentication from "*Bibelens klare Ord*" his critics are thereby also impugning the Bible itself. (There is nothing new in Grundtvig's suggestion that there are people who would quite readily impugn the Bible. He had long believed that the rationalists and biblical-textual scholars were tearing down the Bible from its exalted position, leaving the common people in confusion and doubt as to the integrity and authority of the Book). (4) Hence his two-pronged strategy of rhetorical questioning: "What else have they found to blame upon *my book*?" (Implicit answer: Nothing – this attack on his dutiful and faithful Christian reading of history is the sole sum and object of their criticism) and "What else could they be impugning other than *that book* [the Bible]?" (Provisional implicit answer: "Nothing" – the sole, logical object of their destructive criticism is the Bible, as source of revealed truth). (5) *But* (he says) there *is* one more possible motivation discernible in these critics: If they think that Grundtvig would stand by and let both the Bible and his Christian faith be thus condemned without making a defensive response [*Gienmæle* – a neat warning of defiance, for this the term he used in the title of his defence of the Church (*Kirkens Gienmæle*, 1825) against Professor H. N. Clausen] then they are also impugning him personally (as a coward and man of little faith). Hence the extension to the second question: "what else could they be impugning other than that book [the Bible] – unless they were to expect that I should allow it [the Bible] to be torn down and my faith scorned without making a response?

4. *Beowulf* and Snorri's *Heimskringla* (Sagas of the Norse Kings).

5. 1 Thessalonians 4:13-14: But I would not have you to be ignorant, brethren, concerning them which are asleep, that ye sorrow not, even as others which have no hope. [14] For if we believe that Jesus died and rose again, even so them also which sleep in Jesus will God bring with him (King James Bible).

6. Grundtvig was not yet at this time subject to *censur* [censorship] (first imposed upon him in 1826), but equally ironic is the image of a somewhat sterile and enclosed dialogue (or rather, performance and adjudication) suggested by the other two usages of the term *Censor* – '(academic) examiner' and 'reviewer.'

7. To prime-sign was (especially in the early Church) to make the first sign of the cross upon one who was thereupon or subsequently to be baptised.

8. Grundtvig echoes Matthew 11:5.

9. Psalm 104:30.

44. Nyaars-Morgen (1824), Fortalen (Preface), pp. xi-xviii; GEEG Stk. 44, pp. 66-69; US IV, pp. 243-246.

"How vain it is to wrestle with the old troll-witch whose true name is Indifference, that is, spiritual insensibility." This realisation Grundtvig reached after almost succumbing himself to "the pestilence of the age" – that spiritual indifference which he often blamed upon the insidious spread of Rationalism – in the period before his call to Præstø. Revitalised by the God-sent opportunity to preach from his own pulpit, first in Præstø then in Christianshavn, and regardless of the spiritual indifference he continued to encounter in the capital, he addressed himself to his work at Vor Frelsers Kirke borne upon a surge of optimism, conviction, creativity and ambitious goal-setting. The great goal was nothing less than "the revitalising of the Heroic Spirit of the North [*Nordens Helte-Aand*] to Christian exploits, upon a field appropriate to the needs and conditions of the age."

Nyaars-Morgen, published in 1824, is a remarkable and lengthy poetic expression of this powerful spiritual ferment: it is visionary, at times mystical, sometimes in tone and spirit reminiscent of the more consolatory prophets of the Old Testament uttering their glimpsed revelations to the chosen people of God, complex to the point of obscurity in its abundant metaphorical idiom. As elsewhere, Grundtvig uses the term *Nyaar* to mean not solely the start of the calendar year but also the dawning of a new age. The vision once so formed remained with him long; ahead lay the achievement of a crucial personal affirmation of his beliefs in what became known as his *mageløse Opdagelse* [incomparable realisation]; but the hope of building some kind of consensus around the goal of a national spiritual regeneration was all too soon to be calamitously dashed.

I felt with horror how dead I had become, and even physically I felt myself close to the grave, when the hour struck which I had never indeed ceased to hope and trust in, although eventually I had ceased to long very fervently for it: I was called again to be a pastor – and, in the way it happened, so completely against my will that not for a moment could I doubt that it was quite definitely according to God's, and this gave me courage to fight the death within me and about me with hope of the resurrection.[1] The Lord gave me strength and, among friendly people in the friendliest natural surroundings my eyes had seen, I came back to life again so that I was able with optimism and pleasure to complete the translation of the chronicles of the North! No sooner was the work completed than that came to pass which many would surely never have thought, but which I [GEEG p. 67] had never doubted, would happen if I gave it time: I got a benefice in the capital!

My old compulsive wish to be able – in that city from which unbelief spread itself across the land, and whence everything which is going to spread itself across the land must flow – my old wish, here to be able for a time, uninterrupted, in peace, to proclaim the Gospel of Christ as that which for the many millions has been, for me is, and evermore shall be, a God-sent force for salvation, now began to be fulfilled and soon it was fulfilled; for if two annual cycles of Christian sermons here effect nothing worth speaking of, then according to my conviction twenty such can effect only the most awful indifference – can perhaps indeed increase the total of church-goers, but certainly not that of believers. Truly, were I to have declared upon my conscience, after a whole year's preaching, whether I had any reason to believe I had accomplished anything, I should have had to answer: yes, I have an unshakable reason to believe it; for I have preached God's Word, and it stands written: My word shall not return unto me void but, as the snow and the rain, it shall accomplish the thing whereto I sent it [Isaiah 55, 10-11]; but I must honestly acknowledge that this is also the only reason, the one with which I may defy much that seems to testify to the opposite. This was perhaps the hardest trial I have yet been through, because my reborn hope in the present generation and consequent engagement in its intellectual weal and woe was still as a new-born babe for whom indifference can be sufficient cause of death; but, God be praised! that danger too I have overcome – not because the world yet looks any better to my eyes but because what God wills, shall live and cannot die but is strengthened and grows with every struggle through which it passes. One is certainly not going to be comforted or pleased by seeing what has constituted Danish literature in recent years; for if one excludes what always must be excluded – that which nobody reads unless they are forced to – then it has completely lived up to its history; and I have near cudgelled my brains to death, fathoming out a way whereby one could still cause a little stir in the dead sea. I therefore worked with all my strength on an apologia for Christianity which was to show as clear as day both how defensible it is and how entirely indefensible every objection against, as well as indifference towards it is; and this work was by no means in vain, for it exposed the lukewarmness [GEEG p. 68] in my own breast and gave it its death-wound; but I could never achieve satisfaction over the form because, however drily I started out, it soon became so poetic that I found it was not at all fitted to make an appearance upon the dead sea, and when eventually I managed to make it transparent I saw with horror that the life had vanished from it; but I also felt with joy that I myself had come alive again and was filled with a living hope of seeing the same miracle of God in many thousands in the North. As priest I had felt this ever since the beginning of the church year when it went through me like a lightning-bolt that *the night was far spent and the day is at hand* [Romans 13:12]; but as writer I first felt it when I seized the rhymster's staff which had lain idly by me for a long time now, among all the other antiquities I thought I would have to take with me to the grave: then I first felt, thoroughly aglow with life, that for me there had come round a blessed New Year's morn in midsummer whose rays I, by then so long accustomed to the darkness and chill of the grave, had striven for a time to obscure by the rush-light within myself – that is, by dull, half-hearted deliberations and a thousand doubts as useless as they were superfluous. In the midst of this joyous discovery, whose fruits, with God's help, no mockery shall rob me of, I received Ingemann's *Kong Valdemar* and although for a moment it deeply pained me to see that Martyr and Patriarch of Denmark's history, our glorious Saxo, depicted as a pedantic bookworm [*Bog-Orm*] and dust-dry academic, this incomprehensible delusion of the eye could not possibly spoil my heartfelt joy over hearing so vital a Danish-historical voice as has not sounded in the field for many centuries; for such a thing I call, in all seriousness, a resurrection of the hero, the beginning of a new succession of heroic deeds of the Danish heart which shall transfigure and consummate its achievements! So now I saw, also outside of myself, the hope I always nourished attain its fulfilment, and so well might my morning-greeting be, at least for my own part, a morning hymn!

What I now still have to do, it is surely too early in the day yet to say anything certain about; for one always wishes in the course of the day to see one's precious morning-dreams happily fulfilled and yet one must be aware this is not to be banked upon especially if the dreams are, like mine, a wee bit grandiose; but yet I now feel, with God's help, fit to continue the ancient chronicles of the North, to renew and, I hope, augment the old-time Danish hymns and in general to help a number of [**GEEG p. 68**] good old friends, with the help of the rhymster-staff to crawl out of the grave in the hope, with loving care from the tender Danish womankind, of gathering strength for a new lease of life. This is more or less what I have to do, and I ought to be deeply ashamed of myself if, despite all that has happened to me, I can have doubts, even occasionally, of finding a friendly little spot in the North where I can have peace and good cheer for this my daily labour. No doubt it is pardonable if I doubt of finding such a spot in the flat unwooded land to which the whole of Copenhagen seems these days spiritually to belong; but, so what? Amager is after all not the whole of Denmark; soon, God willing, the stone will be rolled away which for many years lay so heavy upon my heart,[2] and then when I have proclaimed the Gospel as well as I can in the capital city of Denmark, then, I feel, I shall be free as the bird in the sky, and I can take my seat in the North wherever it shall be, where God will prepare me a place! Truly it is my hope – unreasonable maybe, but not therefore unfounded – that God, after the eighteen years of trial endured (badly, for sure, in the eyes of God, but not in the eyes of the world), will grant me a little spot where I can preach what I believe, sing what I please and tell what I see, without being afflicted by that boorish sarcasm, that mindless self-opinionatedness, that laughable haughtiness, that frigid hair-splitting, in short, that whole dead state of being which is the pestilence of the age and had hitherto been both within and without my torment! How vain it is to wrestle with the old troll-witch whose true name is Indifference, that is, spiritual insensibility – this Thor learned in ancient days from Udgaards-Loke, but it is one of those things no one believes before he has tried it; now, on the other hand, when I have learnt that one soonest falls when one does battle with nothing, now I yearn quite fervently for a little circle of friendly collaborators who, not caring about the witch, trust in the Lord and fix their eye constantly upon the great goal he surely wills shall be achieved: *the revitalising of the Heroic Spirit of the North* [Nordens Helte-Aand] *to Christian exploits, upon a field appropriate to the needs and conditions of the age!!*

1. Grundtvig refers to his appointment (unsought) to the incumbency of Præstø with Skibbinge (February 1821) followed by his appointment (November 1822) as *kapellan* [curate] at Vor Frelsers Kirke in Christianshavn, Copenhagen.

2. Grundtvig alludes to the great burden of his historical translations (Saxo, Snorri, *Beowulf*) over the period 1815-22.

45: Sermon in Vor Frelsers Kirke, Ninth Sunday after Trinity, 31 July 1825
US IV, 386-94; not in GEEG.

At the end of July 1825 Grundtvig, enlightened by writings of the Church Father Irenaeus, came to an understanding of the unique significance of the Apostles' Creed for the Church. This understanding, which he believed by-passed what he held to be the destructive rationalisations of many contemporary theologians and church historians, is what came to be called his great realisation or discovery – *den mageløse Opdagelse*, which formed a foundation for the theology of the Living Word [*Det levende Ord*] as he was henceforth to develop it. He first outlined this perception to his congregation at Vor Frelsers Kirke in a sermon delivered on Sunday 31 July 1825. In reasserting traditional doctrine of the Trinity against modern rationalists, he appealed to the authority of the Apostles' Creed which (as Irenaeus attests in what Grundtvig calls "*det mageløse Vidnesbyrd*" [that peerless testimony]) has been confessed by Christians as long as Christians have existed, that is, from the time of the Apostles; thus these words, spoken at Baptism and before the Lord's Table, form an irreducible and irrefutable core of truth and authority in the Church's possession; they are the living word, the life and the guarantor of every faithful Christian congregation. The first part of the sermon has been on the subject of Old Testament prefigurations of Baptism and Eucharist, on false teachers and idolatry and on true teaching and honouring the Trinity, and on the comfort of the messianic prophecies. Grundtvig casts himself in the role of prophet. See also the headnote to item 9.

***

Christian friends! If this is a dark saying to you, you know not how the Lord comforts his people and puts an end to doubt, reveals his glory that they all may see it, great and small, wise and foolish, that He, that Jesus Christ, is our God, the God of the Christians with honour and to His Father's honour, as long as the world shall stand; you know not how the Lord puts them to shame who say it is unChristian and idolatrous to worship Him, to honour the Son as one honours the Father, and to call Him God; you know not how He has caught the wily in their own snare, in the snare they laid in His Church for His congregation, how they themselves are fallen into the pit they [US IV, p. 392] dug, descended to the uncircumcised, to all blatant enemies of the Church. If you still do not know it, then hear me carefully, then hear how the Lord has taught me to comfort the Lord's people and to speak comfortably unto Jerusalem; then hear what I have learnt to reply to those who call themselves Christ's apostles, the servants of Jesus Christ, and yet will rob Him of His divinity's honour, rob His body, that is His congregation, of its Head in heaven and thereby of its certain hope, its eternal comfort. Or do you know it all, did you perhaps know it long before I did, who, after having suffered shipwreck of my childhood faith, was found like a corpse upon the naked seashore and for a long time could not rightly decide where I was when I woke up in the church, and long imagined that I had been far away in foreign lands and had half walked with pilgrim-staff, half been carried back to my home, to the motherly bosom of the Church; for a long time could not understand that it was all a dream, a dreadful dream [...]

[US IV, p. 393] Thus then I answer those who say that it is both idolatrous and unChristian to call Jesus Christ God with the Father and to worship Him. You make an extraordinary mistake, at least when you say it is unChristian, for it is obvious to you as it is to me, it is obvious to us all that as long as there have been Christians, just as long have there also been people who were baptised in the name of the Father, the Son and the Holy Spirit, just as long have there also been people who confessed that Jesus Christ was the only-begotten Son of God, God with the Father, in whose Word they let themselves be baptised, in whose name they knelt, in whose name at baptism they received God's Spirit with forgiveness of sins, in community with whose Body and Blood they found everlasting life, as God's gift of grace in Him, in Christ Jesus, our Lord. See! this is what you cannot deny without becoming a laughing-stock to each other, to the congregation; this is what the Church's foes affirm just as loudly as its friends; this is the profession of the Apostolic belief which is sealed with the blood of all those who have shed it in witness of our Lord Jesus Christ; this is that Creed which we still find among all Christian congregations, which was also pronounced for you when you received baptism as a bath of rebirth and renewal by the Holy Spirit; this is the Creed you have yourselves adopted – unless, by despising the Lord's Table, you have excluded yourselves from His congregation.

46. Om Religions-Frihed. (Tredie og Sidste Stykke). Af N. F. S. Grundtvig; conclusion of an article in Theologisk Maanedsskrift, vol. 8 (Copenhagen 1827, suppressed by censor same year, eventually published 1866); US V, pp. 130, 149, 153; not in GEEG.

In 1825, the publication of Professor H. N. Clausen's *Catholicismens og Protestantismens Kirke-forfatning, Lære og Ritus* [Constitution, doctrine and rites of Catholicism and Protestantism] contributed to changing the course of Grundtvig's life, coming close, to all immediate appearances, to ending his career as a writer, blocking his vocation as priest and jeopardising hopes of any other form of future public appointment. Grundtvig (in *Kirkens Gienmæle*) had furiously denounced Clausen's understanding of the Danish Church and declared Clausen himself unfit to teach since his teachings denied the very authority upon which his own status in Church and University rested. Clausen sued for libel and the authorities discerned an offence against regulations governing the press. Grundtvig was fined and placed under lifelong censorship. His intention to publish a lengthy self-vindication in 1827 (in *Om Religions-Frihed* [On freedom of religion]) was stifled by the censorship imposed upon him by the courts, so his account of the *mageløse Proces* [unparalleled, extraordinary process], as he called the law-suit, did not appear in print until 1866 when laws controlling the press had been changed in the wake of democratisation. The following are brief excerpts from his account. See further item 35 and the Index entries *Clausen*, Henrik Nikolai; *Kirkens Gienmæle; censur*).

⌇

[US V, p. 130] Shall I speak of that unparalleled process [*denne mageløse Proces*] or shall I be silent? I can do both and would rather do the latter if only I were sure it would nevertheless remain unparalleled; but since I cannot possibly be that, and yet would be just as reluctant for Denmark's sake as for my own that it should ever lose this designation [i.e. that the process should cease to be unparalleled], I must gather into a brief summing-up what happened, as a legal curiosity of the nineteenth century. Since I have been declared null and void as a writer and an ex-pastor withal, it is plainly no delusion, that I speak of the whole thing as something which happened in old days, as irrelevant to both me and my fellow-citizens as anything human can be to human beings who strive to avoid the mistakes of the past and to learn from the hurt of others.

[Gr gives a lengthy, detailed and technical, as well as polemical, account of proceedings, representing the issue as one affecting not him alone but Denmark, its priests, its poets, its patriots; but unquestioningly obedient, in the end, to the authority of the *enevælde*, he vows to lay down his pen as he has done his priestly office.]

[US V, p. 149] So then I here lay down my patriotic pen at the foot of the throne, as I laid down my office;[1] and although I had hoped to wield it in Denmark until my death, yet will I dip it no more since it does not please His Majesty [*Majestæten*], of whose grace I hope, on the other hand, that I be allowed without prosecution to write these words for printing which, without complaint, I could have uttered orally before the throne of Majesty [*Majestætens Throne*] in the Supreme Court – if I had been summoned there to give an account of the conduct of my office and of the connection between that and *Kirkens Gienmæle*!

[US V, p. 153] Speak then, my pen![2] and in your shackles bow deeply before His Majesty, just as I, the deeply bowed priest, poet and citizen bow when His Majesty speaks! Nik. Fred. Sev. Grundtvig.[3]

1. Though Grundtvig here associates his resignation from the curacy at Vor Frelsers Kirke (1826) with the Clausen libel case, there were other weighty factors involved. One was the success of Clausen's father (*Stiftsprovst* H. G. Clausen) in securing a ban on the use of hymns which Grundtvig had written to be sung on Whitsunday 14 May 1826 when the Danish Church was to celebrate its thousand-year anniversary; Grundtvig was deeply wounded and disgusted by the deviousness of his superiors. Another was Grundtvig's growing disillusion with the discipline and integrity of a Church which required him to minister to people without faith who casually used the church merely to fulfil social and legal obligations.

2. But Grundtvig hoped too much of the authorities: the article was suppressed.

3. Grundtvig's main account of his *Kirkekamp* [Church Struggle] around 1825, which chronologically speaking belongs here, forms part of the very lengthy retrospective narrative in his *Kirke-Speil* [Mirror of the Church] (1871), excerpted as item 59 below. It has been thought best to leave it in that context.

The visits to England 1829-1831

47: Article in Grundtvig's periodical *Danskeren I* (1848), pp. 585-586; GEEG Stk. 45, p. 70.

To all outward appearances, the second half of the eighteen-twenties had been disastrous for Grundtvig, the happiest event being, perhaps, Lise's safe delivery of a daughter, Meta, in 1826 (she was to prove a great consolation to Grundtvig in years to come) – but the family lived in straitened circumstances on an uncertain income. Convinced of the need for a Christian revival in Denmark, certain of the Christian truths he desired to preach, and increasingly aware of the need for reform within the Church, he had nevertheless been without a pulpit of his own since his resignation from Vor Frelsers Kirke, and prospects for advancement within the Church looked dim. As a writer, he faced the humiliation and constraint of having to get an official *imprimatur* for anything he wished to publish. It was therefore a shrewd move to turn back to scholarship, to Northern antiquity and to Danish legend-history in the form of the Anglo-Saxon epic poem *Beowulf* and other Anglo-Saxon writings which might be tracked down in the libraries of England. In an audience with the king (Frederik vi) he was advised to apply for a royal grant to enable him to visit England, and this he subsequently received. In fact, he received support for three successive summer visits. His encounter with England and English culture, both ancient and modern, proved to be of very great consequence to him and to his country.

⌒

[GEEG p. 70] Englishmen are not among those people who accommodate themselves to foreigners, so if one wishes to go among them one must needs learn to stick one's finger in the soil and sniff out where one is; and of this I got a foretaste even before I set foot ashore – and in such a funny way that even if it was in itself a triviality it still amuses me to think about it. When one sails up the Thames to London one in fact takes on board a customs officer who has to see to it that one does not smuggle anything in; so we also got one, and since the lady wife of this same customs officer had come out in order to visit him, the skipper or captain I was travelling with was naturally polite enough to invite her to eat dinner with us, which she accordingly did; but when the captain noticed that she did not help herself to the potatoes we had with the meat he did the best he could in his broken English to let her know that the potatoes were well worth eating; and so then she took a couple, but with a very condescending demeanour and with the words: But I know in advance they are not as good as the English ones. At this, the captain was very offended – and sea-folk are rarely sensitive; but since after all he did not want to fall out with the Customs Office he made do with saying to me in Danish: *Den forbandede Mær!* The damned bitch! how can she say that my potatoes are not just as good as the English ones before she has even tasted them? Naturally, I agreed with the captain, both that the Custom-wife's Englishness was a little excessive and that it had burst out very discourteously; but still, by examining more closely how far ahead the Englishman has got with the belief that there is nothing to match Old England or things English in all of the world, I have reached the conclusion that when it comes to the pinch a nation should much rather, like Englishmen, idolise all that is their own, than, as we long have done, idolise almost everything foreign and disparage or even utterly forget one's own.

1. Named in Grundtvig's Almanac for 1829 as Andresen from Altona near Hamburg.

48: *Mands Minde (1838, 1877); GEEG, Stk. 46, pp. 70-1; MM, pp. 460-461.*

See the first paragraph of the headnote to item 3. When one has a good anecdote to tell, to such an audience and on such a jovial occasion as the *Mands Minde* lectures quickly became, one has a licence to embroider the facts a little. Upon the censor-freed platform of these lectures, Grundtvig, now in his mid-fifties, was about the task of self-portraiture to a new, mainly young generation of Copenhageners. Naturally enough, it was to be a portrait about which disciples might thereafter build myths: here that of the Danish viking (a metaphor Grundtvig liked to apply to himself in contexts relating to his English visits of 1829-31) cocking a snook at pompous, chauvinistic and bumbling English antiquarians and librarians, and finally panicking them into protectiveness towards their national treasures. Among the facts pardonably suppressed for the sake of the story is that as early as 1814 John Josias Conybeare (1779-1824), Professor of Anglo-Saxon and Professor of Poetry in the University of Oxford, had communicated papers on Anglo-Saxon poetry drawing attention to the Exeter Book and to *Beowulf*, with some transcriptions and analyses of the alliterative mode of composition, to the Society of Antiquaries of London who then published them in their journal *Archæologia*, vol. xvii. The journal appears among the acquisitions of the Royal Library in Copenhagen from that period. Then in 1826 a volume collecting Conybeare's pioneering work on Anglo-Saxon poetry was published posthumously (and also purchased by the Royal Library), in which Conybeare advocated a programme of publications of Anglo-Saxon texts: it was in fact used by Grundtvig in preparation for his visits to England as his own notes in the Arkiv show. Meanwhile several other English scholars were already at work on England's early literature and language, including Benjamin Thorpe (1782-1870) who ultimately published the *editio princeps* of the Exeter Book, having resided in Copen-hagen 1826-30 in order to study Anglo-Saxon with the outstanding Danish linguistic scholar Rasmus Rask (1787-1832). However, the myth of English antiquarian ignorance and negligence is well set up by Grundtvig and has sturdily endured.

The first summer I was in England – for just like the first Danish vikings I made only sum-mer expeditions to the Thames and packed up before winter – the first summer, then, the Englishman viewed me as a half-crazed poet who had got the notion that there [GEEG p. 71] lay great treasures buried in the ancient barbaric tomes, which they laughed at mightily, seeing me sitting there daily and rummaging in them, and they told me with an air of importance that there was nothing there.

The second summer on the other hand, when they saw that I really had returned and noticed that I, who had now become better familiarised with both them and the language, was really making fun of them and deploring their lack of discrimination – that they gar-nered glass beads and cast away the jewels – now they plainly began to harbour doubts that after all things might not be so much of a piece as regards the judgment [David] Hume and their other historical oracles had passed, without examination, upon the Anglo-Saxon period; and with regard to this I must tell you a characteristic episode which says more than many words. Down in *Exeter* in Devonshire there lay a book of Anglo-Saxon poetry which it was known had lain there in the ancient diocesan library ever since Exeter got its first bishop at the end of the eleventh century; and one of the first things I asked after in the British Museum was, naturally, whether they did not have there a faithful transcription of this remarkable book; but with a condescending smile they answered me that one did not bother with such things. The next summer it was of course my resolution to go to Exeter, and having furnished myself with a recommendation from the Archbishop of Canterbury in order to gain access to the firmly closed diocesan library I told them this in the British Museum; but now they were far from laughing; on the contrary they looked very serious and thoughtful and enquired several times as to whether I really meant to put myself to this great inconvenience, to which I naturally answered with a smile: "Yes, I am obliged to, since that is trash to you what to me is a great treasure." A couple of days after, the Secretary of the Museum came briskly up to me with the words: "Now you don't need to journey to Exeter; we have written to them down there, to borrow the famous manuscript and have it transcribed." "Really?" I said, "That was handsomely done of you; but it will be a bit of a slow process, so I can't spare myself the journey."

49. Mands Minde (1838, 1877); GEEG, Stk. 47, pp.71-73; MM, pp. 427-428.

See the first paragraph of the headnote to item 3. Grundtvig's letters from England to his wife confirm his shock and depression when in the summer of 1829 he first wandered forth from his ship, rather poorly prepared either practically or psychologically, into the vastness and indiffer-ence of England's capital city. Yet it is testimony to his inner resources (and the conviction that all was within the Lord's good purposes) that he rose above depression, humiliation, loneliness and frustration, built up a circle of acquaintances, worked upon his scholarly mission, returned again in two further successive summers and used his diverse experiences to form critical per-spectives, amusingly sketched but with sober implications, not only upon the English but also upon his own country and culture; as is glimpsed in the following excerpt.

⌐⌐

England, in my experience, is a tedious country to be in if one does not have one's house and home and daily business affairs there, to keep one amused; for everybody there is so inordinately *busy*, each with his own, from the ministers of state to the pickpockets, the public houses are so unpleasant, and private houses so thoroughly locked and fortified that the stranger is either entirely left to himself [**GEEG p. 72**] like an owl among crows or else he immediately gets tired of seeing what an effort it costs and what a sacrifice it is for an Englishman to devote half, not to mention a whole, hour to him. I have therefore never been closer to despairing than when I first came to England, to which it definitely contrib-uted to some extent that I was already somewhat elderly when I, so to speak, first came out into the world, and that I arrived there, so to speak, headfirst by boarding a Danish ship out here at the Customs House and landing directly at the Customs House in London, which inevitably seemed to me like arriving as a complete stranger in another world.

However, I conclude that the reason for my desperation lay more outside me than within me, or rather more in my Danishness than in my bookworm nature [*Bogormevæsen*], from the fact, among other things, that I once met in London a much younger, fitter and already well-travelled countryman who, before he could get started at work, became so desperate that he believed if it had not been for the sake of his wife and children here at home he would have jumped straight into the Thames. I also have a strong suspicion that a great deal of desperation lies at the bottom of this inordinate English busy-ness; for with them it is not at all as with the Germans, that they pursue industriousness as a virtue for its own sake; work seems on the whole not to give them any pleasure, and even though self-interest is the commonest driving force nonetheless one sees many Englishmen who are just as busied in gadding about the world as others are in working, or just as busied in squandering money as others are in earning it.

But just as tedious as on the whole I found England to be in, just as pleasing I have since found it to think about, when one comes home to Denmark where folk usually allow themselves good time for everything, so that one can properly size up all that busy-ness at leisure and view it from both sides, the bright as well as the dark; and the more I do this the clearer it becomes to me that we might wish a goodly portion of it for ourselves, if by this Copenhagen would become a far more agreeable place for foreigners to stay than it now has a reputation for being and indubitably is. For even with regard to foreigners we should much prefer them to say: "True enough, we were bored in Copenhagen, but we took away with us the picture of a great and [**GEEG p. 73**] vital industriousness which we would not have missed at any price" than that they should say, as is now usual: "Copenhagen is a very beautiful and amusing city, but with that you have said everything, for the culinary arts and entertainment seem to be the only things pursued with any vigour and zest."

50. Introduction to Phenix-Fuglen. Et angelsachsisk Kvad. Førstegang udgivet med Indledning, Fordanskning og Efterklang [The Phoenix. An Anglo-Saxon poem. Published for the first time with introduction, Danish version and an afterword] (1840), pp. 10-12; GEEG, Stk. 48, pp. 73-75.

Grundtvig's decision to publish an edition of the Anglo-Saxon poem *The Phoenix* in 1840 is in itself an example of the way he would put to use in a contemporary context the materials he had gathered from his visits to England (in this case poetry he had transcribed from The Exeter Book). In 1839 Frederik VI died, having been king since 1808 and having in effect wielded royal power from 1784; in 1840 Christian VIII, a well-educated and cultured man with a particular interest in history and literature, was crowned amid great expectations that a new era in Danish national life would now begin. The poem's theme of triumphant rebirth from the ashes of the funerary pyre was therefore apposite, and Grundtvig used the lengthy preface partly to remind people of his longstanding service to the study of Danish history and historic Danishness, and to literature, and partly to air contemporary hopes and aspirations in the dawning of the new age. Christian's queen, Caroline Amalie, was, and would remain for the rest of Grundtvig's life, a faithful supporter and patroness of his work, particularly in the educational field. Here Grundtvig tells a version of the story of his decision (1828) to travel to England.

⌒

It was in the year 1828, when I was standing, so to speak, idle in the market-place, that King Frederik the Sixth on one occasion asked me what I was working upon and I answered: Nothing, your Majesty! and I really do not know what to do at the moment, unless it might please his Majesty to let me travel to England and examine the Anglo-Saxon manuscripts more closely, which are also of great importance for the illumination of Denmark's antiquity but are entirely disregarded in their homeland.[1] The King received this speech with lively interest and the consequence of it was my English journeys 1829-31, which so far appear to have yielded no return at all but which as I shall endeavour to show were in no way useless. This fact would surely not have required fresh proof if the 'Angelsachsiske Bibliothek' [Anglo-Saxon library][2] for which I provided a prospectus in English, had not been strangled at birth,[3] but now it looks like a ceremonial caress as compensation for everyday coldness which I, far from being able to invoke it, rather have difficulty in defending.

The story however is this: that when I came to England the first time and with barbaric eloquence waxed expansive over the beauty of Anglo-Saxon literature and its unhappy fate, all the answer I got was a pitying smile over my poor taste, since all the experts would know at first hand that what I praised to the skies as a faery-queen [*en Ælve-Dronning*] was an ancient wrinkled hag who with her black arts and with her barbaric mode of thinking had fully deserved the kicks and contumely with which [David] Hume, [Thomas] Warton and other gentlemen of the finest classical education had found it necessary to fend off her blandishments. Naturally, this annoyed me, not merely for the subject's sake but particularly for my own, and I then availed myself in the cruellest way of the unfamiliarity of those involved with what they condemned, to tease them over the great self-denial they showed in so completely leaving to us the historical and poetic queen of the new Europe, together with all that world-historical renown that we Danes, as her feeble, maybe, but faithful knights, were sure [**GEEG p. 74**] enough of winning but, out of natural modesty, would willingly have shared with our high-born and splendid kinsmen in Angul's Isle who undeniably had first claim upon the honour. When this, upon my second quite unexpected visit, began to take effect, people urged me, half in jest and half in irritated seriousness, to bring into the light of day this beauty whom I could never tire of extolling, and ensured that my endeavours to shed light upon this murky business should not want for support; and when then the publishers themselves, Black and Young, offered their services I could not possibly refuse to take the step which could well seem to have been abortive and yet served to advance the cause.

So my prospectus was published for an Anglo-Saxon Library, the editing of which by myself no doubt bordered on the impossible but which I knew needed only to attract a little attention in order to find an editor in England itself. In the prospectus, therefore, far from sparing English sensitivity, I strove assiduously to wound it as deeply as possible and said, among the rest, straight out: "If I were an English, instead of a Danish poet and historian, I would address my fatherland in the words of the 'Immortal Bard':

Dorskere er du end Urten, som raadner
Paa Fedme-Jords-Bredden af Lethe i Mag,
Vil du dig ei røre endnu;[4]

but though I am indeed far from able to express myself in English with such terseness, I should not complain that my services were rejected if it should simply appear that it was not the subject but only myself that was viewed with indifference."

For a while, the signs were promising that the subscription would be sufficient and therefore I must needs either shamefully withdraw or attempt the absurdity of residing in Denmark and being the leader of such an undertaking in England, and I still had enough of my poetic audacity without hesitation to choose the latter; but when, in order to get started on it, I came to England for the third time [summer 1831] my prospectus had worked its natural effect so that I was plainly regarded and treated as a Danish Viking who, after the example of my dear forefathers, desired to enrich both myself and Denmark with England's treasures, and the publisher [Black, Young and Young] was on the brink of saying straight out that he did not dare to have anything more to do with me, so as not to be branded a traitor to his country.

[GEEG p. 75] However, let me not be misunderstood, as though I meant to complain over my shipwrecked expedition, for I count those summer months I spent in London and Cambridge[5] as the most agreeable as well as the most educative in my life, and personally I met with all the respect and courtesy I could wish for; but the cause, the publication of the important and precious remnants of the first new-European literature, this had now become an issue of honour for England which could not possibly be given up out of acquiescence to a foreigner. Now since this was precisely what I had desired from the outset, I was not hard to console (although it was a little impertinent of a certain man[6] to declare that the publication of an Anglo-Saxon library was *his* deep idea which I had opportunistically snapped up and now wished to ruin him by implementing), and I have therefore sat very patiently and watched how they publish one portion after another of the work of which I was the herald.

1. It was an innocuous exaggeration to suggest that English scholars showed no interest in or esteem for surviving Anglo-Saxon literature. As recently as 1826 the Anglo-Saxon research and editorial work of John Josias Conybeare (1779-1824), Professor of Anglo-Saxon (1808) and Professor of Poetry (1812) in Oxford, had been published by his brother William Daniel Conybeare (1787-1857) as *Illustrations of Anglo-Saxon Poetry*, which contained work provisionally published by John over a decade earlier in which he had advocated a programme of publication of surviving Anglo-Saxon writings. These publications were in the Royal Library Copenhagen well before Grundtvig put his proposition to the King. Furthermore, even as Grundtvig prepared his first visit to England, the young English scholar Benjamin Thorpe (1782-1870) was in Copenhagen studying Anglo-Saxon with the Danish philologist Rasmus Rask, preparatory to a scholarly career as an Anglo-Saxonist. Since Grundtvig knew Rask well and had discussed with him collaboration on an edition and translation of *Beowulf*, it would be odd if he had heard nothing of Thorpe's presence, work and ambitions.

2. Gr's footnote: *Bibliotheca Anglo-Saxonica. Prospectus. London* MDCCCXXI

3. When Grundtvig returned to London in 1831 (with a royal grant of 300 *rigsdaler*) he found that the Society of Antiquaries (some of whose members had hitherto ostensibly supported his initiative) had formed a Saxon committee and launched their own publication plan, with Benjamin Thorpe as the nominated editor of the first volume.

4. In this account of what he said in his *Prospectus*, Grundtvig quotes Shakespeare (*Hamlet*, Act I, Sc. v, 32-33) in a Danish translation of his own, as given here (of which the literal translation is: More sluggish are you than the weed which rots / on the fat-earth-shore of Lethe at ease / if you still will not bestir yourself). In the *Prospectus* itself the English quotation is oddly punctuated: Duller shouldst thou be than the fat weed / That rots itself in ease on Lethe's wharf / Would'st thou not stir in this?

5. In Cambridge, June 1831, Grundtvig was guest of the hospitable Professor William Whewell (1794-1866) in Trinity College. His experience there subsequently contributed to his ideal of a Danish *folkehøjskole*.

6. By summer 1831 Benjamin Thorpe was already working (with support of the Society of Antiquaries) on an edition of the Anglo-Saxon poems traditionally attributed to Cædmon which he published the following year. There is little doubt that the Antiquaries' initiative followed Gr's, just as there is little doubt that Thorpe's ambitions preceded Gr's initiative; but as for the public advocacy of a publication programme both were preceded by John Conybeare. Nor should the stimulus of Dk's State Archivist G. J. Thorkelin (1752-1829) and the debate launched by his 1815 *editio princeps* of *Beowulf* (*De Danorum rebus gestis secul. III & IV : Poëma Danicum dialecto Anglosaxonica*) be overlooked: his pioneering work was critically noticed in Conybeare's *Illustrations;* in 1835 John Kemble (1807-57), another young English Anglo-Saxonist (whom Grundtvig met in the British Museum), published an edition of the poem; and other editions and translations followed from scholars in various countries. In 1840 Frederic Madden (1801-73), Keeper of Manuscripts at the British Museum (1837-66) and yet another young English medievalist who had encouraged Gr's plans and with whom Grundtvig remained in touch for several years, published for the Society of Antiquaries an edition of Layamon's *Brut* (a Middle English text in which Grundtvig had shown much interest), and in 1842 Thorpe published the Exeter Book to which Grundtvig had undoubtedly drawn fresh attention in 1829 and 1830.

From the later years

With the major exception of his *Kirke-Speil eller Udsigt over den christne Menigheds Levnetsløb* (1871), from which excerpts are given in item 59 below, autobiographical passages are relatively sparse in Grundtvig's later writings. This lack is to some extent compensated by the wealth of reminiscences deriving from those around him, from which a more continuous record of his activities over the later years may be elicited.

51: Mands Minde (1838, 1877); not in GEEG; VU 4, p. 259.

On the source, see the first paragraph of the headnote to item 3. In this lecture Grundtvig speaks in praise of Denmark, Copenhagen, the Øresund coast, and Strandvejen (the coastal road northwards out of Copenhagen), and of that blending of national-historical associations with the idyllic vistas of landscape and sea which had been rediscovered and celebrated by such as Thomas Thaarup (1749-1821) in his poetry and author Frederik Sneedorff Birch (1805-69) in his lectures. Never, he says, was he himself more conscious of all this than when, one evening in Strandvejen, he was inspired to compose his song about Willemoes. This is the song which his audience spontaneously began to sing after his lecture and which students returning from Skamlingsbanken sang in honour of both Willemoes and Grundtvig, as their ship passed Sjællands Odde on 5-6 July 1844.

Although I am a village child from a lovely area where too the sea weds itself to the woodland, yet I am conscious of nothing more surely than this, that the most historical-idyllic mood I know from experience is that in which, thirty years ago, one evening on Strandvejen, I was humming to myself the song about [Peter] Villemoes, which is not unfamiliar to you all: *Kommer hid, I Piger smaa! / Strængen vil jeg røre.*[1]

> 1. Come you here, you lassies small / for I mean to strike the string. From the Strandvej Grundtvig could look out across the Øresund and Kongedybet where Willemoes achieved fame for heroic action against an attacking British fleet (1801). See Index entries **Willemoes, Peter**; and **Rune-Bladet**.

52: Mands Minde (1838, 1877); VU 4, 239; not in GEEG.

On the source, see the first paragraph of the headnote to item 3. Grundtvig argues in this lecture that good fortune is better than intellect (*Lykken er bedre end Forstand*). He refers, of course, not to material prosperity but to *Skjaldens Lykke*, the good fortune granted to the poet whose blessing it is to have the spirit (*Aanden*), ever young, hover over his head even in his grey hairs

– the spirit which controls the word, the winged word which moves hearts as the wind the ocean. An autobiographical dimension is characteristically sustained.

⁓

Yes gentlemen, this good fortune: that the little bird overhead which sang above my poet's-cradle of the rebirth of the warrior-life, of the noble, strong and jovial folk-life, in the North,[1] and especially upon the lovely "spot of earth" which has been apportioned us in "Denmark, loveliest mead and meadow, encircled by ocean blue,"[2] the little bird which sang so that it resounded sweetly in my breast, that little bird is not dead; and if it descended a little it was only so as to settle itself upon the hand, a little closer to the heart; and what an agreeable difference it makes during scholarly endeavours, which always have something in common with the hunt, not to have a hawk or a falcon but a songbird upon one's hand, only they know who have tried it;[3] what consolation it is when one is tempted by despondency in a time of confusion, when almost everything called edification and enlightenment is removed steadily further from life and nature, what consolation it then is to hear a little bird sing of how foolish or how vain it is, when one has a fatherland and is standing in its midst, even more so when one has a Nordic fatherland, unsubjected to foreigners, from time immemorial peopled by siblings and kinsfolk, yes, even when one has Denmark as one's fatherland, of all lovely lands within and without the most homogenous in the world – then to think that one stands alone, to think there is hardly anyone left who is willing to turn back to life and to nature as they involuntarily formed themselves upon this soil, beneath this bit of the sky, actually to turn back, not to the dead remnants of decayed forms which belong to the grave, but to life and nature as they are vitally reborn and truly rejuvenated in every successive generation, in order, through changing forms, to work in that same spirit and approach towards that luminescence at which human life always aims and after which human nature therefore ever longs.

1. Grundtvig evidently has in mind such works as his *Optrin af Nordens Kæmpeliv* [Scenes from the warrior-life of the North] (1809-11) as well perhaps as his song on Willemoes (*Kommer hid, I Piger smaa!*).

2. *Danmarkdejligst Vang og Vænge, / lukt med Bølgen blaa*, quoted here by Grundtvig, are the opening lines of a lyric composed by Laurids O. Kock (1634-91).

3. This image appears to have inspired Rasmus Bøgeberg (1859-1921), whose statue of Grundtvig shows him seated, with a lark taking wing from his hand.

53: Sermon in Vartov Church, Wednesday 1st May 1844; ed. Jette Holm and Elisabeth A. Glenthøj, Grundtvig-Studier 2005, pp. 68-70.

In the Spring of 1844, Grundtvig became quite seriously ill, physically because of an attack of mumps and psychologically as a consequence, no doubt, of this glandular disease and the strain of the diverse burdens he had taken upon himself before, during and after his visit to England in 1843. Also in 1843 his older brother Otto – the last remaining of Grundtvig's four siblings and the one with whom Grundtvig had shared an important period in his life – had died. His depression was exacerbated by the somewhat petty attitude of the bishop, J. P. Mynster, when Grundtvig was obliged to cancel an Evensong at Vartov Kirke. Now in his sixty-third year, Grundtvig felt so weakened that he imagined his death might be drawing near. His preaching from this period depicts him in effect taking leave of his congregation and concerned to put a perspective upon his life's work as he does so – to leave to his congregation, as it were, testimony to the core of his belief and the essence of his teaching. During his convalescence, cared for by family and friends, he was inspired to compose the moving hymn *Sov sødt, Barnlille*. In the outcome, he so well recovered that in July he was able to stir a huge open-air audience with his address on the Slesvig issue at Skamlingsbanken in Jylland and, at sea on his way back home, to draft his poem *Rune-Bladet*. See further the index entries for these two texts and the headnote to item 56 (Preface to *Skov-Hornets Klang mellem Skamlings-Bankerne*).

In this sermon, then – his last before leaving the city to convalesce in less hectic surroundings and possibly, as he himself seems to have feared, his last ever – he speaks to his Vartov congregation of his historic engagement with the Living Word – "the living Word of God which shall last forever."

⌒

In Jesus' Name
Wednesday 1st May 1844

Romans 10, 5: *Moses describes the righteousness of the Law thus, that the man that does these things through them shall live, but the righteousness of faith speaks thus: Say not in your heart, who will go up to the heavens, that is to fetch Christ down, or who will descend into the depths, that is to fetch Christ up from the dead! But what does it say? The Word is close by you, in your mouth and in your heart, that is, the word of faith which we proclaim; for when you profess the Lord Jesus with your mouth and you believe in your heart that God raised him up from the dead, then shall you be saved because with the heart one believes unto righteousness and with the mouth one professes unto salvation. Wherefore the Scriptures say, whosoever believes in him shall not be ashamed! For there is no distinction between Jews and Greeks, since he himself is Lord of all, sufficient unto all those who call upon him, so that each one who calls upon the Lord's name shall be saved! But how should they call upon one in whom they do not believe, or believe in one about whom they have not heard, or hear except what is proclaimed; and how should they make proclamation who are not sent forth, as it stands written: how lovely are the feet of those who proclaim the glad tidings of peace, proclaim* [GS p. 69] *the gospel of goodness! But not all were attentive to the gospel, for Isaiah says: Which of us has believed our ears? Belief, then, comes from hearing, namely the hearing of God's Word.*

Christian friends! These words of the apostle Paul came forcefully to mind when in my youth, a generation ago, I began to think seriously about the proclamation of God's Word and the way of salvation, and it then at once appeared to me as clear as day that what the apostle wished to say was briefly this, that he and his fellow apostles had proclaimed a Word of God which could and which needs must be believed and professed, and which, when it so came to pass, rendered all who believed righteous before God and assured of salvation.

Nowadays few if any would deny it is so, but at that time the plain truth had the whole world against it, and especially the sage and the learned of this world, so that when I demanded aloud: Why has the Word of the Lord vanished from his house?[1] the whole world rose up against me as a miscreant and I had to be prepared to confront it in a battle of life and death over the ancient Word of God, sincere belief in it, and open profession of it, which I declared to be the only genuine Christianity and the heavenly means of salvation upon the earth.

Now, my friends, this good fight I have fought and preserved my faith, but whether I have reached the end of the race, God alone knows and it rests in his hand; but I owe him, and truth, and the Lord's congregation which he bought with his blood, this witness, that it was not I who gave the Word but the Word which gave me strength to strive and to win, and that it was much more faith which preserved me than I who preserved faith; in short, that all that I was, as believing Christian and servant of God's Word, this I was by the grace of God, which I merely endeavoured never to take in vain but to use honestly for my own and for others' salvation in the blessed name of Jesus Christ which is granted and given us to this end.

It was, in the beginning, far from appearing so clear to my eyes as now it stands, what Word of faith and of profession it was to which the apostle bore this great witness, that it gives each believing heart peace and sufficiency so that we ask not who will bring to us the Lord, but feel that he is as close to us as the Word he has sent us with his apostles, just as close to our mouth and our heart as this Word; but yet it was ever a living and audible Word of God – the Lord's, and not our own – to which I bore witness, that is, a Word of God which all Christians, both learned and lay, both wise and unwise, might recognise, own, believe, love, preserve in common in their heart and profess in one voice from their mouth, for thus I found God's saving Word described in Scripture, and thus I felt its power and blessing in my own heart.

Therefore I was glad as one that finds a great treasure – yes, as that merchant who sought after genuine pearls and found one so precious that he [GS p. 70] sold all that he had and bought it – when, in Martin Luther's *Catechism*, in the Christians' three age-old declarations of belief and instruction for children, and above all in the communal profession of the Creed at Baptism, I found the sole Word of God that *all* Christians have heard and with one voice professed, that Word of God which all Christians must believe and profess and by it be justified and saved; for now I could clarify it both for myself and for the congregation that it was not myself but the Lord Jesus Christ whom I proclaimed; not my own invention or my own bookish knowledge and bookish cleverness or my own inward feelings and experiencings that I call God's Word which is mighty in the saving of souls, but that it is a communal Word of belief from the mouth of the holy apostles, heard and professed over the whole of Christendom – hidden maybe from the learned but apparent to babes and sucklings – precisely such a one as the apostle describes in our text, upon which alone I too built my hope of salvation and willingly gave it my lowly witness.

Therefore, you see, I can when God wills it calmly set an end to my preaching and cease my witness; for I know that this Word of faith is God's own witness of his Son so that everyone who has this Word in his mouth and in his heart has, as the apostle John writes, God's own witness within himself, God's witness that he has granted us life everlasting and that this life is in his Son, Our Lord Jesus Christ, so that whosoever in faith has him, has also that life.

In this respect it is a manifest grace of God if he lets the servants of his Word grow old and frail before the eyes of his congregation and the world, for he is in no way a Lord that casts off his servants in the time of their old age or forsakes us when our strength fails;

indeed we find strength in our weakness so that it becomes clear as day that we ourselves stood in great need of God and of his Word, to hold us upright to fight the good fight: only then is the world compelled to see what is obvious to the congregation, that we carry the jewel in a vessel of clay, so the surpassing strength which accompanies the Word is God's and is none of ours. And lo! it was an imperative of our heart when we spoke because we believed, and believed because we felt that only Our Lord Jesus Christ has authority on earth to forgive sins and power to justify and save those who believe and call upon him; yes, it is an imperative of our heart that belief and trust in the matter of salvation must necessarily shift from us who come and go, blossom and wither with the flowers of the field, shift from us and cleave fast to the Word of God which is powerful to save our souls, and which has revealed upon us all its strength in that we were thereby fitted to become servants of the new Covenant – not that of the letter which killeth, but of the Spirit which quickeneth, the living Word of God which shall last forever.

1. *Hvi er Herrens Ord forsvundet af Hans Hus?* [Why has the word of the Lord disappeared from his house?] was the title of Gr's probational or dimissory sermon, preached 17 March, 1810, for the publishing of which he was attacked by Copenhagen clergy and reprimanded by the University.

54: Article in Grundtvig's periodical *Danskeren I* (1848), p. 481; GEEG, Stk. 49, p. 75.

Among the rest, Grundtvig was an able philologist with an interest in the historic forms of Danish and its kindred languages – and ever alert to the untutored idiom of the mother-tongue.

⌒

Some years ago, while I was living out in Christianshavn, I was walking past Børsen [The Exchange] on one occasion at dusk, behind a pair of half-grown ship's lads who were chatting with each other without bothering who was listening to them, and since I have always liked to keep my ears open I noticed at once that the talk was of one of their *comrades* who had not been behaving properly and had had to pay a little corporeal penance; then the one of them asked: "So what happened to him?" and the other answered with the greatest matter-of-factness: "Oh, he had to *stryge Underseilene* [lower the bottom sails]!" This form of speech, '*at stryge Underseilene*' I had never in my life heard before that occasion and therefore I shall remember this little story as long as I live, but yet I understood its meaning instantly because it was in the style of old Danish, so where I was a child they called the same painful event "*at stryge Seil for Kronborg*" [to lower the sails for Kronborg].[1]

1. For some centuries the kings of Dk asserted the right to claim toll from ships passing the fortress of Kronborg at Helsingør, on entering or leaving the Øresund; lowering sail signalled compliance with this authority. The metaphor stands, of course, for lowering the trousers to receive a beating.

55: Sermon in Vartov Church, 11th Sunday after Trinity, 19 August 1855; N. F. S. Grundtvigs Vartovs-Prædikener 1839-60; ed. H. Begtrup (1924), pp. 368-369; GEEG, Stk. 50, p. 76 (extended).

It was in the same year as the event here recalled (1841) that Denmark's new queen, Caroline Amalie, established in Copenhagen the *asylskole* [free school associated with a refuge for orphans] of which Grundtvig was appointed director and where he saw some of his own theories of an education for life implemented. He praised the initiative for offering deprived children the chance of living a happy and fulfilled life, whereas (in his opinion) the traditional, stuck-in-the-mud educational system was responsible for filling the reformatories, prisons and workhouses with delinquents and failures. Though the queen herself ordered the arrangements for the reception of the English Quaker and prison reformer Elizabeth Fry, and asked Grundtvig to join the escorting party, it is clear from the anecdote narrated here that Grundtvig took a less charitable view of the prisoner's lot, where adults were concerned, than did some contemporary prison reformers. As well as comprising a record of an illuminating episode in Gr's public life, the sermon affords interesting illustration of Grundtvig investing personal experience with symbolic significance, and using personal anecdote as material for preaching to his Vartov congregation.

[GEEG p. 76] It befell me [...] a number of years ago [August 1841] that some foreigners came to town here, who were travelling around in order to visit prisoners and to get better provisions made for the humane treatment and reformation of offenders;[1] and assuredly, with us as everywhere, such great shortcomings and mistakes occur that I did not dare to refuse, when I was asked about it, to accompany the foreigners into our prisons and to be their interpreter, since they themselves could not speak Danish. Now on that occasion, the foreigners asked me in conclusion to comfort the prisoners, who are indeed for the most part thieves or worse, with the gospel about the Pharisee and the tax-gatherer,[2] and far from concurring with them in this I greatly shuddered within myself at the thought of how this parable can be misused, and though it is itself as innocent of this as the sun is innocent of all the evil that happens by its light, yet without doubt my affection for it was cooled, so that since then I have not really had so much pleasure from today's gospel as previously, nor laid it so upon my listeners' hearts. For even today when I thought upon it, I felt there was something amiss and upon investigating what it could be, I stumbled upon the impression of that incident in the prison.

I have said that all such misuse arises from not perceiving and applying the parable as a parable but as an historical description of the path of justification, so that he who lives in all sorts of gross vices but now and then smites himself upon the breast and says: God be merciful unto me, a sinner! – he is supposed to be more righteous than one who preserved himself from all gross vices and thanked God for it: which is as outrageous as it is pernicious to think thus, and is bound to confirm all offenders in their wickedness and teach them to despise all reformation.

But it is expressly told us that this story of the Pharisee and the tax-collector is a parable, which the Lord spoke to those who trusted in their own self-accomplished righteousness and despised other people; and that the lesson which he himself drew out of the parable was that whosoever exalts himself shall be humbled but whosoever humbles himself shall be exalted.

So the Lord is in no way comparing here, in the Pharisee and the tax-collector, manifestly decent folk with thieves and robbers, nor saying that the latter are more righteous than the former. Rather, he is comparing the proud with the humble and giving the humble the prize, even if, like the Pharisee in the parable, one actually has something one could take pride in before the world without becoming the object of derision.

1. The foreigners were Elizabeth Fry (1780-1845), Quaker, prison reformer, and her brother Joseph John Gurney (1788-1847), emancipationist, from England. Elizabeth Fry's letter thanking Grundtvig is printed in *Breve* II, 447.

2. Luke 18:9-14. (9) And he spake this parable unto certain which trusted in themselves that they were righteous, and despised others: (10) Two men went up into the temple to pray; the one a Pharisee, and the other a publican. (11) The Pharisee stood and prayed thus with himself, God, I thank thee, that I am not as other men [are], extortioners, unjust, adulterers, or even as this publican. (12) I fast twice in the week, I give tithes of all that I possess. (13) And the publican, standing afar off, would not lift up so much as [his] eyes unto heaven, but smote upon his breast, saying, God be merciful to me a sinner. (14) I tell you, this man went down to his house justified [rather] than the other: for every one that exalteth himself shall be abased; and he that humbleth himself shall be exalted (King James Bible).

56: Preface to Skov-Hornets Klang mellem Skamlings-Bankerne [The ring of the valdhorn among the Skamling-hills] (1844), pp. 11-13; GEEG, Stk. 51, pp. 76-78.

There are many moments in the long life-story of Grundtvig when the biographer is granted a clear view of the feet of clay upon which the great heroic bulk of Grundtvig stood – most obviously, perhaps, in those episodes of mental and emotional breakdown which at intervals afflicted his adult years, in the indignities he suffered when he could no longer master his feelings, thoughts and behaviour; but also in the moments of revealed vanity, self-promotion, blinkered self-righteousness, unfeeling judgmentalism and a sometimes ill-measured tendency to seek confrontation and controversy. Grundtvig is no hero unflawed: there is plenty for detractors to work upon. On the other hand no one, surely, can read (for example) the records of the year 1844 (See also the headnote to item 53: Sermon in Vartov Church, Wednesday 1st May 1844), Grundtvig's sixty-first year, without feeling caught up in the heroic drama of his life, without being touched by the frailty of a man exhausted by a prodigious and long-sustained work-load, sickness and the indifference or hostility of his superiors; without being moved by the humility with which he returned into public scrutiny after these episodes; without (as in this passage) sharing the tearful exhilaration of a man transcending his frailties and finding a new optimism which (in his own account) dawned in the gloom like the dawn that rose over the sea and the green beechwood shores of Sjælland as his ship carried him and "Denmark's youth" back from Skamlingsbanken in Slesvig to the capital city of Copenhagen. If the puritanical moralist finds the taint of human vanity in the account, the rest of us are surely ready to forgive Grundtvig that. It seems fitting that human nature, vulnerable to temporal adversities and vanities and yet capable of the loftiest apprehensions, should be so vividly depicted in the life-records of a man who *trusted* human nature – as not many of his theological-philosophical contemporaries did – and held human nature [*Menneske-Naturen*], in the child, to be " en skjult Skat, der skal drages for Lyset og giøres frugtbar!" [a hidden treasure, which must be drawn into the light and rendered fruitful] through enlightened education.

⌒

The steamship passage through Lillebælt and Øresund, especially on the homeward journey, was so smooth, so cheerful, so jolly without any disturbance, in brief, so genuinely Danish and decent [*dansk og dannis*] that even had I wanted to – but which was far from being the intention – I could not have imagined to myself that the whole thing was a dream, I could not have prevented myself from getting the impression that there is "something new afoot" but only of that sort of new which is called so because it "seldom happens" and is basically only a living renewal of the age-old so that, as even the Frenchman has observed, it is really not the parents but the grandparents who live on in their children! You see, then, that during the journey I came both to grasp this and to feel it in the most beautiful and pleasing manner, and to say it to the young folk in both verse and non-verse style; and the first good opportunity was by Gniben and Sjælland's Rif where we all recalled [Peter] Villemoes and the other doughty and staunch Danish men [*Dannemænd*] who now sleep in Odden's churchyard but once were wide awake for [GEEG p. 77] the honour of old Denmark and closed their eyes in a desperate battle with the superior English force in 1808 when our last ship of the line of the old build, *Prinds Christian*, ran aground and was wrecked and ended its life; because there the young folk tuned up and sang my old ballad of Villemoes for the "lassies small" and with that I got the best opportunity to remind them what appears on the monolith [*Bauta-Stenen*][1] over him and the other *einherjar* or contenders for the life in Valhalla and the Folkvang, in heroic poem and battle-song, and to call for a Danish Hurrah! in their memory. And in this there was a fortunate warning, because the pilot, who could not help listening to the ballad of Villemoes, had almost grounded us fast on Sjælland's Rif, but did not ground us, so we steered doubly happily by the Nakke-Hoved and Kullen lights into the Sound. Here there now presented itself the best opportunity for a friendly exchange of words with "Young Denmark," for as I, still with something of the tears in my eyes which the Villemoes song had coaxed forth, looked out across the ruffled sea with the slight white froth of foam which followed us like a flock of young swans on both sides, I took a sincere desire to let the young folk know how sincerely well I felt in their midst and for that reason I was humming to myself the first verses of *Rune-Bladet*, which was to accompany the Skamlings-speech, and at the same moment the thoughts of the young folk were with me and with old Denmark, as I delightfully got to know when a young man came up to me and asked whether I would not empty a cup with the young people. "With the greatest pleasure" was naturally my answer, "as long as the drink is not too strong for me!" and although I straight away found that all I could cope with was to sip at the cup of youth, yet it already gave me the youthful courage and agility to jump up on to the bench and tell the young folk what I had just been humming to myself, because I now felt that I had much too prematurely grieved that I would doubtless end up taking the larger part of old Denmark's inheritance and freehold, movables and immovables, with me to the grave, now I observed that in the younger generation there were contenders and competitors enough for everything that is beautiful and noble, lofty and deep, of the mind and of the heart and in the end bright and lucid – and did they not all say "Yes!" then I was stone-deaf.

So you see, under these circumstances it came easily to me, or more correctly it came of itself, that in the morningtide, sailing in [GEEG p. 78] the Øresund along the lovely coast of Sjælland, the *Rune-Bladet* came to be more or less what it is, so that off Torbæk I could comfortably stand up on the bench and read from the paper to the considerable amusement of the young folk who had seen with their own eyes that there was no mystique about writing Danish poetry in the Øresund but that it happened just as naturally as when each bird sings from its beak in the "green woodlands"

1. The obelisk, bearing a poetic inscription by Grundtvig, over the common grave of heroes from the Battle of Sjællands Odde, in Odden churchyard, Overby, Sjællands Odde.

57. Article in Grundtvig's periodical Danskeren I (1848), pp. 556-560; GEEG, Stk. 52, pp. 78-80.

Though Grundtvig was slow to accept the arguments for constitutional democracy – not least because he feared both for the future status of the national Church and for national unity amidst the power politics played between parties representing sectional interests where previously the sovereign could mediate impartially and with absolute final discretion between competing interests – when the democratising process formally began he understood his obligation to participate. Elections to the Constituent Assembly [*Den grundlovgivende Rigsforsamling*] were set for 5 October 1848. In Vartov Church they sang *Vor Konge signe Du, o Gud!* [Thy blessing grant our King, O God!] and Grundtvig voiced his anxieties from the pulpit, but resigned the outcome into the hands of God. In the constituency of Præstø, where the National Liberals (primarily a fairly conservative urban and middle-class party), which supported the allocation of 48 out of 193 seats to the king's nominees, were opposed by the Friends of the Farmers Party [*Bondevennernes Selskab*], which challenged the provision for royal nominees, following a confused and somewhat irregular voting procedure the National Liberal candidate Professor Henrik Nicolai Clausen (Grundtvig's adversary in the law-suit of 1826) was first (on a show of hands) declared the winner and then (in a paper vote demanded by the opposition) the loser. Two weeks later the elected representative, the weaver Hans Hansen, over whom an allegation of handling stolen goods was pending, resigned. At a fresh election on 6 November Grundtvig (who had already stood for the constituency of Nyboder and been defeated) was persuaded to stand in Præstø, his opponent being the local parish constable [*sognefoged*] Jens Jensen, strongly backed by the farmers. Unlike Clausen, Grundtvig (his father having long been parish priest at nearby Udby, and he himself having for a short period been curate at Udby and then parish priest in Præstø) had local connections (though not all of them such as would win the approval of the farmers) and a favourable reputation among the electors of Præstø. The outcome is narrated in the following passage. This was the start of Grundtvig's career as politician, first in the Constituent Assembly, then in the *Folketing* and later in the *Landsting*.

On the way to Præstø I got to know that a large number of farmers had resolved to choose from among themselves a much esteemed farmer, the *sognefoged* [parish constable] of the parish of Udby, Jens Jensen from Gromløse, something which I however found very unreasonable, since this good man not only happened to be one of my first and cleverest confirmands but he had always remembered me with affection and a short while ago, when I was first thinking of standing in the constituency, had expressly commended me to the farmers as a steady fellow, who yielded ground to no one. When however I arrived at Nysø, a house of old and faithful friends which I could not possibly shun[1] even though I well knew that all manor houses were at the time regarded with suspicion by the farmers, I now heard that on the face of it the situation had its justification, since so many of the farmers, and probably the majority, would hear of no other *Rigsdagsmand* [member of parliament] than Jens Jensen from Gromløse, and the test ballot gave me no particular comfort because only comparatively few farmers turned up and nobody at all other than myself stood for office, so that it was not until the evening before election day I got to know for certain that the *sognefoged* from my birthplace was my only, but in the circumstances dangerous, rival. It now first struck me, that on this occasion I was playing a risky game; for whilst it could have been supportable for any other well-known man to be ousted by a farmer who plainly could not at all measure up to him in competence as a *Rigsdagsmand*, it was quite otherwise with me, as a long-standing friend of the farmers [*bondeven*], who had always assert against learned folk that the farmers of Sjælland were no geese, even though they were grey, but that what they lacked in knowledge and clear intellect they richly compensated for in deep and true feeling, which may well be more or less asleep in the bulk of them but which could be awakened with a bold but friendly and colloquial [*folkeligt*] word, and would only need to awake in order to have an incomparably happy effect. In fact, it became as clear as day to me that now, since my election as *Rigsdagsmand* depended upon the farmers of Sjælland, [GEEG p. 78] and since I was standing face to face with them in the district where I was born, and had that colloquial [*folkelige*] language and especially the peasant-speech of Sjælland more readily at my command than any other famous person, more or less the whole of my efforts on behalf of the *folkelige* now depended upon what the outcome should be; for albeit I could, if fortune failed me, plead that I had never said that one could *instantly* awaken the deepest Danish sentiment in the bulk of the dreadfully unappreciated, neglected and ill-treated Sjællanders, but yet it was easy to foresee what the whole world would say and I would not be able to deny, that the world would have much more than mere appearances on its side, if the bulk of the farmers in my Sjælland birthplace spurned me as *Rigsdagsmand*, and one of the people who know me best, my own pupil, blocked my election. Even if my faith in the deep and affectionate nature of my closest Sjællandic relations remained unshaken, as far as I could judge my voice in their defence and help would be gagged, my efforts for the *folkelige* if not stifled then grievously crippled.

With these thoughts I was to fall asleep and with them I was to wake, with them I met at the polling place, but yet, God be praised! with a firm courage and with the underlying idea that precisely because so much good was at stake, precisely therefore I definitely had to win; and in this I was wonderfully strengthened by the way (masterly, in a Danish sense) the Election Committee's chairman, the Danish farmer-priest [*den Danske Bondepræst*; Peter Rørdam] from Mehrn, introduced the election process, and by the way, probably unparalleled in our day, in which the farmers received his speech, just as audacious as it was friendly, as to what this deciding ballot signified.

In the full conviction that, as I have always said, a good word finds as good a place among the Sjællanders as anywhere on earth, I now set out the question of my election as openly, as clearly, as boldly and as friendlily as I could,[2] and I could well observe that the farmers both understood my meaning and felt, as one of the opponents afterwards confided in me, that there was something moving inside the skin; but nonetheless my rival stepped boldly forwards and told his electors what he would vote for if he got into the *Rigsdag* and not until he had had his say about this did he change his tone and conceded that it was only with a feeling of sorrow that he could stand in the way of his old pastor and teacher to whom, both as a faithful friend of the farmers and as a liberal-minded man, he must give the finest testimonial – so [**GEEG p. 80**] he would prefer to withdraw and himself ask his electors to vote for me! And behold, this visibly touched the farming-flock far more deeply than anything else, so Jens Jensen's noble-spirited offer was received, so to speak, with popular acclaim, and he withdrew. At a show of hands for me, it also then became clear that the opposition was insignificant; and when, on a half-hearted motion, a vote was taken according to protocol, there were only eleven votes *contra*, against six hundred!

This in itself was hugely pleasing; but the friendly, happy mood which showed itself throughout the day, no less in my rival and the large majority of his following than in the middle classes of Præstø who were the hosts and Lars Larsen, *sognefoged* from Mehrn who had proposed me in a quite superb manner and in his not inconsiderable following of farmers, this was the most pleasing of all and in various other eyes than mine augured for Denmark a uniquely charming and happy solution to its peculiarly complicated problem.

Thus then I came to be elected *Rigsdagsmand* in a wondrously yet at bottom a uniquely smooth and natural manner so that the glitter was quite outshone by the affection; and just as it was for me an indescribable recompense for all the opposition my thinking and speaking on the *folkelige* have met with for nearly half a century, so I also hope that it will remain for me an inexhaustible comfort through all the opposition my Sjælland-Danish thinking and speaking hereafter, both inside the *Rigsdag* and outside, will necessarily meet; for throughout the whole of my life's struggle, a lovely summer sunset, in the sense of both mind and heart, has been my sincerest desire and my fairest prospect, and within the limited scope it could not possibly have acquired a fairer countenance than it had on election day in Præstø and in the evening hour at Nysø where nobleman and priest, warrior, citizen and farmer not only gave each other their hand but found all such differences smoothed out in the deep, loving feeling that all Danes [*Dannemænd*] are the children of one mother, and she the tenderest and most lovable mother under the sun!

1. Gr had been advised, for tactical reasons, not to stay at Nysø in a letter from his close associate Peter Rørdam (1806-83), formerly a teacher in Copenhagen schools, but at this time (1841-56) parish priest in Mern.

2. Gr's published his election address in his weekly periodical *Danskeren* 1 (1848), 545 ff. under the title "Hvad vil N. F. S. Grundtvig paa Rigsdagen?" [What will NFSG do in the *Rigsdag*?].

The visit to Norway 1851

58 (a-e): Article in Grundtvig's periodical Danskeren IV (1851), pp. 389-90, 393-396, 401-402, 403-407, 411-412; GEEG Stk. 53, pp. 80-86.

Danskeren [The Dane] was a weekly periodical published and largely written by Grundtvig, of which four volumes were issued between 1848-51, covering the period of the Three Years' War over the duchy of Slesvig. Launched in direct response to the outbreak of that war, it addressed topical circumstances and issues, domestic and international, asserting the national viewpoint and aspiring to raise national morale with prose articles, poems and songs. It is also a major source for autobiographical comment by Grundtvig, who felt, with some justification, that the issues which engaged his intellectual and physical energies and commanded his most passionate feelings were also germane to the life and well-being of the nation as a whole. At a time when Denmark stood particularly in need of friends, it was a profound joy to Grundtvig to discern the emergence of a new solidarity between the Nordic countries, led – and this added greatly to his optimism – by the young students of the Nordic universities. In early June 1851 a great gathering of students convened in Kristiania (Oslo) to which Grundtvig was invited as guest of honour of the Norwegian students' association. It is hard to think in what way it could have been any richer an experience for him. The students hailed him, the newspapers greeted him, the Norwegian Parliament suspended its sitting so that members might hear him preach; he spoke informally from the top of a tumulus to an open-air gathering in the countryside and formally from the pulpit of Kristiania's cathedral; he met old friends and made new ones, walked among the crowds and talked with individuals both young and old and learned and simple; he was taken to view some of the most spectacular scenery of Ringerike, and there trod in the footsteps of Saint Olaf whose Life he had translated among the 'folk-books' of the North; on one day he joined in celebrating the lively folk-culture of Hallingdalen, on another (8 June) he celebrated the day of Pentecost when the Holy Spirit breathed life into the Church. If the 'divorce' from Norway in 1814 had always pained him, the events of 1851 did much to restore his confidence in *Nordens Aand*, the spirit of the North. Although in fact nothing came of this to change the course of history in his lifetime, Grundtvig retained a special affection for Norway, always welcomed visiting Norwegians, and hoped to the end of his life that Norway would come to embrace those ideals that he had striven to realise within his own nation.

⌒

58(a): Danskeren IV (1851), pp. 389-90; GEEG Stk. 53, pp. 80-81.

"A genuine bonding, of mind and of heart, between the three Nordic peoples and realms"

It is [...] not my intention to narrate what was said or how much singing and drinking there was in Gothenburg, where I was not involved, nor to enumerate more or less everything, lock, stock and barrel, that I took part in between Copenhagen and Tanberg-Moen, from the welcome on the Norwegian quayside to the farewell on the Danish gangplank; I only wish, [GEEG p. 81] if possible, to record a little of what made the most impression upon me, either because it was closest to hand or because it seemed to be the most remarkable anyway; and even though it is a dubious business, such picking and choosing as one pleases, the gentleman and lady reader are nevertheless best served by it because with the pen as with the mouth it must be pleasure which motivates the work if it is to proceed enjoyably.

For me as well, the main thing about the journey to Norway in which I was so intensely involved is in fact that it was Swedish and Danish students who as a group and in fraternal association visited the Norwegian students, just as the Norwegian and Swedish six years ago visited the Danish, and that Kristiania vied with Copenhagen, Norway with Denmark to make the hospitality and foster-brotherhood of 1851 yet more admirable and more unforgettable than that of 1845, for it both augurs and promises, foreshadows and affirms what has indeed long been spoken of and sung about but which is still often jeered at and sneered at: a genuine bonding, of mind and of heart, between the three Nordic peoples and realms, so that in conflict with foreigners they may stand shoulder to shoulder with each other and routinely look to each other for all the help, variety, increment, enjoyment and rivalry that they desire and need; while, precisely so that they can find in each other what they more or less lack in themselves, and also because they honour the humanity and love the freeborn pride in each other, they heartily desire and wish for each other all the freedom, individuality and independence that they desire and wish for themselves.

58 (b): Danskeren IV (1851), pp. 393-396; GEEG Stk. 53, pp. 81-83.

"Norway has opened its embrace; come then beloved bard! your name the brother-land blesses"

Although I dare say that the chief reason for my participation in the journey to Norway, especially during Whitsuntide, was my wish and hope of the most heartfelt alliance, the friendliest intercourse and the most joyous fellowship in the North that has ever taken place among close-related but noble, brave, freeborn peoples, yet it would be just as dishonest as unreasonable if I were to say that N. F. S. Grundtvig, the personality, was on that occasion and during the whole of this journey a matter of complete indifference to me, or that all the great attention and friendly reception I everywhere met I credited without the smallest deduction to the account of the new foster-brotherhood. No; for one thing, none of us is so pure and perfect as to do so, and for another, N. F. S. Grundtvig – as a priest of forty [GEEG p. 82] years' standing within the Church common to Norway and to Denmark, as one of the few Danish authors who has retained a goodly portion of Norwegian readers, as a grey-haired skald who sang at their cradles while they were still keeping time with each other as twins, and as a link in a youthful chain of Norwegian friends which did not break before, like *Drypner*, it had propagated itself – had a relationship with Norway quite his own, for which reason he was also personally invited by the Norwegian student association, and therefore throughout the whole journey had to do what he certainly all too eagerly desired to do, not only to remember and to speak about what was common to both but to combine with this, as best might succeed, that which is special to each, just as we must desire and wish all those dwelling in the North, the small along with the great, amicably to combine the common with the special so that the whole may blossom and all, each individually, can draw benefit from it and rejoice in it.

Already on the Fjord I was most pleasantly surprised by Norway's smile; for I had hardly come up on deck in the early morning when we set sail after an overnight anchorage off Vallø, before I was handed a letter from there, which was that welcome in verse which could later be read, a little lengthened, in the *Norske Rigstidende* (no. 47), and of which the closing lines in particular:

Norge aabnet har sin Favn,	Norway has opened its embrace;
Kom da, elskte Skjald! dit Navn	come then beloved bard! your name
Broderlandet signer,	the brother-land blesses,

addressed me in the friendliest way. Moreover, it now so luckily chanced that at the same time there had come on board a pretty little Norwegian girl, just to go with us a little further up the Fjord to keep *Pindse-Helgen* [the Whitsun holiday], and since she was standing there quite alone we soon got into a little conversation which, because of its lovely natural expressiveness so exceedingly delighted me that I call it Norway's live morning-smile [*Norges levende Morgen-Smil*] to me.

How I was now received in Kristiania, not only by a friend and colleague of many years' standing,[1] by the children and the relics of deceased friends and by the association of students but, so to speak, by all that I met; how they competed to make the long summer days brief, abounding in delights and unforgettable for me; how old and young colleagues came flocking to me; how the capital's church[2] opened itself to me with a multitude of hearers; how even the Storthing [Parliament] and the Statsraad [Government] showed me the most honorific attention; and finally how [**GEEG p. 83**] invitations from Bergen and Trondhjem came jostling against each other – this, with yet much besides, floats before me like a most agreeable dream, almost too flattering and too much like a fairytale to be mentioned here, so that I cannot wax expansive upon it; but since it is after all a real fact, and since I, as luck would have it, am nothing in this world but an old Vartov-priest, rhyme-smith and bookworm, with a dash of the young parliamentarian bringing up the rear, nevertheless it testifies as clear as day in my eyes on behalf of Kristiania and Norway that – God be praised! – it is far from being the case *there* that the body (material interests), as has so often been rumoured, has swallowed up the spirit [*Aanden*], for among all the renowned men of the North there is none that more exclusively than N. F. S. Grundtvig owes to activities of the spirit [*aandelig Virksomhed*], spoken and written, all his renown![3]

1. Wilhelm Andreas Wexels (1797-1866).

2. Vår Frelsers Kirke (Church of Our Saviour), Kristiania (Oslo): here, after the excursion into Ringerige, Gr preached on Friday 13 June, when the Norwegian parliament (Stortinget) suspended its sitting in order that members might attend.

3. Grundtvig's argument seems to be that Norway has proved its enduring commitment to spiritual-intellectual values by so warmly receiving one (namely himself) whose sole claim to fame is his pursuit of those values in his preaching and writing.

"Everything that shall properly reach us to the heart must reach us through the woman!"

When I think back to what, during that week of living in Norway, made the most vivid impression upon me, it was, as always with poets, old as well as young, the smiles upon beautiful lips that, with more or less justification, I take into account, so that even the lively impression which the whole of the reception, as cordial as it was grand, of the young people of the southerly North [that is, from Denmark] on the evening of Whit Sunday inevitably made upon me as upon all of Norway's guests, first became truly vivid when on the Monday I casually asked a pretty little girl whether she too had been present and how she had felt about it, and she then answered with a beautiful smile that she had been present in two places and had near "*graatet*" [wept]; but although, according to the poet's and I believe according to mankind's nature, such a little intermediary is needed so that we are able to take a lively impression home with us alive for our daily use, yet none the less uplifting for this was the impression, in its broad generality, of when I took an active part in the triumphal procession of joyous Nordic youth through Norway's capital, all the way from the ancient Aggershuus to the new Kongeborg; and if in retrospect I choose to let my eye rest upon the pretty little girl who had near "*graatet*" this is doubtless not least because the eye prefers to rest upon the beautiful which greets us with a smile, but perhaps just as much because experience has taught me – and my grey hairs have given me the courage to say it aloud – that as a rule everything that shall properly reach us to the heart must reach us through the woman!

"To speak now of the famous excursion to Ringerige"

[GEEG p. 84] To speak now of the famous excursion to Ringerige; I must at once confess that when I took an active part in it and not only rejoiced in it at the time but still rejoice and shall often rejoice over it as long as I live, it was and is neither for the so-called "King's Prospect" from the top of Krog-Kleven, which I was too lethargic to climb, nor for the so-called "Queen's Prospect" on Flakkebjerget which I only enjoyed very fleetingly in pass-ing, nor for anything of all that which is usually called "beautiful prospects" – for maybe, especially as a skald, I am what is called "a fool for beautiful prospects" but it is not for those beautiful prospects that can be hunted down on Krog-Kleven or in the Alps, but those one can just as well experience by, according to the proverb, "staying on the plain and praising the mountains" as I did recently when in *Danskeren* I rhymed about *Skjaldelivet i Danmark* [The poet's life in Denmark];[1] and besides, that Wednesday morning when the excursion was to start, the nearest prospects to Kristiania were only grey and nearly black so that I was very doubtful as to what extent I should risk two whole days of my Norwegian Whit-week on the very dubious and even, by all accounts, rather dangerous adventure. I would therefore probably not have gone with them to Ringerige at all but would have missed all the many glorious moments and friendly memories this excursion gave me, had not one of my elderly Norwegian acquaintances and colleagues[2] come up from the Mosse area in order kindly to have a meeting with me, and had invited me sit up alongside him in his small covered trap with a pair of pretty 'blue' horses which up here they call *Abildgraa* [dapple-grey] – so the prospect on the strength of which I travelled to Ringerige was plainly this, that however things turned out as regards the weather and the splendid prospects from Kleven, it was the living, human aspect of Norway, which hereby found opportunity to unfold itself to me, that would make the journey just as much worthwhile inwardly as the Norwegian people with generosity and pleasure made it worthwhile outwardly. Therefore even though, immediately after the difficult and slow descent from Kleven, I was quite sincerely delighted to see the evening sun shining softly across the Steensfjord, and from the friendly parsonage at Norder-Houg to see the morning sun illumine the beautiful Ringerige and cast a splendour upon the distant snowcaps, yet this folk-life continued to be what I particularly fixed my eye upon, and this folk-life's happy evolution with its deep prime tone in all its [GEEG p. 85] picturesque beauty, this was the beautiful enchanting prospect which first and last rejoiced my eye, and which, through the excursion to Ringerige, acquired a definite form with an unfading colour which I am sure will often, when I am least expecting it, visit me and delight me.

This prospect was the one that first properly opened itself before me in Tanberg-Moen, that lovely birchwood grove where Ringerige's farmers were hosts to the youth of the North, where folk and land merged together before my eyes in the soft evening light, where there really was no night, and where the blaze from Gyrihougen became for me the image of Norway's splendour which, in the evening of time, shall shine abroad in the world as a beacon upon a mountain top!

Under these circumstances, I find it quite fair what I read in a newspaper, that the couple of words I spoke from the tumulus in Tanberg-Mo, where the folk-flocks of both sexes had encamped so beautifully upon the slopes around a little stage for the Halling-dance, were some of the most beautiful I spoke in Norway; for even if I can only remember very little of the details yet I know from experience it testifies that I must have been happy enough in that moment almost entirely to forget myself and all the details in favour of the whole, which is therefore also unforgettable to me.

It had in fact been said to me in passing that here in the neighbourhood it was thought that Sigurd Syr's royal manor had stood, and I knew that in all events it stood both in Norway and in Ringerige – and instantly Snorri Sturlesøn's incomparable *Kings' Chronicle*, with the whole of that Norwegian folk-life which it does not describe but paints, then appeared before me large as life, whilst the eye rested with real delight on the crown upon the work, which is the saga of Olav the Holy, and especially the portrait of Olav's homecoming from his long and daring viking-journey which has always given me indescribable pleasure.[3] The remembrance of this I would encourage with a warm and audacious word wherever it was to be found awake; and where it slumbered I would awaken it; and if this succeeded then it would be not only beautiful but enlivening; and in myself I can feel that it has succeeded, for I always measure that vitality which wakens or grows in the remembrance according to that enlivening which thereby descends upon hope; and I feel that my hope for Norway's future was mightily enlivened in the birchwood grove, so now I quietly hope what I can remember I audaciously declared: that just as St Olav, when he visited Ringerige with a claim upon Norway's throne as his patrimony, achieved his goal so that all the petty kings became farmers, just so should the spirit of the North [*Nordens Aand*], [**GEEG p. 86**] which was now visiting Ringerige with the same claim, also achieve its goal, but at the same time turn the farmers into petty kings!

1. *Danskeren* was a weekly periodical currently being issued by Grundtvig; The poem mentioned is in IV (1851), 225 ff. (*PS* VII, 392 ff.).

2. Pastor U. Sundt from the parish of Rygge near Moss, Norway (*GEEG*).

3. Gr's rendering of the saga is in his *Norges Konge-Krønike af Snorro Sturlesen* [Norway's Chronicles of the Kings by Snorri Sturluson], vol. ii (1819), 1-372; the account of Olav's homecoming from his exploits in Scandinavia, France and England – a baptised Christian with the intention of bidding for kingship in Norway – is in the same work, pp. 26-27.

58 (e): Danskeren IV (1851), pp. 411-412; GEEG Stk. 53, p. 86.

"This conversation, to me unforgettable, cannot possibly have been fruitless"

It befell me beneath the open sky on the way homewards from Ringerige, whilst the blue horses were resting at Klev-Stuen, that a youngish Norwegian colleague engaged me in an open conversation on the relationship both between body and soul and between divine and human things; and here is the source of that stream of light which in manifold rivulets shall permeate human life and scatter the darkness which conjuration has laid upon it, so this conversation, to me unforgettable, cannot possibly have been fruitless. It could also have near cost me my neck, because certainly it at least contributed to fortifying the "Hurra" with which I was bidden farewell, and when a gun-salute was added the blue horses down the hill became barely manageable, so that I think my reverend protector-patron can still feel what it cost him to keep control.

If now the Spirit gets its Northern Light properly lit over Norway then Happiness will come of itself, and this is what I was thinking of when, at the farewell banquet on Friday evening, they still wanted to hear a word from me, and I briefly told them what on the Wednesday I had heard from a Norwegian farmer at Jonserud who cast doubt upon whether all this hullabaloo would bring "*Glædja*" [Happiness] to Norway, for I agreed with him that this was the big question, but I would by no means concede to him that the answer was in doubt, and whoever saw the happy folk-gathering that was listening, and the still far greater one which next morning sadly escorted us aboard, must at least acknowledge that all indicators must prove false if the student sortie [*Studenter-Toget*] of 1851 were not to gain a place in Norway's history as a *happy* event!

Reflections upon the church

59 (a-h): Kirke-Speil eller Udsigt over den christne Menigheds Levnetsløb (1871); GEEG Stk. 54, pp. 86-112; US X, pp. 334-61.

While Grundtvig's radical ideas on education were very largely converted into practice, modified and developed by others – he himself having rather little practical involvement after his early years as a tutor, and beyond his occasional visits and inspirational talks to a few particular schools including *Grundtvigs Højskole* at Marielyst – his engagement in the church struggle [*Kirkekampen*], to combat rationalism in all areas of faith, worship and teaching where its effects had taken hold, and to free priest and congregation, church-member or sectarian, believer and unbeliever alike, from a range of official compulsions which insulted conscience, was direct and practical in a whole variety of ways. Out of it, in his own lifetime, grew *Grundtvigianisme* – whose title was not of his choosing though "it can hardly fail to be acknowledged that in this latter generation there has indeed established itself the kernel of a Danish Christian free congregation which, since it adheres exclusively to the Apostolic Creed and the Lord's own institutions, can surely least among all the now so-called Christian Church-societies justifiably be called a sect (an off-cut) and given a nickname after one of the Lord's and its own servants; but which yet, right enough, has *this* churchly singularity – that of demanding consensus only over what has been common to *all* who have believed and been baptised, and of seeking only a new life of the spirit within *The Word* given to us from the Lord's own mouth, through his own institutions."

His *Kirke-Speil* – its title echoing the medieval encyclopaedic title *Speculum Ecclesiae* [Mirror of the Church] – is the clearest and most important exposition he made of his overview of Danish church developments in his lifetime. In various respects it might be thought of as the church-historical equivalent of Grundtvig's *Mands Minde*. It began life as informal talks given in his home over the winter of 1860 at the request of a group of young students, the Norwegians Olaf Arvesen and Herman Anker and Ernst Trier, which then turned into lectures given over three successive winters, attracting a large attendance (see items 114, 115). Grundtvig wrote down these memoirs over the winters of 1862-63 and they were finally published in book form in 1871. Other important expositions of his view of the Church are in *Om Religions-Frihed* [On freedom of religion], third section, 1827 (published 1866, *US* V, 97 ff.), chiefly concerned with circumstances surrounding the clash with H. N. Clausen, 1825-26; *Den christelige Børnelærdom* [Christian instruction for children], 1868, 253 ff. (*US* IX, 504 ff.); and, in very brief survey, *Aabent Vennebrev til en Engelsk Præst*, 6 ff. (*US* VIII, 194 ff.). For convenience of access, this very long extract from *Kirke-Speil* (covering the period up to Grundtvig's appointment to Vartov Kirke) has here been broken up into a number of shorter passages, with footnotes after each passage.

Grundtvig recalls the stagnancy of the Danish Church during his young years in Udby and
Thyregod. "The only new thing in the church was Balle's *Lærebog*"

How I, during the renewal of the seemingly moribund Danish church-struggle, discovered
the ancient tracks (which they call the church's new path) through *folkelighed*, freedom and
historical education, this I shall endeavour to set forth, perhaps not as flatly as Laaland but
at least as much on the level as are Sæland and Denmark as a whole;[1] and I dare to hope that
this will succeed because I have become convinced that the path, despite appearances and
despite all objections, is nevertheless in accord with the Danish heart.

Nikolaj Edinger Balle became bishop in Sæland the same year that I was born; and
I was among the first Danish children to be baptised without the Exorcism [*Besværgelsen*]
which Luther had retained only because he was afraid that it had nevertheless perhaps
originally belonged to Baptism, and which Christian the Fourth, when he did away with it
for the royal children, may well have thought the Danes found indispensable, but of which
Balle immediately recommended the abandonment, and thereby sufficiently indicated that
he was not at all what he was later called, extremely orthodox (hyperorthodox), but rather
disposed to conform happily to the taste of the times and notions from Göttingen [*gøttingske Begreber*]; so that it was only the stormy reactions which subsequently frightened him
so that he did not dare any further to touch the sacraments, as the apple of the Lutheran
congregation's eye.

So when in the Nineties Balle himself got his very unLutheran and only marginally
Christian textbook[2] introduced into the *Almueskoler* [elementary schools] throughout the
realm, and throughout his diocese got the Kingo hymnal replaced by the (so called, merely)
"Evangelical" hymnal (as lacking in heart as it was in spirit), and when finally he got established a teachers' training college[3] with downright unChristian teachers, then church
history must count him a subverter rather than a defender of the Lutheran State-Church;
although *we* who knew the man owe him this testimony, that he honestly believed the
opposite, and only went so extraordinarily wrong because he credited himself with the
spiritual judiciousness which he lacked, and he confused that Christian gentleness and
forbearance which he, above any contemporary bishop, desired to practise with that turning of a blind eye which only makes opponents more reckless and preserves appearances
at the cost of the reality.

As sincere and Christian as indeed was Balle's constant assertion that he would not
call upon the secular authority in defence of the realm of the spirit, yet just as unChristian
and thoughtless was his actual conduct in allowing the theological professors unhindered
to inoculate their students with doubt and [GEEG p. 88] unbelief, and to allow the priests
to preach as wrongly and to administer the sacraments as badly as they wished, without
taking steps towards the repeal of the civil mandatory laws which bound all those who
wanted to be priests to the theological professors in Copenhagen, and bound all members
of the congregation to their parish priests; and if then the people were robbed of their old
prayerbooks and hymnbooks and the country was oversown with puffed-up and for the
most part unbelieving schoolmasters, it had little or no relevance to life how well or how

badly one wielded the pen in feuding with the, in any case, few and mostly anonymous persons who in our little reading-world attacked and mocked the Bible and Christianity;[4] so it hardly repays the effort to compare [Otto] Horrebov's *Jesus og Fornuften* [Jesus and Commonsense] with Balle's *Bibelen forsvarer sig selv* [The Bible is its own Defence]. That on the other hand the royal confessor [*den kongelige Skriftefader*], the capital's foremost spokesman for the Church and in the Eighties the most read Danish author, Kristjan Bastholm, constantly justified the Bible and Christianity as indispensable first aid to the sensual and the senseless multitude and proposed a brand-new form of worship, as over-dramatised and theatrical as possible – *this* was an ecclesiastical declaration of bankruptcy which, since it was not put to shame by the clear demonstration of mind and strength, could only extenuate indifference and provoke mockery, which is why in the Nineties Bastholm was also publicly asked "whether it was right to lie to the common folk."[5]

In the parsonage on the Jylland heath where I once wore out my childhood shoes and learned Latin in the best old-fashioned way according to Aurora and Donatus, without regular grammar and rod, everything still followed in the old track, with sleepy but honest churchgoing, with Kingo's hymn-book and Luther's *Katekismus* [Catechism], which among other things I learned by heart in Latin; so the only new thing in the church was Balle's *Lærebog*, of which the kernel and main section, the sixth chapter concerning Duties, was for the most part omitted, together with the commentaries; but I, who had already learnt childhood instruction in Christianity [*den kristelige Børnelærdom*] from my mother back home in Sæland, had read Holberg's *Kirkehistorie* [History of the Church] for her and a great deal of the Bible for myself, I now also read a little in *Jesus og Fornuften* and more in *Bibelen forsvarer sig selv* and in the other Copenhagen periodicals which through a reading club in Vejle floated around on the heath; and without my taking it any further to heart I thought it would perhaps be worth helping Bishop Balle a little, who stood so much alone, by delivering a lecture to the upstarts and disparagers [*Spyttegjøge og Spottefugle*].

1. Dk presents a relatively flat landscape, its highest point (Yding Skovhøj in central Jylland) achieving no more than 173 metres; Laaland (modern spelling Lolland), Dk's fourth largest island, situated in the Baltic, rises to only 25 metres above sea-level.

2. N. E. Balle (in collaboration with C. Bastholm), *Lærebog i den evangelisk-christelige Religion* [Text-book in the Evangelical Christian religion; 1791]. Authority required the introduction of the book into schools by 1794.

3. *Et Skolelærer-Seminarium.* From the year of its establishment and for more than two decades (1789-1814) Balle, along with such other leading figures in Danish life as the enlightenment-inspired reformer Christian Ditlev Reventlow, sat on *Kommissionen til de danske Skolers bedre Indretning* or *Den store Skolekommission* [The Commission for the better ordering of Danish schools; The great School-Commission], a major initiative, both pragmatic and humane, in the state's provision of educational opportunity and control of quality of teaching and content of curriculum. Balle particularly argued the need for state-authorised seminaries for the training (including Bible-based Christian instruction) of teachers – the first fruit being the Blaagaard Statsseminarium established (1791) in a former royal residence outside the city-walls of Copenhagen. Gr had made allusion to this institution in his juvenile satirical comedy *Skoleholderne* [The schoolmasters] (1802). Compulsory education from the age of seven until Confirmation (which had been obligatory since 1736) was enacted in 1814.

4. One example of the many contemporary periodicals hostile to the church was *Repertorium for Fædrelandets Religionslærere* [Repository for the fatherland's teachers of religion] (*GEEG*).

5. The challenge came from Otto Horrebow (1796): *Er det en christelig Lærers Pligt at lyve for Almuen? et Spørgsmaal Dr. Bastholm helliget* [Is it a Christian teacher's duty to lie to the common folk? a question dedicated to Dr Bastholm]. By 'Christian teacher' is of course meant preacher, priest.

59 (b): Kirke-Speil eller Udsigt over den christne Menigheds Levnetsløb (1871); GEEG Stk. 54, pp. 89-91; US X, pp. 336-38.

"Thus ended my so-called academic course, without intellectual gain and without faith". "Doubtless it was only the bombardment of 1807 that saved us from that awful new liturgy."

[GEEG p. 89] When Napoleon Bonaparte was fighting with Admiral Nelson at Abukir and making his pilgrimage to the Pyramids, I for my part moved to the Latin School in Aarhus, and even though it lasted for only two years I there forgot not only Napoleon and the newspapers but church history, churchgoing and childhood learning, in the face of boredom, pipe-smoking, card-playing and loafing about with schoolbooks under my arm; so when in the year 1800 I came to Copenhagen and became a student, there was not a thought within me of ever setting foot inside a church except when on the family's behalf I participated in escorting the body of Bishop Balle's wife over in Frue Kirke.[1]

The ecclesiastical pen-feuding had died out of its own accord when the Press Ordinance [*Trykkeforordningen*] of 1799 put a stop to more or less all printing except that of almanacs in German and Danish, posters and ordinances, the Berling newspaper, *Politivennen* [The friend of (public) polity] and translations of Lafontaine's stories and Kotzebue's comedies. True enough, [K. L.] Rahbek's *Minerva* and [L. N.] Fallesen's *Teologisk Maanedsskrift* continued to drag themselves along until 1808 and 1809, but commanded the attention of no one, not even of the editors.

When, without any desire to do so, according to the will of my elderly parents, I had to read for the *Attestat*s, as they at that time still rightly named what is now called studying Theology even though it is one and the same thing, naturally I did not enquire what the theological professors but only what the most reasonably-priced tutors were called; and I listened to none of the theological lectures except that for fun on one single occasion I went to hear the detractor [C. F.] Hornemann who then stood in the vanguard and was amusing himself, when I heard him, over the Epistle to the Romans, both with what Paul thought and with what he ought to have thought. Otherwise there were the High German [D. G.] Moldenhawer who ran the factory, and was renowned in the capital as a Latin orator but was otherwise called "The Jesuit" because he did not deny but circumvented the faith of the Church; [Bishop Friederich] Münter the *hjemtysker*, famous for his ecclesiastical-historical learning, from which however neither he himself nor others gained any benefit, but known to us only for his muddle-headedness; and finally the very nice, polite Copenhagener, P. E. Müller, a completely fresh-baked professor without any decided opinions and as yet without any influence at all. His lectures I therefore did not read, and in those I read I found, naturally, no Christianity; so when I presented myself [1803] the professors, naturally, found nothing in me either, but they found all Moldenhawer's lectures and a bit of Münter's [GEEG p. 90] natural theology and history of dogma, and with this they were well pleased except for P. E. Müller who had to keep silent where Moldenhawer spoke.

However, I was awakened a little out of the school-stupor from quite other quarters: partly by the powerful cannonade in the Kongedyb by which the hero of Abukir [Nelson] fired in the century of national-mindedness [*folkelighed*];[2] and partly through the ancient chronicles of the North which a comrade in the student-corps, the Bornholmer [P. C.] Skougaard, pushed under my nose; and finally by the frightful uproar my half-German cousin, Henrik Steffens, caused at Ehlers' Kollegium, so that Regensen was close to collapsing; and I found it quite implausible, certainly, but yet quite extraordinary what he, in his bold free-speaking, called undeniable: that everything which we in Copenhagen read and wrote and praised to the skies was German and French trash, that France, with its whole revolution and with all its wisdom and beauty was merely an imitation of the Roman hell with Nero in the high seat, and that if one wished to know what poesy was then one should just read Shakespeare and Göthe, whom I had never heard mentioned, and if one wished to get an idea of philosophy then one should listen to Steffens and read Schelling.

Thus ended then my so-called academic course, without intellectual gain and without faith, and although I tried to remain in the capital and go in for Icelandic and Nordic antiquities, it would not work out so I had to go out to pasture and went then [1805] to Langeland as residential tutor in a manor-house where, following baronial example, they preferred to speak German, which I had not learnt at school but now had to teach myself, although they never got me talking it. Here, naturally, I found nothing of Christianity either, but practically empty churches with somnolent priests and with Kingo's hymnal because the old bishop, Tønne Bloch in Odense, could not abide the Evangelical Hymnal, and he had only recently died. Here there was good opportunity to preach freely upon virtue and enlightenment,[3] and since I readily allowed myself to be heard and was readily listened to, I preached vigorously against Kingo's hymn-book, against all kinds of superstition and other vices; but in order to compensate a little for the somnolence, the German and the coarseness, which I did not share, I soon got a reading association set up, through which readable Danish books from the previous century and new things from this century, German as well as Danish, first gained admittance to Langeland.[4] By this means, Øhlenschläger's poetic writings from 1805 came to my notice, and since I had recently been touched upon that tender spot whereby *everything* that lies within us wells up,[5] so also there welled up [GEEG p. 91] ancient memories in me, and I avidly accepted all the new impressions which, especially in *Vaulundur* and *Aladdin*, came my way.

Now, in my own eyes and in those of the world I was new born in spirit, so when I preached for example upon the two questions: Do we possess justification? Do we have faith? and the answer was: Neither – it was found on Langeland to be the ancient orthodoxy, albeit with a new cut, so it got itself an audience, and they were not asleep. Just at that time (1806) people were squabbling in the periodicals over the Lolland bishop [P. O.] Boisen's proposal for a new liturgy, which, at the recommendation of the Chancellery, was under consideration by a Commission where, certainly, Bishop Balle occupied the high seat but where unbelief and indifference undoubtedly had the most voices, so that there was a danger that the Baptismal Covenant and the Sacramental word as a whole would be, if not totally thrown out, at least garbled. For sure, neither I nor anyone else took this very seriously, but yet I felt myself driven to join in the discussion and to lay stress upon "Baptism and the Lord's Supper" [*Daaben og Nadveren*] as the focal points of the whole liturgy, from which rays of light must needs go out to all sides. This paper "On Religion and Liturgy"

[*Om Religion og Liturgie*] was included in Fallesen's *Maanedskrift* when it was on its last legs, and it caused a certain stir in the capital; but although the moralising priests got their set pieces said, yet the whole thing was so declamatory and the triumph of rationalism so much a foregone conclusion that not a single dog barked at it, and doubtless it was only the bombardment of 1807 that saved us from that awful new liturgy.

1. The funeral was that of Balle's second wife (died 11 April 1802), daughter of his predecessor Ludvig Harboe (Bishop of Sjælland 1757-83); Balle had previously been married to Friderica Severine (1747-81), sister of Gr's father.

2. Gr alludes to the British fleet's assault on Copenhagen (The Battle of Copenhagen, or of Reden) 1801 which, he believed, had the effect of awakening, not only in the University's student body (which formed a defence corps) but in the country more widely, a previously wanting sense of common purpose and of national pride.

3. Gr preached his sermons in the large and handsome church at Bøstrup, Langeland (where the grave of Constance Leth is now to be found).

4. Gr's draft *Protokol for Langelands Læseselskab* [Protocol for the Langeland reading association] was subsequently published by Johan Grundtvig in *Den Danske Højskole* III (1903), 146-186 (*GEEG*). The prospectus was circulated in November 1805 and the association founded February 1806.

5. Editors of *GEEG* appear to believe that Gr refers here to the impact which Oehlenschläger's *Smaadigte* of 1803 had earlier made upon him; but the familiar Romantic idiom also suggests that he may be alluding to his love for Constance Leth, Lady of Egeløkke. Pages covering March to September 1805 have been torn out of his surviving diary, but Gr himself says elsewhere (see, for example, items 29, 30, 32) that the experiencing of this love saved him from his previous cold, cloddish and conceited self, and opened his eyes to profounder aspects of existence (such, one may confidently add on Gr's behalf, as Oehlenschläger's poetry so preeminently intimated).

59 (c): Kirke-Speil eller Udsigt over den christne Menigheds
Levnetsløb (1871); GEEG Stk. 54, pp. 91-95; US X, pp. 338-43.

The probational sermon. Udby. "A sign that Our Lord had not utterly smitten the hand from off me."

The year 1807 was for Denmark, in worldly respects, the year of the great shipwreck, when both its naval fleet and its merchant fleet perished in one and the same storm, and an ill-fortuned seven years' war began which was to end with State Bankruptcy, divorce from Norway, the kingdom's slavish dependence upon its hereditary enemies and, inevitably stemming from all this, a despondency which in so womanly [*kvindelige*] a people as the Danes must needs border closely upon a mute despair; and this was a warning for the future which foretold anything but a resurrection of the folk and a golden year corresponding to the days of Fredegod, Denmark's time-honoured age of gold, renowned throughout the whole of the North and never completely forgotten; so that if for a while now the signs have nevertheless not been unpromising of a happy [**GEEG p. 92**] season of New Year among us, then there must have occurred a miracle of God in our church history which one would least have expected.

When [N. E.] Balle [1808], deeply oppressed beneath his own and the fatherland's misfortunes stepped down from the bishopric of Sjælland and handed over the high seat to the bookish, muddle-headed, bombastic, good-natured but impotent and faint-hearted *hjemtysker* and freemason, Frederik Münter, it then also became plain, before two years were out, that *Lutheran* Christianity, far from exercising an absolute authority in Denmark, had there lost its citizenship to a higher degree than anywhere in Germany, and that the forbearance (Toleration) which the rationalists had enjoyed in full measure under Balle and which indeed they made a profession of, this they abandoned even before Balle came to his grave, as soon as they thought they themselves had no need of it; and, since it was my probational sermon [1810] which gave rise to this very grievous discovery, this same probational sermon, though given before an empty house in the Regens-Kirke, has thereby attained a church-historical importance to which, in itself, it is in no way fitted. How things really connected with each other in all this, naturally no one can clarify as well as I, if only I can regard the affair as a matter not personally concerning myself; and this costs – at any rate now, after the passage of half a century – not the slightest effort.

This probational sermon with its (on paper) undeniably provocative title, *Why has the Word of the Lord vanished from his House?* [*Hvi er Herrens Ord forsvundet af hans Hus?*] is in fact not at all, as someone out in the world might suppose, the passionate outburst of some Lutheran-traditionalist hothead by which he wished to indict or provoke either Copenhagen's or the whole of Denmark's rationalist clergy; rather it was a very tame and innocent occasional speech by a young speaker and author who, poetically immersed in the antiquity of our High North, yet felt ashamed that his old father, in the year in which he became a jubilarian [*Jubel-lærer*], was forced to lay down his office because his youngest son, even though he had achieved his *Attestats* and the age of ordination, would not give up his glittering prospects in the capital by becoming personal curate in his little birthplace in South Sjælland.

I had in fact come [1808] to Copenhagen where I immediately became an alumnus in Valkendorfs Kollegium and history teacher in the most famous Institute [Det Schouboeske Institut], and found my experiments in writing in *Minerva* and [L. N.] Fallesen's monthly regarded with rather wide eyes, and in the college I found intelligent companions, especially in [S. B.] Hersleb and [F. C.] Sibbern, who introduced [**GEEG p. 93**] me to the capital's most brilliant circles, at the home of Anders Sandø Ørsted, married to Øhlenschlæger's sister, and at the home of the renowned Norwegian professors [Niels] Treschow and [Georg] Sverdrup. By my essays in *Kjøbenhavns Skilderi* which the Jew [Salomon] Soldin kept open for everything that could find readers, by my *Nordens Mytologi* [Mythology of the North; 1808] and the first *Optrin af Kæmpelivet i Norden* [Scenes from the warrior-life in the North; 1809] I had gained quite a respectable name in our little reading-world; and for the sake of a much greater name *there* and a matching chair in the university I had so completely lost sight of the Church that I did not even get myself heard in any of the capital's churches, let alone contemplate contending with the capital's ecclesiastical oracle, [H. G.] Clausen, curate of Frue-Kirke, for either palm or precedence. When I had to preach my probational sermon in an empty place I wanted only to express my perception of the tendency of the Church's thinking of that period, and since this was all in all not nearly as severe as in the treatise on "Religion and Liturgy" [*Om Religion og Liturgie*; 1807] it never occurred to me that anyone would fulminate against it or that the rationalist priests who had recently flattered themselves as having no other term of divinity than 'Reason' would ever take it ill to be reminded of this. For me then it was completely unexpected that the sermon would be carried off and read by the whole capital, and when it was rumoured that the capital's priests, excepting the old Greenlander, Bishop [Otto] Fabricius, with Professor [H. G.] Clausen in the vanguard, would set heaven and earth in motion to get me hanged or burnt – then those all around me laughed and I laughed with them, as one can still see in my first New Year's gift *Idunna* which was then [late 1810] going through the press. A. S. Ørsted said that if the priests sought to prosecute me for it, it would be just as wise as if the whole generation sought to prosecute [J. G.] Fichte for his *Grundtræk af Nutiden* [Outline of the present time], and it was said for certain that when Clausen spoke about the case with Kristjan Colbjørnson, who was then *Justitiarius* [presiding judge] in the Supreme Court, Colbjørnson had urged him to be wary of the law-courts which according to law were obliged to adjudge Grundtvig to be in the right. In any case, both Bishop Münter and the University administration wanted the law-courts, to which I submitted myself, to be avoided; and the deletion from the *Candidat*-list with which the Bishop threatened me if I was unwilling to accept a stiff reprimand from himself or from the University Senate, also fell through, even though I fought against the reprimand as long as I could; and the reprimand really did not turn out to make any impression at all since it consisted merely of the *Rektor* [Vice-Chancellor] of the University reading aloud to me from the royal resolution that [GEEG p. 94] I was to receive a reprimand because I seemed to reveal the intention of seeking attention. [C. F.] Hornemann himself felt pity for me, so he went down with me in the *Studiegaard* and exhorted me to shrug my shoulders at this mishap, as [Jacob] Langebek too had done. [D. G.] Moldenhawer, who was after all the moving spirit of the University's administration, wept over me like an ancient Roman at the thought of Fortune's fickleness; and [F. J.] Kaas who was President of the Danish Chancellery assured me that both the King and he knew I was in the right, so it would not in the least way harm me, but that one had to do a little on behalf of the clergy and he had himself, more often than not in vain, advised them to preach a bit more biblically – all this because they thought that it was on account of this laughable matter that I was close to sinking into the ground.

On the contrary, it was a serious matter of a different sort, which it was thought at that time could at best happen in Copenhagen to a *Candidat* Maalø, the *herrnhuter*, and to the old *herrnhuter* Gerhard Seberg, the unfrocked priest from Norway, or to the Norwegian *Bygde-Prædikant* [itinerant preacher], Hans Hauge who at that time was every so often placed in the pillory of the *Lærde Efterretninger*; but which in fact actually happened to the young northern poet and antiquarian in Valkendorfs Kollegium in the Autumn of 1810. I still well remember how it began; for I was sitting alone one evening and reading in Kotzebue's History of Prussia which was the most recent thing on this country and which, although I deeply despised the name, I felt as a teacher of history I must dutifully make use of; but I had got no further than the thirteenth century when the German knights invaded and christened Prussia by the sword, for here Kotzebue had planted one of his poisonous flowers beneath what he called "the withered Cross" – and with this a chill ran down my spine so that I not only threw the book from me but leapt up as though gripped by some mighty spirit which was calling me to become a reformer. Thereupon followed a couple of months of proud but quiet religious zeal in which for the first time since my childhood I read the Bible in earnest, especially the Prophets, and the hymns of Luther and Kingo, and prayed and pondered over

Reflections upon the church

how, especially with pen and ink, a reformation might in our times be accomplished. In the literary sphere, *Nyaars-Nat* [New Year's Eve] is the sole trace of this life of religious zealotry, for it was abruptly ended when all at once I was shattered by the questions: Are you yourself a Christian? and do you have forgiveness of your sins? – questions of conscience, which fell like stones, yea like rocks upon my heart. Then I closed all my books, let all proud plans go by the board and hurried [**GEEG p. 95**] home to my old father, who had laid down his office since at that time, far from doing honour to a jubilarian priest [*Jubel-Lærer*], they would not even allow him to take on his son as his curate because there were unemployed curates in the diocese. Meanwhile, I had now gained courage precisely to be a curate, if Our Lord would only accept me as the minister of his word, and as soon as my mind had become a little calmer I took it as a sign that Our Lord had not utterly smitten the hand from off me if, against all reasonable expectation, I could get my father back his office and be his helpmeet. Doubtless it was mainly through Bishop Balle's influence with Kaas and the King that it turned out well; at all events, turn out well it did both outwardly and inwardly so that I became priest and could happily both settle down in peace with our three old articles of faith and for the rest let the Holy Spirit and the Bible decide; for *this* I quickly learned: that it was not nearly so much belief in "The Son" as in "The Holy Spirit" that had been completely lost among us, whereby both the Faith and the Scriptures had become dead and impotent; so that when, with Luther, both were received again at first hand – from the Spirit who bestows life – then they too became living and were set in force. Meanwhile, I also learned at Udby that, at least among Sjællanders in particular, it was the new *Textbook* [Balle's *Lærebog*, 1791] and the *Evangelical Hymnal* [1798] which had delivered the frail inherited faith its death-wound; for it was not with my father and his Sjællandic listeners as with the stubborn Jutlanders [*de stærke Jyder*] who staged a revolt; so even though my father, not otherwise of a soft disposition, would shed tears when he thought about the way these dry and insipid books had robbed him of all his joy in both church-service and confirmation-teaching, yet he had not only immediately obeyed the royal decree concerning the *Textbook* but had soon given in to Bishop Balle's wishes as regards the *Hymnal*, and most of his listeners, who missed their old hymns and could not be bothered with struggling to read the new, stayed at home and threw the old books, like a forbidden fruit, far away from them, so that when I would have my confirmands learn Kingo's festal hymns, certainly I found *them*, especially the girls, very happy about it but they found it very difficult to get hold of an old hymnbook, even though it was only ten years since it had been abandoned. When, either in sermon or at confirmation, I let the old strains sound forth, then I could hear the old people sobbing around me; but I did not notice that my old parents, though both had good voices, got the courage to sing once more their old favourite hymns, so it would hardly be the case with anyone at all.

1. This is the father, *Kapellan* and later *Stiftsprovst* H. G. Clausen, who was named titular professor in 1809, not the son, Professor H. N. Clausen.

59 (d): Kirke-Speil eller Udsigt over den christne Menigheds Levnetsløb
(1871); GEEG Stk. 54, pp. 96-100; US X, pp. 343-49.

The passage tellingly describes how close Grundtvig came to defeat at the end of the "seven lean years" and before he was at last called to ministry in the Church, at Præstø.

[GEEG p. 96] It was in this situation that I wrote my first *Verdenskrønike* [World Chronicle] [1812], which looks so peculiar not, as was said, because I more than all other writers of history lacked skill and taste, but because the book was actually begun at Valkendorfs Kollegium as a little overview of world history which I found was badly needed in school; but when then I came to the Reformation it seemed to me that I, as a Christian scholar, needs must grasp the opportunity of portraying especially the ungodly eighteenth century, both abroad and at home, with the blackest colours. When I then furthermore, from my strictly Lutheran-Biblical standpoint, by the naming of names, mercilessly gave our then-living writers, theologians and other famous men their testimonials in black and white, it was no wonder that in our otherwise stagnant, sleepy reading-world the Chronicle was regarded by all so-called "sensible people" as nothing more nor less than a spiteful lampoon whose fluent and not unwitty style only made it the more venomous and atrocious. The Chronicle came out right at Christmas [1812], the impression was sold out in a few days, and my Copenhagen friends quickly informed me that I would surely have had a dozen libel-cases hanging round my neck had not the State immediately after New Year gone completely bankrupt and thereby given the Copenhageners something else to think and to fuss about. But now out of the whole thing there came only a dull and long-protracted pen-feuding [*Pennefejde*];¹ though what of a more spiritual character could have come out of it under any circumstances I could never myself have said; for, even if it had been particularly by the pen that the Church had been torn down, yet it was clear that not by the pen could it be built up again, and I did not for a moment share that superstitious faith in the literal text [*Bogstav-Skriften*] which began as late as the nineteenth century to be traceable amongst us as well, through the Bible Societies – of which I have never once become a member. It was besides not at all to be expected, especially amongst us, that a serious pen-feud concerning the faith and the content of the Bible could be raised, since the times were so estranged from both of these and so indifferent towards all spiritual life-issues that the controversy would inevitably come to concern itself either with the good name and repute of individual persons or with the high worth of so-called 'Science' [*Videnskabelighed*] which, our renowned physicist H. C. Ørsted in particular asserted upon this occasion, I had frightfully insulted with this monstrosity of a world-history and wanted to excite the superstitious populace into burning books and scientists as in the darkest days of the papacy. [GEEG p. 97]

I had in fact endeavoured to make the point that when this so-called 'Science' and its so-called great light which in the eighteenth century either made mock of all things divine and human or at least pushed them aside in order to throw themselves into the minute scrutiny of the material world and the building of castles in the air, then not only was this the sign of an ungodly way of thinking but also all sense of the spirit [*Aandelighed*] was then at its last gasp and would soon, just as formerly in Greece and Rome, lose itself in brutishness and barbarism; and this, naturally, was something one could quarrel about until Doomsday.

What had dimly floated before me was however the possibility that king and statesmen might become observant that this unbelief and ungodly enlightenment led in every way to the dissolution of human society, so that they would again raise up the Lutheran State Church as a dam against the flood of corruption just as Napoleon had endeavoured to raise up the Catholic Church in France; for I saw well enough that neither would the way of thinking become the more spiritual, nor Christianity the more alive by this, but I thought that then Our Lord could and maybe would decide the outcome by some miracle or other. Since I, like Luther, had the feeling that the written word would not suffice when – through the living voice – the Spirit did not proclaim the Gospel to the people as a divine force for salvation, I decided after my father's death not to turn away from the capital nor spare my voice; but when [H. G.] Clausen, who was now become *Stiftsprovst*, soon got all Copenhagen's priests to refuse me their pulpits I completely gave up hope [1815] of being able for the time being to work with hand or voice for the reformation of the Danish State-Church.[2] Upon Norway's divorce from Denmark it was pretty nearly the case that my bosom friend [S. B.] Hersleb who became the first theological professor in the new university in Kristiania drew me up there with him; and since I stood in a friendly relationship with a number of the Haugians [*Haugianerne*] it would have been reasonable to give the church-history of the North a quite independent redirection; but it was not God's will, and over a span of years [until 1821] it was exclusively labours within the spirit of the North [*Nordens Aand*], such as the periodical *Danne-Virke* and the translation of Denmark's and Norway's chronicles and of *Beowulf* [*Bjovulfs-Drape*] which absorbed my time and my activity. But that in no way did I give up the hope of a renewal of Christian life in the North, this was heard in my farewell sermon in Frederiksberg [1815] on "Resting [**GEEG p. 98**] beneath the wings of Christ" [*Hvilen under Kristi Vinger*] but both in my published biblical sermons [1816] and in the new edition of my *Verdens-Krønnike* [1817][3] I was profoundly gripped by this feeling, that neither writing skill nor speaking talents, and even less worldly power, would now suffice to remedy the agony of the Church, since what was needed was no less a miracle than the Lord's resurrection from the dead with a new transfigured body. "Here we stand" – so it said among much else – "There is to be seen but a hair's breadth between death and life but yet this is a chasm which none can overleap. We can peer in upon the Patriarchs; the sheen bedazzles our eye, but the sheen is devoid of strength.[4] We see this distinctly: it is a Life-force that we lack; we see it so very distinctly, that if we could touch the Patriarchs, come in spiritual contact with them, then we would be helped; but this seems impossible, it will demand a miracle which we cannot possibly comprehend before this happens within ourselves; for what we have not felt we can never comprehend; and so the question is whether we are willing to believe what we absolutely do not comprehend, hope for the unreasonable, in hope in him who can awaken the dead and precisely render the impossible possible, fill the empty and render the powerless strong." "*This* is the true, historical art, which performs miracles and which only he understands who raised up Jesus Christ from the dead but which also he will indubitably perform. The question is only where and when? – and at this we can only guess."

Thus then I acknowledged, in the very year of Luther's jubilee [1817], that my attempt over the previous seven years to repair, with God's help, the collapsing Lutheran State-Church in Denmark had completely failed not only outwardly, since I was become a priest without a church and a speaker without a voice, but also inwardly, since I had not been able to find that spiritual chain which vitally links Christians with the Lord and with each other.[5] So it could not at all console me that another Lutheran priest, who had both churches and audiences in abundance, namely Claus Harms in Kiel, in the same year of jubilee stepped up as Martin Luther the Second with his famous Theses or Apples of Discord, to be fought over in German; for I neither believed that Luther could revive in Germany nor could anyone convince me that that would succeed for Harms which failed for me, who in quite another way had dedicated myself to the spirit of Luther both with a simple faith in the triune God, with a firm trust in the means of salvation according to [GEEG p. 99] the Lord's own institutions, and with the strains of Lutheran hymnody in *Et Barn er født i Bethlehem* [A babe is born in Bethlehem] and *Dejlig er den Himmel blaa* [Lovely are the heavens blue], *Der sad en Svend i Blaamænds Land* [There sat a youth in Ethiope], etc.

However, that I had not lost hope that Lutheran Christianity would waken, prevail and endure is to be seen, among the rest, in my jubilee-year song to the memory of Luther, which reads (*Danne-Virke*, vol. 3):

Ja, *o Luther!* vil i Blinde	Yea, O Luther! if, in blindness,
Dine Fodspor trindt man sky,	widely men your footsteps shun,
Altid skal dog en Kjærminde	yet forget-me-not shall ever
For dig gro i Bøge-Ly,	bloom for you in beechwood shade,
Gro, til sidste Bøg henvisner,	bloom until the last beech withers,
Sidste Dane-Hjerte isner:	the last Danish heart grows icy:
Med Guds Hjælp, til Domme-Dag.	with God's help, to Judgement Day.[6]

Since the time of New Year is in general a time of self-awareness then not only the individual but also the people who have lived to see the time of New Year and had a decent life must happily become self-aware; and such a popular self-awareness indeed conspicuously flourished at the Reformation in the sixteenth century; but yet even among us it seems to be strangled at birth through that crabwise progress in the mother tongue, which the Latin School induced and daily advanced. In the eighteenth century then, *folkelighed* was almost as dead and impotent as Christianity, so that all the so-called sensible and enlightened folk rested their honour upon having elevated themselves above all races as true citizens of the world (Kosmopoliter [Cosmopolitans]), the High German "Mann, wie er sein sollte"[7] [Man as he should be]; but then here too nature proved stronger than nurture and in the nineteenth century it became clearer day by day that all the folk in Christendom more or less felt an instinct to rise up from the dead; so it was only a question of whether it would turn out to be more than nightly haunting and spectral reappearance, whereby the resurrection-instinct should first manifest itself in the reading-world and on the stage. Already at the end of the eighteenth century such haunting began here at home, so that Danishness, especially in P. A. Heiberg, really seemed to tweak the nose of the prevailing Germanness; but that this was only the apparition of ghosts one saw, among the rest, from the fact that "*Niels Ebbesen*'s implausible author" ([L. C.] Sander) was himself a German; for the strongest expression of Danishness at that time was [GEEG p. 100] that, when the tragic drama *Niels Ebbesen* was performed, the pit burst into laughter at *Grev* Gert's death and shouted: "That's the German down and out!" In the dawning of the nineteenth century on the other hand, not only did the battle in the Kongedyb serve a warning about the achievements of the Danish folk; but in the midst of Denmark's deepest humiliation (1807-14) the woodland seemed to echo with a popular reborn hymnody to which the whole North listened and which even the Germans had to heed; and even if the keynote in Oehlenschläger was more Norwegian, and in Grundtvig more Old Norse than Danish, yet on the other hand the keynote in Ingemann was so exclusively the Danish of the islands and in [Steen Steensen] Blicher so broad Jutlandish, that a later enlightened generation will be thoroughly surprised over such a rare display of the *folkelige*. For certain, the whole of that poetic movement in the first generation of the nineteenth century – which, speaking in human and *folkelige* terms, was nowhere more devoid of life and achievement than in Denmark – seemed to be so completely restricted to a very narrow reading-world and a very obscure stage that it had to be regarded as a nightly haunting; for which reason also, *Dagen* and all that belonged to its regime (just as *Dagbladet* still) crossed itself almost as devoutly against the whole of this poetic fooling about with old superstition and ancient monuments as for my raving mad berserk-gang, *Bededag*-sermonising and dirge-singing [*Dødninge-Sang*]. I may well have still had the courage in 1815, when I gave up the church-struggle for the time being, to pick a paper quarrel in the periodical *Danne-Virke* with all the Germanicising here at home, and to devote full seven years to the revitalising of Nordic *folkelighed* by translation into Danish of the nordic heroic poem *Bjovulfs Drape*, of Saxo the runemaster's *Danmarks Historie* and Snorri Sturlesøn's Chronicles of Norway; but with these I also seemed to have exhausted my powers, whilst indifference towards everything of the spirit and even for the land of our fathers seemed to inundate us all so that I was also close to despair over the saving of the communal life [*Folkelivets Redning*],[8] as can still be seen from the Foreword to my *Nyaarsmorgen* [New Year's Morn] (1824); and it is therefore quite reasonable that (as I heard) it was said, spitefully enough, on that occasion: "Now Grundtvig means to emigrate, with Saxo under the one arm and Snorri under the other."

1. Episodes in this feud included a review in P. E. Müller's influential journal *Dansk Litteratur-Tidende* (1813) by theologian and historian Professor Jens Møller (1779-1833) – a scholar noted for unaggressive and fair-minded judgments (and incidentally the man whose frivolous treatment of *Skirnirs Reise* in *Ny Minerva* 1806 had so incensed Grundtvig); Grundtvig's response in *Nyeste Skilderie af København* (17, 21 and 24 August 1813); forthright criticism in a letter from philologist and historian Christian Molbech (1783-1857) and a subsequent article which so offended Grundtvig that their friendship was broken off for a while; and a lengthy exchange launched by H. C. Ørsted (1777-1851) when he took the opportunity to condemn the work in the course of writing a review (in *Dansk Litteratur-Tidende*, 1814, nos. 12 and 13) of Grundtvig's *En mærkelig Spaadom ogsaa om Dannemark efter en gammel Haandskrift* [A remarkable prophecy also concerning Denmark, from an old manuscript; 1814], to attack what he perceived to be Grundtvig's anti-scientific polemic; see Index entries **Galilei,** Galileo; **Vanini,** Giulio Cesare (Lucilio); and **Roskilde Landemode**.

2. Having preached a farewell sermon in Frederiksberg Kirke (26 December 1815) Grundtvig announced that he would not preach again in any Copenhagen church until he was formally appointed to an incumbency. He is at pains to point out however (below) that the Frederiksberg sermon, far from being an admission of total despair, still reflected his faith and hope that there would yet come a Christian spiritual renewal in the North.

3. *Udsigt over Verdens-Krøniken, fornemmelig i det Lutherske Tidsrum* [Survey of world history principally in the Lutheran era].

4. 'the sheen' – Grundtvig's word is *Skinnet*, the outer surface, the (mere) appearance.

5. Grundtvig refers to his distinctive view of the role of the sacraments (eucharist and baptism) together with the associated words of institution, profession and prayer handed down in unbroken oral tradition from apostolic times, which guaranteed the historic fellowship of the Church and embodied the mystical union of Christ with his church.

6. Verse 6 of Grundtvig's 18-verse poem *Morten Luthers Minde* [In remembrance of Martin Luther] published in his periodical *Danne-Virke* (1817). The nine verses (6-10 and 15-18) he actually quoted in his lecture are all printed in *US* X, 346-47. The beechwood, a characteristic of the Danish landscape, here stands, as often in poetry, for the land itself, Denmark.

7. Grundtvig apparently alludes, sceptically, to the precept of Johann Wolfgang von Goethe: "Treat a man as he is and he will remain as he is. Treat a man as he can and should be, and he will become as he can and should be."

8. This echoes his earlier statement concerning his failure to find "that spiritual chain which vitally links Christians with the Lord and with each other." The significance to Grundtvig of this dramatic conceptualisation of a dying *folkeliv* may be clarified by recalling his characterisation of the supremely heroic status of Beowulf in his introduction to *Bjovulfs Drape* (1820) where he says that Beowulf, by ending the ravagings of the dragon even at the cost of his own life, saved the dying *folkeliv* of his people.

59 (e): Kirke-Speil eller Udsigt over den christne Menigheds Levnetsløb
(1871); GEEG Stk. 54, pp. 100-103; US X, pp. 349-51.

Kirkens Gjenmæle: "An only half miscarried, first giant stride in the whole church-movement." The calls to Præstø and to Vor Frelsers Kirke.

⌒

Kirkens Gjenmæle which came out the next year was presumably the thing which most likely moved Frederik the Sixth to his famous witticism: "Grundtvig is a fire-spouting mountain" – for there can be found a certain, even if distant, likeness between Vesuvius, which between its [GEEG p. 101] eruptions patiently lets itself be ploughed and tilled as a vineyard, and a combative author, who for a stretch of years can sit as quietly as a mouse and then rear up again like a lion on paper, as I of course reared up in my contentious tract against *Clausen* the younger, at that time the youngest professor in our University but even so our proper instructor of priests since of the two Møllers (whom Baggesen called "the water-miller" and "the wind-miller")[1] the one had no opinion and the other no authority. Since however the so-called "Church's Retort" [*Kirkens Gjenmæle*] by pen and ink now appears in my eyes as an imprudent leap into the air and a piece of desperate risk-taking – whilst with its terse title, its remarkable content and its unhappy fate (in the short term) it appears to most people an only half miscarried, first giant stride in the whole church-movement which is now a matter of joyous fact – then perhaps it is worth the inconvenience of explaining how this book – imprudent but at least extraordinary, so-called fire-spouting but yet only glowing with the Northern lights – came into the world.

Maybe I did somewhat indiscreetly confide in the Royal Danish Chancellery that I was unwilling to take any incumbency outside the capital; and through its very indiscreet head, Excellency [F. J.] Kaas, the Chancellery confided back to me that within the city-walls, right in the face of the bishop and the senior clergy, and especially after the frightful clash at the Roskilde *Landemode* [diocesan convention], I would receive no appointment: but all the same both things came fully to pass.

As early as 1818 one of the Chancellery gentlemen[2] wrote to me that if I were willing to apply for the vacant resident curacy in Aalborg then I should be appointed; and even though it was very much against my inclinations, yet for God's sake I did not dare to refuse to mount a proffered pulpit, not even when Kaas confided in me that naturally he had first enquired of his good friend, His Excellency F. Moltke in Aalborg and received assurance that the diocesan authorities had nothing against my appointment. So it even got as far as a party being arranged for me and one of Aalborg's dignitaries, in order that my nomination, as hot as it was, should come directly from 'Kabinettet' [the Cabinet] and be welcomed with a toast to the curate; but there came no offer, and it now transpired that the King had taken a stand against the Chancellery and declared emphatically that Grundtvig should not leave the city.

However, that the King had herewith been thinking of my work with [GEEG p. 102] the folk-books [*folkebøgerne*],³ which he genuinely interested himself in and had, as he said, created a living wage for, *this* is to be seen from the fact that quite unexpectedly (1821) upon his own initiative he nominated me as parish priest in Præstø; and notwithstanding that precisely at that time I felt myself just about as dispirited, dead and listless as Denmark as a whole, yet I did not dare to set myself against what seemed to me was God's call, and I just confided in His Majesty the hope that since in this I yielded to *him*, he would also yield to *me* when opportunity arose, and would call me back to the capital. It may be noted, as a curiosity, which however has certainly also had some small significance, that Copenhagen's priests (though not those at Frue-Kirke) competed in offering me their pulpits,⁴ so I preached round about, including for the first time in Vartov, by way of taking my leave, and this with such a reputation that Queen Marie had me invited as preacher in 'Kabinettet' [the Cabinet] and when, following the gospel concerning the Canaanite woman, I asserted that only in the potency of faith does that which the good heart wills come to pass, she praised my eloquence to the skies and most graciously enjoined me that when I came to the city and could stay over the Sunday then I should let her know this; indeed, I was apparently within an ace of being named as court-preacher. However, I took good care not to invite myself; and when after the course of one and a half years the King really did summon me to be curate at Frelserens Kirke in Christianshavn my court favour came to a disastrous end, without my being able to this very day to find out or fathom out what aroused the Queen's indignation in my Cabinet-sermon on the gospel for the second day of Christmas concerning the persecution of Christianity, first with violence, then with stealth and finally with both, but yet all in vain.

It was naturally a great amusement for Copenhageners to storm Vor Frelsers Kirke on the First Sunday in Advent in order to hear how *Stiftsprovst* Clausen would induct Grundtvig; but they after all went home with long faces since both Clausen and I had sufficient tact to keep quiet about our well-known opinions about each other – which perhaps presented the *Stiftsprovst* with a little difficulty but nevertheless fell out quite well, with this turn of phrase: that Grundtvig, as he drily remarked, had, both by the spoken and the written word, made himself sufficiently well known. Incidentally, if I had not previously known old Clausen's extraordinary effrontery in quoting the very pithiest of biblical passages without making the slightest application of them, I would have had to be highly astonished [GEEG p. 103] that at my induction, without the slightest fear of tripping up, he waded into the words of the first Epistle to Timothy [1 Timothy 4:16]: "Take heed unto thyself, and unto the doctrine; continue in them: for in doing this thou shalt both save thyself, and them that hear thee" but now I merely found that it was a counterpart to that effrontery with which at my ordination he had shriven me without absolution, upon the words in the first Letter to the Corinthians: "I constrain myself, so that I, who preach to others, shall not myself be repudiated."⁵

1. Professor Peter Erasmus Müller (1776-1834), editor (1805-30) of *Dansk Litteratur-Tidende*, and Professor Jens Møller (1779-1833), frequent reviewer in the journal.

2. Christian Magdalus Thestrup Cold (1754-1826).

3. Gr refers to his translations of Saxo, Snorri and *Beowulf*, produced during his "years in the study" (1815-22). His usage of the element '*folk-*' here does not imply that these books are the written record of an oral, preliterate peasant culture, but rather that they are 'national' books, definitive (one might suggest) of the historic identity of the Danish folk as the confessional books are definitive of the national church.

4. Gr was invited to preach, for example, at two prestigious Copenhagen churches, Holmens Kirke (by Lorenz Nicolai Fallesen, 1757-1824) and Trinitatis Kirke (by Frederik Carl Gutfeld, 1761-1823) as well as at the Harboeske Enkefruekloster (a charitable foundation for unmarried ladies and widows from the first five of the nine *rangklasser* [official ranks in the honours system]) in Stormgade. He preached for the Queen on 18 March 1821.

5. The allusion is to 1 Corinthians 9:27; others as well as Grundtvig took Clausen to task for failing to practise what he preached.

59 (f): Kirke-Speil eller Udsigt over den christne Menigheds Levnetsløb
(1871); GEEG Stk. 54, pp. 103-106; US X, pp. 351-55.

1825: The *mageløse Opdagelse* – "It struck me in a blest moment that the peerless testimony [*det mageløse Vidnesbyrd*] I so laboriously sought after in the whole world of the spirit, *this* rang out as a voice from heaven through the whole of time and of Christendom *in the Apostolic Creed at baptism.*"

Now I had achieved my old wish, to be priest in the capital city; but I soon found the position there, with indiscrimate Communion [*Altergangen i Flæng*][1] and with the marrying of divorced persons [*fraskiltes Vielse*], nearly intolerable, especially since, far from observing that anything was coming to life in my listeners, I found that the life within my own self was wasting away and I found the indifference of the age as stiff-necked as Grendel's Mother, the troll-wife in *Bjovulfs Drape* [*Beowulf*]. However, when I soon found myself once more as revitalised as one can see I was in the poem *Nyaarsmorgen* (1824), then the hope was also revitalised of yet eventually prevailing, by biblical sermon and writings, over my fellow-countrymen's indifference, and to awaken the faith of their childhood in them; and to this revitalisation the unpredictable contributed – that the two most learned younger men in the land, Dr [A. G.] Rudelbach and *Adjunkt* [J. C.] Lindberg attached themselves to me and asked me to be a joint-editor of a theological monthly[2] which was gestating within them. What a comfort and joy it is, when for a span of years one has stood quite alone against the whole world, then to get oneself two brothers-in-arms, surely only he rightly knows this who has experienced it; but that it must be gratifying and strengthening anybody can understand; and therefore when I advised the young warriors rather to take Dr [J. P.] Mynster as their leader it was naturally only because I knew that *his* name and not mine would bind together in collaboration all the friends of the old Christianity in the land. When therefore Mynster would have nothing to do with the enterprise, I of course immediately threw my name into the ring; but even with that, it was only by hook and by crook that a publisher was found; for the Danish book-trade, whilst I was working on the ancient writings, had almost totally come to a standstill, and [C. A.] Reitzel, who was now the only publisher one could think of, did not dare, because of the men of high learning, touch anything that was aimed against them. [J. F.] Milo the bookbinder however let himself be talked into risking his skin, the monthly periodical came out, and the broadsides from my learned collaborators manifestly scared the older rationalists so that [GEEG p. 104], not daring to risk a public fight, they merely strove in dumb desperation to stir up the secular authority against the upholders of church law, to the advantage of those in breach of it.

Under these circumstances, surely it will at least be found sufficiently reasonable and responsible of me to have attacked without any compunction the first rationalist who ventured into the field in order either to force a decisive war of the written word [*Penne-Fejde*] or to compel the Government to investigate whether *we* or our opponents had Church-laws on our side. Now it so chanced that the most junior professor of Theology [H. N. Clausen] was the first who stepped forward with a bold rationalistic text; after the most senior professor of Theology [C. F. Hornemann] had laid a charge in the Chancellery against the Lutheran priest [Heinrich] Egge for fanaticism [*Fanatisme*], *etcetera*; and so neither did I hold back from the sharpest attack I could contrive to make.

Thus far everything was in order, since I was prepared to gamble either that the young author would regard it as beneath his dignity to give this intellectual attack a juridical turn or that the courts would allow laws which in their eyes were antiquated to count for more than public opinion and their personal persuasion; and yet the venture was inexpedient, in that I had recently reached an awareness that in order to revitalise the Christian congregation something else was needed, quite different from pen-feudings or High Court judgments.

I had in fact fallen into deep thought over the desperate position into which Christ's congregation and especially all its children and unlearned members had come by virtue of the fact that almost all the clever scripturalists [*de skriftkloge*] obstinately maintained that not only were the origin, canon and authenticity, and the correct interpretation, of the Holy Scriptures matters of great uncertainty, but that the basic doctrine of the Church concerning the Trinity, the divinity of Christ and the atonement, if one were competent in the original languages and investigated properly, were simply not to be found in the Bible, which nevertheless was for all Protestants the sole warranty of the Faith. No matter how aware in fact I myself was, that the rationalists' Biblical criticism and Scriptural interpretation were more or less equally ill-based and dishonest, yet I could neither ignore that Christian children and layfolk fared equally badly nor forget that even my own Bible-knowledge would not suffice to defy the legion's testimony if I did not also have knowledge of church-history and, before all things, did not have the Spirit's testimony within my inner self, which was able to defy the whole world. Just as it now became to me clear as daylight that *he* who gave witness that [GEEG p. 105] the mystery of salvation was hidden from the learned and clever and revealed to babes and sucklings could not possibly, without plain self-contradiction, bind the faith of the unlearned to the testimony of the learned, so it became for me equally clear as daylight that *if* Scripture were the Christian congregation's rule of Faith then unbelief (since almost all the Scripture-scholars paid homage to this) would now have a far stronger and more valid testimony than the Faith to which only a few individual scholars bore witness; and so my conclusion was that as surely as Jesus Christ was God the Father's only-begotten Son, as surely then there must also be found within the Church a far stronger and more valid testimony of the authentic original Christian Faith than the literal text [*Bogstav-Skriften*] could in any way be for women and children and all the unlearned. When then I unceasingly meditated, read and wrote, with prayer and supplication, lo, it struck me in a blest moment that the peerless testimony [*det mageløse Vidnesbyrd*] I so laboriously sought after in the whole world of the spirit, this rang out as a voice from heaven through the whole of time and of Christendom *in the Apostolic Creed at baptism*.[3]

With this the light was lit for me and the lot cast; for "Immersion in the Word" [*Vandbadet i Ordet*] – that is, the Word at Baptism – is the Christian well of life; this Luther had straightway taught me; and that he who himself had instituted Baptism as the bath of rebirth and renewal in the Holy Spirit had himself also determined in what faith baptism should take place if by "Faith and Baptism" one would be sure of one's salvation, this, I saw at once,[4] is so manifestly undeniable that whoever will not allow the word of faith at baptism to have validity as a word given us from out of the Lord's own mouth must either deny the Lord as being the instituter of baptism or deny baptism as being the well of life, and thereby place himself outside the Christian congregation.

From this moment on it had to be my sole pastoral care to get all those who had a heart to believe upon Jesus Christ to make fast their Christian faith to the word of the Lord's mouth as being, by his own institutions, the Word of Life; and above all to the word of faith at baptism, as being the conjoined testimony of the Lord and the congregation.

With this, the rationalists' Scriptural criticism and Scriptural interpretation in my eyes necessarily lost their sting and all their danger to the congregation; and now to start up a pen-feud or appeal to the judgment of a secular High Court would indeed be a great irrationality which must sooner serve to confuse than to clarify the Church-cause and the Church-struggle. What nevertheless [GEEG p. 106] moved me to this irrational piece of daring was right enough, as I expressly declared, first and last Clausen's position as a preeminent teacher of priests in our compulsory State-Church with the parochial tie [*Sognebaand*]; but nevertheless I really hoped by precisely such a controversial piece of writing to force upon the reading world that attention to the Creed at baptism which I quite rightly foresaw would be very difficult to achieve.

It is well enough known how bitterly I was disappointed in my expectations, when *Kirkens Gjenmæle* was popularly perceived only as a spiteful and vengeful attack upon the son for the fault of the father and brought only a vexatious libel-process as a consequence, whereby my voice as priest was stifled, my pen was shackled and the Church-movement was in no way advanced but on the contrary was held back.[5] However, the reason why I resigned my office, notwithstanding that Bishop [Friederich] Münter insistently urged me to keep it, was simply and solely because the position of the priest within the State Church seemed to me altogether insufferable when the authorities sided with the manifest enemies of the State Church, and when I, as a born hater of litigious processes, had to be persecuted with the most vexatious of all processes, where one's civil honour was at stake; and so it determined the issue that Frederik the Sixth, when I personally set the matter before him, answered me quite soberly: "I can do nothing about it; I have stood by you as long as I could." On the other hand, the fact that I resigned office a week before the Ansgar celebra-tion[6] – which I had actually conceived and had inaugurated and looked forward to the whole winter – was the trick *Stiftsprovst* [H. G.] Clausen played upon me over *Den signede Dag, som vi nu ser* [The blessed day which we now see], notwithstanding that the choice of hymns for the anniversary festival had formally been made a free matter.

Reflections upon the church

1. Grundtvig's objection was to the gross debasement of the sacramental occasion of the celebration of the Lord's Supper when the priest was obliged to give the sacrament to communicants who attended not of their own volition but by constraint, and who recited the general confession and received the absolution and were received at the altar whether they were genuinely believing Christians or not and whether they led a godfearing or a plainly ungodly life. He observed (*Den christelige Børnelærdom* [Christian instruction for children]; 1855-61, 1868, 1883; ch. 16) that many layfolk felt compelled to leave the *Folkekirke* because they were offended by such indiscriminate absolution and admission to the Lord's Table.

2. *Theologisk Maanedsskrift*, from 1825.

3. The "blest moment" of Grundtvig's realisation of "that peerless testimony [*det mageløse Vidnesbyrd*]" – of the Apostles' Creed spoken in the sacrament of Baptism – appears to have fallen within the week preceding Grundtvig's statement of the idea in his sermon in Vor Frelsers Kirke on the Ninth Sunday after Trinity (31 July), 1825. In August he was able to express the insight clearly in a letter to B. S. Ingemann (*GEEG*).

4. In this retrospective account, Grundtvig appears to have pushed back in time the moment of achieving his conviction that the Apostles' Creed was given to them by Christ himself: a year later, in 1827, he was still attributing the formulation of the creed to the Apostles themselves (*GEEG*).

5. In summary, then, Grundtvig's dual aim with *Kirkens Gjenmæle* was, he says in this retrospect, first to object to destructive rationalism being taught at the highest level to future clergy whose congregations statutorily had no choice but to listen to them preaching it onwards; but also to create debate around his new understanding of the oral profession of the Creed within the sacrament of Baptism as the cornerstone of the historical apostolic Church. In the event, he says, it suited his opponents to evade constructive debate on both issues by sneering at the publication as an act of spite against H. N. Clausen's father and Grundtvig's old adversary, H. G. Clausen.

6. Whitsunday, 1826; the thousandth anniversary of the introduction of Christianity into Dk by Ansgar; see Index entries **Ansgar celebration** and **Den signede Dag**, *som vi nu seer*.

59 (g): Kirke-Speil eller Udsigt over den christne Menigheds Levnetsløb
(1871); GEEG Stk. 54, pp. 106-109; US X, pp. 355-57.

"A Christian free congregation in Frederiks Kirke in Christianshavn" – "What a triumph it after all was for the vexatious priest."

There passed, as is well known, thirteen years [1826-39] from when I resigned my office as priest within the State Church until I took it up again as priest in Vartov; and in that interval the course of my life would really have had nothing to do with the history of the Church if, in seven of these intervening years, outside the State Church so to speak, I had not striven to gather a Christian free congregation [*Frimenighed*] in Frederiks Kirke in Christianshavn; but this was both so novel and had such diverse consequences that Danish Christians at least will afford it some attention and wish to know the true facts of the situation. [GEEG p. 107]

To establish a Free Church [*Frikirke*] which in its doctrine could well adhere to the Augsburg Confession but yet would keep doctrinal statements sharply distinguished from the common faith and would make free use of Scripture's "things old and new" and make the church service far more alive, as regards the Lord's own institutions, sermon, prayer and hymn-singing alike, than it had been for many centuries – this was now my desire; but since permission for this had been utterly refused[1] I had no mind whatsoever to bid defiance but to await an opportunity which it always seemed to me must come in God's good time; and when on one occasion I again got to speak to the King [Frederik VI] and he very sympathetically asked what I was now doing it occurred to me to reply: "Nothing, your Majesty! and I do not even know what I might be doing, unless your Majesty would send me to Engelland to examine the Anglo-Saxon manuscripts which can be of importance to Denmark too." Against all presumption, the King took me at my word and only expressed regret that the public travel subsidies for the current year were all allocated so I would have to wait until next year, to which I replied that there was no haste at all, since I at my age was not much bent upon travels abroad; but still the consequence was my three journeys to England [1829-31], during which I seemed to have utterly forgotten the desperate issue of the Church but was in fact being prepared precisely to get properly to grips with it. In England, in fact, I first learned in respect of freedom as of all things human to lay the whole weight upon reality, with deep contempt for the empty exterior and for pen-pushing and the bookworm's existence [*Bogormsvæsenet*] in every regard; for though I in no way found Englishmen free from all this, yet among them I found life and death by the side of each other: life, wherever men strove *freely* to make use of their vital forces, and death, wherever the living were tormented in honour of the dead.

My followers here at home had meanwhile found it intolerable to forego all assembly for collective edification and so had begun to hold what were called "devotional assemblies" [*gudelige Forsamlinger*] under the leadership of [J. C.] Lindberg and the catechist at Frederiks Kirke, [Lorenz] Siemonsen, who was Danish-born in Flensborg and seemed amongst us to thrive upon the mother-tongue [*Modersmaalet*], although time showed that this had no substance.[2] In this, certainly, I took no part since I do not look favourably upon such assemblies which almost inevitably lead to a self-constructed congregational life with a self-constructed sanctimoniousness that has nothing to do with Christ; but so much the less could I [**GEEG p. 108**] show indifference towards them, and was bound to find them indispensable if the gospel did not come to be properly proclaimed again; and I therefore went to [P. C.] Stemann who was then President of the Royal Danish Chancellery to see whether I could not get a church in which to preach to a free audience. I found him, however, as could have been expected, as stubborn as a mule and so prejudiced against all freedom that he merely laughed at all my panegyrics upon this with regard to things spiritual, and let me know that if it mattered so much to me to preach then I should have hung on well to the church when I had it: now there was nothing to be done about it. Even when I directed His Excellency's notice to the devotional assemblies which I knew that he hated, and remarked with emphasis that I could no longer, as hitherto, advise against them when a pulpit was denied me, it seemed to affect him not at all, for he remarked contemptuously that no one had asked me to advise against "devotional assemblies" which, as long as they kept themselves strictly within the law, were a matter of complete indifference to him. So I took my leave with the assurance that hereafter I should certainly take good care not to advise against what I now heard was, in the eyes of the Chancellery, entirely innocuous; and the next Sunday I turned up at the assembly myself; but when I got the impression that they were at risk of straying into the wrong tracks I decided myself to step to the fore.[3] As soon as it was rumoured, however, that I had not only been at the assembly but had hired a loft which was fitted out as an assembly-room, then the indifference vanished and [C. J. C.] Bræstrup, the chief of police, had a busy time interviewing Lindberg, Siemonsen and myself.

The discussions in the Office of Police make no claim upon immortality and I shall not make the effort of perpetuating those I had to hold with Bræstrup, who was quite unable to enter into my view of the matter: that what I would use my rooms for was nobody's business until it was seen that something unlawful was going on, and that where I would proclaim the word of God was not the business of the police since I was ordained with royal leave to proclaim it freely both in the light of day and behind the scenes ("privily and openly");[4] so I will only add that upon his recommendation I went to the bishop in order to come if possible to an understanding with him. The bishop, P. E. Müller, who where antiquarianism was concerned was otherwise one of my few admirers and in the ordinary run of things a very mild man, I now found very agitated; but after an hourlong conversation, during which I industriously [GEEG p. 109] strove both to convince his mind and to touch his heart, he at least promised to do his best to secure me permission for an assembly in the loft, as long as I would neither distribute communion nor in the (incidentally, free) hymn-singing use Lindberg's *Sions Harpe*. Meanwhile, the bishop recommended the Government instead to make the vacant Frederiks Kirke available to me for the service of evensong, and because they could not get the royal licence properly undersigned before the Friday evening, Bræstrup held up the *Adresse-Avisen* until my name could appear among the preachers, without thinking what a triumph it after all was for the vexatious priest [*den ærgerlige Præst*].

1. Grundtvig must be alluding to the rejection of efforts made before 1829 (the year of his first visit to England). It was after his return from his third summer in England that on 24 November 1832 Lindberg and others submitted the formal application to Chancellery for permission to establish a congregation at the near-redundant Frederiks Kirke in Christianshavn with Grundtvig and Lorenz Siemonsen as its ministers, independent of the restraints of *Sognebaandet* [the parochial tie], that is, a free church – which was rejected on 28 January 1832. See also Index entry **Rolighed**.

2. Grundtvig presumably alludes to the fact that much later, in the Three Years War over Slesvig, when Danish troops entered Husby where Siemonsen was then parish priest, he fled to the side of the pro-German Holsteners (rebels from the Danish viewpoint) and was consequently dismissed from his incumbency.

3. Grundtvig, seeing the bid to take over Frederiks Kirke blocked by intransigent authorities, decided to speak for the first time at one of Lindberg's devotional gatherings on Sunday 12 February 1832.

4. Grundtvig here invokes the rite of Ordination.

59 (h): Kirke-Speil eller Udsigt over den christne Menigheds Levnetsløb
(1871); GEEG Stk. 54, pp. 109-112; US X, pp. 357-61.

Twenty-five years on, Grundtvig looks back to his appointment to Vartov ("It was in a difficult moment I once again received a post within the State-Church") and takes satisfaction in "the impact which the Vartov assembly with its congregational singing under its nickname '*Grundtvigianism*' has made not only in the capital but in the whole of Denmark."

The seven years [1832-39], in the course of which I, so to speak, proclaimed the gospel every Sunday as freely as any teacher in apostolic times and wrote, as well as my *Haandbog i Verdenshistorien*, my little book on the Danish State-Church and compiled the *Sang-Værk* for the Danish Church,[1] were certainly years of tribulation to the extent that not only did I find it difficult to exist with wife and children in the capital but I myself as well as my faithful followers found it hard to be deprived of the proper use of the sacraments and even by stealth – I know not whose – to be committed to the vacuous, so-called Evangelical Hymnal; but yet they were far from being years of unfruitfulness, for my position was sufficiently apostolic to affirm that I spoke only because I believed; my free preaching and [J. C.] Lindberg's *Nordiske Kirketidende* [Nordic Church News], which I was delighted to support, manifestly paved the way for the new perception of the basis for a living Church and of churchly freedom;[2] and even the tedious squabblings with *Stiftsprovst* [H. G.] Clausen over his home-made Baptism confirmed both that the dissolution of parochial ties [*Sognebaandets Løsning*] was a necessity and that it would contribute immeasurably to peace within the State-Church which was the goal of all the secular authority's wishes for the Church.

Only one thing at length made this position unbearable, and this was enforced confirmation; and when my own sons reached the age of confirmation it lay so heavy upon my heart that I realised this tie must be dissolved or burst asunder; for although I personally could have evaded the struggle by having my sons confirmed by a friendly priest in the country, yet I found it almost unbearable to be priest and not to dare to confirm one's own children, and uncharitable, now that [J. P.] Mynster had become bishop, to let my Christian friends in the capital remain in that anguish which they could not avoid nearly as easily as I. [GEEG p. 110] I therefore petitioned the King for permission to confirm my own children and those of good friends, and found the King not unfavourably disposed towards this; but since I knew well enough that it would depend mainly on Bishop Mynster's pronouncement and that I could not expect any favours from him, I asked our present Dowager Queen [Caroline Amalie] to put in a good word for me with the bishop and to prepare the ground. This however did not help, for when on the last day of 1838 I presented myself to the bishop in order to set before him as clearly and earnestly as possible this matter dear to my heart I found him not only so unbending but so bitter and hostile that after an hourlong conversation on the sofa I had to go away with a contemptuous dismissal and – I do not deny it – in a mood of indignation to which I gave free vent.[3]

When, however, on that beautiful winter's day, in order to regain my equilibrium, I walked round the city fortifications and through *Kongens Have* [The King's Garden] where the small birds were chirrupping so friendly, then it came into my mind what the Psalmist sings of that God who begrudges neither sparrow nor swallow a nest at his altar to hatch their young;[4] and then I walked calmly home and put my thoughts into rhyme as it can presumably still be seen in one of the first *Kirketidender* for 1839.[5] In the same year, then, as is well known, I actually became priest at Vartov, and this in such timely wise that I could properly prepare and confirm my two eldest sons at Michaelmas.

Now how that came to pass Danish Christians at least will want to know; and since Bishop Mynster has given a misleading account of it which has found acceptance I must assiduously correct it without wishing to deny that Mynster may very well have thought that his information was correct, so that it actually was he who had to persuade our old King against his will to make me priest at Vartov, because the bishop assured him that I could do more harm outside the State-Church than within it.[6] Frederik the Sixth in fact secretly let me know, through *kammerjunker* [H. C.] Reedtz and my English friend, Legation-Secretary [Peter] Browne, that if I wished to apply for Vartov I should get it. For a long time now I had had my eye on Vartov as the sole corner in the State-Church where I as an enlightened Christian priest could endure the position as long as it might be, because there I could not easily find myself constrained to something which conflicted with my conscience, and yet had the opportunity to perform the priestly [**GEEG p. 111**] office in its fullest extent and above all to confirm the children of all those Christian parents who desired it; but I would not apply for it merely upon secret intelligences, which I was old enough to know are seldom entirely reliable. I therefore went to the King myself, and in the antechamber I met my predecessor [Niels Gissing Wolff] in both Præstø and Vartov who was there to thank the King for a good promotion and told me, when he came out, that to his great astonishment the King had asked him whether he believed that Grundtvig, were he to become priest in Vartov, would disturb the peace of the Church. So when I got to speak to the King I immediately said to him that I had it in mind to apply for the Vartov incumbency, but only if His Majesty would give me hope of getting it. "I never give any hope" was the King's short answer; but when I then responded: "Well then I shall certainly not apply for it, because I am too old now to be made a fool of in the Chancellery" the King answered very kindly: "Well then, you can give your application to me" and to this I declared myself willing. Then shortly afterwards I handed in my application in the antechamber and although our present Dowager Queen humoured me by enquiring about the case with the King she brought me only an evasive answer, so in the end, when I was informed by the Chancellery that my application had not reached there, I really believed that by some peculiar misfortune it had been lost; but when I got someone to enquire in the Cabinet I received the answer that it was in good care and the reason was that the King had considerately kept the application to himself until he could see from the disposition of the Chancellery that there was nothing in the way of my nomination.

It was however in a difficult moment I once again received a post within the State-Church; for, after a petition from Copenhagen's clergy with *Stiftsprovst* Clausen at the forefront, the Service Book issue [*Alterbogs-Sagen*] was once again started up, and Bishop Mynster, in privy association with the *Stiftsprovst*'s son-in-law [P. C. Stenersen Gad],[7] a downright rationalist, had produced a proposal for a new Service Book [*Alterbog*] which was to be communicated only to those whom the Bishop found worthy of it and then judged by a commission of which the Bishop himself was president. It could not but strike me as very suspicious, and therefore when [P. C.] Stemann admonished me to keep the peace as best I could, I indeed assured him of my readiness to do this, but warned him that the new Service Book would very likely provoke a quarrel which would make peace impossible. His Excellency however confided in me that he would prefer to see things remain as they were and that when I received the book I could [**GEEG p. 112**] write against it as harshly as I wished; and when I remarked that when it came to Bishop Mynster forming a friendship circle *I* was pretty sure to be excluded, the old man remarked that he dared bet me that the Bishop would send the book even to me. And naturally so it turned out, and I then saw with astonishment that Bishop Mynster, in line with Professor [H. C.] Clausen's proposal in the book on Catholicism and Protestantism,[8] wanted to have the Baptismal Covenant [*Daabspagten*] completely removed from infant baptism and yet still have infant baptism made a compulsory matter, so that hereafter in the Danish State-Church the Baptismal Covenant should be set up only with those Jews who might possibly want to enter into it. The whole thing was so casually and carelessly handled there in the spirit of thraldom [*Trældoms Aand*],[9] that my *Frisprog* against it could not but be thoroughly radical. However, since Frederik the Sixth's death occurred just then, the Service Book issue forthwith died, fortunately, because a contemptuous dismissal was the sole answer Mynster gave my *Frisprog*, but he had indeed got quite a lot passed through under the old King which would at least have made the priest's position in the State-Church more burdensome and the church service stiffer and deader than it already was.

If God wills that I shall live until Whitsun next year, then I shall have completed twenty-five years in Vartov's church; and were I to calculate it according to the number of confirmands then its efficacy in a living Christian respect must appear insignificant in the extreme; but according to the impact which the Vartov assembly [*Vartov-Forsamlingen*] with its congregational singing under its nickname 'Grundtvigianism' has made upon the world, not only in the capital but in the whole of Denmark it can hardly fail to be acknowledged that in this latter generation there has indeed established itself the kernel of a Danish Christian free congregation [*Frimenighed*] which, since it adheres exclusively to the Apostolic Creed and the Lord's own institutions, can surely least among all the now so-called Christian Church-societies [*kristne Kirke-Samfund*] justifiably be called a sect (an off-cut) and given a nickname after one of the Lord's and its own servants; but which yet, right enough, has this churchly singularity – that of demanding consensus only over what has been common to all who have believed and been baptised, and of seeking only a new life of the spirit within The Word given to us from the Lord's own mouth, through his own institutions.

1. *Haandbog i Verdenshistorien* [Manual of Universal History], published 1833-43]; *Den danske Stats-Kirke upartisk betragtet* [The Danish State-Church impartially viewed], 1834; and *Sang-Værk til den danske Kirke* [Song-work, or Carillon, for the Danish Church], vol. 1, 1837.

2. Lindberg also used his periodical *Maanedskrift for Christendom og Historie* [Monthly journal of Christianity and history], published between 1830-32, to draw attention to and challenge alterations to ritual introduced by individual rationalist clergy, including modifications made by the *Stiftsprovst* [Archdeacon or Dean] H. G. Clausen himself. See Index entries **Daabspagten** and **Alterbogs-Sagen**.

3. According to Mina Grundtvig, wife of Gr's eldest son Johan, Mynster snapped scornfully at Gr: Do you suppose that we can grant every jumped-up curate [*forfløjen Kapellan*] permission to confirm? Gr retorted: Well, since I appear to the Right Reverend Sir to be a jumped-up curate, then I have nothing more to say.

4. Psalm 84:3.

5. The poem in which Gr expressed both his pain and his consolation was printed in J. C. Lindberg's periodical *Nordiske Kirketidende* 1839, 1 (6 January).

6. Bishop Mynster published his account of the process of Grundtvig's appointment by Frederik VI in his *Meddelelser om mit Levnet* [Information concerning my life; 1854] where he represents the King as remaining unimpressed by Grundtvig's claims to a pastoral incumbency, "very learned man" though he was. As Gr here correctly recalls, Mynster claims to have overcome the King's serious doubts by arguing that Gr would be more of a troublemaker out of office than in.

7. In his *Meddelelser om mit Levnet* Mynster says he had no real collaborators in his work.

8. Gr refers to H. N. Clausen's *Catholicismens og Protestantismens Kirkeforfatning, Lære og Ritus* [Constitution, doctrine and rites of Catholicism and Protestantism; 1825] – the study which provoked him to respond with *Kirkens Gienmæle* and led to his prosecution and punishment by censorship; now Gr is in effect asserting that he was right to warn against insidious rationalism at that time.

9. *Trældoms Aand* ("the spirit of bondage" – King James Bible) is contrasted in Romans 8:15-17 to "the spirit of adoption" – "[15] The Spirit you received does not make you slaves, so that you live in fear again; rather, the Spirit you received brought about your adoption to sonship. And by him we cry, '*Abba*, Father.' [16] The Spirit himself testifies with our spirit that we are God's children. [17] Now if we are children, then we are heirs – heirs of God and co-heirs with Christ" (New International Version). The allusion indicates how dangerous Grundtvig believed Mynster's proposed interference with the sacrament of baptism to be – dangerous not only to the Danish Church but also to its author – in its implicit disregard of 'adoption to sonship.' I owe the reference to Professor Jakob Balling.

Part two – Memoirs of Grundtvig

Student years 1800-1803

60. Henrik Steffens (translated from the German Was ich erlebte I-X, 1840-44, *by Frederik Schaldemose, 1840-45),* Hvad Jeg Oplevede; nedskrevet efter Hukommelse *[What I have experienced, written down from memory], IX (1845), pp. 247-48; GEEG Stk. 1, p. 115.*

In 1792 the nine-year-old Grundtvig was sent to Jylland to begin his formal education first in private tuition then in Aarhus Cathedral School until September 1800 when he was admitted to read Theology in Copenhagen University, whence he gained a first-class degree in October 1803. Notable among his academic experiences were philosophy lectures delivered in Copenhagen during the winter of 1802 by Henrik Steffens, who happened to be Grundtvig's cousin, though Steffens, as he observes here, barely knew Grundtvig. Later, a long-enduring friendship would develop between the two. The opening reference is to Steffens's mother's sisters.

[GEEG p. 115] The eldest of them was wife of [Johan Ottesen] Grundtvig the priest; my mother [Susanne Bang] was the youngest of them all. Late in her life, the priest's wife [Kathrine Marie Bang] had given birth to a boy who, when I earlier came back from Germany to Copenhagen, had just left school to go on to the University. My wife and I met him at the home of the old Professor [F. L.] Bang with whom we often dined. He sat there, shy and timid, and I had no idea of the stir which he would later cause. My public philosophy lectures, which at the time met with such lively participation in Copenhagen, made – as the young man himself admitted – a great impression upon him. I did not know he was attending my lectures; to me he remained a stranger; during this time I did not get to know him at all.

61. Peter Frederik Adolph Hammerich: 'Henrik Steffens i Forhold til den nordiske Udvikling' [H. S. in relation to Nordic development] in For Literatur og Kritik, *III (1845), p. 171; GEEG Stk. 2, p. 115.*

Frederik Hammerich (1809-77), Professor of Church History in Copenhagen University from 1859, a lifelong and steadfast if sometimes wary and not uncritical friend of Grundtvig, is an important source of Grundtvig anecdotes, many of which he had from Grundtvig himself: here a comment on Grundtvig's earliest encounters with Henrik Steffens.

[Grundtvig] was at that time a young student who often dined together with Steffens[1] at the table of their common maternal uncle, the elderly [F. L.] Bang. He was very reserved and spoke but little. "Are you also attending my lectures?" Steffens once asked him. When Grundtvig answered the question affirmatively, Steffens exclaimed: "But then, do you understand them?" "Oh yes. Somewhat." replied Grundtvig drily.

1   Henrik Steffens (1773-1845), in guest-lectures on philosophy, literature and aesthetics, given (1802) in Ehlers' Kollegium Copenhagen, in effect delivered a manifesto for Romanticism to a young generation. That Grundtvig understood something of the lectures, at least to his own satisfaction, is evident from a diary discussion he holds with himself in 1805, on the nature of poetry, in which he endorses Steffens' Romantic concepts. The cousins were to become firm friends and exchanged correspondence over many years.

Langeland 1805-1808

62. Carl Steensen Leth: extracts from a letter dated 7 January 1873, communicated by T. Graae in Dagens Krønike II (1890), pp. 535-7; GEEG Stk. 3, pp. 116-117.

After graduating in Theology Grundtvig took employment from March 1805 to April 1808 as residential tutor to the Steensen-Leth family at the manor-house of Egeløkke on the southern Danish island of Langeland where he developed and sustained a love for Constance Steensen Leth, the young mother of his seven-year-old pupil Carl (see items 28-34). Commentators have variously analysed the affair in terms of real if immature sexual passion, a semi-fiction tellingly Romantic in circumstances and expression, and a symptom of that psychological instability which periodically afflicted Grundtvig throughout his life. After ending the hopeless situation by quitting his post, Grundtvig immersed himself more deeply in the study of Romantic philosophers and of Norse mythology, but for some years he nurtured the romantic memory of an idealised Constance. The record-straightening thrust of Carl's memoir, written after Grundtvig's death, is to be understood in the light of all this.

⌐

[GEEG p. 116] When Grundtvig says that German was spoken at Egeløkke, it would only have been when the gentlefolk from the castle were there, for these were all German.[1] And when the many German gentlemen who at that time stayed at the castle came riding now and again of a morning to Egeløkke, then German would be spoken, as is understandable: but, as sure as God is in heaven, never at any time in daily use was there uttered one German word. Really, I should like to know with whom German should have been spoken.

Grundtvig was a peculiar character in his youth, forbidding, domineering and demanding, hard-hearted, etc. so I believe that in his earliest youth he had no friends. [J. L.] Heiberg published a little pamphlet against Grundtvig where he gives him a dressing down: it is worth reading.[2]

As regards country priests, well we all know that as speakers they were everywhere much the same; but for that matter we still have priests now who are no better than priests were then – and this in our own capital city [...]

⌐

When he talks about empty churches, well this claim is also untrue since countryfolk actually distinguished themselves by a true religious piety. If the churches in town are full, well that is just as much curiosity, fashion, etc.

Grundtvig could hardly have written his memoirs in his younger days, because then he must surely have known how falsely he has gone about it. All that he has put into print like this will now turn into the truth in the fullness of time [...]

An elderly bigoted lady visited me at Christmas. She had read Grundtvig's biography which she offered to me to read but which however I did not accept. She held forth about the frightful ungodliness on Langeland, and much else about the priests. For sure, this is hardly the first time that [Frederik] Barfod without further ado writes about things he loosely takes from out of other books[3] [...] [GEEG p. 117]

Grundtvig was my tutor whom I could never as such have reason to criticise. He instructed me indefatigably, but he was also an irascible man and certainly treated me strictly – which all the same I will not complain over, for it could have been deserved.

1. In *Kirke-Speil* (1871), 364 ff.

2. Johan Ludvig Heiberg (1791-1860) satirised Grundtvig, who had by then published several books intended for the education of children, in his *Ny A-B-C-Bog i en Times Underviisning til Ære, Nytte og Fornøielse for den unge Grundtvig* [A new ABC-book for an hour's instruction, to the honour, use and pleasure of the young Grundtvig; 1817]. It was conceived as a blow in a minor feud which was then being waged within Danish literary circles.

3. (Povl) Frederik Barfod (1811-96), in *Grundtvigs Levned* [Life of Grundtvig; 1872] based his account of Grundtvig's time at Egeløkke wholly on Grundtvig's own account in *Kirke-Speil*.

63. *Povl Frederik Barfod:* Grundtvigs Levned. Nicolaj Frederik Severin Grundtvig, et løst Udkast *[The life of Grundtvig. N. F. S. G., a rough draft] (1872), p. 12; GEEG Stk. 4, p. 117.*

Frederik Barfod worked closely with Grundtvig, despite occasionally severe misunderstandings, over many years, and he and his family were family friends of the Grundtvigs. His "draft" of a Life of Grundtvig is the work scorned by Steensen Leth in the passage above but nevertheless Barfod was in a position to gather much material at first hand, including illustrations of Grundtvig's often caustic wit. In the following anecdote, the person inviting Grundtvig to compare Langeland with Biblical Canaan presumably has in mind the tradition also expressed in the English hymn "Fair waved the golden corn in Canaan's pleasant land." Typically, Grundtvig's repartee invokes the fuller Biblical account. Abram and his seed are promised possession of the land of Canaan for ever and Abram built an altar there to the Lord. But "the Canaanite was then in the land" (Genesis 12:6-7); and later the Lord enjoins Moses: "after the doings of the land of Canaan, whither I bring you, shall ye not do: neither shall ye walk in their ordinances" (Leviticus 18:3). The land was lovely but its inhabitants profligate and ungodly.

There is an anecdote from Langeland which especially over there is so well-known that we really ought to include it. At a party, Grundtvig was asked what he thought of the island: "Is it not indeed a land of Canaan?" "Yes" he answered "and the Canaanites have not been driven out: they are still here."

Valkendorfs kollegium 1808-1811

64. Povl Frederik Barfod: Grundtvigs Levned. Nicolaj Frederik
Severin Grundtvig, et løst Udkast [The life of Grundtvig. N. F.
S. G., a rough draft] (1872), p. 12; GEEG Stk. 5, p. 117.

In May 1808, after leaving Egeløkke, Grundtvig returned to Copenhagen to look for a new teaching post. After the fire-bombardment of Copenhagen by the English in 1807, as an incident in the Napoleonic wars, there was a severe shortage of habitable accommodation in the city, but Grundtvig successfully applied for a place in Valkendorfs Kollegium, a residence in the university quarter of Copenhagen where over three years he was to meet many who would become prominent in Danish and Norwegian cultural life. Barfod's anecdote deftly affirms both the earnestness and the abrasive wit of the young Grundtvig.

⌐

At Valkendorfs Kollegium there was a drinking-party in his shared quarters, through the sitting-room of which he had to pass when, late in the evening, he came home. In order to tease him, one of the guests stood up as he entered and in strong language proposed a toast "To Reason – the only light upon our path." When he had finished, someone else asked Grundtvig what he thought of the toast, and got the answer: "It is handsome of you, gentlemen, to remember absent friends."

65. Frederik Christian Sibbern: 'Notits af F. C. Sibbern om hans
Rejse med Grundtvig til Udby Præstegaard i December 1810' [Note
by F. C. S. concerning his journey with Gr to Udby Parsonage in
December 1810], communicated by G. Sibbern, Personalhistorisk
Tidsskrift 4, *Rk. III (1900), pp. 211-12; GEEG Stk. 6, pp. 117-118.*

In November 1808 Grundtvig secured a teaching position at the Schouboe Institute in Copenhagen. At Valkendorfs Kollegium he continued to study and write for publication in a wide variety of genres and fields. Particularly notable is his *Nordens Mythologi* [Mythology of the North] (1808), attempting by metaphorical treatment to elicit a religious and moral world-view from the myths concerning Asgard preserved in Icelandic, which he called 'asa-læren,' the teachings of and about the Æsir. Grundtvig later spoke of the period as the time of his '*asa-rus*' – intoxication with '*asalæren*'. His publications also led to stressful controversy and reprimand: six Copenhagen priests lodged official complaints against his published probational sermon (May 1810) in which he blamed the clergy for neglecting the Christian message in their clever, showy sermons. Sibbern, subsequently a Professor of Philosophy in Copenhagen University and examiner of the doctoral thesis of Søren Kierkegaard, became one of Grundtvig's most valuable and valued friends during this period, standing by him at the time of his mental breakdown and spiritual crisis, of which this "Note" is an important document. Grundtvig's crisis in 1810 shared various characteristics – labelled by modern commentators as bipolar disorder (manic-depressive syndrome) – with those which occurred in his later life (May 1844 and April 1867), including vivid and overwhelming hallucinations expressed in a religious idiom and no doubt reflecting, albeit with dramatic exaggeration, his daily conceptualisation of a world under God's providence and his own doubts, calling, mission and struggle within it. Christian Sigfred Ley (1806-74) recorded in his diary (1829; published in *Danskeren* V, 1891, 236; noted in *GEEG*) an account of Grundtvig's illness as it was witnessed by a contemporary in Valkendorfs Kollegium, the later judge and politician Niels Møller Spandet (1788-1858): "In the autumn of 1810 Grundtvig's mental illness began. He was attending holy communion and all at once began to weep aloud. When with the other communicants he came up into the chancel and the front row knelt down at the altar, he was behind, but yet he threw himself on his knees and wept aloud. After that occasion, people said he had gone mad. He would often sit and stare at one spot, would often break off a conversation and sob and would not uncommonly fall to weeping etc. Once he also walked down the middle of the street with a long pipe which he was holding by the mouthpiece in one hand and a bottle in the other."

I lived a great deal together with Grundtvig at Walchendorphs Kollegium where he got a place after the bombardment of Copenhagen, when he came from Langeland where he had been resident tutor with a Fru {Constance] Leth. He was tutor in History in Schouboe's Institute, and wrote his first *Nordens Mythologie* [Northern Mythology] which was very poetic, and a great deal of which I liked. Remarkably enough, the underlying idea is in a Christian spirit: for Odin here arrives at his divine might through a kind of fall from grace or apostasy. I used to call on Grundtvig a lot of an evening: he often sat up far into the night. It was said of Grundtvig at that time that his faith was the Asa-faith [*Asatroen*], which [GEEG p. 118] naturally was not so.

But now we – [S. B.] Hersleb and I together with the rest – experienced a major change which occurred in Grundtvig. This was in December 1810. He remained in bed in the morning and lay in such a state that we sent for his uncle, the old *Etatsraad* [F. L.] Bang, father of the present Oluf Bang (Balfungo), but he declared that this was no physical sickness he was suffering from, but that he lay in an inward struggle for his soul's salvation. So I took it upon myself to drive with him to his old father who was priest in Udbye on the road to Vordingborg. Unfortunately I cannot recall the least detail of what then must have been spoken between us on the journey. At that time, the country road between Køge and Vordingborg meandered a great deal and Udbye lay a long way from it into the country. We therefore decided, when in the evening we arrived at Vindbyeholt, to stay there in the inn until dawn the next day. We went to bed, but Grundtvig sat and worked at his farewell poem[1] to the pupils of Schouboe's School, while I fell asleep.

But far into the night I awoke; Grundtvig was down on his knees in a corner of the room and was praying with such a loud voice that it must surely attract attention in the house. I tried to calm him down but it went on for a long time. Eventually, when it had grown light, we got into a carriage and drove to Udbye. On the way, Grundtvig told me that he had felt the Devil as a serpent twisting itself about his body. At Udbye I was somewhat surprised that the father, when I gave him an account of the son's condition, quickly composed himself. My son is suffering from *anfægtelser* [doubts], he said; and thereby knew what he was facing.

I very much regret that I remember almost nothing and have not for many years recalled to mind what was said. December 21st was one of the days I was away from town with Grundtvig. I know this, because that year I was not at A. S. Ørsted's on his birthday, although otherwise I was one of those who would gather at his home on that day.

1. Conflicting views have been held as to when Gr formally resigned his post in Schouboes Institut, whether before or after his illness reached its crisis point. Sibbern here implies a date at the beginning of December 1810 (unless Gr was writing his farewell poem in early anticipation of a not yet submitted resignation); Svend Grundtvig suggests a date after the crisis, in Spring 1811, which could have been as late as May (Frederik Nielsen), by which time Gr was well on the way to recovery. The text is in *PS* I, 319-22.

66. *Bernth Christoph Wilkens Lind Hjort:* Nicolaj Gottlieb Blædel. Et Livsbillede *[N. G. B. A life portrait] (1881), pp. 26-27; GEEG Stk. 7, pp. 118-119.*

W. Hjort (1830-1911), who matriculated 1848 from the Metropolitanskole, Copenhagen, and graduated from Copenhagen University 1854 as *cand. theol.*, was dismissed from his incumbency as priest in Slesvig following Prussian occupation of the duchy in 1864, and eventually settled (1870) as parish priest and subsequently *provst* [rural dean] in Nyborg on Fynen. He is remembered particularly for his initiative in the founding of Soldiers' Institutes [*Soldaterhjemme*] across the land but he also published occasional contributions to liturgical and cultural-political issues and biographies including that of Nicolaj Gottlieb Blædel (1881) from which this passage is drawn. Blædel (1816-79) was son of Anna Elisabeth (born Dons) and married his first cousin, Henriette, daughter of Povel Dons. Priest at Garnisons Kirke in Copenhagen 1859-79, he published (1873) two polemical works critical of Grundtvigianism: *Grundtvigianismen og den danske Folkekirke* and *Grundtvigianismens Katekismus.* Hjort appears to have drawn upon oral or written tradition in the Blædel-Dons families, though as documentation it lacks secure substantiation.

On each occasion of his illness, it was Grundtvig's good fortune to have steady friends about him, and his bad luck (and sometimes their misfortune too) that some of these friends and family were predisposed – increasingly as over time he acquired a great following of devotees and a reputation for inspired and prophetic utterance – to nourish their own need for signs and revelation with an overheated religious fervour sometimes called in Danish 'sv*ærmeri.*'

⌒

Probably no one followed Grundtvig so closely during these years as [Povel Dons], but his [Grundtvig's] way of thinking soon became too powerful for him; it overwhelmed him; his nature was too sensitive and delicate, and since, without heeding his own limitations, he would unceasingly follow him up to the mountain-tops – it was shattered. Justly, Grundtvig writes about him: [**GEEG p. 119**]

Gjennemrystet, gjennemsuset,	Throughly shaken, throughly blasted,
gjennemluet, overspændt,	throughly fire-swept, overstrained,
svimled han som en beruset,	like a drunken man he fainted,
blussed som en selvantændt.	like one self-ignited blazed.[1]

The first blow, however, he received through an act of love towards Grundtvig. When in 1811 the latter suffered an attack of insanity, Dons did not budge from his side, but nursed him night and day – indeed, when the madness took the upper hand, would even struggle with him so that often they both sank exhausted. Grundtvig eventually recovered, but Dons had heard and seen far too much ever to forget it. The impression had been too strong for him, and one is not far wrong in dating his decline from this period [...] In the years 1811-1820 he in fact disintegrated more and more. In the beginning it was hardly noticeable and, perhaps to his own harm, he acted as proofreader of Grundtvig's books. But gradually he became more sickly and his relationship with Grundtvig became more tense. The latter was unyielding and Dons was weak. They had violent collisions when Grundtvig wished to point the high-flying, volatile [*sværmeriske*] Dons back into his proper limitations.

1. From Grundtvig's poem on the death of Povel Dons, April 1843; the text is in PS VI, 459-62.

67. *Fredrik Schmidt:* Provst Fredrik Schmidts Dagbøger. Udgivne i Uddrag ved N. Hancke (1868), *pp. 123-24; GEEG Stk. 8, pp. 119-120.*

In the days of royal absolutism before the granting of a democratic constitution, when both publication and public assembly were strictly controlled by essentially repressive laws, social gatherings in the homes of private individuals played an important role in the dissemination of new ideas and the formation of alliances between the like-minded. Later on in life, Grundtvig's own home became the customary gathering-place for his collaborators, disciples and visitors, but in the earlier years he was to be encountered, as here by the Norwegian-Danish cleric Frederik Schmidt (1771-1840), in such salons as that of the Norwegian Niels Treschow, Professor of Philosophy in Copenhagen University. The anecdote records Grundtvig's deep-seated antipathy to German-influenced Rationalism which was to contribute to his unfortunate collision with Professor H. N. Clausen in 1825.

It was on [Niels] Treschow's sofa that I first encountered Grundtvig, whom I now [1 April 1811] saw for the first time. He was involved in a deep Christian-philosophical conversation with Treschow during which, among other things, he put to him this question of conscience: whether a philosopher can believe in himself. The manner in which these two good men set forth their different opinions on mysteries – about which, though, one never reaches clarity – was very interesting and humane. Treschow sought to formulate them according to – and bring them into harmony with – the ideas of Reason, but Grundtvig stuck so rigidly to the system that in respect of Trinitarian doctrine he did not even tolerate the slightest deviation from the Athanasian formula. It is beyond doubting that Grundtvig's faith in Christ, as the one he, according to his [Grundtvig's] conviction, has declared himself to be, as a divine being and Redeemer [*Forsoner*] of the world (he would not allow himself to make do with the title Deliverer [*Forløser*]), is warm, sincere and unfeigned. In him this is the result of a vain speculation and exertion in order to reach his goal by some other way, and he feels himself fortunate in this faith. [GEEG p. 120]

In his dark eyes and the lively features of his pale face there is something intense, but at the same time something mild. Instead of what I had resolved, to leave at once, I was detained until ten o'clock and even then I had to cut the matter short.

I will just briefly note: that during this conversation Treschow repeated his observation – which I had already heard from him some years ago – about the connection between the Christian religion and that of the Essenes; and that Grundtvig, when I told him the main thesis in [J. A.] Eberhard's *Geist des Urchristenthums*, namely that "der griechische Sinn und das orientalische Gefühl" [Greek thought and oriental feeling] are fused within it, replied: "So once more, a Christianity without Christ"; and also that the thread in this conversation was so often broken and rejoined that I cannot give what I otherwise would have wished, some coherent summary of it. Treschow declared on this occasion that he subscribes to and endorses [Friedrich] Schelling's system of identity.

68. *Fredrik Schmidt:* Provst Fredrik Schmidts Dagbøger. Udgivne i Uddrag ved N. Hancke (1868), *pp. 125-26; GEEG Stk. 9, pp. 120-122.*

After his severe breakdown in 1810 Grundtvig had returned to Copenhagen possessed of new Christian convictions and undiminished intellectual zest. Turning now against the orthodox Romanticism to which Steffens had once pointed him, in part because its ideological trust in the capacity of the individual to redeem himself demeaned the role of Christ as sole redeemer, he cultivated an identification of the poet with historical-biblical revelation and prophecy, an identification he subsequently found wondrously confirmed in the figure of the Anglo-Saxon Cædmon and which he increasingly extended to himself. Alongside his highly active participation as poet and critic in the contemporary literary scene (including the area of religious lyric in the form of hymns, to which he was eventually to make an outstanding historic contribution) he was developing ideas on education which he would later consolidate into some of his most original and important contributions to Danish and European cultural history. Schmidt usefully records an encounter with this ferment of a mind in remarkable metamorphosis.

At two o'clock (8 April 1811) I went to [Niels] Treschow's. Since Grundtvig, who had also been invited, was somewhat delayed in coming, Hansen was sent express to fetch him. Hardly had he come in through the door before he and Treschow were again deep into philosophy and theology, although at the table this alternated with poetry. Grundtvig's physician Ole Mynster has advised him to refrain from all literary work which demands exertion but rather to occupy himself with such things as, without demanding much independent thought, still engage his mental powers, for example in translating, and he had now almost decided that he would like to translate [F. L. Z.] Werner's *Weihe der Kraft*, whereas Treschow and I sought to persuade him to set about *Die Söhne des Thales*. He makes much of [Friedrich] Schiller, especially his *Braut von Messina*,[1] in which Treschow was in agreement with him, but I was not. *Don Carlos* is, and for ever will be, in my eyes, his masterpiece. On [Adam] Øhlenschlæger, Grundtvig felt that he was now in a state of transition to a new system, since a great poet, according to Grundtvig's opinion, always worked worst when he was at such a turning-point, and he was therefore inclined to draw the conclusion from Øhlenschlæger's latest compositions that he was at such a turning-point or conversion. Grundtvig had heard only the first part of Øhlenschlæger's lectures,[2] where he laid the foundation-stone [GEEG p. 121] of his aesthetic system, which Grundtvig found was laid too loosely and Treschow not deeply enough. When the conversation subsequently turned to the latest theories of education and upbringing, Grundtvig told about someone in Copenhagen who had been brought up on [J.-J.] Rousseau's *Emil*, but unfortunately in such a way that he had become half mad. When occasion was taken from this to demolish Rousseau's *Emil*, someone else is supposed to have remarked that the aforementioned half-mad person had been brought up on *the Danish translation* of *Emil*.[3]

After the meal there was discussion of the shopkeeper mentality and bad public servants; and about the way in which integrity vanishes with religiosity; and finally about freedom and necessity; on which occasion Treschow and Grundtvig united themselves against me and freedom and wished to have the latter exchanged for an inward necessity, and Grundtvig likewise found that it was surely not *determined*, but *foreseen*, by God how this person or that *must needs* be a scoundrel and eternally damned – for he maintained that he, as a good and logical Christian, could not, by the same token, do away with eternal punishment.

When I went to the piano he sneaked off, perhaps because he cannot endure music. Various beautiful things by [F. L. Æ.] Kunzen and 'Natten' [The Night] by [Daniel] Steibelt were played and sung. On his return, Grundtvig nevertheless had to put up with the music again and I rejoiced him with 'Stusle Søndagsqvællen' [The lonesome Sunday evening]. The remainder of the evening was spent in theological discussions, principally between Treschow and Grundtvig, to which I now and again contributed my mite, especially when Grundtvig began to defend the Devil, over which we got rather seriously into dispute so that at table Grundtvig asked me to excuse it if in the heat of the quarrel he had been overhasty, which however was not the case.

In appearance Grundtvig has a great likeness with [Jens] Baggesen but is indubitably a much better person. There is as mentioned something disturbed in his eyes: these he sometimes closes after a strenuous conversation, as if he would gather himself again. He is very dissatisfied with our Evangelical-Christian Hymnal[4] and remarked – as I feel, with reason – that it is a significant deficiency in it that it has no historical hymns and that, instead of examples from life, dry moralising is offered. Conceivably, miscarried expectations, humbled pride and the persecution by some of Copenhagen's priests to which he has been subjected[5] – and which does not exactly do these any credit – as well as bodily weakness, have some part in his present views upon Christianity. But that they are nevertheless primarily [GEEG p. 122] grounded in the feeling of his own need for a reassuring certainty, as well as in the conviction that the wretchedness of the age can be helped only by true devotion to religion, and that this finds its secure ground only in a faith in Christianity's divine authority – of this one is steadily more persuaded by hearing that enthusiasm with which he speaks about this, his and humankind's most important concern. Upon closer examination, he might perhaps find he has not sufficiently separated out the authentic teaching of Christ from the system, and that the teaching remains the same even if the form of the teaching is different.

1. A few years previously (1806) during his time at Egeløkke Grundtvig had read Schiller's *Die Braut von Messina oder die feindlichen Brüder* [The bride of Messina or The enemy brothers], then recently published (1803), and in his diary had used quotations from it to give expression to his own emotional drama: see item 30.

2. Lectures on the Danish poet and dramatist Johannes Ewald (1743-81) and on the German poet, philosopher, historian, and dramatist Friedrich Schiller (1759-1805) given by Oehlenschläger as Professor of Aesthetics (appointed December 1809) in Copenhagen University.

3. From note in *GEEG*: The Danish translation (1796-99) by Johan Werfel (1764-1831) of Rousseau's *Emile* [*Émile ou De l'éducation*; 1762] was far from error-free but was particularly notorious for the excessive quantity of corrective and often laughable notes and comments deriving from the German educationalists and the translator.

4. Grundtvig's complaints against the Evangelical-Christian Hymnal were no doubt at his finger-tips, since he published them in a prose introduction to his hymn *Dejlig er den Himmel blaa* [Lovely are the heavens blue] in Knud Lyhne Rahbek's weekly journal *Sandsigeren* [The soothsayer, truth-teller] 12, 10 April 1811.

5. Schmidt alludes to the complaint then recently lodged by six Copenhagen clerics against Grundtvig's alleged affront to the clergy in the printed version of his dimissory sermon, 1810.

Curate in Udby 1811-1813

69. Carl Joakim Brandt: from his edition of Grundtvig's
Kirkelige Lejlighedstaler *[Occasional church addresses]*
(1877), p. 353; GEEG Stk. 10, p. 122.

In May 1811, having previously failed to secure appointment in the Church, Grundtvig was permitted to take office as his father's curate at Udby, an arrangement more earnestly desired by the father than by the son; but while Grundtvig continued to study and write for publication over the two years he was there, he also proved his pastoral dedication as priest. Grundtvig's attachment to, and apparently successful propagation of the hymns of the Danish bishop Thomas Kingo (1634-1703) is symptomatic of his attachment to the spirit, idiom and form of a traditional Danish hymnody preceding the currently used Evangelical-Christian Hymnal with which he was deeply dissatisfied. The informant here, Carl Joakim Brandt, many years later succeeded Grundtvig as pastor of the Vartov congregation.

An old woman who as a widow lived in a house close to Rønnebæk *præstegaard* [Parsonage] was among the girls who in that year [Spring 1812] was confirmed in Udby. She told me with what zeal "the young Grundtvig" prepared the children and, especially the last time he had them gathered around him, how, having talked with them and to them for several hours, as was his wont, and admonished them in the most sincere fashion, he fell on his knees in the midst of their circle and prayed for them with a loud voice and many tears: that the Lord might preserve them, that they might continue in his covenant. After this he stood up, deeply moved, and went into a side room, but they could clearly hear how on his own there he continued to pray.

Old Dorthe Hansdatter,[1] in the days of her grey hair, still thanked the young priest who in her childhood has taught her those hymns of [Thomas] Kingo which she had to read for him from the floor of the church and which she still knew by heart when she passed away close to eighty.

> 1. *GEEG* notes that the list of Grundtvig's confirmands in April 1812 does indeed include the name of Dorthe Hansdatter.

70. Ludvig Peter Schrøder: N. F. S. Grundtvigs
Levned *(1901), p. 46; GEEG Stk. 11, p. 122.*

A number of the anecdotes recorded of Grundtvig demonstrate that even in post-Reformational Lutheran Denmark a feeling for, indeed a talent for, hagiography lived on: this didactic little story would have graced a medieval Saint's Life. Schrøder (1836-1908) was and remains one of the most outstanding principals in the history of the Danish folk-highschools established upon Grundtvig's inspiration, where oral 'story-telling' of this kind had its own distinctive educational function.

⌒

In his desire to look after the poor [Grundtvig] once gave away the corn which was to have been sown in the glebe-field. When the old pastor, who had heard his farmhand grumbling over it, asked his son how this had come to pass, he merely got the reply: "But, Father, what do we preach about?"

71. Daniel Peter Smith: from Daniel Smith Thrap, 'Provst Daniel Peter Smiths Erindringer fra hans Skolegang og Læretid i Roskilde' [Provst DPS's memoirs from his schooldays and time as teacher in Roskilde] in Kirkehistoriske Samlinger, Series 3, IV (Selskabet for Danmarks Kirkehistorie, Copenhagen 1882-4), pp. 679-680; GEEG Stk. 12, pp. 123-124.

During his time as curate at Udby, Grundtvig continued to write, notably upon world history (*Kort Begreb af Verdens Krønnike betragtet i Sammenhæng* [A Concise Outline of a World Chronicle viewed in Context], 1812) and national history (*Roeskilde-Riim* [The Roskilde Rhymes], 1812), where his contentious aims were to demonstrate that the providential hand of God controls the course of human affairs and to call the Danish Church and people back to emulation of the exemplary achievements of their forebears. There ensued, largely within the pages of Copenhagen's various weekly magazines, fierce sparring with objectors such as the distinguished physicist H. C. Ørsted and Grundtvig's friend from Valkendorf days, the literary critic Christian Molbech. Quarrels with both of these men were eventually patched up, but Grundtvig was developing a reputation as a controversialist, indeed as a trouble-maker. Though Smith, in this anecdote, presents a delightfully comic account of Grundtvig's lengthy readings from his work-in-progress, the *Roeskilde-Riim*, to clerical worthies gathered at the diocesan conference in Roskilde (October 1812), Grundtvig's polemical contributions to the main agenda of such meetings were deemed provocative and no doubt contributed to his subsequent difficulty in securing an appointment in one of the Copenhagen churches.

Daniel Peter Smith (1782-1871), teacher, priest, *Provst* in several successive deaneries, was Grundtvig's friend and his host during the meeting at Roskilde. The words from Grundtvig's reading of *Roeskilde-Riim* remembered by Smith do not exactly correspond to the text as published (1813), though Grundtvig does indeed take the opportunity a couple of times to rhyme the phrase "fra Palladius til Balle" with the word "alle". For Grundtvig's references to Münter's father, see the Index under **Baltzer's son**. *Af Provst Daniel Peter Smiths Optegnelser* [From the memoranda of *Provst* D. P. S.] was edited and published by Daniel Smith Thrap (priest in Kristiania) in 1886.

⌒

[GEEG p. 123] [Grundtvig] was in Roskilde at the diocesan assembly – with which Bishop [Friederich] Münter had associated some scholarly proceedings and to which all theologians had access, and where also I, the little schoolmaster, dared to read a thesis on 'The boundaries between pulpit and theatrical oratory,' squeezed into the proceedings) – in order to do a reading of his splendid book *Roeskilde-Riim*,[1] in which his masterpieces, Bishop Vilhelm and Ole Vind, are found. He lodged at my place and loaned me his manuscript to read, so that I had twice the benefit from hearing him as good as sing it out in a steady rise and fall with his deep monotone voice.

The other proceedings were ended, the good priests had enjoyed a fine meal, taken a pipe with the coffee but alas! no Siesta. They had to go up again to the diocesan assembly hall, and at 9 o'clock in the evening our poet and curate began. He was sitting by the side of *Amtsprovst* [M. F. G.] Bøgh, our mutual patron, who with the patience of an angel relit the candles every time Grundtvig's enthusiasm blew them out. Münter was less patient, and got up and walked about and leafed through the library books. But with the other rural deans, nature prevailed over upbringing: they slept, and *Provst* [Eiler] Hammond, along with others, was snoring foully.

But then Grundtvig raised up his voice of thunder, when on his poetic journey he came to "the church gallery, where he saw lights, summoned up his courage and entered, and to his wonderment sees bishops and chivalric crosses pinned on priestly garb[2] and all the bishops' portraits on the wall." Then he declaimed even louder: "Sit comfortably, bishops all, from Palladius down to Balle" – and then he addresses the Bishop as "old Baltzer's son." The Bishop [Münter] dropped the book from his hand, the deans all woke up, and if Hammond had had any hairs they would now have risen from fright above his staring eyes.

It got late into the evening and it was close to midnight when Grundtvig put his manuscript into his pocket: and now we had to go in half-darkness down the twisting of the murky spiral staircase before we could reach the church, where in the moonlight the paintings moved as though awakened by the sorcerer Grundtvig. The wonderful haste with which the deans pushed past each other definitely indicated some heart-palpitations, so I and Grundtvig followed up in the rear and I could not resist whispering to him: "You have given the good prelates a fright and they [**GEEG p. 124**] are thinking: 'He who comes last gets put in the black pot'!"[3] Grundtvig roared with laughter, and we went home to bed.

The next day he remained over at my place. At that time he was going through his most extreme orthodoxy and we came to talk about Inspiration and because, despite his eagerness to convert me, I would not admit that *every word* in the whole of Scripture was inspired by God, "dictated by the Holy Spirit," he left me, after a disputation from seven o'clock to one o'clock, violently weeping, and he prophesied that there would come a time when I would deeply bewail my unbelief. That time has certainly not come but, on the contrary, the remarkable time has come for him, that he has publicly declared that one may abandon the whole idea of Inspiration and, instead of sticking to the Word of God, commit oneself firmly to the Baptismal Creed.

1. However, neither by this reading nor by other contributions did Grundtvig gain inclusion in the published proceedings (*Videnskabelige Forhandlinger ved Sjællands Stifts Landemoder* [Learned proceedings of the diocesan conventions of the diocese of Sjælland], 3 vols., 1812-18) – perhaps a consequence of the discord between him and Bishop Münter. His collected contributions to various *Landemoder* (1811-14) are listed in the *Bibliografi*, item 168.

2. *Ridderkors paa Præstekjoler*: the chivalric insignia of the Order of Dannebrog worn with clerical dress. Irony is doubtless intended against the bishops who are "sitting comfortably" adorned with their symbols of worldly rank and status. Vilhelm Birkedal (*GEEG* p. 203) records that (1864/65) Grundtvig "acknowledged with me the deplorable situation of these badges of distinction having been randomly scattered as it were to be scrambled for, and having come to hang on many robes which concealed only an empty hollow soul – yes, that there were knights with whom all true knights would be ashamed to walk in procession" and argued that the grounds for each award should be publicly declared upon the nomination, "because then it would become impossible for the King or the Government to hang the cross upon an unworthy or completely insignificant man." For his portrait of 1843 by C. A. Jensen (1792-1870) Grundtvig wore his recently (1840) bestowed *Ridderkors* on his *præstekjole*, as proper for formal dress.

3. "*Den som kommer allersidst, skal i den sorte Gryde*" – Smith is quoting from a Danish children's game and song, *Bro, bro, brille*, which like the English *Oranges and Lemons* has two children forming a snare with their arched arms under which the others pass in a chain; the child passing under the bridge when the song reaches 'the pot' is the one ensnared.

The "seven lean years" 1813-1820

72. Carl Otto: from Pennetegninger *[Pen drawings], selection edited by Julius Clausen, in the periodical* Tilskueren *1929 II, 206-207*

Carl Otto (1795-1879), doctor of medicine, editor of medical journals and associate member of various foreign learned societies, was appointed (1825) physician to the prison-reformatory (Tugt-, Rasp- og Forbedringshuset) in Christianshavn at the time Grundtvig (with whom his acquaintance went back some eight years) was living in Strandgade with his young family. Otto was by then related by marriage (to Anna Friis, daughter of *Grosserer* [import and export merchant] Hans Friis) to Grundtvig's wife Elisabeth. From 1832 he held an appointment as professor in the University of Copenhagen with a special interest in phrenology until, in effect left behind by modern advances in medicine, he resigned (1862), though he continued in his practice as a physician. He cultivated a great interest in literature, was a co-founder of the reading club Athenæum and of the Reading Association for Manual Workers [*Læseforeningen for Haandværkere*], and member of the Classenske Litteraturselskab. He wrote autobiographical accounts including *Livserindringer fra mine Reiser* [Life-memoirs from my travels] (1875), *Af mit Liv, min Tid og min Kreds* [From my life, my times and my circle] (1879), as well as the *Pennetegninger* (here excerpted from the version published in the periodical *Tilskueren*, 1929). Increasingly engaged in freemasonry and inclining steadily further to conservatism in politics, he was neither socially nor temperamentally predisposed to nurture his early friendship with Grundtvig, though he was evidently pleased, near the end of his life, to be able to record the connection.

⌒

Although very remotely, I am related to this famous and in many respects remarkable man. Grundtvig's first wife [Elisabeth (Lise) Blicher] and mine [Anna Elisabeth Friis] were first cousins. When in 1817 my engagement was celebrated in the home of my parents-in-law, he, together with the whole of the rest of the family, was present with his fiancée. As it so happened that there were three other engaged couples in the house, Grundtvig, whom I had already seen there on an earlier occasion, took the opportunity after supper of delivering a poem about, and addressed to, all the engaged, himself included.[1] Naturally, it was, as everything from his pen, extremely powerful with many beautiful images and expressive; but I dare say that only a few of those present understood it since it was delivered in his usual manner: scanning it in those rising and falling rhythms which to a great extent deprived it of its beauty. One could however feel with what high esteem he was already regarded, for during the performance so deep a silence prevailed that one could hear a pin drop. In general he already possessed a name as a poet, historian and theologian – and therefore the family naturally regarded it as an honour to be able to count him as *one of their own*. But at that time too he was [GEEG p. 125] just as peculiar in his ways as he has later shown himself to be; and since it has been said again and again that he was so placid a character, I would not dare to deny it. But it is certain that everyone in the family was fearful of contradicting him, since he would always grow vehement about it and would defend what he had once said, very sternly and irascibly.

When he got married there was a general murmuring in the family over the way in which he lived. He was in fact so irregular that he would not allow himself to be disturbed for anything when he was working at his desk. At every meal the food had to be left standing until his book allowed him to eat it – and that was often half the day. Sleep he took only when it sneaked up on him in his armchair, at his worktable; his wife could almost never get him to bed, never, at least, at the right time, except when by chance his work was ended by bedtime; otherwise he would always pick up where he had left off, until he fell asleep from exhaustion. Whether he continued this extraordinary way of living, so damaging to health, all through his life, or for how long a period, I do not know. During his first marriage no change occurred, and one must be really surprised that he reached so great an age and had not already lost at an early stage the strength which, remarkably enough, he was able to enjoy to the last.

I was many times together with him during the days of my engagement. But he was obviously bored in the extreme in these family circles since he neither played cards nor put the slightest value upon the trivial conversation which is ordinarily maintained on such occasions. He would therefore talk only with this person and that, in whom he could expect if not an affinity of intellect then at least an amenability to "learned discussions." And yet he could often laugh heartily when one or another laughable situation in town was on the line – just as he did not at all display any discrimination or reservedness even with those who ranked lowest in intellect. I was often honoured with his conversation and when I undertook my first journey abroad in 1819 he wrote a beautiful poem in my album.[2] Later our paths did not lead us together. But I am proud and glad just to have known him.

1. Probably Grundtvig's poem *Jaordet* [The word 'Yes'], composed 1 June 1817 and published in the first part of Vol. III of his periodical *Danne-Virke* (July 1817); printed in *PS* IV, 461-63.

2. The poem, dated 24 October 1819, is printed in *PS* V, 61.

Priest in Præstø with Skibbinge 1821-1822

73. Nicolai William Theodorus Bondesen: from Minde om Nikolai Frederik Severin Grundtvigs Præstegjerning i Aaret 1821 *[Memorial of NFSG's ministry in the year 1821] (1874), 4-6; GEEG Stk. 14, 126-27.*

Though Bondesen (1823-96), appointed parish priest in Præstø 1872, biographer, poet, was not born until two years after the date of which he is here writing, and published this short work after Grundtvig's death, the value of his account lies in the fact that it is based upon the testimony of people still living who had known Grundtvig while he was serving as parish priest in Præstø, February 1821 to November 1822. Already, however, the process of popular mythologising was at work, as demonstrated by Th. Helveg in an article on '*Sagndannelser*' [legend-makings] in Bondesen's account, published in *Højskolebladet* 1903, cols. 563-68 (*GEEG*); and thus, as in traditional Saints' Lives, the anecdotes sometimes tell more about the religious sensibilities and needs of the devotees, and the legacy of enthusiasms inspired by the subject, than about the subject himself.

***

[GEEG p. 126] During Grundtvig's ministry the church was constantly attended by large numbers; his sermons were lively and affecting, and he himself was often very intensely moved so that the tears ran down his cheeks. Sometimes his sermons were very long but they were always followed with concentrated attention; if however their duration dragged out rather too long the schoolmaster – in all likelihood according to agreement – would walk quietly down the church and then Grundtvig would end his sermon. Only once did he hold a confirmation here in Præstø. The confirmands, twenty-four in number, were prepared only during the winter period; then they studied Monday, Thursday and Saturday from nine o'clock until towards three without any break but yet, according to one old woman's account, did not grow tired nor felt hunger or thirst. Each time they would sing a hymn first; then Grundtvig would say a prayer; then each child would read at his table a piece of the Bible, the content of which he would then talk to them about; next would come an examination together with an explanation and account of those things which belong to the kingdom of God; finally they would end with a hymn and a prayer. Among the hymns sung, the old people especially recalled the pleasure with which they would sing *Et Barn er født i Bethlehem* [A babe is born in Bethlehem].[1] Most of the hymns they learned by heart – and they learned many – were not to be found in the hymnal then current, and they would then have to borrow hymnbooks from the old ladies in the Almshouse.[2] For instruction, Balle's textbook was used,[3] but special weight was laid upon the teaching of the Catechism and they diligently used the so-called *Pavekatechismus* [Pope Catechism] on the title-page of which is found a portrait of Luther with the well-known verse: "Hear me, O Pope! I fain would be, etc" [*Hør mig, o Pav! jeg være vil*]. Besides the Bible history which was studied in school, the confirmands also used the *Bible-History* [*Bibelkrøniken*].[4] Although the schoolmaster in Præstø was a capable man, yet the children were wanting in knowledge of Bible history and the Catechism. Grundtvig would sometimes complain about this to the teacher; and the latter, who was strict and severe, then used to hand out corporal punishment in school to those concerned. Grundtvig himself worked tirelessly with [**GEEG p. 127**] his confirmands and took on several who were already grown-up, and year after year had been turned away. While the teaching was going on, he would not be disturbed or interrupted, and whoever came would have to go away with their business un-accomplished, whether they were high-born or low. It had particularly made an impression on the children that even the owner of the neighbouring baronial seat [Stampenborg] once had to leave without success; just as they never forgot to tell me how all the genteel folk who were present on the confirmation-day and had seated themselves in the choir had to leave it so that the children could come up to the altar and kneeling make their promise.

There were indeed genteel folk present that day, among others the Duke of Augusten-borg and the Prince of Noer. That confirmation-day all those I have spoken with recall very vividly. Grundtvig's first address to the confirmands was so moving that all without exception were intensely affected; he had to ask them to calm down and cease their tears – indeed, he even had to make a long pause on account of their sobbing.

Just as Grundtvig showed himself throughout to be a serious and zealous priest, so also with respect to the Communion. The young people had to meet at his place the day before, one by one, and those who had forgotten what they had learnt before confirmation about the Lord's Supper and its signification were not allowed to go to the Lord's table.

1. Grundtvig published his own reworking of this ancient Christmas hymn in 1820. It is not known whether his confirmands learned his version or whether they sang it in the sixteenth-century version by Hans Tausen.

2. The unavailable hymnal was the Evangelical-Christian Hymnal of 1793; the old ladies in the almshouse clung to the old hymnal of Thomas Kingo.

3. *Lærebog i den evangelisk-christelige Religion* [Textbook in Evangelical-Christian Religion], 1791.

4. Grundtvig's *En liden Bibelkrønike for Børn og Menigmand* [A little Bible-history for children and the common man], 1814.

Curate at Vor Frelsers Kirke Copenhagen 1822-1826

74. Christian Sigfred Ley: Extracts from his diaries, published in
Frederik Nygaard, Minder om Grundtvigs præstevirksomhed i
Kiøbenhavn 1813-15 og 1822-26 *[Memorials of Grundtvig's ministry in*
Copenhagen etc], in Danskeren II, 1889, 380-81; GEEG Stk. 15, 127-28.

After returning to Copenhagen following his father's death (and therefore the termination of
his curacy) in 1813, Grundtvig preached by invitation in a number of city churches and began
to build up a circle of friends and disciples. Among these was the family of Christian Sigfred
Ley (1806-74), young son of a master tailor. In due course, the enthusiastic and impressionable
Ley was to become a lifelong devotee of Grundtvig. His diaries provided biographical materials for Frederik Nygaard (1845-97), priest, historical author and biographer, who made various
contributions to the biographical record of Grundtvig. Here Ley records the allegation that
Grundtvig was encouraged to challenge Professor H. N. Clausen by Bishop Münter – who then
left Grundtvig to his fate when Clausen had recourse to the law.

When Grundtvig had read [H. N.] Clausen's book[1] he went out to the bishop [Friederich
Münter] and told him that the Professor of Theology had written this book in which there
appeared this and this. The bishop was then very angry about this and said: Yes, this was
indeed frightful. Grundtvig then said to him that he had in mind to take Clausen on over
this. "Yes, do just that" said Münter, "He really does deserve [GEEG p. 128] a serious trounc-
ing! It also pains me that he has dedicated this book to me." "Yes" said Grundtvig, "I can
well believe that it must pain you that he wants to make you a pillar of his rotten church."
"Yes indeed" said the bishop.

1. H. N. Clausen, *Catholicismens og Protestantismens Kirkeforfatning, Lære og Ritus* [Constitu-
   tion, doctrine and rites of Catholicism and Protestantism], 1825.

75. Hans Brun: Biskop N. F. S. Grundtvigs Levnetsløb udførligst
fortalt fra 1839 *[Bp NFSG's Life recounted in fullest detail*
from 1839] (2 vols., 1882), I, 77; GEEG Stk. 16, p. 128.

Hans Brun (1820-90) was Grundtvig's first major bibliographer. His study covers the years of
Grundtvig's ministry at Vartov (1839-72). In this anecdote, Grundtvig shrugs off student support
for Clausen.

During lectures there circulated [in September 1825] among theological students a declaration of gratitude to [H. N.] Clausen in connection with the *Gjenmæle*.[1] When someone told Grundtvig that eighty-eight had now subscribed to it, then he just answered: "Put a line straight through it and then you have four noughts."

1. That is, in support of Clausen after Grundtvig's attack on him in *Kirkens Gjenmæle* [The Church's retort], 1825.

76. *Jakob Christian Lindberg: from Niels Lindberg, Af* Jak. Kr. Lindbergs Papirer *[From J. C. L's papers] in* Historisk Maanedsskrift V *(1885), 84-86; GEEG Stk. 17, pp. 128-9.*

Lindberg was among those who stood closest by Grundtvig during and after the traumatic events of 1826. Here he records that it was upon hearing the King condemn Grundtvig's attack on the younger Clausen that Grundtvig resigned his post at Vor Frelsers Kirke – though a major contributory factor was the elder Clausen's prohibition of the use of Grundtvig's specially composed Whitsun hymns on the day of the thousandth anniversary of Christian Denmark.

Now [in 1826] the thousandth anniversary of the introduction of Christianity by Ansgar was at hand. Naturally, we looked forward to this, those of us for whom it was to be kept – since it was obviously not a celebration of the abolition of Christianity. Grundtvig wrote those lovely Whitsun-hymns[1] and *Kong Harald og Ansgar* [King Harald and Ansgar], and ended his sermon on the last Sunday before Whitsun [7th May] by wishing us: "Happy festival! Happy festival!" On the Monday [8th May] he took the hymns and *Kong Harald og Ansgar* to the King, and I met him, as previously mentioned, in the antechamber. But *Provst* [H. G.] Klavsen had already forbidden that these hymns might be sung, and Bishop [Friederich] Münter, who as a bishop was far more measly than as a scholar he was great and esteemed, was agreed upon this. Grundtvig received an audience and talked for a long time with the King and he departed from him as though nothing were the matter.

In the evening I came to Grundtvig longing to hear what the King had said. *Licenciat* [Jens] Holm […] and *candidat* [Peter] Fenger […] were with him. They were waiting for him because he was talking with his brother, *Provst* Otto Grundtvig, priest out by Bagsværd [in Gladsaxe]. He [Grundtvig] came in to us and told us that he had today tendered his resignation. We were struck dumb. Dr [A.G.] Rudelbach joined us and heard it from us. He with us was struck dumb. Then came the old [Jens] Hornsyld. He met Grundtvig himself – noticed nothing. Grundtvig said nothing to him, and they had a very cheerful conversation; though Hornsyld said a couple of times to us silent folk: "Well now, where did you lose your tongues?" When later we left Grundtvig we told him the reason for our silence. The [GEEG p. 129] old man was so shocked or astounded that he almost slipped from my grip – I was holding him under the arm – especially since from Grundtvig's cheerfulness he had suspected nothing. What however had happened with the King was this: that he had indeed given Grundtvig a good reception but nevertheless during the conversation had given him to understand that he regarded Grundtvig as guilty of libel. Grundtvig had replied: "Your Majesty's word is to me more than a judgement of the High Court" and the same morning he tendered his resignation. Bishop Münter's good-naturedness showed through here as well, in that he sent an urgent message to Grundtvig's brother [Otto] the *provst*, that he should persuade him to withdraw his application.

1. Lindberg refers to the hymns – *Den signede Dag* [This blessed day], *Tusind Aar stod Christi Kirke* [A thousand years Christ's Church has stood] and *Klar op, du Sky paa Øien-Bryn* [Clear up, you cloud upon the brow] – which Grundtvig composed to be sung in Vor Frelsers Kirke on Whitsunday (14 May) 1826 when the Danish Church was to celebrate the thousandth anniversary of Ansgar's Christian mission to Denmark. He published them in advance on 28 April 1826 as a 16-page booklet, *Danske Høitids-Psalmer til Tusind-Aars Festen* [Danish festival hymns for the thousandth anniversary]. However, their use was obstructed by *Stiftsprovst* H. G. Clausen.

Public and private life 1826-1832

77. *Hans Brun:* Biskop N. F. S. Grundtvigs Levnetsløb udførligst fortalt fra 1839 *[Bp NFSG's Life recounted in fullest detail from 1839] (2 vols., 1882), I, 134; GEEG Stk. 18, p. 129.*

Brun, Grundtvig's first major biographer, was a Norwegian settled in Kristiania (Oslo). He was in a good position to gather material originating in Norway or among Norwegian visitors to Grundtvig in Copenhagen. This anecdote is meant to raise a smile. Brun's readers knew that Wilhelm Andreas Wexels (1797-1866), priest in Vor Frelsers Kirke, Kristiania, was later to become Grundtvig's most vigorous Norwegian supporter in the Church Struggle [*Kirkekampen*] over the first half of the 19th c., acknowledged by Grundtvig as his "friend of many years and brother in office." See further the Index entry for **Wexels,** Wilhelm Andreas; and **Moravians**.

⌐

Wexels had been in Copenhagen [summer 1827], and at that time he was no better known than that Grundtvig took him to be a priest of Moravian tendency. I think it was one of the Fengers (or maybe Dr [A.G.] Rudelbach) who then accompanied him to Grundtvig. [W.A.] Wexels happened to express something from which Grundtvig concluded that Wexels must believe that "the Devil's children" could become "God's children" and when Grundtvig asked Wexels whether he really believed this, "then I answered" – related Wexels once – "as I had learnt: Yes, when they repent." "The Devil's children become God's children! God preserve me!" Grundtvig exclaimed, went off, knocked out his pipe and didn't talk to him any more.

78. *Frederik Ludvig Bang Zeuthen:* Mine første 25 Aar *[My first 25 years] (1866), pp. 121-24; GEEG Stk. 19, pp. 129-31.*

F. L. B. Zeuthen (1805-74) is a fair representative of the many Danish intellectuals of Grundtvig's day who found their abiding home in German speculative philosophy. He was particularly inspired by the writings of Friedrich Wilhelm Joseph Schelling (1775-1854) and, on the visit to Grundtvig recorded here, noted (with a touch of scepticism?) that Grundtvig was currently reading one of Schelling's publications and thought it a good book; but unlike Henrik Steffens (1773-1845) – to whom both he and Grundtvig were related and whom he visited on his academic travels, and who shared Zeuthen's proselytising zeal for German philosophy – he found little common ground with Grundtvig. Zeuthen, by his own account, is unbendingly stern, earnest and dogmatic in this exchange, and Grundtvig's jovial dismissiveness falls upon stony ground; but it is partly upon such published accounts as this (and by no means upon his educational ideology alone) that Grundtvig and Grundtvigianism developed a reputation, still current, of being anti-intellectual. See also item 85.

⌒

During the years under discussion, from 1827-1830, I visited him [Grundtvig] now and again of an evening. He had resigned as priest at Frelsers Kirke and was leading a quiet life with his family. One hardly knew what he lived on, but there was no sign of any poverty.[1] One will perhaps be surprised to hear that at that time he did not contradict me much when I praised [J. P.] Mynster, indeed agreed with me to a great extent; and that he read *German* authors and talked with interest [GEEG p. 130] about the powerful minds out there. He once expressed himself with enthusiasm about Jean Paul's *Vorschule der Æsthetik* [Primer in aesthetics] which he was reading just then. He made the remark that while witticisms normally tend to reveal a certain coldness, yet in the witticisms of Jean Paul an amiable heart seemed to express itself. When I found his witticisms rather contrived, Grundtvig would not go along with this: "What does one achieve without contriving it?"[2]

However stimulating conversations with Grundtvig could be for me, nevertheless, especially when it came to a dispute, they still had a great deficiency which arose from the fact that in the ideas which were put forward he did not sufficiently respect that mutuality [*hiint Fælles*] of which I spoke above.[3] I found it impossible to bow to his authority; and therefore I was to be won over to a viewpoint only in so far as either it could be brought into harmony with that which I brought with me – my pre-existing conceptual scope – or else I was convinced, by a closer investigation of the matter, that what I previously thought was incorrect. Therefore I could not be persuaded to acknowledge his famous "discovery" [*Opdagelse*] to be a real discovery as such.[4]

However astonishing an eye for the deeper truths Grundtvig could bring to light, he was not much of a judge of deeper *ideas as such, in the form of ideas*. I will clarify this by an example, which is at the same time indicative of an important side of Grundtvigianism. Grundtvig once said: "The Devil is a great arithmetician." Undeniably, a deep truth can be intimated by this. That which comes out by calculation has lost its centre, that which exists of itself, the absolute; and it moves only within the relative, within relationships; and therefore it enters into the indeterminate, into that which [G.W.F.] Hegel calls sheer infinity [*den slette Uendelighed*]. In this there is a restlessness without repose or peace, a hunger and a thirst without satisfaction. And in this there is manifested a significant peculiarity of evil or of the Evil One.[5] But Grundtvig did not show himself to be in command of this truth as an *idea* in its abstraction, for use in concrete instances – as one will see from the following. In Hegel's *Logik* (I, 188) there is discussion of a description of eternity by the Swiss [Albrecht von] Haller. Hegel declares that what [Immanuel] Kant called this "*schauderhafte Besch-reibung der Ewigkeit*" [atrocious description of eternity] used to be particularly admired – but not often from the side [GEEG p. 131] which constitutes its true merit. In his poem, Haller adds in richly imaginative fashion quantity upon quantity, worlds upon worlds, millions upon millions; but if, in this frightful aggregation or likewise construction, one sees a description of eternity, then one is overlooking the fact that the poet himself declares this moving about in the infinite in time and space to be something fruitless, and that only by giving up this empty infinite process can the true infinity achieve immediacy. Indeed, Haller ends with this point:

Alle Macht der Zahl vermehrt zu Tausend mahlen
Ist nicht ein Theil von dir!
Ich ziehe sie ab und du liegst ganz vor mir![6]

This *indirect* relationship between the eternal and the finite preoccupied me much in those days. When I now came with these thoughts to Grundtvig I therefore found him altogether unreceptive. I clearly recall how, when I quoted to him those words of Haller: "I take them [the numbers] away and you [eternity, the Eternal] lie right before me!" he had nothing to reply, other than what any person who lacks a sense or understanding of a higher spiritual state of things would also answer, namely: "*Then* there is nothing at all!" And that was that, despite the fact that, since it is the Devil who is *really* the great arithmetician (according to Grundtvig), the numbers must still, in one way or another, be done away with (as the first premise) in order to come to God and Eternity.

That Power which has the possibility of numbers and of finites within itself is infinitely greater than the finite magnitudes themselves: this is the Power of Eternity. The former must be removed if the latter is to become apparent. But in the very act of removal this Power of Eternity reveals itself as having mastery over finitude.

"*Then* there is nothing at all," said Grundtvig. If faith has moved mountains, is there then nothing at all? If those motions within the human soul which wander in unboundedness are overcome by the power of the Spirit, and a stillness before God has entered instead, is there then nothing at all, as in the sluggish and apathetic?

I should hardly have dwelt upon this saying of Grundtvig however, if a deficiency did not express itself therein which seems to me characteristic of Grundtvig and his followers. They have no sense for, nor understanding of that powerful affirmation [*Bekræftelse*] which there can be in the denial [*Benægtelsen*], and neither therefore of the ideal significance of limitation [*Begrændsningen*].

1. *GEEG* notes that though Grundtvig received no pension upon his resignation from Vor Frelsers Kirke (1826), he was granted an annual royal bursary to support his historical studies which he held until his appointment at Vartov (1839); he also received grants from the royal purse *Ad usum publicum* [for public purpose] to reside in England in the summers of 1829-31; and furthermore had some income from his publications. However, Marie Blom, writing of the Grundtvig household over this period, hints at stringencies and observes that, though Grundtvig himself appeared to pay little attention to the domestic economy, his wife Lise was "orderly and thrifty in the extreme" and "could lay on a fine spread even with the most frugal materials."

2. Zeuthen's footnote: "Schelling's book *On Academic Study* he was also reading with satisfaction at the time I visited him. He called it a good book." Zeuthen refers to *Über die Methode des akademischen Studiums* (1803) by the German philosopher Friedrich Wilhelm Joseph Schelling (1775-1854).

3. Zeuthen refers to a previous point in his text where, having recorded some reminiscences of Bishop J. P. Mynster, he remarked: "Usually, a younger person's debate with important men ends up on the latter's side in a monologue where that respect for mutuality, which is required of every proper converse, does not receive its due."

4. Zeuthen alludes to Grundtvig's so-called *mageløse Opdagelse* [matchless discovery]. In this rejection of a true "discovery" Zeuthen shared the opinion of another of Grundtvig's entrenched critics, Søren Kierkegaard – though Kierkegaard too came in for polemical attack from Zeuthen.

5. Zeuthen's footnote: "*Divine* calculation is a disciplined, serviceable one. *Dum Deus calculat, fit mundus* [When God calculates, a world is framed], says Leibniz."

6. Correct version of Zeuthen's quotation from Haller's poem *Unvollkommenes Gedicht über die Ewigkeit* [Incomplete poem upon Eternity], published in *Versuch* (1732), is: "Ist alle Macht der Zahl, vermehrt mit tausend Malen, / Noch nicht ein Teil von dir; / Ich tilge sie, und du liegst ganz vor Mir." – Haller in his persona as scientist and mathematician deals in huge numbers, piles age upon age, world upon world, "(And when from that awesome height, fainting, I look again upon you) *all that power of numbers, a thousandfold increased, is not even a particle of you. I blot it out, and whole you lie before me.* (O God, you alone are the foundation of all! You, Son, are the measure of measureless time […] In you, eternity is one single Now!)." See further Index entry **Haller,** Albrecht von.

79. Christian Sigfred Ley: Extracts from his diaries, published by Frederik Nygaard in Danskeren IX, 1893, p. 4; GEEG Stk. 20, p. 132.

[GEEG p. 132] When Johan [Gr's eldest son] was quite small, he liked to come in to Grundtvig of an evening, in the half-light; and he would then ask him to put letters together and spell without a book. Once when [F. L. B.] Zeuthen was with Grundtvig Johan came bounding in and said: "I have got it now." "Really?" said Grundtvig, "Let me hear then." So then he began: "This asserts Beda, that right honest man," etc.,[1] but he didn't know it properly and had to go away and learn it all over again.

> 1 *Det siger Beda, den ærlige mand.* The lines derive from *Den danske Rimkrønike* [The Danish Rhyming Chronicle] published as Denmark's earliest printed book in the Danish language by Gotfred af Ghemen (Copenhagen 1495): Thet syer Beda, then ærilighe man, / Thet ær well giort, i hwo thet kand, / Ath skriffuæ forælderes gerningher allæ / Ere the ondæ man maa thennom fly, / Ere the godæ, man maa thennom thy, / Och engælunde fraa thennom fallæ. They were memorised by Johan, no doubt, in a modernised form: Det siger Beda, den ærlige Mand, / Det er vel-gjort, af hvem der kan, / At skrive Forældres Gierninger alle; / Ere de onde, maa man dem flye, / Ere de gode, dem giøre paa Nye, / Og dem ingenlunde frafalde! [This asserts Beda, that right honest man: / it is well done of him who can / to write down all of his forebears' deeds. / If they are evil, then one must shun them, / if they are good, repeat them anew / and seek to fall short of them never]. This precept of the 8th-c. English historian (from the dedication of Bede's *Ecclesiastical History*, 731) Grundtvig used as the motto on the title-page of his translation of Saxo's *Danmarks Krønike* (1818).

80. Marie Blom: Minder fra N. F. S. og Fru Lise Grundtvigs Hjem 1830-50 [Memories from N. F. S. and Mrs Lise Grundtvig's home], published in H. P. B. Barfod's Minder fra gamle grundtvigske Hjem [Memories from old Grundtvigian homes], I (1921), pp. 11-27; GEEG Stk. 21, pp. 132-43

Marie Blom (1824-1901) was daughter of a friend of Grundtvig's youth, *Oberst* H. J. Blom (1796-1864), who at this time was living in the military barracks in Sølvgade, Copenhagen. As children, she and her brother Vilhelm (who was eventually to die in the Battle of Isted, 1850, fighting for Danish Slesvig) often visited the Grundtvigs' home to play with the children there, Johan, Svend and Meta. The rest of the relevant facts are well covered in the excerpt itself. These reminiscences were written down in 1888 on the prompting of Lavra Grundtvig, widow of Grundtvig's second son, Svend, by which time, no doubt, some of the stories had become well-honed through frequent retellings, and enhanced by the hindsight of the 64-year-old author; but none the worse for all that, they offer engaging glimpses of family life in the Grundtvig household across the water in Christianshavn – where Grundtvig is already the rather awesome *paterfamilias* and Lise and Aunt Jane Blicher keep the hospitable household running.

In the last years of the Twenties and until Grundtvig became priest at Vartov Church, he lived with his family out at the west end of Strandgade in Christianshavn, right up by Frederik's German Church.[1] The courtyard-house was the last dwelling in the street, but after that there still came a couple of quite big warehouses which extended right down to the church's very low enclosure. Directly opposite was a wall with an imposing entrance gate which led to shipyards, rope-walks, a soap-factory and heaven knows what else, which all went together under the common name *Pladsen* [The Square] and which together with the aforementioned courtyard-house belonged to "the King of Christianshavn" – that is to say, the merchant-king Jakob Holm. This magnate had his offices on the ground-floor and lived with his various broods of children,[2] which were just as many as Grundtvig's later became, on the first floor, while the interior which I will try to describe here was on the second floor.

The courtyard-house, which was impressive but without architectural character, was built according to the type which had become commonplace after the great fires. The facade to the street was taken up with three rooms – a four-windowed drawing-room and two minor rooms; but because space was more plentiful in this outer part of the city the two minor rooms at the sides were here replaced by two spacious three-windowed living-rooms. As usual, the front wing of the house towards the courtyard was taken up by the spacious staircase and by a small one-windowed room which formed the actual entrance to the apartment, whereas the space above the portal on the other side of the staircase made way for one – here, two – small rooms behind the furthest three-windowed living-room. In the angle with the side-wing there lay a so-called *Smigstue* with its solitary window placed in the corner;[3] after [GEEG p. 133] this, the big larder and the very big kitchen, then the back staircase and finally the maid's room.

But Grundtvig did not use the apartment in this regimented fashion. For a start, the Holms had reserved the three abovementioned rooms on the left side of the staircase, those closest to the church, for their large household; and moreover the considerable library of the master of the house already at that time demanded so great a space that he had to have the large four-windowed room divided by a partition for his sole use. Thus, apart from the small entrance-hall, the family had only two rooms – which on the other hand were much larger than folk of the middle class at that time commonly lived in. Through the abovementioned anteroom, which served the boys Johan and Svend as a bedroom, and into the *Smigstue* came all those who wished to visit the women,[4] and this is how I made my 'joyeuse entrée' into this house in the year 1830 or 1831.

I came there with my mother, and what moved this very stay-at-home woman to walk this long way, and into the bargain with me hand in hand, I cannot remember; whereas I do clearly recall that Fru Grundtvig was ill and lay in her bedroom which was in fact in this corridor room. I clearly remember that the beds were four-poster beds with red and white striped cotton hangings; that the dressing table was built out of an enormous console table with a small oval mirror above it; that in addition to this, a small spindlebacked sofa, once the open side had been turned to the wall in the evening, served the only daughter, the youngest child Meta, as a sleeping place. But furthermore this spacious room was furnished with a Bornholm-clock, two equally large oilcloth-covered folding tables, a cupboard for tableware, also more chairs than were actually needed in a bedroom, for in the same room the family always made their dining room. Here the morning, midday and evening food was brought in from the kitchen next door.

Fru Grundtvig cannot have been very ill. She was perhaps convalescent after a serious illness, but she talked gaily with my mother and her sister, *Frøken* Blicher, Aunt Jane, and with another lady with a little girl who came at the same time. These were the wife and daughter of [Niels Møller] Spandet who later became so well-known; a short while afterwards, through another route, they became my friends until the daughter died, twenty-two years old. Fru Spandet had brought Marie with her so that she could see Meta's [GEEG p. 134] English doll. The "English" doll was apparently a French fashion-doll, which Meta's father on his first journey to England had been given over there for his little daughter. Thus it was probably the *first* blandishment Meta received for her father's sake. It was indeed brought out, and I still see it before my eyes with its waxen face, its glass eyes, its coiffure of real hair, styled *à la Titus*,[5] and its costume of white satin swathed in gauze of a light violet colour, decorated with small white posies of flowers – an absolute dream for the three small girls; but for actually playing with, this belle of the ball was no use, and so without regret we saw her disappear in her box into the larder.

After this visit I dare say I saw the Grundtvig children a few times, most likely at the home of Grundtvig's brother-in-law, [Christian] Schmidt the wholesaler in Nyhavn; but I do not believe I was there in their house earlier than Christmas Eve 1832. The day before, my mother had been buried, and I and my brother Vilhelm who during her illness had been taken in by the Schmidts were still there in the house and accompanied the whole huge family of Schmidts and Glahns and whoever else there was of unattached and unengaged Blichers,[6] out there. The half-flattering, half-hurtful feeling which the company's sympathetic attention aroused in me, I well remember; but when one of the Grundtvigs – probably the little girl – asked me why I had a black dress on, I could not answer for weeping, and I did think it was really nice of the mother to call her into a corner and reprove her.

That evening I know that I got to see the living room the way it remained almost unaltered until 1840. The walls were light blue, oil-painted, but, according to the fashion of the period, covered in canvas nailed on frames between the wainscotting; three windows out to Strandgade; and, on the two piers between them, two mahogany chests of drawers – as best I remember bowed but not scrolled, on tall thin legs. On the long wall nearest to Brogade stood the sofa of rather pale birchwood; like all sofas then, it was designed to give room for three people. The covering was quite dark green, of a cloth-like, presumably home-woven, material. Six chairs, matching it; and, in front of it, a mahogany folding table over which, on Sundays and on other solemn occasions there was spread a fine dark-green tablecloth adorned with a stylised flower-border in orange. This wall was divided into three sections and in each one hung a rather large oil-painting – portraits of the master of the house and his wife on the [GEEG p. 135] wings, and the latter's mother, old Fru [Mette] Blicher, in the middle. By the wall nearest the church stood the stove and its appendage

– an enormous firewood-basket with beech-logs. Next to this was the door into "Father's room" and nearest the window a bureau of mahogany with a bowed drop front and on top three bowed cupboards as its upper portion. This room's finest furniture belonged to Aunt Jane. There were a couple more polished tables, and later on the room became not a little more decorative with yet another small painting depicting Sorø lake with the Academy in the background, and an enormous sofa-cushion upon which Louise Schmidt had sewn an "*Edelfräulein*" in Düsseldorf-style, which at that time was admired beyond all moderation: the tapestry work was quite definitely done with much taste and expertise. The floor was painted – which was a great rarity at that time – and in winter a carpet lay in front of the sofa. Originally, I believe, the curtains were white muslin ones, both summer and winter; later there were some brown and yellow ones whose background was reminiscent of tiger-skin, while the border consisted of ornamentations which framed human figures of three or four inches in height.

But to get back to that Christmas Eve: I know for sure that the whole party in the living room got tea and Christmas cake, which were available in rustic overabundance, but that the Christmas tree was lit in the bedroom. The children were full of wonderment and the adults pretended to be so, but the master of the house poked fun, albeit amicably, because there were candles only on the one side of the tree, that which turned towards the public, and talked, if I do not remember incorrectly, about an elfin-maiden who was hollow-backed, and Aunt Jane cheerily defended her arrangement. Christmas presents were also distributed but my ungrateful soul has quite forgotten what fell to my share. On the other hand three campstools, suited according to the ages (ten, eight and six years) of the three small boys, stand clearly before my eyes. Such chairs were at that time regarded as an infallible means of getting children to be straight-backed. One has subsequently come to think differently. The chairs were used by all three of them until they were in an all too great disproportion to the height of their persons. Johan and Svend became straight-backed, Vilhelm, despite his military career, stooped rather much with his head.

The boys were very satisfied with their portable seats and were incessantly putting them up and folding them together. Already at that time Svend revealed himself to me to be an extraordinarily lively young person who was everywhere he was not supposed to be, and where the grown-up cousins, male and female, [GEEG p. 136] would rather have been free of him; Johan was well brought up and well-behaved; Vilhelm was a small, pale, sickly and tearful boy, but who already at that time, just six years old, not only could read but did read, as soon as he could get at it.

In the rear room the children and the young ones were later assembled to play Christmas games. It seemed to me that none of us was specially amused by it – a characteristic I find they had in common with most later Christmas games I have participated in. We all ate together in the bedroom and were served porridge. Apart from the customary quiet table-prayer there were absolutely no other religious ceremonies.

The Grundtvig household no doubt remained for a while as I have tried to describe it here; and it was probably not until the next autumn that I went out there one morning with my father and my brother and found the house totally transformed. Father did not think that the arrangement which the lady of the house showed us was at all surprising but it surprised us rather more. The bedroom was now *only* the dining room, "Father's room" had become the bedroom, the rear room the study, and – how peculiar – a door which we had not specked to exist, since it was concealed by the large bookcases, had been opened up into a quite unknown room, the three-windowed room at the other end of the house, which plainly enough served the double purpose of being the library and the boys' bedroom. Here were standing the two familiar beds with the stitched blankets for bed-curtains, and along the walls the tall bookcases with books of which the white vellum bindings were ghastly enough but not so fear-inspiring as those which sometimes allowed their titlepages, printed with a red colour, to be seen; and in the middle of the floor a table with the aforementioned camp-stools. But we entered still further into the mystery, because behind the drawing room two further bedrooms opened up, and it was first from Fru Grundtvig's conversation with my father that we understood that the house out there had gained three new residents as boarders: the then small Barons [Henrik and Holger] Stampe, and their, Johan's and Svend's shared tutor, Mr [Carl] Muus.

No doubt Mr Muus was neither respected nor loved in any very high degree by his pupils, or else they would surely have grown tired of always using his name as the starting-point for their impertinent scurrilities, which culminated when, in all likelihood, Svend got the witty notion of placing a mousetrap in the tutor's slipper – an idea which amused us beyond all measure, but which I believe Mr Muus was [GEEG p. 137] sensible enough to ignore. The eldest Stampe, Henrik, was a nice little lad with more polished manners than we were otherwise accustomed to among our contemporaries, but probably without any very great talents. The younger, Holger, I can remember only as being at that time a somnolent lethargic lump.

How and why this arrangement was brought to an end I am completely ignorant about, but it seems to me not to have lasted even for the full year. The two courtyard rooms to the left of the staircase were handed back to the landlord, and Mr Muus and his charges disappeared; but what remained was "the Drawing-Room." To this room – which now, it is to be noted, was linked to the rest of the apartment only via the bedroom and "Father's room" – we five children would always gravitate on the Sundays which the Blom children spent out there. That first the lady and then the learned man of the house put up with this traffic highly astonished me at the time and is still a puzzle to me, but I have never noticed a single remark that indicated that we were a nuisance. The beautiful red beds, the great console-table, the spindlebacked sofa etc. had now been moved into the room to the street where, arranged with Fru Grundtvig's good taste, they formed a particularly pleasing (despite the through-way) and extremely decorative room.

Not quite so Grundtvig's room. Here there stood a long broad sofa between the window and the door into the drawing-room, and in front of the sofa a table with a jumble of books, manuscripts, inkhorn, pens, tobacco pipes, half-empty tea and coffee cups. Otherwise, all the walls here too were taken up by bookcases, and had only one ornament ... : a bright, and according to my notion at the time, strange picture, where, through the tobacco smoke, one glimpsed Christ and the Apostles. The picture was most likely an etching after some Old Master.

It was clear enough that Grundtvig's real workplace was in the sofa behind the table, but I have only seldom seen him here. When I and companions, albeit subdued, dashed through the room, Grundtvig was usually standing at the back of the room with one arm on the second stage of the not very high stove, smoking his pipe and staring out in front og him. He was certainly tall and strongly built, but strikingly pale, which was indeed not remarkable since in these years there were no doubt many weeks when his only walk in the open air was the short walk every Sunday afternoon to Frederiks Kirke, where he preached at Evensong. Otherwise he passed the whole day outside mealtimes, and very often the night [GEEG p. 138] too, in the described room, where book-dust and his uniquely strong Dutch tobacco formed an atmosphere like a dense fog. Within his family it seems to me he was always properly dressed, in accordance with his position. In his own room he was in a multicoloured chintz dressing-gown. Of the manifold portraits which exist of him, of which admittedly I have seen not very many, it seems to me that a pen drawing, drawn by [P. C.] Skovgaard in 1845-46, resembles him best. The sweetly-pious and the venerable which is found in [N. W.] Marstrand's picture was certainly not to be found in him in my time. He was a very serious man. In his house, to see him was to obey him. He seldom smiled, and his laughter often had an almost harsh ring which, the worse for the one at whom it was directed, would be joined in by the whole family (called "the laughter chorus" between my brother and me). I do not think I have ever heard him laugh from heartfelt delight at anything comical or joyous. At the same time, let it not be said that he was always moody and unapproachable. At his table he was, if not affable, then certainly a friendly and hospitable host, and if there were no more distinguished persons present he would converse with the children, both with his own and with us, the outsiders. Gradually not only my brother but I too learnt to put up with his seriousness and satire, and certainly we sometimes answered back outspokenly in a way that only our immaturity could excuse. If there was a little sense in the childish talk, then he would willingly join in with us. Fru Grundtvig on the other hand often thought that our remarks were too cheeky and she would sermonize that "Vilhelm (Svend, Marie or Johan) really should not have said that."

Great were the requirements which Grundtvig imposed upon his wife if she was to fulfil his not exactly great but inflexible pretensions for his personal comfort and solicitude for all those people he invited to share in daily life together, for Grundtvig was a very hospitable and charitable man. But it does really seem to me that he paid very little attention to the economic side of things, and left it to his wife to feed the multitude with "five loaves and two small fishes." However, it is certain that he could not have found anybody who was more fitted for this, for apart from being orderly and thrifty in the extreme, she had that beautiful gift of nature that she could lay on a fine spread even with the most frugal materials. It goes without saying that to this end she complied with the three precepts which much later were printed in the front of Madame Mangor's Cookery Book. And all this sprang out of her [GEEG p. 139] loving and, in the best sense, humble disposition, coupled with a grace which she and her sisters must have received as a christening gift. It was clear from the children's stray remarks – they have never talked about it directly – how many difficulties she had in being allowed to undertake the essential cleaning in her husband's room, which for long periods he occupied day and night, not to mention getting him to put on a complete change of clothing at least once a week. From that big, not at all conveniently used apartment I cannot remember the slightest disorder of any kind whatsoever, even though we so to speak looked around us in every room, including attic and boxrooms, almost every time we were there. Fru Grundtvig managed everything without appearing busy and without that injured air of martyrdom by which every domesticity vitiates its reward. Although her sons not infrequently contradicted her, they no doubt loved her much more highly than they did their father. Vilhelm and I also esteemed her very highly, but we all four thought that she spoiled Meta unduly.

Fru Grundtvig's sister, Tante Jane, was undoubtedly just as noble a character and a better and livelier mind. She gave more attention to us children and to the other guests who came; had acquired some education for herself; understood German somewhat and was mad about Schiller whose works she owned, and with whose portrait she claimed, a little affectedly, she could talk. She resembled Fru Grundtvig but was in general on a bigger scale, taller and had a less delicate face. She carried her forty years and unmarried status with much dignity, which indeed she could so much the better do because, as was generally known, five priests had sought her hand in marriage. Occasionally though we found that she rated herself and her sex rather highly. and between ourselves my brother and I called her jestingly "*Frauenwürde*."[7]

Then there were the three children. It gets difficult for me to pin them down for the simple reason that there development over the course of years makes the picture less secure. When I came into contact with them, Johan was a very handsome tall ten-year-old boy, the beauty of whose face was only marred by the fact that he never could or did look straight at people. Svend was less handsome but livelier and with an openness of expression, which later acquired a somewhat too self-important, overbearing expression. Meta was a pretty little five-year-old girl, spoiled by the father who doubtless could see no faults in her, and by the mother, who saw them but indulged them. [GEEG p. 140]

What specially marked these children out from others was, in the case of the two boys not their ignorance but their total lack of schoolroom skills. I will not quite claim that as early as 1832-33 they were reading the Gospel of St John in the original language, but I do know that they practised this sort of thing long before one had sought to impart to them the "little table"[8] or taught them to write copy-book script in a prescribed writing-book. When the abovementioned Mr Muus and the Stampes came into the household, the teaching presumably became more methodical; but this only lasted a short while, and for a long time it was at least the plan that the boys, after having been to prayers with their father in the morning were for a determined period incarcerated behind Grundtvig's room in the above-mentioned drawing-room and there they were admonished to learn as much of the books given to them as they were capable of. Since the father very rarely stood the door ajar and even more rarely went into the drawing-room, and as they were both quick to learn – Svend, moreover, to a high degree – they had a different understanding of the business and practised all kinds of tomfoolery alongside, or more correctly, during the reading. What Johan busied himself with, I cannot remember, but can in contrast remember the small card-like leaves on which Svend wrote riddles and rebuses. Besides his many other gifts he must doubtless have had a talent for drawing. I still see in spirit those small, primitive but extremely confidently sketched figures, which were exhibited on Sundays as the fruit of the day's industry.

Of course, it is really only from Sundays that I know the Grundtvig house. My brother and I would make the long journey from the Sølvgade Barracks out to Frederiks Kirke and would get to the Grundtvig house around their dinnertime, at 4 o'clock. Even though strict holy day observance came in much later,[9] the whole of Copenhagen was very quiet; and once one had crossed the Knippelsbro not even the most orthodox Jew or the most strictly observant priest could imagine a more perfect Sabbath peace. The little church with its disproportionately high tower at the end of the street seemed directly to insist upon this quiet.

When the priest came from his evensong we would eat, and there was very often a couple of guests besides us – Peter Rørdam was regularly one such, over a long period – but no sign of what might be called a banquet. After the hushed grace, the father of the household would distribute, at first to our great astonishment, three small pellets to each member of the family, and I could not help ascribing this to some mystical religious practice or other, until my [GEEG p. 141] inquisitiveness or chance eventually furnished the information that the pellets were white peppercorns which had been recommended to the household – which had earlier been suffering from agues – as a beneficial preventative. If Rørdam or some other such were present, Grundtvig would converse with him and we others would listen very attentively; but if there were no visitor, or only ladies such as Madam Grundtvig and her daughter or a *Jomfru* [unmarried lady of rank] from the Duebrødre Kloster out in Roskilde, then Grundtvig would often address the conversation to the children and would listen very amicably to our childish answers and even to our counter-opinions. One gradually got used to his not altogether pleasant laughter, and I do not recall that he ever became angry on such occasions. After the very plentiful but modest meal, coffee would be drunk in the sitting-room, and if there were, as indicated, one of Grundtvig's own guests, then the interesting conversation would continue there, during the winter in the light of an astral lamp[10] – a modified Corinthian pillar without fluting and with a Doric capital, with lilac-grey lacquer and gilded pilaster strips, for which a new shade could not be found when the first one had been broken, and which had therefore been provided with a green crape shade of Fru Grundtvig's workmanship; and the children would again listen from the corners in the half-darkened room.

These conversations revolved around much that one would not have expected in that house. Thus I remember with certainty that I, on hearing a conversation there between the later Bishop [Peter Christian] Kierkegaard and Grundtvig, learned that "un lion" was the Parisians' name for a dandy and "un rat" was a wretched youngster who was trained to dance in the great opera.. Only one thing disturbed for me the agreeableness of these hours, and that was the horrible tobacco smoke. What kind of plant could it have been that Grundtvig burned in his pipe? I have otherwise never been troubled by such a thing, but this continually caused me coughing fits.

This was during the winter. In the summer even the most famous speakers we waved goodbye and went to *Pladsen* [the Square] whose extensive territory we had at our complete disposal on a Sunday afternoon. How many stacks of timber were climbed, and how one showed one's skill at walking along the wharf-edges and now and again falling into the water it would become too long-winded to describe. It was really only the boys who practised foolhardy tricks, and even then very moderately. Svend was the most daring, and we two girls were no doubt two timorous wretches; but the hours [GEEG p. 142] passed enjoyably by in the fresh air.

Sometimes for a change we would go over to the courtyard and play hide-and-seek in the warehouse lofts. O joy! when we found a disgusting dried-up prune in a barrel or an almond in a box, however bitter. If there were snow in the winter we would also go sledging in the big courtyard, in which I had the advantage over Meta's timidity which forbade her to sit on the sledge which the boys were pulling. Most of the time, the boys and I ganged up against Meta who the rest of us found spoilt and suspected of telling tales. But sometimes the roles were otherwise apportioned. Thus I remember one summer's day Vilhelm and I found the two brothers very incensed against the sister whom, as soon as none of the adults could observe it, whispering or aloud, they regaled with these ugly words: "Down with the beast!" Vilhelm at once joined in their pact but when I saw that it was really hurting Meta I allied myself with her. As we could not be left in peace anywhere, we took refuge up in the attic where old furniture and old toys gave us enough material for our amusement. But when we incautiously went near the window there at once rang out a three-voiced "Down with the beast!" from far down in the bottom of the courtyard, with a persistence which might have been worthy of a better cause. I can well remember that I saw the Grundtvigs quarrel and fight among themselves but never that there was any real animosity between the Christianhavners and those from out of the far East.[11] On the other hand, that foul spirit, Boredom, could set in now and again, when of an evening we sat in the big dining room and my father allowed himself to be detained far too long by the ladies, before he would set off home with us. Then discussion would get going about every possible thing between heaven and earth, although mostly about that wisdom each believed himself brought up with. Svend composed himself in a true Grundtvigian posture with arms crossed, and asserted that nothing would come of "you lot," nothing would come out of such a hothouse-upbringing. "Don't you think," asked Vilhelm "that better fruit will come out of the hothouse?" Or else the two families' pronunciation of words would also come under discussion: we knew no better way of defending the fact that we pronounced the very ordinary word '*kartofler*' [potatoes] as '*kartufler*' than by letting them know that they said '*undt*' instead of '*ondt*' [bad] and 'olle' for 'olie' [oil]. But also we found endlessly much to criticise in each others' sentence-structure. We said that the Grundtvigs talked "sloppily" and they said we talked "pedantically."

"I will tell you a myth" [**GEEG p. 143**] Svend began. "When the gods created the world out of the giant Ymer's body, it was such a lucky thing that within his brain, from which they formed the clouds, they found a dictionary and a grammar book. Wasn't that good? Because previously even the high gods had not been able to speak purely!" I still see Svend's triumphant expression at this fancy, and we allowed him to have the last word.

If I had to characterise in a few words these children's relationship with each other, then I should say that Johan represented common sense, Svend poetic enthusiasm and Vilhelm a reflective criticism – expressions which no doubt sound very odd about young people of whom the eldest was then not yet sixteen years, the next fourteen years and the youngest not twelve years old. But then they were not like others of their age. As far as I myself am concerned, I am afraid that my role was like that of Momus in the old comedy. I would eagerly find out the weak point and would laugh merrily, more than was proper.

1.   The house and church (now renamed Christians Kirke) are still there, though not 'Pladsen'.

2.   Jacob Holm, founder of the firm Jacob Holm & Sønner, had children from three marriages – as Grundtvig also eventually did.

3.   A diagonally-set corner room, with (only) one window in the diagonal wall.

4. Marie Blom uses the word *Damerne*, then notes in parenthesis ('Fruentimmerne' kaldtes de *altid* dengang [At that time they were *always* called the *Fruentimmer*]) that a more archaic term was at that time regularly used. The women were Grundtvig's wife Elisabeth (Lise) and her unmarried sister, Jane Blicher, known to family and friends of the family as Aunt Jane.

5. Hair *à la Titus* was worn short and curled.

6. One sister of Grundtvig's wife Elisabeth (born Blicher), Anna Pouline (1785-1880), was married to Christian Schmidt; another, Bodil Marie Elisabeth, was married to Pastor Poul Egede Glahn (1778-1846). The fourth Blicher sister was Jane who was unmarried; and there were two brothers.

7. The German word meaning 'womanly dignity' is, as applied to Aunt Jane, a jocular title (Her Worshipful Ladyship?) by which the children are also perhaps mocking the ponderous ideas and idiom of the German-speaking households in Christianshavn.

8. Multiplication tables from 2 to 10.

9. By an order of 26 March 1845 concerning the mandatory observance of Sundays and holy days, Christian VIII required that all non-essential labour and all entertainments should cease from the morning onwards, and especially during the time that divine services are held, until four in the afternoon.

10. Lamp with a ring-formed oil-container, so that only a small shadow was cast downwards.

11. Marie Blom's jocular reference to her own home territory in the eastern quarter of the walled city.

81. *Lavra Grundtvig: from her reminiscences published in H. P. B. Barfod's* Minder fra gamle grundtvigske Hjem *[Memories from old Grundtvigian homes], I (1921), pp. 44-50; GEEG Stk. 22, pp. 143-148.*

"*To work and to be obedient.* This Svend and Johan learned in their father's school, whatever else could be said about it." Lavra Grundtvig (1837-91), widow of Grundtvig's second son, Professor Svend Hersleb Grundtvig (1824-83), puts together, from Svend's reminiscences and other reliable information, an account of the pedagogic principles which Grundtvig applied to the early education, at home, of his own children. On Barfod and his *Minder* see Index entry **Barfod, Hans Peter Gote Birkedal.**

⟽⟾

According to Grundtvig's way of thinking, children belong at home. *Teaching* should tie itself in with the domestic and the familiar. Children should have command of *the mother-tongue* [*Modersmålet*] before they are introduced to the foreign. The supremacy which the foreign has in the schools, at the cost of the mother-tongue, was in his eyes *an unnatural phenomenon* which he fought to the utmost.

Patriotic enlightenment in the mother-tongue [*En fædrelandsk Oplysning på Modersmålet*] was the target he strove after.

It was not his intention that children should learn nothing. He thought, quite to the contrary, that children ought to learn *a lot*, as long as the learning was organised for them in such a way that they could experience enjoyment of it. The only thing that mattered was to give children nothing but what was suited to their age, so that they could accept it with relish. "Even the best children become naughty when they are bored" he always said. Boredom was in his eyes the root of all evil. In contrast to the school of that time he wanted to protect the childhood state, a healthy and natural development of the child's abilities and spiritual life. It therefore lay close to his heart to free his children from "boy-scholarliness" [*Drengevidenskabelighed*] as he called the school's attempt to pack into the childhood years all that [GEEG p. 144] knowledge which a person later on in life could have use for: "Only the bud, fresh, green, in early Spring, / the flowers' profusion in the warmth of Summer."[1] Grundtvig wanted to show himself and the world that knowledge of books and true education and competence could be achieved without following the beaten track through school with its stultification and examination mentality. In the hope that he would succeed, he took it upon himself to be his sons' tutor.

So how did Grundtvig fare as a practical educationist? Was he a good teacher?

The majority would no doubt answer negatively to this question, and probably be right. Whoever knew him must surely say that *it was not his way* to fall in with others' way of thinking. To place himself on a level with the child surely did not come naturally to him, however much he, according to his theory, wanted to do it. To carry out in practice, on a small scale, his own great poetic thoughts probably lay outside his proper mission. Only love for his children and for what was to him a matter of both heart and conscience forced him to take upon himself this onerous work. But as a teacher too, *he was his own man.*

His powerful personality, filled with ideas, characterised by a high seriousness, had to have an enthralling effect upon Svend's kindred nature, an educative and disciplining effect upon his receptive mind. The father's enormous assiduousness and industry demanded assiduousness of the sons. The great power of the example influenced them immediately in this direction. The question was not whether they felt like doing something, only whether what they were reading was something they could be interested in and profit from.

Many of Grundtvig's friends and disciples who felt themselves in their hearts attracted by his poetic view of the teaching of children have subsequently, at his word, broken with "the black school" [*den sorte Skole*] and tried to lay down this way of thinking of his as the basis of their children's teaching in a free school [*Friskole*] or in the home. But though the force of truth which lay in Grundtvig's educational thinking may undeniably have helped *indirectly* to bring more light and life into the school he so hated, yet it is striking that the *direct* endeavours which were made by his friends to bring his ideas into reality have often born poor and unripe fruits. The reason for this may well be that the disciples have indeed followed in the steps of the master in so far as it was a matter of freeing their children from the pressure and coercion of the school and in their [GEEG p. 145] endeavours to make the teaching as enjoyable as possible for their children, whereas they have not striven in the same degree to teach their children two things: *to work and to be obedient. This* Svend and Johan learned in their father's school, whatever else could be said about it.

To give a detailed description of the teaching which Grundtvig gave his sons, after the space of more than half a century, would not now be possible without guesswork. In the following, therefore, will be found only what could be gathered from reliable information in supplementation of Svend's oral communications of his schoolday reminiscences.

Svend doubtless made great haste to get through his ABC with his mother, in order to get to read with his father together with his big brother. That as early as Spring 1829 he had begun his schooling with his father can in fact be seen from a letter to Peter Fenger in which Grundtvig writes that he hopes to get Ludvig Christian Müller to read with the boys while he himself was in England that summer, "sufficiently, that they should not forget what I have taught them."[2] Svend was then only in his fifth year, so it was in good time that Grundtvig had his sons start their home schooling.

The teaching took place in the father's study and would begin with a morning prayer. Grundtvig would recite the Creed, say the Lord's Prayer and after that read a piece of the Old or New Testament. As the boys grew bigger, he also let them take part in this reading aloud. They learned a number of hymns by heart but there was no hymn-singing. There was probably not much of this in general at that time, even in Christian homes; and anyway musical aptitude was but weak within the Grundtvig family.

As little as the teaching followed a previously determined timetable, as little did it begin or end at a precise time. It had to adjust itself somewhat to the priest's time and convenience, but even so it proceeded on the whole fairly steadily and regularly, and usually commenced early in the morning.

Just as the teaching on the whole had a predominantly historical character, so also it was especially through the oral recounting of Bible history that the boys received their religious teaching. When the priest, there in that quiet room, with true spirituality and the warmth of belief, in all [GEEG p. 146] simplicity told his children the holy saga, it must surely have been able to enthral the soul of a child and make a deep and unforgettable impression.

To what had been recounted were linked biblical-historical hymns which were in part learnt by heart according to [L. C.] Hagen's collection;[3] and in Grundtvig's little *Bibelkrønike*[4] they had a brief epitome of what had been orally recounted to them.

History and geography were read as one. Grundtvig began by teaching them to recognise on the map: first, all the historical lands around the Mediterranean, as the arena for the history of the ancient world; and thereafter the lands around the Baltic as the places where the north-dwellers and especially the Danes had their world.

Once they had made themselves thoroughly at home in these regions, then he recounted quite thoroughly to them the principal events in the historical life which had unfolded there, whereas the lesser events with the many dates and names were only cursorily or not at all touched upon.

How close this lay to Grundtvig's heart, and to what great effort he put himself in order to give a vivid presentation of history, suited to the child's need, can be seen, among the rest, from the preface to *Krønikerim* where he gives a very interesting presentation of this method of his.

It was of course also to supply the presumed want of suitable reading-books to support oral tuition that at that time – in the course of 1829 – published *Krønikerim* as well as *Kort Udsigt over Verdenskrøniken*[5] and the historical *Udsigtstavle* [Tabular prospect] which he called *Tidens Strøm* [The stream, or river, of time].

The objective of the rhyming chronicles – in a pleasurable way to fix in the memory what was communicated orally – was, for Svend's part, completely achieved. He learned them by heart with great enjoyment, and those of them which as a boy he had found particularly amusing and beautiful he still knew by heart in his old age.[6] Svend was also very fond of *Tidens Strøm*; he had the impression even from his boyhood that it fulfilled its purpose remarkably well: to make graphic the course of historical evolution through the ages.

Of foreign languages they learned only one, namely Greek. Herodotus was read, and Homer's *Odyssey* and *Iliad*. Grundtvig would read it to them and have them read it after him in Greek and would then very meticulously translate for them into Danish what had been read. There was as yet no question of any grammatical explanation. Grammar was and remained for them, as children, a [GEEG p. 147] complete *terra incognita*. But what, after mature reflection, he presented to them in this way as, in his opinion, the best translation, he also expected to get back verbatim from the boys; and if they blundered when they were to present their reading, then Grundtvig would get angry and give the sinner one on the ear – which especially when it was given with the back of the right hand to the one who sat to the right of him could come with such force that it sometimes resulted in tears. They also read *Æsop's Fables* and these they had to translate in writing, Johan in prose but Svend in verse. Svend early on showed a facility for making verse which the father much encouraged. There still exist a couple of booklets from 1837 in which these rhymed translations of *Æsop's Fables* are neatly copied out and furnished with notes and indices.

Schooltime was not however restricted to the shorter or longer period in which Grundtvig himself read to or talked with the boys, but when this was over they took their places at their own table in the drawing-room, where for a certain number of hours they then had to sit quietly and read. They were not given anything specific to do but only a general injunction to read as far as they could get in the given time. So there they would read onwards in Saxo and Snorri's *Heimskringla*, from which they used daily to read something aloud for their father; and there the above-mentioned text-books published by their father would be read through and the verses learnt by heart.

Since the drawing-room was reached via the father's room, to which the door would stand ajar, the boys were of course compelled to stay on the spot and to remain quiet for the fixed period. Otherwise they were left completely to themselves. It was only seldom that the father, standing in the door, would throw a cursory glance in to them. It could happen that these quiet reading hours could seem a little wearisome to both Svend and Johan, and they could long to escape to their games in the open. Johan says that he was often quite dreadfully bored. Svend better understood how to hold boredom – that foe so intensely feared by Grundtvig – at bay. If he grew tired of reading, he would cheat by writing verses or would devise riddles or draw rebuses, in which he was very talented. These productions were kept in the table drawer until Sunday when Vilhelm and Marie Blom came. Then they were enjoyed together, and in the greatest secrecy, in a lumber-room or in one of the warehouse lofts, and they were usually much admired.

Occasionally Grundtvig got a little help towards the boys' tuition [GEEG p. 148] from one or another of the younger theologians who at that time belonged among his regular followers in the church, and who also personally attached themselves to him and visited him in his home, where they always met with the most friendly reception. Thus L. C. Hagen was for a time tutor in writing, and Christian Sigfred Ley did sums with them and also talked to them about this and that. Ludvig Christian Müller was also their teacher for a time, especially during Grundtvig's journeys to England.

1. The quotation is from a verse in Grundtvig's *Aabent Brev til mine Børn* [Open Letter to my Children], published 1841 in Frederik Barfod's periodical *Brage og Idun*: *Kun Spiren frisk og grøn i tidlig Vaar / Og Blomsterfloret i den varme Sommer, / Da Modenhed imøde Planten gaar / og fryder med sin Frugt, naar Høsten kommer!* [Only the bud, fresh, green, in early Spring, / the flowers' profusion in the warmth of Summer: /then to maturity the plant will grow / and by its fruits delight, when Autumn comes]. The sense of the compact verse is: If only

the freshness of childhood and blossoming of youth are left to flourish unspoilt by artificial cultivation (for example by Latin School education) then the individual will safely mature into one who yields rich returns to the common good.

2. The arrangement was indeed made and Grundtvig's letters home from England (summers of 1829-31) often ask for reports and exhort the boys to apply themselves assiduously to their studies and their mother to see that the arrangement is working properly.

3. *Historiske Psalmer og Riim til Børne-Lærdom* [Historical hymns and verses for children's learning] (1832). Hagen was for a time tutor in the Grundtvig household, and the collection of hymns published under his name was in fact much shaped by Grundtvig's involvement with composition and compilation – as confirmed in item 84.

4. Refers to first edition of Grundtvig's *En liden Bibelkrønike* [A small Bible-history]. Grundtvig issued a revised edition in 1828.

5. The correct title of the work mentioned is *Historisk Børnelærdom* [Historical instruction for children] (1829). The text was an excerpt from the preface to his *Krønikerim* [Rhyming Chronicle] (1829).

6. Svend Grundtvig's own testimony to his affection for this work from earliest childhood onwards is found in a postscript to his 1875 edition of his father's *Krønikerim*.

82. Christian Sigfred Ley: Extracts from his diaries, published by Frederik Nygaard in Danskeren VII (1892), pp. 44-45; not in GEEG.

Frederik Nygaard's *Dagbogsoptegnelser af Sigfred Ley om Grundtvig, Baggesen, Martensen m. fl.* [Sigfred Ley's diary entries concerning Grundtvig, Baggesen, Martensen and others] appeared in *Danskeren. Tidsskrift for Land og By* [The Dane. A periodical for country and town], ed. F. Jungersen, F. Nygaard and L. Schrøder, and contributed to the increasing quantity of biographical material concerning Grundtvig published in the decades following his death as posterity set about putting into perspective a life which was seen to have helped shape (for better or for worse, according to standpoint) the nation which was now passing through the close of the turbulent nineteenth century. The first substantial biography, *Biskop N. F. S. Grundtvigs Levnetsløb udførligt fortalt fra 1839* [Bp NFSG's Life recounted in fullest detail from 1839], in two volumes, had by this time already been published by H. Brun in 1882. as had Frederik Rönning's *Hundrede Aar. Et Mindeskrift i Anledning af Hundredaarsdagen for Nic. Fred. Sev. Grundtvigs Fødsel* [One hundred years. A commemorative volume in connection with the hundredth anniversary of the birth of NFSG] (1883). The monumental eight-part biography by Rönning still lay in the future. Now, at the beginning of the twenty-first century a new comprehensive biography of Grundtvig is a major *desideratum* in the Danish and European cultural sphere.

Here, the 25-year-old Ley, in the privacy of his diary (which nevertheless he envisages being read one day by a friendly eye), reveals something of the emotional religiosity which was often focussed by his followers upon Grundtvig the man. Friends commented upon Grundtvig's brusqueness (in contrast to the sincere affection his written words could reveal) towards such emotionally volatile disciples as Poul Dons, and here Ley evidently observes a similar discrepancy; but the extract may also (unintentionally) hint at Grundtvig's good sense in handling with restraint the enthusiasm his charisma generated in the young men and women who gathered round him. Søren Kierkegaard mentions Ley as a specialist in the kind of overblown rhetoric which (in Kierkegaard's view) characterised Grundtvig's circle.

Oh could I but portray Grundtvig in his house, the dear Grundtvig. He is not as tender as folk mostly are, oh but yet he is loving, this *Gothe*[1] who has endeared his way into Denmark's love. And then his wife, his Elise, with the sharp but yet sweet eyes (she sometimes punishes the children with a smack; Grundtvig certainly never does this, or almost never); and then Johan with eyes full of the joys of life and Svend with his father Grundtvig's tear-cheeks[2] and then the pretty, lively Meta and *Frøken* [Jane] Blicher (she too has her proper home in the house). Oh shame upon me that I cannot write anything really adequate. Yet perhaps a friend in the field will see what I have written and feel about it (my pen can manage so little and especially now this evening least of all), and will extend the picture. Spirit will be needed for this, but then may God never let his good holy spirit turn away from Denmark. Oh in Denmark good memories are dear and may God let it always be so. Grundtvig, Svend, Johan, Muus, Ludvig Müller, Lindberg (why do I sigh?),[3] Laurent, Hagen, Jensen, Hass, dear teacher Rudelbach (you are in Germany)[4] […] February 1832. Chr. Sigfr. Ley.

1. The name generally signified a member of the *Gothones*, the Germanic tribe (Ostrogoths and Visigoths) involved in overrunning the Roman Empire, but in Ley's day could be used for inhabitants of Götaland (Sweden), as in the official title of the kings of Denmark (*Venders og Gothers konge* [King of the Wends and Goths]) and thus (poetically, with conscious allusion to heroic Nordic antiquity, as here) for a *Nordbo* [North-dweller, Northerner, Scandinavian] in general.

2. One may guess that Ley's unusual word *tårekinder* (literally 'tear-cheeks') – in the somewhat *sværmerisk* (emotional-devotional) spirit of the passage – alludes to Grundtvig's strong cheekbones over which tears might conspicuously flow when the preacher was moved to weeping (as was sometimes reported of Grundtvig).

3. Presumably Ley alludes to his anxiety that Lindberg, in his determination to press ahead with unlawful religious assemblies at his home, risked not only prosecution by the authorities but a split with Grundtvig: "Lindberg […] otherwise one with Grundtvig in matters of importance, here went directly against his views and serious admonition" (Fr. Nygaard). In the end, however, Grundtvig supported Lindberg and the outcome was Grundtvig's appointment as preacher at Frederiks Kirke where in effect a 'free' congregation could gather, at least for preaching and prayer, whilst remaining within the state church.

4. Svend Grundtvig, Johan Grundtvig, C. A. H. Muus, L. C. Müller, J. C. Lindberg, L. C. Hagen, Rasmus Jensen (probably), L. D. Hass, A. G. Rudelbach.

83. Christian Sigfred Ley: Extracts from his diaries, published by Frederik Nygaard in Danskeren VII (1892), pp. 45-51; GEEG Stk. 23, pp. 148-52.

Ley's somewhat breathless reports to his diary, punctuated with alternately fearful and pious exclamations, convey some of the drama surrounding J. C. Lindberg's confrontation with the authorities over the right to hold religious devotional gatherings in his home. An initial impetus had been the desire of Grundtvig (recently returned from his third visit to England over the summer of 1831) and his would-be congregation of supporters to secure a pulpit of his own – a desire which the ecclesiastical authorities so far showed no sign of intending to gratify – but an issue of major principle was also coming into sharp focus as a consequence: the shackles imposed upon freedom of conscience by laws tying individuals to their own parish church. When Lorenz Siemonsen, priest serving a dwindling congregation in Frederiks Kirke next door to Grundtvig's home in Strandgade, Christianshavn, indicated his willingness to share with Grundtvig the pastoral care of a free Danish-German congregation there, a solution seemed to be to hand. However, the authorities continued to be stubborn. Grundtvig, initially cautious about joining Lindberg's confrontational gatherings (which the police were known to be observing), but exasperated and insulted by the face-to-face intransigence of both secular and ecclesiastical authorities, dramatically brought the conflict to crisis point by himself resolving to address one of the gatherings. Ley tells the story.

Today [Sunday 12 February 1832] my aunt Ovene came home from Lindberg's meeting and reported that Grundtvig had spoken there for half an hour when Siemonsen's sermon was over.[1] It looked as though Siemonsen was much astonished when Grundtvig patted him on the shoulder and said: "Now let me say a couple of words!" He was extremely moved, with tears in his eyes. Today was the first time that Grundtvig was there at the meeting. I dare say he was with [P. C.] Stemann yesterday and discussed with him why the Chancellery has refused in the matter of the church, so this has no doubt prompted him to go to the meeting today. God in heaven help us all. I am glad – a little fearful but for the most part glad – that this has happened.

6th Sunday after Epiphany [12 February 1832]: "It is good to be here," Grundtvig began today. I have the foregoing from [L. D.] Hass and Ovene. Now Jensen tells me that Hansen had told him that on Saturday Grundtvig talked for half an hour with Stemann, who had ended: "this is nothing and will come to nothing." Whereupon Grundtvig parted from him with these words: "Oh yes, this both is something and shall come to something!" God in heaven grant that it may come to something good in his eyes.

13th February 1832: The meetings at Rolighed did not please Stemann; but as they were under supervision (by Pastor Rothe) they were left alone. Grundtvig said Yes, he would rather not have set foot out there: but now… Grundtvig also talked to him about the judgment of posterity. Ah! posterity, [GEEG p. 149] what is that? said Stemann; the time we live in, that is what concerns us. Grundtvig begged his pardon: he was an historian. (This Ludvig Gøricke told me, from Siemonsen). I then talked with Grundtvig this evening. He had done only that which he could not leave undone. He is not willing to preach in a church – he feels himself too divorced from the State Church for that – and he also wishes that other people shall see this. He is not thinking immediately of a separation of the sacraments from the State Church. He does not believe that Christians can at the moment bear the consequences. This would be to do God shame, he says. But that enlightenment which he can deliver by the spoken word he will not withhold. We shall desist from all prejudgments, he said; one must be glad if one knows what one has to do for the present moment. God will look after the future.

Grundtvig looked anxious, but yet amiable. O God, what shall become of this? Grundtvig will carry on preaching at the meetings. O, the Father of our Lord Jesus Christ will surely enough bring all things to the best, he, the dear, ever-gracious God. May he give succour through his good Holy Spirit, amen!

My father talked this evening with student [P. C.] Pedersen. He was somewhat shocked, and it also shocked my father a bit. He says he will not go to the meetings.

O Father, be near us with your Holy Spirit, as we pray in the Lord's Prayer.

13th February 1832

On Sunday [19th February] Grundtvig preached at Rolighed. [H. A.] Laurent and Hanne and some of the others were there. I also went out there at 10.30 but then there were already just as many streaming back as heading out there. It was of course a frightful heat and crush to be sitting out there. Grundtvig said that he would rather, much rather, have met with them before the altar than in this place, but really this was the Lord's will. It was actually Septuagesima Sunday.[2] And he said that the congregation must not be offended at his strange conduct. Indeed it might well appear odd, he said, that he should come at the third hour and work a little, and go away again, and come back a little at the sixth, then at the ninth, and now again at the eleventh. Just as quietly as he had last time gone from his work, because it was the Lord's will, just as surely did he now go to it again, because the Lord had called him. And maybe he would soon go from it again, when the Lord let him know it was for the [GEEG p. 150] best. It is required of servants that they be faithful. (Grundtvig was really confident in his cause, that it is the Lord who has bidden him speak this time. I also noted this the last time I talked with him). He believed, incidentally, that this really was the eleventh hour. "The sound of the grinding is low."[3] Now the world would vilify him because he had begun to speak at Lindberg's meetings; but how should that touch him, who from his youth upwards was accustomed to bear the vilification of the world?

Who has rejected this application concerning the church? he also asked. It is He up above. Incidentally, the Danish people would surely unanimously grant us our request, directly it became as obviously about everyone as about him; that we made the application solely for salvation's sake; and that we gladly wish for all the same freedom which we ourselves have desired.[4]

Grundtvig had no desire to be a martyr; of his nature, he had so much against it, nor did he feel he could become properly qualified for it. Nor was it good for the people and the land where martyrs were created.[5] Certainly he had an appreciation of the glorious crown of martyrdom. Unwarranted martyrs, we can get plenty of those.

26 February 1832

Now that the police have had [C. C.] Harmsen's Amager-meetings stopped, they fancied that they have won the game. The bishop[6] has sent a request to the police to prevent the others as well. Siemonsen, summoned to Bræstrup,[7] has promised to desist until he gets a request for permission handed in to the Chancellery and a reply to it. This evening there was also a police officer standing outside his door and chasing people home. Lindberg was also summoned, but he put Bræstrup in his place and went from him to the bishop, who said ten times over that he was a fanatic [en sværmer], and admitted that it was he who had sent the request to the police. What kind of bishop are you? Lindberg then said.

Should you not have come out and preached to those who were allegedly on the wrong path, rather than use police batons? *No, he himself stuck to the law!* Yes, I have that on my side too, said Lindberg. *Yes, you are a fanatic* [en sværmer], *etc.* This went on for two hours. Lindberg threatened and begged, and finally promised the bishop that he would go to the King and procure permission. To Bræstrup Lindberg also said that he would put a stop to his meetings when it was properly permitted Grundtvig to preach, not otherwise. *No,* said Bræstrup, *it had to be prevented altogether.* Yes, I will hold meetings in my house and it will mean [GEEG p. 151] a lawsuit if you do anything against it. *No, he did not want to have a lawsuit with Lindberg. And there had also been preparations made to prevent it.* Yes, Lindberg would certainly show him that he let himself be judged only by the law of the land. And, as said, Bræstrup spoke conciliatory words and promised that he would talk with the bishop. (After Hass, who had it from Lindberg himself).

Whilst Lindberg – doubtlessly without Grundtvig knowing – did battle with the law, Grundtvig proceeds calmly onwards and looks neither to right nor left: for the Lord has called him. And then he was summoned. He asked Bræstrup whether he had done anything wrong, since he had to go to the police. Yes, it was the rumour about these meetings. Yes, rumours! wait until you have something to make a charge over! Incidentally, it is true I want to hold a meeting, and that is that. In no way shall I defer it, said Grundtvig to Ferdinand Fenger. (After Laurent and Fenger, who had it from Grundtvig himself).

Copenhagen, 1 March 1832

28 January: Petition for a free congregation rejected by a resolution of the Chancellery.

12 February: Grundtvig at Rolighed for the first time (Siemonsen preached; Grundtvig afterwards spoke for half an hour).

19 February: Grundtvig preached at Rolighed; Harmsen on Amager for the first time.[8]

Between 19th and 26th February: The police interrupt the meetings on Amager (Pastor Brun, *amtsforvalter* [District Revenue Officer] Frydensberg).[9]

26 February: Siemonsen preaches at Rolighed.

27 and 28 [February]: Siemonsen was three times, and Grundtvig twice, summoned before Bræstrup, without Lindberg getting to know anything about it.

29th [February]: Lindberg was before Bræstrup and before the bishop. He expected to be arrested.

1 March: The King sat in the Supreme Court and the Order in Council was drawn up.

2 March, 1.45 in the afternoon: the licence was with Stemann for signature. At the same time I got to know of the matter. At six o'clock I talked with [GEEG p. 152] Lindberg at [J. F.]

Milo's and went with him to the police office where he received the resolution.

3 March, morning, it is now, as I write this.

Between the 12th and the 19th [February]: Lindberg was in Roskilde and talked with the farmers [*bønder*].

⌒

Yesterday afternoon, when I came to Grundtvig's and greeted his wife, he opened his door and gave me his hand and drew me into his embrace. He was overjoyed.

"It is a blessing, it is wonderful, that after all I still get to see happiness in my grey hairs," he said.

He recounted the matter to me thus: On 28 February he was with the bishop. If Pastor Grundtvig wanted to be parish priest in Vor Frelsers Kirke then there would be nothing in the way of it; but he could not give his consent to the holding of such meetings. He had nothing against the petition in its substance but in terms of its form it was a slur upon the clergy. However, in the end Grundtvig was so far successful that the bishop promised to request the King for permission for meetings under the name of prayer-times. He could call them what he liked [replied Grundtvig]. So on the 28th the bishop also submitted his proposal and recommendation, as is seen from the licence, where there expressly appears the 28th. That is, Lindberg's law-sermon[10] [*lov-prædiken*] on the 29th can in no way have influenced the whole thing, but Grundtvig readily believes that it can have hastened it.

The fact that it was Frederiks Kirke we received, both Grundtvig and Lindberg attribute, after God, to our kindly King.

Today he preached there for the first time. It is Quinquagesima Sunday.[11] He spoke of the importance of baptism, of his hope and his joy and the prophetic words which had found life within him: "For Zion's sake I will not hold my peace, and for Jerusalem's sake I will not rest, until the righteousness thereof go forth as a brightness, and the salvation thereof as a lamp that burneth."[12] Finally, he also praised the gracious magnanimity of Frederik VI. The church was full to bursting, but for that very reason the hymns resounded like cottonwool, for the church is poorly built.

But our Father in heaven is rich in mercy and grace. Praised be he, the God of my salvation!

Copenhagen, 4 March 1832.

1. Footnote by Ley's editor Frederik Nygaard: "As Grundtvig had promised J. K. Lindberg to speak at his meeting at the '*kalkbrænderi*', Lindberg asked whether he should not send a cab for Grundtvig's wife Elise and her sister. But Grundtvig answered: The women will probably rather not. F. N."

2. Septuagesima Sunday is the ninth Sunday before Easter and the gospel text of the day is Matthew 20:1-16 concerning the workers in the vineyard whom the lord hires at the various hours of the day up to the eleventh hour. Preaching at Rolighed, Grundtvig makes use of the parable with reference to his own employment in the Lord's vineyard, that is in his preaching ministry. He believed, as Ley notes, that this really was the eleventh hour, and that he had been summoned to this work by the Lord. Similarly, his references to martyrdom echo the Epistle of the day (Paul's First Letter to the Corinthians 9:24-27).

3. *Røsten i møllen bliver svag.* This appears to be a reference to Ecclesiastes 12:4 (King James Bible – the sound of the grinding is low; Christian VI Bible – *naar Røsten i Møllen bliver lav*), which is also echoed in Jeremiah 25:10 (King James Bible: Moreover I will take from them the voice of mirth, and the voice of gladness, the voice of the bridegroom, and the voice of the bride, the sound of the millstones, and the light of the candle; Christian VI Bible – *og jeg vil lade borte fra dem Fryds Røst, [...] Møllers Røst*), and in Revelation 18:22 (King James Bible – the sound of a millstone shall be heard no more at all in thee; Christian VI Bible – *og Møllens Lyd ikke høres i dig mere*). All three metaphorically worded biblical sources treat of the eleventh hour. Ecclesiastes warns of personal decline in old age; Jeremiah prophesies the enslavement of Judah to Babylon, and Revelation apocalyptically warns of the violent overthrow of the great city of Babylon itself. All would fit with the dramatised perception Grundtvig, Ley and other participants had of the crisis that was unfolding in Copenhagen.

4. The preceding passage suffers a little from Ley's hectic style. Grundtvig reiterates his conviction that events, whether seemingly favourable or unfavourable, express the will of God; it must be within God's purposes that the authorities have rejected the application for permission allowing Grundtvig to take over Frederiks Kirke. As far as the Danish people as a whole are concerned, they would wholeheartedly support such a new departure in church practice once they clearly understood that the application was not exclusively for Grundtvig's own advancement but in the general interest: the applicants are motivated solely by genuine religious convictions and they desire that the advantage they seek should be extended to all.

5. Perhaps Grundtvig still had in mind the admonitions of Revelation (18:24). There, one justification declared for the violent overthrow of the great city Babylon is that she has martyred her prophets and saints (King James Bible: "And in her was found the blood of prophets, and of saints").

6. Bishop of Sjælland Peter Erasmus Müller (1776-1834).

7. Christian Jacob Cosmus Bræstrup (1789-1870), Chief of Police, Copenhagen, and Minister of Justice.

8. Ley's intended meaning is fairly certainly that Harmsen *preached* on Amager for the first time that Sunday. Ley will not have been unaware that on the previous Sunday, 12 February, Harmsen had alarmed the authorities and the police by heading a throng of a hundred supporters from Copenhagen and Christianshavn to join an unlawful religious assembly on Amager. There was real drama in the steady escalation, here chronicled by Ley, of the stand-off between the religious revivalists on the one side and the authorities of church and state on the other.

9. If this 'Pastor Brun' is Carl Bruun (1805-83), appointed curate at Taarnby on Amager in 1832 upon the Bishop's recommendation of him as a steady hand, his presence at the police dispersal of the assembly may be as a representative of the authorities rather than as a supporter of the organisers. Carl Bruun was later appointed *provst* [rural dean] for Hammer-Tyberg in south Sjælland where he was entrusted by Bishop Martensen with duties of visitations to parishes. If 'Pastor Brun' is at the assembly to represent the authorities, then probably so too is the royal official '*amtsforvalter* Frydensberg' who may be the 'Skifteforvalteren paa Kongens Gods Justitsraad og Amtsforvalter Frydensberg' whose name appears in official documents relating to courts of probate on the King's estate [*Kongens Gods*] on Amager over this period.

10. The term *lovprædiken* 'law-sermon' or 'preaching the law' has a specialised meaning in theological discussion, alluding to the preaching of a false gospel, especially one which belonged in substance or spirit to the age of the Law such as Paul reproved the backsliding Galatians for entertaining (Galatians 1:6) and such as Luther too condemned and Lutherans were alert in guarding against; but in more popular usage it acquired the sense of 'laying down the law' or sermonising in a pontificating manner about any subject. Since Lindberg's declared and confident stance was that he would let himself be judged only by the law of the land.(*GEEG* p. 151), and he was now actually arguing the law (canon and secular) with the custodians of the law (Bishop Müller and Chief of Police Bræstrup), Ley's use of the term *lovprædiken* for Lindberg's peroration has multiple and ironical resonances.

11. The seventh Sunday before Easter, and the Sunday preceding the start of Lent.

12. Isaiah 62:1.

Evensong preacher at Frederiks Kirke 1832-1839

84. Christian Sigfred Ley: Extracts from his diaries, published by
Frederik Nygaard in Danskeren IX (1893), p. 10; GEEG Stk. 24, p. 153.

The creative ability to "sit down in this way and dictate lovely new verses from out of one's head" remained with Grundtvig to his life's end, as witness Trier's anecdote in item 126. On Laurits Christian Hagen (1808-80) and his published collection *Historiske Salmer og Riim til Børne-Lærdom* (1832), see endnotes to item 81 and Index entry for **Hagen,** Laurits Christian.

[**GEEG p. 153**] [L. C.] Hagen is getting real satisfaction out of visiting Grundtvig at this time [September 1832]. He says which hymns he wants to have altered. Then Grundtvig sits himself down in a corner of the sofa and composes and Hagen writes it down. While Hagen is away, then Grundtvig also produces new hymns or makes changes to the old ones. It is indeed remarkable that one can sit down in this way and dictate lovely new verses from out of one's head. Recently, [Lorenz] Siemonsen criticised Grundtvig because he altered the old hymns. Grundtvig defended this a little, but said in the end: "Well, Siemonsen, it is all one – for when someone comes to me and bids me do my best, then I do not dare to say no!"

85. Frederik Ludvig Bang Zeuthen: Et Par Aar af mit Liv [A couple
of years of my life] (1869), pp. 13-19; GEEG Stk. 25, pp. 153-57.

"Though after that I visited him now and again until my journey abroad [1833], inwardly I was more and more distanced from him and therefore felt myself less and less encouraged to a declaration which already, as a consequence of the great difference in age and so much else, was not at that time natural to me. It would hardly have led to anything but wrangling. Later, as priest, I have not kept silent, and my declarations then provoked much agitation from the Grundtvigian party's side. I have somewhere ventured to deny Grundtvig's capacity for scholarly thinking." Zeuthen continues his analytic criticism of Grundtvig and Grundtvigianism. See also Item 78.

As has previously been recounted,[1] as a young *candidat* I regularly visited the Grundtvig house. When later [in the 1830s] things had changed, this was not at all because Grundtvig had changed his relationship to me. I was continually received with friendliness by him as well as by his *first* wife (his later wives I have not known). When I came in to him of an evening he would immediately lay his work aside and then we would usually sit together on a small sofa and converse mostly about scholarly subjects. However lively our conversations could be at times, yet there could also intervene very long pauses, longer than otherwise tend to occur when two people are sitting together during a visit. Perhaps Grundtvig's thoughts would turn back to the work which he had abandoned on my arrival, and I, who seldom had anything new to communicate and had no gift for making a lengthier narrative of my communications and did not want to talk about the weather, would also fall silent, until I would begin thinking about the silence itself, which to me became oppressive, but the more I [GEEG p. 154] thought about it, the more difficulty I naturally had in finding a suitable subject with which to terminate it. Most people doubtless know to a great or lesser degree this oppressive feeling. Especially with Grundtvig I have sometimes had it to a very high degree. What always awakened his lively interest was whatever had to do with language, the Danish language, old Danish words; and here polemical feelings did not come into play in the way that so easily happened when the conversation turned to the theological, the ecclesiastical, even the aesthetic. [Christian] Molbech had given him his new edition of the old Danish *Rimkrønike*[2] and I saw with my own eyes how Grundtvig could quite justifiably be called a bookworm [*Bogorm*], even though I had earlier heard him in the strongest terms dissociate himself from this title, and surely with complete justice when it is taken in a pejorative sense. But when I saw this *Rimkrønike*, which Grundtvig had received as new a few days earlier, already so worn, almost as if gnawed, I could not but think of a bookworm; but I could only admire this love of the old, the old language (it was doubtless this that especially made the book so important to him) which therein revealed itself. If Grundtvig could have been more observant of his own self, then he would not, in the way he did, have used *Boglærdom* [book-learning] almost as a term of abuse. Naturally, this was not without occasion on the part of the scholars. For there are indeed such book-learned scholars as seem to be without a sense of real life and, forgetting the issue itself in favour of what are only the means towards knowledge of it, seem to get bogged down with all their interest in *books*. This is that tendency which Grundtvig presumes to be present when he speaks mockingly of "the learned" [*de Lærde*] and "book-learning." But has he not permitted himself such presumption everywhere that thorough and meticulous learning have got in his way, when his idiosyncratic assertions have offended against that to which the contents of the books testified?

In the years 1831-32 Grundtvig was occupied with the authorship of his great mythology of the North [*Nordens Mythologie*] of which, in my foreign travels of 1833 I took a copy to Jakob Grimm in Gøttingen, in which Grundtvig had written: "With long-standing esteem to Jakob Grimm who does not despise to read Danish." One evening Grundtvig read me the Introduction to the Mythology [*Nordens Mythologi*] right through. In this he gives it an essentially poetic origin, in that he regards it as the metaphorical language of the peoples. During the reading [GEEG p. 155] he himself seemed agitated by entering into that agitation of the soul which according to his view expresses itself in the myths. It really pained me that I could not sympathise with him any more than I can with the purely prosaic view of mythology (such as Finn Magnussen's in the translation of the *Edda*). At that time, the aboriginally religious [*det oprindeligt Religiøse*] was for me already – before I yet knew Schelling's way of looking at things – the primary and the essential in mythology.

What distanced me more and more from Grundtvig was naturally no more a lack of sympathy in this case than in any other case of a merely theoretical kind, as for example when Grundtvig, in connection with [J. P.] Mynster's review of [Henrik] Hertz's *Gjengangerbreve*[3] declared that he had previously credited Mynster with aesthetic sense and taste, but now he had to deny him it. As a matter of fact, I had found this review excellent, so excellent, I believe, that I rated it above the *Gjengangerbreve* themselves. Naturally, Grundtvig found them unworthy of the praise which Mynster granted them, although this was by no means unqualified. It was understandable enough that Grundtvig had to despise the weight which Hertz and Mynster placed upon the form. Mynster however does not omit to take exception to this overweighting at the expense of the idea, the substance, as though one "could let the butchers shut up shop because one ought to be able to cook a good soup from next to nothing just as well as from a hunk of meat, if only one has a good cook."

It was not a lack of agreement or sympathy with this or that which changed my relationship with Grundtvig, but truly antipathetic feelings that stirred within me in certain circumstances. Thus I recall a couple of things. First of all it could gall me to hear Lindberg's, as it seemed to me, slanderous stories about the behaviour of various priests and Grundtvig's mocking laughter over it.[4] If it were true, it sooner seemed to me something to weep over than to laugh at. Next (and this is the most important), I found myself in a very oppressive atmosphere when at Grundtvig's place I was together with many of the younger people who had become his followers. Then I got a vivid impression of a party, which had [GEEG p. 156] Grundtvig as its leader. On such an occasion, there was almost no one who spoke but Grundtvig, or, when they did express themselves, then it was, as it seemed to me, with far too great a deference.[5] In my thoughts in such company there prevailed no intellectual freedom, however much, otherwise, freedom is always demanded on Grundtvig's side. It was not in and of itself Grundtvig's superiority which was the cause of this, but the fact that he brought his superiority to bear in such a way that, instead of going as far as possible into thoughts which were not quite correct or in conformity with his own, either, laughing mockingly, he would dismiss them, or he would answer them only with a play on words, whereby he got laughter on his side. Already at that time, perhaps, it also seemed to me that Grundtvig's personality did not benefit from followers. He seemed of his nature all too strongly disposed to be a party-leader for the relationship between him and his followers to be kept pure, free and noble, so that the follower's individuality should not suffer by it, or so that from their side there could occur a profitable responsive effect upon him. On the contrary, it seemed to me that the more followers there gathered about him, the greater their circle became, the more he consolidated himself within the circle of his own peculiar thoughts and views. I have always had a loathing for everything party-political and so I felt myself more and more alienated from the Grundtvigian spirit. Once indeed I stayed away from Grundtvig's house for a very long while until one evening when I sat and tutored at Borchs Kollegium he came in to me and asked very amicably whether I could not manage to visit them any more. Then he invited me for the next day. Had I on that occasion been alone in my room I might have told him the cause of my absence. But on that occasion there was no opportunity and, though after that I visited him now and again until my journey abroad [1833], inwardly I was more and more distanced from him and therefore felt myself less and less encouraged to a declaration which already, as a consequence of the great difference in age and so much else, was not at that time natural to me. It would hardly have led to anything but wrangling. Later, as priest, I have not kept silent,[6] and [GEEG p. 157] my declarations then provoked much agitation from the Grundtvigian party's side. I have somewhere ventured to deny Grundtvig's capacity for scientific thinking [*Evne til* videnskabelig *Tænkning*]. By this I meant the

Evensong preacher at Frederiks Kirke

same as Bishop [H. L.] Martensen has later expressed in an interesting way, in that he has attributed to Grundtvig "the frequent use of the category of the sudden leap."[7] From that time on I long had to endure the most violent attacks from all the most important of his followers, as though I had trampled underfoot all that modesty, humanity and humility on which I myself had written dissertations. So my visits to Grundtvig's house necessarily ceased as it were of their own accord, especially since his domestic circumstances had become quite altered from what I had earlier known.[8] But just once since that time I have been at his place. This was perhaps ten or twelve years ago when, as priest in Sorø I heard a sermon by Grundtvig in Vartov which appealed to me greatly. It concerned the woman who, when she has born a child, is no longer mindful of her travail because of her joy that a child is born into the world (*John* 16 [:21]). He preached not about the bath of rebirth [*Gjenfødelsens Bad*] but about the spirit of rebirth [*Gjenfødelsens Aand*], of that "little human being" [*lille Menneske*] in faith and in the joy of faith born to new life within us, over whom we must watch and keep guard as we must do with other "little persons" [*smaa Mennesker*] (children), so that they do not fall and come to harm. It surprised me that Grundtvig could talk about new life without mentioning baptism, and it was pleasing to me, and unexpected, to hear the weight he laid upon what pertains to *sanctification* [*helliggjørelsen*].[9] The day after hearing this sermon I again visited him (after several years' interval) and thanked him for the sermon. Despite the unconstrained opinion I had publicly expressed about and against Grundtvig, and for which I had had to listen to very ugly things from his friends, yet in this case I was conscious of no ill-will and could approach him with a clear brow and an open countenance. I found him indeed his old self, as though nothing had happened: but how new to me and how altered his whole milieu on that occasion! This will perhaps have been the last time we talk together in this life.

1. Part of Zeuthen's account alluded to here, relating to the years 1827-30, is given above.

2. Christian Molbech's edition of the Danish *Rimkrønike* was published in December 1825 and was the subject of a detailed review by Grundtvig in April 1826.

3. J. P. Mynster's review of the *Gjengangerbreve eller Poetiske Epistler fra Paradis* [Letters of a revenant or poetic epistles from Paradise], by Henrik Hertz (1797-1870) but published anonymously 1830, appeared in the periodical *Maanedsskrift for Litteratur* V (1831, 197-222).

4. Zeuthen's footnote: "As a whole, Grundtvig's expression of mockery was often distasteful to me. Yet he himself wrote the words: Mockery is an evil weed which grows upon Love's grave."

5. Zeuthen's footnote: "At the Friends' Meetings [*Vennemøderne*] now many do indeed speak out without contradiction from Grundtvig; but is not this because they have all now essentially learnt to speak *like Grundtvig*?"

6. Zeuthen's footnote: "In my two open letters to P. C. Kierkegaard (now Bishop), my monograph on the so-called concept of the church [*kirkelige Anskuelse*], etc."

7. Martensen, in his *Til Forsvar mod den saakaldte Grundtvigianisme* [For a defence against the so-called Grundtvigianism] (1863), says: "As soon as his talents give him an eye for the beginning, he looks onwards to the end, but what lies between in the prospect is leapt over" (p. 99) and "One may compare his gift of language with an instrument which has all the tones in the high and the low registers, but on which harmonies can hardly be elicited because of a deficiency in the middle tones" (p. 101).

8. Zeuthen presumably refers to changes following Grundtvig's second marriage. At the time of the visit "ten or twelve years ago" (1857-59) next mentioned, Grundtvig would have been married to his third wife, Asta.

9. If Zeuthen's dating of "ten or twelve years ago" is correct, the sermon in question may be that given by Grundtvig on the Third Sunday after Easter (15 May) 1859 where he used the metaphor of the mother's care for her new-born child and spoke of the sanctification of the spirit and heart when the Gospel of Christ finds living access. "Sanctification consists in the soul's refoundation upon the image of Jesus Christ" [Helliggjørelse bestaar i […] Sjælens Omdannen efter Jesu Kristi Billede] (Monrad); "The Holy Spirit will make none glad who is not willing to be sanctified" [Den Helligaand gjør ingen glad, / Som ej vil helliggjøres] (Grundtvig).

86. Povl Frederik Barfod: Et Livs Erindringer [A life's reminiscences], ed. Albert Fabricius (1938), pp. 183-208; GEEG Stk. 26, pp. 157-78.

Frederik Barfod (1811-96) wrote down his reminiscences in the last two years of his long, busy and combative life, in a series of letters (hence the dates heading each section) to his grandson, Olaf Ostenfeld Barfod (1871-1940). Their style is therefore relatively informal and anecdotal; recall of dates and sequentiality of events can be vague; and particular stories or characterisations can naturally have ripened in their preservation over so long a time; but not many of his generation were so engaged with such tenacious vigour in such a range of causes as he, and his reminiscences and abundant other writings are in that respect a treasury of documentation of the turbulent century through which he lived. His relationship with Grundtvig, steadfast from his side over most of four decades, also had its periods of turbulence, as the following excerpts narrate. Deferential though he may have been to his admired elder, Barfod was always his own man. In all his involvements he had his own robust convictions and lived up to them, sometimes at considerable cost when, for example, he outspokenly criticised dignitaries and institutions of State and Church from the King downwards. To some he was an easily mocked figure (and mockery was a tactic much used between factions in 19th-c. Copenhagen's rather narrow confines) especially in his later years when he could be made to appear the last home of various lost causes – an echo of this, but sympathetically sounded, is in the memoir of their chance meeting by Edmund Gosse (1849-1928; see headnote to item 125). Many nevertheless admired him for his contributions to Danish life and on his eightieth birthday he agreed to have his portrait painted for the National Museum in Frederiksborg. His contemporary H. F. Rørdam wrote of him, in the 1877 edition of the Dansk Biografisk Lexikon: "The whole of B's public activity has had a thoroughgoing idealistic character. If many, particularly in earlier times, disapproved of his reckless pronouncements, hardly anyone has called into doubt his love of truth and his patriotic spirit." All of these qualities contribute towards making Barfod a biographer of Grundtvig to whom it is worth listening. Barfod's chapter on Grundtvig was separately published in Gads danske Magasin 1925, 439-61 (GEEG).

29 April 1895

In October 1827 I was in Copenhagen to see and hear how the matriculation examination proceeded.[1] I stayed the whole time at Provst [GEEG p. 158] [A. P.] Bregendahl's. But on October 16th it was removal-day[2] and the Provst was to move into the adjacent house (in Prinsessegade in Christianshavn). Now this was not so strange, but stranger was the fact that he, the priest at Vor Frelsers Kirke, was to move into the apartment which the curate at the same church, N. F. S. Grundtvig, occupied, whereas the latter was to move into the *Provst*'s apartment.³ Between the two courtyards there ran a high dividing-wall of planks, and through the big gate in this partition all the possessions from both sides could be moved without a scrap of it coming out on the street. So we were busily occupied the whole day with the removal, young and old, men and women, and Grundtvig himself moved all his books. I knew Grundtvig from his translation of Saxo and Snorri and indeed at that time he was on everyone's lips in connection with his *Kirkens genmæle*, but which I myself was hardly likely to have read. I had a great desire to exchange a couple of words with him, but how should this best come about? We indeed kept on bumping into each other while we were each carrying his bundles (I also met Fru Grundtvig once on the stairs; she had the twenty-week-old little Meta on her arm); but, as said, it was not enough for me to see him and doff my hat to him: I also had to speak with him, even if it were only a couple of words. And I hit upon a plan. He had already carried various of his books down to his new apartment and placed them in the bookcases, but he still had many left. So I would make myself impertinent, take a book out of the bookcase, allow myself to be surprised as I was looking in it, and so get the opportunity to make him an apology. And it went as calculated. What we talked about, I no longer recollect, only that Grundtvig politely accepted my apology and asked me whose son I was. When I told him this, he did not personally know my father but had heard him spoken of as a capable and respectable man.⁴ With that the conversation was ended; we were both busy, and besides, what was I supposed to be able to talk to him about! But I was pleased that my stratagem had worked out so well.

Some eight years passed before I again spoke to him. I had of course heard him many times in 1832 etc, when he preached in Frederiks Kirke, but I stood so far from him in theological views (if I may so express myself, since I myself knew theology only by name, as another matter of curiosity) and thus could not think of going to him after the church-service. But I had often felt a desire to get closer to him – not to the theologian but to the historian and [GEEG p. 159] the Dane – but people had advised me against any attempt; Georg Aagaard especially did so: he knew him of course from his repeated visits to Iselinge but, as the following will show, he did not know him to the full.

30 April 1895

Then at the end of 1834 Grundtvig published a little pamphlet: *Om sognebåndets løsning og hr. professor Clausen* [On the dissolution of parochial ties and Professor Clausen].⁵ I read this at Gjorslev where I again spent Christmas. Over one sentence in it (as far as I recall, towards the end) *kammerraad* [J. F. S.] Dorph and I disagreed, as we each understood it in his own way. "I will have that question cleared up" I then said. "How so?" "When I get to Copenhagen I will ask Grundtvig which of us is right." "Do you know Grundtvig?" "No." "Well then, it seems to me you ought to think twice about putting such a question to him." "Why? An author of course wants to be understood and not misunderstood, and he must surely be pleased to be able to correct it when he hears that he is misunderstood." Dorph still had reservations, but no sooner said than done. As soon as I got back to Copenhagen after Christmas I called on Grundtvig one morning in his home. I found him standing and working at his desk, went up to him and told him who I was and what my business was:

"In your last little pamphlet there occurs a remark which has been understood by some as though you regretted that in *Kirkens genmæle* you had not far more sharply tackled Professor Clausen; while I have understood it as though you regretted that you handled the case in a way which was not fully worthy either of yourself or of Clausen. Which of us is right?" "You can find that out by reading it!" answered Grundtvig quite shortly; but nevertheless went to a bookshelf at the other end of the room, pulled out a small book and read attentively in it. After being silent for some time he said: "Yes, unfortunately the expression has actually come out ambiguously, but *you* are completely right, and I shall certainly say it more clearly when opportunity arises." It was this, the young person's impertinent (not to say shameless) approach to the renowned author, which gave rise to my longlasting relationship with him. He liked the unusual, and I also think he liked my unusual outspoken candour; and in a short conversation he asked me to come again when I had anything on my conscience. And I did indeed soon become a friend of the family, came to him morning and evening, [**GEEG p. 160**] and had manifold, not only instructive but cordial conversations with him, even though I did not conceal that in everything to do with Christianity I was completely estranged from him; was besides so indiscreet as to say about one of his historical poems (pretty certainly one on the history of the fatherland) that he had no doubt written it to order, *invita Minerva* [at the invitation of Minerva = against one's natural inclination] (which however he denied ever having done); accompanied him into his family where I soon became good friends with his wife, his sister-in-law ("Aunt Jane") and with all his three children, especially the then eleven-year-old Svend.

Now you must not expect of me any strictly chronological exposition. The many precious memories almost run together into one single big one. I shall give you only a single incident here and there, mainly for the illumination of Grundtvig's personality.

Thus I once wanted to get him to contribute to *Nordisk Ugeskrift* [Nordic weekly], the publication of which I managed on behalf of "the Society for the Promotion of an improved Orthography" [*sælskabet for en forbedret retskrivnings udbredelse*]. He had nothing against the journal itself and nothing in particular against its orthography, but since, in accordance with its objective it would only accept contributions in *this* orthography, he was not willing to contribute to it, since he believed that we ought to have an open enough mind to let everyone retain his own orthography, and that it was not this that mattered but the spirit and content of the contributions. In this he was quite right, and yet wrong, since *we* had only just set it as our journal's objective to work towards a more rational orthography than the senseless one which had hitherto been used (is in part still used).

Another time I came to him and he was very excited. I believe that it was Prince Christian who had lost his librarian and therefore had to have a new one (though I am not sure whether it was not King Frederik himself). Such a position must really be something for me, since I loved to dabble with books, and my royalist viewpoint must make it doubly attractive to me and make me particularly acceptable to the relevant person. I must therefore immediately apply for the position; he would give me a written recommendation to enclose with the application and would himself orally plead my cause. I did indeed receive the recommendation and I well remember that I blushed to read it; but whether the application was handed in, I do not recollect; if it were, it came too late, for the exalted relevant person had bustled about and found himself another librarian, and this, as far as I know, even before Grundtvig had tipped me the wink.

On one occasion I visited him and found him against all custom sitting in [GEEG p. 161] the sofa and writing – but it is quite possible that this was some years later. He was depressed and I sat myself down on the sofa by him. He complained that in recent days he had not been able to work. "But still you are writing!" "Yes, I am copying out some of my old things, but that is not really working, and I cannot manage anything else." I do not need to say what an impression this made upon me; even [L. A.] Kramer, who was in no way a Grundtvigian, was deeply moved when I told him this. He repeated it to a couple of other friends with the exclamation: "Imagine! that Grundtvig is now reduced to being a copyist." Luckily, this condition of weakness did not last long; he went off to the country, no doubt to his bosom friend Gunni Busck and in the lap of nature he won back his old strength again.[6]

On the 14th November 1841 my father died at an age of nearly seventy-two years. From reputation, Grundtvig had formed a respect for his honesty, his quiet but steady industriousness; and when, after his burial, I visited again I had to tell him something about my father's life and death. I concluded more or less thus: "One can see from this that tireless industry does not at all wear out prematurely either bodily or spiritual strength; and that a restless zeal for the objectives one has made one's own does not do so either." This was water to Grundtvig's mill, and he exclaimed spiritedly: "No, that is for certain!" But dear Fru Elise Grundtvig was not at all so content with this conclusion of mine; she feared, and with every justification, that her husband was really doing too much with his incessant toil and that by this he would prematurely break down his iron constitution. She then gave us both a gentle admonition, the most serious she was capable of.

A little event [1839] in which I do not myself participate I will record here anyhow. Professor [Carsten] Hauch in Sorø was having a child baptised and as godparents had invited Grundtvig, [B. L.] Ingemann, [Bertel] Thorvaldsen and [Adam] Øhlenschlæger. Before they went to the church Ingemann said to Grundtvig: "Why should you be standing as godparent? I think you ought rather to be baptising the child!" "Yes, that is what I would also prefer: but what would Sommer, the priest [incumbent in Sorø], say to that?" "I shall sort that out with him alright" said Ingemann, and it was then arranged as he wished. When teatime arrived in the evening, Ingemann and Grundtvig were standing and talking together and Fru [Anna] Hauch, who wanted to do the very best for her guests, came in and said: "May I ask you, Pastor Grundtvig, [GEEG p. 162] do you prefer to sleep with an eiderdown or blankets?" Grundtvig was at a loss to answer her, and Ingemann gave her a nudge, drew her aside and said: "But dear Fru Hauch, how could you put that question to Grundtvig? Did you not see how embarrassed he was by it? Do you not know that he never goes to bed, so he could not choose between what you offered him." Over many, many years Grundtvig really did not ever go to bed; he would sit beside his lamp in the sofa and work; when he got tired he would turn the lamp down a bit and lean back, ready to turn it up again and tackle his work afresh when he awoke from the short nap. He did not know what comforts either eiderdown or blankets promised him and therefore could not possibly choose; but this secret was *his* secret and must never be mentioned in his hearing.

3 May 1895

I was almost as one of the family at the Grundtvigs: I came there at all hours of the day and was always welcome. We talked with each other about every possible thing, though more rarely on religious questions which he himself never broached, neither directly to me nor to anyone else, but always willingly joined in if one brought them up oneself. It was in such a conversation (although it was possibly not until some years later) that he once said to me:[7] "You are no Christian, Barfod, and perhaps you will be slow to become one, but yet I have no anxiety for you because you are a truth-loving person and you will therefore also find the truth, here or beyond." It was these warm and gentle words, "here or beyond", which made so affecting an impression upon me. I have once heard them more precisely developed by him in a sermon in Vartov. I had in my home felt myself powerfully affected by the hymn *I kvæld blev der banket på helvedes port* [This night came a knock at the portals of Hell]: it was the doctrine of the possibility of a conversion *after* death which, before any other doctrine, won *me* over to Christianity. The idea had troubled my feelings as a crying injustice, that all those dear people whom I knew both from history and from life should be eternally damned if – here below, in the brief journey of the earthly life – they had not learnt to know the faith and accepted it. Now I saw that there was indeed another possibility, and was glad, I can earnestly say: both for their sake and for our Lord's. Even so there were [GEEG p. 163] to pass several years yet, before I could really accept Christianity. Grundtvig had to find a supporter in my Emilie.

As mentioned, I had already become as one of the family at the Grundtvigs, and not only with him but with his quiet, delightful and lovable wife and with her sister, the eminent "Aunt Jane." The children grew closer little by little and to them too I felt myself attached, especially to the lively Sven who was probably more than thirteen years younger than I, but from early on was developed far beyond his age. He and I had many enjoyable conversations before he was yet fourteen years old.

4 May 1895

Grundtvig had the habit, when strangers visited him, of walking up and down the floor with them; he never invited them to sit down, indeed did not even offer them a pipe although he himself, as is well known, always went about with a pipe in his mouth. This was not a lack of hospitable feelings; it was simply just a thoughtlessness which had become a habit with him. If they were complete strangers, he moreover had difficulty in getting a conversation started: the visitor himself had to see to this. All this his wife and sister-in-law had long since discovered, but it was of no help that afterwards they would tease him and scold him; he could see alright that it was wrong but in this area he was incorrigible. When we were become more closely acquainted, they would therefore regularly send a message to me if they knew that he was getting a specially interesting visit (such as Peter Hiort Lorenzen, the first time he was in town) and would ask me to come in order to get everything moving. And this I would do; and when I had then got one topic or another under way I knew that I could quietly withdraw, since the ice was broken and there was no danger at all that the open water would close over again. But first I would ask the visitor whether he would not like a pipe or a cigar, and "Would you not rather sit down, because if you wait for Grundtvig to suggest it to you, you will wait in vain." Whether the visitor accepted my offer or not, Grundtvig would still nod approvingly and laugh a little.

But I could have other business with Grundtvig. Thus it was I (in collaboration, I think, with Frederik Hammerich and a third person)[8] who exhorted him to hold the series of lectures at Borchs Kollegium which first made him famous as a lecturer and filled both the lecture-hall itself and the adjacent rooms and corridors with [GEEG p. 164] an attentively listening audience. He immediately agreed to our proposal with pleasure and quickly made up his mind on the chosen topic; but was subsequently sorry that he had fixed the first lecture (but which he was thereafter unwilling to change) right on the day when we celebrated the fifty years' anniversary of the freeing of the peasantry,[9] out at Bellevue, with the consequence that he himself could not take part in a celebration which would have pleased no one more intensely than him, and nor could I be present at the first lecture, since I (at [Orla] Lehmann's exhortation) had written songs for the celebration and was also to make a speech at it.

The draft of the lectures, as is well known, came out after his death under the title *Mands Minde*, edited by his son Sven, but this was only the undeveloped notes which as such gave only an imperfect, if evocative, impression of the lectures themselves. And at this opportunity I shall observe, since I do not know whether it has previously been observed by anyone else, that Grundtvig *never* gave any lecture without previously having carefully prepared himself. This held good not only for this lecture (and the successive series), but also for every speech he meant to give in public, on Skamling [Skamlingsbanken], for example, or, later, in the *Rigsdag*, indeed, even for a toast within a circle of friends. He wrote them all down. It could of course happen with the bigger lectures that time forbade him from writing them out completely so that he was obliged more or less to extemporise, but he did not do this without reluctance. It therefore also goes without saying that he wrote out *all* his sermons, but it could well happen that on the way to the pulpit he would get a new thought and not use a word of what was written down but either gave a completely new address or elaborated upon and extended that which was already written down. His collected sermons do not therefore always contain what he actually delivered but only what in his study he had intended to deliver. That both in the *Rigsdag* and elsewhere he could suddenly make a speech without having thought about it in advance is something quite different, and neither invalidates nor contradicts the rule.

5 May 95

Another exhortation to Grundtvig was also issued through me but this was some years later. When the Convention of Copenhagen's clergy, chiefly through the influence of *Stiftsprovst* [E. C.] Tryde, had rejected Grundtvig's draft for a new hymnal, I wrote a little poem in *Dansk Kirketidende*.[10] [GEEG p. 165] It created something of a stir, and this was probably the reason why – since the congregation nonetheless wished that Grundtvig should publish his draft, which might thus get authorisation to be used in Vartov – there were chosen, at a meeting which I did not attend, three men who in conjunction were to exhort him to the desired publication.[11] To my surprise not only was I one of the chosen three, but was into the bargain chosen as their spokesman. So I carried out the task assigned to me, but when I had said my piece old [H. C.] Hansgaard set to, with all his warmth and fervour, and indeed he certainly could rather have been called upon to act as spokesman (who the third man was I no longer remember). Of course, Grundtvig was visibly pleased at the exhortation but even so he could not accept it there and then. He was not himself satisfied with the hymnbook proposal; it was not homogenous; it had been adapted in many ways according to the Convention-members' divergent theological and aesthetic views, and the Convention had been constantly surprised by how co-operative and accommodating Grundtvig had been when he, to whom the real editorship had been assigned, had to mediate between the conflicting opinions and yet produce something which was answerable in both Christian and aesthetic terms. That is, he was not willing to publish a hymnbook, in effect composed by him, tabled by the Convention, and adopted item by item, but now rejected in its entirety by the same Convention (if I am not much mistaken, it was the general opinion that it was Pastor [P. J.] Spang's death occurring during those days which brought about the rejection). On the other hand, he told us that he had already thought of another way out, which in consequence of our exhortation he would take into the most serious consideration. The outcome of his considerations was Vartov's *Kirke-salmebog* (*Festsalmerne*), of which the fourteenth impression (1880) is lying in front of me, though doubtless quite a few more impressions have come out.

But if I could thus, by exhortation, occasionally have *some* influence on Grundtvig, he of course constantly had a ten and twentyfold greater influence upon me. I have, I think, already occasionally indicated this in various places and will, I hope, come to indicate it further. Since I dare not rely upon it that I shall find time to do it later, I will here provisionally point to one particular, even if less significant yet for me decisive step, which he got me to take. [GEEG p. 166] It was in fact chiefly at his exhortation that I began publication of *Brage og Idun*, just as it was he who gave it this name.[12] He exhorted me to this, and I also approached Orla Lehmann who repeated the exhortation. I was full of anxiety, I who was so to speak foreign to the whole reading and writing world and would now have to turn to authors and readers of the whole of the North for support. I went many times to and fro between Grundtvig and Lehmann but they, although not in conjunction, outplayed me, no doubt mostly in order to find me a steady occupation, and I obeyed them. That it was Grundtvig and Lehmann who worked together in this (without knowing it) hardly anyone suspected.

The first volume of *Brage og Idun* came out in the new year, 1839. At my instigation, on 18 April in the same year was founded *Det Skandinaviske Selskab* [The Scandinavian Society] in Copenhagen of which Grundtvig became the chairman whilst I became its treasurer and secretary.[13] But I should like to devote a more detailed account to this society, if the opportunity falls to me. Here I must make do with having mentioned it. Still in the same year, on 3 December, King Frederik VI died. I was sitting at my table in the morning and working when my landlady's daughter, an oldish girl always ready to laugh, came grinning into my room and told me about it. I was strongly affected and immediately went out to see Grundtvig who long before my arrival had himself received the news. He too was strongly affected but he had far better opinions of Christian VIII than I did and was therefore not so deeply shaken as I was. On one thing though we were fully agreed: "God be gracious to old Denmark!"

I had thought to go to the Lord's Table before I brought home my bride, and a month previously I was sitting in the sofa together with Grundtvig and said this to him. He was not entirely unwilling to comply with my wish but still he bade me delay this until I myself was more certain that it was really the Lord's very body and blood he delivered to me. When that time had come I could come to him again and he would do it with joy. By mutual agreement I had in fact to delay it until, next Spring, I came to him together with my wife.

[GEEG p. 167] I had in fact already got married. But before I could do that I not only had to see to all kinds of equipment, both indoors and out, [but also] had to pay organist Wiuff a half year's rent in advance, had to see to furniture for the house as well as to all the manifold articles which were necessary for running a household. My bride had certainly been as unassuming as in any way possible, but nevertheless all my few sources were completely emptied. I had even had to borrow a hundred *rigsdaler* from [Abraham] Wessely, the loss adjuster, one of the editors of *Fædrelandet*. A couple of days before the wedding I did not own a penny and did not know where I was to raise them. Then I remembered that Grundtvig once – indeed, several times – had said that I must not fall into distress: in that case I was to let him know in time. So I went to him and asked him to lend me thirty *rigsdaler*; with these I expected to be able to cover the priest and the parish clerk and still be able to fund our moving in. I did not know at that time how modestly placed he himself was. Without a single objection he went and fetched a fifty *rigsdaler* note, which he gave to me. God knows where he had got it from! And my anxiety was quenched.

After we had settled down, we were in Vartov Church almost every Sunday and after the service would very regularly go to Grundtvig's for lunch. My Emilie was indeed hand in glove with his womenfolk and not infrequently we were invited there either to dinner or for the evening. We were still just the two of us and therefore we had our full freedom. Grundtvig, who was a good walker, also came regularly out to us in Frederiksberg, and we had many cosy conversations. At that time I would still usually stand at my desk and work, but the sun shone on it and so it would never fail that as soon as he arrived Grundtvig would immediately roll the blind down with a stern warning that I should protect my eyes. But one particular anecdote I must tell: on one occasion Grundtvig was getting ready to go again. I asked whether there was such urgency, whether we could not talk a little more. "Yes, we could indeed, if you had either a pipe or a cigar; but the sad fact is that you do not have either." "No, true enough, I don't – though I recently found a bundle of cigars in my desk; but they have no doubt lain there since my father owned the desk and they are surely dried out. Only I did not have the heart to throw them out because they had without a doubt been his." Grundtvig laughed: "So you do not even know that cigars get better [GEEG p. 168] the longer they are kept! Let us see one of them!" And I took the bundle, he tried one, found them excellent, and stayed. It goes without saying that I carefully kept the rest – some twenty – and took good care that no one else got access to them, but that they remained there for Grundtvig until he had used up the last one. What happened after that, I cannot say. It is only clear to me that I knew nothing about buying either tobacco or cigars.

11 May 1895

Grundtvig was enormously naive: he himself practised no deceit and therefore did not suspect it in others. Yet it could happen with him as with various other naive people (as an example I have only to mention [A. F.] Tscherning): there could suddenly spring up a misconception in him almost without one having any idea of the cause; and his whole constitution carried with it a tendency for him, at such a moment, to become undiscriminatingly impetuous. In the Spring of 1848, I was to become the object of such a misconception. We had spent a lovely Sunday at his place. He had been in an excellent humour, had as usual been gently teasing his wife and sister-in-law and making fun with the rest of us. It had got very late before we broke up, but as we were all standing with overcoats on Grundtvig gave me an article which he wished to go into *Berlingske Tidende* and he asked me to see to what needed doing. It was past midnight when we got home but I went straight up to *Berlingske Tidende*'s office and performed my errand (at that time we lived in the same courtyard in Nørregade as [M. L.] Nathansen, and during the war the office was open the whole night). Nathansen promised me to print the article, and with a good and peaceful conscience I went to bed. But Grundtvig's article did not appear in Monday's paper and on Tuesday morning early Grundtvig came over to us. He did not come to my entrance door however, but went diagonally across the courtyard to the kitchen door. My Emilie was standing in the kitchen but he did not greet her. He went straight past her, through our living room and into my study where I was standing at my desk. But neither did he greet me with more words than these: "If you did not want to do what I asked you to, you could have said no and not given me your promise," and he flung the door open and vanished without any farewell. Undoubtedly the situation was that Grundtvig had thought that Nathansen would be so pleased to receive an article from him that he would print it [**GEEG p. 169**] immediately; he was disappointed and could then think of no other cause than that I had forgotten my promise. But Nathansen too had his vanity: no one was to think that he was ever anxious to get hold of material or that one did him a service when one wrote an article for his paper; it was he who did a service to the person concerned when he printed his article; therefore one had to wait patiently until there was space; and Grundtvig could certainly wait until the next day. And indeed, unless I am extraordinarily mistaken, it came out as early as Tuesday evening. When Grundtvig and I met a couple of days later we were just as good friends and this little interlude was not mentioned at all.

12 May 1895

Grundtvig tolerated no constraint upon his own convictions but nor did he wish to lay constraints upon those of others. To this extent he was the most independently minded person one could imagine; could also relate in friendship to people who nurtured views which were dead opposite to his. Among others I will mention *Oberst* [Colonel] H. J. Blom, even though they were in disagreement on every second issue that was of significant importance to themselves. I mention this with reference to the disturbed year of 1848.[14] He [Grundtvig] certainly did not like the mass procession to the palace of Christiansborg on 21 March nor, therefore, *my* participation in it, but he put up with it without letting me hear a word. (Whether his own sons participated in it I do not remember, but I should think it fairly likely; it is at least certain that they participated in the Casino-meeting on the previous evening). Then came the war. Over this we were certainly in complete agreement and were constantly proud of our brave Jenses (Grundtvig indeed sang one fine song after another about them)[15] – even if we could now and then disagree over the way in which it was being conducted. It could nevertheless result in points being raised about which we were not in agreement. I am not thinking of the Ejder frontier, for Grundtvig wished with me[16] that we might be blessedly and safely quit of Holstein and Lauenburg; but it was a different matter when the discussion touched upon Germany's unity, which I sincerely desired but Grundtvig desired to preserve us from. In excuse of myself, though, I must say that I never dreamed that Germany would become a 'unity' under a half-Vendish (that is, non-German) Prussian leadership. I was [GEEG p. 170] only enthusiastic for national unity here as in other places and never dreamed that this could become dangerous for the North, which also must become a unity. This danger Grundtvig saw and he dreaded it. Whether he also saw that what is now called "German unity" would be a huge lie, in that it only turned out to be an entanglement of Germans and Vends (Slavs), is not clear to me, since I do not remember that this possibility was particularly brought to the fore when discussion turned to "united" Germany.

After the war came the deplorable armistice and then – the elections to the Constituent National Assembly [den grundlovgivende Rigsforsamling]. Here again there was disagreement between us, and I especially remember that the conflict grew heated when I (be it said to my own shame!) wished that A. S. Ørsted might get eliminated in the elections. Ørsted had never and in no respect been a friend of Grundtvig, but all the same he [Grundtvig] warmly declared that a man with Ørsted's talents, skills, experience and honourable character should hardly be found absent when the future constitution of the state was to be negotiated. There were also other persons over whom we disagreed, not to mention the objective of the negotiations themselves.

Both he and I were members of the National Assembly. We were very far from standing on the same side, since I was a zealous 'farmers' friend' [bondeven] whilst he comprised a party to himself and was what is called a løsgænger [independent]. But the negotiations of the National Assembly I shall not enter upon here. If you want to know in more detail about our participation in it I refer you to the little book by L.K.D.,[17] about which I know that Grundtvig said in his home that it was a good and truth-loving book, but that he would wish and hope that it was not, as rumour alleged, written by Barfod (why he wished this my confidant, his son Sven, could not tell me). One thing, however, I must tell you, which could not be included in that book, and which pleased me greatly: According to the rules of procedure, the same speaker could speak to the same issue once only, unless it were for a short "personal" observation. It now chanced that Grundtvig had already spoken, but I had not, and yet there was still something he wanted to have said. He walked the long way from his seat to mine in order to ask me to say it. In this way I was more than once his spokesman, most commonly of course in questions on which we were completely agreed.

On 14 January 1851 died the pious and lovable first Fru [Lise] Grundtvig. [GEEG p. 171] I *believe* that it was missing both her sons that laid her in the grave.[18] She had not wished to keep them from taking up the sword in the fatherland's defence; she saw them go; but from that moment there lay as it were a darkness over her mood. When one came there, one constantly found her in the sons' room, busying herself with their things and with the map of Sønderjylland in front of her. It did not relieve, did not lift the mother's mood that both of them, first Sven then Johan, won themselves with honour the cross of the Order of Dannebrog. She could not look upon the horrors of war with the same eyes, the same hope and faith, as Grundtvig.[19] Certainly she too was resigned to the will of God, she too loved the fatherland and was convinced of its good and just cause; but first and foremost she was a mother.

On 25 October 1851 Grundtvig married Fru Marie Toft, a strong, warm-blooded and well-born woman. I knew her already from Rønnebæksholm, when in 1849 she had asked me to work for the election of F. Boisen. The first time I greeted her as Grundtvig's wife she received me in friendly and cordial manner and our relationship became extremely good. But it was no longer the old Grundtvigs' house for us, especially not for my Emilie: she so deeply missed both the former Fru Grundtvig and Aunt Jane; I missed them with her, missed also Meta who a couple of years earlier married Peter Boisen, and Johan and Sven who had both said goodbye to the home. But Grundtvig himself still remained and, as I said, I was in good standing with the new Fru Grundtvig.[20]

In October 1852 I founded "The Danish Association" [*Den danske Forening*] of *Rigsdag*-members, the aim of which was to oppose both the projected introduction of an inheritance law and the moving of the customs frontier from the Ejder to the Elbe. This is what I alluded to in *Tænkt og følt* II, 81, but which I want to go into in more detail, if I manage to give an account of my political work. At the dissolution of the *Rigsdag* on 13 January 1853 I ceased to be a *Rigsdag*-member but still thought that "The Danish Association" could do some good, and there were others who thought the same. So I got a meeting summoned at which it was refounded for both *Rigsdag*-members and non-*Rigsdag*-members, for the whole people, and Grundtvig was elected chairman on 7 March 1853. It was agreed to publish a journal, [**GEEG p. 172**] *Dannebrog*, and I was elected as its editor. As such I was given a completely free hand: I could publish it either once or twice a week, I could issue it as a half-sheet or as a broadsheet, according as I found material, and I was my own censor. I was really pleased with this undertaking which allowed me still to have a certain political influence; and what others thought of my journal I do not know, but from Sven I know that his father was very pleased with it, and that in the father's hearing one was not allowed ever to make fun of it (which Sven could well have felt like doing now and again). Thus things went for eight months, I think, but my happiness was swiftly to be converted into the most bitter pain, the deepest grief. I wish that I could tear out this page from both Grundtvig's history and my own, but I cannot, for I must speak the truth and only the truth.

Karl Moltke, as "Minister for Slesvig" issued a proclamation (or whatever it was called) to the inhabitants of the duchy which I did not like at all. I expressed this in the opening section of a longer article. When this opening section was published I got word from Grundtvig that he wanted to speak with me. I had a suspicion what it was about for after all I knew Grundtvig's views, but I just sat and worked on the continuation, which I wanted to take to the printers the same day; and besides I thought that there was no urgency. So I finished writing my article and took it to the printers. Next day I was again at the printers: the whole of my article – that is, also the ending of the piece about Karl Moltke – had been typeset, but the printers informed me that Grundtvig had also been in touch – and had laid an embargo upon the publication of my paper. So I got only a proof-copy which they pulled off for me, to take home. (This proof-copy with all its corrections I have subsequently given to my grandson Olaf). On the same day I received a very hard letter from Grundtvig in which he handed me my dismissal as editor.[21] My feeling was that a violent offence had been committed against me (after all, Grundtvig had not appointed me and therefore could not dismiss me out of hand), and over the next seven months I exchanged neither spoken nor written word with Grundtvig, whereas at the *Rigsdag* on the same evening I wrote a farewell letter to his wife, to whom I sent with thanks the thirty *rigsdaler* which she had lent me in the first days of September [GEEG p. 173] when my son Ludvig lay critically ill. I was deeply offended and I was overwrought. I wandered up to the Mill[22] to Grundtvig's son-in-law Peter Boisen, at whose place I by chance met Carl Brandt, Ludvig Helveg and one or two more. What did I want there? And who raised the subject of what had happened? Was it me or someone else? I do not know; but this I do know, that both my pain and overwrought state came out in the conversation, that I spoke of Grundtvig's high-handedness and arbitrariness, and that I used the expression that "if the worst came to the worst, I would rather have Karl Moltke as my superior than Grundtvig." It goes without saying that the others neither wholly agreed nor wholly disagreed with me, and that they tried affectionately to calm me down.

Grundtvig himself now took over the editorship. He scrapped not only the unprinted number and the one which had given offence but furthermore one or two of the immediately preceding numbers, and replaced them with new. In those numbers I had written something on matters concerning large estates which could well have been uncomfortable for the estate owners. Out of this the suspicion formed within me, which however I kept to myself, that possibly it was his wife [Marie Toft], the owner of Rønnebæksholm, who had stirred up his anger against me. (A year later I met her brother, the *hofjægermester* [Master of the Royal Hunt] [H. R.] Carlsen, on Holmensbro. He came up to me and assured me, without the remotest prompt from my side, that "if I had suspected his sister of having given rise to the rift – but *I* had never spoken to him of any "rift" – then I did her an injustice." Maybe he was right in his assertion but I admit that it strengthened my suspicion). Grundtvig issued only a couple of numbers of *Dannebrog*, then he handed over the editorship to [Carl] Brandt. Not until long after the rift did I get to know that my Emilie, who saw how it pained me, had gone straight to Grundtvig to tell him this and to beg him to be more kindly disposed towards me, but had been unable to achieve anything, so embittered was he by my "defiance". Granted he was polite towards her but nothing could soften him, and she left without having seen his family. Good that a scar had grown over the wound before this was confided to me!

13 May 1895

As mentioned, for over seven months I exchanged not a word, either with Grundtvig or with his wife. Indeed, her I never saw again: barely two months after giving birth to Frederik she died on 9 July 1854. She [GEEG p. 174] was a strong-willed, intelligent woman who could share and really did share all her husband's opinions – religious, aesthetic, *folkelige* and political.

As Fru [Marie] Toft, she had held religious gatherings at Rønnebæksholm from a wide area and from all social classes. Already at that time she loved Grundtvig's hymns which she herself would sing with a beautiful and strong voice. (In one of his hymns she got him, among other things, to make an alteration so that she could use it as her daily evening-hymn. My memory would much disappoint me if it were not the hymn *Julen har englelyd* [Christmas brings angel-song], in the second verse of which he rewrote the four last lines so that they came to say as they now say: *Gik ned for os i døden / som sol i aftenrøden, / og stod i morgengry / op for os påny* [For us he descended into death as the sun in the glow of evening, and for us he rose again in the breaking of the day]. She was also a good honest woman who had room in her heart for a great many things. She always received me with friendship and I had many pleasant conversations with her. I have told in *Tænkt og følt* II, 82-83, in what way she partially characterised herself, but I have added that her "self-assessment I will neither endorse nor refute." My suspicion of the lady of property [*godsejersken*] I have expressed above.

After she had died [1854] I went straight over to Grundtvig's and was received by him as an old, good friend. He was affected and I was affected and without anything being said on either side our differences were settled.[23] Sometime afterwards I was at a clerical convention away from the capital: I do not recall where, and neither do I recall any of the others present except for Peter Fenger. They all knew of my earlier relationship with Grundtvig but fortunately did not know that there had been a rift between us. People thought that I might be able to tell them something which they themselves did not know, and so Fenger asked me to tell about her Fru Grundtvig's last moments. But I could only tell what I had from Grundtvig himself in our last conversation: that as she lay and groaned, again and again she prayed Jesus Christ to assuage the heavy pains, but without her feeling any relief – until she prayed "Our Lord Jesus Christ" to help her, whereupon the pains ceased. Fenger could not understand this any better than the others, nor could I; but – how little indeed we do understand!

During Grundtvig's loneliness I visited him regularly and thus not infrequently met a woman quite unknown to me. This was Fru Asta Reedtz, widow of *Gehejmekonferensråd* [Privy Councillor] Reedtz, former Foreign Minister. [**GEEG p. 175**] I had known the husband a little from the *Rigsdag* and from the royal dinners, but had not exactly felt myself especially attracted by him. The widow was now entering into her twenty-ninth year, while Grundtvig was seventy-one. She was no beauty, a small, insignificant and unassuming creature; she hardly had particularly many talents or much knowledge but she was good-natured and friendly, and it was obvious that she hung on Grundtvig's lips when he spoke. A couple of years went by. One day I was sitting in my place as secretary in the *Rigsdag* and Rotwitt in the chairman's seat, when he leaned over to me and asked: "Is it true as rumour runs that Grundtvig is getting married next week to Fru Reedtz?", but in good faith I answered him an absolutely definite no. All the same, on 16 April 1858 Fru Asta Reedtz became Fru Grundtvig.

It has been suggested that Grundtvig said about his three marriages: the first was an idyll, the second a romance, the third a fairy-tale; and it is not implausible that he really did say this.[24] A more beautiful idyll than the marriage with the love of his youth it would be difficult to find, and just as truly could the second well be called a romance and the third a fairy-tale; but all three women made him happy, each in her own way, for they really were devoted and loyal to him; and even if they could not all follow him equally easily upon his soaring flight yet they all had a will to do so and all nursed him equally lovingly in his grievous illnesses, the last [Asta] until he closed his weary eyes.

Our relationship continued through all the years that remained. Grundtvig may no longer have visited us – he was too old for this and walking was too difficult for him – but I constantly visited him and was always received with the same trust and sincere kindness. Grandmother, I think, visited more rarely; her house had become too big, and the new Fru [Asta] Grundtvig was a *relative* stranger to her. All our children, however, were confirmed by Grundtvig except for Ludvig who wished to be confirmed by [J. C. R.] Frimodt, which we dared not oppose. Sofie [Reedtz], Fru Grundtvig's daughter from the first marriage, was contemporary with our Hulda which resulted in their visiting each other and becoming friends. Sofie regularly visited us, and Hulda her, and several of the other children followed suit. One winter (1858-59?),[25] Grundtvig held a series of historical lectures in his home, primarily intended for the theology [GEEG p. 176] students, but many more came and every evening our Agate was an unfailing listener. Fru Grundtvig herself would open the door to her and from start to finish Agate was her specially welcome guest. Our small children especially were playmates with her children and they could spend whole or half days together in her or our garden, or go with her on picnics.

At Constitution Day celebrations in Tivoli and the Alhambra Grundtvig and I were constantly invited as speakers and Grundtvig once gave me his wife's arm and asked me to escort her into the beautiful grounds while he himself remained in the festival arena.

It became the custom that on Grundtvig's birthday folk would gather in large flocks outside the house which he now occupied in Gammel Kongevej (later at Tuborg on Øster-bro), and of course I was never absent; but once, on the way there, I bumped into a largish throng of youths who asked me to bring him "a greeting from the young folk"; another time I received in writing a request from *Provst* [P. G.] Ahnfeldt of Skarhult to bring Grundtvig a warm greeting with a lengthy poem from him; and of course I carried out both these requests and doubtless more like them. It goes without saying that we were present at Sofie [Reedtz]'s wedding with the physician Sparrevohn, and our daughter-in-law Mine and our daughter Hulda were among her bridesmaids. Other festive occasions I will pass over.

It could not however be otherwise than that Grundtvig's political standpoints and mine diverged considerably, indeed more and more so; however, no sharp expression of disagreement was ever uttered, not from either side. The sharpest was probably the joke about the word 'ennobled' [*adlede*] which I have discussed in *Tænkt og følt* II, 83. As though by tacit agreement, we left each other in peace.

His last long and grievous illness (1867?)[26] I shall not comment upon, any more than upon any of the earlier ones. I will tell just one anecdote which few know: he had become well again and one Sunday the carriage was waiting outside the door, which was to take him to the church. But there was a coating of ice and when he went down the front steps he fell and hurt his one side. But he was determined to go to church and with some difficulty they got him into the carriage. He held out for the whole service, preached as usual and drove home again. When he got home the physician was called. His side was so swollen that the physician could not ascertain whether a couple of ribs had been broken or not, but he could well understand that the fall had caused him much pain. "But Bishop Grundtvig, how could you preach under the circumstances?" "Well, you see, if I had [GEEG p. 177] had to preach with my side it would hardly have worked, but I always preach with my mouth."

Before the physician left, he ordered Grundtvig to be put to bed, but when he had left, Grundtvig said: "Really, if you think I am going to bed! Once I was taken to bed I would probably never get out of it again." And he remained for several days sitting in his armchair, night and day as in previous times, but he recovered and lived for some years yet.

I clearly remember when I stood as godfather to Asta, Sofie Sparrevohn's eldest daughter. We spent supper and the evening at the Sparrevohns' together with Fru Grundtvig, Niels Lindberg and his wife,[27] as well as a couple of other friends. When it was time to go home again, we looked for a skovvogn[28] and so walked past Grundtvig's windows. He had no blinds pulled down but inside the window he was sitting at his work-desk. This was without doubt the last time we saw his white head. If I do not remember incorrectly, he died the next day. His son Frederik (of the second marriage) had read aloud to him from [E. G.] Geijer's *Svenska folkets historia*, but the father asked him to pause a little, and he went out for the space of an hour. When he came in again, his father was sitting dead in the armchair; the pipe had fallen out of his mouth and stood by his side, still warm. (This pipe I was supposed to have received as a memento of him, but since I had no use for it and believed besides that my days would soon be over, I asked his widow to give it to my son Hans Peter. So he owns it. Our Frederik received his desk.

15 May 1895

Talking of Grundtvig's death, I am reminded of a conversation I had with him many years earlier. He declared that he was too old for some task or other, but that it could be something for me. "Nonsense" I said, "You are younger than I am." This he could not understand, and I had to present the proof. "Yes, because, you see, it is not worth talking about the time which is past: that is both buried and forgotten. No, we are talking about the time which in all probability can still be left, and then people in your family regularly get to be over eighty, while the average in my family is fifty-five or fifty-six years. Thus there is the likelihood that you have more years left than I." He found the proof "ingenious" but still would not permit himself to be convinced. However, he told it later to Gunni Busck, for whom I had to repeat the proof on the day when he had ordained Hans [GEEG p. 178] Rørdam as his curate. But time proved that my calculation was inaccurate. To be sure, he reached eighty-nine but *I* was not only present in the great funeral procession which escorted him from *Frelsers kirke* to the little tomb in the grove in Gammel Køgegaard; eleven years later I was again present in the great circle of friends [*den store Vennekreds*] who celebrated the centenary of his birth in his birthplace, Udby. Since then, getting on for twelve years have passed and here I am still sitting in my armchair and writing down a few memories of the man who had so powerful and blessed an influence not only upon me but upon the whole of our nation. I did not come to a stop at fifty-five but have managed to get beyond eighty-four. "Man proposes but God alone disposes."

After Grundtvig's death, the relationship with his widow continued: we came to her from time to time, and she to us (though perhaps still more frequently to our son Hans Peter), and so she was present at our daughter Hulda's wedding. By and by, however, she associated herself more and more with radical circles (with [C. P.] Berg, [S. M.] Høgsbro, etc) and she herself became more and more radical, and our dealings therefore became less frequent. But

I still visited her especially in the mornings when I had a greater likelihood of meeting her on her own. And so I still had many a pleasant conversation with this friendly woman, who faithfully preserved her dead husband's memory as a sanctuary of the heart. The last time we met her was in Frederiksberg gardens where she was being wheeled along in a small invalid chair by her housekeeper and admiring friend, Filippine Larsen. We were really fond of this pious and cordial woman, and the news of her death made no small impression upon us.

1. *Studentereksamen*: matriculation – the university-administered examination by which, in Barfod's and Grundtvig's day, transition was achieved between school and university. Grundtvig, having been prepared at Aarhus Latin School, was examined in October 1800 shortly before his seventeenth birthday. In October 1827 Barfod was halfway through his sixteenth year and was being privately prepared for the examination which he took the following year, though he subsequently left the University after sitting the second University examination, without completing a degree course.

2. *Flyttedag*, removal day, was the official day for changing domiciles and undertaking removals and occurred twice a year. H. C. Andersen made it the topic and title of a story. Characteristic of the day were the piles of discarded belongings left in the streets to be picked over by scavengers. The exchange of dwellings between the Bregendahls and the Grundtvigs appears to have been a more discreet and orderly affair.

3. In fact, Grundtvig had resigned as curate at Vor Frelsers Kirke in 1826. The family continued to live in Strandgade (Christianshavn) until 1840 when they moved to Vimmelskaftet 49 in the inner city. See Index entry **Grundtvig's Copenhagen addresses**.

4. Barfod's father, Hans Peter Barfoed (1770-1841), priest and principal of a teacher training college, was offered but declined (1833) the bishopric of Ribe.

5. Published April 1834 (*Bibliografi* item 529), the article was to some extent a continuation of Grundtvig's dispute with Professor H. N. Clausen over the character and ordering of the Danish church.

6. Barfod refers to the physical illness, depression and spiritual crisis, exacerbated by a certain lack of sympathy from his bishop, J. P. Mynster, suffered by Grundtvig in the Spring of 1844. Grundtvig, in his sixtieth year, spoke to his congregation as one who was saying a final farewell but with the support of friends, especially of Gunni Busck (1798-1869) in whose home he convalesced (and composed the moving hymn *Sov sødt, Barnlille*), he made a remarkable recovery, and in July could address a mass-gathering at Skamlingsbanken.

7. Barfod's footnote: " *Tænkt og følt*, I, 23." *Tænkt og følt* [Thought and felt] I-II were two booklets containing various reminiscences including some relating to Grundtvig, published by Barfod 1882-83 under the pseudonym Palle Jyde.

8. These were the lectures, marking the lifting of personal censorship upon Grundtvig and firmly reestablishing him as a powerful and respectable voice in free public debate, which were subsequently published (edited by Svend Grundtvig) under the title *Mands Minde* [Within living memory]. With Barfod in the approach to Grundtvig were in fact P. C. Kierkegaard and H. P. N. Købke. Frederik Hammerich whom Barfod misremembers as being one of the three was instead among those who formally thanked Grundtvig at the end of the series, 26 November 1838.

9. The fiftieth anniversary of *Stavnsbaandets Ophævelse* – the repeal of the law of 1733 which tied peasantry to the district of their birth – was on 20 June 1838; see index entry **Stavnsbaandet**.

10. Barfod's footnote: "'Kingo-Grundtvig', *Dansk Kirketidende* 1846 Nr. 24." In March 1844, the Copenhagen Clerical Convention's Hymn Committee charged a working party including Grundtvig and H. L. Martensen with compiling a specimen anthology of hymns, preparatory to replacement of the old Evangelical-Christian Hymnal. Grundtvig, though ill through much of the first half of the year and a temperamental member of the party, made a major contribution to the anthology which was published in January 1845; but a year later it was

vetoed wholesale by the Convention. Bishop H. L. Martensen's account of events in this working party, and an analysis of Grundtvig's merits and failings as poet and hymnwriter, are given in items 98 and 99 below.

11. An exhortation to publish the collection as submitted to the Convention would have been redundant, since it had already been in print since January 1845. The deputation's mission seems rather to have been to encourage Grundtvig to put his own draft (free of the compromises made in committee) into print in the name of the Vartov congregation. This is what eventually happened.

12. Barfod's footnote: "Grundtvig constantly made contributions to the periodical, the first volume of which was prefaced by his poem *Brage og Idun*."

13. Barfod's recollection is inaccurate: it was the Danske Samfund [Danish Society], not Det Skandinaviske Selskab [The Scandinavian Association] which he founded in April 1839. He did not manage to write the "more detailed account" mentioned.

14. Barfod refers to the peaceful events leading to Frederik VII's renunciation of royal absolutism and acceptance of constitutional democracy, 1848. The mass procession to the palace of Christiansborg was intended to make clear to the King the people's expectations. By the time the deputation of its spokesmen was admitted to an audience with the King, he had already acted upon their wishes. See the Index entry **Grundloven**.

15. Some of Grundtvig's songs relating to the war of 1848 were published in special editions, others in his weekly periodical *Danskeren* [The Dane]. Texts are printed in *PS* VII.

16. Barfod's footnote: "*Tænkt og følt*, II, 44." See note 5 above.

17. Barfod's footnote: "Den grundlovgivende Rigsforsamlings Historie [The history of the Constituent Assembly] by L. K. D." Barfod, its author, formed his pseudonym from the final letters of his three names.

18. When Grundtvig's first wife Elisabeth (Lise) died, an armistice had just come into force in the Three Years' War over Slesvig and Holsten; but her two sons Johan and Svend were still on active service. Their close childhood friend Vilhelm Blom had been killed at the Battle of Isted in the previous year.

19. Barfod's footnote: "*Tænkt og følt*, II, 78-79."

20 Barfod's footnote: "*Tænkt og følt*, II, 82-83."

21. Barfod's footnote: "The last number of *Dannebrog* to be edited by Barfod is no. 35 for 22 November 1853. The next number (36 for 2 December) and the rest of the year is edited by Grundtvig himself."

22. Store Kongens Mølle, substantial house, outbuildings and windmill on the Vestervold [Western ramparts], Copenhagen, where (1846-64) Queen Caroline Amalie's Charity School was housed and where Peter Boisen taught (from 1851 as its principal) and he and his wife Meta (Grundtvig's daughter) had their home.

23. Barfod's own account of the reconciliation, shortly after the death of Grundtvig's second wife Marie on 9 July 1854, raises interesting questions about a mythologising tendency in Vilhelm Birkedal's anecdote (*GEEG* p. 206 below) which associates the reconciliation with Svend Grundtvig's wedding (December 1858) and attributes the initiative to Grundtvig ("a small victory he had won over himself").

24. Grundtvig's poem *Til min Asta* [To my Asta] says something similar (*PS* VIII, 294-95). Although it was not published until 1891 it most probably dates from the year of the marriage (1858) and could have been known at least by report to many beyond the immediate family circle.

25. In fact, it was in the winter of 1860-61 that Grundtvig gave the first of his series of lectures on church history in his home in Gammel Kongevej, Copenhagen. Two more series followed, in the winters of 1861-62 and 1862-63.

26. Barfod refers to Grundtvig's breakdown on Palm Sunday 1867. See Index entry **Palm Sunday 1867**

27. Barfod's footnote: "Clara Cathrine Lindberg, f. Monrad."

28. A *skovvogn* was a hire-carriage in which people sat in rows of seats behind each other, typically used for carrying people to, around and from the woods outside the city, especially those along the Øresund coast including *Dyrehaven*.

87. *Hans Brun:* Biskop N. F. S. Grundtvigs Levnetsløb udførligt fortalt fra 1839 *[Bp NFSG's Life recounted in fullest detail from 1839] (2 vols., 1882), I, 133.*

"He could be somewhat curt when someone he did not know came and interrupted him."

There emanated from him [Grundtvig] a sort of awesomeness, especially earlier on when he was deeply engaged in his greatest scholarly labours. In the midst of his busy industriousness night and day, he could be somewhat curt when someone he did not know came and interrupted him and did not exactly register that there was something serious going on. Thus there was a mason or some such who, in the beginning of the Thirties, went up to him and started somewhat awkwardly saying that it seemed to him the Church was so topsy-turvy these days. Grundtvig: "Oh really? you would perhaps prefer the spire to point downwards. I must send for you when something goes wrong with my stove."

88. *Hans Brun:* Biskop N. F. S. Grundtvigs Levnetsløb udførligt fortalt fra 1839 *[Bp NFSG's Life recounted in fullest detail from 1839] (2 vols., 1882), I, 134; GEEG Stk. 28, p. 179.*

Another of Brun's anecdotes amusedly illustrating the hazards of approaching Grundtvig in his den.

[GEEG p. 174] A man, who was not in the slightest way given to drinking *akvavit* took a little dram to strengthen his courage one day when he was to go and talk with Grundtvig. Grundtvig notices his breath and instantly dismisses him: "I don't talk with people whose breath reeks of *akvavit*."

89. *Peter Frederik Adolph Hammerich:* Frederik Hammerich. Et Levnetsløb *[A life] ed. Angul Hammerich (1882), I, pp. 271-72; GEEG Stk. 29, p. 179.*

Frederik Hammerich (1809-77), like Frederik Barfod, spent four decades in close association with Grundtvig and, like Barfod, was a sympathetic but astute and not uncritical observer of Grundtvig's strengths and weaknesses. Unlike Barfod, however, Hammerich secured himself a distinguished place in the establishment of the day, as Professor in Church History in Copenhagen University (from 1859), the first of Grundtvig's circle to gain such academic preferment. He was to play a significant part in the dissensions over the political stance of Grundtvigianism especially around the time of Grundtvig's death. Grundtvig followed his academic work with

interest and from time to time made his contributions to it. Here Hammerich recalls their earliest meetings, and adds to the record of a certain shortage of social graces in Grundtvig from
which Hans Christian Andersen took insult – though it is also Hammerich (*Et levnetsløb*, 1882)
who records a chance, and apparently amiable, meeting between Andersen and Grundtvig many
years later when both were old men and Grundtvig sat smoking his pipe one summer evening
on the Øresund coast.

About that time[1] I ventured for the first time to call on Grundtvig […] [He] received me
with much friendliness. We talked, I remember, about modern Greek and the universal-
historical importance of Greece; and he offered me a pipe, something he could easily forget
to do. It was not always easy, by the way, to get him talking: rather one had, so to speak, to
wind him up, and this I could do because I was determined to. After a while he would then
start conversing fluently and when he really got into the spirit, it was a joy to listen to him.
At that time I liked to turn the conversation to historical and poetic subjects which were
especially on my mind, and I thank him for many an enlightenment, many a consolation,
many a characteristically ingenious, teasing utterance.

If on the other hand one sat silent with him, he in response could sit just as silent.
Unlike Harms, he did not instantly come forward on the spot with a thoughtful idea; on the
whole he was afraid of opening himself up and delivering something other and more than
that which stirred within him at that moment. Never would he offer people mere pleasant-
ries; he was far more likely to give someone or other offence. At a tea-party with Christian
VIII, H. C. Andersen was on one occasion going to read something aloud. Grundtvig walked
out. Andersen could never forgive him for this, and called him "a rude old man."[3]

1. Sometime in the eighteen-thirties.

2. Claus Harms (1778-1855), in some respects Grundtvig's counterpart in Kiel (duchy of Holsten, then under Danish sovereignty), opposed rationalism, battled for the cause of 'true'
   Lutheranism (publishing his own ninety-five theses in 1817) and gained the popular title of
   'the second Luther.'

3. Walking out on the social performances of others was an old habit of Grundtvig's, according
   to Fredrik Schmidt (item 68). He himself enjoyed having an audience, whether in reading his
   own poetic composition to the gathered clergy in Roskilde (item 71, Daniel Peter Smith) or
   on more formal occasions; but doubtless he would have drawn a distinction between events,
   upon the criterion of substance and its potential to edify rather than merely to entertain.

90. Hans Lassen Martensen: Af mit Levnet [From my life], II (1883), pp. 49-58; GEEG Stk. 30, pp. 179-184.

H. L. Martensen, Bishop of Sjælland 1854-84, was described by the English writer Edmund
Gosse (1849-1928) as the greatest philosophical genius that Europe's Protestant Church owned.
Though Gosse was not necessarily the ultimate authority upon such matters, it is a fact that
Martensen's international standing was high and it is therefore a considerable accolade when
he writes of Grundtvig and Bishop J. P. Mynster (1775-1854) as "these men who, in this century,
in Christian and ecclesiastical respects are the most important in our Fatherland." But similarly
his criticism of some of Grundtvig's key ideas must also be allowed to carry weight, and not

least his reasoned rejection of Grundtvig's "so-called peerless discovery [*hans saakaldte mageløse Opdagelse*]" quoted below, where he writes, with characteristically generous acknowledgment of what he found attractive and admirable, of his earlier friendship with Grundtvig.

If I am now to talk about my personal relationship to Grundtvig and [J. P.] Mynster, these men who, in this century, in Christian and ecclesiastical respects are the most important in our Fatherland, then I will begin with Grundtvig. We must go back to the year of the Reformation Jubilee, 1836, because in that year I went to him for the first time. As mentioned earlier, [P. K.] Marheineke had come here as a deputy. He desired to make Grundtvig's acquaintance, and that I should escort him. True enough, I did not know [GEEG p. 180] Grundtvig at all, but nevertheless it was arranged, I do not now remember how. Grundtvig gave indication that it would be a great pleasure for him to receive us. So we set off for his place one evening. He was living in Christianshavn in the vicinity of Frederiks Kirke, himself opened the door to us and received us, even my lowly self, very amicably. A great deal of the conversation was of minor significance; it concerned itself with the Reformation Jubilee festival and the speeches which had been held there, about which – and especially about Clausen's speech – Grundtvig expressed himself dismissively, in that he viewed them as reverberations (*Nachhall*)[1] from times which had more or less vanished and had no spiritual vitality. But after that the discussion turned to Speculation and speculative theology which Marheineke greatly commended as that of which the age stood in need. Grundtvig would have no part in this and declared that he would be afraid to have any part in it. "Why would you be afraid?" said Marheineke. Grundtvig replied: "I am afraid for myself. For me, the principal antithesis [*Hovedmodsætning*] is the antithesis [*Modsætning*] between Life and Death." That is, he wished to make it clear that life could be lost or suffer harm through this submission to speculation, to what he used to call *Hjernespind* [literally 'brain-spinning' – intellectual fabrication]. Marheineke treated the matter jocularly and declared that the difference between life and death was indeed a considerable difference, but that one might perhaps get back to logical antitheses here, and considered as the chief antithesis, from out of which one had to proceed, the antithesis between Thinking and Being. Grundtvig answered good-humouredly: "You great philosophers forget Life in the erection of your intellectual edifices." This, roughly, is what he said. I restricted myself to listening, and even though I could not undertake to give up Speculation yet I could not help but find – and it accorded with my own earlier experiences – that in his antithesis between Life and Death there was something very striking, it was one of those philosophical flashes which Grundtvig often had and in which he could sometimes express a whole life-view. By this he wanted to say that those antitheses which for us are the most important and which determine our undertakings and our enigma, are far more than logical or intellectual antitheses, but are what have also been called existential antitheses [*existentielle Modsætninger*]. I have found a comparable statement in Steffens, who says in his *Religionsphilosophie*: "All philosophy must have an ethical significance. It is not the dialectic between Being and Nothing; it is the struggle between Heaven and Hell and the first already determined victory, which constitute [GEEG p. 181] the proper subject of all scientific enquiry [*Videnskab*]." The saying reminds me also of Franz Baader. In later times I have often thought back to the flash of light which shone forth in that conversation when Grundtvig said: "Mein Gegensatz ist Leben und Tod." [For me the antithesis is Life and Death]. With the years and growing experience, these words – which are indeed also those of the Scriptures – have gained a new and deeper power for me.

From first to last the conversation proceeded in German, and it was interesting to me to observe how Grundtvig expressed himself in this tongue. His pronunciation was not particularly good but I had to admire the way in which he always chose the most powerful, the most charged and the most suggestive expressions and phrases. This was that great genius for language which could not belie itself. Although he spoke German, one knew that it was Grundtvig who was talking. As we left, he was so friendly as to ask me in Danish to visit him more often, adding in that incomparable manner by which he was able to win over younger people when he wished: "We could both get something out of it."

On the way home Marheineke expressed his great satisfaction and pleasure over this visit, at the same time, however, as being unable to refrain from the observation that natures such as those of Grundtvig and [Henrik] Steffens – to whom he saw well enough that Grundtvig was related – always came back to Life instead of sticking to antitheses of Thought [Tankemodsætninger]. Marheineke just like [G. W. F.] Hegel would have everything logical.

From that time on I visited Grundtvig more frequently and always found him friendly and welcoming. In ordinary conversation he had an admirable eloquence which was often mingled with wittiness and humour. I have conversed with him on many of the most interesting subjects. I got him to express himself about Danish poetry, about [Adam] Oehlenschlæger, [Jens] Baggesen, [B. S.] Ingemann, and sometimes also about his own poetry, always to my enjoyment and instruction. On mythology and revelation, on the folkelige and the Christian I have heard him express in speech what I already essentially knew from his writings. In history, we would often return to the Middle Ages and we talked at various times about Ansgar and his dreams. Grundtvig had a particular predilection for the Middle Ages, and declared that still in our own days there were characters who basically belonged in the Middle Ages; and I sometimes took the impression that he regarded himself as a medieval character. In theology proper or dogmatics he engaged himself hardly at all, [GEEG p. 182] even if he could on the odd occasion engage himself with an individual point such as Mellemtilstanden[2] or the thousand-year kingdom,[3] when he expected that the prophet Elijah would return in the flesh. With Grundtvig the hymn took the place of dogmatics; in the hymn he found and expressed the teachings of the Faith. But I always detected in him that lofty Christian outlook which I had admired from the beginning. There was especially one point where I sympathised utterly and with all my heart: his conception of corporeality. Although the spirit was for him the foremost, indeed in truth the sole reality, yet he could not think of the spirit without corporeality, and a spirit from which all nature and corporeality were excluded was for him merely a vapid spirit, the Rationalists' spirit, with which he could have nothing to do. Thus he had within his outlook a loftier spiritual realism, which was indeed also to be found in Lutherdom, particularly in the sacramental doctrine. Here I could entirely agree, and likewise also in the great significance he attached to that metaphorical language which had for him a greater truth and reality than abstract designations, and whose loftiest form he found partly in the Holy Scriptures, in the sayings of the prophets and of Christ, partly in the myths, in the symbolic language of the North. The language of metaphor was not to be played about with, and he quite often declared that genuine poets treated metaphorical language seriously and through it expressed the truth of their understanding of life.

On the Christian sermon I had various conversations with him. I declared it as my conviction that the Christian sermon was the highest spiritual product a person could bring forth, higher than the poet's, higher than the philosopher's, because the sermon is a work of the entire, undivided personality, compressed into itself, to which all else spiritual is the means. In none of the other productions is the whole undivided personality entailed. In a way he went along with this, but at the same time he set the condition that the sermon must then have a *prophetic* character, which I did not find essential even if I was by no means willing to have my characterisation applied to each and every mediocre sermon. Once when we were talking about sermons Grundtvig said: "Mynster has written *Om den Kunst at prædike* [On the art of preaching]. If I were to write, I would write: Preaching is no art." For the composition of a sermon he gave this excellent rule, that everything here depends upon having [GEEG p. 183] a fertile starting-point, from which a small entity can emerge. One must have an egg out of which there can come a bird. When I once suggested that no doubt he did not need to write out his sermons like others, he answered that in fact he wrote out his sermons with great care.[4] But true enough he gave for this the extremely curious reason, that he was obliged to write them out since otherwise he would not be sure of catching the right *folkelige* expression.

He was undeniably attractive to me, indeed captivating. And yet I was also to experience the off-putting. Naturally, I neither could nor would avoid talking with him about his so-called "peerless discovery" [*hans saakaldte "mageløse Opdagelse"*] which has been decisive for what people here in this country have presumed to call *den kirkelige Anskuelse* [the view, or concept, of the Church]. Of course I had to acknowledge what I still acknowledge, that he has drawn attention to the Apostolic Creed, that profession of facts, in such a way that not in a long while will it be possible to forget it among us. Indeed in other countries too, independently of Grundtvig, people have been led by an inward necessity to the Apostolic Creed as being, alongside the Scriptures, the oldest testimony about the original and authentic Christianity. I say expressly 'independently of Grundtvig' because with the exception of Denmark and a portion of Norway the whole of the rest of Christendom has paid no regard at all to the discovery; even if it knows of it, it has not found that any significance can be attached to it. Of course I for my part could do no other than sympathise with the joy over a collective profession from the Church's most distant antiquity in which all Christians could meet irrespective of their confessional differences. But a strong resistance stirred within me when I was supposed to accept that in the forty days after the resurrection Christ presented to the Apostles this formulation as containing all the conditions for salvation, nothing more nor less. Christ thereby came to appear to me as a new Moses, and regardless of all talk of freedom we were led back into a thraldom of the Law and the Letter. And a resistance no less strong stirred in me when I was supposed to regard this formulation as belonging with the institution of baptism. To the institution of the sacraments belongs neither more nor less than what the Lord himself has said and done. But the Church has never known anything about the Apostolic Creed belonging to the institution of baptism. Many baptismal proceedings are carried out without the Apostolic Creed and without their validity for that reason being [GEEG p. 184] denied by the Church. I realised that this assertion, if it were to be taken seriously and were consistently implemented, must lead to a Sect. I shall not however expound any further here what I have expounded in detail in other contexts.[5] Here I shall merely observe that at that time this difference did not bring an end to the friendly relationship. Grundtvig let me talk and set forth my objections, and I listened with patience to the "God preserve us" [*Gud bevares*] which he uttered many times in connection with my false reasonings and my blindness. But I had a suspicion, a premonition, that here was an issue which could lead to a schism, lead to my distancing myself from him; for it appeared clear to me that I belonged to quite another camp than that into which he would lead us. In the best and most propitious case he could only lead me into that old-catholic Church in the second and third centuries with Irenaeus and Tertullian, while the Church of the Reformation was for me something far deeper and loftier. Notwithstanding that Grundtvig maintained he was in true unity with the Reformation, and notwithstanding that he had preserved within his purview many good reminiscences from his earlier Lutheran period, yet – I could not see it otherwise – the *Principle* was breached.

1. The German word in parenthesis to the Danish term *Efterklange* is supplied by Martensen.

2. The condition in which, according to a certain theological view, the soul waits during the period between death of the body and judgment of the soul.

3. Refers to the thousand-year reign of the saints and the imprisonment of Satan which John says is 'the first resurrection' (Revelation 20:4-7). At the end of the thousand years Satan will be loosed and there will be a general resurrection of the dead and judgment (Revelation 7-15).

4. Written texts of more than 3000 of Grundtvig's sermons survive.

5. Martensen's most significant discussion of Grundtvig and Grundtvigianism is in his *Til Forsvar mod den saakaldte Grundtvigianisme* [For a defence against the so-called Grundtvigianism] (1863).

91. Carl Joakim Brandt: from a diary entry (1839), published in Danske Kirketidende [Danish Church News] (1893), cols. 232-33; GEEG Stk. 31, pp. 184-85.

To Grundtvig, universal history necessarily meant the exposition of that Christian understanding of history which a Christian historian must necessarily expound: on it rested much revelation and prophecy. Concerned as he was with the place of the Danish congregation in the universal plan, it was natural that he should wish a Danish historical society to set its objectives widely enough to accommodate the universal context. In this way, such a society would vitally engage itself and the public in issues of spiritual reality and immediacy rather than wasting its efforts and opportunities upon dead words. Molbech was of old an opponent of Grundtvig's approach to historical writing, as (apparently) was a majority of other quite distinguished persons present at the meeting which Molbech convened in February 1839 in order to launch the *Dansk Historisk Forening*. The student C. J. Brandt (1817-89) is to be seen as typical of the young generation Grundtvig had won over to himself in Copenhagen with his recent well-received 'Mands Minde' lectures in Borchs Kollegium. Brandt's scorn for the cultural establishment of the city (including his employer, Kolderup-Rosenvinge) – more interested (he suggests) in society offices and rules than in the great search for truth and things of the spirit – declares him to be a worthy follower of the old campaigner who had just left the meeting, apparently insulted by an accusation that he was merely pursuing self-interest. Over this period, Brandt was studying at the University and developing an interest in church and literary history, with a particular interest in medieval Danish texts, in which field he was later to publish. Just over thirty years later he was to become Grundtvig's successor at Vartov; see further the Index entry **Brandt**, Carl Joakim.

⁓

[Christian] Molbech has founded a "*dansk historisk Forening*" [Danish Historical Association] which will publish a periodical besides major national undertakings in history, geography, etc. On Friday [22 February 1839] I was present when the provisional administration's draft of laws for the Society were to be debated in Auditorium 3 of Studiegaarden.

Against the first paragraph Grundtvig voiced opposition. After a little introduction, as to how the Society's objective to awaken historical "Spirit and Interest" was as though spoken from out of his own heart, he complained that the Society wanted to set its limits at collecting only "*Danish* historical monuments" and at publishing only works relating to "Denmark's" history, geography, etc. After a quite vehement dispute with Molbech and several of the Committee, he got "Danish" removed from the first place by a majority vote, but after even more vehement debate on the second he had to endure his proposition on the latter falling through. Shortly afterwards he got up [GEEG p. 185] and left, and it was clear that he was not exactly very satisfied. I could almost believe that someone had been churlish enough to remind him that he himself was working on a Universal History, so his proposition could have a self-interested appearance; at any rate, I heard him say: "God preserve us! surely I cannot be held in suspicion!" No, certainly not! of self-interest? not by your blindest, most stupid enemy!

I cannot deny that he behaved obstinately, but it is after all a case of one man being worth the lot of them; he bounds up like a lion and fills the hall with his *Bjarkemaal*,[1] whilst the manikins take fright.

It was amusing to see how as it were the tied tongues of all the little ones burst free once he was gone. They were not at all at ease in his presence. Naturally, Rosenvinge[2] was also among his opponents and he recounted afterwards that Grundtvig had spoken to him about how the Society ought to work with "the living word instead of the dead pen, etc." of which, however, he had understood almost nothing; but it is to be seen from this that Grundtvig had in mind to oppose more than paragraph 1, and that it was not his original intention to leave immediately.

After his departure there was discussion back and forth for a couple of hours, but not about "Danish and universal-historical but about the living word or spirit and life" – no, but whether the Governing Body should be elected by Peter or by Paul, about Honorary Members and Committees and suchlike curious matters, until finally five members of the Governing Body were chosen by vote.[3]

1. Brandt shows himself a faithful follower of Gr in this use of Nordic heroic allusion; see Index entry **Bjarkemaal**.

2. J. L. A. Kolderup-Rosenvinge (1792-1850) was a professor of law at the University and a distinguished legal historian, for whose family Brandt, while at university, worked as private tutor. On grounds for antipathy between him and Grundtvig's supporters, see endnote 18 to item 93.

3. Brandt's rather elliptic statement of the theme of discussion after Grundtvig's departure seems to mean that the assembly did not continue discussing Grundtvig's argument – namely, that the issue under debate was nothing as paltry as that of 'Danish history' versus 'universal history' but was rather the more radical and comprehensive issue of central Christian truth and realities (living word, spirit, life) versus blinkered conformity with conventional scholarly categories ("the dead pen"). Instead the assembly spent two hours discussing offices and rules. The committee elected comprised Christian Molbech, L. Engelstoft, J. L. A. Kolderup-Rosenvinge, J. N. Madvig, and Pastor P. C. S. Gad.

Priest at Vartov 1839-1872

92. Hans Brun: Biskop N. F. S. Grundtvigs Levnetsløb udførligst
fortalt fra 1839 *[Bp NFSG's Life recounted in fullest detail from
1839] (2 vols., 1882), I, 134-36; GEEG Stk. 32, pp. 185-7.*

The abundant circumstantial detail in many of Brun's anecdotes, gathered in from many sources
in Denmark and in Norway, can communicate a graphic impression of the increasing profusion
of demands made upon Grundtvig, now in his late fifties and firmly established as a prominent
figure in Denmark's cultural life. The juxtaposition in which Brun places the earnest young
seminarist Andresen calling to thank Grundtvig for his sermon and the plump *Provst* calling
with greetings and gossip from Nysø and angling for a dinner invitation, all set against the
background of domesticity in Christianshavn, is telling.

⟡

At that same time [1839] – or perhaps the year after – there also visited him a quite young
seminarist,[1] [P. R.] Andresen, a South-Jutlander [*Sønderjyde*] by birth, but resident tutor
in Tvedestrand in a house where the wife or the grandmother was Danish and where they
therefore looked for their resident tutors in a teachers' training college in Fyn. Andresen,
who was not without poetic talents, will be known, at least by name, to all who know of
Den Norske Folkeskole from about 1850, as up until his death (1853) he was [GEEG p. 186]
one of its co-editors. In '39 (or '40) he had come to Copenhagen with a sailing-ship and had
not as yet much explored Grundtvig's "persuasions" and knew only a few of his poems, but
nevertheless had heard so much about him that he wanted to go to Vartov. The preacher
however corresponded so little to his preconception of the famous man that he had to ask:
Was that really Grundtvig? No, Grundtvig had gone away, to southern Sjælland.

Next Sunday on the other hand Andresen was in no doubt, and on Monday morning
he goes to call on Grundtvig who then still lived out in Christianshavn in the neighbourhood of Frederiks Kirke, on the third floor. He rings the bell, and Grundtvig himself comes
out in his shirtsleeves. "Thank you for the sermon yesterday!" says Andresen. "Oh, so you
were in church. Please come in!" So they went into a longish room from which one could
see at least something of the sea and where there stood a writing-desk, standing by which
he had written so many a page. His sons, wearing blouses, were sitting at a table with Peter
Syv's *Kæmpeviser* in front of them. Grundtvig says: "There you see my boys. You can go
now, lads" and he was so jovial, friendly and pleasant to the young man that he stayed
there for quite a long time. Meanwhile there enters a very fat *provst* [dean],[2] with a greeting
to Grundtvig from [Bertel] Thorvaldsen who was staying at Nysø Manor. Grundtvig exchanged some words with him and then says: "Will the Dean not be so kind as to come back
and eat dinner?" The fat Dean excused himself and left. "That's a man who likes his food,
that one" said Grundtvig. "Yes, I am not inviting you to come here to dinner, but won't you

be so kind as to come here tomorrow evening, then we will go to the Danish Society [*Det danske Samfund*] together." Naturally Andresen returned, and was to become so intimate with Grundtvig that he showed him a number of Christmas hymns he had written, which Grundtvig had likely enough kept from the first visit and which he thought quite well of, but remarked about one of them that it was "too polemical." They drank tea, and Andresen also saw his daughter Meta in the red dress. At the Danish Society that evening was also [Adam] Øhlenschlæger, to whom Grundtvig presented Andresen – who therefore called on the 'King of Poets' next day, but found him stiffer to approach than the other great man. It was not Grundtvig who spoke at the Danish Society that evening but, according to the description, probably the present bishop P. C. Kierkegaard, who visited [**GEEG p. 187**] Grundtvig a lot, and had even made "the Living Church-Word" to some extent the subject of his disputation for the Licentiate's degree.[3]

When Andresen is bidding farewell, Grundtvig says: "Sea-folk do not always ride the day they saddle; if you are staying longer down here you must be so good as to visit me again." In the house, Grundtvig presented him with his *Prøver af den Gammel-Danske Rim-Krønike* [1834] in its revised form, in which he also received his autograph in the words: "To Mr Andresen from the Author."

1. Though in English the term 'seminarist' is commonly reserved for a student training in a theological college or seminary, I use it here as an alternative to the cumbrous 'student in a teacher training college [Danish '*seminarium*'].

2. Brun's footnote: "Pavels from Sandefjord." Possibly *Provst* Peter Pavels: see Index entry **Pavels,** Provst Peter.

3. Kierkegaard's thesis, which introduced Grundtvig's ideas into the theological argument, was entitled *De theologia vere Christiana* [On true Christian theology].

93. *Schøller Parelius Vilhelm Birkedal:* Personlige Oplevelser i et langt Liv *[Personal experiences in a long life], II* (1890), pp. 39-63; GEEG Stk. 33, pp. 187-206.

When Bishop J. P. Mynster (1775-1854) did his best to disparage Grundtvig and his proposals concerning the dissolution of parish ties [*Sognebaandsløsning*] in Roskilde in January 1839, the bid was, in one significant point at least, counterproductive: it lost him the loyalty of Vilhelm Birkedal (1809-92) who wrote: "My mind was tormented and agitated during Mynster's ruthless, unjust and bitter assault upon a man who always appeared to me as one of our nation's noblest, most spiritually endowed personalities, whom I may not previously have followed but whom I felt did not deserve so uncharitable and iron-hard a condemnation." Before long, Birkedal had made direct contact with Grundtvig and was to become one of his most active allies in the 'church struggle' to achieve Grundtvig's ideal vision of free congregations gathered round free priests: "To establish a *Free Church* [*Frikirke*] which in its doctrine could well adhere to the Augsburg Confession but yet would keep doctrinal formulations strictly apart from the common faith and would make *free* use of Scripture's 'things old and new' and make the church service far more alive, as regards the Lord's own institutions, sermon, prayer and hymn-singing alike, than it had been for many centuries – *this* was now [1832-39] my desire" (Gr). At Ryslinge on Fyn (where Christen Kold had Birkedal's support in setting up his Grundtvigian-backed folk-highschool in 1851), after much prolonged agitation and an eventual change in the law (1868) , Birkedal became Denmark's first *valgmenighedspræst*, appointed by the free choice of his congregation, which nevertheless remained within the national church. Later he entered politics, allying himself with the more conservative of the Grundtvigian politicians; and he published various pieces in support of Grundtvig and Grundtvig's view of the Church and universal history. His reminiscences of a career in alliance with Grundtvig constitute key documents in the archives of Grundtvigianism.

⌒

I am now to give a picture, in approximate chronological sequence, of my contact with the man whom I have named in the title. But I feel a natural embarrassment about tackling this undertaking; partly because there exist so many biographies of and contributions about this most renowned spokesman of the Danish Church that my contribution thereto will only be an extremely poor one; and partly because I myself in a general way have sought to give an outline of his portrait as a Christian witness and a chieftain of the people [*folkelig Høvding*] in my book *De syv Folkemenigheder* [The seven national congregations], which I can mention as my perception of his public character and importance. I cannot entirely bypass him in these pages which are supposed to tell about my relationship to the more important personalities in the course of my life, nor indeed have I promised to give a comprehensive and exhaustive account of the *whole* life and actions of those concerned, but only to point to what I myself have *personally* experienced in a more or less fruitful coexistence with them. There have been many who have been able to enjoy a quite differently intimate and thoroughgoing acquaintance with Grundtvig; but even so I have had not a little to do with him, and of the different experiences I had during a friendly – from his side paternal, from my side filial – involvement with him there are perhaps various ones of interesting and characterising worth which can add some traits to his spiritual character or confirm what others have to a fuller extent pointed out as being peculiar to him.

Already as a pupil at school and later as a student I was, as earlier recounted, influenced by him, by his preaching in Vor Frelsers Kirke and Frederiks Kirke as well as by his writings, especially his *Roskilde-Rim* and his *Nordens Sindbilledsprog*. But he did not become my chief mentor [**GEEG p. 188**] at that time. I became priest in 1837 as an adherent of [J. P.] Mynster. Then came the transmutation in me, by virtue of two powerful spiritual influences from different sides – the one repelling, the other attracting.

The first consisted of Mynster's and the scriptural-theologians' [*Skriftteologernes*] process against Grundtvig and his tendency, especially in the Roskilde *Stænderforsamling* [Assembly of the Estates of the Realm] during the handling of the proposal for the dissolution of the parochial tie [*Sognebaandets Løsning*].¹ I have previously indicated how my mind was tormented and agitated during Mynster's ruthless, unjust and bitter assault upon a man who always appeared to me as one of our nation's noblest, most spiritually endowed personalities, whom I may not previously have followed but whom I felt did not deserve so uncharitable and iron-hard a condemnation. The second influence came from probing Christian discussions with a neighbouring priest, [C. F.] Hassenfeldt, who had long since committed himself to Grundtvig and who caused me more and more to feel that he had solid ground under his feet, while my scriptural theology was at bottom without firm footing. Amidst these two spiritual cross-currents I wrote my judgment of the Assembly's handling of the issue mentioned. Shortly afterwards I came to Copenhagen and my friends thought that I ought to visit Grundtvig (1839). When, that first time that I saw him in his house, I stepped in through the door he ended a conversation with a man, a Norwegian I think, with these closing words: "It depends not on what we say or think about Christianity, but on the words of the Lord to us." Strangely enough – for in these words lie, as in a bud, the whole Grundtvigian [*Grundtvigske*] view.[2] Granted, I had expected a more welcoming reception that the one I was offered. I had, after all, accorded Grundtvig a deep appreciation in my book,[3] and he, in a published letter to an English priest,[4] had expressed his pleasure over my defence of him and his viewpoint, indeed, in much stronger terms than I deserved for this, my first very deficient participation in the Church struggle. I gave him my name but the first minutes' conversation was extremely reserved and non-committal. Finally he offered me a chair and a pipe, and beneath the smoke of the tobacco developed little by little a lively conversation; he invited me to dinner with him and was then extremely communicative and entered into quite deep-going ecclesiastical subjects, which I now no longer recall, and in which I was indeed principally only a listener.

Grundtvig has been attributed, from a certain quarter, with a great weakness for flattery, and has been blamed for desiring to hear people echo his own words. [GEEG p. 189] First of all I would ask: which of us dares declare himself completely free of this weakness; doubtless Grundtvig too had to pay his due to this household imp. But his vanity was in any case of quite another sort than the ordinary. For it is otherwise usual that the vain person shrinks from thrusting his admirers away by immediately and strongly attacking them when they see fit to express themselves wrongly and untenably about that which counts as truth for the person concerned. One compromises, keeps quiet, or speaks half ambiguously in order not to forgo the admirer's goodwill or allow him to notice that one quite disagrees with him. Grundtvig was not so: even in those moments when he was being most highly exalted by the person or persons present, privately or publicly, he was always prepared for the fray and ready to strike his blow right in the middle of that train of thought when he thought it conflicted with the viewpoint he had upon the matter; and I have not seldom been witness to the way in which he, right in the middle of fervent demonstrations of homage, would throw a bomb into the ranks of the eulogisers and in one stroke reduce them to silence and embarrassment. There will perhaps be an opportunity later in these communications of mine to present examples of this. It was also the case with him, that at bottom he was averse towards every obsequiousness and every parroting of his words. Even though he was often vehement and almost offensive during an exchange of words on important matters, and could burst out: "But God preserve me, how can you say such a thing?" as though one had come from a fools' paradise with one's observations, nevertheless he always esteemed one's spirit and candour when one stood up against him, and it always ended with one coming closer to him than previously after such a skirmish, whilst the parrots sank in his esteem when he saw and felt that it *was* parrotry they came with. For his was a warrior-spirit and he respected an honest open challenge. But quite definitely, as I perceived him, he had no special talent for judging the individual, and not infrequently allowed himself to be paid lip-service without noticing it. There has been none among us like him for judging great minds on the grand scale: in world history, in the annals of the Church he has had a clear eye for the conflicts between the various combative and catalysing forces and has been able to separate the genuine ore from all the fool's gold. He was long-sighted and sharp-sighted when it came to scanning across the ages and that which stirred and filled them. But he was shortsighted as regards the individual personalities who [GEEG p. 190] approached him, and he was often not good, in his personal relationships, at distinguishing the parasitic plant from the thought-flower rooted in the soil of truth. Not a few who knew how to come out with Grundtvigian phrases, whether concerning people or church, were able to ingratiate themselves and play a role with him without his discovering for a long time the hollowness of these so-called supporters. But it was not because they appeared to pay him homage, but because in his unsuspiciousness he took much to be honest goods in the individual, which were not.

This freedom from the desire merely to please also revealed itself in Grundtvig in his capacity as proclaimer of the Word. Never did he allow himself, out of regard for any external thing, to be tempted away from his unostentatious, even manner of preaching the gospel. It never happened – as not so infrequently does perhaps happen with priests – that on particular occasions when there were unusual listeners of greater or lesser intellectual rank around his pulpit he would aim to speak in a loftier and more so-called intellectual tone of voice than was otherwise in daily use. When, on the Sunday after the Scandinavian church assembly [det skandinaviske Kirkemøde] in Copenhagen in [July] 1857, he preached in his church where there were present men and priests from Sweden and Norway, I recall that Fr[ederik] Boisen[5] thought and secretly wished that Grundtvig would have spoken then in such a way that the strangers could get a grand impression of a grand proclamation, he wanted to see Grundtvig preach on this occasion with a mightier flight than was otherwise usual. That he could let the Word's rushing wings of the spirit go forth across the congregation and the crowds, so that the soul's ocean would heave and something would glimmer before the eye – this he had demonstrated, and when one reads his *Søndagsbog* [Sunday book] then one gets the feeling that a mighty force and great visions pass before one. But in his later years as priest at Vartov the rough turbulence had abated – the spiritual vitality in him had sought for itself a deeper level and the powerful organ-tone had quietened down to a gentler tone as in the eventide when the storm has abated and the waves speak of peace and love. Then it was as though in the clear waters one could view the deep bottom. But this was not a decline but an advance in his witness, as truly as "the quiet Spirit's incorruptible being"[6] is Christianity's innermost core and yet in the end is stronger and more lastingly effectual than the rushing and beating of wings which often perhaps pass over the hearers and can momentarily bend them but yet often not reach to the deepest place in their hearts. The testimony which Grundtvig bore sank deep [GEEG p. 191] where there were ears with which to hear. On that occasion in 1857 Boisen was disappointed; for Grundtvig appeared as usual with his quiet but deeply inspiriting words and there was absolutely no aim of making anything other and more out of his sermon than he was accustomed to do; he had apparently just not considered it, that that day he was to have strangers listening, who perhaps had come with a claim to something especially distinguished. It was just the same when in the year 1851 he preached in Kristiania. That day the Parliament went into recess in order to hear the famous Danish man preach; many of them, I have been told, went away extremely dissatisfied and could not understand that this man was the great proclaimer of the Spirit, because he avoided thumping on the big drum, which Norwegians especially are so accustomed to demand to hear in the pulpit. He spoke steadily and quietly, and the deep undercurrent of the gentle rushing of the Spirit they did not really have an ear to notice. Such was Grundtvig. He would never be anything except himself and he never glanced to right or to left to look for people's approval. He had his responsibility before God and for the preservation of his own personal veracity. If then he was vain, then it was a vanity which was quite different from the common sort.

It was often that on a visit to Grundtvig one went from him without any particular profit, or could be with him for several hours without the conversation elevating itself particularly above the ordinary; either it was his rest-period after heavy work, or perhaps he was into a train of thought which one did not happen to touch upon. He never forced himself upon one with his persuasions; but if, perhaps by chance, one did fall in with his thoughts, or if one came to him with a serious question with a desire to have a matter clarified, then one would often get valuable information and an answer; and at such a time he could then express or develop thoughts in a coherent discourse and shed light upon regions of the spirit which hitherto lay in obscurity for the listener, so that one went from such a visit enriched with something good and distinguished. One had to admire not only his lively spiritual vision which could find a solution to many problems, but also his wide-ranging knowledge, gathered from far and near, over which he had complete mastery and which he always used in life's service.

He was a *folkelig* man of the genuine ore. For a long time now much nonsense has been talked about "*Folkelighed*", so help us God. [GEEG p. 192] Nowadays, a *folkelig* man has to be someone who is transparent and understandable to the masses and can rally them about himself, often because he goes no further in his conduct and in his speech than that the stolid householder-class can stay within their depth in it, a *folkelighed* without colour, without flourish, which could just as well be French, German or Chinese as Danish. This then means that the *folkelige* and the "popular" [*det "Populære"*] are one and the same. But in so far as *Folkelighed* first and foremost consists in this, that the characterising spirit of the people articulates itself in word and deed, and that the people's heart has given itself into the power of this spirit and permits itself in love and in hate to be impelled by this spirit – then two-thirds of that which is now called *folkeligt* must be ejected from the latter's circle and directed to the abode of the empty and the flat, there to find its keep and its poor relief. This kind of *folkelighed* was not Grundtvig's; for the people's spirit was upon him in a mighty abundance, and the people's heart beat its warm pulses within him; but he was not in the ordinary sense populist [*populær*]; for he was not transparent like water – there were in him, as there always are with the spirit, depths and heights which not everyone as directly and effortlessly can achieve. Catchpenny philosophers and catchpenny champions of the *folkelige* stood outside and could peer in through the window at him, where many of them picked up some misunderstood and incoherent phrases which they then palmed off as "Grundtvigianism". But those who had a really true, even if unconscious attraction towards the *folkelige*, because it was the bedrock within their own selves, they had an in-describable blessing from being in his proximity and listening to his talk; did not perhaps understand everything – maybe not even most of it – but yet felt that in contact with him there fell a refreshing dew upon that bedrock and that a dawning broke over them with streams of light. And then there was that *folkelige* aspect to him, that he never made distinc-tion between people. I have seen his drawing-room full of high and low, gentlemen and aristocratic women among peasants and peasant women, of which last no small number spent whole weeks in his house as cherished guests day and night, and he was always ready to take up with anybody who approached him. And there was weight in his words. When he spoke about Christianity, one always had a vivid feeling that the words came from a man who had experienced what both sin and grace are, and with whom the Spirit had filled his words so that they sank down into the receptive soul. When he spoke of *folkelige* and human things, one felt [GEEG p. 193] likewise that they were spoken out of a great heart which loved humanity and loved the people.

[H. L.] Martensen speaks in his autobiography[7] of the rumour which had frightened him away from visiting Grundtvig in the last years of the latter's life, the rumour that Grundtvig was surrounded by so many women who impeded every confidential conversation and therefore he kept himself away. I have often been at Grundtvig's, and in his last years; I often met him alone with his wife and children, and I often also found the house more or less full of guests; but I never remember that it was especially women who surrounded him; it was an equal mix of both genders that came visiting him, and it was never so, that one lacked access to hold a confidential conversation with him when one really wished it. Sure enough, there were women who sometimes, in an unengaging manner, put their admiration and love for him on display. On the day of commemoration of his fifty years of ministry [29 May 1861], when [D. G.] Monrad[8] had brought Grundtvig's nomination as Bishop a woman of high standing (not the Dowager Queen [Caroline Amalie], who was also present), exclaimed with hysterical rapture, while she practically fell at his feet: "O, our bishop!" Grundtvig received this message from the Minister with much sobriety, and after he had expressed thanks in a few friendly and serious words for this recognition from the King he shortly afterwards added, jestingly: "I also rejoice over this because my wife thus becomes "*Naadigfrue*,"[9] which after all she was in a way born to." But he received in seriousness the homage which a gathering of priests, with Dr [C. H.] Kalkar as spokesman, brought him. One noticed that he felt deeply the difference between the situation now and that of generations ago, when particularly the priests of Copenhagen, to a man, one could say, were his bitter enemies, indeed denied him their pulpits. Now this clergy sent him their reverent and appreciative greeting for his beneficial activity within the Danish Church. His answer was short but with a heartfelt ring, and he did not forget to give God the glory and to thank him who had allowed him to experience such a festival day.

His home life and matrimonial life with those nearest to him was stamped with his personality and, according to my experience, extremely loving, even though a change could be traced in the different phases of the development of his life. He has himself characterised his relationship to his dear wives [GEEG p. 194] with the three words: "Sisterly, Motherly and Daughterly".[10] During his first marriage, according to what I could judge, there was still to be traced in my time a reverberation in the tone of the house, from his strenuous fight for Christianity and the Faith of the Church: there was a seriousness at times mixed with some bitterness in his manner, which could cast something of a shadow over his home life. Indeed he still stood at that time in an extremely tense relationship with the Bishop of Sjælland, Mynster, and his bride from those young days stood steadfast at his side as a beautiful womanly figure who self-sacrificingly and altruistically provided him with all the support she could, but was probably not always in a position to share his vision and way of thinking. She was to him as a sister who believed in his noble struggle for truth and for Christianity but probably without completely being able to grasp the innermost driving force and the singularity of his view of human and Christian life, although always ready to bear what she could of his burdens and of the often bitter consequences of the struggle.

In his second marriage he had a co-worker who in the most proper sense could understand and follow him. If Elisabet Blicher was a devoted, beautiful woman who supported her husband with her love, strength and will to bear the burden, Marie Carlsen was a high-minded, singular and independently aware figure of a woman, who could reach to the very depths of Grundtvig's way of thinking and his view on life, a personality who could also make her powerful contribution to the Christian and human management and fulness of the household's life, as well as to the deepening of that vision of human life in the strength of the Lord's spoken word, which was the core of her husband's outlook. She was, I suppose, mother to many new and lively spiritual children, begotten of her by Grundtvig. And in another respect it could also be that she protected him in a motherly fashion. I had an impression that although life in the house was characterised by a greater spiritual communication between man and wife than previously – there was greater mutual give and take – yet it was also the case that the home became more exclusive, less open to all and everyone; she kept it more closed as though to have him for herself alone, and perhaps, like a mother, to keep away the many disparate influences, for the protection of his and her and their home life's *Hjerteblomst* [heart-flower]. There was something beautiful and refreshing about coming there at a good moment when she urged Grundtvig to read something or other aloud, for example a poem which he had newly composed, and then to be [GEEG p. 195] witness to the way in which the two of them would sit on the sofa holding each other round the waist whilst he read the poem aloud, often in an emotional voice. But one could also observe that she, with her forceful nature, could sometimes herself intrude thoughts and viewpoints into him which showed rather little consistency with his own original outlook. It was certainly not completely unfounded when it was said that under her influence Grundtvig picked up the additive of a sort of aristocratic tint. She was the daughter of a noble family who, though with genuine Danish blood in her veins and with a democratic spirit in her,[11] yet could not do other than share, to no small degree, the feelings of the manor house towards the common folk, and in no way looked upon the Danish rural class – as Grundtvig did both before and afterwards – as the one which not least nursed the future in its bosom and would have to be summoned forth as future spokesmen and bearers in the task of freedom. This influence of hers upon Grundtvig was traceable in the short time they lived together; but that it had not penetrated into his innermost self revealed itself clearly when, after her death, in this area too he resumed his old activity – of fighting for the common people's advancement to liberty and participation in power when it was ripe for this; and to the acquiring of this ripeness Grundtvig contributed not least, but for a long time more or less alone, by working towards peasant high-schools for the enlightenment and uplifting of the agricultural class, so that it might worthily assume its place in the development of the nation [*Folket*].

In contrast to Fru Marie Grundtvig, Fru Asta Grundtvig, born *Komtesse* Friis, threw the house wide open, and in her time there was certainly the most lively bustle and concourse in that home; and I believe it was then that, for the first time outside his ministry as priest and activity as writer, Grundtvig became for countless people a living spring to whom one went and got a fine impression from the personal contact with him. She was not as spontaneous as Elisabet Blicher, nor so private a nature with her own personal spiritual life as Marie Carlsen; she invariably accepted all her husband's ideas without opposition and without any particular contribution of her own, and probably for that reason did not, like Marie Carlsen, sound out the depths of what was communicated to her by Grundtvig. But in compensation, she bestowed upon his domestic life and upon him the warm and loving radiance of sunbeams when the lark sings lively, and cheerful pastime; she looked up to him as a daughter to her father, and never had any doubt as to the utter infallibility of his thoughts and words, even when we others had to take a different position from his. So it was at the time when Grundtvig, during his [GEEG p. 196] mental breakdown in the Sixties, became wildly over-excitable: it was a long time before she opened her eyes to the fact that it was a brain disorder involved here, and no healthy, spiritual condition. But she devoted to him the wonderful and loyal love of a woman with unparalleled self-sacrifice and self-effacement, happy as a child to create comfort around him and make his old age bright and mild. It was touching to see how this highborn and basically delicately built woman could bend herself to daily nursing and get down on her knees to bandage Grundtvig's swollen and ulcerated feet. Their shared life was extremely loving, and Grundtvig was towards her as a father can be towards his beloved daughter. More often than before, his gentle warmth would break through. Thus I remember one time when I was sitting with him in his room and his wife came and called us to the dinner-table: "Hillemænd!"[12] he said, "If it is that time, then I had better put another jacket on." "Oh no," she replied, "just come in the old jacket." "Yes, that's all right with me, but what will *the parish* say?" And then he told the story about the crofter in the Bækkeskov manor field[13] both of whose legs were cut off by the reaper's scythe which was following behind him; and when the others came crowding round to express pity for him, the legless one said: "Yes, it's all right with me, but what will the parish say, because now I'll be going on the poor relief?" To Grundtvig's witticisms just one must be added here: A man sent him a poem entitled 'Peter on the Water' and now asked him what his opinion of it was. Grundtvig answered: "Not bad; but the title should have been 'The water on Peter.'"[14]

After Grundtvig had gone, Fru Asta came into a fundamentally difficult situation. She bore the great name, with which there were associated not only great memories, but also great future promises. She was carried by him while he was alive, but when this prop was taken away from her, she was capitalised upon by the extreme *Venstre*-folk, without their stopping to think that the name she bore was not as a matter of course a surety that she was a custodian of his views upon things.

It was not at all to the liking of the Friends [*Vennerne*] when the announcement went round: Grundtvig is marrying again. Already after the first period of widowerhood heads were shaken among us when the 69-year-old man married Fru Marie, and even less did it suit us when, into his seventies, he brought home as his bride *Gehejmeraadinde* Reedtz.[15] It [GEEG p. 197] was not for the reason which Martensen contended that we were upset – because it was aesthetically graceless to marry a third time whilst on the other hand the second marriage can often much better match up to its ideal (Martensen himself was married a second time). No, it was because we felt that our old Mentor[16] should have lived out his eventide in personal tranquillity now that God had called from him the bride of his youth, occupied only in busying himself with the one thing needful and regarding the Danish flock as his bride, communicating the fruit of what God's Spirit whispered to him – even though we could not deny that no injunction, divine or human, stood in the way of his doing what he did. Yes, this is the way it appeared to the majority, no doubt, of the Friends [*Vennerne*]. But then when we saw that Grundtvig in the days of his old age was as though rejuvenated through his life together with an honourable wife, whereby there came a cosiness and light and warmth into his home so that we had a vivid sense that years had been added to his days by this changeover for him from the lonely and sad widower's life to a loving and lively home-life – then we came to feel sure that this had not happened without Our Lord's gracious blessing and goodwill, and we rejoiced over it. I visited Grundtvig the year after Fru Marie's death; he was then living at the *Forgyldte Nøgle* [Gilded Key] in Nørregade; but what an impression I got of human desolation and sad loneliness. The whole of his outward environment appeared so neglected and repellent. No one was creating any comfort around him, and he himself looked grievously bent and more than ordinarily decrepit with the aura of an imminent decease. Things looked different and happier when I later visited him as father of his family and I could not but be grateful to his wife, next to God, who contributed to our keeping him for so long. It was touching to see his relationship to the two children which were granted to him in his old age: Frederik Lange Grundtvig was now the apple of his eye, and sometimes one might see the famous man sitting and rocking the little Asta when his wife was away.

Whilst I am writing here about Grundtvig's home-life I must also recall the morning and evening devotional act he held in his home with his wife, children, servants and whoever else was present. I stayed for some days as guest in the house and was witness to this beautiful gathering around creed, hymn and prayer.[17] There was a weightiness of spirit and heart in Grundtvig's voice during this devotional act, and one felt that he was wholly and fully engaged. In his last years, when he was more [GEEG p. 198] infirm, he used a rather long prayer composed by himself into which the Creed, the Lord's Prayer and the eucharistic words were woven; but to Melbye and me it seemed too long and that, repeated daily, it must lose some of its fervency of tone. His wife would sit by his side when his memory failed him during this long prayer learnt by heart. One curiosity I must also mention here though. On one occasion one of his own baptismal hymns was sung: *O, lad din Aand nu med os være!* When the singing was ended, Grundtvig asked whom the hymn was by, and was surprised when the answer came: "But it is by you yourself."

After these reminiscences concerning Grundtvig's domestic circumstances or the inside of his private life, I turn to telling various things about the way in which he could let drop repartee in his dealings with third parties – words which testified to his sparkling wit and his quick-wittedness to all sides. I was once commanded to the Dowager Queen's table where in a large and mixed circle I also met Grundtvig. The conversation turned to the mother tongue, and then Grundtvig declared that those intellectual concepts for which a people had no expression in their own language were basically something alien to this people's understanding, and could never become their property. The Lord Chamberlain [*Hofchefen*], *Grev* Tramp, objected that this could surely not be said without qualification, and stated – naturally without understanding the nub of the matter – that the Germans did not have a word to describe the business of '*at more sig*' ['enjoying oneself']. So they had to borrow the expression from French and say '*sich amüsieren*.' "Yes," replied Grundtvig, "and what follows from this, Count, except that the Germans do not enjoy themselves?" With this the Count was disarmed. Some time after this, I myself had the opportunity of testing the validity of this pronouncement when in Germany I associated with many different Germans and had to admit the truth of his jesting declaration. Either they floated *entzückt* [overwrought] among the clouds in regions of powerful feelings or else they went around being speculative with great or small intellectual problems on their mind; but this straightforward 'enjoying oneself' was basically unknown to them. Incidentally, there at the Dowager Queen's table I was witness to a piece of bad taste from a high-born spinster. The conversation had later turned to the Greek church and its perverseness; the lady then addressed herself to Grundtvig with the question: "But is it not a good thing about this division of the Church that a priest belonging to it may not marry more than once?" (Grundtvig was then married for the second or third time). Grundtvig dismissed this question with a movement of his head. At the Queen's table, it would [**GEEG p. 199**] not do to give back "uncooked for raw." Another time, Grundtvig was to dinner at Minister [C. C.] Hall's together with *Etatsraad* [State councillor] Professor Kolderup-Rosenvinge, and there was a discussion going about the strife between the two Swedish historians, [E. G.] Geijer and [A.] Fryxell.[18] The *Etatsraad* was shocked over the harsh blows and the offensive tone which were being exchanged in the battle between the two great men. To this Grundtvig replied: "Yes, *Hr. Etatsraad*, he who cannot wield Thor's hammer must needs let it lie." This was much too mythic for the learned professor.[19] At the great public celebration for the *Sønderjyder* [South Jutlanders] visiting us in 1865 at the Slesvig stone in Dyrehaven, where among others Grundtvig and [Orla] Lehmann were to speak, but it was impossible to be heard by the crowd of thousands which had gathered, Lehmann consoled himself that the speech could at least be read the next day in the newspapers. "Yes, that is a consolation for deaf mutes, but not for speaking and hearing people" objected Grundtvig.

I was also present once at Hall's where Grundtvig and [B. S.] Ingemann were sitting together at table and exchanging words with each other in earnest and in jest. It was captivating to listen to these two bosom friends whose eyes were shining with the brightness of old memories. They would joke with each other and then laugh so heartily at the recollection of some little incident from days gone by which was rather indicative of the life of friendship and love they shared. "Do you remember, Grundtvig, how you once insulted me and made your insult almost public by getting all the school-children in all the *Almueskoler* [elementary schools] to read a lampoon upon me in the handwriting textbook?"[20] "What do you mean?" asked Grundtvig. "Well, you write in a poem there how you are driving through the gate into Sorø and you go through all the great memories from the Middle Ages which attach themselves to this town. When you approach the Academy building where for forty years I have had my occupation and in whose immediate vicinity my residence lies then you say in the verse to the coachman:

> … Turn!
In there there's *nothing of concern.*

I ask the company present whether this was not also the most studied insult of myself." "Ho-ho-ho" laughed Grundtvig.[21]

I did not belong to Grundtvig's nearest and no doubt dearest circle of friends, like Gunni Busck or Peter Rørdam, P. Fenger and others and did not come like them to stand in a particularly close relationship with him. But he looked upon me in friendly fashion and acknowledged with pleasure the small contribution I [**GEEG p. 200**] was able to throw into the struggle over the Church for his philosophy of life. I have two letters from him, written to me in kind thanks for two pieces of writing I had sent forth into the world[22] – the one, *Kirkeaaret som et Spejl for den kristelige Livsudvikling* [The Church's Year as a mirror of advancement in Christian living] and *Alvorligt Svar paa haard Tiltale* [A sober response to a harsh indictment] against Pastor H. Knudsen, who had issued a strong challenge to us. These two letters are precious to me: in them he calls me "Dear friend" and there breathes there a fatherly friendliness and recognition, which did me so much good when I was standing in the heat of the fray and yearned for a reviving word which, most of all from him to whom I looked up as my soul's benefactor, was precious to me. But his good thoughts about me and his confidence in me did not hinder him from sharp-shooting when it seemed to him that I was acting wrongly and came out with statements which went against his view upon the issue that had been broached. When, in connection with the negotiations set up concerning clerical freedom, I had written a piece in *Dansk Kirketidende* in which I asserted that clerical freedom (*præstefrihed*) in the sense of an unconditional right of the parish priest to turn away from himself every man in the parish with whom, in his view, he did not stand in faithful communion, could never be achieved and accepted by the residents of a parish unless the priest on his side made the sacrifice of renouncing the tithe and all contributions from those whom he thus turned away. Then Grundtvig was displeased in high degree and spoke sternly to me when I visited him shortly afterwards. He thought that the difficulty with the tithe should and could be removed by the priest being put on a regular remuneration so that the congregation did not end up in a *personal* remunerative relationship to him. But worse was that in this article I had mentioned something which particularly concerned him. He had in fact publicly claimed that he could only minister in the *Folkekirke* because he stood in an almost totally free status as priest in Vartov, and had given us others to understand that our position as ministers of the Word was fundamentally insupportable. I had thrown down an objection against this and declared that my place as parish priest in Ryslinge was for me a happier one than his in Vartov, and had let him understand that I would not exchange my congregation with his actual *Folkekirke*-congregation which consisted of the aged and for a great part decrepit inmates of the Hospital who from the outset could not be perceived as particularly hopeful subjects for Christian influence. This he counterattacked with much vehemence. "I have no baptism to perform for children at random – you do. I do not have to confirm all children that are sent to me – you must. I do not have to marry all kinds of folk – you have to" [**GEEG p. 201**] he said. "But then Holy Communion," I objected. Yes, here he could not but admit that this was the weak point in his position. When, moreover, I now thought and said to him that it had pained us that in his last pronouncement in this matter he had as it were separated himself from us other faithful priests, as though we were not in a Christianly justified position and that basically he alone could have a good conscience as priest and also added: "Do let us stand shoulder to shoulder with each other as an entirety and a unity" he burst out: "That is precisely what Denmark's clergy are not; we do not stand in unity with each other." And in this he was no doubt right. This conversation was conducted with much heat from my side, with great vehemence and some bitterness from his. But yet it ended with him giving me his hand and saying mildly: "Come and eat dinner with us!" This is how he was: inconsiderate and often harsh even towards friends, but in the end good and kindly when he had got over his outburst; and basically one always rose in his estimation when one had had the courage to contradict him. He did not have much patience with yes-men, once he had discovered that that is what they were. But this, as previously mentioned, he did not always see.

In the March-days of 1848 I was in Copenhagen with a deputation from the Jutlanders which was there to pray the King not to give way to the Slesvig-Holsteners, [but rather] to dismiss the old ministers and to take up the fight. There was great commotion: what we were supposed to pray for was already done. The King had anticipated the people, war stood at the door and a free constitution was in close prospect. We were all carried away by "the spirit of 1848" and wherever one betook oneself in the city one saw exaltation and soberly joyous faces. Naturally then I visited Grundtvig: but he was not happy, on the contrary strangely and feverishly irritated. He did not at all trust the popular commotion and the great mass demonstration which aimed to get the King's absolute rule replaced by a so-called constitution [*Konstitution*]. This conflicted far too much with his old political watchword:

| Kongehaand og Folkestemme, | Kingly hand and people's voice, |
| begge stærke, begge fri. | each one strong and each one free.[23] |

During those days he was like a lion fuming in its cage. No one – least of all I – could say anything to his liking. He flew at everyone and everything that came near him and gave rein to his resentment even against the verbal expressions one came out with. When, at the dinner-table, I declared about something – I do not remember what or in what context – that [**GEEG p. 202**] it was 'demoralising' [*demoraliserende*], he said fiercely: "That is not Danish," and when I asked him how one should express what I had wished to express by this word, he answered: "It's fodder for vanity" [*Det er til Næring for Forfængelighed*]. It was of course quite natural that a shift in the Danish form of government from absolute monarchy to democracy could not fail to touch him upon that sore spot, since he had always seen the people's future best secured by a free and loving collaboration between people and monarch, both strong, unconstrained, and least of all by a cold written document, a constitution, between them. He *never* became a particularly enthusiastic supporter of the more modern Constitution-thing [*Konstitutionsvæsen*]; for him personal freedom in the world of both spirit and body was best assured by good simple laws; and that freedom, he thought, could best be achieved by a somewhat moderated absolutism influenced by the voice of the people. Nor does one need to feel shocked over the so-called sea-change [*den saakaldte Grundforandring*] in him, which took place once it had been determined that now we were going to have a free constitution, as though a total revolution had happened inside him in the wake of which he came to stand in the foremost ranks of those who demanded liberty and liberties. It is in fact psychologically quite explicable that he, once the old absolutism fell, had to look to the sole place of support for what he had always demanded as the innermost core in the growth of a people – personal freedom – under those conditions which were created by the State Constitution, and to do his bit so that this cherished and stubborn thought of his could be fulfilled as well as possible through the constitution, and especially that absolute monarchy should not be transformed into ministerial government which he hated, but that the centre of gravity should be located in the people themselves whom he loved and credited with every good thing, now that the King was giving up *his* power to stand sturdily on guard for the common people. It could well be – and I myself believe it – that he went too far in his confidence, not in the Danish folk-spirit but in the Danish population, such as it was then and still is, and in his demand for liberty; but a real reversal of his fundamental views it was not: before and after the granting of the constitution it was the same goal for which he strove, only under the various conditions which prevailed.

I sat in the Danish *Rigsraad* [Council of State] which in 1864 and 65 had to debate the (bitter) Peace Settlement, as well as the alteration to the constitution, and during that time was regularly in Grundtvig's house and was witness to his pain and resentment [GEEG p. 203] over what had happened and would happen. But I cannot recall a great deal of what he declared in the many conversations which were held at his place. Just one thing stands out clearly for me, because it bore the stamp of a remarkable idea of his, an idea which could *only* have occurred to him. This was when the question of the revision of the constitution, and in particular the composition of the new *Landsting* [Upper House], were being debated in the *Rigsraad* and in the *Rigsdag*. He then advised me to propose that those eligible to vote on this issue should be only those who wore the Order of Dannebrog in all classes from Dannebrogsman to the Grand Cross. When I objected that this chivalric badge was surely an all too inadequate indicator of genuine Danishness and nobility of soul in its bearers, he thought that it could become this if no such nomination should be apportioned to anyone without the grounds on which the person concerned was thus honoured being publicly declared upon the nomination, because then it would become impossible for the King or the Government to hang the cross upon an unworthy or completely insignificant man. For indeed he acknowledged with me the deplorable situation of these badges of distinction having been randomly scattered as it were to be scrambled for, and having come to hang on many robes which concealed only an empty hollow soul – yes, that there were knights with whom all true knights would be ashamed to walk in procession.[24] I mention this idea of Grundtvig's because, however impossible it was to effect in reality, it yet bears witness to his idealistic, perhaps his romantic, pattern of thinking, his trust that by and large there was a nobility of spirit among the people, and to his love for that Danish banner from which those badges take their name. On another occasion I heard Grundtvig in conversation with Professor [Carsten] Hauch express another idea but which, naturally, was only proposed in jest. The rebelliousness of the Slesvig-Holsteners was being discussed. "Would it not" said Grundtvig "be helpful if one moved all the Slesvig-Holsteners up to Iceland and the Icelanders down to Sønderjylland [South Jutland]. It would certainly be a long time before the latter were infected by things German, and they could be a good frontier guard on Dannevirke."[25]

I received the notification of my dismissal as priest in Ryslinge whilst, in the year 1865, I was home from the *Rigsraad* in order to confirm the young ones of the congregation. When I returned to Copenhagen to occupy my place in the Council my first excursion was naturally to Grundtvig. He received me with great emotion, and when I told him of my congregation's bearing under this vicissitude, how [GEEG p. 204] their affection had blazed up and had been reflected in magnificent generosity – then the dear old Chief [*den kjære gamle Høvding*] broke out weeping and for a time he could not speak. Then we naturally entered into the question: "What should I now do?" I have earlier explained in my account of my dealings with Bishop Martensen what opinion Grundtvig had from the start about the position I should occupy from now on. He could only envisage it as a free priest's in a free congregation. I went from him weighed down with my thoughts, because I shuddered at the thought of such a thing. When I visited him again after having talked with Martensen, and told him that I had now reached my decision: I would remain in my ministry in Ryslinge but not resign from the Folkekirke, and thus let it depend upon what the church-management would do – Grundtvig burst out animatedly: "Yes, this is a way out, this is the right way; through this, if you hold on to this post, we shall get a *freedom within the Folkekirke* for which we might otherwise have battled for thirty years." This is to stand as a testimony from Grundtvig's last years that he was far from seeing it as best for the faithful to resign from the *Folkekirke*, but that he wanted to preserve this church in the context of the whole people, both for its own sake and for the sake of the believers who were exposed to many dangers by formally separating themselves from that same context. Concerning myself personally, he said: "I see a good omen for the matter in this that it is you this lot falls upon, because you of all my younger friends have expressed the greatest love for the *Folkekirke*. Therefore you will be able, with God's help, to navigate the rocks." These words too witness that Grundtvig as little as possible wished for a formal schism in the church.

Before I left Copenhagen in order to tackle the resolution of this task, I had several conversations with my old fatherly friend on various matters relating to the unusual state of affairs and he gave me several good counsels. On one however we were in disagreement. He thought that I should immediately introduce a congregational council, a kind of body of elders, by nominating or causing to be elected to this duty the best men in the congregation.[26] I was afraid of this, because I had a feeling that we were far from being able in a fitting manner to create such apostolic arrangements on the strength of a theory which in itself could be right enough but presupposed that a society was mature enough to sustain such a thing. I feared that such an instantly [**GEEG p. 205**] and precipitately introduced council of elders could easily have the effect that a spirit of pride could insinuate itself in the chosen few. It would have to come about by itself as a development from within at the right time, not on the strength of a decision from without. Grundtvig did not convince me nor I him.

The last time I saw this unforgettable Mentor [*Lærefader*] of mine was in the year 1871 when he was present in the forest where Danes and Norwegians were gathered for a *folkefest* [folk-celebration].[27] But by that time he was grievously in decline and I suspected that he would soon be leaving us. But it was at a good time for him that he departed. He did not see the disorder which subsequently burst in upon his church-circle, in the course of which many committed a mortal sin in allying themselves with some of the giant-species [*Jættevæsen*];[28] nor did he see the internal fragmentation which was to befall the folk and the fatherland he loved.

And if I am now asked whether I really could not then, or cannot now, see some frailty, some blemish or wrinkle in this great Chieftain of the North [*denne Nordens store Høvding*], then I would wish to reply first, that when I stand by the grave where rest the remains of my nation's and my own benefactor, blessed by God, then I have no desire to dwell upon anything but the bright and rich memories which attach themselves to this resting-place, no desire to profane the love and the gratitude by dredging up that which I cannot remember with joy. But anyway I hardly need to spell it out, that he like all of us was a frail and sinful man, and if I were to write his *history* as a whole that I would also have to point to the shadows which followed him and which are the more conspicuous precisely in a great personality, for such a one always casts a great shadow. What is said about Luther who is praised to the skies by all, thanks to his more than three hundred years distance from our time? I have moreover let it be understood in the preceding pages that I could by no means follow Grundtvig in each and every point. He was like Luther headstrong and inconsiderate in many matters, he sometimes got a distorted view and was all too one-sidedly obsessed with his love of the Danish folk, whom he was not far from seeing as a model folk. He had a strongly passionate warrior-nature which, had he not bowed before the Saviour of the world, would have made him, as one of his friends said, a mighty viking in ancient times, if he had lived then. But he was humble before God even if he did not find it easy to bow before men. [GEEG p. 206] But I was once witness to one of his victories over himself. He had deeply wounded Frederik Barfod by dismissing him from the editorship of the journal *Dannebrog* because he (Barfod) had written articles in it which went against Grundtvig's opinions.[29] Barfod would not go soliciting a renewed friendly relationship and Grundtvig made no approach to him. Then they met together at Svend Grundtvig's wedding.[30] They kept themselves distant from each other but when Grundtvig was leaving the party and saw Barfod at the other end of the hall, then he stopped: I saw that something was stirring within him. It was a battle between his natural pride and the feeling that he owed the insulted person a redress. Suddenly he turned about, walked quickly over to Barfod, gave him his hand and said something to him which once again restored the old relationship. It was a small victory he had won over himself. But we know besides that he too was able in great matters to acknowledge his mistakes. Indeed he has often publicly confessed that here or there he has managed things badly or awkwardly, in contrast to so many others who pay homage to the principle that if one has said A then one must also say B, and in particular can never persuade themselves to revoke and beg pardon for what in culpability has been done or written. Thus the bishops Mynster and Martensen, who, one might suppose, saw themselves as nearly infallible in each and every thing, however much in theory and in their sermons they acknowledged that they were sinners.

1. January 1839. The proposal for the dissolution of the parochial tie [*Sognebaandets Løsning*] was defeated on this occasion by a majority of seven votes out of the 63 votes cast (28 for, 35 against).

2. Birkedal presumably has in mind the dependency of Grundtvig's theology and conceptualisation of the Church and the congregation upon words given by Christ to his disciples, as spoken in unbroken continuity thereafter amidst the congregation of the faithful at the sacramental rites of baptism and eucharist – his doctrine of the Living Word: "I demand only *one* prerequisite, that is, belief – but Christian belief, of course, which has its peculiarity in this, that it believes in the Lord not only as he was eighteen hundred years ago […] but as he *is*, present in amongst us and as near to us as the Word on our lips and in our heart." (Grundtvig to Ernst Trier, see item 114).

3. *Om Stænderforhandlingerne i Roeskilde* [On the Estates-transactions in Roskilde], 1839.

4. Grundtvig's *Aabent Vennebrev til en Engelsk Præst* [Nugent Wade] (June 1839).

5. Editors of *GEEG* identify 'Fr. Boisen' as 'Pastor Frederik (Frede) Boisen' whose dates they give as 1808-82, and whom they name as editor of the periodical Budstikken. In fact, the Fr. Boisen whose dates are 1808-22 and who was editor of Budstikken was Frederik (Frits)

Boisen, father of Frederik (Frede) Boisen. Frede was born in 1841 so would have been only sixteen in the year of the Scandinavian church assembly to which Birkedal here refers. It seems more likely, then, that it was the father, Frits, who was present and disappointed by Grundtvig's restrained preaching.

6. In I Peter 3, the apostle advises that the true Christian's ornament should not be external decoration, "[4] But let it be the hidden man of the heart, in that which is not corruptible, even the ornament of a meek and quiet spirit, which is in the sight of God of great price" (King James Bible).

7. Bishop H. L. Martensen, *Af mit Levned* [From my life] III (1883), 85-86.

8. D. G. Monrad (1811-87), in his office as *kultusminister*, Minister for Church Affairs and Education.

9. Literally 'Gracious Lady' – form of address accorded to wives of bishops and to female aristocrats of which Grundtvig's third wife Asta was born one. Her formal rank was that of *Komtesse*, a title accorded to the daughter of a count, corresponding approximately to the English 'Lady'.

10. In his poem *Til min Asta*, not published until 1891 but probably written for his third wife in 1858, the year of their marriage (*PS* VIII, 294-95).

11. Birkedal, who like other commentators lacks an established political vocabulary, uses the somewhat florid idiom *med Folkets Aand over sig*, literally "with the spirit of the people upon her."

12. An oath, by '*de hellige mænd*' [the holy men, the saints].

13. Grundtvig's term is *Hovmark*, signifying land worked under obligatory service from peasant to landlord (*Hoveritjeneste*).

14. The gospel narrative of the disciple's experience on the Lake of Gennesaret is in Matthew 14: 28-31.

15. The feminine form of the title (*-inde*) designates her as spouse (actually, the widow) of Privy Counsellor (Holger Christian) Reedtz.

16. *Lærefader* (literally 'teaching-father'), expressive of both affection and discipleship, was a term widely used of Grundtvig among his followers in the later years.

17. Among the various places in which the text of Grundtvig's daily household devotions has been printed, is the periodical *Dansk Kirketidende* [Danish Church News] 1910, cols. 561-64.

18. The politically-coloured strife between the Swedish historians Erik Gustav Geijer (1783-1847) and Anders Fryxell (1795-1881) over the interpretation of historical record was fought out between 1845-51.

19. Professor J. L. A. Kolderup-Rosenvinge (1792-1850), an eminent legal historian, was notably conservative in his view of the proper structure and government of the national Church, a standpoint which was bound to create antipathy between him and Grundtvig; see also endnote 1 to item 91.

20. The *Skriftlæsningsbog* was a textbook used in the teaching of handwriting, containing literary passages for copying. The lines (mis-)quoted here (*Sving! / thi inden for er der ingen Ting*; correctly *sving! / Indenfor er Ingenting*) are from Grundtvig's *Munkeburet i Soer* [The monastery in Sorø], first published 1855.

21. Birkedal's Danish representation of Grundtvig's laughter (*Haahaahaa*; rather than conventional *Hahaha*) is phonetically closer to English 'Ho, ho, ho' than to 'Ha-ha-ha' ("The difference is not entirely trivial" – Professor Jakob Balling, to whom I am indebted for the observation).

22. The two monographs were published in 1843 and 1855. In this account, Birkedal has misremembered the first title which in fact had '*Billede*' (image) where he has now substituted

'*Spejl*' (mirror) – thus interestingly echoing a title-usage [Mirror/*Speculum*] of very ancient antecedents. The two complimentary letters from Grundtvig to Birkedal are 472 and 633 in *Breve* I.

23. First lines of a song published by Grundtvig 1839 (*PS* VI, 232-34).

24. Others in Grundtvig circles shared this scepticism over the honours system. Frederik Barfod, in an article ironically entitled *Naadens Overflødighed* [The abundance of grace, Grace abounding] published 1845 in *Skandinavisk Folkekalender* (which he edited 1845 and 1846), listed the honours distributed by Christian VIII in the seventy months of his reign to date. On average not one day had passed without his bestowing an honour; he had honoured one-and-one-seventh men per day; every four days he had created a *Ridder af Dannebrog*, and in the higher ranks of the Order, every five days a *Dannebrogsmand*, and every eighteen days a *Kommandør af Dannebrog*.

25. The idea cropped up again in Grundtvig's disturbed state during his breakdown in 1867, when he wrote to the authorities proposing that the Finns be settled in the ancient Danish frontier zone of the Dannevirke, and the Germans moved from there to Finland.

26. Grundtvig's suggestion was not a new idea: the establishment of parochial church councils began in Denmark in 1856, though the first related legislation was not passed until 1903.

27. The Friends' Meeting [*Vennemøde*] in Copenhagen at Pentecost 1871 also marked the sixtieth anniversary (Monday 29 May) of Grundtvig's ordination with a meeting in Casino on Wednesday attended by some 2000 people and a gathering of some 1300 people at the Slesvig Stone in the Dyrehave [Deerpark] at Klampenborg on Thursday 1 June, where the 87-year-old Grundtvig made a speech.

28. Birkedal uses the metaphorical language based upon Norse myth, promoted by Grundtvig and much used , in earlier days, among the folk-highschools. The *jætter* were the formidable adversaries of the Æsir and were involved in the final catastrophe of Ragnarok.

29. Frederik Barfod's own account of this episode is included in item 86.

30. At the cost of impugning a moving anecdote, it has to be noted that Barfod himself says that Grundtvig and he were reconciled well before Svend Grundtvig's wedding which took place on Friday 10 December 1858.

94 (a-c): Søren Aabye Kierkegaard: from Papers (VI B 29), Afsluttende uvidenskabelig Efterskrift til de philosophiske Smuler af Johannes Climacus [Concluding unscientific postscript to the Philosophical Fragments of J. C.] (1845; finalised version of the work was published 1846), ed. Niels Thulstrup, Søren Kierkegaards Papirer, 16 vols. (Copenhagen, 1968-78), vol. 6.

In juxtaposition to Vilhelm Birkedal's appreciation of Grundtvig and his achievements it is appropriate to be reminded of the opposition to the same which was mounted and sustained by Søren Aabye Kierkegaard (1813-55). Kierkegaard has been in some respects the most damaging of Grundtvig's adversaries: partly for the stringent philosophy he set up against the kind of Christian life (and life-style) preached by Grundtvig (which, however, contemporaries such as Hans Christian Andersen – who found the hybrid 'Edda-Christianity' of Grundtvig and the cold, dank 'stalactite cave' of Kierkegaard's cleverness equally uncongenial – could take or leave at will), partly for the abundance of catchily-comical terms of ridicule of Grundtvig and Grundtvigians which flowed so easily from Kierkegaard's pen into popular circulation, but also for the fact that on the back of his worldwide repute such mockery of the man and the movement has been carried so far through time and space. In recent years, appropriately for the turn of the millennium, anciently-rooted antipathies have been largely put aside and Danish scholars are increasingly finding the predictable profit of studying together these two monumental figures who were formed, broadly speaking, from the same cultural roots and influences, under the same system of governance by State and Church, in the same small capital city of Denmark, during the same period of time in the turbulent 19th century. Basically polarised though their essential stances are – Grundtvig's commitment to the congregational and the *folkelige*, Kierkegaard's to the inward subjective struggle of the discrete individual – there is more common ground between them than a cursory judgment allows. Identifiable references to Grundtvig in Kierkegaard's writings are numbered in hundreds rather than scores, spanning Kierkegaard's whole working life, and often it is upon the basis of a refutation of Grundtvig's ideas and philosophical procedures that Kierkegaard frames and defines his own. For his part, Grundtvig opposed Kierkegaard in sermons and in writings, both implicitly and explicitly. "It took no great skill for Søren Kierkegaard, with the world's loud applause, to describe the whole of our so-called Christian preaching and Bible-reading and divine service, baptism and communion, as one great nonsense, as a merry comedy which however became tragi-comic, indeed, not only hugely lamentable but extremely blasphemous, in that many folk believed what we so-called priests, we "black-cassocks" taught them to believe: that if only they would listen to us and say Yes to it, and let their children be baptised and themselves go to the altar once in a while, then they would be taking, in an admittedly somewhat obscured and to us incomprehensible manner, yet a nevertheless quite proper part in the Christian, spiritual and eternal life which Our Lord Jesus Christ had led on earth and promised to share with all his faithful followers everlastingly. No, that took no great skill, but [...] he thus plainly thereby put his own honour and the New Testament into pawn" [Det var [...] ingen Kunst for Søren Kierkegaard, med Verdens højrøstede Bifald, at beskrive hele vor saakaldte kristelige Prædiken og Bibellæsning og Gudstjeneste, Barnedaab og Altergang, som en stor Narrestreg, som en lystig Komedie, der imidlertid blev tragi-komisk, ja, ikke blot uhyre sørgelig, men højst bespottelig, derved, at mange Folk indbildte sig, hvad vi saakaldte Præster, vi »Sortekjoler«, indbildte dem: at naar de blot vilde høre paa os og sige Ja til det, og lade deres Børn døbe, og selv gaa til Alters en Gang imellem, saa tog de, paa en vel aldeles skjult og os ubegribelig Maade, men dog ganske rigtig, Del i det kristelige, aandelige og evige Liv, som Vorherre Jesus Kristus havde ført paa Jorden og lovet at dele med alle sine tro Efterfølgere evindelig. Nej, *det* var ingen Kunst; men [...] saa har han derved aabenbar sat sin egen Ære og det ny Testamente i Pant] (*Den christelige Børnelærdom* [Christian instruction for children]; 1855-61, 1868, 1883; ch. 10). Something of Kierkegaard's exasperation with the bulky figure of Grundtvig which loomed so large in contemporary Copenhagen can be read in the following extracts.

⌒

94 (a): Søren Kierkegaard; Thulstrup p. 101-102.

It appears to have been Kierkegaard who (mockingly) attached the overdone epithet *mageløs* (matchless, peerless, unparalleled, incomparable) to the 'discovery' (*Opdagelse*) made by Grundtvig in 1825 (see the Index entries: mageløs; mageløse **Opdagelse,** den; and **mageløse Vidnesbyrd,** det). Ironically, it passed into acceptance among Grundtvigians at face value – for the realisation achieved by Grundtvig as he read Irenaeus was indeed presented from the outset as recognition of a truth which had nothing to beat it. As is made clear in the following passages, Kierkegaard held in contempt what he deemed to be Grundtvig's enthusiastic absoluteness, his utter lack of dialectical integrity, his habit of substituting poetic vagueness, catchwords, bombast and histrionic mannerisms in place of any "proper progression through thinking" and precision of discourse.

⌣⟶

As a poet, essentially; as an original and resonant hymnwriter, usable outside the party if the public authorities are willing to bear the cost of having him shaved; as a sturdy nature even if so sturdy that it seems to demand strife and opposition; as a deep-minded man whose assertions are now and then confirmed in a remarkable way; as [p. 102] a witnessing man who, having been strongly moved in an instant passion, has toiled day and night with a rare stamina; as a man with many, many proficiencies, even if they are not exactly always controlled – Grundtvig will always maintain his importance […]

As a thinker, Grundtvig is a Genius; but so instantly a genius that the ingenious impulse or the Ingenious One's experiencing during the idea has, in respect of the mental constitution, something in common with what an apoplectic seizure is for the corporeal. An idea seizes him, he is astonished, is affected, he wants to render the whole of humanity happy with his matchless discovery [*mageløse Opdagelse*]: however, he lacks the dialectic flexibility for a reflective relationship in order to look into what it is he has discovered, whether it is something great or something void. While therefore his ideas are many, are extremely various and of exceedingly varying quality, they all have one common characteristic, a birthmark whereby one immediately recognises them: that of absoluteness, undialectic or apoplectic absoluteness [*den udialektiske eller apoplektiske Absoluthed*]. Everything that Grundtvig says is absolute. The moment he has an opinion, no matter what, it is the absolute, the matchless [*den mageløse*], the sole source of blessedness. Sometimes the idea, because the thought-process is broken off, does not really come to anything; but it remains a subject for lyrical outpourings in which the poetic in unmistakable, whether it be his depiction of the foul ignorance of the age or his radiant prospects into a matchless future, or ingenuous wonderment over his own self, that once again he has made a matchless discovery.

94 (b): Søren Kierkegaard; Thulstrup pp. 109-110.

Systematically interrogating the concept of Grundtvig's *mageløse opdagelse*, Kierkegaard comes round to asking: Is it a dogmatic discovery?

⌣⟶

When there is talk of the Living Word [*det levende Ord*], the speaker's enthusiasm mounts thus: the Living Word, Life and Spirit, the Mother-Tongue, the Heart of Woman, Denmark Loveliest Field and Meadow,[1] the Word of the Church, Martin Luther, the Matchless Discovery [*den mageløse Opdagelse*], the Word Which in the Beginning Was. The last, as everyone knows, is an [p. 110] allusion to the first chapter of John's Gospel. Now an allusion to this is not exactly an unparalleled discovery [*en mageløs Opdagelse*] restricted to a universal-historical genius; nor, the more's the pity, is the neo-Platonic-gnosticising mishmash unparalleled [*mageløst*]. Just as there have been times when idolatry was cultivated using the number, just as a lottery-player still concentrates his entire guesswork upon the number, so also the word has been used and is used – the Word which from the beginning was – in order, merely by mentioning it with a hollow voice, to elicit an effect of deep-mindedness. Everywhere that the dialectical and a proper progression through thinking are absent, there a through-road is conveniently opened up to the most hopeless opposite: the deep-mindedness of the deep-minded thought is made obvious by furrowing the forehead, by yodelling with the voice, by shooting up the brow, by staring ahead of one, by hitting the low-F in the bass-scale.

1. *Danmarkdeiligste Vang og Vænge* is the opening line of a lyric composed by Laurids O. Kock (1634-91), about 1685. It was indeed emotively quoted by Gr, for example in his lectures at Borchs Kollegium 1838 subsequently published under the title of *Mands Minde* [Within living memory].

94 (c): Søren Kierkegaard; Thulstrup pp. 111-112.

"One can be a Genius and become a geriatric without learning the least thing from life, existentially."

Naturally, our age, which is so vigorously agitated and in ferment, always has use for someone above the ordinary, a seer, a prophet, a strong man, a wielder of authority, a martyr, etc. And if then it so fortunately chances that one man can undertake this whole repertoire of extraordinariness with equal bravura – and Grundtvig, whose life has never suffered from uniformity, can do so in a manner which must utterly satisfy our age – is it any wonder that he is esteemed? Now with the apostolic aura of sanctity about his [p. 112] transfigured countenance, now unrecognisable in his Old-Nordic hairiness, always a clamorous individuality, godly, worldly, Old-Nordic, Christian, High Priest, Holger Danske, now exultant, now lachrymose, always prophetic even when it so ironically chances that he becomes contemporaneous with a fulfilment first glimpsed in far-off ages, Grundtvig is a not unremarkable phenomenon. It is a different question to what extent it has benefited Christian orthodoxy to be defended with every ounce of his vitality by such a fairytale figure as, in the capacity of Defender of Orthodoxy, can readily provoke offence. Every calmer anxiety over the religious, every more inward understanding which in fear and trembling is kept under restraint by anxiety over the self, easily feels itself painfully affected by that absence of restraint which heedlessly busies itself only with grand visions and matchless discoveries [*mageløse Opdagelser*]. And he who thinks that one shall learn by living, and that to exist is an art, will not exactly rejoice over the Grundtvigian outcome: that one can reach the age of sixty-five[1] and yet still remain just as undialectical within one's own self, just as externally-orientated, just as clamorous as in one's youth; that is, that one can be a Genius and become a geriatric without learning the least thing from life, existentially.

1. In fact, Grundtvig did not reach the age of sixty-five until 8 September 1848.

95. Richard Petersen: Henrik Steffens. Et Livsbillede [HS. A life portrait] (1881), pp. 374-75; GEEG Stk. 34a, pp. 206-207.

Richard Petersen (1838-1905) was a priest (of Grundtvigian inclination) and author of a number of biographical accounts of notable historical and contemporary figures including Henrik Steffens, Thomas Kingo, Madame de Staël, Fredrika Bremer, B. S. Ingemann and Frederik Barfod. He cites no source for the anecdote which, like the one in item 96, relates to the summer of 1840 and Grundtvig's visit to Nysø.

During the week [13-20 July 1840] [Henrik] Steffens spent as her [Baronesse Christine Stampe's] guest, there was gathered a small select circle at Nysø, since Øhlenschlæger, Grundtvig and [F. C.] Sibbern also went out there. Thus there was an interesting communal life between these great men of intellect, and in particular Grundtvig and Steffens had much to debate between them. Especially the relationship between Danish and German, which had started to become a burning issue, seems to have been a chief theme in their conversation, and it is easy to understand that they must have a different perception of this. They could both become heated, especially Grundtvig, so that on one occasion he is even supposed to have got up, thrown his chair on to the floor, and as soon as he had declared his opinion in blunt words, had gone his way. Otherwise it proceeded [**GEEG p. 207**] more peaceably. When on one occasion these two were carrying on a long interesting conversation at table, Øhlenschlæger wanted to make some remarks but Thorvaldsen, who was sitting by his side, is supposed to have held him by the arm and said: "No, listen, look here! when sensible folk are speaking you really ought to keep quiet!"

96. Johan Borup: N. F. S. Grundtvig (1943), pp. 134-35; GEEG Stk. 34b, p. 207.

Borup gives no source for this anecdote which must relate to the summer of 1840. Grundtvig, who was at that time newly installed as priest at Vartov, visited Nysø near Præstø, the handsome country house and estate of the Stampe family (whose sons had for a time been tutored with the Grundtvig children in the Grundtvigs' home), in the summers of 1839 and 1840.

One day [Oehlenschläger] was explaining to Thorvaldsen how disgracefully Baggesen had treated him after the publication of En Rejse [A Journey] – the one which Baggesen called Æderejsen [The eating trip][1] – "Yes, you really must read it because that is where the whole quarrel starts." Grundtvig, who was sitting and listening, then turned to Thorvaldsen: "You shouldn't read that book at all, because it is real rubbish." "Rubbish?" Øhlenschlæger exclaimed. "Perhaps you, Grundtvig, have never written any rubbish?" "Yes, I dare say I have; but I do not require that anyone shall read it."

1. Outrage at Jens Baggesen's scathing critique of Oehlenschläger's substantial work En Reise, fortalt i Breve til mit Hjem [A journey, narrated in letters home], 2 vols., 1817-18, gave rise (1818) to the quarrel [Strid] mentioned – namely, the penne-fejde [pen-feud] known as the Tylvtestrid led by the group of students known as Tylvten [The twelve].

97. *Peter Frederik Adolph Hammerich:* Frederik Hammerich. Et Levnetsløb *ed. Angul Hammerich (1882), I, p. 272; GEEG Stk. 35, p. 207.*

Hammerich neatly narrates another brief anecdote illustrative, ostensibly, of Grundtvig's some-times unmannerly treatment of people who did not interest him. A more probing biographer might have asked himself what the poem (*Til Karen Biørns Minde* [In memory of KB]), now ac-cidentally published as another man's work, might have meant to its author, Grundtvig. In fact, Grundtvig was moved to write it in 1813 – barely five years after the emotional metamorphosis he underwent in Egeløkke – upon reading a poem of the same title published in memory of Karen Bjørn (died 1785) by her husband, Tyge Rothe. In his poem Grundtvig depicted Rothe as forerun-ner of a new age of richer emotional relationships between married partners. Subsequently he reworked it as a kind of love poem for his fiancée Lise Blicher and published it in his collection *Kvædlinger eller Smaakvad* [Little lays or Short songs] (1815) – together with a short note declaring that he addresses his poem not to those who would gleefully use his own words against him, but to those noble persons, whether known to him or not, with whom, through his writings, he has borne a friendship; such friends his words will confirm in the conviction that he is not "that arrogant, egotistical man I am proclaimed to be" [den hovmodige, egenkærlige Mand, jeg udraabes for] on account of his obedience in putting the love of God above all; for such friends he will speak open-heartedly of himself: "of my outlook and my progress, my talk, my faults and errors" [om mit Syn og min Gang, mit Mæle, mine Fejl og Vildfarelser]. Wulf's adventitious revival of the poem may have stirred in Grundtvig more poignant recall than he or indeed Hammerich understood.

⌁

One day I saw *Kommandør* C. Wulf come up to visit him. Grundtvig received him at the door with his pipe in his mouth, whereupon Wulf grew even more awkward than his errand in itself made him. He meant to apologise for an error that had crept into the publication of his father's writings.[1] Grundtvig's poem on Karen Bjørn had in fact been included in it because he had found it copied out in his father's hand and had therefore supposed that his father had composed it. Grundtvig listened to the apology, said now and then: "I see, I see" and nothing more, did not even invite Wulf further into the room. There followed a long pause, Wulf stared at the floor in front of him and I felt positively embarrassed; at last he bowed and removed himself.

And as it befell Wulf so it has befallen many besides him. One cannot therefore be surprised that especially lay-folk should be a little afraid when they had to visit such a man, for whom they nurtured so deep an awe.

1. *PoetiskeArbeider ved Peter Frederik Wulff. Udgivne efter hans Død* [Poetic works of P. F. W. published after his death], 1844.

98. *Hans Lassen Martensen:* Af mit Levned *(1882), pt. 1, pp. 64-67 and 69. [Not in GEEG].*

Bishop Martensen's experience of working with Grundtvig in the (ultimately aborted) task of preparing a new hymnal for the Danish Church (1844-46) well qualified him as a critic of hymns written or reworked by Grundtvig himself, such as were under consideration – and in dispute – among the committee. Here, in retrospect and upon a rereading of Grundtvig's *Sang-Værk til den danske Kirke*, Martensen makes a probing analysis of what he deemed to be Grundtvig's strengths and shortcomings as poet and hymn-writer. However justified some of his observations may have been, he was wrong in his prediction about the popular appeal of Grundtvig's hymns. To take as a guide only their respective representation among the approximately 800 items in *DDS* 2002, including reworkings with original compositions: Thomas Hansen Kingo (1634-1703) is represented there by some 80 items (about 10%), Hans Adolph Brorson (1694-1764) by some 115 (about 14%), and Grundtvig by some 250 (about 31%). See further item 99, with its more detailed account of the often stormy proceedings of the working-party; also Frederik Barfod's reference to the same episode (item 86; see endnote 10).

⌐⌐

Through collaborating with Grundtvig and through the closer acquaintance I formed with his renowned *Sang-Værk til den danske Kirke* [Song-work (or Carillon) for the Danish Church] my judgment of him as hymn-writer was not a little modified, and this judgment has reinforced itself for me right up to the present day, in that, with the encouragement to take a retrospective view which this present work necessarily offered me, I have once again gone through the *Sang-Værk* in its new, very comprehensive edition. To this extent, I cannot agree that Grundtvig is the great hymn-writer many take him to be; I cannot agree that he is the greatest hymn-writer in the Danish Church; and even less can I agree that he is the world's or the Christian Church's greatest hymn-writer – a foolishness which F. Hammerich has committed himself to and left to posterity in his *Levnetsløb*. It is my conviction, which I have also once allowed myself to express to Grundtvig himself, that if the question is solely that of poetic talent as such – of poetic strength, richness and abundance – he is a far greater poet than both [Thomas] Kingo and [H. A.] Brorson; but that as a hymn-writer he will never be able to gain access to the people in the manner of these two, least of all in the manner of Brorson who even more so than Kingo has won the people's hearts and wondrously sung his way into them. I am not talking about the lapses of taste in Grundtvig which after all could also be found in the older writers. That which is lacking lies deeper. P. Hjort used to say of Grundtvig: "He is not pious enough and not humble enough to be a hymn-writer." I would rather say: His gift for the historical-poetic led him off in that objective direction to great visions, but it was not granted him to return from these intellectual visions into the interiority of the life of the soul. He took for sure a powerful grip upon the golden harp, but not all its tones stood at his disposal. His strength is the church-historical, the biblical-historical, the struggle and the victory of God's kingdom through the ages; but what is so often wanting there is precisely the Brorsonesque, the life of the individual soul in its relationship to God. We could also say: What is so often wanting there is the practical aspect of Kingo. For even though Kingo has an emphatic historical inclination, he never neglects its practical application to the individual soul. No one will deny that there is something admirable in the Grundtvig hymns such as *Kirken den er et gammelt Huus* [The Church it is an ancient house], *Paa Guds Jerusalem det ny* [In God's Jerusalem, the new], *Foragter ei de ringe dage* [Scorn not the days of lowly toil] and the like. But however admirable such hymns may be, however much they may be acknowledged as genuinely churchly, yet they are not sufficient to satisfy the religious requirement, as long as other tones are lacking. Within a congregation there are many individual moods in souls which require that their yearning shall be satisfied. If one should perhaps answer me that what I require is provided, and if one should point out such hymns as *Sov sødt, Barnlille* [Sleep sweet, little baby] or *Urolige Hjerte, hvad fattes dig dog?* [O heart ever-fretful, what is it you lack?] or so many a twilight sigh of old age and whatever else can be associated therewith, then I answer that my censure is not to be understood as absolute but as relative. But broadly speaking, I believe I remain in the right when I suggest that his hymn-writing is altogether too objective and thereby acquires an abstract, altogether commonplace character. Often one is moving among merely commonplace appositions, such as Life and Light, Life and Death, without anything individualised emerging. Grundtvig is often renowned because he is an opponent of Pietism. But pietism can be taken in more than one sense, and we believe that one might wish his hymns held rather more pietism. With many of his hymns the demand that asserts itself is: More piety, more awareness of sin. Here he is often excelled by both [B. S.] Ingemann and [C. J.] Boye.

But that which in particular must call forth opposition is not so much his own original hymns as his reworking of the hymns of other writers [...] In his publications on hymnody, [A. G.] Rudelbach, as a chief point in Grundtvig's hymn-writing to be protested against with fullest vigour, has emphasised this rewriting and recomposing, this supplanting of other writers' individuality. He similarly emphasises that in quite a lot of hymns Grundtvig intrudes his error concerning the Word from the Lord's own mouth and what attaches further to "The Discovery" [*Opdagelsen*], and that one must protest against the inclusion of such in a hymnal of the Evangelical-Lutheran Church. To these protests we must needs agree. The friendly personal relationship with Grundtvig was not breached. Not until a later point in time, when his ideas on freedom, especially his ideas on clerical freedom (*præstefrihed*), grew too wild for me, when the room grew too confined for me and the atmosphere too oppressive, did I then withdraw myself somewhat. It first came to a breach and public conflict when I had become bishop.

99. *Hans Lassen Martensen:* Af mit Lefnet *[From my life]*, *II (1883), pp. 58-63; GEEG Stk. 36, pp. 207-08.*

Following a commission from the Copenhagen Clerical Convention's Hymn Committee in March 1844, a working-party tackled in August that year the compilation of a Specimen Volume (*Prøvehæfte*) of new hymns which might replace the existing Evangelical-Christian Hymnal. After much conflict of taste and wills, the *Prøvehæfte* discussed here in Bishop Martensen's memoir was published in January 1845 but in 1846 was rejected outright by the Copenhagen Convention, and Bishop J. P. Mynster instead authorised a Supplement (uninfluenced by any Grundtvigian tone) to the existing Hymnal. Meanwhile the Roskilde Convention took over the initiative of compiling a new hymnal for the church. Though Martensen here frankly realises the difficulties of working in harness with Grundtvig and declines Grundtvig's suggestion that they should work on even without official support, he is a sympathetic and fair witness to the rare gifts which Grundtvig brought to the task.

It was an unconditional necessity that the Danish congregation got new hymns, since the Evangelical-Christian Hymnal from the period of Rationalism was altogether too lack-lustre and lacking in content to be capable of satisfying the congregation's religious requirement. Bishop [J. P.] Mynster also [**GEEG p. 208**] recognised this and had a supplement compiled and introduced, which to some extent relieved the prevailing need. Meanwhile, the idea was stirring not only within myself but in many that it would still be a fine thing to get a complete hymnal. Our Church had after all had a Kingo-hymnal and now that we had a renowned hymn-writer among us, should it then be impossible to have a Grundtvig-hymnal for our time? Certainly we knew how much there was to give offence – lapses of taste, idiosyncrasies and obscurities of expression. But should it not be possible to get the offending matter removed, as long as Grundtvig would collaborate with men who were benevolently disposed towards him and his hymns, and as long as he would allow himself to be influenced by their advice and observations? To give the Danish Church a new hymnal was after all a great and praiseworthy undertaking. Thus the matter stood at that time, for me and for many. The Clerical Convention of Copenhagen, of which I was a member, took up the idea and established a committee: Grundtvig, [J. H. V.] Paulli, [P. J.] Spang, [E. V.] Kolthoff and myself. We were charged with compiling a sample booklet of hymns, which would be submitted to the Convention's judgment, as to whether it would permit such a hymnal to be compiled. I was full of hope, which afterwards certainly showed itself to be sanguine and illusory.

Committee meetings were held in the evening [in Autumn 1844] at Paulli's, who lived in Nørregade. The principles both for the selection of hymns and for their reworking are discussed in the foreword to the sample-booklet, and on this present occasion I will not go into closer detail about this. The various trends in Danish hymn-writing which upon Christian and church-related grounds had found admittance in the congregation were to be represented here. Also a few hymns from the Evangelical-Christian Hymnal were to be adopted.

In these meetings Grundtvig was indeed captivating. It was edifying to hear him read aloud a hymn he had newly composed, for example the fine poem *At sige Verden ret Farvel* [To bid the world a fit farewell] or the beautiful ordination-hymn, *Idag paa apostolisk Viis* [This day in apostolic wise]; it was instructive to hear him express himself about the older hymn-composition in our Church, indeed, on hymn-writing in the Christian Church and in the various ages of the Church in general, with which he was very familiar; it was gripping to hear him quote passages from the old hymns by which he himself was gripped, as when he once, deeply moved, repeated Kingo's: [**GEEG p. 209**]

O hør os Jesu milde	O hear us gentle Jesus
Og dan vort Hjerte saa,	and fashion so our heart
At aarle det og silde,	that it both late and early
Dit Tempel være maa.	your Temple may become.
Du selv vort Hjerte vende	Do you yourself our heart turn
Fra Verdens kloge Flok	from this world's clever herd
Og lær os dig at kjende	and teach us that we know you,
Saa har vi Viisdom nok.	we wisdom have enough.[1]

Sometimes we would make a little digression and moved away from the hymns to more general considerations relating to the church, when we readily listened to him.

Naturally, difficulties entered when we asked for adjustments, whether it was to his own hymns or whether it was in his reworkings. Here he could be somewhat unyielding. In the poem 'At sige Verden ret Farvel' [To bid the world a fit farewell] there is mention of the icicle-hand of death. When we would have liked to have the icicle changed, he declared that this was out of the question. He had written this hymn for himself and we must either take it as it was or leave it out completely. So thus the icicle was forced upon us.[2] On other occasions he would change nothing "because he could not give up his viewpoint and outlook to please us." Sometimes the volcanic element in his nature came to the fore: he would get angry, would depart from us and go out of the room. Then Spang would have to go after him and bring him back, and we would get him round again. I must also testify for him that sometimes after a long battle he would permit the adjustments after all, which he would then carry out with great care and diligence. But the unfortunate thing was that when he removed tasteless elements from one place then he would introduce new tasteless elements in other places as a consequence of the adjustments made, and we could surely not go on battling with him into eternity, as a result of which he might indeed have completely lost interest. P. Hjort to whom I told this, said: "I can imagine that it is the same with his hymns as it is with an eiderdown that has got into a tangle. When you squash it down in one place it bulges out in another."

[GEEG p. 210] Eventually the specimen volume [*Prøvehæfte*] was finished, for we toiled unrelentingly, especially Grundtvig who had the real work. I suppose that no one will deny that this specimen volume bears the hallmark of unusual proficiency, spirit and originality. This was also the judgment of the Convention – and yet nevertheless it was rejected. It was found that Grundtvig's individuality, even when it showed itself with genius, was far too one-sidedly obtrusive, not only in his own hymns but in particular in the reworking of those of other writers, whose individuality he to some extent obliterated in order to impose his own instead. We his collaborators, who had had such great battles, could only declare that we had not managed to produce a substantial alternative to what was now submitted and felt unable to promise that a complete hymnal would have a substantially different character from this, and that one was now able to know what the committee in association with Grundtvig would be able to present. After various discussions and deliberations it was then decided that it was not that sort of hymnal that was wanted, however reluctant they were to drop it. Grundtvig took this rejection very badly and wanted to continue the task with the committee on his own responsibility. He had several conversations with myself and Paulli and earnestly tried to talk us into working with him upon a hymnal. But we could not let ourselves in for this. Our eyes had been opened, and we knew that we would be unable to accomplish anything, or at any rate accomplish anything that would lead to something.

---

1. The verse is from Thomas Kingo's hymn (1689) *Hvor stoor er dog dend Glæde* [How great indeed that joy is] (*DDS* 2002, no. 139). Martensen adds in a footnote, with reference to Grundtvig's reworking of Kingo's text: "The last four lines he [Gr] subsequently spoiled: *Hvor Du er selv tilstede* / I Ordet af din Mund, / Med Liv og Lyst og Glæde / Nu og i allen Stund [Where you yourself are present / *in the Word from your mouth*, / with life and pleasure and joy / now and at all times] This is 'the discovery' [*Opdagelsen*; that is, Grundtvig's *mageløse Opdagelse* concerning *det levende Ord*, the living Word], which is here being put into Kingo's mouth."

2. The final verse (9) in *DDS* 2002 begins: *Før døden med sin istap-hånd / gør skel imellem støv og ånd* [Before death with its icicle-hand / makes separation between dust and spirit].

100. Hans Brun: Biskop N. F. S. Grundtvigs Levnetsløb udførligst fortalt fra 1839 [Bp NFSG's Life recounted in fullest detail from 1839] (2 vols., 1882), I, 208-209; GEEG Stk. 37, pp. 210-11.

Brun's affectionately humorous anecdote about Grundtvig's well-known habit of remaining silent until a guest came out with an interesting topic of conversation also serves to illustrate the connections Grundtvig maintained with Norway, chiefly by welcoming (in his own way) visitors to his home.

⌐

Where in his young years Grundtvig had stayed with [K. L.] Rahbek and his "Kamma" at Bakkehuset he took a summer residence that year and at least in the following one [1845 and 1846], but moved back to Vimmelskaftet in the autumn.

Out here he had visits from several Norwegians,[1] among them one from [Amund] Helland, the merchant from Bergen to whom (which was not very frequently the case) he had also said something about his recently recounted mental experience.[2]

Then one day [S. B. C.] Welhaven went out there. "I had," the professor recounted [GEEG p. 211] many years afterwards, "nothing particular to talk to him about but I then suddenly remembered about Kamma and Rahbek and their circle out there." "Yes," said Grundtvig, "there has been nonsense in plenty prattled there."[3] And then Welhaven obliged with a number of stories from the school at Bergen where in his day one did more or less as one wanted, whether one intended to study further or not. "Yes," answered Grundtvig and slapped him on the shoulder, "Thank God that you went to a poor school, and therefore came through it alive!"

I have a story about a third Norwegian's visit from the visitor himself, and that was the visit of the late *Rektor* [Hans] Holmbo from Bergen. Grundtvig receives him politely and invites the *Rektor* [Headmaster] to be seated on the sofa but then says – nothing. The *Rektor*, who was a forthright man, then tries to get a conversation going: "Just to get started with something – is there anyone in Bergen Pastor Grundtvig knows and wishes to hear something about?" Gr.: "That would have to be Sagen." Holmbo then tells a little about *Overlærer* [senior teacher] Lyder Sagen, and there is another hiatus. H.: "You know Helland the merchant; hasn't he visited you?" Grundtvig replies: "Yes" and adds a few words of a favourable inclination concerning the person mentioned. There is then again a pause of such protracted duration that the Rektor feels he must make his farewells. Grundtvig accompanies him out and says upon parting: "But *Hr. Rektor*, this must not be the end of it. Will the *Rektor* not be so kind as to come here one day and eat dinner!" H. (quite bewildered): "Yes, thank you; but I shall be here for a while; Pastor Grundtvig must be so good as to say when is convenient for you." Yes, tomorrow…there was some impediment, but the following day. "We eat at 4 o'clock." So the *Rektor* came and this time Grundtvig was prepared, so that his guest stayed with him the whole day until 11 o'clock, and then Grundtvig even accompanied him right into town. They very likely also talked much about the education system.

---

1. Brun's footnote: "To one of the visitors from here [Norway] who offered an apology for his visit, Grundtvig said: I gladly see Norwegians."

2. Brun alludes to the severe depression, probably connected with physical illness and over-work, which Grundtvig suffered in 1844.

3. Grundtvig reveals a degree of impatience with the conversations of the diverse opinion-forming personalities who gathered at Bakkehuset, evidently regarding them as (to use a modern label) 'the chattering classes' of contemporary Copenhagen society.

101. Carl Joakim Brandt: 'Rejse med Grundtvig i Sydsjælland' [Journey with G in South Sjælland], letter of 24 September 1846, published in Dansk Kirketidende [Danish Church-news] 1893, cols. 233-35; GEEG Stk. 38, pp. 211-13.

Carl Joachim Brandt (1817-89), who at the time of this narrative was co-editing with Ludvig Helveg (1818-83) an anthology of Danish hymns, *Den danske Salmedigtning* [Danish hymnody] (1846), was to become a noted medievalist, an energetic supporter of Grundtvig's *kirkelige anskuelse* [concept of the Church], first principal of Grundtvig's highschool, Marielyst, and eventually Grundtvig's successor as pastor of the Vartov congregation. It is a well-observed and well-told account Brandt presents here, portraying Grundtvig in a jovial mood, notwithstanding the rainy weather, as he travels through his old home territory of south-west Sjælland towards his destination, the romantic manor-house of Rønnebæksholm. No less tellingly portrayed is the appearance of the young widow Marie Toft of Rønnebæksholm, Grundtvig's hostess whom five years later he was to marry.

⌐

I had hardly expected to be making any more journeys round the country this year [1846] and yet the day before yesterday I got home from one into south-west Sjælland.[1] The reason for this was that the Danish Society [*Det danske Samfund*] in Næstved, a society which like the others of the same name was established in order to disseminate a sense of and love for everything pertaining to the fatherland, had this year invited [GEEG p. 212] Grundtvig to come down there on the King's birthday [Christian VIII; 18 September] in order to enliven the intended festivity with his presence. Fru [Marie] Toft from Rønnebæksholm, a mile[2] from the town, had invited him to stay at her place. He promised he would, and prepared her for the fact that he would be bringing some of his younger friends with him. On Thurs-day morning [17 September] Grundtvig, his eldest son, P. Boisen and I drove in an open landau to Næstved and had a really pleasant day; the Old Man was jovial and entertaining the whole way; if we got tired of discussing serious things we discussed inconsequential things – and he does of course have it in common with all great men that bagatelles are transmuted into erudition in his hands, so that nothing remains trivial. On the way he took a fancy to visit [J. G.] Willemoes in Herfølge, a brother of the naval hero. He is a *forsamlingspræst*[3] and therefore he has long kept himself distant from Grundtvig: it was as though Grundtvig stretched out a hand to him, and he took it with joy. The priest was not at home when we arrived, but his wife and a considerable and very talkative flock of daughters entertained us until he arrived. It was a beautiful parting. By chance, the priest's family had formed a half-circle about the old Bard: immediately opposite stood Willemoes, a stately, mild, gentle, priestly man with a velvet calotte, by the side of his wife, two daughters on each side. Willemoes offered Grundtvig his hand in farewell and added: "One word you must take away with you: finish for us that hymn-book you have started on."[4] It merely sounds banal in the telling, but all those present felt themselves gripped by the moment; I saw tears in their eyes. If one knows the situation a bit more closely it is easy to explain, but it would be too much of a digression to expand upon and anyway I have already intimated it.

The journey was now resumed, in continuous conversation, to Rønnebæksholm. The Old Man was in high spirits, he knew every spot, pointed out for us by name every church and manor-house: here he had been on one occasion, there on another. Many old memories came back to him, little tales which it amused him to tell and us to hear. He laughed so heartily when he remembered, at one house where he had once come riding along lost in his own thoughts and in an old green coat, that a man had come chasing after him and shouting Wasn't he the pig-gelder from Olstrup? Meanwhile it had grown dark, none of us knew where the manor-house lay, it was raining, so every moment we had to ask our way onwards; if we were able to get really good information well [GEEG p. 213] expressed in the local dialect then it was doubly good, for we had first the content and then the form to discuss, especially when some proverb or another was thrown in. It was getting towards nine o'clock before we reached the manor-house. Rønnebæksholm is a new manor, completed a few years ago but built in an old style with gothic gables. The main entrance is in such a gable with pointed arches on the doors and windows. In the open door stood the hostess, simply dressed in black, like a knight's wife from bygone days, with waxen candles in a silver candelabrum to receive her guests. She looked like a Fru Inge, and Fjennesløv[5] never offered greater hospitality, piety and good cheer than that manor; there was an overabundance of everything, both spiritual and material. She has been led by wondrous ways, she has passed through the eye of the needle; herself young, beautiful and wealthy she made a wealthy match, was married for half a year. The husband on his sick-bed became gripped by Christianity; he died, but she kept the pearl which he had found in the eleventh hour. She now lives with her little daughter, her mother – a woman I took the whole evening to be a sister or sister-in-law of the same age but later heard was getting on for seventy – and two sisters; and her home is open to all that is Christian but also, right enough, for all that calls itself Christian.

Next day was the celebration. Pastor F. Boisen from Skørpinge spoke first, on the Danes' love for their king, which he supported with examples from the history of the fatherland. It is remarkable with this man, the change and the progress that has happened to him in the past couple of years. As he himself acknowledges, it was seemingly God's guidance that he should stay a while longer where he was and where he has a wide field. From being the president and idol of the *forsamlinger* he has become their sober leader and damper, which people such as Lars Møller and his [followers] don't like, who think in their spiritual pride that they are spiritually pure who have no Fatherland here below, and think that that Christianity they can drag out of the Bible is God's word, etc.

After Boisen Rørdam spoke, and finally Grundtvig held a powerful speech about the mother-tongue and its importance to us; and various songs were sung besides.[6] After the celebration there was a *"Zweckessen"* [festive meal] where several toasts were drunk. The next night we stayed again at Rønnebæksholm, where Grundtvig remained for a couple of days more, preached on the Sunday in Rønnebæk and returned home by way of Nysø.[7] I accompanied the brothers Boisen to Skørpinge on Saturday morning.

1. Christian VIII's birthday was celebrated on 18 September.

2. That is, a Danish mile, approximately equal to 4.7 English miles.

3. Grundtvig was known to be generally sceptical about the *gudelige forsamlinger*, revivalist meetings held outside the framework of the Church, often with a lay preacher leading them; though there came to be various significant figures among Grundtvig's supporters who were also associated with such revivalist meetings and were themselves *forsamlingspræster*. Grundtvig had special reasons for this gesture of friendship: Willemoes was brother of Grundtvig's former friend, the naval hero Peter Willemoes; and (a more immediate reason, perhaps) he had been the agent of the religious awakening of Marie Toft, Grundtvig's hostess on this occasion and his future wife.

4. Grundtvig had recently been working with H. L. Martensen and others to draft a new hymnal for the Danish Church but the initiative had stalled, partly upon disagreement as to the role of Grundtvig in determining its character (see items 98, 99).

5. Brandt alludes to the legend-history of Asser Rig and his wife, whose great manor was at Fjenneslev between Ringsted and Sorø in Sjælland. See the Index entry **Inge,** Fru.

6. See Index entry **modersmaal**.

7. Nysø, near Præstø, was the seat of Baron Henrik Stampe whose wife Christine maintained a kind of salon of artists, writers, politicians and other notable persons.

102. *Carl Koch:* Grundtvigske Toner *[Grundtvigian tones]* *(1925), p.7; GEEG Stk. 39, p. 214.*

[GEEG p. 214] There was someone who told me that he had seen Grundtvig and Søren Kierkegaard walking together in Østergade.[1] Grundtvig strode out, placid and expansive; Kierkegaard, dodging restlessly about, was now on the one side of his companion, now on the other, all the while in lively conversation. So they came to the door where Grundtvig was to go in; he just raised his hat; Kierkegaard bowed deeply and removed his hat with great reverence.[2]

1. Koch does not name his informant. Østergade is a street in central Copenhagen, forming part of Strøget (then called *Ruten* [The route]) a string of streets crossing the central city.

2. In 1841 Sophie Henriette Glahn, daughter of Grundtvig's brother-in-law Poul Egede Glahn, married Peter Christian Kierkegaard, Søren's brother, though this linkage of the Grundtvigs with the Kierkegaards is little more than a matter of the merest curiosity.

103. *Hans Brun:* Biskop N. F. S. Grundtvigs Levnetsløb udførligst fortalt fra 1839 *[Bp NFSG's Life recounted in fullest detail from 1839] (2 vols., 1882), I, 134, 292-293; GEEG Stk. 40, p. 214.*

At the time [1848] the present Professor [Svend] Grundtvig was eagerly and earnestly preparing himself to go voluntarily into battle,[1] one of his acquaintances, a young Norwegian, came to visit him and, though they could both of them play jokes, Svend Grundtvig was not in the mood for such things. The Norwegian however could not repress himself but says: "I say, Svend, do you know that folk in town are not singing "the valiant Land-Soldier" [*den tappre Land-Soldat*] now but "the valiant Tin-Soldier" [*den tappre Tin-Soldat*]."[2] This of course was a joke of the Norwegian's, but Svend Grundtvig could not know this, and when they come in to lunch where the Old Man was he says: "I say, father! N. says that now folk in town are singing the valiant Tin-Soldier instead of Land-Soldier."[3] "That is the irony of the folk-spirit, my son" answers the Old Man's deep voice. 'Irony' here means jocularity and this jocularity Grundtvig found highly appropriate since he always felt that – "necessarily for the sake of discipline," of course – one should treat soldiers more as dead things than as living persons. Concerning the same young Norwegian, Svend Grundtvig says to his father: "Do you know that N. now makes so much of Søren Kierkegaard?" The Old Man, who of course did not at that time credit the Norwegian with any particular judgment in this matter, just says laconically: "Good Lord! does he really!" [*Herregud, gjør han det!*] in the relevant party's hearing.

1. During the war over Slesvig-Holsten (1848-50) many volunteers joined the armies of both sides. The citizen's mandatory duty to bear arms as required by the State was first introduced as a provision of the free constitution of 1849.

2. The title *Landsoldat* originally attached to the peasant levies who alone (until general conscription was introduced in 1849) were bound to perform military service, but came to designate any soldier in the national army. The sentimental-heroic song *Den tappre Landsoldat* [The valiant soldier-man] by Peter Faber (1810-77) was specially distributed on 10 April 1848 in time to celebrate the Danish victory in the first engagement of the war, at Bov, the previous day. H. C. Andersen's popular story *Den standhaftige Tinsoldat* [The steadfast tin soldier] had been published in 1838.

3. Brun's footnote: "The mentioning of the matter to the Old Man so caught the Norwegian by surprise that he did not manage to say in the heat of the moment that he had spoken in jest. This little anecdote I have from the Norwegian himself in his maturer years."

104. Hans Brun: Biskop N. F. S. Grundtvigs Levnetsløb udførligst fortalt fra 1839 [*Bp NFSG's life recounted in fullest detail from 1839*] (2 vols., (1882), I, 298-303; GEEG Stk. 41, pp. 214-20.

A classic Brun-anecdote, this excerpt narrates the 28-year-old Brun's first visit on his own to Grundtvig's home in Vimmelskaftet, Copenhagen. It is 1848 and the eve of elections to *Den grundlovgivende Rigsforsamling* [The national Constituent Assembly]. Grundtvig is up for election in the Nyboder constituency. On the Sunday morning before the election Brun is in Vartov church where Grundtvig warns his congregation of the seriousness of unfolding events but urges them to entrust all to the safe hands of God. In the afternoon Brun resolves to call on Grundtvig at home. He is made unhesitatingly welcome and immediately caught up in the flurry of the public and domestic activities of his host. He hears about Grundtvig's involvement in educational initiatives and discusses educational and religious affairs in Norway; makes a quick excursion to visit Peter Boisen (recently married to the Grundtvigs' daughter Meta), and returns with them to Vimmelskaftet for dinner with various other young guests. Though the dinner-table conversation naturally revolves much around the forthcoming election, Grundtvig, in Brun's account, is prompted by female company to reminiscence about a certain unforgettable Englishwoman he had met many years previously in London.

I went to Copenhagen the Saturday before the 'Election-Thursday' [5th October 1848] for the election of members of the *Rigsdag* for the passing of the constitution. [GEEG p. 215]

On Sunday, the fifteenth after Trinity [1 October], I was naturally in Vartov. The Matins hymn – *Vor Konge signe Du, o Gud!* [Thy blessing grant our King, O God!] from the Evangelical-Christian Hymnal already indicated that in his sermon Grundtvig would take notice of the important issue which was to be decided on Election Thursday. He began with the words "Take therefore no thought for the morrow"[1] and declared that it is a blessing when the spirit of the Lord, the Holy Spirit, reposes these words in the hearts of us his disciples. For every sober person naturally feels an anxiety about the unknown future, and indeed there is also often a particular day in the future over which one is especially anxious, and if nothing else then the day of our death confronts us all. And now in the coming week a day confronts us which all Danish hearts must be concerned about and not least those of Danish Christians, because there shall be elected men who are to assemble in order to give the kingdom of Denmark a new constitution; and Danish Christians also have grounds to feel concern for this important issue, that in the constitution there shall also be incorporated provisions for the status of the congregation within the kingdom. "And I cannot conceal the fact," he said, more or less, "that those who are holding forth most loudly among us – not only do they rarely ask 'after God's Kingdom and his righteousness' alone [Matthew 6:33], but they ask little or nothing after what, in temporal terms, pleases the Danish heart; so that I was quite inconsolable when I thought upon Election Day, until the spirit of the Lord reposed this blessing within my heart: Take therefore no thought for the morrow! do you take no thought for Thursday, for the Lord shall take thought! only remember that today is the Lord's Day, and let the congregation repose these blessed words within their hearts: Take therefore no thought for the morrow!"

He dwelt upon what he had often said, that the Danish people are a people of the heart, and it is the heart that God holds in regard, this is what he wants us all to be. And then he spoke of how to resign oneself, with one's heart, into the power of the heavenly Father who will not only outwardly clothe us as the flower and feed us as the bird but also inwardly clothe the flower and feed the bird with eternal life in Christ Jesus our Lord.

This is what stands out for me about the morning in the church; and later in the afternoon I felt the wish to go out and pay my regards to him where he was living, in Vimmelskaftet.

This was the first time I was to visit Grundtvig on my own, and they had more or less said up there that he did not look kindly on people disturbing him in his work if they did not have [GEEG p. 216] something definite to talk to him about. But I set out with the same thought with which an old woman from Trøndelagen, who got the finest reception, had visited him: "*Hajn Gruijndtvik e no dejn Màin, hajn è, holleds 'n tàr imot Dæ.*"[2] I rang the bell, and asked the maid to announce that it was a Norwegian theology graduate who would like to greet him, but that I had no particular business, so I did not wish to trouble the Pastor if it was not convenient. Immediately afterwards Grundtvig himself came out with the most friendly face, and in his room there was – not for professional reasons but apparently as a Danish-Christian friend – a shoemaker[3] with whom he was discussing the forthcoming *Rigsdag*. Grundtvig looked and behaved as one who was become inwardly comforted, inwardly at ease and happy (he would laugh really heartily now and then), after having been distressed, exactly as the sermon had expressed it in the morning.

When the shoemaker had left, I had proof of his excellent memory. There was an old Christian woman living near to Kristiania – the Quaker Eriksen's wife and sister of Hans Hauge – who I think had visited Grundtvig in 1816 or 17 and had a very serious conversation with him. She asked me to give him a greeting, if he could recall her, but I had barely said her name before Grundtvig says: "Is *she* still alive!" After a conversation about Wexels and about the Herrnhuter and the Haugians who in Trondheim seemed to have united in opposition to Bishop [P. O.] Bugge, even though, as Grundtvig observed, "there were otherwise differences enough between them", we got into the issue of the Folk-university [*Folkehøjskole-sagen*]. We have seen that Grundtvig's thinking at that time was: the immediate establishment of a splendid Folk-university, from which enlightenment should subsequently spread across the whole land and that this was his idea with regard to Norway just as it was with regard to Denmark. I now gave my opinion that in the longer run this would not work in Norway, and he listened mildly to my objections; but when I also said "We do not have the resources to set up just one such establishment!" then he answered with a gentle smile: "But if you do not have resources to set up one, then you do not have resources to set up several." This did not knock me back though, because what I meant was that it would impose a bigger burden with one such great establishment for the whole kingdom; but I said no more, and now Grundtvig told me what again I have previously recounted, about his approach to King Christian on the King's last birthday, and he ended: "But then the King died [GEEG p. 217] and the Ministry was determined to have county-schools." I asked him after that about *Dronningens Asylskole* [The Queen's Charity-School] where his son-in-law P. O. Boisen, whom I wanted to visit, was teacher, and he gave this testimonial to the school: "You will enjoy going there; there are really lively things happening there" and when he heard that I meant to go directly to Boisen at his residence, he says: "Boisen is coming here this evening, so will you not be so good as to accompany him back?" I did not wait to be asked twice. So then I go over to Boisen's but I find him much preoccupied with the school's accounts which he had to have ready for the Dowager Queen, so I had to sit and wait a goodly while. Then his wife – at that time a good walker – also appeared and once more my path lay over to Vimmelskaftet, where Grundtvig's successor C. J. Brandt (at that time *candidat*) and *candidat* Theodor Fenger had also arrived – and what discussion there was there too, as everywhere in Copenhagen, which was only to be expected, about the election to the *Rigsdag*. But when, after some while had passed, we were invited by the lady of the house to tea and *smørrebrød* in an inner room and had seated ourselves at the table, then other matters were also discussed. There was also a young woman there, dressed in mourning, who sat at the table-end by Grundtvig's side and whom he treated with much attention, and the conversation soon came round to women in general. Then Grundtvig told us that the last time he was in England, at a party, after the meal he came to sit with a young woman with whom he entered into an enjoyable conversation,[4] and when they had been sitting a long while together the host comes over to them and says: "What can you be talking so much about?" So then she good-naturedly lifted up her eyes and answered: "We can talk about everything!" And – continued Grundtvig – it is true: with ladies one can talk about everything but not with gentlemen; with them one can talk only about what they have studied and acquainted themselves with scientifically, but then it depends upon getting hold of the matter from the right side, which is the side of the heart, of taste. Holding a disputation with women, that doesn't work; they do not take in what is presented to

Priest at Vartov

them in that manner; and so it is indeed with all of us, that anything we are going to feel happy about must involve our heart – but women always take it in a quite different way, intuitively, with the heart. While he was talking further about woman as the expression of human nature, his son-in-law interrupted once with the remark that "That all sounds very pretty" – then Grundtvig immediately turns to him and replies: "Yes, but it is also true." Such pertinent formulations [GEEG p. 218] were so common with him. He deftly championed the woman's freedom of heart as against men's desire to conform her nature, but added, seriously, that if anyone thought that what he said applied to external relationships "then that would be a misunderstanding, then that would be a misunderstanding! for on the outside, women can most certainly conform themselves with their men."

He continued his development of the relationship between man and woman with a smooth and lively and sometimes somewhat jocular surface, but with the depths of human life perceptibly beneath it, without using Bible references, right up until its consummation upon earth when we know that it is Christian prophecy that human life within the congregation shall have its most vital expression in 'the Bride.'

"That is a man who can talk," said his son-in-law to me when we had got up from the table, and I could not then and cannot now at this moment help thinking: Should there not also be written down 'Table-discourses' or more properly 'Domestic-discourses' from the Church-chieftain of the North [*Nordens Kirkehøvding*], just as from his closest predecessor in church history – the *Høvding* [Chieftain] in Saxony?[5]

After the evening meal we went out into his study again where one of the guests spotted the opened Greek Testament and asked whether it was X's edition. Gr: "No thank you. For daily reading I always use the *Complutenser*. So a discussion began on source-texts and manuscripts and various ways of reading and a little on Bible-translations, about which he said that the current translations sometimes suffer from a false clarity, and this was particularly the case with the Epistle to the Romans, which he himself had therefore also translated, in part at least,[6] and he wanted obscure passages to be obscurely translated so that one beckoned to others to do it better. In connection with 'ways of reading' he referred to Ephesians 5:9 where in one manuscript can be found "the fruit of the spirit" and in another "the fruit of light in all goodness" etc., and here he proposed as his conjecture that originally both of them existed so that the passage read: "the fruit of the spirit is light in all goodness" etc., "for," he added in manner so fervently good, so heartfelt and grateful, "when the Spirit of the Lord is upon us, then we find light in everything that is good."[7]

Then we got on to the Church-issue in the new constitution, and what Grundtvig was most afraid of in this was: that in it an obligation might be fixed upon the symbolic books as a condition of attaining priesthood. It was in fact impossible [GEEG p. 219] that all who desired to become priests could honestly swear upon them: "Christianity must have been working upon one for a long time before one can accept the Augsburg Confession as one's creed." He foresaw the danger as being so great that he considered turning his back upon the *Folkekirke* if the members of the *Rigsdag* agreed on this. "If they do that then I for my part will say goodbye," I can well remember him saying. Then he threw himself down in the sofa-corner and began to talk about how, in the course of his own life also, appearances had been the most hindrance in his Christian development – in particular, wanting to force life into moulds which it was not yet matured and developed to fit into.[8] "I well know that I seem more worldly in my old age, but I also know that when we let go all appearances, then things go better for the work within us." And then he talked about wanting at our stage to give relationships in the congregation the same form as in Apostolic times, and uttered among the rest the following remarkable words: "If I were offered a liturgy which it was possible to prove to me was from the Apostles themselves, I would have to answer: No, we cannot use it yet; we have not matured enough for that."

The lady of the house now engaged me for a while so I did not get to hear everything that he subsequently said on the reason why the Papists did not proffer the chalice to the laity, or his statement on proffering the eucharist to a single individual. But with regard to the first I did hear this much, that he believed it arose from the fact that when, by violence and force, the so-called church had been filled with believers and unbelievers alike, and yet the faithful in the priestly class felt the need for spiritual and heartfelt communion, then they tried themselves to create a communion in this completely crazy fashion. The thought that the priesthood were the real spiritual class is naturally a precondition of this error, but this precondition I hardly think he found it necessary, on this occasion, to point out. With regard to the eucharist proffered to a single individual, he praised the old custom that on the priest's visit Christian relatives or other Christian friends should share communion with the sick person.

I think it was immediately after we had got up from the dining-table that he was asked what he thought about women authors. To this he answered that if they emerged early within the evolution of a people then "this is not a good sign" but if they first emerge when the evolution was far advanced then "it is they who impose taste upon" what has evolved. It was probably in the full flight of this that when we got back into the study [GEEG p. 220] he declared that it was a misunderstanding if one believed that Scripture forbade all public utterance by women in all circumstances. He also mentioned on this occasion the word of prophecy: Your sons and daughters shall prophesy.[9]

1. The sermon takes its text and allusions from Matthew 6, of which verses 31-34 read (King James Bible): (31) Therefore take no thought, saying, What shall we eat? or, What shall we drink? or, Wherewithal shall we be clothed? (32) (For after all these things do the Gentiles seek:) for your heavenly Father knoweth that ye have need of all these things. (33) But seek ye first the kingdom of God, and his righteousness; and all these things shall be added unto you. (34) Take therefore no thought for the morrow: for the morrow shall take thought for the things of itself. Sufficient unto the day [is] the evil thereof.

2. Brun footnotes: "Grundtvig is still the man he is, no matter how he receives you."

3. The shoemaker was probably J. P. Mouritsen.

4. This was the infamous Mrs Clara Bolton. Grundtvig perhaps had a narrower escape from scandal than he ever came to realise: see the Index item **Bolton**, Clara.

5. Brun means Martin Luther. This is one among various contemporary references to Grundtvig as a latter-day Luther, a continuator of the Reformation of the Church.

6. Fascicule 147 in the Grundtvig Arkiv contains portions of a translation of the Epistles of Paul including part of the first chapter of the Epistle to the Romans.

7. The different readings are reflected in the differences between, on the one hand, the English King James Bible (For the fruit of the Spirit [is] in all goodness and righteousness and truth) and, on the other, the Latin Vulgate version (fructus enim lucis est in omni bonitate et iustitia et veritate) and the currently authorised (1992) Danish Bible (for lysets frugt er lutter godhed, retfærdighed og sandhed) [for the fruit of light is all goodness, righteousness and truth].

8. *Skinnet*, the exterior, externals, appearances, in their relation to the inward, the spiritual, the real, the true, the highest eternal, were long a preoccupation with Grundtvig. They could belie or betray that which resides within; but the embodying externals were not to be viewed with unqualified revulsion and rejection. To some extent such views were formed out of his encounters with the philosophers he read in his immediate post-university years, including Fichte, Schelling and Steffens; to some extent they were an expression of his concept of freedom – here freedom from legislated conformity in matters which properly belong with the individual conscience.

9. The reference is *either* to Peter's words at Pentecost, Acts 2:16-18 (King James Bible): [16] But this is that which was spoken by the prophet Joel; [17] And it shall come to pass in the last days, saith God, I will pour out of my Spirit upon all flesh: and your sons and your daughters shall prophesy, and your young men shall see visions, and your old men shall dream dreams: [18] And on my servants and on my handmaidens I will pour out in those days of my Spirit; and they shall prophesy; *or* directly to Joel 2:28-29 (King James Bible): [28] And it shall come to pass afterward, that I will pour out my spirit upon all flesh; and your sons and your daughters shall prophesy, your old men shall dream dreams, your young men shall see visions. [29] And also on the servants and on the handmaids in those days, I will pour out my Spirit.

105. *Sofus Magdalus Høgsbro:* Mit Forhold til Grundtvig, Tscherning og Monrad *[My relationship with G., T. and M.]*, ed. Svend Høgsbro (1902), p. 12.

Sofus Høgsbro (1822-1902) was a dedicated supporter of Grundtvig, primarily in the field of education and politics (including church politics and political journalism). Some forty years younger than Grundtvig, he reached adulthood in an age already markedly different from that which had shaped Grundtvig's values and causes. The monolithic cohesion, absolutes and fidelities of the *enevælde* [royal absolutism] were fast crumbling away; the post-Napoleonic complexity of international politics had put new perspectives on local issues like the sovereignty of Slesvig-Holsten; in that winter of 1848-49 the inauguration of a democratic constitution was imminent in Denmark; the industrial revolution was in full spate in Britain and elsewhere and was making its inevitable impact upon Denmark; science was advancing both as a material reality in daily life and as a challenge to religion, philosophy, art and poetry alike. Even a Grundtvig could get annoyed when the convictions of his own younger days were contradicted by the youth of today. Høgsbro, the future politician, understands the importance of tact and knows when to yield and when to be stubborn. He would keep his respect for Grundtvig's *persona*, record and status throughout the two decades which remained of Grundtvig's life, consulting him and informing him to the last. His own great struggles were still to come.

⌒

As far as I recall, Svend [Grundtvig] was at home during the winter [1848-49], and I visited them much, as usual. We rejoiced over the termination of the truce, but when news came of the disaster at Eckernförde Grundtvig was indignant that *Kommandør* [F. A.] Paludan had hauled down the flag to the Germans: he could, like [Ivar] Hvitfeldt, have caused the ship to be blown up with it. When I however found it explicable that he should wish to save the crew, Grundtvig grew so vehement that he – who was walking about with his pipe behind the chairs on which we were sitting at table – came up behind me and in his ardour so vigorously waved about the arm holding the pipe that he was on the brink of hitting me on the cheek with the end of the tube. In general my views on the conduct of the war and the diplomatic negotiations were often rather divergent from his, whereas my mother rejoiced over the articles she read every week in *Danskeren*. However, I knew that a battle of words with him would not get anywhere, and as a rule I therefore restricted myself to expressing doubt and asking for closer explanations from him, and in this he was ever willing.

We were also very much at odds with regard to physical science. Grundtvig stuck to the word of the Bible, that the sun moved round the earth (the words of Joshua [10:12]: "Sun, stand thou still upon Gibeon") and appealed to Tycho Brahe and some minor writings published during those years by Aschlund (as far as I recall the name).

Once when, at table, I told how the earth's interior, according to the more recent opinions of physicists, was a melted fluid mass, and that in relation to this the solid crust of the earth with all its mountains and valleys was no thicker that the wrinkled skin on an apple, he dismissed this statement with a somewhat derisive remark that we had better stick to the course we were supposed to be eating. For the physical sciences he had on the whole no regard. The life of the spirit was everything to him. When [J. J. A.] Worsaae showed that Finn Magnussen's runic inscription on the rock in Blekinge was only an effect of natural forces, he would not forgo the satisfaction of the significance of the runes for ancient history and was convinced that Finn Magnussen would be reestablished by some later scholar.

1. The loss of the Danish warship *Gefion* – trapped under fire at Eckernförde in 1849 and surrendered by Paludan to avoid wholesale loss of life among crew – was a bitter blow to Danish hopes of an early victory in the Three Years' War.

2. *Danskeren* (volumes I-IV, 1848-51) was the weekly periodical published by Grundtvig in direct response to the outbreak of war over Slesvig, the majority of articles being penned by Grundtvig himself.

3. Arent Aschlund (1797-1835) published (1830) a work upholding an anti-Copernican view of the universe held by the Danish astronomer Tycho Brahe (1546-1601).

4. In this conviction Grundtvig was deluded; see the Index entry **Magnussen**, Finn.

106. Alvilda Andersen: From an interview in the Berlingske Aftenavis [Berlingske Evening Paper], 11 December 1935; GEEG Stk. 43, p. 221.

[GEEG p. 221] I remember Constitution Day, the very day, that is, when the Constitution was granted, the fifth of June [1849]. I was in the gardens of Frederiksberg with my parents. It was the loveliest weather and in front of the castle there was gathered an enormous throng of people. A meeting was going on. We heard Grundtvig speak. I still recall the words he said at the beginning. "Here I come," he said, "I come last like the thin beer; but thin beer is better than a dry bung." Yes, that is how he began.

107. Christen Mikkelsen Kold: from a speech at the Vennemøde, September 1866; in Kristen Køster, Det kirkelige Vennemøde i Kjøbenhavn 10de og 11te September 1866 *[The church-related Friends' meeting in Copenhagen, 10th and 11th September 1866], 1866, pp. 67-71; GEEG Stk. 44, pp. 221-23.*

Christen Kold, splendidly his own man ("I have always been sure in my cause, even when I have been wrong"), unintimidated by Grundtvig, and in his element when addressing the audience of *Vennerne* [the Friends, supporters of Grundtvig], recalls (to an audience of Grundtvig's supporters gathered to mark his birthday) negotiations (1849) with the Grundtvigians, establishing him as founder of the free-school at Ryslinge. The opening of the school on 1 November 1850, which marked Kold's arrival as a shaper of Danish free-schools was a milestone in the history of Danish education. See the Index entry **Kold,** Christen Mikkelsen.

There had been a number of so-called Grundtvigians gathered in Copenhagen [in 1849] to deliberate what should be done to educate the Danish agricultural class [*den Danske Bondestand*] so that it could make use of the civil liberty [*den borgerlige Frihed*] it had been granted, and the Spirit apparently also had its fingers in the game at that time, for when it had been agreed that something should be done and the question had been asked what man they should get to carry out this enterprise, Ludvig Christian Müller answered: "I know of no one but Kold" and they all found that this was indeed the right man. It was most extraordinary, for I was not much qualified for it at that time; now I am much better qualified for it, although I am not yet near being fully so. So they wrote to me[1] that I should come over to them and deliberate with them what could be done for the education of the folk [*folkeoplysningen*]; they thought that I could travel around Jylland and work on the young schoolteachers there, so that a better kind of teaching could be introduced there, but I answered that I already knew what I wanted to do: I wanted to set up a so-called Higher *Bondeskole*,[2] to which they answered that I could in that case count upon their subsidy. It was a remarkable day for me when I received this letter. However, over a year went by during which I had no need of any subsidy because I first had to make my preparations. I first had to be a year with Birkedal in order to prove how far the four pupils I had could be inspired and whether I could at all inspire youths at the age at which I now thought to teach them. When this year had gone I had become less confident in my beliefs: strangely enough I always have become so just shortly before [**GEEG p. 222**] I was to start upon an enterprise, and I also become so when I have to get up and speak. I prayed to Our Lord that he however would not lead me into something which I possibly could not carry through, but then there came a definite order: that it would have to be now or never. I could not find it in myself to say yes to its never happening and so I had to say: then it must be now.

The house about which I previously spoke had meanwhile been sold and had become available again. I went up to the man who had it for sale and asked if he would wait eight days while I journeyed to Copenhagen because I did not dare to buy it before I had got to know whether I could get any subsidy over there, and he promised me then to wait eight days. With that I marched off next morning to Copenhagen and walked the whole way. When I got to the city [May 1850] I went over to Algreen who at that time was at Regensen, I stayed with him and spent the night on his sofa. It was however only poor consolation I got from him because he answered me: "What are you talking about? the Grundtvigians are not the sort of folk who remember this year what they decided last; they have quite different ideas now and this will doubtless come to nothing; but I will come with you to see Grundtvig." When we came in to him he was standing and smoking his pipe and resting his arm on the stove. "This is Kold from Fyn" said [P. K.] Algreen. "Oh" said Grundtvig, "is it?" and we immediately fell out with each other. I wanted to have my lads in school when they were newly confirmed, at the age of fourteen, fifteen, sixteen, but Grundtvig said: "It won't work before they are eighteen." I well remember that I said: "Grundtvig cannot know how the peasants are over there because by the time they are eighteen they have already begun to play at sweethearts, smoke tobacco, deal in pipes and watches, and so we cannot get them inspired. "Yes," answered Grundtvig, "certainly we can." "No," I said, "according to my experience of the matter, my opinion is the only right one." I have always been sure in my cause, even when I have been wrong. However, Our Lord saw to it that we got people both over and under eighteen years of age to teach, and then I immediately discovered by experience that those who were eighteen and above we could achieve something with while we could achieve nothing with those that were under eighteen years. But the quarrel between Grundtvig and me was settled, though by means of Grundtvig giving way, and otherwise nothing would have come of the whole thing, because I would not have given way. With that, I came forward with my errand, namely, that I should now get hold of the subsidy that was promised me. "Yes," said Algreen, "what [GEEG p. 223] are we going to do about that, how is that going to materialise, because Grundtvig himself knows that there is nothing in the kitty." "Oh yes," said Grundtvig, "it will materialise alright." With that, he asked me how much subsidy I thought I needed. I have got five hundred *rigsdaler* myself, I said; if I get six hundred *rigsdaler* more – but it will have to be as a gift because I dare not promise to pay them back – then I shall have eleven hundred *rigsdaler* and with that I shall get by. "Yes," answered Grundtvig, "six hundred *rigsdaler* and five hundred *rigsdaler* are eleven hundred *rigsdaler*; but what will you be able to do with them?" "Well, if something can't be done with a little," I answered, "then it can't be done with a lot, but it can't be done with nothing at all." With this, Grundtvig said to me: "Go home and draft an appeal to people of goodwill, in which you ask them to subsidise you in this undertaking, and bring it up to me then I shall sign it first and then we shall see what effect my name can have!" I can remember this as though it happened yesterday. When we got outside, Algreen grabbed me by the coat and said: "You are fortune's favourite; now your cause is won; when Grundtvig involves himself with it in this way, then it is safe." And indeed the six hundred *rigsdaler* were collected: Grundtvig himself gave fifty *rigsdaler*, Fru [Marie] Toft one hundred *rigsdaler* and our good old friend Gøricke, that I spoke with yesterday, fifty *rigsdaler*.

1. The nomination of Kold came from Ludvig Christian Müller, Vilhelm Birkedal and Peder Kjellerup Algreen; and the letter inviting Kold to put his ideas to a planning meeting in Copenhagen was written by Algreen on 27 August 1849.

2. "en saakaldet høiere Bondeskole" – Terminology presents its usual problem to the translator. In this context, the terms 'peasant' and 'farmer' (as a translation of *Bonde*) are each too exclusive of the other to cover the mix of rural classes served by the school. The comparative form *højere* [higher] suggests a position in an educational hierarchy higher than the established elementary and secondary schools, but not as high as the *højskole* (a term which, as Professor J. N. Madvig sharply reminded the National Constituent Assembly in 1848, properly

meant 'university' and should therefore be applied only to the University in Copenhagen)
– though nevertheless *højskole* was historically the title which attached to free-schools on the
Grundtvig-Kold model.

108. *Hans Brun:* Biskop N. F. S. Grundtvigs Levnetsløb udførligst fortalt fra 1839 *[Bp NFSG's Life recounted in fullest detail from 1839]* (2 vols., 1882), I, 452; GEEG Stk. 45, p. 223.

Over the period around Whitsun 1851, Grundtvig made the visit to Norway which so revitalised his consciousness of the ancient cultural ties between the two peoples and strengthened his hope of their sharing a common future destiny. It was naturally with some misgivings that he listened in to, and discussed with Norwegian visitors to his home, the vigorous contemporary debate on what form of the language Norway should adopt as its official standard. At least one of the motives among reformers was that the language should be purged of its Danishness and restored to its ancient Norse character. Others doubted whether a language artificially constructed by linguistic scholars would actually be adopted into common use. Grundtvig, who had a lifelong interest and competence in language, feared that such a language might prove to be stillborn.

It was this year [1851], towards the autumn, that Grundtvig had a visit from the young Norwegian educationist [*Oplysningsmand*] Ole Vig, who first called on him one day but was then invited back to dinner another day. Among the issues which were discussed at table was also the language-issue [*Maal-Sagen*],[1] whereupon Grundtvig asked, a little sceptically, about the population in the mountain districts: "But do they *really* not understand the ordinary literary language?" to which Vig could not definitely give an answer; but when somebody present attacked the establishment of a new Norwegian written language as proof of an almost total insanity, Grundtvig asked simply: "Why?" – even though he certainly did *not* believe that it could turn out advantageously without conditions which were not in place.

1. From the mid-19th c. onwards momentum had been gathering in Norway for the creation of an independent national standard written language (*landsmaal*) distinct from previously dominant Danish. This, it was held, would enhance Norwegian internal cohesion and assert Norwegian national identity and autonomy against both Denmark and Sweden. See further the Index entry **Maalstræv**.

109. *Olaus Arvesen:* Samliv med landskjendte mænd *[Life in the company of nationally famous men]* (1915), pp. 10-12, 14-17; GEEG Stk. 46, pp. 223-28.

"It is after all about Grundtvig and not about the Uppsala-expedition that I am writing" declares the Norwegian Olaus Arvesen (1830-1917), later (1864) pioneer of the Grundtvigian folk-high-school in Norway – but the gathering of 20 June 1855 in Tivoli gardens in Copenhagen, narrated in some detail here, was a continued expression of the bond nurtured between the Scandinavian lands by students at the respective national universities, declared at the great Uppsala gathering from which Arvesen was just returning, and supported, with quite earnest commitment, by Grundtvig who four years previously had been received with unforgettable Norwegian hospitality at a similar great gathering in Kristiania (Oslo). The Danish king himself, Frederik VII, recognised the political significance of this movement among the young elite of Scandinavia, and patronised an open-air lunch for them in the Deer-park – though despite the zealous Scandinavianism of such as Frederik Barfod (in the face of the blows which the inter-Scandinavian history of the period delivered) the bond never came to the constitutional embodiment for which some hoped. Arvesen set a seal on his elated weekend by attending Sunday service at Vartov Church to hear Grundtvig preach and to join in "Vartov's famous hymn-singing." "As a rule it was Grundtvig's own hymns or hymns reworked by him which were sung, and in his hymns, as all well-informed people know, there is a content, a strength and a poetic amplitude and loftiness as in few other hymnwriters since the earliest days of the Church. In this even his opponents have been agreed." See also the headnote to item 115.

We Norwegians who were involved in the expedition[1] were invited to Copenhagen on the way back and here it was that for the first time I saw and heard Grundtvig, at the great student festivity which the Copenhageners [GEEG p. 224] held for us in Tivoli. This was in the last days of June [1856]. We had in fact on the same day been to a great luncheon with King Frederik the Seventh out at Eremitagen [The Hermitage] in the Deer-Park. This excellent festivity was held out in the open field where the horseshoe-shaped tables in great multitude were placed for the numerous crowd and where everything proceeded with liveliness and enthusiasm but which did not pass by without a certain amount of clashing of patriotic currents. I should have liked to describe these a bit more closely, but apart from one single episode, of which more later, I must let this pass on this occasion. It is after all about Grundtvig and not about the Uppsala-expedition [*Uppsalatoget*] that I am writing.

As mentioned, we were invited in the evening to a festivity in Tivoli. Besides the great crowd of Danish students there were also various of Copenhagen's great men gathered, and among these Grundtvig. He was at that time seventy-three years old. However, no one could have believed he was so old, briskly and agilely as that broad-built figure went about among us and talked now with one and now with another of the Norwegians. Five years previously he had for the first and last time visited Norway for the student march and there was delighted both to see some of the places he so often had dreamed of as historian of the North, and to see the people whose sagas he ranked highest of all – at least as high as even those of the Greeks who, as is well known, were definitely his favourite nation. The Norwegian people's warlike and magnificent way of life he had both studied and described over many years. Grundtvig, as is well known, was one of the most knowledgeable men in the antiquity of the North in those days. Even our own nation's great scholar in the field of history, P. A. Munch, during a violent scholarly battle over *Beovulfs drapa* gave him this testimonial, that among the antiquarian experts of the North there "were not many who were worthy to unloose Grundtvig's shoestrings."

When Grundtvig mounted the speaker's rostrum in Tivoli Garden, he was received with the greatest enthusiasm. I remember that men such as [J. S. C.] Welhaven, [D. G.] Monrad, A. Munch and a whole lot of the older Norwegians who had been on the Uppsala-expedition crowded close in below the speaker's rostrum. Grundtvig's speeches – I recall that he gave two – were as ever short, plain and calm. I remember only a couple of points from them now. He began by saying that just as his memories from the Norway-visit had been a great pleasure to him so recently he had again derived a pleasure from up there, from reading Ivar Aasen's just-published "Norwegian Proverbs." It [**GEEG p. 225**] was always a great delight to him to read a people's collections of proverbs, for these, next to the people's myths, reflect most clearly of all the people's character. Its experiences, purified through the generations. Its yearnings and its hopes are mirrored most deeply in its myths and most clearly in its proverbs. After having made a number of appropriate remarks upon the importance of these sources of enlightenment to a people, he continued and concluded with a comparison between Aasen's Norwegian collection and the Danish ones; he had found a lot of similarities but also a quantity of differences – these latter, though, especially in their form. Thus when we Danes say: "As one shouts in the forest, so one gets answer," in Norway it runs: "As one shouts in the mountains, so one gets answer." Now he would desire, both on his own behalf and on behalf of Denmark and the whole of the North, that the many young people who had come down here might receive just as good and pleasing a response from the Danish beechwoods as the Danes recently received from the Norwegian mountains.

To his speech was then added a spring song, full of feeling, which he had written for the young folk's festivity. In it he likens the youth of each of the three countries with a rose-garden to which each one individually will bring his portion, to the happiness of the common folk-stock. The song ends with the verse:

Høinordens rosengaard,	Rose-garden of High-North,
jo tiere du seiler, des fastere du staar,	the oftener you sail forth the steadfaster you stand,
des rikere blir rosens flor,	the richer is the rose's bloom,
des mere liflig dufter den søtt i gamle	Nord. the livelier its fragrance spreads, sweet in the ancient North.[2]

At the festivity in Tivoli another episode occurred which in its way was illustrative even though it was so brief that it almost belongs among instantaneous photographs. After Grundtvig's speech about Norway Volrath Vogt, in those days very well known, stepped up with a speech about – well, I don't remember what but I think it was about good co-existence in the North or somesuch. This same Vogt was a big well-built man, a genuine Norwegian lad, but in his way a little extraordinary – if not in precisely the same style as my table-companion, [H. H. S.] Schulze, then at least such that he immediately upon his appearance had to awake attention among those who did not know him.. He always came across as a bit rough and arrogant, so that those who did not know his good heartedness might get the impression that he was a man of strife who wanted to be up [**GEEG p. 226**] and do battle. On top of this he had a powerful voice and a sort of torrential fluency of speech which, especially when he performed publicly, gave the impression of the roaring of a waterfall, with thundering and din. And so it was this time. We who "knew him" were aware that he only meant it well, for he was a man of honour from top to toe, but all the other hundreds of listeners apparently did not understand what was happening. I recall that he began with a description of the Norwegian mountains and how barren and naked, intimidating and confrontational they stood there, and gave warning to all foreigners who came sailing in between them. Grundtvig, who with the other guests of honour was sitting by the side of the speaking rostrum's wide curtains, immediately got up at the start in order to hear what this stout Norwegian had to say; but as soon as it appeared that it was starting to brew up for a bout of violence he instantly disappeared behind the curtain. But one could tell that he went on listening, because as soon as the speaker had become calmer and began to describe how, behind these mountains and intimidating pinnacles and mountain peaks there are found fertile fields, leafy slopes, and flower-adorned dales still as a church, and as with the natural environment so also with the people who live there – they can appear rugged and hard but if you enter more closely into their life you can find both kind-heartedness and warmth – during these words Grundtvig bounded forth again and shouted: "Hear, hear! it is true, every word that he speaks!" Here again, the same as in the proverb: "As one shouts in the forest, so one gets answer."

⌒

During these days I got both to hear and to converse with Grundtvig. A good old friend of his, the glover [N. F.] Larsen, accompanied me out to his house on the Saturday morning. To begin with, I was a little apprehensive towards the great renowned man, but I was soon cured of apprehension. Grundtvig at once offered me a chair and then began to enquire about various matters in Norway, particularly about the Lammers controversy which right at that time was at its most intense,[3] together with the violent conflict of Gisle Johnson versus [W. A.] Wexels which had then just begun. The observations he made on these things were striking, and the description he gave of Pietism which at that time had started up in our country, caused me to understand that he knew this spiritual tendency better than I did. Among the rest he observed: "Where Pietism is allowed a free hand, it stunts the thriving of the folk and that development within the folk which must above all form the basis of [GEEG p. 227] the work of Christianity; it renders Christianity inhuman and thereby unviable."

I had at various times had the best opportunity, and later gained still more, both from knowledge of my own native town and a couple of years later of the capital itself and from far and wide in the country, to gain experiences which entirely confirmed the truth of these observations.

The day after, I visited Vartov Church or, if you like, Vartov 'old women's hospital' [*kællinghospital*], a big redbrick building in the lowest storey of which the church is located. Whether it should be called a church or just a meeting-hall is not easy to say. It was a very large old-fashioned room with a huge chiming-clock up on its rear wall. The institution itself was a kind of home for old 'crones'; I think it is officially called *Helligaands Hospital* [Hospital of the Holy Spirit]. This was the only church with which Grundtvig, at long last, was favoured and he kept it until the day of his death. This appointment was doubtless the least that could be found for him (the annual salary was only 800 *rigsdaler* – 1600 *kroner*). However, one would be mistaken if one believed that these old women were his sole congregation. There were certainly many of them, but as a rule only a few of them gathered for his sermons and those who gathered liked to sit up in a gallery and bicker about anything and everything, now about their seat, now about private differences. The hall itself on the other hand was jammed full of listeners from outside, men and women of all classes of folk, right from the Dowager Queen Caroline Amalie who through all these years until her death was an admirer of Grundtvig's preaching, and down to the manual labourers and petty folk. Priests, professors and prominent politicians were regularly to be seen among the great crowd of listeners. Many Norwegians and Swedes also gathered there: they wanted to hear this remarkable man.

Grundtvig's sermons were always short, at any rate now in the days of his old age; they seldom lasted above half an hour, but they were at the same time clear and incisive. Despite the quiet manner in which they were done, there was a fire and a fervour in the content which could not possibly do anything but grip the audience. Then on top of this there was Vartov's famous hymn-singing. This was the most lively and sonorous church singing I have ever heard. [Bjørnstjerne] Bjørnson, who in those days very often stayed in Copenhagen and would then constantly visit Vartov Church, would often declare that "that hymn-singing is more powerful than any mission." As a rule it was Grundtvig's own hymns or hymns reworked by him [GEEG p. 228] which were sung, and in his hymns, as all well-informed people know, there is a content, a strength and a poetic amplitude and loftiness as in few other hymnwriters since the earliest days of the Church. In this even his opponents have been agreed.

1. Arvesen refers to *Uppsalatoget*, the expedition (1856) to a pan-Scandinavian gathering in Uppsala in Sweden, by student supporters of the Scandinavian movement. The return reception in Tivoli gardens in Copenhagen was on 20 June 1856.

2. Grundtvig's poem *Høinordens Rosengaard* is printed in *PS* VIII, 135-36 in six-lined verses, here presented by Arvesen as four-lined; see the Index entry.

3. The Lammers controversy was a conflict within the Norwegian church over the teachings of the pietistic preacher Gustav Adolf Lammers.

110. *Hans Brun:* Biskop N. F. S. Grundtvigs Levnetsløb udførligst fortalt fra 1839 *[Bp NFSG's Life recounted in fullest detail from 1839] (2 vols., 1882), II, 236; GEEG Stk. 47, p. 228.*

There were doubtless many clerics and other respectable people in mid-19th-c. Copenhagen, where the rates of death from postnatal complications, tuberculosis and the intermittent epidemics of the age were high, who married a second time; but a third marriage, especially when one was in one's seventies and one's intended bride was forty years younger, was held by some to be indecent and undignified. Even among Grundtvig's loyal followers some were dismayed at news of his engagement to the widowed Asta Reedtz. Brun's anecdote of the weeping young woman perhaps gives a glimpse of the nature of Grundtvig's charisma among one section of his congregation.

Naturally, there were at that time too [1857] those who disapproved of the engagement,[1] and there were those who sneered at it. A young woman of Grundtvig's acquaintance, it is told, came weeping up to him when she had received the news and asks whether it was true he was going to be married? Yes, it was – and he asked her what there was about the matter which caused her such pain? Well, she could not but think that when he took this step then he must needs stand with one foot in heaven and with the other on the ground. "Naturally I am standing with both feet on the ground" replied Grundtvig and talked with her so gently about the matter that she was apparently already becoming pacified and later also had to join in praising the new wife in the house.

1. Brun's footnote: "Gr's engagement with his third wife to be, Asta Reedtz, born *Komtesse* Krag-Juel-Vind-Frijs."

111. *Morten Eskesen:* Minder og Udsigter fra 40 Aars Skoleliv *[Memories and perspectives from 40 years' school-life]* (1881), pp. 180-81, 192; GEEG Stk. 48, pp. 228-29.

Generally speaking, Grundtvig left the actual implementation of his educational ideas to gifted and pioneering teachers such as Christen Kold, Ludvig Schrøder and Ernst Trier. In 1856, however, *Grundtvigs Højskole,* largely funded by a gift from Danish and Norwegian subscribers to mark Grundtvig's seventieth birthday, was inaugurated in a property close to Copenhagen named by Grundtvig Marielyst after his deceased wife, Marie Toft. Its first principal was C. J. Brandt (1817-89). In this school Grundtvig took much practical interest, visiting it with the Dowager Queen Caroline Amalie and other dignitaries, making speeches there upon educational issues, and from time to time holding classes – of which Morten Eskesen (1826-1913), a young teacher at the school, gives the following account.

[At Marielyst Highschool, during the winter of 1857-58, I taught] ballads and geography;[1] but arithmetic teaching, which I thought [Jeppe] Tang could better carry than I, especially since the teaching of adults was concerned, I wriggled out of – which I was later sorry for, since [C. J.] Brandt would then get stuck with it; but I got my great joy from being present, as far as was possible, in Brandt's lessons, especially when, relying upon the Rhyming Chronicle,[2] he taught World History. But still Grundtvig was Grundtvig and when he came we really got something out of it. The lads would sit round an elongated round table and Grundtvig would place himself at the furthest narrow end where, gripping the edge of the table with his hands, he would stand and talk simply and yet so profoundly about the mysteries of human life, for he much dressed his speech in the old Nordic metaphorical language. Individual points took particular hold on me. Thus: [GEEG p. 229]

"The human heart is the most wonderful thing God has created; for it is so little that it can be contained within a human breast and yet so great that it can contain all heaven and all hell and usually some of both!"

"There is a sort of conflict which arises out of misunderstanding as did that of the Aesir and Vanir, and it needs must end in reconciliation; but there is also a conflict which can only cease when one of the combatants is annihilated. Such is the conflict between Truth and the Lie (Thor and the Midgard Serpent), Life and Death (Odin and Fenris), Light and Darkness (Freyr and Surt)."

"Books are to be compared with Mimir's head which, when the Spirit gives them life, can bring news from the realm of the dead."

"Unenlightened ingenuousness is like the blind Høder, and can easily go astray as did he when Loki put the mistletoe into his hand."

"The educated person is one who can think what he feels, say what he thinks, and knows what his mouth is saying."

At the highschool we often had guests and sometimes distinguished guests. Of such I recall particularly the Dowager Queen Caroline Amalie, *Gehejmeraadinde* Hall [Privy Councillor Hall's wife], Bishop D. G. Monrad and Bishop P. C. Kierkegaard. One day the Dowager

Queen arrived with Grundtvig and as the door opened I heard her say "We have seen only so little of it as yet!" "Yes, Your Majesty," said Grundtvig, "yet we have seen something; but our children shall see more." "Yes, but we are eager to see something more." Brandt spoke the same day about Iceland and Grundtvig himself read the Rhyming Chronicle[2] *Isklædt med Ild i Barmen* [Ice-clad with fire in its bosom] and in such a way that it had real effect.

1. The somewhat uncommon term *jordkundskaben* used here by the folk-highschool teacher Eskesen, rather than the term *geografi* (already in technical use in Danish in the eighteenth century), appears to be an example of ideological substitution of Danish-derived words (cp. German *Erdkunde*) for words derived from Greek and Latin.

2. Grundtvig's own *Krønnike-Rim til levende Skolebrug* [Chronicle-rhymes for living school-use].

112. *Peter Rørdam:* H. F. Rørdam, Peter Rørdam, *III* (1895), pp. 103-04; GEEG Stk. 49, pp. 229-30.

On Wednesday [30 March 1859] all we priests who customarily visit the Queen[1] were there to a large reception, including [H. L.] Martensen and Rasmus Nielsen. But the disparities of viewpoint were so great that no general conversation took place; everyone talked with his neighbour and it proceeded quietly onwards right to the end when Grundtvig and Rasmus Nielsen[2] clashed together over Mathematics which R. N. thought was of great use with respect to "the Eternal"[3] [GEEG p. 230] – to which Grundtvig first remarked "Yes; you no doubt mean the Infinite" and when R. N. answers "Yes, the Infinite!" then says Grundtvig: "I could tell you meant the Infinite – the desolate and empty – for one can no doubt infer nought from nought, but one cannot infer the greater from the smaller unless within the smaller from which one starts out there is something wherein the smaller resembles the greater." R. N. grew pale; but Martensen laughed so that he positively chortled.

1. The Dowager Queen Caroline Amalie, widow of Christian VIII, who patronised, financially supported and regularly participated in a wide range of religious, intellectual, social and charitable activities.

2. Rasmus Nielsen (1809-84) was a professor of philosophy in Copenhagen University, a mathematician and much more: altogether a remarkable and formidable figure.

3. There is an echo here of the topic in which, many years previously, F. L. B. Zeuthen to his frustration proved unable to engage Grundtvig (see items 78 and 85), leading him to deny Grundtvig's capacity for scientific thinking [*Evne til* videnskabelig *Tænkning*].

113. *Olaus Arvesen:* Oplevelser og erindringer *[Experiences and reminiscences] (1912), p. 165; GEEG Stk. 50, p. 230.*

One day [in 1859] we[1] met the two aforementioned Norwegian priests[2] who had been to lunch out at Grundtvig's. One of them, the elderly unostentatious Faye, then came over to me and told me a little about the meeting. They had both had much pleasure from talking with the "Old Man" but, added F[aye], in that house speech is certainly free with a vengeance, and during lunch the old man and both his sons got into a vehement dispute about freedom of belief – they had in fact had a conversation about it. The sons (the professors Svend and Johan Grundtvig) protested vehemently against their father: "But there has to be some constraint involved, father, for how otherwise would it work? Everybody could then believe what they themselves wished." Then the old man got vehement: "You have no understanding of belief, my son, if you think that anybody can be constrained to it!" "I was getting quite fearful as I sat there" said Faye, "and I could not help thinking about the ancient viking-times, because then it was not rare for father and sons to do battle with each other." They disputed a long while about this, but apparently it had no influence upon the good relationship otherwise. "The old man has grown accustomed to stating his opinion, and he has doubtless also brought up his sons to state theirs."

1. Arvesen (1830-1917) and Herman Anker (1839-96) who later collaborated in establishing the first Grundtvigian folk-highschool in Norway..

2. Pastor Andreas Faye (1802-69) and *Provst* J. W. C. Dietrichson (1815-83).

114. *Ernst Johannes Trier:* Erindringer fra Grundtvigs Hjem in Frederik Rönning, Hundrede Aar. Et Mindeskrift i Andledning af Hundredaarsdagen for Nic. Fred. Sev. Grundtvigs Fødsel *[One hundred years. A commemorative volume in connection with the hundredth anniversary of the birth of NFSG] (1883), pp. 17-20; GEEG Stk. 51, pp. 230-35.*

Ernest Trier (1837-93) had long been established as principal of the folk-highschool at Vallekilde when he gave these memoirs to Grundtvig's biographer Frederik Rönning for publication in a commemorative volume (1883) one hundred years after Grundtvig's birth. They benefit therefore from his mature perspectives and hindsight. At the same time, they recall with some vividness the experiences of a young student, earnest, impressionable, who – admitted to private conversation with Grundtvig as freely as any important personage of church or state – learned by trial and error how to set flowing the huge reservoirs of wisdom and polemic stored in that venerable (and now 76-year-old) head. Such an article does not lend itself to great depth or extensive detail of anecdote – yet Trier has usefully recorded his recollection of Grundtvig's views on Education, on the problem of Sin and Evil, on Belief in the presence of Christ in the living word, and on the history of the Church. He is also a witness to the Grundtvig who would give time to help a young student through his examinations and a young tutor through his first lectures, who would lay on a course of *ad hoc* lectures in his own home when a group of young people showed interest (and would eventually turn the lectures into a book, *Kirke-Speil* [Mirror of the Church], 1871), and who, after the disasters of 1864, "most of all showed the way forward towards those tasks which right at that moment lay ahead in uplifting the Danish folk anew."

⌣

In Autumn 1859, upon an invitation from Fru [Asta] Grundtvig, I came for the first time into Grundtvig's house. I found him in his dwelling in Gammel Kongevej in the big library facing the garden with double-doors out to it. In this room what immediately caught the eye were the many bookshelves from floor to ceiling along all the walls and on both sides of the sofa right out into the floorspace with books on both sides. In front of the sofa [GEEG p. 231] stood a large table and again on this one observed piles of books. By the window sat the old man himself at his little table, quite covered with books and papers, in front of him. Never will one forget, once one has met him, the impression which his powerful personality made upon one. There was something great, in truth venerable, investing his figure but, at any rate in his old age, it was matched by something unusually mild and amicable. I had got to know that he never of his own accord entered into conversation with those who were visiting him, so that it would only get going when the visitor himself had questions to set before him, and it was lucky for me that I had got to know this in advance because it proved to be absolutely right: he received me amicably and offered me a seat opposite him but not a word did he otherwise have by way of introduction to the conversation. But since I was now prepared for this, I had taken care in advance to have my questions ready to hand on those matters on which I would wish to know his opinion, and so now I came out with them one after the other. But it did not sound as though he thought very much of them. He answered mildly for sure, but only with a 'Yes' or a 'No' or a 'So-o-o' or something like it; and when after the space of half an hour I realised that my store of questions would soon be used up, I began to get embarrassed and disappointed with the thought of having to break up without having got anything out of my visit. Then I don't know how it came about that I came to mention the Latin school and how resentful I was over the teaching that was offered us there: he began at once to be all ears; now *he* took over the talking and went on for two and a half hours. (In the space of that time his wife arrived and invited us in to the coffee-table; there he continued the conversation; afterwards he invited me back into his library and carried on). Then it was for the most part he alone who did the talking; he set out for me the contrast between the Latin school's teaching and that which he favoured; and he showed me his vision of good, genuine education. I cannot describe how astonished and thrilled I was over the richness in his talk which here came pouring forth, the clarity he conveyed to me in the matter, the certainty of conviction which manifested itself, the greatness which I had encountered here.

This was the way it often worked for me subsequently, for from that time I visited him not infrequently: if there were questions over which I had trouble in reaching clarity I always turned to him. If I have learnt much through his preaching [GEEG p. 232] and his writing, yet it seems to me that I have gained even more from conversations with him, when the words would fall so wondrously steadily from his lips and he would listen with remarkable patience to one's questions and would help to put one to rights. When the time drew near for me to take my Final Examinations in Theology, he offered to go over with me afterwards, from time to time, what I had been doing for my Theology tutor. What rich evenings did I not come to spend with him through this! Here where I cannot possibly take the opportunity to tell about these in their entirety I will just report an episode from a single one. He was not well that evening but still wished that I should come in to him. When I arrived he was sitting with closed eyes in the sofa-nook and remained sitting thus. I began something like this: "Since I was with you last time, I have been reading, in Dogmatics, the section about Sin." "So; have you indeed?" was all that he replied, and now we sat silent for a while. At length I continued by observing that there was much in it I could not understand. Then he at last opened his eyes and said: "Yes, I'll readily believe that; but if you fancy getting down to the bottom of Hell I would have you know that I don't fancy escorting you." At this answer I started laughing. "What are you laughing about?" he asked. To this I replied that he very well knew that I did not want to go to the bottom of Hell and did not wish to have him with me. But now he grew animated and drew himself up to his full height and now he set to: "Yes, yes" he said, "that will be the consequence of it, if we follow all those learned folk who want to investigate the origin of Sin and Evil." And now he expounded for me how we mortals can never know anything about something which lies beyond the ambit of our experiencing, so if, since Sin has come to us through the Devil, we were really to know something about how Evil originates we should have to participate in it, in the experiencing of the Evil One. It was as though something cold ran down my spine as he depicted to me the horror there is even in that kind of enquiry, and he finally burst out: "But God preserve us from it!" Then he went through for me what we can learn from Holy Scripture as to how Sin came about among human beings and the seduction by the Devil.

It was always in the afternoon I had these conversations with him; I would then normally stay for the evening meal afterwards, where he was almost always jocular, exceptionally sparklingly witty [*mageløs spillende vittig*], and rich with an [GEEG p. 233] abundance of ideas and anecdotes which he came out with in an indescribably amusing manner. But if after the evening meal we went back into his library, it was strange to observe the deep seriousness which almost always then spread over him as witness to the fundamental character of him. It was remarkable how he could hold out in this way through a long evening and continue to be fresh and lively in holding forth. I recall one evening after such a long conversation, when it was already past ten o'clock and I was standing by him, hat in hand, to say goodnight to him, that I quite casually let fall a little remark that his sermons were difficult to understand. He then threw himself anew, animatedly and heatedly, into discussion; he asserted that I was mistaken; but I stuck by my assertion and finally, in order to support it, I put forward the fact that often many prerequisites were needed for the understanding of his sermons. "No" he then finally said, "I demand only *one* prerequisite, that is, belief – but Christian belief, of course, which has its peculiarity in this, that it believes in the Lord not only as he was eighteen hundred years ago, or as he one day will come, which the Jews also believe, but as he *is*, present in amongst us and as near to us as the Word on our lips and in our heart."

However, it was not only thus as I have hitherto narrated, through conversations when the two of us were alone, that I received instruction from him in his home. I would later come to be there in a largish, and finally in a large, circle. About this I can report the following. In Summer 1860, at the behest of the Norwegians Olaf Arvesen and Herman Anker, I had discussed with him whether in the course of the autumn and winter he would not lecture on church history. He then said definitely no, with the comment that for this he now lacked two things: fluency and memory. However, when the two aforementioned Norwegians came here in the autumn and gathered one evening with some other young theologians, there arose a dispute among us concerning the consecration of priests. In the end we agreed to take Grundtvig as arbitrator and therefore one evening shortly afterwards we all went out to him together. He now clarified the question for us splendidly; we spent a grand evening with him and were ever so pleased because he offered that we might come again next week if there were further questions we would like to hear his opinion upon. We did not wait to be asked twice and we came again the next week. Meanwhile several others – women, in fact – heard about [GEEG p. 234] this and came along next time. The conversation then went haltingly and in conclusion Grundtvig said: "If you are coming next time it would probably be best that I myself choose the subject on which I can give you my opinions." And so it was, but this time he referred consistently to church history as though it were a given fact that we all had both knowledge of it and views upon it. When he was finished we therefore pointed out to him that he could not take such a thing for granted and that there was nothing we needed him to help us with more than a survey of church history. "Alright then, let me have a go" he said. So the next evening he began that series of lectures which he continued over the course of three winters and which he long afterwards [1871] published under the title of *Kirkespejlet*. But now the circle of listeners had grown so much that both his library and the adjacent rooms were completely filled with listeners, men and women.

Although over these years Grundtvig, because of physical frailty, was tied to the home, yet he thus exercised an influence upon many from there. And from there he followed everything that was happening in the country with great attention and took a lively interest in what was going on round and about. There was something very remarkable in this, that he who spent most of his time in his library nevertheless found opportunity to intervene effectually in a whole host of situations in our land. But from my own relationship with him I can, with regard to this, pick out the following.

A couple of weeks after I had taken my Final Examinations I was to begin a new job as teacher at Blaagaards Seminarium[1] and as such give lectures on Bible history. Tired out after the strain of the examinations, I could not gather my thoughts for this. The day before I was to begin I still had no idea as to how I was to tackle it. So I betook myself, as was my way on such occasions, out to Grundtvig and asked him to help me – but then got much more than I had expected. After a brief time for reflection, he in fact gave me in broad survey a complete introduction to Bible history. At the forefront of this he placed the Mosaic-Christian perception of the human being as the creature created in God's image – fallen into sin – destined to be raised up again; and with all the weight that lay in his words he imprinted upon me that day that it is enlightenment in *this* which must be made the foundation of all genuine and true popular enlightenment [*Folkeoplysning*]. But he did not content himself with helping me this one time; he diligently asked [GEEG p. 235] me what else I was undertaking as teacher and went through with me the greater part of what I was supposed to be doing at the Seminarium.

Unfortunately he was far from managing to go through the whole of Bible history for me. The war of 1864 broke out. For a time I was called away from Copenhagen as an assistant field-chaplain. Nevertheless, when I came back, it was he who most of all showed the way forward towards those tasks which right at that moment lay ahead in uplifting the Danish folk anew. It was he who then lifted as it were a veil for me and allowed me to see that it was not through the (national) children's school but on the contrary through the independent school for mature youths that something great was to be accomplished in that regard. And it was he who gave me the final push so that I got the occupation that I now have. I told him in fact that there had been some talk that Frederik Boisen was supposed to have started his work here in the county of Holbæk but had now changed his mind so that he went to

Møen; and that [Villiam Johan] Hoff, the priest from Vallekilde, had complained of this in a letter to me. "Yes" said Grundtvig then, "I should be very mistaken if it is not precisely in that part of Holbæk county that the next folk-highschool should be established. If Ludvig Schrøder is not successful in getting started up in Askov I shall advise him to get going out there. Or perhaps", he continued, "there is another young person who has the courage, talent and inclination to make a start, who can move out there." These words so took root in my soul that it provided the grounds of my coming to Vallekilde. With great sympathy he followed the development of the school here over the coming years.[2] I was always sure of getting good advice and a good word which helped to sustain cheerfulness.

This is how things turned out for me in my relationship with him; but things also turned out thus for many others. Often on a visit to him, even after his grievous illness in 1867, I have been astonished at how remarkably well-informed he was about everything that was going on round about the country, how attentively he followed it in detail, how often he had the opportunity to have an influence upon what happened.

1. Teacher training college; not to be confused with a seminary for the training of priests.

2. The folk-highschool at Vallekilde opened in November 1865.

115. Olaus Arvesen: Samliv med landskjendte mænd *[Life in the company of nationally famous men]* (1915), pp. 18-21; GEEG Stk. 52, pp. 235-37.

Olaf Arvesen (1830-1917) and Herman Anker (1839-96) were notable among the many Norwegians who, long after enforcement of the so-called 'personal union' *[personalunion]* with Sweden divorced Norway from Denmark (1814), and notwithstanding a persistent consciousness that Denmark had long been the country's often-resented overlord, continued to look to Denmark for cultural fellowship. Grundtvig for his part valued and nurtured his Norwegian connections and particularly after the overwhelming experience of his reception in Kristiania in 1851 nursed warm feelings for the country and the people, and welcomed visiting Norwegians to his home. Arvesen's expression of a sense of exhilaration experienced in the presence of Grundtvig – brightness, happiness, fellowship, intellectual and spiritual enlightenment – is matched in a host of other witnesses. In more volatile characters it could become the *sværmeri* [fanaticism] which sober churchmen looked on with distaste; in many an individual and congregation it seemed to affirm those Christian assurances which Grundtvig preached, and to confer strength, motivation and solidarity in both material and spiritual, personal and congregational life (of which one abundant source of documentation is H. P. B. Barfod's *Minder fra gamle Grundtvig'ske Hjem* [Memories from old Grundtvigian homes], 8 vols., Copenhagen 1921-28). Here Arvesen makes valuable record of the informal lectures Grundtvig gave in his home over the winter of 1860 – which were eventually redrafted and published as *Kirke-Speil eller Udsigt over den kristne Menigheds Levnedsløb* [The mirror of the Church or Survey of the life-history of the Christian congregation] (1871) – of their content, of ensuing debate and of the typical composition of their audiences: almost half of them women, including the Queen Mother Caroline Amalie, plus professors, businessmen, tradesmen, students, distinguished politicians and parliamentarians and clergy – such, says Arvesen, as regularly formed the Vartov congregation. See also the headnote to item 109.

It was in the middle of September 1860 that we travelled down there [from Norway to Copenhagen] and we then stayed there the whole winter [GEEG p. 236] until well into the Spring of 1861. It was a glorious period which provided us both from the first day to the last with many bright and happy times, and not only many acquaintanceships and friend-ships and much excellent help in the examination-reading we were pursuing and which we intended to get finished with down there, but first and last Grundtvig's lectures every Tuesday evening, and then not forgetting Sundays in Vartov Church. These were the most glorious Sundays we had ever experienced. Grundtvig's lectures were held in his two rooms – the big work-room of which the four walls were all filled with books, and the living-room by the side of it. There was a large open folding-door between the two so everybody heard well. Grundtvig's speaking was always calm, I might even say gentle; but since he had powerful lungs and a strong voice hardly a word was lost to any of the listeners. There were regularly as many listeners as the two rooms could accommodate. As a rule it was the same people who came back each time and for the most part it was those men and women who were seen each Sunday in his church: a couple of professors, businessmen and tradesmen, several students and at one time or another also distinguished politicians as for example Carl Ploug, individual old parliamentarians over from Jylland and suchlike, and as a rule several priests. The Dowager Queen Caroline Amalie was also sometimes present. Towards half of those gathered were women.

Grundtvig would sit in his big armchair in front of his work-table and hold his lec-tures. These would usually last an hour and were, as we could see, worked out in advance. In fact he would have a pile of handwritten quarto sheets in front of him and on rare occa-sions he would peer down with his big magnifying-glass at the manuscript. The lecturing was otherwise quite free and did not for one moment give the impression of being tied to the papers. The lectures gave a survey over the life of the Church from the first ardent days in the Hebrew congregation, from the strongly religious-philosophical days in the Greek congregation, from the centuries of powerful administration in the Church of Rome, etc. He pointed to the kind of folk and the folk-character which lay behind the reception which Christianity got and was bound to get in the seven different congregational circles through which, on its triumphant journey through the national churches, it had progressed. Anyone who wants to have more detailed information of the content of these important lectures I refer to his book *Kirkespejl* [The Mirror of the Church, *Speculum Ecclesiae*] or "Udsigt over den kristne Menigheds Levnedsløb" [Survey of the life-history of the Christian congrega-tion].

After the lectures there usually followed some question or another, in some cases [GEEG p. 237] concerning this or that point in the lecture which the questioner had not understood, in some cases concerning such ecclesiastical or religious subjects in general as might be on the mind of someone in the gathering. Both men and women were among the questioners and Grundtvig gave his clarifications with the greatest forbearance. I remember especially that nimble little pastor Peter Rørdam as a man eager to know "how", "why" and "wherefore." Thus on one occasion he wanted to get it sorted out what attitude "we priests and layfolk" are supposed to take when there is something or other in the Bible which we feel we cannot quite agree with. He then mentioned several such trifles, among them these words of Paul that women must not speak in the assembly. Grundtvig's answer was brief: "We must follow Paul and the other biblical authors respectfully but freely; what Paul said about women was appropriate to that time and corresponded to the feelings of the people he was talking to!" On another occasion Rørdam asked how far freedom of belief could and ought properly to stretch and whether there ought not to be some *constraint*. Grundtvig's reply this time was if possible even shorter and certainly more forceful: "Anyone who can talk seriously of a constraint upon believing cannot possibly have grasped for himself what belief actually is."[1]

1. The question concerning freedom of belief raised here by Peter Rørdam is elsewhere reported by Arvesen (who had the anecdote from Pastor Faye; see item 113) to have been raised over lunch in the Grundtvig home by the Grundtvig sons, Svend and Johan. Grundtvig's answer is the same in both anecdotes.

116. *Jakob Holm: article in* Danske Kirketidende *[Danish Church-news]* 1909, col. 744; GEEG Stk. 53, p. 237-38.

Like Grundtvig's son Frederik Lange, Holm crossed to America to serve there (1876-81) as pastor to Danish-Lutheran congregations of immigrant origin in Chicago. He was also one of the increasing number of contributors, in the decades following Grundtvig's death, to the growing corpus of biographical reminiscences – often culled from the dwindling company of those who had personally known '*den Gamle*' [the Old Man] – of Grundtvig and of the formative years of Grundtvigianism.

One of Grundtvig's older friends, the well-known elderly free-school teacher Jens Hansen in Broby by Sorø, visited me the other day and shared with me his rich memories from old Grundtvigian times.[1] He was with Grundtvig a lot in his home on Gammel Kongevej, and also at the *Vennemøde* [Meeting of Grundtvig's Friends] of 1863 when several of the friends were gathered one afternoon and the conversation lit upon the Word and Scripture. It ended with Grundtvig going over and laying his hand on the Bible which usually lay opened on a table in his work-room, and then he said: "I dare to say that *I believe everything that is written in this book*. Doubtless there is much that I do not understand; but it is my conviction that everything that I need for the sake of my own development and for the enlightenment and guidance of the congregation, this the Spirit will gradually clarify for me. It is not granted one individual generation or age to understand Scripture in its entirety for it extends to the end of time." [GEEG p. 238] Grundtvig added: "I make bold to ask: how many of our Scriptural-theologians [*Skriftteologer*] can say that?"

This testimony to the infallibility and the indispensability of Scripture needs no comment – only the observation that it is of course with Jens Hansen's permission that I report it here.

1. Jens Hansen (1827-1914), old friend of Grundtvig, was at this time aged about 83.

Crisis of Palm Sunday 1867

117. Peter Frederik Adolph Hammerich: Frederik Hammerich. Et Levnetsløb, *ed. Angul Hammerich (1882), II, pp. 204-10; GEEG Stk. 54, pp. 238-43.*

Frederik Hammerich (1809-77), being an ordained priest as well as professor of Church history at the University and, not least, a trusted friend of Grundtvig, was better placed than any, excepting alone his younger colleague Pastor Frederik Helveg (1816-1901), to give an account of what happened in Vartov Kirke on Palm Sunday 1867 when during the celebration of Holy Communion, in the presence of the Dowager Queen Caroline Amalie and a rapidly growing congregation, it became evident that Grundtvig was undergoing a breakdown. Hammerich's account appears to report incidents accurately: it corresponds closely with the account subsequently submitted by Helveg to the *Kultusministerium*. One might perhaps register a note of circumspection when Hammerich (prudently?) assigns to Helveg the judgment on the basis of which they resolved to step forward and assist Grundtvig in administering the sacrament at the altar, that "Yet nothing has so far occurred that conflicts with the faith" [*Der er alligevel ingen ting endnu kommen fræm, som strider mod troen*]. Another witness, the young Hans Peter Barfod (1843-1926), confirms (see item 118) "no significant disagreement" with Hammerich's published account – but tellingly remarks that "from Hammerich one gets the impression of an uncomfortable atmosphere [*Indtryk af Uhygge*], whilst I had an impression of a special sublimity [*Indtryk af en særlig Højhed*] across these hours." Others present reflected a similar, but sometimes more extreme, divergence in interpretation of events, ranging from the banal and medical to the exalted and mystical; and of course rumour and gossip flew round Copenhagen which, whether sympathetic or hostile, traded rather in the sensational than the factual and in the bizarre rather than the clinical. Though it might easily be demonstrated that there was more order and sense in Grundtvig's disarrayed talk than witnesses understood or chose to elicit, and though a more understanding attitude has since developed towards the bipolar disorder from which Grundtvig seems to have suffered, Grundtvigians have on the whole preferred to forget the episode. Grundtvig's proffered resignation was set aside after the Vartov congregation had formally expressed their desire that he should remain their pastor, and he returned after convalescence to continue as such until his death in 1872. For further discussion, see the Index entry **Palm Sunday** 1867 and additional entries listed there.

⌒

At this time Grundtvig himself was stricken by a severe vicissitude. He had long been suffering from swollen legs, for which reason he went about with a *fontanelle*; this now closed itself and the water settled on his brain. Plausibly, mental grounds were also contributory, grief over Denmark's misfortunes – this, at least, gave his delirium its colouring. It began with his being unusually talkative and lively and physically brisker than at any point within more recent time; the swollen legs had recovered their natural appearance. So came Palm-Sunday 1867.

As was his custom, he made his summons to confession in front of the altar. There was an over-effusive fervency in it, and he ended by inviting everybody to the Lord's table: "those who do not wish to join in here" he said "are to be shown out of the church: the sexton must see to this!" A great part of the congregation obeyed the call, then he turned to the Dowager Queen's pew; she was still listening to him: "But where is Denmark's queen?" he cried. "The queen of Saba came to listen to Solomon's wisdom, and here there is truly more than Solomon!"[1] With that the Dowager Queen stepped out of her pew and knelt down in front of the altar and as he pronounced over her the absolution of sinners he added: "And herewith are all Denmark's sins absolved." After a pause while the altar was filled up anew he said further: "Now just let the king of the Prussians come, for now Denmark has peace!" I recognised immediately what was going on, and like various others, I wanted to remove myself but was held back by the pleas of my wife and a couple of female friends.

He went into the pulpit and when he had prayed the Lord's Prayer he said: "You must not believe that the first three petitions here are an act of servility [hoveritjeneste]. But we must cross our hands over our breast: this is so as to shut fast the chamber, and this lock the devil himself cannot get through. This I have learnt today: isn't it a good teaching?" After the gospel-reading he told his listeners: "Well, I have just read that with these [GEEG p. 239] old glasses of mine which otherwise I haven't been able to read a single word with. Isn't that good progress?" There were a couple more words before the sermon began: "Yesterday I was sick unto death" he said "and yet I got quite a decent sermon from Our Lord. But how shall I be able to deliver it? I said. Just leave that to me, he replied, and now today I have got this far."

The sermon, which was delivered in a tone of exaltation, was the most wondrous mixture of madness and inspired thoughts. "What people through all the ages have puzzled over, the Lord had devised – a vital unstillness (*perpetuum mobile*) in the human heart, and the squaring of the circle (quadrature of the circle [*sirkelens kvadratur*]) in the foursquare heavenly Jerusalem, measured by a man's measure."[2] "There had been many impediments to the Lord's coming, for the intellect [*Aanden*] and the heart [*Hjærtet*] had become separated. The intellect God had planted in the east on the hill of visions [*synernes høj*] and the heart here on the Danish islands. But now they have at last been reunited and now Jordan flows out into the Øresund, now the Lord is riding into his city. The foal of an ass which bears him has grown up among us, but first its mother must be set loose, and that is what I am doing today."

Thereupon he spoke more about the Lord's coming and what should precede it, that is, that an antichrist-king should first enter into the world's chief city. "Indeed, the foe has already entered in, although his time is short. And even as there was heard weeping and sighing without end when the walls were broken down about Jerusalem so shall there be unending jubilation and joy now that they are being built up again." After the sermon there again followed various casual remarks.

While the congregation was singing Grundtvig send a message and asked me to help with the communion. It was a painful moment for me, but was it not straightforwardly a duty to step into the breach here? There was no time for reflection: I would therefore have to act upon an immediate feeling, and it did not let me down. But not in any circumstance would I be alone with Grundtvig at the altar. I therefore first turned to [Kristen] Køster the curate, who appeared as though he did not know whether he was coming or going, and

Crisis of Palm Sunday 1867

thereupon to my friend Pastor F[rederik] Helveg. "This is going rather far over the mark," I said, "so what are we going to do now? Dare you participate in the communion, and dare I?" "All the same," replied Helveg, "nothing has yet emerged that conflicts with the faith. And I for my part have always been prepared for it, that Grundtvig's exit from the world could, despite all the differences, have a similarity to Søren Kierkegaard's."³ "Then" said I "let the two of us [GEEG p. 240] go together, in God's name!" We did so, and each donned his priest's vestments in the sacristy.

Meanwhile Grundtvig had held a baptism; at it he had chatted with the baby and in general behaved himself strangely. From that he came back to his seat. "I don't know from one moment to the next" he said to us "what I have to do: I am granted everything on the spot. I am therefore thinking of submitting my resignation; and we must all do this, for we cannot be priests within the State Church in this fashion." I asked whether at communion he did not mean to use the Lord's Prayer and the words of institution. "Yes, naturally" he replied, "but an informal address." The altar-service began and I stuck to his side with the intention of breaking off proceedings if anything unseemly should supervene. Helweg did the same.

Grundtvig's informal address was beautiful. In everything else he followed the ritual. Among the very numerous altar-guests were to be seen the Dowager Queen, himself and his wife, four of his confirmands who were to be confirmed immediately after Easter, and his youngest son, a bright boy of thirteen. After the communion he embraced and kissed Helweg and me, and is supposed also to have kissed the Dowager Queen and said that in February next year she would give birth to Holger Danske.

He invited us out to his home for dinner, and at table there his speech now became quite wild. He talked about the holy kiss, and that the woman who received it would give birth to a sinless child in nine months. In 1844, he said, it went more or less the same with him as now, but people called him mad, and he let himself be frightened then; however this would not happen again because now the Lord who had sought him for eighty-four years had at last found him, and now he was a *Kristoforos* who bore his Lord. He proposed and drank a toast to Christ and all his congregation.

Tales about what had taken place in Vartov were soon on everybody's lips and found their way into the daily papers. A couple of days afterwards *Stiftsprovst* [P. C.] Rothe called to see me and asked whether I thought Grundtvig could deliver his resignation-sermon on Good Friday. He had in fact in the meantime applied for retirement without a pension; his Order of Dannebrog, he wrote, he would like to keep but on the other hand not his ranking with the Bishop of Sjælland.⁴ To this question I replied to Rothe that in my opinion Grundtvig ought to be prevented from delivering a sermon which could easily give very great offence, and that in any event I wanted to talk with others of his congregation about this.

[GEEG p. 241] I hurried off out and on the way met the *seminarium* [teacher training institute] principal, [Jeppe] Tang, whereupon we accompanied each other over to P. Fenger's. Fenger had advised Grundtvig against the sermon in question but he would not go along with deliberately placing impediments in his way. "He is my friend," he said, "and I will not act against him." But we two would: for it was indeed a deed of love towards a friend in his condition. We therefore went to the *Stiftsprovst* and gave it him in writing that both we and many others of the congregation were much opposed to the resignation sermon Grundtvig wanted to deliver. He wanted to send these few words to Grundtvig in a letter in which he also asked for information as to what had happened in Vartov.

On Thursday of Holy Week a number of Grundtvig's friends assembled: all were full of anxieties about the imminent sermon and I then wrote down a brief declaration concerning his "unpredictable" state of mind, which the others then co-signed. The member of parliament [J. H. T.] Hasle and I set off with it to the *Stiftsprovst*, who just at the same moment had received information from Grundtvig concerning the communion. "The Queen" it said here "thanked me with an angelic smile which shall not be forgotten in this world or the world to come. Though I must add that I saw the same angelic smile on Ane-Marie from Grundtvig's Highschool (the baby he baptised) but she afterwards cried, as I can understand, because her hip went out of joint" – an allusion to Jacob's struggle with the Lord.

When in the name of many we asked Rothe to block the resignation sermon he perhaps hung back a bit, but still promised to do it – if he might also send our written declaration to Grundtvig. This we permitted. While we were still talking about this, [H. L.] Martensen arrived directly from the King, who had also desired that Grundtvig should be kept away from the pulpit. Martensen had arrayed himself in his fullest episcopal dignity and was less complaisant; he talked of the fact that children had been taken to the altar on Palm Sunday: "Practically the whole congregation apparently took leave of their senses," he said, "But this can be investigated later as well as what is then to be done further about it." His bitterness against Grundtvig really gave vent to itself so we did not part in the most friendly mood. The prohibition of the sermon was now executed, and in *Berlingske Tidende* I inserted an account of what had taken place on Palm Sunday.

On Easter Day Grundtvig again wanted to preach and would in no way allow himself to be talked into better sense; therefore his son Svend and one of his [GEEG p. 242] friends had to hold him back by force while he grabbed his stick and struck out: "That's the way to give it to the louts!"

Two false imaginings turned up again and again – the already mentioned one about the holy kiss which begets children without sin, and the other about a new attack from the side of the Prussians. He wrote "a verbal note concerning the unity of the North" to the administrations's chairman, *Grev* [Christian Emil] Frijs. In it, it said that the Finns must be settled in the area of the Dannevirke, and the Germans then moved from there over to Finland. For a long time his third wife, born *Komtesse* [Asta] Frijs, was unable to see what fundamentally was going on and believed in all seriousness that he was experiencing revelations.

She went to see the *Grevinde* [Thyra Valborg] Frijs and read out to her a couple of poems he had written in his deranged condition. When the prohibition of the resignation-sermon arrived, backed up with our written declaration, she was beside herself with indignation. "Just don't forget, wife" Grundtvig is supposed to have said "that these are my oldest and best friends who have written this! They cannot truly mean me any malice; but for the moment they are looking at the matter from their side." One night she sat up with him at their place in Gammel Kongevej and awaited the Prussians who would come ashore, he had said, at Kallebodstrand. Thereafter the battle would be pitched outside his garden, and *candidat* [C. M.] Kragballe was to engage with them and slay them. Thus delirium sported with his otherwise so lucid mind.

Finally the doctor got Fru [Asta] Grundtvig persuaded of her husband's derangement; she burst into violent weeping, and now Emil Fenger was also consulted. The delirium increased, and Grundtvig wanted to have the circumcision of Jesus added to our baptismal covenant. Lust, he said, sat behind the ears and it had to be washed away or cut away.[5] One was fearful, not without reason, of what it might occur to him to do, so there was talk of taking him to Oringe. Then a young doctor,[6] one of his friends, offered to move out with him to Frederiksdal, remain in the house there and supervise the cure; and so it happened. At the time Grundtvig was driven away he believed that he was to be hidden from the Prussian king just as Luther was hidden from the emperor at Vartborg [Wartburg].

Out at Frederiksdal he lived in complete peace and quiet where no one had access to him. The delirium gradually abated so that he grew calmer, and after a six-month period the illness was over. The swollen legs now returned again and the fontanelle with all the infirmities of old age which, during his illness, had been as if it were blown away. [**GEEG p. 243**] [P. C.] Kierkegaard, the minister at that time, allowed him to resume his office even though this met with strong opposition in higher places. Concerning the church-service on Palm Sunday both Helveg and I had meanwhile received enquiries from the *kultusministerium* [Ministry for Church Affairs and Education] and in the reply we cleared ourselves completely and maintained that what we had done was correctly done. The minister, [C. P. T.] Rosenørn-Teilmann, must have realised this since we heard no more of the matter.

1. "*[…] her er sandelig mere end Salomon!*" Though they have sometimes been treated as if, in what would then be an expression of breathtaking vanity, Grundtvig was applying them to himself, these words are an explicit paraphrase of Matthew 12:42 and allude in all orthodoxy to the mystical presence of Christ in the sacramental event. On this and other allusions made by Grundtvig on this occasion, see the Index entries **Solomon**; and **Palm Sunday** 1867.

2. The reference is to Revelation 21:16-17.

3. Helveg's perception of some kind of similarity between Grundtvig's seemingly terminal disintegration and the death of Søren Kierkegaard (1813-55) appears to rest on a popular view that Kierkegaard's physical frame could no longer support the extraordinary energy of the intellect, and that body and brain were suddenly and dramatically burnt out together. In fact, Kierkegaard, after a period of encroaching illness, collapsed while walking in a Copenhagen street on 29 September 1855. He entered Frederik's Hospital on 2 October, suffered a steady physical deterioration while his mind remained as orderly as could be expected in the circumstances, and died there nearly six weeks later on 11 November. Grundtvig, though now in his eighty-fourth year, recovered and continued preaching in Vartov for five more years.

4. Grundtvig had been granted the title of Bishop and the same rank as the Bishop of Sjælland (as had other distinguished clerics before him), on completion of fifty years of ministry in May 1861. During the era of the *enevælde* [absolute monarchy] an extremely elaborate system of titles (*Rangforordningen*) had developed, ranking those within it, from the King downwards, in a series of nine classes with numbered subdivisions in each. Many titles which had originally related to real functions within the state eventually became merely honorific, determining precedence, and in some cases the distinction was made explicit between *virkelige* [real] positions and mere titles (thus, for example, *Etatsraad* [Councillor of State] could be a 'real' appointment or merely titular). The Bishop of Sjælland was in Class 2, no. 10, with precedence over the *Confessionarius* [Chaplain Royal] in Class 2, no. 11. Other bishops were a whole class below, in Class 3, no. 9. In comparison, Ordinary Professors in the Universities of Copenhagen and Kiel ranked in Class 4, no. 3; while Doctors of Philosophy of the two universities were ranked in Class 8, no. 2. The listing was published annually in the *Kongelig Dansk Hof- og Stats-Calender* [Royal Danish Court and State Calendar].

5. *lysten[...] sad bag ved ørene*: the archaic idiom suggests an image of Lust sitting like an evil spirit whispering in the ears: that is to say, lust can be provoked by listening to lewd talk. The spiritual bath of baptism coupled with symbolic recall of the circumcision of Jesus should be used, Grundtvig suggests, symbolically to wash or cut away this tempter. Once again, there may be found to lie a time-honoured orthodoxy of Christian thought and imagery (in this case, from long-standing penitential doctrine) behind the events reported by observers who, whether wilfully or obtusely, settled for the more sensational narrative.

6. J. A. Sparrewohn, son-in-law to Fru Asta (Reedtz), Grundtvig's third wife.

118. *Hans Peter Gote Birkedal Barfod:* Minder fra et langt Liv *[Memories from a long life] (1928), vol. VIII (1928) of his own series Minder fra gamle Grundtvig'ske Hjem [Memories from old Grundtvigian homes] (8 vols., 1921-28), pp. 102-12; GEEG Stk. 55, pp. 243-50.*

Hans Peter Barfod (1843-1926), later to become a doctor of medicine, was the 24-year-old son of Povl Frederik Barfod (1811-96), so his account of Palm Sunday 1867 allows us a glimpse of the response of two successive generations of a family fairly intimate with the Grundtvigs to the persona and the image of the leader of the now well-established Grundtvigians within the Danish Church. "The whole mood and manner in which it took place" he judiciously wrote "was such that it could not have shocked me, and nor has it shocked anyone to whom I have subsequently talked, except for Father. But I have later realised that it will no doubt give rise to offence and that is a serious matter. For this reason I also believe that it was wrong, what happened." Of his own intuition, he is less sceptical, more accepting of the unshakeably established prophet-preacher of Vartov than was his parent's generation, even if in the end he is still deferential to their judgments. His sensitive and on the whole sympathetic yet sober account makes for an interesting comparison with the accounts of Frederik Hammerich and other more established figures.

⌒

In 1867 occurred an incident which stirred up a great deal of attention across the whole country, namely the divine service in Vartov Church on Palm Sunday, the fourteenth of April, when Grundtvig's temporary mental illness erupted. This service has been described by individual witnesses, among others, copiously, by Professor Frederik Hammerich in his autobiographical memoirs, *Et Levnedsløb* [A life]. The following day, the fifteenth of April, in a letter to my betrothed, I tried to describe the incident according as I saw and experienced it. Although my account largely coincides with what is already available, there are nonetheless some divergences, and what happened has so much significance that I want to give my description here, in the letter alluded to. One ought to bear in mind that it is written by a young person under the overwhelming impression of that moving incident.

"It is certainly going to be a strange letter you get today, but when you have read it you will understand the reason for this. I shall not get round to speaking of much else but Old Grundtvig, who in all probability will be dead when you get this letter: that anyway is how it looks to human eyes. On Friday the incisions in his legs closed up, and from this originates everything extraordinary that has happened since. He had no bodily pains but his mind was in an unceasing agitation from early morning to late at night, and this gave him a bodily strength which he has not had in the last seven years. He threw away his stick and walked briskly around the rooms and in the garden without any support and he talked unceasingly about Our Lord Jesus and about the battle which will apparently soon face our little fatherland. There came many people to see him that day and for each one that came he started again from the beginning to explain the Scriptures and prophesy about the times to come. In the evening Hulda and Sjarlotte [Barfod] were there, and he was then still talking with a youthfulness, liveliness and strength which they had never seen in him. When the visitors were about to leave he said to them that he wanted to kiss them on the eyes so [GEEG p. 244] that they would gain their sight and would then be able to see God's Wisdom and Mercy; and he wanted to kiss them on the hands in order to draw them to Christ. And this he did to each single one. He also said that a battle would soon take place in the Sound here off Copenhagen, and that Our Lord would give us the victory. Previously he was almost blind and had got a pair of very strong glasses, but during the night Fru [Asta] Grundtvig dreamed that she had kissed a blind man on the eyes and that he had gained his sight. So Grundtvig asked her to kiss his eyes, and now he can use his old glasses again and can now see much better with them than previously with the strong ones. In short, he had a strength and a fervour which were altogether remarkable. The day before yesterday, Saturday, he was, as he said in church yesterday, more dead than alive: "he was sick and grieved unto death, as Christ in Gethsemane." Naturally, the previous day had much exhausted him. Fru Grundtvig had said to him he must not kiss his friends on eyes and hands any more, for it gave rise to scandal and one must not do that. This had pained him, and the whole of Saturday he sat quietly apart and he said yesterday that he had searched his heart and asked Our Lord whether he had behaved improperly but the Holy Spirit had answered him that he should just do that which it bade him to, for this was right. And when in the evening he had folded his hands and prayed, he suddenly became strong and fit again.

Yesterday the service did not begin before the church was full. Grundtvig delivered the exhortation to confession [Skriftetale], in which he addressed himself to the entire congregation, but I was so completely thunderstruck by his bearing that I could not properly follow. You know well the bent old man who would come slowly in and, supported on his stick, go up to the altar – and so you can well understand the impression it made now to see the same white-haired old man come forward upright and strong and walking with sure and firm steps into the church and up to the altar. It was as though Our Lord had struck out the past thirty years, extinguished his old age and given him his youth back again. But when the exhortation to confession was ended, there began the most wondrous and the most gripping divine service I have ever attended and perhaps ever shall attend. When he had pronounced the absolution to the altar-guests he said to the congregation: "If there are still any that need the gracious forgiveness of their sins, in the name of Father, Son and Holy Spirit, then let them come hither. Here I stand as the servant of the Lord and have authority [GEEG p. 245] from my Lord to give this to all of you. Come hither, all you that labour and are heavy laden, I will give you rest for your souls, says the Lord!" Then many, many came streaming up, and amongst them I myself. It was for me as though Our Lord, on the last occasion he was going to allow Grundtvig to proclaim the Word, would also let his grace stream out more abundantly upon us through his old, faithful servant, whom he has, through all the many years, so wondrously favoured with his grace. Now for half an hour here at the altar he went about and laid hands on us. But many hung back since apparently they were afraid that Grundtvig would drop dead under the strain. But when he noticed that it had begun to thin out he cried: "Come! come! come! Are there not more who need the Lord's grace? See! I am ready in the Lord's name. And you must all understand this, that when the communion begins all those must leave who do not wish to be at the Lord's table, for they must not stay here!" So people streamed forward from all over the church and he carried on with undiminished strength administering the absolution.

Since there were now no more coming, Grundtvig raised himself up to his full height and strength and spoke across to the Dowager Queen who was sitting in her pew: "Where is the Queen of Denmark? Will she not come? Behold, the queen from the south came to hear the wisdom of Solomon; here there is more than the wisdom of Solomon!" Then the Dowager Queen came up to the altar and knelt down. Grundtvig laid his hand on her head and said in a voice which rang through the whole church: "And to you the gracious forgiveness of all your sins in the name of Father, Son and Holy Spirit! And herewith be all Denmark's sins forgiven!" Then he added with a lowered voice: "Right then; now just let the Prussian king come."

At that, the service proper began with hymns 687 and 852.[1] When Grundtvig had read the gospel he said, as he held out his old glasses: "Look, God has made me strong in the days of my old age. These are the glasses I have not been able to see with for many years. Is this not good progress?" He began his sermon with an explanation of the first three petitions in the Lord's Prayer, but I will not try to repeat it because I cannot clearly recall his own words, and that would be necessary in order to understand it properly. "But now" he said "I shall tell you what Our Lord has first taught me today, and what I am so heartily glad of. I have never been able to understand what it was supposed to mean, that in prayer we should go into our closet and lock the door in order to speak with God. Why must we do that, I would ask; Our Lord is everywhere, so why should I go in there in order to speak [GEEG p. 246] with him? But now I know what is meant by this. Look, this is what we have to do." Here he folded his hands and pressed them in against his heart. "In Jesus' blessed name we are to fold our hands before our hearts and pray Our Lord to go in there with us; and when in Jesus' name we press our folded hands against our breast then we are locking the door so that no one, no one can hear what we are talking to Our Lord about but he and ourselves alone; and when we do that then the Devil and all that is evil is utterly unable to come near us or touch us with a single finger. See, this is what Our Lord means in saying that we must go into our closet and lock the door."

You can surely imagine how wondrous it was to see the old man press his hands against his heart as he said this; and then he added: "I am so happy! For eighty-four years now I have toiled to get out of myself and let Our Lord move in and now today he has accomplished this for me so that I can sing: "Death, where is thy sting? Hell, where is thy victory? Thus has God taught me today to sing, and thus should you all learn to sing with me!" You doubtless know that Grundtvig has always nursed a great horror of death, so that he has even been unwilling to go to bed when he was ill. But now it seems that Our Lord has taken that horror from him, so that for the last three nights he has again gone to bed.

In his sermon, Grundtvig spoke about the coming of the Lord which he believed was not far off, and he closed with a warm and sincere prayer for the Church, the country and the folk; and he ended with praise for God's grace towards himself over the many years. As he delivered the blessing he also explained it beautifully. But I cannot repeat it for you. Overall, the day was so rich that it is only so infinitely feeble, what I have been able to sketch for you.

Before communion there was a baptism. It was a small baby which lay and waved its arms about like a little bird its wings. I was standing right up close and saw and heard everything. Precisely as the baptismal ritual was about to begin, the baby reached out both arms towards Grundtvig and smiled at him, and Grundtvig exclaimed: "Yes, just you be happy, little one, for what is now about to happen to you! Now I am going to say something to you which you shall rejoice over, and that is that it is exactly such small children as you the kingdom of heaven belongs to, so you will be alright, little one. And none can enter therein except they become as a little child as [GEEG p. 247] you are now." What, by the way, I did not like was that he used only the renunciation, the articles of faith and the Lord's Prayer from the baptismal rite, but otherwise his own words – which were nevertheless for the most part beautiful and moving.

After the baptism, the communion began in which probably towards eight hundred people participated. He had also called young children to confession and now also led them to the altar, among them his son Frederik, who was thirteen years old. Father and brother Ludvig were not present in church but otherwise we were all there and all participated in going up to the altar. I saw also Povl [la Cour] and the Harald Jensens.[2] At first I had understood Grundtvig to mean only that the congregation should go to confession, and not that he was exhorting them to the regular communion, and what gave me the courage to go now to the altar as well were the words he said: "Verily, Our Lord accepts you *as you are!*" I so sincerely wished that you, dear friend of mine, had been present in those hours. Such an alive and abundant congregational life as that which blossoms in Vartov I have only imagined in the apostolic congregations where all were one soul and one heart.

Already before the sermon, Grundtvig had asked Professor Frederik Hammerich and Pastor Frederik Helweg to assist him at Holy Communion with the distribution and they then sent word for their vestments. Grundtvig and his curate [Kristen] Køster distributed the eucharist to the first three tables; Hammerich and Køster to the fourth and in this one Grundtvig, his wife and Frederik participated; to the fifth and sixth Grundtvig and Hammerich distributed and at this one Helweg and Køster went to the altar; at the seventh table Hammerich received the sacrament from Helweg and Køster. These three now alternated at the distribution until the communion was ended. How many children participated in the Holy Communion I do not know.[3] Some more besides Frederik were there, sure enough, but it would not have been many. This did not shock me at all at the time, and the less so because the three priests besides Grundtvig did not hesitate to give the children the eucharist, and the whole mood and manner in which it took place was such that it could not have shocked me, and nor has it shocked anyone to whom I have subsequently talked, except for Father. But I have later realised that it will no doubt give rise to offence and that is a serious matter. For this reason I also believe that it was wrong, what happened. And yet, confirmation is a purely human institution, something over a hundred years old, merely, here in this country; so even if it conflicts with civil regulations it cannot conflict with Our Lord's, and that is the chief issue. But [GEEG p. 248] one has to have been there oneself to understand it properly. It was past 2.30 p.m. when the service ended.

Yesterday evening we were all prepared to receive news of Grundtvig's death. Since we knew how exhausted he has always been after an ordinary service, we thought it must be impossible for him to be able to endure such exertion and mental upheaval as this. But with God nothing is impossible. For most of the evening all my three sisters were over there and he, who had rested the whole day, was robust and strong, talked of Our Lord, of our fatherland and many other things; but all the same it seemed to the sisters that sometimes he came out with, as it were, disturbed utterances. This morning he awoke at six o'clock and when Sjarlotte was over there at nine o'clock he had been talking incessantly the whole time, often confused. Svend Grundtvig now believes he is mentally ill. His body, on the other hand, was strong and free from pain. Now this evening he is quite his old self. There have been many people with him in the course of the day. Pastor Gunni Busck is there now, and Grundtvig is talking completely sensibly about everything, though he is not talking as much as yesterday and this morning even though he is if anything still stronger. Our Lord is taking good care of things for our dear old priest!

I will only just add that today Grundtvig has handed in his letter of resignation. He says that it is his duty since he has broken with the discipline of our Church, but he could have done nothing else. When on Saturday, mortally sick as he felt, he intended to send word that he could not come to the church on Sunday, it seemed to him that Our Lord said to him: "You must not do that. I shall help you." And upon this promise he drove to church on Sunday morning without having had the strength to prepare himself as to what he should say, just as he was also first inspired while he was delivering the exhortation to confession, to take the whole congregation to the altar. On Friday, Good Friday, Grundtvig will deliver his resignation sermon."

This then is my young self's understanding and account of what went on in Vartov that Palm Sunday. When I compare it to what Frederik Hammerich has written in *Et Levnedsløb* [A Life] there is no significant disagreement. I only feel that from Hammerich one gets an impression of the sinister, whilst I had an impression of a special sublimity across these hours. But indeed I was very young at that time and therefore more easily carried away with Grundtvig's inspired [GEEG p. 249] even if, as I subsequently saw, ill condition. But one does not understand that Hammerich could, as he says, at one and the same time be clear about Grundtvig's mental disorder and also, by himself participating in the service at the altar, assume shared responsibility for what could possibly occur by way of impropriety: for the fact that he and Helweg placed themselves at Grundtvig's side before the altar at that time certainly made the congregation feel secure.

On the Thursday of Passion week, the eighteenth of April, I wrote to my betrothed: "Unfortunately it will be a sad Easter for the Vartov congregation. Dear old Grundtvig is mentally ill. He is calling himself the Angel Gabriel and says that every word he speaks he speaks not of himself but it is Our Lord who is speaking through him. And the distressing thing is that his wife and whole household believe the same and are allowing people in vast numbers to beleaguer the house in order to hear him. He has prophesied to his wife that she will give birth to Elias and she believes it. He prophesied to the Dowager Queen that she would give birth to Holger Danske when he kissed her. She allowed him this not because she believes in it but out of sympathy with him, in order not to hurt him. Yesterday he wrote to the Admiralty that it must deploy the fleet out by Reden because the Prussians would come last night. He, Fru Grundtvig and Karoline Larsen[4] sat up the whole night to await what would happen and when nothing had happened by six o'clock Grundtvig said that Our Lord must have delayed it to show that Grundtvig was after all only a human being who could make a mistake about the time, for come the Prussians soon would, etc. There has been great movement to get him to desist from preaching tomorrow, but neither Peter Rørdam, Gunni Busck, Helweg, Fenger, Hostrup, Hammerich nor anyone else has been able to persuade him to give it up, mainly no doubt because he is supported by his wife and other zealots. Today however he has received an injunction against it from *Stiftsprovst* [P. C.] Rothe, but whether he will conform with it is perhaps questionable. But may Our Lord not let this condition last long but either clear his understanding or call him home!"

On Good Friday, April 19th, I wrote: "Today Vartov Church has been closed by the authorities. God be praised! At least this way a scandal has been avoided because all the world's riffraff, the genteel as well as the rough, had together come rushing to get a seat as early as 7.30. It would certainly have been horribly difficult if such a scandal had involved Grundtvig. All this has caused sister Hulda's and Grundtvig's daughter Sofie's [GEEG p. 250] trip to be put off. How *Sofie* dares to think of a trip at all none of us understands.[5]

April 30th: "Now Fru Grundtvig too sees that he is mentally ill but she first saw it after Sofie had left. The day before she left, Sofie was still saying, here at home with us, that the more people said that her father was confused the firmer those at home simply became in the belief that this was not true. *But Grundtvig says himself at times that he is mentally ill.* Now he has travelled to Frederiksdal together with his wife and Frederik, and they have taken a young doctor with them.[6] Poor Fru *Grundtvig*! She is so oppressed with grief and self-reproach because she has for so long closed her eyes to Grundtvig's illness and by this brought him further and further into those sickly ideas. By the way, the Government has not been willing to grant him the resignation he had applied for but has only suspended him for the time being. This is indeed a very handsome show of respect."

The peaceful stay at Frederiksdal, and the fact that he was protected from all those harrowing visits he had incessantly been the object of here in town, soon brought an improvement in Grundtvig's condition. Completely cured even if bodily weak, in the autumn he once again took up his priestly office.

1. Hymn 687 was *Jesus! aldrig nogensinde / Korsets Træ mig gaae af Minde* [Never, Jesus, may the Cross-tree ever go from my remembrance] and 852 *Fryd dig, du Christi Brud* [Rejoice, thou bride of Christ]. Both were hymns by Grundtvig, the former loosely based upon the *Stabat Mater*, the latter inspired by Matthew 21:1-9. Both had been included (from 1851, 3rd imprint) in the hymnal for use in Vartov Kirke produced over a number of years by Grundtvig and subsequently collected into one edition (*Grundtvigs Kirke-Salmebog. Festsalmer*, 1873) by C. J. Brandt. The former hymn used three verses of a text which had earlier been published by Grundtvig in his *Sang-Værk*, vol. I; it survives as part of no. 195 in *DDS* (2002), *Naglet til et kors på jorden* [Nailed upon a cross on earth]. The latter had also first appeared in an earlier version in *Sang-Værk* I; a version of it is retained in *DDS* (2002) as no. 81.

2. Barfod's footnote: "Povl la Cour from Skærsø and lithographer Harald Jensen and his wife Andrea Lønborg, our close friends."

3. Barfod's footnote: "Fr. Hammerich declares in *Et Levnedsløb* that it was in all four who were all to be confirmed immediately after Easter."

4. Barfod's footnote: "A young girl from Tøstrup in Jylland who for many years lived in the Grundtvig household both before and after his death and who played a large role as confidential friend of *Fru* [Asta] Grundtvig and the daughters [Asta Marie Elisabeth Grundtvig (1860-1939) and Sofie Vilhelmine Henriette Reedtz (1849-1906)]."

5. Sofie was the daughter of Grundtvig's third wife Asta by her previous marriage to Holger Christian Reedtz.

6. Barfod's footnote: "Antonius Sparrewohn, who had offered to nurse Grundtvig during his illness. He was married in 1868 to Sofie, *Fru* Grundtvig's daughter from her first marriage with Foreign Minister H. Chr. Reedtz."

119. Thomas Skat Rørdam: from a letter of 9 May 1867 to Otto Møller, published in H. Skat Rørdam, Otto Møller og Skat Rørdam. En Brevveksling. [O. M. and S. R. An exchange of letters], 1 (1915), pp. 123-27; GEEG Stk. 56, pp. 250-54.

Thomas Skat Rørdam (1832-1909), later Bishop of Sjælland, was among the most prominent supporters of Grundtvig's principles regarding the Church in the second generation of Grundtvigians, but had no sympathy with what he saw as the delusions of Grundtvig's wife Asta and members of the Vartov congregation in their ready disposition to expect charismatic manifestations about Grundtvig. Accordingly, his account of events around Palm Sunday 1867 voices distaste and exasperation which are all the more explicitly expressed for being in a private letter.

Even though I feel no inclination at all to write about what has been occurring over here in recent days, yet I can imagine that you, like other out-of-town people who live away from the capital, could wish to hear something closer about it and I will therefore set about overcoming my disinclination to write.

As far as I can discern from your letter you have already by now received rather good information on what passed in Vartov Church on Palm Sunday and immediately thereafter, but otherwise you can hardly imagine what an impression it made to be in church that day.

I came to church without suspecting that anything unusual was afoot. But as soon as I entered I saw that this was the case. One batch after another was going to the confession (I arrived just after the exhortation to confession), and Grundtvig was speaking the words of absolution with so strong a voice as I have never before heard him use. [GEEG p. 251]

I soon heard tell that his legs had recovered their mobility and that his sight had become again as in his young days, and naturally also that this was a miracle never before seen and suchlike; but I felt the whole time a certain fear that something wrong was afoot; there was something strangely disturbed and impetuous about Grundtvig's whole conduct, which I had never seen before. So I sat myself down and awaited what might happen and I was not willing in the doubt in which I was placed to permit myself to go to the altar.

After the course of half an hour Grundtvig made the threat that those who would not come to the altar should be shown out – "they *must* not be here" – and my feeling then was that I would leave immediately. But, thinking about the custom of the Early Church, I stayed, and since my wife was eager to go to the altar I conceded and resolved to try what it was like, going to the confession, which I indeed made bold to do without any hesitation. But when I had been to the confession I had completely made up my mind that it was not

God's Spirit but insanity which was driving Grundtvig and I decided not to go to the altar and I left the church immediately after the sermon.

[…] Later in the day and especially next day I got more precise information as to how Grundtvig's derangement was manifesting itself at home. It was a perfectly ordinary satyriasis that he was suffering from. It has developed through the water from his dropsical legs forcing its way up to the brain.

Now it is doubtless the correct view of derangement to view it like every other illness, but all the same there is something beastly about such a man becoming deranged and especially in such a manner. Everything however could have gone off very quietly if Grundtvig had not had so many blind votaries, not only among his closest circles but also in the congregation as a whole. For despite the fact that they well understood what Grundtvig was doing and well sensed that this was not right, yet they could in no way tolerate it being said that he was deranged.

It can have contributed something to this situation that, amidst the most utterly crazy things, Grundtvig could still give expression to the most sublime and the most profound, but the main issue was that they *would not* see the truth, because they had hitherto *believed in Grundtvig* and viewed him as the [GEEG p. 252] authentic mediator between God and men. That this has been the case with the whole of that admiring circle which constantly visited Grundtvig now appears absolutely clear to me. I cannot tell you what a lamentable impression it gives, that the great majority of the congregation to which Grundtvig has now preached for so many years have thus at a stroke been turned into fanatics [*Sværmere*].[1]

Gradually, since those around him said Yes and Amen to everything, Grundtvig naturally got his derangement systematically organised. He himself was the Angel Gabriel, and the Holy Spirit was to be communicated by kissing so that those women who were kissed by him were supposed to conceive by the Spirit just as the Virgin Mary, and thus there would arise a new generation and a complete new and sinfree congregation of God in Denmark, etc. Everything he hit upon was "unparalleled" [*mageløs*] and "inspiring." When he sat and lectured on the nature of the relationship between man and woman, young women and old stood in troops around him with folded hands and exclaimed more or less vociferously in enthusiastic exclamations about how beautifully he spoke, and husbands and sweethearts said Amen to this.

When I became clear over how matters stood, I thought that I ought to do what I could to avert the scandal of his coming to preach on Good Friday. And after having talked with various people I got a number of the older and more sober-minded members of the Vartov congregation assembled on the Tuesday with the idea that we should send a deputation out to him to ask him to postpone his resignation sermon.

But this was unthinkable. It was objected: How could it be that God should abandon his old servant? This was not derangement! Much had happened that was strange, but we should wait and see what mysteriously great thing God would bring out of it, and other similar objections. To want to obstruct Grundtvig from preaching was pure unbelief. There was nobody that spoke as sensible persons except [N. J.] Termansen and P. Fenger, and even he conspicuously held his tongue despite his having seen Grundtvig in exactly the same condition twenty-three years ago. (Grundtvig in fact had an attack of the same derangement then, but which became known only to his closest friends). N. Lindberg too was well aware the whole time how matters stood but he is not among those who speak at such meetings.

Here, then, nothing was achieved. I then made a last attempt, in that [GEEG p. 253] I strove to persuade Svend Grundtvig to close the house to visitors and get Grundtvig under treatment from a doctor; but by that time he had already been shown the door with very harsh words from his father and with "Get thee behind me, Satan" from Fru Grundtvig, so he did not think he could do anything. Meanwhile I had to travel home to Hammer to help father[2] (who had had a chest infection) with preaching over the Easter-days; but after I had left there were various people who came to an acknowledgment that Grundtvig was out of his mind, in that he was now nakedly declaring himself to be Gabriel. But then instead of going to Grundtvig himself (which I can only explain as fear of the man) they addressed themselves to the *Stiftsprovst* [P. C. Rothe] who then, sure enough, played the trick on them of sending their (written) request to him out to Grundtvig as a supplement to his prohibition or admonition against his resignation sermon.

You are surprised that my uncle[3] did not do anything. He did what he could, but he was shown the door by Grundtvig because of his attempt to make him listen to reason; and Fenger only escaped the like by listening in silence to everything that Grundtvig said.

Finally, after about fourteen days of scandals he was taken out to Frederiksdal where he is now in the care of a specialist in mental sickness, [J. A.] Sparrevohn. In the end in fact his wife also acknowledged that it was derangement, since he began to strike the people around him and suchlike. He is now out there in complete tranquillity; naturally it is not a good thing that his wife and especially his poor son, whom he has made almost half-crazy, are out there; but as regards the first it is perhaps necessary. The doctor has not given up hope of his being cured but he thinks that even if it should get that far a relapse will be much to be feared (Sparrevohn by the way is a man of faith, came regularly to Vartov).

According to what I hear, Grundtvig is now quiet and calm but still has the same deranged ideas as earlier. And the same, unfortunately, must also be said of the majority of the Vartov congregation. [Kristen] Køster has lit upon the dogma that this trial has befallen the congregation in order to test whether they will continue to hold together; and a distinction is drawn between those who are harsh and the kindly. The first are those who say that Grundtvig is deranged and therefore what he has spoken in his derangement can have no divine truth but in this regard he stands on the same footing as other mentally ill people (to this group belong, [GEEG p. 254] among the rest, I myself and other heretics). The "kindly" ones think sure enough that because of bodily sickness Grundtvig has fallen into some aberrations but that he nevertheless continues to be a prophet of God as previously, if not an even greater one.

1. Skat Rørdam's term is *sværmere*. A *sværmer* can be a visionary; but in a religious context the term commonly expresses more or less distaste in a range between 'enthusiast' and 'fanatic' depending upon the attitude of the user towards religious zeal. Grundtvig's followers included both those who rather easily slipped into *sværmeri* and those (like Skat Rørdam) who mistrusted this aspect of the Grundtvigian ambience and found it vulgar. Luther, using the equivalent German term, warned against the self-delusions of the *Schwarmgeist* (though his adversaries declared that he was one himself); and debate on charismatic behaviour can still polarise around the question *Heiliger Geist* [Holy Spirit] or *Schwarmgeist*? See also the Index entry **sværmeri**.

2. Thomas Skat Rørdam's father was H. C. Rørdam, priest in Hammer with Lundby in south Sjælland.

3. His uncle was Peter Rørdam, priest in Kongens Lyngby.

The last years 1868-1872

120. *Hans Brun: Biskop N. F. S. Grundtvigs Levnetsløb udførligt fortalt fra 1839 [Bp NFSG's Life recounted in fullest detail from 1839] (2 vols., 1882), II, 606-07; GEEG Stk. 57, p. 254-5.*

From among Grundtvig's many and welcome Norwegian visitors in Copenhagen Brun collected various interesting anecdotes concerning Grundtvig's educational ideas, for both Denmark and Norway. Here the 84-year-old Grundtvig declares, of folk-highschools in Denmark: "If you want to know our highschools then you must visit Kold's and Schrøder's." He rejects a suggestion that the Norwegian Kristoffer Bruun (1839-1920) could not run a successful school because he was inadequately educated in matters Christian, but he has misgivings over Bruun's policy of promoting the *maalstræv* (Norwegian language issue) through the school. He fears (according to Brun's sources) that supporters "would toil away upon a new language which they imagined was a living one, 'even though it is dead.'"

He regularly received visits. Thus on *Fastelavn* [Shrove Tuesday; 1868] [Lars] M. Bentsen, the present *Storthingsmand* [Member of Norwegian Parliament] and highschool teacher in Stjørdalen, came out to Tuborg together with Pastor [Kristen] Køster. In with Grundtvig were Bayer, the glover from Odense, and another Fyn-dweller, and discussion revolved around the issue of the *Valgmenigheder* [Elective congregations] concerning which meetings "for and against" were at that time being held in Denmark.[1] Køster took up the conversation. Grundtvig who, as remarked, could see but poorly sat with closed eyes; it looked as though he was asleep but one discovered well enough that he was wide awake and was following in the liveliest manner when he threw in his strikingly enlightening and sometimes jovial and witty observations. Køster soon steered the conversation over to Bentsen himself who was just then in a state of transition from business to highschool. Grundtvig asked when he had visited any of the Danish highschools. Besides Marielyst, where by chance there was no teaching the day he wanted to go there, Bentsen named a couple of others. About these Grundtvig said nothing but when B. then said that he intended to go out to Vallekilde, Grundtvig says: "Yes, Vallekilde is not bad, but if you want to know our highschools then you must visit Kold's and Schrøder's."[2] Which of the two he named first Bentsen did not recall however: therefore they are placed in alphabetical order. Then Grundtvig asked about the folk-highschools here in Norway, and when Bentsen also named Kristoffer Bruun's, Køster thought that Bruun probably could not achieve anything much since he had not acquired for himself an education in matters Christian. Grundtvig replied: "Oh yes, he can very well do so, if only he has an eye for the human." But for Grundtvig it was questionable whether Bruun did not make the so-called "*Maalstræv*"[3] too much of a principal objective of the school. Now Køster was so totally against the *landsmål*-cause that Bentsen would have liked to get away from it: he felt they had discussed it enough previously. However, he did not escape, but he then merely opined that there must surely come some good out of it. Then Grundtvig says briskly: "Yes, *that* [GEEG p. 255] you may be confident of, that there will come some good out of it," but he was a little afraid that they would toil away upon a new language which they imagined was a living one, "even though it is dead." It would be another matter, he remarked, since the Norwegian folk-speech lay so close to Icelandic,[4] if it were a development from that.

1. This debate led up to the passing of the law, 15 May 1868, authorising and regulating elective congregations [*Valgmenigheder*].

2. The principal of Vallekilde folk-highschool was Ernst Trier (1837-93); Chresten Kold (1816-70) was principal of Dalum folk-highschool, and Ludvig Schrøder (1836-1908) was principal of Askov folk-highschool.

3. *Maalstræv* was 'the *landsmål* movement' – a movement for the definition of a Norwegian national language.

4. Bruun's footnote: "Which had formerly been in living use as the language of Church and school, that is, for the expression of the deepest matters of mind and of heart, Grundtvig naturally meant."

121. Hans Brun: Biskop N. F. S. Grundtvigs Levnetsløb udførligst fortalt fra 1839 [Bp NFSG's Life recounted in fullest detail from 1839] (2 vols., 1882), II, 657-8; GEEG Stk. 58, p. 255.

It was after Gunni Busck's death and possibly in the same year, 1869, that Frøken Busck[1] one day asked Grundtvig: Do you fear death? Grundtvig then answered: I don't exactly fear it; "but" – he added with great seriousness as he looked at her – "it is an enemy."

1. Presumably the sister of Grundtvig's old friend Gunni Busck.

122. Louise Skrike: Et Tilbageblik. Nogle Livserindringer af Louise Skrike [A retrospect. Some life-reminiscences of LS], in Vraa Højskoles Aarsskrift 1931, 14-36 (continued in 1932, 7-43 and 1933, 14-38); 1931, p. 23; GEEG Stk. 59, p. 255.

Louise Skrike (1842-1935), was daughter of *geheimelegationsraad* [title and rank accorded former diplomats] Jacob Samuel Skrike (1786-1859) and a member of the Vartov congregation who became personally acquainted with Grundtvig in the final three or four years of his life (see also item 130). Along with many others in Denmark, Grundtvig hoped for a French victory in the war with Germany (1870-71), which would curb the rising power of Denmark's southern neighbour and historic foe; but this was not to be.

Grundtvig took the outcome of the war between Germany and France very hard. While it was going on he said once to his wife and me: "Yes, you would no doubt like to join in there." But after the outcome he never mentioned the conflict.

123. *Evald Tang Kristensen:* Minder og Oplevelser *[Memories and Experiences], II (1924), p. 84; GEEG Stk. 69, pp. 255-56.*

Evald Tang Kristensen (1843-1929) was to become established as Denmark's leading collector of folk-stories and other forms of folk-tradition including sayings and proverbs. Svend Grundtvig also worked in these fields. Between them they published a number of internationally esteemed collections. Grundtvig himself had a lifelong interest in proverbial sayings and folk idiom, though on this occasion his guest evidently failed to elicit much from him.

On Sunday then [7th May 1871] at 3.30 I turned up at Klampenborg station according to arrangement and we then travelled a distance by train and then we walked to old Grundtvig's home at Store Tuborg and Svend Grundtvig showed me in to his father who was sitting in his library in an armchair and smoking his pipe. He looked very old and appeared to be very decrepit. The son said who I was and Grundtvig talked a little with me about the folk-ballads, but I got no real impression that he was actually engaged. Immediately afterwards we had to go in to the dinner-table and the old man, who had bad feet, had to be guided in by their taking him under the arm. But he participated a little in conversation at the table and there he showed that he was well engaged and had good recall. I was sitting among totally unknown people and naturally said nothing except when I was asked. There were also topics treated which I was unfamiliar with, namely literary questions and about literary persons. But otherwise the lady of the house and all of them were on the whole very friendly towards me. Afterwards we had a [GEEG p. 256] cup of coffee in the library and I marvelled much at the enormously big collection of books the old man had gathered. Not only were all the walls filled with bookshelves but here and there bookcases stood out at right angles into the floorspace. It was indeed a really memorable afternoon.

124. *Johan Borup:* N. F. S. Grundtvig *(1943), pp. 298-300; GEEG Stk. 61, pp. 256-58.*

Johan Borup (1853-1946), highschool principal, writer, here records closely observed details of custom and atmosphere in Vartov Kirke in Grundtvig's last years. Unlike various other witnesses, he was not drawn by devotion or curiosity towards the persona of Grundtvig but "dropped in there by chance one Sunday" and to that extent his account is characterised by a valuable objectivity. Like Edmund Gosse, he is impressed by the aura of "incredible agedness" about the near-nonagenarian and is romantically conscious of his burden of sixty years of struggle and self-sacrifice; and (again with Gosse) he likens him not to one of the venerable patriarchs of Christian art and story but to a "warrior of heathen antiquity who, full of days, hastens towards his grave-mound."

The one who is writing this remembers [Grundtvig] from his last year in the church. It was not in fact for his sake that I visited Vartov. I dropped in there by chance one Sunday. But there in that low-ceilinged unadorned church with the narrow pews there was a completely different life and mood from that in the other churches. In there, all joined in the singing, all belonged together as friends, no stiffness or solemnity, but a quiet feeling of belonging together prevailed therein, and was seen in the open countenances.

The service began every Sunday with the ancient hymn by Luther which Grundtvig had recast: *Nu bede vi den Helligaand* [Now pray we to the Holy Ghost]. It ended:

Da er Sorgen slukket,	Then is grief extinguished,
Da er Perlen fundet,	then is the pearl found,
Parades oplukket,	Paradise unlocked,
Døden overvundet,	Death defeated:
Hør vort Hjertes Bøn.	hear our heart's prayer.

A hymn or two more, and then he would emerge, old and white-haired, up in the lofty pulpit above the altar. The clerk [*Degnen*][1] would secure a board behind him upon which he could lean; then the door was closed behind him and he was alone. He would then recite in his sepulchrally deep voice, clearly, only with a slight aspiration on the *D* in the pronunciation of *Du*, similar to English *th*:

Kom, Sandheds Aand, og Vidne giv,	Come, Spirit of truth and witness bear
I os at Jesus er vort Liv,	in us that Jesus is our life,
Og at ej Du af andet ved	and that you know of none but he
End ham vor Sjæl til Salighed.	to be our soul's salvation.
Kom Lysets Aand, og led os saa,	Come, Spirit of light and lead us so
At vi paa Klarheds Veje gaa,	that we in lucid paths may tread
Men aldrig dog fra Troens Grund	and never from faith's solid ground
Et Haarsbred vige nogen Stund.	one hair's breadth stray at any time.

[GEEG p. 257] These two verses are, with a couple of minor alterations, Kingo's. But then he added a third of his own. And there would come a warm resonance into his deep voice as he concluded:

Gud Faders Aand, kom til os ned	God-Father's Spirit, come down to us
Med Himlens *Ild*, Guds Kærlighed,	with heaven-fire, the love of God;
Læg paa vor Tunge Naadens Røst	lay on our tongues the voice of grace
Med Livets Ord til evig Trøst.	and Word of Life, to comfort aye.

This "*Himlens Ild*" [heaven-fire] would come out with such strength that it cast a downright radiance about him.

After this he would recite a long prayer, always the same, word for word, so that everyone knew it by heart. When this was ended he would bring out a small black magnifying glass and bending over the service book he would read the text of the day, then close the book, settle himself upon his seat and begin his sermon, which was always short, worked out and written down as it was in advance. It would hardly last much more than ten minutes, maybe a quarter of an hour. Whilst he spoke, he would not move from the spot. His hands would lie on the lectern, and his only movement would be, when he emphasised something, then to turn the palms of his hands upwards and a moment later to lay them back in position again. His sermon was more of a soliloquy than an address, and it surely went over most people's heads, involved as it was in the explanation of The Word, the significance of the spoken Word, which he steadily repeated Sunday after Sunday. At any rate, it went over my head; and when I once told this to Otto Møller in Gylling he replied that it was the same with him when in the Fifties he heard him preach in Vartov.

But then it was not what he said, but it was the sublimity and certainty that emanated from his person when he stood up there, old and white-haired, and bore witness to the same he had borne witness to against opposition and with self-sacrifice over sixty years – it was this which made an impression.

I remember one Sunday when I was standing in the middle aisle of the homely little church. The sermon was over. And the hymn-singing was stilled. In the silence I suddenly hear a hard ring of iron against stone and in the same instant, with staff in hand, he comes striding briskly past, down the church to the font. This was the only time I got [GEEG p. 258] to see him at close quarters. Previously he had stood distant and elevated on his pulpit up there; now I got to see for the first time that he was a real person like the rest of us. But never in all my life did I see or imagine anything so ancient of days. The long white hair and beard flowed down over his shoulders and breast; the high forehead criss-crossed with deep furrows, the large clear eyes beneath the leonine brows, the wide stern mouth; and as in this instant, thick-set and heavy of body, supported by his staff which struck hard against the tiles, slightly bowed, he slipped past, he most of all resembled, in his incredible agedness, a warrior of heathen antiquity who, full of days, hastens towards his grave-mound.

1. The *Degn* (or *Kordegn*) has no exact counterpart in the English Church. He carried some of the duties of a parish clerk including responsibility for official records of the church but also represented a lay presence in services, speaking an opening prayer, leading the singing and attending upon the officiating priest.

125. *Edmund William Gosse:* Two Visits to Denmark
1872, 1874 *(1911), Ch. V, pp. 78-87.*

The English critic, writer and poet Edmund William Gosse (1849-1928) played a significant role in mediating modern Scandinavian literary culture to his contemporary English-reading public – not least in being among the first English critics to appreciate the work of the dramatist Henrik Ibsen (1828-1906). In 1872 he travelled from Germany through Denmark and resided for a period in Copenhagen as guest of *Provst* Bruun Juul Fog (1819-96), regarding whom see the relevant Index entry. The narrative of Gosse's visit to Vartov Church in 1872 was written up long after the event and is not to be trusted in detail – though Gosse is by no means alone among Grundtvig's lesser and greater biographers in adjusting fact for the advantage of the anecdote. His brief account of Grundtvig, even if it occasionally veers towards the literary-gothic, is far from unsympathetic towards the man, and not without true perspective. It remained the most widely known pen-portrait of Grundtvig in English until relatively recent times. Gosse's book was translated into Danish by Valdemar Rørdam (1912) and it was from that translation that the editors of *GEEG* took their excerpt (*GEEG* Stk. 62, pp. 258-60). The following excerpt is taken from Gosse's original English text.

⁓

It is difficult to-day, it was almost impossible forty years ago, to discover the immediate past history of a little country like Denmark from the latitude of London. The domestic incidents of immediately recent years are chronicled in no book of reference that is within reach of a foreigner. Hence it was on the mere presumption that a man born ninety years before was not likely to be still alive, that I said at breakfast this morning, 'How I wish I had come to Denmark during the lifetime of Grundtvig!' There was a shout from every one, 'But he *is* alive, and he still preaches every Sunday morning in the Workhouse Church!' 'This is Sunday morning – I *must* listen to a poet who was born five years before Byron, and who recollects the execution of Louis XVI. Where is this Workhouse Church?' But thereupon there fell a silence, and my friends looked at one another with a dubious and deprecating expression. [Gosse, p. 79]

The North at that time contained no more extraordinary man than Nikolai Severin Grundtvig. He was born, in 1783, in the country parsonage of Udby, in the strictest odour of orthodoxy, a typical child of the manse. He entered the church early, but did not become a parish priest until 1821. By that time he had formed the view that the Danish ecclesiastical system was too precise and too frigid, and he determined to amend it. Pharisaism and rationalism – those were the two bugbears of his long fighting career. He attacked them in high places, in the person of [H. N.] Clausen, then the leader of official theology in Denmark. The immediate result was that Grundtvig was driven out of his incumbency in 1826. He now became a species of outcast, in a protestant society which did not tolerate nonconformity, and he entered upon nothing less than a war with Church and State. He called for the formation of a 'People's Church' outside the State, and for complete liberty in liturgical and dogmatic opinion.

Not more than the briefest outline of an extremely interesting career must be attempted here. Grundtvig had something primitive about his character, an intensity of purpose which made him maddening to those whom he opposed, an object almost of idolatry to those whom he [Gosse, p.80] hypnotised. Denmark had languished under an ecclesiastical bondage too grievous to be borne in its puritanical coldness and formality. It was Grundtvig who first gave expression, often in violent and illogical language, to the popular sense of sacerdotal oppression. There was nothing, as I understand it, very dogmatic about his teaching. He went straight back to the Bible, and indeed almost exclusively to the Gospels. He took the Lord's Prayer and the Sermon on the Mount as a basis of practical Christianity. But he was a passionate lover of liberty, and his sympathy for those whom orthodoxy treated as rebels was incessant. He was, in consequence, himself treated as a rebel. All the fires of orthodoxy and formalism were concentrated on his head. But he was a magnificent fighting man; he never consented to give way; he wrote, and preached, and hurried from parish to parish, while in process of time he gathered about him a cloud of passionately devoted disciples. There was a faint resemblance between his career and that of John Wesley.

Like all prophets, Grundtvig was intensely and exclusively national. He was not merely a leader of religious reform; he was a mythologist, because in the old faith he saw evidences of natural piety; he was an editor of the ancient sagas, because Danes [Gosse, p. 81] ought to know the primitive history of their race; he wrote hymns and patriotic poems, because the Christian should mightily rejoice in God with a loud noise of singing. As the Church would grant him no incumbency, he appealed to the people, and he became a radical politician, who sat successively, and spoke often, in the Folkething and in the Rigsdag. He was a violent partisan of Denmark against Germany upon every occasion, and his enemies said that his object in religious controversy was mainly to turn the German theology out of the teaching of the schools. Occasionally, like a prophet of old, Grundtvig would make a sudden appearance at the courts of kings, and he had the art to command respectful attention there. The priests were his enemies, he said, not the monarch; and indeed he so impressed Frederick III[1] that in 1861 that King appointed him titular bishop, without a see, to the intense vexation of the real bishops, who continued to exclude him from all the pulpits in their dioceses. It was to an earlier monarch, indeed, that Grundtvig owed the power to preach at all. Christian VIII, on his accession in 1839, finding that the poet-prophet had no place for the sole of his foot in any State church, appointed him chaplain to the Vartou, or Workhouse. There he remained, never making peace [Gosse, p. 81] with the ecclesiastical authorities, until the close of his long life.

He was preaching at the Vartou one Sunday in 1867, when his gestures became more and more extravagant, and he went mad in the pulpit. But after a short period of retirement he recovered self-control. Perhaps an element of not perfect mental health in his extreme individuality was required to enable the divine *logos* in him to breathe through his speech articulately. His disciples, at all events, cared not whether he were sane or insane. He held up before them over and over again, with passionate vivacity, the ideals of his life – perfect love, perfect liberty, enthusiasm for the Fatherland, hope for the future of Denmark. From the Workhouse Church, a new sect, soon calling themselves Grundtvigians, extended all over the country, and even over Norway and Sweden. The pedagogic instinct was strong in Grundtvig, and he fostered the didactic spread of his own opinions. Encouraged by King Christian VIII, against the united wish of the Bishops and the Government, he began to set up 'folk-schools' in every direction. His disciples became the more devoted to him the more that the sanhedrin derided him. He must have been lovable to be so ardently beloved, but he was not less ardently detested. [Gosse, p. 83] The priests were his natural enemies, and the whole energy of a multifarious career may be summed up in saying that he succeeded in breaking down the despotism of Scandinavian official religion. He tore away from men's consciences all the obligatory tests and the deadening formulas, all the *totafoth* and *zizith* of the scribes and Pharisees.

The writings of Grundtvig, whether in prose or verse, have never been attractive to me. They are so exclusively national as to be scarcely intelligible to a foreigner; they lie, if I may say so, outside the European tradition. But as a human being, as a documentary figure in the history of his country, no one could be more fascinating. That he should still, at the extreme age of ninety, be existing and visible seemed an element on which the youthful adventurer might warmly congratulate himself. So fragile an apparition, so incredibly delayed (as it seemed) on my particular behalf, might, at the smallest sign of neglect, be inevitably and finally withdrawn. I conceived my Genius, with awful finger uplifted, saying, 'You might have heard Bishop Grundtvig preach, and were too idle to do so. Very well; he expires to-night!' It was evident that, at all hazards, Grundtvig must be visited. But how to do it without giving offence to my generous host I knew not, since Dr. Fog [**Gosse, p. 84**] had been one of the reformer's most determined opponents.

Miss Aline Fog forestalled my apologies by saying, 'Of course you can go alone to hear Bishop Grundtvig preach. But I am afraid you must not expect us to countenance such a dangerous schismatic.' The Dean was in one of his statuesque attitudes; in his violet eyes curiosity, it suddenly struck me, was contending with a sense of propriety. 'Aline,' he said, 'I don't feel sure that we ought to say "schismatic." I have always strenuously opposed his teaching, as Clausen did and as [Bishop H. L.] Martensen does; but I admit, when we take away the personal elements, the irritating manner, and the false rhetoric, that the differences between Grundtvig's creed and ours are only just enough to keep the party flag flying. And the passage of time – he is so old! I declare I feel tempted to accompany our young friend to the Vartou myself!' 'Impossible, my brother!' said the ecclesiastically agitated spinster. 'On the contrary, not only possible, but now decided upon,' replied the Dean. 'I do not preach to-day. I have not set eyes on Grundtvig for years and years. We must indeed make some haste or we shall not see him now'; and he rose to put on his clerical dress. [**Gosse, p. 85**]

We arrived, however, so far as seeing the great man was concerned, in most ample time at the little Workhouse Church, opposite the trees and still waters of the western ramparts. We found seats with difficulty, the chapel being crowded with communicants, doubtless attracted by a rumour that this would be the last time that the aged prophet would address his disciples. After sitting more than half an hour, surrounded by strange, fanatic faces, and women who swung themselves backward and forward in silent prayer, the word was passed round that the Bishop would probably be unable to come. The congregation began to sing hymns of his composition in a loud, quick, staccato manner invented by the poet, which was very little like the slow singing in the State churches. Suddenly, and when we had given up all hope, there entered from the vestry and walked rapidly to the altar a personage who seemed to me the oldest human being I had ever seen. Instantly an absolute silence prevailed throughout the church, and then there rose a sound as though some one were talking in the cellar below our feet. It was the Bishop praying aloud at the altar, and then he turned and addressed the communicants in the same dull, veiled voice. He wandered down among the ecstatic worshippers, and stood close at my side for a moment, while he [**Gosse, p. 86**] laid his hands on a girl's head, so that I saw his face to perfection. For a man of ninety, he could not be called infirm; his gestures were rapid and his step steady. But the attention was rivetted on his appearance of excessive age. He looked like a troll from some cave in Norway; he might have been centuries old.

From the vast orb of his bald head, very long strings of silky hair fell over his shoulders and mingled with a long and loose white beard. His eyes flamed under very beetling brows, and they were the only part of his face that seemed alive, for he spoke without moving his lips. His features were still shapely, but colourless and dry, and as the draught from an open door caught them, the silken hairs were blown across his face like a thin curtain. While he perambulated the church with these stiff gestures and ventriloquist murmurings, his disciples fell on their knees behind him, stroking the skirts of his robe, touching the heels of his shoes. Finally, he ascended the pulpit and began to preach; in his dead voice he warned us to beware of false spirits, and to try every spirit whether it be of God. He laboured extremely with his speech, becoming slower and huskier, with longer pauses between the words like a clock that is running down. He looked supernatural, but hardly Christian. If, in the body of the church, he had reminded me of a troll, in the pulpit he looked more like some belated Druid, who had survived from Mona and could not die. It was an occasion of great interest to me. Had I missed hearing and seeing Grundtvig then, I should never have heard or seen him, for he took to his bed a few days later, and in a month the magnificent old fighting man was dead.[2]

1. Thus Gosse; actually Frederik VII.

2. Gosse's anecdotal architecture determines there shall be a closure of this sort; it is however incorrect, for Grundtvig, far from being confined to his bed for the last month of his life, continued, though infirm, to preach in Vartov until the day before his sudden death on Monday 2 September 1872.

126. Ernst Johannes Trier: Erindringer fra Grundtvigs Hjem *in Frederik Rönning,* Hundrede Aar. Et Mindeskrift i Andledning af Hundredaarsdagen *for* Nic. Fred. Sev. Grundtvigs Fødsel *[One hundred years. A commemorative volume in connection with the hundredth anniversary of the birth of NFSG] (1883), pp. 17-20; GEEG Stk. 63, pp. 260-61.*

On the important figure of Ernst Trier (1837-93) see the relevant Index entry and the headnote to item 114. The following moving anecdote has conferred a special status upon the closing lines of the poem concerned: they are seen by many as the closing lines of Grundtvig's life-story itself, a self-written epitaph. See also items 84 and 127.

The last time I visited him – on a warm day in August 1872, two to three weeks before his death, I again had something to request of him. I was in process of gathering songs for the song-book which I later published under the name of *Sange for den kristelige Folke-Skole* [Songs for the Christian Folk-school; 1874]. I had with me the first forty songs for it. For about three hours he endured going through them together with me. So attentively did he keep abreast that when I had read No. 5 for him with all its twelve verses (as it is to be found in the second part of his *Sang-Værk*[1] as No. 1, from verse 25 to the end) he said: "You will have to correct what appears in the second verse (in *Sang-Værket* verse 26) "skin Lys *ud af* Mørke!" [shine light out of darkness!] to "skin Lys *gjennem* Mørke!" [shine light *through* darkness] – for I assure you that light never comes out of darkness." When I came to the series of songs which have a bearing on education about the four ages of man I pointed out to him that when we communicated this to the young people we lacked a song for it – and to give him an idea of what line it should follow I read aloud to him from the poem that under the title "Open Letter to my Children" [*Aabent Brev til mine Børn*²] is to be found, written by himself, in [Frederik] Barfod's *Brage og Idun* 1841 from verse 33. [GEEG p. 261]

Et jævnt og muntert, virksomt Liv paa Jord	A plain and cheerful, active life on earth,
Som det, jeg vilde ej med Kongers bytte,	as this, I'd not exchange for life of kings -
Opklaret Gang i ædle Fædres Spor	treading, illumined, one's noble fathers' track,
med lige Værdighed i Borg og Hytte.	with equal dignity in hall or hut,
Med Øjet, som det skabtes, himmelvendt,	with eye, as it was shaped for, fixed on heaven,
Lysvaagent for alt skjønt og stort herneden,	awake to all things lovely and great below
Men, med de dybe Længsler velbekjendt,	but, well familiar with those longings deep,
Kun fyldestgjort af Glans fra Evigheden.	satisfied by eternity's light alone.
Et saadant Liv jeg ønsked al min Æt,	A life like this I've wished for all my kin,
Og pønsed paa med Flid at forberede.	and studied to achieve by diligence;
Og naar min Sjæl blev af sin Grublen træt,	and when my soul, from brooding so, grew tired,
Den hviled sig ved "Fadervor" at bede.	in praying to "Our Father" it found rest.
Da følte jeg den Trøst af Sandheds Aand,	Then felt I the comfort of the Spirit of Truth:
At Lykken svæver over Urtegaarden,	that blessing hovers over this garden here,
Naar Støvet lægges i sin Skabers Haand,	when dust is laid in its Creator's hands,
Og al Ting ventes i Naturens Orden.	and all is awaited in Nature's ordered round.
Kun Spiren frisk og grøn i tidlig Vaar	Only the bud, fresh, green, in early Spring,
Og Blomsterfloret i den varme Sommer,	the flowers' profusion in the warmth of Summer,
Da Modenhed imøde Planten gaar	then to maturity the plant will grow
og fryder med sin Frugt, naar Høsten kommer!	and by its fruits delight, when Autumn comes.

When I had read this for him he said at once: "If I now gave you four more lines then it would be a song with three eight-lines verses." I had to read the four last lines aloud for him again. For a little while he sat and gazed out through the open garden door. I shall never forget what a beautiful expression there was upon his face, and what deep emotion there was in his voice when he said: "Write on:

"Om kort, om langt blev Løbebanen spændt,	Though short, though farflung, be the course we run
Den er til Folkegavn, den er til Grøde;	it is for all men's gain, it is for growth;
Som godt begyndt er Dagen godt fuldendt,	as day is well begun, so well it ends,
Og lige liflig er dens Aftenrøde."	and just as bright with life its sunset-hour.

1.   *Sang-Værk til Den Danske Kirke-Skole* [Song-work (or Carillon) for the Danish Church-School], 1870.

2.   The full text of the poetic *Aabent Brev til mine Børn* is in *PS* VI, 242-247 and *VU* VIII, 145-149. These extra lines composed extempore by Grundtvig in August 1872 contend with the *Sidste Digt* (*Gammel nok jeg nu er blevet / Mellem Vugge min og Grav* [Old enough I now am grown / 'twixt my cradle and my grave]) as Grundtvig's last piece of poetic composition.

127. Hans Brun: Biskop N. F. S. Grundtvigs Levnetsløb udførligst fortalt fra 1839 *[Bp NFSG's Life recounted in fullest detail from 1839] (2 vols., 1882), II, 780; GEEG Stk. 64, pp. 261-2.*

See the headnote to item 126.

⟨⟩

[Ernst] Trier travelled [to Copenhagen] in Summer 1872, presumably in August since by the end of July he was finished with his girls' school for the year,[1] and he then discussed with Grundtvig the song-book alluded to, which he had in progress.[2] In the course of this, he came on one occasion to read a couple [**GEEG p. 262**] or more songs of [Bjørnstjerne] Bjørnson. Grundtvig was then very tired and was gasping loudly, and when the song 'Undrer mig paa, hvad jeg faar at se' [I marvel at what I get to see] was read, he said "That one's no use." So Trier reads 'Løft dit Hoved, du raske Gut!' [Raise your head up, O doughty lad!] then Grundtvig says: "That was better."

Whether it was on the same occasion I don't know but Trier was talking about hymns and songs by Grundtvig himself which he wanted to include and he mentioned among others 'Ordet var fra Arilds Tid' [Since time began the Word has been]. "No," he ought not to include that one. Says Trier: "But you wrote it yourself!" "Yes," replied Grundtvig, "But I have written much that is no good." It was especially the refrain he was displeased with and he himself disapprovingly attacked individual phrases in it, for example: "The phrase *som en Havfru-Sang* [like a mermaid-song]" in the context in which it occurs. Nevertheless Trier included the song.

1. Trier and his wife Marie pioneered classes for female students at Vallekilde folk-highschool in NW Sjælland.
2. *Sange for den kristelige Folke-Skole* [Songs for the Christian Folk-School], 1874.

128. Peter Frederik Adolph Hammerich: Min sidste Samtale med Grundtvig *[My last conversation with Grundtvig] in Dansk Kirketidende (1872), cols. 675-76; GEEG Stk. 65, pp. 262-63.*

On Frederik Hammerich, see the relevant Index entry and the headnotes to items 89 and 117. Hammerich had an eye for the symbolic occasion and of this one it might be said that if it had not existed one would have wished it to be invented: Grundtvig takes the Anglo-Saxon poem *The Ruin* to be symbolic of the "truly proud ruin" which the remains of Anglo-Saxon literary culture constitute, while Hammerich delicately transfers the image of this noble ruin to the person of Grundtvig himself. Grundtvig has now sustained his interest in, and feeling for, Anglo-Saxon poetry through almost six decades. It is fitting that it holds its place among other epitaphs upon the long life of one of its 19th-c. pioneers, now drawing to its close.

⟨⟩

In his last years Grundtvig got about more than he had otherwise been accustomed; he liked to go for a drive after dinner and on that occasion he would visit another of his friends. So I had the pleasure of seeing him regularly at our home on Strandvejen, where he would find a seat in a gazebo with the Sound immediately in front of him, light his pipe and stay for the space of an hour. This year he liked to come once a week, and since I was then occupied with work on the earliest church-literature of the Gothic peoples we would quite often talk on such topics.

Grundtvig, as is well-known, had a long-standing love of the Anglo-Saxons. Right from the start he was at home in their writings. He has translated *Bjovulfs Drape* [*Beowulf*] and pieces by Cædmon, both published and translated *Føniks-Fuglen* [*The Phoenix*], studied and transcribed their manuscripts on his journeys to England, proposed plans, in English, for an edition of them and thereby driven and egged on the Englishmen at last to get to work upon the rich remnants from antiquity. The last time he was at my place, the Wednesday [28 August 1872] five days before he died, he had recently had sent a small English monograph about an Anglo-Saxon poem, 'An ancient Saxon poem, by J. Earle'. There was no one in his closest circle who could read it for him. His son, Professor S. Grundtvig was away, and Professor [George] Stephens he had [**GEEG p. 263**] not found at home. All this he told about. Otherwise he was well, indeed sat out by the shore until darkness fell, because that day he had come to us late.

The following Friday, three days before his death, I therefore went over to Tuborg[1] to look at the small monograph and inform him what it contained. He had not been quite well after the visit to us but he felt himself better now and wanted to preach the next Sunday, which he indeed did. I went through the monograph, gave him the main contents and read some of it for him. There was nothing new in it, except the conjecture that the city in ruins which the ancient poem so picturesquely describes could be Bath. The poem, said Grundtvig, he knew well from [George] Hickes' *Thesaurus*. Among the rest I read him the opening of it, where it says (I keep in translating as closely as possible to the text):

Du vældige Stenvold,	You formidable stone wall,
Styrtet af Skjæbnen!	toppled by Fate!
Rokket og rævnet	Shaken and fissured
Er ringmurens Kjæmpeværk,	is the ring-wall's gigantic work,
Tagene borte,	roofs are gone,
Taarnene rave,	towers totter,
De mægtige Porttaarne;	the mighty gate-towers;
Murværket rimslaget,	the masonry rime-covered,
Brustne Skandserne;	breached the fortifications;
Brudt ned, styrtet alt,	broken down, all tumbled,
Undergravet	undermined
Af Ildens Magt!	by the power of fire!

"Yes," said Grundtvig, "There is something of the monumental here, in which the English have always had their strength. On hearing this, one cannot help but think of the whole of Anglo-Saxon literature: for it is itself a truly proud ruin and therefore it can well be likened to the city in ruins of which the ancient poet has sung." We talked a little more about the

Anglo-Saxons and he gave me the poem to take home with me. So I left him – and little suspected that this would be the last time I should see him in this life.

1. Hammerich refers to the home at Store Tuborg on Strandvejen, close to the shore of the Øresund, established for Grundtvig by his third wife, Asta, following his breakdown in 1867.

129. *Hans Brun:* Biskop N. F. S. Grundtvigs Levnetsløb udførligst fortalt fra 1839 *[Bp NFSG's Life recounted in fullest detail from 1839] (2 vols., 1882), II, 802-04; GEEG Stk. 66, p. 263.*

Following the granting of the Constitution in 1848, Grundtvig's political involvement, both direct, as a member of the *Rigsdag*, and indirect, through his supporters and associates in the *Bondevenner* party and, from 1870, in *Det forenede Venstre* (United Left) party, continued until the end of his life. Neither by conviction nor by temperament was he a natural party-politician. His independent stance, especially during the crisis of 1866 when conservative amendments to the 1849 Constitution were being driven through the *Rigsdag*, exasperated many; and it is arguable that he could have achieved more in the *Rigsdag* if he had been able to justify to himself the compromises and strategic alliances other more pragmatic politicians took for granted as part of the process of policy-achievement. The political scene, both national and international, was shifting fast over these decades – and Grundtvig was becoming an old man. Nevertheless, it is a fact that up to his last day his home remained a meeting-place for political leaders such as Sofus Høgsbro (1822-1902) where Grundtvig was kept informed of – and indeed consulted over – current events within *Det forenede Venstre* (for the emergence of which he claimed some credit) and dealings between the party and other like-minded groups in Scandinavia. The meeting here described took place on 1 September 1872. Grundtvig died suddenly, late in the following afternoon.

On the same day there was a dinner-party at the Grundtvigs where several *rigsdagsmænd* [GEEG p. 264] were present. Most of them left as the afternoon wore on but at least *statsrevisor* [auditor of public accounts] [Sofus] Høgsbro and a Sønderjyde [South Jutlander][1] remained behind. Grundtvig himself raises the subject of what was recently written about him in *Fædrelandet*, both on the question of enlightenment and education and of his activity on behalf of civil society in general and then particularly of his independent activity as *rigsdagsmand* in 1866 which, as we know, the 'National-Liberal' [*national-liberale*] newspaper[2] was much against. Høgsbro asks whether Grundtvig has read (naturally, had read to him) what appeared in the newspaper about him. Yes, he had; and – he said – "It was as one could have expected from that quarter; Ploug[3] is correct only in the fact that my approach to the King together with Tscherning gave impetus to the *Forenede Venstre* even though we were not thinking of that."[4] With talk of the *Forenede Venstre* Grundtvig then asks whether it is true, as again had been said to him, that they constrained members to have no other convictions than those of the majority? To this Høgsbro replied that it was completely untrue, as the proceedings of the *Rigsdag* show. He mentioned as an example the question of clergymen's stipends, in which a single member of the *Venstre* put forward a motion in opposition to the majority's, and several members spoke to it and sought to push their idea through; and Høgsbro added that it often happened like this. "Oh, I see," Grundtvig replies; it was just the old gossip still doing the rounds. Then Grundtvig asks why the *Venstre* had expelled Dinesen,[5] and to this Høgsbro answered that Dinesen was working dead against the rest of the members in quite another spirit, so that it had come to the point at which old Jens Jørgensen himself had said: "Either I or Dinesen must get out of the *Venstre*" and "So," said Høgsbro, "You can well understand that things were far gone." "Yes, that is for sure" replied Grundtvig, who knew Jens Jørgensen to be one of the most level-headed, peaceable and honest farmers in parliament.

After that, Høgsbro told about his very recent journey to Norway, and they then came to talk about various distinguished men up here, whereupon Grundtvig declared that it seemed strange to him that Kristoffer Bruun could not develop an eye for education concerning the church [*den kirkelige Oplysning*][6] since it was after all the same thing – namely the Living Word – for which he had striven in both respects, the *folkelig* and the *kirkelig* [ecclesial].

In the course of discussion of the Hammar Convention [*Hammar-Mødet*] up here that year, the conversation also came round to [S. A.] Hedlund, the editor from Gøteborg, who was also present at [GEEG p. 265] the meeting there and who, even though his religious disposition is rationalistic, was nonetheless pleased by all of Grundtvig's *folkelige* efforts. With that, Høgsbro read out a number of those pieces in Hedlund's *Gøtheborgs Handels- og Søfartstidende* [Gothenburg's Business and Maritime News] which had led Ploug to call Hedlund a "Dane-hater" and "the most characterless phrasemonger in the whole of the North" etc, etc. Høgsbro now asked Grundtvig whether he found anything in the pieces by Hedlund which insulted Denmark and which we ought to repay in the same fashion. Grundtvig: "No, not at all. We must remember he is Swedish and cannot possibly look at the circumstances with the same eyes as we Danes." With talk about Hedlund, thoughts then moved easily to [Bjørnstjerne] Bjørnson who had been in Sweden, and Grundtvig expressed his pleasure that perhaps Bjørnson could be the instrument of getting the Swedes to give attention to his work, since it had been a matter of regret to him that he had been so little known in Sweden.

Høgsbro asked whether, in the event of Russia and Germany going to war, and Sweden out of an old grudge for Russia allied with Germany, whether the Danes should then go against Germany and Sweden. To this Grundtvig answered emphatically: "No, we must *never* do that; Denmark must never ever go against Norway or Sweden, but ought in such a case to seek to be neutral, unless Germany first gave us back the Danish portion of Sønderjylland, then there could certainly be talk of allying with Germany and Sweden."

"But," said Høgsbro, "what now if England allies with Germany and Sweden?" "Ah well, then we have to go with them" answered Grundtvig, very emphatically.

What more was discussed between Grundtvig and *statsrevisor* Høgsbro I do not know, but at their leave-taking the *statsrevisor* said: "Life will surely win through!" – a hope to which Grundtvig did not leave his *Yes* wanting. Whether they talked about Bishop Monrad's election as *Rigsdagsmand* I likewise cannot say for certain but I know it from a household friend of the Grundtvigs that in the evening Grundtvig was very anxious to find out whether [Bishop D. G.] Monrad (who, for example, wanted to have a "Church Council" or Synod) had been elected or not. He waited as long as there was the least point in waiting for a young man, who was to give him intelligence in this respect, to come out to Tuborg. The young man [GEEG p. 266] however had been delayed, but Grundtvig's strong desire achieved its fulfilment: Bishop Monrad went down at the election.

1. By this date, old Nordslesvig (North Slesvig) had long since been annexed by Prussia and was commonly referred to in Denmark as Sønderjylland (South Jutland); thus, to identify a visitor in terms of his being a Sønderjyde was to draw attention to the possible political implications of the visit. Sønderjylland was reunited with Denmark on the basis of a plebiscite in 1920.

2. The daily newspaper *Fædrelandet* [The Fatherland].

3. Carl Parmo Ploug, 1813-94, owner and executive editor of *Fædrelandet*.

4. Grundtvig alludes to the attempt he made (1866), together with democratic politician Anton Frederik Tscherning (1795-1874) to gain an audience with King Christian IX in order to urge the king not to undersign proposed constitutional revisions undoing provisions of 1849 Constitution: no audience was granted.

5. Lars Dinesen (1838-1915).

6. Christoffer Bruun (1839-1920), Norwegian folk-highschool founder, followed Grundtvig in his convictions that history and poetry must form the core of a *folkelige* education and that teaching must give primacy to the living, spoken word rather than the book; but Grundtvig appears to be puzzled that Bruun is not teaching the kind of universal history which others of Grundtvig's followers espoused since it was simultaneously the history (in effect) of the Living Word, a concept to which Bruun did adhere.

130. *Louise Skrike:* Et Tilbageblik. Nogle Livserindringer af Louise Skrike *[A retrospect. Some life-reminiscences of LS]*, in Vraa Højskoles Aarsskrift 1931, 14-36 *(continued in 1932, 7-43 and 1933, 14-38); 1931, pp. 29-30; GEEG Stk. 67, p. 266.*

"I grieved from my most inner heart and felt that never again could I be truly happy here on earth." On Louise Skrike, see also the headnote to item 122.

⌐⌐

And so the day came when we lost Grundtvig. Because his sight was poor, Fru Grundtvig would read for him, and often from his own works, and he could say, so pleased about something or other, "No! Did I really say that?"

On 2 September 1872, Grundtvig had read to him the gospel concerning the birds of the air and the flowers of the field, the text for the following Sunday which usually he did not ask for until the Friday. Fru Grundtvig then went out of the room for a moment and when she came back in he was sitting lifeless with foam about his mouth. A summons was immediately sent to Professor [C. S. M. N.] Engelsted and he confirmed that death had occurred suddenly, the consequence, said Engelsted, of a flaw in the heart which he must have had from his youth. I grieved from my most inner heart and felt that never again could

I be truly happy here on earth now that his voice was taken from me; though this, praise be to God, turned out not to be the case.

131. *Hans Brun:* Biskop N. F. S. Grundtvigs Levnetsløb udførligt fortalt fra 1839 *[Bp NFSG's Life recounted in fullest detail from 1839] (2 vols., 1882), II, 804-05; GEEG Stk. 68, pp. 266-67.*

"Just before his eighty-ninth year, on 2 September, a little after 5 in the afternoon, without any perceptible death-struggle, the course of his rich life was completed."

At household devotions on Monday morning[1] he was indeed somewhat afflicted by a phlegmy cough, but this was nothing unusual. His wife asked him whether he would not like to send word after the doctor but he did not find this necessary and his general condition was such that his tender and faithful wife had no misgivings about going, according to plan, for a walk in *Dyrehaven* [the Deerpark] with the children.[2] The only unusual thing was that he had the gospel for the following Sunday[3] read to him in order to make a start on his sermon, which he would not customarily do until the Friday. Later in the day his curate Pastor [Christian] Jørgensen and his son Frederik read for him from [E. G.] Geijer's *Svenska folkets historia* and from *Historisk Arkiv*. At about 3 o'clock he said to his son that he was now tired, so he could leave for the time being. When Fru Grundtvig got home she asked him whether he would like a cup of coffee – he had declined dinner. Fru Grundtvig notices that he is somewhat changed in his appearance. He enjoys [**GEEG p. 267**] a mouthful from his cup, hands his pipe to her, throws himself abruptly to one side in his chair and settles down to rest. He looked mildly at her when she first spoke to him; later he apparently opened his eye a little but now it was completely glazed and dull. Fru Grundtvig leaves the room for a moment; Professor Engelsted is summoned. When Fru Grundtvig came back his head was sunk across his arm. He had long suffered from a heart disease and by a heart attack, perhaps during a fit of phlegmy coughing, he had his petition to God fulfilled – not to lie lingering in his sick-bed. It was fulfilled later than could have been expected: just before his eighty-ninth year, on 2 September, a little after 5 in the afternoon, without any perceptible death-struggle, the course of his rich life was completed.

1. Monday 2 September 1872; Grundtvig's ninetieth birthday was six days away.

2. Frederik Lange Grundtvig (Grundtvig's son with Marie Toft) was at this time eighteen years old, and Asta Marie Elisabeth (Grundtvig's daughter with Fru Asta) was twelve years old. Fru Asta also had a son (Holger) of an age with Frederik Lange who was confirmed by Grundtvig in 1868, along with Frederik Lange, and a daughter Amalie Reedtz, confirmed 1871. Sofie Vilhelmine Henriette Reedtz (also Fru Asta's daughter from her previous marriage) had left home in 1868 when she married J. A. Sparrevogn.

3. The fifteenth Sunday after Trinity.

Obsequies 1872

132. Jens Kristian Madsen: N. F. S. Grundtvigs Jordefærd og det kirkelige Vennemøde den 11te og 12te September 1872 [NFSG's funeral and the ecclesiastical Friends' meeting 11-12 September 1872] *(1872), 39-42, 55-56; GEEG Stk. 69, pp. 267-8.*

Kristian Madsen (1839-83), having graduated in theology 1868, was appointed *kataket* [Catechist] at Grundtvig's old church, Vor Frelsers Kirke, Christianshavn, in 1869. In 1873 he secured a post as principal of a teacher-training institution and was appointed parish priest at Jelling. Working closely with P. A. Fenger (1799-1878) he played a considerable role in preparing the new edition (1868) of Grundtvig's *Sang-Værk*.

In 1853 Grundtvig had consecrated a small private cemetery (Claras Kirkegaard) on the family estate of his brother-in-law H. R. Carlsen at Gammel Køgegaard. On that occasion, Grundtvig had envisaged that his wife Marie (born Carlsen) and he himself might be buried there. Tragically, Marie died the following year. In 1855 a crypt was built in the cemetery and Marie's body laid in it. It was natural to observe Grundtvig's wish that he too should eventually lie there. Accordingly, his funeral service was held in Copenhagen on Wednesday 11 September at Vor Frelsers Kirke and the coffin was then escorted through the streets of the city to Vartov and the railway station and so to Gammel Køgegaard. On the carved oakwood coffin was a silver plate, the gift of the Vartov congregation, inscribed with a verse by B. S. Ingemann: *Med Sagastav og Pederssværd i Haand, / Han arved Saxos Blik og Kingos Aand. / Fra gamle Nord han skued imod Østen, / Og Aander har han vakt med Kjæmperøsten* [With History's-stave and Peter's sword in hand / he inherited Saxo's vision and Kingo's spirit. / From ancient North he gazed towards the East / and spirits he awakened with his mighty voice]. The spacious church was packed and admission had to be restricted. Card-bearing *Venner* [Friends, gathered for the September *Vennemøde*] had their place, as did representatives of the Royal family, Government, University and students. About a quarter of all the land's clergy were there, says Madsen. At the front sat the Bishop of Copenhagen, H. L. Martensen, with Grundtvig's one-time adversary Professor H. N. Clausen on his right. The officiating priest was Grundtvig's friend and collaborator, Peter Andreas Fenger. Leading figures in Grundtvig circles, State and Church made addresses. The final hymn sung before the cortège moved off was Grundtvig's own *Sørger ei for dem, der sove / Med Guds Fred i Gravens Skjød!* [Sorrow not for those who slumber / with God's peace in grave's embrace] from *Sang-Værk til den danske Kirke* I (1837), no. 563 in *DDS* 2002, inspired by 1 Thessalonians 4:13-18.

When this hymn had been sung, some twenty younger priests [carried the coffin] out of the church;[1] outside the door it was received by citizens and farmers from all regions of the country, who placed it upon the hearse […] The cortège thereupon began moving off, with the students at the head. Behind the hearse walked a great number of priests, but gradually people became more mingled with each other. The cortège passed along Dronningensgade, Kristianshavns Torv, Overgaden over Vandet, Langebro, along Ny Vestergade into the city, along Frederiksholms Kanal, through Løngangsstræde to Vartov. On both sides of the cortège stood a close, almost boundless multitude of people; there was hardly a window the cortège passed by but was filled. The ships flew their flags at half-mast and the same was the case with not a few private houses; also the Industrial Exhibition building, where the cortège later passed by, was hung with a considerable number of flags at half-mast. There was something magnificent in seeing all, high and lowly, old and young – a big proportion of [GEEG p. 268] the biggest private schools in Copenhagen, for instance, had given the day free – gathering to honour the man who in earlier days was loved by few, ridiculed by many, hated and feared by various people: his cortège through the streets of Copenhagen was in truth kingly […]

When the cortège reached Vartov it halted outside the church. The door was standing open, the organ was playing and soon *Krist stod op af Døde* [Christ arose from the dead] sounded forth from the swelling multitude. When those who stood nearest the coffin had ended, the last lines were still sounding forth from the furthest end of the cortège. It has been remarked with justice in many places that this was the most poignant moment of the whole solemnity here in the city, just as it has been said, apparently also with reason, that such a multitude of hymn-singing people has probably not walked through the streets of Copenhagen for many centuries.[2] From Vartov, where all the windows were full of the old women, the cortège passed to the railway station. *Dejlig er jorden* [Lovely is this earthly place] and *Op dog, Sion, ser du ej* [Up, O Sion! seest thou not?] was heard from the close-packed crowds. At the railway station most people took their leave, but some six to seven hundred people, men and women of all social classes and from all regions of the country, travelled with the special train which carried Grundtvig's body to Køge. On the route one saw many men standing with heads uncovered as the train steamed past.

At 4.30 the train arrived at Køge, which had decked itself in mourning dress. The church-bells were ringing; a great number of houses were flying the flag at half mast. The Craftsmen's Association and the Køge *Vaabenbrødre*[3] went with their banners in the van-guard, and the whole route – a littler short of a quarter of a mile[4] – out to *Aasen* [The Ridge] where Grundtvig was to be interred by the side of his second wife whose resting-place he himself had consecrated seventeen years ago, was strewn with flowers.

Various hymns were sung on the way and it sounded beautiful across the field when the brass band, whilst the cortège slowly processed up towards the consecrated spot, per-formed various hymn-melodies, for example *Fred til Bod for bittert Savn* [Peace as balm for bitter loss].[5] In the cemetery itself, which is a prettily-lying little spot and enclosed by a ring-wall, only a small part of the people could be accommodated. The coffin, which for most of the way had been transported on a small hearse but was carried up the last slope below the cemetery, was then set down just inside the entrance, and by its side stood the men who spoke so that they could be heard by the few within and the many without […]

[The committal began with the singing of 'Ved Biskop N. F. S. Grundtvigs Jordefærd' [At Bishop NFSG's interment], composed by Grundtvig's friend, the poet and priest Jens Christian Hostrup (1818-92); there followed various addresses by Frederik Hammerich and others, and further hymns, and finally (Madsen p. 55; not in GEEG) the leave-taking]

The whole cortège now filed slowly past the brickbuilt vault, the entrance to which was surrounded with flowers and greenery and where the coffin had now been deposited. After a great part of the cortège had thereafter been up at Gammel Køgegaard where the owner, *Hofjægermester* [H. R.] Carlsen, in whose family burial-ground Grundtvig thus came to rest, had provided refreshments, at about eight o'clock the special train carried the participants in the cortège back from Køge to Copenhagen.

It can confidently be said that those who were involved that day – not only in spirit as doubtless the greatest part of the Danish people was, but personally present – experienced a day they would never forget. Sure enough it was a sorrowful occasion as needs must be when children escort their elderly father, who died at a great age, full of days, to the grave. But it was an occasion of sorrow as needs must be when those who grieve grieve not as those who have no hope[6] but who securely trust that:

Kristi venner ingensinde	Never do the friends of Christ
ses sidste Gang,	meet for a last time.[7]

And that there was something of this hope present, the cheerful mood bore witness, and the lively songs which sounded forth from every carriage upon the journey back. It was evident that the lamentation over what Grundtvig's friends had lost by his death fell silent before the joy over what they had gained by his life.

1. Vor Frelsers Kirke in Christianshavn, where fifty years previously (1822) Grundtvig had taken up his first clerical appointment in the city.

2. Three years later the city saw another huge public funeral, that of Hans Christian Andersen (11 August 1875).

3. Literally 'brothers in arms' – members of the local branch of *De danske Vaabenbrødre*, the Danish War-veterans Association.

4. A quarter of a Danish mile was equal to a little more than one English mile.

5. Melody by Ludvig Mathis Lindeman (1812-87), 1871.

6. Madsen makes allusion to the final hymn (by Grundtvig) sung before the cortege left Vor Frelsers Kirke, and to its Scriptural source, 1 Thessalonians 4:13-14: But I would not have you to be ignorant, brethren, concerning them which are asleep, that ye sorrow not, even as others which have no hope. [14] For if we believe that Jesus died and rose again, even so them also which sleep in Jesus will God bring with him (King James Bible).

7. In summary, sorrow was tempered by certainty that the friends were only temporarily parted, would meet again in heaven and would never part again: a sentiment echoing various New Testament texts. Jens Nicolai Ludvig Schjørring (1825-1900), 1857 assistant pastor to Vilhelm Birkedal at Ryslinge, subsequently parish priest in Hodde with Tistrup north of Varde in Jylland, and later in Ørslev near Skelskør, author of hymns and religious songs including *Kærlighed fra Gud* [Love from God] (no. 494 in *DDS* 2002), published (in journal *Dansk Kirketidende* 1866, and in his own *Sange og Rim, Gave til Venner og Frænder* [Songs and poems, a gift to friends and relations] 1898), an *Afskedssang* [leave-taking song; funeral hymn] beginning (with quotation): "*Herrens Venner ingen Sinde / Mødes skal for sidste Gang*" [The Lord's friends shall never meet for a last time] (no. 546 in *DDS* 2002), which rapidly became popular across the country, sung to a melody composed by Ludvig Mathias Lindeman.(1862). Its final verse in particular anticipates Madsen's sentiment: *Når til afsked tårer rinde, / syng det ud med liflig klang: / Herrens venner ingen sinde / mødes skal for sidste gang!* [When at parting tears are flowing, / sing it loud in lively tone: / Never shall the Lord's friends ever / meet together a last time].

Part three: Index

Index

The special characters Æ/æ, Ø/ø (and Ö/ö), Ü/ü and Å/å (Aa/aa) are treated as occurring in this order at the end of the alphabet. Numerals in italic following stemmata refer to pages. Abbreviations: c. = century, Dk = Denmark, Gr = Grundtvig. In the following notes, extensive reference is made to *Krønnike-Rim*. This alludes to the glossary Gr appended to his *Krønnike-Rim til levende Skolebrug* (literally 'Chronicle-rhymes for living school-use' but translatable as 'History in verse for use in the school for life'), 1st edition 1828, augmented 2nd edition 1842, 3rd edition 1875. Though Gr's definitions and opinions did not all remain unchanged throughout his long life, there is some value in consulting this work in which, especially in the augmented 2nd edition, he reveals what values and viewpoints he would like to see inculcated in young Danes in a truly 'living' Danish school (as against the 'dead' or stultifying Latin school) in the period of the founding of the first Danish folk-highschools.

A

Abildgraa *151*; 'apple-grey' cited by Gr as Norwegian (Ringerike) term for horse of dappled colouring; but also ancient Scandinavian poetic name for 'horse.'

Ab(o)ukir, battle of *81, 156, 157*; Napoleon's triumphant action against Turks, temporarily securing his dominance in eastern Mediterranean; to young Gr "remarkable in the extreme" as event in outside world, in contemporary history, but ignored in Latin School at Aarhus. Subsequently, Nelson (Battle of the Nile, 1-2 August 1798) destroyed in Aboukir (Abu Qir) Bay the anchored French fleet which had brought Napoleon to Egypt, ending Napoleon's eastward aspirations and giving Britain preponderance in Mediterranean.

Absalon *103*; *ca.* 1128-1201; Bishop of Roskilde (1158), Archbishop of Lund (1177); one of great shapers of medieval Dk; effectively founder of Copenhagen for mercantile and military domination of entry to Baltic and passage to Danish territories across Øresund and on southern Baltic coast; active supporter of foster-brother King Valdemar the Great, notably in suppression of Vends in Rügen and destruction there of effigy of great heathen deity Svantevit; in effect ruler of Dk during early reign of Knud VI; commissioned his secretary Saxo Grammaticus to write *Gesta Danorum* and dictated much material to Saxo; both Gr and his cousin Henrik Steffens believed their maternal lineage derived from Hvide family (most powerful dynasty in medieval Dk after royal house) to which Absalon and his father Asser Rig and brother Esbern Snare belonged, and whose progenitor, Gr believed, was Palnatoke, great chieftain in Dk who justified heathen creed against Christian in debate with Odinkar in court of King Harald Blatan [Bluetooth] (*Optrin af Kæmpelivets Undergang i Nord* [Episodes from the downfall of the warrior-life in the North], 2 vols., 1809-11); Absalon, Esbern Snare, Asser Rig and Fru Inge his wife, and various other family members lie buried in Cistercian abbey-church at Sorø (where Gr aspired to found new folk-university); see also **Inge,** Fru; **Valdemar den store**.

absolutism; see **Enevælde**.

Address to the Swedish people *105*; *Er Nordens Forening ønskelig? Et Ord til det svenske Folk* [Is the Union of the North desirable? A word to the Swedish People]; pamphlet by Gr published 1810; in Gr's own account, marks point at which his interest turned irresistibly to history; in writing it, "my perspective upon the history of the North developed itself, especially through the viewpoint upon the Kalmar Union [Union of Denmark, Norway and Sweden under one sovereign though with separate laws, signed 1397 at Kalmar, Sweden, collapsed 1448, formally dissolved 1523] which I then formed." Gr maintained, with varying intensity and through various involvements, lifelong advocacy of Scandinavian fellowship and belief in special destiny (under God) for the North.

addresses, Grundtvig's, in Copenhagen; see **Grundtvig's Copenhagen addresses**.

Adjunkt *168* and passim; teacher; as for example J. C. Lindberg at the Metropolitanskole in Copenhagen.

Adresse-Avisen 173; newssheet published in Copenhagen, officially titled *Kiøbenhavns kongelige allene priviligerede Adresse-Contoirs Efterretninger* [Announcements from Copenhagen's exclusively royal-privileged Address Office], founded by J. F. von der Osten 1706; survived until 1908; primarily carried advertisements for goods, services, properties, new publications and such, as well as official announcements such as public appointments; until abolition of censorship, an organ largely at disposal of authorities; had its counterparts in various other regional centres in Dk such as Adresse-Contoirs in Odense and Ribe; a similar *Adresse-Avisen* was founded in Norway in 1767.

Aggershuus *150*; *Akershus*, in Kristiania (Oslo), Norway; castle and former fortress from late 13th c.; substantial rebuilding begun under Danish king Christian IV completed by Frederik III and Christian V; still a dominant shape in city profile; gave its name to administrative district north of Kristiania.

Agricola, of Tacitus; see **Tacitus**.

Ahlefeld, Grev *67*; Ahlefelds originally from Slesvig-Holsten established estates on Langeland from 1672, united with Norwegian family of Laurvig (Larvik) 1785; this *Grev* [Count] Ahlefeld is mentioned as previous employer of Bertel Faurskov (schoolmaster at Udby); a *Grev* Ahlefeld-Laurvig, commander-in-chief of the *Landeværn* (Home guard) on Langeland when English landing was feared (1807), appointed Gr (though not as yet ordained) military chaplain.

Ahnfeldt, P. G., *243*; 1808-63, Swedish priest and *provst* from Skarhult (mid-Skåne, Sweden; imposing 16th-c. mansion, seat of Danish Huitfeldt family), writer; cultivated support for Gr;

wrote substantial biographical account of Gr in Swedish journal *Samtiden* [The present age] (1859), reprinted in his *Studentminnen* [Memoir of student years] I (2nd edition, 1882), 287-318.

Aladdin *100, 113, 157*; character in Oehlenschläger's play (1805) of that name.

Aladdin *100, 113, 157*; *Aladdin eller Den forunderlige Lampe* [Aladdin or The Magic Lamp] five-act play by Adam Oehlenschläger (1779-1850) published 1805 in his *Poetiske Skrifter*; romantic-exotic story derived ultimately from *The Thousand and One Nights* (*Arabian Nights' Tales*) but more immediate source named by author himself was Ludvig Tieck's *Kaiser Octavianus* (1804).

Algreen, Peder Kjellerup *293, 294*; 1807-77; priest; like his younger contemporary and eventual colleague Christen Kold (1816-70), grew up in NW Jylland, graduated (1826) from Snedsted Seminarium there; in 1830s began holding unlawful *gudelige forsamlinger* [religious gatherings not within a church] for which (1840) he was prosecuted but at which Kold first experienced spiritual conversion; career in teaching being blocked (as was Kold's) by authorities, he moved (1844) to Copenhagen to study Theology; became member of Vartov congregation, deeply committed to Grundtvigian ideas, particularly of folk-enlightenment, and was partly instrumental in securing Grundtvigians' nomination (1849) of Christen Kold as principal of Ryslinge folk-highschool; graduated 1854; 1855 appointed chaplain and tutor at Nykøbing School, NW Jylland; 1859 took parish of Vrejlev and Hastrup, diocese of Aalborg; 1867 priest at Aaker on island of Bornholm until death.

Alhambra *243*; Copenhagen concert hall and theatre evoking Moorish pleasure-palace in style then fashionable in various European cities, opened 1857 by Georg Carstensen, used for large public meetings but, unable to compete with Tivoli, closed after some twelve years; see also **theatre and drama**.

Almuebøger *73*; popular books, folk-books, written and printed for the *almue* 'the common folk' who, being largely illiterate in Gr's time, would usually hear them read aloud, at a gathering; an element in Gr's alternative education while at Aarhus Latin School.

Almueskoler *154, 265*; elementary schools, maintained at public cost for the *almue* (in 18th-c. and 19th-c. usage, the 'common people, humble folk' whether urban or rural, but especially peasantry; sometimes less specifically 'the common throng'); when, influenced by Enlightenment philosophy, *Den store Skolekommission* [The great School Commission] began work (1789), objective was to educate good, happy and useful citizenry but by the time decrees were published, 29 July 1814, the educational aim expressed was rather that useful, Christian citizens supportive of the absolutist system of government be thus created – that "the State's maturing youth be timely taught to recognise what each owes God, himself and others, and how, by properly using his talents, he could become useful to the society of its citizens" [Statens tilvoxende Ungdom betimeligen læres at kiende, hvad Enhver skylder Gud, sig Selv, og Andre, og hvorledes Han, ved rettelingen at bruge sine Evner, kunde blive gavnlig for Borgersamfundet]; national school-system was thus established 1814 by two decrees, the *Anordning om Almueskolevæsenet i Købstæderne* [Decree concerning Elementary Education in Towns] and the *Anordning om Almueskolevæsenet på Landet* [Decree concerning Elementary Education in the Country], providing universal free but mandatory elementary education between ages of seven and fourteen; Dk divided into school-districts charged with building schools and employing permanent teachers; seminaries for the training of teachers established; intention was that State should provide free education to all children, girls and boys alike, but this proved excessive economic burden which was then alleviated by using older pupils to teach younger, thus enabling one teacher to oversee as many as 100 pupils; system was challenged in mid-19th c. by success of initiatives of Christen Kold (1816-70) and Gr towards establishment of *friskoler* (independent schools) often founded by groups of like-minded parents desiring a certain kind of education for their children, as part of wider Gr-led movement towards gaining liberty in church and in education, and nurturing a national historical and *folkelig* consciousness; *almueskoler* remained official title for public-maintained elementary schools between 1806-99; in bigger towns so-called *borgerskoler* [commoner-citizens' schools], with broader objectives and curricula, enjoyed the greater prestige; *almueskoler* eventually superseded, along with radical restructuring of whole state education system, by *folkeskoler*, national schools; see also **sorte Skole,** den; **friskole**.

Alterbogs-Sagen *175, 176*; the Service Book issue; ongoing contention at time of Gr's appointment to Vartov (1839) over revision of the *Alterbog*, official service book of Danish State-Church containing collects and scriptural readings for church-year; essentially a struggle, conducted partly through items published by J. C. Lindberg and Gr, between Rationalist reformers and traditionalists, relating particularly to baptismal ritual (notably revision or abandonment of 'interrogation' concerning renunciation of Devil, and omission of sign of cross); two of chief activists for revision, J. P. Mynster Bishop of Sjælland and *Stiftsprovst* H. G. Clausen, suffered setbacks; in Copenhagen, Clausen initiated an altered ritual, supported by most Copenhagen clergy but a Royal Resolution of 22 April 1834 expressed disapproval and ordered him to restore official ritual; Mynster, charged with gathering views of clergy across whole country, drafted revised *Alterbog*, submitted it for Royal and official consideration (1839), responding only with "a contemptuous dismissal" (Gr) to Gr's *Frisprog mod H. H. Hr. Biskop Mynsters Forslag til en ny Forordnet Alterbog* [A free-speaking discourse against the Right Reverend Bishop Mynster's proposal of a newly ordered Service Book; 1839]; though 300 copies were printed for public consideration, King (Frederik VI) was disposed to favour judgment of bishops and academic theologians; however, following death of King (1839), Mynster's proposed revision was, to his bitter resentment, eventually shelved.

Amager *125, 222, 223*; island in Øresund adjacent to Copenhagen; its northern extremity incorporated within bastions of fortified city; in Gr's day linked across harbour to Copenhagen proper by two bridges, Langebro and (via Christianshavn which developed in 19th c. as suburb of city) Knippelsbro; here, beyond Christianshavn, was one of city's places of execution where beheading and quartering by axe continued far into 19th c., adding association of barbarousness to that of backwardness in eyes of such as Søren Kierkegaard who thought Langebro [long bridge] fitly named because having crossed it on to Amager one was suddenly a long, long way from Copenhagen.

Amtsprovst *194*; ecclesiastical rank, corresponding very approximately to rural dean in English Church, having authority over district called *amt*, roughly corresponding to English 'county.'

Andersen, Hans Christian *76, 245, 248, 272, 286, 341*; 1805-75; author, poet, dramatist; most significant for his renewal, in form of his *eventyr* [fairytales], of art of *fortælling* [story telling, narration], bridging oral and literary – making interesting contemporary parallel to role of *fortælling* in educational theory of Kold-Grundtvig folk high-schools, to Gr's use of Northern myth as symbol and metaphor, and to Søren Kierkegaard's pervasive use of parable as metaphorical didactic instrument; Andersen more widely travelled, more widely known and esteemed outside Dk, in lifetime and since, than Gr; enjoyed distinguished patronage in Dk especially in later years; though Gr was among many whose encouragement he solicited in early years, and he got tuition from L. C. Müller (tutor to Gr's sons); in his *Vignetter til danske Digtere* [Vignettes of Danish poets; 1832; p.17] his characterisation of Gr reads: *Stolt synger Bølgen gjennem Issefjord, / Om Kjæmpelivets Undergang i Nord, / Fra Roeskild'-Kirke toner det paa Vang, / Som Bølgen og som Org'let, er din Sang* [Proud sings the breaker down the Isefjord, of warrior-life's eclipse here in the North, from Roskilde's church the sounds rings o'er the lea: like breaker and like organ is your song]; but his own somewhat idiosyncratic religious views were much at odds with both Gr's "Edda-Christianity" and Kierkegaard's "stalactite cave spring of humour and cleverness" (tr. Elias Bredsdorff) – in line with views of his patrons, the patrician Collin family; Gr was equally impatient with Andersen's scene-stealing at royal court and Kierkegaard's first published work was a scathing attack on one of Andersen's publications; Frederik Hammerich (*Et levnetsløb,* 1882) mentions a chance meeting between Andersen and Gr after many years, now both old men, one summer evening as Gr sat smoking his pipe on the Øresund coast – but records no conversation.

Andresen, Captain *129*; named in Gr's diary for 1829 as captain (from Altona) of ship which took Gr to England on first visit 1829; indignant defender of Danish potatoes against English criticism.

Andresen, Peter Rasmussen *22, 255, 256*; 1814-53; Danish teacher; born in Sønderjylland, *seminarium*-educated in Fyn, employed as house-tutor by family with Danish origins resident in Tvedestrand, Norway; co-editor 1850-53 of educational periodical *Den Norske Folkeskole*; author of devotional writings, hymns; visited (1839), and warmly received by Gr.

Ane-Marie *312, 317*; baby girl baptised by Gr amid events of his breakdown Palm Sunday (14 April) 1867; described by Frederik Hammerich as "from Grundtvig's Highschool" (Marielyst Højskole, inaugurated November 1856, funded by 70th birthday gift to Gr from contributors in Dk and Norway); Vartov's baptismal register records for that day christening of "Ane-Marie Hansen, datter af forpagter Ole Hansen og hustru Anne Kathrine Hansen, født Hansen" [A-M. H., daughter of tenant O. H. and his wife A. K. H., née Hansen].

anfægtelser *187*; diagnosis of Gr's mental and spiritual crisis (1810-11) made by his father upon Gr's return home to Udby vicarage (December 1810); Danish cognate of German *Anfechtung*, onslaught, affliction, trial, temptation; concept has very strong Lutheran associations, since Luther himself, particularly in early struggle to realise his vocation, famously suffered *Anfechtungen* – spiritual struggles within his soul, often envisaged as the assaults of Satan, manifest in, e.g., doubts relating to faith, bodily temptations, self-reproach for idleness and lack of achievement, and guilt over being unworthy of esteem received from family and friends; weapons of counter-attack are prayer and Word of God; "Without the Word of God the enemy is too strong for us. But he cannot endure prayer and the Word of God" (Luther); Gr emerged from spiritual crisis ("the strange metamorphosis") with altered view of life; the pattern was repeated in his severe mental illness Spring 1844, compounded by an attack of mumps; see also *Verdens-Krønike*.

Anglo-Saxon fable *120*; when Gr alludes to *Beowulf* as "et ditto [= halvhedenske] angelsachsisk Æventyr" [a half-heathen Anglo-Saxon fable] the noteworthy point is that, unlike other early *Beowulf*-scholars, he gives status to the Christian content of the poem and places the unknown poet on a par with Saxo Grammaticus (monk and secretary to archbishop Absalon) and Snorri Sturluson (Christian-educated mythographer who rationalised the Norse gods and myths as originating in real events involving human protagonists); see ***Beowulf***.

Anglo-Saxon literature *27, 133, 134, 172, 189, 335*; "Grundtvig, as is well-known, had a long-standing love of the Anglo-Saxons. Right from the start he was at home in their writings." (Frederik Hammerich, 1872); see **Anglo-Saxons**; **Anglo-Saxon manuscripts**; *Beowulf*; **Exeter Book,** The; ***Phoenix, The***; **Bede,** The Venerable; **Cædmon**; **Hickes,** George; **Stephens,** George.

Anglo-Saxon manuscripts *62, 133, 172*; manuscripts (majority probably produced and initially preserved in monastic communities) of Anglo-Saxon poetry, chronicles, laws, charters, homilies, saints' lives, liturgical books, translations of the Bible and of seminal Latin patristic texts, recipes, charms, etc., surviving in English libraries, at that time largely unpublished, which Gr was enabled by royal grants to study (summers 1829-31) in expectation (based on evidence of Danish antiquarian scholars Langebek, Suhm, Thorkelin) that they would augment sources of early Danish and Northern history and literature; though English scholars – notably John Josias Conybeare (1779-1824), appointed (1808) Professor of Anglo-Saxon and (1812) Professor of Poetry in the University of Oxford; published series of communications on Anglo-Saxon poems of the Exeter Book and on *Beowulf* in *Archaeologia* xvii (1814), journal of Society of Antiquaries of London; his work on Anglo-Saxon poetry was published posthumously (1826) by his brother William Daniel Conybeare – had already proposed and begun work towards their publication, Gr's prospectus (*Bibliotheca Anglo-Saxonica*, London 1830) certainly galvanised English scholarly establishment resulting notably in Benjamin Thorpe's editions of scriptural narrative poems, poems of Exeter Book and Anglo-Saxon metrical paraphrases of Psalms; thus, and by virtue of substantial textual and interpretative work on *Beowulf*, Gr established a place among pioneers of modern Anglo-Saxon scholarship; see also ***Bibliotheca Anglo-Saxonica***; **medieval character,** Gr as.

Anglo-Saxons *144, 334*; "*Anglo-Saxons* is the common name for the Danish and Frisian vikings who in the fifth and sixth centuries occupied Britain except for Wales and called it England, and from the eighth century became tutors to both Germany and the North in Christianity and the art of writing in the mother-tongue. Their language (its own blending of German and Nordic) was the first that, after the Roman jurisdiction, became a language for writing, and even though there are still but few Anglo-Saxon books in print, there are many in manuscript" (Gr in *Krønnike-Rim* 1828 and 1842); historically, migrants primarily originating from regions at southern end of Jylland peninsula who from mid-5th c. began colonising former Roman province of Britannia; socially organised on basis of kingship; underwent christianisation from late 6th c. onwards; dominant cultural orientation towards continental Christian Europe, but a very significant cultural orientation towards Christian Ireland ensured distinctive identity of regions north of Humber in earlier period; Bede's *Ecclesiastical History of the English People* (completed 731) played major role in consolidating an 'English' identity and history; from 8th c. onwards Scandinavian raiders and settlers also impacted upon development of English culture; under Alfred (849-901) and his successors concept and political reality of an English nation emerged; despite vicissitudes, a rich literary culture, extensively expressed in the vernacular language rather than Latin, was maintained from beginning to end; militarily and politically, Anglo-Saxon state ended with conquest by William of Normandy 1066; sense of English identity and English language itself survived period of 'Norman' kings, subsequently to emerge dominant; legendarily, according to (Danish) tradition recorded by Saxo Grammaticus, 12th-c. Danish historiographer, and used by Gr in poem prefacing *Beowulfes Beorh* (edition of *Beowulf*, 1861), founding-fathers of Danes and Angles were two brothers, Dan and Angul; evidence that Anglo-Saxons preserved traditional memories of neighbouring Danish legend-history may be afforded by poems *Widsith* and *Beowulf*; to these ancient legendary and historical identities and affinities Gr appealed in conviction that England and Dk could and should share common destiny within the High North; the Anglo-Saxons he referred to as "these unknown creators, as it were, of the modern civilized world" (letter to Sir Frederic Madden 1839) and their literature he called "the first New-European literature" and "the historical and poetic queen of the new Europe." See also **Angul's Isle**; **Denmark**.

Angul's Isle *133*; England; so called by Gr with reference to legend recorded by Saxo Grammaticus (*Gesta Danorum*, Book I), thus translated from Saxo's Latin (and Saxo's commendation of Bede no doubt heartily endorsed) by Gr: "Dannemarks Krønike begynder med Humbles Sønner: Dan og Angel, som baade vare de første navnkundige Høvdinger i Riget ... Fra denne Angel skal, efter Sigende, det engelske Folks Navn have sin Oprindelse, thi det Landskab han raadte over, kaldte han Angeln, og slap derved paa en nem Maade til et udødeligt Navn, thi da hans Efterkommere siden indtoge Britannien, skildte de tillige Øen ved sit gamle Navn, og satte deres eget Fædrenelands, nemlig Angelns, isteden ... Herom kan man læse hos Beda, som var selv en Engelskmand, og velberømt for sine gudelige Skrifter, thi han indlemmede med Flid sit Fædrenelands Krønike i sine dyrebare Bøger om Troen og Lærdommen, fordi han tænkde, som sandt var, at det er ligesaavel en Kiærligheds-Gierning at tænde Lys i sit Fædrenelands Krønike, som at udlægge Guds Ord; det Ene skal giøres, og det Andet ikke forsømmes. Det var nu Angel, men fra Dan nedstammer, efter Forfædrenes Vidnesbyrd, vort gamle Kongehuus, saa Konge-blodet er fra ham, som et Kildespring, rundet giennem Slægten lige til den Dag i Dag." [The chronicle of Dk begins with Humble's sons, Dan and Angul, which two were the first renowned chieftains in the land ... From this Angul, according to tradition, the name of the English people has its origin, because he called the territory over which he ruled Angeln and thereby in an easy way hit upon an immortal name, for when his successors subsequently conquered Britain they also stripped the island of its ancient name and imposed instead that of their own fatherland, namely Angeln's ... One can read about this in Bede, who was himself an Englishman and famed for his religious writings, for he assiduously incorporated his fatherland's chronicle in his valuable books on the faith and on scholarship, because he believed, which was right, that it is as much a work of love to give light to his fatherland's chronicle as to set forth the word of God. The one must be done, the other must not be neglected. So much for Angul. But from Dan descends, according to the forefathers' testimony, our ancient royal house, so the blood royal has flowed from him, like a spring, down through the lineage until this very day] (*Danmarks Krønike af Saxo Grammaticus*, 1818, p.1). "Angler kaldes Hovedstammen hos Angel-Saxerne, og af dem har endnu landskabet Angeln ved Slesvig sit Navn" [The chief ethnic group among the Anglo-Saxons is called the Angles, and from them Angeln, the region around Slesvig, takes its name] (Gr in *Krønnike-Rim* 1828 and 1842).

Angul's Song *120*; the Anglo-Saxon heroic epic *Beowulf*; so called by Gr in allusion to Saxo's legend of Angul; see **Angul's Isle** and ***Beowulf***.

Anker, Herman *153, 301, 304, 306, 307*; 1839-96; Norwegian educationist; *cand. theol.* 1863; spent study-period in Dk with Olaus Arvesen with whom (1859-60) he was visitor to Gr-home; with Arvesen, was among those who prompted Gr to give series of winter lectures at his home, eventually published as *Kirke-Speil* (1871); inspired by Gr's ideas, collaborated (1864) with Arvesen to establish and lead first Norwegian folk-highschool at Sagatun, his property near Hamar, which became model for others; with his marriage to Marie Elisabeth (Mix) Boisen (1842-92), daughter of Frederik (Frits) Engelhard Boisen and Eline Birgitte Heramb, he joined 'Grundtvigian' family Boisen into which Gr's daughter Meta also married; a daughter Katti Anker Møller, became noted feminist; see also **Arvesen,** Olaus; **folk-highschools.**

Ansgar *170, 201, 250*; *ca.* 801-865; archbishop of Hamburg-Bremen, missionary, honoured as Apostle to the North after baptising the exiled Danish king Harald Klak 826 and accompanying him back to Dk; driven out again along with the king, he carried his mission on to Sweden; according to his biographer Rimbert Archbishop of Hamburg and Bremen (d. 888) he was guided throughout his life by dreams in which, Rimbert (citing Acts of the Apostles VIII:29) says, mental enlightenment came to him from the Holy Spirit; in one such dream he stood by St Peter as a group of people begged Peter to send them a teacher and pastor – to which Peter replied with irritation "Did I not tell you that he should be your teacher who stands before you? Why do you doubt? Did you not hear the voice of the Holy Spirit that came for this purpose, to consecrate a pastor for you?" (tr. Charles H. Robinson) – these dreams of Ansgar were of great interest to Gr; on Jelling Stone, at Jelling Church, Jylland, king Harold Blatan [Bluetooth], who succeeded to his father Gorm *ca.* 940, claims credit for first making Danes Christian; but the Danish Church celebrated its thousand-year anniversary on Whit Sunday 1826.

Ansgar celebration *170, 201*; official celebration (Whitsunday, 14 May 1826) of thousandth anniversary of introduction of Christianity into Dk by Ansgar, archbishop of Hamburg-Bremen; for which Gr (then under threat of H. N. Clausen's litigation against him) had made preparations and written a hymn *Den signede Dag, som vi nu seer* [The blessed day which now we see], but he resigned his curacy at Vor Frelsers Kirke a week before the event and permission to use his hymn was withdrawn, to Gr's deep and lasting bitterness; see also ***Den signede Dag,*** *som vi nu ser*; and **Ansgar.**

Anskuelse, den kirkelige; see **kirkelige Anskuelse,** den.

Apostles, Apostolic times, apostolic profession *138, 139, 290*; Luther's rejection of latter-day accretions to Christian doctrine and Rationalism's challenge to integrity of scriptural tradition led Gr and others to look to the days of the Apostles for warranty of creed and practice; central to Gr's "peerless discovery" [*mageløse opdagelse*] (1825) was a supposition that in the forty days between resurrection and ascension Christ taught the Apostles the form of the Creed preserved by the Church as expression of the Living Word, which Gr crucially associated with sacraments of baptism and eucharist; Gr held preaching to be an apostolic activity, regarded religious ministry as apostolic profession, though conscious that Danish clergy did not stand in the continuous lineage of apostolic succession; his views opposed by such as Bishop H. L. Martensen ("the Church has never known anything about the Apostolic Creed belonging to the institution of baptism") as tending towards the sectarian; yet while Gr himself had reservations as to the spiritual capacity of the modern age to order the Church upon truly apostolic principles (as also did Vilhelm Birkedal in debating circumstances at Ryslinge with Gr, 1865), yet witnesses could report of Vartov that "Such an alive and abundant congregational life as that which blossoms in Vartov I have only imagined in the apostolic congregations where all were one soul and one heart" (H. P. B. Barfod); see also **Apostles' Creed**; **mageløse Opdagelse,** den.

Apostles, picture of in Gr's study *95*; sole ornament in Gr's study in Strandgade, according to Marie Blom, was picture of Christ with the Apostles – an interesting priority in light of Gr's central theological placement of the living word descending through the Apostles; see **Apostles,** Apostolic times, apostolic profession.

Apostles' Creed *16, 18, 125, 126, 139, 153, 168, 170, 176, 194, 217, 251, 264*; the *Symbolum Apostolorum*, which evolved between second and ninth centuries, the earliest known text of its current form being recorded by Caesarius of Arles (died 542), was traditionally held to have been written down by apostles immediately after Christ's ascension, and indeed each of its professions is founded in formulations current in apostolic times; regarded by Gr as a profession of belief taught directly to apostles by Christ, it was, when congregationally professed within the sacramental acts of baptism and eucharist, central to his theology of the Living Word (*Det levende Ord*); see also **Apostles,** Apostolic times, apostolic profession; **mageløse Vidnesbyrd,** det; **Irenaeus**; **sacraments**.

Aristokraternes Katekismus; see **Bruun,** Malthe Conrad.

Arvesen, Olaus (Olaf) *24, 153, 295, 296, 301, 304, 306, 307*; 1830-1917; educationist, politician; *cand. theol.* 1862; spent study-period in Copenhagen with Herman Anker, with whom he was visitor to Gr-home; played part in prompting Gr (1860) to embark upon lecture series on Church history eventually published as *Kirke-Speil* (1871); returned to Norway inspired by Gr's ideas on church, education and *det folkelige*, which he worked to further in Norway; through 1860s edited Gr-sympathetic periodical *Kirkeligt Folkeblad*; 1864 together with Anker founded Norway's first Grundtvigian folk-highschool, at Sagatun, Ankers' property near Hamar; sole principal 1873-91; dedicated friend of Dk, proposed health of Dk and Slesvig at meeting of Nordic *folkepartier* [people's parties] at Sagatun (1872); member of Norwegian Storting 1891-97; see also **Anker,** Herman; **folk-highschools**.

Asatroen *186*; the Asa-faith; belief in the gods of Norse myth which some of his critics derisively attributed to Gr with the publication of his *Nordens Mytologi* (1808); but his close friend F. C. Sibbern more perceptively discerned that "the underlying idea is in a Christian spirit: for Odin here arrives at his divine might through a kind of fall from grace or apostasy." See **Aser, Vaner**; *Nordens Mythologi.*

Aschlund, Arent *292*; 1797-1835; surveyor and author; defended, in *Om Verdens-Bygningen* [*On the Construction of the World*] (1830), Tycho Brahe's view of solar system against that of Copernicus – Gr's approval of which was indicated by 4-lined verse he contributed to accompany engraving of Brahe.

Aser, Vaner *43, 98, 185, 272, 300*; Icelandic Æsir, Vanir; two principal groupings of gods in northern mythology; extant northern origin-myths, largely dependent on Snorri Sturluson's synthesisations and rationalisations in his *Edda* and *Heimskringla*, are cryptic and sketchy, and stories become somewhat clearer once these two groupings of gods have emerged; after Óðinn led Æsir into war with Vanir, hostages were exchanged bringing Vanir Njörðr, his son Freyr and daughter Freyja into Ásgarðr, home of Æsir, and sending Æsir Mímir and Hænir into Vanaheimr; but peace failed and many stories relate directly or indirectly to continuing rivalry and strife between them, some of it fomented by Loki, son of a giant from Jötunheimr, and all contributing eventually to doom of gods at Ragnarök; much of all this Gr reworked in major 19th-c. appropriation of Norse myth (*Nordens Mythologi*, 1832) aspiring to furnish contemporary North with a native resource of metaphor parallel to those of Greek and Latin tradition; see also *Nordens Mythologi.*

Askov *306*; folk-highschool, Vejen, Jylland; school originally established (1844) at Rødding, North Slesvig, on initiative of Christian Flor (1792-1875), professor in University of Kiel (before the loss of Slesvig-Holsten in 1864, one of Denmark's two universities), as first ever materialisation of educational innovations sought by Flor, Gr and Christen Kold (1816-70), to promote historical cultural Danishness against German cultural rivalry, to advance education of a largely rural population and to encourage Scandinavianism; under fourth principal, Sophus Magdalus Høgsbro (1822-1902; principal 1850-62), objectives were broadened and modernised, particularly in pursuit of Gr's educational aspirations; after Denmark's loss of Slesvig in war of 1864, Flor raised money enabling fifth principal, Ludvig Peter Schrøder (1836-1908; principal from 1862) to lead resettlement at Askov, north of new frontier on river Kongeåen, as continuing beacon for Danishness on both sides of frontier; foundation still flourishes as Askov Højskole and Askov Efterskole, declaring its aim to be what it always was, *livsoplysning* [life-enlightenment] with respect to the fundamental conditions of existence, and *folkelig oplysning* concerning the important issues of the age and of society; see also **Høgsbro**, Sophus Magdalus; **Schrøder**, Ludvig Peter.

assemblies, devotional; see **forsamlinger**

Assembly of the States General; see **Constitutional history**.

asylskole *141, 288*; free school for orphaned and deprived children; see **Dronningens Asylskole**.

Athanasius *188; ca.* 296-373; Alexandrian Patriarch giving name to the formulation (in refutation of Arian theology) of the Creed of the Christian Church which among the rest lays emphasis upon Trinitarian doctrine of three persons, Father, Son and Holy Spirit, being of one substance, in one God; to which orthodoxy Gr is reported as rigidly adhering in 1811.

At sige Verden ret Farvel *280, 281;* To bid the world a fit farewell; hymn (1843, 1845) by Gr (*DDS* 2002, no. 538), on dying, death and resurrection of the body; admired by (Bishop) H. L. Martensen.; see also **hymns**.

Attestats (**attestatus**) *61, 66, 86, 156, 159;* examination (person qualified by examination), especially Theological, particularly intended to qualify men to hold offices of State and, since Reformation, to minister and hold office in State Church; extended to Law 1736; system consolidated and standards assured by institution of external examination 1788; in 19th c., normal culmination of university education; see also **cand.** (*=candidatus*); **matriculation**.

Augsburg Confession *119, 171, 256, 289; Confessio Augustana,* Lutheran profession of faith, originally drafted by Melancthon, read in *Rigsdag* at Augsburg, 25 June 1530; foundational document in international Lutheranism (though not adopted by all 'reforming' churches – not, for example, by English); establishing distance from Zwingli as well as from Pope; first of two main sections deals with faith – God, original sin, the Son of God who liberates from sin; on justification by faith, and the well-springs of faith – Word and Sacraments; on good works as fruits of faith; on Oneness of the Church; on efficacy of sacraments not being dependent upon merits of their administrant; on individual sacraments; on ordering of secular civil responsibility and Christ's return to Judgment; on curtailed freedom of human will; on cause of sin, on good works; on cultivation of saints; second main section deals with specific abuses; Danish (Lutheran) Church is confessionally bound by the three Creeds of the primitive Church, the Short Catechism of Luther and the *Confessio Augustana;* over the last, Gr expressed certain misgivings.

Augustenborg, Duke (*Hertug*) of *199;* seat at Augustenborg on island of Als, formerly within Slesvig, now part of Sønderjylland, Dk; Christian August of Augustenborg (1798-1869), though closely related to Danish royal house, being son of Frederik VI s sister Louisa Augusta, raised as Danish-speaking prince, and host at his homes in Augustenborg and Graasten to such Danish cultural celebrities as Oehlenschläger and H. C. Andersen, became (with brother Frederik, Prince of Nør) identified with cause of duchies (*hertugdømme*) of Slesvig-Holsten against Dk (1846 onwards); see also **Frederik,** Prince of Nør.

Aurora Latinitatis *67, 155;* 'Dawn of Latinity,' Latin word-book for beginners published in Dk 1638 by Professor Thomas Bang; still a standard work in period of Gr's early education.

Axel og Valborg *101;* tragic drama in five acts by Adam Oehlenschläger (1808), in style of French classical tragedy; based upon folk-ballad in the book (1695) of two hundred ballads on Danish kings and heroes by Peder Syv (1631-1702).

B

Baader, Benedict Franz Xaver von *249*; 1765-1841; German professor in Munich, philosopher of religion, Roman Catholic but independent thinker; opposed declaration of papal infallibility; strongly interested in social reform; argued that all true philosophy must be religious ("Not to begin with God is to deny him") and divided philosophy into a religious metaphysics, a religious natural philosophy, and a philosophy of spirit, the last focussing particularly upon revelation of the human spirit within societal interactions.

Bacchus *76, 90*; Latin name given to Greek god Dionysos; becomes jocularly-learned symbol of excessive indulgence in wine and good living, just as Venus becomes symbol of sexual indulgence; to neither could the impoverished student Gr, whatever other principle may also have restrained him, afford to offer sacrifice; see also **Venus**.

Baden, Gustav Ludvig *106*; 1764-1840; historian, jurist; his uncircumspectly assertive and quarrelsome temperament and recklessness in managing his financial affairs are held to have ruined his promising career in public office and led to huge debt, dispersal of his assets including his library, imprisonment and eventually lifelong censorship; but amidst all adversities he continued to study, write and publish mainly historical works including five-volume *Danmarks Riges Historie* [History of the Kingdom of Dk], 1829-31; his proposal (*Dr G. L. Baden til Hr Geheimconferenceraad F. v. Moltke om vor danske Histories Fader Saxo Grammaticus og Trangen til en ny Udgave af ham* [... concerning the father of our Danish history Saxo Grammaticus and the need of a new edition of him] (1809) was challenged by Gr in article in *Nyeste Skilderie af Kjøbenhavn* (22 August 1809).

Baden, Jacob *81*; 1735-1804; Professor of Rhetoric Copenhagen University 1780; philologist, critic, with significant influence upon contemporary Danish usage, especially spoken; author of Latin-Danish dictionaries, and of a Latin Grammar which was standard text-book in Danish schools over half a century; see also **Saxo,** new translation of.

Baggesen, Jens Immanuel *83, 113-115, 164, 166, 190, 250, 276*; 1764-1826; Danish poet who often wrote in German, professor of Danish language and literature in the University of Kiel 1811-14; from impoverished origins, was encouraged by patronage of poet Christian Henriksen Pram (1756-1825) co-founder with K. L. Rahbek (1760-1830) of influential monthly periodical *Minerva* in which Baggesen published; under patronage of Holsten aristocracy travelled widely and wrote travel-accounts in spirit of Lawrence Sterne's *Sentimental Journey*; made a mark (1806) with his 'verse-letters' (*rimbreve*) of an autobiographical and often satirical character, including *Min Skygge* (My Shadow), and (1807) with his Danish poem-cycle *Giengangeren* (The Ghost, the haunting spectre); early works read, but half-dismissed, by Gr ("the jesting is good enough but all of life's serious questions are passed off in jest") but later works seriously philosophical, striving for a more pictorial, metaphorical language of philosophy; settled in Copenhagen 1813-20 as major figure in cultural circles, controversial theatre-critic and author, notoriously engaged in protracted *pennefejde* [pen-feud] following his criticism of work of contemporary Danish poet Adam Oehlenschläger to which Peder Hjort, literary critic to periodical *Athene*, responded with destructive analysis of Baggesen's own literary achievement; left Dk 1820, eventually died abroad in unhappy circumstances; see also **Tylvten**; *Rimelige Strøtanker*; **pennefejde.**

Bagsværd *201*; in 19th c. a village 10 km north of Copenhagen, today a suburb of city.

Bakkehuset *282*; 'house on the hill', home of Rahbeks, Kamma and Knud Lyhne, on Valby Bakke near Frederiksberg outside Copenhagen; became (though Rahbeks had difficulty with economy of an open house) gathering-place for leading figures in 19th-c. Danish cultural life, such as poets Adam Oehlenschläger (married to Kamma's sister Christiane), Jens Baggesen, B. S. Ingemann, Christian Winther and Johan Ludvig Heiberg, scientist H. C. Ørsted and jurist and minister A. S. Ørsted; though K. L. Rahbek was not, in his own poetry, plays and novels, caught up by tidal wave of 19th-c. Romanticism, and retired (1799) as professor in aesthetics partly perhaps because he felt no sympathy for new Kantian philosophy of period, he and Kamma – through Bakkehuset's role as meeting-place of diverse personalities – effected some continuity and cohesion in Danish intellectual and cultural life notwithstanding radical new departures; Gr also visited in younger years but later characteristically dissociated himself from such fashion-following. See **Rahbek,** Knud Lyhne and **Rahbek,** Kamma.

Balder hin gode *101*; *Baldur hiin gode* [Baldr the good], tragic drama by Oehlenschläger, published in his *Nordiske Digte* (1807) within new vogue for Nordic subjects in literature and other arts; in Norse myth Baldr is son of Óðinn and Frigg, most loved by gods but killed by trickery; his character, death and subsequent return to world purged of strife gave scope for Gr, among others, to draw parallels with Christ; Gr, who enthusiastically though not uncritically reviewed *Baldur* in K. L. Rahbek's *Ny Minerva*, December 1807, hailed Oehlenschläger as the first authentic Nordic poet for almost a thousand years and as "hine Navnløses Frænde, fra hvis Læber Eddas hellige Qvad udstrømmede" [kinsman of that nameless one from whose lips streamed forth the sacred songs of the *Edda*]; see also ***Nordens Mythologi***.

ballads, folk; see **folk-ballads**.

ballad of Villemoes *136, 143*; Gr's song *Kommer hid, I piger smaa* [Gather round, you lassies small] to commemorate heroic death of Peter Willemoes in Battle of Sjællands Odde 1808; see **Willemoes,** song for.

Balle, Johanne Frederikke Harboe *156*; 1756-1802; second wife (1782) of Bishop N. E. Balle, daughter of Bishop Ludvig Harboe, grand-daughter of Bishop Peder Hersleb; related by this marriage to Gr who attended her funeral (11 April 1802).

Balle, Nicolaj Edinger *62, 69, 103, 154-156, 158, 159, 161, 193, 194, 198*; 1744-1816; professor of theology, Copenhagen (1772), Bishop of Sjælland (1783); *kongelig confessionarius* [chaplain royal] 1800; while studying in Germany, attended lectures of church historian Christian Wilhelm Walch (1757-1784) and philosopher and orientalist Johann David Michaëlis (1717-91) and absorbed from them and from writings of German theologian Johann Salomo Semler (1725-91), transitional figure between Pietism and Rationalism, the new theological critical-historical method popularly called *Neologi*; also much influenced by theology of German Christian Wolff especially as regards synthesis between reason and revelation; even so, strenuous in defending Christianity against contemporary rationalism which he perceived as damaging not only to religious faith and practice but to divine authority of royal absolutism on which Danish monarchic rule had been founded since 1660; to revitalise church-going, instituted Sunday evensong in Copenhagen with huge success; was nevertheless regarded by Gr and others as overly rationalistic; his *Lærebog i den Evangelisk-Christelige Religion* [Textbook in Evangelical-Christian Religion; 1791], mandatorily introduced into state schools, drew scorn from all sides for preoccupation with bourgeois morality at expense of Christian teaching; the new Evangelical-Christian Hymnal (1798) compiled by a commission under his chairmanship was widely regarded as expression of rationalism; but he himself strove to counter extremes of rationalism which held, for example, that Jesus was no more than an enlightened teacher of the rational, issuing weekly serial publication *Bibelen forsvarer sig sel.* [The Bible is its own defence] (1797-1802) scrupulously addressing every attack upon Bible and Christianity; his role in a commission reviewing the liturgy (1806) was, in Gr's view, ineffectual; despite much contumely throughout his career his earnestness and conscientiousness shine through accounts; he retired (1808) "deeply oppressed beneath his own and the fatherland's misfortunes" (Gr), perhaps having finally exhausted himself comforting and encouraging population during terror of British bombardment of Copenhagen 1807; his first wife was Frederikke Severine, sister of Gr's father who gave Gr his three names after this couple; see also **Bastholm,** Christian.

Balle, Peder Hansen *68*; 1777-1835; son of Bishop N. E. Balle; was taught together with Gr (his cousin) by Laurits Feld in Tyregod; became major in Danish army.

Baltzer's son *194*; Bishop Friederich Münter (1761-1830), addressed at length in Gr's *Roeskilde-Riim* (1814), and present at Gr's reading of it to clerical convention in Roskilde (1812); lines in published text are "Nej, du Bisp, med Arv saa skjøn ... Vakre Baltsar Münters Søn!" and again "Fromme Baltsar Münters Søn" [Nay, thou bishop, with heritance so fine ... fair B. M.'s son!; pious B. M.'s son]; though praise of father is not ultimately intended as flattery of son, for Gr more or less scorned him. Bishop Münter's father was Balthasar Münter (1735-1793): born in Lübeck, studied at university in Jena; moved to Copenhagen 1765 where as pastor to German community in Sankt Petri Kirke he was greatly esteemed as preacher whom younger theologians such as Christian Bastholm (1740-1819) took as rhetorical model; freemason of high rank; it was his duty to prepare Johan Friedrich Struensee (1737-72), imprisoned in Kastellet, Copenhagen, awaiting public execution (1772) for crime of *lèse majesté*; he subsequently published conversations with Struensee which were then translated into all principal European languages; see also **Münter,** Friederich Christian Carl Hinrich.

Bang, Carl Vilhelm, *76, 87*; 1754-1806; brother of Gr's mother; officer in militia; called by Gr "my extremely rich uncle Captain Bang" who, implicitly, could have afforded Gr a more generous student allowance than two *rigsdaler* a month.

Bang, Frederik Ludvig *76, 181, 182, 186*; 1747-1820; Doctor of Medicine, professor, *Etatsraad* [Councillor of State; honorific title]; Gr's maternal uncle; his two sisters were the mothers of Gr and of philosopher Henrik Steffens (1773-1845); by his first marriage became step-father to brothers Ole and (later bishop) Jacob Peter Mynster (1775-1854); resident in Copenhagen, he gathered about himself a circle of young students, including nephew Gr, who would later make their mark in Danish ecclesiastical and cultural life; it was in his home that Gr first met both his older relatives, Mynster (later his bishop and opponent) and Steffens.

Bang, Kathrine Marie *61, 63, 108, 116*; 1748-1822; Gr's mother; born and raised in Egebjerg, Odsherred, NW Sjælland, daughter of Niels Christian Bang overseer of royal estates in Odsherred, Sjælland; commemorated by Gr in stone erected at Egebjerg, depicting her teaching him to read, and in his poem upon her death (*Nyeste Skilderie af Kjøbenhavn*, 1822): O Moder-Støv og Moder-Aand! / Mit Hjertes Tak Du have, / Som lærde mig, i Lede-Baand, / Paa Herrens Ord at stave, / At stave, grunde, bygge paa / Det Ord, som aldrig skal forgaae!! [O mother, dust and spirit both, / with all my heart I thank you, / who taught me, still in infant reins, / to spell upon the Bible, / to spell, to found and build upon / the Word which never shall decay]; her younger sister Susanne (b. 1751) was mother of philosopher Henrik Steffens (1773-1845); her elder brother professor, Dr Frederik Ludvig Bang (1747-1820) was step-father to later bishop (and Gr's adversary) J. P. Mynster (1775-1854).

Bang, Niels Christian *61*; 1697-1760; Gr's maternal grandfather; *forvalter* (overseer) of Crown estates in Odsherred, NW Sjælland; *Kammerraad* (Counsellor, minor honorific title).

Bang, Oluf Lundt *186*; 1788-1877; son of Frederik Ludvig Bang; doctor, subsequently professor, Privy Councillor; published on treatment of cholera and on aesthetics and wrote poems under whimsically rearranged name Balfungo.

Bankruptcy, State (Statsbankerot) *99, 108, 158, 162*; Dk suffered State bankruptcy in 1813 as consequence of involvement in Napoleonic Wars, including pre-emptive destruction of Danish naval and mercantile fleet by British naval force (1807); between 1816-20 in Copenhagen alone some 250 concerns went bankrupt; gave rise to acute hardship (and bitter anti-British sentiment) in both Dk and Norway; led to establishment of Dk's National Bank, to secure separation of monetary system from direct state control.

baptism *126, 127, 139, 154, 157, 165, 168, 170, 171, 174, 176, 177, 194, 224, 229, 251, 264, 266, 270, 273, 311, 313, 314, 317*; see also **sacraments**; **Daabspagten**.

baptismal covenant; see **Daabspagten**; **sacraments**.

Barfod, Agate *243, 318*; daughter of (Povl) Frederik and Emilie Barfod, attended historical lectures given by Gr in his home (1858-59), befriended by Fru Marie (Toft) Grundtvig.

Barfod, Emilie Birkedal *234, 237, 238, 240, 241*; sister of (Schøller Parelius) Vilhelm Birkedal (1809-92); wife of (Povl) Frederik Barfod; married 11 September 1841.

Barfod, Frederik *120*; son of (Povl) Frederik and Emilie Barfod.

Barfod, Hans Peter Gote Birkedal *215, 244, 314*; 1843-1926; son of (Povl) Frederik and Emilie Barfod; historical writer, doctor; right-wing, royalist Grundtvig-adherent; his copious anthology, *Minder fra gamle Grundtvigske Hjem* [Reminiscences from old Grundtvig-adherent homes; Copenhagen, 1921], is a valuable record of devotion to Gr's ideals as a way of life among families in various parts of Dk.

Barfod, Hulda *243, 244*; 1850-78; adoptive daughter of (Povl) Frederik and Emilie Barfod; playmate of, later bridesmaid to, Sofie daughter (by previous marriage) of Gr's second wife Marie (Toft); Barfod family lived in Frederiksberg Allé 55, near Gr's house (1859-67) in Gammel Kongevej; Hulda married (1873) Povl la Cour (1846-1908), one of most distinguished teachers at Askov folk-highschool where she herself had been a student (1867).

Barfod, Ludvig *241, 243, 317*; son of (Povl) Frederik and Emilie Barfod; his critical illness in 1853, when his father had to turn to Fru Marie (Toft) Grundtvig for loan of 30 *rigsdaler*, was one of traumas of unhappy year for Barfod family.

Barfod, Mine *243*; daughter-in-law of (Povl) Frederik and Emilie Barfod

Barfod, Olaf Ostenfeld *230, 241*; 1871-1940; grandson of (Povl) Frederik and Emilie Barfod; bookseller.

Barfod, Povl Frederik *64, 184, 185, 218, 230, 239, 245, 247, 270, 272, 276, 296, 314, 332*; 1811-96; historical writer, politician, member of *Rigsdag*; teacher upon whose initiative charitable boys' school (later called Frederik Barfod's School) was established 1834 where he taught unpaid; librarian in a succession of appointments, Royal Library Copenhagen 1861-66; originally supporter of royal absolutism, joined active Venstre political group which included such activists as Vilhelm Birkedal (1809-92) and C. C. Hall (1812-88) and was strongly influenced by Gr; working closely with Gr, he founded (1839) Danske Samfund, society for promoting Danish culture, which published periodical *Brage og Idun* 1839-42; free expression of liberal ideology in daily paper *Fædrelandet*, especially demands for freedom of press, cost him heavy fines and censorship; 1848 his championing of farmers' claim to representation in new *Rigsdag* won him election to Constituent Assembly [*Den grundlovgivende Rigsforsamling*; for determination of the new Constitution] where he achieved constitutional assurance of press-freedom; 1853 appointed as editor of new journal *Dannebrog* but peremptorily dismissed after political collision with Gr; subsequently moved politically towards right but exercised no great influence; prolific historical writer with special interest in personal history; chief work was *Fortællinger af Fædrelandets Historie* [*Stories from the history of the fatherland*], I-II (1853); driving causes were spiritual and intellectual freedom, Scandinavianism, combatting German cultural imperialism; strenuous critic of Bishop J. P. Martensen; encounter with Barfod (1872) is jocularly described by Edmund Gosse (1849-1928) in *Two Visits to Denmark 1872, 1874* (1911); married (11 September 1841) Emilie Birkedal, sister of his political colleague Vilhelm Birkedal; his sister Anna was for some years housekeeper in Grundtvig household.

Barfod, Sjarlotte *318*; daughter of (Povl) Frederik Barfod; with sister Hulda, household friend of Grundtvig family; Barfod family lived in Frederiksberg Allé 55, near Gr's house (1859-67) in Gammel Kongevej.

Bastholm, Christian *155, 156*; 1740-1819; leading Danish rationalist theologian in tradition of 18th-c. Enlightenment, one of the so-called 'neologists' disliked by Gr, with later reputation for reducing theology to the banal and lifeless, and for florid rhetoric; after period as missionary priest in Smyrna and priest in Kastellet, Copenhagen, appointed preacher to royal court and

(1782) *kongelig confessionarius* (chaplain royal); his *Forsøg til en forbedret Plan for den udvortes Gudstjeneste* [Attempt at an improved plan for the outward divine service] (1785) aroused opposition – not least from N. E. Balle (*Vej til Hæderlighed for Geistlige* [The way to honesty for clergy], 1785) – and major liturgical controversy which carried over into 19th c.; but subsequently collaborator in Balle's *Lærebog i den Evangelisk-Christelige Religion* (1791) which was appointed for mandatory instruction (by rote-learning) in Danish schools after 1794; see also **neologists**.

Bath *334*; city in SW England notable for fine remains of Roman baths, possible inspiration of Anglo-Saxon poem *The Ruin*, known to and commented upon by Gr.

Bauta-Stenen *143*; term derived from Icelandic for large free-standing stone raised as memorial; here referring to monolith erected on Sjællands Odde by Captain L. Fribert, with poetic inscription by Gr, to commemorate heroic Danish dead of the *Prins Christian Frederik* destroyed in a three-hours engagement with five English ships off Sjællands Odde, 22 March 1808, as last gesture of annihilated Danish fleet in Napoleonic Wars; on its plinth is inscribed verse by Gr: *De Snekker mødtes i Kvæld paa Hav / Og Luften begyndte at Gløde. / De leged alt over den aabne Grav / Og Bølgerne gjordes saa røde. // Her er jeg sat til en Bautasteen / At vidne for Slægter i Norden. / Danske de vare, hvis møre Been / Under mig smuldre i Jorden, / Danske af Tunge, af Ære og af Id, / Thi skal de nævnes i løbende Tid / Fædrenes værdige Sønner* [The vessels met on the sea at eve / and the air it began to smoulder. / They sported all over the open grave / and the billows were rendered so ruddy. / Here I am set as a monolith / to attest to the North's generations: / Danish they were, they whose crumbling bones / moulder in earth underneath me, / Danish of speech and of honour and deed, / thus, though time passes, still shall they be named / worthy, the sons of their fathers].

Bayer *323*; a glove-manufacturer from Odense who visited Gr (1868) to discuss current issue of *valgmenigheder* [elective congregations]; typical of the *jævne folk* [ordinary folk] who had been Gr's main adherents from early days: "His circle consisted mostly of ordinary folk: craftsmen, grocers, small shopkeepers and suchlike. Among better known folk can be mentioned : J. C. Lindberg, theology student C. C. Harmsen who had attracted attention in the meetings at 'Rolighed', *cand. phil.* Parmo Carl Petersen (teacher at the Borgerdydsskole in Copenhagen), *assessor* [judge] N. M. Spandet, H. C. Hansgård (*fuldmægtig* [principal] in the Admiralty), *institutbestyrinde* [institute-director] Susanna Klingenberg, theology student C. S. Ley, master shoemaker J. Mouritsen, schoolteacher A. D. Wimmer, apprentice smith P. F. Cato, brewer C. J. Westberg, master carpenter A. Grundtvig, Hr. Kierkegård [probably P. C. Kierkegaard, brother of philosopher Søren, but could be their father M. P. Kierkegaard or L. K. Kierkegaard, dealer in silk and fabrics], *justitsråd* [senior ranking civil servant] Hjorthöj, *assessor* Hamgård, British Legation Secretary Browne" (tr. from Frederik Rönning, *N. F. S. Grundtvig*, 1911; describing Gr's supporters at Frederiks Kirke, 1832).

Beda, *21, 206*; 673-735; The Venerable Bede, Anglo-Saxon monk of Jarrow (Northumbria, England) and scholar; author of *Ecclesiastical History of the English People* (731); known to Gr from *c.* 1815 onwards through English editions and translations in the Royal Library Copenhagen; significant influence on Gr's view of 'universal history' and perceived as major historian of early Northern Christianity; "*Beda*, en angelsaxisk Munk (700 eft. Kr.), var i sin Tid vel den lærdeste

Mand i hele Kristenheden, og har iblandt andet efterladt en Historie om Kristendommens Ind-
førelse og Skæbne i Engelland, som er ubetalelig, og bekjendt under Navn af *Bedas Kirke-His-
torie*" [Bede, an Anglo-Saxon monk (A.D. 700), was in his time probably the most learned man
in the whole of Christendom, and left to posterity a history of the introduction and fortunes of
Christianity in England, which is priceless, and known under the name of *Bede's Ecclesiastical
History*] (Gr in *Krønnike-Rim* 1828, 1842); the *Ecclesiastical History* was translated into Danish
(1864) by Gr's follower, Christian Kragballe, with Gr's active encouragement.

Bededag *165*; 'Intercession Day,' day of special observance in Danish Church, fourth Friday after
Easter, called *Almindelig* [general, universal] or *Store* [great] *Bededag*; instituted 1686 as national
day of fasting, penance and prayer; originally strictly observed, an occasion for cautionary sermons; on Gr's ironical reference to his *Bededag*-sermonising; see also **berserk-gang**.

bees *69*; "these wonderful insects which from my childhood I have loved as much as I hated the
others" (Gr); aged nine, boarder at school in "Jylland's dark heathlands," Gr amused himself
among Jutish peasants, the bees, and his books; in lectures later published as *Mands Minde* he
found in bees a natural metaphor for England's everyday industriousness as he observed it in
his visits 1829-31.

Bellevue *235*; park and beach at Klampenborg north of Copenhagen, popular resort from early
18th c. and used for public gatherings such as commemoration of emancipation of peasantry.

Bentsen, Lars M. *323, 324*; 1838-1919, businessman, member of Norwegian *Storthing*, educational
pioneer; having visited Gr and folk-highschools in Dk, established (1868) folk-highschool in Re,
Stjørdalen, becoming its principal.

Beowulf *110, 111, 114, 120, 130, 134, 168*; Anglo-Saxon poem of some 31,000 lines surviving in unique
manuscript (London, British Library Cotton Vitellius Axv) datable *ca.* 1000; poem has ancient
roots in legend-history of NW Europe, particularly of Dk and Sweden, therefore attracted attention of 18th and 19th c. Danish historians; first fully transcribed, edited, published (1815) by
Danish State Archivist G. J. Thorkelin; publication directly inspired Gr to learn Anglo-Saxon,
to engage with Thorkelin (*via* periodical articles, acrimoniously) in the first ever substantial
critical discussion of *Beowulf* text, to read widely (1815 onwards) in extensive surviving Anglo-Saxon writings, and to make three successive visits to England (1829-31) with significant
consequences for his subsequent life's work; Gr published both a Danish 'translation' (*Bjowulfs
Drape. Et Gothisk Helte-Digt fra forrige Aar-Tusinde,* 1820) and an edition (*Beowulfes Beorh,*
1861), both with important introductions and prefatory poems in Danish and Anglo-Saxon;
he also published lengthy interpretation of poem in his periodical *Danne-Virke* (1816-19), in
universal terms of struggle between Truth and the Lie in history, under providential God; *Beowulf*'s central concern with kingship and community and struggle between order and chaos in
a providentially God-governed universe furnished Gr with both affirmation of and inspiration
for his distinctive notions of universal history, and with themes, motifs and idiom useful in expression of his national-romantic perception of Danish national identity and communality; for
Gr, it has been suggested, "*Beowulf* was the *missing link* which linked the antiquity of Dk and the
North to the mainstream of universal-historical progression from Babel, Hellas and Rome – by-

passing Germany, preceding Luther!" (tr. after Ole Vind, 1999); Gr's response to *Beowulf* and the Anglo-Saxon legacy as a whole comprises one of the most striking examples of creative cultural appropriation of medieval antiquities in the 19th c. and its legacy among Danish scholars is evident in work of such as Peter Frederik Adolph Hammerich, Ludvig Peter Schrøder, Frederik Rönning and Andreas Haarder; see also **Schrøder**, Ludvig Peter; ***Bjovulfs Drape***; **Munch**, Peter Andreas; **Grendel's Mother**.

Berg, Chresten Poulsen *244*; 1829-91; teacher, politician; having started working-life as shepherd's boy, was guided by parish priest into education, qualified as teacher; emerged from constitutional struggle of 1848 as active political supporter of Gr's bid for greater freedoms in civil and ecclesiastical spheres, became (1870) leading architect of *Det Forenede Venstre* [The United Left] parliamentary grouping and author of its programme; collaborated in establishment of number of *Venstre*-orientated provincial newspapers which enhanced independence of provincial press from opinion-dominating Copenhagen press; with such as Sophus Høgsbro, remained radical activist and in tussle to inherit Gr-mantle after Gr's death gained support of Gr's widow Asta; after split with Sophus Høgsbro and others in March 1877 he quit the *Det Forenede Venstre* and with 27 colleagues formed *Folketingets Venstre* [Parliamentary Left]; see also **Høgsbro**, Sophus Magdalus.

Bergen *149, 282*; Norway's second largest city, earlier its capital; harbour established in 1070, protected by Bergenhus castle; became a Hanseatic port with links to Germany, Holland, Iceland, England, Scotland; thus developed as important cultural centre, prosperous in 19th c. as Norway's largest town; leading intellectuals reacted against the imposed union with Sweden (1814).

Berling's newspaper *66, 156*; *Berlings-Avisen*; originally *Kiøbenhavnske Danske Post-Tidende*; Danish newspaper founded 1749 by Ernst Heinrich Berling (1708-1750); at first published twice weekly with parallel French and German editions; under absolutist rule with press censorship, rose to pre-eminent status, being privileged to report foreign news and appointed as journal in which Sjællanders obligatorily placed their announcements; 1808 government-nominated co-editor was installed, and name changed to *Danske Statstidende*; 1833 began publishing every weekday, renamed *Berlingske Politiske og Avertissements-tidende*; 1834 distinguished editor M. N. Nathanson oversaw great increase in circulation; modern descendant is *Berlingske Tidende*.

berserk-gang *165*; berserk-attack, reckless assault by frenzied warriors, often mercenary shock-troops, usually in a gang, as described in various Icelandic sagas; the frenzy sometimes attributed to possession by Óðinn; the term is used ironically by Gr, with reference to his writings before 1815, to echo the terminology of his detractors' scorn for "this poetic fooling about with old superstition and ancient monuments as for my raving mad berserk-gang, *Bededag*-sermonising and dirge-singing [*Dødninge-Sang*; literally 'corpse-song']" (Gr); references appear most probably to be to his *Roskilde-Riim* (1812; "old superstition and ancient monuments"), *Optrin af Kæmpelivets Undergang i Nord* [Episodes from the downfall of the warrior-life in the North; 2 vols, 1809-11] ("berserk-gang"), his dimission (probational) sermon (1810) and his Christian-didactic, judgmental and moralising *Kort Begreb af Verdens Krønike* [Concise view of universal history; 1812, 1814] ("*Bededag*-sermonising") and perhaps his *Mindesang paa Fædres Gravhøj* [Memorial song upon the fathers' grave-mound; pub. 1815] ("dirge-singing, corpse-song"); see also **Bededag**.

Besværgelsen *154* , also named *Exorcismen, Djævle-Besværgelsen, Djævleuddrivelsen*; the exorcism, expulsion of devils, element in baptismal rite in both Greek and Roman Catholic tradition, one of several rituals which medieval church performed at church door; initially (1521) excluded by Luther from reformed rites, subsequently reintroduced by him in shortened form; opposition to its use by Christian IV (1606), who had it omitted from baptism of daughter Elisabet, was successfully countered by Hans Poulsen Resen (1561-1638, Bishop of Sjælland 1615-1638); abolished in parts of Slesvig and Holsten 1736 and finally (1783) in Denmark and Norway with acceptance of Bishop N. E. Balle's revision of baptismal ritual, so that Gr was among very first Danish children to be baptised without Exorcism; see **Daabspagten**; **Balle,** Nicolaj Edinger; **Brorson,** Christian Frederik

Bibelen forsvarer sig selv *155*; The Bible is its own defence; periodical issued (1797-1802) by Bishop N. E. Balle in item-by-item refutation of rationalist attacks on Bible by Otto Horrebow; see **Balle,** Nicolaj Edinger; **Horrebow,** Otto.

Bibelkrøniken *199*; *En liden Bibelkrønike for Børn og Menigmand* [A little Bible-History for children and the general reader], published by Gr 1814 and used by him in preparation of confirmands.

Bible, The *85 and passim*; first Danish-language Bible after Reformation was that of Christiern Pedersen for Christian III (1550), based upon Luther's German Bible; revised versions of this were promulgated by subsequent kings; the first Danish Bible translated directly from the original languages was made by Hans Poulsen Resen (1607) revised 1647 by Hans Svane, which remained, through numerous revisions, the authorised text of the Danish Bible until completely new translations were issued in 1931 (Old Testament) and 1948 (New Testament); currently authorised Bible, another new translation, was issued 1992. Gr was brought up on (taught by his mother to read upon) Christian VI's Bible (1740), where the Old Testament chapters are headed by references to their fulfilment in the New Testament, imparting a view of scriptural history as a tissue of providentially ordered prefigurations and fulfilments, a view which, powerfully sustained by the Church's cycles of liturgically ordained readings, reached back into medieval biblical exegesis and could still in the 19th c. warrantably furnish a model for a methodology of historical writing. In the light of Gr's long drawn out battle against rationalism and rationalist approaches to scriptural scholarship, and of the development of his own theology of the Living Word, it was an over-simplification by Edmund Gosse to report of Gr to an English readership that "He went straight back to the Bible, and indeed almost exclusively to the Gospels. He took the Lord's Prayer and the Sermon on the Mount as a basis of practical Christianity." See also **Luther,** Martin; **Bang,** Kathrine Marie; **Complutenser**; **Balle,** Nicolaj Edinger; **Bible is its own Defence,** The; **Hornemann,** Claus Frees; **Horrebow,** Otto; **neologists**; **skriftteologer**; **mageløse Opdagelse,** den; **Word, The Living**.

Bible and rationalism *155, 162, 169*

Bible, arbitrary interpretations of *118, 284*

Bible, Gr's use of *25, 120, 155, 160, 161, 169, 198, 289, 292, 307, 308, 328*

Bible, history *199, 217*

Bible is its own Defence, *The 155*; see **Bibelen forsvarer sig selv**.

Bible, rationalist mockery of *155, 162, 169*

Bible, translations *289*

Bible-History; see **Bibelkrøniken**.

Bible societies *162*; The Danish Bible Society (*Bibelselskabet for Danmark*) was established in 1814 with aim of disseminating the Bible; in 1886 it was granted right to print authorised version of Danish Bible and churches were officially ordered to devote New Year's Day collection to its support – though from beginning it had derived income from collections organised by individual churches as well as from subscriptions to membership.

Bibliotheca Anglo-Saxonica *133, 134, 334*; Gr's "Prospectus, and Proposals of a Subscription, for the Publication of the most valuable Anglo-Saxon Manuscripts, illustrative of the early Poetry and Literature of our Language. Most of which have never yet been printed" (Black, Young and Young, Foreign Booksellers to the King, Tavistock Street, Covent Garden, London, 1831), proposing and justifying comprehensive selection in 10 volumes; earlier English and Danish scholars known to Gr had urged publication of Anglo-Saxon England's rich legacy of writings but Gr's active presence in London (three visits 1829-31) and his Prospectus galvanised Society of Antiquaries to launch rival programme spearheaded by Benjamin Thorpe (1782-1870), resulting in string of major editions; though his labours in reading and transcribing were enormous, he published (independently, and later) only *The Phoenix* (1840) and *Beowulf* (1861).

Billed-Sprog *227, 250, 251, 257, 272, 300*; metaphor, literally 'picture-language.' "*Billed-Sprog* kalder man det, naar man med Navnene paa Dyr, Fugle, Træer og alle Haande synlige Ting, ikke mener disse Ting selv, men noget usynligt og aandeligt, som de tænkes [at] ligne og paa en Maade svare til" [It is called 'Billed-Sprog' when, by the names of animals, birds, trees and all kinds of visible things are meant not those things themselves but something invisible and spiritual which they are thought to resemble and in some way answer to] (Gr in *Krønnike-Rim* 1842). Fundamental to Gr's self-expression is his deep-seated mental habit of seeking and of coining metaphor, in a manner and to an extent worthy of the medieval exegetes and Christian Neoplatonists. His contemporary, Bishop H. L. Martensen, wrote with much insight: "There was especially one point in which I sympathised utterly and with all my heart: his conception of corporality [*Legemligheden*]. Although the spirit [*Aanden*] was for him the foremost, indeed in truth the sole reality [*det eneste i Sandhed Virkelige*], yet he could not think of the spirit without corporality, and a spirit from which all nature and corporality were excluded was for him merely a vapid spirit, the Rationalists' spirit, with which he could have nothing to do. Thus he had within his outlook a loftier spiritual realism [*en høiere, aandelig Realisme*], which was indeed also to be found in Lutherdom, particularly in the sacramental doctrine. Here I could entirely agree, and likewise also in the great significance he attached to that metaphorical language which had for him a greater truth and reality than abstract designations, and whose loftiest form he found partly in the Holy Scriptures, in the sayings of the prophets and of Christ, and partly in the myths, in the symbolic language of the North. The language of metaphor was not to be played about with, and he quite often declared that genuine poets treated metaphorical language seriously and through it expressed the truth of their understanding of life." Gr's discourses, especially his poetry, therefore have an inexhaustible richness and complexity of nuance, sometimes to the point of impenetrability; thus his associate Frederik Barfod (1811-96), whilst seeing Gr as "the personified spirit [*Aand*] of the North, the North's pathfinder [*Nordens Anfører*] since none saw as clearly as he which way the spirit of the North is going and leading" also felt obliged to add that "Grundtvig has the misfortune that almost no one, not even his best friends, understands what he means." See also **Aand**; *Nordens Mythologi* eller *Sindbilled-Sprog*.

Birch, Andreas, *88*; 1758-1829; theologian, studied ancient biblical manuscripts in Rome, launched upon major new edition of New Testament; failing to secure academic preferment, entered ministry, rose to become Bishop of Lolland-Falster 1803, translated to Århus 1805; offended by Gr's interference in educational matters on Falster.

Birkedal, Schøller Parelius Vilhelm *22, 256, 257, 271, 272, 293*; 1809-92; *cand. theol.* 1834; teacher, priest, author, hymnwriter; at Borgerdydskole, Christianshavn, taught by such notables as P. A. Fenger (1799-1878), J. C. Lindberg (1797-1857) and L. C. Müller (1806-51), there befriended such as the later politician C. C. Hall (1812-88), much enthused as student (1830s) by national Romanticism ('poetry, the fatherland, liberty'); engaged P. C. Kierkegaard (1805-88) as his *manuduktør* (tutorial assistant to students especially of theology, law); attended Gr's sermons in Vor Frelsers Kirke and Frederiks Kirke; sympathetic to Gr's outlook, championed his causes in print, consulted closely with Gr in own disputes involving *præstefrihed* (pastor's freedom to teach according to own best understanding, and without restriction to own incumbency) and *sognebaandsløsning* (freeing of individual parishioner to join congregation other than that of own parish priest); 1849 appointed as parish priest to Ryslinge but his activism led to dismissal 1865 (his bold response was "*Kongen har dømt; Folket skal dømme*" [The King has passed judgment; the people shall pass judgment] – that is, it is the people who shall in the end decide); became *valgmenighedspræst* (priest appointed by congregation's own election, though remaining within the national church) in Ryslinge after change in law (1868) provoked largely by his case; took lead in establishing Grundtvigian folk-highschool in Ryslinge, where Christen Kold (1816-70) was appointed principal (1851-53) under Birkedal's tutelage, "to educate the Danish agricultural class so that it could make use of the civil liberty it had been granted" (Kold); taken to Supreme Court (1877) and fined for ordaining a priest to serve Danish-sympathetic congregation in (German-controlled) North Slesvig; strongly pietistic, uncompromisingly *ejderdansk* in nationalistic political stance, demanding recognition of River Ejder as Dk's natural and historical southern frontier; with Gr, saw Danes as a chosen people; to the end, vigorously and controversially pursued conservative objectives in theology and in politics; editor (1879-82) of *Dansk Folkeblad. En Røst til og fra Folket* [Danish folk-paper. A voice to and from the people]; arguably Gr's most influential disciple; author of *Om Stænderforhandlingerne i Roeskilde* [On the Estates-negotiations in Roskilde] (1839), concerning political negotiations in Stændertiden [The Estates period] 1831-48 and *De syv Folkemenigheder i Lyset af Herrens Spaadomsord* [The seven congregations in the light of the Lord's words of prophecy] (1877) concerning Gr and universal-historical ideas; see also **Ryslinge**.

Bjarkemaal *253*; *Bjarkemál* was an ancient Norse poem, surviving only in several reworkings or retellings; in 12th c. freely rendered in Latin in Saxo's *Gesta Danorum*; free rendition also occurs in medieval Icelandic *Hrólfs saga kraka* [The saga of Hrolf Crow] (this saga being in part an analogue of story told of early Danish kings in Anglo-Saxon poem *Beowulf*, and Böðvarr Bjarki, foremost of King Hrólf's warriors, for whom *Bjarkemál* is named, being an analogue of Beowulf); poem represents rallying call of Hjalti for Hrólf's warriors to make last stand around their king against overwhelming battle odds; poem was sung by court poet of King Olaf Haraldsson at Battle of Stiklastad (1030) to rally Olaf's men in battle in which he lost his life; this highly charged poem was reworked by Grundtvig in *Danne-Virke* III (1817) as song *Sol er oppe* [The sun is up] with its rallying-cry "Vågner, vågner, danske helte!" [Awake, awake, you Danish heroes!]; proverbially, a '*Bjarkemaal*' is therefore a stirring call to heroic deeds in defence of all that is most precious; Gr's vigorous advocacies were jocularly likened by C. J. Brandt to the *Bjarkemaal*.

Bjovulfs Drape *120*; Anglo-Saxon poem rendered in Danish verse (1820) by Gr; subtitled *Et Gothisk Helte-Digt fra forrige Aar-Tusinde af Angel-Saxisk paa Danske Riim ved Nik. Fred. Sev. Grundtvig Præst* [A Gothic Heroic Poem of the previous Millennium from the Anglo-Saxon in Danish Verse by NFSG Priest]; dedicated to his patron Privy Councillor Johan Bülow (1751-1828); furnished with skilful Danish and pastiche Anglo-Saxon verse introduction, lengthy prose introduction discussing text and interpretation, notes (some being original contributions to Beowulf text-scholarship), and name-list; rendition is in variety of metres, strophic forms and rhyme schemes; aspired, albeit in vain – so Gr wrote in his article *Folkelighed og Christendom* in *Dansk Kirketidende* 107 (1847) – to *opvække Folkeligheden fra de Døde* [awaken *folkelighed* from the dead], and to enrich national historical awareness and to be healthful reading for children, but achieved only disappointing sales; see ***Beowulf***; also **Schrøder**, Ludvig Peter.

Bjørn, Karen *277*; 1742-1795; subject of a poem Gr was moved to write (1813) on reading small work (Til Karen Biørns Minde, 1795) published in her memory by her husband Tyge Rothe (1731-1795), widely travelled poet, philosopher, land-reformer, prominent figure in 18th-c. Copenhagen intellectual and cultural life; Gr's poem of same title, turned by a short supplement into kind of love-poem (published in his collection *Kvædlinger eller Smaakvad*, 1815) to Elisabeth Blicher who after courtship of seven years became his first wife (1818), represents Rothe as forerunner of new age of more expressive emotional relationship between partners in marriage.

Bjørnson, Bjørnstjerne Martinius *299, 333, 336*; 1832-1910; Norwegian author; Nobel prizewinner for literature (1903); though he studied and worked (theatre, journalism) in Oslo and spent periods abroad in Copenhagen (including frequent visits to Vartov where he found the hymn-singing "more powerful than any mission" and to Gr) and in Rome (where he wrote innovatory issue-focussed drama anticipatory of his contemporary Ibsen), his most popular writings (plays, novels, short stories, poetry) remained rooted in Norwegian history and folk-life, often expressed strong nationalistic and Scandinavian allegiances; enthusiast for Danish-Norwegian folk-highschool ideals; revolutionary thinker, polemicist, social reformer, involved in politics; caused furore with speeches in 1872 (including one at Vennemøde in Vartov, days after Gr's death), proposing that after French defeat by Prussia (1871) Scandinavia should put out new 'signals' changing traditional disposition of hostility towards Germany; thereafter regarded by many Grundtvigians with deep suspicion, compounded by his growing enthusiasm for European positivism and the cultural radicalism of Dane Georg Brandes (1842-1927) who included Bjørnson among *Det moderne Gjennembruds Mænd* [Men of modernity's breakthrough; 1883]; symptomatic of late 19th c. European secularisation, Bjørnson's subsequent break with church and Christian faith did not damage his status as one of the shapers of modern and independent Norway.

black school, the; see **sorte Skole,** den.

Black, Young and Young *133, 134*; London publishers, Foreign Booksellers to the King, at time of Gr's negotiations over editing and publishing Anglo-Saxon texts; having published (1830) Gr's *Prospectus, and Proposals of a Subscription, for the Publication of the most valuable Anglo-Saxon Manuscripts, illustrative of the early Poetry and Literature of our Language, Most of which have never yet been printed* Black surreptitiously entered into rival arrangement led by Benjamin Thorpe (1782-1870) backed by London Society of Antiquaries, which went ahead; Gr recalls English deviousness and embarrassment with amusement in *Mands Minde*; seven of their letters to Gr are preserved in Arkiv Fasc. 448.3 See also ***Bibliotheca Anglo-Saxonica***; and **Milo,** Jacob Frederik.

Blekinge; see **Magnussen,** Finn.

Blicher family *62, 88, 208, 211*; family of *Provst* (Rural Dean) Didrik Nicolai (1746-1805) and Mette (Poulsen) Blicher (1751-1826) in Gundslev, Falster; four daughters – Bodil Marie Elisabeth, Anne Pouline, Elisabeth Kirstine Margrethe, Jane Mathia – and two sons – Peder, Hans Jakob; visited by the young Gr while staying with his brother Otto (priest in neighbouring Torkild-strup); Gr, though initially more interested in Bodil Marie Elisabeth (called Marie by family and friends; subsequently married Poul Egede Glahn) later (1818) married Elisabeth Kirstine Margrethe (Lise).

Blicher, *Provst* Didrik Nicolai; see **Blicher** family.

Blicher, Elisabeth Christina Margaretha; see **Grundtvig,** Elisabeth Kirstine Margrethe.

Blicher, Jane Mathia *207-209, 212, 220, 224, 232, 234, 240*; 1792-1853; 'Aunt Jane' [Tante Jane]; un-married sister of Gr's first wife, Elisabeth (Lise) who lived for a period with the Grundtvigs until Lise's death; evidently much esteemed by family and friends.

Blicher, Mette *208*; wife of *Provst* Didrik Blicher, mother of Gr's first wife Elisabeth (Lise).

Blicher, Steen Steensen *164*; 1782-1848; priest, poet and author; transitional figure in the development of literary realism, noted particularly for short stories often recounted through an I-narrator or observer, with plot-motifs reflecting Romanticism's interest in folk-legacy – stories of hauntings, madness induced by love denied, noble-spirited robbers (*Røverstuen* [Robbers' kitchen], *Hosekræmmeren* [The Hosier]); but typically set in vividly characterised heathlands of Jylland (Jutland), concerned with lives of peasantry, travellers and such, tending to express a dark fatalism (*En Landsbydegns Dagbog* [Diary of a country parish clerk]), reproducing dialect speech of regions regarded from distant Copenhagen as semi-barbarous wilderness (*E Bind-stouw* [A knitting-parlour]); common great-grandfather with Lise (Blicher) Grundtvig; resident in Valkendorfs Kollegium Copenhagen (1808-09) same period as Gr though no special friendship arose.

Bloch, Tønne *157*; 1733-1803, Bishop in Fyn (1786) who according to Gr was so averse to *Evangelical-Christian Hymnal* of 1798 that he retained in use old hymnal of Thomas Kingo – against which (and "against all kinds of superstition and other vices") Gr therefore preached in the spiritual desert (as he saw it) of Langeland (1805).

Blom, Hans Jørgen *206, 238*; 1796-1864; Colonel in Danish army; friend of Gr's youth; father of Marie Blom, friend of Gr's children.

Blom, Marie *205-207, 210, 211*; 1824-1901; daughter of Colonel H. J. Blom (1796-1864), friend of Gr's youth; she and brother Vilhelm were childhood friends of Gr's children, of which period she has left an account.

Blom, Vilhelm *206, 208-212, 214, 218*; 1826-50; son of Colonel Hans Jørgen Blom, friend of Gr's youth; brother of Marie Blom, childhood friend of Gr's children; as child, boarded for a period with Grundtvigs to be tutored with Johan and Svend; later lieutenant in Danish army; following his death at Battle of Isted (1850) in Three Years' War over status of Slesvig and Holsten, Gr wrote memorial poem *Søn af Vennen fra de unge Dage* [Son of my friend from the days of youth], published in periodical *Danskeren* III, 1850, 540-41 (*PS* VII, 304-06).

Boglærdom *227*; book-learning, bookish scholarship; see **Bog-Orm**.

Bog-Orm *110, 124, 132, 149, 172, 227*; bookworm; Gr's attitude towards the written word and bookish scholarship [*Boglærdom*] is ambivalent; in some contexts he is famously scornful of the moribund character of learned books and those bookworms, denizens of the study, who pore over them, disengaged from vital realities; in transcribing the Anglo-Saxon Exeter Book it suited him to find a riddle with the agreed solution 'Bookworm' in which the worm devours many words but is not a whit the wiser, and a riddle with his proposed solution 'Word and script' where, when the Word says it is sometimes overcome by sleep, Gr notes "nemlig naar Ordet skrives" [namely, when the word is written down]; but for his own part he was content to accept that "jeg […] ei er andet […] end en gammel Vartous-Præst, Rimsmed og Bogorm, med en Smule ung Rigsdagsmand paa Enden" [I am nothing but an old Vartov-priest, rhyme-smith and bookworm, with a bit of a young parliamentarian at the end]; for books, despite their abuse, retained an important place in support of the living word and the national historical culture, and Gr the bookworm is not, as his detractors would have it, fundamentally anti-intellectual; see also **Bogstav-Skriften**; **Ordet**; **Ord,** det levende.

Bogstav-Skriften *162, 169*; alphabetic writing, literal text; strictly speaking, writing system distinguished (by use of alphabetic letters) from alternatives such as pictographic; but for Gr having various further specific connotations and associations; since Rationalist scholarship had undermined trust in literal word of Scriptures Gr sought divine authority in the spoken word, the living word; while in the field of secular education he found parrot-learning and recitation of prescribed texts stultifying, and championed instead oral dialogue; often he echoed St Paul's words, that 'the letter killeth' and he could describe *bogstavskrift* as a 'mummified' (*balsameret*) form of the spoken word; closely linked with this was his fundamentally poetic cast of mind which exalted the metaphorical, with its rich creative pliability, in both his reading and his writing; therefore he "did not for a moment share that superstitious faith in *Bogstav-Skriften*" which prevailed among others; nevertheless, Gr often referred to himself as a *Bog-Orm* [bookworm], though it was with some justice remarked: If Grundtvig could have been more observant of his own self, then he would not, in the way he did, have used "book-learning" almost as a term of abuse (Zeuthen); see also **Ordet**; **Ord,** det levende.

Boisen, Frederik (Frits) Engelhardt *240, 259, 284, 305*; 1808-82; son of Bishop P. O. Boisen of Lolland-Falster; *cand. theol.* 1830; priest in various parishes including Skørpinge near Skælskør (west Sjælland) and Vilstrup (Sønderjylland); steadily more attracted to Gr's concept of Church and of *folkelighed*; for farewell ceremony on B's move from Sønderjylland, Edvard Lembcke (1815-97) wrote *Vort Modersmaal er dejligt* [Lovely is our mother-tongue], quickly established in repertoire of nationalist song; popular and powerful speaker, for a time (from 1837) associated with *de gudelige forsamlinger* (popular religious gatherings held in locations other than church, breaching laws restricting acts of worship to churches and priests to their own congregation), though regarded as moderating influence; from 1845 one of Gr's most active supporters, politically attached to the *Venstre*; member of Constituent Assembly (*Den grundlovgivende Rigsforsamling*) drafting Constitution of 1849; as elected member of the *Landsting* (1866) strenuous opponent (with Gr) of conservative revisions to Constitution; editor (1852-79) of periodical *Budstikken til oplysning og opbyggelse* [The Courier for enlightenment and education], mouthpiece for Grundtvigian ideas; wife Eline (1813-71) wrote private memoirs from 1856 onwards (excerpts published 1985 as *Men størst af alt er kærligheden* [But the greatest of these is love] and the whole published 1999 as *Eline Boisens Erindringer* [EB's memoirs]) vividly documenting subordinated role and status of wives and mothers in her lifetime, and notably critical of idealised image of family life within Grundtvigian circles.

Boisen, Peter Outzen *157*; 1762-1831; Bishop of Lolland-Falster; as priest (1787) in Vesterborg, under patronage of reformer *Grev* [Count] Johan Ludvig Greve (1751-1801), brother of statesman *Grev* Christian Ditlev Frederik Reventlow (1748-1827), established *seminarium* for training teachers; emerged as gifted proponent of rationalism; appointed (1805) Bishop of Lolland-Falster diocese; thereafter remained more interested in education than in church, though issued (1806) a *Plan til Forbedring ved den offentlige Gudsdyrkelse* (*Plan for the improvement of public divine worship*) containing proposals for new liturgy, subject of much public wrangling; six of his sons became priests, most notable being Frederik Engelhardt Boisen and Lars Nannestad Boisen.

Boisen, Peter Outzen *24, 240, 241, 283, 284, 286, 288, 289*; 1815-62; son of Bishop P. O. Boisen (1762-1831); *cand. theol.* Copenhagen 1841; from his youth, a great admirer of Gr and his ideas on education and church; after serving as teacher in Queen Caroline Amalie's Charity School [Asylskole] established 1841 for orphaned children in Copenhagen (of which Gr was a director), became its principal (1851); appointed as Gr's curate at Vartov (1854); gained repute as pastor of children and the poor; contributed to cause of *folkelighed* and consolidation of national identity through role of song, especially on traditional and historical Danish themes suitable for use in Grundtvigian folk-highschools; associated with publication of song-collections (precursors of the *Højskolesangbog* [Highschool Songbook] which has been repeatedly republished since first edition 1894) and collaborated with Christian Bull in publication of melodies to these texts in *100 Melodier til 'Nye og gamle Viser af og for Danske Folk' samlede for en Deel efter mundtlig Overlevering* [100 melodies to *New and old ballads by and for Danish folk*, collected in part from oral transmission] (Copenhagen, 1852); married (1847) Gr's daughter Meta; Boisens archetypally exemplify distinctive life of the 'Grundtvigian' family; a sister was first wife of P. C. Kierkegaard; Boisen's early death was great grief and loss to family and congregation.

Bolton, Clara *286, 288, 290*; 1805-39; briefly prominent figure in London society; dazzled Gr, who met her in London 1830 at a reception in home of Charles Heaton, with her readiness and capacity to talk about "everything" in way of which men were incapable; invited Gr to visit her at home, but when, on his way there, Gr called in at Heaton's house to brief himself more fully he learned that not only was she married but that her husband had been present at same reception; Gr decided immediately that not having been introduced to husband he could not respectably call upon wife, which sense of etiquette saved him from potential embarrassment, for Mrs Bolton was wife of a society physician who reputedly condoned her infidelities as means of gaining high-class clients; for a period in early 1830s she was lover of Benjamin Disraeli (1804-81) and then mistress of Disraeli's political patron, Sir Francis Sykes. Back in London following year, Gr wrote home to his wife Lise to assert that despite teasing from Heatons he had neither seen Mrs Bolton nor would even remember what she looked like; nevertheless she is one of three women he celebrated in poem *Smaa-Fruerne* [The little women; 1844] as having been (other than his wife) the loves of his life, and biographers have generally accepted that, whether in reality or whether in Gr's symbol-seeking imagination, meeting with her effected some kind of significant revelation and liberation in him; see also **Ælve-Dronning**; **kvindelige**, det; **Hjertet**.

bombardment of 1807 *18, 79, 99, 156, 158*; British fleet-based assault upon Copenhagen, intended to prevent Dk (allied with Napoleon) from aiding Napoleon's policy of crippling Britain by blockading British shipping-routes; from 2nd to 5th September, following military siege of city since 15 August, British troops fired Congreve's rockets (delivering explosion and fire) from batteries beyond defensive lakes to west of city, sighting particularly on spire of Vor Frue Kirke; reportedly the church's carillon played as tower burned and cheering from British batteries was heard inside city as it fell; estimated 1600 civilians killed, 1000 wounded, over 300 houses destroyed as well as major public buildings; cultural losses such as destruction of manuscripts and books in the University Library and elsewhere were irreparable; when 72-year-old General Ernst Peymann, entrusted with defence of city, negotiated capitulation to end slaughter and destruction, regent Crown Prince Frederik (later Frederik vi) had him court-martialled and dismissed service without pension; Danish fleet was carried off or destroyed, leaving Dk with only two ships of war which were not in port at that time; consequences of British action for Dk's national economy was catastrophic, contributing to National Bankruptcy (1813); as assault on civilian population, bombardment was widely viewed by contemporaries in England and elsewhere in Europe as dishonourable and barbarous.

bonde *294*; peasant, peasant-farmer; when 19th c. opened, nearly 80% of Dk's population of 926, 000 (census 1801) were country-dwellers (11% of population lived in Copenhagen, 10% in market-towns); most owner-farmers and some tenant-farmers lived reasonably well but many *husmænd* (farm labourers, their income often dependent upon daily hire, their house or smallholding subject to insecurities of tenancy conditions) lived at merest subsistence level; until Constitution of 1849 imposed duty of military service upon all able-bodied male citizens, only men in these agricultural classes had obligation to train for and perform military service when called upon to mobilise, though they were permitted to pay for another to serve in their stead; in last quarter of 18th c., significant abolition of ties upon peasantry was enacted and modest educational initiatives were undertaken, but country-dwellers remained largely underprivileged, uneducated and looked down upon (unless romanticised by poets and painters) far into 19th c.; see **bondestand, den danske**; **Bondefriheden**; **Stavnsbaandet**; **Bondeskole**, Higher; **Bondevennerne**.

Bondefriheden *235*; freeing of the (male) peasantry from restrictions upon their freedom of movement (and thus also upon their freedom to market their labour), with particular reference to *Stavnsbaandets Ophævelse* (20 June 1788); see **Stavnsbaandet**.

Bondesen, Nicolai William Theodorus *20, 198*; 1823-96; *cand. theol.*; priest; 1863 appointed tutor to royal children at palace of Fredensborg, Dk; 1872 appointed to incumbency of Præstø-Skibbinge south Sjælland; published (1874) *Minde om N. F. S. Grundtvigs Præstegjerning i Aaret 1821*, brief memoir relating to Gr's incumbency at Præstø-Skibbinge (1821-24); some suspicion of mythologising subsequently cast upon some portions.

Bondeskole, Higher *24, 293*; innovatory kind of 'peasant-school' to extend duration of education for peasant population, advocated by Christen Kold (1816-70), pioneer of Danish *friskole* [independent school], and realised when (1849) financial support from leading Grundtvigians committed to improving education of peasant class established him as principal of school at Ryslinge (opened 1 November 1851); he stubbornly maintained his original conviction that boys should enter at age of 14-16 against Gr's insistence that effort would be wasted on youths under 18, but later found and admitted that Gr was right; see also **Ryslinge**; **bonde**.

bondestand, den danske *293*; the Danish peasant class, agricultural class, who were not finally divested of near-feudal ties until 19th c. and whose well-being and advancement supporters of Gr pursued educationally and politically, particularly after the granting of the Constitution of 1849; see also **bonde**; **bondefriheden**; **Bondevennerne**.

bondeven; see **Bondevennerne**.

Bondevennerne *144, 145, 239*; members of Danish political association, *Bondevennernes Selskab* [Association of friends of the *bonde*], formed 1846 under leadership of Anton Frederik Tscherning (1795-1874), Danish officer and democrat opposed to privileges and class distinctions; aim was to use political means to free the *bonde* (plural *bønder*, peasants and farmers), from impositions, obligations and differentials, relating to persons and to land, which substantially disadvantaged them relative to other social groups (especially of course big landowners), including still-surviving villeinage and widespread copyholder status; the *bondebevægelse* [peasant movement] was partly rooted in religious *forsamlinger* (devotional gatherings held outside framework of, and to some extent in defiance of, established Church) and its causes chimed with ideals of *folkelighed* as propounded by Gr and implemented by such of his followers as Peter Rørdam, priest at Mern in south Sjælland; ideals also attracted urban supporters such as co-founder Orla Lehmann (1810-70), leader of National Liberals in *Folketing* 1851-53 and *Landsting* 1854-70, champion of civil liberties, scandinavianism, status of Danish language; notable leaders were Balthasar Mathias Christensen (1807-82) and Jens Andersen Hansen (1806-77); *Bondevennerne* achieved strong representation in Constituent Assembly (*Den grundlovgivende Rigsforsamling*) and thereby contributed to strongly democratic character of Constitution of 5 June 1849 (later curtailed in conservative revisions of 1866); see also **bonde**; **bondestand**, den danske.

bookworm; see **Bog-Orm**.

Borchs Kollegium *64, 89, 99, 108, 228, 235*; founded in Copenhagen 1689 by Ole Borch (1626-90; historian, philologist, chemist, court physician, botanist, professor in University of Copenhagen) as free residence for 16 students; together with Valkendorfs Kollegium has played significant role in Danish intellectual life; locale for Gr's lectures (1838), following his release from censorship (1837), subsequently published as *Mands Minde* [*Within Living Memory*].

borgerlig *84, 103, 154, 170, 293, 317, 335*; adjective sometimes applied to urban middle class and middle-class culture, approximately in sense of 'bourgeois' but used more commonly with broader sense of 'public' or 'civil' as in 'civil liberty' as when Christen Kold (1816-70) urged address to question of "what should be done to educate the Danish agricultural class [*den Danske Bondestand*] so that it could make use of the civil liberty [*den borgerlige Frihed*] it had been granted."

Bornholm *80, 83, 157*; Baltic island *ca.* 588 sq. km south of Sweden, forming part of Kingdom of Dk, notable for medieval round churches, major fortress of Hammershus, granite quarries, scenic beauty; birthplace of Gr's university friend Peter Nikolai Skougaard.

Borup, Johan *276, 325, 327*; 1853-1946; folk-highschool principal, writer; trained in theology, he chose to make education his career, having been early attracted to the folk-highschool concept; in 1891, after many years employment in teaching, he established a modest school to provide "Videregaaende Undervisning for ikke-studerede Herrer og Damer" [Further tuition for Gentlemen and Ladies who have not studied], which gave educational access to working-class men and women who often needed instruction in basic reading, writing and calculation; in 1916 Borups Højskole was formally constituted which by 1926 was able to move into the spacious and dignified premises on Frederiksholm Kanal in central Copenhagen it still occupies; its success as city-based school lay in Borup's bridge-building between Gr's vision of the folk-highschool, workers' education and urban intellectual circles in Copenhagen; notable among his other achievements was publication (1914) of his *Dansk Sangbook* [Danish songbook]: while it contained many traditional texts (pride of place being given to those by Grundtvig), it also included more recent lyrics which composer Carl Nielsen (1865-1931) set to music and together with separate volume of melodies by Nielsen is credited with having helped renew currency of Danish *sangskat* [treasury of song] and revive popularity of communal singing.

Boye, Caspar Johannes *279*; 1791-1853; priest, poet, dramatist and leading Danish hymn-writer of 19th c.; parish priest in Søllerød 1826, Helsingør 1835, where he published *Aandelige Digte og Sange* [Spiritual poems and songs], I-IV, 1833-36 and two further volumes 1840-43, republished in augmented edition 1847-54; appointed 1847 incumbent of Garnisonskirke, Copenhagen; published four volumes of his *Udvalgte og samlede poetiske Skrifter* 1850-51 [Selected and collected poetic writings]; died in cholera epidemic 1853; in view of bishop H. L. Martensen, he and Bernhard Severin Ingemann (1789-1862) often excelled Gr as hymn-writer; a number of his hymns remain favourites in the current Danish Hymnal.

Brage og Idun *236, 332*; *Brage og Idun, et nordisk Fjærdingårsskrift, udgivet, med Bistand af Danske, Svenske og Normænd, af Frederik Barfod, Student*; [Bragi and Iðunn, a Nordic quarterly published with contributions from Danes, Swedes and Norwegians by F. B., student]; periodical launched by Frederik Barfod upon exhortation of Gr and Orla Lehmann; so named, according to Barfod, by Gr who prefaced first volume (new year 1839; publication ceased 1842) with his poem *Brage og Idun*; journal intended as practical step in furthering cultural unity and interchange among Scandinavian countries, one of several contemporary initiatives involving Gr and Barfod (which as far as Barfod himself was concerned grew into lifelong commitment to Scandinavianism); Bragi, in Snorri's *Edda*, appears as Nordic god of poesy, son of Óðinn, though little is known of him from other sources; his wife was Iðunn, also featured in Snorri's *Edda*, as custodian of golden apples which Æsir eat to retain perpetual youth; in 19th c. Scandinavia, motif of Bragi and Iðunn was popular symbol of poesy's eternal divine preeminence as in Danish *Kunstforening*'s commemorative medal (Harald Conradsen, 1851) for Oehlenschläger.

Brage og Idun *246*; poem by Gr prefacing first volume of Frederik Barfod's journal of same name (1839).

Brahe, Tycho (Tyge) Ottesen *292*; 1546-1601; Danish astronomer born in Knutstorp, Skaane (now Sweden); studied law at University of Copenhagen from age of 12, and at Leipzig, Wittenberg, Rostock and Basel; from 1560 became increasingly absorbed by astronomy and alchemy; over period of 20 years constructed globe which by 1595 depicted precisely calculated position of 1000 fixed stars (globe destroyed by fire, Copenhagen 1728); though initially educated in Aristotelean concept of immutable universe with fixed and impenetrable planetary spheres, his observation (1572) of a supernova in Cassiopeia (and later observations of comets) forced reconsideration of received authorities; his *De nova stella* [Concerning the new star; 1573] established his European reputation; he accepted invitation of Frederik II to settle in Dk on island of Ven between Skaane and Sjælland where Uranienborg, residence and observatory, was constructed for him 1576-80 and where over 20 years he built instruments, made observations, theorised and published, bringing scientific principle to bear upon an understanding of the universe hitherto based upon antiquity and conformity with Bible and theology; hugely privileged status ended in dispute with Christian IV and Brahe left Ven (1597), moved eventually to Prague where astronomer Johannes Kepler (1571-1630) became his collaborator (and later modified the Tychonic universe, not least by establishing planetary orbits as elliptical) and where he died 1601; in his final view of the universe (a mediation between tradition and scientific observation) he opposed Copernicus by sustaining ancient (and theologically endorsed) concept of earth as static centre about which sun and moon circle, but held that the circling sun is orbital centre to the five other planets, located in space through which comets can freely pass; Gr is said to have cited authority of Brahe and Arent Aschlund (1797-1835), in holding to the word of the Bible, that the sun moves round the earth (Joshua 10:12, "Sun, stand thou still upon Gibeon"); see also **Aschlund,** Arent.

Brandt, Carl Joakim *23, 192, 241, 252, 283, 288, 300, 301*; 1817-89; priest, scholar; *cand. theol.* 1841; while student, worked as private tutor to family of Professor J. L. A. Kolderup-Rosenvinge; church and literary historian with interest in medieval Danish texts which he studied in manuscripts in Stockholm and Uppsala; published with Ludvig Helveg important anthology and study of Danish hymns (1846-47); *Lucidarius* (1849) and various other editions and studies of medieval literature, also (1850-55) five volumes of Danish writings of 16th-c. Danish historian and lexicographer Christiern Pedersen; 1856 (to 1859) first principal of Gr's *højskole*, Marielyst folk-highschool; 1849 co-founder of *Selskabet for Danmarks Kirkehistorie*;from 1845 founder-editor of *Dansk Kirketidende* with brother-in-law R. T. Fenger; 1860 parish priest in Rønnebæk and Olstrup; six days after Gr's death (2 September 1872) at annual gathering in Vartov to mark Gr's birthday (8 September) Brandt preached outdoors to congregation too large for church; at *Vennemødet* day after Gr's funeral (11 September), Brandt as chairman pacified meeting upset by speech of Bjørnsterne Bjørnsen urging Scandinavian rapprochement with Germany; on 30 November appointed by the Vartov Free Congregation as Gr's successor in Vartov Church; congregation, at heart of Grundtvigian way of life, continued to flourish; he oversaw establishment of funds for social assistance, and contributed, by editing and original compositions, to maintenance of Vartov's distinctive tradtion of hymn-singing, therefore often regarded as first among Gr's successors in history of Danish hymnody; was succeeded at his death by son-in-law Jørgen Herman Monrad.

Brandt, Karl; see **Brandt,** Carl Joakim

Bregendahl, Albert Philip *230, 231*; 1771-1835; *provst*; parish priest at Vor Frelsers Kirke when Gr was curate there (1822-26); exchanged apartments with Gr family, October 1827.

Brevet, 87; 'The Letter;' four-act comedy by Gr begun December 1802, completed July 1803 when, he says, lethargy, reading history books and summer heat distracted him from theology in which his final examination imminently loomed (October 1803); piece did not get as far as being considered by the selection committee of the Royal Theatre, Copenhagen (as, unsuccessfully, was his three-act *Skoleholderne*) but was staged (1803) as amateur production with Gr playing male lead; manuscript is in Fascicule 491 in the Gr Arkiv, Royal Library Copenhagen; see also *Ulfhild*; *Skoleholderne*.

Brevveksling mellem Nørrejylland og Christianshavn 116; An exchange of letters between North Jylland and Christianshavn; Gr's draft (1823-24) of an apologia for Christianity, repeatedly reworked but never completed, partly in the form of (fictive) letters exchanged between him and a serious and open-minded correspondent from Jylland.

Bride, the Church as; see **kvindelige,** det.

Brief Outline of World History; see *Kort Begreb af Verdens-Krønike i Sammenhæng.*

British Museum *131*; national museum of Great Britain, established in consequence of Act of Parliament authorising state purchase of library and natural history specimens of Sir Hans Sloane (died 1753), purchase of manuscript collections of Robert and Edward Harley, Earls of Oxford, and proper care of collection of Sir Robert Cotton (already in state ownership), to which George II transferred custody of Royal Library (containing collections from time of Henry VII to Charles I); opened 1759 in Montague House, Bloomsbury, London; subsequently established as copyright library; Gr gives account of ill-lit, uncomfortable working conditions in manuscript reading room in visits during summers of 1829-31 to study manuscript of *Beowulf* and other Anglo-Saxon and medieval manuscripts in great collections; he also suggests initial indifference of Museum officials to his search for Exeter Book (which proved to be in Exeter), though various distinguished scholars in medieval antiquities were working there (including Richard Price, Frederic Madden, Benjamin Thorpe, John Kemble); but major development of library and public reading room awaited appointment of Anthony Panizzi (keeper of printed books 1837) and building of great rotunda opened as reading room 1857; presentation copy of *Beowulfes Beorh* (1861), Gr's edition of *Beowulf*, is still accessible to readers, with Gr's handwritten dedication: "Til Det Brittiske Museum Bjovulfs-Drapens Arnested i taknemmeligt Minde fra 1829-31. Fra N. F. S. Grundtvig Kiöbinghavn 1861 Nov. 4." [To the B.M., the *Beowulf*-epic's inglenook, in grateful remembrance from 1829-31. From N.F.S.G., Copenhagen, 4 November 1861].

Brogade *208*; street in Christianshavn (obliterated in replanning 1938) leading to Knippelsbro; here, not far from Gr's residence in Strandgade, author and critic J. L. Heiberg and bishop and politician D. G. Monrad lived.

Brorson, Christian Frederik, *90*; 1768-1847; 1793 appointed curate and 1815 parish priest in Garnisons Kirke, Copenhagen; 1808 named titular professor; 1843 upon completing fifty years as priest, was granted rank of bishop (a matter of honorific status not to be confused with consecration as bishop of a diocese); 1828 while baptising child of *Assessor* Niels Møller Spandet (1788-1858; friend and supporter of Grundtvig) he omitted renunciation of the Devil and some other words over which omission Spandet complained to bishop Münter who reprimanded him and, to Gr's temporary satisfaction (temporary, for the issue broke out anew and dramatically in 1832 over the formulaic adjustments of no less a person than *Stiftsprovst* H. G. Clausen), issued directive to priests to keep precisely to prescribed formulas; he was intermediary in negotiating Gr's appointment as resident tutor to Steensen-Leth family at Egeløkke, Langeland (1805-8); see **Daabspagten**; **Besværgelsen.**

Brorson, Hans Adolph *23, 278*; 1694-1764; dean (1737) then bishop (1740) of Ribe, hymnwriter and poet; born of clerical family in Slesvig to which region and its culture he remained deeply attached throughout his life though also unswervingly loyal to Dk's absolute monarchy; vulnerable (like Luther before him and Gr after) to *anfægtelser* (attacks of spiritual doubt), he was attracted temperamentally as well as theologically to German-originating pietism, whose zeal for congregational singing inspired him to express in hymns of his own composition remorse and sorrow for the world's sinful and transitory nature, and humility, gratitude and joy over the certainties of salvation, in affective poetry which drew upon late baroque, reformational and medieval traditions; of which published collections were *Nogle Jule-Psalmer* [Some Christmas hymns] 1732, *Troens rare Klenodie* [The rare jewel of faith] 1739, *Svane-Sang* [Swan-song] post-humously 1765; see also **hymns**.

Browne, Peter Dennis *175*; Secretary of the British Legation (*Det engelske gesandtskab*) in Copenhagen; 1829 furnished Gr with letter of introduction to connection in England (Reverend Mr Parsell, to whom he explained Gr's difficulties with church in Dk and Gr's complete unfamiliarity with world outside Dk and especially British part of it), and with advice on London accommodation (1829); attended Gr's Sunday afternoon services in Frederiks Kirke while Gr was licensed to preach there (1832-39); he and wife Catherine joined Gr's circle of personal friends (extending to friendship between Gr's son Svend and Browne's son Dennis) and entertained Gr at their residence where (November 1834) Gr met the Legation Chaplain Nugent Wade; through Legation duties, Browne and wife were well and widely connected in Dk with responsibility for receiving and entertaining distinguished visitors from England such as Joseph Gurney and Elizabeth Fry (1841) whom Gr was also enlisted to assist; Gr records that Frederik vi used Browne to advise him secretly that, should he apply for position at Vartov (1839), he would get it; some 50 letters to Gr from Catherine and Peter Browne are preserved in Arkiv (*Registrant* XXIV, p. 188).

Brun, Hans *200, 203, 219, 247, 255, 282, 285, 286, 295, 299, 323, 324, 333, 335, 338*; 1820-90; *cand. theol.* 1847; teacher in Kristiania (Oslo); Grundtvigian; author of first substantial biography of Gr, *Biskop N. F. S. Grundtvigs Levnetsløb udførligt fortalt fra 1839* [Bp NFSG's Life recounted in fullest detail from 1839], 2 vols., 1882.

Brun, Pastor *223*; possibly Carl Bruun (1805-83), curate [*kapellan*] at Taarnby, Amager,1832; present at unlawful religious gatherings on Amager (February 1832), together with the *amtsforvalter*, Frydensberg. See footnotes to item 83.

Brun, Thomas Christopher; see **Bruun,** Thomas Christopher.

Bruno 96; *Bruno, oder über göttliche und natürliche Principien der Dinge, ein Gespräch* (1802), work by Friedrich Wilhelm Joseph Schelling (1775-1854) which made impact upon Gr in turbulent period of his infatuation with Constance Steensen-Leth at Egeløkke (1805-08); "I dared to acknowledge the truth: Reality holds no joy for me ... I forsook life with Schelling in his Bruno" (Gr); Giordano Bruno, philosopher deemed heretical (supported Copernican view of universe, theorised its infinite extension and number of worlds, was regarded as pantheist and atheist) and burned at stake in Rome 17 February 1600, came quickly to be regarded as martyr to cause of liberal thought especially in anti-Catholic circles; gained increasing status mid-18th c. following Friedrich Heinrich Jacobi's translation of selection of his writing, subsequently used by Schelling to write *Bruno*, dialogue in Brunian manner, which Gr read; see **Schelling**, Friedrich Wilhelm Joseph von.

Bruun, Christoffer *323, 336*; 1839-1920; Norwegian sympathiser with Gr's ideas on education and the *folkelige* ("All humane education must be founded upon history and poetry, because human life possesses no more powerful educative forces" – Bruun, *Folkelige Grundtanker* [Fundamental *folkelige* ideas], 1878); founded (1867) folk-highschool at Sel in Gudbrandsdal which moved (1871) to Gausdal, some 25 km NW of Lillehammer and subsequently (1875) to Vonheim,

Aulestad, Lillehammer, where Bjørnstjerne Bjørnson (1832-1910) made his home and lectured at the school; Gr dismissed suggestion that Bruun could not succeed because he lacked education in Christian matters, but was less enthusiastic over Bruun's promotion, through school, of movement for definition of a Norwegian national language, and later seems to have come to share misgivings about Bruun's notion of religious education; Bruun remained leader of school until 1893, becoming central figure in Norwegian national *folkeliv*.

Bruun, Malthe Conrad *68*; 1775-1826; geographer, writer, literary critic whose work grew increasingly politically radical; publication (1796) of *Aristokraternes Katekismus eller kort og tydelig Anviisning til den aleene saliggjörende politiske Troe. Med et Anhang af aristokratiske Salmer, til Troens Bestyrkelse hos de enfoldige og de vantroendes Omvendelse* [The Aristocrats' Cathechism or a short and plain guide to the one saving political faith, with a supplement of aristocratic hymns, for the strengthening of faith among the simple and the conversion of unbelievers], a kind of parody on the Lutheran Catechism, satirising privileges of absolute monarch and aristocracy with such new Commandments as "Thou shalt not make presumptuous testimony of any form of government superior to the existing one," was reported to the Chancellery by Bishop N. E. Balle, led to his prosecution, eventually dropped because of his young age; but for publication of fresh satirical writings offending against royal absolutism he was finally exiled from Dk (1800).

Bruun, Thomas Christopher *68, 79*; 1750-1834; author, professor of English in Copenhagen University; his *Mine Frie-Timer* [My Leisure Hours], reworkings of Boccaccio and Fontaine, was officially suppressed (1783) and he was summoned before Bishop N. E. Balle to answer charge of frivolity and to prove his Christian sobriety; at time of greatest published criticism of Danish royal and ecclesiastical establishment (soon to be suppressed by new restrictions of freedom of press) he continued, in spirit of Voltaire, to publish long verse satires against royal power and dogmatic religion, including *Særsyn* [Rare Sights] 1797; canvassed for renewal of theology based on critical study of Scriptures and Church history; his *Skriftemaalet* [The confession] (1798) was read by Gr over winter of 1801-02; he had some stylistic influence on Gr's early literary efforts; but Gr later (1812; tr. from *Kort Begreb af Verdens Krønike*) wrote: "Thomas Bruun has sullied many a page with ungodly and lewd jesting ... Many a man must curse the sweet poison which as a youngster he sucked in from those evil flowers; and even now in his old age he in his blindness persists in building himself a burial-place of indecency" (alluding to Bruun's publication of his collected writings, 1812).

Bræstrup, Christian Jacob Cosmus *173, 222, 223*; 1789-1870; Chief of Police, Copenhagen; Minister of Justice; as official responsible for civil order and therefore also for upholding laws relating to State Church, came into face-to-face conflict with J. C. Lindberg, Gr and others (1832) over right to hold gatherings for religious observance (*Andagtsforsamlinger*) elsewhere than in churches, and those to which priests concerned were appointed.

Bue Digre *83*; Bue the Stout (Icelandic: Búi Digri); died *ca.* 986; "Bue, a warrior hard as stone from Jomsborg, supposed to have been a Bornholmer and regularly called Bue Digre or the Stout by the Icelanders" (Gr's note in his translation of Saxo Grammaticus); according to *Óláfs saga Tryggvasonar* in *Heimskringla*, Bue joined with Jomsvikings in expedition to Norway to kill or expel Hakon Jarl; but fleet was tricked into trap and their leader Sigvald Jarl fled; Bue fought on but was grievously sword-hacked in face; seizing chest of plundered gold under each arm, calling upon his men to follow, he leapt overboard from his ship, was never seen again; in a characteristic use of Northern legend-reference, Gr likened his student friend, robustly independent-minded Bornholmer Peter Nikolai Skougaard, to Bue, of whom Palnatoke says, in Gr's *Optrin af Kæmpelivets Undergang i Nord* [Episodes from the downfall of the warrior-life in the North; 1809], "You are of steel, and steel never yields before it is utterly broken asunder; may Jomsborg never want for the like of you; but it would soon be laid waste if *all* were the like of you!" [Du est af Staal, og Staalet viger / Ei før det hel er sønderbrudt; / Gid Jomsborg aldrig dine Lige / Maa mangle! men den ødtes fluks, / Hvis Alle vare dine Lige].

Bugge, Peter Olivarius *288*; 1764-1849; Norwegian bishop (1803) in Trondheim (Nidaros); vigorous activist in politics of Norway's separation from Dk (1814), close advisor to Christian Frederik (King of Norway May to October 1814 and later Christian VIII of Dk); aroused some ill-feeling over way in which he addressed countrymen in coronation sermon; contributed to drafting of Constitution; member of first Storting (Norwegian parliament), later president of Odelsting (upper house); as bishop, in conflict with nonconformist groups, followers of Hans Nielsen Hauge (1771-1824) and Wilhelm Andreas Wexels (1797-1866) as well as Hernhutter.

Bugge, Thomas *78*; 1740-1815; professor of mathematics and astronomy in Copenhagen University; one of Gr's examiners April 1801 and *rektor magnificus* of University at time of Gr's reprimand in the *Consistorium* (12 January 1811), concerning publication of his probationary sermon.

Busck, Gunni *233, 244, 265, 318, 319, 324*; 1798-1869; priest; born into wealthy family, first marriage was into clerical family, father-in-law Frederik Carl Gutfelt (1761-1823), *Provst* at Holmens Kirke, Copenhagen, who helped him find his calling to ministry; graduated in Law 1820 but then turned to Theology; appointed 1824 to incumbency of Stifts-Bjergby and Mørke near Holbæk; strong ally of Gr, by both spoken and written word, in clash with H. N. Clausen (1826); 1835, after death of first wife (1832), remarried; 1844 appointed incumbent of Brøndbyøster and Brøndbyvester near Copenhagen; remained Gr's lifelong friend, confidant and sounding-board, as correspondence testifies, judicious, loyal, generous to extent (for example) of financially assisting Gr to devote himself to compilation of his *Sangværk* (1837; Gr dedicated the work to him and to Peter Fenger); active in supporting Gr's causes, for example with pamphlets against Bishop Martensen (1863) and Bishop Brammer (1867), but a milder polemicist whose role was often to temper Gr's more combative dispositions, for example in trying to encourage a friendlier disposition towards Bishop J. P. Mynster; Gr wrote a memorial poem upon Busck's death (28 March 1869).

Bygde-Prædikant *160*; village preacher, itinerant lay preacher; see **Hauge,** Hans Nielsen.

Byron, George Gordon Noel *26, 328*; 1788-1824; 6th Baron Byron; leading English Romantic poet, contemporary of P. B. Shelley, John Keats; Edmund Gosse, visiting Dk 1872, felt compelled to go to Vartov to hear Gr – "a poet who was born five years before Byron."

Bækkeskov *263*; Mansion and estate north of Præstø, Sjælland; present main building erected by English-born Baron Charles Joseph Selby (1796-1798); locale for jocular story told by Gr.

Bøgh, Matthias Frederik Georg *194*; 1762-1831; studied at Odense School and University of Copenhagen; resident tutor to Peter Erasmus Müller (1776-1834; subsequently philologist, historian, professor and Bishop of Sjælland); priest at Præstø and Skibbinge 1797; *amtsprovst* [rural dean] of Præstø district (1807); *amtsprovst* of Bjeverskou and parish priest of Herfølge and Sædder 1822; concerned with standardisation and regulation of Danish orthography, based upon precept that "Brugen er øverste Lov" [Usage is the supreme law]; published in periodical *Minerva* (1805) his *Forslag til en Lovkommission for det danske Sprogs Retskrivning* [Proposal for an official Commission on the Orthography of the Danish Language]; in 1807 *Almindelig dansk orthographisk Undersøgelse* [General enquiry into Danish orthography]; and in 1822 *Dansk Retskrivningslære foredraget som selvstændig videnskabelig Lære. Et Forsøg* [The Teaching of Danish Orthography, set forth as independent scholarly teaching. An essay]; it was *amtsprovst* Bøgh who patiently relit candles puffed out by Gr in vigorous declamation of his *Roeskilde-Riim* to clerics gathered at Roskilde (1812).

Børsen *140*; The Exchange; building on Slotsholmen, Copenhagen, adjacent to palace of Christiansborg, erected 1619 onwards by Christian IV as key element of king's mercantile policy, housed rentable business offices and storerooms, and trading hall; still standing, distinguished by Dutch renaissance style architecture in red brick and stone with green copper roofs and twisted dragon spire.

C

Cabinet *167, 175*; *Kabinettet*; French-derived term, originally for small room, also called *gemak* in Danish; in 18th and 19th c. more intimate reception chamber in great house or palace, also antechamber in royal court where royal business was dispatched; thence by extension to advisory body closest to king's person through which abolute royal will was executed.

Cabinet-sermon *167*; sermon preached at royal command in *kabinet* (semi-private chamber rather than royal chapel or church), by invited clergy; Gr's early repute as preacher secured him invitations (1821) from queen Marie who at first praised him to skies but later unexplainedly took offence.

Cambridge *16, 62, 134*; younger of England's two medieval universities, founded 13th c. on River Cam some 55 miles north of London; comprised of self-governing residential colleges (in Gr's time, for men only); University and college libraries (notably that of Corpus Christi College) held large collections of Anglo-Saxon manuscripts sought out by Gr in 1831 when, on basis of chain of introductions initiated by internationally-known Danish scientist, H. C. Ørsted, he was befriended by Professor William Whewell of Trinity College and accorded hospitality there; impressed by his (somewhat romanticised) perception of benefits of residential community of teachers and students, which contrasted with his (somewhat soured) perception of his own university of Copenhagen, Gr took home ideas leading to his mission of creating a folk-university (*folkehøjskole*) for Dk.

Canaan, Canaanites *184*; Biblical land, later called Palestine, named after a son of Noah (Genesis 4); promised by the Lord to Abraham and his seed for ever, though the profligate Canaanites had first to be crushed by the Israelites (Genesis 12); the Lord subsequently enjoins Moses: "after the doings of the land of Canaan, whither I bring you, shall ye not do: neither shall ye walk in their ordinances" (Leviticus 18:3).

Canaanite woman *167*; subject of sermon preached by Gr before Queen Marie, based on gospel of Matthew 15:21-28: Canaanite woman, begging Jesus to heal her possessed daughter, is at first rebuffed on grounds that bread intended for children (Israel) should not be cast to dogs (Canaanites) but when she replies that even dogs are permitted to eat crumbs from master's table, Jesus replies her faith has earned her what she desires.

Cancellie, Det Kongelige-Danske *15, 112, 157, 160, 166, 167, 169, 172, 175, 221-223*; The Royal Danish Chancellery; state secretariat responsible for much of domestic administration of kingdom; established 1523 upon reconstruction of earlier chancellery; had until 1660 sole responsibility for home affairs in Dk north of Kongeåen (the Tyske Kancelli [German Chancellery] being responsible for duchies of Slesvig and Holsten and bulk of foreign affairs) and in Norway, Iceland and the Faroes; after establishment of absolute monarchy 1660 its responsibilities restricted to administration of legal, ecclesiastical and educational affairs in these areas; at times governed collegiately, but president (F. J. Kaas, 1804-27, during Gr's difficult earlier years) wielded very considerable influence in relevant areas of public life; underwent major overhaul in 1800; dissolved 1848 in move to constitutional democracy when its responsibilities were distributed among ministries (Justice, Home Affairs, Finance, Church); see also **Kaas,** Frederik Julius; **Stemann,** Poul Christian.

cand. (= *candidatus*) *passim*; Danish-used Latin designation ('clothed in white' said to derive from custom of *toga candida*, white toga, worn by Romans seeking selection to public office) given to those who have passed *kandidateksamen* at university within particular faculty, thus for example in Theology (Divinity) *candidatus theologiae* (*cand. theol.*) and in Law *candidatus juris* (*cand. jur.*); qualification to public office including (when supplemented by other mandatory qualification including satisfactory preaching of a dimissory or probational sermon) church ministry; junior to Danish *magister* (Master) degree; see also **Attestats** (*attestatus*).

Cand. S. S. Minist.*67*; *candidatus sacrosancti ministerii*; equivalent of *cand. theol.*; see **cand.**

Canterbury, Archbishop of *131*; William Howley (1766-1848) was archbishop (1828-48) during all four of Gr's visits to England; drafts of Gr's letters to him, requesting letters of commendation for his initial visit, and mentioning Gr's own status as priest ordained without apostolic succession, are in the Grundtvig Arkiv.

Carillon for the Danish Church; see ***Sang-Værk til den danske Kirke.***

Carlsen, Hans Rasmussen *241, 339*; 1810-87; Danish politician; landowner (Gammel Køgegaard, Sjælland); brother of Gr's second wife Marie (Carlsen) Toft and to Jutta, wife of Gr's disciple Peter Rørdam; married (1841) Clara Sophie, *Komtesse* Krag-Juel-Vind-Friis (died 1852) to whose family *Komtesse* Asta, Gr's third wife, belonged; much influenced by Gr in causes he pursued; committed to establishment of constitutional democracy in Dk to replace absolutism; 1841 member of *Stænderforsamling* [Assembly of Estates of the Realm] for Sjælland; from 1854 member of various national assemblies; briefly Minister of the Interior in Monrad's ministry of 1864; of the party advocating defence of the River Ejder as Dk's southern frontier; leading opponent of the conservatively-reformed Constitution of 1866; buried in the private family cemetery on Gammel Køgegaard estate where Gr himself and his wives Marie and Asta also lie; see also **Gammel Køgegaard**.

Carlsen, Marie *262, 263*; Gr's second wife; see **Grundtvig,** Marie (Toft).

Caroline Amalie *132, 141, 174, 175, 261, 264, 265, 288, 298, 300, 301, 306, 307, 309-312, 316, 318*; 1796-1881; princess of Augustenborg, of the Oldenborg dynasty, sister to Christian August Duke of Augustenborg and Frederik Prince of Nør; married (1815) to Prince Christian Frederik (later Christian VIII); as Enkedronning (Dowager Queen) was active as member of the Vartov congregation, devoted follower and generous patroness of Gr and his initiatives (a devotion matched by Gr's spiritual solicitude for the queen which, particularly in 1840s, had intensity of a courtship); concerned herself with educational, charitable and humanitarian issues, for example receiving visit of Quakers Elizabeth and Joseph Fry (Copenhagen, August 1841) to discuss prison reform and abolition of slavery; funded Gr's visit to England (1843) to meet John Henry Newman and other churchmen involved in the Tractarian controversy; cast by Gr's disordered imagination, Palm Sunday 1867, in key role in securing Dk's triumph, under God, over her foes; considerable number of her letters to Gr are in Arkiv Fasc. 450; correspondence relating to Gr's visit to England 1843 was published in periodical *Danskeren* V (1891).

Casino *239*; Copenhagen's first private theatre (1846), opened by impresario Georg Carstensen, used also for public meetings – a functional association reflecting more than mere economic practicality for since late 18th c. theatre had served significant role (for want of wide range of other permitted places of public concourse and forums for debate) in formation of currently prevailing taste and opinion; notable for major political 'Casino-meetings' (*Casino-møderne*) in 1848 triggered by expectations of dissolution of royal absolutism and rumours of rebellion in Slesvig-Holsten, and initiated by national-liberal Committee, leading to mass demonstration and concession of constitution (March 1848; see **Martsministeriet**); again in 1863 national-liberals calculatedly used meetings at Casino to secure popular backing for Slesvig policy; on both occasions events led to war; see also **theatre and drama**.

Cathechesis *68*; primary (oral) instruction in Christian faith such as given to catechumens; prescribed textbook in Latin schools, already studied by Gr at Tyregod under Pastor Laurits Feld, was that of Ove Høegh-Guldberg, *Den naturlige Theologie* (1765); particular attention given to study of Luther's *Lille Katekismus* (Short Catechism) of 1529, established as one of the confessional books of the Danish State Church as of the post-absolutist Folkekirke; see also **Katekismus**.

Catechism; see *Katekismus*, Luther's; and *Aristokraternes Katekismus*.

Catechism, Luther's; see **Katekismus**

Catechism, Aristocrats'; see **Bruun, Malthe**

Catholicism and Protestantism, book on *176;* H. N. Clausen's *Catholicismens og Protestantismens Kirkeforfatning, Lære og Ritus* [Constitution, doctrine and rites of Catholicism and Protestantism], 1825; see **Clausen,** Henrik Nicolai.

censorship; see **censur**.

censur *16, 62, 64, 68, 127;* censorship; a regular concomitant of absolutist rule, designed to assert sovereignties of Crown and Church, Danish censorship of the presses nevertheless long fluctuated in severity of application and was briefly abolished in 1770, but with dissolution of old orders gathering momentum in Europe as in America, constraint of free expression was reviewed (1798) by commission resulting in decree (1799) generally stifling printed criticism of authority, forbidding anonymity and imposing censorship (and, for extreme cases, exile) upon offenders; did not necessarily mean total suppression of offender's publishing activity but enforced submission of all intended publication to police scrutiny and *imprimatur;* Gr, held guilty of libel against H. N. Clausen by publishing *Kirkens Gienmæle* [The Church's Retort] (1825), was penalised with over ten years of censorship (not lifted until 1837) though he appears to have been refused permission to publish in only one instance; especially in increasingly politically-conscious decade between concession of *Stænderforsamlinger* (regional advisory assemblies; 1835-36) and establishment of Constitution (1849), periodicals with such titles as *Raketten* [The Rocket], *Lynstraalen* [The Thunderbolt], *Skjærsilden* [The fire of Purgatory] afforded some debate of public and political issues, but were locked in continuous and costly tussle with censors; see also **Press Ordinance; Trykkeforordningen**.

Cervantes Saavedra, Miguel de *85;* 1547-1616; most renowned of Spanish writers, already enjoying, like Shakespeare and Goethe, pre-eminent status in early 19th-c. European literary canon, chiefly on basis of his two-part novel *Don Quijote de la Mancha* (1605, 1615), translated into Danish in 18th-c.; but Gr's admiration was particularly aroused (1802) by lectures of Henrik Steffens, and with light self-irony his diary refers to his visit (1804) to Elisabeth Blicher, his future wife, as *donkisjotske,* Don Quixotic.

Chancellery; see **Cancellie,** Det Kongelige-Danske.

Charity-School, Queen's; see **Dronningens Asylskole**.

Charlemagne, Chronicle of *61;* Carolus magnus, 742/747-814; son of Pepin, king of Franks; succeeded with brother Carloman as king of Franks (768); on death of Carloman, king of all the Franks (771); waged war against neighbouring peoples, especially heathens, including Danes, extending Christendom and his imperium; crowned emperor in Rome (800); vigorous reformer and nation-shaper; presided over brilliant (Christian) cultural renaissance deliberately emulating model of late Roman civilisation; engaged distinguished Europeans in his service including Einhard (his biographer) and Alcuin of York (master of schools in Aachen and Tours, liturgist);

subsequently assumed legendary character in European heroic and chivalric literature, with which legendary Danish hero Holger Danske is also associated, and in same spirit has been presented by some historians from own time onwards as *pater Europae*, father of Europe; from Einhard, through *Chanson de Roland*, the 13th-c. Icelandic *Karlemagnússaga*, and Danish translations and reworkings, *Kejser Karl Magnus Krønike* [Chronicle of the emperor Charlemagne] and *Kong Holger Danskes Krønike* [Chronicle of king Holger Danske] of Christiern Pedersen (*ca.* 1480-1554), the Charlemagne legend became part of Danish heritage; along with P. F. Suhm's *Om Odin og den hedniske Gudelære* [On Óðinn and heathen mythology], these medieval legends of Charlemagne and Holger Danske were Gr's refuge from boredom at Aarhus Latin School.

Christian IV *154*; 1577-1648; King of Denmark and Norway from 1596; son of Frederik II; brother of Anne who married James VI of Scotland; uncle to Charles I of England; though at one time among richest of European princes, dissipated resources not least through military conflict with expansionist Sweden; nevertheless invited foreign craftsmen, engineers, merchants and artists into Dk, undertook major projects and buildings (a number still gracing Copenhagen); considerably extended central administration and body of law; at times autocratic as if under divine right, yet hindered by inherited institutions (including privileges of aristocracy), his rule was erratic; but despite personal and national misfortunes remains among most prominent of Danish sovereigns.

Christian VIII *132, 236, 248, 283, 285, 288, 329*; 1786-1848; King of Dk 1839-48, of Norway May to October 1814; successor to Frederik VI; last Danish sovereign to be anointed and crowned; well-educated, engaged in intellectual and cultural currents of the period; supported establishment of new University of Kristiania (Oslo) 1811; secured free constitution for Norway when sovereignty handed to Sweden by Treaty of Kiel (1814) but remained committed to absolutism in Dk; Gr saw accession as inaugurating a "new year" for Dk, as hailed in his edition of Anglo-Saxon poem *The Phoenix* (*Phenix-Fuglen. Et angelsachsisk Kvad* [The phoenix-bird. An Anglo-Saxon poem], 1840), but Christian rejected every suggestion of a democratic constitution, to bitter frustration of liberals and reassurance of landed gentry and aristocracy, and tightened censorship laws, as illustrated in case of political agitator Orla Lehmann (1810-70) and Meir Aron Goldschmidt (1819-87), editor of the satirical journal *Corsaren*, both jailed (1842, 1843 respectively) for taking liberties with the law; however, Christian (partly through good offices of Gr's friend and supporter Dowager Queen Caroline Amalie) did lend his patronage to Gr's plan for a folk-university at Sorø, but his untimely death from blood-poisoning was a fatal blow to scheme; succeeded by Frederik VII.

Christian IX *335*; 1818-1906; King of Dk 1863-1906; reign characterised by early catastrophic loss of duchies of Slesvig and Holsten in war (1864) with Prussia, and by the *Forfatningskamp* [Constitutional struggle] beginning with bitterly fought reactionary revision (July 1866) of 1849 Constitution, assigning King power to nominate 12 of 66 members of the *Landsting* and granting great landowners and major taxpayers special electoral privileges, thus ensuring solid conservative entrenchment in upper chamber; ending 1901 with *Systemskiftet* [The System-change] whereby democratic principle was finally asserted, that freely elected majority in the *Folketing* should form Government; Gr who had enjoyed some favour with Frederik VI, Christian VIII and Frederik VII found himself politically at odds with Christian IX and (though he retained friendship of Dowager Queen Caroline Amalie) was rebuffed by him when he attempted directly to petition King to refuse to undersign constitutional amendments of 1866; see also **Grundloven**.

Christian, Prince, poem upon *105*; *Sørgekvad ved Prinds Kristjans Død* [Elegy upon the death of Prince Christian]; see **Christian August**, Prince.

Christian August, Prince *105*; 1768-1810; Christian August, Prince of Slesvig-Holsten-Sønder-borg-Augustenborg; achieved prominence during conflict between Dk and Sweden within context of Napoleonic wars resulting (April 1808) in Swedish invasion of Norway, against which, appointed by Danish king Frederik VI, he successfully led Norwegian-Danish army, sharing hardships of battlefield with his soldiers to his great popular credit but at cost to his health; in complex political machinations following deposition of Gustav IV Adolf of Sweden (March 1809), he was invited from Swedish side to submit for election as successor; he remained ostensibly loyal to Danish strategy of achieving Scandinavian union with Frederik VI as head, but July 1809 accepted (with Frederik's endorsement) election as Swedish Crown Prince (taking name Carl Augustus), in which month also Frederik VI (despite mistrust of his conduct) named him *Statholder* [Viceregent] of Norway; his death (May 1810), disappointing political significance of which prompted Gr to write his *Sørgekvad ved Prins Kristjans Død* [Elegy on the death of Prince Christian;1810], ended such prospects as there were of Scandinavian unification, and Treaty of Vienna (1815) transferred Norwegian sovereignty from Dk to Sweden.

Christian August, duke; see **Augustenborg**, Christian August, Duke of.

Christianity as mythology *118, 119*; in a retrospective rationalisation of his early development, referring to "everything I wrote before 1811" Gr explains the sense in which "Christianity was for me neither more nor less than a *complete mythology*" during his "mythological phase" which preceded his "theological" and "historical" phases – though, far from implying that Christianity is fictionalised, he rather suggests that myth is well seen as a vehicle of truth, "a map of the kingdom of the spirit and of the route to it." See also **mythology**.

Christiansborg *238*; founded in 12th c. by Bishop Absalon as fortress securing Copenhagen harbour, subsequently royal residence with substantial rebuildings; suffered two major fires 1794, 1884; present chief buildings from 1906; seat of Danish Parliament (*Rigsdag; Folketing*).

Christianshavn *18, 22, 62, 116, 123, 140, 167, 171, 207, 230, 249, 255, 341*; naval, mercantile and residential enclave of Copenhagen across the harbour from Christiansborg and Gammel Holm, on northern extremity of Amager but enclosed within city fortifications; laid out with docks, wharves, warehouses 1618, linked to city proper by Knippelsbro and Langebro; here were located both Christianhavn's Borgerdydsskole [Civic virtues school] and the Tugthus [House of Correction]; here Gr lived while serving in Christianhavn's two chief churches, Vor Frelsers Kirke (1822-26) and Frederiks Kirke (1832-39).

Chronicles 114; Gr's translation (1818) of Saxo's *Gesta Danorum*, under title *Danmarks Krønike af Saxo Grammaticus*, criticised by philologist Rasmus Rask (1787-1832) for outlandish language resulting from Gr's attempt to rehabilitate ancient or invent new words from Scandinavian roots; the edition seriously failed to achieve sales expectations.

Chronicles of the North; see **Saxo, Snorri.**

Church Assembly, Scandinavian 259; periodic gathering of representatives of Nordic churches; July 1857 held in Copenhagen.

Church-chieftain of the North; *Nordens Kirkehøvding*; reference to Gr; see **Høvding**.

Church council; see **synod**.

Church, Danish *18, 102, 103, 119, 127, 129, 144, 148, 153-156, 159, 162, 163, 170-176, 193, 221, 247, 257, 261, 269, 278-281, 289, 311, 314, 316, 328-330*; constitution of Danish Church was originally *Kirke-ordinansen* [The Church Ordinance] of 1537; following Dk's constitutional change to absolute monarchy, *Kongeloven* [The King's Law, royal law] of 1665 affirmed Lutheran doctrine as belief of the Danish Church; 1683 Christian v's *Danske Lov* [Danish Law] assembled the somewhat diverse lawcodes governing kingdom's several regions and thereby became *Landslov* [national law] which also codified ecclesiastical laws hitherto pertaining; in 1685, laws were supplemented by first Danish *Kirkeritual* [church ritual] though this was not fully worked out until newly or-dained *Alterbog* [altar-book, service-book] of 1688, which with various revisions then remained in use until 1895; at promulgation of parliamentary Constitution (1849) religious freedom was established, State became formally secular, and intention was declared that affairs of national Church be regulated by law, implying kind of free Church with own representation and constitu-tion, but such constitution has never been agreed, resulting by default in Parliament remaining supreme authority of Danish Church, exercising authority through ministry. In the glossary to his *Krønnike-Rim*, augmented 2nd edition 1842, Gr asserts: "*Kirke* [Church] is a word with not merely two but three significations, and since it is also from a foreign root, it is forever being misunderstood when it is used of anything but the tangible gathering-place of Christians; thus the priesthood [*Præsteskabet*] usually mean by 'the Church' themselves, yet nevertheless make claim of its authority over all Christians, which only has any basis if one understands by 'the Church' the whole Christian community [*hele den kristne Menighed*] to which every member must naturally subordinate himself. To make the Church-issue really complicated, the jurists claim into the bargain that in all church matters people must obey the clergy [*Gejstligheden*], though not for the clergy's own sake but for that of the secular authority which has the right, if it wishes, to create a new Church every year, which has sovereignty as long as it lasts. On the other hand, if one ignores the haggling over words, the matter is extremely simple; for the business of soul and salvation is unquestionably each person's own business, in which none can prescribe him anything, unless he voluntarily enters a church-society whose laws he must naturally observe if he does not wish to be excluded. Thus a Church which claims the right to gain itself members by compulsion and to lock them in thereby declares itself indifferent to soul and salvation, unless it is foolish enough to believe that souls can be brought to salvation directly against their will." See also **symbolic books, the; Augsburg Confession; Folkekirke; kirkelige Anskuelse, den; Church struggle,** The; **Sognebaandsløsning; Kultusministeriet.**

Church, Early, custom of *320*.

Church, Free; see **Frikirke**.

Church, Greek; see **Greek Church**.

Church, historical *117-120, 169, 280*.

church, history *156, 157, 158, 246 (note 25), 289, 304, 305*.

church, law *169*.

church-literature of the Gothic peoples *334*; study by Frederik Hammerich on ancient Christian epic poems of Gothic peoples (1873); see **Goths**.

Church, the living *174, 256*; see also **Ordet**; **Ord,** det levende.

Church, People's *328*; Gosse's translation of *Folkekirke*; see **Folkekirke**.

Church, of Reformation *252*; see **Church,** Danish; **Folkekirke**.

Church, Roman Catholic *127, 162, 176, 200, 252 (old catholic)*.

church struggle, The *128, 153, 203, 256, 258*; *Kirkekampen*; perception of entrenched struggle against upholders of absolutist-orientated State Church, held by Gr and supporters of bid to put into effect Gr's *kirkelige anskuelse* [view (concept, purview) of the Church], his distinctive conception of the history, character, status, role and organisation of the Danish Church, especially around period of polemical clash with H. N. Clausen (1825) and thereafter: "Christianity consists neither in holding the right faith, nor in certain religious experiences, nor in a particular ethic, but is God's dealings with man: in baptism when the Christian life is born, and in the Eucharist when it is sustained. Christianity has become ritual drama again. The word of God is not the Scriptures but 'the living word' which is heard at baptism and in Holy Communion (in the sacraments). At the same time Gr attached small importance to the clerical office, for which reason Grundtvigianism is markedly ecclesiastical and sacramental but not High Church, if anything definitely Low Church" (Hal Koch). See also **Church,** Danish; **Folkekirke**.

Church, view; see **kirkelige Anskuelse**.

Cicero, Marcus Tullius *71, 81*; 106-43 B.C.; Roman writer, orator, statesman; major figure linking European Middle Ages back to intellectual tradition of Rome and Greece; significance renewed in Renaissance especially in matters of rhetoric but also seen as forerunner of humanism.

circumcision of Jesus *313, 314*; "And when eight days were accomplished for the circumcising of the child, his name was called Jesus" (Luke 2:21); Jewish ritual of removal of foreskin signified participation in covenant established between the Lord and Abraham (Genesis 17:10); but, following Paul's argument (Romans 4) that righteousness rests not upon observance of the law but upon faith (for Abraham had "the righteousness of faith" *before* he was circumcised, and received sign of circumcision as seal upon this righteousness), Christians have taken circumcision of Jesus as symbolic of 'true circumcision of the spirit; that, our hearts, and all our members, being mortified from all worldly and carnal lusts, we may in all things obey thy blessed will" (Collect for 1 January, Book of Common Prayer); in early Church, liturgical celebration of event developed on Octave of Nativity (January 1), which day was already dedicated to celebration of "the fruitful virginity of blessed Mary" (Collect for Feast of Circumcision 1 January), asserting reality of Mary's motherhood and reality of Christ's manhood (as affirmed at Council of Chalcedon A.D. 451); all mainstream Christian liturgies preserve some degree of both commemorations for 1 January; Gospel commonly appointed for day (Luke 2:21) itself links both, while text commonly used as Epistle of day (Galatians 3:23-29) links Abraham's justification by faith, and baptismal promise to his seed and heirs, with gentile-Christian baptism; Gr had just performed a baptism, had recently experienced revelation of spiritually fructifying, even nationally redemptive, effect of holy kisses (and was reproved for it, by Asta, from mundane fear of scandal); here he expresses conviction that symbolism of circumcision ought to be incorporated in baptismal rite; his declaration that carnality "had to be washed away or cut away" is orthodoxly agreed by Circumcision liturgies ("cleanse us by thy heavenly mysteries" "Purge us from guilt" – Prayer, Feast of Circumcision, 1 January, Book of Common Prayer); despite Gr's colloquial idiom of lust sitting "behind the ears" (like Óðinn's raven, whispering?) his mind might well be more intelligently and coherently focussed upon a collocation of liturgical ideas and their meaning than Hammerich and others had enough willingness, or insight, to see; see also **Palm Sunday** 1867.

Citadel *112*; fortification in Copenhagen called Citadellet Frederikshavn or more commonly Kastellet, forming northerly point of city's defences; comprising fortress contained within complex of moats and bastions, close to Øresund shore and anchorage called Reden; also provided high-security prison facilities for notable State prisoners; built 1662 for Frederik III, decommissioned as fortress in 1850s but kept in use as barracks with own church; to the young Gr, seeking appointment to a city church, an "unenviable position" (he applied, and was rejected, thrice), though a succession of notable clerics served there.

Clausen, Henrik Georg, *111, 159, 163, 167, 170, 174, 175, 201, 330*; 1759-1840; *Stiftsprovst* [diocesan dean, corresponds approximately to English archdeacon or dean] in Vor Frue Kirke, Copenhagen; titular professor 1808; weighty figure in city's ecclesiastical circle and social life; moving force behind complaint of Copenhagen clergy (1810) against Gr's probational sermon, contributor to pressures leading Gr to resign his curacy at Vor Frelsers Kirke (1826); thereafter, lifelong adversary of Gr; father of H. N. Clausen.

Clausen, Henrik Nicolai *20, 64, 111, 127, 144, 160, 166, 169, 170, 175, 188, 200, 201, 231, 232, 249, 328, 339*; 1793-1877; academic, politician; son of Gr's adversary *Stiftsprovst* [diocesan dean] H. G. Clausen; Professor of Theology Copenhagen from 1822; publication of his *Catholicismens og Protestantismens Kirkeforfatning, Lære og Ritus* [Constitution, doctrine and rites of Catholicism and Protestantism; 1825], informed both by rationalism and by teaching of German Protestant theologian, Friedrich Daniel Ernst Schleiermacher (1768-1834); there conceptualised Church in somewhat abstract and relative terms as community defined by its commitment to advancement of general religious observance, and having guarantor in Holy Scriptures, as established and authenticated by modern (rationalist) biblical scholarship; provoked Gr's protest in *Kirkens Gienmæle* (1825); Gr intemperately called Clausen false teacher who confused and seduced the people and undermined the Church he purported to serve; *Kirkens Gienmæle* was adjudged libellous and led (1826) to Gr suffering a substantial fine (actually paid by his defence lawyer, F. W. Treschow), and his being placed under censorship (1826-37), and resigning his curacy at Vor Frelsers Kirke; Clausen subsequently emerged as leading national-liberal politician campaigning for free constitution (including freedom of the press); appointed as member of the 'March-ministry' (1848) set up on collapse of absolutism, and of *Den grundlovgivende Rigsforsamling* [the Constituent Assembly, charged with establishing Constitution]; committed to incorporation of Slesvig in Kingdom of Denmark and to ideal of Scandinavian unity; thus shared much common ground with his former adversary Gr and they were thus, for example, joint guests of honour when Copenhagen students hosted great reception (1845) to celebrate ideals of Scandinavian unity and nordic fellowship; enjoyed long and successful career with esteem of such pupils as Søren Kierkegaard; see also **Kirkens Gienmæle**.

Clausen, Peder 62, 1545-1614; Norwegian-born cleric; initial education in Stavanger but no university education; never travelled outside Norway; author of historical-topographical works (descriptions of Iceland 1580, Færoes 1592, Greenland 1596) and saga-translations as well as works on natural history of Norway; translations of Snorri's sagas of Norse kings, though begun 1599, were not printed until 1632 and 1633, edited by Danish antiquarian Ole Worm (reprinted 1727 and 1757); these editions consolidated Snorri's status as historical source and Clausen's as historian of Norway, and were among Gr's intensive reading in early historical literature of Scandinavia inspired by university friendship (begun Summer 1801) with P. N. Skougaard.

clerical convention 235, 236, 242, 279-281; *præstekonvent*; *geistlige Convent*; synod of clergy – though it is to be stressed that these regular and formal assemblies of clergy of the various regions such as Copenhagen and Roskilde, though empowered to debate, form resolutions and initiate certain actions, including publication, were not part of a conventional synodal structure of church government (a mode of government still resisted in the Danish Church); see also **Church,** Danish; **synod**.

clerical freedom; see **præstefrihed**.

Colbiørnsen, Christian 160; 1749-1814; Norwegian-born statesman, *Justitiarius* (Presiding Judge) in Danish Supreme Court; collaborated with *Grev* [Count] Christian Ditlev Reventlow (1748-1827), statesman and reforming landowner, seeking to improve rights and status of peasantry; as Secretary of Land Commission (1786) played considerable part in dissolution of the *stavnsbaand* (law of 1733, tying male peasantry to the district of their birth) in 1788; his widow and daughter, wrote H. C. Andersen autobiographically, "were the first ladies of high rank who cordially befriended the poor lad; who listened to me with sympathy, and saw me frequently." (Andersen, translated Mary Howitt, 1847).

Cold, Christian Magdalus Thestrup *166, 168*; 1754-1826; Jurist, professor (1788), from 1799 onwards held leading positions in the Danish Chancellery; advised Gr to apply for church post in Aalborg (1818).

colloqvier *67*; colloquies, dialogues in Latin (sometimes also with vernacular) designed to exercise schoolchildren (including young Gr) in use of Latin language; genre reaches back through Middle Ages to classical antiquity.

Come, Spirit of truth; see *Kom, Sandheds Aand.*

Complutenser *289*; the *Complutum*, edition of Bible published (1515) Alcala, Spain; used by Gr for his daily readings.

Constantinople *65*; city founded by Constantine the Great (330) became ancient capital of Byzantine Empire, conquered by Turks 1453; 18th and 19th c. ambition of Russians (regarding themselves as true heirs of Byzantine legacy) to seize it from Turks had major strategic implications for western European nations; but more stirring to young Gr in 1789, when Russians seemed close to success, was romantic and religious aura of its name in newspaper reports (read and discussed in Udby parsonage on Sunday afternoons); report of fall of Otschakov (Oczakov) in *Kiøbenhavns Tidender*, 16 January 1789, concluded with speculation that "this intelligence will help (God grant it) to promote peace, otherwise a Russian fleet will no doubt be making a visit to Constantinople in the Spring."

Constituent National Assembly; see **Rigsforsamling,** den grundlovgivende.

Constitution, The; see **Grundloven**

Constitution Day *24, 243, 292*; *Grundlovsdag* (5 June), Danish national holiday on which national flag is flown on public buildings, commemorating undersigning of first Constitution by Frederik VII (1849); Gr was invited speaker at *Grundlovsdag*-festivities in Tivoli and Alhambra, Copenhagen.

Convention; see **clerical convention**.

Conybeare, John Josias *130, 134, 135*; 1779-1824; Professor of Anglo-Saxon and Professor of Poetry in the University of Oxford; communicated to Society of Antiquaries of London (who then published them in their journal *Archæologia*, vol. xvii for 1814) papers on Anglo-Saxon poetry of the Exeter Book and other manuscripts (with some transcriptions); this journal appears among acquisitions of Royal Library Copenhagen from that period; collection of Conybeare's pioneering work on content and form of Anglo-Saxon poetry was published posthumously (*Illustrations of Anglo-Saxon Poetry, edited together with additional notes, introductory notices, &c., by his brother William Daniel Conybeare*, London 1826; included extracts and translations from the Exeter Book and from *Beowulf* and "Hymns of Cædmon and of Bede") and was also purchased by the Royal Library and used by Gr in preparation for his visits to England; in it Conybeare advocated a programme of publications of Anglo-Saxon texts as Gr himself did in 1830.

Copenhagen *passim*; Danish København (older Kjøbenhavn); founded on small holm between Sjælland and island of Amager, on Sjælland's Øresund coast, as fortress and merchants' harbour, by Absalon (died 1201), warrior-archbishop (also popularly called Axel, hence Gr's allusion to city as Axelborg); became in Middle Ages Dk's capital, seat of sovereigns, and eventually ecclesiastical capital (see also **Sjælland,** Bishop of); university city 1479; prior to 19th c., period of greatest expansion and adornment was reign of Christian IV (1588-1648), but by 1830s city was still contained within ramparts and moats (military authorities opposed development outside walls) and, with some 120,000 inhabitants occupying less than five square kilometres, was grossly overcrowded; major fire of 1795 destroyed quarter of city; British incendiary-bombardment in Napoleonic Wars (1807) left more than 300 buildings ruined; advancing awareness of health considerations and growth of trade and industry made city ripe for major redevelopment and expansion mid-19th c. onwards so before century was out, boundaries reached far beyond old defences and population had more than doubled; capital status, presence of court, aristocratic residences, patronage, major churches, university, libraries, theatres, port with international traffic, etc., and little competition from elsewhere in country, guaranteed Copenhagen's cultural preeminence throughout 18th and 19th c. – yet it was a small stage for the many large personalities which would strut upon it, and a strikingly determinant factor in the daily lives of its principal players was the tight, institutionalised and almost infinitely hierarchical complexity of Copenhagen society.

Copenhagen, battle of *81-83*; 1801; Battle of Reden; event in Napoleonic wars; Dk-Norway, with significant mercantile fleet, entered into armed neutrality pact with Prussia and Sweden under auspices of Russia, creating threat to England's war-economy, swiftly answered by assault upon Copenhagen by English fleet under Admiral Hyde Parker, second in command being Horatio Nelson, renowned for recent destruction of French fleet at Aboukir (Battle of the Nile, 1798); after brief skirmish passing Kronborg Slot at entry to Øresund (30 March 1801), English fleet took up positions in Kongedybet, channel off Copenhagen; ensuing sea-battle (2 April 1801) known in Dk as Battle of Reden (*Reden* being 'the road' used for anchorage off Copenhagen but also offering scope for pun on word for 'the nest' and notion of 'defending the nest'); militarily, outcome was not clear cut; Danish fleet was, in words of Crown Prince Frederik's adjutant, General Lindholm, caught by surprise, short of officers, under-manned, crewed partly by inexperienced volunteers, and comprised of old and decaying ships, but despite losses it held out long enough for 24-hour ceasefire to be negotiated and to spare city from bombardment; England gained goal of forcing Dk to withdraw from pact of armed neutrality; most important from Danish viewpoint, defence of Copenhagen at sea and on land (brigades of volunteers were formed, one of university students including Gr) was perceived in Dk as success and triumph for a people rediscovering their old national cohesion and pride, so popular historians have spoken of Battle of Reden as country's national and democratic birthday; in contrast stands poem *Battle of the Baltic* by Thomas Campbell (1777-1844) attributing to Nelson not only victory "by the wild and stormy steep, / Elsinore" but also magnanimity in offering Denmark truce ("Ye are brothers! ye are men! / And we conquer but to save"): "Then Denmark blessed our chief, / That he gave her wounds repose; / And the sounds of joy and grief / From her people wildly rose, / As death withdrew his shades from the day, / While the sun looked smiling bright / O'er a wide and woeful sight, / Where the fires of funeral light / Died away." See also **bombardment of** 1807.

Copenhagen University *61, 63, 71, 78, 80-82, 86, 100, 115, 154, 159, 160, 166, 181, 185, 188, 247, 295*; founded by Christian I as Dk's first university in 1479 (second, founded 1665, was at Kiel in Holsten until loss of duchies in 1864) some thirty-five years after Copenhagen replaced Roskilde as royal centre of Dk (1443); like other medieval European universities, served Theology as the supreme study to which other liberal arts and sciences were handmaids; underwent reformation along with other principal institutions of Church and State 1537, consolidating its major role of qualifying priests for ministry but also advancing and gradually modernising study of law and medicine, particularly by substantial reorganisation and modernisation in 1840s and 1850s; in Gr's day, male students (only) were admitted by examination from Latin Schools and private tuition (many of them living in residential colleges, such as Regensen, in university quarter) and were required to submit for examination to gain degree (all faculties having instituted degree examinations by 1788); its buildings were severely damaged under British bombardment 1807, and new principal buildings not inaugurated until 1836; Copenhagen and Kiel (which exercised considerable influence especially as cultural link between Germany and Scandinavia) were sole universities of Denmark-Norway until establishment (1811) of Norwegian university at Kristiania (Oslo); in 1800 the University was organised in four faculties (Theology; Philosophy – which as well as general philosophy, metaphysics and logic, also covered History, Geography, Mathematics, Astronomy, classical and oriental languages; Law; Medicine); Theology had four professors (Claudius Frees Hornemann, Daniel Gotthilf Moldenhawer, Nicolai Edinger Balle, Friederich Münter), Philosophy eight professors (Abraham Kall, Börge Riisbrigh, Thomas Bugge, Nicolai Cristoph Kall, Jacob Baden, Lauritz Sahl, Jeremias Wöldiche, Andreas Gamborg), Law three professors, and Medicine four professors; there were in addition various 'Extraordinary' and 'Honorary' professors; Gr's opinion of Copenhagen University was never very high (in 1801 "the University was stone dead") and he came to believe fervently in need for an alternative 'folk-university' in Sorø or a pan-Scandinavian university in Göteborg (Sweden).

corporeality, Gr's concept of *250*; wholeheartedly endorsed by Bishop H. L. Martensen.

Corregio 101; tragedy in three acts by Oehlenschläger (1811) first written in German then redone in Danish by author himself; plot concerns Italian painter Antonio Allegri Correggio (1494-1534) through whom author projects own romantic *angst* over uncertainty of sustaining artistic creativity beyond brilliant youthful beginnings.

Council of State; see **Rigsraad**.

Court law; see **Hof- og Stadsretten**.

Creed, Apostolic; see **Apostles' Creed**.

crusades *105*; holy wars waged by medieval European Christendom against Mohammedan occupiers of Christian holy places in Middle East; exact number of qualifying expeditions varies among informants, but between 1095 and 1270 some eight major campaigns were undertaken in the Holy Land; historians broadly agree with Gr's view that papal foreign policy, formulated under Leo IX and Gregory VII (whom Gr admired and taught his pupils at Schouboe's Institute to admire, 1808-11), restored discipline and unity of Christian vision and purpose to fragmented secular states of Europe; thus 1810 Gr read zealously in history of crusades, which seems to have answered to a latter-day crusading spirit in himself and certainly led him to a belief informing his own historical writings, namely "the necessity of Christianity in the history of the nations."

currency, Danish *passim*; The Danish (silver-standard) currency system dating from 1625 comprised three units of denomination: the *rigsdaler*, the *mark* and the *skilling*, with 6 marks to the rigsdaler and 16 skillings to the mark (thus 96 skillings to the rigsdaler). However, the value of a sum when made up of small coins came eventually to be quoted at *courant* rate which was lower than the *species* rate quoted for a sum made up of silver rigsdaler (thus from 1713 to 1813 one rigsdaler *species* was worth 120 skillings *courant*. In 1813 following Napoleonic wars Dk suffered State bankruptcy and *Rigsbanken* [State Bank] was constituted to establish a single monetary system for the whole kingdom: the unit of currency was the *rigsbankdaler*, divided into 96 *rigsbank skilling* and fixed at value of one-half of the *rigsdaler species* (which continued to be issued as silver coin) or 6 *rigsdaler courant*. In 1854 the *rigsbankdaler* was renamed *rigsdaler* and the *rigsbank skilling* was renamed *skilling rigsmønt*. In 1873 Dk, along with Sweden and (1875) Norway, changed from silver standard to gold standard and to decimal coinage based upon the *krone* (divided into 100 *øre*). In 1818 the *Rigsbank* was reformed as an independent share-based institution, *Nationalbanken*, which in the course of time became the banker to the country's smaller banks and financial institutions. Over 19th c. and especially in second half, growth of *Sparekasser* [Savings banks], empowered to make loans, played important role in emergence of farmers into economic and political significance. Incomes varied dramatically widely. In 1820 when he was arrested for embezzlement Christian Birch (1760-1829), a highly-placed official in central financial administration, was being paid 2300 rigsbankdaler a year; at same period a docker in the Admiralty shipyards in Copenhagen was paid 2 rigsbankdaler for a six-day week and a retiring schoolmaster in North Sjælland was granted a pension of 200 rigsbankdaler a year. In 1799 Gr, by singing in Aarhus Cathedral choir, earned a stipendium amounting to 30 rigsdaler over the year, offsetting his school fees; at university he found it hard to get by on an income of 20 rigsdaler a month, eked out by free dinners and food supplies sent from home; his first appointment at Egeløkke earned him a salary of 150 rigsdaler a year on top of lodging and keep; to enable him to live while devoting himself to work on Saxo and Snorri he was granted an annual pension of 600 rigsbankdaler, sufficient to give him security to marry; for his visit to England 1829 he was awarded a grant of 2000 rigsbankdaler; on appointment as priest at Vartov his starting salary is said to have been "only 800 rigsbankdaler." In 1850 Christen Kold felt able to set up a school at Ryslinge for 1100 rigsbankdaler. In that year, a cobbler in Roskilde could earn 7 rigsbankdaler a week. In 1864 H. C. Andersen's declared income was 1820 rigsdaler, his assets were calculated to be 10039 rigsdaler (corresponding to more than one million Danish kroner in today's currency), and his quarterly tax bill was 12 rigsdaler and 48 skillings (Johan de Mylius); in the same year Richard Petersen was paid an annual wage of 400 rigsdaler "og en Offerdag" [and an offerings-day] in his first church appointment as personal curate near Randers in Jylland. One estimate of inflation over the century suggests that it was 30% between 1820-36, 50% between 1835-50 and 50% between 1850-70.

Cædmon *135, 189, 334*; Anglo-Saxon poet, first Christian poet of the English language (before A.D. 680); his miraculous acquisition of gift of oral composition of poetry is narrated by 8th-c. English historiographer, the Venerable Bede, in *Ecclesiastical History of the English People* (completed

731); little if any surviving Anglo-Saxon poetry can now be safely attributed to him, but contents of Anglo-Saxon poetic codex Oxford Bodleian Library MS Junius 11 were once attributed to Cædmon, published by Franciscus Junius as *Cædmonis Monachi Paraphrasis Poetica Genesios ac praecipuarum Sacræ Paginae Historiarum, abhinc annos M.LXX. Anglo-Saxonicè conscripta, & nunc primum edita* (1654); Gr's encounter (from *ca.* 1815) with this earliest of all documented Northern poets – a Christian poet to whom attached this testimony of direct inspiration by the Holy Spirit – contributed to his own self-identification as a Northern *skjald* (skald, poet) singing, like Cædmon, to a harp handed down from David the psalmist, and consolidated his philosophy of history as the record of God's purposeful and providential dealings with world; he prepared (but never published) a transcription of this codex together with his own verse preface composed partly in Old English (Grundtvig Arkiv Fascicle 320); among the rest, the Cædmonian narrative of Christ's harrowing of hell particularly struck him, inspired him to write two hymns, *I Kvæld blev der banket paa Helvedes Port* [This night came a knock at the portals of Hell] and *Kommer, Sjæle, dyrekøbte* [Come you souls so dearly purchased], and inspired his followers to translations, poems and pictures; see also **hymns**.

D

Dagbladet *165*; 'The Daily Newspaper' first published 1851 by S. B. Salomon in Copenhagen; under leadership of politician Carl Steen Andersen Bille (1828-98) paper gained much influence and broke new journalistic ground, taking advantage of telegraphic communications; maintained National-Liberal (conservative) stance and in particular waged crude propaganda against the *Bondevenner* (favoured by Gr and followers); Gr mentions (1862) that paper was dismissive of his writings just as former daily *Dagen* had been; title finally disappeared 1891.

Dagen *165*; 'The Day' daily newspaper published from 1803 by K. H. Seidelin in Copenhagen; apart from Berling's already established daily, *Berlingske Tidende*, with which it shared official privilege of publishing foreign intelligence, most important daily until decline 1841; edited 1811-14 by K. L. Rahbek, reflecting his interest in literature and culture; edited 1822-35 by Frederik Thaarup, reflecting his concern with national economic statistics; Gr puns somewhat mockingly on its name when referring to its exorcising critique of contemporary (early 19th-c.) literature including some of his own.

Dane- (Danne-) *143*; prefix (*Dane-* being regarded as having more solemn or formal ring than *Danne-*) frequently used by Gr (and 19th-c. Romantic authors such as B. S. Ingemann) as equivalent of 'Danish' particularly with reference to antiquity as in *Danedrot* [Dane-king], *Dannebrog* [Dane-banner, national flag], *Dannevirke* [Dane-ramparts, frontier fortification; also name symbolically given to weekly paper launched 1838 to promote cause of Danishness in duchy of Slesvig]; but in some compounds, notably *Dannemand, Dannekvinde* (used by Gr especially to refer to archetypal Danish man and woman), first element has alternative derivation and sense related to *dannis* 'decent, worthy, honourable' permitting authors a calculated ambivalence (Danish/honourable), as in *Dane-hjerte* [(honourable) Danish heart]; Gr describes atmosphere on ship returning from great nationalistic gathering at Skamlingsbanken (1844) as *saa ægte dansk og dannis* [so genuinely Danish and decent]; see also **Dannevirke**.

Danedrot *114*; 'Dane-king,' archaic-poetic term typical of vocabulary devised, revived or revitalised by Gr following his immersion (particularly 1815 onwards) in ancient literary culture of North (Saxo, Snorri, *Beowulf*); this new-antique vocabulary within the *modersmaal* [mother-tongue], sometimes mediated by Gr through translations and their introductory poetical pastiches which he hoped would take their place as reading for children at home and in schools, tacitly claimed honourable continuity from, and appealed to authority of, Northern heroic legendary antiquity to endorse contemporary institutions and concepts, social and political, especially as related to king and folk, as conveniently summarised in his characterisation of blest (Danish) community ruled by king Scyld Scefing (Skjold) in *Beowulf*: "Skjold, den Landets milde Fader, og det ham kiærlig, tro hengivne danske Folk" [Skjold, mild father of the land, and the Danish folk, affectionate, faithful and devoted towards him].

Dane-Hjerte; see **Dane-**.

Dane-king; see **Danedrot**.

Danish Association, The; see **danske Forening**, Den.

Danish Historical Association; see **Dansk historisk Forening**.

Danish Society; see **Danske Samfund, Det**.

Danish State-Church impartially viewed, *The*; see **Den danske Stats-Kirke upartisk betragtet**.

Danmark dejligst Vang og Vænge *137, 274*; *Danmark dejligst Vang og Vænge, / lukt med Bølgen blaa* [Denmark, loveliest field and meadow / enclosed by ocean blue] are the opening lines of a lyric composed by Laurids O. Kock (1634-91), around 1685, since when it has held a place among Denmark's most popular patriotic songs; quoted by Gr in lectures at Borchs Kollegium 1838, its use as part of Grundtvigian rhetoric was mocked by Søren Kierkegaard.

Danmarks Historie *165*; The *Gesta Danorum* of Saxo Grammaticus, translated by Gr along with other Northern legendary-historical texts after 1815 "when I gave up the church-struggle for the time being" (Gr); see **Saxo Grammaticus**.

Dannebrog, Order of *62, 240, 268, 311*; Danish chivalric order founded 1671 by King Christian v (1670-1699); its symbol derived from the red banner ('red-coloured' is probable original meaning of word *dannebrog*) with a white cross, the national flag of Dk which legend says fell from heaven (1219) when Valdemar Sejr confronted heathens at the battle of Lyndanise, Estonia; honour may be granted to nationals and non-nationals for distinction in civil or military service; originally comprised single class of knight but reforms (1808) by Frederik vi established two classes, Grand Commander and Commander – subsequently (1864) divided into two grades; investment with silver cross as badge of honour of Dannebrogsman also instituted (1808), to be granted without regard to recipient's formal title and status; these changes followed by considerable increase in numbers decorated.

Dannebrog, *240, 241, 270*; weekly periodical of Dansk Forening , society formed by Gr and friends May 1853 to promote "fatherland, mother-tongue and everything *folkelig* [pertaining to sense of national communality]," its first editor being Frederik Barfod whom Gr subsequently and summarily sacked following disagreement on editorial viewpoints.

Dannemænd *143, 146*; 'Danish men' with implication of true Danish heroes; Gr's term for the Danish seamen who died fighting with Captain C. V. Jessen and Gr's friend Peter Willemoes off Sjællands Odde (1808); see **Dane-**.

Danneskjold, Christian Conrad Sophus *114*, 1774-1823; *Grev* [Count] of Samsø, Grand Cross of Dannebrog, *amtmand* (corresponds roughly to archaic English High Sheriff) of Præstø; aristocratic descendant of illegitimate offspring of Danish kings with seat at Gisselfeld, some 25 km north of Gr's parental home, Udby, and similar distance northwest of Præstø; "Elskeligt og aabent var hans Hjerte, utrættelig hans Gavnelyst; hans Glæde var Godgiørenhed, hans Haab var Gud" [Amiable and open was his heart, untiring his generosity; benefaction was his delight, and God his hope – Gr 1824]; subject of Gr's elegy *Forsetes-Kvide ved Grev Danneskjolds Grav* [Forsete's lament at the grave of Count Danneskjold]] drafted around 1824, of which a portion was published 1828 (whole text published 1883 in *Poetiske Skrifter* 5 under title *Danneskjolds-Drape*); name Gisselfeld appears to have prompted Gr to association, via old Danish *gissel*, ray of light, to mythological Glitner, the radiant, name of gold and silver hall in home of the gods, Ásgarðr (mentioned in Icelandic *Grímnismál*) where Forsete, son of Baldr and Nanna, had his judgment seat, the best among gods and men, and by his just judgments restored peace where there was strife (Snorri's *Edda*); poem's lament is not only for dead benefactor but for decadence into which times have sunk in Dk; see also **Nordens Mythologi**.

Dannevirke *268, 272, 312*; Fortification lying between River Ejder and Slien (The Schlei), probably dating back to 7th c., developed 808 by Danish King Godfred to control and secure trade routes on southern frontier; subsequently consolidated as military frontier, notably (according at least to Saxo Grammaticus) by Thyra (*circa* 930), queen of Gorm den gamle [the Old], who (legend says) set up residence there for three years to oversee the work, and by Valdemar (1162); the military retreat from Dannevirke 1864 was one of the great traumas of Danish history, and gravely affected Gr along with others; the frontier was never recovered and the remnants of Dannevirke now lie within Germany; "*Dannevirke* is what, in metaphorical language, we call everything which guards true Danishness and decency [*ægte Danskhed og Dannished*] against that which is alien [*det vildfremmede*], which continually insinuates itself and has often brought Denmark to the brink of her ruination" (Gr in *Krønnike-Rim* 1842); its name was adopted by Gr as symbolic title of his periodical (1816-19) *Danne-Virke* (with its mission of asserting Danish cultural frontiers against foreign, particularly German, cultural encroachment) and by editors of a weekly newspaper *Dannevirke* (asserting a more specifically Slesvig-focussed political-geographical mission), founded in Haderslev by Peter Christian Koch (1807-80), leading pro-Danish activist, granted royal privilege to publish through influence of Christian Flor (1792-1875, professor of Danish, Kiel University; see also **Dane-** (Danne-).

Danne-Virke *110, 120, 163-165, 197*; *Danne-Virke, et Tids-Skrift af N. F. S. Grundtvig*; periodical written and published by Gr in Copenhagen 1816-19, in which "personal experience and psychology, Christianity and history are melded into a complex universe" (J. I. Jensen); contains essays, poems and other items by Gr, largely didactic and polemical; verse epigram on title-page well conveys flavour: *Klokken i den danske Kirke / Det er Sagas klingre Skjold, / Til at bygge Danne-Virke / Vække den hver Dane bold! / Ret den klinger dog i Vangen, / Kun i Chor med Kirke-Sangen / Under Thyra Dannebod!* [The bell in the Danish church, it is Saga's ringing shield; to the building of Dannevirke may it rouse every bold Dane! Yet rightly it rings in the meadow only in chorus with the singing in the church under Thyra Dannebod] – where *Saga* is personification of (national) legend-history, Dannevirke is Dk's ancient southern frontier fortification built (according to legend-history) by Queen Thyra, and *Dannebod* or *Danmarks Bod* [Denmark's adornment? Denmark's succour?] is soubriquet given to Thyra – daughter of King Æthelræd I of England (Saxo) or of Jutish king Harald Klak (medieval Icelandic saga tradition), wife of Gorm the Old and mother of King Harald ("who won for himself all Denmark and Norway and made the Danes Christian") – according to the inscription (*tanmarkaR but*) on the smaller of the two 10th-c. runestones at Jelling in Jylland; in retrospect Gr characterised *Danne-Virke* as the arena where he would "throw down the gauntlet to anyone who would do battle with me in the field of history, over the honour of the Church and the integrity of my Christianity."

danske Forening, Den [The Danish Association] *44, 240*; society established by Frederik Barfod (October 1852) for like-minded members of *Rigsdag* opposed to mooted law of succession affecting duchies, and to mooted policy of moving customs frontier from Ejder to Elbe; but after dissolution of *Rigsdag* (January 1853) it was refounded (March 1853) with Gr as president; its aim now was to work for advancement of 'Danishness' among the people, through, for example, lectures such as Gr's series of twelve *Forelæsninger over Højnordens Historie* [lectures on the history of the high North] (Spring 1854) and weekly paper *Dannebrog* edited 1854-55 by C. J. Brandt, which published (23 June 1854) Gr's final lecture in series, and (13 and 20 January, 23 March, 8 June and 6 July 1855) series of five articles by Gr on *Den Danske Sag* [The Danish Cause]; a particular objective of Association, to found a people's university (*en dansk folkelig Højskole*), progressed when, with fund started by large monetary donations honouring his 70th birthday (8 September 1853), Gr bought Marielyst, property near Copenhagen, where *Grundtvigs Højskole* opened Autumn 1856.

Danskeren *129, 140, 144, 147, 148, 150, 152, 292*; weekly periodical published (volumes I-IV, 1848-51) by Gr, majority of articles being by Gr himself; in direct response to outbreak of war over Slesvig, it addresses topical circumstances and issues, domestic and international, asserting the national viewpoint; also used for publication of poems and songs by Gr, as for example his *Slesvigsk-Dansk-Minde-Sang* [Slesvig-Danish commemorative song], I (1848) on legendary King Vermund and son Uffe who rallied to fight Germans on Ejder frontier, and *Skjaldelivet i Danmark* [The bardic life in Denmark], IV (1851).

Danske Samfund, Det [The Danish Society] *256, 283*; Society founded (18 April 1839) by Frederik Barfod, following success of Gr's lecture-events at Borchs Kollegium (June-November 1838), the texts of which were subsequently published as *Mands Minde* [In Living Memory]; aim was to advance 'Danishness' at *folkelig* level through same format of lecture on Danish subject plus communal singing of Danish songs; format eventually used widely around the country and is still used; gave rise to Society's publication (1840) of dedicated song-book, *Viser og Sange for Danske Samfund* [Ballads and Songs for the Danish Society].

Dansk historisk Forening [The Danish Historical Association] *22, 253*; Association founded 14 February 1839 on initiative of Gr's friend, librarian, historian, philological scholar Christian Molbech (1783-1857) with objective of awakening (particularly national) historical "Spirit and Interest" and promoting (particularly Danish) historical studies; Danish-national restriction opposed, unsuccessfully, by Gr who desired to promote own universal-historical principles; besides periodical *Historisk Tidsskrift* Association published various individual studies.

***Dansk Kirketidende** 70, 235, 245, 266*; Danish Church-news; weekly periodical edited by R. T. Fenger and C. J. Brandt, launched 1845, devised as mouthpiece for Gr's stance on the church and the *folkelige*; carried many items by Gr himself; still continues, published by Kirkeligt Samfund, promoting values of freedom in Danish spiritual life.

***Dansk Litteratur-Tidende** 160, 165*; periodical (until 1811 titled *Kjøbenhavnske lærde Efterretninger* [Learned news from Copenhagen]) edited 1790-1804 by Rasmus Nyerup (1759-1829), literary historian, professor, embodiment of 18th-c. Enlightenment values, dedicated through wide range of his professional undertakings to enlightenment, liberty, civic virtues, scholarly collaborator with K. L. Rahbek, in whose journal *Minerva* he published many articles; edited 1805-30 by P. E. Müller; Gr refers to "the pillory of *Lærde Efterretninger*" which (around 1810) put to scorn activities of such as populist and pietist itinerant preacher, Norwegian Hans Hauge.

dansk og dannis *143*; Danish and decent; see **Dane-** (Danne-).

Danz's *Grammar 71*; presumably the "Dansii Grammatik" which Gr lists among books he studied at Aarhus Grammar School is the Hebrew grammar, *Compendium Grammaticæ Ebraicæ-Chaldaicæ* (Jena, 1699), of German theologian and Hebraist and professor of Oriental languages at University of Jena, Johann Andreas Danz (1654-1727), translated into German as *Hebräische und Chaldäische Grammatik* by G. Kypke (Breslau, 1784), which enjoyed a very long life as a standard text-book.

Davout (Davoust), Louis Nicolas *108*; 1770-1823; French marshal (1804) serving Napoleon, highly distinguished in series of battles; governor of Hamburg from 1811; following retreat from Russia (1812) he recaptured Hamburg, governed it with great severity, surrendered it only after Napoleon's fall; in 1813 commander of French forces and auxiliaries (including Danish auxiliary corps) north of Elbe, during which period Napoleon lost battle of Leipzig and Allies under Bernadotte pushed Danish troops northwards, took Glückstadt and Rendsborg and overran Jylland as far north as Kolding Aa [Kolding river].

***Dejlig er den Himmel blaa** 164*; *Lovely are the heavens blue*; Christmas lyric by Gr, written December 1810 shortly before his breakdown; published under title *De hellige tre Konger* [The three holy kings], with preface by Gr justifying this kind of 'historical-Christian' hymn, in *Sandsigeren, eller den danske Huusven, et Ugeskrift. Udgivet af Prof. K. L. Rahbek* [The Truth-teller or the Danish Household Friend, a weekly journal published by Prof. K. L. R.], No. 12 (April 1811); as first drafted, comprising 19 verses and deliberately addressed as to congregation of children; melody later furnished by Thomas Laub (1852-1927); revised 1853 with 7 verses, melody furnished by J. G. Meidell (1778-1857); later version has become one of most loved of Danish Christmas hymns; no. 136 in *DDS* 2002; see also **hymns.**

Dejlig er jorden, *340*; *Lovely is this earthly place*; hymn written (1850) by Bernhard Severin Ingemann (1789-1862), set to 18th c. melody from Slesvig; no. 121 in *DDS* 2002; example of popular durability of St Augustine's image of earth, created in its beauty by God, as place of (spiritual) pilgrimage towards the heavenly homeland; sung by throng processing through streets of Copenhagen in Gr's funeral cortège, 1872; see also **hymns.**

Den christelige Børnelærdom *153, 155*; Christian instruction for children; title of work published by Gr 1868 in which, among the rest, he outlines his perception of the Church; but also the regular term for that primary instruction in the faith, as for example epitomised in Luther's Short Catechism, which parents and godparents were enjoined in the baptismal rite to provide; taught to Gr by his mother at home in Udby; see also **Katekismus,** Luther's.

Den danske Stats-Kirke upartisk betragtet *174, 176*; *The Danish State-Church impartially viewed* (1834); major step in Gr's ongoing opposition to H. N. Clausen's published and taught concepts of Christianity and Church: Christianity is an unalterable historical fact, but State Church is a construct of government which government can alter or even dissolve; however, to argue that Church should be emancipated from State is to confuse Church with School and faith with churchly institutionalism; ruins of medieval church-state certainly still need clearing away and the motivation and zeal for this will be achieved only by granting freedom of religious conscience and of religious practice, not by conformity enforced by secular and ecclesiastical authorities – not a hair should be harmed of the head of a heretic; Gr wants not dissolution of State Church but a free State Church with a free congregation; see also **Church,** Danish; **Folkekirke; Frikirke; Clausen,** H. N.; *Kirkens Gienmæle; Frisprog;* **Early Church,** custom of; **forsamlinger; Church struggle,** The; **Birkedal,** Schøller Parelius Vilhelm; **præstefrihed; sognebaandsløsning.**

Denmark *passim*; In his *Krønnike-Rim til levende Skolebrug* (literally 'Chronicle-rhymes for living school-use' but translatable as 'History in verse for use in the school for life'), 1st edition 1828, augmented 2nd edition 1842, 3rd edition 1875, Gr supplies a glossary of definitions relevant to the study of Danish history, presenting the perceptions he wished should be promoted in a properly conceived and taught educational programme; the entry for 'Danmark' reads: "*Denmark* is our tiny but age-old, and in antiquity highly renowned, kingdom and fathers' land, whence went forth the Angles who christianised and enlightened the whole of the North. Nowhere are the ancient legends of the people better preserved nor the fathers more lovingly and constantly besung, so Denmark is justly called in metaphorical language the Fortunate Isles (*Sæl-Land*) [pseudo-etymology of Sjælland, name of Denmark's chief island, as though derived from archaic word *sæl*, 'blest by fortune, happy'], where people lived on after death." Similarly the entry for 'Danskhed' [Danishness] reads: "*Danishness* counts in the world for nothing at all, but yet has defended itself against the world for a couple of thousand years."

Den Norske Folkeskole *255*; Norwegian educational periodical; see **Andresen,** Peter Rasmussen.

Den signede Dag, *som vi nu seer 170; The blessed day which now we see;* hymn by Gr (1826); no. 402 in *DDS* 2002; based upon a medieval *Dagvise*, morning-hymn; Danish Church celebrated thousand-year anniversary on Whitsunday, 14 May 1826, in honour of which Gr wrote *Kong Harald og Ansgar. Rim-Blade af Danmarks Kirke-Bog til Jubel-Aaret* [King Harald and Ansgar. Verse-pages from Denmark's church-register for the year of jubilee] and new festal hymns including *Den signede Dag* and *Tusind Aar stod Kristi Kirke* [A thousand years Christ's Church has stood; no. 343 in *DDS* 2002] which he publicly announced would be sung on Whitsunday morning in Vor Frelsers Kirke where he was curate; though it had already been decreed that, while texts for festival-day were prescribed, priests could decide own choice of hymns, archdeacon of Copenhagen H. G. Clausen immediately wrote to Gr warning him that only hymns from authorised Evangelical-Christian Hymnal were permitted; bishop Friedrich Münter supported Clausen's action and condemned Gr's new hymns, asserting that they lacked proper hymn-like character, all contained obscure and tasteless passages, and one (*Den signede Dag*) did not even have a melody (in fact, a melody by C. E. F. Weyse (1774-1842) accompanied the text in second edition late in same month); thus Münter persuaded Danish Chancellery to issue resolution that hymns from authorised Hymnal alone might be used; Gr, already awaiting outcome of his prosecution for libel (in connection with *Kirkens Gienmæle*, 1825) against professor H. N. Clausen (son of *Stiftsprovst* H. G. Clausen), was deeply wounded and resigned his curacy at Vor Frelsers Kirke a few days before Whitsunday; he was therefore not in office to celebrate the great festival he had been involved in planning, nor were his hymn-offerings sung; in October same year, he was fined and placed under censorship and court costs were awarded against him, for Clausen libel; but though associated with so much personal trauma for Gr himself, *Den signede Dag* in reworked form, suited to celebration of every new morning, every Sunday, every festal day of the Church's year, subsequently entered Danish Hymnal and remains among most popular of all Danish hymns; see also **hymns**.

Der sad en Svend i Blaamænds Land *164; There sat a youth in Ethiope,* also entitled *Kammersvenden fra Morland*, narrative poem of a serving-lad who, inspired by story of queen of Sheba's visit to Solomon, finds his way to Christian truth; composed 1812, published in his *Kvædlinger* (1815); one of his early compositions in which Gr felt he was faithfully echoing the strains of Lutheran hymnody; subsequently set to melody by J. P. E. Hartmann; *blaamand* (pl. *blaamænd*) (etymologically 'blue-man' but meaning 'black man' – cp. 'Bluetooth' [*Blatan, Blaatand*] as soubriquet of Danish king Harald) was term sometimes used for dark-skinned peoples of such lands as Ethiopia and Egypt.

Descent into Hell *114;* the article of belief that Christ's descent into hell followed upon the crucifixion and preceded the resurrection, professed in Apostles' Creed of western church tradition (though not in some other parts of early church), was stressed by such reformers as Luther and Calvin as of great consequence in accomplishment of redemption, and was so held by Gr who used the literary *topos* (often called the harrowing of hell), which he encountered in Anglo-Saxon poetry, as basis for hymns (*I Kvæld blev der banket paa Helvedesport* [This night came a knock at the portals of Hell] and *Kommer, Sjæle, dyrekøbte* [Come you souls so dearly purchased]), and inspired his followers to translations, poems and pictures; he also used phrase metaphorically to describe fate of literary culture when offended parties turned to libel litigation with backing from the courts; see also **Cædmon; hymns**.

Det Skandinaviske Selskab *236*; The Scandinavian Association, founded in Copenhagen 1843 at instigation of Frederik Barfod (treasurer, secretary) with Gr as chairman; expression of growing cultural and political Scandinavianism of period, aimed to promote fellowship between Dk, Norway, Sweden; collaboration in society led to improved relationship between Gr and his old adversary Professor H. N. Clausen, a main figure in the society.

dictata *105*; notes made by Gr for own use as teacher (1808-11) at Schouboe's Institute; *Registrant* Fasc. 211.

Die Bestimmung des Menschen *96*; The destiny of man (1800) by Johann Gottlieb Fichte (1762-1814); Fichte had previously argued that philosophy could not and did not need to postulate a supernatural authority in order to endorse human moral law, and this severe restriction upon the legitimate scope of religious philosophy (as distinct from the historical claims of revealed religions) was regarded by some, in the context of the then current debate on atheism, as atheistic; in *Die Bestimmung des Menschen* (sharing its title with a publication (1748) of German philosopher Johan Joachim Spalding, 1714-1804, and thus inviting juxtaposition) he attempted to answer his critics by expounding a conceptualisation, going beyond the subjective phenomena of finite nature, of human life as self-revelation of divine presence of God; read by Gr (who found it a "fine book") while resident tutor at Egeløkke and immediately prior to his sudden new departure (1806) into Nordic antiquity; see also **Fichte,** Johan Gottlieb.

Die Söhne des Thales *189*; *Die Söhne des Thales, ein dramatisches Gedicht* [The sons of Thales, a dramatic poem], Part I: *Die Templer auf Cypern* [The Templars of Cyprus] (1803), Part II: *Die Kreuzesbrüder* [Brothers under the Cross] (1804); see **Werner,** Friedrich Ludwig Zacharias.

Die Weihe der Kraft *189*; *Martin Luther oder die Weihe der Kraft. Eine Tragödie* [Martin Luther, or The consecration of strength. A tragedy] (1807); see **Werner,** Friedrich Ludwig Zacharias.

Dietrichson, J. W. C. *302*; 1815-83; Norwegian *provst* (rural dean); one among many visitors, including Norwegians, who called on Gr when visiting Copenhagen; later changed office to that of postmaster.

Dimis-Prædiken *62, 102-104, 110, 111, 118, 138, 159, 160, 185*; probational or dimissory sermon, formally assessed by auditor-examiner [*Censor*], upon satisfactory completion of university theological examinations, to affirm Theology graduate's fitness to preach; a necessary qualification for taking up a pastoral appointment; thus Gr needed to preach his probational sermon (17 March 1810, in Regenskirken, "to an empty house") in order to become his father's curate at Udby; his sermon was given a distinction by the *Censor*, Professor P. E. Müller, but when subsequently published under title *Hvi er Herrens Ord forsvundet af Hans Hus?* [Why has the word of the Lord disappeared from his house?] it drew complaints from various Copenhagen clergy, as being a libel against their calling as preachers; "Those holy men [of former days] themselves believed the teaching they were called to confess. And is this so with the majority of ministers of the Word in our day? Ah no, and that especially is why the Lord's Word has vanished from his house; this is why belief in Jesus is daily extinguished more and more even amongst the simple, and why Christianity will soon no longer find a home even in those cramped huts to which it fled when it was hounded out of the palaces of the great" [De hellige Mænd troede selv den Lære, de kaldtes til at forkynde. Er det og saa med Mængden af Ordets Tjenere i vore Dage? Ak nej, og derfor var det især, at Herrens Ord forsvandt af hans Hus; derfor er det, at Tro paa Jesus daglig mer og mer udslukkes selv hos den Enfoldige; at Christendommen snart ej længer vil finde noget Hjem, selv i hine snævre Hytter, til hvilke den flygtede, da den udjoges af de Stores Paladser] (Gr's sermon); Gr was formally rebuked by the University authorities, and doubtless the stress of the affair contributed to his breakdown in December of that year; wry comments on then-prevailing standards of candidates and censors are made in diary (19 May 1815) of Claus Pavels (1769-1822) acting as censor in Kristiania (Oslo) shortly before his appointment as Bishop of Bergen: "Just as his discourse lacked life and pith, so there was also wanting clear orderliness. On the other hand the sermon had many well chosen Bible quotations, contained sound ideas, was composed in a good, pure, though not particularly oratorical language and was delivered with dignity even if, as with the majority of student preachers nowadays, with stiffness and coldness. Bearing in mind what one is accustomed to hearing and with what tolerance dimissory sermons are adjudicated both in Copenhagen and here, I voted to give him *Laudabilem* [deserving of praise]."

dimission *102*; *dimis*, formal exit, typically by process of examination, from school or university; see also **Dimis-Prædiken**.

Dinesen, Lars *336*; 1838-1915; politician; student at Grundtvigs Højskole, Marielyst 1859-61; excluded (1872) from Venstre parliamentary party for opposing party line on policies.

Diogenes *77*; Greek philosopher of Sinope, *c.* 400-325 B. C.; cynic who scorned materialism; alluded to ironically by Gr with reference to own sparse, second-hand and unfashionable student wardrobe.

Discovery, The; see **mageløse Opdagelse,** den.

Donatus, Aelius *67, 155*; ca. A.D. 350; Roman grammarian who gave his name (in form 'donat') to medieval handbook on Latin grammar; famed as tutor to Jerome author of Latin Vulgate Bible; but also for *Ars major* and *Ars minor*, textbooks on Latin grammar which became standard works in schools of medieval Europe; an edition of *Ars Minor* was one of first books printed (1493) in Copenhagen; the *Donat* remained a staple of classical study in schools throughout 19th c.

Don Quixotic *91*; Gr's self-ironic diary-characterisation of his visit to Falster (1804) where he called on the Blichers and, on basis of enigmatic bearing, unspoken hints and modest nuances, constructed an "interest" in Elisabeth – whom later he did indeed marry; see also **Cervantes** Saavedra, Miguel de.

Dons, Povel *19, 187, 188, 219*; 1783-1843; Norwegian born writer, educated in law; from youth, bosom friend of Christian Molbech (1783-1857), through whom he met Gr (1808); developed intense friendship with Gr with whom he shared strong religious sensibilities; paid homage to Gr's authorship of *Maskeradeballet i Dannemark. Et Syn* [The masked ball in Denmark. A vision] with a poem in periodical *Nyeste Skilderie af Kiøbenhavn*; his solicitude over Gr's crisis in

1810 affected his own health and stability; assisted Gr in preparing works for publication as Gr acknowledged in dedicating to Dons his *Optrin af Norners og Asers Kamp* [Scenes from the strife of Nornir and Æsir] (1811); shared various friends with Gr including B. S. Ingemann and Gunni Busck; Gr was unsympathetic to him during Dons' periods of disturbed health (exacerbated by increasing dependence upon alcohol) according to observers including Dons' daughter ("While Gr, during Father's periods of frailty, always treated him in a highhanded fashion, Ingemann would come as the balm and the healing power"); eventually forced (1821) to resign modest post in *Enkekassen* (a kind of compulsory insurance and pension fund for civil service) and retired to country; on his death Gr wrote an appreciative memorial poem and in 1875 Ludvig Schrøder augmented and published a memoir left by Kristian Køster (Gr's curate in Vartov), *Til Minde om Povel Dons, Grundtvigs og Ingemanns Ungdoms-Ven* [In memory of Povel Dons, friend of Gr's and Ingemann's youth]; some 40 of his letters to Gr between 1811-39 are preserved in Arkiv Fasc. 453.

Dorph, Jens Frederik Siegfred *231;* 1778-1855; estate-manager from Gjorslev; *Kammerraad* (Exchequer Councillor).

Dowager Queen *passim; Enkedronning;* title used for widowed queen, notably Caroline Amalie of Augustenborg (1796-1881), second wife of Christian VIII; see **Caroline Amalie.**

Drenge-Videnskabelighed *82, 216;* scholarship-for-boys: term used pejoratively by Gr of concept of education pursued in Danish Latin schools of his youth, which was in his view inappropriately intellectual and, because dreary and uninspiring, actually damaging to child's intellectual growth; see also **Hundeklogskab.**

Dronningens Asylskole *141, 246, 288;* The Queen's Charity-School; school founded 1841 by Queen Caroline Amalie, housed until 1864 in Store Kongens Mølle [The King's great mill] on Vestervold in Copenhagen; here Gr was director, and his son-in-law P. O. Boisen was teacher and from 1851 principal.

Dronningens Udsigt *150;* 'The Queen's Prospect,' viewpoint on Flakkebjerget commanding spectacular prospect of Tyrifjorden, some 40 km north-west of Oslo, Norway; named after visit (1825) by Dronning Desideria (1777-1860) wife of Karl Johan, king of Sweden-Norway from 1818; site satisfied both nationalist and Romantic sensibilities in 1851 when 600 participants at pan-Nordic student gathering in Kristiania (Oslo) walked across mountain and stopped here (in rain and fog) for refreshments, choir-led patriotic songs and cannonades. See also **Kongens Udsigt.**

druid *331;* Edmund Gosse visiting Vartov (1872) likened Gr in pulpit to druid (priestly class among ancient Celts of Britain, Gaul, Germany; figures of revived interest in Romantic literature and art of 19th c.) from Mona (Anglesea), ancient residence of druids off northwest coast of Wales, which was savagely attacked by Suetonius Paulinus, Roman commander of Britain under Nero (A.D. 59-62), for nurturing resistance to Romans, when long-haired druids called down vengeance upon invaders.

Drypner *148*; Draupner, in Norse myth, Óðinn's ring of gold, which every ninth night dripped eight new gold rings; symbol of self-propagation; Gr uses reference to symbolise happy relationships with Norway which sprang from his student friendships with Norwegians in Copenhagen, describing himself as "a link in a youthful chain of Norwegian friends which did not break before, like *Drypner*, it had propagated itself "; in *Roskilde-Riim* [Roskilde Rhymes; published 1814] Gr sees Drypner as foreshadowing "Kirkens gyldne Altertavle" [The golden altarpieces of the Church], that is, the Church itself, multiplying and propagating its altars; see also **Nordens Mythologi**.

Duebrødre Kloster *213*; post-Reformational name applied to hospital in Roskilde, Sjælland, formerly maintained by Augustinian-derived order of monks of Helligåndshuset (House of the Holy Spirit) dedicated to establishing hospitals after example of community of Holy Spirit in Rome, known by symbol of Holy Spirit as descending dove, hence popular title 'dove-brethren' (*duebrødre*); after dissolution of monasteries at Reformation, hospital (like others of its kind in Dk) continued under secular patronage providing, for example, sheltered accommodation for such as impoverished widows and gentlewomen; of Helligåndshuset in Copenhagen the church has remained in use as church (Helliggeistes Kirke; from 1881 called Helligåndskirke).

Dyrehaven *265, 272, 338*; Jægersborg Dyrehave [deer-park]; great park close to Øresund 10 km north of Copenhagen; laid out (1669) by Frederik III for hunting purposes; opened to public from 1756; by early 19th c. Copenhagen's chief leisure-park resorted to by all classes of society (including royal visitors) particularly on Sunday afternoons in summer; setting of Adam Oehlenschläger's *Sanct Hansaften-Spil* [St John's Eve (Midsummer night's) Play; 1803] expressing the dramatist's new-discovered joy in nature stirred by literary-philosophical lectures and conversations of Henrik Steffens, though, as the play's chorus of revellers excitedly enumerate, Dyrehaven also offered multitude of exotic entertainments and erotic encounters; Slesvig Stone erected there in 19th c. to commemorate visit to Copenhagen of two deputations of loyalists from Slesvig.

Dødninge-Sang *165*; 'corpse-song, dirge' one of several terms used ironically by Gr to characterise his detractors' scorn for his writings 1812-15; see also **berserk-gang**.

Düsseldorf-style *209*; Artistic style associated (ca. 1820-90) with the Academy in Düsseldorf, noted for its appropriation of motifs from medieval German art with emphasis on historically correct detail, under influence of German Romanticism; visited by various Scandinavian artists.

Daabspagten *157, 176, 313*; baptismal covenant; negative and positive affirmation (forming part of sacrament of baptism) of renunciation of evil and acceptance of word of God, articles of belief and responsibilities of Christian life, by or on behalf of the baptised, in response to special promise, vouchsafed through Christ, of inward grace, regeneration and incorporation into Christ's body, the Church; was retained in Luther's original conservative simplification of traditional baptismal rite, but ritual of renunciation of devil and act of exorcism with which it was earlier associated were widely dropped throughout Lutheran churches during 18th and 19th-c. pietistic and rationalist periods (in Dk and Norway, dropped 1783 in Bishop N. E. Balle's revision of baptismal ritual); along with J. C. Lindberg and others, Gr, in such pieces as *Om Daabs-Pagten. I Andledning af S. T. Hr. Stiftsprovst Clausens Barne-Daab og offenlige Erklæring* [Concerning the Baptismal covenant. With reference to *S. T.* (= *salvo titulo*, meaning formal title omitted) Mr Archdeacon Clausen's Child Baptism and public pronouncement; 1832] and *Fris-prog mod H. H. Hr. Biskop Mynsters Forslag til en ny Forordnet Alterbog* [Free-speaking against the Right Reverend Bishop Mynster's proposal of a new Authorised Service Book; 1839], strongly opposed chief proponent of rationalist revision in Dk, bishop J. P. Mynster, and his support-ers, notably over perceived paradoxical absurdity of abandoning act of affirmation while also retaining mandatory baptism (which could be physically enforced, for example against religious non-conformists, by police); "Baptism is the name of that solemn initiation by which those who will believe in Christ shall be received into his Church's bosom or congregation and so receive the name Christian with promise of everlasting life if they keep the agreement which is called their Baptismal Covenant. Compulsion to this is tyranny." (Gr in *Krønnike-Rim* 1842); see also **Besværgelsen**

E

Earle, John *334*; English scholar; published (1871) 'An Ancient Saxon Poem of a City in Ruins Supposed to be Bath' in *Proceedings of the Bath Natural History and Antiquarian Field Club* II (1870-73), pp. 259-270, including text of Anglo-Saxon poem *The Ruin*, literal English translation and discussion of the association with Bath; Gr's receipt of copy (1872) is recounted by Frederik Hammerich in moving anecdote of Gr's last week of life; four letters he sent to Gr 1848-51 are in Arkiv Fasc. 448.

Early Church, custom of *320*; *Oldkirkens Skik*; Danish heirs of Reformation could distinguish between Church as, in their perception, led astray by Rome in Middle Ages and *Oldkirken*, the ancient or Early Church, perceived as closer to Church founded by Christ and shaped by apostles and early Fathers; latter was accommodated by Gr within his *kirkelige anskuelse* [view (concept, purview) of the Church] and endorsed by such scholarly followers as J. C. Lindberg; Gr's notable encounters with the *oldkirkelige* include his exploration from 1815 onwards of Christian culture of Anglo-Saxons and, crucially, his readings in Irenaeus, 2nd-c. Bishop of Lyons, through whose *Adversus haereticos* [Against the heretics] (arguing authority of unbroken tradition handed down from Apostles which could confidently be found in that which ancient churches held in consensus) Gr reached (1825) his 'matchless discovery' concerning authority – divine, irreducible, unassailable by rationalist criticism – of *Ordet*, the word embodied in the Apostles' Creed and other formulations sacramentally spoken at baptism and the Lord's Supper; on Palm Sunday 1867 Thomas Skat Rørdam (loyal though not uncritical follower of Gr, later bishop) assuaged own anxiety over Gr's invitation to all to receive communion, whether or not confirmed, by recalling *Oldkirkens Skik*, presumably being aware that making Confirmation at age of discretion a precondition of receiving Holy Communion (regulation which in England dates from no earlier than 13th c.) was not custom of early Church.

Ebbesen, Niels *164*; hero of Danish historical ballads; Danish historian Anders Sørensen Vedel (1542-1616) author (1591) of "the first printed edition of ballads in the world" (Frederik Nielsen,

1961), tells how "the honourable Danish hero and noble knight, Sir Niels Jepssøn" (= Niels Eb-besen), amid a nine-year interregnum, rid Jylland of incessant depredations of *Grev* [Count] Gert and his 11,000 Holsteners in great battle at Randers, Jylland, 1 April 1340; Ebbesen became celebrated in early Danish ballads as national hero and was glorified as such on Danish stage in L. C. Sander's tragic drama *Niels Ebbesen* (1797); final verses of Vedel's version afford some explanation of Ebbesen's status within cultural *Danskheden* [Danishness] from end of 18th c. onwards: "God save your soul, Niels Ebbesen, / a Dane, a hero, you! / full eager out of your fatherland / those foreign guests you threw! // And Christ bless each good Danish lad / who with both tongue and hand / sober, modest, with toil and faith / will serve his fathers' land!"

Eberhard, Johann August *189*; 1739-1809; German theologian and philosopher of the Enlighten-ment; professor in Halle; challenged the philosophy of Kant; first volume of his *Handbuch der Aesthetik* (1803-05) was translated into Danish by Knud Lyhne Rahbek as *Haandbog i Æsthe-tikken* [Handbook in Aesthetics; 1803]; his *Geist des Urchristenthums* [The spirit of primitive Christianity] was published Halle 1807-08.

Eckernförde *291*; Danish Egernfjord; fortified harbour on fjord 28 km northwest of Kiel in Sles-vig; on 5 April 1849 ship of the line *Christian VIII* and frigate *Gefion*, trapped in fjord by contrary wind, were lost in engagement with two German shore-batteries; Gr was indignant that *Gefion's* commander Frederik August Paludan hauled down flag to Germans when he could, like Ivar Huitfeldt captain of ship *Danebrog* in battle with Swedes in Køge Bugt 1710, have suffered ship to be blown apart (and many crewmen killed) rather than surrender; loss left unaltered Danish naval control in Baltic but was great blow to Danish optimism which had characterised early phase of Three Years' War with Prussia (1848-51); Paludan, after short time as German prisoner, was tried by Danish tribunal over loss of *Gefion* and sentenced to three months' military deten-tion.

Edda *62, 83, 97, 118, 227*; name of uncertain meaning, possibly related to Icelandic *óðr* 'poem, poetry' which word may also relate to name of god Óðinn [the spirit, divinity, inspiration], thus sense would be 'Poetics' though as much signalling poetry as divinely inspired utterance as poetry as compositional technique; 'eddaic' poetry (Danish: *eddadigtning*), in contrast to other chief genre of medieval Icelandic poetry, skaldic poetry (Danish: *skjaldedigtning*), is of simpler form and less characterised by elaborate poetic diction; name *Edda* applied (1643) by Bishop Brynjólfur Sveinsson to unique 13th-c. codex of Icelandic mythological, heroic, didactic poems he sent (1662) to Copenhagen to his king, Frederik III of Dk (hence subsequent designation of manuscript as *Codex Regius*); Sveinsson gave contents title which has since attached, *Edda Sæmundi multiscii*, on presumption they were work of Sæmundr (1056-1133), called *inn fróði* ('the learned, wise'), Icelandic scholar and founder of school at Oddi, Iceland; book also known as The Poetic Edda and The Elder Edda; name *Edda* also given to textbook on poetry (so-called *Snorra Edda* or *Prose Edda*) by Icelander Snorri Sturluson (1179-1241); *Prose Edda* appears to draw heavily upon (a version of) *Poetic Edda* for substance; between them the two *Eddas* form the foundation of Norse mythology as known to post-medieval ages and have achieved com-mensurate iconic status (especially from period of 19th-c. Romanticism and Scandinavian na-tionalisms onwards) as symbol of Nordic antiquity and Icelandic-Norwegian-Danish identities; attracted Gr's early attention, resulting in *Lidt om Sangene i Edda* [A little about the songs of the *Edda*, 1806], *Om Asalæren* [On the doctrine of the Æsir (= Norse mythological lore), 1807], *Nordens Mytologi* [Mythology of the North, 1808], *Optrin af Kæmpelivets Undergang i Norden* [Scenes from the decline of heroic life in the North, 1809], *Optrin af Norners og Asers Kamp* [Scenes from the strife of Nornir and Æsir, 1811] and much more, published in period of what Gr later jocularly called his *asa-rus* [Æsir-mania], culminating in maturity and profundity of *Nordens Mythologi eller Sindbilled-Sprog* [Mythology or symbol-language of the North, 1832] and lifelong commitment, inherited by Grundtvigians especially in folk-highschools, to use of Northern myth and legend as resource of metaphorical reference comparable to Greek-Roman myth and legend, a massive act of 19th-c. cultural-historical appropriation comparable to, and related to, Gr's huge appropriation of Anglo-Saxon culture; see also **Northern literature**, ancient; *Nordens Mythologi*.

Edsberg, Johan Henrik *89*; born 1781; distant relative of Gr, contemporary student in Copenhagen, who helped find him position as house-tutor at Egeløkke 1804.

Egeberg *61*; small estate in Odsherred, northwest Sjælland, home of Gr's mother, Cathrine Marie Bang, daughter of *Kammerraad* Niels Christian Bang.

Egeløkke *13, 19, 62, 84, 89, 90, 92, 97, 101, 104, 157, 158, 183-186, 191, 277*; mansion and estate lying towards northern end of island of Langeland where Gr was residential private tutor (1805-08) to young son of family Steensen-Leth; Gr developed strong passion for the boy's mother, Constance, six years older than himself; ending in his resignation; "the hopeless love at once humbled and awakened his heart; through struggle and suffering he achieved self-awareness as a man, a poet and a preacher" (Poul Dam).

Egge, Heinrich *169*; 1796-1843; German Lutheran priest, studied philology and theology Kiel 1819; curate 1820 at Frederiks Tyske Kirke [Frederik's German Church] Christianshavn (Copenhagen); 1825 subject of charge of fanaticism [*Fanatisme*] laid against him in Chancellery by Professor C. F. Hornemann, who was consequently attacked by Gr; later priest in deanery of Gottorp, in Slesvig.

Ehlers' Kollegium *109, 157*; residential college for students in Copenhagen University; one of several forming university complex in central Copenhagen; founded 1691 by *Etatsraad* [State Councillor] Jakob Ehlers (1647-1692) in memory of two children, Eggert and Sophie, who died in catastrophic opera-house fire at Amalienborg, 19 April 1689; here (winter 1802) philosopher Henrik Steffens gave renowned series of lectures which set in motion Danish national-romantic movement.

einherjar *143*; in Norse myth, warriors who having died in battle go to Valhalla to live well there and train as Óðinn's support in the mighty battle at Ragnarök; imagery used by Gr (1844) in extempore commemoration of Willemoes and other crew of the *Prinds Christian*, who died in sea-fight against superior force of English ships off Sjællands Odde 1808; see also *Nordens Mythologi*.

Ejder *239, 240*; river flowing 188 km from Kiel westwards via Rendsburg to Friedrichstadt into the German Bight; boundary between Slesvig and Holsten; Dk's first established geographical frontier (9th c.), later regarded as natural frontier to be held against Germany, thus became central issue in the political strife over defensible Danish southern frontier in 1840s.

Ejderpolitik *239, 240*; National frontier policy of Danish National Liberals from 1842, seeking to make Ejder natural southern frontier, entailing incorporation of dukedom of Slesvig into the kingdom, and resignation of Holsten to German Federation; policy disregarded strongly German character (language and culture) of southern Slesvig and conflicted with ancient and rooted principle nurtured especially in southern Slesvig and Holsten that the two duchies should be everlastingly joined; but in any case foundered upon unacceptability to major European powers; revival of Ejderpolitik in 1863 contributed to war with Germany (1864) and resulting disastrous loss of both dukedoms.

Elbe *240*; major river flowing from Prague north-west though Magdeburg, Wittenberg, Hamburg into German Bight at Cuxhaven; southern boundary of duchy of Holsten.

Election-Thursday *287*; *Valg-Torsdagen*; 5 October 1848, day appointed for election of representatives to the *Rigsforsamling* [National Assembly] to enact the passing of the Constitution.

elementary schools; see **Almueskoler**.

Elias *250, 318*; Elijah, Hebrew prophet (1 Kings xvii-xxi; 2 Kings i-iii) called Elias in New Testament; disappeared from earth in fiery chariot; in Jewish tradition his reappearance will herald Messiah's coming; his bodily return was also allegedly part of Gr's eschatological beliefs.

Elijah; see **Elias**.

Elmqvist, Adolf Frederik *115*; 1788-1868; leading figure in Århus literary circles; bookprinter, bookseller; opened first bookshop in Århus 1810; published works of Steen Steensen Blicher, B. S. Ingemann, H. C. Andersen and other leading names; held literary salons; published and edited newspaper *Aarhus Stiftstidende*; major undertaking, though seen by Gr as sad evidence of supine literary readership in 1820s, was his *Læsefrugter, samlede paa Literaturens Mark* [Reading-fruits, gathered in the field of literature], 1818-33 and 1839-40, in 66 volumes.; see also ***Læsefrugter***.

Enevælde *127, 128, 144, 267, 291, 313 and passim*; absolute monarchy; following Denmark's military eclipse by Sweden in war of 1657-60, entailing concession of Scania (southern Sweden), loss of sole control over Øresund, and state bankruptcy, alliance of burghers and peasants seized opportunity to disempower aristocracy which was largely blamed for failures, and in 1660 supported Frederik III (first cousin to the executed Charles I of England, whose son resumed royal rule as Charles II in 1660) in assumption of absolute power for himself and heirs, endorsed by Church (already under state control); led to extensive modernisation of government and moves (legislative, fiscal, administrative) towards national unification, aimed at greater equality between king's subjects; ultimate dependency of all offices and liberties upon absolute jurisdiction of sovereign ensured that *enevælde* permeated and conditioned virtually every aspect of Danish life; also created expectations of advantage in middle classes and peasantry which were slow in fulfilment so that, despite spread of 'enlightenment' in 18th c., it came to be felt as oppressive and repressive; in wake of 19th-c. popular liberation movements across Europe, and under pressure of Prussian ambitions and revolt in Holsten (1848), Frederik VII was persuaded to relinquish absolute power and grant liberal Constitution (1849); Gr, despite himself falling foul of some of consequences of absolutism (notably curtailments of liberties), nourished at heart concept of "Kingly hand and people's voice, / each one strong and each one free" and played his part in promoting image of king as father of his people from Danish antiquity; though he worked for democracy once established; Gr's misgivings over ill-considered clamour for 'freedom' [*Frihed*] are expressed in the glossary to his *Krønnike-Rim*, augmented 2nd edition 1842, thus: "*Freedom is a word as slippery as an eel*, so that it is never any use thinking or talking about it without first knowing which forces' freedom is meant, and why they desire freedom; for civil society is founded upon the verity that, whilst the freedom for all honourable and beneficent forces to develop themselves and work undisturbed is human nature's necessary requirement, just so is the free working of bestial, wild and disruptive forces human nature's plague; so that only those laws are truly good which promote and protect the free working of all beneficent forces. Therefore people still fight blindly over 'freedom' as though it were not a question of what forces the freedom attaches to, and how it is won and defended, but rather which individuals – those who comprise the authorities or the government or the mob – shall have the right to do exactly what they want, or to bully or oppress each other in turn."

Engelland *172*; England; form of name sometimes used by Gr poetically, or perhaps ('Angle-land') to emphasise that the English derived ethnically from the Angles of Angeln (Slesvig) and were therefore Danish; in the glossary to his *Krønnike-Rim* 1842 Gr declares: "*Engelland*, in more recent times almost the only free arena for human life [*næsten det eneste fri Spillerum for Menneske-Livet*], has thereby become, in the eighteenth and nineteenth centuries, not only the richest spot in the whole world but also the richest in learning. Furthermore, just as Christianity and the art of writing once came from there to Germany and the North, just so was the Ox-fordian Wycliffe in the fourteenth century "The Reformation's Morning Star"[*Reformationens Morgenstjærne*]; and finally it was the English poets, especially the incomparable Shakespeare [*den mageløse Shakspear*] from Queen Elizabeth's days, who at last awakened the spirit [*Aanden*] in Germany and the North; so to our kinsmen on that island we really stand profoundly in debt – upon which we shall have the pleasure of paying high interest."

Engelsted, Carl Sophus Marius Needergaard *337, 338*; 1823-1914; professor, doctor in the Kommunehospital in Copenhagen; attended at Gr's death.

Engelstoft, Laurits (Lars) *254*; 1774-1851; *cand. theol.*; historian; teacher at Skouboe Institute and professor; *Justitsråd* and *konferenceråd* (distinguished, largely honorific titles bestowing social rank); member of governing body of Copenhagen University.

England *16, 27, 62, 69, 70, 101, 129-134, 137, 143, 172, 175, 184, 185, 205, 208, 216, 218, 258, 288, 326, 334, 336*; Gr used the name both for England proper and for Great Britain (officially designated *Storbritannien* in Danish state documents) as whole; naturally, G's attitude to 'England' developed in response to his dealings with country, history and people; early perceptions were coloured by conventional history and contemporary events in Napoleonic Wars including British acts of war against Dk (1801, 1807); some reorientation prompted by lectures (1802) of Henrik Steffens expressing Romantic estimation of poetic genius of Shakespeare, and by own programme of English reading (including Shakespeare, Locke) on Langeland (1805-08); by 1812 (*Verdenshistorie*) he was aware of distinguished English literary tradition from first English Christian poet Cædmon (pre-680) through Spenser and Shakespeare; 1815 encountered *Beowulf*, learned Anglo-Saxon, read in Bede's *History*, accommodated English pagan and Christian antiquity within his emergent concept of North and *Nordens Aand*; undertook (with royal support) four visits to England; 1829, studied Anglo-Saxon manuscripts in British Museum in expectation of finding materials relevant to Danish history and culture; 1830, transcribed much of Anglo-Saxon poetic codex, the Exeter Book, was encouraged by support among English antiquaries and London publishers to issue prospectus inviting subscriptions for serial publication of extant Anglo-Saxon manuscripts; 1831, found many previous supporters of *Prospectus* now backing rival scheme; completed transcriptions of Exeter Book and other manuscripts but in effect conceded to rival plan; meanwhile took home new perspectives and various fertile ideas arising from exposure to English life, subsequently critically aired in hugely popular retrospective lectures (Borchs Kollegium, Copenhagen, 1838) in series known as *Mands Minde* [Within living memory]; thereafter maintained English friendships and interest in current English affairs including developments in English Church; 1843, fourth visit with son Svend, under patronage of queen Caroline Amalie, to make contact with Newman and Pusey, leaders of Oxford Movement, though failed to make any significant impact and thereafter rather cool towards latter-day Anglicanism; but refreshed acquaintance with English collegiate system at Cambridge which stimulated his ideas for a Danish 'folk-university' (*folkehøjskole*); travelled extensively in England and Scotland observing not only church life but economic change and social and political trends in early period of British Industrial Revolution; published editions of Anglo-Saxon poems *The Phoenix* (1840) and *Beowulf* (1861), was reading Anglo-Saxon poetry until week before his death; 'England' remained, in ideal terms, despite exasperating waywardness, land of the brother-folk betokened in Saxo's legend of Dan and Angul, whose people had played a crucial role in dissemination of Christianity to the North and whose eventual rediscovery of *Nordens Aand* within themselves was enduringly a matter of faith and hope, and sometimes perhaps love; see also **Angul's Isle**; **Anglo-Saxons**; **London**.

English, Englishman; see **England**.

English priest; see **Wade**, Nugent.

Enkedronning *passim*; title used for widowed queen, notably Caroline Amalie of Augustenborg (1796-1881), second wife of Christian VIII; see **Caroline Amalie**.

Ephesians, Epistle to *289*; given by Gr as example of "ways of reading" variants in biblical text.

Epistles, of Cicero; see **Cicero**.

Eremitagen *296*; The Hermitage; royal hunting-chateau in Dyrehaven [The Deer-park] north of Copenhagen; built 1734-1736 by court architect Laurids de Thurah (1706-1759) in late baroque style for Christian vi; underwent 19th and 20th c. restorations; commands views over hunting terrain and Øresund; though chateau was always reserved for royal use, it has formed backdrop to many gatherings and outings in Deer-park itself, one of Copenhagen's most charming popular gathering-places since 19th c.

Eriksen's wife *288*; sister of Norwegian pietistic lay-preacher Hans Nielsen Hauge (1771-1824), wife of Quaker, from Kristiania (Oslo), therefore belonging to persecuted minority – there being only one woman and three men joining Kristiania Meeting when Norwegian Society of Friends was set up in 1818, a year or two after her visit to Gr; see also **Hauge,** Hans Nielsen; **Quaker.**

Eskesen, Morten *300, 301*; 1826-1913; *folkelærer* [teacher within folk-highschools, outside state educational system], remarkable witness to spirit of Grundtvig-Kold educational initiatives especially among hitherto ill-served rural population; born in Ulbæk, Vestjylland, by age of 14 he was teaching in the *vinterskole* [winter-school; seasonal independent school for working farming population] while, at the start, earning his living in summer as shepherd-boy; encouraged by Ludvig Christian Müller (1806-51), principal of Snedsted-Ranum teacher-training *seminarium*, to qualify formally as teacher; in conformity with views of Gr and Christen Kold (1816-70) he strongly opposed examinations system, resigning as principal of Ut senior *Bondeskole* [peasant-farmers' school] over this issue; appointed teacher at Marielyst Højskole (Grundtvigian *friskole* established on fund gathered by subscription for Gr's 70th birthday), from school's opening (1856) until 1858; moved on to *friskole* [school independent of state system] in Rudme, Fyn (1858-64), then to Odense (1864-84); described by Kold as the best teacher of children he knew; energetic public speaker on nationalist themes; wrote and published songs and poems; author of *Minder og Udsigter fra 40 Aars Skoleliv* [Memories and perspectives from 40 years' school-life] (1881).

Essenes *189*; small religious fraternity of Jews in Palestine before and during the time of Christ, noted for ascetic living and communal ownership of property, and having certain affinities with early Christianity.

Estates of the Realm, Assembly of; see **Stænderforsamling**

Et Barn er født i Bethlehem *164, 198*; medieval Latin carol *Puer natus in Bethlehem* was translated into Danish (1553) by Hans Tausen (1494-1561; a chief architect of Reformation in Dk) and published in a reworked version by Gr in periodical *Nyeste Skilderie af Kjøbenhavn* 23 December 1820 as a *Jule-Sang for Christne Børn* [Christmas song for Christian children]; now one of the best-loved Danish Christmas carols.

eternity, the Eternal *93, 95*; philosophers of 18th- and 19th-c. Romanticism exemplify the familiar human pattern of returning, after a period of dominant rationalistic or scientific interpretation of the world, to acknowledgement of what lies beyond numbers, material quantities, rationalistic proofs and speculative systems, to the accommodation of a more mystical perception of the individual's relationship to existence. Henrik Steffens (1773-1845), for example, brought to Denmark (or at least had unprecedented success in expounding there) Romanticism's modification of the concept of eternity and the eternal which had long been a chief load-bearing pillar of

Christian philosophy: eternity lay beyond existence but the eternal was manifest and intimated in the natural world. Discernment of the eternal was a gift of the poet, and poesy transcended existence and shared in the eternal by virtue of becoming, through the inspired poet's shaping, an embodiment of the eternal. Poesy was everything that embodied within itself something of eternity. To be a poet was to struggle with the vicissitudes of existence in the attempt to glimpse and contemplate the eternal. Romantic love formed a particular arena for such struggle. Ideology of this kind seems to inform Gr's anguished passion for Constance Leth, as recorded in his diaries (see item 32): "Existence can have no worth, no reality in my eyes, except it manifests itself in her whom I eternally adore." Naturally enough, the conventional Christian equation of the Eternal with God was, at the same time (see item 29), active in his mind – "And yet, bold questions: do I, a mite, dare then to dispute with the Eternal? Have I read in the book of the future or seen through His plan?" – but there could be a profane ambiguity to this too: "My life was a song of praise to the Father of love; and, lifted aloft to him above the bounds of time, I dreamed myself into eternal pleasure" (see item 30); and later (writing 1823-24; see item 43) he admits that during his 'mythological period' "even the view, more peculiar to Christianity, of this temporal existence as a preparation for the eternal, was with me more *eddic* than *biblical.*" Much of this changed after the events of 1810. When in the period 1827-30 the young F. L. B. Zeuthen tried to engage him in discussion of Infinity and Eternity, Gr was impatient with the abstractions. Two decades onwards (see item 112), in table-talk, he was ready to trip up the professor of philosophy and mathematician Rasmus Nielsen over the same topic. The concepts of existence (and the existential) and eternity were of course central to the philosophy of Søren Kierkegaard – and a subject of serious controversy with Gr and his followers.

Et Særsyn i det nittende Aarhundrede *88*; 'A rare sight in the nineteenth century' was Gr's first published work, significantly on the issue of rural access to education; articles printed in numbers 299 and 301 (not 300, as Gr inaccurately recalled) of *Politievennen* [Friend of (public) polity], 1804, drawing attention to neglect of a school on Falster (where Gr's brother Otto was parish priest of Torkildstrup), which for ten years had been lacking a teacher; articles drew a letter of rebuke from Bishop Andreas Birch of Lolland-Falster; articles and correspondence with the bishop are printed in *US* I, 38-9 and 34-5 respectively.

eucharist *165, 264, 290, 317*; see further **sacraments and liturgy**.

Europe, the new *133, 134*; Gr's designation of post-classical Europe, within Christian-providential universal-historical view of world history he had developed between 1808-14; in this view, Anglo-Saxon literature, especially its Christian poetry first uttered by inspiration of Holy Spirit from Cædmon's mouth, which Gr began to study intensively in 1815, was "the *first* new-European literature" and a providential manifestation of transfer of Christian succession from Latin-Roman to northern peoples and mother-tongues.

Eusebius *120*; *c.* 265-339; bishop of Caesarea, theologian and historian of early Church; his *Ecclesiastical History* was a model for other early medieval Christian historians such as Gregory of Tours and Venerable Bede.

Evangelical-Christian Hymnal; see **Hymnal, Evangelical-Christian**.

Evangelical Hymnal see *Hymnal, Evangelical-Christian*.

Exeter *16, 62, 131;* cathedral town in southwest England; 11th-c. bishopric whose first bishop, Leofric, donated books to monastic library including The Exeter Book, codex of Anglo-Saxon poetry; this book Gr journeyed to Exeter in 1830 to read and transcribe; his visit to Exeter was a happy experience not least because of hospitality of family (father and two sisters, Anne and Lucy Jane) of John Bowring (1792-1872) some of whose correspondence with Gr between 1829-43 is in Arkiv Fasc. 448.4.

Exeter Book, The *16, 130-132;* Exeter, Cathedral Chapter Library, MS 3501; The Exeter Book, Anglo-Saxon codex from late 10th c., principally comprised of poetry in Old English; one of the four major Anglo-Saxon poetic collections surviving (the others are MS Cotton Vitellius Axv in the British Library, MS Junius 11 in the Bodleian Library Oxford, and MS cxvii in the Biblioteca Capitolare del Duomo di Vercelli Italy); Gr journeyed to Exeter (1830) to transcribe it though his hope of publishing the *editio princeps* was thwarted by London antiquaries and the honours went instead to Benjamin Thorpe whose edition was eventually published 1842; Gr's transcriptions of the Exeter Book are in Fasc. 316 in the Grundtvig Arkiv, Royal Library, Copenhagen (see Introduction, Abbreviations, *Registrant*); see also **Anglo-Saxon literature**.

existential *23, 249, 275;* of or relating to existence, particularly human existence, and particularly human life lived out in individual autonomous interaction with ethical, moral, religious and spiritual concepts and situations; relating especially to philosophy of Christian existentialism developed by Søren Kierkegaard (1813-55), encapsulated in the "*existentielle Modsætninger*" [existential antitheses; H. L. Martensen's phrase (1883), see item 88] most famously represented by Kierkegaard's "*Enten-Eller*" [Either/Or; his book of this title published 1843]; for Gr, in contrast, the great existential antithesis was (he declared) that between Life and Death, and the way to the great resolution lay essentially in the congregational sacramental life of the church and in secular *folkelighed* rather than in the individual's subjective inwardness; but Gr's life's work proved to Kierkegaard only that "one can be a Genius and become a geriatric without learning the least thing from life, existentially."

Exorcism, The; see **Besværgelsen**.

F

Fabricius, Otto *160;* 1744-1822; missionary to Greenland; zoologist, linguist; priest at Vor Frelsers Kirke Copenhagen from 1789; titular professor 1803, titular bishop 1818; the one priest in Copenhagen who, according to Gr's jocular speculation, did not wish Gr hanged or burnt for his dimissory sermon (1810) – his comment on Gr's attack on failure of contemporary (rationalist) clergy to preach healthful Word of God being: I find that he speaks of the generality of teachers of religion, and therein I do not feel the cap fits myself; born in Rudkjøbing, Dk, his name fashionably latinised from 'smith' (his father's trade), he was not, as it suits Gr's jocularity to call him, a 'Greenlander' unless by virtue of his dedication to continue missionary work of his hero, 'Apostle to Greenland' Hans Egede (1686-1758); see also **Greenlander**.

faery-queen; see **Ælve-Dronning**.

Fall, The *68, 69*; *Syndfaldet*; Gr recalled that Lutheran doctrine of Fall and of Free Will were stumbling-blocks to him as boy disputing with tutors at Thyregod; his later theology was distinguished by conviction that God's created likeness in his human creation was not wholly destroyed at Fall, and by belief in human Free Will (*Menneskets fri Villie*).

Fallesen, Lorenz Nikolai (Nissen) *156, 158, 159*; 1757-1824; editor; *første residerende Kapellan* [first resident curate] in Vor Frue Kirke Copenhagen until its destruction in British incendiary bombardment 1807, thereafter priest in Trinitatis Kirke (1808); belonged with friend H. N. Clausen (Gr's adversary in *Kirkens Gienmæle* 1826) to theologically liberal, rationalist wing of Church; significant figure in early development of theological debate in Dk through periodical journalism; founded first proper Danish theological journal, *Religionslærere* [Religious instructors] I-VI (1793-1797) which continued as *Magazin for Religionslærere* I-VI (1798-1802); thereafter published *Theologisk maanedsskrivt for Fædrelandets Religionslærere* [Theological monthly for the fatherland's religious instructors] I-XII (1803-08) of which Gr wrote dismissively: "True enough, Rahbek's *Minerva* and Fallesen's *Teologiske Maanedsskrift* continued to drag themselves along until 1808 and 1809, but commanded the attention of no one, not even of the editors") and *Theologisk Qvartalsskrivt for Fædrelandets Religionslærere* [Theological quarterly for the fatherland's religious instructors] I-II (1809); editorially, he aspired to hold middle way between orthodoxy and heterodoxy though committed to communicating to fellow priests awareness of new directions in, for example, biblical textual scholarship.

Falster *62, 76, 79, 81, 88-90*; Danish island lying off southern tip of Sjælland, its principal town being Nykøbing; Lise Blicher, Gr's first wife, lived at Gundslev Falster where her father D. N. Blicher was rural dean and where Gr met her while staying with brother Otto's family at neighbouring Torkildstrup vicarage; for drawing public attention (1804) to educational shortcomings on island, Gr incurred displeasure of bishop, Andreas Birch.

fatherland *329*; Gosse, writing in English of Gr's distinguishing ideals, uses term 'Fatherland' ("the ideals of his life – perfect love, perfect liberty, enthusiasm for the Fatherland, hope for the future of Denmark"); Gr commonly uses *Fædrelandet* (literally 'the fathers' land'), a term rare in 18th c. Danish but increasingly used over first half of 19th c., carrying nuance of 'ancestral, of the forefathers' with which may be compared German *Vaterland* (literally 'the fatherland') which carries popular nuance of land-as-father; Gr's perspectival emphasis on the ancestral, the heritage from the forebears, he makes explicit in frequent use of such forms as *Fæderne-Landet* (literally 'the land of the fathers') and *Fædernelandskjærlighed* (*31*, literally 'love of the land of the fathers'); consistently with this, Gr's acute awareness of history as a motivating and cohesive, binding and obligating force in his own life and the life of the Danish folk and the peoples of the North he repeatedly expresses in allusions to 'the fathers' – as is encapsulated in his *Krønnike-Rim* [Rhyming Chronicle] 1842: "A *Fæderneland*, properly speaking, belongs only to that people which lovingly remembers its forefathers and dedicates itself to their mother-tongue; and whosoever does not do so thereby loses his *Fæderneland*, though he have a thousand ancestors of doughty lineage."

Fathers of the Church *119*; as "Christian mythologists" (Gr); see also **Irenaeus**.

Faurskov, Bertel *67, 80*; 1729-1807; *cand. theol.*; appointed 1788 as schoolmaster in Udby during Gr's childhood; his special enthusiasm was for French language and affairs – with the result that, as Gr notes in his draft of *Mands Minde*, his mother-tongue had so far deteriorated "that the peasant lads were highly astonished when once in a while they heard him talk; but this happened only seldom because at that time there were no fines for missing school so the children habitually stayed at home; and I, who had to remain on parade, can affirm that they lost nothing thereby." The anecdote of course tacitly served Gr's polemic on the use, abuse and neglect of the mother-tongue – a theme in his *Mands Minde* which struck a chord with his audiences (see headnote to item 3).

Faye, Andreas *301, 302*; 1802-69; Norwegian priest, historian; among Gr's various visitors from Norway; startled by vigour and bluntness of exchanges between father and sons at Gr's lunch-table: "I could not help thinking about the ancient viking-times".

Feld, Laurits *61, 67, 68, 71, 76, 116*; 1751-1803; private tutor and parish priest; was for a period teacher in Udby (as was his elder brother Christian) where he taught the young Grundtvigs; continued to prepare private pupils for admission to grammar school, including Gr's elder brothers Jacob and Niels, when called to incumbency at Hirsholmene (Frederikshavn, Jylland); appointed 1790 to parish of Thyregod (30 km. north-west of Vejle, Jylland; at that time, more than a week's journey from Udby) where 9-year-old Gr was placed for tuition (1792-98) in care of bachelor pastor and his sister Tryfona; like a kindly godfather, he gave young Gr a silver watch to mark graduation from village school to private tuition, and made Gr allowance of two *rigsdaler* a month when he entered university.

Fenger, Carl Emil *313*; 1814-84; brother to P. A., J. F. and T. Fenger; politician, physician; after graduating spent several years travelling abroad; subsequently held senior posts at Frederiks Hospital, appointed Professor of Pathology Copenhagen University, significantly contributed to advances in medical practice and public hygiene in Dk; entered political life, became Finance Minister and was involved in peace negotiations in Vienna after 1864 war with Prussia; was consulted during Gr's illness 1867.

Fenger, Johannes Ferdinand *223*; 1805-61, *cand. theol.*, brother of P. A., C. E. and T. Fenger; though well qualified for academic appointment, was denied it, doubtless because of early close association with Gr; long career as priest, opposed Gr over issue of *præstefrihed* [clerical freedom], undertook support of missionary work in Danish colonies.

Fenger, Peter Andreas *201, 203, 216, 242, 265, 311, 319, 321, 322, 339*; 1799-1878; priest, notable contributor to Danish hymnody (to him – and to Gunni Busck and the Danish congregation) Gr dedicated his *Sangværk* (1837), editor of hymns of Thomas Kingo; son of Rasmus Fenger whom Gr was appointed to assist as curate in Vor Frelsers Kirke 1822, and brother of Johannes Ferdinand, Carl Emil and Theodor Fenger; while still at university became devoted supporter of Gr following Gr's strife with Clausen; subsequently Gr's close friend and collaborator, for example, together with Ferdinand, discussing in detail Gr's work on *Psalme-Blade til Kirke-Bod*

[Hymn-pages for Penitence] (1843) intended to counter Bishop Mynster's *Udkast til et Tillæg til den Evangelisk-Christelige Psalmebog* [Draft proposal for a supplement to the *Evangelical-Christian Hymnal*] (1843); his own supplement to the Evangelical-Christian Hymnal (1880) grew into hymnal in own right; 1827-55 priest in Slots Bjergby, S. Sjælland, where he allied himself, not entirely to Gr's liking, with *de gudelige vækkelser* (pietistic religious revivalist meetings); for his silver wedding Gr wrote wedding song *Det er saa yndigt at følges ad* [It is so lovely to walk side by side] (1855), no. 703 in *DDS* 2002; 1855 appointed to Vor Frelsers Kirke; got leading composers including C. E. F. Weyse (1774-1842) and H. Rung (1807-71) to provide new melodies for Gr's hymns; remained close to Gr during Gr's illness 1867 though criticised by Thomas Skat Rørdam for keeping silence; officiated at Gr's funeral in Vor Frelsers Kirke 1872; see also **hymns**.

Fenger, Theodor *288*; 1816-89; brother of P. A., J. F. and C. E. Fenger; member of Gr's circle.

Fichte, Johan Gottlieb *62, 84, 96, 160*; 1762-1814; German philosopher, professor in Jena and later Berlin, resident in Copenhagen 1807; influenced by Immanuel Kant (1724-1804), moved towards more theoretical enquiry into relationship of consciousness to the external world; after 1800 (*Die Bestimmung des Menschen* [The destiny of man]) relinquished a former principle concerning the autonomy of the "I" and made the "I" dependent upon a divine ultimate, from which position of "an idealism relative to God" he challenged the later Schelling and Kierkegaard; Gr declares, in poem (*Gottlieb Fichte*) apparently written 1814, he can never forget "at du varst mig kjær / At mig glædede din Kæmpestemme; *Den* mig vakte af min falske Ro, / Den mig vækkede til Tvivl og Tro, / Vækkede mig til at ihukomme / Sandheds Lys og Kærlighedens Blomme // Jeg forfærdet ved *dit* Lynglimt saa' / Sig Fornuften i sig sel. forvilde; / Af *dit* Ord jeg kunde grandt forstaa: / Kun ved Tro vi naa til Livets Kilde." [that you were dear to me, that your gigantic voice rejoiced me; *this* wakened me from my false tranquillity; this wakened me to doubt and belief, wakened me into remembering the light of truth and the blossoms of love; I saw reason, affrighted by *your* lightning flash, get lost within itself; by *your* word could I clearly understand that only by faith do we reach the well-spring of life]; A. S. Ørsted observed that for the priests to prosecute Gr for his probational sermon (1810) assessing current state of preaching of God's word in Dk would be as pointless as for the whole generation to prosecute J. G. Fichte for his *Die Grundzüge des gegenwärtigen Zeitalters* (called by Gr *Grundtræk af Nutiden* [Outline of the present age]; 1806); see also *Die Bestimmung des Menschen*; and **Dimis-Prædiken**.

Finland, Finns *272, 312*; in his disturbed mental state, Easter 1867 (third anniversary of calamitous Prussian invasion of Sønderjylland 1864), when Prussian threat to Dk was an *idée fixe*, Gr wrote to Government proposing scandinavianisation of Slesvig-Holsten by moving Germans thence to Finland, putting Finns in their place; appears to be variant upon idea Gr once jocularly proposed to Professor Johannes Carsten Hauch, involving replacing Germans by Icelanders who would be resistant to 'infection' by Germans, therefore excellent defenders of Dannevirke; see **Hauch,** Johannes Carsten.

Fjennesløv *23, 284*; Fjenneslev, town between Ringsted and Sorø in Sjælland, 75 km west of Copenhagen; notable for medieval church with two towers marking (according to tradition) birth of brothers Absalon (later archbishop of Dk in Lund, founder of Copenhagen) and Esbern Snare. See **Inge,** Fru.

Flakkebjerget *150*; mountain region overlooking Tyrifjorden, north-west of Oslo, Norway. See **Queen's Prospect**.

Flensborg *172*; German Flensburg, now German town in Slesvig-Holsten, just south of Danish border, on fjord giving access to Baltic; originated as trading centre in 12th c., by 1450 chief town in Danish-ruled Slesvig and by 16th c. leading mercantile centre in kingdom; but always subject to influence of German culture and language; passed under German control with breakaway of Slesvig-Holsten and outbreak of Three Years' War 1848, and permanently lost to Dk at Prussian annexation of Slesvig 1864; strong Danish loyalties remained, and support, both material and spiritual, for Danishness in Slesvig remained a powerful issue in Dk throughout Gr's lifetime and beyond; Edmund Gosse (*Two Visits to Denmark 1872, 1874*, London, 1911) gives account of dejected atmosphere of Flensborg in decade following peace settlement in Vienna 1864.

Fog, Bruun Juul *327, 330*; 1819-96; bishop of Århus (1881), then of Sjælland (1884); matriculated 1837 from Metropolitanskolen in Copenhagen and as theological student at university was drawn to teaching of Gr's close friend from student days, F. C. Sibbern (1785-1872), and of H. L. Martensen (1808-84), though also much absorbed by classical literature and philosophy; took the Theologiske Embedsexamen (examination qualifying him for church appointment) 1843; after teaching and junior church appointments, and achievement of doctorate in philosophy (1856), called (1857) as resident curate to Holmens Kirke in Copenhagen and named (1867) as *Holmens Provst* (archdeacon for area of city including base of Danish fleet, and splendid and prestigious Holmens Kirke elegantly sited on Holmens Kanal, adjacent to Christiansborg's parliamentary buildings, Stock Exchange and other major public buildings); esteemed as outstanding preacher of his time, noted for penetrating psychological insight; consecrated as bishop in Århus 1881, but upon death of Martensen (1884) succeeded him as Bishop of Sjælland; conservative in enactments, always an opponent of Gr and Grundtvigianism; retired 1895; familiar with England from a number of visits; highly spoken of by Englishman Edmund Gosse who resided with Fog and his sister Aline on visits to Dk 1872 and 1874 and was accompanied by Fog to Vartov Kirke for the experience of seeing Gr not long before Gr's death in 1872.

folk, folket *passim*; the folk, the people, the nation; as used by Gr, term essentially tied in with Danish and national-romantic ideology; though it may in context, and in compounds such as *folkefest* [folk-festival], suggest idea of 'the popular' its implications are far more extensive and diverse than modern English (American) term 'folk' (folk-festival, folk-song, folk-dancing); thus English 'folk' is rarely an adequate translation of Danish *folk*; see **folkelige,** det; **folkelivet**; and other terms under the stem **folk-**.

folk-ballads *325*; *folkeviser*; Dk's traditional ballads and songs which some believed comprised genuine and original literature of the folk, others saw as more aristocratically originating literature, subsequently appropriated, orally circulated and recreated by peasantry; surviving in early written and printed sources; their collection in Dk, particularly from 1810 onwards, was as in England and Scotland an aspect of Romanticism but also served to express and nurture emergent nationalism; notable studies and publications include those of (from 1840) A. P. Bergreen, (after 1850) Svend Grundtvig, and (from 1868) Evald Tang Kristensen (1843-1929) whose collections from Vestjylland were especially copious; though in principle Gr treasured such unaffected expression of the *modersmaal* (mother-tongue), Kristensen, visiting (1871) with Svend, was disappointed that Gr (now old and tired) had little to say on the topic.

folk-books *147, 167; folkebøgerne:* see **folk-chronicles** of the North.

folk-chronicles of the North *111, 114;* works of Saxo Grammaticus and Snorri Sturluson; see **Nordens Folke-Krøniker**.

folkefest *1871 269;* in 1871 major popular celebratory gatherings around Gr were held in Whitsun-week, both in connection with a meeting of the 'Friends' [*Vennerne*] and in honour of the sixtieth anniversary of his ordination; on Monday 29 May, the anniversary day, he was driven to church in new closed carriage presented to him by friends and admirers, while a carpet made by Grundtvigian women was laid in his study; in the evening a dinner for over 100 guests was held at Store Tuborg at which Frederik Hammerich and other leading supporters of Gr spoke, followed by further celebrations in the gardens where among other guests was a group from Sagatun folk-highschool in Norway; on Wednesday an assembly of some 2000 people gathered in the Casino in Copenhagen; and on 1 June some 1300 people assembled in Dyrehaven where Gr (then 88 years old) spoke at *den slesvigske Sten* (the Slesvig Stone; an inscribed stone erected 1865 to commemorate visit of deputation of Danish loyalists from Slesvig following Prussian occupation 1864); see also **folk**.

folkehøjskole-sagen *288, 329;* the folk-highschool issue; in 1837, while still under censorship in Dk, Gr published in Norway *Til Nordmændene om en norsk Højskole* [To the Norwegians concerning a Norwegian highschool], proposing establishment of folk-highschool upon principles he had outlined but not yet brought to realisation in Dk; ideas aired there were further developed *Skolen for Livet* [The school for life; 1838] and in periodical *Brage og Idun* (1, 1839) and a series of other publications on education; Dk, Norway and Sweden should each have their own *folkelige Højskole* and, because the three Scandinavian nations were informed by one spirit [*Aand*], they should have one single *videnskabelig Højskole* [scholarly highschool, university]; first Norwegian folk-highschool (Sagatun, near Hamar, 1864) was not established until twenty years after the first Danish one (Rødding, 1844); dream of a single pan-Scandinavian folk-university met with scepticism from outset, and though location in Göteborg, Sweden, was debated, it was never realised; see also **folkelige**; **folkeoplysning**; **Kold,** Christen Mikkelsen; **Askov**; **Anker,** Herman; **Arvesen,** Olaus (Olaf); **Hammar-Mødet**.

Folkekirke *266, 269, 289, 328;* In Danish church-history, useful distinction can be made between *Statskirken* [The State Church] and *Folkekirken* [The National Church]; with Reformation (1536) a *statskirke* was declared in Dk, in which King assumed responsibility for Church and was its head; this status was consolidated with establishment of absolutism (1660) when Church was confirmed as being evangelical-Lutheran church confessing three creeds of early Church plus Augsburg Confession and Luther's Short Catechism, and directly governed by royal authority, all clergy being appointed by sovereign and all Danish subjects (with defined exceptions such as Jews) mandatorily members; with granting of Constitution (1849) *Statskirke* was reformed as the established *Folkekirke* of which membership was matter of individual choice and which was supported economically and legislatively by enactment of elected government; further extensions of religious freedom allowed for elective congregations (called *valgmenigheder*) to select (and pay) own pastors outside parochial framework while remaining within *Folkekirke*; but Constitution's declared principle that internal governance of Church was to be ordered according to law (*"ordnes ved lov"* – with implication that Church should be essentially self-governing) was never defined in operative detail; thus, while individual church has its *menighedsråd* [congregational council], *Folkekirke* has no synodal structure, nor may bishops singly or collectively act in name of whole Church, and constitutionally speaking ultimate authority over *Folkekirke* is exercised by government minister responsible to *Folketing* which allocates Church budget.

folkelige, det *passim*; that which pertains to the *folk* and to *folkelighed*; social-cultural-political concept, in Dk particularly associated with 19th-c. national-romanticism, Gr and Grundtvigianism, and mid-19th-c. emergence of democratic government (*folke-styre*); 19th-c. national-romanticism, influenced by German philosopher J. G. Herder (1744-1803), idealised notion that one national state be comprised of one *folk* with common mother-tongue, national history, own discrete culture, and, among some advocates, one race; "In Denmark it is none other than Grundtvig who mediates Herder's ideas and changes them into genuine politics of culture" (Flemming Lundgreen-Nielsen); 1815-20, following long period of severe national political and economic setbacks and, in his view, inertia, Gr turned to translation of monuments of national (legend-)history (works of Saxo, Snorri and *Beowulf*), began using term *folkelighed*, presented *Beowulf* (in which concept of 'the folk' is very prominent) as symbolic poem celebrating Northern hero who "saved the dying *folkeliv* [folk-life]" (1820); on this Danish-historical perspective Gr also brought to bear Christian universal-historical ideas envisaging God working providentially through the destinies of appointed nations; "*Folkelighed* is the necessary precondition of living Christianity" [*Folkelighed er levende Christendoms nødvendige Forudsætning*] (Grundtvig, *Om Folkelighed og Dr Rudelbach* [Concerning *Folkelighed* and Dr R.], in *Dansk Kirketidende* 124, 1848); personal collisions and travel abroad sharpened his dislike of Danish prescriptive authoritarianism, in church, school and civil spheres, disposed him towards a more *folkelig* distribution of responsibility and liberty; like the influential German philosopher J. G. Herder (1744-1803), Gr could not view urban élites as defining model of *den fælles folkeaand* [the common folk-spirit, folk-mentality], hence his hostility to élitist embrace of German culture in Dk, his commitment to founding a *folke*-university to confront Copenhagen's élitist University and his role in establishing *folkehøjskoler* [folk-highschools] open to all and dedicated to educating people for life, and a life lived in *folkelige* awareness, rather than qualifying them for jobs in public administration. These values and objectives were embodied in first Danish *folkehøjskole* (1844, Rødding, north Slesvig), model of Danishness (language, culture) and of Danish *folkelighed* (communal life, teaching relationships and methods, subjects addressed) confronting German education system, culture and language, established by Christian Flor (1792-1875, professor, Kiel University, Gr-sympathiser); in Dk, similar schools were pioneered by Christen Kold (1816-70) who aspired to assist former peasantry to greater equality within society (which Gr, reconstruing '*folkelighed*' ['folkly-ness'], sometimes called '*folke-lighed*' '[folk-parity]'); Grundtvigians subsequently pursued cause of peasantry's advancement politically (as *Bondevenner*); ideals of *folkelighed* and associated Danishness also earnestly pursued in urban *borgerlige* circles among Grundtvigian congregations, in public life and within family life; in Gr's poem (1848, year preceding granting of democratic constitution) *Folkeligheden* (beginning, not without a touch of irony, "Folkeligt skal alt nu være" [Everything has to be *folkelige* now]) is, as put, liberal in its inclusiveness: *Til et folk de alle høre, / som sig regne selv dertil, / har for modersmaalet øre, / har for fædrelandet ild; / resten selv som dragedukker / sig fra folket udelukker, / lyse selv sig ud af æt, / nægte selv sig indfødsret* [To a *folk* all those belong who count themselves part of it, have an ear for the mother-tongue, feel passionately for the fathers' land; the rest, as men of straw, exclude themselves from the *folk*, repudiate the family, deny themselves their birthright]. The range of nuances of *folke-* terms defies precision of definition but it is a safe generalisation that one of the most distinctive legacies of Gr and Grundtvigianism in Danish national life is a sense of consensus in the *folkelige*.

folkelighed *157 and passim*; see **folkelige, det.**

folkelivet *100, 101, 165, 166*; the life, or the thriving, of the nation, the communal life; not to be confused with the concept expressed by English 'folk-life' alluding to a primitive or rustic and largely oral culture distinct from a urbane literary culture; a key concept in Gr's ideology of the *folk* and the *folkelige*; characteristically, Gr perceived the great heroic accomplishment of King Beowulf to be (at the cost of his own life) his saving of "the dying *folkeliv*" of his nation; see also **folk,** folket; and **folkelige,** det.

Folkemenigheder, *De syv* [The seven Congregations] *257*; book by Vilhelm Birkedal; see **Birkedal.**

folkeoplysning *305*; popular enlightenment, education of the people; lifelong ideal of inclusiveness vigorously advocated (in various writings; for example, a key theme in *Christenhedens Syvstjerne* [The seven stars of Christendom], 1860) and pursued by Gr; ideal shared by his contemporary, Swedish historian Erik Gustav Geijer (1783-1847) who associated it (after 1838) with cultivation of sense of nordic nationhood and with political trends towards democracy and universal franchise (developments over which, however, as far as Dk was concerned, Gr expressed substantial misgivings), shared also by Christen Kold (1816-70) who, invited by Grundtvigians (1850) to discuss (in effect) proper inclusion and integration of Danish agricultural class in exercise of civil freedoms constitutionally granted, proposed establishment of a *højskole* [highschool] for the *bønder* [peasantry and small farmers] – realised at Ryslinge 1851; ideal of popular enlightenment thus rooted by Gr remains to this day a dynamic not only among professed adherents to Gr's ideals but within Danish society at large; see **folk; folkelige.**

Folke-Repræsentanter *121*; people's representatives; Gr saw it as one of the ills of his day (in 1823-24), and it would remain a misgiving about democracy throughout his life, that those who clamoured for the people's representation in government, being deaf to counter-argument, would pursue only prejudice and self-interest.

Folkething, The *144, 329*; Edmund Gosse's anglicisation of Danish *Folketing* (19th-c. title of lower house of *Rigsdag* [parliament]; title of parliament itself after 20th-c. constitutional reform).

folk-highschools *193, 257, 293, 294, 300-302, 305, 306, 323, 324, 333, 337*; The folk-highschool did not spring, Athena-like, fully formed and armed from Gr's brow. His crucial role was, over some years, to formulate and advocate with quite remarkable effectiveness – particularly through his many educational-polemical writings such as the milestone preface to *Nordens Mythologi* (1832) – the concept of such a school; but in the practical establishment and management of actual schools the role of other talented men and women was equally crucial to the emergence of the educational system which evolved as a Danish alternative to traditional objectives, methods and organisation of the Latin schools and state-ordered system. Pedagogically rooted in Gr's experience-based conviction that conventional curricula and teaching methods not only killed off any enthusiasm for learning but did nothing to prepare pupils to realise their own capacities in their individual lives thereafter, and modelled partly upon the learning-communities Gr met in the colleges of Oxford and Cambridge, Gr's concept of the ideal school quickly developed to meet other perceived secular needs of the times (the teaching roles of Church and School he believed in keeping separate): the nurturing of what might now be called 'national identity' (through, for example, cultivation of national history and the mother-tongue; and in particular against the rivalry of German speech, culture and political affiliations in the duchies of Slesvig and Holsten), the nurturing of a sense of *folkelighed* (an inclusive, national, social and cultural cohesiveness), and the preparation of the proportionally huge rural underclass to exercise and extend the social, economic and political liberties gradually being yielded to them. Myth-breaking modern historians would have it noted that the first folk high school in the Danish realm was established in 1842 by the Germanophile upper classes in Rendsborg on the Slesvig border with Holsten to educate the peasant-farmers of the Assembly of the Estates in Slesvig (Vagn Wåhlin, *Grundtvig Studier* 2006). Two years later Christian Flor (1792-1875), professor in the University of Kiel when Holsten was still under formal Danish sovereignty, established the first free (independent of the State) school of a broadly Grundtvigian kind at Rødding in North Slesvig, quite overtly as a flagship of Danishness in that mixed cultural and politically unstable region. The direction the school took thereafter depended on the vision, ideals, administrative and diplomatic skills of such as Sophus Magdalus Høgsbro (1822-1902), principal 1850-62, who broadened and modernised its objectives, and especially Ludvig Peter Schrøder (1836-1908), principal from 1862, who led its relocation at Askov after 1864 and who remains one of the towering figures in the history of the movement. The development of the Grundtvigian folk-highschool took one of its most consequential steps forward when in 1850 a committee of Grundtvigians called in the remarkable Christen Kold (1816-70) to establish a folk-highschool dedicated to Gr's ideals at Ryslinge and subsequently (1862) in Dalum (both on Fyn) where 112 young men were enrolled for the winter session and almost as many young women for the summer sessions which he initiated in 1863. Kold's school set the model for most succeeding folk-highschool establishments (elsewhere in Scandinavia as well as in Dk). Typically they have been independent schools for young adults, with residential facilities for students and staff (creating an important but largely unsung domestic and pastoral role for the wives of principals and teachers), 'schools for life' rather than career-orientated training schools, free from examinations and offering no certifications, prioritising oral communication and teaching by *fortælling* [narrative] over book-learning and learning by rote; emphasising history, the mother-tongue, song, and Northern mythology, symbolically understood and used as a source of metaphor. They are generally agreed to have played an important role in Denmark's political, social and economic transformation from 19th-c. absolute monarchy to modern democracy and they have furnished a broad model and inspiration to both developed and developing countries and to emergent democracies across the world. A century and a half onwards, such hall-mark characteristics are still sustained in some of the Danish folk-highschools, though in the closing years of the 20th c. the number of surviving folk-highschools significantly dropped as a result of falling recruitment and rising costs, student demand for qualifications as the objective of study, and broader trends such as internationalisation and globalisation. See further **Latin schools**; **black school, the**; *Nordens Mythologi eller Sindbilled-Sprog*; **friskole**; **Kold**, Christen Mikkelsen; **Høgsbro**, Sophus Magdalus; **Schrøder**, Ludvig Peter; **Trier**, Ernst Johannes; **Anker**, Herman; **Arvesen**, Olaus; **Bruun**, Christoffer; **Ryslinge**; **Vallekilde**; **Marielyst**; **Folkehøjskole-sagen**.

folk-highschool issue; see **folkehøjskole-sagen**.

folk representatives; see **Folke-Repræsentanter**.

folk-university issue; see **folkehøjskole-sagen**.

Folkvang *143*; Idasletten or Idavolde; in Norse myth (as in Icelandic *Edda*-poem *Völuspá*), the plain on which Æsir gathered to build Ásgarðr; here they would once sit in the grass, playing chess with golden chess-pieces; here the *einherjar*, warriors killed in battle and gathered by Óðinn's valkyries into Valhalla, fight daily, exercising in anticipation of the last mighty battle at Ragnarök, but at evening are healed of all wounds while the field is cleaned of all blood; here, after Ragnarök, the gods will once more gather, find again the golden chess-pieces and sit in the grass playing chess in harmony and peace; Gr speaks (poetically) of Peter Willemoes and those who died with him in battle off Sjællands Odde as "*einherjar* or contenders for the life in Valhalla and the Folkvang." See also *Nordens Mythologi*; **Valhalla**.

fontanelle *309, 313*; artificially induced wound kept open with intention of draining excessive fluid from body; treatment given to Gr's condition 1867.

Foragter ei de ringe dage *278*; Scorn not the days of lowly toil; hymn by Gr based on Zechariah 4:6-10; published in *Sang-Værk til den danske Kirke* 1837; appears as 350 in *DDS* 2002; see also *Kirken den er et gammelt Huus*; *Sov sødt, Barnlille*; **hymns**.

Forenede Venstre, Det *335, 336*; literally 'The United Left' but *Venstre*, in Danish political spectrum, was not and is not 'leftwing' in more international sense, rather a centrist liberal grouping; political party formed 1870 as one of series of realignments of broad grouping of *Venstre* politicians, to which many Grundtvig-adherents belonged; standing principally for more equitable distribution of tax burden, reform of *fæstevæsenet* (system governing status and obligations of tenant farmers) and institution of *parlamentarisme* (system of Cabinet responsibility and accountability; government emanating from popularly-elected assembly) with return to Constitution of 1849; on this manifesto (election of 1872) they won absolute majority in *Folketing*, under leadership of distinguished politician, farmer's son and Grundtvigian, Christen Berg (1829-91); Gr held that his own personal appeal to king, made (1866) jointly with A. F. Tscherning, to block reactionary changes to 1849 Constitution, though unsuccessful, gave impetus to formation of *Det Forenede Venstre* grouping, and he was monitoring party's progress closely, in consultation with leading parliamentarians, right up to his death; further political realignments followed, but concept of united *Venstre* agenda held good until major constitutional reform (*Systemskiftet*) of 1901; see also **Venstre**; and **Tscherning**, Anton Frederik.

Forgyldte Nøgle, Den *264*; The Gilt Key, block of apartments named after hostelry which formed part of it, at Nørregade 5 (now 7) Copenhagen, close to University, where Gr was living 1856-57 following death of second wife Marie.

forsamlinger *172, 284, 285*; *de gudelige forsamlinger* religious gatherings, often laity-led outside regular framework of Church, manifestation of revivalist movements which were later called *de gudelige vækkelser* ['the godly awakenings'], whose adherents were widely referred to as *de vakte* ['the awakened']; to some extent in spirit of early Pietist assemblies in 17th c. Lutheran Germany; emergence of such early revivalist movements led by lay preachers caused Christian VI to issue *konventikelplakat* (1741) forbidding gatherings of more than three people for religious purposes unless with previous permission and ideally supervision of incumbent priest; 1804 Hans Nielsen Hauge imprisoned for not only lay-preaching at gatherings in Norway and Dk against established (rationalist-inclined) Church but agitating against economic tyranny of big merchants; 1821 Chresten Madsen (popularly called apostle from Fyn) imprisoned for preaching at unlawful gatherings, and force of *konventikelplakat* officially reaffirmed; *forsamlinger* were organised by various distinct religious groupings, *herrnhuter* who had established settlement in Christiansfeld in Jylland, Baptists whose children could be forcibly baptised into the *statskirke, de stærke Jyder* [the strong (stubborn) Jutlanders] resisting new religious instructional and devotional books including Bishop N. E. Balle's catechism (1791) and the *Evangelical-Christian Hymnal* (1793); women as well as men spoke and testified at such meetings; *forsamlinger* therefore tended to be viewed by establishment as threat to public order and social decency as well as to *Statskirken*; but others within Church – and not least Gr and his supporters (for Grundtvigianism itself was essentially a revivalist movement and Gr formed many important links with revivalist priests) – welcomed broad revivalist movement, the challenge and alternative it offered to inroads of cold, intellectual and (in Gr's view) spiritually sterile rationalism within Church, and pressure which *forsamlinger* brought to bear in struggle for *sognebaandsløsning* [dissolution of parochial ties; that is, freeing individuals from obligation to seek pastoral ministrations solely from their own parish priest]; thus, Gr's close collaborator J. C. Lindberg arranged *forsamlinger* at his home 'Lille Rolighed' near the *Kalkbrænderi* [lime kilns] in Copenhagen suburbs (1832) provoking police intervention and confrontation with bishop; though Gr was known to be mistrustful of *forsamlinger* and *forsamling*-priests in general, he published an article in *Nyeste Skilderie af Kjøbenhavn* (12 February 1825) asking why the State regulated "godly" gatherings more stringently than "ungodly" ones (as at taverns for drinking and gambling), he spoke at Lindberg's meeting and was instrumental in achieving subsequent compromise with authorities; while Lindberg campaigned, not least in his journal *Nordisk Kirke-Tidende* (1833-40), for religious freedom, the Danish Chancellery issued circular (1835) reminding religious and secular officials that 1741 *konventikelplakat* was to be strictly observed; but tide of freedom was running and eventually Constitution of 1849 permitted *forsamlinger* though reserved right of police to oversee them; see also **Pietism**; **forsamlingspræst**; **Jensen,** Rasmus; **Frederiks Kirke**.

forsamlingspræst *283, 285*; priest supportive of religious gatherings (pietistic, revivalist, etc), outside regular framework of Church; such (among many) as Pastor Frederik Boisen (1808-82), priest (1837) in Skørpinge near Slagelse, Sjælland; and Pastor Joachim Goske Willemoes (1781-1858) in Herfølge, Sjælland who was instrumental in religious 'awakening' of both Marie Toft and Asta Reedtz, Gr's second and third wives; see **forsamlinger**.

Forsetes-Kvide *ved Grev Danneskjolds Grav 114*; Forsete's lament at the grave of *Grev* Danneskjold; elegy by Gr; see **Danneskjold,** Christian Conrad Sophus.

Franco-Prussian war *325*; war 1870-71 between France under Napoleon III and Prussia led by Bismarck; Gr and like-minded Danes hoped outcome would be defeat for Prussia which would ease Prussian grip on Slesvig-Holsten and generally weaken Dk's menacing southerly neighbour; therefore ensuing humiliation of France on battlefield and at conference table, followed (1871) by foundation of German Empire with king of Prussia as emperor, was grave disappointment and augmented threat.

Franks *66*; collective name for federation of Germanic tribes which seized advantage of collapsing Roman Empire (5th c.) to conquer former Gaul, their original Germanic language giving way to dialect of Latin (now French); shaped into kingdom and state under Pepin and especially (8th c.) Charlemagne on Christianised model of late Roman culture and institutions.

fraskiltes vielse *168*; marriage of divorcees; to the Scripture-based principle concerning marriage – that "what God hath joined together, let no man put asunder" and the pre-Reformation view of marriage as a sacrament – Reformation and Christian v's *Danske Lov* [Danish Laws; 1683] brought some limited relaxation, mainly on basis that marriage was no longer viewed as a sacrament; divorce cases were put to special ecclesiastical court, *Tamperretten*; church ritual authorised in 1685 made few changes to earlier marriage ritual though in preliminary debate provision for marriage of divorced persons had been advocated; by late 18th c., in spirit of Rationalism, marriage was increasingly seen as civil contract (though not until after 1851 was strictly civil marriage [*borgerlig vielse*] possible), and divorce (by decree of 1797 disbanding *Tamperretten* and referring cases to ordinary civil courts, though also imposing inhibiting conditions including three years of prior separation, and both spiritual and secular mediation) was made matter of legal termination, thus further diminishing ideological objections to new marriage of divorced persons; divorce and remarriage were also known in royal house; but no general authorised provision for church marriage of divorcees had yet been made by Gr's time, nevertheless he was required by law to marry divorcees in his first post at Vor Frelsers Kirke and seems to have found the indiscriminate situation intolerably typical of the spiritual indifference of clergy and laity alike, and on these grounds (among others) resigned his curacy in 1826; subsequently, Gr and supporters joined with liberal politicians in seeking to make marriage an essentially secular civil process with consequence that divorce would be termination of civil contract, not of church-sanctified bond; since 1922, church-marriage of divorced persons in Dk has been left to conscience of individual priest; see also **præstefrihed**.

Fredegod *158*; Frode Fredegod, Frode the *sagtmodig* [mild, meek, gentle]; legendary Danish king of Skjoldung dynasty depicted in *Gesta Danorum* of Saxo Grammaticus and Icelandic saga-literature, and mentioned in *Beowulf*, his name [Old Icelandic fróðr 'wise', friðr 'peace'], sharing the element *Frede-* with the Danish royal name Frederik [peaceful and powerful, powerful for peace], defining him as symbol of ideal kingship exercised in wisdom and guaranteeing peace; to his rule, which he extended far and wide in neighbouring lands, is attached traditional testimony of peace-bringing authority, that precious objects placed by highway are never stolen; hence *Fre-degods-Dagene*, golden age of days of Fredegod; medieval sources chronologically associate this age with period of Roman *Pax Augustana* and therefore with time of Incarnation of Christ; Gr poetically used legendary aura of Skjoldung kings to give historical and heroic lustre to (absolute) kingship of his own day – as in his *Krønnike-Rim* 1842: "*Fredegod* er hos Dannemænd, med deres mageløse Fredsommelighed, det folkeligste Tilnavn for en Konge" [Fredegod is, amongst Danes, with their unmatchable peaceability, the most *folkelige* appellation for a king], and (as a compliment to the late king) "*Frederik* is the royal name which in the Oldenborg dynasty has regularly alternated with Christian and in Frederik the Sixth fused together with *Fredegod*."

Frederik VI *15, 21, 62, 103, 107-112, 129, 132, 133, 160, 161, 167, 170, 172, 174-176, 201, 223, 224, 232, 236*; 1768-1839. King of Dk 1808-39, Norway 1808-14, son of Christian VII (who suffered from insanity) and his English queen Caroline Mathilde (exiled 1772 for adulterous relationship with leading statesman Johan Friedrich Struensee); brought up in spartan circumstances on principles of Rousseau; as Crown Prince during Dk's period of absolute monarchy, took over government by coup 1784 until accession (upon king's death) 1808; oversaw major agrarian reforms including ending (1788) of *stavnsbåndet* (feudal ties of peasantry); also oversaw Dk's shift from armed neutrality to pro-Napoleonic confrontation with Britain and allies, leading through preemptive and punitive military strikes against Copenhagen (1801, 1807), destruction of fleet (1807) and national bankruptcy (1813) to ceding of Norway to Sweden (1814).

Frederik VII *195, 261, 267, 268, 296, 329, 331*; 1808-63, king of Dk 1848-63, son of Christian VIII and first wife (divorced 1810 for infidelity) Charlotte Frederikke; acknowledging direction of events in Europe and at home, was quick to concede end of royal absolutism (1848) and granting of constitution (1849); partly for this reason, partly because of popular sympathy for his steadfast relationship with Louise Rasmussen (later named as *Grevinde* [Countess] Danner though never officially accepted as royal consort; popularly seen as a guarantor of king's commitment to democracy), partly because of a bluff amiable presence, remembered as 'the people's king;' but his resistance to any settlement of Slesvig-Holsten crisis which involved partitioning the duchies contributed to outbreak of war 1848-51; and his death without offspring (after two formal marriages dissolved) ended the Oldenborg dynasty which had ruled through 16 kings over 415 years; succeeded by Christian IX, son of dukes of Glücksborg.

Frederik, Prince of Nør (Noer) *199*; 1800-65; seat at Nør between Eckernförde and Kiel in Slesvig-Holsten; brother of Christian August, Duke of Augustenborg; though closely related to Danish royal house, being descendants of House of Oldenborg, sons of Frederik VI's sister Louisa Augusta, brothers to Christian VIII's queen (and Gr's later patroness) Caroline Amalie, and raised as Danish princes, both became identified (1846) with cause of 'indivisible' duchies of Slesvig and Holsten (where they claimed hereditary rights) against Dk, Prince of Nør taking lead, eventually militarily with occupation of garrison town of Rendsborg (1848).

Frederiksberg *163, 237, 245, 292*; district west of the walled city of Copenhagen historically forming part of the city's outer defences; named after Frederik IV who built there (1699-1703) a royal residence, further developed through the 18th and 19th centuries and provided with handsome gardens and parkland; the palace left unused by royalty after 1852 became (1868) military officer-school; *kommune* [public-administrative district] granted (1858) independent status; developed and retained reputation as fashionable residential area.

Frederiksdal *313, 319, 322*; rural area north of Copenhagen lying between lakes (Lyngby Sø and Furesø) where old highway crossed Mølleåen; in 17th c. Frederik III built a small *maison de plaisance* here, and area subsequently became popular resort for Copenhageners; here Gr was taken for convalescence after breakdown in 1867, accompanied by physician Dr J. A. Sparrewohn, son-in-law of his third wife Asta.

Frederiks Kirke *18, 21, 62, 70, 171-173, 207, 211, 212, 224, 231, 249, 255, 257*; Originally Frederiks Tyske [German] Kirke, erected in Christianshavn (Copenhagen) 1755-59 to serve the German community; outstanding example of a Protestant church designed with the centrality of preaching in view; subsequently (1901) rededicated as Christians Kirke; coffins and tombs of various distinguished personages in its remarkable mortuary-crypt; notable memorial to Gr in porch; virtually redundant church until Gr was grudgingly authorised (by royal resolution 1 March 1832) to hold evening services here (and to preach but categorically not to administer sacraments); by this move, authorities, yielding to pressure from Jakob Christian Lindberg, Gr and others, hoped to stop *forsamlinger* (religious gatherings held elsewhere than in church) such as had recently gathered, with some support from Gr, in Lindberg's home; but in effect gave some unintended substance to idea of a *frimenighed* (congregation within the national Church but formed about a minister of their choice at church of their choice, unrestricted by parish ties) and to this extent the arrangement, which lasted until 1839 when Gr was appointed to Vartov, was a gain for Gr and his sympathisers in the church struggle being fought over this period; Gr, who had been offered no clerical appointment after his resignation from Vor Frelsers Kirke 1826 and thus felt gagged as preacher, opened his first sermon at Frederiks Kirke with text from Isaiah (62:1): For Zion's sake I will not hold my peace, and for Jerusalem's sake I will not rest; see also **forsamlinger**.

Fred til Bod for bittert Savn *340*; Peace as balm for bitter loss; hymn by Gr (1843, 1845), *DDS* 2002 no. 426; melody composed 1865 by Johan Peter Emilius Hartmann (1805-1900); played by brass band accompanying Gr's funeral cortège at Gammel Køgegaard, 11 September 1872; see also **hymns**.

free church; see **Frikirke**.

free congregation *18, 171*; *Frimenighed*; see **Frikirke**.

freedom *68, 70, 99, 104, 117, 148, 154, 172, 174, 190, 222, 228, 251, 266, 267, 267, 269, 279, 289, 302, 308, 328, 329*; *Frihed*; "perfect love, perfect liberty, enthusiasm for the Fatherland, hope for the future of Denmark" were "the ideals of [Gr's] life" – "he was a passionate lover of liberty, and his sympathy for those whom orthodoxy treated as rebels was incessant" (Gosse); and it was through "Folkelighed, Frihed og historisk Oplysning [cultivation of the *folkelige*, freedom and historical edification]" (wrote Gr himself) that he rediscovered "the ancient paths" fit to be followed by a Christian society; his appreciation of freedom as a first and indispensable principle was much sharpened by his visits to England 1829-31, though Europe as a whole was shaken by universal demand for liberty during Gr's lifetime; his early concern for freedom of expression especially in print was augmented by a major lifelong concern for freedom of religious conscience, clerical liberties, freedom of congregations to choose their own pastor and, increasingly, political and civil freedoms which he long believed, notwithstanding his radical engagement in democratic government, were best guaranteed by moderated royal absolutism; freedom (and necessity) in more abstract, philosophical and theological terms also much concerned him; he never lost hope of "a genuine bonding of mind and of heart between the three Nordic peoples and realms" which, "because they honour the humanity and love the freeborn pride in each other, [...] heartily desire and wish for each other all the freedom, individuality and independence that they desire and wish for themselves." As regards legislative achievement of Gr's (and the Grundtvigians') specific objectives for the Church, the compulsory 'parochial tie' of parishioners to their own parish church (the *sognebaand*) was ended 1855, mandatory baptism into the national Church was abolished 1857, the formation of elective congregations within the national Church was legalised 1868, and the freedom of priests to accept charge of a congregation within another priest's parish was established 1872.

Freemasons *159*; freemasonry, essentially 18th-c. phenomenon though with claims to greater antiquity, founded in England, spread in same century to Germany and Dk, advantaged by its strongly rationalist character; in Gr's lifetime, Frederik vi, Christian viii, Frederik vii were all freemasons; Gr, ever opposed to Rationalism as it affected bible, theology and church, puts 'freemason' alongside '*hjemtysker*' (literally 'home-German' – Dane of German origin and cultural affiliations) and a string of other pejorative adjectives in dismissive evaluation of Bishop Friederich Münter (1761-1830).

free school *216*; school established and maintained independently of public provision and regulation; see **friskole**.

Free Will (*Menneskets fri Villie*); see **Fall,** The.

Frelserens Kirke; see **Vor Frelsers Kirke**

Frelsers Kirke, Kristiania; see **Vår Frelsers Kirke,** Oslo.

French Revolution *66, 80, 84, 157*; 1789; a political issue in Gr's village of Udby mainly because of fierce opinions of newly-arrived schoolmaster, formerly a teacher of French in Copenhagen, of extremist republican (Jacobin) views; but unsurprisingly six-year-old Gr was more concerned with 'revolution' this arrival effected in his own awareness of wider world – upon which he began reading *Berlings-Avisen*.

Freyr and Surt *300*; Gr uses Norse myth of Ragnarok, where the fire-giant Surtr kills Freyr (one of the Æsir and god of fertility, sun, rain, harvest), before hurling fire across the earth and consuming all the world, to symbolise principles of Light and Darkness; see also **mythology**; **Thor and Midgard Serpent**; **Odin and Fenris**.

Friends, The; see **Vennerne**.

Friends' Meetings, The; see **Vennerne**.

Friend of public polity *156*; Danish popular weekly newspaper over first half of 19th c.; see *Politi(e)vennen*.

Friis, *Komtesse 262*; title *Komtesse* (corresponding approximately to English 'Lady') was used of unmarried daughter of a *Grev* [Count], whereas wife of a *Grev* was conventionally titled *Grevinde*; see **Grundtvig,** Asta.

Frijs, Grev *312*; Christian Emil Krag-Juel-Vind-Friis, 1817-96; *Lensgreve* [Count] of Frijsenborg, major estate northwest of Aarhus in Jylland; from 1858 to 1880, member of *Rigsraad* [Parliament]; supported Danish unitary state constitution [*helstatsforfatning*] of 1855, incorporating the duchies, which led to secession (1858) of Holsten and Lauenborg; became *konsejlpræsident* [prime minister] 1865 and was thus in office when Gr, during breakdown at Easter 1867, wrote to government warning of (imagined) new Prussian plans to invade Dk; Gr's third wife (from 1858), Asta Reedtz (1826-90), was of the family of Krag-Juel-Vind-Frijs whence her title *Komtesse* (corresponding approximately to English 'Lady' – thus Lady Asta Tugenreich Adelheid Krag-Juel-Vind-Frijs).

Frijs, *Grevinde 312*; born Thyra Valborg Haffner, 1821-81; wife of *Lensgreve* Christian Emil Krag-Juel-Vind-Friis thus related by marriage to Gr's third wife, Asta (born *Komtesse* Asta Krag-Juel-Vind-Friis) who sought to involve the *grevinde* in consequences of Gr's breakdown (1867), as Gr himself (with different matters in mind) had sought to involve the *Greve* (at that time Dk's prime minister).

Frikirke *18, 171, 256*; 'free church' associated with 'free congregation' (*Frimenighed*); as 16th-c. Lutheran reformation reflected will of various national churches to be free of governance by Rome, so emergence of free-church thinking from 17th-c. onwards reflected will of congregations to be free of governance by state authority; in Dk, Gr and followers pioneered, after bitter struggle with absolutist authorities, an optional 'free' status for priests and congregations while formally remaining within national Church; "To establish a *Free Church* [*Frikirke*] which in its doctrine could well adhere to the Augsburg Confession but yet would keep doctrinal formulations strictly apart from the common faith and would make *free* use of Scripture's 'things old and new' and make the church service far more alive, as regards the Lord's own institutions, sermon, prayer and hymn-singing alike, than it had been for many centuries – *this* was now [1832-39] my desire" (Gr); important steps towards ultimate (though protracted) fulfilment included *forsamlingler* (religious gatherings) organised (1832) at J. C. Lindberg's home in defiance of law and police action, permission Gr wrung out of authorities to preach to 'free' congregation in Frederiks Kirke Copenhagen (1832-39), and (1866) establishment in Ryslinge of Dk's first *valgmenighedskirke* (church of elective congregation, opting to elect own pastor but remaining within the established Church) with Vilhelm Birkedal as pastor.

Frimenighed; free congregation; see **Frikirke**.

Frimodt, Jens Christian Rudolph *243*; 1828-79; priest, founder of the *Indre Mission* [Home Missionary movement; strongly evangelical branch of Church of Dk] in Copenhagen; in early years much caught up in politics and nationalistic movement; close friend of H. N. Clausen.

friskole *216, 295*: school independent of state educational provision; around mid-19th c. *friskoler* were providing for well over fifty percent of Copenhagen children in education, reflecting low reputation of public provision; but simultaneously with public school reform and improvement in 1840s, public education system was further challenged by success of initiatives of Christian Flor, Christen Kold and Gr towards establishment of *friskoler* whose organisation, programmes and methods served specific contemporary objectives including assertion of Danish historical national identity and mother tongue, advancement of oppressed and disadvantaged rural population, and reeducation of society towards *folkelig* cohesion; greatest legacy was proliferation of folk-high-schools for young adults, through Dk, Norway and Scandinavia more widely, though very few have managed to survive until today without state financial subsidy; see also **sorte Skole,** den; **Almueskoler**; **Kold,** Christen Mikkelsen; **Bondeskole,** Higher; **Ryslinge**; **Schrøder,** Ludvig Peter.

Frisprog 176; *Frisprog mod H. H. Hr. Biskop Mynsters Forslag til en ny Forordnet Alterbog* [Free-speaking against the Right Reverend Bishop Mynster's proposal for a new Authorised Service Book; 1839]; Gr's critique of Mynster's proposed changes; in particular a vigorous defence of the Interrogation at baptism, with which Mynster desired to dispense; to his bitter resentment Mynster subsequently saw his proposals completely shelved; see also **Daabspagten.**

Frue Kirke; see **Vor Frue Kirke.**

Fry, Elizabeth *141*; 1780-1845; English prison reformer, daughter of Quaker family; shocked by visit to London's infamous Newgate Prison into forming association to press for amelioration of prison conditions; with brother Joseph Gurney (activist for emancipation of slaves) also promoted their causes abroad, being received by kings of France and Prussia; visited Copenhagen August 1841, under patronage of Queen Caroline Amalie who asked Gr (as English speaker with some experience of England) to join group escorting them round city prisons; "She spoke with marvellous effect. The pathos of her voice was almost miraculous, and melted alike the hardest criminals and the most impervious men of the world. Cool observers who had witnessed the effects of her appeals in Newgate prison could hardly describe the scene without tears." (Dictionary of National Biography); Gr was less readily carried away, but though he was suspicious of rationalist Quakers and fashionable soft-heartedness towards convicts, he admired Fry as person and acknowledged serious shortcomings in humane treatment of prisoners; at request, he says, of 'the foreigners' he "comforted the prisoners with the gospel concerning the Pharisee and the tax-gatherer" (presumably Luke 18:10-14), an experience which left him ever afterwards troubled by potential of this text for misconstruction.

Fryd dig, du Christi Brud 319; Rejoice, thou bride of Christ; hymn by Gr sung on Palm Sunday 1867; see endnote 1 to item 118.

Frydensberg, *amtsforvalter 223, 225*; present February 1832 at public religious revivalist meetings on Amager, near Copenhagen which, being held in location other than a church, were deemed illegal and led to police intervention; one in series of deliberate confrontations with authorities over church liberty, one outcome of which was the authorities' reluctant licensing of Gr to preach at evening service in Frederiks Kirke. See **Brun,** Pastor; and footnotes to item 83. See also **forsamlinger**; **Frederiks Kirke.**

Fryxell, Anders *265*; 1795-1881; Swedish priest, dr. theol., historian, author (1823-81) of monumental 46-volume History of Sweden, priest; headmaster of Maria Skolen in Stockholm, appointed professor 1833, member of Swedish Academy 1840; entered into furious politically-coloured dispute with historian Erik Gustaf Geijer (1783-1847) over interpretation of Swedish history; see **Geijer**, Erik Gustaf.

Fyn *66, 92, 255, 294, 323*; second largest of Danish islands, lying between Sjælland and Jylland, rich agricultural region; among its chief towns are former royal residences, strongholds and administrative centres, Odense, Nyborg and Svendborg.

Fædrelandet *237, 335, 337*; Danish newspaper; founded 1834 in dying years of absolutism as weekly (daily from 1839) by Professor Christian Georg Nathan David (1793-1874) and Johannes Dam Hage (1800-37) to voice emergent moderate liberalism and responsible concern for public affairs; like other papers risking free speech and satire such as *Kjøbenhavnsposten* [The Copenhagen Post] and *Corsaren* [The Corsair], persecuted by authorities with fines, dismissals from office (David), personal censorship (Hage); other liberals joined editorial board, including Abraham Wessely (1800-75), Orla Lehmann (1810-70) and Carl Parmo Ploug (1813-94) who as executive editor from 1841 campaigned on agenda, later taken up by National-Liberal party, of nationalism, a Danish Slesvig, and scandinavianism; censorship ceased with Constitution of 1848, paper became leading forum of political debate, distinguished also for cultural content; during 1850s played main part in highly divisive debate over status of Slesvig, advocating confrontation with Germany rather than concessions, which policy led to calamitous war of 1864; thereafter, paper's hitherto defining agenda being in ruins, Ploug took it steadily towards conservatism and abusive opposition to sovereignty of parliament, growing democracy and Grundtvigian manifestations of *det folkelige*; Ploug sold paper 1881 and it closed 1882.

Føniks-Fuglen; see **Phenix-Fuglen**.

G

Gabriel, archangel *318, 321, 322*; fantasy of identity suffered by Gr during 1867 breakdown; but like other aspects of that painful episode, perhaps less outlandish and irrational than it has suited scandalised commentators to acknowledge; Thomas Skat Rørdam, impatient friend, was on the trail ("Gradually, since those around him said Yes and Amen to everything, grundtvig naturally got his derangement systematically organised. He himself was the Angel Gabriel, and the Holy Spirit was to be communicated by kissing so that those women who were kissed by him were supposed to conceive by the Spirit just as the Virgin Mary, and thus there would arise a new generation and a complete new and sinfree congregation of God in Denmark, etc."); Gr had long since developed (especially in hymns and poems) a complex quasi-theology of *kjærlighed*, love, the human capacity which is proof of the surviving likeness of God in fallen Man; its residence is the heart; women speak the language of the heart more naturally than men and, like the Marys of the gospels, fulfil a kind of sublime ministry of the heart; the Danish mother-tongue is a language of the heart, indeed the Danish folk are distinguished from other peoples as a folk of the heart and in that (complimentary) sense are a 'womanly folk' (et *kvindeligt folk*) and thereby have a warranty as God's people; in his sermon for Palm Sunday (commemorating Christ's symbolic entry into Jerusalem) Gr had already said that "there had been many impediments to the Lord's coming, for the spirit and the heart had become separated. The spirit God had planted in the east on the Mount of the Seers and the heart here on the Danish islands. But now they have at last been reunited and now Jordan flows out into the Øresund, now the Lord is riding into his city" (Frederik Hammerich); thus the Øresund was to become a great Scandinavian baptismal font, Copenhagen was Jerusalem; spirit and heart were conjoining to beget "a new generation and a complete new and sinfree congregation of God in Denmark, etc" (Skat Rørdam); disordered though his stricken mind had grown, Gr surely glimpsed here (whether or not delusorily) an ecstatic vision of the Lord's coming which had its coherence in, and consummated, a theology of love long since formulated and richly articulated by Gr the poet and psalmist; the doctor however diagnosed "a perfectly ordinary satyriasis." See also **kvindelige**, det; **Palm Sunday** 1867.

Gad, Peter Christian Stenersen *175, 254*; 1797-1851; priest, later (1845) bishop in Lolland-Falster and (1848) in Fyn; views on religion and church influenced by father-in-law H. G. Clausen and brother-in-law H. N. Clausen; along with Clausen circle as a whole was critical of ritual of Danish Church (and himself made changes in it, for example in omitting from the celebrant's prescribed words, after distribution of bread and wine, reference to "remission of all your sins" accomplished through Christ's gift of his body and blood, holding that published ritual was only a guide which individual priest could adapt) and was therefore in continual conflict with Gr's party and supporters; "en plat Rationalist" [a crude rationalist; Gr]; strove with Clausen for radical overhaul of teaching methods and organisation in public-funded *almueskoler*, and for replacement of absolutist rule with democratic government; among other public involvements, he was a founder-member of *Den danske historiske Forening* [Danish Historical Association], reflecting his strong nationalistic interests.

Galilei, Galileo *165*; 1564-1642, persecuted by Church for challenging medieval conceptualisation of universe by scientific observation and reasoning; came to be seen as archetypal martyr to Church's obscurantism in face of scientific enquiry; see **Vanini**, Giulio Cesare (Lucilio); and **Roskilde Landemode**.

Gamborg, Anders *78*; 1753-1833; moral philosopher, professor of philosophy in University of Copenhagen; one of Gr's examiners April 1801.

Gammel Kongevej *243, 302, 308, 312*; main road linking city of Copenhagen westwards to major suburb of Frederiksberg; here Gr lived 1859-67 in villa 'Gladhjem' [Happy home; Gr's chosen name for official 'Christianshvile,' 'Christian's repose'], a short walk from palace and gardens of Frederiksberg; after trauma of Gr's illness Easter 1867 family moved to villa 'StoreTuborg' [Great Tuborg], Strandvejen 123, on Øresund shore some 4 km north of central city.

Gammel Køgegaard *244, 339-341*; imposing manor-house and estate adjacent to Køge, Sjælland, 30 km south of Copenhagen; medieval and 17th c. origins; neo-classical rebuild when (1775) estate taken over by Rasmus Carlsen Lange, forebear of Marie (Toft) Grundtvig, born Carlsen, Gr's second wife; name Lange preserved in latter's son by Gr, Frederik Lange Gr; a private cemetery on the estate was first consecrated 1853 by Gr for burial of Clara Carlsen (born Krag-Juel-Vind-Frijs, wife of Hans Rasmussen Carlsen, died 1852), "but also for the dust of those who would wish to lie here by her side, and such would wish not only you, my friend [Carlsen], who with loving hand have prepared for your spouse's dust this beautiful and peaceful resting-place, as she desired for herself, but you also would wish it, my soul's beloved [Marie, Gr's wife, sister of Hans Rasmussen Carlsen]! and in what spot of earth should I then rather wish that my own dust might rest until the Lord comes, but here where our dust can mingle" (Gr, quoted by Frederik Rönning); soon afterwards it indeed became resting-place of Gr's second wife Marie (died July 1854, shortly after birth of Frederik Lange) and eventually of Gr himself and of his third wife Asta (born Krag-Juel-Vind-Frijs, foster-sister to Clara, died 1890).

Geheimeraad *112, etc.*; Privy councillor; title conferring rank in civil list (1st Class), rather than office; wife of such (after Danish convention of designating wives by feminine version of husband's occupational title) was accorded title *Geheimeraadinde*, as was Gr's third wife, Asta Reedtz, widow of *Geheimekonferensraad* H. C. Reedtz.

Geijer, Erik Gustaf *244, 265, 338*; 1783-1847; Swedish historian, poet, exact contemporary of Gr; like him, influenced by early visit to England and, like him, inspired through study of history to a nordic nationalism, often expressed through medium of his poetry; shortly after appointment (1810) as *docent* [lecturer] in Uppsala University (of which he was distinguished graduate) founded *Götiska Forbundet* [Gothic Association], promoting ancient- Nordic-based nationalism partly through publication of its journal *Iduna*; professor of history Uppsala 1817; published 1825 brilliant critical study of mythical and legendary sources of Swedish history in his *Svea Rikes häfder*, contributing further to 19th-c. nationalist-romantic identification of Swedish national character against background of nature; 1832-36 published second great work, *Svenska folkets historia* [History of the Swedish nation]; instinctively conservative, strongly royalist ("Sveriges historia är dens konungers" [The history of Sweden is the history of her kings]), reflecting a deeply religious, though not orthodox, nature; after 1838, influenced by contemporary emergent Scandinavian liberalism, he shifted allegiance from political conservatism to liberalism, committing himself to cause of *folkeoplysning* [popular enlightenment] and to demand for universal franchise; his deprecatory review of role of aristocracy in Swedish history led to extremely bitter feud with Swedish historian Anders Fryxell (1795-1881); as historian and as poet, one of Sweden's greatest spirits and in some respects a remarkable counterpart to Grundtvig – who esteemed his work and was listening to reading from Geijer's *Svenska folkets historia* on day he died; see also **Fryxell,** Anders.

German and French trash *157*; Henrik Steffens' provocative evaluation (Copenhagen lectures 1802) of what Copenhagen "was reading, writing and praising to the skies;" remedy was to read Shakespeare and Goethe; see **Steffens,** Henrik.

Germany, German *passim*; Dk's southerly neighbour, increasingly powerful over 19th c., had long been barely more than a geographical expression deriving from Roman designation *Germania*; despite participation in Holy Roman Empire, multiplicity of small states wielded little political or military power until Federation of German States formed, following Napoleonic Wars (1815), to be replaced (1866) by North German Federation excluding Bavaria and southerly states; emergence of Otto Eduard Leopold Bismarck (1815-98) as chief minister to Vilhelm I of Prussia marked start of expansionist policies resulting in crushing of Austria (1866) and France (1870) and formation of German Empire (1871) with Prussian king as emperor and Bismarck as chancellor; Dk too, after more or less successful conflict 1848, catastrophically lost territory of Sønderjylland in war of 1864, and threat of further Prussian designs on Dk haunted Gr and others thereafter; but Gr saw German culture (or undiscriminating affectation of it in upper strata of Danish state and society) as equally insidious threat to Danish identity and independence, and was lifelong opponent not only of German Rationalism within Church and University but of any preference of German language over Danish mother-tongue or German cultural models over Danish; inculcation of Danishness was one objective of Grundtvigian folk-highschools; given the long-standing German integration in Slesvig-Holsten all these were problematical as national commitments; see also **Slesvig-Holsten**.

giant-species; see **Jættevæsen**.

Gilt Key, The; see **Forgyldte Nøgle**, Den.

Gjor(d)slev *231*; mansion and estate in Sjælland, 17 km SE from Køge; episcopal seat until 1536, Crown property until 1540, various private owners but passed again to Crown 1678; 1793-1923 owned by Scavenius family; south wing erected 1843 contains interiors executed by internationally eminent Danish sculptor Bertel Thorvaldsen.

Gladsaxe *201*; in 19th c. a community 10 km north of Copenhagen; today a suburb.

Glahns *208*; family of Poul Egede Glahn, 1778-1846, married to Bodil Marie Elisabeth Blicher , sister of Gr's wife Elisabeth; it was in Glahn's parsonage in Olstrup near Udby that Gr had begun wooing Elisabeth Blicher; the Glahns thus formed part of large kinship group Gr entered into by marriage; the Glahns' daughter Sophie Henriette married Gr's supporter (and later Bishop in Aalborg), Peter Christian Kierkegaard.

Glykstad (Glückstadt) *108*; town in Slesvig-Holsten on north shore of Elbe estuary; originally Danish, founded 1616 by Christian IV as fortified mercantile centre intended to compete with Hamburg; its fortifications destroyed when town captured (1813) by Allies in Napoleonic wars; lost permanently to Prussia 1864.

Gnav *76*; domestic table game involving exchanging of cards or pieces.

Gniben; see **Sjællands Odde**

Gosse, Sir Edmund *230, 248, 327, 328*; 1849-1928; English critic, author, poet; see headnote to item 125.

Goths *114, 334*; grouping of Germanic peoples whom Roman records locate in regions north of Donau river and Black Sea whence large part was stampeded to take refuge within Roman imperial frontiers by assault of Huns (*ca* 375); divided by 5th c. into Ostrogoths, who moved into Italy and for a time ruled Rome, and Visigoths who conquered Spain; their place in early development of Christian vernacular poetry was studied by Gr's friend Professor Frederik Hammerich in *De episk-kristelige Oldkvad hos de gothiske Folk* [The ancient Christian epic poems of the Gothic peoples; 1873]; they feature conspicuously in epic-legendary tradition of NW Europe along with Huns, being mentioned in Anglo-Saxon *Beowulf* and *Widsith*, Icelandic poetry (e.g. lays relating to Völsungs and to Atli) and sagas (e.g. *Þiðriks saga*, *Völsunga saga*) and in German *Nibelungenlied*; but were to some extent confused both with Swedish Götar from Gottland who appear in *Beowulf* as *Geatas*, to which people the hero belonged, and with Jutes of Jutland (Jylland); *rex Gothorum*, king of the Goths, became part of the titles of kings of Sweden and Dk; see also **Visigoths**.

Gothenburg *147*; Göteborg, Swedish city founded 1619 on more ancient settlement site on Kattegat coast at mouth of Göta river; here at centre of the three chief Scandinavian lands Gr long hoped to see established a great Nordic university (*Højskole*) to rival Oxford; "naturally not one where civil servants are to be fabricated but where the whole human world of knowledge shall be seen through high-Nordic eyes and cultivated with high-Nordic strength for the increasing and multiplying enlightenment of human life and all its circumstances" (Gr); but the vision never achieved realisation; city's modern university began as University College 1891, formally founded as independent university 1954.

Gothenburg's Business and Maritime News *336*; *Gøtheborgs Handels- og Søfartstidende* (*Göteborgs Handels- och Sjöfarts-Tidning*); see **Hedlund**, Sven Adolf; **Hammar-Mødet**.

Greece, universal-historical importance of *248*; topic discussed at first meeting (1830s) of Frederik Hammerich with Gr.

Greek Church *25, 265, 307*; the second 'congregation' (*menighed*) out of the seven phases, corresponding with the seven churches of *Revelation* 1:20, into which Gr divided history of God's revelation to world, as expounded particularly in his *Christenhedens Syvstjerne* [The seven stars of Christendom]; informal lectures given by Gr in his home over winter 1860-61 (to large gatherings sometimes including Queen Caroline Amalie) "gave a survey over the life of the Church from the first ardent days in the Hebrew congregation, from the strongly religious-philosophical days in the Greek congregation, from the centuries of powerful administration in the Church of Rome, etc." according to Olaus Arvesen's exhilarated report; Gr's universal-historical schematisation was also basis of Vilhelm Birkedal's *De syv Folkemenigheder i Lyset af Herrens Spaadomsord* [The seven congregations in the light of the Lord's words of prophecy] (1877); Vilhelm Birkedal recalls provocative mention of Greek Church's 'perverseness' (*Forvendthed* – in the sense of Paul's Letter to the Philippians 2:15 "den vanartige og forvendte Slægt" – "a crooked and perverse nation") at Dowager Queen's tea-party where Gr's marital history was target of malicious remark; out of courtesy, Gr declines to respond.

Greek congregation *25, 307*; *grækermenighed*; see **Greek Church**.

Greek language and literature *72-74, 81, 100, 101, 217, 248*; in Dk, classical as distinct from New Testament Greek first became mandatory part of theological study with 16th-c. Reformation; by early 19th c., around Gr's university period, and partly under influence of new humanistic trends from Germany, classical (Greek and Latin) philology was recognised as discipline and became, as in public schools and universities of England, a cornerstone of higher education; Gr learned Greek and Latin with Laurids Feld at Thyregod, these being essential for admission to Latin School at Aarhus where he studied principal classical authors; performed only moderately well in examinations on admission (1800) to Copenhagen University, felt unjustly assessed by examiners especially in Latin; recalled being struck, in Henrik Steffens' renowned lectures (winter 1802), by view that fallen world was as though celestially consoled by Greek Muses and Graces, though ungodly Romans were summed up in Nero and crucifixion of Christ; also saw to it that own sons studied Greek in their programme of home tuition, though Marie Blom asserts they were taught no grammar at that time; he could discuss modern Greek and significance of Greece to universal history with Professor Frederik Hammerich; but Olaus Arvesen observed that Gr ranked the Norse sagas "at least as high as even those of the Greeks who, as is well known, were definitely his favourite nation" and indeed Gr held that giving priority to writings of ancient Greeks and Romans over native Scandinavian myth and legend was an unnatural prejudice; see also **Latin schools**; *Nordens Mythologi*.

Greek Muses and Graces *85*; presented in Henrik Steffens' historical perception of human life as offering fallen humanity "celestial consolation" – an idea Gr found impressive.

Greek New Testament *289*; for daily reading (1848) Gr used Greek text in *Complutum*, edition of Bible published (1515) Alcala, Spain; see **Complutenseren**.

Greek thought *189*; commenting on J. A. Eberhard's characterisation of early Christianity as having fused "der griechische Sinn und das orientalische Gefühl" [Greek thought and oriental feeling], Gr observes (1811): "So once more, a Christianity without Christ."(Schmidt).

Greeks, ancient *98, 101*; Gr's passion for Northern antiquity, rekindled by his ill-starred love for Constance Leth, set a vision of the Eternal before his eyes like that of the Olympian Jupiter before the eyes of the ancient Greeks.

Greeks, Gr's favourite nation *296*; thus O. Arvesen; as reflected widely in Gr's writings and lectures, classical education against which he campaigned had nevertheless imprinted him with sense of eminence of Greek culture, alongside that of ancient North.

Greenlander *160*; Bishop Otto Fabricius (1744-1822); Greenland, having by then been partly inhabited for some 3,000 years, was discovered (*ca.* 985) and precariously settled by the Norwegian-Icelander Erik the Red (Eiríkr rauði) and his son Leif, christianised in line with conversion of Iceland (1000), and given a bishop (*ca.* 1110); like Iceland, it passed into Norwegian control in 13th c., and was thus eventually united with Norway to the Danish crown, then retained by Dk when Treaty of Kiel (1814) forced Dk to cede Norway to Sweden; long neglected, it was in effect colonised afresh when Christianity and commerce took renewed interest, beginning 1721 with Christian mission of 'Apostle to Greenland' Hans Egede (1686-1758) whose son Paul Egede (1708-89) translated New Testament into Inuktitut language; see **Fabricius,** Otto.

Gregory, Pope *105*; Pope Gregory VII (*ca.* 1020-85; pope from 1073), formerly Hildebrand; regarded as one of greatest of Roman pontiffs; after distinguished early career in service of Church, which took him on various occasions to France and Germany, and eventually popularly elected to papacy at time when Christendom was in acute state of chaos and flux, he set about reforming and strengthening the Church and asserting first independence of papacy from secular sovereigns and later supremacy over them, often against strenuous opposition on all fronts; 1074 sought to promote (though unsuccessfully) what would have been the first crusade, to free Christians in East from Turkish domination; prolonged struggle over authority against German emperor Henry IV, involving excommunication of the latter, finally led (1084) to Gregory's "exile" from Rome to Salerno where he died; came to Gr's attention when Gr was writing (1810) on history of Henry IV; and in his teaching notes compiled for pupils at the Schouboeske Institute (where he taught 1808-10) Gr calls Gregory, for his monumental efforts to restore the order of Christendom in a chaotic world, "en af de største Aander, historien kender" [one of the greatest spirits known to history]; and in doing so, Gr is dissenting both from the Enlightenment's conventional view of the middle ages as a period of unrelieved darkness and from a legacy of Protestantism's battle with Rome which saw the middle ages as a period of ignorance and superstition under papal tyranny.

Grendel's Mother *168*; in Anglo-Saxon poem *Beowulf* which Gr began studying in 1815 and published in Danish translation (*Bjovulfs Drape*, 1820), Beowulf liberates Heorot, great hall of Danish king Hrothgar, from humanoid monster Grendel but is then confronted by devastating act of vengeance from Grendel's monstrous mother who symbolises stubborn perversity of offspring of Cain threatening happiness and advancement of human community under Scyldings' benevolent kingship in Heorot; on several occasions Gr utilises this Anglo-Saxon legend alongside stock of northern myth and legend used by him as metaphorical language – for example, as metaphor for stiff-necked indifference of the age in Copenhagen of early 1820s, or (in his *Krønnike-Rim* 1842) for destructive forces to which the nation will succumb if not awake in the spirit: "*Grendel* is, according to *Beowulf*, the name of the loathsome monster which devoured Danish men in their sleep and unfortunately did not die childless." See also **Beowulf, Bjovulfs Drape**; **Nordens Mythologi**.

Grimm, Jacob Ludvig Karl, *227*; 1785-1863; German language scholar, pioneer in Germanic philology (including definition of Grimm's Law); folk-tale collector with brother Wilhelm Grimm (1786-1859), published *Kinder- und Hausmärchen* [Children's and household tales] 1812-15; having studied law became librarian in Kassel, subsequently professor in Göttingen but dismissed for political association with liberal circles; member of Academy of Sciences Berlin 1841; member of National Assembly in Frankfurt 1848; to him Gr sent copy of his *Nordens Mythologi* (1832) inscribed "Med gammel Agtelse til Jakob Grimm, som ikke forsmaaer at læse Dansk" [With longstanding respect to JG who does not disdain to read Danish].

Grundloven *144, 188, 238, 239, 246, 267, 268, 287, 289, 292, 329*; the Constitution. From establishment of Sovereignty Act (*Kongeloven*) of 1665 which fixed king's right to absolute power, until 1849 when Danes gained first free constitution (*Grundloven*), Dk was autocratically governed. Significant developments followed upon Dk's unlucky involvement in Napoleonic Wars. Ahead of ceding Norway to Sweden (1814) by terms of Treaty of Vienna, the (Danish) king of Norway (later Christian VIII of Dk) granted a constitution there. In 1816 royal power particularly in fiscal matters began for pragmatic reasons to pass to the colleges which administered them. However, final erosion of autocracy seriously began with so-called July Revolution (1830). Frederik VI and ministers were forced by threat of civil war to implement promise (embedded in 1814 Kiel treaty ending Dk's involvement in Napoleonic Wars) granting Duchy of Holsten (by then a member of German Confederation) its own constitutional assembly. Concession was now also evenhandedly extended to the provinces of the kingdom of Dk itself -four *provinsstænderfor-samlinger* [provincial consultative assemblies] were established, in Roskilde serving the islands, in Viborg serving northern Jylland, in Slesvig serving duchy of Slesvig, in Itzehoe serving duchy of Holsten; franchise, dependent on value of property owned (or for tenant farmers value of their copyhold), was thus restricted to barely 3% of the population. Role of these provincial consultative assemblies was, as name indicates, not autonomous and executive but only consultative. An experiment in limited local government 1837-41 created municipal councils (*kommuneraad*), but voting rights were again restricted, here to major landowners and taxpayers. More significant effect of these assemblies and councils was to give a platform and a better defined agenda to those who, alert to broader European trends, would argue for constitutional reform, to sharpen popular political awareness, and thus to create eventually unstoppable momentum towards achievement of real democratic government. In March 1848 mass meetings in Copenhagen culminated in peaceful march to palace to sue for a free constitution. Frederik VII was ready with proclamation renouncing his absolute powers, declaring himself a constitutional monarch, and placing responsibility for government upon his ministers. A Constituent National Assembly (*Rigsforsamling*) was elected (electorate consisting of all independent males over 30) the same year (Gr was elected in Præstø, S. Sjælland), and a constitution drafted which was signed on 5 June 1849. A Parliament (the *Rigsdag*) was established comprising a lower house (the *Folketing*) and an upper house (the *Landsting*), to legislate for the Kingdom of Denmark (supplemented 1854-66 with revived *Rigsraad*, partly to accommodate governance of the duchies of Slesvig, Holsten and Lauenburg). Judicial authority was vested in independent courts; legislative authority jointly with King and Parliament (*Rigsdagen*), executive authority with King who however might perform no acts of state except upon responsibility of a minister; taxes could be levied only by consent of Parliament. Right to vote for membership of both chambers was restricted to independent males over 30 who comprised only 14.5% of population; moreover, eligibility for election to the *Landsting* was more exclusively restricted than eligibility for election to the *Folketing*. It had been a source of contention among democrats that right was reserved to monarch to nominate a quarter of the members of the Constituent Assembly and this composition of the two chambers also came to be seen as an obstruction in the way of government by the democratically elected majority (the *Bondevenner*). Emergence of political parties (though such as Gr had deep misgivings over partisanship in government) was inevitable. Conservatives achieved reactionary victory in wake of catastrophic war with Prussia 1864, forcing constitutional amendment (July 1866) whereby King gained right to nominate 12 of 66 members of the *Landsting* and great landowners and major taxpayers were granted special electoral privileges, thus ensuring solid conservative entrenchment in upper chamber. By 1870 democratic parties held majority in the *Folketing* and demanded that Government should on principle be formed from this elected majority; however, conservative majority in the *Landsting* prevailed and conservative Governments continued to be called until 1901 when King accepted a change of system (the *Systemskifte*) and thenceforth appointed governments on basis of prevailing majority in the *Folketing*. Against this background, Gr (who looked lingeringly back to concept of Enlightened Absolutism by which King was 'Father of the nation' who would listen to his subjects' advice and desires, and then decree his judgments with a strong hand) served several periods as *Rigsdagsmand* and was consulted to the end of his life by political leaders of the *Bondevenner* and the United Left alliance. Of great concern to Gr and supporters in 1848-49 was the governance of the national church [*folkekirken*] under a constitutional dispensation; but in the event, though the Constitution declared the intention that "Folkekirkens Forfatning ordnes ved Lov" [The constitution of the national church shall be ordered according to law], such an ordering was never effected. See also **Rigsraad**; **Monrad**, Ditlev Gothard; **Lehmann, Peter Martin Orla**; **Bondevennerne**; **Venstre**; and **Forenede Venstre**, Det.

Grundtræk af Nutiden 160; *Die Grundzüge des gegenwärtigen Zeitalters*, 1806; see **Fichte,** Johan Gottlieb.

Grundtvig, Asta *242-245, 261-264, 271, 299, 302, 303, 311-313, 315, 317-320, 322, 325, 337, 338*; Asta Tugenreich Adelheid Krag-Juel-Vind-Frijs Reedz;1826-90; born of aristocratic family (hence bearing title *Komtesse*, corresponding approximately to English 'Lady'), wealthy widow of Holger Christian Reedtz (died 1857) with children, married Gr 1858 (in his 75th year) as his third wife; marriage aroused various degrees of criticism and misgivings among family, friends and foes, not least because Asta was 43 years his junior; she was sometimes referred to as Bispinde [bishop's wife]; was dedicated to creating stable, comfortable domestic and working environment for Gr but was also strongly disposed to treat him as inspired visionary, to respond to perceived charismatic about him, which in particular added to difficulties in Gr's breakdown of 1867; outlived him by eighteen years, after marriage lasting fourteen years of which one child was born, Asta Marie Elisabeth (1860-1939), named after Gr's three wives; after Gr's death was (perhaps naively) involved in struggle among religious and political factions to inherit true mantle of Gr; "She was carried by him while he was alive, but when this prop was taken away from her, she was capitalised upon by the extreme Liberals, without their stopping to think that the name she bore was not as a matter of course a surety that she was a custodian of his views upon things" (Vilhelm Birkedal).

Grundtvig, Asta Marie Elisabeth *264, 319, 338*; 1860-1939; Gr's fifth and last child, daughter with Asta (formerly Reedtz); named after Gr's three wives; father and daughter between them span 156 years, and her grandfather Johan (Grundtvig) was born 205 years before her death.

Grundtvig, Elisabeth Kirstine Margrethe (Christina Margaretha) *13, 90, 129, 174, 207-213, 220, 231, 233, 239, 240, 261*; 1787-1851; known as Lise, daughter of *provst* (rural dean) D. N. Blicher of Gundslev on island of Falster; Gr's first wife; after engagement of seven years, married 1818; marriage spanned some of the most difficult and impecunious times in Gr's life when Lise stood ready to share any hardship rather than allow exigency to force him to betray his beliefs; managed home and family during Gr's four prolonged absences in England; suffered much when both sons served in war in Sønderjylland (1848) though both returned safely; her children grown up, she perhaps felt herself increasingly lost in the milieu of intellectual and church-political controversy that accompanied Gr's advancing status; died in her mid-sixties, buried in Christianshavn, Copenhagen, at Vor Frelsers Kirke where Gr had held his first clerical appointment in the capital (1822-26); many contemporary commentators speak affectionately of her role in the Gr home;

Vilhelm Birkedal, recalling Gr's own characterisation of his three matrimonial relationships (Lise, Marie, Asta) as "Sisterly, motherly and daughterly" says of Lise that she "self-sacrificingly and altruistically provided him with all the support she could, but was probably not always in a position to share his vision and way of thinking. She was to him as a sister who believed in his noble struggle for truth and for Christianity but probably without completely being able to grasp the innermost driving force and the singularity of his view of human and Christian life."

Grundtvig, Frederik Lange *244, 264, 308, 311, 317, 322, 338*; 1854-1903; Gr's son with second wife Marie Toft (who died shortly after son's birth); privately educated, partly under care of Gr's third wife Asta; was at Gr's side throughout traumatic period of Gr's illness and convalescence 1867 and read to Gr in last hours of his life; entered University of Copenhagen 1876, took examinations in economics 1881; same year married and moved to America where (1883) he became pastor of Danish community in Clinton, Iowa; took leading part in Danske Folksamfund, society dedicated to preservation of Danish language and tradition in America; intended remaining there permanently as pastor and teacher in church-school in Des Moines, Iowa, but during visit to Dk (1900) misunderstandings delayed appointment and he was offered position, which he accepted, with Kirkeligt Samfund af 1898, newly founded society dedicated to maintenance and furtherance of Gr's concept of Church; his name Lange commemorated aristocratic family from which his mother (Marie, born Carlsen) was descended and it was intention of last survivor of line, Emmy Carlsen (1842-1912), to make Frederik heir to family estate of Gammel Køgegaard (where Gr's tomb was erected 1872) but he predeceased her and she established instead charitable foundation, Carlsen-Langes Legatstiftelse.

Grundtvig, Jacob Ulrich Hansen *67*; 1775-1800; Gr's brother; second of Johan Ottesen's four sons to survive infancy; prepared by Pastor Lauritz Feld at Hirsholmene (islands off Frederikshavn, Jylland) for admission to Viborg Latin School whence he matriculated to Copenhagen University; having signed up as missionary priest in order to qualify for bursaries to help pay his way through university he was posted (as was also his younger brother Niels Christian Bang) to Danish colony on Guinea coast where, like Niels Christian and an alarming tally of other Europeans, he died young of disease; his daughter, Cathrine Marie Grundtvig (1799-1823), lived with Gr's mother in Præstø after the death of Gr's father.

Grundtvig, Johan Diderik Nicolaj Blicher *21, 62, 116, 206-219, 239, 240, 302*; 1822-1907; eldest son of Gr and first wife Lise; earliest education at home, by parents and tutors; *cand. theol.* Copenhagen; volunteer (with brother Svend) in war of 1848; married Oline Vilhelmine Christiane Stenersen (called Mina, daughter of theology professor and friend of Gr's youth, Stener Stenersen in Kristiania (Oslo), Norway); studied Danish history, appointed 1860 in archives of *Indenrigsministeriet* [ministry of home affairs], moved to Kongerigets Arkiv (national archive, amalgamation of various ministries' archives, from 1861), eventually advancing to become head of archives; contributed to *Grevefejdens Historie* (1871; history of feud leading to civil war, between *Grev* [Count] Christoffer of Oldenburg and Danish king Christian II, 1534-36); committee member of *Den danske historiske Forening* 1873-88; admitted to *Danske Selskab* 1876; elected to *Folketing* 1858-61 and 1864-66.

Grundtvig, Johan Ottesen *14, 19, 61, 62, 71, 76, 77, 102, 103, 107, 108, 159, 161, 163, 181, 186, 192, 193;* 1734-1813; Gr's father; born on Sejerø where his father Otto Jørgensen Grundtvig (1704-1772) was parish priest; educated at Roskilde School in ancient cathedral town and royal seat of Roskilde; studied four years in Copenhagen, took theological *Embedsexamen* qualifying him for clerical appointment; 1760 curate in Egebjerg, Odsherred, NW Sjælland, where he met his wife, Gr's mother, Kathrine Marie Bang (1748-1822); 1766 parish priest in Odden, northwest Sjælland; parish priest (1776-1813) of Udby and Ørslev, some 8 km north of Vordingborg, south Sjælland where Gr was born and subsequently served as father's curate; published (1779) *Katekismi Forklaring efter Saliggjørelsens Orden* [Explanation of the Catechism according to the order of salvation] in the form of 741 questions and answers; completed fifty years of ministry 1810; his religion was rooted in pre-rationalist 18th c. and Gr described him as a man "med øre for Salmer som Kingoer sjunge – med Barnet i Hjærte og Skriften på Tunge" [with an ear for hymns which lovers of Kingo sing, with a child in his heart and scripture upon his tongue]; his sister was first wife of Bishop Nicolaj Edinger Balle (1744-1816).

Grundtvig, Kathrine Marie; 1748-1822; Gr's mother; see **Bang,** Kathrine Marie.

Grundtvig, Lavra *21, 206, 215;* 1837-91; wife of Gr's second son Svend.

Grundtvig, Marie (Toft) *240, 241, 242, 244, 261-264, 283-285, 294, 339, 340;* 1813-54; Gr's second wife; born Ane Marie Elise Carlsen at Gammel Køgegaard, Sjælland, married (1840) Harald Peter Nicolai Toft (1812-41) owner of estate of Rønnebæksholm, Sjælland, with whom she had daughter Haralda Judite Johanne Margrethe Toft (1841-92; subsequently heiress to Rønnebæksholm); on husband's death inherited estate, managing it efficiently and according to liberal ideals (granting tenant farmers rights of copyhold and, later, opportunity of self-ownership); "The husband on his sick-bed became possessed by Christianity; he died, but she kept the pearl which he had found in the eleventh hour" (C. J. Brandt); inspired to religious awakening by Joachim Goske Willemoes (1781-1858), priest at Herfølge, Sjælland, and *forsamlingspræst* [pastor ministering to revivalist religious gatherings held elsewhere than in churches], she and Willemoes made Rønnebæksholm a centre for orderly and respectable *forsamlinger* (which were nevertheless condemned by Church authorities and had initially been treated with suspicion by Gr); an enthusiast for Gr's hymns, she came into contact with Gr in 1840s and invited him (with son and two friends) to stay at Rønnebæksholm while on visit to Næstved (1849); married to Gr October 1851 by Gr's lifelong friend Gunni Busck in latter's church in Brøndbyvester, following death of his first wife Lise in same year; to disapproval and distress of some of Gr's circle of family and friends, she changed Gr's domestic and social milieu and his accessibility, and undoubtedly influenced his thought and actions in religious and political spheres, though, despite her liberal record, as substantial landowner she was held in suspicion by some of Gr's political associates; shortly after giving birth to Gr's son, Frederik Lange (1854-1903), she died; was laid in crypt within private cemetery at Gammel Køgegaard, where Gr's body was also later laid.

Grundtvig, Meta Catherine Marie Bang *129, 206, 208, 212-214, 220, 231, 240, 256, 286;* 1826-87; Gr's daughter; during his period of mental illness 1844 was her father's dearest consolation; of Gr's poem of gratitude, *Til min egen Meta* [To my own Meta], composed to mark her wedding (1847), J. P. Bang observes: "Digtet *Til min egen Meta*, et af de dejligste Digte i dansk litteratur – men hvormange kender det?" [The poem *To my own Meta*, one of the loveliest poems in Danish literature – but how many know it?]; married to Peter Boisen, Gr's curate at Vartov Kirke 1854-62.

Grundtvig, Niels Christian Bang *67, 87*; 1777-1803; Gr's older brother who after education with Pastor Lauritz Feld at Hirsholmene (Frederikshavn, Jylland), then at Viborg Grammar School and Copenhagen University became a priest in Danish colony in Guinea, where he died (as had his older brother, Jacob Ulrich); arranged for Gr, as student, to receive monthly subvention of four *rigsdaler*.

Grundtvig, Otto Jørgensen *76, 79, 81, 88, 90, 116, 137, 201, 202*; 1772-1843; Gr's older brother; educated at Herlufsholm school and Copenhagen University, was appointed (1800) to incumbency of Torkildstrup and Lillebrænde on island of Falster, where Gr stayed on various occasions and where he met his future (first) wife Elisabeth Blicher (1787-1851); 1805 *Provst* [rural dean] for northern district of Falster; 1823 moved to incumbency of Gladsaxe, Sjælland, where he died 1843; married to daughter of his uncle Bishop Nicolaj Edinger Balle (1744-1816).

Grundtvig, Otto Krabbe Jørgensen *61, 107*; 1704-1772; Gr's paternal grandfather, son of Jørgen Hansen Grundtvig and Anna Isachsdatter; priest on Sejerø, island 10 km long, 2 km wide, south of Sjællands Odde, whose population had ancient reputation for quarrelling with their priests; later appointed to incumbency of Vallekilde-Høve, NW Sjælland.

Grundtvig, Svend (Svenn, Sven) Hersleb *21, 65, 206, 207, 209-218, 220, 232, 234, 235, 239, 240, 270, 272, 283, 285, 286, 291, 302, 312, 318, 322, 325, 334*; 1824-83; second son of Gr with first wife Elisabeth (Lise); named after Gr's friend Svenn Hersleb, Professor of Theology in the University of Kristiania, Norway; philologist; Professor of Nordic Philology in University of Copenhagen; moving force behind ground-breaking publication of Dk's ancient folk-songs (*Danmarks gamle Folkeviser*); did much to organise archive of Gr's papers for posterity; died before completing publication of Gr's poetic works (in which he assumed the right to make textual alterations); married to Lavra.

Grundtvig, Ulrikke (Ulrica) Eleonora *64, 65, 94*; 1782 -1805; one year older sister of Gr, his playmate and rival in infancy, whose early death he formally lamented while privately noting that since she lacked beauty, accomplishments and a fortune her future had in any case looked drear.

Grundtvigian(ism) *18, 21, 22, 24, 34, 173, 176, 204, 214, 226, 228, 233, 247, 257-260, 293-295, 306, 308, 309, 314, 320, 329;* movement, with both religious and secular dimensions, developing out of Gr's distinctive concept or purview of the Church (*kirkelige anskuelse*) as initially defined in his *Kirkens Gienmæle* [The Church's Retort; 1825, year of his "peerless discovery"], and out of his equally distinctive poetical-historical concept utilising myth and legend of North as metaphorical account of Northern search towards Christ, and as resource of metaphor uniquely competent to articulate Northern preoccupations and sensibilities, as defined in his *Nordens Mythologi* (1832); terminology came into use in Gr's own lifetime, often hostilely used with intent to brand it a religious sect, a charge which Gr robustly dismissed with an argument of radical catholicity and ecumenism, that it "has *this* churchly singularity – that of demanding consensus only over what has been common to *all* who have believed and been baptised, and of seeking only a new life of the spirit within *The Word* given to us from the Lord's own mouth, through his own institutions" (Gr); "The word of God is not the Scriptures but 'the living word' which is heard at baptism and in Holy Communion (in the sacraments). At the same time Gr attached small importance to the clerical office, for which reason Grundtvigianism is markedly ecclesiastical and sacramental but not High Church, if anything definitely Low Church" (Hal Koch); Grundtvigianism is also characterised by commitment to the *folkelige*, a concept and agenda too diverse to be summed up briefly, but fundamentally expressive of an ideal of inclusive (not exclusive) communality, in congregation, family, school, society, nation; though particular Grundtvigian values and formulations have come to permeate Danish society as a whole, Grundtvigianism proper still finds its fullest expression in the *valgmenigheder* (congregations within the State Church but granted freedom to elect – and pay – own pastor) and the folk-highschools; the English term 'Grundtvigian' serves, sometimes misleadingly, to translate both *grundtvigsk* (that which re- lates more directly and individually to Grundtvig) and *grundtvigiansk* (that which relates more broadly to the movement which took his name) – though the Danish terms themselves are not always used with careful discrimination. The enrichment to their austere lives and the means of self-advancement gained by many of agricultural working-class through involvement in the religious revivalist movement and spread of Grundtvigianism is movingly recorded (My trans- lation from H. P. Berthelsen, *Østjydsk Hjemstavn* (1947), 33-47; online source, *Aner til Lauritz Thomsen*, www.poul.tuknet.dk/291.htm, November 2006) by weaver Lauritz (Laust) Thomsen (1837-1928) who, aged 19, got employment as a farm-labourer with Jens Kjær, substantial farmer in Vrønding, Tamdrup parish near Skanderborg, central Jylland: "It was a tough job as regards work and the food was not as good as in Myllerup [his previous job]. But all the same it was a good place to come to for a young person. One got accustomed to working and making use of one's time [...] In Tamdrup at that time there was a religious revival [*en religiøs Vækkelse*]. We had a priest who was called Funder [P. F. J. Funder (1823-1912), curate in Tamdrup 1849-60; subsequently married a daughter of Otto Arenfeld Reedtz (below)]. He was only the curate. The old priest was not up to much. I went to church more or less every Sunday. It was something I was happy with. Going to church suited Jens Kjær and his wife. We gladly went along with them. Someone had to stay at home of course, and this was usually the girl; she didn't care for church-going. But it was also particularly Pastor Funder's Bible-readings in Vrønding School every Tuesday evening. It was especially the singing which was attractive to me. It was led by the old *Kammerherre* from Bisgaard [*Kammerherre* (Lord-in-waiting; honorific title) Otto Arenfeld Reedtz who owned nearby manor of Bisgaard , central Jylland, 1848-89; brother to diplomat Holger Christian Reedtz (1800-57) who was first husband of Asta, Gr's third wife] and two of his daughters, Nanna and Marie. They sang splendidly and it was in fact at that time when Grundtvig's hymns began to get known, and these the two young ladies sang with might and main. Those evenings I shall never forget. It could also happen that Nanna would read aloud one of Grundtvig's sermons [...] When I had served Jens Kjær for 3 years I moved from there to learn a trade [weaving]. In those three years I had earned 25 *rigsdaler* and good clothes. I had to provide my own tools for my trade." Later Laust Thomsen was introduced to the congregation at Jelling, central Jylland: "There I came into contact with many good men and so I became a *Sognebaandsløser* [one who broke the parish tie by joining a congregation other than that of his own parish church] to Pastor Svendsen, the famous teacher-training college principal [Hans Jørgen Marius Svendsen, 1816-72, parish priest in Jelling and principal of Jelling Seminarium (teacher training college) 1856-72]. I was a *Sognebaandsløser* with him for six years. There came [Vilhelm] Birkedal, Svejstrup [Hans Kristian Janus Nikolaj Balthasar Krarup Sveistrup, 1815-93], [Mads] Melbye from Asperup, Leth from Middelfart [Andreas Peter Martin Leth, 1822-1905], [Frederik (Frits)] Budstikke-Boisen, P. Skræppenborg from Dons [Ole Peter Holm Larsen (Skræppenborg), 1802-73], etc. It was good company to be among. One always went away from these meetings happy and uplifted and never noticed that the road was long because we were always many who accompanied each other. They were happy days and rich in blessings and it is a great pleasure and blessing to recall that time now I am an old man [...] It was a beautiful time and rich in blessings when Grundtvig's name and deeds became known all across the land. For I mixed with many of the Grundtvigian folk." see also **Irenaeus**; **mageløse Opdagelse**; *Kirkens Gienmæle*; **Church struggle**; **Folkekirke**; **Sognebaandsløsning**; **Frikirke**; **folkelige**; *Nordens Mythologi*; **Nordens Aand**; **Kold,** Christen Mikkelsen; **Marielyst**.

'Grundtvigianism' acknowledged by Gr *18, 173, 176*; though Gr sought to attach no personalised label to the set of principles and values accepted from him by his followers, he acknowledged the *øgenavn* [nickname] 'Grundtvigianism' which came to be used by friends and foes alike; looking back over 25 years as priest in Vartov he rests his sense of accomplishment not in having augmented Church membership by the modest total of confirmands he had prepared, but in "the impact which the Vartov assembly" – he pointedly uses the term *forsamlinger* associated with the controversial and formerly unlawful religious gatherings which had helped force reluctant authorities into liberalising laws governing church affiliation – "with its congregational singing, under its nickname *Grundtvigianism*, has made upon the world, not only in the capital but in the whole of Denmark." See also **hymns**.

Grundtvig's Copenhagen addresses *207, 208, 243, 282, 287, 288, 323, 325, 334, 337, 340*; It has been estimated that Gr lived for shorter or longer periods at some 25 different addresses in his adult years; most were in Copenhagen, including: 1816-17 Kronprinsessegade 44; 1818 Vingaardsstræde 9; 1819-20 Løngangsstræde 29; 1821 Kronprinsessegade 12; 1823 Torvegade 25; 1824 – 27 Prinsessegade 52; 1828 Prinsessegade 50; 1828-40 Strandgade 4; 1840-50 Vimmelskaftet 49; 1851 Stormgade 17; 1852 Nybrogade 12; 1853-55 Frederiksholms Kanal 16; 1856-57 Nørregade 5; 1858-59 Larslejsstræde 12; 1860-67 Gammel Kongevej 148; 1868-72 Strandvej 123 (Store Tuborg).

Grundtvig's Highschool; see **Marielyst**.

Guds Godhed ville vi prise *70*; *Helft mir Gotts Güte preisen*, hymn used at New Year written by Paul Eber (1511-1569); translated from original German into Danish by Rasmus Katholm (unknown date of birth; matriculated from Aarhus Latin School to study theology in Copenhagen; appointed Professor of Rhetoric 1563 and priest at Vor Frue Kirke 1574 where he earned distinction as preacher; died 1581); hymn remembered from his years in Jylland and much esteemed by Gr who reworked it 1845; no. 716 in *DDS* 2002; see also **hymns**.

Guinea *87*; Danish colony established 1658 on Gold Coast (modern Ghana), West Africa, for trade in gold and slaves (transported to Danish West Indies, another Danish colonial settlement, sold to USA 1917, now US Virgin Islands); came under Danish royal administration from 1792 when trading in, though not ownership of slaves was forbidden; slavery was abolished 1848, and remaining Danish rights in Guinea were sold to England 1850; pastors, missionaries and teachers were sent out to Guinea from Dk; two of Gr's brothers (pastors), like so many others, died there prematurely of disease; Gr was member of anti-slavery committee 1839-48 and met with Joseph Gurney, English emancipationist, and his sister, the Quaker and prison reformer Elizabeth Fry, in Copenhagen (1841); see **Fry,** Elizabeth.

Guldberg, Ove Jørgensen Høegh- *68; 1731-1808;* author of *Den naturlige Theologie* [Natural Theology] (1765), textbook prescribed in Latin schools for primary instruction in Christian faith, promoting a 'natural' or rationalist theology not dependent upon revelation and revelation-based dogma; studied by Gr at Tyregod (1792-98) with Pastor Laurits Feld; *cand. theol.* in Copenhagen 1754; professor of rhetoric Sorø Academy 1761-64; various scholarly publications including (1761) *Tanker om Milton og den saakaldte religiøse Poesi* [Thoughts upon Milton and so-called religious poetry] and (1768-72) three volumes of a *Verdens Historie* [World history]; but began rise to fame and power when appointed tutor (1764), later private secretary, to heir presumptive Frederik, son of Frederik v; was a chief architect of indictment (1772) of Johann Friedrich Struensee for crime of *lèse majesté*; thereafter succeeded effectively, though not formally until 1784 (and then only for eight days), to Struensee's office as *Statsminister* [chief minister of state], reversing various of Struensee's liberal reforms; president of royal commission resulting in *Forordning angaaende Skoele-Væsenets Forbedring ved de publiqve Latinske Skoeler* [Order concerning improvement of educational system in public Latin Schools] (11 May 1775), which required that textbooks, especially in religion, be in Danish and that pupils be taught, by reading in best Danish authors and by written and oral exercise, to enhance their competence in the Danish mother-tongue; after losing office 1784 retired to various public posts in Aarhus in Jylland, where he was still living whilst Gr was (as he put it) squandering his time "on chewing over, *usque ad infinitum*, the Catechesis, Guldberg's revealed theology and everything connected with this commonsense-destroying apparatus."

Gun(d)slev *62, 88, 91;* village in north Falster about 200 km south of Copenhagen where D. N. Blicher, father of Gr's first wife, Elisabeth (Lise), was rural dean [*Provst*]; close to Torkildstrup vicarage where in his bachelor years Gr often stayed with the family of his older brother Otto Jørgensen Grundtvig (who moved to Gladsaxe in 1823).

Gyrihougen *151;* Gyrihaugen, conspicuous peak and rock formation overlooking Ringerike and Krokskogen, north-west of Oslo, Norway; legend tells of giantess Gyri who, enraged by bells of King (St) Olaf's new church, tore off leg to throw at it, was therefore turned into stone by saint-king; site of symbolic bonfire on Gr's visit (1851) to Nordic student and folk gathering at Tanbergmoen.

Gøricke, Ludvig *221, 294;* 1804-88; priest serving (much reduced) German community at Frederiks Tyske Kirke (later renamed Christians Kirke) in Christianshavn (Copenhagen), active supporter of J. C. Lindberg's (illegal) *forsamlinger* [religious gatherings] and of Gr, his offer of resignation from his near-redundant church helped clear way for Gr's authorisation (1832) to preach there to adherents on Sunday evenings; presumably son of, and successor to, Christian Georg Wilhelm Göricke (1762-1829), born at Ranzau in German-speaking Holsten, who moved with family to Copenhagen 1810 as priest serving German community in Christianshavn at Frederiks Kirke; if so, then he was also brother to Adolf Wilhelm Theodor Gøricke (1798-1885), doctor specialising in treatment of mental illness in Odense and Copenhagen, titular professor 1847, active in establishment (1863) of Den danske Diakonistiftelse, hospital located in Frederiksberg; uncertain whether Ludvig or (more likely) Adolf Wilhelm Theodor is the benefactor called (by Christen Kold) "our good friend, old Gøricke" who donated 50 rigsdaler to Kold's planned free school (1849); see **Frederiks Kirke.**

Goethe, Johan Wolfgang *62, 85, 157*; 1749-1832; born Frankfurt, educated Leipzig, Strasbourg; moved away from practice of law to literature, art, science, though served as adviser to Duke Carl August of Saxen-Weimar; wrote novels, lyric poetry, drama, markedly enriching German literary language; much influenced by friendship with Schiller; immense literary impact throughout Europe, notably through his *Faust* (1832), felt also in Denmark, where earliest translators included Adam Oehlenschläger and Knud Lyhne Rahbek.

Gøtheborgs Handels- og Søfartstidende *336*; Gothenburg's Business and Maritime News; see **Hedlund,** Sven Adolf; **Hammar-Mødet.**

Göttingen *154*; German university town in Lower Saxony; university, established 1737, notable for extensive libraries; reputation of its professors soon attracted foreign students, including Danes such as Nicolaj Edinger Balle (1744-1816), later bishop of Sjælland (1783-1808), *kongelig confessionarius* [chaplain royal] and author of standard works used in church and school, who was influenced by theological critical-historical method popularly called *Neologi,* expounded there; Gr wrote dismissively of Balle's "gøttingske begreber" [Göttingen concepts]; see also **neologists.**

gøttingske begreber *154*; Göttingen concepts, notions disseminated from the University of Göttingen; see **Göttingen**; also **neologists.**

H

Hagen, Laurits Christian, *21, 217, 218, 220, 226*; 1808-80; *cand. theol.*, priest; friend of Gr and, while at University, private tutor to Gr's children; published 1832 collection of *Historiske salmer og rim til børnelærdom* [Historical hymns and verses for the teaching of children], with significant collaboration and contributions from Gr (*Bibliografi* item 502A), who used the collection in preparation of his own children for confirmation.

Hake (correctly, Haken), Johann Christian Ludwig *105*; 1767-1835; German theologian, historian; author of *Gemälde der Kreuzzüge etc.,* [Pictures of the crusades] I-III (1808-20); Gr, feeling (Summer 1810) urgent need to study the crusades more closely, got Haken's account (vols I-II, 1808-19) "which naturally much exasperated me" because of its unsympathetic prejudices (rooted in Enlightenment values) concerning the Middle Ages: "To be sure, Gr had not been completely untouched by the view of 'the age of enlightenment' upon the Middle Ages, hierarchy and papal power; this was after all a perception which had its roots further back, in Protestantism's hostile feelings towards Catholicism. But he had begun to make himself independent of the inherited historical lenses" (Frederik Rönning).

Hakon hin Rige *101*; *Hakon Jarl hin Rige* [Earl Haakon the mighty], tragic drama about Norwegian Haakon Sigurdsson (killed 995), for a time ruler of Norway; by Adam Oehlenschläger; premiered Royal Theatre, Copenhagen, 1808; see also **Oehlenschläger, Adam Gottlob.**

Hall, Carl Christian *265*; 1812-88; Norwegian-born; Doctor of Law; school friend of C. E. Fenger, Vilhelm Birkedal; other friends from youth included Frederik Barfod, Georg Aagaard, D. G. Monrad; took residence in Copenhagen, model of educated professional middle-class; helped by considerable personal charm, won great popularity as National Liberal politician, in forefront with D. G. Monrad; Church and Education minister 1854-57; *konseilpræsident* (prime minister) 1857-59 and 1860-63, also foreign minister 1857; his widely-supported Ejder-policy, inherited by Monrad's administration of December 1863, ended perhaps inevitably in the calamitous war with Prussia, 1864; see **Ejderpolitik.**

Hall, *Gehejmeraadinde 300*; wife of privy councillor and prime minister C. C. Hall, named among distinguished persons, including Dowager Queen and bishops, who patronised Marielyst Højskole (Grundtvigs Højskole), the "*Folkelige Højskole*" founded by Gr with money subscribed in Dk and Norway to mark his 70th birthday, inaugurated November 1856.

Haller, Albrecht von *204, 205*; 1708-1777; polymathic Swiss author, botanist, scientist, doctor, philosopher; advocated the superiority of a life of nature over a life of culture; his German-language instructive poetry, furnished with factual and scientific footnotes, was much esteemed by Goethe and other leading German poets; his poem *Die Alpen* [The Alps], published in his collection of descriptive and reflective poems *Versuch Schweizerischer Gedichten* [Attempt at Swiss poems] (1732), did much to inspire interest in Alpine region; his grand-daughter Sofie was wife of Danish poet Jens Baggesen; Gr's reportedly banal response to Haller's poetically embodied philosophical ideas on finitude and eternity, as put to Gr in 1820s by F. L. B. Zeuthen (1805-74), disappointed Zeuthen and prompted him to criticise the perceptual *uformuenhed* [poverty, deficiency] of Gr and his followers; Gr was perhaps impatient with Haller's poetical paradoxes.

Halling-dance *151*; *Hallingdandsen*; Norwegian folk-dance belonging to Hallingdalen (region between Oslo and Bergen); solo male dancer executes steadily more athletic leaps and somersaults culminating in *Hallingkast* in which feet are supposed to kick ceiling; performed at Tanberg-Moen as part of festivities organised (1851) by Norwegian students, where Gr was honoured, and deeply affected, guest; the dance features in Edvard Grieg's music (1876) to Henrik Ibsen's *Peer Gynt* (1867).

Hamburg *108*; ancient German town on Elbe river, immediately south of southern frontier of duchy of Holsten, seat of 9th-c. archbishop Ansgar of Hamburg-Bremen, apostle to Denmark; seized (1811) and governed by Napoleon's marshal Louis Nicolas Davout until fall of Napoleon; see **Davout** (Davoust).

Hammar Meeting; see **Hammar-Mødet**.

Hammar-Mødet *336*; meeting (1872) of leading representatives of the three Nordic national *folkepartier* [folk-parties] at Sagatun folk-highschool, Hamar, Norway, attended by Sophus Høgsbro, leader of Danish *Forenede Venstre* [United Left]; discussed political objectives of each party (all broadly concerned with improving democratic representation and *folkelige* participation) and desirability of union of the three national parties; described in Høgsbro's letters as festive Nordic occasion with dancing, singing, eating, speeches by Sagatun's co-founder Olaus Arvesen (proposed toast to Dk and Slesvig), Norwegian poet Bjørnstjerne Bjørnson (toast to Sweden), Sven Adolf Hedlund, Swedish editor of leading Göteborg newspaper (much praised by Bjørnson; his speech reported by Høgsbro as being "about as sympathetic to the farmer, as Nordic and as *folkelige* [*bondevenligt, nordisk og folkelige*] as one could have desired" though Høgsbro could understand why he was caricatured as a *Frasemager* [phrase-monger]); speech by Høgsbro himself (proposed toast to "the young Norway" and spoke of need for "a voluntary union of that which is now divided, for the discharge of its special calling in history" [en frivillig Sammenslutning af det nu skilte til Løsning af dens særegne Kald i Historien]), and by the Norwegian Kristoffer Bruun, Grundtvigian folk-highschool founder and principal (proposed health of Gr); generally deemed satisfactory show of Nordic political solidarity around the *folkelige* agenda; all this subsequently reported back to Gr in Copenhagen by Høgsbro; possibly the last account Gr received of the contemporary Nordic political-cultural scene, for he died a few days later; see also **Hedlund**, Sven Adolf; **Høgsbro**, Sophus Magdalus.

Hammerich, Peter Frederik Adolph *64, 181, 235, 247, 248, 277, 278, 280, 309, 314, 317-319, 333*; 1809-77; priest, historian, theologian; *magister* in Theology; Professor (1859) in Church History Copenhagen University; influenced by religious instruction of J. C. Lindberg and Gr's preaching, became strong adherent of Gr; first of Gr-circle to receive academic recognition; deeply affected by experiences as volunteer field-chaplain in war with Germany 1848-51; much travelled in Scandinavia (resulting in strong enthusiasm for scandinavianism) and England (making close contact with figures in 'High Church' Oxford Movement, attempting to influence them with Gr's *kirkelige anskuelse* (concept or purview of the Church); established a Lutheran Association (1852) intended to nourish Christian life in Danish society but pulled out disappointed by conflict between priests and layfolk provoked in part by publications of Søren Kierkegaard; had formal responsibilities in Vartov Church and congregation, was called on by Gr to assist at eucharist, Palm Sunday 1867, and by ecclesiastical authorities to assist in resolution of ensuing scandal; subsequently critical of Gr's advocacy of *præstefrihed* [clerical freedom] and of Grundtvigianism as political movement; published on Church history, mystical and scholastic theology, religious poetry of 'Gothic' peoples including (inspired by L. C. Müller) the Anglo-Saxons; in last years strongly opposed cultural radicalism then taking rooting in University; an autobiography *Frederik Hammerich: Et Levnetsløb* was edited and published (1882) by his son Angul Hammerich; see also **Palm Sunday** 1867.

Hammond, Eiler *194*; 1757-1822; priest; from 1820 *amtsprovst* (dean exercising authority within administrative region called an *amt*, corresponding approximately to English 'county') in Roskilde and rector in Roskilde Cathedral; well-meaning, moderate, liberal man of the 18th c., esteemed by Bishop N. E. Balle (figurehead of the old certainties of the pre-19th-c. Danish Church) but with little grasp of new theological currents of 19th c.

Hanne *222*; one of supporters of J. C. Lindberg's religious gatherings at Rolighed 1832; see **Laurent**, Harald A.

Hanrej *65*; 'cuckold' – card game of type which leaves loser with one unpaired card.

Hansen *189*; unidentified person present (1811) in home of Professor N. Treschow (1751-1833), sent to find Gr who was late for meal; perhaps simply generic name for a servant.

Hansen *221*; apparently a supporter of J. C. Lindberg and Gr over *forsamlinger* (unauthorised religious gatherings not held in church) at Lindberg's home, Rolighed, Copenhagen, 1832, but otherwise unidentified, and conceivably a token name, together with Jensen, approximately equal to "Tom, Dick and Harry" and standing for vehicle of gossip, hearsay, rumour; see also **forsamlinger**; **Jensen,** Rasmus.

Hansen, Jens *308*; 1827-1914; for forty years a *friskolelærer* [teacher in independent school] mainly in Broby, near Sorø, having gained some of his teaching experience in Gr's highschool Marielyst; old friend of Gr; source of reminiscences, including occasion of *Vennemødet* [the gathering of (Gr's) friends] on Gr's 80th birthday (8 September 1863).

Hansgaard, Hartvig Christian *236*; died 1855; *fuldmægtig* [chief administrator] in an office of the Admiralty; *Justitsråd* (largely honorific title within honours-system, bestowing official rank); member of 'free' congregation which gathered round Gr at Frederiks Kirke from 1832; typical of the *jævne folk* [ordinary folk (Rönning)] to whom Gr's conception of the church and the Christian life increasingly appealed; zealous advocate of a special hymnal to be compiled by Gr, after Gr's proposals for a revision of the official Church hymnal were rejected (1846).

Harms, Claus *163, 248, 121*; 1778-1855; German priest, archdeacon of Kiel (university town and administrative capital of duchies of Slesvig and Holsten, under Danish sovereignty until 1864), with great repute as preacher, who on 300th anniversary of symbolic start of Reformation republished (1817) Luther's 95 theses together with 95 more composed by himself, his aim being through these 'Apples of Discord' to denounce rationalism and also the "Prussian Union" whereby Friedrich Wilhelm III of Prussia planned formally to unite the Lutheran and Reformed Churches in his kingdom; much controversy arose but Gr was sceptical of capacity of this "Luther the Second" or even of Luther himself to restore true Lutheranism in Germany, and in Gr's view things were at that time little better in Dk; Gr visited Harms on his return journey from England 1829 and on his outward journey to England 1830; Frederik Hammerich found Harms a more forthcoming conversationalist than Gr was.

Harmsen, Claus Christian *222, 223*; 1805-39; born in Treia, Slesvig; *stud. theol.* [student of theology; formally enrolled student not yet proceeded to final examination] Copenhagen University; "et ungt og uklart brushoved" [a young and muddled hothead] (Frederik Nygård), determined supporter of J. C. Lindberg (1797-1857) in confrontation with church and secular authorities over freedom to hold public religious meetings for worship elsewhere than in a church; attended and preached at such *forsamlinger* in Christianshavn and (February 1832, accompanied by a throng of supporters from Copenhagen and Christianshavn) on Amager which greatly alarmed the authorities and were subsequently stopped by intervention of police; quickly became an embarrassment to Lindberg who attempted with small success to restrain Harmsen's supporters (especially those who preached without licence to do so) on Amager; published *Politische Betrachtungen mit einem Blick auf Dänemark und Holstein, von N.F.S. Grundtvig. Deutsch herausgegeben von C. Harmsen* [Political reflections of NFSG with regard to Denmark and Holsten. Published in German by CH], Copenhagen 1831; see also **forsamlinger**.

Hasle, Jørgen Henrik Theodor *312*; 1816-89; farmer, long-standing member of *Rigsdag*; *Statsrevisor* [member of Public Accounts Committee]1864-75; involved, along with Frederik Hammerich and others of Vartov congregation, in official negotiations to contain consequences of Gr's breakdown, Palm Sunday 1867.

Hass, Ludvig Daniel *220, 221, 223*; 1808-81; priest; closely involved in Lindberg's 'free' gatherings of a congregation (*forsamlinger*) at his home, 'Lille Rolighed' on outskirts of Copenhagen, February 1832, at which Gr also preached, leading to clashes with authorities which continued at intervals, and for various causes, throughout his life; travelled 1842 as missionary to Smyrna, Turkey, on behalf of Det danske Missionsselskab [The Danish Missionary Society]; took as tutor to his children Christen Kold (later educational pioneer, allied with Gr) who, however, bitterly disappointed in Hass's self-indulgent life-style and servile treatment of him, left his service, made own way back to Dk, mainly on foot; Hass returned to Dk from completely unfruitful mission 1847; as priest he was enthusiastic supporter of Gr; later politician elected to *Rigsdag*, supporting a Grundtvigian range of causes including freedom within Church and school and political objectives of *Bondevennerne* [friends of the peasant farmer] against alliance of middle-class urban professionals and greater landowners.

Hassenfeldt, Carl Frederik *257*; b. 1800; *cand. theol.* 1828; appointed incumbent priest in Vellinge, Fyn 1830 and in Holmsland in Ribe Diocese, Jylland, 1841; apparently the 'neighbouring priest' sympathetic to Gr's views on theology and church who was influential in bringing Vilhelm Birkedal (1809-92) round to a Grundtvigian view thus initiating Birkedal's lifelong dedication to Gr's principles and causes; published *Sendebrev til Professor Theol. Dr. H. N. Clausen, i Anledning af "Betragtning over Ritualsagen"* [Letter to theology professor H. N. C. concerning "Reflections upon the Ritual Issue"] in *Folkebladet*, Copenhagen 1840; see also **Birkedal**, Schøller Parelius Vilhelm.

Hauch, Anna *233*; Anna Brun-Juel, 1811-96, wife of Johannes Carsten Hauch; as hostess at her daughter's christening (Sorø, 1839) her well-intended question to Gr about his sleeping preferences was turned into embarrassment by Ingemann who could not resist telling her what everyone was supposed to know, that Gr never went to bed.

Hauch, Johannes Carsten *233, 268, 137*; 1790-1872; Danish poet, novelist, dramatist, professor; after studying at Det Schouboeske Institut in Copenhagen (where Gr taught history and geography 1808-10) had gained doctorate (zoology) at university by 1821; travelled extensively abroad

1821-27; though educated, for a time under H. C. Ørsted (1777-1851), in natural sciences which from 1827 he also taught at Sorø Academy, he was active as poet, dramatist and novelist writing under influence of the great figures of contemporary Romanticism, and belonged in circle of leading cultural figures in Dk; appointed professor of Nordic languages and literature at Kiel (1846), and (honorary) professor of aesthetics in Copenhagen (1851); associated with direction of Royal Theatre Copenhagen 1855-71; at christening of his daughter Albertine Louise in Sorø (26 July 1839), godparents were Ingemann, Thorvaldsen, Oehlenschläger and Gr (who in the event performed the baptism).

Hauge, Hans Nielsen *104, 160, 288*; 1771-1824; Norwegian pietistic lay-preacher, founder of revivalist movement called Haugianism; journeyed round Norway and Dk preaching to (unlawful) gatherings, on sin and saving grace; effective in stirring considerable revivalist movement; critical of rationalist-permeated clergy within the *statskirke*, regarding them and institutionalised religion as superfluous (they in turn therefore persecuted him), also of economic hold of town merchants; published various writings including *Betraktning over Verdens Daarlighet* [Meditation upon the iniquity of the world] and *Grunnsætninger i Christendomens Lære* [First principles of Christian teaching]; efficient businessman and early industrialist (Eker papermill); held under arrest 1804-11 pending judgment and sentence (delivered 1813) of imprisonment with hard labour in irons though sentence commuted to fine; with friends' support bought farm where he lived quietly until death; left quantity of writings; followers known as Haugians mostly peasants and farmers but those in towns often worked way up to position of wealth by self-education, industriousness, modest living as taught by H; regarded sympathetically by English Quakers (who, tradition says, exported organised Quakerism into Norway in 1814 with a small number of ex-prisoners-of-(Napoleonic)-war to whom they had ministered in captivity), he himself married one of the few (maligned and persecuted) Norwegian Quakers; the survival of Haugianism in teeth of dogged official opposition (which even tacitly encouraged Haugian and Quaker emigration to America), was for Gr evidence of uselessness of State persecution of religious minorities; from about 1850 Haugianism was gradually absorbed into the *Indremisjonsbevægelse* [Home mission movement]; see also **Quaker**; **Eriksens's wife**.

Haugians; see **Hauge**, Hans Nielsen.

heart, the; see **Hjertet**.

heathlands, Jylland *61, 73, 80, 81, 116*; *den jyske hede*; much of Jutland (Jylland) peninsula was, in Gr's childhood, only sparsely cultivated heathland, often described by travellers as wild, dark, depressing terrain, difficult of access; here were some of Dk's most backward regions, and character of landscape, remoteness from Copenhagen, strong Jutish dialect, all contributed to popular view of *det mørke Jylland* [dark Jutland], endorsed by such stories as that of Michael Kierkegaard, father of Bishop Peter Christian Kierkegaard and philosopher Søren Aabye Kierkegaard who as 10-year-old shepherd-boy in Vestjylland (West Jutland) was so tormented by crushing loneliness of the heath and hunger and cold that he stood on a hillock and cursed God and was never thereafter free from fear of having brought a curse upon his family, even his children, by committing a sin against the Holy Spirit; reciprocally, Jutlanders were conscious of own history, tradition and custom, law, and were often stubbornly resistant to impositions from central government whether secular or religious, giving rise to soubriquet *de stærke Jyder* [the strong, or stubborn, Jutlanders]; Gr boarded for education in parsonage at Thyregod, Jylland (1792-1798) before moving to grammar school in Aarhus (1798-1800); in striking contrast of personality and temperament to those of Michael Kierkegaard, Gr found good material for the constructed story of his life in pathos of lonely boy delighting in heathland bees, in firsthand encounter with authentic folk-life and folk-culture, in his emergence from spartan obscurity and provincialism into national distinction; writings of Gr's distant relative Steen Steensen Blicher (1782-1848) projected a new image of stoicism, comedy, tragedy of common Jutish folk including heathdwellers, into 19th-c. Danish literature, often using dialect; modern reclamation of heathlands began with state investment 1759 in area west of Vejle, but developed in earnest following territorial losses to Prussia (1864) with foundation of *Hedeselskabet* [The heathlands society] (1866).

Hebrew congregation *25, 307*; first of the seven congregations or churches in Gr's schematisation of world history; see **Greek congregation**.

Hedlund, Sven Adolf *336*; 1821-1900; Swedish journalist, polemicist, politician; expressed early the perception that "It is through the power of the word that the publicist reshapes the entity of the state, that he transforms the people from a raw and unthinking mass into a thinking and educated community of fellow-citizens which looks after its own welfare and no longer, like the blind, lets itself be led into ruin by false do-gooders [...] A free and independent press is a country's crowning glory, it is its defence even in times of peril, for the power of bayonets is as naught against that of the press, if it is wielded by competent and strong hands" (Hedlund, quoted by Harald Wieselgren, *Bilder och Minnen* [Images and Memory] 1899; Projekt Runeberg 2004; my translation); experience (as journalist) of 1848 uprising in Paris convinced him that Swedish working class must be given weapon of education in its struggle for economic and political justice; found his platform in 1852 as editor in chief of *Göteborgs Handels och Sjöfarts-Tidning* [Göteborg's Business and Maritime Intelligence], campaigning among the rest for electoral reform, freedom of conscience and civil liberties, improvement of the status of women, drastic reduction of state's spending on regular army, separation of education from church, abandonment of traditional 'Latin school' and organic educational structure from primary school to university; expressed much sympathy with Gr's ideas on *folkelighed*, though he was denounced in Danish journal *Fædrelandet* by conservative C. M. Ploug (1813-94) as "Dane-hater" and "the most characterless phrasemonger in the whole of the North; "he is still honoured, along with Gr, as a main source of spirit and ideology of Göteborg University, first established as university college in 1891 as free, open and nordic centre of enlightenment, differentiated from traditional state universities; see also **Hammar-Mødet**.

Heeren, Arnold Herman Ludwig *105*; 1760-1842; German historian, professor of philosophy, subsequently of history, Göttingen; pioneered study of economic imperatives in history of the ancient world; his *Versuch einer Entwickelung der Folgen der Kreuzzüge für Europa* [Attempt at an explication of the consequence of the crusades for Europe] (Göttingen, 1808) was issued same year in French translation as prize essay of the Institute of France; eagerly read (1810-11) by Gr who admired his great perspicuity with regard to broad historical learning but regretted his lack of a religious-historical eye, which meant that he saw clearly in detail but dimly in the entirety.

Hegel, Georg Wilhelm Friedrich *204, 250*; 1770-1831; German philosopher, professor in Heidelberg and Berlin; identified, like J. G. Fichte and F. W. J. von Schelling, with German post-Kantian Idealism; is perhaps most significant philosopher from that period; conceived of study of logic as investigation into fundamental structure of reality itself; taught that all logic is dialectical in character (Thesis – Antithesis – Synthesis); consequently, reality is also conceived of as logically structured, dialectically analysable system; clearly demonstrated in his teleological account of history, an account which was later adapted by Marx to produce materialist theory of historical development; the element of Hegelianism most relevant to theology is perhaps that reality as such can be comprehended as a systematised body of objective knowledge; what is real is intelligible, and only that which is intelligible may be considered real; after his death, his ideas became a highly significant, often dominant strain within western philosophy; in Dk (1840s and 1850s) Hegelianism took firm root within academic and religious philosophy, with J. L. Heiberg and H. L. Martensen as proponents; Hegelianism and responses to it (notably its rejection by Søren Kierkegaard) came to define much of intellectual climate of later part of cultural 'Golden Age' (ca. 1800-50) of Dk; Gr vents his scorn for Hegel in the glossary to his *Krønnike-Rim*, augmented 2nd edition 1842: "Hegel, the latest German brooder to cause a stir, was nothing more nor less than a great hair-splitter (Dialectician) to whom it was a trifling matter (...) both "to be and not to be"; and he proved more than he meant to, namely that one cannot deny the existence of eternal Truth without thereby confirming it and slapping a permanent sticking-plaster over one's mouth."

Heiberg, Johan Ludvig *183, 184*; 1791-1860; son of exiled writer Peter Andreas Heiberg; author of vaudevilles and romantic plays, particularly renowned for *Elverhøj* [Fairy hill] (1828); poet, notably of *Nye digte* [New poems] (1841) containing religious-philosophical pieces; critic distinguished for his Hegelian aesthetic and his mediation of Hegel's speculative philosophy in Dk; director (1849-56) of Royal Theatre Copenhagen, remaining until his death a *censor* (assessing submitted scripts for theatrical viability); married to leading actress and authoress Johanne Luise Heiberg (1812-90); his *Ny A-B-C-Bog i en Times Underviisning til Ære, Nytte og Fornøielse for den unge Grundtvig* [A new ABC-book for an hour's instruction, to the honour, use and pleasure of the young Grundtvig; 1817] satirised Gr who had by then published several 'brief views' of world history, Christianity and Biblical history for children and the general reader.

Heiberg, Peter Andreas *40, 68, 84*; 1758-1841; writer, outspoken critic of various official Danish orthodoxies during late 18th c., "that golden age of the freedom of the pen" (Gr), but fell immediate victim to subsequent reassertion of press censorship; sentenced (1799) to exile from Dk for libelling a state official in course of agitating in print against absolutism and censorship of press; his subversive publications were read and enjoyed by adolescent Gr in library of his tutor Laurits Feld at Thyregod; see also **censur; Trykkeforordringen.'**

Heimskringla 218, 122; the world-circle; medieval Icelandic history of kings of Norway; translated by Gr and studied at home by his sons; see **Snorri Sturluson.**

Helland, Amund *282*; 1786-1870; substantial merchant in Bergen, Norway; followed with interest Gr's fight against Rationalism; corresponded with Gr (whom he occasionally also supported financially) and leading Grundtvigians.

Helligaands Hospital *298*; Hospital of the Holy Spirit; see **Vartov**.

Helveg, Hans Frederik *309, 311, 313, 317-319*; 1816-1901; priest, appointed principal of pioneering Rødding Højskole 1846 but upon outbreak of war 1848 volunteered as military chaplain; from 1850 held church appointments in Haderslev but was deprived of incumbency when Prussians occupied Slesvig 1864; moved to Copenhagen and took on editorship (1864-65) of political weekly *Danmark*; strong supporter of Gr; with Frederik Hammerich, assisted Gr at Holy Communion on Palm Sunday 1867 and submitted important witness-evidence of Gr's breakdown, affirming that despite various irregularities no invalidating breach of core ritual had been committed; though briefly threatened, as consequence of this involvement, with exclusion from clerical appointment, he was nevertheless granted (1867) incumbency of Kjøbelev (Lolland) and subsequently appointed (1886) archdeacon [*Stiftsprovst*] for Lolland-Falster diocese; published various books (deemed by contemporaries to be excessively obscurely written) including *Spaadommene eller Gud i Historien* [The prophecies, or God in history] (1855-62, 3 vols.) and translations and interpretations of biblical books, and contributed to ongoing public debate on national and religious issues (including Grundtvigianism); brother of Ludvig Nicolaus Helveg; see also **Palm Sunday** 1867.

Helveg, Ludvig Nicolaus *241*; 1818-83; priest, church historian, hymnologist, member of circle about Gr; collaborated with C. J. Brandt in publication of *Den danske Salmedigtning* [Danish hymnody] (1846), two volumes anthologising Danish inheritance of vernacular hymns; brother to Frederik Helveg.

Henry IV *105*; 1050-1106; Heinrich, German king 1056-1105, Holy Roman Emperor 1084-1106; his history studied by Gr in connection with his teaching at Det Schouboeske Institut in Copenhagen (1808-10); see also **Gregory,** Pope.

Hermitage, The; see **Eremitagen**.

herrnhuter *288*; members of the *Unitas Fratrum* [Union of Brothers, Brotherly Congregations], branch of followers of reformer Johan Hus, originally (15th c.) from Moravia, settled from 1721 in German town of Herrnhut (hence their Danish name *herrnhuter*) under patronage of *Grev* [Count] N. L. Zinzendorf (1700-1760), subsequently made settlements in Denmark (notably at Christiansfeld in Jylland but also in Stormgade in Copenhagen where Michael Kierkegaard regularly took his sons Peter Christian and Søren Aabye) and in Norway; see **Moravians**.

Herodotus *72, 217*; *ca.* 484-424 B.C.; Greek historian; his History in nine books treats of Persia, Lydia, Egypt, but main theme is struggle between Greeks and Persians; staple author in 19th-c. classical studies.

Hersleb, Svenn (Svend) Borchmann *62, 99, 100, 102, 159, 163, 186*; 1784-1836; close friend from Gr's early years in Copenhagen, alumnus (contemporaneously with Gr and F. C. Sibbern) of Valkendorfs Kollegium 1805-10; witness to Gr's crisis in December 1810; subsequently Professor of Theology and Hebrew, University of Kristiania (Oslo), Norway; Gr named second son after him.

Hertz, Henrik (Heymann) *227, 228*; 1797-1870; Bachelor of Law; distinguished novelist and playwright; author (1830) of *Gjengangerbreve eller poetiske Epistler fra Paradis* (Letters of a revenant, or poetic epistles from Paradise), anonymously published rhymed letters purporting to be from the late Danish poet Jens Baggesen, constituting a kind of manifesto against the preoccupation of contemporary writers (such as H. C. Andersen) with content to the neglect of form.

Hickes, George *334*; 1642-1715; English priest, scholar, non-juror, titular bishop of Thetford; published (1703-1705) monumental *Linguarum veterum septentrionalium thesaurus grammatico-criticus et archæologicus* in two volumes with lengthy dedication to Prince George of Denmark, commonly called Hickes's *Thesaurus*; first volume being grammatical compilation and exposition of Anglo-Saxon, Old Norse and other ancient northern tongues, runic alphabets, etc., second being analytical description of Anglo-Saxon manuscripts in English libraries by Humphrey Wanley, librarian of Bodleian Library, Oxford, thereby presenting comprehensive documentation of Anglo-Saxon Church and spirituality and some of oldest Christian poetry of northern world, looking back to early Church and Church Fathers; *Thesaurus* remained through 18th and most of 19th centuries definitive portrait of Anglo-Saxon Christian-literate culture; copy in Royal Library Copenhagen, was used by Gr for study of Anglo-Saxon (1815 onwards), who thereby experienced major early encounter with the *oldkirkelige* [old-churchly, pertaining to early Church] within northern literary-cultural inheritance; in last days of his life Gr recalled reading Anglo-Saxon poem *The Ruin* in Hickes's *Thesaurus*; see also **Anglo-Saxons**; **Anglo-Saxon manuscripts**.

hill of visions *310*; *Synernes Høj*; reportedly mentioned by Gr in his Palm Sunday discourse, 1867; perhaps a conventional phrase meaning much the same as "ivory tower" – the rarified environment of intellectuals, philosophers, visionaries and prophets, exalted above the workaday world; thus when Gr, on appointment to Vartov, takes up residence (1840) in Vimmelskaftet in the midst of the teeming city, "He has descended into his contemporary world, enters into it and takes a busy part in its work for the people's welfare! The visionary from the hill of visions finishes up as member of parliament and sits on the committee for the bakery industry" (Frederik Rönning); perhaps more specifically the Biblical Sinai; but in I Samuel 10:1-13, Samuel, having anointed Saul, instructs him to go to Gibeah to "the hill of God" (probably Tell-el-F l, north of Jerusalem), where is a garrison of Philistines and where, as one of three signs confirming him as the Lord's anointed, "thou shalt meet a company of prophets coming down from the high place … and they shall prophesy; And the Spirit of the Lord will come upon thee, and thou shalt prophesy with them, and shalt be turned into another man. And let it be, when these signs are come upon thee, that thou do as occasion serve thee; for God is with thee." Saul then defeats the Philistines, the invaders. In his address to the Vartov congregation, Palm Sunday 1867, Gr declares that previously intellect [*Aanden*] and heart [*Hjærtet*] had been separated, the intellect being planted by God upon the hill of visions, the heart in Dk (Sinai, where Moses received the Commandments, was also used – for example by H. A. Brorson (1694-1764) in his hymn *Guds igienfødde, nye, levende Siele!* [God's born-again, new, living souls!] (*Samlede Skrifter* I, no. 107, v. 7) – as symbol of the Law juxtaposed against Golgotha as symbol of Redemption, so these polarised death-and-life concepts may also have been active in Gr's mind); now today, Palm Sunday 1867, intellect and heart are reunited, Jordan's baptismal waters are flowing into the Øresund and Christ is riding into his city (Copenhagen = Jerusalem); there were undoubtedly those in Gr's congregation that day who believed that the Spirit of the Lord had come upon him, that he was prophesying with the prophets from Gibeah, and was turned into another man, that he could only do as occasion served him, for God was with him; see also **synernes høj**; **Palm Sunday** 1867.

Historisk Arkiv 338; *Historisk Archiv: Et Maanedsskrift for populaire Skildringer af historiske Personer og Begivenheder* [Historical archive: A monthly journal for popular portrayals of historical personages and events]; published in Copenhagen 1869-88, principal editor and regular contributor of original articles, redactions and translations was Frederik Carl Herman Granzow; items from journal read to Gr by his curate (young South-Jutlander Christian Jørgensen) and son Frederik Lange in his last hours.

History of Prussia; see **Kotzebue**, August Friedrich Ferdinand v.

History of Switzerland; see **Müller**, Johan von.

hjemtysker (hjemmetysker) *156, 159*; term (literally 'home-German') used particularly from 1840s onwards and particularly (though by no means exclusively) with reference to mixed-cultural region of Sønderjylland (North Slesvig), to designate Danes who were of German extraction and regarded as being *tysk-sindede* ['German-minded'] and as identifying themselves with German culture; clearly, in Gr's usage, a pejorative term; thus he calls Bishop Frederik Münter "the bookish, muddle-headed, bombastic, good-natured but impotent and faint-hearted *hjemtysker* and freemason."

hjerteblomst *262*; heart-flower; *Dicentra spectabilis*, called in English Bleeding Heart or Lady's Locket; has a gracefully drooping stem off which are hung a dozen or more small red and white heart-shaped flowers, set off against delicate soft foliage; typical cottage-garden flower; associated with love and serviceable for poetical metaphorical use and embroidery motif; used by Vilhelm Birkedal to characterise domestic happiness of Gr and Marie (Toft).

hjertet *15, 17, 18, 93, 98, 103, 107, 115, 124, 125, 140, 141, 143, 147, 148, 150, 154, 161, 164, 167, 170, 174, 242, 259-261, 264, 270, 279, 280, 287, 289, 300, 304, 310, 316, 324, 326*; the heart; a concept in which, for Gr, romantic, spiritual and theological overlapped; heart, ear and mouth symbolised for Gr the human creature's capacity, given by the Creator, to answer to the love of God – the ear to hear his word; the heart to ponder and nurture the received word of truth and to be the seat of *Aand* [spirit] and the human creature's prompt to godliness in thought, word and deed; and the mouth to profess and proclaim the word and the perceived truth, goodness and love of God; Gr's theology (following St Paul) embraced the assertion that the Lord is "present in amongst us and as near to us as the Word on our lips and in our heart" [*nærværende midt imellem os, og os saa nær som Ordet i vor Mund og vort Hjerte*]; for Gr it was no chance, but an act of Providence, that the heart stands among the heraldic symbols of the kingdom of Denmark, for *det danske Folk er et Hjerte-Folk* [the Danish people are a people of the heart], Denmark's mother-tongue was a language of the heart and especially when it was upon the lips of Denmark's womenfolk, since the heart was a domain more readily and intuitively accessed by women than by men; and in his semi-mystical vision of a great Christian revival in the North, Denmark was the heart to which the Spirit would return to take up its abode; see also **Aand**; **modersmaal**.

Hjort, Bernth Christoph Wilkens Lind [W.] *187*; 1830-1911; priest, biographer; see headnote to item 66.

Hjort, Peder *278, 281*; 1793-1871; Danish literary critic; son of Viktor Christian Hjort, poet and Bishop of Ribe; professor in German at Sorø Academy 1822-49; as young literary critic to periodical *Athene* (edited by Christian Molbech) published highly critical studies *Digteren Ingemann og hans Værker* [The poet Ingemann and his works; 1815] and *Tolv Paragrapher om Jens Baggesen* [Twelve paragraphs about Jens Baggesen; 1816]; engaged in notorious *pennefejde* [pen feud] between poets Jens Baggesen (1764-1826) and Adam Oehlenschläger (1779-1850), contributing damaging analysis of Baggesen's work; reported to have thought Gr insufficiently pious and humble to be a hymn-writer, and to have compared Gr's hymns to a lumpy eiderdown.

Hjort, W.; see **Hjort,** Bernth Christoph Wilkens Lind.

Hoff, Villiam Johan *306*; 1832-1907; priest, born Rendsborg in Holsten, attended grammar school Viborg, mid-Jylland, graduated Copenhagen University 1857; committed himself early to Gr's conception of the church; 1860 curate in Vallekilde and Hørve, north Sjælland, where he was at centre of religious revivalism; worked with E. J. Trier when latter opened folk-highschool (1865) at Vallekilde; confirmed (1873) as *valgmenighedspræst* [priest of congregation within Danish Church but authorised to choose own pastor] in Ubberup with Vallekilde where new *valgmenigheds*-church, Bethlehemskirken [Bethlehem church], was dedicated (1873); moved (1894) to Vartov Kirke, remaining there until his death; his devotional work in two volumes, *Fra Kirken og fra Lønkammeret, kristelige Læsestykker til hver Dag i Aaret* [From church and closet, Christian readings for every day in the year] was popular enough to go into second edition (1891); see also **Trier,** Ernst Johannes, **Holbæk.**

Hof- og Stadsretten *114, 115*; name of the ordinary court of first instance for Copenhagen from 1771 (when *Hofret*, law-court for protection of court and persons of rank since 1682, was amalgamated with *Stadsret*, civic or municipal law-court, in 'law-court for court and city') to 1919; this was the court which heard the case brought against Gr for publication of *Kirkens Gienmæle* (1825), and passed sentence (1826) of fine of 100 *rigsdaler*, court costs and indefinite term of censorship; see also **censur.**

Holberg, Ludvig *61, 63, 64, 69, 83, 85, 97, 117, 155*; 1684-1754; Danish-Norwegian born in Bergen; travelled in France, Italy; historian, novelist, essayist, dramatist, Denmark's most notable writer of comedy; gained much influence in Royal Theatre after accession of Frederik V ended supremacy of pietism in Danish public life; his writings, such as *Niels Klim*, covertly full of contemporary satire and challenging to contemporary political, social, religious convention, were reading for Gr through boyhood and youth and one of his few reading satisfactions in university years, endorsed by Henrik Steffens' lecture commendation of Holberg as a master in his genre.

Holbæk *305, 306*; substantial town in NW Sjælland on Holbækfjord, at southerly end of Isefjord; area of much religious revivalist activity in 1860s; Grundtvigian sympathies in region led, for example, to establishment of *valgmenighed* and folk-highschool in Vallekilde; see also **Hoff,** Villiam Johan; **Trier,** Ernst Johannes.

Holger Danske *61, 275, 311, 318*; first appeared in *Chanson de Roland*, medieval French *chanson de geste*, as knight (named Olgerus or Otgerus) of Charlemagne; developed life of his own in *Chevalerie d'Ogier* by Raimbert de Paris (12th c.) and subsequent northern literature, notably 13th-c. *Karlamagnussaga*, in Danish chronicles and related works, in widely disseminated *Mandeville's Travels*, celebrated for exploits against Saracens and in India, and in folk ballad *Holger Danske og Burmand* (15th c.); figure consolidated as Danish national hero by Christiern Pedersen's *Olger Danskes Krønike* (1534); Jens Baggesen wrote libretto for opera *Holger Danske* (1789); Poul Martin Møller wrote comic ballad *Holger Danske og Skrædderne* [HD and the tailors] (1816); B. S. Ingemann composed epic poem-cycle *Holger Danske* (1837); H. C. Andersen's tale (1845) immortalised tradition that Holger Danske sleeps beneath Kronborg Castle, Elsinore, to awake in Denmark's hour of greatest need.

Holm, Jakob *207, 214*; 1770-1845; merchant dealing in general merchandise, part-owner of many ships, property owner, "the King of Christianshavn"; founder of Jacob Holm og Sønner specialising in ropes and cables; had offices and stores and lived with offspring of three marriages in Strandgade 56 (now 4) where the Gr-family rented rooms late 1820s.

Holm, Jakob *308*; 1845-1923; priest; for five years (1876-81) served as pastor to Danish-Lutheran communities in America (where Danish emigrants had been settling since 17th c., with great increase in numbers – and inevitably a growing factionalism over divergent affiliations to other emigrant Lutheran groups and over contending confessional traditions – through 19th c.); returned to Dk as parish priest (1882) in Vadum by Nørre Sundby and (1893) in Tølløse, Sjælland; edited journals and continued to work for Danish-American church connections; contributor of anecdote on Gr to *Dansk Kirketidende* (1909).

Holm, Jens *201*; 1779-1861; *lic. theol.* [Licenciate in Theology], priest.

Holmbo(e), Hans *282;* 1798-1868; *Rektor* (Head) of Bergen Cathedral School, Norway, 1830-62.

Holmens Bro *241*; bridge in central Copenhagen, adjacent to Holmens Kirke, connecting city with *Slotsholmene*, the island(s) on which Christiansborg Palace, the Stock Exchange (*Børsen*), Christian iv's Brewery, and more recently the Royal Library, stand.

Holste(i)n, Holsteiners; see **Slesvig-Holsten**.

Homer *217;* Greek was included in tuition of his sons which Gr undertook at home; in particular, translation of passages from *Odyssey* and *Iliad* though not, according to informant Marie Blom, grammatical analysis ("Grammar was and remained for them, as children, a complete *terra incognita*"); Blom's account suggests that Gr's personal teaching methods at that time (1830s) were curiously prescriptive and entailed much learning by heart.

Horace (Quintus Horatius Flaccus) *71*; 65-8 B.C.; Roman poet educated in Rome and Athens; introduced by Virgil to Maecenas who gave him farm on Sabine Hills; spent rest of life between there and Rome writing, notably *Satires, Odes, Epistles*; accommodated Greek literary traditions into Latin composition; gained prescriptive status for his analytical discussion of theory and practice of literary composition, celebrated for sharp lapidary style; therefore a model for writers both before and, particularly, after Renaissance and a major figure in western European school curricula.

Hornemann, Claus Frees *156, 160, 169;* 1751-1830; professor (1776) in Theology Copenhagen University; rationalist who had studied under Johann David Michaëlis (1717-91) in Göttingen and was notorious for his irreverent remarks on biblical topics; showed some sympathy for Gr when required to reprimand him (1810) for his *Dimisprædiken* [probational sermon]; but was subsequently branded in print as 'detractor' and 'blasphemer' by Gr (for which Gr's friend, theologian S. B. Hersleb, reproved him in vain) on account of his 'meddling' with the Bible; in 1825 he sharpened Gr's sense of conflict with establishment's application of church law by laying in Chancellery a charge of fanaticism against Lutheran priest Hinrich Egge, curate in Frederiks ('German') Kirke, Christianshavn.

Hornsyld, Jens *201;* 1757-1840; pastor; born in Jylland, became early staunch supporter of Gr's causes, though could be dismayed at Gr's abrasive mode of debate as when (January 1816) he wrote to Gr on behalf of a number of friends reproaching him for handing adversaries opportunities to scorn both him and true religion in recent polemical publications including Gr's *ad hominem* ridicule of G. J. Thorkelin's edition of *Beowulf* (1815).

Horrebow, Otto *103, 155;* 1769-1823; Danish writer, scurrilous polemicist, strongly influenced by Voltaire; his *Harleqvin Præst* [Harlequin the priest] (1796) was a scornful satire on Sjælland's bishop, N. E. Balle (1744-1816); used position as editor (1797-1801) of weekly periodical *Jesus og Fornuften* [Jesus and Rationality] to challenge conventional Christianity on grounds that faith and rationality are mutually untenable opposites and that Jesus was no more than an enlightened teacher of the rational; to counter this, Bishop Balle published (1797-1802) his weekly paper *Bibelen forsvarer sig sel.* [The Bible is its own defence].

Hospital of the Holy Spirit; see **Vartov.**

Hostrup, Jens Christian *319;* 1818-92; priest, poet; while studying theology in Copenhagen, emerged, along with Carl Ploug, as talented contributor to *Regensens Sangbog* (songbook for use in Regensen, University hall of residence); soon after graduating (1843) wrote comedy *Genboerne* [The neighbours] about two cultures in then-contemporary Dk (educated professional establishment and uneducated and uncultured classes), runaway success in Royal Theatre Copenhagen and still in classical repertoire; as priest (1856) in Silkeborg, Jylland, showed keen interest in Gr's ideas, particularly in advancement of folk-highschools (for which he also wrote suitable songs); noted as excellent preacher; 1862 appointed parish priest in Frederiksborg; associated with prominent circle of Gr's friends and colleagues and involved in efforts to contain consequences of Gr's breakdown in Vartov 1867; in retirement from 1881 lived in Frederiksberg keenly interested in politics.

Hoveritjeneste *271, 310;* obligatory field-service due from peasant to lord; term used (in sense of 'act of servility') on Palm Sunday 1867 when Gr, after saying Lord's Prayer from pulpit, told congregation: "You must not believe that the first three petitions here are *Hoveritjeneste*" [namely,

Hallowed be thy name; thy kingdom come; thy will be done]; though much on this occasion was expression of manic disorder overtaking Gr, by no means all of his observations, noted by informants, were without potentially sound and viable doctrinal value; see also **Palm Sunday** 1867.

Hrothgar *Danedrot 114*; Hrothgar, king of Danes; in *Beowulf*, son of Healfdene, brother of Heorogar and Helge, within Scylding (Danish *Skjoldung*) dynasty; successful warrior-king who builds great hall Heorot in order there to share with his people all that God has granted him, but is powerless to stop depredations of monsters Grendel and mother; Beowulf from royal house of Geatas (*Götar*, from Götarike, southern Sweden) kills monsters, but poet indicates that Heorot will be burnt down following feud with Hrothgar's son-in-law Ingeld and hints at future usurpation of succession by Hrothgar's nephew and co-regent Hrothwulf; Hrothgar is same figure as Roar in Danish legend tradition, king at Lejre in Sjælland and founder of nearby royal township of Roskilde (etymologised as *Roars kilde*, Roar's spring), though in Icelandic *Hrólfs saga kraka* it is Hrólf (*Beowulf*'s Hrothwulf) ruling in great hall when it is freed from monster by Beowulf-counterpart (Böðvarr Bjarki); these are figures Gr desired "to tempt or to drag up from the gravemound into the light of day" with his translations (1817).

Huitfeld, Arild *61, 73, 97, 117*; 1546-1609; historian of Dk; born at Bergenhus in Norway; aristocratic feudal landowner; educated abroad in Strasbourg, Tübingen, Orleans; became diplomat and (1586) Chancellor of realm; though antiquarians were employed by state no general history of Dk had been written since Saxo's (1200) subjective account, a situation Huitfeldt made good by publishing his didactic (and aristocratically orientated), *Danmarckis Rigis Krønnicke* [Chronicle of the kingdom of Denmark] (1595-1604) in ten quarto volumes, which long remained authoritative; childhood reading for Gr "on the Jylland heath" (1792-1798).

Huitfeldt, Ivar *291*; 1665-1710; Norwegian-born captain in Danish fleet; when Swedish fleet attacked Danish fleet at anchor in Køge Bugt south of Copenhagen 1710, Huitfeldt's ship *Danebrog*, one of finest vessels in Admiral Gyldenløve's fleet, came into firing line, caught fire; but with ship disabled by loss of masts, blaze out of control, and strong wind blowing, Huitfeldt dropped anchor to prevent drifting among other Danish ships; continued to fire cannon against Swedes until finally ship's magazine exploded, destroying ship; all but nine crew, said to amount to 600 men, perished; their bodies were then washed ashore along coast; memorials to heroism were erected in Køge and on Langelinie in Copenhagen where bronze cannon salvaged from wreck by speculative divers in 1870s were incorporated; wreck relocated 1978, now protected site; Huitfeld's heroism became legendary; Gr felt exigencies of war required such sacrifice, and was therefore angry at *kommandør* Frederik August Paludan's decision at Eckernförde (1849) to save crew by surrendering ship *Gefion* to Germans; see **Eckernförde**.

Hume, David *131, 133*; 1711-76; Scottish philosopher and historian; though the bulk of his writings was on philosophy (controversially characterised by his substitution of pragmatic utilitarianism in place of any divine authority as imperative for morality, by his rejection of the ostensibly miraculous and his treatment of religion as superstition, and by his distaste for self-serving and hypocritical clergy, both Roman and Protestant), he also published *The History of England from the Invasion of Julius Caesar to the Revolution in 1688*, in 4 volumes (1754-62), the fourth being *The History of England from the Invasion of Julius Cæsar to the Accession of Henry VII* (1762) which Gr condemned for its dismissive treatment of the Anglo-Saxon legacy, a failure in critical perception which Gr blamed upon author's classical education.

Hundeklogskab *82*; ironical opposite of *hundegalskab* 'canine insanity, rabies' meaning such cleverness as might characterise a trained dog: term used by Gr for kind of low-grade cleverness, lacking in humane vision and spirituality, which moved into vacuum left by ineffectual Latin school education; elsewhere Gr associates it pejoratively with brutish intelligence (*Jættekløgt*) of giants of Norse mythology, with *Drengevidenskabelighed* (such pedantry as was drilled into the heads of boys in grammar schools) and with 18th-c. 'enlightenment' and rationalism.

Hvitfeld, Arild; see **Huitfeld,** Arild.

Hvitfeldt, Iver; see **Huitfeldt,** Ivar.

Hymnal, Evangelical-Christian 154, 157, 161, 174, 190, 192, 279, 280, 287; Evangelisk-Christelig Salmebog, samlet af et Selskab og udgivet som et Forsøg [Evangelical-Christian hymnal compiled by a committee and published as a trial], published in two parts 1793, 1795, and followed by the *Evangelisk-Christelig Salmebog til Brug ved Kirke- og Huus-Andagt* [E-C hymnal for use in worship in church and home]1798; officially sanctioned hymnal in Danish Church, much influenced by Bishop N. E. Balle, published in wake of Balle's *Lærebog i den Evangelisk-Christelige Religion* (1791) [Textbook in the Evangelical-Christian Religion] which had been appointed as mandatory learning in Danish schools; Gr strove for replacement of this (as he saw it) rationalist-coloured and spiritless hymnal (just as Christen Kold opposed rote-learning of Balle's textbook in school), not least by publishing collections of his own original hymn-texts, notably in his *Sang-Værk til den Danske Kirke* [Song-work, or Carillon, for the Danish Church] (1836-37), but Balle's hymnal with supplements and revisions retained its identity beyond publication by the Roskilde church-assembly of the *Salmebog til Kirke- og Huus-Andagt* [Hymnal for worship in church and home] (1855); meanwhile Gr's Vartov congregation adopted its own hymnal; see also **hymns**.

hymns *12, 14, 19, 23, 24, 70, 108, 124, 125, 128, 154, 155, 157, 160, 161, 164, 170, 172-174, 184, 189-192, 198, 199, 201, 202, 217, 224, 226, 234-236, 241, 242, 245, 250, 256, 264, 274, 277-281, 284, 287, 296*; Dk shared with rest of Europe's pre-Reformation Church a rich tradition of Latin hymnody, and symbolically a Latin hymn (part of office honouring Knud Lavard, canonised 1169) is Dk's earliest surviving piece of polyphonic music; but in post-Reformation Lutheran Church the vernacular hymn quickly came to flourish and in 1569 an official hymnal was authorised, *Den danske Salmebog* [The Danish hymnal] of Hans Thomissøn (1532-73), containing hymns of his own composition and his reworkings of Latin and German originals; more poetically talented were ballad-influenced hymns of Hans Christensen Sthen (*ca.* 1540-1610) published in his *En liden Vandrebog indeholdende adskillige smukke Bønner og trøstelige Sange* [A little travelling-book containing various beautiful prayers and comforting songs] (*ca.* 1590) and elsewhere; to reflect evolving character of public worship and new order of absolute monarchy, a century after first fervour of Reformation, a new hymnal was commissioned of Thomas Kingo (1634-1703) of which the final authorised outcome (1699) was commonly known as *Kingos Salmebog*; notable among other hymn-writers of 18th c. were Hans Adolph Brorson (1694-1764) whose pietist and often intensely affective hymns reflected his personal spirituality, and Ambrosius Stub (1705-58) known both for jovial drinking-songs and for pietist hymns on perilous voyage of earthly life; despite authorisation of '*Guldbergs Salmebog*' (*Psalme-bog eller En Samling af gamle og nye Psalmer*) [Hymn-book or A collection of hymns old and new] (1778), Kingo's Hymnal remained popular, so its displacement by rationalism-permeated *Evangelisk-kristelig Psalmebog* [Evangelical-Christian Hymnal] (1798) caused much sorrow among conservative congregations especially in rural parishes; it was as a consequence of church authorities' rigidity over new hymns composed by Gr for thousandth anniversary of Dk's christianisation that Gr resigned his position at Vor Frelsers Kirke (1826); and it was to re-endow Danish Church with a treasury of hymnody drawing widely upon traditions of the universal Church through the ages, as well as to teach theology of the Living Word, that Gr undertook monumental compilation of his *Sang-Værk til den danske Kirke* [Song-work, or Carillon, for the Danish Church] (1837); though Gr was appointed (1844) to committee planning new authorised hymnal, conflicting interests doomed the enterprise and as one consequence Vartov Church developed its own (Grundtvigian) hymnal and, according to some observers, its own distinctive style of congregational singing; in various memoirs, their authors assert that it was a particular hymn by Gr or the experience of congregational singing in Gr's Vartov, which kindled or rekindled their faith; Gr's hymns which, together with the closely-linked sermons, held a major didactic and devotional position in his ideal of congregational worship ("With Grundtvig the hymn took the place of dogmatics; in the hymn he found and expressed the teachings of the Faith" – H. L. Martensen; see item 90), have long comprised the largest authorship group in successive authorised Danish hymnals; leading composers who provided music for Gr's hymns included Christian Ernst Frederik Weyse (1774-1842), Andreas Peter Berggreen (1801-80), Henrik Rung (1807-71), Ludvig Mathias Lindeman (1812-87), Johan Peter Emilius Hartmann (1805-1900) and Christian Barnekow (1837-1913); since the *Fuldstændig Choral-Bog som indeholder alle gamle, saavelsom nye Melodier af den nye Kirke-Psalme-Bog saaledes som de udi den Kongelige Slots-Kirke bliver brugte og nu til Kirkernes Brug i Dannemark og Norge med Bass og behövende Signaturer forsynet [etc.]* [Comprehensive Chorale-book which contains all old as well as new melodies of the new Church hymnal and likewise those which are used in the Royal Palace-Chapel, and now for the use of the Churches in Denmark and Norway furnished with bass and necessary signatures, etc.] (1764), compiled with royal authorisation by Frederik Christian Breitendich (1702-75) and drawing upon the *Graduale* (1699) of Kingo and the Hymnal (1740) of Erik Pontoppidan (1698-1764), the Danish Church has had an authorised chorale-book (now in form of *Den Danske Koralbog*) for use of church-musicians as well as clergy, choirs and individuals; see also **Kingo,** Thomas; **Brorson,** Hans Adolph; **Boye,** Caspar Johannes; **Ingemann,** Bernhard Severin; **Hymnal, Evangelical-Christian**; *Sang-Værk til den danske Kirke*; *Sions Harpe*; **Fenger,** Peter Andreas; **Rørdam,** Peter; **Hagen,** Laurits Christian; **Helveg,** Ludvig Nicolaus; **Hansgaard,** Hartvig Christian; **Paulli,** Just Henrik Voltelen; **Vartov's** *Kirke-Salmebog*; and entries under various hymn-titles.

Høder *300*; in Northern myth, blind god in Ásgarðr, home of the Æsir; unintentional killer of god Baldr; see also *Nordens Mythologi*.

Høgsbro, Sophus Magdalus *244, 291, 335, 336*; 1822-1902; *cand. theol.*; fourth principal (1850-62, following Frederik Helveg, Christian Flor and Johan Wegener) of Rødding folk-highschool (founded 1844 to promote Danishness in Slesvig and encourage Scandinavianism); though, like

Christen Kold, dedicated to education of old peasantry, yet he opposed moves to give Rødding character of agricultural college once Danishness seemed secure in Slesvig, and was in important respects more a man of his times than Kold, ready to add modern political processes to means of furthering Grundtvigian mission of awakening and uplifting the nation; member of *Rigsdag*; editor of political weekly *Dansk Folketidende* [Danish Folk News] (founded 1865 with support of Gr); collaborated closely with Gr (his eldest son was educated with Gr's youngest son Frederik Lange); became major player in the struggle for freedom in the *Folkekirke* (constitutionally established national church); worked for Scandinavian unity; as *folketingsmand* [member of the 'lower' house in parliament] held various prominent offices including *statesrevisor* [auditor of public accounts]; politically, aimed to unite all *Bondevenner* (political supporters of farmers) in common front, of which he expected Grundtvigians to emerge as natural leaders, an aim in which he at last broadly succeeded with formation (1870) of majority grouping, *Det forenede Venstre* [The United Left], opposed to right-wing National Liberals (traditionally party of professional middle class centred on Copenhagen, now with support of landowners resisting political and economic rise of smaller farmers [*bønderne*]); however, an historic split followed within the Grundtvigian movement as consequence; he lived to see parliamentary reform (*Systemskiftet* [Change of system], 1901), long advocated by *Venstre* groupings, which in effect undid anti-democratic modifications (1866) to original Constitution of 1849 and ensured that thereafter king could not appoint a government opposed by a majority in the *Folketing*; see also **folk-highschools**; **Berg,** Chresten Poulsen; **Venstre**.

Høinordens Rosengaard 297; *Høinordens Rosengaard (Ved et Besøg af norske Studenter paa Veje fra Upsal i Tivoli d. 20. Juni 1856)* [Rose-garden of the High North (for a visit by Norwegian students on the way from Uppsala, in Tivoli 20th June 1856)]; published separately and in the daily newspaper *Berlingske Tidende*; a small (five-verse) *tour-de-force* of Grundtvig's symbolism and mixed metaphors (There is a summertime of flowering on plain and high fell [Dk, Norway] called The Age of Youth; in Northern parts, a flower-garden of youth which "goes up and down" like billows on the sea, and wins the prize for singing; a rose-garden surrounded by four-leafed clovers which foretell its good fortune; it is in the good hands of the Norns [the Fates in Norse mythology], watched over by Northern lions [heraldic reference to the arms of the three chief Scandinavian nations, all containing lions]; its plants are the Spirit of the North [*Nordens Aand*]; a marvel has occurred, this rose-garden has been seen to steer forth over the salt sea [the Norwegian students visiting Denmark] like Óðinn on his horse; the more often this rose-garden thus sails over the sea, the more firmly it stands and spreads its vital fragrance across the High North).

Høvding 257, 268, 269, 289; 'chieftain, leader' used by H. Brun of Gr ("*Nordens Kirkehøvding* [Church-chieftain of the North]") comparing him with Luther ("the *Høvding* in Saxony"), and by Vilhelm Birkedal of Gr ("this Christian witness and *Høvding* of the people" and "this great *Høvding* of the North"); see also **Luther,** Martin; **Lærefader**.

Haandbog i Verdenshistorien 174, 176; *Haandbog i Verdenshistorien. Efter de bedste Kilder. Et Forsøg af N. F. S. Grundtvig* [Handbook on universal history according to the best sources: an attempt by NFSG], 1833-56; Gr's three-volume work (*Oldtiden* [Antiquity], *Middelalderen* [Middle Ages], *Nyaarstiden* ['new-year period,' Modern Age]), his most thoroughgoing bid to be recognised as historian; begun after publication of *Nordens Mythologi* (1832) the work, together with compilation of his *Sang-Værk til den danske Kirke* (1837), "saa godt som udelukkende" [as good as exclusively] (Gr) occupied the decade 1833-43; third part (modern period up to end of 17th c.) not published until 1856; revised edition 1869 allowed Gr opportunity to add supplement outlining principal events of 18th and 19th c.; essentially a Christian-polemical reading of history in spirit of earlier German scholars including G. E. Lessing (1729-81), J. G. Herder (1744-1803), J. G. Fichte (1762-1814), but characteristically recast in conformity with his own distinctive concepts and principles (such as that of the Living Word); accepted traditional chronology of Scripture (Creation of Man 3761 B.C.); despite contemporaries' scepticism over assumptions and procedures of Christian universal historiography, particularly its implicit optimistic premise that the world was advancing through predicted and predictable phases towards a just resolution of all things for all people at some future date within God's providence (a philosophy starkly challenged by Søren Kierkegaard's existentialist account of the individual's crucial choices in the present moment; while H. L. Martensen also delivered weighty criticism, more concerned with the integrity of the historical validation of the Grundtvigian thesis) the *Haandbog* was enthusiastically adopted in folk-highschools (such as Ludvig Schrøder's Askov) and remained for some generations a key text.

I

I marvel at what I get to see; see **Undrer mig paa, hvad jeg faar at se.**

Ice-clad with fire in [my] bosom; see *Isklædt med Ild i Barmen.*

Icelandic book-treasure *62*; in referring (with theological idiom jocularly suggesting sacramental experience) to "the Real Presence of an Icelandic book-treasure from the Middle Ages" Gr indicates that alongside published editions of early Scandinavian literature (A. S. Vedel's translation of Saxo Grammaticus 1575, P. Clausen's translations from Snorri Sturluson 1599, B. C. Sandvig's translation of *Edda* 1783-1785), he also got to know at first hand the treasury of Icelandic manuscripts held in Copenhagen which included collection of Icelander Arne Magnusson (1663-1730) and unique 13th-c. Codex Regius containing Elder or Poetic *Edda*; his zest for this non-curricular reading being inspired by university friendship (begun Summer 1801) with Bornholmer Peter Nicolai Skougaard (1783-1838), whom Gr called "one of the few who both loved and knew" history of North; see also **Northern literature**, ancient; **medieval character,** Gr as.

Idag paa apostolisk Viis 280; This day in apostolic wise; hymn (1843, 1845) by Gr (*DDS* 2002, no. 486), for ordination of priests; admired by (Bishop) H. L. Martensen; see also **hymns**.

Idunna. En Nytaarsgave 160; *Iðunn. A New Year gift*, published by Gr late 1810, in which Gr jocularly refers to ongoing furore caused by his dimissory (probational) sermon (1810), *Hvi er Herrens Ord forsvundet af Hans Hus. Dimisprædiken* [Why has the word of the Lord vanished from his house? Dimissory Sermon]; Iðunn is wife of Bragi, Norse god of poesy.

I Kvæld blev der banket paa Helvedesport *234*; This night came a knock at the portals of Hell; composed by Gr under inspiration from Anglo-Saxon poem on the Harrowin g of Hell (associated with ancient liturgy of Saturday of Holy Week and Vigil of Easter); phrase *i Kvæld* is ambivalent, used by Gr to signify both 'this evening' and 'last evening' (equivalent of archaic English ballad-word 'yestreen'), therefore the hymn could apparently serve as well for Easter Day as for Saturday of Holy Week – though there is some evidence that in Grundtvigian homes it was particularly associated with "Påske Lördag Aften" [Easter Saturday evening] in which case the opening perhaps deliberately echoes ancient liturgical practice of beginning commemorations of scriptural events with "*Hodie ...*" or "*Haec nox est in qua ...*" ['Today ...' or 'This is the night in which ...'] as though the event were (re-)occurring in present time; Frederik Barfod records that its apparent assurance of possibility of conversion *after* death (a possibility entertained by Gr) won him over to Christianity; see also **Cædmon**.

Industrial Exhibitions Building *340*; the imposing *Industriudstillingsbygningen*, Copenhagen; built 1870-72 for the *Industriforening* [Industrial union] in Vesterbrogade after 19th c. demolition of Copenhagen's medieval ramparts; one of most impressive of modern buildings in its day (architect Vilhelm Klein,1835-1913)and striking symbol of Dk's participation in the new industrial age; hung with flags at half-mast for Gr's funeral (1872).

Inge, Fru *23, 284*; Lady Inge, historical figure in Danish ballads and Adam Oehlenschläger's national-romantic poem *De Tvende Kirketårne* [The twin church-towers; 1811]; lady of *Finnesløv* (Fjenneslev); wife of wealthy and powerful Asser Rig (?1080-1151); mother of Absalon (later archbishop of Dk in Lund, founder of Copenhagen) and Esbern Snare (later supporter of King Valdemar and Absalon in consolidating Danish kingdom; builder of the massive Kalundborg Kirke); foster-mother of Valdemar; when Asser Rig left pregnant Fru Inge to go campaigning he bade her add a spire to their church if she bore a daughter, a tower if she bore a son; returning home he was confronted by two new towers (for, in this folk-story, Absalon and Esbern were twins, though in fact Esbern was the elder); Fjenneslev church with typical pair of Romanesque west towers (though actually modern additions) stands 8 km. east of Sorø, Sjælland; when C. J. Brandt likened Marie Toft's reception of Gr at Rønnebæksholm (September 1846) to Fru Inge's reception of Asser Rig, he most probably had in mind the illustration of Asser's homecoming by Lorenz Frølich (1819-1909) recently published (1844) in a special edition of Oehlenschläger's poem – perhaps (in view of the central place of babies in the Inge anecdote) not an entirely tactful allusion.

Ingemann, Bernhard Severin *15, 62, 115, 124, 164, 233, 250, 265, 279, 339*; 1789-1862; Danish Romantic poet and novelist, friend of Gr; early poetry marked by religiosity and sentimentality to some extent inspired by his enthusiasm for German Romantic poet Novalis but as early as 1811, resident in Valkendorfs Kollegium in Copenhagen, he gained popularity with songs celebrating Danish history and nature; critics (Christian Molbech, Peder Hjort, J. L. Heiberg among them) rounded upon him after performance of his tragedy *Blanca* 1816, Gr alone defending him; he travelled widely with royal grant 1817 onwards; returned to become (1822) teacher in Danish language and literature at Sorø Akademi; morning and evening hymns exuding a child-like simplicity were popularly prized (though neither he nor Gr thought greatly of them) but contemporaries esteemed him most as writer of historical novels and poems related to Danish history, particularly admired by Gr was poem *Valdemar den store og hans Mænd* [Valdemar the Great and his men] (1824) with its stirring opening: Tungt Herrens Haand over Folket laa; / Det var som Dannemarks Tid var omme, / Som skulle Gudherrens Dom nu komme, / Og Folk og Rige og Navn forgaa. / – Stig op af Graven, du Slægt, som døde! / Forkynd dit Fald og afmal din Brøde! / Advar os for Udslettelsens Dom, / Og vis os, hvorfra din Frelse kom! / Men I, som lyste i Tider dunkle, / Som klare Nordlys ved Midnat funkle! / I store Aander, som over Jord / Med Frelsens evige Banner foer, / Der Herren mægtig sin Haand udstrakte / Og Folkeaanden til Liv genvakte! / Lys atter for os fra natlig Tid, / I Aandekæmper i Herrens Strid! [Heavy the Lord's hand lay upon the folk; it was as though Denmark's time was done, as though the Lord God's judgment should now come, and folk and realm and name perish. Rise up from the grave, you generation that died! confess your fall and delineate your guilt! Warn us of the judgment of annihilation, and show us whence your salvation came! But you who shone in ages dark, as the clear Northern lights glimmer at midnight, you great spirits who over all the earth with the Saviour's eternal banner went forth, where the Lord mightily outstretched his hand and awakened the folk-spirit to life again, shine once more for us from night-dark time, you spiritual soldiers in the Lord's fight!]; his historical novels written between 1824-36, including *Valdemar Sejr* [Valdemar the Victorious] (1826), answered with unerring intuition to the needs of the age as Denmark adjusted to painful consequences of Napoleonic era; and during war of 1848-50 Ingemann outshone even Oehlenschläger as mirror of Danish nationalism; see **Valdemar den store og hans Mænd**; **medieval character,** Gr as.

Irenaeus *16, 120, 125, 126, 252, 273*; born between A. D. 140-160, died *c.* 200; Bishop of Lyons, Father of Church whose eastern-rooted theology engaged Gr in 1820s when he read Irenaeus' chief work, written against Gnosticism, *Adversus haereses* (in Latin translations *Contra omnes hæreses*, 'Against all heresies,' Danish *Mod kætterne*, 'Against the heretics') and translated Bk. v of Latin text and published it in *Theologiske Maanedsskrift* (1827) under title 'Om Kjødets Opstandelse og det evige Liv' [On the resurrection of the body and the life everlasting]; in the face of erosion of older convictions by rationalist theology and biblical textual criticism, Gr asked with Irenaeus the radical hypothetical question: If we did not have the Scriptures to guide us, where should we make our appeal on issues of truth and of authority? in Irenaeus' answer Gr recognised supreme revelation: To the Apostles who were the first appointed mediators of the meaning of Christ's revelation and who in unbroken tradition taught their representatives and successors, the bishops, and thus implanted within the living apostolic churches the essential formulations of truth and faith, above all, the Apostles' creed and sacramental words spoken at Baptism and at the Lord's Supper, as handed down into the present age; these are an expression of the Living Word (*det levende Ord*); concomitantly, the Church is the historical congregation of believers gathered about this living Word; Gr dates *Kirkens Gienmæle* [The Church's Retort], his response (deemed libellous) to H. N. Clausen's *Catholismens og Protestantismens Kirkeforfatning, Lære og Ritus* [The ecclesiastical constitution, doctrine and ritual of Catholicism and Protestantism] 26 August 1825, Irenaeus' commemorative day in the calendar of the Church; see also **mageløse Opdagelse,** den.

Iselinge(n) *231*; mansion and estate immediately NE of Vordingborg, south Sjælland, named after Baron Reinhard Iselin (1714-81); owned in 19th c. by Aagaard family; under patronage of Judge Holger Halling Aagaard (1785-1866) house became gathering-place for leading figures in Danish intellectual and cultural life.

Isklædt med Ild i Barmen *301*; Ice-clad with fire in [my] bosom; poetic description of Iceland, dramatically quoted by Gr on visit to Marielyst Højskole (opened 1856), from his own poem in *Krønnike-Rim til levende Skolebrug*, (literally 'Chronicle-rhymes for living school-use' but translatable as 'History in verse for use in the school for life'), augmented 2nd edition 1842, 3rd edition 1875; persona 'Iceland' speaks in own voice, expressing pride in birth of Northern poetry and in sagas, against background of stark ruggedness of landscape; poem of 49 strophes, introduced into second edition, is item 56 in third edition, preceding poem on Snorri Sturluson.

J

Jacob *312*; Old Testament patriarch, son of Isaac; in place he called Peniel, "for I have seen God face to face, and my life is preserved" (Genesis 32:24-32), Jacob, though his hip became dislocated, wrestled throughout night with an angel he would not release until he received a blessing; angel therefore renamed Jacob ('supplanter') Israel ('perseverer with God') and blessed him; thereafter Jacob was new man with new name and renewal of life; story traditionally taken to symbolise spiritual tenacity of people of Israel, obligating Christians to tenacity in upholding the new covenant symbolised particularly in sacrament of baptism; Gr alludes to this Old Testament type in baptism of baby girl in Vartov Kirke, Palm Sunday 1867; in his hyperactive state of mind on that day, Gr was throwing out allusions and comments faster and more randomly than his audience could keep up with; see also **Palm Sunday** 1867.

Jacobin *66*; originally association formed at French Revolution, diversely including such reformist nobility as La Fayette, extreme republicans and usual opportunists; label came to attach to republicans desiring certain degree of social equality but maintaining right to ownership of property; later used pejoratively of people regarded as fanatical revolutionaries.

Ja, o Luther! vil i Blinde *164*; Yea, O Luther! if, in blindness; poem *Til Morten Luthers Minde* [To the memory of Martin Luther] on 300th anniversary of Reformation; published by Gr in his periodical *Danne-Virke* III (1817); see also **Luther**, Martin.

Jason *86*; statue (1802-03) by Bertel Thorvaldsen (then in Rome) depicting Greek legend-hero bearing Golden Fleece; established Thorvaldsen's preeminence; statue now in Thorvaldsens Museum Copenhagen; symbol for Gr of the cult of 'the colossal.'

Jensen, Harald *317*; 1834-1913; notable Danish lithographer (one of his best-selling portraits was that of Christen Kold of which original is in Thisted Museum, Jylland), and as such representative of socially-conscientious professionals, manufacturers and skilled tradesmen comprising significant part of Vartov congregation; he and wife Andrea Lønborg mentioned as close friends of H. P. B. Barfod; present in Vartov Kirke on Palm Sunday 1867.

Jensen, Jens *144*; *sognefoged* (constable, minor public order officer with responsibility for parish) for Udby at time of elections (1848) to the Constituent Assembly [*Den grundlovgivende Rigsforsamling*] for the determination of the forthcoming Constitution (1849), when he was popular choice of farmers as parliamentary candidate for Præstø County's 4th Electoral District but in effect stood down out of deference to his rival, Gr; presumably the same *sognefoged* Jens Jensen from Grumløse who had been appointed as an official of the fire insurance syndicate for Præstø area formally established 1846 by a collective of farmers; as such, he affords a striking model of mid-19thc. radical social and political reorganisation of Dk's rural population, and witness to image and status of Gr (and Grundtvigianism) among the increasingly organised, economically and politically rising class of small farmers (*bønderne*) – as illustrated in anecdote of Gr's election to the seat in 1848.

Jensen, Rasmus *220*; master shoemaker in Løngangsstræde, Copenhagen, at whose home Copenhagen's first small *gudelige forsamlinger* (revivalist religious gatherings in breach of law governing acts of worship within state church) were held, 1820-26; probably the Jensen named by Christian Sigfred Ley alongside Gr, Jakob Christian Lindberg and Andreas Gottlob Rudelbach as being among dearest friends in Dk; see **forsamlinger.**

Jensen and Hansen *221*; Danish surname Jensen, like Hansen, is commonly occurring, thus "Jensen informs me that Hansen had told him" is a way of describing second-hand hearsay, rumour or gossip; see also **Jenses.**

Jenses *239*; ordinary soldiers; *Jens* (*Johannes*, John), commonly occurring name in Dk; equivalent of English *Tommies.*

Jerusalem *105, 224, 278, 310*; "the four-sided heavenly Jerusalem" mystical reference in Gr's discourse, Palm Sunday 1867, associated with liturgical theme of day, Christ's triumphal entry into Jerusalem; throughout this extraordinary service, Gr presented his recovery of strength, sight and physical well-being as here-and-now testimony to the creator-God who can accomplish all things which have defied human competence and capacity, such as perpetual motion (in the vital unstillness of the Spirit working within the human heart) and the squaring of the circle (in the framing of the heavenly Jerusalem): "I am so happy! For eighty-four years now I have toiled to get out of myself and let Our Lord move in and now today he has accomplished this for me so that I can sing: "Death, where is thy sting? Hell, where is thy victory? Thus has God taught me today to sing, and thus should you all learn to sing with me!" See also **Palm Sunday** 1867.

Jesuit, The *156*; nickname attributed to "the High German Moldenhawer who ran the factory" in Gr's ironical account of state of Copenhagen's Theology Faculty at start of 19th c.; so called "because he did not deny but circumvented the faith of the Church." See **Moldenhawer,** Daniel Gotthilf.

Jesus! aldrig nogensinde *319*; *Jesus! aldrig nogensinde / Korsets Træ mig gaae af Minde* [Never, Jesus, may the Cross-tree ever go from my remembrance]; hymn by Gr sung on Palm Sunday 1867; see endnote 1 to item 118.

Jesus and Reason 103, 155; *Jesus og Fornuften*; see **Horrebow**.

Jews and Greeks 138; reference to St Paul's teaching that gentiles and Jews are all one under the Lord.

John, the Baptist 107; *Johannes Døberen* in Danish; proclaimed the coming of the Messiah in Jesus; imprisoned and finally executed by Herod Antipas; his imprisonment, mentioned in the gospel-reading of the day, was recalled by Gr's dying father, Johan ("I too am called John, and prisons are of many kinds and I too am in prison").

John, St; evangelist 139; the Gospel of St John was a text of particular significance to Gr, for its opening verbal association with Genesis offering a link between God's creation of the world and Christ's Incarnation as re-creation, and for John's unfolding of the mystery of the Word which is life and light and dwells among those who dwell in Christ..

Johnson, Gisle Christian 298; 1822-94; Norwegian theologian, professor at university of Kristiania (Oslo); as pietistic-orthodox Lutheran theologian, he was zealous opponent of Grundtvigian concept of church, which he attacked (*ca.* 1856) in polemical feud with Wilhelm Andreas Wexels (1797-1866), preeminent personality in Norwegian Grundtvigianism, who had welcomed Gr on his deeply moving visit to Norway 1851.

Jordan 310; mentioned by Gr in sermon ("the most wondrous mixture of madness and inspired thoughts" – Frederik Hammerich) within liturgy (Palm Sunday 1867) commemorating Christ's triumphal entry into Jerusalem; Gr's lifelong yearning for massive spiritual rebirth of Sixth Church or Congregation (the Scandinavian) had virtually become conviction that this rebirth was imminent; as if in preparation, in Palm Sunday service he shrives the whole congregation and, through Queen Caroline Amalie, the whole Danish people, and bids them all into one fellowship at the Lord's table; now the Lord is riding into his city (Copenhagen is a new Jerusalem) and now Jordan flows into the Øresund (the waters between Denmark, Sweden and Norway – over which, in his poem *Rune-Bladet* (1844), Gr had symbolically envisaged *Nordens Aand* (the Spirit of the North) hovering – is become one huge baptismal font); it is a grand and visionary imagination that is here running away with Gr in his sickness; see also **Palm Sunday** 1867.

Jubel-Lærer 103, 159, 161; term, now archaic, used after Reformation in Dk and Norway to designate one in certain professions, especially priesthood, who had completed fifty years' service or ministry.

Julen har Englelyd 242; Christmas brings angel-song; hymn by Gr. which Frederik Barfod believed Gr's second wife, Marie Toft, adopted as her daily evening-hymn, for which purpose Gr (1851) made slight revisions; see also **hymns**.

Jutland; see **Jylland**.

Jutish pot 77, 78; derisive nickname for a Jutlander; see **Jydepotters Land**.

Jutlanders *108, 161, 267*; though the years Gr passed in Jutland (Jylland), boarded out for his education, were in various respects dark and painful, he refers with esteem to Jutlanders (Jutes) and their traditional stubborn integrity; in 1813 when Dk stood to lose both Norway and Jylland "it was only among the students, especially the Jutlanders, that things began to heat up ... they really had the courage to go through fire for Jylland's honour and for the foster-brotherhood with ancient Norway" (Gr); in 1848 Gr joined deputation of Jutlanders to urge King to hold fast against demands of schleswig-holsteiners; traditional phrase *de stærke Jyder* [the strong, or stubborn, Jutlanders], originating with 19th-c. revivalist movement in Horsens area which was particularly opposed to prescribed adoption of Bishop Balle's *Lærebog* [Textbook] and the Evangelical-Christian Hymnal, expressed both admiration and exasperation; see **heathlands,** Jylland; **Jydepotters Land**; **Jørgensen,** Jens.

Juvenal *81*; Decimus Junius Juvenalis, lived approximately A.D. 65-135; Roman poet known for his sixteen *Satires*, satirising contemporary citizens of Rome and their frailties.

Jydepotters Land *77, 78*; land of Jutish pots; in marginal heathlands of Jylland meagre incomes were traditionally augmented by home-manufacture, usually by women, of low-grade clay pots, unglazed, dark-coloured and three-legged; in jocular-pejorative speech a *Jydepot* was a Jutlander, and *Jydepotters Land* a way of referring to Jylland.

Jylland *61, 70, 73, 76, 80, 81, 108, 116, 155, 293, 341*; Jutland; peninsula lying between North Sea and Danish islands, its southern region (Sønderjylland) historically comprising Duchy of Slesvig; middle and northern Jutland's great wastelands of sandy heath (until large-scale reclamation began in 19th c.) caused it to be traditionally regarded by Copenhageners as dark and backward, but it has a past distinguished in history and legend and celebrated for example by Gr in *Et Blad af Jyllands Rimkrønike* [A page from Jylland's rhyming chronicles; 1815] and, in very different style, by Gr's contemporary Steen Steensen Blicher; see also **Jutlanders**; **Jydepotternes Land**; and **Blicher,** Steen Steensen.

Jættevæsen *269*; 'giant-species,' Norse mythological figure used, in fashion characteristic of Gr-circle, as metaphor and symbol; in Norse creation-myth, first humanlike creature to exist was the *jætte* Ymer, destroyed by Óðinn and the Æsir; the father of Night was a *jætte*, and the wolflike monsters pursuing and trying to swallow Sun and Moon were offspring of a *jættekvinde* [giant-ess]; the *jætter* made their abode and fortress Útgarðr in Jötunheimr on the shores of the great ocean surrounding Miðgarðr, the world; most notorious of them was Loki, handsome without but malevolent within, son of a *jætte* and himself father of monsters, who having insinuated himself into community of Æsir in Ásgarðr treacherously contributed to the ultimate downfall of the Æsir; see also *Nordens Mythologi*.

Jødelæsning *74*; Gr's jocular-pejorative term for study of Hebrew.

Jørgensen, Christian *338*; compelled (1870) to give up his position in Sønderjylland following Prussian annexation (1864), became Gr's last curate at Vartov; would read to Gr in his home; subsequently appointed pastor in Visby, Thy, Nordjylland.

Jørgensen, Jens *336*; 1806-76; farm-owner, politician; from 1833 friend of *vækkelsesprædikanten* [revivalist preacher] Peder Larsen Skræppenborg who preached at *gudelige forsamlinger* (unauthorised, unlawful religious revivalist gatherings) organised by Jørgensen at his home in Holtum, Jylland; unwavering upholder of constitutional cause as member of *Den grundlovgivende Rigsforsamling* [National Constituent Assembly] 1848, determined to stay in Copenhagen to counter any reactionary moves by opposition, even while his wife lay dying in Jylland; from 1849 committed himself as supporter of Gr, and proved in many respects an archetype of Grundtvigians among the self-made, religious-minded and public-spirited farmers who benefited from early liberalisation of laws governing peasantry and eventual granting of free constitution, and themselves fought for liberty of individual; prominent among *de stærke Jyder* – the strong or stubborn Jutlanders, opponents of rationalist-orientated church reforms, including revisions of Danish hymnal; attempted in vain to get Thomas Kingo's hymnal officially restored to use; set up local free school in spirit of Kold and Gr; sat for many years in both *Folketing* [lower chamber of the *Rigsdag*] and *Landsting* [upper chamber]; as member of the *den forenede Venstre* [The United Left] grouping his integrity was for many a benchmark.

K

Kaas, Frederik Julius *112, 160, 161, 166*; 1758-1827; Danish politician, *statsminister; cand. jur.* Copenhagen 1782; 1792-1802 held several high public offices in Kristiania (Oslo), Norway, at time when Norwegian coasts were being fortified against possibility of British attack in Napoleonic wars; recalled to Dk 1802 and named judge in Supreme Court; appointed President of Danish Chancellery 1804; his machinations to secure election of Frederik vi as heir to Swedish throne, even after election of Prince Christian August, ended in embarrassment and his dismissal (1810) from Norwegian posts; but he remained personal and trusted friend of Frederik vi and President of Danish Chancellery until death in 1827, during which period he handled Danish negotiations with Napoleon and served as Justice Minister (1813) and *geheimestatsminister* (principal minister of state under *enevælde* [absolute monarchy]; 1814-26); over traumatic decades in Danish history, little in area of public life did not come under his eye and influence; Gr regarded him as "very indiscreet head" of Chancellery, and some contrast may be discerned between the power he exercised domestically and the humble pie which was often his diet in international diplomacy; see also **Cancellie**, *Det Kongelige-Danske*.

Kabinet *167*; see **Cabinet, Cabinet-sermon**.

Kalkar, Christian Andreas Hermann *261*; 1803-86; priest; from Jewish family, baptised 1823; parish priest (1843-68) in Gladsaxe, Sjælland; chairman (1860-72), Det danske Missionsselskab [The Danish Missionary Society]; leader of deputation of priests congratulating Gr on occasion of his 50 years as priest and nomination as titular Bishop ranking with Bishop of Sjælland.

Kall, Abraham *67, 72, 112*; 1743-1821; Danish historian; *cand. theol.* 1762, Copenhagen; professor of Greek and history 1770, of history and geography 1781, in Copenhagen University; professor of mythology and art history at Kunstakademiet [Academy of arts], Copenhagen, 1781; author (1776) of *Den almindelige Verdenshistorie* [The universal history of the world], translation and adaptation of J. M. Schröckh, *Lehrbuch der allgemeinen Weltgeschichte* (1774), which, though eventually adjudged to have lost sight of the wood for the trees and to lack any capacity for imaginative stimulation, was widely adopted as textbook in Latin schools, and was early reading for Gr, who valued the foundation it laid for him; Gr was later (1817) supported by Kall in his applications for clerical appointment.

Kallebodstrand *312*; Kalvebodstrand; waterfront area of Copenhagen, accessible from sea, lying beyond southwest corner of ramparts not far, in Gr's time, from Gammel Kongevej where he was living in 1867 but subsequently much built up; here Gr, in his disturbed state following Palm Sunday, apparently feared party of Prussians would land with objective of taking him prisoner; sense of persecution he felt at this time echoes persecution of Martin Luther who, in danger of his life, was conveyed (1518) from Augsburg into protection of Elector Frederick III of Saxony; it may also reflect Gr's deep-seated and lifelong apprehension of standing threat German language, culture and political-military aspirations posed to survival of Dk and Danishness; see also **Palm Sunday** 1867.

Kalmarunionen *105*; The Kalmar Union (1397); historic treaty of union between Dk, Norway, Sweden, settled at Kalmar, Sweden, by which Erik of Pomerania (1382-1459), 15-year-old nephew of Danish regent, Queen Margrethe 1 (1353-1412), was crowned king of the united kingdoms; the union was to be governed "in perpetuity" by same king, and to stand together in peace and in war, but each land would keep own laws and be ruled by native-born men; union finally disintegrated in 1523 amid rebellion, economic crisis and religious conflict; in his pamphlet *Er Nordens Forening ønskelig? Et Ord til det svenske Folk* [Is union of the North desirable? A word to the Swedish people; 1810], Gr sees Kalmar Union as defining moment in concept of Nordic unity, which, in form of Scandinavianism, remained through much of 19th c. an active issue on political and cultural agenda to which Gr lent some support; see also **Barfod,** Povl Frederik; **Lehmann,** Peter Martin Orla; **Monrad,** Ditlev Gothard; **Det Skandinaviske Selskab**.

kammerjunker *175*; Groom of the Chamber; title originally designating role and status within hierarchy of Danish royal court but eventually simply a title according rank (Class 4, no. 2), before mid-19th c. reform of civil list; carried for example by Secretary in Foreign Ministry; "When a Dane comes to Hamburg, and they don't know his title in the hotel, he is called *Kammerjunker*" (Hans Christian Andersen).

kammerraad *61, 231*; Danish title originally attached to membership of state fiscal college but eventually simply a title in civil list according rank (Class 6, no. 2), before mid-19th c. reform of civil list; carried for example by Gr's maternal grandfather, Niels Christian Bang of Egebjerggård, as steward of royal estates in Odsherred, Sjælland.

Kancelli; see **Cancellie,** Det Kongelige-Danske.

Kandidat; see **cand.**

Kant, Immanuel *84, 204*; 1724-1804; German philosopher; Professor of Philosophy (1770) University of Königsberg; founder of modern critical philosophy, notably through three works, *The*

Critique of Pure Reason, The Critique of Practical reason, The Critique of Judgment; Gr alleges that in his time at University "our theologians knew but very little about Kant" but Copenhagen lectures of Henrik Steffens 1802 were catalyst to new interest in German philosophy; scientific thinkers such as H. C. Ørsted found inspiration in Kant's position between materialism and idealism; in field of literary aesthetics, K. L. Rahbek imported into debate ideas of J. A. Eberhard, opponent of Kant; theologically, Kant furnished substance to those who would rationalise religion as being of exclusively ethical character without reference to revelation and could espouse his proposition that each person possesses consciousness of a general ethical imperative which it is an obligation to follow – ideas not, as such, congenial to Gr.

Katekismus, Luther's *139, 155, 198, 199*; Martin Luther issued (1529) a 'Greater' and a 'Short' Catechism, in form of instruction in essentials of the Faith by means of question and answer in four areas, Commandments, Creed, Lord's Prayer and Sacraments (Baptism, Eucharist), together with instruction on private confession; the Short Catechism, which is in fact a considerable theological treatise, together with the three Creeds of the primitive Church and the *Confessio Augustana*, is confessionally binding upon the Danish (Lutheran) Church; as priest in Præstø (1821-22) Gr laid much emphasis on teaching confirmands through the *katechismus*, using a translation of Short Catechism made for children by Bishop Hans Poulsen Resen (1561-1638; Bishop of Sjælland from 1615), printed in very many editions, popularly called *Pavekatechismus* [Pope Catechism] because its title-page bore image of Luther and a quotation from Luther's foreword, beginning "Hør mig, du Paw!" [Hear me, thou Pope!] as though Luther were catechising the Pope; another edition of Catechism for use in schools and confirmation classes, published 1841 by Gr's close friend and collaborator P. A. Fenger (1799-1878), went to thirteenth reissue (1868), when it was attacked by Nicolai Gottlieb Blædel (1816-79) in article *Grundtvigianismens Katekismus* [The Grundtvigian Catechism; 1873] for alterations Fenger had made to Luther's text, after which its use as text book was forbidden (1874); see also **catechesis**.

Kierkegaard, Peter Christian *213, 229, 256, 300, 313*; 1805-88; theologian, politician, bishop; brother of philosopher Søren Aabye Kierkegaard; educated in Borgerdydskole and University of Copenhagen, graduating 1826; travelled, studied patristics and scholasticism in Germany, attending lectures of leading German philosophers and theologians including Schleiermacher and Hegel; doctor of philosophy in Göttingen; experienced barricades in Paris 1830; in thesis publicly defended (1836) for licence to teach theology in university, championed Gr's theology of the Word, revealed strong influence of Gr's understanding of sacraments, creed and scripture; emerged, especially through substantial scholarly and periodical publications, as apologist for Gr and remained thereafter his sturdy supporter; 1842-57 parish priest at Pedersborg and Kindertofte near Sorø, Sjælland, where his refusal to enforce baptism into state church upon children of Baptists helped focus demand for religious freedom (vigorously fought for by Gr) which was soon afterwards embodied in Constitution of June 1849; briefly (1849-53) involved himself in politics (elected to *Landsting* [upper chamber of *Rigsdag*] 1849); appointed as Bishop of Aalborg, north Jylland, 1856, distinguishing himself as speaker and debater, ever the apologist and champion of a Grundtvigian concept of the church, notably in first Scandinavian Church Convention (1857) when he refuted critique of Gr by Andreas Gottlob Rudelbach (1792-1862); 1867 appointed *Kultusminister* [Minister for Church Affairs and Education] and as such helped smooth over crisis of Gr's illness that year, but resigned 1868 when his proposals for law relating to the *valgmenighed* [congregation opting to elect and employ own minister while remaining within state church] aroused great opposition and fellow bishops unanimously dissented; in later years he was much troubled by mental instability and afflicted by sense of self-condemnation apparently inherited from depressive father, Michael Pedersen Kierkegaard (1756-1838); concluding himself unworthy of high pastoral office, resigned as bishop 1875, sank ever deeper into self-castigating depression, and finally hastened his death by penitentially starving himself; his many writings have been adjudged as mirroring a spirit and intellect which were of a kind with, and yet different from, those of his brother; see also **Kierkegaard,** Søren Aabye.

Kierkegaard, Søren Aabye *24, 185, 205, 285, 286, 311*; 1813-55; Dk's most widely renowned and studied philosopher, outstanding exponent of (Christian) religious individualism, regarded as father of existentialism; younger brother of Gr's dedicated supporter Peter Christian Kierkegaard (appointed Bishop of Aalborg the year after Søren's death). Though in early years attracted to Gr as potential catalyst for radical redefinition of the individual Christian life, once freed from the prerogatives of State and Church to enforce public worship and constrain the individual conscience by law and dogma, he was disappointed by Gr's adherence (notwithstanding his dedication to individual liberty) to an institutionalised national church and commitment to the congregational and collective which he validated by appeal to history and by his theology of the Living Word. Unrestrainedly in his private papers (which sometimes read like literary exercises in the rhetoric of abuse), and arguably with somewhat more restraint (and therefore thrust) in publications, Kierkegaard ridiculed Gr for his *mageløse opdagelse* [incomparable discovery, matchless realisation] and his theology of *Ordet* [the Word], his addiction to universal history and primitive Nordic culture, his brawling polemical manner, his dialectical vapidity, and more; he in turn was denounced as a dangerous enemy of religion and the church, and corrupter of the faith of the common man and woman by Gr, who called him one of "those ice-cold detractors who always hang like icicles under the roof of the church" (*de iiskolde Spottere, der altid hænge som Iistapper under Kirketaget*). He was himself a man easily mocked, and repeated satire upon his person, his personal history and his views in the often scurrilous paper *Corsaren* [The Corsair] seems both to have goaded him onwards and taken a toll upon his mind and bodily health. When H. L. Martensen publicly spoke of the newly deceased Bishop J. P. Mynster (1775-1854) as "*et af de rette Sandhedsvidne*" [one of the real witnesses unto truth], Søren Kierkegaard launched – through his volume *Øjeblikket* [The moment] and various more ephemeral publications – a scathing attack upon 'official Christianity' for falsifying and deserting the precious essentials of New Testament Christianity, so that true successors of Christ were no longer to be found. After collapsing in a Copenhagen street he suffered a slow decline in Frederiks Hospital and died on 11 November 1855. See also **Kierkegaard,** Peter Christian.

Kingo, Thomas Hansen *19, 23, 154, 155, 157, 160, 161, 192, 245, 278, 280, 281, 326, 339*; 1634-1703; Danish bishop and hymnwriter, of Scottish ancestry; priest Slangerup 1668; 1677 Bishop of Fyn; 1669 first collection of hymns representing the Baroque style in Dk; his hymns have given him reputation, rivalled perhaps by Gr alone, as Dk's greatest hymnwriter; his *Aandelige Siunge-Koors Første Part* (1674) was small collection of original hymns for domestic singing (*Husandagt*), distinguished by traditional Lutheran certainty of belief and understanding of his calling; the Second Part (1681) shows more introspective penitential mood and greater interest in individual's condition and feelings, especially lowness of individual before God; his form of Christianity has been called 'reform-orthodoxy'; Kingo was appointed to compile new hymnal reflecting new order of *enevælde* [absolute monarchy], wrote majority of hymns; first part (*Vinter-Parten* [The winter-section]) was authorised 1690 but shortly afterwards revoked by king; subsequently large portion of it published in *Dend Forordnede Ny Kirke-Salme-Bog* [The new appointed church-hymnal] (1699) also called *Kingos Salmebog*; still held in esteem and affection a century later, Kingo's hymnal was nevertheless replaced (1798) by rationalist-coloured *Evangelical-Christian Hymnal* – to widespread dissatisfaction, especially of rural congregations; Gr, who was gifted interpreter of K's hymns and reworked a number of them for his *Sang-Værk til den danske Kirke* [Song-work (or Carillon) for the Danish Church; 1836-37], records that at Thyregod parsonage (Jylland) where (1792-1798) he received childhood education "everything still followed in the old track, with sleepy but honest churchgoing, with Kingo's hymn-book and Luther's *Katekismus*, which among other things I learned by heart in Latin." See also **hymns**.

King's Prospect, The *150*; see **Kongens Udsigt**.

Kings' Chronicle *151*; *Heimskringla*, *Saga of the Norse Kings*; see **Snorri Sturluson**.

King Valdemar *124*; historical poem by B. S. Ingemann; see **Valdemar den store og hans Mænd**; and **Ingemann,** Bernhard Severin.

Kirkehøvding, Nordens *289*; church-chieftain of the North, *ad hoc* title given Gr; see **Høvding**.

kirkelige Anskuelse, den *229, 251, 257, 283* and *passim*; Gr's concept or purview of the church; distinctive conceptualisation of the historical and living, universal and national Church and its ministry, role and ordering, gradually formulated by Gr, basis of the church-struggle (*Kirkekampen*) engaged in by him and his followers, and of historical Grundtvigianism; one foundation stone of which was Gr's *mageløse Opdagelse* [incomparable discovery, unique realisation] concerning the fundamental authority of the historical church; see **Church,** Danish; **Folkekirke**.

Kirken den er et gammelt Huus *278*; *The Church it is an ancient house*; hymn by Gr published in *Sang-Værk til den danske Kirke* 1837, now divided into two hymns (323 and 329 *Give da Gud, at hvor vi bo*) in *DDS* 2002, one of several of Gr's hymns meeting taste and criteria of Bishop H. L. Martensen (1808-84) who regarded others as too abstract, too generalised, lacking in pietism of better sort, thus in need of "More piety, more awareness of sin!" (Martensen); others approved were *Foragter ei de ringe dage* [Scorn not the days of lowly toiling; *DDS* 350], *Paa Guds Jerusalem det ny* [thus Martensen; hymn appears as *På Jerusalem det ny* (In the new Jerusalem) in *DDS*

332], *Sov sødt, Barnlille* [Sleep sweet, little babe; *DDS* 674] and *Urolige Hjerte, hvad fattes dig dog?* [O heart ever-fretful, what is it you lack?; *DDS* 44]; see also **hymns**.

Kirkens Gienmæle *18, 62, 127, 128, 166, 170, 328*; [The Church's Retort] 1825; monograph, short but monumental, published by Gr in heated response to comparative study of ecclesiastical constitution, teaching and ritual of Roman Catholicism and Protestantism published (1825) by (in Gr's view) rationalist-tainted professor of Theology in Copenhagen, H. N. Clausen, who there conceptualised Church in abstract and relative terms as community dedicated to broad nurturing of religious values with guarantor in Scripture as clarified by modern textual and exegetical scholarship; Gr responded to what he castigated as Clausen's assertion of an "exegetical papacy" wielded over the faithful by learned scriptural-textual professors, with his first publication of a particular view of the Church which he had been developing for some time (inspired in part by reading in Irenaeus) – that the Church is a real, specific, historical congregational entity in continuous existence since apostolic times with its guarantor in *det levende Ord*, the living Word, particularly Apostles' Creed and formulations spoken sacramentally at baptism and Lord's Supper; when Clausen, confronted by personal and professional denunciation by Gr, sued for libel, judgment (30 October 1826) of the *Hof- og Stadsretten* [Court for (Royal) Court and City] found Gr's charges against him offensive, groundless and void, and imposed fine of 100 *rigsdaler* (to be paid to the city's poor-laws administration), court costs and an indefinite term of censorship (eventually lifted December 1837) for abuse of press; see also **censur**; **Clausen,** Henrik Nikolai; **Lindberg,** Jacob Christian; **Spandet,** Niels Møller.

Kirke-Salmebog *236, 319*; Church Hymnal; also called *Festsalmerne*; hymnal drafted by Gr for, and (1846) rejected by Hymnal-committee of Copenhagen's *Præstekonvent* [Convention of Clergy], subsequently long used in Vartov Church; see also **hymns**.

Kirke-Speil *25, 153, 302, 305-307*; *Kirke-Speil eller Udsigt over den kristne Menigheds Levnedsløb* [The mirror of the Church or Survey of the life-history of the Christian congregation]; Gr's survey of Church history (published 1871); originating in lectures given in his home, winter 1860 onward; title echoes Latin title-element *Speculum* widely used among medieval encyclopaedists (as in the title *Speculum ecclesiae* – Mirror of the Church), where encyclopaedists intended, as no doubt Gr does here, to condition reader's expectations of the work, by alluding to 1 Corinthians 13:9-10, 12: For we know in part and we prophesy in part. But when that which is perfect has come, then that which is in part will be done away with. [...] For now we see in a mirror, dimly [Latin Vulgate: *Videmus nunc per speculum in aenigmate*], but then face to face (New King James Version).

Kirketidender; see ***Nordiske Kirke-Tidende***.

Kjøbenhavns Skilderi; see ***Nyeste Skilderie af Kjøbenhavn***.

Klavsen, Provst; see **Clausen,** Henrik Georg.

Klev-Stuen *152*; Ringerike, Norway; place for refreshment on Gr's visit to Krokkleven 1851, where his extempore homily upon life and death, divine and human, earned him upon departure enthusiastic cheers and gun-salute which almost caused horses drawing his carriage to bolt; see **Krog-Kleven**.

Klim, Niels *61*; eponymous Norwegian hero of satirical story by Ludvig Holberg written in Latin, published 1741, translated into Danish by Jens Baggesen 1789; exploring mountain cavern, Klim falls into Utopian underworld governed as enlightened despotism without aristocracy, with freedom of religious conscience and all public offices open to both genders; childhood reading for Gr as boarding pupil (1792-1798) at Laurits Feld's parsonage, Thyregod, Jylland.

Knippelsbro *212*; bridge connecting city of Copenhagen (*Slotsholmene*) to Christianshavn (docks and residential suburb) and island of Amager, first established 1619 under Christian IV.

Knudsen, Hans *266*; 1813-86; priest, author, philanthropist; *cand. theol.* 1836, ordained on same occasion as Vilhelm Birkedal (1809-92); missionary in Danish colony of Trankebar 1837 but forced by ill-health to return to Dk 1843; incumbent of Gjerlev with Enslev 1846-53 and of Bregninge with Bjærgsted (1853-65), and (1869-72) minister to Diakonissestiftelsen (order of 'deaconesses' established in Dk 1863, on German and Swedish models, for women dedicated to helping the needy, the sick, children and women released from imprisonment); 1872 established own philanthropic society dedicated to care of crippled children; author of various works of biblical commentary and three volumes of an incomplete *opus*, Om Jesu Christi Person og Liv (1880-86), also of hard-hitting open letter (1854) against Gr, Birkedal and Grundtvigianism, as vigorously answered by Birkedal (*Alvorligt Svar paa haard Tiltale*, 1855); Gr's letter of appreciation to Birkedal is Brev 633 in *Breve fra og til NFSG*, II (ed. Georg Christensen and Stener Grundtvig, Copenhagen, 1926).

Koch, Carl Frederik *285*; 1860-1925; priest, author; prolific lecturer, writer of articles and books, chiefly on religious, philosophical or church-related topics; among earlier exponents of Kierkegaard's philosophy, he published *Søren Kierkegaard* (1898), *Søren Kierkegaard og Emil Boesen. Breve og Indledning* [SK and EB. Letters and Introduction] (1901) and an anthology of Kierkegaard's writings (1908); also *Fuglen Føniks. Et Sindbilledes Historie* [The Phoenix. The history of a symbol] (1909) and (1925) *Grundtvigske Toner* [Grundtvigian tones – that is, Grundtvig-related rather than concerning Grundtvigianism]; see item 102.

Kold, Christen Mikkelsen *24, 26, 257, 293-295, 323*; 1816-70; pioneer of Danish *friskole* [independent school] and *folkehøjskole* [folk-highschool]; born Thisted, NW Jylland, son of master cobbler; at nearby Snedsted *seminarium* (teacher-training college) captivated by national-historical romantic novels of B. S. Ingemann, experienced spiritual conversion at *gudelige forsamlinger* [religious gatherings] on island of Mors led (1830s) by P. K. Algreen; following graduation (1836), appointment as teacher in state school on Mors blocked by authorities hostile to unlawful *gudelige forsamlinger*; employed to teach children of a group of farmers, was soon in trouble with bishop and Danish Chancellery for rejecting (officially mandatory) rote-learning of Bishop N. E. Balle's *Lærebog*, prompting him to formulate and publish his own pedagogic principles; in this, he was encouraged by pastor Ludvig Daniel Hass (ardent supporter of J. C. Lindberg and Gr in Copenhagen in 1830s) whose household he joined as house-tutor; as such, accompanied them (1842) to Smyrna, Turkey, when Hass undertook missionary work there; disappointed with Hass's indolence and servile treatment of him, Kold returned to Dk on foot, his belongings on a handcart; reading in Gr's *Haandbog i Verdenshistorien* [manual of universal history] and constitutional revolution of 1848 fired him with zeal "to get folk to believe in the love of God and the prospering of Denmark" (Kold); great breakthrough came 1849 when invited by Vilhelm Birkedal to become house-tutor in his parsonage at Ryslinge (island of Fyn), where (1851) leading Grundtvigians opened folk-highschool dedicated to Gr's ideals, to which Kold was appointed principal; as initial roll of 15 pupils grew, Kold moved school to larger premises, finally (1862) building school in Dalum parish near Odense, Fyn, for roll of up to 112 young men in winter session and almost as many young women in summer sessions which he initiated in 1863; Kold's school set model for most succeeding folk-highschool establishments; see also **folk-highschools.**

Kolderup-Rosenvinge, Janus Lauritz Andreas *253, 254, 265*; 1792-1850; jurist, professor in Copenhagen University, *Etatsraad* [State councillor]; published first systematic exposition of Danish legal history, ancient laws and judgments; published also on canon law; holder of various public offices and member of various committees and commissions and of learned societies; founding member (1839), with Christian Molbech, Gr and others, of Dansk historisk Forening [Danish Historical Association] when Gr contentiously (and unsuccessfully) pressed for Association's brief to accommodate universal history and "Naturally, Rosenvinge was also among his opponents" [C. J. Brandt]; as when Rosenvinge skirmished with Gr on another social occasion, the dismissive Grundtvigian line was that the learned jurist (the law?) was too obtuse to grasp Gr's ideas and wit; Molbech and many other contemporaries witness, nevertheless, to a much-esteemed, congenial and cultured personality, and antipathy between him and Gr's supporters evidently has more to do with his very conservative principles with regard to structure and government of the Church.

Kolding River *108*; Kolding Å; river running through Kolding, town on east coast of Jylland dominated by medieval fortress of Koldinghus; until Prussian annexation of Slesvig in 1864, river was boundary between Kingdom of Dk and Duchy of Slesvig.

Kolthoff, Ernst Wilhelm *280*; 1809-90; teacher, cleric; born in Germany, raised in Dk; various degrees in theology (doctorate 1852), taught at Sorø Academy, lectured (1835) at University of Copenhagen; resident curate at Vor Frue Kirke (1837), Holmens Kirke (1843); priest in charge of Helligaandskirke (1856); married to niece of professor H. N. C. Clausen; member (with Gr, J. H. V. Paulli, P. J. Spang and H. L. Martensen) of Hymnal Committee of Copenhagen clergy in ill-fated attempt (1844) to revise hymnal; see also **hymns.**

Kom, Sandheds Aand 326; Come, Spirit of Truth; hymn by Gr (1826, 1837, 1864), based upon verses by Thomas Kingo (1699); no. 300 in *DDS* 2002; a version of Kingo's hymn is no. 281 (*Nu nærmer sig vor Pinsefest* [Our feast of Pentecost draws nigh]) in *DDS* 2002; see also **hymns.**

Kommer hid, I piger smaa! 136, 137, 143; Hither come, you lassies small!; song for naval hero Peter Willemoes composed by Gr in profound "historical-idyllic" mood; achieved iconic status for Gr himself and for Danish contemporaries as celebration of latter-day manifestation of ancient heroic spirit of North; see **Willemoes,** Peter.

Kongeborg *150*; *den ny Kongeborg*; the new king's castle; Gr's light-hearted romantic designation of new royal palace in Kristiania (Oslo) completed two years before his visit to Norway, June 1851 when he joined procession from Akershus (medieval royal fortress) to palace; procession along this route to palace, where King would appear on balcony to receive people's greeting, was initiated by Norwegian poet Henrik Wergeland to mark granting of Norway's free Constitution (17 May 1814), and in 1836 gained official recognition by Parliament; in 1870, on advocacy of poet Bjørnstjerne Bjørnson, children joined annual procession, which still continues, chiefly as event for children.

Kongedybet *82, 83*; anchorage off Copenhagen, location of sea-battle between Dk and England 1801; in Gr's view, battle served as symbolic warning to Dk's enemies concerning the achievements of the Danish folk; see also **Copenhagen, battle of**.

Kongens Udsigt *150*; 'The King's Prospect,' Krokkleven, some 40 km north-west of Oslo, Norway; higher and more dramatic of two spectacular mountainside viewpoints (other being Dronningens Udsigt) over Tyrifjorden and its islands and holms; see **Krog-Kleven**; **Dronningens Udsigt**; and **Klev-Stuen**.

Kong Harald og Ansgar *201*; *Kong Harald og Ansgar. Rim-Blade af Danmarks Kirke-Bog til Jubel-Aaret* [King Harald and Ansgar. Verse-pages from Dk's church-register for the year of jubilee]; poem composed by Gr in honour of thousand-year anniversary (May 1826) of Dk's acceptance of Christianity; Harald Klak, baptised (A.D. 826) in exile by Ansgar archbishop of Hamburg-Bremen, returned to Dk accompanied by Ansgar (who was subsequently honoured as Apostle to Dk), briefly regained power before being once more driven out.

Kong Valdemar *124*; historical poem by B. S. Ingemann; see ***Valdemar den store og hans Mænd***; and **Ingemann**, Bernhard Severin.

Kort Begreb af Verdens-Krønike i Sammenhæng *193*; Gr's 'Concise Outline of World History in Context' published December 1812, over-hastily written product of the period (1810-13) Gr spent in Udby as his father's curate; starts from premise that "ethvert Folks *Bedrift* maa have været og blive en Frugt af dets Tro ... af Menneskets Tankegang; men hvad bestemmer denne uden Menneskets Hovedtanke om Forholdet mellem Gud og Verden, det synlige og usynlige?" [every people's achievement must have been and remains a fruit of its beliefs ... of human thinking; but what determines this, other than humankind's primary thinking about the relationship between God and the world, the visible and the invisible?]; becomes a subjective, somewhat arbitrary and sometimes factually erratic attempt to prove the truth of Christianity by tracing (in a way reminiscent of the medieval patristic philosopher-historians such as Augustine) the providential purposes of God manifest in history; Gr's judgmental characterisations of living as well as departed Danes and his doomsday pronouncements upon the present age earned him scathing reviews and recriminations and among the rest ended for a time his friendship with Christian Molbech (1783-1857); Gr however embarked upon a revision though because of physical and nervous exhaustion had to publish it uncompleted in 1814; see also **universal history**.

Kotzebue, August Friedrich Ferdinand v. *106, 113, 156, 160*; 1761-1819; German dramatist, satirist, influenced by Voltaire; studied law, combined career (which took him to Russia) with involvement in theatre and writing of satirical comedies; in Russia (1800), his Jacobin sympathies earned him brief prison sentence in Siberia; back home in Weimar waged satirical feud (through periodical *Der Freimüthige*) against Goethe and brothers August Vilhelm and Friedrich Schlegel (champions of new German philosophy of nature); upon Napoleon's victory (1806) fled into Estonia and waged polemical war through anti-Napoleonic periodicals *Die Biene* and *Die Grille*; published *Preussens ältere Geschichte* (1808) which, after Napoleon's defeat (1813), secured him status in Prussia and opportunity to involve himself again in theatre; published (1814-15) *Geschichte des Deutschen Reiches von dessen Ursprunge bis zu dessen Untergange*; 1817 founded weekly *Litterarische Wochenblatt*, polemicised against demands, especially within student movement, for press freedom and democratic government; murdered 1819 in Mannheim by member of student association; his plays were popular in Dk especially in period 1801-15, to which Oehlenschläger's satire of German philosophy of nature in his *Sanct Hansaften-Spil* (1803) significantly contributed; Gr read A. F. F. von Kotzebue's History of Prussia for teaching purposes, but was decisively alienated (1810) by his irreverent treatment of Christian history.

Kragballe, Christian Malta *312*; 1824-97; *cand. theol.*; priest; teacher at various schools, with noted talent for narrating biblical stories to children; close associate of Gr; translated among other works *Ecclesiastical History* of Bede with Gr's active encouragement; editor of periodical *Kirkelig Samler* (1855-62) used as mouthpiece by Gr; but fell foul of Bishop H. L. Martensen who refused to ordain him as curate to P. Rørdam; hindered from incumbency in the *folkekirke* until 1888.

Kramer, Ludvig August *233*; 1808-65; fellow-student of Gr's friend, Georg Aagaard (1811-57), though no Grundtvigian; *Kancelliraad* (assessor or judge within one of 'colleges' under which public administration ordered; later a purely honorific title within civil list).

Krarup, Thure *71, 74*; 1739-1808; Rektor (principal) of Aarhus Latin (or Grammar) School 1775-1805, where Gr was pupil; by this time barely in control of discipline, "this funny old man" who was "no mere dabbler in the Lord's own language" (Gr) was only moderately successful in teaching Gr Hebrew; he was assisted by a *Konrektor* [deputy principal], Jens Stougaard (1761-1838).

Kristiania *17, 147-150, 163, 259, 288, 296*; viking-age settlement on Oslo Fjord, Norway; from middle ages, major Scandinavian trading-port and religious centre; designated capital of Norway from 1814 when Norway disjoined from Dk in post-Napoleonic adjustments to balance of power; university established there 1811 when various Norwegian academics (including Gr's "bosom friend" S. B. Hersleb) moved from posts previous held in Copenhagen; despite earlier political centralisation upon Copenhagen, Kristiania developed own distinctive cultural eminence, to some extent marked by an English orientation in contrast to German cultural orientation of Copenhagen; Gr's reception there (invited by students supportive of Scandinavianism and nordic fellowship, 1851), when Parliament went into recess to hear him preach, deeply moved his pan-Scandinavian feelings: "*Kristiania* vied with *Copenhagen*, *Norway* with *Denmark* to make the hospitality and foster-brotherhood of 1851 yet more admirable and more unforgettable than that of 1845" (when Copenhagen students had hosted a spectacular reception); renamed with its ancient name of Oslo in 1925.

Kristoforos *311*; Christopher, bearer of Christ; like other references made by Gr in his disturbed condition, Palm Sunday 1867, his self-association with Christopher was not without meaning; in medieval *Golden Legend*, a giant swore to serve only the mightiest master, whom he at first believed was Satan; but finding that Satan feared Christ he vowed instead to serve Christ; a hermit instructed him to do so in humility and service, by carrying travellers across a river; one passenger, a mere child, grew so heavy that midstream the giant feared both would drown; the child then revealed himself to be Christ, bearing upon his own shoulders the world and its sins; the giant, now called Christopher, bearer of Christ, thereafter preached and converted in Lycia (Asia Minor) until arrested, tortured and beheaded by Romans in reign of Decius (3rd c.); alluding to a previous disturbance, Gr reportedly said "In 1844 ... it went more or less the same with him as now, but people called him mad; ... however this would not happen again because now the Lord who had sought him for eighty-four years had at last found him, and now he was a Kristoforos who bore his Lord" – the burden now afflicting him was the privilege of bearing in humility, service and witness the Christ who himself bore the sins of the world; see also **Palm Sunday** 1867.

Krist stod op af døde *340* ; Christ arose from the dead; ancient Easter hymn reworked by Gr in several versions between 1815-45 (no. 218 in *DDS* 2002); one of series of his festival hymns (others for Christmas, Ascension and Pentecost) having format of three verses with refrain; congregationally effective in its simplicity; each verse begins with triumphant proclamation of Christ's resurrection, followed in second and third verses by simple statement of one of joyous consequences; refrain bids Christ's congregation everywhere to sing angels' Christmas song (Luke 2:14); concludes with additional *Halleluja*-refrain; at Gr's funeral (1872) when huge cortège reached Vartov Kirke which stood with open doors and organ playing, this hymn was taken up by crowds; "It has with justice been remarked in many places that this was the most poignant moment of the whole solemnity here in the city, just as it has been said, apparently also with reason, that such a multitude of hymn-singing people has probably not walked through the streets of Copenhagen for many centuries" (J. Kristian Madsen); see also **hymns**.

Krog-Kleven *150*; famous mountain viewpoint over Tyrifjorden, Ringerike, Norway; see **Kongens Udsigt**.

Kronborg *140*; fortress and royal castle in Dutch renaissance style at Helsingør (Elsinore), Dk, commanding entrance to Øresund and access to Baltic Sea and its ports; built by Frederik II between 1574 and 1585 to replace older castle of Krogen, in enforcement of right claimed by Danish kings from 15th c. onwards to take toll (major source of royal revenues) from ships passing through Øresund; by tradition ships passing Kronborg dipped their flag in salutation; Gr suggests "to lower the sails for Kronborg" meant, in popular speech, to drop trousers in order to receive beating.

Krønnike-Rim til levende Skolebrug *301*; literally 'Chronicle-rhymes for living school-use' but translatable as 'History in verse for use in the school for life,' 1st edition 1828, augmented 2nd edition 1842, 3rd edition 1875; see note introducing the Index; see also **universal history**.

Kullen Light *143*; Kullens Fyr, lighthouse standing on coast of Skåne (Sweden) at entry to Øresund, visible across Kattegat; from 1560 one of chain of lights, also including lights on Sjælland coast at Skagens Rev and Nakkehoved, established by command of Danish King Frederik II to aid safer navigation along north coast of Sjælland into Øresund.

kultusministerium, kultusminister *261, 271, 309, 313*; Danish government ministry and minister responsible for cultural polity including Church affairs, Education and such national institutions as the Royal Theatre; see **church,** Danish; and **Folkekirke**.

Kunzen, Friedrich Ludwig Æmilius *190*; 1761-1817; composer born in Lübeck, notable admirer of Mozart, appointed (1795) composer to Danish court and *Kapelmester* (orchestral conductor) at Royal Theatre Copenhagen; introduced Mozart into operatic repertoire; wrote comic operas showing influence of Mozart (*Dragedukken* 1797) and operas on national historical subjects, showing influence of Gluck, to libretti by Jens Baggesen (*Holger Danske* 1789; *Erik Ejegod* 1798); composed incidental music to plays on Scandinavian legend by Oehlenschläger (*Stærkodder, Hagbarth og Signe*), an oratorio to words by Baggesen (*Skabningens Halleluja* [The Creation-Halleluja] 1797), cantatas and songs; thus established as major figure in Danish literary and musical Romanticism; reportedly, at a *soirée* Gr would leave room when such playing and singing began, evidently impatient to return to discussion of theology.

kvindelige, det *18, 90, 93, 150, 158, 289*; 'the feminine, womanly' – when Gr uses phrase "so *kvindelige* a people as the Danes" he intends not reproach (for effeminacy) but compliment; he alludes to his own preached and published conviction that Danes are essentially a people of the heart and that the beneficent workings of the heart (above all, openness to Christ, a divine capacity for love which constitutes part of the likeness of God residual in humankind after the Fall, a maternal intuition to cherish the inherited formulations of Christendom especially those in the mother-tongue, and to cherish the mother-tongue itself as the optimum language of the heart) are supremely exemplified in woman, in *Dannekvinden* [the Danish woman]; "I Herrens Huus er Varmen / Den dybe Kiærlighed, / Som har i Kvinde-Barmen / Sit rette Arnested!" [In the Lord's house the warmth is that deep love which has in woman's bosom its proper hearth] (Gr, *Kvinde-Evangeliet* [The women's gospel], 1842, v.1); "Experience has taught me – and my grey hairs have given me the courage to say it aloud – that as a rule everything that shall properly reach us to the heart must reach us *through woman!*" (Gr); his poetry and hymns in particular can celebrate women (in Christian story, notably Mary mother of Jesus, in Danish history, in the Danish family, in his own life, in literal and in metaphorical forms) and distinctively use idiom and imagery of the heart to articulate their often complex theology and spirituality; "Og naar Maria glemmes, / Hvor Jesus nævnes end, / Da Hjertet overstemmes / Af Hjernespind hos Mænd!" [And when Mary is forgotten where yet Jesus is named, there the heart has been outvoiced by the intellectualisations of men] (*K-E*, v. 4); "It is Christ's prophecy that human life within the Church shall have its most vital expression in 'the Bride'" (H. Brun reporting conversation with Gr); "I Taare-Bække! rinder / Kun stride over Støv, / For Kirken uden Kvinder,

/Som Lunde uden Løv!" [Ye streams of tears, flow freely, yea, pour forth over dust, for the Church devoid of women, as a grove devoid of leaves], (*K-E*, v.54); "He ingeniously championed the woman's freedom of heart as against men's desire to conform her nature" (Brun); his personal relations with women, notably his three wives, the Dowager Queen Caroline Amalie, his daughter Meta, Constance Steensen-Leth and even Mrs Clara Bolton, form a highly significant strand in his life both internal and external, domestic and public, and in the development of Grundtvigianism; his third and even his second marriage caused family and friends misgivings and his adversaries material for salacious or sanctimonious gossip; but to think (as his doctor, 1867) that all is sufficiently explained by a medical diagnosis is to ignore in Gr a complex integration of outward and inward life, corporeal and spiritual, experiential and mystical, registered within himself and inculcated by him in others, which is sometimes more easily describable and analysable in terms of medieval spirituality (such as *compunctio cordis* [compunction of the heart, *penthos*] ·and devotion to the Virgin) than in conventional Lutheran post-reformational and post-rational categories; see also **Gabriel,** archangel; **Hjertet**; **sexuality,** Gr's.

Kvædlinger eller Smaakvad *277*; *kvædling* (plural *kvædlinger*) is diminutive of *kvad* (cognate with Old Icelandic *kvæði* [poem, song]), therefore meaning same as *smaakvad* [little poem]; principally a gathering of Gr's earlier lyrical poems published 1815, notably including his *Maskeradeballet i Dannemark. Et Syn* [The masked ball in Denmark. A vision], *Til Karen Biørns Minde* [To the memory of KB], but with addition of newly-composed *Thryms-Kvide* [Lay of Thrym] in which loose retelling of story of theft of Thor's hammer in *Þrymskviða* from Icelandic *Edda* (Codex Regius) is used as vehicle for polemic, theological and political (with reference to Sweden's annexation of Norway after Treaty of Kiel, 1814).

kællinghospital *298*; hospital for old women, Vartov; *kælling*, originating as term of affection (*kærling*, dear one; cp. English 'old dear'), can still be used, in Gr's time, half-affectionately, though depending on context and tone can also be used disparagingly; and Vartov Hospital or almshouse for impoverished elderly women was indeed disparagingly labelled by Gr's detractors; the young Vilhelm Birkedal, in moment of pique, refers uncharitably to "the aged and to a great extent decrepit inmates of the Hospital who from the outset could not be perceived as particularly hopeful subjects for Christian influence." See **Vartov.**

Køge *186, 340, 341*; ancient Danish market town and harbour on old coastal road between Vordingborg and Copenhagen, *ca.* 40 km south-west of the capital, having some 1500 inhabitants in 1801; on Gr's road between Udby and Copenhagen; subsequently on railway by which Gr's body was carried to burial-place; see also **Gammel Køgegaard.**

Køster, Kristen (Hans Kristian Ørsted), *310, 317, 322-324*; 1836-71; priest; soon after leaving Randers Latin school, joined the 1856 *studentertog* [student sortie, rally] to Uppsala in support of Scandinavian unity; as theology student in Copenhagen, influenced by ideas of Gr; taught, while still at university, in Velgjørenhedsselskabets Drengeskole [Benevolent Society Boys' School] Copenhagen; gained theological *attestats* 1858 and appointed house-tutor with eminent Grundtvigian Vilhelm Birkedal (1809-92) at Ryslinge, subsequently teacher at Sødinge Højskole and ordained assistant in Vedersø church; 1862 succeeded P. O. Boisen (1815-62) as Gr's curate in Vartov where until his premature death in 1871 he gave faithful and long-suffering support to Gr not only in church and in daily attendance at Gr's last home at Store Tuborg, but with publications in various periodicals, and in the turbulent events surrounding Gr's illness in 1867 (though Thomas Skat Rørdam reproaches him for encouraging Vartov congregation to find divine purpose in Gr's breakdown); contributed to P. O. Boisen's songbook *Et Hundrede danske Sange* [One Hundred Danish Songs] (1865); carried main load of organising *Vennemøder* (Friends' meetings, gatherings associated with Gr's birthday) established in 1863 (Gr's eightieth birthday), and collaborated with clerics Gunni Busck and Peter Rørdam and politicians H. R. Carlsen and Sophus Høgsbro to uphold and advance Grundtvigian concept of the church.

L

La Cour, Povl *317, 319*; 1846-1908; professor, physicist and meteorologist, folk-highschool teacher, sometimes called 'the Danish Edison' for work on Danish telegraph system; in 1878 appointed by Ludvig Schrøder to teach science at Askov folk-highschool, confirming major shift away from traditional curricular foundations; married to Hulda, adoptive daughter of Frederik and Emilie Birkedal Barfod; close friend of brother-in-law H. P. B. Barfod; member of Vartov congregation; present in Vartov Kirke on Palm Sunday 1867.

Lafayette, Joseph *66*; 1757-1834; La Fayette, French aristocrat, general, politician; appointed commander-in-chief of new national guard after fall of Bastille (1789); Gr first (1791) became aware that "whole world was in commotion" through impact upon his French teacher of news filtering into Udby village from post-Revolutionary France.

Lafontaine, Jean de *156*; 1621-95; French author, noted for his tales and fabliaux; Gr records with some scorn that Danish Press Ordinance of 1799 put a stop to more or less all printing except that which was officially authorised or harmless – almanacs in German and Danish, posters and ordinances, the Berling newspaper, *Politievennen* [The friend of (public) polity (good order)] and translations of Lafontaine's fabliaux and A. F. F. von Kotzebue's comedies.

Lammers, Gustav Adolf *298*; 1802-78; Danish born, though brought up, educated in Norway; appointed (1827) hospital priest in Trondheim where he was supporter of Herrnhuter and Haugians; priest (from 1848) in Skien, Norway; zealous pietistic preacher, notably successful revivalist, almost inevitably, therefore, came into conflict with doctrines (including that of confession) of State Church and was obliged to resign office 1856; his controversial response was to leave State Church and establish a free congregation with its own profession of faith written by him; all this was followed with great interest by Gr in Dk who mistrusted pietism; when later his congregation split over rebaptism of the born again, which he rejected, he renewed adherence to Augsburg Confession, returned to State Church though was not given appointment; it has been suggested he was in part model for Henrik Ibsen's *Brand*.

landsmaal-cause *323, 324*; controversial 19th c. campaign in Norway for definition of independent national standard language; see **Maalstræv.**

Landsting *144, 268*; upper chamber of Danish Parliament, established by Constitution of 1849 upon dissolution of absolute monarchy; represented from start concession to old establishment of powerful and wealthy in so far as election was indirect and conditional among other things upon a certain level of income, and this character was consolidated in conservative revision of Constitution in 1866 which placed 12 seats (out of 66) at disposal of royal nomination and made changes of electoral procedure (attempting to grant electoral power in proportion to taxes paid) which further favoured major landowners; in legislative matters the two chambers had parity, though second chamber, the *Folketing*, had tactical advantage that Budget was presented there before going to *Landsting* for consideration.

Langebek, Jacob *160; 1710-75*; Danish historian, dedicated to publishing sources of Danish and Norwegian history; published 1737-39 *Dänische Bibliothek*, meanwhile also collaborating with Frederik Rostgaard (1671-1745) in planning modern Danish dictionary; 1745 founded Det kongelige danske Selskab for Fædrelandets Historie og Sprog [The Royal Danish Society for the Fatherland's History and Language]; 1745-53 initiated publication of periodical devoted to historical source materials, *Danske Magazin*; from 1748 State Archivist; began publication 1772 of great collection of source-texts for Danish-Norwegian history, *Scriptores Rerum Danicarum Medii Ævi* [Historians of Danish affairs of the medieval age], which it was left to his successor Peter Frederik Suhm (1728-1798) to complete; compiled transcriptions of charters and such documents with aim of producing a Danish diplomatarium, which form basis of substantial manuscript diplomatarium in Rigsarkivet [State Archive, Public Records Office], Copenhagen; similarly his numismatic drawings (produced 1753-1754) are important holding in Royal Coins and Medals Collection, Copenhagen; when Gr was formal rebuked from University *Konsistorium* [Senate] for offence caused by his probational sermon (1810), Professor C. F. Hornemann urged him to bear with misfortune as Langebek had when (1746) he was rebuked by *Konsistorium* for alleging (actually with justification) inaccuracies in work of Eric Pontoppidan (author of *Den danske Atlas*, 1763) – a comforting comparison, since two years later Langebek was appointed State Archivist.

Langeland *19, 62, 89, 90, 99, 102, 103, 157, 183, 184, 186*; small island SE of the island of Fyn some 200 km from Copenhagen, in Gr's time linked only by sea to Fyn and Sjælland. See also **Egeløkke** and **Canaan, Canaanites**.

Larsen, Karoline *318*; young girl from Jylland, in Gr-household, friend of wife Asta; one of circle of women attending on Gr during illness Palm Sunday 1867 and reading to him when his sight failed.

Larsen, Filippine *245*; 1843-1911; sister of Karoline Larsen, engaged in Gr household 1870 as teacher to Asta (daughter of Gr and Fru Asta); one of number of people who would read to Gr when his sight failed; remained devoted friend of Fru Asta after Gr's death.

Larsen, Lars *146*; like Jens Jensen (Gr's temporary political rival in parliamentary election, Præstø 1848), Larsen was a *sognefoged* [constable, paid officer responsible for good order within parish], from Mern parish near Præstø, and accordingly wielded local influence among middle-class townsmen and farmers (who were deeply suspicious of landed gentry from manor-houses, as Gr – who himself was familiar guest at Nysø manor, Præstø – comments) and made a decisive proposal-speech on behalf of Gr in Præstø election; by day's end, Gr had emerged as unifying figure, and benign effects of *folkelighed* were manifest ("in the evening at Nysø ... nobleman and priest, warrior, citizen and farmer not only gave each other their hand but found all such differences smoothed out in the deep, loving feeling that all Danes are the children of one mother, and she the tenderest and most lovable mother under the sun!"- Gr); election gives revealing glimpse of power-base of Gr (and Grundtvigianism), at least in Sjælland.

Larsen, Niels Frederik *298*; 1814-81; though on father's death his family was so impoverished that he had to be placed in orphanage, he learned trade of glove-making and came to be prosperous glove manufacturer, owned tannery in Viborg, exported to England, won various international prizes for his products; property-owner in Copenhagen; city councillor Copenhagen 1858-67; typical of substantial citizens with reserved family pew in Vartov Kirke in Gr's time; made his home a gathering-place for Gr-circle; involved with other leading members such as P. O. Boisen, C. M. Kragballe, shoemaker P. Mouritsen, brewer J. Vestberg, master-tailor C. H. N. Vinther, in establishing relief fund (1854) for members of Vartov congregation suffering hardship ('20 – 30 families'), and, as "a good old friend" (Arvesen) of Gr, in negotiations following Gr's breakdown in 1867.

Latin *64, 67, 72, 74, 155, 156*; Lutheran Reformation, and its promotion of vernacular, detrimentally branded Latin as tool of Roman Church's control of access to Scripture, liturgy and theology, but in education Latin remained indispensable key to classical literature and philosophy, and basis of philological and other foundational studies deemed essential to training for professional career in Church or State; hence long-sustained status of 'Latin school' or 'grammar school' in Dk as in England; but Gr's lifelong hostility to Latin (one reason why his educational legacy has sometimes been branded as fundamentally anti-intellectual) was at heart hostility to concomitant institutionalised disregard for mother-tongue and common, native cultural inheritance embodied in mother-tongue, and hostility to attendant cultural elitism which stood in the way of a *folkelig* unification within a truly Danish national identity; his own Latinity was painfully founded (from age of seven) on indifferent or downright poor teaching and (he believed) unfair assessment at university; hence his later scorn for the pomposity of delivering "a mouthful of cloister-Latin" and hence the provocative definition of '*Barbarer*' [barbarians] in his *Krønnike-Rim* 1842: "*Barbarer* kaldte Græker og Romere alle dem, hvis Sprog de ikke forstod, og derfor kalde vor Latinere, naar de er aandløse, deres egne Landsmænd saa, for de ikke kan Latin; men med rette kalde vi kun de aandløse saaledes, fordi de aldrig kan lære Aandens Sprog" ['Barbarians' is what the Greeks and Romans called all those whose language they did not understand, and therefore our Latinists – since they are devoid of *Aand* [spiritual life-force] – call their own countrymen so because they do not know Latin; but rightly we call only those devoid of *Aand* thus, because they can never learn the language of *Aanden*]; see also **Latin schools**; **Aand**.

Latin schools *11, 61, 81, 82, 85, 117, 156, 164, 302, 303*; type of school maintained in Dk between Reformation and 1903, of which there existed some twenty in towns across Dk in Gr's early days; approximately equivalent to English grammar schools; descendants of monastic and cathedral schools of Middle Ages; emphasis on Latin "quia Deus sine hoc studio non cognoscitur" [because without this study God cannot be known] (Olaus Theophilus, rektor of Metropolitanskole, Copenhagen, 1565-75) and Greek because they gave access to heritage of western Christian and classical learning and literature; lectures and examinations in Copenhagen University were conducted in Latin until about 1840; Latin school (also known as *den lærde Skole* [the learned school]),was intended to prepare young men for university and so for offices in Church and State; Christian instruction and classical learning, including Latin, Greek and Hebrew, were core of curriculum, to which, especially in 19th c., were added such subjects as Danish, German, French, history, geography and mathematics; much criticised by Gr and followers for deadening teaching methods, classical bias of curriculum, social exclusiveness, exclusion of girls, narrow orientation towards university and civil service; in Gr's parlance, such schools (as compared with his ideal of a 'school for life' which the Grundtvigian folk-highschools aspired to be) were 'dead' in sense of his definition in his *Krønnike-Rim* 1842: "*Død* betyder i Billed-Sproget Skilsmissen mellem Sjæl og Aand, som giør, at man ingen levende Forestilling har om, hvad er aandeligt og evigt" [*Death* means in metaphorical language the divorce between soul and spirit with the result that one has no living notion as to what is of the spirit and eternal]; such grammar schools were superseded in radical reforms of state provision in 1903; whether or not he learnt it at school, Gr was able to astonish audience at a public doctoral disputation 1836 by opposing in fluent Latin; see also **Aarhus**; **folk-highschools**; **Aand**.

Lauenburg *239*; dukedom on north bank of Elbe River, adjacent to southern border of Holsten, SE of Hamburg; because of position amidst contending political and ethnic groupings, frequently changed hands from 8th c. onwards; conquered by Danish King Valdemar Sejr 1202 and thereafter entangled in politics of Slesvig-Holsten; occupied by Napoleon 1803, annexed to France 1810; with Napoleon's defeat, restored to Hannover 1813, forthwith relinquished to Prussia who conceded dukedom to Dk (1814) in exchange for recognition of Prussian title to Pomerania, though Lauenburg continued, like Holsten, to belong to German federation, which Slesvig did not; 1858 seceded with Holsten from the Danish unitary state constitution [*helstatsforfatning*] and (1863) was occupied by German troops; 1864 Dk forced to concede Lauenburg to Austrian-Prussian alliance; 1865 Prussia secured sole sovereignty; Gr had always wished that Dk might be "blessedly and safely quit of Holsten and Lauenburg" though (with justification as events proved) he feared German unity; see **Slesvig-Holsten**.

Laurent, Harald Anton *220, 222, 223*; 1809-59; *cand. theol.*, priest (1837); while at university tutored (as did L. C. Müller, C. A. H. Muus, L. C. Hagen and C. S. Ley) Gr's children and subsequently two sons of Baron Stampe of Nysø; participant (1832) in J. C. Lindberg's *forsamlinger*, religious gatherings other than in church, in defiance of law preventing priests from ministering except in own appointed incumbency; married to Hanne, sister of Christian Sigfred Ley .

Lehmann, Peter Martin Orla *235, 236, 265*; 1810-70; Bachelor of Law, advocate; emerged early (1836) as supporter of policies to assert Danish culture (against German) in Sønderjylland (Slesvig); on accession of Christian VIII (December 1839), optimistic for liberal reforms, Lehmann collaborated in relaunching weekly paper *Fædrelandet* (founded 1834 by C. N. David and Johannes Hage) as daily, with National-Liberal agenda; same day he presented student address to new King, asking for free Constitution; city councillor Copenhagen 1840; for speech in Nykøbing, Falster, 1841, urging peasants to demand free Constitution, gaoled for three months; in other highly effective speeches over this period (including address to nationalistic gathering at Skamlingsbanken, Jylland, 1844), argued for status of Danish language in legislative assemblies etc, for holding Danish frontier at Ejder River, for Scandinavianism; co-founder (1846) of *Bondevennernes Selskab* [Association of friends of the peasant farmers]; 1848-61 *amtmand* (chief administrative official) in Vejle, east Jylland; leader of National Liberals in *Folketing* 1851-53 and *Landsting* 1854-70; 1861-63 Minister of Interior [*Indenrigsminister*] in administration of C. C. Hall, fighting for so-called *Novemberforfatningen* (common constitution for kingdom of Dk and Duchy of Slesvig; effectively making Ejder Dk's southerly frontier); secession of Holstein-Lauenburg, ensuing war with Prussia (1864) and loss of all three duchies in Vienna peace-negotiations ended period of National-Liberals' and Lehmann's supremacy; shared various common interests (primarily political, national-cultural) with Gr; speaker, with Gr, in popular ceremony at Slesvig stone in Dyrehaven (1865) to welcome loyalists from Sønderjylland.

Leibniz, Gottfried Wilhelm *84, 206*; 1646-1716; German diplomat, philosopher; made significant contributions in fields of philosophy, theology, mathematics, physics, jurisprudence; believed with his age that God created the world which, in so far as it is a created and finite thing, is imperfect but yet the best of all worlds; since God created the world by calculation (*Dum Deus calculat et cogitationem exercet, fit mundus* [When God calculates and exercises thought, a world is created]), scientific calculation has power to reveal secrets of creation.

Leofric *16, 131*; first bishop of Exeter; died 1072; a number of Anglo-Saxon books survive from Leofric's donation to monastic community at his cathedral, including Exeter Book, collection of Anglo-Saxon poems, studied by Gr in Exeter 1830.

Leth, Captain C. F. Steensen; see **Steensen-Leth,** family of.

Leth, Constance; see **Steensen-Leth,** Constance Henriette.

Levnetsløb *278*; *Frederik Hammerich: Et Levnetsløb*; Hammerich's autobiography, edited, published (1882) by son Angul Hammerich; valuable account of life extensively overlapping Gr's, by a Gr-sympathiser who, unlike Gr himself and most of his supporters, managed to gain university appointment; Bishop H. L. Martensen, not well-disposed towards Gr, dismisses Hammerich's judgment of Gr's hymns with words: "I cannot agree that he is the greatest hymn-writer in the Danish Church; and even less can I agree that he is the world's or the Christian Church's greatest hymn-writer – a foolishness which F. Hammerich has committed himself to and left to posterity in his *Levnetsløb*."

Ley, Christian Sigfred *20, 21, 186, 200, 206, 218-220, 224-226*; 1806-74; son of master tailor Ley in Copenhagen; matriculated 1827, studied theology but did not submit himself for examination; teacher; private tutor to Gr's sons Johan and Svend; author of articles (1836, 1839) on educational conditions; 1857-70 teacher in Sønderjylland; during Danish-Prussian war (1864) taken by Prussians as prisoner to Polish border; his diaries record friendship established between his family and the young curate Gr, preaching (1813-15) in various Copenhagen churches, and his personal lifelong admiration of Gr (intermittent letters to Gr between 1831-68 are in Arkiv Fasc. 422); Søren Kierkegaard cited Ley's admiring imitation of Gr's style as evidence of how easily (even if inadvertently) parodied that style was.

Liberals *146*; after establishment of parliamentary democracy (1849), label associated with *Venstre* groupings in Danish parliamentary politics; in Dk, early 19th-c. ideology and terminology of liberalism derived historically from French Revolution but, as more analytic commentators complained, terminology was used and abused with little clear definition; some liberals saw themselves as defending enlightenment values against reactionaries; others were more specifically preoccupied with ousting of absolutist system; for more conservative spirits, 'liberal' was pejorative term synonymous with 'revolutionary'; outside the political sphere it kept common connotation of 'generous' so that in 1827 Gr could refer to "the Danish government's incomparably liberal spirit" – in an article immediately suppressed by the censor; see **Venstre**; also **Minerva**.

licentiat *201*; *licentiatus theologiæ, medicinæ, juris* (commonly abbreviated to *lic. theol., lic. med., lic. jur.*) person who has achieved university grade of licentiate in Theology, Medicine or Law; stage between *baccalaureus* (Bachelor) and doctoral grade; conferred right to give lectures in university and practise profession; abolished for medicine 1854, for law 1872, for theology 1917.

Life and Death *249, 250, 279, 300*; antithesis fundamental to Gr's theological conceptualisation and understanding of the earthly condition, widely expressed in his sermons, prose, poetry and hymns. When theologian Marheineke commended speculative theology and the conceptual poles of Thinking and Being to him, Gr "declared that he would be afraid to have any part in this. Why would you be afraid? asked Marheineke. Grundtvig replied: I am afraid for myself. For me, the principal opposition is the opposition between Life and Death ... You great philosophers forget Life in the erection of your intellectual edifices." H. L. Martensen (1808-84), witness to the discussion (and later Bishop of Sjælland), was struck by Gr's thought ("Grundtvig said: "Mein Gegensatz ist Leben und Tod." [For me the antithesis is Life and Death]. With the years and growing experience, these words – which are indeed also those of the Scriptures – have gained a new and deeper power for me.") but was more dismissive of Gr's capacity to articulate the antithesis: "Often [in Gr's hymns] one is moving among merely commonplace appositions, such as Life and Light, Life and Death." See also **Odin and Fenris; mythology**.

Light and Darkness *279, 300*; without difficulty, Gr found this ancient and powerful conceptual opposition embedded in Norse myth as it is in Christian, and took advantage accordingly in his metaphorical use of indigenous myth; see **Freyr and Surt; mythology**.

Lillebælt *143*; The Little Belt; narrow strait between island of Fyn and peninsula of Jylland, ultimately linking Baltic and North Sea; see also **Øresund**.

Lindberg, Jakob Christian *21, 70, 168, 172-174, 201, 220-224, 228*; 1797-1857; priest, internationally recognised Orientalist scholar, "a loyal friend, an outstandingly doughty worker and a warrior of renown in Our Lord's good cause" (Gr) and crucial figure in furtherance of Gr's *kirkelige anskuelse* [concept or purview of the Church]; born, schooled in Ribe, university in Copenhagen 1815; resident in Valkendorfs Kollegium, studied Theology, also numismatics; 1822 graduated as *cand. theol.*, entered employment as teacher at Copenhagen's Metropolitanskole (resigned 1830 because of lawsuit, living for next fourteen years without public appointment) and published Hebrew primer and grammar and grammatical analysis of Genesis; 1824, with publication of study of Punic coins, seemed destined for high academic appointment; but, zealous to combat inroads of rationalism in Theology and Church, joined (1825) with Gr and A. G. Rudelbach in publication of *Theologisk Maanedsskrift* [Theological Monthly], thus launching lifelong polemical career; stood up for Gr's cause against Professor H. N. Clausen (published short tract December 1826, *Den kgl. Lands-Overrcts samt Hof- og Stads-Rets Kjendelse og Dom i Sagen Dr. Prof. Theol. H. N. Clausen contra Pastor N. F. S. Grundtvig, bedømt af Jac. Chr. Lindberg* [The verdict and sentence of the Royal Supreme Court and *Hof- og Stads*-Court in the case of Doctor Professor of Theology HNC versus Pastor NFSG, judged by JCL], prefaced by letter from N. M. Spandet) and, keeping hair's-breadth within law though at cost of academic preferment, harassed Clausen in print for five years; while Gr still restricted by personal censorship, Lindberg took on battle with leading rationalist clergy (for example over their unauthorised 'rationalisation' of baptismal rite) in pamphlets and his *Maanedsskrift for Christendom og Historie* [Monthly journal for Christianity and history;1830-32] and *Den nordiske Kirketidende* [Nordic church times; 1833-40] to which he likewise contributed various weighty scholarly studies on aspects of early Church; saw *de gudelige forsamlinger* [religious gatherings] in Jylland and Fyn as grassroots rejection of Clausen's kind of Church, published hymnals for such use (*Nogle danske og tyske Salmer til Brug ved Husandagt* [Some Danish and German hymns for use in house-devotions], 1831; *Zions Harpe* [Sion's harp], 1831; and *Rosen-Kjæden* [Rose-chain, rosary] which included 183 hymns by Gr, 1843); himself began (1832) holding (unlawful) *forsamlinger* at his home 'Lille Rolighed' outside Copenhagen which led to police intervention and face-to-face confrontations between Lindberg and authorities, ecclesiastic and civic, but eventually to permission to use Frederiks Kirke (Christianshavn) on Sunday afternoons with Gr as preacher, further major step towards Gr's realisation of his view of Church [*kirkelige anskuelse*]; endured much persecution, popular vilification and lampooning in press, approaching demonisation; 1844 appointed parish priest Tingsted, Falster where as priest he won admiration for care of cholera-stricken parish 1853, and as scholar he continued and completed (1837-53) translation of Old and New Testaments intended for *folkelige* use; politically, experience of repressive authority converted him (as it did Gr) from conservative esteem of absolutism to democratic liberalism; 1853 elected to *Rigsdag* where he frequently spoke and sat on parliamentary committees; died 1857 shortly after moving to parish of Lille Lyngby with Ølsted in N. Sjælland.

Lindberg, Clara Cathrine *247*; wife of Niels Lindberg, daughter of *Provst* L. V. and Elisabeth Margrethe Monrad.

Lindberg, Niels, *244, 321*; 1829-86; priest; son of Jacob Christian Lindberg; *cand. theol.*, having also studied mathematics, oriental languages; took various teaching posts in Copenhagen, including that of private tutor to Frederik Lange Grundtvig, Gr's son by Marie (Toft) Grundtvig; editor 1860-72 of periodical *Dansk Kirketidende* through which he vigorously supported Grundtvigian positions; subsequently chosen as *valgmenighedspræst* (priest to congregation electing to choose and employ own pastor while remaining within State Church) in Kerteminde, Fyn; following divisions among Grundtvigians after Gr's death, he aligned politically with those who joined the *Det Forenede Venstre* [The United Left]; married to Clara Cathrine Monrad, daughter of *Provst* L. V. and Elisabeth Margrethe Monrad.

Lindholm, Hans *90*; 1757-1821; *Generaladjutant* (officer serving as aide-de-camp), obliquely involved in appointing Gr as private tutor (1805-08) to Steensen-Leths at Egeløkke manor-house, Langeland; his wife, also involved in appointment, was sister to Constance Steensen-Leth, lady of Egeløkke, with whom Gr was to fall in love.

liturgy *18, 156-159, 290*; given Gr's distinctive theological views it is not surprising that his chief liturgical interest lay in sacramental rites of baptism and eucharist and in the office of the word (preaching); in his sermons but particularly perhaps in his hymns (a notable and remarked-upon feature of liturgical performance in Vartov Kirke) he voiced responsiveness to, and elicited teaching from, the cycle of liturgical seasons of Church's year; his (very early; 1807) *Om Religion og Liturgie* expressed alertness to symbolic function of liturgical performance and accessories; he and his supporters fought hard and long against liturgical reform which sought primarily to implement Rationalist agenda; but yet "If I were offered a liturgy which it were possible to prove to me was from the Apostles themselves, I would have to answer: No, we cannot use it yet; we have not matured enough for that" (Grundtvig); see also *Om Religion og Liturgie*; **Ord, det levende**; **sacraments**; **Alterbogs-Sagen**; **Daabspagten**; **Besværgelsen**; **Boisen**, Peter Outzen; **Apostles**, Apostolic times, apostolic profession; **hymns**.

logos, the divine, in Grundtvig *329*; Edmund Gosse (1849-1928) in his (entirely derivative) account of Gr's breakdown on Palm Sunday 1867, as in his account of attending Gr's preaching in Vartov 1872, is dedicated to shaping a good anecdote; yet he (or his informant – though unlikely to be his host Provst Bruun Juul who opposed Gr's teachings and his "false rhetoric") is open to possibility that "Perhaps an element of not perfect mental health in his extreme individuality was required to enable the divine *logos* in him to breathe through his speech articulately" (Gosse); it might certainly be argued, simply on exegetical grounds, that contemporary Danish commentators made too much of the disorder and too little of the articulacy in Gr's discourse that day; see also **Palm Sunday** 1867.

Loke *300*; Icelandic Loki ; in Norse myth, son of giant but resident in Ásgarðr, characterised by Snorri Sturluson (*Prose Edda*) as slanderer of Æsir, father of lies, disgrace and harm of gods and of men; responsible for various betrayals and treacheries, worst of all his part in death of Baldr, son of Óðinn and Frigg; when all nature was sworn not to harm Baldr, most loved of the gods, humble mistletoe was overlooked; evil in his jealousy Loki took opportunity of gods' sport of shooting (harmless) arrows at Baldr, to give arrow of mistletoe to blind Höðr who then shot and killed Baldr; could all nature have been persuaded to weep for Baldr, Hel would have returned him, but one old hag (Loki in disguise) refused; hence one of Gr's cited pronouncements, drawing upon Norse mythological analogy: "Unenlightened ingenuousness is like the blind Høder, and can easily go astray as did he when Loki put the mistletoe into his hand." See also *Nordens Mythologi*.

London *16, 62, 129, 132, 134*; though initially (visit of 1829) bewildered and deeply dispirited by London's vastness, ceaseless activity and seeming indifference to the individual, Gr used well his introductions to establish (summers of 1829-31) a social network and research connections and routines and came to enjoy his flirtation with London society; but more deeply, London was for him symbol of England's freedoms; he sometimes called the city *Elve-Dronningen*, borrowing the title of Edmund Spenser's 16th c. poem *The Faerie Queene*, as defined in Gr's *Krønnike-Rim* 1842: "*Elve-Dronningen (The Fairy Queen)* among capital cities may London well be called, though only because there prevails there a civil freedom which is wanting in all other capitals; for this fairy alone can thus set all the forces of human life in motion; and although these forces are by no means everywhere as great as in England, yet, as history witnesses, freedom works miracles wherever there are people who desire something other than drunkenness and riotousness, ostentation and flirtation, or brawling; so it is simply a question as to whether the authorities will and the people can cope with it." London, like life itself, is full of oppositions, "life and death, light and shade, old and new, town and country, wealth and destitution, kindheartedness and cruelty" and therefore, Gr says (*op. cit.*), "it sheds light on life far better than all German books." See also **England**.

Lord's Prayer *217, 222, 264, 310, 311, 316, 317, 328*; Edmund Gosse told his English readers that Gr took Lord's Prayer, along with Sermon on the Mount, as basis of practical Christianity; Gr recited Lord's Prayer with Creed, and read Biblical passage with his children at start of their morning's tuition; late in life he incorporated it with Creed and Eucharistic words within lengthy prayer of own composition for morning household devotion; Palm Sunday 1867 he taught congregation that first three petitions are not expressions of vassal-relationship [*hoveritjeneste*] with God; despite other unpredictable behaviour Gr properly used Lord's Prayer and words of institution at altar that day, and no formal charge of canonical breach was upheld against him; see also **Hoveritjeneste**.

Lord's Supper *26, 199, 266, 290, 310-312, 316, 317, 321*; holy communion, eucharist; see **sacraments**.

Lorenzen, Peter Hiort *234*; 1791-1845; Danish politician and businessman; 1834-40 leading left-wing agitator in representative group for Slesvig, demanding free constitution for Slesvig-Holsten in union with the Danish crown; 1841, following dealings with liberal leader in Dk, Orla Lehmann, elected from Sønderborg to lead Danish party in the *stænderforsamling* (Assembly of the Estates) in Slesvig where as political gesture he would speak in Danish, resigning seat when king decreed only those unable to speak German were permitted to use Danish; remained activist and leader of Danish interests in Sønderjylland until his death.

Louis XVI, execution of *26, 328*; Edmund Gosse, in Copenhagen 1872, felt impelled to visit Vartov Church to hear Gr preach because "I *must* listen to a poet who was born five years before Byron, and who recollects the execution of Louis XVI."

Luckner, Nikolaus *66*; 1722-1794; German soldier, fought with distinction for Prussians in Seven Years War 1756-63; gained Danish nationality 1778 as owner of estates in Holsten, ennobled as Danish count 1784; joined French army, promoted to marshal, but after Revolution dismissed (1793) under suspicion of treason, guillotined 1794; affairs in France were first contemporary international events of which Gr as child became aware (1791).

lust *313*; one of Gr's random preoccupations during delirium following breakdown on Palm Sunday 1867, contributing to physician's somewhat facile diagnosis of problem as priapism; see also **circumcision of Jesus**; **Palm Sunday** 1867; **sexuality,** Gr's.

Luther, Martin *18, 70, 103, 155, 159-164, 169, 170, 198, 250, 252, 270, 279, 313, 326*; 1483-1546; German theologian, religious reformer; born Eisleben in Saxony; educated Magdeburg, Eisenach and Erfurt where, having originally intended career in law, entered Augustinian monastery; 1508 sent to Wittenberg University as lecturer, there gained theological doctorate and repute as preacher; meanwhile, impelled to radical revaluation of medieval theology, developed doctrine of salvation at variance with that of Church; 1517 challenged friar John Tetzel to debate his business of selling papal indulgences; pinned 95 theses on church door in Wittenberg as basis for debate, this act being subsequently regarded as symbolic start of Reformation; his challenge to doctrine of Church also attracted supporters alienated by scandals and abuses within Church; 1520 he publicly burned papal bull condemning him; his *De captivitate Babylonica ecclesiae praeludium* [Prelude concerning the Babylonian Captivity of the Church; 1520] in effect called upon Roman clergy to defect from papal authority, radically challenged medieval theology, concluding, for example, that only two of Rome's seven sacraments (baptism, eucharist) were valid; his *Von der Freiheit eines Christenmennschen* [On the freedom of the Christian; 1520] asserted key Lutheran precept that Christian individual is unconstrained in faith by any human requirement but, by Christ's own commandment, is bound to love of neighbour; when summoned to repudiate his teachings at Imperial Diet of Worms (1521) he maintained his position with "Ich kann nicht anders" [I cannot do otherwise] for which he was outlawed by imperial decree and excommunicated by Pope; in danger of his life, he was spirited away by Elector of Saxony to protection in Wartburg fortress, there spent a year, translating New Testament into German; 1525 married former nun Katharina von Bora who bore him several children; as breach with Church of Rome spread in German states, and his ideas began to take root among Northern humanists, he devoted himself – crucially supported throughout by Philipp Melancthon (1497-1560) who compiled exposition of protestant dogmatics, *Loci communes* (1521), and drafted *Confessio Augustana* (1530) – to shaping confession, teachings, structure and territorial organisation of a reformed church, by writing (including hymns), preaching, and visitations; 1529 issued a 'Greater' and a 'Short' Catechism, instruction in essentials of Faith by means of question and answer; 1534 published first edition of German Bible which he continued revising for remainder of his life; 1535 dean of theological faculty at Wittenberg; increasingly overburdened, ill and subject to depression, he grew more virulent and coarse in polemical writings such as tracts against Jews (1543) and against Papacy (1545); died suddenly while visiting town of his birth, Eisleben, February 1546; Gr, needless to say, esteemed Luther highly, but was indifferent enough to hero-worship to be able to write (*Krønnike-Rim* 1842): "*Luther* was the sixteenth century's hero but precisely therefore cannot be the nineteenth's; and whether one kisses or fights with a shadow one wins just as much." See also **Augsburg Confession**; *Katekismus,* Luther's; **anfægtelser**; **hymns**.

Lutheran *164*; pertaining to Luther and Lutheranism; designation used of essential confession and teachings of Martin Luther (1483-1546) as also of adherents (individuals, churches) of Luther's essential confession and teachings; official adherence of Danish State Church and *Folkekirke* from 1537 onwards; itself founded in part upon rejection of humanly-constituted authority in domain of faith, 'Lutheran' inheritance, in Dk as elsewhere, was ever open to degree of reconstruction, pluralism or fragmentation (as in emergence of pietism, or conflict with ec-clesiastical and secular authority over laws perceived as restricting preachers from freely preach-ing); 19th c. rationalism entailed adjustments to aspects of Lutheran heritage (one characteristic controversy being that over baptismal rite); movements for reform were routinely countered by conservative movements to preserve the authentic and original, or at least traditional (as exem-plified in resistance to revision of Danish service books, hymnals); Gr had own problems with some Lutheran theology, and with aspects of contemporary German Lutheranism; nevertheless 'Lutheran' remained definitive through 19th c. against 'catholic' (whether Roman or Anglican-Tractarian); see also **Luther,** Martin; **Augsburg Confession;** *Katekismus,* Luther's; **Church,** Danish; **Palladius,** Peder; **Kingo,** Thomas; **Daabspagten; Folkekirke; Frikirke; Rudelbach,** Andreas Gottlob; **Hammerich,** Peter Frederik Adolph; and **Fall,** The.

Lutheran hymnody *164;* congregational hymn-singing was major feature of reformed worship and Dk has distinguished lineage of hymn-writers in this tradition – with which Gr consciously and centrally identified himself; see **hymns..**

Lutherdom; see **Luther,** Martin; and **Lutheran.**

Luther the Second; see **Harms,** Claus.

Lyskander (Lyschander), Claus Christoffersen *64, 97;* 1558-1624; Danish historian who after publishing several works on national history was appointed (1616) Christian ɪᴠ's historiogra-pher royal; planned but never realised an all-embracing history of Dk in 116 books; his *Synopsis historiarum Danicarum, en kort Summa offuer den danske Historia, fra Verdens Begyndelse til Christian IVs tid oc Regemente* [Synopsis of the histories of Denmark, a short review of Dan-ish history from the beginning of the world to the time and reign of Christian ɪᴠ], published 1622, was short-titled *De danske kongers slectebog* (Genealogy of the Danish Kings) which, in the conventional manner of medieval historiographers, linked historical figures to legendary, and legendary to biblical, thus taking ancestry of Danish kings back to Adam; the work formed part of Gr's earliest childhood reading.

Lærde Efterretninger *160; Kjøbenhavnske lærde Efterretninger* [Learned news from Copenha-gen]; see *Dansk Litteratur-Tidende.*

Lærebog, Balle's *161;* Bishop N. E. Balle's *Lærebog i den Evangelisk-Christelige Religion* [Textbook in Evangelical-Christian Religion; 1791], written in conjunction with *kongelig confessionarius* Christian Bastholm (1740-1819), mandatorily introduced into state schools; Gr was sceptical of Balle's reputation for orthodoxy, charging him rather with following rationalist fashions brought back from Germany; see **Balle,** Nicolaj Edinger; **Göttingen.**

Lærefader 269; teacher-father, mentor; solemn title accorded to great teachers (*Ordbog over det danske Sprog* exemplifies with names of Cicero, St Irenæus, Philipp Melancthon) who have com-manded a following; used of Grundtvig among his most dedicated disciples; see also **Høvding.**

Læsefrugter 115; *Læsefrugter, samlede paa Literaturens Mark* [Fruits of reading, gathered in literature's meadow; title puns upon sense derived from German *lesefrüchte* 'windfalls']; series of literary anthologies published in magazine form 1818-33 (and continued 1839-40, totalling sixty-six issues) by A. F. Elmqvist (1788-1868), printer in Aarhus; included new work by contemporary writers such as Steen Steensen Blicher; see also **Elmqvist**, Adolf Frederik.

Løft dit Hoved, du raske Gut! 333; *Raise your head up, O doughty lad*; vigorously optimistic lyric by Norwegian winner of Nobel Prize for Literature, Bjørnstjerne Bjørnson (1832-1910); Øyvind's song from Bjørnson's novel, *En glad gut* (1860).

M

Maalstræv 323; Norwegian *målstrev*; supporters sometimes labelled *maalstræverne*; Norwegian movement, beginning mid-19th c., which aimed to create independent national standard written language (*landsmaal*); bid to assert Norwegian national identity, cohesion and autonomy against domination by either Denmark or Sweden; though it was in some respects a cause entirely at home within a folk-highschool agenda and consistent with a certain ideal of literary language, Gr himself had misgivings over zeal of Kristoffer Bruun (1839-1920) founder (1867) of folk-highschool at Sel in Gudbrandsdal, fearing that such a constructed written language would be stillborn: better to draw upon the Norwegian folk-speech which was closer to Old Icelandic and was therefore, like Old Icelandic, Old Danish and Old English, of authentic descent (Gr liked to believe) from the parent *Old-Nordisk* language; see also **Aasen**, Ivar.

Maaløe, *Kandidat 160*; possibly H. W. L. Maaløe (1761-1840; *candidat* degree 1787, later priest); Gr, in a late retrospect (written down 1862-63) upon his crisis of Autumn 1810 (hounded by Copenhagen clergy for his probational sermon, threatened with exclusion from *candidat* list at University, formally reprimanded by Rektor upon royal resolution) characteristically found a pattern and a timing in events, and cast a particular light upon his own circumstances by associating them with similar historical instances; in this case with "*Kandidat* Maaløe, the *herrnhuter*" and two well-known Norwegians, one also a *herrnhuter*, the other an itinerant preacher, all penalised for religious radicalism; but, he says, the Copenhagen establishment failed to discern in him what it could readily believe of the other three, namely that his crisis was one of personal faith, in which he was "as though gripped by some mighty spirit which was calling him to become a reformer"; and it indeed proved a turning-point in his life.

Maanedskrift, Fallesen's *158*; *Teologisk Maanedsskrivt* [Theological monthly]; see **Fallesen**, Lorenz Nikolai.

Madvig, Johannes Nicolai *254, 294*; 1804-86; professor of philology Copenhagen, University Librarian 1828-48; *Kultusminister* [Minister for Church Affairs and Education] from 1848, resigned 1851 over Slesvig-Holsten issue; special interest in *retskrivning* [correct form of written Danish]; his *Bemærkninger om Behandlingen af den danske Retskrivning i de lærde Skoler* [Observations upon the practice of Danish orthography in the grammar schools] was answered by philologist, lexicographer, librarian Christian Molbech in his *Nogle Ord om det, man kalder "Retskrivn-*

ing", (Orthographie) og om de for samme opstillede Grundregler: med et Tillæg, vedkommende
hr. Etatsraad, Prof. Madvigs "Bemærkninger om Behandlingen af den danske Retskrivning i de
lærde Skoler" [A few words about what is called 'correct writing' (Orthography) and about the
ground-rules set up for the same; with a supplement concerning State Councillor, Professor M's
etc.] (1855); member of founding committee of Dansk historisk Forening [Danish Historical
Association] initiated by Molbech (1839); his opposition in the *Rigsforsamling* (1848) to Gr's
advocacy of 'Danishness' (and condemnation of Latinity) and to Gr's concept of the *højskole* (a
term Madvig insisted could apply only to the University in Copenhagen) is perhaps the most
concise, cogent and polarised contemporary expression of a 'European' viewpoint, as alternative
to Gr's 'Nordic' orientation (which Gr then scathingly defended in *Danskeren* 40 (1848).

mageløs 22, 23, 111, 126, 127, 168, 170, 171, 249, 251, 274, 275, 279, 304, 321; 'incomparable, unparalleled, peerless, matchless, unrivalled' – adjective, not uncommon in Gr's day, used (and perhaps
overused) by Gr himself of things, events and circumstances he held to be of great significance;
thus, for example, the Icelandic *Edda*-poem *Völuspá* is "*dette mageløse Digt*" [this incomparable
poem] in *Nordens Mytologi* (1808), Gr found the accessibility and naturalness of Frederik VI
both *mageløs*, the lawsuit against him in 1825 was a "*mageløs Proces*"; but most notably applied
(apparently first, and ironically, by Søren Kierkegaard) to Gr's *opdagelse* [discovery] through
Irenaeus of the significance of 'the living Word' (*det levende Ord*); adopted with enthusiasm by
Gr's followers to honour the prophetic wisdom discerned in him, and therefore also subject to
ridicule by foes (as, repeatedly, by S. Kierkegaard) and by more sceptical friends ("Everything
he hit upon was 'incomparable' [*mageløs*]" – Skat Rørdam, of the indiscriminate enthusiasm of
those about Gr during his breakdown in 1867); but, semantically speaking, not too much should
be made of the word which often carries little more force than 'remarkable, wonderful'.

mageløse Opdagelse, den 22, 23, 123, 125, 249, 251, 274, 275, 279; often translated as 'the matchless,
unparalleled, discovery'; the realisation or conviction Gr reached (1825), partly inspired by reading in Irenaeus, "that God's *word* to man is not to be found first and foremost in the written, biblical word but in the word that is spoken at baptism and Holy Communion. Throughout history,
he argues, the written word has been subjected to the divergent interpretations of theologians.
The living word from the Lord himself – that is, the Creed, the words of personal address at
baptism and the words of initiation [institution] at Holy Communion – have by contrast been
heard and remained unchanged since the days of the early Church. Thus the Christian's firm
foundation is not to be found in the Bible but wherever a congregation gathers around God's
spoken word at baptism and in Holy Communion ... The fundamental element of Grundtvig's
view ... was the unity created by the Holy Spirit between the risen Christ and the Word of Faith
confessed by the Church." (Anders Pontoppidan Thyssen and Christian Thodberg); see also
mageløs; **Irenaeus**; **mageløse Vidnesbyrd**.

mageløse Vidnesbyrd, det 126, 168, 170, 171; peerless, incomparable testimony; testimony Gr
"so laboriously sought after in the whole world of the spirit" affirming unbroken continuity of
sacramental authority of Church from apostolic times; "*this* rang out as a voice from heaven
through the whole of time and of Christendom *in the Apostolic Creed at baptism*" (Gr); see also
mageløs, **mageløse Opdagelse, den**; **Ord,** det levende.

Magnussen, Finn *227, 292*; 1781-1848; Finnur Magnusson, Icelandic lawyer, antiquarian scholar, professor in Copenhagen; appointed (1829) as Privy Archivist (*Gehejmearkivar*); leading published authority on Icelandic medieval literature especially the poetic Edda and northern mythology; in 1833, accompanied by distinguished Danish geologist Johan Georg Forchammer (1794-1865) and Gr's friend , philologist and librarian Christian Molbech, visited Runamo in Blekinge, southern Sweden, to examine a rock believed from time of Saxo Grammaticus to bear a major (though indecipherable) inscription in runes; in *Dansk Ugeblad*, June 1834, he announced decipherment of a fragmentary text achieved by reading the runes backwards, which he construed as an incantation carved by Danish king Harald Hildetand before (semi-legendary, 8th c.) battle of Bråvalla, invoking Óðinn against his enemy Sigurd Ring; but in 1844 young Danish antiquarian J. J. A. Worsaae examined the stone, found Magnusson's illustrations inaccurate and in any case showed convincingly that the marks were not man-made but a commonly occurring natural geological phenomenon. In eyes of most scholars, Magnusson's reputation was irreparably damaged; but, revealingly of his own enthusiasms, Gr long continued to trust Magnusson's judgment and believed that it would one day come back into scholarly acceptance. See also **Worsaae,** J. J. A.

Mands Minde *61, 69, 130, 235, 245, 275*; literally 'Man's memory' usually translated as 'Within living memory' – series of fifty-one public lectures, delivered by Gr in Borchs Kollegium Copenhagen over second half of 1838, comprising review of historical events in his own lifetime, as they impacted upon him both materially and spiritually; therefore of particular importance as autobiographical material; not published in printed form until edition based on Gr's handwritten drafts was undertaken by Svend Grundtvig in 1877; title is essentially Gr's own, being written on first lecture and elsewhere, though in hyphenated form *Mands-Minde*; see also headnote to item 3 and list of Contents.

Mangor, Madame (Anne Marie) *211*; 1781-1865; author of *Kogebog for smaa Huusholdninger indeholdende Anviisning til forskjellige Retters og Kagers Tillavning med angiven Maal og Vægt* [A cookery book for small households containing directions for making various dishes and cakes with specified measure and weight] (1837) and, among others, *Kogebog for Soldaten i Felten* [A cookery book for the soldier in the field] (1864), donated in several thousand copies to the army as her patriotic contribution to national cause in crisis of 1864; also celebrated for "Madam Mangor's three domestic spices"- namely, definite and precisely kept mealtimes; snow-white tablecloth with correct table-setting; and housewife's friendly gentle face.

Manual [Handbook] of Universal History; see *Haandbog i Verdenshistorien*.

Marengo *81*; Italian site of one of Napoleon's earliest and greatest victories (14 June 1800), following his heroic crossing of Alps, against superior forces of Austria; Gr who as a boy had avidly followed Napoleon's career says he was so deeply buried in stultifying classical learning at Aarhus grammar school that he barely noted the latest great dramatic events in contemporary European history.

Marheineke, Philipp Konrad *249, 250*; 1780-1846; German professor of dogmatic theology, Berlin; earlier under influence of Schelling, later Hegel; in his conservative Hegelianism, found sympathiser in H. L. Martensen (who was largely responsible for mediating Hegelian philosophy in Dk); visited Copenhagen and was escorted by Martensen to call on Gr (1836); Gr engaged in vigorous dispute (in impressively articulate German) on merits of speculative theology; they parted amicably but no closer in convictions.

Marie, Queen *167*; Marie Sofie Frederikke of Hessen-Kassel (1767-1852), wife of Frederik vi of Denmark; initially enthusiastic over Gr's preaching in period before his incumbency at Præstø but later took offence at his Cabinet-sermon "on the gospel for the second day of Christmas concerning the persecution of Christianity, first with violence, then with stealth and finally with both, but yet all in vain."

Marielyst *283, 300, 312, 323*; country property near Copenhagen, originally Tagenshus but renamed by Gr after his deceased wife Marie (Toft), bought 1855 for 21,000 *rigsdaler* by Gr with fund including 7000 *rigsdaler* gift from Danish and Norwegian subscribers marking his 70th birthday (September 1853), expressly for foundation of a "*Folkelige Højskole*"; inaugurated 3 November 1856 as *Grundtvigs Højskole*, fulfilling objective of Den Danske Forening [The Danish Association] founded Spring 1853 by Gr, C. J. Brandt (Marielyst's first *forstander* [principal] 1856-59, assisted by Morten Eskesen and Jeppe Tang) and others to promote 'Danishness' among the people; initially took only male pupils but summer courses for females were initiated ten years later; Gr's speeches at Marielyst, though little noted in contemporary public press, represent the final and maturest development of Gr's educational thinking regarding role of the *højskole* in *danskhed* [Danishness], *folkelighed* [sense of national cultural solidarity and participation] and *livsoplysning* [true enlightenment for living a proper human life].

marriage of divorcees; see **fraskiltes Vielse**.

Marstrand, Nicolaj Wilhelm, *211*; 1810-73; prolific Danish painter; professor in the Kunstakademi, director 1863-73; "Of the manifold portraits which exist of [Grundtvig], of which admittedly I have seen not very many, it seems to me that a pen drawing, drawn by Skovgaard [Peter Christian Skovgaard, 1817-75] in 1845-46, resembles him best. The sweetly-pious and the venerable which is found in Marstrand's picture [1862] was certainly not to be found in him in my time" (Marie Blom, alluding to 1830s); see **portraits** of Grundtvig.

Martensen, Hans Lassen *23, 229, 248, 261, 263, 268-270, 277, 279, 301, 312, 330, 339*; 1808-84; Bishop of Sjælland 1854-84; his interest in philosophy having been stirred by the same F. C. Sibbern who was Gr's close and cherished friend from student years onwards, his career is in striking counterpoint to that of Gr; associated admiringly with Gr in 1830s to extent of supporting idea of a Grundtvig hymnal; but eventually, perhaps under influence of conservative Bishop J. P. Mynster (Gr's dogged adversary) he steadily moved away from Gr's position, finally aligned completely with Mynster and ecclesiastical and secular establishment, opposing contemporary tendency towards individualistic interpretations of nature and role of Church; consistently with this stance, he published (1863) *Til Forsvar mod den saakaldte Grundtvigianisme* [In rebuttal of the so-called Grundtvigianism] which long stood as the most thorough critique of Grundtvigian conceptualisation of the Church; similarly, along with all other bishops, publicly protested (though unsuccessfully) against law permitting establishment of *valgmenigheder* (congregations electing and employing own pastor while remaining within the State Church); was also unsuccessful in proposing institution of a synod for Danish Church; but despite various major defeats he gained various signal honours and distinctions; he became distinguished speculative theologian seeking accord between believing and understanding; principal mediator of Hegelian philosophy in Dk, achieving honoured international status for his scholarship (Edmund Gosse declared him to be the greatest philosophical genius that Europe's Protestant Church owned); his *Den christelige Dogmatik* [Christian dogmatics] was published 1849; succeeded Mynster as Bishop of Sjælland 1854, securing nomination over H. N. Clausen who was preferred candidate of national-liberal groupings and king; when, in a sermon delivered a week after Mynster's death, Martensen spoke of Mynster as "*et Sandhedsvidne*" [a witness unto truth], Søren Kierkegaard unleashed his fierce and radical attack upon "official Christianity" to which Martensen responded in a single article, thereafter holding himself aloof from Kierkegaard's denunciations; when in 1861 Gr (to mark his 50-years jubilee and his life-service to Danish Church) was granted title of Bishop, protocol ranked him alongside Martensen (Bishop of Sjælland); his autobiography *Af mit Levnet* [From my life], vol. 3 (1883) describes his relationship with Gr.

matriculation *40, 68, 71, 74, 77, 156, 187, 230, 245; at blive student* [to become a student]; *studentereksamen*; process of admission to University from the *Latinskoler* (also called *de lærde skoler* [grammar schools] which were governed under the same state-appointed *Direktion* [board of governors] as the University); in Gr's day, the examination, called *examen artium* [examination in Arts] was administered not by schools but by University and was assessment of both scholarly knowledge and fitness for admission to University community as academic citizen; first year at University was then devoted to somewhat basic classroom study and concluded with *examen philosophicum* [examination in Philosophy], commonly called *anden examen* [the second examination], after which student moved into chosen specialist field (such as Theology or Law); see also **attestats (attestatus)**; **students**.

medieval character, Gr as *250*; Gr's "particular predilection for the Middle Ages" (H. L. Martensen, 1883) is indeed marked, not only in his interest in medieval history and the medieval literatures of Iceland and England, but in the mind-set in which he approached history and the dynamic role of poetics in the articulation of theology and Christian thought; though it was by no means an expression of mere Romantic historicism nor an exclusively aesthetic literary preoccupation but could provide him with a relativistic basis for comment upon contemporary issues and values, of which a notable example is his pronouncement upon medieval monasticism in *Krønnike-Rim* 1842: "*Kloster* [monastery] means a cloister or enclosure for monks; and these monasteries became, in the later Middle Ages, real pests in the land because they teemed with loafers who wanted to eat without working; but originally the monasteries had everywhere been the only plant-nurseries of Christianity and book-based arts; and when the Protestants would not suffer even those monasteries which laid a burden upon no one, then that was tyrannical of them; and in the end our compulsory Poor-law provision is very much worse than the monastic provision" – an opinion given more ideological expression by Gr's one-time collaborator and supporter A. G. Rudelbach (1792-1862) who (in 1849, the year of Dk's conversion to a democracy) blamed the Church for abandoning the poor to the secular administrators of the Poor-laws and reformatories and thereby helping to create the modern Proletariat (*det moderne Proletariat*) which was perceived as a threat to the stability of the state.

Mehrn *145, 146*; Mern, village in south Sjælland some 11 km south of Præstø where Gr successfully canvassed for election as *Rigsdagsmand* [member of Constituent Assembly] (1848) and where Peter Rørdam (1806-83), admirable chairman of the Election Committee, was priest (1841-56) and married to Jutta Carlsen (sister to Marie Toft who was heiress of Rønnebæksholm and subsequently Gr's second wife).

Melbye, Mads *264*; 1817-79; *cand. theol.* Copenhagen 1840; after short periods as residential tutor and curate in various parts of Dk, ministered as incumbent of Asperup and Orslev on Fyn 1845-79; from student days onwards, devoted follower of Gr; close friend of Carl Joachim Brandt (1817-89; active and powerful supporter of Gr, and Gr's successor in Vartov Church 1872), Ludwig Nicolaus Helveg (1818-83; collaborator with C. J. Brandt in publishing *Den danske Salmedigtning* 1846), and Vilhelm Birkedal who said of him that he was "en hedningekristen af reneste vand" [a heathen-Christian of the purest water] because the Nordic in him was in a special way clarified in his Christianity; zealous in expressing his sense of Danish identity, conceived of a national angel appointed to watch over Danish folk; habitually supported common folk against any kind of aristocratic imposition; it was Melbye who, when Asta, widow of Holger Christian Reedtz (died 1857), sought spiritual counsel in her loss, suggested she should visit and talk to Gr – whom she then married the following year.

Metamorphoses, of Ovid; see **Ovid**.

metaphor, metaphorical; see **Billed-Sprog**.

Milo, Jacob Frederik *168, 224*; 1795-1865; bookbinder, proprietor of Wahlske Boghandel [bookshop, publishing house] in Copenhagen; Milo family, 18th-c. immigrants from East Prussia, were bookbinders, printers, publishers in Odense – notable among them Johan Milo (1788-1861) who published, for example, translated novels of Charles Dickens (1850s) and religious-educational and popular historical works of distinctly Grundtvigian character; for many years (1820s-1850s) Gr's publisher; "This is the distinguishing factor between the book business and all other businesses, that there is a quite different interaction between intellectual interests and trading from that of any other business; ideally, a bookstore is the focal point of intellectual life in a people ... such 'proper' book businesses were operated in those years [1840s] by the big Gyldendal firm, Andr. Fred. Høst, P. G. Philipsen, Schubothes Boghandel, Soldenfeldt, and the Wahlske Boghandel ... Other proper bookstores did not exist ... but they were all far surpassed by G. A. Reitzel's concern" (Otto Bernhard Wroblewski, 1827-1907, *Ti Aar i C. A. Reitzels Boglade* [Ten years in C. A. Reitzel's bookstore], Copenhagen 1889).

Mimir's head *300*; example of Gr's use, in teaching at Marielyst School, of Norse mythological figures metaphorically to convey truths about life; Mimir, wisest of Æsir, was sent to Vanir in exchange of hostages to end war but Vanir, suspecting bad exchange, decapitated Mimir and sent head back to Æsir; Óðinn preserved head and uttered spells over it so it continued to speak deep wisdom to him when consulted; other metaphors used there included strife between Æsir and Vanir, Thor and Midgard Serpent, Óðinn and Fenris Wolf, Freyr and Surtr, and blind Höðr tricked by Loki into shooting Baldr; see also *Nordens Mythologi*.

Minerva *156, 159*; monthly social-political and literary journal founded 1785 by Knud Lyhne Rahbek (1760-1830) and Christian Henriksen Pram (1756-1825), published in Copenhagen; spanning period of French Revolution, it served both as a main source of information from Europe and as a forum of Danish public opinion stirred by liberal movements abroad; survived, though increasingly out of contact with main new philosophical and literary currents of Romanticism, until eventually, according to Gr (though he himself had published there, as for example his *Lidet om Sangene i Edda* [A little about the songs of the *Edda*], 1806), it "commanded the attention of no one, not even of the editors" and ceased publication 1808; title was revived 1819-39; see also **Lærde Efterretninger**.

Mirror of the Church *307*; *Kirke-Speil eller Udsigt over den kristne Menigheds Levnedsløb* [Church mirror, or Survey of the life-history of the Christian congregation]; Gr's *speculum ecclesiae*; see **Kirke-Speil**.

modersmaal *73, 90, 140, 172, 215, 274, 284*; mother-tongue; central to Gr's concept – to some extent influenced by ideas of German philosopher J. G. Herder (1744-1803) – of Danish historical and contemporary identity and of a *folkelige* cohesion of Danish people; correspondingly central to his educational philosophy, both in 'free' schools (folk-highschools) and in home; for same reasons, object of passionate and politicised feelings in and over Slesvig; but also linked inextricably with more mystical concept of the 'heart' of the Christian Danish folk ("the Danish people are a people of the heart" and the *modersmaal* is the language of the heart) through which the Spirit worked, and of the Living Word spoken amid the congregation at Baptism and Eucharist; summarised in lines from his *Christenhedens Syvstjerne* (1860): Folke-Tungen, Moders-Maalet, / Aandens Spejl og Hjertets Sprog, / hverken laant, ej heller stjaalet, / elsk det! favn det! kys det dog! / Kun i det, som Moders-Livet, / Ordet er af Gud os givet, / bliver Kød for os og Aand! [Folk-tongue, mother-speech, / neither borrowed nor stolen, / love it! embrace it! kiss it indeed! / Only in this as womb / is the Word given us from God, / and becomes for us flesh and spirit!]; celebrated in various still-popular 19th-c. Danish songs including Gr's *Moders Navn er et himmelsk Lyd* [Mother's name is a heavenly sound] (1837), Kristen Karstensen's *Længe nok har jeg Bonde-Pige været* [Long enough have I been a peasant serving-wench] (1850; referring to status of Danish language in Slesvig) and Edvard Lembcke's *Vort Modersmaal er dejligt* [Our mother-tongue is lovely] (1859); see also **Hjertet**; **folkelige**, det; **folk-highschools**; **Skamlingsbanken**.

Molbech, Christian *22, 61, 73, 76, 93, 97, 193, 227, 253, 254*; 1783-1857; librarian, professor at Sorø Academy, one of the directors of the Royal Theatre Copenhagen, philologist, lexicographer, with particular interest in historical and dialectal forms of Danish and English; published material from early Danish writings (such as 13th c. herbals of Henrik Harpestreng, 15th c. *Rimkrønike*, 16th c. Danish Bible, 16th-17th c. letters of Christian iv), major works of lexicography notably his Danish dialect dictionary (1841) and his landmark Dictionary of Danish (1859); maintained contact, especially through his position in Royal Library Copenhagen, with English and other European scholars; visited England, France; publisher of monthly periodical *Athene* (1813-17) with leading contributors in fields such as language, history, ancient Nordic literature, myth and legend; founder of Dansk historisk Forening [The Danish Historical Association] 1839 and editor of *Historisk Tidsskrift* 1840-54; friend of Gr from 1808 except for period after 1813 following his hostile review of Gr's *Verdens Krønike* (1812) to which Gr retorted (*Skal vi tro paa Gud eller paa Athene? eller om Tro og Fornuft* [Are we to believe in God or in Athena? or, on faith and reason; Gr is punning on title of Molbech's periodical], Copenhagen, 1814) by accusing Molbech of being in conflict with Christian doctrine; friendship eventually restored, he corresponded with Gr in latter's visits to England (1829-31) particularly over purchase and exchange of books on behalf of Royal Library; 1847-48 Molbech was again in conflict with the Grundtvigs, this time with Gr's son Svend when Samfundet til den danske Litteraturs Fremme [Society for the promotion of Danish literature] supported publication of Svend's edition of Danish ballads and folksongs rather than Molbech's; Molbech, indignant that Svend had traded upon Gr's name and influence, published own rival collection and a critique of Svend's work; Molbech's correspondence with Gr collected by son Christian Frederik Molbech (1821-88), published 1888 by Ludvig Schrøder under title *Christian Molbech og Nikolai Frederik Severin Grundtvig. En Brevvexling.*

Moldenhawer, Daniel Gotthilf *156, 160*; 1753-1823; German-born theologian, professor (1783) Copenhagen University; renowned ("in the capital" adds Gr, ironically) for delivering his lectures in Ciceronian Latin; "but was otherwise called The Jesuit because he did not deny but circumvented the faith of the Church" (Gr); as head of Royal Library Copenhagen, he considerably increased its holdings and (1793) made it accessible to public; Rektor [Vice-Chancellor] of University 1799-1800, when Gr began studies and found Theology Faculty hardly more than a manufactory for turning out examination-guaranteed clergy-material, while Moldenhawer "ran the factory" (Gr).

Moltke, Frederik *122, 166*; 1754-1836; member of aristocratic family originating in Mecklenburg, traceable from 13th c. in Dk and in royal service; from 1799 president of Danish Chancellery but removed 1803 because of his opposition to prime minister Christian Ditlev Reventlow (1748-1827; agrarian reformer, who brought in Forestry Act 1805 controlling Danish forestry management) and Christian Colbiørnsen (1749-1814; leading reformer of law relating to peasantry and landownership rights); appointed Privy Councillor 1810 but forced to resign when, following transfer of Norway from Dk to Sweden (1814), letter he wrote sympathising with Norwegian resistance caused diplomatic embarrassment with Sweden; 1815 appointed *Stiftamtmand* (representative of royal authority in area approximately corresponding with diocese; roughly equivalent to Lord Lieutenant in England) in Aalborg, north Jylland.

Moltke, Carl *240, 241*; 1798-1866; member of aristocratic family originating in Mecklenburg, traceable from 13th c. in Dk and in royal service; *Grev* [Count] with family seat in Holsten; jurist, statesman; opponent of *schleswig-holstein* movement; wished to see Slesvig and Holsten in close association according to ancient declaration, but unified with Dk; 1846 appointed president Slesvig-Holsten-Lauenburg Chancellery to implement Christian VII's resistance to separatist movement in duchies; 1848 *gehejmestatsminister* [prime minister, under absolute monarchy]; 1852-54 Minister for Slesvig; 1864-65 Minister without portfolio; article criticising Moltke's Slesvig policy, written (1853) by (Povl) Frederik Barfod as editor of new journal *Dannebrog*, in foundation of which Gr was involved, led Gr peremptorily to suppress article and dismiss Barfod, who then said bitterly to friends that he would rather have Moltke as his superior than the high-handed Gr.

Momus *214*; *Momos*, figure in Greek myth, god of insult and accusation, faultfinding and mockery, finally thwarted when he could find no imperfection in Aphrodite; Marie Blom, childhood friend of Gr's children, casts herself in classical role amidst the Norse mythologising of the household.

Mona *331*; Anglesea, off northwest coast of Wales, ancient home of druids; see **druid**.

monetary upheaval 1813 *108*; see **Bankruptcy, State**

Monrad, Ditlev Gothard *261, 271, 296, 300, 336, 337*; 1811-87; Bishop, politician; student of oriental languages; in early years, influenced by scientific philosophy of H. C. Ørsted, temporarily lost Christian convictions; entered political activity as editor of *Fædrelandet* (The Fatherland), later of *Dansk Folkeblad* (Danish Folk-paper), and author of political pamphlets supporting National Liberalism and scandinavianism; gained significant ministerial positions; appointed Bishop of Diocese of Lolland 1849 but dismissed on political grounds by administration of A. S. Ørsted (1854); thereafter held a further series of ministerial positions culminating in his brief premiership 31 December 1863 to 11 July 1864; bore responsibility (with former prime minister C. C. Hall) for Danish policy towards Slesvig-Holsten and Prussia (see **Ejderpolitik**) leading to catastrophic and psychologically crushing Danish defeat (1864); emigrated with family to New Zealand but returned 1869, resumed calling of priest; reappointed Bishop of Lolland Diocese 1871; noted for keeping his distance from the major Church movements of the period, the Indre Mission and Grundtvigianism.

Moravians *20, 203*; members of the *Unitas Fratrum*, branch of followers of reformer Johan Hus, originally (15th c.) from Moravia, settled from 1721 on land granted them in Saxony and established township of Herrnhut (hence their Danish name *herrnhuter*), following radical pietist principles in worship, upbringing and way of life; zealous in establishing missions, including one to Danish West Indian colonies (1732) and to Greenland (1733); established meeting-house in Stormgade, Copenhagen, 1739, subsequently attended by respectable and substantial citizens such as Michael Pedersen Kierkegaard (1756-1838) with his family; in 1771 established notable settlement at Christiansfeld in Jylland (became headquarters of Danish brotherhood in 1773), in purpose-built township with population of 756 in 1806, though numbers declining towards mid-19th c.; in 1839 officially delegated by Danish state to supply teachers to schools for native children in West Indian colonies; established themselves also in Norway.

Moses and the Law *138, 140*; Gr's conventional Christian rejection of the sufficiency of the Law to ensure justification before God, and of the letter of the Law which "killeth" associates productively with his theology of *det levende Ord* [the living Word]; see for example his Vartov sermon on 1 May 1844.

mother-tongue; see **modersmaal**.

Munch, Andreas *296*; 1811-84; Norwegian poet, one of a number of artists honoured in period of Norway's 19th-c. emergence into cultural independence from Dk by being appointed professor at Oslo University; probably the A. Munch mentioned by Olaus Arvesen as attending great rally in support of Scandinavian movement, Tivoli, Copenhagen 1856.

Munch, Peter Andreas *296;* 1810-63; distinguished historian of Norway, regarded as a founder of Norwegian nationalist historicism; lecturer in History University of Kristiania (Oslo), professor 1841; one of earliest non-catholic researchers in Vatican Library; among various significant publications, 8-volume work *Det norske Folks Historie* and *Nordens gamle Gude- og Helte-Sagn* [Ancient legends of gods and heroes of North; 1840]; argued against the *fornorskning* [norricising] of the language and for continuing common language with Dk; nevertheless praised work of Ivar Aasen towards standard Norwegian written language; during scholarly clash over *Beowulf,* nevertheless gave Gr testimonial that among antiquarian Nordic experts there "were not many who were worthy to unloose Grundtvig's shoestrings."

municipal lawcourt; see *Hof- og Stadsretten.*

Muus, Carl Augustin Høffding *210, 212, 220;* 1796-1885; *cand. theol.;* church historian, author, librarian; private tutor, while at Copenhagen University, to Henrik and Holger, two sons of Baron Henrik and Baronesse Christine Stampe, of Nysø; lodged briefly, with Stampe boys, in Gr household, also tutored Gr children; methodical, long-suffering of Gr boys' fun over his name (= mouse); under Gr's influence was led to Luther but subsequently in Germany converted to Rome, adopted name Augustine; appointed in University of Würzburg; retained lifelong respect for Gr as spiritual force in whom he and others found a 'catholicising' tendency.

Mynster, Jacob Peter *22, 137, 168, 174-177, 204, 205, 227, 228, 248, 249, 251, 256, 257, 261, 270, 279, 280;* 1775-1854; Danish theologian; *kongelig confessionarius* [chaplain royal] 1828; Bishop of Sjælland from 1834; with brother Ole, brought up by stepfather Professor Frederik Ludvig Bang (1747-1820), Gr's uncle to whose home Gr, as student, came for meals and met Mynster; strong adherent to concept and principles of *enevælde* [absolute monarchy], opponent of rationalism, critical of Hegelianism; like his father-in-law, Bishop (of Sjælland) Friederich Christian Carl Hinrich Münter (1761-1830), was deeply hostile to Gr's concept of Church, and unsympathetic to revivalism and the *folkelige*; though Gr earlier held some esteem for him, a series of major confrontations hopelessly embittered relationship; Mynster refused Gr permission to confirm his own sons, pursued policy of compulsory (and physically enforced) baptism into State Church of children of Danish Baptists; clashed with Gr over *Sognebaandsløsning* (dissolution of parochial ties) and proposed radical revision of baptismal rite anathema to Gr; regarded as able administrator of his office, esteemed preacher, published collections of sermons, also *Om den Kunst at prædike* [On the art of preaching; 1812], though Gr retorted that preaching is no art, and Søren Kierkegaard profoundly disapproved of his sermons as witness to Christian truth; his two-volume *Betragtninger over de christelige Troeslærdomme* [Meditations upon the Christian doctrines; 1833] was among major Danish devotional works of 19th c.; gradually weaned H. L. Martensen (1808-84) away from early adherence to Gr, so when Martensen succeeded him as Bishop (1854) Gr could still expect no support from that quarter; but Mynster's posthumous image was coloured at least as much by Søren Kierkegaard's violent attack (1854-55) upon him and upon the Church, following Mynster's death.

Mynster, Ole Hieronymus *189*; 1772-1818; doctor; physician to Gr around period of his break-down (1810) and to other notable literary figures of the period; brother of Bishop J. P. Mynster.

mythology *73, 100, 118, 159, 183, 185, 186, 227, 250*; "By mythology I understood a map of the kingdom of the spirit and of the route to it, which could be more or less incomplete" (Gr); this remained, in very broad sense, Gr's view, though early and unsatisfactory attempts to harmo-nise Northern myth with Christian story and theology yielded to later more poetic-linguistic perceptions of myth as indigenous (rather than externally borrowed) metaphorical language, usable as was Greek myth or Biblical story poetically to articulate and thus advance real life and contemporary ideas, values, issues, especially as outlined in the highly important Introduction to *Nordens Mythologi* 1832; intellectually and poetically remarkable though his accomplishments in this field were in their 19th c. setting, it can hardly be claimed that his attempts thus to enrich Danish language and culture bore particularly significant lasting fruits, other than in Grundtvi-gian folk-highschool tradition, where it is also fast disappearing; see also ***Nordens Mytologie***; ***Nordens Mythologi***; **Christianity** as mythology.

Mythology of the North 1808; see ***Nordens Mytologie***.

Mythology of the North 1832; see ***Nordens Mythologi***.

Møen *306*; Møn, Danish island lying between Sjælland and Falster, noted for its white chalk cliffs.

Møllers, the two *166*; professor of theology Jens Møller (1779-1833), reviewer for periodical *Dansk Litteratur-Tidende*, and professor of Theology Peter Erasmus Müller (1776-1834), editor of same journal, substantial scholar and later Bishop of Sjælland; punning on names (both mean 'miller') Jens Baggesen slightingly called them 'water-miller' and 'wind-miller' in verse polemic published in *Nyeste Skilderie af Kiøbenhavn* (5 December 1818) as sortie in literary feud with *Tylvten*, The Twelve; see **Müller,** Peter Erasmus.

Møller, Jens *97, 98*; 1779-1833; theologian, historian; early enthusiast for Northern myth and legend, competed (1801) with Adam Oehlenschläger for University essay prize on topic "Var det gavnligt for Nordens skiønne litteratur om den gamle nordiske mythologie blev indført og af vore Digtere i Almindelighed antaget i Steden for den græske?" [Would it be profitable for Northern fine literature if ancient Norse mythology were introduced and in general accepted by our poets in place of the Greek?] (he argued it would be profitable); 1802 won University gold medal for philological dissertation; while employed as teacher in Slagelse school won (1806) gold medal of Videnskabernes Selskab [Royal Danish Society of Science and Letters] for histori-cal dissertation and also wrote (1806) *Skirners Reise eller Kiærlighed Gudernes Straf, en Fortælling* [Skirnir's journey or Love, the punishment of the gods, a narrative tale], a frivolous version of Icelandic poem *Skírnismál* in *Poetic Edda* which, published in periodical *Ny Minerva* (May 1806), aroused Gr's ire; subsequently professor of theology in Copenhagen and major reviewer for P. E. Müller's journal *Dansk Litteratur-Tidende* of which he eventually became editor (1830-33); see ***Skirnirs Rejse***.

Møller, Lars *284*; mentioned by C. J. Brandt (Gr's successor as pastor of Vartov Kirke), when recalling events from 1846, as exemplifying a self-righteous, unpatriotic and self-concocted Christianity nurtured by zealotry of the *forsamlinger* [religious revivalist gatherings].

Møller, Lars Otto *327*; 1831-1915; priest in Gylling; author; much influenced by Gr though he could be critical of Gr's sermons (in 1850s) for going over heads of congregation; never called himself 'Grundtvigian' and could exclaim "God deliver us from happy Christianity" [Gud fri os for den glade Kristendom]; his voluminous correspondence with clerical contacts all round country, including Bishop Thomas Skat Rørdam, constitutes major source for contemporary history of Danish Church.

Müller, Johannes von *105, 106*; 1752-1809; author of a history of Switzerland, *Die Geschichte der Schweizer* (1780), which Gr read 1810-11, finding himself "for the first time in the company of a comparatively historical mind" which sowed seed of Gr's conviction "concerning the necessity of Christianity in the history of the nations."

Müller, Ludvig Christian *216, 218, 220, 293*; 1806-51; priest, teacher, popular historian, philologist with outstanding expertise in Hebrew, competent in Syrian language, Icelandic and Anglo-Saxon (published *Collectanea Anglo-Saxonica*, Copenhagen 1835, based on Gr's transcriptions of the Exeter Book); while at University (*cand. theol.* 1827; alumnus at Borchs Kollegium thereafter) earned income as private tutor – like Laurent, Muus, Hagen and Ley – to Gr's children (and others including, 1827-28, Hans Christian Andersen who was belatedly acquiring further education in Copenhagen and who called Müller "one of the noblest and most lovable people [...] this unspoiled, gifted young man who was of just as peculiar a nature as I was"); published (1831; *Bibliografi* item 498A) a small collection of hymns influenced by his friendship with Gr; became committed to Gr's educational ideology, was later principal of Snedsted-Ranum *seminarium* [teacher-training college]; "few held me in such affection" Gr wrote of him.

Müller, Peter Erasmus *156, 173, 222-224*; 1776-1834; Doctor of Theology, philologist, historian; 1801 Professor in Ethics and Dogmatics, Copenhagen; Bishop of Sjælland (1830-34); leading scholar in field of early Scandinavian literature; his *Sagabibliothek* (1817-20) was landmark in modern scholarly study of Icelandic sagas; editor (1805-30) *Dansk Litteratur-Tidende*; identified by Gr and supporters in 1820s as pillar of theological Rationalism, therefore often target of their attack; his favourable review of Thorkelin's *editio princeps* of *Beowulf* (1815) provoked Gr's attack in series of articles in *Nyeste Skilderie af Kiøbenhavn* (1815).

Münter, Friederich Christian Carl Hinrich *156, 159, 170, 193, 194, 200-202*; 1761-1830; church historian and archaeologist, Bishop of Sjælland (1803-30); born in Gotha, Thuringia (Germany), where his father Balthasar (1735-1793) was chaplain to ducal court; educated privately in Copenhagen after father moved there 1765 to become pastor in Sankt Petri Kirke serving German congregation (including many leading German figures in Danish society and religious and cultural life); nurtured by father for priesthood (being provided, as young boy, with home pulpit in which to learn art of preaching), his own interests also included archaeology (he made considerable collections of antiquities over his lifetime) and poetry; graduated with distinction from University (philology, theology) 1781; after fashion of period, travelled in Germany, securing meetings with Goethe and other distinguished men, and studied further at Göttingen where for a time subjects inspired by his Freemasonry attracted him; researched in medieval church history; doctor of philosophy (Fulda, Germany) 1784; travelled in Italy, forming friendship with prominent figures in Roman church and finding nurture to his interest in antiquities; 1790 appointed professor in Copenhagen and same year achieved doctorate in theology there, emerging as adherent of Rationalism; published 1798 *Theses over den naturlige Theologie* [Theses upon natural theology] and 1801-04 *Haandbog i den ældste christelige Kirkes Dogmehistorie* [Handbook in the history of dogma of the earliest Christian Church; 2 vols.]; his historically-inclined writings, on theology, church history, national history gained him wide recognition at home and abroad and contributed to his appointment (1808) as Bishop of Sjælland to succeed N. E. Balle (1744-1816); but many, including Gr ("Münter the *hjemtysker* ['home-German' – Dane of German origin and cultural affiliations], famous for his ecclesiastical-historical learning, from which however neither he himself nor others gained any benefit, but known to us [students] only for his muddle-headedness" and "the bookish, muddle-headed, bombastic, good-natured but impotent and faint-hearted *hjemtysker* and freemason, Frederik Münter"), were disappointed by his combination of dry bookishness, lack of deeper philosophical understanding and engagement, and remoteness from ordinary folk; his one significant contribution to liturgical character of *folkekirke* was a reworking, along conservative Anglican and Roman Catholic lines, of ritual for consecration of bishops, which thereafter caused much disquiet within the Danish church; worked to improve education and pastoral efficacy of priests; being unsympathetic, as responsible bishop, to Gr's *Kirkens Gienmæle* (1825) challenging rationalism in form of Professor H. N. Clausen's *Catholicismens og Protestantismens Kirkeforfatning, Lære og Ritus* [Constitution, doctrine and rites of Catholicism and Protestantism; 1825], he responded (after initially ambiguous reaction to Gr's complaints; and while at the same time urging Gr not to resign his curacy at Vor Frelsers Kirke) with encyclical making plain assertion of rationalist stance, and implicitly defending secular and ecclesiastical establishment against dissidents within; his son-in-law was J. P. Mynster (1775-1854), Bishop of Sjælland from 1834, who continued the establishment's opposition to Gr, of which Münter had set the tone; see also **Baltzer's son**.

N

Nakke-Hoved Light *143*; Nakkehoved Fyr; two lighthouse towers built 1771-1772 on north coast of Sjælland to assist (in conjunction with Kullens Fyr on coast of Skåne) navigation into Øresund; easterly lighthouse, disused from 1898, stands as one of world's few surviving coal-fired lights; see **Kullen Light**.

Napoleon Bonaparte *81-83, 86, 108, 156, 162, 185*; 1769-1821; Gr recorded his youthful fascination with the great achiever Napoleon; charted his own obscure early career (ironically) against the Napoleonic drama ("When Napoleon Bonaparte was fighting with Admiral Nelson at Abukir … I for my part moved to the Latin School in Aarhus"); deplored the stultifying lack of interest in the great European struggle he met at Aarhus Grammar School; made Napoleon a norm for metaphorical reference ("the whole of world history was so familiar to him [*P. N. Skougaard*] and thus seemed to have been conquered by him like a Napoleon in the world of books"); was conscious of the impact of Napoleon and Nelson upon Denmark's and his own sense of national identity; devoted significant space in his lecture series *Mands Minde* (1838) to Napoleon; and though labelling him a "godless tyrant" always retained for him a certain awe, seeing him as an instrument of God's will within European history.

Nathansen (correctly Nathanson), Mendel Levin *238*; 1780-1868; born of Jewish family in Altona (Duchy of Holsten), brought to Copenhagen as child, established career within commercial concerns of family; established own wholesale business at age of 18, in 1799 set up trading connections with England where he thereafter often visited and where his earlier enthusiasm for France, the Revolution and Napoleon began to yield to sympathy for English constitutional government, liberty, commercial enterprise and cultural life including literature and theatre; dedicated to securing civil rights for Jews and encouraging their integration in Danish national life, founded freeschool for Jewish boys 1805, participated in establishment of *Carolineskolen* [The Caroline School] for Jewish girls 1810, had considerable influence on law of 1814 granting Jews civil rights; cultivated interest in Danish theatre and opened his home to many leading figures on Danish cultural scene including Jens Baggesen, Henrik Hertz; wrote on issues of national economy; editor of leading Danish newspaper (and, during absolutism, mouthpiece of government), *Berlingske Tidende*, during two turbulent periods in Denmark's political and military history (1838-58 and 1865-66); "Nathansen too had his vanity: no one was to think that he was ever anxious to get hold of material or that one did *him* a service when one wrote an article for his paper; it was *he* who did a service to the person concerned when he printed his article" [Frederik Barfod]; named as *Etatsraad* [State councillor; honorific title]1860.

National Assembly *239*; *den grundlovgivende Rigsforsamling*; assembly which debated and passed Constitution of June 1849, replacing absolute monarchism with parliamentary monarchism; see **Rigsforsamling**, den grundlovgivende.' [Note to editor: the displacement caused here by this change will be largely readjusted by changes to be made to the entry '**Rigsforsamling**, den grundlovgivende' - see below]

naturalism *117, 118, 156*; *den naturalistiske tankegang, naturalisme*; the naturalistic way of thinking, naturalism; Gr counted this naturalism as a form of heathenism, but it was not (in his view) a belief-system based solely upon acceptance of a mechanistic universe subject only to the laws of physics, for it was alert to a spiritual dimension of some sort, though this alertness is not pursued in thought to a true conclusion (that is, to an acceptance of the Christian understanding of eternal truths); more formally the term covered the philosophy that man can save himself by natural means, by his own powers; but conscience alone, says Gr, taught him at the age of 22 that "it is hot air, all that is said about our natural powers of satisfying the unalterable law of purity and love."

Nelson, Horatio *81*; 1758-1805; English admiral, achieved fame (1798) by destroying French fleet at Aboukir (Abu Qir), event known in British naval annals as Battle of the Nile, whereby Britain gained control of Mediterranean; as second in command to Admiral Hyde Parker took part in assault on Copenhagen 1801 to disable Dk as ally of Napoleon; killed in sea-battle off Cape Trafalgar 1805.

neologists *68*; *Neologerne*; dismissive name given by opponents to adherents of new theological criticism entering Dk from German universities *ca.* 1740-80, transitionally between Pietism and Rationalism; advocated renewal of theology by non-denominational critical study of Scripture and Church history, opposing fashionable deism and naturalism, upholding faith in Christ as divine incarnation and in immortality of soul, but sceptical of other traditional theology such as that of original sin and Christ's making satisfaction for sins of world; Gr spoke dismissively of Bishop N. E. Balle's *gøttingske Begreber*, notions acquired in Göttingen where he had been influenced by critical-historical methods of church historian Christian Wilhelm Franz Walch [1726-84] and orientalist Johann David Michaëlis (1717-91); also influential upon Balle was work of Johann Salomo Semler (1725-1791), theology professor I Halle, who stressed role of historical criticism in study of Bible and its teachings, interpreted its supernatual revelation as expression of moral truths consistent with reason and offering basis for personal religion, to be construed by Church and theologians according to needs of contemporary society.

Nero *85, 157*; Nero Claudius Drusus Germanicus; A.D. 37-68, Roman emperor from A.D. 54, demonised for his depravities and brutal persecution of Christians; Gr's deep resentment of dominant Latin-based culture and religious aversion to Rome were both served by historical perspectives of Henrik Steffens who, in his Copenhagen lectures, saw the divine in human life as having been "crucified by the uninspired, downright ungodly Romans who achieved in Nero, as the ultimate, that devilish perfection they had aspired to and fought for" and who shocked his Danish audiences by declaring that "France, with its whole revolution and with all its wisdom and beauty was merely an imitation of the Roman hell with Nero in the high seat."

New School in Germany *85*; newly emergent German Romantic movement, mediated in Dk through lectures by Henrik Steffens in Ehlers' Kollegium Copenhagen, winter 1802; Gr records that Steffens had been in close association with leading figures of new movement, philosopher Friedrich Schelling (1775-1854), authors Ludwig Tieck (1773-1853) and Novalis (Friedrich von Hardenberg, 1772-1801) and authors and critics, brothers August Wilhelm Schegel (1767-1845) and Friedrich Schlegel (1772-1827) who were otherwise previously little known in Dk. "except by rumour – as a raving mad antithesis to the whole of the eighteenth century's Poesy, History, Physics, Philosophy, Theology, Art and Science" [Gr].

New Year's Eve; poem by Gr (1810); see **Nyaars-Nat**.

*New Year's Morn; poem by Gr; see **Nyaars-Morgen**.*

Nielsen, Rasmus *25, 301*; 1809-84; Danish philosopher; *cand. theol.*; professor of philosophy (1841) in Copenhagen, concerned with problems of faith and knowledge, student of mathematics, chemistry, physiology; distinguished lecturer, productive writer (including *Grundideernes Logik* [Logic of fundamental ideas] 1862-64, *Religionsphilosophie* 1869); one of circle of clergy, theologians, philosophers which Dowager Queen Caroline Amalie gathered about herself; originally, together with Hans Lassen Martensen (later Bishop), a Hegelian, but subsequently, powerfully influenced by philosophy of Søren Kierkegaard, changed his understanding of theology; perceived the religious life as a form of existence grounded upon the will and basic personality and quite independent of the principle of knowledge; he formulated proposition that "Tro og Viden ere som Principer absolut ueensartede" – belief (*tro*) and knowledge (*viden*) are absolutely discrete principles which can therefore be maintained together within one and the same consciousness without contradiction – and "Den larmende Strid mellem Aabenbaring og Fornuft, Religion og Videnskab, beroer paa en Misforstaaelse" [The clamorous conflict between revelation and reason, religion and science, rests upon a misconception]; likewise, "Uenigheden mellem de forskjellige Kirkepartier hos os er [...] ingenlunde saa betydelig, som man efter de Toneangivendes stærke Udtalelser ligefrem skulde formode. Ved at besinde sig paa Forholdet mellem Troesprincipet og Troens Indhold vil man efterhaanden komme til at indsee, at Troesindholdet ikke kan tilføres Menigheden udenfra gjennem officielle Lærebøger og store Dogmatiker, men maa udvikle sig organisk indenfra – af Troesbekjendelsens enfoldige Grundord" [Disagreement between the various church parties among us are in no way as significant as one might immediately assume from the stark pronouncements of the trendsetters. By reflecting upon the relationship between the principle of belief and the content of belief one will eventually come to see that the content of belief cannot be conveyed to the congregation from without, through official textbooks and great dogmatists, but must develop organically from within, from out of the simple basic words of the creed] (Nielsen, 1869); thus he came into heated and protracted conflict with both dogmatic theologians such as H. L. Martensen (whom he metaphorically damned as dogmatist and objectivist in a Dantesque allegory set in the underworld, *Et Levnetsløb i Underverdenen* 1853) and free-thinkers such as Georg Brandes – and, whilst at same time offering much that was grist to Gr's mill, with Gr himself.

Noer (Nør) *199*; ancient estate and aristocratic seat between Eckernförde and Kiel in Slesvig-Holsten; see **Frederik,** Prince of Nør, and **Augustenborg,** Duke of.

Nohr, Christian Valdemar *65, 66, 80*; parish clerk (*Degn*) at Udby, Gr's childhood home; b. 1751; matriculated student 1771; took Part I of philosophy examination at Copenhagen University; appointed at Udby 1776.

Nordens Folke-Krøniker *111*; folk-chronicles of the North; like *folkebøgerne*, Gr's designation of legendary-historical works of Saxo Grammaticus and Snorri Sturluson which, together with *Beowulf*, he translated and published between 1815-22; here *folke-* probably signifies 'national' rather than 'popular, of the people' though the nuances easily shaded into one another in Gr's usage; see also **Saxo Grammaticus; Snorri Sturluson.**

Nordens Kirkehøvding *289*; Church-chieftain of the North; reference to Gr; see **Høvding.**

Nordens Mythologie *118, 159, 185*; *Nordens Mytologi eller Udsigt over Eddalæren for dannede Mænd der ei selv ere Mytologer* [Mythology of the North or an overview of the Edda-lore for educated people who are not themselves mythologists], published 1808, shortly after Gr's return to Copenhagen from Egeløkke, expresses the comprehensive (and idiosyncratic) quasi-religious understanding of the *Asalære* [Æsir-doctrine] Gr had constructed during phase of intensive reading in Old Icelandic literature especially the Edda-poems; he later wrily diagnosed his state at that time as an *Asarus* [Æsir-intoxication, Æsir-frenzy]; his study of the same myths in 1832 vividly reveals how far and fundamentally his thinking had shifted in the critical intervening years.

Nordens Mythologi eller *Sindbilled-Sprog 227, 257*; Mythology, or Symbolic Language, of the North, one of Gr's most important writings (1832). Though sharing part of its title with work Gr published in 1808, far from being a revised edition of that work, it is rather a wholesale replacement of it, reflecting radical intellectual restructurings entailed in Gr's personal spiritual crisis (1810), the *mageløse Opdagelse* (1825), the clash with Clausen and rationalism over the church (1826) and the visits to England (1829-31), and representing Gr's fundamentally changed perception of the meaning and utility of northern myth – seen now as the legacy of a phase in the historical cultural evolution of the North within the universal-historical frame of Christendom's conquest of heathendom. In Gr's exposition, the myth (now also incorporating Anglo-Saxon matter), though defunct as embodiment of a religion, remains a brilliantly conceived and articulated repository of abiding Northern values, spiritual and worldly, which – taken metaphorically or symbolically – can still serve uniquely well, in conjunction with that other great communal possession of the *folk*, the mother-tongue, to give creative and poetic expression to the Danish heart and mind. It is a primary resource, like the mother-tongue itself, for individual self-identification with the historical identity of the whole *folk*, which should therefore be taught to each rising generation; and indeed the lengthy preface to the work is in effect a manifesto – one of Gr's most important propositions to his age – in which he is radically preoccupied with the educational development of the whole human being in the context of human community, upon which the nurturing of the more specifically Christian engagement with life can follow. Such use of northern myth in education has been a hallmark of the Grundtvigian folk-high-schools and has left maxims in Danish common parlance such as "Justice for Loki as well as for Thor." See also **Aser, Vaner**; *Balder hin gode*; **Danneskjold,** Christian Conrad Sophus; **Drypner**; *Edda;* **einherjar; Folkvang; Greek language; Grendel's Mother; Grundtvigian(ism); Høder; Jættevæsen; Loke; Mimir's head; Odin; Snorri Sturluson; Suhm,** Peter Frederik; **Udgaards-Loke; Vaulundur; Vaulundurs Saga; Ymer.**

Nordens Sindbilledsprog; see *Nordens Mythologi.*

Nordens Aand *16, 123, 125, 147, 152, 163*; Spirit of the North; Gr's concept of an informing spirit distinguishing and uniting people of North, surety of a noble destiny; embodied in mother-tongue, manifest in history, in Northern myth and legend and, potentially, in all spheres of human activity, in war and peace, but especially in matters of heart and mind, religion, literature, and all that is truly *folkelige*; closely associated with Christianity; Anglo-Saxon (and Norman) England had crucial role in its nurture: "Thi det var i England, baade Kristendommen og Levningerne af Oldtidens Vidskab fandt et Fristed, da de var husvilde paa Jorden; det var jo engelske Præster, som kristnede baade Tyskland og Norden, og det var jo den angelsaksiske Literatur, som den første i Folkeverdenen, der blev Moder baade til den frankiske og den islandske. Det var altsaa Nordens Aand, i Forbund med Kristendommen, som ved de nordiske Udflyttere paa Øen skabte vor Folkeverden" [For it was in England that both Christianity and the remains of antiquity's scholarship found sanctuary when they were homeless upon the earth; it was English priests who christened both Germany and the North, and it was Anglo-Saxon literature, as the first in the world of the *folkelige*, which became mother to both Frankish and Icelandic literatures. That is to say, it was the Spirit of the North, in conjunction with Christianity, which, through the northern migrants into the island, shaped our world of the *folkelige*] (J. P. Bang summarising from *Nordens Mythologi* (1832), Gr's great exposition of *Nordens Aand*); Gr long nursed hope that England, having gone astray after Norman period, would yet be moved by residual spirit of North to return to Northern fold; see also **Northern literature**, ancient.

Norder-Houg *151*; Norderhov, Ringerike, Norway; *præstegaard* [parsonage], visited by Gr 1851; associated with Norwegian national heroine Anna Kolbjørnsdatter (1665-1736) whose resourcefulness and courage helped save Norway from Swedish conquest in wars of 1710-20.

Nordic antiquity and antiquities *14, 83, 96-98, 102, 117, 124, 133, 157*; Gr's interest in northern antiquities more widely was a natural concomitant of his particular interest in the northern literary antiquities to which he was awakened at University by P. N. Skougaard; though his intention to study them in Copenhagen after graduating was thwarted by need to earn living as tutor at Egeløkke he shared in 19th-c. perception of national antiquities as component in definition of national identity and as sources and verifications of national history; thus he retained lifelong interest in such antiquities as (supposed) runes at Runamo in Blekinge, southern Sweden, and sites associated with St Olaf in Norway; see also **Suhm,** Peter Frederik; **Magnussen,** Finn; **Stephens,** George; **Northern literature**, ancient.

Nordic Church News; see **Nordisk Kirketidende, Den**.

Nordic Weekly; see **Nordisk Ugeskrift**.

Nordiske Digte *101*; collection of poems published 1807 by Adam Oehlenschläger; included *Thors Reise til Jotunheim, et episk Digt* [Thor's journey to Jotunheim, an epic poem], *Hakon Jarl hin Rige, et Sørgespil* [Earl Hakon the Mighty, a tragedy], and *Baldur hin Gode, et mythologisk Sørgespil* [Baldr the Good, a mythological tragedy]; its preface declared, in the new spirit of the times, that the greatest concerns of the poet were historical and national; its content celebrated "the ancient North which he ... had visited upon the wings of an eagle and surveyed with the eye of a falcon" [Gr].

Nordiske Kirke-Tidende, Den *174, 176*; weekly periodical 'for church and school' edited 1833-41 by J. C. Lindberg to promote views and values of Gr who was regular contributor; Gr says periodical, together with his own preaching, manifestly paved way for new perception of basis for a living Church and churchly freedom; first issue (6 January) for 1839 contains poem Gr wrote in self-consolation after Bishop Mynster refused him permission to confirm own sons.

Nordisk Ugeskrift *232*; Nordic weekly, mouthpiece of movement for language-reform advocated by distinguished linguistic scholar Rasmus Rask, published for Society for Promotion of an improved Orthography [*Sælskabet for en forbedret retskrivnings udbredelse*]; co-edited 1834-37 by Peter Ludvig Møller (1814-65) who wrote in it (1837) a lengthy biographical memorial poem to Rask; also co-edited (1837-38) by Frederik Barfod who records that Gr, though in principle not opposed to journal, would not contribute an article if his orthography had to be brought into conformity with journal's.

Norske Rigstidende *149*; Norwegian journal published in Kristiania (Oslo) between 1815-82; published (in issue No. 47) a verse welcome to Gr on his visit to Norway (1851).

Northern literature, ancient *25, 27, 62, 63, 83, 89, 96, 133, 151, 152, 296, 329, 334*; " Saxo and Snorri, the Eddas and the whole range of Iceland's sagas·which I knew only by name were a sphere of knowledge in which he [P. N. Skovgaard] moved about as freely and easily as in his own home territory" and through Skovgaard the student Gr's historical and literary sensibilities were stirred and one of the great preoccupations of his life was established; justly he recognised Copenhagen's great collection of Old Norse (Old Icelandic) manuscripts bequeathed by Arne Magnusson for public use (1730) to be "an Icelandic book-treasure from the Middle Ages" [*en Islandsk Bogskat fra Middelalderen*]; but ancient Northern literature also comprised writings in Latin, Danish, Swedish, and Anglo-Saxon (which Gr regarded as having migrated from a northern home in Slesvig); certain that within this literature resided both the historical record of *Nordens Aand* [the spirit of the North] and the latent potential of this spirit to breathe a new vitality into contemporary Northern life, Gr became, through his translations, interpretative and critical writings and original poetic compositions one of the greatest mediators of this ancient literature to the 19th c. See also **Icelandic book-treasure**; **Snorri Sturluson**; **Saxo Grammaticus**; ***Edda***; **Olav,** Saint; **Nordic antiquity**; **Nordens Aand**; ***Nordens Mythologie***; ***Nordens Mythologi***; ***Svenska folkets historia***; **Fredegod**; **Goths**; *Beowulf*.

North, spirit of the; see **Nordens Aand**.

Norway, Norwegians, Norwegian *passim*; ancient kingdom of Norway was in union with Denmark from 1380 to 1814 when by Treaty of Vienna Dk paid part of price for allying with Napoleon by being compelled to cede Norway to Sweden; despite historical tensions between Dk and Norway, a gathering of Norwegians at Eidsvold resisted the so-called 'personal union' [*personalunion*] with Sweden, proclaimed a free constitution and elected the Danish viceroy, Prince Christian Frederik (later Christian VIII of Dk) King of Norway; Swedish armed intervention forced acceptance of Vienna terms (though the constitution and continuation of the Storthing [parliament] were secured by negotiation) and the union lasted until its dissolution in 1905; the Danish-Norwegian divorce was traumatic for many on both sides and dream of reunion in one form or another remained a motivating force in Scandinavian cultural, religious and political life for some generations, though there were also strong movements towards separation of Norway's linguistic, cultural and political identity from those of both Denmark and Sweden (articulated by such as Norwegian historian and poet Henrik Wergeland (1808-45) who ridiculed Norwegian 'Danomanes' for desiring to keep Norway "a literary province of Dk" and for "rehashing Gr's old songs on the Danes as Scandinavia's leading nation in ancient times, and on the universal sovereignty of the Danish language"); Gr, while at university in Copenhagen, made valued friends and acquaintances among Norwegians there, a number of whom moved to new University of Kristiania (Oslo) after 1814; and, particularly conscious that much historic testimony to *Nordens Aand*, spirit of the North, was resident in rich early literature of Norway (and of Norwegian settlement in Iceland), Gr retained throughout his life a special affection for Norway ("the foster-brotherhood with ancient Norway"), greatly enhanced by his profoundly moving reception there on invited visit 1851; see also **Norwegian circle**; **Bjørnson,** Bjørnstjerne Martinius; **Arvesen,** Olaus (Olaf); **Anker,** Herman.

Norwegian circle *100, 148, 151, 159*; the Norwegian circle of friends "which at that time was the ornament of our university" to which Gr was introduced as student in Copenhagen; in part accounts for Gr's feeling throughout his life that he "had a relationship with Norway quite his own" (Gr) ; included his bosom friend S. B. Hersleb (1784-1836) after whom Gr's son Svend Hersleb was named, the subsequently distinguished philosopher F. C. Sibbern (1785-1872), both alumni of Valkendorfs Kollegium where Gr resided, N. Treschow (1751-1833), professor of Philosophy in Copenhagen (1803-13), subsequently in newly-founded University of Kristiania (Oslo), and philologist G. Sverdrup, professor of Greek in Copenhagen (1805-13), subsequently in Kristiania; see also **Norway**.

Norwegian Parliament; the *Storthing*; see **Norway, Norwegians, Norwegian**.

Novalis *84, 85*; 1772-1801; pseudonym for Friedrich von Hardenberg; leading figure, together with friends Friedrich Schlegel and Ludwig Tieck, in emergence of German Romanticism; successful student of jurisprudence in Jena (where influenced by philosophy lectures of Johan Gottlieb Fichte), Leipzig, Wittenberg; studied geology and mining, gained high post in salt-mining concern; but early death from tuberculosis furthered his projection to literary public as romantic, unworldly, dreaming visionary, notably through his six *Hymnen an die Nacht* (1800), blending mystical with erotic; his *Die Christenheit oder Europa* (1799) contributed to characteristic interest of Romantic artists in Christian Middle Ages; his work, placed alongside that of Shakespeare, Cervantes, Goethe and Tieck, was first made known to Gr through lectures of Henrik Steffens in Copenhagen 1802.

Now pray we to the Holy Ghost; see *Nu bede vi den Helligaand*.

Nu bede vi den Helligaand *326*; Now pray we to the Holy Ghost; 12th c. German hymn reworked by Martin Luther 1524, entered Danish use in translation 1529, reworked by Ove Malling (1798) and Gr (1836; published in *Sang-Værk til den danske Kirke*, 1837); example of a Danish *lejse* (loanword derived from shortening of Middle High German *kyrleise*), hymn originating in Middle Ages as vernacular addition to liturgical petition *Kyrie eleison* [Lord, have mercy!] sung in Mass, but eventually developing into free-standing text to which the Greek words are a kind of refrain and can be replaced, as here, by their vernacular translation; remained in popular use after Reformation; no. 289 in *DDS* 2002; see also **hymns**.

Nyeste Skilderie af Kjøbenhavn *110, 165*; twice-weekly Copenhagen periodical edited and published (1804-25) by Salomon Soldin (1774-1837) which Soldin "kept open for everything that could find readers" (Gr); carried articles, sometimes ongoing debate, by Soldin and such prominent literary figures as K. L. Rahbek, Christian Molbech and Gr whose exchanges there (1815) with *Gehejmearkivar* [Privy, or State, Archivist] G. J. Thorkelin (1752-1829) over latter's *editio princeps* of *Beowulf* (1815) constitute first scholarly (if acrimonious) debate on Anglo-Saxon poem's text and interpretation.

Nygaard, Frederik Sextus Otto Alfred Petersen *200, 206, 219, 220, 224, 226*; 1845-97; Danish priest, folk-highschool teacher and principal, historian especially of Grundtvigianism, editor of diaries of Christian Ley (*Danskeren* VII, 1892, 45-51); was earlier attached to Indre Mission movement but influenced by preaching of Peter Rørdam moved towards Grundtvigianism and joined

Vartov congregation; commitment to Grundtvigian ideas strongly affirmed when he became teacher at Ryslinge folk-highschool (1870-72) under influence of Vilhelm Birkedal.

Nysø *145, 146, 255, 276, 284*; estate forming part of Stampenborg, north of Præstø, South Sjælland; seat of the baronial family Stampe; under patronage of Christine and Henrik Stampe, a resort for leading figures in Danish cultural life – among others, sculptor Bertel Thorvaldsen, artists P. C. Skovgaard and N. W. Marstrand, poets Adam Oehlenschläger, B. S. Ingemann, Jens Baggesen and H. C. Andersen, architect M. G. Bindesbøll, art critic N. L. Høyen, philosophers Henrik Steffens and F. C. Sibbern, and Gr (from his time at Udby and Præstø onwards); there Gr, asked to find name for studio built in grounds for Thorvaldsen's use, proposed *Völunds Værksted*, Wayland's workshop, after the fabulous smith of Norse legend (whose story Oehlenschläger had revived in his prose narrative *Vaulundurs Saga*, 1805.

Nyaars-Morgen *123, 165, 168*; New Year's Morn; poem by Gr published 1824 which, according to his foreword, is a series of visions evoked by a desperate, almost crushed and yet now resurgent yearning for regeneration of the North ("Indifference towards everything of the spirit and even for the land of our fathers seemed to inundate us all so that I too was close to despair over the saving of the communal life [*Folkelivets Redning*], as can still be seen from the Foreword") and, according to a letter to Ingemann, was a God-given revelation; highly poetical in both form and expression though the work is – regarded by some as his highest poetical utterance – revelation is not an appropriate term for the mystical, obscure, and self-referential tissue of allusions, the elucidation of which, in an attempted commentary, Gr himself abandoned.

Nyaars-Nat *161*; *Nytaars-Nat eller Blik paa Kristendom og Historie* [*New Year's Eve or A Glance at Christianity and History*], published by Gr Christmas 1810; collection of poems including one on *Sorø Kirke* and one on his father's fiftieth anniversary of ordination; reflecting brief period of his "*Sværmer-Liv*" [life of religious enthusiasm] when, disturbed by Kotzebue's account of violent 13th-c. christianisation of Prussia and reference to "the withered Cross," he characteristically sought refutation in Christian-orientated historicism, and was fired with zeal to reform and revitalise Danish Church ("especially with pen and ink") on foundation of Bible and hymns of Luther and Kingo; but by time *Nytaars-Nat* came out he was instead slipping irreversibly into deep crisis of personal faith.

Nør (Noer); see **Frederik, Prince of**.

Nørregade *238, 264, 280*; street in central Copenhagen, close to Vor Frue Kirke, University and student quarter; Gr lived here (1856-57) in rented apartment in *Den Forgyldte Nøgle* (The Gilt Key), following death of second wife Marie.

O

O, lad din Aand nu med os være! *264*; O, be thy Spirit with us now!; *DDS* 2002, 446; baptismal hymn by Gr, published in his *Sang-Værk* (1837); based upon English hymn by Edward Bickersteth (1786-1850), evangelical and anti-Tractarian editor of *Christian Psalmody, A Collection of above*

900 *Psalms, Hymns and Spiritual Songs* (London, 1841), whose declared zeal for congregational singing, endorsed by Scripture and Fathers, was a worthy counterpart of Gr's own; Vilhelm Birkedal was surprised when Gr failed to recognise his own hymn, sung in his own home; see also **hymns**.

Oczakov *65, 66, 80*; Ochakov, ancient Greek town and naval harbour in Ukraine at Black Sea mouth of River Dnieper east of Odessa; held as Turkish fortress during war against Russia; successfully stormed (1787) by Russians led by Field Marshal Potemkin and field officer (later Count) Levin August von Bennigsen, conceded by Turks to Russia 1792.

Odense *157, 323*; anciently-settled town on island of Fyn, commercial and administrative centre with cathedral (dedicated to martyred king, Knud the holy), castle, Latin school, asylum for mentally ill, publishers Milo, theatre and concert facilities; at beginning of 19th c., Dk's second largest town ("Little Copenhagen") with some 6000 inhabitants; birthplace of Gr's contemporary Hans Christian Andersen (1805-75).

Odin; see **Óðinn**.

Odin and Fenris *300*; Gr uses Norse myth of Ragnarok, when Óðinn is swallowed by Fenris Wolf (sibling of the Midgard Serpent and Hel, begotten by Loki upon giantess Angraboda), to symbolise struggle between principles of Life and Death; see also **mythology**; **Thor and Midgard Serpent**; **Freyr and Surt**.

Oehlenschläger, Adam Gottlob *14, 23, 84, 96, 99-101, 113, 114, 157, 159, 189, 190, 233, 256, 276*; 1779-1850; "a poetic star of the first magnitude has risen over our fatherland with this century" (Gr); deemed, and (1829, in Lund University and Cathedral) laurel-crowned as, greatest poet of Dk's 'Golden Age'; in 1791, showing early precocity in verse-writing, attracted notice of Edvard Storm (1749-1794), poet and principal of Efterslægtens Skole in Copenhagen where he was subsequently enrolled and, from Storm himself, learned Scandinavian mythology; 1800 submitted University prize-essay responding to set subject "Var det gavnligt for Nordens skiønne Litteratur om den gamle nordiske Mythologie blev indført og af vore Digtere i Almindelighed antaget i Steden for den græske?" [Would it be profitable for Northern fine literature if ancient Norse mythology were introduced and in general accepted by our poets in place of the Greek?] with enthusiastically affirmative essay *Om betimeligheden af en digterisk udnyttelse af den nordiske mytologi* [On the timeliness of a poetic utilisation of Norse mythology]; gained *entrée* into circle of artists and other prominent Danes gathering at Rahbeks' home at Bakkehus (he later married sister of Kamma Rahbek); with decisive encouragement of Henrik Steffens (1802) and under patronage of Ørsted brothers emerged as mediator of national-Romanticism in Danish literature, attracted by humanism of Goethe and Schiller and new German philosophy of nature, and much influenced by travels (1805-10) and meetings with artists, philosophers, in Germany, France, Italy; no weighty philosopher himself, but celebrating in his plays natural piety and lofty public spirit, often finding themes in Nordic mythology and legend-history such as his *Nordiske digte* [Nordic poems], tragedies *Hakon Jarl hin Riges* [Earl Haakon the wealthy] and *Baldur hin gode* [Baldr the good], the lengthy narrative poem *Thors rejse til Jotunheim* [Thor's journey to Jotunheim], and tragedies *Palnatoke* and *Axel og Valborg* (all successively published between 1807-10); other notable works include *Sanct Hansaftenspil* (*A Play for Midsummer Eve*) premiered 1819, choreographed by Poul Funck (1790-1837), and *Aladdin eller Den forunderlige Lampe* [A. or the wonderful lamp] premiered at Royal Theatre, Copenhagen, 1839, with music by Friedrich Kuhlau (1786-1832), choreography by August Bournonville (1805-79); from university days onwards, known to Gr who greatly (though not uncritically) esteemed his work.

Olav, Saint *147, 151*; Olaf Haraldsson; 995-1030; Norwegian king 1015-1030; born after father Harald Grenske killed by Swedes; mother Asta married Sigurd Syr, petty king in Ringerike where young Olaf was raised; a main source of information is *Saga of Olaf the Holy* in Snorri Sturluson's *Heimskringla*; colourful story of viking and mercenary adventure, partly in England under Anglo-Saxon king Æthelræd and Danish king Cnut, with serious theme of Olaf's conversion to Christianity (baptised in Rouen) and mission to rule as sole king over a Christian Norway; Olaf succeeded in establishing sovereignty but made enemies including Cnut who effectively imposed Danish domination of Norway from 1028 and connived in Olaf's eventual overthrow; though his evangelical methods could be brutal Olaf consolidated Norwegian Christianity, built churches, was cultivated as saint soon after being killed in battle (Stiklestad, 29 July 1030), his shrine being in Trondheim (Nidaros) where site of his death was miraculously marked by a spring; traditionally regarded as founder of Norwegian nation and Church, and patron saint of Norway; on visit (1851) to Stein, farm in Ringerike traditionally identified as the *kongsgaard*, seat of Sigurd Syr, Gr was much moved by historical consciousness in treading sites of saga he had translated years previously.

Om den Kunst at prædike; On the art of preaching; see **Mynster,** J. P.

Om Religion og Liturgie *157-159*; 'On religion and liturgy' – substantial article by Gr published in *Theologiske Maanedsskrivt* IX (1807); prompted by Bishop P. O. Boisen's proposals (1806) for revision of liturgy of State Church; Gr, fearing victory for rationalism at sacramental heart of liturgy, vigorously defended Baptism and Lord's Supper "as the focal points of the whole liturgy, from which rays of light must needs go out to all sides" though when Boisen's proposals failed it was, Gr suggests, less a triumph of principled opposition than a consequence of disruption following British incendiary bombardment of Copenhagen (1807); see also **Katekismus,** Luther's; **Grundtvigian(ism)**; *Kirkens Gienmæle*; **mageløse Opdagelse,** den; **Church struggle,** The; **Alterbogs-Sagen**; **Daabspagten**; **Frisprog.**

Om Religions-Frihed *153*; On freedom of religion; written by Gr 1827, in context of libel-suit brought against him by H. N. Clausen but, because of censorship imposed on him by court and because of the work's criticism of restrictions upon freedom of conscience in religious matters, not published until 1866.

On Freedom of Religion; see *Om Religions-Frihed.*

On Religion and Liturgy; see Om Religion og Liturgie.

On the Art of Preaching; *Om den Kunst at prædike*; see **Mynster,** J. P.

Op dog, Sion, seer du ei *340*; Up, O Sion! seest thou not; hymn by Gr (*Festpsalmer* 833, 7th edition 1857; a version having been published in *Dansk Kirketidende* 1851) sung by crowds as Gr's funeral procession passed through streets of Copenhagen, 1872; also entitled *Livets Vej* [The way of life], and set to music by J. P. E Hartmann; beginning: Op dog, Sion! seer du ei / Seirens palmestrøede Vei / Til Guds Huus i Himmerig! / Den er og beredt for dig. [Up, O Sion! seest thou not / the palm-strewn path of victory / to the house of God in heaven! / For thee too it is prepared]; see also **hymns**.

Opdagelsen; 'the discovery' – see **mageløse opdagelse,** den.

Open letter of friendship to an English priest; see ***Aabent Vennebrev til en Engelsk Præst***.

Open letter to my children; see ***Aabent Brev til mine Børn***.

Optrin af Kæmpelivet i Norden *137, 159*; title so phrased by Gr in *Kirke-Speil*; see ***Optrin af Nordens Kæmpeliv***.

Optrin af Nordens Kæmpeliv *159*; Scenes from the warrior-life of the North; though Gr's original plan was to write major poetic characterisation of spirit informing Northern antiquity, drawing upon myth, legend and history, and written as dramatic dialogue in manner of some of Edda-poems, he published only two parts of opus envisaged: *Optrin af Kæmpelivets Undergang* [Scenes from the decline of the warrior-life] (1809; based upon three episodes in early Danish history) and *Optrin af Norners og Asers Kamp* [Scenes from the strife of the Norns and Aesir] (1811; drawing upon history of Volsungs and Gjukungs or Niflungs preserved in saga and *Poetic Edda*) which he designated as, respectively, parts 2 and 1 of work under collective title *Optrin af Nordens Kæmpeliv* [Scenes from the warrior-life of the North]; around Christmas 1810 Gr underwent profoundly significant psychological, spiritual and religious upheaval of which one outcome was interpretation of struggle between Aesir and Norns in Christian historical terms; two other related pieces survive: *Om Odins Komme til Norden* [On Óðinn's coming to the North] (unpublished in Gr's lifetime; prompted by Snorri Sturluson's account in *Prose Edda*) and *Om Sværdet Tirfing* [On the sword Tyrfing] (published in *Idunna* (1811); based on account of fateful sword in *Hervarar saga ok Heiðreks konungs* [Saga of Hervor and king Heiðrek] and in its embedded poem usually called *The Waking of Angantýr*.

Ord, det levende *16, 85, 125, 126, 138, 140, 163, 170, 264, 274, 279, 281, 302, 311*; the Living Word; teaching propounded by Gr, his most distinctive contribution to theology and ecclesiology; "In his earlier years, he had been of the opinion that the Church's whole foundation was the Bible, but now [early 1820s] he arrived at the view that it was the Church itself, and its tradition, especially as expressed in the apostolic confession at baptism, that was the basis of Christian faith ... It is in the congregation, at baptism and communion, that Christ speaks his living word to the community, the word that creates what it names. The congregation had always existed even before the Bible was written." (Poul Dam); "The church of Christ is founded upon and with the loud and living word of God in the mouth of man, long before a Christian book was [...] penned" (Gr; summarised in *Registrant* XXIV, p. 102, from English draft of letter to Edward Irving between 1825-27); for Gr the living Word was also to some extent an active dimension of the

New Covenant as set against the letter of the Law which "killeth" [St Paul]; it was fundamentally and inextricably bound up with the essential and definitive signs of spiritual life in a Christian congregation: "Not until we have discovered the living expression of the Christian Faith in the profession of the Creed at Baptism, and the living expression of Christian Hope in the Lord's Prayer, both at Baptism and at Holy Commumion, and the living expression of Christian Love in Christ's words of affection to his believers, or his declaration of love to his Bride at Holy Communion – not until then can we, in congregational life, boast a Christian profession, preaching and praise which are the peculiar and unmistakable life-signs of Christian Faith, Christian Hope and Christian Love [Først naar vi har opdaget den kristne *Tros* kristelige Liv-Udtryk i Tros-Bekjendelsen ved Daaben, og det kristelige *Haabs* Liv-Udtryk i Herrens Bøn, Fadervor, baade ved Daaben og Nadveren, og den kristelige *Kjærligheds* Liv-Udtryk i Kristi Hengivenheds-Ord til sine troende, eller hans Kjærligheds-Erklæring til sin Brud, ved Nadveren – først da kan vi i Menigheds-Livet opvise en *kristelig* Bekjendelse, Forkyndelse og Lovsang, som er ejendommelige og umiskjendelige Livs-Tegn af den kristne Tro, det kristelige Haab og den kristelige Kjærlighed] (Grundtvig, *Den christelige Børnelærdom* [Christian instruction for children]; 1855-61, 1868, 1883; ch. 10); but in a less theological, though still related sense, Gr distinguished sharply between the spoken (living) and the written (dead) word: "*Balsamere* bruges, billedlig, om Bogstav-Skrift, hvori den mundtlige Ord endnu efter Døden, som en Mumie, bevares fra Opløsning" ['To enbalm' is used, metaphorically, about alphabetic script, in which the spoken word even after death, like a mummy, is preserved from dissolution] (Gr in *Krønnike-Rim* 1842); hence the status accorded the oral discourse as against the printed word, in the Grundtvigian folk-highschools; see **Ordet**; **sacraments**; also **mageløs, mageløse Opdagelse, den; mageløse Vidnesbyrd, den; Irenaeus**; various **word** entries; **Moses** and the Law.

Ordet *17, 138-140, 281*; The Word; concept fundamental to Christian theology in all denominations, a key concept in Luther's reformed doctrines, central to his sacramental theology, as it therefore also is to Gr's exposition of a theology of *det levende Ord*, the living word, which has precedence over the written word of Scripture; in Gr's usage, *ord* covers a wide semantic range – the Word that is God and was in the beginning with God, the creative *fiat*, the word of the patriarchs and prophets and of Christ and the apostles and evangelists, the Living Word by which Christ is truly present in his congregation and upon which depend the life and the authority of the Church, the word which lives in the hearts and upon the lips of the Christian congregation, the sacramental word, the word of prophecy and the word preached, the royal word, the word which is a 'riddle-picture' and "old Danish words" and the words which comprise the mother-tongue, the spoken word by which enlightenment is communicated from teacher to taught, and more; routinely and purposefully Gr gives the term an ambivalence, sometimes a multivalence, of significations, so that it is rarely unfruitful, when reading Gr, to look beyond the primary contextual signification to the hierarchical and organic structure of nuances invested in the term; "*Ordet* er Aandens Legeme, vel usynligt, men ikke usanseligt, da vi i Hørelsen har Sans for det" [*The word* is body of *the spirit*, invisible for sure, but not unsensory, since in hearing we have sense for it] (Gr in his *Krønnike-Rim* 1842); see also **Ord, det levende**; **sacraments**; **Bogstav-Skriften**.

Ordet var fra Arilds Tid *333*; *Since time began, the Word has been*; text which Gr published as no. 55 in *Sang-Værk* I (1837) but himself later criticised ("I have written much that is no good"), particularly for its mention of mermaid-song in refrain.

Oringe *313*; hospital for psychiatric patients, near Vordingborg, south Sjælland.

Orthography, Society for the Promotion of an improved; see **Society for the Promotion of an improved Orthography**.

Óðinn *61, 73, 186, 300*; in Norse myth, name (perhaps meaning 'the spirit, divinity, inspiration') of chief god among Æsir in Northern pantheon, cultivated particularly by warrior-nobles and their retainers and by poets; god of battle-lust and victory, wisdom, wealth, poetic inspiration and eloquence; sacrificed himself to himself, hanging on tree, to secure wisdom of runes for humankind; possessed of many names, including All-Father, and identities, especially during his visits to human world; commonly represented as mysterious one-eyed ancient-looking figure (eye given as pledge for securing drink from Mimir's well of wisdom), with two ravens on shoulders, Thought and Memory, which fly round the world each day reporting what seen; as battle-god, strong and handsome riding on eight-legged horse Sleipnir; served by valkyries, gathers fallen heroes to Valhalla to prepare for final doom of gods (*Ragnarok*), in which cataclysmic battle he is to be devoured by the Fenris Wolf; symbolic significance much developed by Gr (*Nordens Mythologi*, 1832) in his effort to harmonise Norse myth with a Christian reading of Northern and universal history; see also ***Nordens Mythologi***.

Otto, Carl *196*; 1795-1879; physician, professor; married to Anna Friis who was cousin to Lise Blicher (Grundtvig); see headnote to item 70.

Ovene *221*; aunt of Christian Sigfred Ley (1806-74), family friend of the Grundtvigs, one among the many women of bourgeois class who enthusiastically supported J. C. Lindberg's (unlawful) religious *forsamlinger* [gatherings] at his home 'Lille Rolighed' near the *Kalkbrænderi* [lime kilns] in Copenhagen suburbs (1832).

Ovid *71, 81*; Publius Ovidius Naso, 43 B.C.- A.D. 17; Roman poet in Latin 'golden age' of Emperor Augustus; his poetry regularly studied in medieval and post-Renaissance schools as exemplary classical Latin composition; his *Amores* and *Metamorphoses* had major influence on European literature of all periods to present; the *Amores* translated into Danish by J. L. Heiberg (1791-1860).

Oxford *62*; Gr visited Oxford in 1830, primarily to look at Anglo-Saxon and later medieval manuscripts, and in 1843, primarily to make contact with leading figures in the High Church Oxford Movement; was impressed not only by collegiate life in England's oldest university but by long history of city and university; was disappointed however in hope of playing some part in outcome of Tractarian crisis 1843.

P

Palladius, Peder *194*; 1503-1560; Danish Lutheran theologian; born in Ribe, educated in grammar school there, taught in Odense, studied 1531-1537 in Wittenberg under tutelage of Luther and Melancthon; appointed 1537 by Christian III as first of seven 'superintendents' (equivalent to, soon renamed as, 'bishops') consecrated in the Danish reformed, Lutheran church; thus was first Lutheran bishop of Sjælland, though authority extended over Norway, Iceland, Faeroes, Gotland and Rügen; was hugely active in establishing and consolidating evangelical-Lutheran character of Danish Church, by visitations and by publication of consuetudinary, didactic and devotional books; professor in Copenhagen University.

Palm Sunday 1867 *25, 309, 312-314, 318, 320*; last and most serious of Gr's several so-called manic-depressive attacks (others in 1810 following ill-fated infatuation with Constance Steensen-Leth and official recriminations over probational sermon, and 1844 when illness was less publicly manifested); in a different age, a charismatic interpretation of occasion might have commanded more credence and respect, but rationalism, social proprieties, distaste for vulgar religious enthusiasm, and some straightforward hostility towards Gr, thorn in the flesh of clerical establishment, have ensured its tag as an embarrassment in the life-records, and a disinclination to examine the striking facility for illuminating exegetical association, and the visionary landscape of Gr's disordered discourse; see also **Hammerich,** Peter Frederik Adolph; **Helveg,** Hans Frederik; **Rørdam,** Thomas Skat; **Rothe,** P. C.; **Rosenørn-Teilmann,** Christian Peder Theodor; **synernes høj**; **Jerusalem**; **Jordan**; **Jacob**; **Solomon**; **Saba,** Queen of; **logos,** the divine in Grundtvig; **Kristoforos**; **Gabriel,** archangel; **circumcision of Jesus**; **Hoveritjeneste**; **Kallebodstrand**.

Palnatoke 101; tragedy in five acts by Adam Oehlenschläger, written 1807 in Paris, published 1809; in keeping with new interest in historical and national themes, Oehlenschläger looked to Saxo Grammaticus and Icelandic saga for story of Danish legend-hero, Toke Palnesøn, founder of viking fortress of Jomsborg, opponent of adoption of Christianity under Danish king Harald I (Bluetooth), eventually slayer of his lord and king during revolt led by Harald's son, Svend Tveskæg (Forkbeard), whom Palnatoke had fostered.

Paludan, Frederik August *291*; 1792-1872; commander of Danish ship *Gefion* trapped under fire at Eckernförde 1849 and surrendered to Germans to spare wholesale loss of life among crew; Gr wished stoic-heroic example of Ivar Huitfeldt's sacrifice (Køge Bugt, 1710) had instead been followed, as presumably did military tribunal also, which sentenced Paludan to three months' military detention; see **Eckernförde**.

papists and chalice *290*; Doubtless Gr knew more and better of Roman Catholic doctrine and dogma than the somewhat mischievous fabricating reported of him by Brun who, admittedly, was distracted by his hostess in mid-exposition but was nevertheless well in sympathy with what he caught of it.

Parnassus *113, 114*; the Greek mountain consecrated to Apollo and the Muses, regarded therefore as mountain of poetry and poets; symbolically used to signify the poetic world within a particular (western) culture or society, as when Gr speaks (with some irony) of "our Parnassus" which in "the new [19th] century" gave no home to the poet Jens Baggesen, though it conceded Gr himself his "little corner."

parochial ties, dissolution of; see **Sognebaandsløsning**.

Paul, Jean *204*; Johann Poul Friedrich Richter, 1763-1825; German author, partly influenced by writing of English author Laurence Sterne, himself influential transitional figure in German literature during early 1800s; regarded, by virtue of subjective element in his writing, as forerunner of Romantic prose writing; notably for his *Vorschule der Aesthetik* (1804).

Paul, St *138, 139, 156, 308*; author of Epistle to the Romans, subject of lectures by rationalist professor C. F. Hornemann (1751-1830), known for his irreverent remarks, whom Gr, as student at Copenhagen University, went to hear, just once, and for fun.

Paulli, Just Henrik Voltelen *280, 281*; 1809-65; Danish priest, chaplain to court; married to daughter of J. P. Mynster (Bishop of Sjælland from 1834); close friend of H. L. Martensen (Bishop of Sjælland from 1854); but despite broadly conservative theological position and closeness to Mynster and Martensen, was not altogether unsympathetic to Gr, nor to pressure for reform in Church; esteemed for having remained in Copenhagen (when many who could retreated into country) to minister to dying and bereaved during 1853 cholera epidemic; member of committee, with Gr, Martensen and others, for drafting new hymnal (1844), completion of which, if a triumph of diplomacy and patience of Martensen and Paulli in accommodating Gr's hefty convictions on matters of content and style, was nonetheless followed by its rejection; see also **hymns**.

Pavekatechismus 198; the Pope-Catechism; popular designation of short catechism for children composed by Hans Poulsen Resen (1561-1683), Bishop of Sjælland from 1615, author of first Danish translation of Bible from original tongues (1607); see further **Katechismus**, Luther's.

Pavels, Provst Peter (?) *255, 256*; cleric from Sandefjord, Norway; corpulent and food-loving visitor to Gr's home (*ca.* 1840) and evidently, like Gr himself, associated with circle of distinguished names (notably sculptor Bertel Thorvaldsen) welcomed by Baronesse Christine Stampe at manor house of Nysø near Præstø, south Sjælland; apparently Provst Peder Pavels, born 1769, from Bergen matriculated Copenhagen University 1788, married in Copenhagen 1801 to Anna Elisabeth Pflueg, priest in Sandeherred, died in Sandefjord 1855.

Peace Settlement *268*; proceedings in Danish parliament (1864-65) consequent upon ending war with Prussia; fifty years after loss of twin-kingdom of Norway, Dk was again engaged in traumatic accommodation of defeat, loss of territory and further fragmentation of the ancient kingdom; for Gr who feared as much cultural as political and military threat of Germany, a time of great pain, bitterness and anxiety for future.

Pedersen, Parmo Carl *222*; 1786-1859; *cand. phil.*; adherent of Gr, participant in J. C. Lindberg's religious assemblies (the *Kalkbrænderi-forsamlinger*), 1832, at which Gr preached; described as having "a great propensity towards the ceremonial, the grandiose and the militaristic attitude"

(Lindberg); later teacher in Hvidberg and in Hillerslev, Thy, Nordjylland where he was noted for not making particular use of Grundtvig-Kold methods in his teaching; esteemed *kirkesanger* [parish clerk; leader of congregational singing in church], poet, song-writer; occasional preacher at *forsamlinger* [religious gatherings] in region.

pen-feud *15, 113, 156, 162, 169*; see **pennefejde**.

pennefejde *15, 113, 156, 162, 169*; 'pen-feud(ing)' was recognised and familiar 19th c. phenomenon especially within Copenhagen academic and literary circles, in which periodicals such as weekly *Nyeste Skilderie af Kjøbenhavn*, K. L. Rahbek's periodical *Minerva* to which Jens Baggesen was provocative contributor, and Christian Molbech's monthly *Athene*, as well as occasional pamphlets, were used to sustain debate, often acrimonious and abusive, over controversial issues, whether secular or religious (such as the contest between Otto Horrebow and N. E. Balle in 1790s); to some extent a symptom of stifling control over public meetings prevailing before granting of freedom of expression in Constitution (1848), but at same time overtly or tacitly an assertion of right to free speech and freedom of pen (and therefore also closely watched and if necessary acted upon by authorities); fury of some pen-feuds, over issues of little concern to public at large, was satirised as in cartoons such as C. W. Eckersberg's engraving (1818) ridiculing protracted *pennefejde* between supporters of Adam Oehlenschläger and supporters of Jens Baggesen in which Athene's owl looks on from one side and a model Sphinx (alluding to Baggesen's riddle-poems) from the other, while protagonists hurl pens and inkpots at each other; but penalties for overstepping limits of public order and libel laws extended to fines, censorship and even exile; see also **Baggesen,** Jens; **Tylvten**; **censur**.

pension *62*; pensions and grants from the fund *ad usum publicum* were a principal instrument of patronage under the *enevælde* [absolute monarchy]; citizens contributing to life and prosperity (material or spiritual) of the state might be granted royal pension; citizens of distinction or potential distinction might be given grants enabling them to travel both for experience and to represent Denmark abroad; people of status and wealth also recognised responsibility of exercising patronage (as famously exemplified in life-story of Hans Christian Andersen); Gr received pension from 1818 "as a national writer" and 1829-31 public grants facilitating three lengthy stays in England to study Anglo-Saxon manuscripts forming part of the heritage from Northern antiquity, as well as receiving assistance from one of the most generous patrons of that period, "Den store Forfremmer af boglig Kunst" [the great promoter of literary art] (Gr), Privy-councillor Johan Bülow of Sanderumgaard (1751-1828); similarly, in 1843, it was with funds found for him by Dowager Queen Caroline Amalie that he was able to go to England for meetings with leaders of the Oxford Movement.

People's Church *328*; Edmund Gosse's rendition of the Danish term *Folkekirke*; in fact the Danish term, in general usage, signifies 'national church' – the church of the whole *Folk* – rather than a church of exclusively demotic character.

people's representatives; see **Folke-Repræsentanter**.

personal curate *112*; *Personel-Kapellan*, ordained but non-established assistant to particular priest, as Gr to his elderly father (1811-13); when in 1838 Gr, at that time priest without a parish, petitioned King and personally requested Bishop Mynster for permission to confirm his own sons, Mynster's "haanlig Afvisning" [contemptuous dismissal] (Gr) was: "Tror De da vi kan give enhver forfløjen Kapellan Lov til at konfirmere?" {Do you then think that we can give every fanciful curate permission to confirm?] (Mina Grundtvig).

Peter on the Water *263*; poem concerning Peter's attempt to walk on water of Lake of Gennesaret made subject of a witticism by Gr.

Pharisaism *328;* hypocrisy, sanctimoniousness; alluding to New Testament accusations against Pharisees of hypocritical observance of the letter of the law whilst evading its spirit; diagnosed by Edmund Gosse as being, along with Rationalism, "the two bugbears of his long fighting career."

Pharisee and the tax-gatherer *141 142*; Luke 18:10-14; topic of Gr's extempore address to prisoners at prison-reformer Elizabeth Fry's request on her tour of Copenhagen prisons, 1841; but Gr was disturbed at thought of how this parable could be abused, and remained so whenever thereafter he preached upon it as gospel of the day.

Phenix-Fuglen *132, 334*; also written as *Føniks-Fuglen*; Gr's edition (1840) of Anglo-Saxon poem *The Phoenix* from Exeter Book, *editio princeps* of full text, with title *Phenix-Fuglen. Et angelsachsisk Kvad. Førstegang udgivet med Indledning, Fordanskning og Efterklang* [The Phoenix. An Anglo-Saxon poem. Published for the first time with introduction, Danish version and an afterword]; characteristically, Gr's motive is not objective scholarship for its own sake but polemical application of antique northern and Christian poesy to current circumstances in Danish national political and spiritual life, namely accession (1839) of Christian VIII upon whom many pinned hopes of various kinds of rebirth.

Phoenix, The *132, 334*; Anglo-Saxon poem from the Exeter Book, edited and translated by Gr (1840); see **Phenix-Fuglen**.

Pietism *279, 298*; popular religious movement reaching Dk from Lutheran Germany; dissatisfaction felt by Philip Jakob Spener (1635-1705) with whole exterior and interior Christian life as enabled and supported by state-authorised religion led eventually to founding (Halle, Germany, 1690s) of model community stressing sanctification of daily life, inward cultivation of spirituality and outward manifestation of gospel values in love and support of neighbour (schools, hospitals, homes for orphans, poor, aged); characterised by conventicles, gatherings for prayer, bible-readings, for mutual support and exhortation; spread to Dk with conventicles in Copenhagen, strengthened by establishment of pietistic *herrnhuter* (Moravians) in Stormgade, Copenhagen (1739) and in own new-built township at Christiansfeld, Jylland (1773); though pietism began to influence king and court and Frederik IV appointed pietistic priest to court and Christian VI enthusiastically promoted it, for example by introducing (1736) rite of confirmation into Danish Church, closing theatres, forbidding entry of actors and street-entertainers into Dk, educational initiatives, establishment of orphanage in Copenhagen, it was also perceived as potential threat to state Church and social good order, and laws, strengthened under Christian VI (1741), forbade private religious gatherings (i.e. conventicles); meetings (*forsamlinger*) organised (1830s) by J. C. Lindberg and others, with some support from Gr, were perceived and treated in this light by state authorities; pietism for its part also rigidified into austere code of public puritanism, mandatory observances, intolerance of spiritual liberty; see also **forsamlinger**.

pig-gelder from Olstrup *284*; subject of anecdote told by Gr about himself; Olstrup was a village in south Sjælland, east of Næstved.

Pindse-Helgen *149*; Whitsun holy-day, so called by Norwegian girl met by Gr on his memorable visit to Norway, 1851; that year, Pentecost was celebrated on Sunday, 8 June.

Pladsen [The Square] *207, 213, 214*; a square by Jakob Holm's property, Holms Plads, Christianshavn, between Strandgade (where Gr-family had apartment) and harbour, used for storage of timber and such.

Ploug, Carl Parmo *307, 335, 336*; 1813-94; journalist, political activist, poet who contributed to Danish *sangskat* ['song-treasure'- treasury of song] some of Dk's best songs of patriotic *genre* and (among much else) composed verse for memorial stone to Christian Flor (1792-1875) on Skamlingsbanken in Slesvig; from 1841, as executive editor of daily newspaper *Fædrelandet* [The Fatherland], campaigned powerfully on agenda (later to become platform of National-Liberal party) of nationalism, Danish Slesvig, and scandinavianism; 1845 headed student committee which organised gathering of some 600 Scandinavian students in Copenhagen, and as principal speaker at 1856 *studentertog* to Uppsala urged union of Scandinavian kingdoms); after termination of censorship with 1849 Constitution his paper, whilst also notable for its cultural content (and for being one of the best edited and printed Danish papers in its day), agitated influentially for confrontation rather than compromise with German federation over status of Slesvig, backing National-Liberal government's policy which ended in disastrous war of 1864; thereafter Ploug used paper to express support for conservative revision (1866) of 1849 Constitution and, often abusively, opposition to sovereignty of *Rigsdag*, consolidation of democracy, Grundtvigian manifestations of *det folkelige* and Gr's advocacy of his educational ideas; 1878 denounced proposed public petition (1878) for reconsideration of Gr's plan for new university where "Folkelighed, Fædreneland og Modersmaal" [nurture of the *folkelig*, fatherland and mother-tongue] should be vital centrepoint of education and enlightenment; Ploug sold *Fædrelandet* 1881 and it closed 1882.

Poetiske Skrifter, Oehlenschläger's *100* ; published 1805; see **Oehlenschläger,** Adam.

Politi(e)vennen 88, 156; The friend of polity (or police); that is, friend of good order, loyal supporter of official public polity, law and order; popular weekly paper (*almuesblad*) published in Copenhagen 1798-1846 (with short breaks 1811-16 and July 1845); first editor, Calus Henrik Seidelin (1761-1811), astutely made of it an organ for venting criticism and complaint about day-to-day governance of state and city from matters of education down to clearing of gutters and dangerous driving by cabbies, which nevertheless contrived to avoid intervention of fairly stringently operated press censorship during period of absolute monarchy and especially after the restrictive Press ordinance of 1799, and indeed served to keep king and authorities informed of what was on the popular mind; here Gr made his first appearance in print (nos. 299 and 301, January 1804) with *Et Særsyn i det nittende Aarhundrede* [A rare sight in the nineteenth century], an exposé of poor educational provision on island of Falster, which at least galled the bishop of Lolland-Falster into a reply.

portraits of Grundtvig *166*; portrayals of Gr include (listed by date): 1820, Christian Frederik Christensen (1798-1882), painting (Det Nationalhistoriske Museum [Museum of National History] Frederiksborg); 1829, Christoffer Wilhelm Eckersberg (1783-1853), drawing reproduced as copperplate engraving by Carl Wilhelm Erling Eckersberg on title-page of *Christelige Prædikener eller Søndagsbog* [Christian Sermons or Sunday-Book] 1831; 1831, Christian Albrecht Jensen (1792-1870), painting (Ny Carlsberg Glyptotek, Copenhagen), also reproduced as engraving by H. Olrik (Det kongelige Bibliotek, Copenhagen); 1841, Peter Christian Skovgaard (1817-75), pen drawing (Det kongelige Bibliotek, Copenhagen); 1843, Christian Albrecht Jensen (1792-1870), painting (Den Hirschsprungske Samling, Copenhagen); 1843, Johan Thomas Lundbye (1818-48), sketch of Gr lecturing in Borchs Kollegium, Copenhagen (Frederiksborg Museum); 1844, Johan Vilhelm Gertner (1818-71), drawing (Kirkeligt Samfund, Copenhagen); 1847, Peter Christian Skovgaard (1817-75), pen drawing (Frederiksborg Museum); 1847-48, Carl Christian Constantin Hansen (1804-80), painting (Davids Samling, Copenhagen), also reproduced as engraving by Hans Peter Hansen (1829-99) (Det kongelige Bibliotek, Copenhagen); 1847-48, Herman Wilhelm Bissen (1798-1868), bust (Ny Carlsberg Glyptotek, Copenhagen; Statens Museum for Kunst, Copenhagen); Date uncertain, Otto Frederik Theobald Evens (1826-95), marble bust (Nordjyllands Kunstmuseum, Aalborg); 1846, Nicolai Wilhelm Marstrand (1810-73), drawing of Gr among other celebrities listening to Oehlenschläger reading at Nysø (Thorvaldsens Museum, Copenhagen); 1848, Andreas Martin Petersen (1813-75), engraving, collage of Gr among 14 Danish poets (Det kongelige Bibliotek, Copenhagen); 1861-65, Carl Christian Constantin Hansen (1804-80), painting of some 150 members of *Den grundlovgivende Rigsforsamling* [The Constituent Assembly of 1848-49] (Frederiksborg Museum); 1862, Nicolai Wilhelm Marstrand, painting (Frederiksborg Museum); 1867, Georg Rosenkilde (1814-91; presented volume of his portrait photographs of notable Danish artists, poets, philosophers, composers to Carl XV and Dronning Louise of Sweden, now in Frederiksborg Museum), photograph (Det kongelige Bibliotek); 1868, Christen Dalsgaard (1824-1907), painting of Gr seated in Vartov Kirke with son Frederik Lange during hymn-singing (Frederiksborg Museum); 1869, Budtz Müller & Co. (Bertel Christian Budtz Müller, 1837-84, became court photographer 1870), photograph (Det kongelige Bibliotek, Copenhagen); 1872, Adolf Lønborg (1835-1916; Fotografisk atelier, Østergade 16, Copenhagen), photographs (Det kongelige Bibliotek, Copenhagen); 1905, Rasmus Bøgeberg (1859-1921), model for statue of Gr seated with lark flying from hand exhibited Charlottenborg, Copenhagen, 1905, statue never actually made, model believed destroyed, photograph in Jakob Marstrand, *Grundtvigs Mindekirke paa Bispebjerg* [Grundtvig's memorial church on Bispebjerg], Copenhagen 1932; 1907-08, Niels Skovgaard (1858-1938) and Karl Schrøder (1870-1943), polychrome ceramic portrait bust (Skovgaard Museum, Viborg); 1910, Niels Skovgaard, ceramic bust (Det kongelige Bibliotek, Copenhagen); 1912-14, Niels Skovgaard (1858-1938), models for statue of Gr and *Livskilden* [The fount of Life] (Statens Museum for Kunst, Copenhagen; the monumental granite statue itself is in the courtyard of Vartov, Copenhagen); portraits of other members of the Grundtvig family may be found in the *Portrætsregistrant* of Det kongelige Bibliotek, Copenhagen; see also **Marstrand,** Nicolaj Wilhelm.

postfører, Norsk 67; post-courier in Norway; in early 19th c. settlements were so widely scattered, roads few and commonly precarious, weather conditions often severe, and mails sometimes subject to robbery and hold-ups, so couriers rode armed or at times escorted by soldiers; thus when Bertel Faurskov (Gr's first teacher at Udby) claimed (as Gr alleges) to have formerly been a *Norsk Postfører* ("etc. etc. etc.") it was as though the village schoolmaster boasted of having once ridden for Wells Fargo.

President of the Chancellery; see **Cancellie,** Det Kongelige-Danske; **Kaas,** Frederik Julius.

Press ordinance; see **Trykkeforordningen; censur.**

Prinsessegade 230; street in Christianshavn, in which Vor Frelsers Kirke, where Gr was curate 1822-26, is located; here Gr's funeral cortège passed on its procession from church into city 1872.

probational sermon; see **Dimis-Prædiken.**

provsti 112; ecclesiastical administrative subdivision of diocese, in care of a *provst* (crown-appointed ecclesiastical official, responsible to bishop; approximately corresponding to rural dean in English Church); see also **stiftsprovst.**

Prussia 106, 239, 310, 312, 313, 316, 318, 319; region bordering south-east Baltic shore, south of Gotland; its earlier population (Borussi) forcibly christianised or slaughtered by invading Teutonic Knights in 13th c.; entered modern history 1701 when Elector Frederick III (1657-1713) of Brandenburg declared himself first King (Frederik I) of Prussia; efficiently organised as absolutist regime and powerfully militarised by Frederick William I (1688-1740; king 1713-40), its territories and influence increased, despite intermittent setbacks (as during Seven Years War and Napoleonic Wars); it emerged in early 19th c. as relatively progressive state implementing ideals of Enlightenment and with a modernised army; having joined coalition leading to defeat of Napoleon it made major gains at Congress of Vienna (1815); played leading role in German Confederation of States which maintained ongoing dispute with Dk over status of duchies of Slesvig, Holsten and Lauenborg; surged forward as European political and military power (and threat to Dk) with appointment of Otto von Bismarck (1815-98) as chief minister; in wars of 1848 and 1864 contended with Dk over duchies, culminating in 1864 military seizure of Slesvig; subsequently, to great disappointment of Gr and Dk, Prussia was victorious in war with France (1870-71) and in 1871 Wilhelm I of Prussia was proclaimed Emperor of Germany; thus the Prussian political and military menace on Dk's southern border, added to long-standing cultural threat from German cultural eminence, understandably lent *Tydsken* [the German] a demonised character in Gr's mind (as witness his fear, during his breakdown in 1867, of being snatched by Prussian raiders) and writings; see also **Slesvig-Holsten.**

Prussia, History of; see **Kotzebue,** August Friedrich Ferdinand.

præstefrihed *266, 279*; clerical freedom; essentially concept that (within certain reasonable parameters) priest should be licensed and constrained by conscience, not by law or State, in offering pastoral ministry and administering rites and sacraments of the church; including, in particular, principle that oaths required of priest be confined to oath of witness and oath of allegiance; that priests be freed to teach according to their own best understanding of Scripture, and to administer sacraments – subject to fundamental invariables – with liturgical discretion; that priests be obliged by State to officiate only in civil ceremony of marriage, reserving Church's blessing upon marriage only to those who set true store upon it and whom the Church can in all good conscience bless; and that priests be free from restriction of ministry solely to parish of which they are incumbent (free,that is, to serve free congregations); over decades, following his first-hand experience (1829-31) of English religious liberties, vigorously striven for by Gr and his followers against traditionalist and conservative parties within both established church and state; but an issue with many ramifications and a bearing on various other issues of contention over individual liberty within state church; to be understood in part as a bid from within the clergy to loosen oppressive institutionalised authoritarianism exercised by clergy of State Church over the people which had, paradoxically, come (in tandem with royal absolutism) to replace papal authoritarianism overthrown in Luther's Reformation; Gr's vision of the *Folkekirke* [national church, people's church], requiring both *sognebaandsløsning* [dissolution of parochial ties] for the people and a corresponding *præstefrihed* [clerical freedom] for the clergy, was of free congregations gathered round free priests; see also **Baptismal Covenant**; **Birkedal,** Schøller Parelius Vilhelm; **Frederiks Kirke**; **free church**; **free congregation**; **Kierkegaard,** Peter Christian; **Lammers,** Gustav Adolf; **Lindberg,** Jakob Christian; **Lutheran**; **marriage of divorcees**; **Mynster,** Jakob Peter; **Pietism**; **religious gatherings**; **Service-Book Issue**; **Sognebaandsløsning**.

Præstø *15, 18, 20, 62, 112, 116, 123, 144, 146, 166, 167, 175, 198, 199, 276*; small town on Præstø Bugt [Bay] some 60 km south of Copenhagen and some 12 km north-east of Gr's parental home and father's church at Udby; Gr named to the living of Præstø and Skibbinge February 1821, held until he moved (November 1822) as *kapellan* [curate] at Vor Frelsers Kirke in Christianshavn, Copenhagen; here his first son, Johan, born; Gr's mother buried here and close by is the manor of Nysø, seat of the Stampe family and gathering-place for leading figures in Danish life.

Paa Guds Jerusalem det ny *278*; *In God's Jerusalem the new*; title thus cited by H. L. Martensen but correctly *På Jerusalem det ny* (332 in *DDS* 2002); Gr's adaptation of 7th c. Latin *Urbs beata Ierusalem*; published in *Sang-Værk til den danske Kirke* 1837; see also **Kirken den er et gammelt Huus**; **Sov sødt, Barnlille**.

Q

Quaker *141, 288*; member of Christian society (Society of Friends) founded in England mid-17th c. by George Fox (1624-1691), their sole authority being 'the inward light' and the sufficiency of Christ dwelling within each believer; no priesthood, nor sacraments; at various times persecuted, but also won respect and influence for their pacifism, sobriety, modesty and industriousness; found followers abroad including Scandinavia; Quaker Thomas Shillitoe (1754-1836) who sought audience with various European heads of state is said to have received assurances from

Frederik VI (1821) that in Dk Quakers would be guaranteed freedom of conscience and exemption from military service; Norwegian cleric Claus Pavels, later Bishop of Bergen, notes (Diary, 9 March 1815) "curiosity" that "a Quaker by name of Tønnes Johnsen has been exempted from swearing the oath of citizenship and doing military service" and that "a couple of the Norwegian prisoners of war have come home from England as Quakers" though Norwegian Quakers trace their formal organisation from 1818; prominent among English Quakers was Elizabeth Fry (prison reformer) who visited Copenhagen with brother Joseph (emancipationist) August 1841, under patronage of Queen Caroline Amalie who asked Gr to help escorting them round city prisons; though Gr disliked what he saw as rationalist tendency in Quakers he respected Elizabeth Fry and her convictions; see also **Hauge,** Hans Nielsen; **Eriksen's wife.**

Queen's Charity-School; see **Dronningens Asylskole.**

Queen's Prospect; see **Dronningens Udsigt.**

Quintilian (Marcus Fabius Quintilianus) *72*; *ca.* A.D. 35-98; Roman rhetorician, successor to Cicero in advocacy of view that what (rhetorically) offends the ear cannot persuade the listener; much studied in schools before and after Renaissance, in Denmark as elsewhere, and therefore widely influential in all fields where rhetoric, oratory, elocution, general power of language relevant.

R

Rahbek, Knud Lyhne *68, 93, 97, 156, 282*; 1760-1830; author, literary historian, critic, professor in aesthetics; leading critical authority of his time and arbiter of public taste; though unsympathetic to 19th-c. Romanticism and its philosophical foundations, his literary influence resurfaced in 1820s cultivation of poetic realism, and was exercised through board of management of Royal Theatre Copenhagen (appointed 1809); married to Kamma Rahbek (1775-1829); their home Bakkehuset became meeting-place for diverse leading figures of period; main published critical work a loose critical commentary on Holberg's drama, and contribution to *Udvalgte Danske Viser fra Middelalderen* [Selected Danish Ballads of Middle Ages] (1812-14); co-founded (1785) with Christian Henriksen Pram (1756-1825) influential periodical *Minerva* (published 1785-1808) which put into public debate issues of liberalism raised across Europe by French Revolution; called 'The Squirrel' by wife because of red hair and habit of stealing hempseed from his canary.

Rahbek, Kamma (Karen Margrethe), *282*; 1775-1829; together with husband, literary critic and scholar Knud Lyhne Rahbek (1760-1830), held open house for gifted and fashionable figures in Copenhagen cultural life at their home Bakkehuset; sister-in-law to poet and dramatist Adam Oehlenschläger; charmed young Hans Christian Andersen when visitor to "Bakkehus, where lived the poet Rahbek and his interesting wife. Rahbek never spoke to me; but his lively and kind-hearted wife often amused herself with me. I had at that time again begun to write a tragedy, which I read aloud to her. Immediately on hearing the first scenes, she exclaimed, "But you have actually taken whole passages out of Oehlenschläger and Ingemann." "Yes, but they are so beautiful!" replied I in my simplicity, and read on" (Andersen, translated Mary Howitt 1847); gifted writer of letters in which J. L. Heiberg found more poetry than in anything else I have read."

Rask, Rasmus Christian Nielsen *114, 130*; 1787-1832; Danish pioneering philologist; after studying in Copenhagen, appointed to librarianship in University Library; following publication (1811) of his Introduction to Grammar of Icelandic and other Ancient Northern Languages, made Member of the Arnamagnæanske Kommission (founded under direction of Copenhagen University to implement will of Arne Magnusson, 1730, bequeathing his collection of Icelandic manuscripts to public use) and undertook editing of an Icelandic lexicon (1814); with royal grants, undertook prolonged visits to Iceland (1813-15), and (from 1816) Sweden, Finland, Tartary, Russia, Persia, India and Ceylon, acquiring command of some 25 ancient and modern languages and knowledge of many more, significantly advancing modern study of comparative philology and collecting manuscripts for University library; to such prodigious field-work he added astonishing published output; notably, an Anglo-Saxon Grammar (1817, translated 1830 into English, under his supervision, by his student – and Gr's later Anglo-Saxonist rival – Benjamin Thorpe), an essay (1818) expounding descent of Icelandic and Scandinavian languages from common ancestry with other European languages and with Latin and Greek, editions of the Elder (Poetic, or Sæmund's) Edda and the *Edda* of Snorri Sturluson (1818), grammars of Spanish (1824), Frisian (1825) and Italian (1827), an essay on controversial issue of Danish orthography (1826), and studies of ancient Egyptian and Jewish chronology (1827, 1828), as well as learned papers on various western and oriental languages and significant periodical reviews; his proposal (1816) to edit text of *Beowulf* (to be accompanied by Gr's translation, with intention of making good the many flaws of Thorkelin's edition of 1815) was frustrated by Rask's journeys abroad, but in any case Rask came to doubt Gr's approach to such translation and criticised idiom adopted by Gr in translations of Saxo and Snorri; poorly rewarded for outstanding services to international scholarship, and to his king, university and country (though belatedly appointed professor), plagued by ill-health and some mental instability, Rask prematurely died 1832.

Rationalism *116, 123, 125, 158-160, 169, 170, 175, 188, 250, 280, 328, 336*; philosophical standpoint associated with 18th c. European Enlightenment, with roots in Pietism – Johann Salomo Semler (1725-91), widely regarded as father of rationalism, was professor of theology in Halle (Germany), historical centre of Pietism; major force through much of 19th c., holding reason to be proper foundation of understanding; therefore opposed philosophically to empiricism which was unreliably founded upon evidence of senses; in religion, opposed to unreasoning acceptance of authority (such as biblical, doctrinal, liturgical), and disposed to modernise Church by shedding traditional formulations which reason could not endorse; therefore absolute reverse of medieval prioritising of faith ("Let be thy Wit, let be thy Wonder; for Faith is above and Reason under") but also challenge to various aspects of Lutheran Reformational heritage; resistance to (German-originating) rationalism gave rise in Dk to so-called "church struggle" [*kirkekamp*] between 1825-32 in which J. C. Lindberg prominently figured, and helped define Gr's concept of Church [*kirkelige anskuelse*] which Lindberg espoused; in Norway too, similar opposition to rationalism of such academics as Niels Treschow (1751-1833), professor in Kristiania (Oslo), often found its stance in Grundtvigian positions and was expressed, as in Dk, in revivalist movement and *de gudelige forsamlinger* [religious gatherings], inspired by such as Hans Nielsen

Hauge (1771-1824); Gr lyrically declared the subordinacy of reason to that which is taught by the Spirit in *Er du skriftklog paa Guds Rige* (*Sang-Værk til den danske Kirke*, 1837): if, as regards the kingdom of God [*Guds Rige*], you are *skriftklog* [learned, smart] by virtue of having been taught by the Spirit of the Lord [*Herrens Aand*], you are entitled to speak of it and to urge others to seek it and live its life, but "If you're merely smart through thinking / thoughts that spin within your brain, / in dead waters cast your anchor! / Of the world speak fair and fine! / But shut up about God's kingdom: / what that means you've no idea. / Speak not of eternal life! / Deeps of God, just as his *Fiat*, / only God's mind fathoms" [*Er du skriftklog kun paa Tanker, / Som i Hjernen de gaae rundt, / I det Smulle kast da Anker! / Tal om Verden smukt og sundt! / Men tie stille med Guds Rige, / Du ei veed hvad Det vil sige! / Tal ei om et evigt Liv! / Det Guds Dyb, alt som hans Bliv, / Kun Guds Aand randsager!*]; see also **Aand**; **Münter,** Friederich Christian Carl Hinrich; **Clausen,** Henrik Nicolai; and **Rudelbach**, Andreas Gottlob.

Reden *78, 79, 318*; shipping roads in Øresund off Copenhagen; strategic area in sea-defence of city and harbours; feature of Gr's illness 1867 was anxiety over Prussian landing from sea, prompting him to write to Admiralty; see also **Copenhagen,** battle of.

Reedtz, Asta; widow of Holger Christian Reedtz; see **Grundtvig,** Asta.

Reedtz, Holger Christian *175, 242, 320*; 1800-57; *Geheimekonferensraad* [Privy councillor], diplomat, Secretary in Danish Foreign Affairs Department, later Foreign Minister; the *kammerjunker* through whom Frederik VI privately encouraged Gr to apply (1839) for post at Vartov; his ancestral manor was at Palsgaard, east Jylland; his widow *Komtesse* Asta Reedtz, became Gr's third wife.

Reedtz, Sofie Vilhelmine Henriette *243, 244, 319, 320, 338*; 1849-1906; daughter of Gr's third wife Asta by previous marriage to Holger Christian Reedtz; see **Sparrewohn,** Sophie.

Regensen *157, 159, 293*; *Collegium Domus Regiae*; residential college including chapel or church (*Regenskirken*) erected 1618-23 on initiative of Christian IV to accommodate 120 students of University of Copenhagen; like older foundation of Valkendorfs Kollegium where Gr resided 1808-11, Regensen formed community of young men who would become leaders of Danish society; colleges and student community as whole formed significant body of opinion and action in 19th c., for example at time of English attack on Copenhagen 1801, of partition of Norway from Dk 1814, and of struggle for Constitution of 1849; Christian IV's foundation was further provided with adjacent church (*Trinitatis Kirke* which, because of its function as church for nearby University and student population, also became known, confusingly, as *Regenskirken*), dedicated 1637 to Holy Trinity though not completed until 1656, its round tower (topped by University's astronomical observatory) a city landmark and its upper floor housing (1657-1861) University Library; in Regenskirken (whether this was the chapel inside Regensen or Trinitatis Kirke seems unsettled) Gr delivered his controversial probational sermon (*dimisprædiken*) because usual venue, Vor Frue Kirke (Copenhagen's cathedral), lay in ruins after English bombardment of 1807.

Regens-Kirke; see **Regensen**.

Rein, Jonas *86*; 1760-1821; Norwegian priest, poet, politician; studied in Copenhagen, frequented Rahbeks' gatherings at Bakkehuset, and Det norske Selskab [The Norwegian Society]; priest in Bergen (1808), elected as one of four parliamentary representatives for Bergen, all fiercely opposed to union with Sweden imposed 1814; one of contemporary poets whose works Gr read, along with many novels, during his second year of studying theology; for a time corresponded with Gr who (1812) praised Rein's latest poem for not having treated Jesus merely as a teacher of the virtuous "which he had least expected of a poet from the period in which Rein had been formed" (that is, the period of Rationalism); when Rein wrote back that it was appropriate for a Christian teacher to show more mildness than Gr expressed towards people of other opinions, Gr responded with a two-page assertion that mildness was all very well in its proper time and place, but in a misguided age one had to declare the truth loud and emphatically (Claus Pavels, later Bishop of Bergen, Diary, April 1812).

Reitzel, Carl Andreas *168*; 1789-1853; leading publisher and bookseller in Copenhagen over first half of 19th c., dealing in foreign as well as Danish literature; esteemed by Gr at time when Copenhagen book-trade was in doldrums; but Gr found him unwilling to take on new theological journal under Gr's editorship, intimidated (Gr alleges) by academic and ecclesiastical establishment.

Religion and Liturgy; see ***Om Religion og Liturgie***.

religious gatherings; see **forsamlinger**.

Rendsborg *108*; town in Slesvig-Holsten near Ejder, 27 km west of Kiel; originally fortress built by dukes of Holsten where Hærvejen (ancient military road) crossed river; by end of 17th c. had become Danish monarchy's most important fortress outside Copenhagen, key to defence of southern frontier; seized (1813) by Allies in Napoleonic wars; seized by Slesvig-Holsteners in revolt against Dk 1848 and permanently lost to Dk.

revealed theology; see **Guldberg**, Ove Jørgensen Høegh-.

Rigsdag; Danish parliament; see **Grundloven**.

rigsdaler, passim; see **currency**, Danish.

Rigsforsamling, den grundlovgivende *24, 144, 239, 246, 286*; the National Constituent Assembly, called October 1848 to deliberate upon *Danmarks Riges Grundlov*, the Constitution of the Kingdom of Dk, which it formally accepted 25 May 1849 and which finally came into force with King's signature 5 June 1849; membership of Assembly was to be determined by popular election (electors being reputable male householders over 30) but controversy arose when government added one *kongevalgt* [king's nominee] for every three elected members; some, like Gr, welcomed inclusion of national worthies of whom disinterested concern for Dk's good might be expected; others, including many of Gr's friends and associates, were already looking towards pursuit of party political goals (though formal parties did not yet exist); the *Bondevenner* (Friends of the peasantry) emerged from election as largest group but distribution of *kongevalgte* members ensured approximately equal size of centrist National-Liberal and right-wing Conservative groupings; draft Constitution (modelled particularly on Constitutions of Norway and Belgium) was framed by D. G. Monrad, refined into Danish conformity by Orla Lehmann, and finally adopted by large majority of Constituent Assembly, 25 May 1849; Gr himself was elected to Assembly from constituency of Præstø (South Sjælland) but, true to own principles, accepted no political whip in deliberations; see **Grundlov; portraits** of Grundtvig.

Rigsraad *268*; Council of the Realm; deriving from Middle Ages, Danish supreme legislative council composed of officers of state, clergy and nobility, with responsibility of electing and constraining power of king; modified at Reformation 1536 with clergy's loss of political status and again with establishment of *enevældet* [absolutism] 1660 when it ceased function; reformed in 1854, within terms of constitutional settlement of 1849, partly in order to accommodate governance of the duchies of Slesvig, Holsten and Lauenburg which were not part of the Kingdom of Denmark but, following 1864 peace-treaty at Vienna when Dk ceded the duchies to Prussia and Austria, finally abolished in 1866 revision of 1849 constitution; see also **Grundloven**.

Riisbrigh, Børge *78, 84*; 1731-1809; Professor of Philosophy, University of Copenhagen; though influenced by Immanuel Kant (1724-1804), he defended empirical science and distanced himself from contemporary Kantianism; described by Gr as confining himself strictly to philosophical tradition of Wolffianism (Christian von Wolff, 1679-1754, German Professor of Mathematics, Halle and Marburg, on basis of philosophy of Gottfried Wilhelm Leibniz, 1646-1716, developed position combining empiricism with rationalism, which for some decades was prevailing philosophy taught in northern European universities); Riisbrigh's textbook *Praenotiones philosophicae* [First principles of philosophy; 1775] was, in Gr's day, a standard introduction to academic philosophy; it was Riisbrigh's assessment of Gr's examination performance in Mathematics and Astronomy (April 1801) as *laudabilis præ ceteris* [commendable beyond others, above average] which tipped balance of judgment in his favour; however, Gr suggests that Copenhagen visiting lectures (1802) of Henrik Steffens (1773-1845), though so revelatory to him, made little impact upon resident philosophers and theologians in University.

Rimelige Strøtanker 114; Gr's *Rimelige Strøe-Tanker ved Kalundborgs i Livet vel meriterede Stads-Satyricus Jens Baggesens Grav* published anonymously (in *Nyeste Skilderie af Kjøbenhavn*, 11 November 1815 and subsequent numbers) as intervention in literary feud being waged between poet Jens Baggesen and Adam Oehlenschläger and his supporters; *rimelige* allowed sense of 'rhyming' as well as 'reasonable, equitable' perhaps as pun in spirit of Baggesen's own riddling strategy; *strøtanker* are '*obiter dicta*, thoughts by the way, jottings, aphorisms' thus title "Equitable aphorisms at the grave of Jens Baggesen, well-merited in life as Kalundborg's town-satirist" is intentionally irreverent; yet though Baggesen's disrespect for Oehlenschläger and contemporary Danish poesy at large also implicitly extended over Gr, *Strøtanker* acknowledged Baggesen's merits while challenging his judgments; Baggesen (who early in November 1815 had sent Gr an inscribed copy of his poem *Drømmen i Kronprindsessegade No. 390* [The dream in 390 Kronprinsessegade]) cursed his anonymous critic as this Martin Luther in reverse (*den bagvendte Morten Luther*) sent by the powers of darkness, but subsequently, particularly after Gr revealed his identity as author of *Rimelige Strøe-Tanker*, came to recognise something of a fellow-spirit in Gr the poet; see also **Tylvten**.

Ringerige *18, 147, 150-152*; Ringerike, historic district in Norway northwest of Oslo about Tyrif-jord; in 10th-11th c. a petty kingdom under Sigurd Syr, stepfather to King Olaf the Holy whose life is narrated in Snorri Sturluson's Sagas of the Norse Kings, which Gr translated; area rich in viking-age art of distinctive style; in 19th c. a focus of Norwegian national-romantic interest; visited in 1851 by Gr who was profoundly moved by reception and experiences there where both natural scenery and antiquities affirmed the historical narratives Gr had handled.

Risbrigh; see **Riisbrigh**.

Rochambeau, Jean Baptiste Donatien de Vimeur *66*; 1725-1807; French aristocrat; marshal in army; distinguished service in Seven Years War (1756-1763); commanded auxiliaries sent by revolutionary France to assist Americans in war of independence against British.

Roeskilde-Riim *193, 194, 257*; 'Roskilde rhymes,' lengthy poetic work by Gr, read by him to con-vention of Sjælland's clergy at Roskilde 1812 (published in substantially revised version 1814), on national historical themes, companion-piece to his *Kort Begreb af Verdens Krønike betragtet i Sammenhæng* [A concise view of universal history examined in context; 1814]; both works demonstrate Gr's thesis that history reveals God's Providence at work, both didactically set the achievements of "our forebears" before the present generation as example to Church and to people; features commentary-tour of sites and monuments in Roskilde, Sjælland, legen-dary seat of Danish kings, anciently a leading ecclesiastical centre, its fine cathedral housing tombs of various Danish kings and of Margrethe I; lengthy section of poem is direct address and exhortation to then incumbent bishop, Friederich Münter; accompanied by *Roskilde-Saga til Oplysning af Roskilde-Riim* [Roskilde-Saga in clarification of Roskilde-Riim; 1814]; see also *Verdens-Krøniken*; **berserk-gang**.

Rolighed *221-223*; 'Lille Rolighed' was J. C. Lindberg's house on Kalkbrænderivej, outside Co-penhagen's walls, where despite regulations preventing priests from freely ministering except within appointed incumbency, and laity from joining any congregation but that of the church of their own parish, public gatherings for religious services were held in Autumn 1831 (with Gr's knowledge but not, initially, his involvement), conducted by Lindberg and Lorenz Siemonsen (originally *kateketen* [catechist] in Frederiks tyske Kirke, but from 1829 priest for the church's dwindling German congregation); in November 1831 they sought King's permission to establish free Danish and German congregation with Gr and Siemonsen as priests, but application was rejected January 1832; on 11 February Gr, initially much disturbed by Lindberg's confrontational initiatives, had unrewarding audience with P. C. Stemann, Chancellery president; in calculated defiance, Gr spoke next day for first time at 'Lille Rolighed' and again following Sunday to hugely increased gathering; new meeting place was hired in Jakob Holm's property adjacent to Frederiks Kirke but after special meeting with Gr, Bishop P. E. Müller made recommenda-tion to Chancellery leading to Gr's authorisation to hold Sunday evening service and sermon at Frederiks Kirke though his appointment as formal incumbent was not granted; nevertheless Gr had succeeded to a limited degree in establishing a free congregation, within the State Church;

but final resolution of the issue of parochial ties was not enacted until 1855; see **Forsamlinger**; **Sognebaandsløsning**.

Romans, Epistle to the *289*; cited along with Ephesians 5:9 in discussion of Gr's view that some Biblical translations effect a false clarity and that obscurity in source-text should be reflected in translation.

Romans, ungodly *85*; characterisation of ancient Rome gleaned by Gr from philosophy lectures given (winter 1802) by Henrik Steffens, Ehlers' Kollegium, Copenhagen, placing Nero's Rome within a Christian, Scriptural-analogous perspective of human history; this schematic view doubtless endorsed Gr's view of papal Rome and contributed to the universal-historical position he assumed in later writings.

Romanticism, German; see **New School** in Germany.

Rome, ancient *72, 162*.

Rome, Church of *25, 307*.

Rose-garden of the High North; see ***Høinordens rosengaard***.

Rosenørn-Teilmann, Christian Peder Theodor *313*; 1817-79; jurist and politician; 1865-67 *kultusminister* (Minister for Church affairs and Education); 1867-68 Justice Minister; responsible for official enquiry into Gr's conduct during Palm Sunday service at Vartov church, 1867; see also **Palm Sunday** 1867.

Roskilde *107, 166, 193, 213, 224, 256, 257, 279*; cathedral town at south end of Roskilde Fjord, Sjælland, some 30 km west of Copenhagen; predating Copenhagen as royal and ecclesiastical 'capital' in Sjælland; legendarily associated with king Roar (so Saxo Grammaticus; Hrothgar in the Anglo-Saxon poem *Beowulf*), historically with Absalon (warrior-bishop, founder of Copenhagen) and other eminent figures of the medieval Church in Dk; cathedral has served as mausoleum for Margrethe I and other Danish sovereigns since Middle Ages.

Roskilde Landemode *107, 166*; biannual diocesan convention in Roskilde, Sjælland, previously a *Provstesynode* [synod for deans] but reformed by Bishop Friederich Münter to provide assembly for whole clergy at which he also introduced custom of reading of learned papers (published as *Videnskabelige Forhandlinger ved Sjællands Stifts Landemoder* [Learned proceedings of the diocesan conventions of the diocese of Sjælland], 3 vols., 1812-); plenary meetings gathered in *Riddersalen* [Great hall] in Roskilde Cathedral; occasion of serious clash between Gr and Münter, bishop of Sjælland, October 1814; Gr had recently published small piece, *En mærkelig Spaadom ogsaa om Dannemark efter en gammel Haandskrift* [A strange prophecy also concerning Denmark, after an ancient manuscript], one of several works over this period in which Gr, serving (1811-13) as his father's curate in his home village of Udby, expressed a biblical-orthodox, pietistic view of providential world history, Church and people, which led him also to challenge reputation of various distinguished figures past and present including scientists and liberal philosophers (including F. W. J. Schelling, whose philosophy of identity, Gr alleged, unacceptably harmonised the existential contradiction between good and evil); H. C. Ørsted, physicist, anonymously wrote hostile review of *En mærkelig Spaadom* in *Dansk Litteratur-Tidende* 12-13 (1814), concluding "Wake up, all friends of truth and genuine piety! Do you not see that pyre rise again upon which Vanini burned? do you not see that prison again tower aloft wherein Galileo languished?" Gr responded (May 1814) with his publication *Hvem er den falske Prophet? Hvem forvirrer Folket?* [Who is the false prophet? Who is it that confuses the people?] and, at the October *Landemode* in Roskilde, with his address *Om Polemik og Tolerance eller Tvist og Taal* [On polemic and tolerance or dispute and sufferance]; already on 6 October he was required to hand over his text to bishop Münter and to representative of royal authority for diocese, W. J. A. Moltke, and on 19 November he received severe reprimand from bishop; Ørsted subsequently took up dispute with *Imod den store Anklager* [Against the great accuser] (1814) and Gr replied to this with *Imod den lille Anklager* [Against the little accuser; 1815], whose title continued *med Bevis for at Schellings Philosophie er uchristelig, ugudelig og løgnagtig* [with proofs that S's philosophy is unchristian, ungodly and mendacious], to which Ørsted made no published response; see **Schelling,** Friedrich Wilhelm Joseph von; **Vanini,** Giulio Cesare (Lucilio); and **Galilei,** Galileo.

Rothe, Peter Conrad *311, 312, 319*; 1811-1902; priest; *Stiftsprovst* [diocesan dean, corresponding approximately to English cathedral Dean or archdeacon] , Vor Frue Kirke, Copenhagen; educated at Metropolitanskolen, Copenhagen (matriculated 1828); *cand. theol.* Copenhagen 1833; for his *Licentiatgrad* (1840) wrote thesis on Life of English saint, Anselm of Canterbury (1033-1109); influenced by dogmatics of Professor H. N. Clausen and especially (Bishop) H. L. Martensen, and found Gr's views and polemic distasteful; 1840-42 travelled in Italy, France, Germany where he spent time with Søren Kierkegaard following lectures of F. W. J. von Schelling (1775-1854); on return was appointed (1843) curate at Vor Frue Kirke, Copenhagen; eventually *sognepræst* [parish priest] and *Provst* [Dean] there, esteemed for tireless industriousness in pastoral and Church matters, until retirement 1892 when he was raised to (titular) rank of bishop; involved in proceedings following Gr's breakdown, Palm Sunday 1867, and issued injunction against Gr preaching on that Good Friday; see also **Palm Sunday** 1867.

Rothe, Tyge; 1731-1795; see **Bjørn,** Karen.

Rothe, Valdemar Henrik *221*; 1777-1857; matriculated from Aarhus Latin School 1794; after graduating in Theology from Copenhagen (1800), travelled widely in Europe; on return appointed (1809) parish priest in Helsinge, 1818 priest at Vartov, 1822 resident curate at Trinitatis Kirke in Copenhagen and 1830 parish priest there; his supervisory presence at J. C. Lindberg's home during religious gatherings (*forsamlinger*) February 1832 was sufficient to prevent police intervention despite official disapproval of these challenges to position of state church; subsequently (1836) achieved degree of Doctor of Theology, the public defence of his thesis being notable for formal opposition from Gr in fluent Latin.

Rotwitt, Carl Edvard *242*; 1812-60; Supreme Court advocate, *amtmand* (chief administrative officer of county), politician; sympathetic to Bondevennerne [Friends of peasant farmer] grouping; chairman of *Folketing* 1853; as personal friend of Frederik VII, invited to form new administration 1859 in which he held several principal offices; Gr made his funeral oration 1860.

Rousseau, Jean Jacques *190*; 1712-1778; Swiss-French poet, philosopher; his pedagogic principles and ideas of natural human goodness and capacity for happiness – which formal learning and social culturising spoil – were applied to the childhood of Crown Prince Frederik, later Frederik VI, who was raised barefooted in spartan environment.

Royal Theatre, Copenhagen *13, 87*; *Det kongelige Teater*; first Danish playhouse was opened in Copenhagen 1722 under royal patronage primarily as stage for group specialising in perform-ing Molière in translation and Danish (though French influenced) plays of Ludvig Holberg (1684-1754), then professor in University of Copenhagen and traditionally regarded as father of Danish theatre; out of favour during period of national (and royal) pietism under Christian VI (1730-46); replaced 1748 by new theatre built to design of Nikolai Eigtved (1701-54) and under royal patronage (Frederik V, 1746-66), in Kongens Nytorv; this, though altered and extended, was theatre known to Gr, H. C. Andersen and their contemporaries; repertoire at beginning of 19th c. predominantly foreign, A. F. F. Kotzebue (1761-1819) being most performed author, until national drama blossomed again about 1810 with tragedies of Adam Oehlenschläger (1779-1850), vaudevilles and romantic drama of J. L. Heiberg (1791-1860) and comedies of Henrik Hertz (1798-1870); this theatre was replaced on same site by present building 1874, designed by Vilhelm Dahlerup (1836-1907) and Ove Petersen (1830-92); see also **theatre and drama**.

Rudelbach, Andreas Gottlob *168, 201, 203, 220, 279*; 1792-1862; priest, doctor of philosophy; ma-triculated from Metropolitanskolen 1810, studied classical languages at Copenhagen University; won University Gold Medal 1817 for dissertation on classical poetic metre and was involved (1818) in *pennefejde* ['pen-feud'] as one of 'The Twelve' [*Tylvten*] against Jens Baggesen; gained reputa-tion as a *gammellutbersk teolog* [old-Lutheran theologian] and was initially strong supporter of Gr in 'church struggle' and opposition to rationalist theology, notably through collaboration in publication of *Theologisk Maanedsskrift* (1825-26; continued by Rudelbach alone until 1828, after Gr was placed under censorship 1826), though after 1845 their viewpoints were to diverge; university preferment in Dk remaining closed to him despite undoubted intellectual qualities and growing repute as protestant theologian, he served 1829-45 as *superintendent* (bishop within Lutheran church-ordinance) in Glauchau, Saxony, continuing to oppose rationalism; from 1848, having returned to Dk, held benefice as *sognepræst* (parish priest) in Slagelse, Sjælland; surviv-ing letters from his sisters Christine and Juliane, busy observers of their middle-class circle in Copenhagen, provide rich anecdotal comment on events and personalities.

Ruin, The *27, 333-334*; Anglo-Saxon poem from the Exeter Book, transcribed by Gr 1830 and revisited in last days of his life, which he took to be symbolic of the "truly proud ruin" which the remaining monuments of Anglo-Saxon literary culture constitute.

Rune-Bladet 138, 143, 144; *Rune-Bladet med 'Kristian den Ottende' til Det unge Danmark* [Rune-sliver aboard the *Christian the Eighth*; for young Denmark]; poem by Gr, composed at sea 5-6 July 1844; subsequently used in introduction to his *Skov-Hornets Klang mellem Skamlings-Bank-erne betegnet af Nik. Fred. Sev. Grundtvig* [The waldhorn's clarion among the Skamling hills characterised by NFSG; 1844] which contained text of his address to huge audience at open-air assembly on Skamlingsbanken, Sønderjylland, 4 July 1844, on Danish-nationalistic themes;

returning to Copenhagen, aboard *Kristian den Ottende*, ship chartered by Det Skandinaviske Selskab [The Scandinavian Association] and full of students (who, as the ship passed Sjællands Odde, spontaneously began singing Gr's song on the death of Peter Willemoes in the Battle of Sjællands Odde, 1808), Gr was stirred to compose *Rune-Bladet*, asserting that it would be Denmark's youth which, under *Nordens Aand* [the Spirit of the North], would carry a message of rebirth of national solidarity to 'the ancient *Stamme*' (*stamme* is both 'tree-trunk' and 'lineage' as in "there shall come forth a rod out of the *stem* of Jesse" – therefore Gr fairly certainly alludes to the king) in Copenhagen: *Snekken under klaret Sky, / Paa den blanke Vove / Glider ind, i Morgengry / Under grønne Skove, / Bringer med til* Axelstad */ Bredt og boldt et Bøge-Blad, / Tæt med Runer ristet! // Bladet sender* Nordens Aand, */ Fuldt af Runer ramme, / Ved det* unge *Danmarks Haand / Til den* gamle *Stamme, / Risted dem paa Bølgen blaa, / Hvor Aartusinder ham saae / Svæve over Sundet!* [Neath the cloudless sky, the ship / on the gleaming sea-swell / with the dawn comes gliding in / under the green woodlands, / bringing there to *Axel's town* [*Axel* = Absalon, Archbishop of Lund, attributed with foundation of fortress and harbour of Copenhagen], / broad and brave, a beechwood spill, / close with runes engraven. / *Northern Spirit* sends this leaf / filled with runestaves potent, / by the hand of Denmark's *youth* / to the *ancient* tree-trunk, / carved them on the ocean blue / where millennia him saw / o'er the Sound a-floating]; the image of the message-bearing rune-stick, once a tree growing by the shore, now delivered from over the sea by a ship, is strikingly close to that of Anglo-Saxon poems *Riddle 60* and *The Husband's Message* in the Exeter Book which Gr had earlier transcribed and studied; see also **Skamlingsbanken**; **Slesvig-Holsten**; **Willemoes,** song for; **Bauta-Stenen**.

Russia, Russians *65, 66, 336*; events in late 18th-c. wars between Russia and declining Turkish Ottoman empire, involving Russian annexation of Crimea 1783 and Field Marshal Potemkin's capture of Otschakov (Ochakov), naval harbour on Black Sea (reported in newspaper *Kiøben-havnske Tidender* 16 January 1789), were followed (subject to considerable delays in reporting) with interest in the parsonage in rural Udby; see also **Constantinople**.

Ryslinge *24, 256, 266, 268, 269, 293*; town on island of Fyn; distinguished in 1851 by establishment of Ryslinge Højskole, with pioneering educationist Christen Kold (backed by Gr) as principal, though school moved 1853 to Dalby near Kerteminde, Fyn; when incumbent of Ryslinge church Vilhelm Birkedal (who consulted closely with Gr throughout) was dismissed (1865) for attacking government and suggesting abdication of Christian ix after loss of Slesvig and Holsten to Germany, outcome (1866) was establishment in Ryslinge of Dk's first *valgmenighedskirke* (congregation opting to elect own pastor but remaining within the established Church) with Birkedal as its pastor.

Rønnebæk Parsonage *284*; Rønnebæk, near Næstved, South Sjælland is some 15 km northwest of Udby (where Gr was born, and served as his father's personal curate, 1811-13).

Rønnebæksholm *23, 240, 241, 283, 284*; large manor house lying some 3 km southeast of Næstved, South Sjælland, owned and, after husband H. Toft's death, competently managed by Marie Toft (1813-54) whom Gr married 1851; still to be seen in gardens is substantial red-brick pavilion built as study for Gr by Marie 1852; during their short marriage their custom was to spend winter in Copenhagen, summer in Rønnebæksholm whence Gr would make Sunday journeys to Copenhagen to officiate at Vartov.

Rørdam, Hans Kristian *322*; 1842-1924; priest; *cand. theol.* 1868; same year appointed *kapellan* [curate] to Gr's close friend and supporter Gunni Busck (1798-1869) in Brøndbyvester, Sjælland; subsequently *kapellan* (1872-81) to Gr's zealous supporter Frederik Engelhardt Boisen (1808-82); held incumbencies of Holeby with Bursø (1881), Ondløse (1886), Fanefjord 1893-1911; one of his hymns is 547 in *DDS* 2002, *Man siger, livet har bange kår* [They say that life leads through fearsome straits; 1878]; his father was Hans Nicolai Kellermann Rørdam and his son was Danish poet and author Valdemar Rørdam (1872-1946).

Rørdam, Peter *284, 308, 322*; 1806-83; priest, teacher, outstanding disciple of Gr; son of Thomas Schatt Rørdam (1776-1831), brother of Hans Nicolai Kellermann Rørdam (1804-84) and Hans Christian Rørdam (1803-69) whose son was Thomas Skat Rørdam (1832-1909); *cand. theol.* 1829; introduced to Gr's circle while still student; assiduous in attending and speaking at Gr's informal gatherings and eventually a frequent guest in Gr's home, Strandgade, Christianshavn; enthused by Gr's ideas on education, took post as teacher 1835 and 1838 was given charge of Copenhagen's *Asylskole* [charity school]; came to notice of Princess Royal, later Queen and Dowager Queen Caroline Amalie, patroness of many philanthropic initiatives, and formed with her a lifelong friendship and working relationship, notably in founding two new charity schools, one of which he himself directed, implementing Grundtvigian educational values there; 1837-38 travelled abroad, chiefly for health; 1841, desiring for himself greater pastoral role of the ministry, was given not a Copenhagen but a distant country parish (Mern in S. Sjælland), perhaps because of ecclesiastical establishment's chronic anxiety over adding to influence of a Gr-disciple already enjoying patronage of queen; popular priest and effective preacher, he was regarded by Gr as model pastor for his success in nurturing *folkelighed* among his flock; married (1850) Jutta Carlsen (died 1866), sister of Marie Toft (born Carlsen), Gr's second wife (1851); largely through efforts of Caroline Amalie he was granted (1855) incumbency of Kongens Lyngby, close to capital, where he built up large congregation; compiled hymnals for use in Lyngby and in his ministry as volunteer field-priest in war of 1864; devoted and close to Gr throughout his life, he nevertheless dissociated himself from political involvement of Grundtvigians with *Det Forenede Venstre* [The United Left] grouping, and was fearful of consequences of political polarisations and confrontations of his last days; the Rørdams, together with the Boisens, exemplify notable phenomenon of Danish clerical families, producing priests, well-run parsonages and a flourishing parochial life over several generations, and intermarrying to create extensive networks of familial connections within the Danish clergy which have played their considerable part in consolidation and continuation of Grundtvigianism, ever an adherence compatible with and congenial to the family; see also **hymns**.

Rørdam, Thomas Skat *320*; 1832-1909; priest, theological scholar, university tutor and teacher, later (1895) Bishop of Sjælland; son of Hans Christian Rørdam (1803-69); together with brother Holger F. Rørdam (until his death 1906, priest in charge of Taarbæk Kirke in succession to his uncle Peter Rørdam) and church historian Frederik Kristian Nielsen he was among the most prominent followers of Gr in the second generation, loyal but independent; but he found the Vartov response to Gr's illness in 1867 utterly distasteful, and preferred medical to charismatic diagnosis of Gr's breakdown; see also **Palm Sunday** 1867.

S

Saba, Queen of *310*; Biblical Queen of Sheba who "heard of the fame of Solomon concerning the name of the Lord ... and when she was come to Solomon, she communed with him of all that was in her heart" (I Kings 10); her example invoked by Gr, Palm Sunday 1867, to prompt Dowager Queen Caroline Amalie to come to altar to be shriven, for "here there is more than the wisdom of Solomon!" See also **Palm Sunday** 1867; **Solomon.**

sacraments *126, 127, 154, 157, 168, 170, 174, 176, 194, 199, 221, 229, 237, 251, 264, 266, 290, 310, 311, 315-317* "Sakramenterne som den lutherske Menigheds Øjestene" [the sacraments as the apple of the Lutheran congregation's eye] (Gr); for Luther, sacraments remained outward and visible signs of inward and invisible grace, divinely bestowed aids to faith, though salvation comes not through sacraments in themselves nor by works but by faith alone; but in his polemical writings (e.g. *Von der babylonischen Gefangenschaft der Kirche* [On the Babylonian Captivity of the Church], 1520), he rejected medieval catholic acceptance of seven sacraments (baptism, eucharist, penance, extreme unction, confirmation, matrimony, ordination) on grounds that only two (baptism, eucharist) were established of Christ's dispensation, others being devisings of Church (sometimes with unworthily worldly intent and effect of conferring excessive power upon ministrant priests); inseparable from sacraments is The Word (cp. Gr's concept of *det levende Ord* [the living Word]), as is evident in Luther on baptism: "Comprehend the difference, then, that Baptism is quite another thing than all other water; not on account of the natural quality, but because something more noble is here added; for God Himself stakes His honor His power and might on it. Therefore it is not only natural water, but a divine, heavenly, holy, and blessed water, and in whatever other terms we can praise it, all on account of the Word, which is a heavenly, holy Word, that no one can sufficiently extol, for it has, and is able to do, all that God is and can do [since it has all the virtue and power of God comprised in it]. Hence also it derives its essence as a Sacrament, as St. Augustine also taught: Accedat verbum ad elementum et fit sacramentum. That is, when the Word is joined to the element or natural substance, it becomes a Sacrament, that is, a holy and divine matter and sign." Similarly, in Luther on eucharist: "Now, what is the Sacrament of the Altar? Answer: It is the true body and blood of our Lord Jesus Christ, in and under the bread and wine which we Christians are commanded by the Word of Christ to eat and to drink. And as we have said of Baptism that it is not simple water, so here also we say the Sacrament is bread and wine, but not mere bread and wine, such as are ordinarily served at the table, but bread and wine comprehended in, and connected with, the Word of God. It is the Word (I say) which makes and distinguishes this Sacrament, so that it is not mere bread and wine, but is, and is called, the body and blood of Christ. For it is said: Accedat verbum ad elementum, et fit sacramentum. If the Word be joined to the element it becomes a Sacrament. This saying of St. Augustine is so properly and so well put that he has scarcely said anything better. The Word must make a Sacrament of the element, else it remains a mere element. Now, it is not the word or ordinance of a prince or emperor, but of the sublime Majesty, at whose feet all creatures should fall, and affirm it is as He says, and accept it with all reverence fear, and humility." (The Large Catechism, tr. F. Bente, W. H. T. Dau, 1921; Project Wittenberg online); thus the four defining motifs in Lutheran sacramental theology, word, water, bread, wine; and Gr's motifs "Daabens Bad og Naadens Bord" [bath of baptism and table of grace]; see also **Daabspagten; liturgy; Katekismus,** Luther's; **Ordet.**

Saga of Olav the Holy; see **Olav,** Saint.

Sagen, Lyder *282*; 1777-1850; writer, *overlærer* [senior tutor] at Cathedral School, Bergen, Norway; known to Gr; credited with having inspired schoolboy and future Norwegian poet, critic, professor of philosophy Johan Sebastian Cammermeyer Welhaven (1807-73) to pursue talent for arts and poetry and to study classics.

Sahl, Laurits *72*; 1734-1805; *cand. theol.*; professor of Greek Copenhagen University; *Konrektor* [vice-principal] of Metropolitanskolen (Vor Frue Skole) Copenhagen; left reputation of being unsavoury, parsimonious, lacking in taste, but above all a bad translator of both Greek and Latin; Gr read Sahl's Herodotus at school in Aarhus, but when teaching his sons Herodotus at home Gr himself translated for them.

Samsøe, Ole Johan; see **Sander,** Levin Christian.

Sandefjord *256*; Norwegian town at end of inlet on west side of outermost end of Oslo Fjord, its church sufficiently prosperous to support "a very fat dean" (Pavels) who spent time in Dk socialising within distinguished circle centred upon Nysø, seat of the Stampe family.

Sander, Levin Christian *164*; 1756-1819 ; born in Itzehoe, Holsten; teacher and author on educational topics, dramatist, first in German then after moving to Copenhagen (1783) in Danish; tragic drama *Niels Ebbesen af Nørreriis eller Danmarks Befrielse* [N. E. of N. or The Liberation of Denmark] (1797) won great success as earliest Danish national-heroic drama, remained in theatrical repertoire long after Sander's death; collaborated with Knud Lyhne Rahbek (1760-1830) in publishing (1804) translation of Shakespeare's *Macbeth*; Jens Baggesen, evidently out of reluctance to accept 'German' Holstener as author of Danish-nationalistic renaissance, alleged (falsely) that Sander plagiarised sketch of drama on Niels Ebbesen from papers of Ole Johan Samsøe (1759-1796), late poet and friend of K. L. Rahbek, and he called Sander "*Niels Ebbesen*'s implausible author."

Sandvig, Bertel Christian *62*; 1752-86; historian and literary historian; though without a university degree, established distinguished and prolific scholarly career cut off by untimely death; co-founder (1777) and secretary of Genealogical and Heraldic Society; secretary (1781) of Det kongelige danske Selskab (the Royal Danish Society); responsible for associated publications and an impressive number of other works, including (1783-85) his translation of the Elder Edda; one of the series of Danish antiquarians who, ahead of Gr, studied Anglo-Saxon within wider context of ancient northern literatures; brought to Gr's attention during his student years by fellow-student Peter Nikolai Skougaard (1783-1838).

Sange for den kristelige Folke-Skole *331, 333*; 'Songs for the Christian Folk-school' – anthology published 1874 by Ernst Trier (1837-93), principal of Vallekilde folk-highschool 1865-93; included pieces by Gr.

Sang-Værk til den danske Kirke *70, 174, 176, 278, 319, 331, 339*; collection of hymns composed by Gr; first part published 1837 (dedicated to the Danish congregation, his friend and financial supporter Gunni Busck and collaborator Peter Fenger) followed in 1839 by portions of a second part; first part issued in new edition 1868, second part, comprised of songs relating to Biblical and Church history, completed and published 1870 under title *Sang-Værk til den danske Kirkeskole*; of the hymns, finally amounting to some 1500 texts, many are wholly original compositions, others are reworkings of pre-existing texts which Gr's characteristic eclecticism led him to seek not only in post-Reformational German sources but in pre-Reformational Latin, in Anglo-Saxon religious poetry, and in hymns of the Greek Church, so that it may be said that here his eclecticism becomes ecumenism; many were eventually adopted into the official Danish Hymnal and still remain the most substantial single corpus of contributions there; "By the word 'Sang-Værk' Gr alludes to the Copenhagen name for the carillon in Vor Frue Kirke which was destroyed by the bombs in September 1807 – Gr's hymn-writing was to be a recompense for this lost music" (Flemming Lundgreen-Nielsen); see also **hymns.**

Sanhedrin *329*; historically, in Jewish antiquity, highest court of justice and supreme council in Jerusalem; metaphorically, and often ironically, any supreme council, particularly within church establishment.

Satires, of Juvenal; see **Juvenal.**

satyriasis *321*; morbidly exaggerated sexual desire in men.

Saxo Grammaticus *62, 83, 106, 111, 114-116, 120, 123, 125, 163, 165, 218, 231, 339*; 12th-c. Danish historiographer; secretary to the warrior-bishop of Roskilde, Absalon, founder of Copenhagen; author of Latin *Gesta Danorum* [Deeds of the Danes], a part-legendary history of the Danes based upon ancient poetry, sagas, word of mouth from Absalon and other informants, a primary monument in defining and thereafter maintaining Danish national identity; *Gesta Danorum* first translated into Danish 1575, translated by Gr, along with Anglo-Saxon *Beowulf* and Snorri Sturluson's Icelandic *Heimskringla*, during his "years in the study" (1815-22), partly to reassert ancient Danish identity and Nordic communality after loss of Norway 1814, partly in spirit of opposing, as in his periodical *Danne-Virke*, "all the Germanicising here at home" (Gr); see also **Northern literature**, ancient.

Saxo, new translation *106*; a pamphlet by Gustav Ludvig Baden (1764-1840), *Dr. G. L. Baden til Hr. Geheimeconferenceraad F. v. Moltke om vor danske Histories Fader Saxo Grammaticus og Trængen til en ny Udgave af ham* [Dr G. L. B. to Geheimeconferenceraad F. von Moltke concerning Saxo Grammaticus, father of our Danish history, and the need for a new edition of him; 1809] was sharply answered by Gr in *Nyeste Skilderie af Kjøbenhavn* (22 August 1809) who believed Baden unfitted to task; Baden, son of Jacob B., graduated 1784 as *cand. jur.* in Copenhagen, gained doctorate in law at Kiel 1793, published a History of the Kingdom of Denmark (1797) and a History of the Kingdom of Norway (1804), and was currently a public official in Odense; his proposed translation of Saxo did not materialise; Gr published his own specimen translation in 1815 and *Saxos Danmarks Krønike* between 1818-22.

Scandinavian Church Assembly; see **Church Assembly,** Scandinavian.

Scandinavian Association, The; see **Det Skandinaviske Selskab**.

Scenes from the warrior-life in the North; see *Optrin af Nordens Kæmpeliv*.

Schelling, Friedrich Wilhelm Joseph von, *62, 84, 96, 157, 189, 203, 205, 227*; 1775-1854; German philosopher, an architect of German transcendental idealism and of 19th-c. Romanticism; a close friend while at Jena University – where from 1798 he taught alongside philosopher Johan Gottlieb Fichte (1762-1814) – of such as Schiller, Goethe and Schlegel; his *System des transzendentalen Idealismus* (1800) proposed *inter alia* that art is philosophy's most important tool; his *Bruno, oder über göttliche und natürliche Principien der Dinge, ein Gespräch* (1802) addressed the philosophy of identity; concerned, like Fichte, with comparative standing of objective and subjective perceptions, he exasperated Søren Kierkegaard (in Berlin 1841 to hear his lectures) with the 'impotence' of his speculative metaphysics and contributed to Kierkegaard's conclusion that philosophy may properly take its starting point only in the subjective; similarly Gr "forsook life with Schelling in his *Bruno*" only to be saved from deadly rationalism by Fichte's 'subjective idealism' and provision of a proper place for faith ("I saw reason, affrighted by *your* lightning flash, get lost within itself; by *your* word could I clearly understand that only by faith do we reach the well-spring of life"); many other distinguished contemporaries of Gr, such as Henrik Steffens, Frederik Wilhelm Treschow, Hans Christian Ørsted and Frederik Christian Sibbern accommodated Schelling's ideas, thus ensuring various well-marked camps within Copenhagen intellectual life of the period.

Schiller, Johann Christoph Friedrich *62, 95, 96, 189, 212*; 1759 – 1805; German historian (professor of history at Jena from 1789, author of history of Thirty Years' War); philosopher and a leading poet and dramatist of German language (plays include *Wallenstein* 1800, *Maria Stuart* 1800, *Die Jungfrau von Orleans* [The Maid of Orleans] 1801, and *Wilhelm Tell* 1804); "the splendid plays and deep speculations of Schiller" formed part of Gr's reading (along with Shakespeare, Goethe) at Egeløkke (1805-08) by which (he says) "the die was cast for the whole of his future."

Schlegel brothers *84*; the brothers August Wilhelm (1767- 1845) and Friedrich Schlegel (1772-1829), leading architects of German Romanticism and central figures in the philosophical, theological, literary circles from which emanated Romantic idealism, liberalism and general reaction against the imaginative shackles, political oppressiveness and classical conformity of rationalism; through their periodical *Athenaeum* (1798-1800) they set an agenda for new approach to more introspective literature, especially poetry, medieval Gothic architecture, untamed landscape, and other such characteristics of what was to become European Romanticism; August Wilhelm was particularly known in Dk as outstanding translator (into German, 1799-1801) of Shakespeare; lectured and published influentially upon drama; appointed professor of literature Bonn 1818; Friedrich achieved distinction with studies *Die Griechen und Römer* (1797) and *Geschichte der Poesie der Griechen und Römer* (1798), and through influential published lecture series emerged as leading philosopher of Romanticism; Gr, partly inspired by attention given by Henrik Steffens (lectures in Ehlers' Kollegium Copenhagen 1802) to German Romantics, read works of both Schlegels during his period on Langeland (1805-08); notable in the context of Gr's dawning interest in Norse myth (he published *Nordens Mytologi* in 1808) is Friedrich Schlegel's *Gespräch über die Poesie* (1800) where, in section entitled *Rede über die Mythologie*, he defines the capacity of myth to revitalise poetry by leading the poet back to the well-springs of poetic conceptualisations of human ideals.

Schmidt, Christian August *208*; 1780-1853; wholesale merchant; married to Anna Pouline Blicher (1785-1880), sister of Gr's first wife Elisabeth.

Schmidt, Frederik *188, 189, 248*; 1771-1840; Danish-Norwegian priest; born in Dk, son of (later, Bishop) Chresten Schmidt; educated in Kristiania Katedralskole; studied theology in Copenhagen where, himself an aspiring poet, he was associated with the Rahbeks' literary circle at Bakkehuset; though he returned to Norway to become (1797) parish priest in Eker and (1808) *Provst* [Dean] in Kongsberg deanery, he was among those who regarded Dk as historic cultural home and spent much time there, forming friendships with such as Norwegian professors Georg Sverdrup (1770-1850) and Niels Treschow (1751-1833), Adam Oehlenschläger, B. S. Ingemann and Gr; opposed (mainly in his verse writings) transfer (1814) of Norwegian sovereignty from Dk to Sweden, moved to Dk and secured (1820) appointment as parish priest in Himmelev, near Roskilde in Sjælland; gained theological doctorate in Copenhagen 1826, published minor collections of poems; selections published from his diaries usefully record life in these circles.

Schmidt, Louise *209*; member of the Grundtvig family circle in Strandgade, Christianshavn; presumably a member of the 'huge' family of *grosserer* Christian August Schmidt, Gr's brother-in-law.

Schouboes Institut *97, 159, 185-187*; *Det Schouboeske Institut*, small private school for boys, Copenhagen, founded 1794 by Frederik Christian Schouboe (1766-1829), teacher and first principal, and closed by him 1814; offering both classical and modern curricula, thus reflecting educational values of 18th c. enlightenment, with languages, drawing and gymnastics on syllabus, it was regarded as one of city's most modern schools; here (1808-10) Gr taught history and geography; but the leading Copenhagen schools – the Metropolitan School and the Borgerdyd [civic virtues] School – were both essentially Latin schools, where many of Gr's distinguished contemporaries had received their education and in contrast to which Aarhus Latin School appeared to Gr embarrassingly quaint and provincial.

Schrøder, Ludvig Peter *26, 73, 97, 192, 306, 323*; 1836-1908; principal of Rødding Højskole, later of Askov Højskole; inspired in his youth by 19th-c. religious revivalism, attracted by Gr's conception of the Church and confirmed in commitment by hearing P. C. Kierkegaard speaking on this (1857); read theology in Copenhagen (*cand. theol.* 1860); in 1861 appointed teacher, and in 1862 succeeded Sophus Høgsbro as principal, at Rødding Højskole which, following Prussian seizure of Slesvig (1864), moved north of new frontier to Askov (1865); Schrøder adopted Gr's conviction that teaching of history, not least through song, should lie at heart of highschool mission, but from Christen Kold (1816-70), pioneer of Danish *friskole* [independent school] and highschool, he also adopted central role of *den vækkende tale* [the inspiring talk, address] on the inner life of spirit and intellect; was himself an outstanding speaker; author of articles and books (including *Om Bjovulfs-drapen: Efter en række foredrag på folkehøjskolen i Askov* [On the Beowulf poem; after a lecture series at Askov folk-highschool; 1875], witnessing to status Gr's pioneering work had given *Beowulf* though taking an independent critical line), co-editor of several periodicals; under his leadership Askov emerged as definitive model of folk-highschool, and after death of Christen Kold (1816-70) he himself was, over a long period, uncontested figurehead of folk-highschool movement; see also **folk-highschools**.

Schulze, Hans Henrik Schreiber *297*; 1823-73; Norwegian author, trained in law, worked for a period as journalist in Kristiania before establishing himself as lawyer and later member of Norwegian Storting (1868-73); published *Fra Lofoten og Solør* (1865), a characterisation of these Norwegian regions, their people, culture and dialects; and other pieces including one-act comedy *Petter og Inge* and play *Haakon Borkenskjæg*.

Science, so-called; see **Videnskabelighed**.

scribes and Pharisees *329*; self-righteous sticklers for law and custom who, in the Gospels, failed to recognise the Christ and became proverbial symbols of religious establishment's hidebound obstinacy and obtuseness; Edmund Gosse's characterisation of those whom Gr fought; see also ***totafoth*** and ***zizith***.

scriptural-theologians; see **skriftteologer**.

Seeberg, Gerhard *160*; 1734-1813; Norwegian pastor preaching an emotional and sentimental pietism; *herrnhuter*; for a time court preacher in Dk; parish priest to Hans Nielsen Hauge (1771-1824; Norwegian pietistic lay preacher) whom he gave access to his library; unfrocked by Supreme Court 1795 for various unlawful breaches of priestly office; thereafter continued revivalist work with small band of followers known as *Seebergianere*.

Sejerø *61*; island *ca.* 10 km long, 2 km wide, lying in bight south-east of Sjællands Odde with two settlements at Sejerby and Kongstrup; inhabitants long had ill reputation for quarrelling with their pastors; Gr's paternal grandfather Otto was priest on Sejerø.

sermon *21, 22, 26, 70, 103, 119, 123, 138, 141, 161, 163, 168, 171, 198, 229, 230, 234, 235, 251, 255, 259, 287, 298, 299, 304, 310-312, 316-318, 321, 322, 327, 338*

sermon and art of preaching, Gr's view on *251*

sermon, Gr's, Sunday 31 July 1825 *125*; see also **mageløse Opdagelse,** den; **Apostles' Creed**.

sermon, Gr's, Sunday 7 May 1826 *201*; see also **Ansar**; **Ansar celebration**; *Den signede Dag*.

sermon, Gr's, New Year's Day, Wednesday 1 January 1834 *70*

sermon, Gr's, Wednesday 1 May 1844 *137*; see also *Sov sødt, Barnlille.*

sermon, Gr's, Sunday 1 October 1848; *287*; see also **Election Thursday**; **Grundlov.**

sermon, Gr's, Sunday 19 August 1855 *141.*

sermon, Gr's, Sunday 15 May 1859 *229, 230*; sermon on Third Sunday after Easter; apparently the Vartov sermon reported by F. L. B. Zeuthen: "there is no other sorrow going hand in hand with the joy of God's kingdom here below, than that which accompanies a mother's joy over the human being she has born into the world. For this is her loving care which can and must become a heart-felt care when the little human being hovers in danger, above all in mortal danger. For that great joy which Christ's Gospel gives birth to in the believing heart, this is far more like a mother's joy over a human being's birth into the world, than we immediately suppose. For where Christ's Gospel finds living entry, it is a rebirth of spirit and of heart, as human as it is divine, that takes place there, so that there comes into the world a new human life, the Christian human life, which is in the end Our Lord Jesus Christ's own human life, over which all believing hearts in the congregation may feel a motherly joy – which is necessarily accompanied by motherly care for this precious life's preservation and growth, and a motherly heart-felt care over all the misunderstanding, opposition, contempt and persecution that this equally loving and beneficent and innocent human life, this new person-of-God, meets in this sinful world." [der er ingen anden Sorg, der gaaer Haand i Haand med Guds Riges Glæde hernede, end den, som følger med Moderens Glæde over Mennesket, hun har født til Verden. Thi det er jo hendes kiærlige Omsorg, som kan og maa blive til en Hjertesorg, naar det lille Menneske svæver i Fare, fremfor alt i Dødsfare. Thi den store Glæde, som Christi Evangelium føder i det troende Hjerte, den ligner langt mere en Moders Glæde over et Menneskes Fødsel til Verden, end vi straks har Formodning om. Thi hvor Christi Evangelium finder levende Indgang, der er det jo en aandelig og hjertelig, ligesaa menneskelig som guddommelig Gienfødelse, der finder Sted, saa der kommer et nyt Menneske-Liv til Verden, det christelige Menneske-Liv, der igrunden er Vorherres *Jesu Christi* eget Menneske-Liv, hvorover alle troende Hjerter i Menigheden føle en moderlig Glæde, der nødvendig følges af moderlig Omsorg for det dyrebare Livs Bevarelse og Væxt og en moderlig Hjertesorg over al den Miskiendelse, Modstand, Foragt og Forfølgelse, dette ligesaa kiærlige og velgiørende som uskyldige Menneske-Liv, dette ny Guds-Menneske møder i denne syndige Verden] (*VS,* 475-6).

sermon, Gr's, Palm Sunday, 14 April 1867 *310, 316, 317, 321*; see also **Palm Sunday** 1867.

sermon, Gr's Cabinet; see **Cabinet-sermon.**

sermon, Gr's desideratum of prophetic aspect of *251*

sermon, Gr's 'dream', of his suppression *103*

sermon, Gr's, farewell in Frederiksberg 1814 *163*; preached on second day of Christmas, it declared Gr's acceptance of his tacit exclusion from majority of Copenhagen's pulpits and his resolution to preach no more in city until he received royal nomination to formal position;

sermon subsequently published under title *Hvilen under Christi Vinger* [Resting beneath the wings of Christ]; appointment to a Copenhagen church did not come until 1822.

sermon, Gr's intended resignation 1867 *311, 312, 318, 322*; see **Palm Sunday** 1867.

sermon, Gr's, on conversion after death; *234*

sermon, Gr's probational; see **Dimis-prædiken.**

sermons, Gr's, effect on Gr and congregation of *161, 198, 229, 259, 287, 299, 327*

sermons, Gr's, nature and role of *168, 171, 251, 299, 304, 327*

sermons, Gr's published *119, 163*; following granting of his licence to preach Gr published a string of single sermons whilst planning to compose and publish a year's cycle; a collection of 16 sermons appeared as *Bibelske Prædikener, efter Tidens Tarv og Leilighed* in 1816; but opportunities to preach over these years were severely restricted for want of an incumbency and reluctance of clergy to offer so controversial a figure use of their pulpit; in these sermons "I was profoundly gripped by *this* feeling, that neither writing skill nor speaking talents, and even less worldly power, would now suffice to remedy the agony of the Church" (Gr); his sermons from Vor Frelsers Kirke were published in three volumes 1827, 1828, 1830 as *Christelige Prædikener eller Søndagsbog* [Christian sermons or Sunday-book], adorned by portrait engraved by E. C. W. Eckersberg and verse by B. S. Ingemann paying homage to Gr as Christian warrior and champion of the North, heir to both Kingo and Saxo; sermons preached in Frederiks Kirke, Christianshavn, 1832-39 were subsequently published, as were (and continue to be) collections of Gr's Vartov sermons; but of the estimated 88,000 pages of Gr-manuscripts surviving chiefly in the Grundtvig Archive in the Royal Library Copenhagen approximately half are his drafts of sermons and other theological and church-related writings and hymns, of which much remains to be published; see also *Søndagsbog*; **hymns.**

sermons, Gr's, quotation of Kingo's hymns in *161*

sermons, Gr, written drafts of *235, 251*

Service-Book Issue; see **Alterbogs-Sagen.**

sexuality, Gr's *91-95, 313, 318*; Gr's sexuality, as expressed and as sublimated in the life-records, is routinely touched upon – though not as yet exhaustively explored in the context of 19th-c. Danish social and sexual mores and psychological and physiological orthodoxies – in modern accounts, and it is sufficiently clear that it has many important and complex ramifications and implications going far beyond juvenile love-poetry on a girl's enchanting eyes, the struggle to assert reason and economics over adolescent sensuality, the passionate fixation upon Constance Steensen-Leth at Egeløkke, flirtations with Miss Bowring in Exeter and Mrs Bolton in London, the three marriages and the charisma he exercised over the many women who in various ways and degrees participated in his ministry; see also **lust.**

Shakespeare, William *62, 85, 133, 157*; 1564-1616; reading and study of English literature in English (rather than in German or Danish translation) appears to have occupied little space in cultural life of first part of 19th c. in Dk, and Gr's contemporary Christian Molbech (1783-1857) claims to have been first to lecture comprehensively on English literature in Copenhagen University, as late as Spring 1847; but interest in Shakespeare, primarily in translation, developed in Dk from end of 18th c., beginning 1777 with anonymous translation – actually by Johannes Boye (1756-1830) – of *Hamlet*; followed 1790-92 by Nils Rosenfeldt's two-volume translation of *Macbeth, Othello, All's well that ends well, King Lear, Cymbeline* and *The Merchant of Venice*; in 1794 Hans Wilhelm Riber (1760-96) published translation of *King Lear* in Nahum Tate's stage version; in 1804 a translation of *Macbeth* was published by Levin Christian Sander (1756-1819) and Knud Lyhne Rahbek (1760-1830); particularly notable was nine-volume series of translations (1807-25) begun by Peter Thun Foersom (1777-1817), actor in the Royal Theatre Copenhagen who first introduced Shakespeare to the Danish theatre (*Hamlet* was staged at Royal Theatre 12 May 1813), completed by Peter Frederik Wulff (1774-1842); in 1810 Simon Sørensen Meisling (1787-1856; the schoolmaster who terrorised Hans Christian Andersen) published translations of *The Tempest* and *The Merchant of Venice*; in 1816 Peter Foersom (1777-1817) issued his translation of *Macbeth*; and in 1816 Adam Oehlenschläger translated *A Midsummer Night's Dream*; otherwise, the German translation (published 1799-1801) of August Wilhelm Schlegel (1767- 1845) was, in Dk as in Germany, most widely read version of the works; Gr appears to have read some Shakespeare in an English reader (alongside German and French literature) while residential private tutor (1805-08) to young son of family Steensen de Leth on Langeland, having heard lectures by Henrik Steffens (winter 1802 in Ehlers' Kollegium Copenhagen) ranking Shakespeare among literary geniuses of world; Gr appreciated Shakespeare's 'poesy' alongside French 'wit'.

shilling, Danish; see **currency,** Danish.

shoemaker *287*; "a Danish-Christian friend" in whose company Gr could discuss composition of the *Rigsdag* and also become relaxed and jovial; probably J. P. Mouritsen, shoe manufacturer and prominent member of Vartov congregation; signatory of proposal (1854) to establish a charitable fund for relief of hardship suffered by families in Vartov congregation.

Sibbern, Frederik Christian *62, 99, 102, 159, 185, 187, 276*; 1785-1872; philosopher; alumnus (1806-11) of Valkendorfs Kollegium contemporaneously with S. B. Herslev and Gr with whom he shared rooms; belonged, with Christian Molbech and Poul Dons, to Gr's circle of close friends and escorted Gr home to Udby in Gr's crisis (December 1810); belonged also to Ørsted brothers' circle, contributing articles to A. S. Ørsted's *Juridisk Arkiv* (having particular interest in philosophical principles of law) and studying physics with H. C. Ørsted; travelled and resided a period in Germany, making acquaintance of many leading figures in academic and cultural life; as professor of philosophy, teaching logic and psychology, he was one of the examiners of Søren Kierkegaard's doctoral thesis; appointed Rektor [Vice-Chancellor] of Copenhagen University for first time 1845; Gr's poem *Til Sibbern* (1811) gratefully remembers his indebtedness to Sibbern; Sibbern died three months after Gr in December 1872.

Siemonsen, Lorentz *70, 172, 221-223, 226*; 1800-72; Danish-born in Flensborg, Slesvig; *kateket* [catechist], later (1829-31) priest to diminishing German congregation at Frederiks Kirke Copenhagen, who at first "seemed to live up to the [Danish] mother-tongue" (Gr) but later appeared to Gr fickle; collaborated (1827 onwards) with J. C. Lindberg in supporting Gr during conflict with H. N. Clausen; resigned from Frederiks Kirke August 1831; September 1831 joined Lindberg as preacher in (then unlawful) religious gatherings at Lindberg's home, Lille Rolighed, Kalkbrænderivej, Copenhagen; was party to petition (November 1831, but dismissed January 1832) seeking royal permission to establish free Danish-German congregation with him and Gr as pastors; subsequently moved to parish in Husby in Slesvig but when Danish army advanced to Husby in Three Years' War (1848-51) he fled to join Holsteners (to Gr's disappointment) and was dismissed from his ministry.

Sigurd Syr *151*; Norwegian petty king in Ringerike, stepfather of King Olaf the Holy; see also **Olav,** Saint.

Simonsen, Lorentz; see **Siemonsen,** Lorenz .

Sin and Evil *303, 304*; Grundtvig leaned less heavily on the dogmatics of Sin and Evil than some contemporaries in the Church, and condemned "all those learned folk who want to investigate the origin of Sin and Evil" – because (according to Ernst Trier's anecdote) he believed that, since human beings learn through experiencing, such academic studies could bring the unwary into jeopardy; though broadly conventional in his acceptance of the entry of Sin and Death into the world, he dissented from the view that the image and likeness of God were entirely destroyed in the human creature at the Fall; he also suggested the less conventional view that Christ's descent into Hell betokened God's ineffable willingness to accept repentance for sin even after death.

Sions Harpe *173*; *Zions Harpe* [The Harp of Zion], small hymnbook compiled and published (1831) by J. C. Lindberg, containing five hymns by Gr and associated with (then illegal) religious gatherings (*forsamlinger*) at Lindberg's home (1831); Lindberg later (1843) published more comprehensive hymnal, *Rosen-Kjæden* [The Rosary], containing 183 of Gr's hymns; official permission granted to Gr (who then had no church of his own) to hold religious gathering in loft in Strandgade (1832) was conditional upon his not using *Zions Harpe; see also* **hymns**.

Sismondi, Jean Charles Leonard Simonde de *105*; 1773-1842; Swiss historian and social economist; though at first adherent of free-market principles of Adam Smith (*The Wealth of Nations*, 1776), was converted by observation of circumstances in England into fierce critic of free-trade economy; Gr found his *Geschichte der italienischen Freistaaten im Mittelalter; aus dem Französischen* (1807) an excellent study of Italian republics and a work which though lacking "a religious eye" yet showed profundity.

Sjælland, Sjællanders *61, 66, 76, 112, 142-146, 159, 161, 255, 283 and passim*; Sjælland (sometimes anglicised as Zealand or Zeeland) is largest of cluster of islands lying between Jylland peninsula and Sweden, growing in political, ecclesiastical and economic preeminence from 12th c. (when Absalon established harbour and fortress of Copenhagen) onwards, and again from Reformation onwards with concentration of authority in Copenhagen; region of Gr's birth to which he ever retained close and deep sense of cultural attachment, finding source of inspiration in culture and speech of the "dreadfully unappreciated, neglected and ill-treated" rural Sjællanders, the peasantry and the farmers who elected him as *Rigsdagsmand* [member of the Constituent Assembly] for Præstø,1848, though he subsequently met with some suspicion when he married into substantial land-owning family (Marie Toft, owner of Rønnebæksholm, related to Carlsen family, owners of Gammel Køgegaard); landscape and shores of Sjælland feature often in his poetry; see also **Øresund**.

Sjælland, Bishop of *68, 159, 248, 261, 311, 320*; office of Bishop of Sjælland, with origins in Middle Ages, was reestablished at Reformation, though chief residence was no longer in ancient cathedral town of Roskilde but close to royal court in Copenhagen where, in Vor Frue Kirke, Johan Bugenhagen consecrated (1539) new Lutheran bishops of Dk; office of Bishop of Sjælland held a *de facto* primacy until diocese divided 1924, separating out a diocese of Copenhagen, when *de facto* primacy (*primus inter pares*) was vested in office of Bishop of Copenhagen (with authority also over Danish churches outside Dk) and Vor Frue Kirke in Copenhagen was elevated to status of cathedral church; in 1861, to mark 50th anniversary of beginning of his ministry, Gr was granted title of Bishop and, within social structure still marked by old absolutist hierarchy of ranking, ranked with the Bishop of Sjælland; "When I read in the ancient Greeks of the Isles of the Blessed in Ocean, where the noblest, most fortunate souls do not flit about like empty and airy shadows but lead a happy life after death, then I always think of the Danish islands and above all of our lovely Sjælland" (Gr, 1840); see also **Balle,** Nicolaj Edinger; **Bøgh,** Matthias Frederik Georg; **Martensen,** Hans Lassen; **Müller,** Peter Erasmus; **Münter,** Friederich Christian Carl Hinrich; **Mynster,** Jakob Peter; **Palladius,** Peder; **Resen,** Hans Poulsen; **Rørdam,** Thomas Skat.

Sjællands Odde *79, 136, 143*; also Sjællands Rif; narrow peninsula 20 km long on north-west coast of Sjælland, its extremest point called Gniben, dividing Sejerø Bugt and Kattegat, where sea-battle between Danish ship of the line *Prince Christian Frederik* and a squadron of British ships (one of them, ironically, a Danish ship seized by British in 1807) commanded by George Parker took place (1808) as incident in Napoleonic wars; Danes were defeated but strategic objective (of hindering British attempts to block Storebælt and thus prevent transport of Danish troops from Fyn to Sjælland) was achieved and honour and national pride redeemed by tactics and heroism of Captain Carl Wilhelm Jessen (1764-1823) who, utterly out-gunned and trapped, ran stricken ship aground to spare it being towed away as spoil of war; crew including 25-year-old Peder Willemoes, hero of Kongedybet (1801) and friend of Gr, killed in battle; Gr subsequently composed song (*Kommer hid, I Piger smaa* [Gather round, you lassies small]) celebrating Willemoes, and a verse inscription for memorial stone raised in Odden's churchyard where some thirty of the Danish dead were laid in a common grave.

Sjællands Rif *143*; see **Sjællands Odde**.

skald; see **skjald**.

Skamlingsbanken *136, 138, 142, 143, 235*; site among hills reaching 113 m. in height, some 7 km. south of Kolding, mid-Jylland, commanding broad vistas of Lillebælt and the Slesvig landscape;

from 1840s traditional venue for popular mass-meetings in support of a Danish Slesvig, one of which (July 1844) Gr addressed at a time of great optimism over readiness of Danish youth to uphold national cause; here (1863) a 16 m. high pillar bearing names of eighteen eminent Danish *sønderjyder* [South Jutlanders] was raised and, after being blown up by invading Prussians 1864, was erected anew 1866; subsequently memorial stones have been placed there for Gr and others, among them the founder of Rødding highschool, Christian Flor (1792-1875), whose memorial stone bears a verse by Carl Ploug setting the tone of the site: *Vort modersmaal han elsked / Hun var hans ungdoms brud / For hendes ret og ære / At værge drog han ud / Hvor mest hun blev forhaanet / Og trampet under fod / Han hendes ros forkyndte / med frit og frejdigt mod* [Our mother-tongue he cherished:/ bride of his youth she was, / and her due rights and honour / to save he sallied forth. / Where most she was insulted / and trodden under foot / there he proclaimed her praises / with courage frank and free]; a lithograph of the scene on 4 July 1844 is in the Royal Library, Copenhagen; see also *Rune-Bladet*; **modersmaal**.

Skamlings-speech, Gr's; see **Skamlingsbanker**; *Rune-Bladet*.

Skibbinge *116, 125, 198*; small town some 3 km. south of Præstø, southeast Sjælland, coupled with Præstø as living to which Gr was presented 1821 and which he left in 1822 to take up curacy at Vor Frelsers Kirke, Copenhagen.

Skirnirs Reise eller Kiærlighed, Gudernes Straf, en Fortælling; see ***Skirnirs Rejse***.

Skirnirs Rejse *97, 98*; Journey of Skírnir; in Snorri's *Prose Edda* and in poem *Skírnismál* in *Poetic Edda*, Skírnir is servant of fertility god Freyr and undertakes journey to home of giants to arrange Freyr's sexual union with Gerd, daughter of giants, loveliest of all women; *cand. theol.* Jens Møller (1779-1833), then a teacher in Slagelse, published *Skirnirs Reise eller Kiærlighed Gudernes Straf, en Fortælling* [Skírnir's journey, or Love, the punishment of the gods, a tale] in May issue (II, 212-231) of K. L. Rahbek's monthly periodical *Ny Minerva* 1806; stylistically, work looked back to 18th c. fashion of comic verse-narrative; Gr, spontaneously indignant over Møller's perceived trivialisation of Nordic antiquity, published response, *Lidet om Sangene i Edda* [A little about the songs of the *Edda*], in September issue (III, 270-299; 1806) of same journal; Møller's work was seen in retrospect by Gr as timely push resulting in his increasingly intensive preoccupation with ancient Northern literature and mythology.

skjald *101, 110-113, 115, 136, 148-150*; originally Icelandic term for poet (Old Icelandic *skáld*), carrying with it from early Northern cultural context suggestion of recognised (high) social status and role – as repository of community's legend and history, as arbiter of worthy and unworthy conduct among princes and people, and as divinely-inspired prophetic spirit; present in Gr's *Nordens Mythologi* (1832) in figure of Widsith drawn by Gr from Anglo-Saxon Exeter Book poem *Widsith* which asserts presence and role of the poet (Old English *scop*) among all peoples through all history adopted by Gr as his favoured term for himself and other poets in the lineage of the ancient poets of the mother-tongue; "Godly poesy (*poiesis*) is a real Creation and godly imagination is the Spirit, which brings to life, and reveals its power to bring our body also spiritually to life by taking our fleshly tongue into its service, so that it speaks forth not what we ourselves but what God is thinking both about himself and about us [*Den guddommelige*

Poesi (poiesis) er en virkelig Skabelse, og den guddommelige Phantasi er Aanden, som giør levende, og beviser sin Magt til at giøre ogsaa vort Legem aandelig levende ved at tage vor Kiød-Tunge i sin Tjeneste, saa den udtaler ikke hvad vi selv, men hvad Gud tænker baade om sig selv og om os] (Grundtvig, *Den christelige Børnelærdom*, 1855-61, 1868, 1883).

Skjald's Life in Denmark, *The*; see **Skjaldelivet i Danmark** *(En Mundsmag).*

Skjaldelivet i Danmark *(En Mundsmag) 150*; The skald's life in Denmark. A taste; poem published by Gr in four issues of his weekly periodical *Danskeren* IV (1851), the year in which he lost his first wife Lise, visited Norway as guest of Scandinavian students and old friends, and married Marie Toft; Gr celebrates "beautiful prospects" such as the skald is by nature disposed to delight in – not mountainous grandeur of Norway or Alps, but lovely landscape of Sjælland and (exploiting pseudo-etymology of 'Sjælland' as 'island of the soul [*sjæl*]') landscape of Danish spiritual and intellectual life, especially those foreshadowings of Paradise which Christian faith affords, against which pagan myths of eternal youth are vain, and the (feminine) principle of love attested throughout Dk's annals; "as a *skjald*, I am what is called 'a fool for beautiful prospects' but it is not for those beautiful prospects that can be hunted down on Krog-Kleven or in the Alps, but those one can just as well experience by, according to the proverb, 'staying on the plain and praising the mountains'" (Gr).

Skoleholderne *87, 155*; three-act comedy written by Gr 1802, satirising both old fossilised and new faddish ideas in education (naming Blaagaard Statsseminarium, the recently state-established and first school in the kingdom for the training of teachers) and in poetry; fair-copied by Gr's friend P. N. Skovgaard, it was submitted anonymously to Royal Theatre Copenhagen on 28 November 1802 but already returned, rejected, on 4 December; Skovgaard's manuscript is in Fascicule 490 in the Gr Arkiv, Royal Library Copenhagen; see also **Brevet**; **Ulfhild**.

Skovgaard, Peter Christian Thamsen *211*; 1817-75; Danish artist, member of Kunstakademi from 1864, titular Professor 1860; his fine drawing of Gr (1847) is perhaps the most commonly reproduced portrait.

Skovgaard, Peter Nikolai *12, 13, 62, 78, 81-83, 87, 88*; 1783-1838; student from Bornholm whom Gr first met in University student-corps formed 1801 against threat of British invasion; "a man of honest and robust character who cared nothing for examinations or the daily bread but applied himself life and soul to what he fancied" (Gr) and captivated Gr with his knowledge of and enthusiasm for ancient history and legend of North at a time when "the University was stone dead" (Gr) so that "my love of the history of the North awoke again at that time and my real acquaintance with the old gods and heroes of the North was established" (Gr); his critical judgment of Gr's attempts to get plays accepted at Royal Theatre Copenhagen was stringent but constructive; but absolutist establishment could not accommodate such free spirits – for blunt criticism of *enevælde* and establishment he was imprisoned, silenced by censorship, exiled from Copenhagen (1807) and, without having realised the potential his friends had seen in him, died an untimely death in Aalborg.

Skov-Hornets Klang mellem Skamlings-Bankerne *142*; The valdhorn's resonance among the Skamling-hills; poem composed by Gr in connection with Danish nationalistic gathering he addressed at Skamlingsbanken (1844), calling nation to defence of Danishness, particularly in beleaguered Slesvig.

Skriftefader, den kongelige *155*; *den kongelige confessionarius*, the royal confessor, Chaplain Royal; see **Bastholm,** Christian.

skriftkloge, de *169*; the clever scripturalists; a pejorative term, within the Grundtvigian lexis; see **skriftteologer.**

skriftteologer *169, 257, 308*; scriptural theologians; especially within Grundtvigian idiom, a pejorative term for practitioners of *skriftteologi*, the conventional theology of the State Church based upon the written word of Scripture rather than a theology founded upon the orally-transmitted word (the living word given by Christ and spoken among the worshipping and celebrating congregation, as for example in the Creed at baptism) in the spirit of Gr's *kirkelig anskuelse* (concept or purview of the Church); but particularly the rationalist textual scholars who, in Gr's view of the state of affairs in 1820s, were irresponsibly undermining not only the Biblical canon and its perceived authenticity, but also basic doctrine of the Church; Gr reportedly professed belief in, even if not full understanding of, everything written in the Bible, and asked challengingly how many of the text-picking scriptural theologians could say as much; see also **Rationalism**; **Clausen,** Henrik Nicolai; **Kirkens Gienmæle.**

Skydebane *114*; The shooting-range, rifle club; at various times in 18th and 19th c., arming and training the civilian population was discussed as alternative or supplement to formal militia especially for defence of Copenhagen; shooting clubs were formed, as much for sport and social gathering as for training, such as *Det kongelige Københavnske Skydeselskab* (The royal Danish shooting society) with a range established (1751) on Vesterbro, extended 1782-87 with catering facilities and assembly rooms used for public and private banquets; original buildings are still to be seen there; the range is now a small park.

Skørpinge *284*; village and vicarage in west Sjælland; in 1846, when Gr visited region to speak at meeting of Danish Society in Næstved, pastor was Frederik Engelhardt Boisen (1808-82), then emerging as one of Gr's most active supporters.

Slesvig-Holsten *291*; German Schleswig-Holstein; affiliation of two territories originally (*ca.* 1000) sharing frontier on Ejder river with Danes to north in Sønderjylland (southern Jylland; by 13th c. commonly called Slesvig to reflect importance of bishopric and dukedom centred in town of Slesvig, successor to viking-age trading settlement at Hedeby, on Baltic inlet called Slien), and with Saxons and Slavs to south in Holsten. After centuries of fluctuating struggle for dominance between the two, and between them and Danish crown, settlement of 1460 recognised overlordship of Danish king, Christian 1, who was required to agree that Slesvig and Holsten should remain undivided in perpetuity (*"up ewig ungedeelt"*). Holsten was elevated to status of duchy 1474. Despite settlement, partitions followed and over centuries sovereignty fluctuated according to fortunes of war, both internal and international. By opening of 19th c., both Slesvig and Holsten were incorporated within Kingdom of Dk and it had become possible for Danish monarchy to nurture political and cultural concept of one integral state (*Helstaten*). However, among ill consequence of Dk's stance in Napoleonic Wars was new fragmentation: academics of Kiel University led way in promoting opposed concept of 'schleswig-holsteinism,' reinvoking ancient pledge of "*up ewig ungedeelt*" and focussing especially upon desirability of purging Danishness (language, cultural affiliations) from Slesvig. In response, by 1840 a pro-Danish movement had formed in North Slesvig to secure parity of status, and at national level National-Liberal sympathisers formulated "Ejder-policy" [*Ejderpolitik*]: Orla Lehmann (1810-70) led campaign to set and hold (militarily if necessary) limit to German political influence at Ejder; Peter Hiort Lorenzen (1791-1845) from Sønderborg in Sønderjylland became popular hero for insisting on speaking in Danish in the German-speaking regional assembly. At Skamlingsbanken, highest point in Sønderjylland, 6000 people gathered in 1843 to support cause of Danish language in Slesvig but in 1844 Christian VIII ruled that right to speak Danish in regional assemblies extended only to those who did not know German; to second gathering at Skamlingsbanken in same year, with doubled attendance, Gr was invited, spoke and was profoundly stirred by occasion and its issues; 1846, challenged by decision of regional assembly in Itzehoe (Holsten) to accept schleswig-holstein-programme, Christian VIII issued letter patent declaring that royal Danish law governing succession (by male or female line; whereas schleswig-holsteiners admitted only male succession) prevailed in kingdom of Dk, Slesvig and Lauenborg but acknowledging uncertainty over parts of Holsten; Holsten assembly, opposed to the wedge driven between dukedoms, appealed for support to the German federation of states and the Schleswig-Holstein problem began to cause international concern. In 1848 Christian VIII died, his efforts to preserve *Helstaten* [the integral state] having failed; same year revolution in France precipitated revolutionary action elsewhere in Europe and led, in Dk, to peaceful revolution (March 1848) bringing absolute monarchic rule (of Frederik VII) to end; amid constitutional transition and political crisis in Copenhagen, Prince of Nør (brother of Christian August of Augustenborg) sent ultimatum on implementation of schleswig-holstein-programme; in Dk, mobilisation began; 24 March, Prince of Nør led armed contingent which occupied Rendsborg, chief garrison-town in Slesvig, marking start of Three Years' War (1848-51); war settled none of the old issues which through 1850s continued to preoccupy Danish cultural debate and bedevil political life, with various administrations still pursuing idea of *helstaten*; from 1856, Prussia, as member of the German federation of states, began to conceive interventionist role in pursuit of own ambitions, and with Austria complained over Danish diminution of rights of German minority and issued ultimatums over status of Holsten and Lauenborg; with stakes steadily rising, Danish National-Liberal administration moved to adoption of November Constitution (1863), expression of Ejder-policy, affirming incorporation of Slesvig into Kingdom of Dk and making Ejder into frontier facing Holsten and German Federation (dominated by Prussia); two days later Frederik VII died, the new constitution unsigned; the Augustenborg family now raised their claim to succession in the dukedoms; Frederik's successor Christian IX reluctantly signed constitution; Bismarck, on Prussia's behalf, protested and German Federation demanded suspension of new constitution; with Danish National-Liberals (backed by widespread national-romantic sentiment) prepared to contemplate war, final attempts to avert crisis failed and on 1 February 1864 Prussians and Austrians, without declaration of war, invaded Slesvig across the Ejder; in ensuing profoundly traumatic war Dk lost both Holsten and Slesvig. Along with loss of Norway (1814) the loss was felt as Dk's greatest national blow in 19th c. See also **Prussia**.

Slesvig-Holsteners *267, 268*; Danish form of name of adherents to political cause of inseparability of the two duchies, associated with institutionalised precedence of German language and cultural orientation; referred to in this book as 'schleswig-holsteiners' (based upon German spelling); see **Slesvig-Holsten**.

Slesvig Stone, The *265, 272* ; monument erected in the Dyrehave [Deerpark] at Jægersborg near Copenhagen to commemorate two visits (1861, 1865) by loyal deputations from duchy of Slesvig; bears inscription "Intet Danmark uden Slesvig – Intet Slesvig uden Danmark" [No Denmark without Slesvig, no Slesvig without Denmark]; between the two dates inscribed, the disaster feared by Danish loyalists in 1861 befell, and Slesvig was overrun by Prussia; stone remained focus of popular gatherings especially those concerned with status of Sønderjylland; chosen as venue (1 June 1871) for popular gathering to honour 87-year-old Gr on sixtieth anniversary of his ordination; see also **Dyrehaven**.

Smith, Daniel Peter *193, 248*; 1782-1871; contemporary of Gr and, like P. N. Skougaard, fellow-member of Copenhagen University student-corps formed for defence of city in case of English invasion 1801; teacher in Roskilde; subsequently parish priest and rural dean [*provst*] in Lolland and elsewhere; much concerned with educational policy; close friend of Bishop P. O. Boisen; contributor to contemporary cultural history, as in memoirs from his years in Roskilde, containing vivid account of Gr reading his *Roskilde-Riim* to clerics assembled at diocesan meeting.

Snorri Sturluson *83, 106, 110, 114, 120, 151, 163, 165, 218, 231*; 1179-1241; Icelandic chieftain, politician, historiographer, poet; powerful member of Iceland's Althing (parliament) 1215-1218 and 1222-1231; author of four-part textbook on vernacular poetics (so-called *Snorra Edda* or *Prose Edda*), in part seeking to revitalise ancient Nordic practice of preserving in orally-transmitted poetry glory and witness of great men and great events by giving new currency to skaldic verse compositional techniques, traditional poetic language, and (as source of metaphorical imagery especially kennings), heritage of Nordic myth and legend which he drew from such ancient poetry as was preserved in so-called *Elder* or *Poetic Edda*; also attributed to Snorri's authorship are *Heimskringla* [*orbis terrarum*, the circle of the world] (so named after its opening words "Kringla heimsins ..." but otherwise, as collection of narratives of lives of early kings of Norway, better entitled *Sagas of the Norse Kings*), and sagas of Egill Skalla-Grimsson and Olaf the Holy; his kings' sagas rendered into Danish by Gr (1815, 1818-22) whose translations from Icelandic and from Saxo Grammaticus over same period reflect not only emergent enthusiasm for literary-cultural antiquities of Northern world but (Snorri-like?) aspiration to re-invest the mother-tongue with native-Nordic and less Christian-explicit language recovered from or modelled upon most ancient Nordic sources; this *norrøniserende* [norricising] language, at its extreme almost unintelligible to readers without knowledge of Icelandic, attracted censure from leading contemporary Danish linguistic scholar, Rasmus Rask (1787-1832); see also **Northern literature**, ancient; *Nordens Mythologi*; **Danedrot**.

Society for the Promotion of an improved Orthography *232*; *sælskabet for en forbedret retskrivnings udbredelse* [thus Frederik Barfod's orthography]; society seeking rationalisation of Danish orthography, on behalf of which Frederik Barfod edited *Nordisk Ugeskrift* [Nordic weekly]; issue had long been debated in Dk when Rasmus Rask and N. M. Petersen published (1826) *Forsøg til en videnskabelig dansk Retskrivningslære* [Attempt at a scientific theory of Danish orthography], various of whose proposals were taken up by a meeting in Stockholm (1869) seeking standardisation within Danish-Norwegian and Swedish orthography; Barfod himself practised a number of conventions endorsed by Rask-Petersen and Stockholm meeting, but Gr declined to contribute to journal (which required observance of new orthographic conventions) on grounds that people should be free to follow own orthography; see also **Madvig,** Johannes Nicolai; *Nordisk Ugeskrift*.

Sognebaandsløsning *70, 154, 170, 173, 174, 256, 257*; dissolution of parochial ties; establishment of concepts of the free individual or congregation empowered to choose own minister, closely linked with principle of *præstefrihed* (freedom of priests, including lifting of restriction of ministry to their own parochial incumbency, and freedom to deny sacraments to those they justly deemed unfit, and to vary liturgy), strongly fought for by Gr and followers; individuals who attended church of their choice other than their parish church such as those who travelled from all over Fyn to Vilhelm Birkedal's church at Ryslinge, were sometimes called *sognebaandsløsere* ['parish ties looseners']; proposals to effect these ends were defeated in Roskilde *Stænderforsamling* January 1839; after granting of Constitution (1849), law was finally passed (1855) which together with legislation (1868) on elective congregations (*valgmenigheder*) and (1872) on church usage, is regarded as having comprehensively freed Danish *folkekirke* whilst preserving its integrity and identity; Gr's response (1855) to this long-delayed but triumphant outcome of his struggle: Perish thraldom and freedom live! even if all the world's deans, bishops and popes would rather die with thraldom than live with freedom! See also **Church struggle**; **Folkekirke**; **Frikirke**.

Soldin, Salomon *159*; 1774-1837; publisher, journalist; edited (1804-25), wrote for and published (from 1811) *Nyeste Skilderie af Kjøbenhavn*, twice-weekly periodical which he "kept open for everything that could find readers" (Gr) at time when, under absolute monarchy, press could be subject to stringent censorship; significant figure among Copenhagen's Jewish population; founded charitable endowment *Salomon Soldin og hustru Hanne Soldins Legat* now making grants to Copenhagen institutions assisting elderly people; see also **Milo,** Jacob Frederik.

Solomon *310, 316*; king and builder of first Temple in Jerusalem, renowned for his wisdom; when Gr, on Palm Sunday 1867, proclaimed from the altar in Vartov Church that "here there is more than the wisdom of Solomon!" he was proclaiming, in all orthodoxy, the presence of Christ in the sacrament of the Word at the eucharist, using the words of Jesus recorded in Matthew 12:42 – "The queen of the south shall rise up in the judgment with this generation, and shall condemn it: for she came from the uttermost parts of the earth to hear the wisdom of Solomon; and, behold, a greater than Solomon [is] here" (King James Bible) – though it suited some, out of malice or obtuseness, to construe it as an expression of megalomania in Gr; see also **Palm Sunday** 1867; **Saba**, Queen of.

Sommer, Magnus (Mogens) *233*; 1762-1848; priest, doctor of theology; 1798 appointed parish priest in Sorø with view to further appointment to professorship in planned Sorø Academy but it was thirty years before reformed Academy opened and he was not then appointed; persuaded (1839) to hand over a baptism in his church to Gr.

Song-Work for the Danish Church; see ***Sang-Værk til den danske Kirke.***

sorte Skole, den *216*; the black school; Gr's best-known pejorative designation of Latin schools in general and of his school in Aarhus in particular, black because he regarded the traditional education they offered as devoid of light and of life in method, content and consequence; in his poetic ***Aabent Brev til mine Børn*** (1839) he denounced the black school and memorably urged his fellow-Danes to rethink the objectives of child education: "and never be so heartless as, for the sake of a hothouse-growth or the prospect of a secure livelihood, to sacrifice lads with rosy cheeks to Grammar and to certain death" [Og aldrig nænne, for en Drivhus-Grøde, / Og Udsigt til de "visse Levebrød," / At offre Gutterne med Kinder røde / Til Grammatiken og den visse Død; 81-84]; in contrast to the 'black school' which was *paa Dødens Side* [on the side of Death] he saw schools such as Queen Caroline Amalie's Charity School [Asylskole] in Copenhagen as *Plante-Skoler* [plant nurseries] where healthy natural growth was nursed and nourished, whereas (he wrote) "That schools in which physical attendance, the number enrolled, examination, fines for non-attendance, instruction, tables, drilling, spelling, rote-learning tasks and mechanical comprehension-exercises in things great and small, good and ill, were the soul and the primary concern have only yielded fruit for what we call *Børnehuse* ['children's houses' i.e. houses of correction for delinquent children] or penal institutions or workhouses [...] is so crystal-clear that surely the world itself must see that it is rushing towards its ruin by continuing this stick-in-the-muddery, and that there is no salvation under what State Constitution soever, as long as they do not stop fighting against and neglecting human life right from childhood onwards, as though human nature were a devil which must first be driven out, and not, where it is found, a hidden treasure which is to be drawn into the light and made fruitful!" [At Skoler, hvori *Kroppe-nes* Næ[r]værelse, Mandtallet, Mønstringen, Mulkter[ingen], Instruxen, Tabellerne, Afretning, Retskrivning, Udenads-Lexer, og mekanisk Forstands-Øvelse paa Stort og Smaat, Ondt og Godt, var *Sjælen* og Hovedsagen, kun har været frugtbare for hvad vi kalde "Børnehuse" eller Straffe-Anstalter og Tvangs-Huse [...] er saa soleklart, at Verden dog selv maa see, den styrter sin Un-dergang imøde ved at fortsætte det Dødbideri, og at der er ingen Redning under nogensomhelst Stats-Forfatning, dersom man ikke holder op at bekæmpe og forvakle Menneske-Livet ligefra Barndommen af, som om Menneske-Naturen var en Djævel, der først maatte uddrives og ei, hvor den findes, en skjult Skat, der skal drages for Lyset og giøres frugtbar!] (Gr Arkiv 335.6, ed. Ulrik Overgaard, *Grundtvig-Studier 2006*, 10); similarly, the Grundtvigian folk-highschools were founded upon pedagogic principles which rejected stultifying traditions of Latin schools and served instead concept of school *for Livet* [for life]; see also **Aarhus** Latin School; **almueskoler, friskole; folk-highschools; *Aabent Brev til mine Børn*; Dronningens Asylskole.**

Sorø *209, 229, 233, 265, 308*; town in Sjælland some 80 km west of Copenhagen, situated on two lakes, Tuelsø and Sorø Sø; medieval settlement originating in a Benedictine monastery (1140) soon replaced by a Cistercian house (1161) under patronage of Bishop Absalon and his family (the Hvide dynasty from which Gr traced descent on his mother's side) who subsequently used abbey church as family mausoleum; prominence and prosperity of church and town grew, enhanced by becoming final resting-place of three kings of Dk as well as of Queen Margrethe I before her body was translated to Roskilde cathedral; in 1586, town given further preeminence by royal foundation of first of a series of schools and academies, and in 1638 granted charter of municipality; by Gr's time, therefore, a place of natural beauty, considerable distinction and historical and rather romantic aura, both ecclesiastical and secular.

Sorø Academy *209, 265*; status conferred on Sorø by its monastic origins, and patronage by Bishop Absalon and his family and several early kings attracted further patronage of later kings, notably in endowment of schools; in 1586 Frederik II assigned large portion of former monastic properties to establishment of boys' school for 30 nobles and 30 commoners (closed 1737); in 1623 Christian IV augmented foundation with an academy for sons of nobility, to be staffed by resident professors; at Ringsted near Sorø was one of northern Europe's greatest libraries, owned by *Landsdommer* [High Court Judge] Jørgen Seefeldt (1594-1662), an asset (until its seizure by invading Swedes, 1658, as reward to traitor, and Seefeld's enemy, Corfitz Ulfeld) to professors at Academy such as Henrik Ernst (1603-65), German jurist and philologist, tutor to Christian IV's son Valdemar, author of tract attacking John Milton's *Defence of the English People* and consequently recipient of preferment under newly-established absolute monarchy (1660); Christian IV's Academy closed in economic difficulties 1665; in 1747 Academy refounded under Frederik V, partly housed in monastic buildings converted by royal architect Laurids de Thura but despite endowment from dramatist Ludvig Holberg (1684-1754) closed again on economic grounds 1798; following fire in the monastic buildings 1813, erection of existing school buildings began, and Frederik VI's School and Academy opened in 1826 with distinguished tutors including poet B. S. Ingemann (1789-1862); Sorø offered ideal natural setting and intellectual milieu for Danish Romantic movement to flourish, and many leading figures in Danish cultural life were visitors, including Gr (who could allow himself to think of the abbey church as the mausoleum of his medieval ancestors, the mighty Hvide family, powerful in state and church); when the Academy again began to languish for want of sufficient income, Gr and others hoped its resources might be used for foundation there of a new university, upon radically different principles ("Folkelighed, Fædreneland og Modersmaal skal være den levende Middelpunkt for Dannelsen og Oplysning" [nurture of the *folkelig*, the land of our fathers, the mother-tongue must be the vital centrepoint of education and enlightenment]; Grundtvig, address to the king, 1843) from those enshrined in the University of Copenhagen; this plan was vigorously opposed by such as H. C. Ørsted and Christian Molbech (who themselves had widely differing ideas as to the proper future of School and Academy), but in any case royal support for Gr from Christian VIII and Caroline Amalie terminated with king's premature death, and closure of Academy came 1849; Gr's solemn and fervent plea in parliament for the royally-endorsed plan was fruitless but he and supporters continued to promote it; after Gr's death a large public meeting in Copenhagen (April 1878) resolved to petition for it, but the idea was denounced in *Fædrelandet* by Carl Ploug (1813-94) as a guaranteed way of lowering Danish educational standards and achievement, and it never came to fruition; the School however survived and continues to exist as a school within the state education system.

South-Jutlanders; see **Sønderjyder**.

Sov sødt, Barnlille *138, 245, 279*; *Sleep sweet, little babe*; hymn (1844; appears as no. 674 in *DDS* 2002) affording good example of intimate and intricate relationship between Gr's daily material, physical and spiritual circumstances, his sermons, and his hymns; in Spring 1844 he was physically ill, "his strength was failing him and one can clearly see his condition in the altered handwriting; he has to have help in fulfilling his office which causes an unreasonable conflict with Bishop Mynster. Of special significance is his final sermon on 1 May 1844, where he takes leave of his congregation in Vartov, prior to his breakdown, and this colours the genesis of *Sov sødt, Barnlille* during his subsequent convalescent travels and visits to his clerical friends in Sjælland, and gives a strong impression of the succour he receives from his followers" (Christian Thodberg); to this extent Gr's sermons and hymns are much more than literary-rhetorical formulations of doctrine and dogma – they are indeed records of a lifelong pilgrimage; see also **Kirken den er et gammelt Huus**; **hymns**; entries under **sermon**.

Spalding, Karl August Wilhelm, *105*; 1760-1830; jurist, historian; author of *Geschichte des christlichen Königreichs zu Jerusalem*, I-II (1803), used by Gr when (1810) he was seized with "irresistible desire" to read history; but Spalding's "wretchedly low perspective on the crusades" (that is, his failure to perceive and intimate a greater religious-historical pattern in events) exasperated Gr.

Spandet, Niels Møller *208*; 1788-1858; judge, politician; appointed Justitsråd 1831, Etatsråd 1840; alumnus, like Gr, of Valkendorfs Kollegium; from 1811 an acquaintance of Gr (whose breakdown December 1810 he had witnessed) and subsequently family friend and Gr's longtime supporter, especially during law-suit brought by H. N. Clausen against Gr and during Gr's bid (1831) for right to establish a *frimenighed* (congregation outside the established State Church); remarkable for his proposal (debated in Rigsraad 1850) of new law concerning freedom of belief, allowing free choice between civil and church marriage, and freedom of parents to decide whether children should become members of any community of believers and raised according to its teachings.

Spandet, Marie *208*; daughter of Niels Møller Spandet.

Spang, Peter Johannes *236, 280, 281*; 1796-1846; priest; educated Borgerdydskolen in Copenhagen and Copenhagen University; after incumbencies in Jylland and Sjælland, became (1840) resident *kapellan* (curate) and (1845), shortly before his early death, parish priest of Helligaands Kirke in central Copenhagen; regarded as gifted preacher; appointed (1844) to committee (E. V. Kolthoff, H. L. Martensen, J. H. V. Paulli and Gr) set up by *Kjøbenhavns Præstekonvent* [Clerical Convention of Copenhagen] for revision of the Church's hymnal; at same time, member of committee which negotiated certain relaxations in law relating to *gudelige forsamlinger* (religious gatherings in places other than churches); his diplomatic skills seem to have been exercised in both committees, especially, in the former, in dealing with Gr's volatile temperament where his own hymns were in debate; his untimely death (14 January 1846), Martensen suggests, left group without negotiator and precipitated Convention's rejection of Hymnal-committee's recommendations.

Sparrevohn; see **Sparrewohn**.

Sparrewohn, Asta *244*; daughter of J. A. Sparrewohn and Sofie (born Reedtz).

Sparrewohn, Jacob Antonius *243, 244, 314, 319, 320, 322*; 1838-1914; physician; married to Sofie Reedtz, daughter of Fru Asta Reedtz (Gr's third wife) by *geheimekonferensraad* H. C. Reedtz.

Sparrewohn, Sophie Vilhelmine Henriette *243, 244, 319, 320, 338;* 1849-1906; daughter of Gr's third wife Asta by previous marriage to Holger Christian Reedtz; married (1868) to J. A. Sparrewohn (1838-1914).

spirit *passim*; see **Aand**.

Spirit of the North; see ***Nordens Aand***.

spirit of 1848 *267;* convergence of Danish revolutionary and nationalistic impulses in response to national and international circumstances, which sought (by mass demonstration but without violence) constitutional democracy, and urged armed resistance to pro-German encroachments in duchies of Slesvig-Holsten; a spirit of exhilaration among many, which Gr met with deep scepticism and misgivings; resulted (1848) in successful defeat of insurgency in duchies and (1849) in granting of *Grundloven* (the Constitution), though grave disappointments lay ahead (1864 loss of duchies; 1866 reactionary revision of constitution); see also **Grundloven**; **Slesvig-Holsten**.

Spyttegjøge og Spottefugle *155;* birds' names applied pejoratively to people, upstarts and disparagers; used by Gr for those – in particular Otto Horrebow (1769-1823) and contributors to his crudely rationalistic periodical *Jesus og Fornuften* [Jesus and rationality], 1797-1801 – who presumptuously and maliciously disparaged the efforts of Bishop N. E. Balle to propagate a Lutheran orthodoxy; though the young Gr once dreamed of being Balle's champion, he later came to express his own dissatisfaction with Balle's theology and teaching; see **Balle**, Nicolaj Edinger; **Horrebow**, Otto.

Stampe, Christine Marguérite Salome *276;* 1797-1868; author, notable host, patron; wife of Baron Henrik Stampe (1794-1876), owner of manor house and estate of Nysø near Præstø, South Sjælland; patron there of leading writers, artists and other leading figures in Danish society, including Gr whose connection with Nysø arose from his appointment as parish priest for Præstø; in particular, on king's request, she established (1839) a residence at Nysø for internationally renowned sculptor Bertel Thorvaldsen on his return from Italy; she, her husband and her children were models for some of Thorvaldsen's sculptures; sons Henrik and Holger were for a time tutored with Gr's sons in Gr's home by Carl Muus; her memoirs, posthumously published (1912) by Rigmor Stampe Bendix, have importance as outstanding example of women's writing from 19th c., and as cultural-historical document; letters to Gr from Stampe family between 1820s and 1860s are in Gr Arkiv Fasc. 466.

Stampe, Henrik *210, 212, 276;* 1794-1876; baron, owner of manor house of Nysø, South Sjælland, within the estate of Stampenborg; son of *lensbaron* Holger Stampe; husband of Christine Stampe.

Stampe, Henrik *210, 212, 276;* 1821-92; son and heir of Baron Henrik and Baronesse Christine Stampe, of Nysø; with brother Holger, was for a time tutored with Gr's sons in Gr's home by Carl Muus; later (1843-44) had an intense but probably platonic relationship with H. C. Andersen who was for a time a frequent visitor to Nysø; became *lensbaron* Stampe 1876.

Stampe, Holger *210, 212*; 1822-1904; son of Baron Henrik and Baronesse Christine Stampe, of Nysø; with brother Henrik, for a time tutored with Gr's sons in Gr's home by Carl Muus; succeeded brother as *lensbaron* Stampe-Charisius 1892.

Stampenborg *199*; seat of the Stampe family, comprising the manors of Nysø, Jungshoved and Christinelund.

States General; see **Stænderforsamling**.

Statsraad, Norwegian *149*; Council of State for Norway, separate from that of Sweden, though the crowns were united from 1814 onwards, and distinct from Storthing (Parliament), in effect the Government; both Statsraad and Storthing formally honoured Gr on his visit to Norway 1851.

Stavnsbaandet *235, 245*; law of 1733 tying peasantry to district of birth; consequence of establishment (1701; 1733) of a national militia based on obligation of each designated *lægd* (recruitment district) to provide an equipped soldier; evasion of service by moving from one *lægd* to another was thus stopped; extended (1764) to children over age of four; associated with feudal tying of peasantry to land, open to abuse by landowners, unpopular and eventually perceived as unjust; through powerful influence of such as statesman and jurist Christian Colbiørnsen (1749-1814), law repealed 20 June 1788; see **bonde**.

Steensen-Leth, family *62, 89, 90, 92, 94, 183, 184*; family of Captain Carl Frederik Steensen-Leth, 1774-1825; of aristocratic lineage linked with Langeland; husband of Constance Henriette; father of Carl Frederik, Gr's pupil at Egeløkke who later wrote a memoir of Gr contradicting more complimentary accounts, and expressing the recipient's experiencing of Gr's detailed, austere and rote-learning-based programme of tuition (preserved in Gr's notebook from 1806); see **Steensen-Leth,** Constance Henriette.

Steensen-Leth, Constance Henriette *92, 183, 186*; 1777-1827; wife of Captain Carl Frederik Steensen-Leth and lady of idyllically-situated manor-house Egeløkke on small island of Langeland, where Gr took post as resident tutor to her son, Carl Frederik, 1805-08; usually described as beautiful and intelligent, she became the object of young (and inexperienced) Gr's passionate infatuation though there is no good evidence that she repaid or even fully understood his passion; but there is little in his life that Gr does not turn to some kind of gain and he himself says experience saved him from his cold, cloddish, conceited self, and opened his eyes to profounder aspects of existence; thus, though pages covering March to September 1805 have been torn out of Gr's surviving diary, Constance appears elsewhere in various of his writings, prose and poetry, as idealised icon of a romantic devotion, anguished and fruitless, significantly in the spirit of Goethe's *Die Leiden des jungen Werther* [The Sorrows of Young Werther; 1774] though stopping short of self-destruction; instead, Gr turned to study of contemporary German Romantic literature (retrospectively appreciating Steffens's lectures of 1802), and to medieval (Icelandic) literature.

Steensfjord *151*; Stensfjorden, Ringerike, Norway; a lesser fjord off the great Tyrifjord north of Drammen, over which Gr, descending with difficulty from the heights of Krog-Kleven, admired the evening sun.

Steffens, Henrik *13, 18, 19, 23, 62, 84-86, 100, 157, 181, 182, 189, 203, 249, 250, 276*; 1773-1845; Norwegian-born philosopher and physicist who combined scientific ideas with German Idealist metaphysics; contributed to establishment of 19th c. ideas of race and differentials in ethnic superiority; studied at Copenhagen, Kiel, Jena, and Berlin; later professor at Halle and Breslau; influenced by Johan Gottlieb Fichte, Schelling and the brothers August Wilhelm and Friedrich Schlegel; though resident only briefly in Dk, one of the figures whose work marks a watershed in Danish cultural life; mediated in Dk the new cultural currents from Germany, and set in movement, partly through association with the poet Adam Oehlenschläger, partly through public lectures, the Danish national-Romantic movement; his philosophy lectures, delivered during winter 1802 in Ehlers' Kollegium Copenhagen were published as *Indledning til philosophiske Forelæsninger* (Copenhagen, 1803); other contemporaries found him unimpressive: Emil du Bois-Reymond described his university lectures as "beginning with metals and ending with dinner," Karl Varnhagen von Ense said listening to Steffens read his autobiography [*Hvad jeg oplevede* (What I have experienced; 1845)] aloud at Prussian court was tantamount to torture, and Heinrich Heine quipped "Among his ideas ... there is one no one has appropriated, and it is his chief idea, his sublime idea: 'Henrik Steffens, born May 2. 1773, in Stavangar near Drontheim in Norway, is the greatest man of the century.'" (examples cited Gabriel Finkelstein, Harvard 2001); but Gr firmly believed in this greatness : "Him I must name to you as one of the great instruments of the Spirit of the North [*Nordens Aand*] and Denmark's Guardian Angel, without whom, according to my full conviction, even the feat upon Kongedybet [= the Danish fleet's heroic defence against the British assault, off Copenhagen, 1 April 1801] would have been in vain" [*Mands Minde*]; Steffens' mother was younger sister of Gr's mother, and the cousins subsequently corresponded in affectionate terms over forty years (Steffens to Gr April 1837: "I cannot tell you how fervently I long to see you, to talk with you – can you not come to Berlin sometime?").

Steibelt, Daniel *190*; 1765-1823; German virtuoso pianist, composer, whose music was performed in Copenhagen professorial drawing-rooms but did not captivate Gr (1811).

Stemann, Poul Christian *172, 175, 221, 223*; 1764-1855; *cand. jur.*, Danish statesman; as President of the Danish Chancellery 1827, holder of highest office of state during absolutism; rigidly conservative, long opposed movements towards civil liberties but grudgingly acknowledged inevitabilities before finally being dismissed as First Minister in 1848; Gr who was in conflict with him on various occasions over many years found him "as stubborn as a mule and so prejudiced against *all* freedom that he merely laughed at all my panegyrics upon this with regard to things *spiritual*."

Stephens, George *334*; 1813-95; English linguistic scholar and antiquarian; second Professor in English at Copenhagen University 1855-93, following Thomas Christopher Bruun (1750-1834); friend of Gr; among other things, including plays and poetry, he published 1866-84. *The old northern runic monuments of Scandinavia and England*; also (1844) *The King of the Birds, or the*

Lay of the Phoenix, translated into the metre and alliteration of the original and (1860) *Two leaves of King Waldere's Lay* being an edition of two leaves of an Anglo-Saxon epic poem found in the Royal Library Copenhagen; all these works were in Gr's library; passionately if eccentrically committed to an ideal of a pre-viking North heroically characterised by individual freedom and democratic self-government, whose legacy was to be read in Northern runic monuments and in literature of Iceland; a monument to his memory is in St Alban's Church, Copenhagen.

stiftsprovst *passim*; the Danish Church is divided administratively and regionally under the bishops into deaneries (*provstier*); the *provst*, being appointed by the Sovereign and serving also as parish priest; corresponds approximately to the rural dean of the Anglican Church; the *stiftsprovst* [diocesan dean], chosen from among priests of diocese, is connected with cathedral church while remaining vicar of his own parish, has diocesan responsibilities and is authorised to function in place of bishop in certain circumstances, thus exercising roles distributed in Anglican Church between archdeacon and dean of cathedral.

Stjernholm *68*; Rasmus and Christian, sons of *Provst* Niels Christian Stjernholm (1738-1835) of Roeslev, Salling in Jylland, who together with Peder Hansen Balle, son of Bishop N. E. Balle (Bishop of Sjælland from 1783) and Gr's cousin (Bishop Balle's first wife was sister to Gr's father), were fellow-pupils with Gr at Tyregod Parsonage from 1792; of this group of sons of clergy, being prepared by Pastor Laurits Feld for admission to grammar (Latin) school, only Gr went on to university.

Stjørdalen *323*; district near Trondheim in Norway where L. M. Bentsen with H. K. Foosnæs established (1868) a folk-highschool; a glimpse of their task is given in Publications of The Norwegian-American Historical Association, Minnesota, vol. 27: "The years from 1862 to 1865 had been economically poor: taxes and interest rates rose while everything the farmers had to sell went down in price [...] In 1867 the district agronomist delivered lectures in Stjørdalen, but his recommendations had slight effect: 'Most of the people,' he reported, 'seemed so entirely gripped by a desire to emigrate and by America fever that relatively little attention could be expected for the cause I had to champion.'"

Storm, Edvard *86*; 1749-1794; Norwegian poet; 1769 went to Copenhagen to study though never took examinations, cultivating instead a place in literary and theatrical circles; nevertheless, earned living by teaching, developed commitment to education in spirit of age of enlightenment, collaborated in founding Efterslægtens Skole in Copenhagen, where he held appointment; wrote poems in Danish and Norwegian, songs and some pieces of drama; appointed (1794) as a director of Royal Theatre Copenhagen; still an esteemed poet in Gr's student years, and read by Gr over winter 1801-02.

Storthing, Norwegian *149, 259, 323*; see **Norway, Norwegians, Norwegian**.

Stougaard, Jens *61, 71, 74*; 1761-1838; son of carpenter, pupil of Aarhus Latinskole, after leaving there 1783 appointed as tutor there 1789, subsequently became *Konrektor* [deputy principal] to Rektor Thure Krarup (1739-1808); Gr's teacher, subsequently remembered by Gr with considerable esteem for his pedagogic skills and human qualities.

Strandgade *207, 208*; street, closed at one end by Christians Kirke (in Gr's day called Frederiks Kirke, meeting-place for local German community), near waterfront in Christianshavn, forming south-eastern suburb of Copenhagen, in which Gr and family resided (1829-40) in an apartment (then Strandgade 56, now 4).

students *77, 78, 80, 83, 84, 86, 108, 109, 113, 114, 117, 147-149, 152, 156, 157, 182, 201, 222, 243, 257, 296, 307, 339*; during Gr's lifetime the four Scandinavian universities were (Denmark) Copenhagen (1479), (Norway) Kristiania (1811), and (Sweden) Uppsala (1477) and Lund (1666, originally Danish); Kiel (1665) in Holsten was also counted as Danish university until final loss of Holsten 1864; but the bulk of Danish clergy, higher civil service and professional classes all passed through Copenhagen University, and, as Gr himself experienced, friendships or antipathies formed in residential colleges such as Valkendorf's in Copenhagen would often be later translated into consensus and conflict in arena of public polity; in effect, university students were almost separate estate of realm with formal privileges and informal indulgences; apart from maintaining conspicuous presence in general city scene, they were (before constitution of 1849, while public meetings were otherwise strictly controlled by law and sometimes watched by police or police-informers) one of few sectors of society with institutionalised opportunity to gather in debate in their own meeting-places in halls of residence and student union, acting corporately to pay homage to poets, artists, scientists, dignitaries of state, forming military defence brigades in times of emergency; and comprising a loose weight which might slide to tip balance in political actions; notably involved in 19th-c. Scandinavianism through great student gatherings in the three countries; romantic image often associated with them is not wholly without foundation: in severe winter 1838 a crowd of Danish students, crossing ice-bound Øresund to visit Lund, met on the frozen sea a crowd of Lund students heading for Copenhagen, turned back with them and entertained them that night in Copenhagen, and thus began a series of pan-Scandinavian student gatherings or rallies [*studentertog*], at which, in Norway and Dk, Gr was an invited and honoured guest; though Gr was no great friend of the University, his great funeral cortège from Vor Frelsers Kirke through the city to Vartov and on to the railway station ("such a multitude of hymn-singing people has probably not walked through the streets of Copenhagen for many centuries" – Jens Kristian Madsen) was headed by students; see also **Studenter-korps, Studenter-Tog**; **matriculation**; **attestats (attestatus)**.

student-corps; see **Studenterkorps, Studenter-Tog**.

Studenterkorps, Studenter-Tog *83, 113, 148, 152, 157, 297* ; student bodies in university towns such as Copenhagen, Kiel, Kristiania/Oslo and Lund enjoyed in 19th c. a distinctive identity and status lost in more recent times; they could organise themselves (as they did 1820 in setting up a *Studenterforening* [students' union] in Copenhagen in emulation of German students at the Wartburg fortress 1817) to pursue political as well as cultural objectives such as Scandinavian unity, and even, in emergency to form a student military corps for defence of city (as at time of threatened English invasion in 1801 when Gr, as student, was involved with Copenhagen *Studenterkorps*); as expression of pan-Scandinavian student solidarity, student rallies (*Studentertog*; cp. the German students' *Studentenzug* to Wartburg 1817, to mark 300th anniversary of Reformation; the term has faintly military nuance as in *Kors-tog* 'crusades') were organised, hosted successively by national student bodies (thus in 1851 Gr was invited to join *Studentertog* to Kristiania/Oslo – reciprocating *Studentertog* of 1845 when gathering of some 600 Scandinavian students in Copenhagen was organised by Danish student committee headed by Carl Parmo Ploug (1813-94) – which remained one of the most exalted memories of his life); see also **students**; **Uppsalatoget** 1856.

Studiegaarden *160, 253*; area and buildings comprising the University in central Copenhagen.

Sturluson, Snorri; see Snorri Sturluson

Stusle Søndagsqvællen *190*; The lonesome Sunday evening; popular Norwegian national melody.

Stænderforsamling *257*; assembly of Estates of the Realm; Danish consultative-advisory body; first established 1468; subsequently developed as regionally distributed instrument of government notably in period of Enlightened Absolutism 1784-1848; in 1830, answering to pressure for more democratic government, four such *provinsstænderforsamlinger* [provincial consultative assemblies] were established on model of developments in Germany and duchy of Holsten; to the one already established in Itzehoe, serving the duchy of Holsten, were added Slesvig serving the duchy of Slesvig, Roskilde serving the islands, and Viborg serving northern Jylland; though only consultative, and not as effectual in hastening revolution as their precursors in France, they nevertheless proved a significant stage in eventual termination (1849) of autocratic government of the kingdom; see also **Grundloven**.

Stærkodder *101*; tragedy (1812) by Adam Oehlenschläger with incidental music composed by F. L. Æmilius (*kapelmester* at Royal Theatre, Copenhagen), reflecting renewed enthusiasm for material drawn from Danish history and legend, here from the *Gesta Danorum* of Saxo Grammaticus; story of proud and iron-willed warrior Stærkodder (whose legend is associated with various sites in Dk) had earlier (1785) been treated by poet-dramatist Christen Pram (1756-1821).

Suhm, Peter Frederik *61, 72, 73*; 1728-1798; antiquarian, Danish state historian; elected (1749) member of the *Danske Selskab til den nordiske Histories og Sprogs Forbedring* [Danish Society for the Improvement of Nordic History and Language] and dedicated major part of his life to these causes, therein serving as primary inspiration to following generation of 'Golden Age' poets and scholars and to architects of subsequent national-romantic movement; outspoken champion of Norway's right to have a university and other cultural institutions denied by Danish mistrust; author of draft constitution addressed to the King, ignored by authorities but much discussed in liberal circles; scholarly works included *Om de nordiske Folks ældste Oprindelse* [On the earliest origins of the Nordic peoples; 1770], *Om Odin og den hedniske Gudelære og Gudstieneste udi Norden* [On Óðinn and the heathen lore and worship of the gods; 1772] – a work which made a great impact upon the young Gr – and his outstanding achievement of documentation and interpretation, the *Historie af Danmark* (14 volumes, 1782-1828, publication completed posthumously by R. Nyerup); encouraged Jacob Langebek (1710-75) in publication (1772) of Langebek's great collection of source-texts for Danish-Norwegian history, *Scriptores Rerum Danicarum Medii Ævi* [Historians of Danish affairs of the medieval age] and himself continued publication (vols IV- VII) after Langebek's death, opened his vast library of some 100,000 books and manuscripts to public access, and in 1796 donated the collection to Royal Library, Copenhagen;

one of a number of leading Copenhagen citizens whose tombs may be seen in mortuary-crypt of Frederiks Kirke (now Christians Kirke) in Christianshavn where Gr was preacher 1832-39; see also **Nordens Mythologi**.

Sunday and holy days observance *212*; from early in 19th c. Dk had regulations governing conduct of trade on Sundays and holy days but by an order of 26 March 1845 concerning *Søn- og Helligdagenes vedbørlige Helligholdelse* [Mandatory observance of Sundays and holy days] Christian VIII imposed stricter controls, requiring that all non-essential labour and all entertainments should cease from the morning onwards, and especially during the time that divine services are held, until four in the afternoon.

Sunday-eye; see **Søndags-Øje**.

Supreme Court *223*; *Højesteret*; seriousness of confrontation between Lindberg and authorities over unlawful religious gatherings [*forsamlinger*] at Lindberg's home, *Rolighed*, and elsewhere is indicated by fact it required royal resolution to resolve it; compromise solution resulted in Gr, though holding no formal appointment there, being authorised to preach at Frederiks Kirke to his own free congregation – in its nature, if not in its scale, a significant qualification to existing law relating to parochial ties.

Survey of world history, The; see **Udsigten over Verdens-Krøniken**.

Svenska folkets historia *244, 338*; History of the Swedish people by Erik Gustav Geijer (1783-1847), Swedish historian and writer; his work, analysing Swedish national character in terms of nature and with reference to myth and saga, was highly congenial to Gr who was listening to extracts read to him by his son Frederik on the day he died.

Sverdrup, Georg *62, 100, 159*; 1770-1850, Norwegian; philologist; Extraordinary Professor of Greek in Copenhagen University 1805-13; later professor in Oslo.

sværmeri *21, 66, 103, 104, 112, 117, 169, 187, 219, 220, 222, 223, 306, 321, 322*; in religious context, devotional behaviour and attitude of a *sværmer*, religious enthusiast; term often used to express mistrust or scepticism towards those manifesting charismatic behaviour or responding to charismatic behaviour in others, such as characterised (in one commentator's judgment; see endnote to item 119) those immediately surrounding Gr in the wake of his breakdown on Palm Sunday 1867; sometimes permissibly translatable as 'fanaticism' though in more formal accusatory contexts the term *Fanatisme* would be used; Grundtvigians, however, could use the term of themselves with entirely positive connotation of something little more than secular romantic feeling ("Dèr havde vi mangen dejlig Stund både i ensomt Sværmeri og i festlig Glæde" [There we spent many a pleasant hour both in solitary *sværmeri* and in festive joy] – Vilhelm Birkedal's daughter Georgia Lange, recalling enjoyment of the woodland at Ryslinge Parsonage]); the term could also cover an enthusiasm for any sort of personal hobby-horse (one's liberties, mythology, Northern antiquity).

Sweden, Swedes, Swedish *105, 108, 148, 259, 265, 298, 306, 329, 336*; bitter history of mutual aggression between Dk and Sweden and Dk's loss of ancient territories (Halland 1645, Skåne and Blekinge 1658) to Sweden lay behind 19th c. relations which were then further embittered by Sweden's more successful negotiation of turmoil of Napoleonic wars and especially by victors' decision (Congress of Vienna 1815) to hand over Norway (previously under Danish rule) to Sweden; nevertheless advantages of Scandinavian unity in spirit of Kalmar Union (from1397 to effective dissolution 1448, formal dissolution 1523) continued to attract advocates and led to such manifestations of Scandinavianism as student-initiated Uppsalatoget (1856) and reciprocal student gathering in Copenhagen (June 1856); Gr believed history showed that political union under one crown was neither viable nor desirable: "If on the other hand people want to call every friendly connection and firm alliance a union, then I find such union between the Nordic states not only possible but as reasonable as it is desirable" [*Vil man derimod kalde enhver venlig Forbindelse og fast Forbund en Forening, da finder jeg en saadan mellem de nordiske Riger ikke blot muligt, men lige saa rimelig som ønskelig*; Mands Minde lectures 1838]; writings of contemporary Swedish historian Erik Gustav Geijer (1783-1847) were much esteemed by Gr; for a time from 1830s onwards Gr pursued vision of a common Nordic university to be established in Göteborg, Sweden, but it was not achieved; and though Swedes were among visitors to Gr's church in Vartov Gr remained to the end disappointed that rather little interest in his work was evident in Sweden.

symbolic books, the *289*; *de symbolske bøger*, also called *kirkens bekendelsesskrifter*; the confessional books or texts of the Church, definitive of the faith of the Church; in the case of the Danish (Lutheran) Church the three Creeds of the primitive Church, the Short Catechism of Luther and the *Confessio Augustana*; of which Gr remarked that it was impossible that all who desired to become priests could honestly swear upon them ("Christianity must have been working upon one for a long time before one can accept the Augsburg Confession as one's creed"), intimating that if the mooted constitution (1849) were to make such an oath obligatory for the priesthood he would consider leaving the *Folkekirke;* see also **Church,** Danish.

synernes høj *310*, hill of visions; mentioned by Gr, Palm Sunday 1867, in his extempore sermon on the entry of Christ into Jerusalem which Gr seems to have been using as a metaphor, or prefiguration, of the imminent coming of Christ into Denmark and the North, in a massive revival of the Church which would consummate the pattern of universal (providential) history. Christ's coming had been hindered, he reportedly said, because the spirit (*aanden*) and the heart (*hjertet*) had been parted. The heart, sure enough, was "here in the Danish islands" but God had planted the spirit away in the east, on *synernes høj*. Now, however, the time was come that they should at last be united, for now the Jordan was flowing into the Øresund. Just as Christ's disciples had been instructed to seek out the tethered ass and free her and bring her with her foal to him, so Gr was himself busy about that task here and now, and now Christ was indeed riding into his capital city on the foal of an ass. Thus much is reliably reported by Frederik Hammerich. Possibly, Gr meant by *synernes høj* Mount Sinai where Moses had a vision of God and received the tablets of the law. But Jerusalem, whose name is traditionally interpreted as *Visio pacis* 'vision of peace' and which is the site of visions past and to come, is also described biblically as a hill or mount, as in *Isaiah* 10:32 and ch. 11-12 which comprises one of the great Messianic visions of the Old Testament; and indeed Gr himself glosses *Sion* (in his *Krønnike-Rim* 1842) thus: "*Sion* is the hill of Jerusalem which, amongst those familiar with the Hebrew prophets, necessarily awakens thought of their visions; and indeed thereby Sion, in our eyes, towers above the summit of all other mountains of the world." In the New Testament, Sinai and Jerusalem are linked by St Paul (*Galatians* 4:22-31) in a homily upon thraldom under the law and freedom under the spirit: Abraham had a son Ismael by the bondwoman Hagar, and a son Isaac by his wife Sara; Hagar, says Paul, metaphorically represents Sinai, the law, and the present Jerusalem which is in thrall to Rome, but Sara represents the Jerusalem on high, which is our mother and is free; Ismael represents those who follow the flesh, Isaac those who follow the spirit, whose fruits are love, joy, peace, longsuffering, gentleness, goodness, faith, meekness and temperance (*Galatians* 5:22). In patristic exegesis, the tethered ass and the foal of the gospel account of Christ's entry into Jerusalem are also associated with the metaphor of the bondage into which Ismael was born and the promise to which Isaac was born. As with much else reported by witnesses from Vartov church on Palm Sunday 1867, there seems to be the possibility of reconstructing a rather remarkable visionary sermon from the scrambled metaphorical allusiveness of Gr's discourse. Christ's biblical-historic entry into Jerusalem, liturgically relived on this day, proves to prefigure the historic fulfilment of God's purposes in history, with regard to the Church and congregation of the North. The Lord has made his moves: the Øresund is as a great font filled with the baptismal waters of Jordan; and Christ is riding into a new Jerusalem, a Copenhagen free, by God's grace, from (Prussian) thraldom. All is prepared and the time is ripe. The congregation now has only to choose to seek absolution at Vartov's altar and from Gr's hand (while metaphorically, as minister of the word and of the sacraments, he frees the tethered beast of burden), to accept the grace of Christ's liberation of his people from thraldom to sin, and to rally round Christ's banner (*Isaiah* 11:10-12), in order to be gathered together as one folk, as God's own people, to live freely in the fruits of the spirit, in scorn of worldly foes, looking to the heavenly Jerusalem to come. See also **Mount of the Seers**; **Palm Sunday** 1867.

synod *336, 337;* Synodal governance of Church was never adopted in post-Reformation Dk; establishment of "Church Council" or "Synod" was idea favoured by politician and bishop D. G. Monrad (1811-87) but, opposed by Gr and his supporters, failed with Monrad's electoral defeat (1872), leaving final governance of Danish Church with parliamentary secular-political grouping of the day.

Syv, Peder Pedersen *255;* 1631-1702; Danish priest and philologist whose work tracing relationship of Danish to other Germanic languages, *Nogle Betenkninger om det Cimbriske Sprog* [Some reflections upon the Cimbrian language] (1663), may be taken to mark foundation of modern scholarly study of Danish language; his two-volume *Almindelige Danske Ord-Sproge og korte Lærdomme* [Common Danish proverbs and short maxims] (1682-88) presented some 15,000 items, thematically grouped, from Danish and European manuscript and printed sources; his *Danske Viser* [Danish ballads] (1695), which Gr set his young sons to study, comprised a reprint of A. S. Vedel's *Et Hundrede udvalgte danske Viser* [One hundred selected Danish ballads] (1591) plus one hundred texts gathered by Syv himself from oral tradition, manuscripts and printed broadsheets, often somewhat clumsily reworked by himself.

Sæland; see **Sjælland**.

Særsyn; see **Bruun,** Thomas Christopher.

Sølvgade Barracks *212*; Sølvgadens Kaserne; military barracks in Copenhagen, built 1764-71 by architect Nicola-Henri Jardin (1720-99), intended both to improve living conditions for men and reduce friction between soldiers and civilian population in city.

Søndagsbog *259*; Gr's sermons preached in Vor Frelsers Kirke, Christianshavn, published as *Christelige Prædikener eller Søndags-Bog,* [Christian sermons, or Sunday-book] by "*N. F. S. Grundtvig, Ordets Tjener*" [NFSG Minister of the Word], Copenhagen 1827, 1828, 1830; bearing engraving of Gr by Carl Wilhelm Erling Eckersberg (1808-89), based upon drawing by Christoffer Wilhelm Eckersberg (1783-1853) and verse by B. S. Ingemann, honouring Gr's emergence as champion of Danish and Nordic antiquity and as worthy heir to Thomas Kingo (1634-1703), Danish bishop and hymnwriter: Med Sagastav og Peterssværd i Haand, / Han arved' Saxos Blik og Kingos Aand. / Fra gamle Nord hans Öie saae mod Östen, / Og Aander har han vakt med Kjæmperösten [With saga-staff and Peter's sword in hand / he inherited Saxo's vision and Kingo's spirit. / From ancient North his eye gazed towards the East / and spirits he has awakened with his mighty voice] – lines which were later to be inscribed on a silver plaque, gift of the Vartov congregation, on the lid of Gr's coffin; see also various entries under **sermons**.

Søndags-Øje *66*; Sunday-eye; in popular and rustic speech of 19th c., a piece of mirror-glass or pocket-mirror probably so called from its use by *Bønderpigerne* [the peasant girls] on the only day they had time and occasion to don their modest finery.

Sønderjyder *255, 265*; South-Jutlanders; after the loss of Sønderjylland to Prussia (1864) a delegation of Sønderjyder journeyed to Copenhagen (1865) to express loyalty to Dk and raise support for Danishness in the occupied territory; when, at "the great public celebration" at the Slesvig stone in Dyrehaven [the Deer-Park] outside the city, Gr addressed a crowd reportedly numbering thousands; see also **Sønderjylland**, **Slesvig-Holsten**.

Sønderjylland *240, 336*; southern region of Jylland peninsula historically forming part of duchy of Slesvig, one of the many tragically disputed border-zones inside Europe; from Middle Ages linked to kingdom of Dk, but lost, in Gr's lifetime, to Prussia; see **Slesvig-Holsten**.

Sørgekvad ved Prins Kristjans Død *105, 106*; Elegy upon the death of Prince Christian, poem composed by Gr 1810; see **Christian August,** Prince.

Sørger ei for dem, der sove *339*; *Sørger ei for dem, der sove / Med Guds Fred i Gravens Skjød!* [Sorrow not for those who slumber / with God's peace in grave's embrace]; hymn by Gr from *Sang-Værk til den danske Kirke* I (1837), no. 563 in *DDS* 2002, inspired by 1 Thessalonians 4:13-18; sung at his funeral; see also **hymns**.

T

Tacitus, Publius Cornelius *81; ca.* 56 B.C. – A.D. 117; Roman politician, historian; his *Germania* is important document in early history of north-west European peoples though here as in all his historical writing he is also engaged in advancing critique of contemporary Rome; Latin compositional elegance, pithy and laconic style as well as historical content have ensured his place in western educational curricula over the centuries.

Tanberg-Moen *148, 151*; gathering-place in ancient kingdom of Ringerike, Norway, where (1851) Gr was honoured and entertained on memorable visit to Norway as guest of Scandinavian students.

Tang, Jeppe Tang Andersen *300, 311*; 1828-1904; after humble beginnings as shepherd-boy in Jylland succeeded in entering Ranum Seminarium where Ludvig Christian Müller was inspiration to him; gained teaching appointments (1851-56) in Copenhagen where he met and impressed Gr and (1856) was appointed teacher at Gr's new Marielyst Højskole; went on to found (1859) the private Blaagaard Seminarium in Copenhagen (as distinct from the Blaagaard Statsseminarium established in 1791 which subsequently changed its name to Jonstrup Statsseminarium), in order to further Gr's educational ideas; member of *Folketing* and educational committees; significant figure in Vartov congregation, who formally opposed "as a loving act" permission for Gr to hold a retirement sermon following the breakdown on Palm Sunday 1867.

tears, Grundtvig's *14, 91, 95, 103, 104, 143, 192, 194, 198, 199, 220, 221, 284*; the ability and the willingness to weep, and particularly if one is a man, and in public, have always been subject to changing cultural convention; whereas in medieval affective spirituality weeping was a sure sign that healthful *compunctio cordis* [*penthos*; compunction of the heart] was taking place, in the age of Rationalism such emotionalism was not esteemed and, as far as religious expression was concerned, tended to be associated with revivalist meetings and attributed to group hysteria; but there were occasions, according to his own testimony and that of others, when Grundtvig did not disdain to weep, from worldly as well as religious emotion; and by his preaching he could move others to tears. It might be claimed, without facetious intent, that Grundtvig's tears are to be found preserved in Grundtvig Arkiv Fasc. 497; see headnote to item 27 and footnotes to item 35.

Teologiske Maanedsskrivt; see **Fallesen,** Lorenz Nikolai.

Theatre *87*; see **Royal Theatre,** Copenhagen.

theatre and drama *passim*; though there is good evidence (not least in *kalkmalerier* [frescoes] in more ancient Danish churches) of medieval religious drama in Dk, post-medieval, post-Reformation tradition of Danish drama essentially begins with Ludvig Holberg (1684-1754), author of 25 comedies staged (1722-28) under royal patronage in theatre in Lille Grønnegade, Copenhagen, who drew from classical, Italian and French models and remains Dk's chief internationally acknowledged dramatist; by Gr's student days theatre and drama offered respectable career option for aspiring poets though Gr the student-actor and dramatist had no success with his *Brevet* and *Skoleholderne* (1802) but instead explored dramatic form in several later longer poems including *Optrin af Kæmpelivets Undergang i Norden* [Episodes from the demise of the warrior-life in the North; 1809], *Optrin af Norners og Asers Kamp* [Episodes in the struggle of Nornir and Æsir; 1811] and *Ragna-Roke* [1817]; though Gr dismissed Danish stage between Holberg and Oehlenschläger (despite reported jubilation in the pit at fall of 'German' Grev Gert in performance of L. C. Sander's *Niels Ebbesen*, 1797) as presenting merely "nightly haunting" by (rather than desperately needed resurrection of) a sense of Danish *folkelighed*, he recognised great national significance of Oehlenschläger's dramatic themes and poesy; and fact is that 19th c. Danish theatre, in absence of wide range of other forms of public gathering and forums for public debate during period of absolute monarchy, played important role in forming, for better and for worse, Danish cultural values and public opinion; see further: **Brevet**; **Skoleholderne**; **Royal Theatre,** Copenhagen; **Alhambra**; **Casino**; **Andersen,** Hans Christian; **Baggesen,** Jens Immanuel; **Bjørnson,** Bjørnstjerne Martinius; **Ebbesen,** Niels; **Goethe,** Johan Wolfgang; **Hauch,** Johannes Carsten; **Heiberg,** Johan Ludvig; **Holberg,** Ludvig; **Hostrup,** Jens Christian; **Kotzebue,** August Friedrich Ferdinand; **Kunzen,** Friedrich Ludwig Æmilius; **Molbech,** Christian; **Nathensen,** Mendel Levin; **Oehlenschläger,** Adam Gottlob; **Rahbek,** Kamma; **Rahbek,** Knud Lyhne; **Sander,** Levin Christian; **Shakespeare,** William; **Storm,** Edvard; **Wessel,** Johan Herman; **Pietism.**

Theologisk Maanedsskrift *111, 127, 171*; journal edited 1825-26 by Gr and A. G. Rudelbach, and after Gr was placed under censorship (1826) continued by latter alone until 1828; dedicated to opposition of rationalist influence in Danish Church and theology.

This day in apostolic wise; hymn by Gr; see ***I Dag paa apostolisk Viis***.

This night came a knock at the portals of Hell; see ***I Kvæld blev der banket paa Helvedesport***.

Thor *101, 125, 265, 300*; god in Norse mythology characterised by strength and courage, also by a capacity to be duped and placed in embarrassing situations, from which, however, he typically manages to retrieve his dignity and reputation; set off against menial deviousness of Loki, he is subject of Oehlenschläger's heroic narrative in five songs on *Thors rejse til Jotunheim* published 1807 in *Nordiske Digte* which was largely based on Snorri's *Edda*; see also **mythology**.

Thor and Midgard Serpent *300*; Gr uses Norse myth, where Thor fishes in world ocean for Midgard Serpent (sibling of Fenris Wolf and Hel, begotten by Loki upon giantess Angraboda), hooks it but loses it, leaving it to return at Ragnarok to be killed by Thor though at cost of his own life, to symbolise the principles of Truth and the Lie; see also **mythology**; **Freyr and Surt**; **Odin and Fenris**.

Thorkelin, Grímur Jónsson *110, 135*; 1752-1829; Icelandic-born scholar; educated in Latin School at Skálholt, Iceland, and in Copenhagen University, graduating in Law (1776); pursued interest in Icelandic medieval manuscripts; through publication of various early Icelandic texts established reputation leading to appointment (1777) as secretary to the Arnamagnæanske Kommission responsible for Arne Magnusson's bequest of Icelandic manuscripts; named Extraordinary Professor in Copenhagen 1783; travelled extensively, notably in United Kingdom where he sought manuscript sources for Danish history and transcribed manuscript text of *Beowulf*; 1790 was offered post in British Museum but chose to return to Dk to take office as State Archivist (1791); much of his work towards *editio princeps* of *Beowulf* was destroyed in British bombardment of Copenhagen (1807) but he heroically brought edition to publication in 1815, only to be savagely attacked by Gr (newly self-taught in Anglo-Saxon) over erratic character of both transcription and interpretation, in series of articles (1815) in *Nyeste Skilderie af Kjøbenhavn*.

Thorpe, Benjamin *130, 134, 135*; 1782-1870; pioneer editor of Anglo-Saxon texts; studied Anglo-Saxon in Copenhagen with Danish philologist Rasmus Rask (whose Anglo-Saxon Grammar he translated into English) and within two years of return (1830) to England emerged as nominee of Society of Antiquaries – and as Gr's rival – in plan to publish corpus of Anglo-Saxon writings; assisted by civil list pension granted 1835; his publications included 1832 poems traditionally attributed to Cædmon in Oxford Bodleian manuscript Junius 11, 1842 Exeter Book and Anglo-Saxon Gospels, 1855 *Beowulf*, 1861 Anglo-Saxon Chronicles and 1865 Charters.

Thorvaldsen, Bertel *86, 100, 233, 255, 276*; 1770-1844; Danish sculptor; after winning the Kunstakademi's Gold Medal, settled in Rome for next 40 years, quickly establishing international reputation as sculptor; 1838 returned to Dk amid great acclaim and publicity, bringing his collection of sculptures to be bequeathed to Copenhagen in exchange for the erection of a museum to house them; Frederik VI asked Baroness Christine Stampe, who had lived for a period in Italy, to help him resettle; accordingly he was provided with accommodation and hospitality at manor-house of Nysø where Stampes presided over salon attracting many leading figures in Danish society, and where an important collection of Thorvaldsen's work remains.

Thyregod *68, 70, 73, 155*; small town some 35 km northwest of Vejle, Jylland where Gr lived (1792-1798) in household of parish priest Laurits Svindt Feld (1751-1803), receiving tuition from him before moving to Aarhus Latin School.

Tidens Strøm *217*; *Tidens Strøm eller universalhistorisk Omrids* [The river of time or outline of universal history], 1829; Gr's schematic overview of universal history, published as a single folio sheet; the metaphor of the river of time is often used by Gr, usually to signal a universal-historical implication.

Tieck, Ludvig *84, 85*; 1773-1853; German poet, writer, translator; esteemed alongside Goethe, outstanding figure in development of style and language of German Romanticism; close friend of Novalis (Friedrich von Hardenberg) and brothers August Wilhelm and Friedrich Schlegel, and with them influenced by philosophy lectures of J. G. Fichte in Jena; his reputation in Dk largely owed to lectures on new German Romanticism given by Henrik Steffens in Copenhagen 1802; his poetry notably translated into Danish by Adam Oehlenschläger 1838-39.

titles *passim*; under the Danish absolute monarchy a profusion of precisely and finely ranked titles for officers of the Crown (ecclesiastical as well as secular) was developed, many of them purely honorific; see item 117, endnote on title of Bishop granted to Grundtvig in 1861.

Tivoli *243, 296, 297*; pleasure gardens in Copenhagen established 1843 by George Johan Bernhard Carstensen (1812-57) and laid out around city's decommissioned western fortifications, remnants of which are still a feature of gardens; on pattern of similar pleasure gardens established in various European cities from late 18th c. onwards, it offered attractively landscaped surroundings, assembly rooms, concerts, miscellaneous theatrical presentations, illuminations and refreshments; in its first full year it is said to have had over 370,000 visitors.

To bid the world a fit farewell; hymn by Gr; see ***At sige Verden ret Farvel***.

Toft, Marie; see **Grundtvig,** Marie (Toft).

Torkil(d)strup *76, 79, 81, 88, 89, 90*; village in north Falster adjacent to Gundslev, some 200 km south of Copenhagen, where Gr's elder brother Otto was parish priest and where Gr visited as student, crediting his stay there in 1804 with having at least made his manners "a little less unlike those of the more refined world than they previously were." Gr upset Bishop Andreas Birch (1758-1829) by publishing (1804) exposure of educational negligence on Falster.

Tors Rejse til Jotunheim; poem by Oehlenschläger; see **Thor**.

totafoth and zizith *329*; prayer-belt carrying sections of Tora for binding on head and 'threadbare' edging of prayer-shawl, symbolic items of ritual dress worn by strictly observant "scribes and Pharisees;" phrase used by Edmund Gosse to characterise kind of "obligatory tests" and "deadening formulas" despotically enforced by "Scandinavian official religion" – which, he says, Gr "tore away from men's consciences." See also **scribes and Pharisees**.

Tramp, Augustus Sophus Ferdinand *264*; 1810-63; *Grev* [Count] with seat at Kyø, Nordjylland; *Hofchef* [Lord Chamberlain] to Dowager Queen Caroline Amalie; philological sparring-partner to Gr at queen's dinner-table.

Treschow, Frederik Willum (Wilhelm) *62*; 1786-1869; Danish lawyer and politician; conducted Gr's defence against libel charges brought by H. N. Clausen and, when (1826) case was lost, himself paid fine awarded against Gr; 1838 fronted proposal of *Sognebaandsløsning* (dissolution of parochial ties) which however was defeated in Roskilde *Stænderforsamling* 1839; resigned office 1846 dissociating himself from authorities' persecution of Orla Lehmann and other National Liberal activists but after 1849 committed himself to Conservative wing, served as one of king's nominees to the *Rigsraad* 1854-63.

Treschow, Niels *62, 188-190*; 1751-1833; Norwegian-born philosopher, noted rationalist and determinist; resident in Copenhagen as Professor of Philosophy 1803-13, when his home became centre for social gatherings of leading intellectuals; 1813-25 Professor of Philosophy and leading figure in newly-founded university at Kristiania (Oslo); 1814-25 also Minister for Church Affairs and Education Minister in Norway; presided over negotiations concerning Norway's union with Sweden (1814) at cost of losing support among nationalistic-minded circles in Norway and Denmark.

Trier, Ernst Johannes *153, 302, 331, 333*; 1837-93; *cand. theol.*, after serving as field chaplain in calamitous war with Prussia 1864, committed himself to cause of *danskhed* [Danishness] by establishing (with support of the *valgmenighedspræst* [priest chosen by congregation] Villiam Johan Hoff (1832-1907), and with patronage of women of Moltke family at Conradineslyst) a folk-highschool in Vallekilde, NW Sjælland (1865), assisted by wife Marie (Nathalie Marie Abel, 1845-73; married 1867) who, alongside bearing four children, became school's *husmoder* [house mother, matron] as well as teaching various subjects including special classes for female students and thus ranks as one of the women pioneers within folk-highschool movement; Trier remained principal until his death; his 'Erindringer fra Grundtvigs Hjem' [Reminiscences of Gr's home], published in Frederik Rönning's *Hundrede Aar. Et Mindeskrift i Anledning af Hundredaarsdagen for Nic. Fred. Sev. Grundtvigs Fødsel* [One hundred years. A commemorative volume in connection with the hundredth anniversary of the birth of NFSG] (1883) includes various sympathetic anecdotes of Gr's conversations with his visitors on such matters as religious belief and secular education, and of Gr's readiness, even in his old age, to teach and encourage the rising generation; remained a visitor at Gr's home up to Gr's death; while consulting Gr (1872) about a song-book in preparation (*Sange for den kristelige Folke-Skole* [Songs for the Christian Folk-school], published 1874) he elicited from Gr extempore composition of new 4-line ending to *Et jævnt og muntert, virksomt Liv paa Jord* [A plain and cheerful, active life on earth]; published *Femogtyve Aars Skolevirksomhed i Vallekilde* [Twenty-five years of school activity in Vallekilde], 1890; see also **folk-highschools**; **Hoff,** Villiam Johan; **Holbæk**.

Trojel, Jacob Thomas *89*; 1782-1859; Gr's cousin on mother's side, with whom, in Hyskenstræde in Copenhagen, Gr stayed for a short time (late summer 1804) while looking (in vain) for an income to allow him to stay in the capital and work upon a doctoral thesis; it was Trojel who passed on to Grundtvig the offer of a residential tutorial post with the Steensen-Leth family on Langeland.

Trondheim *288*; Norwegian city in northerly coastal district of Trøndelag; first capital of Norway, established 10th c. as harbour and market at mouth of river Nidelva, hence earlier called Niðarós (Nidaros), by King Olav Tryggvason, Christian convert who reputedly desired to build his church far from centres polluted by old heathen practices; its Christian religious history rests largely upon death of King Olaf Haraldsson at Battle of Stiklestad (1030) and cultivation of his grave (Trondheim cathedral) as shrine which made it major pilgrimage-centre throughout Middle Ages; cathedral (long left in ruins after great fire of 1531, subsequently further damaged, extensively rebuilt 1869 onwards) has been traditional setting for coronation and anointing of Norwegian sovereigns since 1814; around 1848, Trondheim was centre of deep conflict between Bishop P. O. Bugge and alliance of Haugians and *Herrnhuter*; see also **Olav,** Saint; **Bugge,** Peter Olivarius; **Hauge,** Hans Nielsen; **herrnhuter**; **Trøndelagen**, old woman from.

Truth and the Lie *300*; the historical struggle between Truth and the Lie becomes central to Gr's Christian philosophy of history, and is a concept he used, for example, in interpreting Anglo-Saxon epic poem *Beowulf* (where Beowulf, serving Truth, is victorious over the Lie embodied in Grendel and Dragon, though at cost of his own life; he found the opposition symbolised in Norse myth and took advantage of it in his metaphorical exposition and application of the indigenous myth; see **Thor and Midgard Serpent**; **mythology**.

Tryde, Eggert Cristopher *235*; 1781-1860; priest, *Stiftsprovst* [diocesan dean] of Copenhagen in succession to H. G. Clausen, enjoying patronage of Bishop J. P. Mynster who among other things highly esteemed his talents as preacher; as student, like others of his (and Gr's) generation, was attracted by lectures of Henrik Steffens (1802) into lifelong interest in philosophy and speculative theology; awarded titular rank of bishop 1854; Doctor of Theology 1857; much more sympathetic than Mynster towards Gr, to extent of supporting principle of *sognebaandsløsning* [freeing of parochial ties]; according to Frederik Barfod, however, was chiefly instrumental, as member of Hymnal sub-committee of Convention of Copenhagen clergy, in rejection of Gr's draft for a new hymnal.

Trykkeforordringen *156*; Press Ordinance, 1799; after brief experiment in liberalisation of press-laws in 1770, administrators of *enevældet* [the absolute monarchy] quickly found it expedient to curtail freedom anew; ordinance issued September 1799 forbade anonymity, restricted criticism of crown and church, and established personal subjection to censorship, along with fines, as penalty for breach; an immediate victim was Peter Andreas Heiberg (1758-1841), on December 1799 sentenced to exile for libelling state official in course of agitating in print against absolutism and censorship of press; thus Dk entered 19th c. with repressive legislation in place, which stifled such as Otto Horrebow (1769-1823) who lampooned Bishop of Sjælland N. E. Balle (1744-1816) and published periodical dedicated to exposing incompatibility between rationalism and faith, and Thomas Christopher Bruun (1750-1834), professorial translator of ribald classics, of whom Gr wrote "Thomas Bruun has sullied many a page with ungodly and lewd jesting;" but legislation of which Gr himself fell foul 1826, when found guilty in court of libelling Professor Henrik Nicolai Clausen (1793-1877); see also **censur**.

Trøndelagen, old woman from *287*; an expression of Gr's abiding concern for Norway was his readiness to receive Norwegian visitors to his home in Copenhagen; Norwegian H. Brun, nervous on his first visit, took heart from saying of a previous caller, an old woman from Trøndelagen (region in northerly Norway, chief town Trondheim): "Gr is simply the man he is, no matter how he receives you."

Tscherning, Anton Frederik *238, 335*; 1795-1874; Danish officer and democratic politician opposed to privileges and class distinctions who nevertheless would leave considerable powers with the monarch; chairman of the Bondevennernes Selskab [Association of friends of peasant farmers] 1846; Minister of War March-November 1848, facing crisis in Slesvig-Holsten; immediately successful in mustering force of 12, 000 men to replenish Danish army which won crucial victory at Bov (April 1848); remained sceptical towards national policy of confrontation with Germany over the duchies of Slesvig-Holsten; sat as royal nominee in the Assembly to frame the Constitution, later an elected and influential member of the *Folketing*; fought strenuously against reactionary electoral changes 1866 and joined Gr in urging the king against undersigning the new Constitution.

Tuborg, Store *243, 323, 325, 334, 337*; Strandvejen 123, villa in northern suburb of Copenhagen, overlooking the Øresund shore; bought by Fru Asta as Gr's home from 1868 following his recovery from breakdown; scene of the great celebrations of Gr's birthdays by the *Venner* [Friends] (some 1100 people gathered in September 1868), and of the sixtieth anniversary (Whitsun 1871) of his ordination when dinner was served to over 100 guests, and evening gathering in gardens included contingent of 190 pupils from Norwegian folk-highschool, Sagatun, led by Herman Anker and Olaf Arvesen; notable also for daily hospitality to visitors calling on Gr so that house could be described as parsonage not for a parish nor even for a city but for many town and country parishes all across Dk and beyond; sold within a year of Gr's death by Fru Asta who had been advised of plans to build major commercial development on land between house and Øresund shore – where various quays, factories and the great Tuborg Brewery now stand.

Turks; see **Constantinople**.

Tvedestrand *255*; town on Skagerak coast, Norway, some 250 km SW of Oslo, 80 km NE of Kristiansand; family with Danish origins there fetched *seminarium*-trained live-in tutors from Dk for children's education. See **Andresen,** Peter Rasmussen.

Twelve, The; see **Tylvten**.

Tylvten (Tylvden) *114*, *276*; The Twelve, initiators of a Copenhagen literary feud when Jens Baggesen published criticism of Oehlenschläger's work; the twelve students of Copenhagen University challenged him (in newspaper *Dagen*, 3 October 1818) to dispute case in Latin; in riposte drafted but not signed by Gr, six other students declared themselves (in *Dagen*, 16 October) supporters of Baggesen; satire and parody were weapons, thus in *Himmelbrevet* [The letter from heaven] Poul Martin Møller (1794-1838), one of The Twelve, parodied Gr's prose ("The verbal parody in *Himmelbrevet* is quite successful. Grundtvig's bulky style gets a couple more kilos added so that the pathetic and the exaggerated are laid bare: *In conclusion I cry yet once more Woe! yea thrice woe! upon the pups who have set themselves up against the Chronicle and me, and me and the Chronicle, and the Chronicle and me. Amen.* (Vilh. Andersen, *Skrifter i Udvalg* II, Copenhagen 1930, p. 67). With his immoderate self-esteem Grundtvig as good as invited this reply to his blustering contribution to the Baggesen feud." – Niels Stengaard, *Poul Martin Møller, Forfatterportræt, Arkiv for Dansk Litteratur* online 2006); see also **Rimelige Strøtanker**; **pennefejde**.

Tyregod; see **T(h)yregod**.

U

Udby *61*, *66*, *73*, *80*, *81*, *87-89*, *102*, *105*, *107*, *108*, *144*, *154*, *159*, *161*, *185*, *186*, *192*, *193*, *244*, *328*; village some 8 km north of Vordingborg, south Sjælland, Gr's birthplace, vicarage of his father Johan Ottesen (1734-1813), where Gr lived until sent to Tyregod Parsonage, Jylland, for education, and where (1811-12) he returned as his father's curate; Udby parsonage is still in use as such, but rooms forming curate's residence are now *mindestuer*, memorial rooms commemorating Gr; likewise a commemorative stone has been raised in the churchyard, where Johan Ottesen's grave is also kept.

Udgaards-Loke *125*; Icelandic Útgarða-Loki; Loki, king of Útgarðr, so distinguished from Loki of Ásgarðr (home of Æsir-gods); in Snorri Sturluson's *Prose Edda*, Thor with Loki of Ásgarðr and others journeys to hall of Útgarða-Loki who scoffs at his puniness, challenges him and his men to contests; Loki proposes eating-match, devours all meat off trough of bones set before him but adversary Logi eats bones and all, so Loki loses; Thor's man Þjálfi proposes running competition, but in three races is easily outstripped by small lad called Hugi, so loses; Thor says he will outdrink all set before him, but though he drinks three huge draughts, he barely lowers contents, so loses; next Útgarða-Loki jeeringly asks if Thor can even lift cat off floor, but though with immense struggle he lifts one paw off floor, he loses; Thor, angry, offers to wrestle all comers, but though his adversary Elli is feeble-looking old man and Thor wrestles mightily, he is brought down on one knee; Útgarða-Loki stops contest, gives Thor and his men a feast; but as Útgarða-Loki escorts him away next morning he reveals he had enchanted Thor and his men, that Logi was insatiable Fire, Hugi was Útgarða-Loki's Thought outstripping any action, drinking-horn's end was in Ocean whose level Thor had for ever lowered, cat was the Midgard Serpent which encircles whole world, wrestler Elli was insuperable Old Age; Thor is furious at deception but before he can strike with his hammer Útgarða-Loki and Útgarðr itself vanish; example of Norse mythology used metaphorically by Gr, here as symbol of "How vain it is to wrestle with the old troll-witch whose true name is Indifference, that is, spiritual insensibility." See also **Nordens Mythologi**.

Udsigten over Verdens-Krøniken *120*; *Udsigt over Verdens-Krøniken fornemmelig i det Lutherske Tidsrum* [Survey of world history principally in the Lutheran era] was published by Gr 1817 as one in complex of works (translations of Saxo and Snorri, essays in *Danne-Virke*, *Bjovulfs Drape*) drawing upon history, legend and myth, and addressing between them both learned folk and the common reader, in implementation of his conviction that "History is something which as far as possible everyone should be familiar with, so that History, which uniquely embraces everything human, can and must connect and interpret it." See also **universal history**.

Ulfhild *87, 88*; unpublished heroic and romantic story written by Gr (1803) around English princess Ulfhild and other figures in Anglo-Saxon and Viking history; the (imperfect) fair copy is in Gr Arkiv Fasc. 492; one of several experimental pieces from Gr's university days when, freed to read widely in literature of his own choosing, he was inspired to test own abilities as poet and dramatist; see also **Brevet**; **Skoleholderne**.

Undrer mig paa, hvad jeg faar at se *333*; *I marvel at what I come to see*; song (dismissed by Gr as "no use") by Bjørnstjerne Bjørnson (1832-1910), Norwegian author, Nobel prizewinner for literature (1903).

universal history *122, 176, 248, 253, 254, 257, 274*; distinctive philosophy of history and historiography founded upon notion that the events whose record comprises history are not random and discrete but give testimony to a cohesive principle, dynamic or purpose, manifest through time and in a multitude of diverse places; central to orthodox Christian historiography which has traditionally held that the Bible models a coherent history of the world from its beginning to its destined end, and that God's purposes and providential interventions in the temporal world are attested in that history, enabling the Christian historian to discern universal truths in history and to some extent to predict (or prophesy) the future course of events; it underpinned Christian theology and exegesis, the liturgy of the Church and religious art and literature – through all of which it was in turn communicated onwards to the faithful. In 19th c., German philosophers espoused more secular (though still highly idealistic) notions of universal history, notable among them being Johann Christoph Friedrich Schiller (1759-1805) whose inaugural lecture as professor at Jena University (1789) was entitled *Was heisst und zu welchem Ende studiert man Universalgeschichte?* [What is the meaning of, and to what end does one study universal history?], the hugely influential Georg Wilhelm Friedrich Hegel (1770-1831) and (influenced by Hegel) Karl Marx (1818-83). In 1806, while private tutor at Egeløkke, Gr wrote his translation of an extract from Schiller's lecture into his notebook (Albeck 1979, 275-82). From 1815 when, according to his own retrospective schematising of his early post-university intellectual and authorial development, his 'historical' period began (and when, incidentally, he encountered the Anglo-Saxon cultural legacy in the poem *Beowulf*, the poetry of Cædmon and the historiography of Bede, all of which works are distinguished by their presumption of a universal dimension to history), Gr committed himself wholeheartedly to expounding history in universal terms and for the rest of his life placed this philosophy of history at the centre of his understanding of the Church and Christendom, and of the destiny of Denmark and the North. See also **Krønnike-Rim til levende Skolebrug**; *Verdens-Krønike*; *Kort Begreb af Verdens-Krønike i Sammenhæng*; *Udsigten over Verdens-Krøniken*.

Universalism; see **Universalisme**

Universalisme *73*; Universalism; outlook which transcends parochial boundaries, whether physical or conceptual, and tends to inclusiveness rather than exclusiveness; in Gr's view desirable quality to be inculcated in young people in respect of home and mother-tongue.

Uppsala expedition; see **Uppsalatoget** 1856.

Uppsalatoget 1856 *295, 296*; expression of enthusiasm, notably among Scandinavian students, for Scandinavian movement; student gathering in Uppsala, Sweden, where political activist and poet Carl Parmo Ploug (1813-94) called for dynastic union between Denmark and Sweden-Norway; in response, King Oscar I (1844-59), receiving the students in Stockholm, declared that hereafter war between the Nordic brothers was impossible, and in a letter to Danish king Frederik VII he offered defensive alliance and 16,000 troops to defend Dk's Ejder-frontier; but offers were rejected; a politically-aligned *Skandinavisk Samfund* [Scandinavian Association] formed in Dk as follow-up to *Uppsalatoget* was banned but Ploug and supporters were able to regroup as the culturally orientated *Skandinavisk Selskab* [Scandinavian Society]; see also **Studenterkorps**, Studenter-Tog.

upstarts and disparagers; see **Spyttegjøge og Spottefugle**.

Urolige Hjerte, hvad fattes dig dog? *279*; *O heart ever-fretful, what is it you lack?*; hymn by Gr (1851); 44 in *DDS* 2002 (with archaic deponent verb *fattes* replaced in modern version by *fejler*); Bishop Hans Lassen Martensen (1808-84) who judged a hymn's ultimate worth by "its practical application to the individual soul" and thus held Gr's hymns often wanting, admitted distinguished exceptions to the generalisation, of which this was one; see also ***Kirken den er et gammelt Huus***; ***Sov sødt, Barnlille***; **hymns**.

V

Valdemar I *78, 115*; 1131-1182, the Great; King of Denmark 1157-1182; son of Knud Lavard (who was later canonised); gained sole rule in Dk with strong support from Jutlanders, and later from the Sjælland family Hvide to which belonged Asser Rig and his sons Esbern Snare and Absalon (and to which Gr believed his maternal lineage could be traced); together with fosterbrother Absalon (later bishop in Roskilde and Dk's archbishop in Lund and founder of Copenhagen), Valdemar led crusade against Vends in Rügen, established Danish rule on continental Baltic seaboard; his reign was in some respects period of national greatness, of which Copenhagen's founding and building of various great churches are surviving memorials, but also period of great strife, marked by internal and external power-struggles, secular and religious; he died in Vordingborg, was buried in Ringsted.

Valdemar den store og hans Mænd *15, 115, 124*; *Valdemar the Great and his men*, historical poem (1824) by B. S. Ingemann, based upon historical-legendary material relating to 12th c. Dk, from Saxo Grammaticus and traditional ballads; in two parts of, respectively, ten and eleven songs; poem, like Ingemann's historical novels, offers history's lesson to present age, that dying national spirit is revitalised by great leaders whom God appoints to their task when need is greatest; Gr was unhappy with Ingemann's portrait of Saxo Grammaticus "as a pedantic bookworm and wind-dried academic" [*en pedantisk Bog-Orm og vindtør Magister* (present text)] and "a clownish pedant" [*en naragtig Pedant* (Verse-letter to Ingemann 3 July 1824)], but forgot criticism in rejoicing that Ingemann ("thermometer of the Danish heart" – Gr) proved Dk was rediscovering its historical heroes and the Danish identity they embodied and symbolised; see **Valdemar** I; and **Ingemann**, Bernhard Severin.

Valhalla *143*; in Norse mythology, *Valhöll*, Odin's Hall of the Battle-Slain, to which the valkyries [choosers of the battle-slain] bring from the battlefield half of the best of dead warriors, to become Odin's select soldiers (*einherjar*), kept in fighting trim for the prophesied cosmic conflict at Ragnarok, while the other half go to Freya's hall, Folkvang; in characteristic application of northern myth to modern Danish history Gr, recording a moving episode aboard ship on his return from Skamlingsbanken (1844), celebrates as *einherjar* Peter Willemoes (1783-1808) and others who died aboard the *Prinds Christian* in an engagement with British ships off Sjællands Odde (1808).

Valkendorfs Kollegium *62, 97, 99, 102, 103, 159, 160, 186*; oldest collegiate residence for students in University quarter of Copenhagen, inaugurated 1589, on site of Carmelite monastic house purchased 1588 by Christopher Valkendorf (1525-1601); where Gr (1808-11) first met many who were to become leading figures in Danish and Norwegian cultural life; together with Borchs Kollegium it has played significant role in Danish intellectual life.

Vallekilde *302, 306, 323*; location of folk-highschool in NW Sjælland established by Ernst Trier 1865; see also **Trier,** Ernst Johannes; **Hoff,** Villiam Johan; **Holbæk.**

valgmenighedspræst *257*; pastor of a free congregation, within the State Church; see **Sognebaandsløsning**; **frikirke**; **Ryslinge**.

Vanini, Giulio Cesare (Lucilio) *165*; 1585-1619; Italian priest, preacher, liberal philosopher who *inter alia* speculated upon human evolution from apes and was burned at stake (1619) for alleged atheism, sorcery but later seen as symbolic victim of Vatican obscurantism over scientific observation and speculation; see **Galilei,** Galileo; and **Roskilde Landemode.**

Vartborg *113, 313*; Wartburg, Thüringen, Germany; fortress-castle of Elector of Saxony where Martin Luther found refuge when, summoned to Imperial Diet of Worms (1521) to repudiate his teachings, he maintained his position with "Ich kann nicht anders" [I cannot do otherwise] and was outlawed by imperial decree, excommunicated by the Pope, and stood in danger of his life; here too he accomplished his translation of the New Testament into German.

Vartou *62, 329, 330*; antique variant upon Danish *Vartov*; see **Vartov**; **Vartov Kirke.**

Vartov *22, 62, 174, 175, 205, 255, 259, 266, 276, 298, 311, 312, 340*; at time of Gr's appointment (1839) as pastor to the community there, Vartov was a charitable home for elderly poor women (in Gr's day, sometimes disparagingly called the *kællinghospital* [gammers' hospital]) just inside the western gateway of the city; origins appear to lie with hospital maintained throughout Middle Ages by the 'Duebrødre' ['Dove-brothers'], Brethren of the Holy Spirit, established in Copenhagen by Jens Krag, Bishop in Roskilde 1290-1300, on site today still occupied by Helligaandskirke [Church of the Holy Spirit]; Helligaandshospital was moved 1607 to crown property outside city and picked up its popular name *Vartou* which stuck to it when the institution settled (1666) in Farvergade where (1724-1744) substantial new two-storey buildings incorporating a small church were erected around a large courtyard, essentially the buildings surviving today; 1930 charitable foundation moved again, leaving buildings in Farvergade (by then raised to three storeys with rebuilt church and unbudgeably known as Vartov) in use as city government offices; subsequently bought (1947) by Kirkeligt Samfund, restored and developed in spirit of continuation of Gr's work; now incorporates public meeting-rooms, student residences, kindergartens, the Grundtvig Library; statue of Grundtvig by Niels Skovgaard erected in courtyard 1932; Vartov now serves informally as living memorial to Gr in Copenhagen.

Vartov Church; see **Vartov Kirke.**

Vartov congregation *138, 141, 192, 266, 283, 306, 309, 317, 318, 320-322, 339*; though Gr was appointed (1839) in then-customary way by royal consent to the church at Vartov, his congregation gathered there from various other parishes in and outside Copenhagen and in effect became, as Gr foresaw, a free congregation (and today constitutes a *valgmenighed*, an elective congregation nominating own pastor though remaining within the *Folkekirke*); dominantly middle-class, it included substantial businessmen, academics, politicians, and their families, and for a long period the Dowager Queen Caroline Amalie, but also craftsmen, small shopkeepers and of course the elderly inhabitants of Vartov Hospital itself; see also **Køster,** Kristen; **Bayer**; **Brandt,** Carl Joakim; **Vartov Forsamlingen**; **Vartov Kirke**; **Vartov**, hymn-singing; **Vartov's** *Kirke-Salmebog*; **hymns.**

Vartov Forsamlingen *176*; Gr's own designation of free congregation gathered about him at Vartov; see also **forsamlinger**.

Vartov gathering; see **Vartov Forsamlingen**.

Vartov, hymn-singing *299*; zest and style of hymn-singing in Gr's church at Vartov was re-nowned, many of the hymns being originally composed or reworked from older texts by Gr and printed in Vartov's own hymnal – "and in his hymns, as all well-informed people know, there is a content, a strength and a poetic amplitude and loftiness as in few other hymnwriters since the earliest days of the Church." (Arvesen); see also **Vartov's** *Kirke-Salmebog*; **hymns**.

Vartov Kirke *70, 176, 207, 229, 286, 298, 299, 307, 314, 319, 320, 322, 327, 339*; spiritual ancestry goes back to church associated from early Middle Ages with Helligaandshospital (whence also Vartov Hospital's origin); present church was incorporated in new buildings in Farvergade 1753-1755 to serve resident community; 1856 all buildings including church raised by one floor, church much reorganised within, additional height later (1935) used to create rooms for congregational use, eventually apartment for priest over church; Gr had preached there by invitation before his call to Præstø (1821), but from 1839 to 1872 Vartov church was centre of Gr's ministry with congregation from far and wide; 1925 constituted, and today still continues, as church of Vartov *valgmenighed* (congregation authorised to choose and remunerate own priest, remaining within national Church); see also various **sermon** entries; **Vartov**, hymn-singing; **Vartov's** *Kirke-Salmebog*

Vartov's *Kirke-Salmebog* *236*; Gr's profound disappointment over rejection (January 1846) by *Kjøbenhavns Præstekonvent* [Clerical Convention of Copenhagen] of draft revision of Church's hymnal drawn up by him and others in committee was mitigated when his own congregation encouraged him to break church regulations (now seemingly in abeyance, but actively enforced in 1826 when Gr's specially composed hymn for the Whitsunday celebration of the thousandth anniversary of the Danish Church was forbidden by Bishop Münter) and bring his own hymns into use in Vartov; he began doing so at Easter 1846 and thus laid foundations for Vartov's own hymnal, *Fest-Salmer*, of which first part was published 1850, and which, augmented, went through many subsequent impressions; see also **Spang**, Peter Johannes; **hymns**.

vassal-homage; see **hoveritjeneste**.

Vavlunder *101*; also Vaulundur; Icelandic *Völundr*, Anglo-Saxon *Weland*: smith of matchless skill in widespread northern myth; see *Vaulundurs Saga*; *Nordens Mythologi*.

Vaulundurs Saga, *96*; prose narrative by Adam Oehlenschläger published 1805 in *Poetiske Skrifter* 2; ultimately based on Icelandic *Edda*-poem *Völundarkviða* [The Lay of Weland]; Völundr is smith of matchless skill who, kidnapped and hamstrung by king greedy for his jewels and skills, takes grisly and brutal revenge by murdering captor's two young sons, raping his daughter and flying away on fabricated wings; story is also known to Anglo-Saxon poets (*Deor, Beowulf, Waldere*) and spread through northwest Europe in much extended saga form; in Oehlenschläger's work, Vaulundur serves as metaphor of Romantic genius, embodying truth that "whatever bears within itself the seeds of corruption must needs perish; but whatever lives in constant peace with itself and whose foes are situated only without, shall at last triumph if with patience and steadfastness it endures the time of affliction" (Oehlenschläger); see also **Nordens Mythologi**.

Vedel, Anders Sørensen *62, 106*; 1542-1616; Danish historian; tutor to astronomer Tyge Brahe 1562-1565, studied in Wittenberg 1566, appointed court chaplain to Frederik II 1568; translated Saxo's *Gesta Danorum* 1575; commissioned 1580, as royal historiographer, to write History of Denmark; this work he never completed and it was handed on to others; when Dr G. L. Baden proposed new translation of Saxo (1809) Gr championed Vedel's merits, published specimens of a revision of his language, eventually himself undertook new translation; Vedel's introduction constitutes valuable contemporary statement on sources of Scandinavian history, influential upon Gr's own historical views: "Her bør de fromme Isslenders flittighed icke at forgettis. Effterdi deris Land er hart oc wfructsommeligt saa giffues dem oc icke stor aarsage til Druckenskab oc Fraazeri men leffue vdi idelige Sparsomelighed oc vende meste parten deris tancker oc idret der hen at giemme oc optegne atskillige Nationers historier. At huad dem brøster paa atskillige liffs lyst oc offuerflødighed det vederlegge de met artighed oc kloge nemme. Thi intet er dem kierere end at de kunde forfare oc vide meget at sige aff vdlendigers vilkor. Oc er dem lige meget huad heller de tale om fremmede dyd eller de selff bedriffue noget merckeligt. Saa haffuer ieg icke bluedis ved at følge saadane forfarne folck effter vdi mange stycker men randsagt oc grandgiffueligen offuerslagen deres Krønicker oc effter deris sandsagn ført meget ind vdi denne min Historie." [Here ought the industriousness of the pious Icelanders not to be forgotten. According as their land is harsh and infertile so are they given no great grounds for drunkenness and gluttony but they live in perpetual frugality and turn the greater part of their thoughts and occupation towards preserving and recording various nations' histories, so that what they lack of various of life's pleasures and superfluity they compensate with good behaviour and wise intelligence. For nothing is dearer to them than to be able to investigate and to know much that can be told of the circumstances of foreign folk. And it is all the same to them whether they tell of the merit of foreigners or whether they themselves perform something extraordinary. So I have not been ashamed to follow such well-experienced people in many items but have ransacked and meticulously translated their chronicles and according to their authentic tradition I have incorporated much into this my history].

Vejle *68, 155*; town at end of Vejle Fjord on east coast of Jylland, some 70 km south-west of Aarhus; historical region includes nearby Jelling with ancient church, royal tumuli and runestones; nearest town to Thyregod where Gr was placed with pastor Laurits Svindt Feld (1750-1803) for his education prior to admission to Aarhus Latin School; from a reading-club there, Feld borrowed books and periodicals to which the young Gr also had free access.

Vends, Vendish *239*; collective designation of a group of West-Slavic peoples formerly inhabiting territories of present day Pomerania and Eastern Germany on southern Baltic seaboard from eastern border of Holsten to river Weichsel including Baltic islands of Femern and Rügen; in early medieval period maintained close trading, cultural and even dynastic links with Dk but in 12th c. Valdemar I (1131-1182) found it necessary to invade Vendish territories to extend his kingdom and crush Vendish heathendom symbolised on Rügen in cult of Svantevit whose great effigy was famously destroyed there (Arkona, 1169) by warrior-bishop Absalon; Vendish territories passed under German domination and in 19th c. were assimilated into unified Germany: "I never dreamed that Germany would become a 'unity' under a half-Vendish (that is, non-German) Prussian leadership ... and never dreamed that this could become dangerous for the North ... This danger Grundtvig saw and he dreaded it" (Frederik Barfod).

Vennerne, Vennemøderne, vennekreds *229, 263, 264, 272, 308, 339*; The Friends (of Gr), the Friends' meetings, the Friends' circle; from early in his career Gr won supporters, friends, devotees and disciples to his causes, as well as enemies; after his 80th birthday (8 September 1863) when some 700 friends gathered (with the Dowager Queen Caroline Amalie in attendance) to honour the day and the man, more formalised annual meetings, the so-called *Vennemøder*, were established where issues and strategies in implementation of a Grundtvigian agenda were aired, but the meeting in 1872, immediately after Gr's death, laid bare tensions and divisions, political, ecclesiastical and religious, and heralded a struggle between competing claims to possession of the true Grundtvigian legacy.

Venstre *263, 335, 336*; label put upon liberal-democratic reformist wing of Danish political spectrum which emerged in parliamentary form with granting of free Constitution (1849), its dissent from absolutist regime reflected in its designation, recalling structure of French national assembly of 1789 with friends of the people on left of chamber, old royalists on right; label first used from 1866 for liberal grouping hitherto usually calling themselves *Bondevennerne* [Friends of the peasant farmers]; its early impetus derived from will of peasant class (and their urban intellectual supporters) to secure, for example, rights and representation claimed by other social classes, reform of employment laws and fairer distribution of burden of taxation; ideologically, it expressed some of spirit and objectives of Gr's concept of *det folkelige* and of educational ideas of Gr and Christen Kold (1816-70); various leading Grundtvigians were prominent among *Bondevennerne*; conservative victory (1866) in securing revision of Constitution (when Gr and Anton Frederik Tscherning (1795-1874) in audience with King failed to persuade him to refuse his signature to revision) led to sharpening of party divisions and splitting of Venstre with emergence of *Det Nationale Venstre* [National-Liberals] led by Sophus Høgsbro and two other groups, one led by A. F. Tscherning, other by Christian Carl Alberti (1814-90) and Jens Andersen Hansen (1806-77); two latter groups merged 1868 as *Det folkelige Venstre*; in 1870, amid much internal conflict which also divided Grundtvigians, parliamentary *Venstre* [Left; but politically a Liberal platform] groups recombined under leadership of Chresten Poulsen Berg as *Det Forenede Venstre* [The United Left]; *Venstre*, subsequently split again into *Det Moderate Venstre* [moderate-liberal] og *Det Radikale Venstre* [radical-liberal, social-liberal], eventually yielded position on ideological left to socialists and social democrats; see also **Bondevennerne**; **Høgsbro,** Sophus Magdalus; **Berg,** Chresten Poulsen.

Venus *76, 90*; goddess of classical myth, symbol of love and sexuality, to whom the student Gr, though (he admits) an idler, card-player and frequenter of public places, avoided (he says) offering sacrifices which would have cost more than his precarious economy could have sustained; see **Bacchus**.

Verdens-Krøniken 105, 163, 193, 217; Gr's *Kort Begreb af Verdens Krønike i Sammenhæng* [Concise view of universal history in context; 1812] was reworking of his *Lærebog i Verdenshistorien* [Textbook in world history, 1808]; was revised, reissued (1814) as *Kort Begreb af Verdens Krønike betragtet i Sammenhæng* [Concise view of universal history examined in context]; together with nationally-orientated and poetic companion-piece *Roskilde-Riim* [Roskilde rhymes; 1814], *V-K* gave expression to Gr's new view of life following mental and spiritual crisis and his return home to Udby parsonage (1810-11); "After the crisis he had returned spiritually to the orthodox, pietistic Christianity of his childhood home. On the basis of this biblical Christianity he had written out of the conviction that the Creation and Christ are the corner-stones of history, and that the overall control by God's Providence is the explanation of its course [...] In both works he sets out to describe "God's control and our forefathers' achievements" in order to revive both the Church and the people" (Anders Pontoppidan Thyssen, Christian Thodberg); judged by some as remarkable for concept, insights and learning, its sweeping judgments of Christian values of distinguished men, living and dead, caused grave misgivings among friends, widespread offence, threats of legal action, led to protracted controversy with H. C. Ørsted and to breakdown of Gr's friendship with Christian Molbech; partly hostile review (1813) by Professor Jens Møller in *Dansk Litteratur-Tidende* ("in individual sections, and especially those which concern Denmark, [it] has all the characteristics which make lampoons the most cherished entertainment of the reading public") was answered by Gr in *Nyeste Skilderie af Kjøbenhavn* 17 (21 and 24 August 1813); see also **universal history**; **anfægtelser**; **Roskilde Landemode**; *Roskilde-Riim*; **berserk-gang**.

Vergil (Publius Vergilius Maro) *64, 72*; 70-19 B.C.; Roman poet; beneficiary, as Horace and others, of munificence of Maecenas enabling him to live on his farm and write, a life celebrated in his most perfected work, the *Georgics*; the *Eclogues* composed to honour emperor Octavian for favours received; his *Aeneid* contributed immeasurably to definition of Roman national legendary-heroic identity both for contemporaries and posterity; enormously influential in western literary tradition on both sides of Renaissance and staple author for study in classics-orientated curricula of the schools, though from 18th c. his poetic supremacy was increasingly challenged by Homer.

Vessel, Johan Herman; see **Wessel**

Videnskabelighed, so-called *162*; 'so-called science'; one of Gr's many jibes at science, scholarship and scholarly cabals, which have left him and Grundtvigian educational tradition with reputation, among detractors, of being anti-intellectual; in part expression of a particular conviction that, in obsession with things material and physical, 19th-c. intellectuals were wantonly undermining belief in and esteem of things spiritual; in part expression of more general conviction that traditional educational system and methods utterly failed to provide *livs-oplysning* 'education for living', an education not reserved to social and professional élites nor restricted to dead languages, rote-learning and book-learning and controlled by graded examinations, but an education mainly based on oral exchange which would itself be an authentic experiencing of real life and would help participants to realise qualitative enrichment of life and encourage *folkelighed*, active sense of national social and cultural community, and in particular knowledge of mother-tongue, history and mythology, in which folk-identity is embodied; Gr was happy repeatedly to refer to himself as a book-worm and the large corpus of his published books demonstrates his own intellect and mastery of intellectual procedures and conventions; his jibes against intellectualism are read at face value only by the wilfully blinkered; see also **Marielyst** and **Kold,** Christen Mikkelsen.

Vig, Ole *295*; 1824-57; teacher in Kristianssund, Norway, author; campaigner for "the sacred calling of *folkedannelsen* [education of the *folk*]", in part by introducing into Norwegian schools educational principles advocated by Gr, whom he visited and consulted; subjects taught should be useful, profitable to the individual; education should be anchored in the received cultural heritage, consolidating historical sense of national identity; education should inspire and enable participation in democratic system; though he died young, his ideals were embodied in great Norwegian school reform of 1860.

Vilhelm, Bishop *194*; d. 1074; earlier a clerk in Bremen, consecrated Bishop of Roskilde from about 1060; English-born, according to Saxo Grammaticus who presents (legend-enhanced) portrait of strong, masterful personality, close friend of king Svend Estridsen (b. 1047 in England, grandson of Svend Forkbeard, d. 1074) whom he appears to have supported in bid to detach North from See of Hamburg and in building of many stone churches (including Roskilde Cathedral) in Dk, though Saxo also tells of punishments and obedience forced by Vilhelm upon king; according to (implausible) legend, bishop and king died at same hour; both buried in Roskilde Cathedral.

Villemoes, see **Willemoes.**

Vimmelskaftet *24, 282, 286-288*; street in central Copenhagen forming with Østergade a portion of *Routen* (now called *Strøget*), a chief place in 19th c. for smarter Copenhageners to promenade; Gr and family moved here (1840, to Vimmelskaftet 49) following his appointment as priest at Vartov.

Vind, Ole (Oluf) *194*; 1590-1646; priest at Helligåndskirke and later Vor Frue Kirke in Copenhagen; 1645 appointed preacher to Court; according to tradition, was reported to Christian IV by courtiers taking offence at his outspoken condemnation of immorality at Court, but having preached the offending sermon again to the king, was appointed Court-preacher and *kongelig konfessionarius* (Chaplain Royal); currency of tradition reinvigorated by Gr's poem on '*Mester Ole Vind*' (1814).

Vindbyeholt *186*; village in SE Sjælland where Gr, in mentally disturbed state, and Sibbern, escorting him home from Copenhagen to Udby, lodged overnight; the inn has subsequently been destroyed by fire.

Virgin Mary *321*; mentioned during Gr's mental disturbance 1867; see **Gabriel,** archangel; **Palm Sunday** 1867.

Visigoths *66*; the West-Goths, distinguished as early as 2nd c. from the Ostrogoths (East-Goths); emerged (from Scandinavia the *officina gentium* 'manufactory of nations' according to highly partisan accounts of Saxo Grammaticus) during great tribal migrations preceding disintegration of Roman imperium; christianised (4th c.) by efforts of Ulfilas who translated Bible into Gothic; in 5th c. occupied western Gaul and Spain; Goths in Gaul conquered (507) by Franks under Clovis and Visigothic kingdom pulled back to Spain, lasting until 711 when last Visigothic king defeated by Moors; aware of Saxo's claim, Gr speaks (lightheartedly) of "the Visigoths who, though distantly, were of our family" and alludes to ill-treatment of them by Franks; see also **Goths**.

Vogt, Henrik Ludvig Volrath *297*; 1817-89; Danish-born theologian and teacher, raised from infancy in Norway; *cand. theol.* 1838, from 1840 teacher (*overlærer*, senior tutor, from 1852) in Kristiania (Oslo) cathedral school; author of school textbooks notably on Bible history, one of which was published in over one million exemplars and subsequently published in America; his *Det Hellige Land* [The Holy Land, 1879] was based on own extensive travels; a speaker, along with Gr, at great Danish-Norwegian student gathering, Tivoli (Copenhagen) 1856.

Voltaire, François Marie Arouet de *84*; 1694-1778; French author, playwright, philosopher; educated by Jesuits, spent some time in England and in Berlin; definitive model of 18th-c. European Enlightenment and rationalism in philosophy, manners, literary engagement and style; advocate of enlightened despotism, lifelong adversary of religious bigotry and every sort of intolerance; reacted against by 19th-c. Romanticism, having been scorned (Gr reports) by "the so-called New School" in Germany (late 18th c.) who spoke (according to Gr) of "that madhouse Voltaire and his cronies had built and called the Temple of Wisdom."

Vordingborg *61, 186*; market town and harbour in south Sjælland where (1167) Valdemar 1 established one of a number of fortresses across Dk (notably including Copenhagen and Kalundborg), designed to assert his rule and defend kingdom again invaders, and where soon trading posts developed, eventually licensed and taxed under royal charters; at beginning of 19th c. town had under 1000 inhabitants but was a chief town in region of Gr's birthplace at Udby, giving access by sea to southerly islands of Dk and beyond.

Vor Frelsers Kirke *62, 70, 111, 116, 123, 126, 129, 166, 167, 205*; Church of Our Saviour, built 1682-1696 in Christianshavn in the deaconry of Vor Frue Kirke (Copenhagen cathedral) as flamboyant baroque gesture of royal absolutism, serving German community as well as Danish; its spire with external staircase ascending to gilded figure of Christ at summit, is conspicuous landmark visible from central Copenhagen; success of Gr's application for appointment as curate (1822, following death of his widowed mother in Præstø) fulfilled his long-thwarted desire for ministry in the capital and created opportunity for study and writing he had sought in his application; by this time, the German congregation had moved to Frederiks Kirke (Christianshavn), the area was degenerating into slums, the church neglected, poorly attended; here Gr quickly achieved following as preacher (sermons subsequently printed); here clarified his perception of the Church as the congregation, preserving its tradition by word of mouth from apostolic times, in which, at baptism and communion, Christ speaks to the community his Living Word, which creates what it names; but Gr's initial conviction that new age was dawning ended, following conflicts with Church establishment and with Professor H. N. Clausen, in his resignation 1826.

Vor Frue Kirke *112, 156, 159, 167*; Church of Our Lady, Copenhagen; the capital's cathedral; one of first churches (earliest mentioned late 12th c.) in newly founded Copenhagen, and among oldest in Dk; here a succession of Danish sovereigns was crowned, including Christian I (1448), Christian IV (1596) and Frederik III, subsequently Dk's first absolute monarch (1648); here also, in cathedral school, Copenhagen University established 1478, and here first seven Lutheran bishops consecrated 1537; in Gr's lifetime the old church was replaced (1811-29) by neoclassical building designed by Christian Frederik Hansen (1756-1845) in which monumental statues of Christ and the twelve apostles by Bertel Thorvaldsen were later installed.

Vor Konge signe Du, o Gud! *144, 287*; Thy blessing grant our King, O God; hymn from *Evangelical-Christian Hymnal*, sung at Matins in Vartov on Sunday of week in which elections to the Constituent Assembly (*Den grundlovgivende Rigsforsamling*), in implementation of granting of constitutional government, were to take place; together with his sermon, its choice reflected Gr's deep anxiety about outcome of this move from benevolent absolutism towards democracy and particularly about the status of the church under the forthcoming constitution; see **hymns**.

Vår Frelsers Kirke, Oslo *149*; Church of Our Saviour, Oslo (formerly Kristiania); now Oslo's cathedral; here Gr preached Friday 13 June 1851, when the *Storting* [Parliament] suspended its meeting so that members might hear him.

W

Wade, Nugent *258. 270*; 1809-93; Irish-born Anglican priest; incumbent of English church in Helsingør (Elsinore), primarily serving as Chaplain to British Legation, from 1833 to 1839 when dwindling congregation led to closure of church; through Legation Secretary, Peter Browne, met Gr (7 November 1834; "had a most delightful & useful interview with Pastor *Gruntvig*: he is decidedly a man of genius & of a first rate order. I don't know that I ever met with so comprehensive a mind, he seems to sweep the whole world history at a glance & philosophise upon it & that soundly & with *one* scope: God & his dealing with man for his Redemption" [diary, ed. Helge Toldberg]); to him Gr addressed his *Aabent Vennebrev til en Engelsk Præst* (1839) [Open letter of friendship to an English priest], calling him "en elskelig Mand, godt inde i det Danske Sprog og vore kirkelige Forhold" [an amiable man, well familiar with the Danish language and the circumstances of our Church]; also befriended B. S. Ingemann and various leading Danish and Norwegian churchmen; around period of his return to England (1839) was engaged in plan to translate some of Gr's historical writing into English, though this never materialised; subsequently at St Mary's Church in Soho, London, and Canon of Bristol; listed among patrons of The Canterbury Association (1849), assisting emigration of respectable Christian working-class families to Canterbury, New Zealand; associated with Anglo-Catholic Oxford movement, supported Gr's visit (1843) to meet its leaders in Oxford and hoped, though in vain, to negotiate on its behalf with Danish Church; friendship with Gr thereafter steadily languished; some correspondence, diaries and papers relating to period 1827-70 are preserved in archives of Pusey House, Oxford; 17 of his letters to Gr between 1838-52 are preserved in Arkiv Fasc. 448.

Walchendorphs Kollegium; see **Valkendorfs Kollegium**.

Warton, Thomas *133*; 1728-1790; historian of English poetry, poet, Fellow of Society of Antiquaries; professor of poetry at Oxford 1757-1767 (he chose to lecture only on classical topics); Camden professor of history at Oxford 1785; Poet-Laureate 1785; his *History of English Poetry from the Close of the Eleventh to the Commencement of the Eighteenth Century etc.* published 1774 was followed by two further volumes (1778, 1781) surveying literature to end of reign of Elizabeth I; envisaged fourth volume reaching to Alexander Pope never appeared; second edition, much revised by Richard Price (1790-1833) came out in 1824; Warton's inadequacy as translator of early English was bluntly criticised by Joseph Ritson (1752-1803) and Gr (who used Price's Warton, and befriended Price himself, in preparation for his visit to England 1829) wrote sarcastically of Warton's classically-biassed contumely for early English literature; but authoritative retrospective view of Warton's work is that "Together with Percy's 'Reliques' it helped to awaken an interest in medieval and Elizabethan poetry ... [and] ... to divert the stream of English verse from the formal and classical channels to which the prestige of Pope had for many years consigned it" (Sidney Lee).

Welhaven, Johan Sebastian Cammermeyer *282, 296*; 1807-73; Norwegian poet, critic, professor of philosophy (1846-66) at University of Kristiania (Oslo); encouraged by Lyder Sagan while at Bergen Cathedral School (where, he told Gr, one otherwise did more or less as one wanted) to pursue talent for arts and poetry and to study classics; read theology (1825) at Kristiania with others who were to become leading figures in Norwegian cultural and political life; there he founded the *Intelligensparti* [Intelligence Party] in opposition to the *Norskhedparti* [Norwegianness Party] of his contemporary, poet and fervent democrat Henrik Wergeland; desired restoration of union between Norway and Dk and Norway's fuller integration into wider European culture; travelled in Germany, France, Italy; his collection of sonnets *Norges Dæmring* [Norway's Dawning, 1834], embodying his aesthetic creed, thereby challenged Wergeland and Norwegian insularism and earned him much unpopularity but, especially after Wergeland's death and own appointment as director of Society of Arts, emerged as leading arbiter in matters cultural; other published collections of his poetry, which place him (notwithstanding classical characteristics) among Norway's significant poets of Romanticism, are *Halvhundrede Digte* (Fifty poems, 1847), *Reisebilleder og Digte* (Travel pictures and poems, 1851) and *En Digtsamling* (A collection of poems, 1859); visited Gr in Copenhagen and (as did Gr) attended great gathering in Tivoli, Copenhagen, June 1856, following *Uppsalatoget* [the Uppsala-expedition] in support of Scandinavian unity.

Werner, Friedrich Ludwig Zacharias *189*; 1768-1823; German Romantic poet, dramatist, preacher; son of professorial Protestant family; studied law and political economy at University of Königsberg, Prussia; impressed by Kant's lectures and philosophy of Rousseau; after father's early death (1782), a period of youthful dissipation, employment in War Office, three divorces, death of highly neurotic mother (1804), amidst which he published first collection of poems (1789) and theatre reviews, and a move to Berlin (1805), he made his way to Rome where (April 1810) he was received into Roman Catholic Church; studied theology and was ordained priest 1814; his sermons (eventually published 1840) gained him some notoriety; briefly entered a religious order before his death; notable works included *Martin Luther oder die Weihe der Kraft. Eine Tragödie* [Martin Luther, or The consecration of strength. A tragedy] (1807), *Die Söhne des Thales, ein dramatisches Gedicht* [The sons of Thales, a dramatic poem], Part I: *Die Templer auf*

Cypern [The Templars of Cyprus] (1803), Part II: *Die Kreuzesbrüder* [Brothers under the Cross] (1804), *Das Kreuz an der Ostsee* [The Cross in the Baltic] (1806), *Der vierundzwanzigste Februar. Eine Tragödie in einem Akt* [The twenty-fourth of February. A tragedy in one act] (1814), and (as a post-conversion corrective to his *Martin Luther*) the poem *Die Weihe der Unkraft. Ein Ergänzungsblatt zur deutschen Haustafel* [The consecration of frailty. A supplementary page to the German *Haustafel* (= term given by Luther to prescription for godly ordering of a household as modelled in, for example, Ephesians 5:21-6:9)] (1814); Gr began but abandoned translation of his drama *Martin Luther* – which was, however, translated into Danish (1818) by Knud Lyhne Rahbek (1760-1830) as *Martin Luther eller Kraftindvielsen* [ML or The consecration of strength].

Wessel, Johan Herman *83, 85-87*; 1742-1785; Danish-Norwegian writer and poet, clergyman's son; settled in Copenhagen as kind of perpetual student, read widely during period of great flux in many departments of traditional European culture; aspired to no particular career but that of writer and poet, taking great delight in language from the street upwards; linked (by Gr and Steffens, admiringly) with Holberg with whom he shared ironical wit and talent for comic narrative, but posterity has not accorded him matching classic status; best-known work (1772), *Kærlighed uden Strømper* [Love without stockings] is burlesque of tragic ballad-opera, performed 1773 with music by Paolo Scalabrini (1713-1803), now regarded as having little more than literary-historical interest.

Wessely, Abraham *237*; 1800-75; Danish politician, jurist; co-founder, co-editor of *Fædrelandet* (The Fatherland), particularly concerned with fiscal issues; left wing of National Liberal Party, *Landsting* [upper chamber of the *Rigsdag*] 1849-66; Auditor of Public Accounts 1851-56; High Court 1854-66.

Wexels, Wilhelm Andreas, *149, 203, 288, 298*; 1797-1866; priest, writer, religious controversialist; born in Copenhagen, educated at the Metropolitan School, read theology at Kristiania (Oslo) University 1814-; appointed (1819) *kateket* [catechist] and (1846-66) resident *kapellan* [curate] in Vor Frelsers Kirke, Kristiania; spent whole of his ministry in Kristiania; though in earlier years sympathetic to Herrnhuter in Norway, from 1831, when he attacked Professor Niels Treschow's *Kristendommens Aand* [The Spirit of Christianity], he emerged as Gr's most vigorous Norwegian supporter in the Church Struggle [*Kirkekampen*] over first half of 19th c.; published 1834-39 periodical *Tidsskrift for Kirkekrønnike og Theologi*; antagonised rising class of evangelised peasantry by suggesting conversion could take place even after death (token of which, as Gr himself suggested, was Christ's descent into Hell) and engaged in controversy with various leading figures in Norwegian life; 1848 declined elevation to rank of bishop; though in 1827, as yet hardly known to Gr, he had been scorned by Gr as a Herrnhuter, by 1851 when he welcomed Gr to Norway he was Gr's "friend of many years and brother in office" (Gr; 18 of his letters to Gr written between 1826-61 are in Arkiv Fasc. 443) and a preeminent personality in Norwegian Grundtvigianism.

Whitsun festival in Norway; see **Pindse-Helgen**.

Willemoes, Joachim Goske *283-285*; 1781-1858; pastor, incumbent of Herfølge, Sjælland; *forsamlingspræst* [pastor ministering at revivalist religious gatherings not held in churches], instrumental in religious awakening of both Marie Toft and Asta Reedtz, Gr's second and third wives; older brother of naval hero Peter Willemoes, who had been Gr's friend before death in sea-battle 1808; knowing Gr's disapproval of *forsamlingspræster* he had long kept distant from Gr but Gr, perhaps influenced by Marie Toft, made rapprochement (1846).

Willemoes, Peter *17, 79, 99, 136, 283, 285*; 1783-1808; Danish naval officer and sea-hero, with whom Gr formed friendship while he was tutor at Egeløkke and Willemoes was transporting Danish troops between Langeland and Lolland; after distinguishing himself and becoming popular hero in naval confrontation with English fleet under Parker and Nelson in Kongedybet off Copenhagen (1801), Willemoes was killed in side-event of Napoleonic Wars, a clash between five English ships and Danish ship of the line *Prinds Kristian*, off Sjællands Odde, 22 March 1808; his body buried with other officers and crew in churchyard at Odden, with elegiac verse by Gr inscribed on memorial erected at expense of Lorentz Fribert, stepson of Gr's "extremely rich uncle" Carl Vilhelm Bang; Willemoes movingly celebrated for his heroic death in song by Gr (*Kommer hid, I piger smaa* [Gather round, you lassies small]); Gr commemorates the dead as *einherjar* (warriors in Valhalla) in impromptu speech to Danish youth aboard ship with him, passing Sjællands Odde (1844).

Willemoes, song for *79, 136, 137*; Verses from Gr's lyrical poem *Villemoes* (1810) in honour of Peter Willemoes, hero of sea-battles off Copenhagen (1801) and Sjællands Odde (1808), became popular as song, *Kommer hid, I Piger Smaa* [Gather round, you lassies small], set to music by C. E. F. Weyse (1774-1842); opportunistically exploiting name of W's ship, *Prince Christian*, Gr makes association between W and King Christian iv whose heroic stand, though wounded, at the high-mast of his ship in battle against Swedes 1644 held iconic status; two verses of Gr's song read: "Han var Dreng, men stod som Mand, / Medens I var spæde, / Stå og slaae for Fædreland / Var den Unges Glæde. / Strømmen gaaer mod Kjøbenhavn, / Kongedyb er Strømmens Navn, / Der blev Helten viet. // Hist i Nord gaaer Odden ud / Mellem høje Bølger; / Der blev Døn af stærke Skud, / Kristian ei sig dølger; / Men som gamle Kristian / Staaer han fast paa danske Strand, / Skjønt hans Blod udrinder." [He was a boy but stood like a man while you were yet infants; to stand and fight for the fatherland, this was the youth's delight. There flows a stream towards Copenhagen, Kongedyb is the stream's name: there the hero was baptised. Up in the north, Odden reaches out between high waves; there was the thunder of heavy gunfire: *Christian* does not hide himself, but like old Christian (King Christian iv) he stands firm on the Danish shore although his blood pours forth]; spontaneously sung by largely student audience after Gr's *Mands Minde* [Within living memory] lectures in Borchs Kollegium (1838); again spontaneously struck up by young Danes aboard ship with Gr when, returning from the nationalistic gathering at Skamlingsbanken (1844), they passed Sjællands Odde, location of the battle and of the grave of Willemoes and other heroes, moving Gr to tears and encouraging him to believe that a rebirth of national historical consciousness and pride was taking place: "Sangen om Willemoës var jo blevet født som folkesang hin Oktober-aften på Borchs Kollegium; nu, der ude over 'den åbne grav', blev den holdt over dåben" [The song about Willemoes was born as a folksong that October evening in Borchs Kollegium; now out there above 'the open grave' it was sung at the baptism] (Frederik Rönning).

Wiuff, Peder Hermand Clausen *237*; 1777-1856; organist at Frederiksberg Kirke, in whose house at Bredgade 10, Frederiksberg, Frederik Barfod and his new wife rented their first apartment.

Wolff, Christian von *84*; 1679-1754; German philosopher, professor of mathematics Halle 1706-1723 and again from 1740; intervening years in Marburg, following dispute with pietistic theologians in Halle; his philosophy, attempting fusion of empiricism and rationalism, founded in part upon philosophy of Gottfried Wilhelm Leibniz (1646-1716), and inculcating Enlightenment's ideals of rational thought and moral rectitude, became known in Dk as *den lebnitz-wolffske filosofi* and Wolffianism, and was long taught in universities of northern Europe, making him one of most influential philosophers of 18th c.; his priority of place in Copenhagen University's curriculum around 1800 confirmed Gr's criticism that "in those days our professors only indifferently kept pace with the times."

Wolff, Niels Giessing *175*; 1779-1848; priest in Præstø-Skibbinge (1813-21), and Gr's predecessor in Vartov (1823-39).

women *passim*; the feminine; see **kvindelige,** det.

women authors *290*; Gr's view; see also **kvindelige,** det.

word of prophecy *290*.

word, immersion in the *170*.

word, the *85, 107, 126, 153, 159, 163, 170, 176, 194, 250, 253, 254, 256, 259, 262, 270, 281, 302, 304, 308, 326, 327, 333, 336*; *Ordet*; concept fundamental to Christian theology in all denominations, a key concept in Luther's reformed doctrines, central to his sacramental theology, as it therefore also is to Gr's exposition of a theology of *det levende Ord*, the living word, which has precedence over the written word of Scripture; in Gr's usage, *ord* covers a wide semantic range – the Word that is God and was in the beginning with God, the creative *fiat*, the word of the patriarchs and prophets and of Christ and the apostles and evangelists, the Living Word by which Christ is truly present in his congregation and upon which depend the life and the authority of the Church, the word which lives in the hearts and upon the lips of the Christian congregation, the sacramental word, the word of prophecy and the word preached, the royal word, the word which is a 'riddle-picture' and "old Danish words" and the words which comprise the mother-tongue, the spoken word by which enlightenment is communicated from teacher to taught, and more; routinely and purposefully Gr gives the term an ambivalence, sometimes a multivalence, of significations, so that it is rarely unfruitful, when reading Gr, to look beyond the primary contextual signification to the hierarchical and organic structure of nuances invested in the term; "*Ordet er Aandens Legeme, vel usynligt, men ikke usanseligt, da vi i Hørelsen har Sans for det*" [*The word* is body of *the spirit*, invisible for sure, but not unsensory, since in hearing we have sense for it] (Gr in his *Krønnike-Rim* 1842); see also **word,** the living; **sacraments.**

word, the, at baptism *126, 170, 194*; see also **word,** the living; **sacraments**.

word, the living; see **Ord,** det levende.

word, the, of God *119, 120, 124, 159, 161, 170, 173, 194, 258, 259, 262, 266, 284, 287, 315, 318.*

word, the, of the Bible *118, 194, 250, 284, 292.*

word, the royal *110, 111.*

word, the spoken *85, 107, 145, 163, 167, 221, 259-262, 270, 304, 318, 327.*

words as riddle-pictures *118;* the worth Gr attached to language as *Billed-Sprog* [picture-language, metaphor] conditions his understanding of scriptural text and northern myth alike and in part accounts for the central place poetic expression has in his own discourses, written and spoken; see also **mythology**; **Christianity** as mythology.

words, eucharistic *264, 311;* see also **word,** the living; **sacraments**.

words of absolution *320.*

Workhouse, The *329, 330;* "The Vartou, or workhouse" – Edmund Gosse's somewhat misleading designation of Vartov; see **Vartov**; **Vartov Kirke**.

Worsaae, Jens Jacob Asmussen *292;* 1821-85; professor of archaeology, Copenhagen, Inspector-General of Antiquities for Denmark; succeeded pioneering archaeologist Christian Jørgensen Thomsen (1786-1865) as director of National Museum of Denmark (1865); had by then already made his own pioneering contribution to international discipline of systematic archaeology by testing (and refining) stratigraphic reliability of Thomsen's schematic division of archaeological time into Stone Age, Bronze Age, Iron Age, by gathering much archaeological field experience in Europe and establishing wider European context of Scandinavian archaeology, and by publication (1843) of his ground-breaking *Danmarks Oldtid oplyst ved Oldsager og Gravhøje* [Denmark's ancient history illumined by antiquities and burial-mounds]; his demonstration (1844) of the errors and misrepresentations of Finnur Magnusson in respect of the Blekinge stone perhaps represented the assertion of scientific objectivity over a self-deceiving enthusiasm towards national-historical antiquities; Gr continued to believe that Magnusson's judgment would find new acceptance; see also **Magnussen,** Finn; **Stephens,** George.

Wulff, Christian Nikolaj *277;* 1810-56; Danish naval officer (*Kommandør*), amateur composer, wrote musical settings of texts by Oehlenschläger and H. C. Andersen; published posthumous collection of his father's poetic works under title *Poetiske Arbeider ved Peter Frederik Wulff. Udgivne efter hans Død* (1844); died of yellow fever contracted while visiting Danish West Indies.

Wulff, Peter Frederik *277;* 1774-1842; Danish admiral, head of *Søkadetakademiet* [Naval cadet academy] 1803-41; wrote and published occasional verse, including *Rimede Smaating og Efterligninger* [Rhymed trifles and imitations; 1813], *Poetiske Skrifter af P. F. Wulff. Udgivne efter hans*

Død [Poetic writings of PFW published after his death; 1844; edited by son, Christian Nikolaj Wulff], which has been deemed of small poetic worth; however, as translator of literary works from English he played important role in progress of Danish Romanticism by rendering accessible both Lord George Gordon Noel Byron (1788-1824) and William Shakespeare (1564-1616), the former in a translation of *Manfred* (1820), the latter in five volumes (1818-25; new edition 1845-50), as continuation of the four volumes of translations published 1807-16 by Danish actor Peter Thun Foersom (1777-1817); also opened his home (official residence in palace of Amalienborg) to the young Hans Christian Andersen (1805-75); his daughter Henriette, to whom Andersen was closely attached, died (1858) in a fire aboard ship bound for New York.

Y

Yea, O Luther! if, in blindness; poem by Gr; see ***Ja, o Luther! vil i Blinde***.

Ymer *214*; primal giant in Northern myth as narrated in Snorri's *Edda*; came into being when heat from Múspellheimr and cold from Niflheimr met in great void of Ginnungagap; killed by Æsir who, from his dismembered body, built cosmos; Gr's son Svend, as precocious child, added own extension to myth to account for correct grammatical speech among gods; see also ***Nordens Mythologi***.

Z

Zeuthen, Frederik Ludvig Bang *21, 203, 205, 206, 226*; 1805-74; priest; related on maternal side to Gr and Henrik Steffens (his mother's brother); educated in Odense and at Copenhagen University; records being impressed by Gr at Vor Frelsers Kirke where as young man he first went to communion in Copenhagen, but gradually grew dismissive of Gr for being more spokesman for Danish antiquity and archaic Christianity than significant preacher and theologian; found greater empathy with Bishop J. P. Mynster (1775-1854) and more substance in his sermons ("he was at that time just about the only respected preacher in Copenhagen" – Zeuthen); 1827 journeyed to Breslau to spend period with his uncle, Henrik Steffens (1773-1845) during which time, and in subsequent travels, he met other leading German philosophers and theologians and ultimately became devoted follower of Friedrich Wilhelm Joseph von Schelling (1775-1854); a vigorous polemicist (though often at expense of making fair acknowledgement of merits of the object of attack), he became lifelong opponent of Grundtvig and Grundtvigianism's *kirkelige Anskuelse* [concept or purview of the church], disputing both in writing and in debates at Roskilde Clerical Convention with such as leading Grundtvigian theologian P. C. Kierkegaard (1805-88) and Frederik Barfod (1811-96).

Zion *224*; originally name of mountain near Jerusalem which eventually become site of Solomon's Temple; name came by extension to stand for Jerusalem, both the earthly and the heavenly; see also **Jerusalem**.

Æ

Ælve-Dronning *133*; faery-queen; term metaphorically used by Gr of Anglo-Saxon literature, no doubt deliberately echoing title of Edmund Spenser's unfinished epic poem *The Faerie Queene* (1590, 1596; known to Gr) thus making Gr by implication a knight facing ogres and detractors (English scholars who scorned and neglected the earliest English literature) as he rode to service of his dispossessed and captive lady; elsewhere he uses the term of the River Thames (punning additionally upon the Danish word *elv* [river]), and (again casting himself as knight of medieval romance) of Clara Bolton.

Æsir, Vanir: see **Aser, Vaner**

Æsop's Fables *218*; prose fables by Æsop, Greek author of *ca.* 550 BC, presumed to have been transmitted orally until written down about 300 BC, with often whimsical subjects commonly drawn from animal world but pointing moral about human frailties and virtues; much used in classical education and in translation as children's reading; included in Gr's programme of home study for his children.

Ø

Øhlenschläger, Adam Gottlob; see **Oehlenschläger,** Adam Gottlob.

Øresund *136, 143, 144, 248, 310, 334*; narrow sound or strait between Sjælland and Swedish coast serving as chief seaway from Baltic into North Sea and Atlantic, therefore having historic military-strategic and economic importance to Dk; its northern entrance guarded on western shore by castle and fortress of Helsingør (Elsinore) and on eastern shore by Kärnan at Hälsingborg; toll or tax levied on all passing ships from 1429 to 1857 when all three straits (Øresund, Storebælt, Lillebælt) in Dk were freed from tolls; Sjælland's Øresund coast a particularly idyllic region much cherished by poets and artists ("in the morningtide, sailing in the Øresund along the lovely coast of Sjælland, *Rune-Bladet* came to be more or less what it is" – Gr, concerning the composition of his poem, 1844); in Gr's disarrayed imagination, Palm Sunday 1867, Øresund seems symbolically to become a baptismal font for all Scandinavia.

Ørsted, Anders Sandøe *62, 99, 159, 160, 187, 239*; 1778-1860; deemed the most talented jurist of his generation, and a chief shaper of modern Danish jurisprudence; member of *Rigsdag* and First Minister; published 1826 a work on ecclesiastical law and priest's obligation to the confessional books which appeared to involve him as an officer of State in the controversial issues raised between Gr and H. N. Clausen; required by king to choose between public office and authorship, chose office; at heart disposed to support enlightened royal absolutism, yet was for a time hailed as a political progressive; later deeply unpopular for reactionary views, voting against the Constitution of 1848; bid by the *Rigsdag* (1854) to indict his administration for breach of the Constitution lapsed when his government resigned; brother to physicist H. C. Ørsted; married to Sophie, sister of Adam Oehlenschläger; home became a meeting-place for intellectuals and artists.

Ørsted, Hans Christian *99, 162, 165, 193*; 1777-1851; internationally recognised physicist, Professor of Physics Copenhagen University and discoverer of electro-magnetism; chemist and discoverer of aluminium; linguist; philosopher influenced by German philosophers Kant, Schelling, Hegel, preoccupied with identifying the pervasive and informing divine principle of creative Reason in the natural world; in conflict (1815) with Gr who regarded such thinking as godless naturalism; following visit to England, established (1824) Selskabet for Naturlærens Udbredelse (Society for the Promotion of Natural Science) dedicated to disseminating public awareness of natural sciences; effectively founder, later Director, of Den Polytekniske Læreanstalt (The Polytechnic Institute) situated adjacent to the University between Studiestræde and Skt. Pederstræde in Copenhagen; brother of A. S. Ørsted and like him a major figure in the cultural life of Dk's 'Golden Age'.

Østerbro *243*; Copenhagen suburb developed outside walled inner city and adjacent to Øresund especially in late 19th c. as fashionable area for more prosperous citizens; from 1868, Gr's home with third wife Asta, at Store Tuborg, Strandvejen 123.

Østergade *285*; street in central Copenhagen forming, with Vimmelskaftet, a section of *Routen* (now called *Strøget*), principal promenade for 19th-c. Copenhageners.

Aa

Aabent Brev til mine Børn *218, 332*; Open letter to my children; printed in Frederik Barfod's quarterly journal *Brage og Idun*, vol. 4, 1841 (and *PS* VI, 242-247); poetic address to his three children (Johan, Svend, Meta), probably written in connection with boys' confirmation Autumn 1839, which was complex emotional occasion for Gr following struggle with bishop for permission to confirm them himself; characteristically polemical piece, to some extent self-justifying but effectively blending expression of fatherly love and solicitude with broader concern for national life and wellbeing, including vigorous appeal for reconsideration of objectives and methods of child-education in Dk; "I look with sorrow on those little lads / whose cheeks are glowing and whose eyes are sparkling / for they too forthwith off to school must go / and steadily diminish as they grow! / There the rose withers in the grave's foul air / before the lovely bloom unfolds its scent; / there fades the eye upon the hearse's straw / ere any stops to think what light is quenched! / Yea, bleed my heart over their fearsome lot / and be not ashamed if weeping chokes your voice! / To Winter is devoted their young Spring, / defrauded of Summer and of Autumntide! / O would but each man living in the land / who has himself endured it, this Black School, / be liberated from the fire and water, / review his footsteps with a falcon's eye / and see the miracles which he can thank / that he with the masses is not bound for hell / ere life has blossomed with the wealth of youth / and youthful vigour's flood come bubbling forth!" [Jeg seer med Vemod paa de Gutter smaa, / Hvis Kinder gløde og hvis Øine tindre, / Thi ogsaa de skal brat i Skole gaae, / Og immer, mens de voxe, blive mindre! / Der visner Rosen i Gravluften kvalm, / Før end til Duft den Deilige oplukkes, / Der brister Øiet paa Ligbaarens Halm, / Før Nogen tænker paa, hvad Lys der slukkes! / Ja, blød, mit Hjerte, ved de bange Kaar, / Og skam dig ei, om Graaden kvæler Røsten! / Til Vintren vies der den unge Vaar, / For Sommeren besveget og for Høsten! / O vilde dog hver Levende i Landet, / Som selv den sorte Skole gjennemgik, / Udfriedes af Ilden og af Vandet, / Sin Bane følge med et Falkeblik, / Og see *Miraklerne* , han det mon skylde, / At ei med Skarerne han foer til Hel, / Før Livet blomstrede i Ungdoms-Fylde, / Og oversprudlende blev Kraftens Væld!; 57-76]; see also **sorte Skole,** den.

Aabent Vennebrev til en Engelsk Præst *258, 270*; Open letter of friendship to an English priest (1839); open letter written by Gr, addressed to the (actually Irish-born) Anglican priest Nugent Wade (1809-93) and giving a brief account of the Danish Church; see further **Wade,** Nugent.

Aagaard, Just Georg Valdemar *231*; 1811-57, Georg Aagaard, national-liberal politician, member of Constituent Assembly (*Den grundlovgivende Rigsforsamling*) drafting Constitution of 1849; friend of Gr; son of Holger Halling Aagaard (who corresponded with Gr over many years; his letters preserved in Arkiv Fasc. 465) whose stately home, Iselinge near Vordingborg, was a gathering-place for leading figures in politics, literature, science; there Gr was introduced to Georg Aagaard's uncle, archaeologist and philologist Peter Oluf Brønsted (1780-1842), who spent several years in Paris and London (where he became, as did Gr later, a great admirer of English liberties: "All forces conspiring against Europe's light and liberty must sooner or later founder upon that rock which is called Britannia" – Brønsted's letter to J. P. Mynster after England visit 1824) and could assist Gr (1827) in researches in Anglo-Saxon literature and (1829) in his preparations to visit England (1829-31) to search out Anglo-Saxon manuscripts (some correspondence with Gr is preserved in Arkiv Fasc. 448.6); thus it seems likely that Gr, in advance of his visits to England, was well alerted to both major aspects of English culture by which he famously returned to Denmark enthused: the Anglo-Saxon literary legacy and the liberties enjoyed by the English people.

Aalborg *112, 166*; prosperous Danish city in northern Jylland, existing at least from early viking period, with monastery from medieval period and bishopric from 1554; well-situated on Limfjord for access to North Sea and Kattegat to develop as market town (charter 1342) and fishing (especially herring) and trading port (especially, up to 1814, trade with Norway); Gr gratefully avoided (1818) appointment to vacant curacy here, so far from Copenhagen; here (1856) Gr's supporter Peter Christian Kierkegaard was appointed bishop, in whose residence the papers of his late brother Søren Aabye were first deposited and sorted.

Aand *136, 149 and passim*; alternative spelling in modern texts *Ånd*; with attached definitive article, *Aanden/Ånden*; together with its derivatives and compounds, a problematical term in the translation of Danish and of the terminology of Gr who attached distinctive theological and philosophical concepts to the term. In a range of respects it is the counterpart of English 'spirit' and like 'spirit' it is etymologically connected with the word for 'breath' (English 'aspirate, inspire, expire'; Danish *aande*, 'breath; to breathe'). The semantic range of *aand* includes 'spirit, mind' (in Danish sometimes also called *sind*, that which is the opposite of body and the corporeal or material); 'inward intellectual or spiritual strength' (as in the sense of English 'genius, spirit'); 'ghost, spirit' (as in English 'the ghost of Hamlet's father' or 'spirits of the vasty deep'); 'the Holy Spirit' (commonly coupled with 'den hellige' but also commonly standing alone as in English 'the Spirit bloweth where it listeth'); 'the essential or characterising intention or disposition' (as in English 'the spirit of the law' or 'the spirit of the age'); 'morale' (as in English 'the morale/spirits of the team was/were high'). Accordingly, the adjective *aandelig* covers the semantic range:

spiritual, intellectual, mental, moral. Among compounds, *aandfuld* and *aandrig* are 'brilliant, witty'; *aandløs* is 'dull, shallow'; *aandsevne* is 'mental faculty'; *aandshistorie* is 'history of intellectual life'; *aandskraft* is 'mental power, strength of mind'; *aandsliv* is 'spiritual life' but also in a more secular cultural sense 'intellectual life'; *aandssvag* is 'psychologically ill, mentally deficient, idiotic'. Of course, in particular philosophical systems most if not all of the phenomena named by *Aand* and its compounds can be seen as linked in kind and in source as the words are linked in etymology. In Gr's discourses, the human creature is essentially resolved into *Aand* and *Støv* [dust]. *Aand* characteristically resides in *Sjælen*, the soul, which can also be referred to as *Sindet*, and (as is of the greatest importance in Gr's imagising of the human individual) in *Hjertet*, the heart. The natural language, indeed the only adequate language of *Aanden*, is poetic and intuitive. "*Aand* er ikke det samme som *Sjæl*, og gribes endnu mindre af Luften, men er *Livs-Kraften*, som Ordet om det *usynlige* nu sædvanlig fattes, men kan dog have, og viser sig da baade *levende* og *kraftigt*, medens alle aandløse Ord om det *usynlige* er døde og magtesløse" ['Aand' is not the same as 'Soul' and even less is it plucked out of thin air, but is the life-force, which talk about the invisible nowadays usually lacks, but yet can have – and then it shows itself to be both living and potent, whilst all *Aand*-devoid talk about the invisible is dead and impotent; Gr in *Krønnike-Rim* 1842]. The concept of *Aanden* was central to Gr's Christian philosophy of life and to his conception of that human condition which by his ministry, writings, and works great and small he sought to help achieve among the Danish people. This Grundtvigian philosophy was encapsulated by Carl Joakim Brandt (1817-89), Gr's successor as priest in Vartov Kirke, in three axioms (quoted by Frederik Rönning) relating to *Aanden*: *Aand er Magt. Aanden virker gennem Ordet. Aanden virker kun i Frihed* [Spirit is power. The Spirit works through the Word. The Spirit works only in freedom]; see also **Rationalism**.

Aarhus *61, 71-74, 83, 156, 181, 245*; Aarhus (Aros – mouth of the river), ancient settlement in eastern Jylland about the minor river which there reaches the sea, was in 1798 (when Gr was sent there to be prepared for university entrance) an important administrative centre, a harbour for both trade and travellers, a gated town with some 4,000 inhabitants, a magnificent medieval cathedral (and several former religious houses) and a Latin School which had produced some notable students but by this time had seen better days; its remoteness from Copenhagen (and Udby) was determined largely by the exigencies of wind and weather (in winter, ice) in crossing the Little Belt [*Lillebælt*] and Great Belt [*Storebælt*] and navigating the Kattegat by sailing ship.

Aarhus Latin School *61, 71-74, 81, 117, 156, 245*; Aarhus Cathedral School, scene (1798-1800) of fourth stage of Gr's education (earliest instruction at home with his mother; then village school in Udby and Laurits Feld's tutelage at Thyregod Parsonage), preparatory for admission to university; scene also of his "*slemme Aar*" [bad years], model of the "*sorte Skole*" [black school] against which he was to be so active in later years; of uncertain origins though evidence points to a school of some sort associated with Church in Aarhus as early as 10th c.; formal association with cathedral (so Gr's school fees were offset by remuneration for singing in cathedral choir) maintained after Reformation; *Rektor* [headmaster, principal] in Gr's day was Thure Krarup (1739-1808) and *Konrektor* [deputy principal] Jens Stougaard (1761-1838); see also **sorte Skole, den.**

Aasen, Ivar *297*; 1813-96; Norwegian poet and language-scholar, largely self-taught; shaper of a standard written form of Norwegian, the *landsmaal*, based upon Norwegian dialects and deliberately differentiated from Danish and from the Danish-based but Norwegian-pronounced language of educated urban speakers which his rival Knud Knudsen (1812-95) favoured as basis for written Norwegian; from 1841, having been granted stipend from State, he researched Norwegian dialects, leading to publication of his *Norsk Grammatik* [Norwegian grammar; 1846] and *Norsk Ordbog* [Norwegian dictionary; 1873] containing some 16,000 items, against background of controversy (in which his direct participation was small) over formation of official standard Norwegian language; his own original literary works and translations served also as exemplifications of the *landsmaal*; his *Norske Ordsprog, samlede og ordnede* [Norwegian proverbs, collected and arranged], published 1856, was commended by Gr in Tivoli speech to supporters of Nordic unity (reflecting Gr's own lifelong interest in proverbs, Danish and English), because, next to a people's myths, they most clearly portrayed a people's character.